Exam AZ-300 & AZ-301 Study & Lab Guide Part 1
Microsoft Certified Azure Solutions Architect Expert

Harinder Kohli

Exam AZ-300 & AZ-301 Study & Lab Guide Part 1
Harinder Kohli

This edition has been published by arrangement with **Kindle Direct Publishing**.

ISBN
ISBN: 9781692760779

Edition: 1st Edition, September 2019

Contact Author

Email: harinder-kohli@outlook.com
Linkedin: www.linkedin.com/in/harinderkohli
Azure Blog @ https://mykloud.wordpress.com

Downloads

Download TOC and Sample Chapter from Box.com
https://app.box.com/s/8keiisj6y6du47qkrq7tmj0xr12x570b

Errata & Updates
Information about Book Errata & Updates will be published at following link @ Box.com.
https://app.box.com/s/ufr65eo89voaedqr00j6gobllpcnzrb8

Contents at a Glance

Contents at a Glance (Contd)

Table Of Contents

Lab Exercises

Lab Exercises (Contd)

Lab Exercises (Contd)

Lab Exercises (Contd)

Lab Exercises (Contd)

Lab Exercises (Contd)

Case Studies

Design Virtual Network and Network Security Groups
Workload Isolation with Hub and Spoke VNETs using VNET Peering
Controlling Access to Database VM using NSG
Access to Database VM using UDR
Access to Azure SQL Database
Designing Disk Solution
Designing Disk and VM Soultion
Design for IOPS and Throughtput for your Application using Different I/O Sizes
Choosing VM size and Designing IOPs
Placement of Virtual Machines in Availability Set
Load Balancing e-commerce server
Highly Available Multisite Website
Design Compute Solution for Image Processing Application
Backup of Azure VM with Managed Disk
Backup of Azure VM with Managed Disk
Backup of Folder in Azure VM
DR for Azure VM
Secure Remote Access to on-premises Application
Identity Management
Licensing Case Study 1
Licensing Case Study 2
Design Role Based Access Control (RBAC)

Introduction

Azure Solutions Architect Expert Certification (AZ-300 & AZ-301) is targeted toward Azure Architects who can Implement & Design Azure Cloud Solutions.

Exam AZ-300: Microsoft Azure Architect Technologies focuses on **Implementation** of Azure Cloud Solutions. Exam AZ-300 focuses both on **Infrastructure Topics** such as Virtual Servers, Networks, Storage, Azure Active Directory, Azure CDN, Azure Key Vault, Monitoring Solutions and **Database & PaaS Topics** such as SQL Database, Web Apps, Containers, NoSQL, Batch Computing & Service Bus. One of the key success points to pass the exam is to work with Azure portal and practice configuring various Azure services.

Exam AZ-301: Microsoft Azure Architect Design focuses on **Design** of Azure Cloud Solutions. Exam AZ-301 focuses on design of Virtual Networks, Compute, Storage, Azure AD, Azure Backup & DR, Security with Azure Key Vault, Azure SQL Database, Web Apps, Containers, Cosmos DB, Messaging Services, Batch Computing, Monitoring with Log Analytics & Azure Automation etc.

Exam AZ-300 & AZ-301 Study & Lab Guide Part 1 & 2 helps you prepare for AZ-300 & AZ-301 Exam. It contains Topic lessons, Lab Exercises & Design Case Studies. It is being published in 2 separate Books.
Part 1 Book (Which is this book) focuses on Implementation and Design of Infrastructure Topics.
Part 2 Book Focuses on Implementation and Design of Database, PaaS, Security, Monitoring and Automation Solutions. It is being published separately but simultaneously with Part 1.

The twin focus of this book is to get your fundamental on Azure Services on strong footing and to prepare you to Implement & design cloud solutions. Topic lessons, Design case studies and lab exercises are all geared towards making you understand Azure fundamentals.

Best of Luck for AZ-300 & AZ-301 Exam.

I would be pleased to hear your feedback and thoughts on the book. Please comment on Amazon or mail to: harinder-kohli@outlook.com.

Harinder Kohli

Topics to read for AZ-300 and AZ-301

Topic to read for AZ-300 Exam

For AZ-300 Exam read all Topics except for following:

1. Topics which are Italicized.
2. AZ-301 specific Chapters. In this book you have three AZ-301 specific Chapters – Chapter 9, Chapter 16 & Chapter 20.

Topic to read for AZ-301 Exam

For AZ-301 Exam, read all topics. AZ-301 exam builds on the theory and Labs covered in Exam AZ-300. For AZ-301 Exam we have also included case studies.

You have common topics between these exams such as Virtual Network Peering, UDR, S2S VPN, Express Route, Service Endpoints, VM high Availability, VMSS, Load Balancing Solutions, Azure AD, Subscription and cost management etc.

In theory we discuss Architecture, components and uses cases. These are all foundation topics for designing.

I am once again stressing that for AZ-301 Exam go through all topics. For example topic VM high Availability is a common topic in both AZ-300 & AZ-301. VM high Availability (Availability Set & AZ) is a good topic for designing highly available VM solutions.

Please note that Common topics for Exam AZ-300 & AZ-301 are not marked with Italics. So for Exam AZ-301 you must go through all topics.

Lab Requirements & Tricks

Resource Naming

In Exercises I keep referring to resources created in previous exercises. My suggestion would be that you name your resources by adding some letter or number to my resource names.
The above suggestion is just for lab exercises in this book and not for your production use case.

Browser Requirements for Lab Exercises

You will require 3 Browsers for completing Lab Activities. I used following Browser options for completing lab activities.

1. **Chrome Browser** was my main Browser. I used it with Subscription User. This was the user with which I signed for Azure Subscription.
2. **Firefox Browser** was used with users created in Azure AD.
3. **Tor browser** was used to simulate suspicious locations.

Custom Domain & Public Certificate Requirement for Lab Exercises

In Part 1 book (This Book) i used domain **mykloud.in**. This was used in 2 Exercises – Azure DNS and Add Custom Domain in Azure AD. I purchased it for around USD 9.

In Part 2 Book i used domain **hksystems.in**. This was used in 2 Exercises – Azure Web App Custom Domain and HTTPS. I purchased it for around USD 7.
For Part 2 Book I also purchased **Public Certificate** from Azure Portal. This was used for enabling HTTPS connection on Web App. I purchased it for around USD 66 with a validity of one year.

How to Save Azure Credits

1. Stop the Virtual Machine in Azure Portal if you are not using it. This will save you lot of money.
2. Delete the resources which you longer require.

How to go to Resource Dashboard

In lab Exercises I will just tell you to go resource dashboard but will not explain how to go. Read below on how to go to Resource Dashboard.

How to go to Resource Dashboard: Preferred Approach

In Azure Portal click the resource type in left pane. For Example if you have to go Virtual Machine or Storage Account or Resource Group Dashboard click the Virtual Machines or Storage Account or Resource Group in left pane and select your Resource in Right pane.

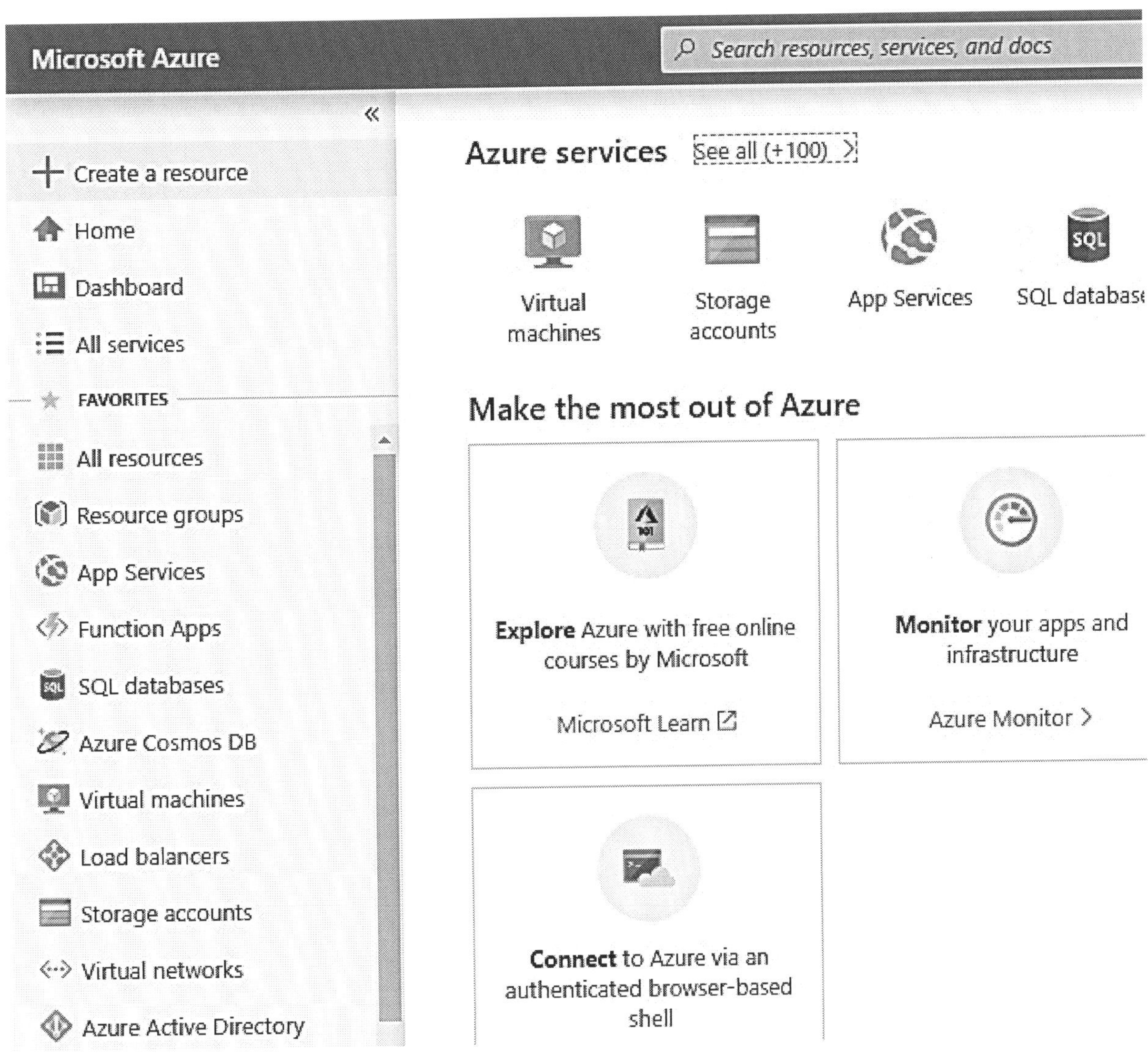

How to go to Resource Dashboard: Option 2

You will not find certain Resources like Azure Automation or Azure DNS etc in left pane in Azure Portal. Click All Resources in left pane. This will show all Resources which you have created till now. Click your resource to go to dashboard.

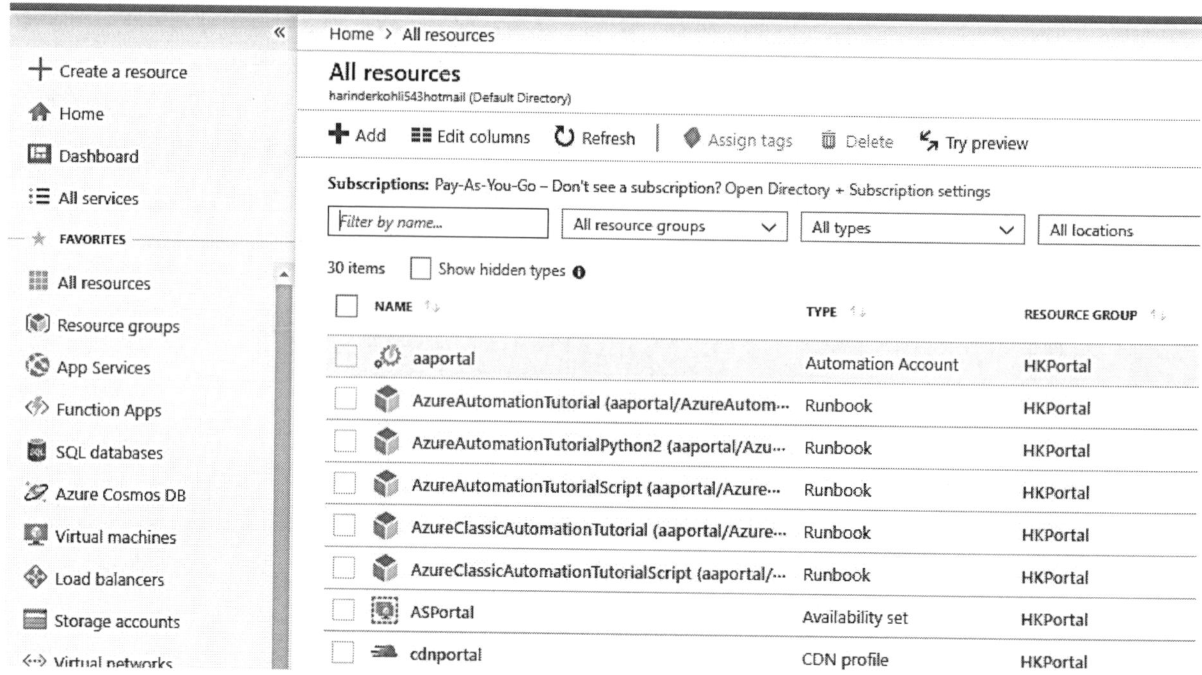

How to go to Resource Dashboard: Option 3

In Azure Portal Click All Services in left pane> In right pane select your resource type. This will open pane for that Resource type. Select your resource to go to its dashboard.

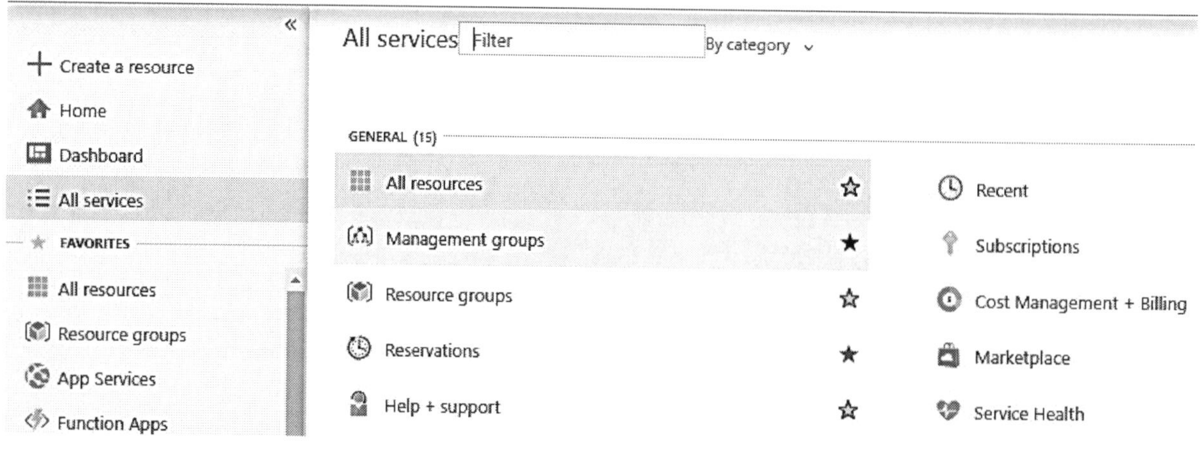

How to Create Azure Resource

How to Create Resource: Preferred Approach

In Azure Portal Click + **Create a resource** in top left pane> Select category of your resource and then the resource itself.

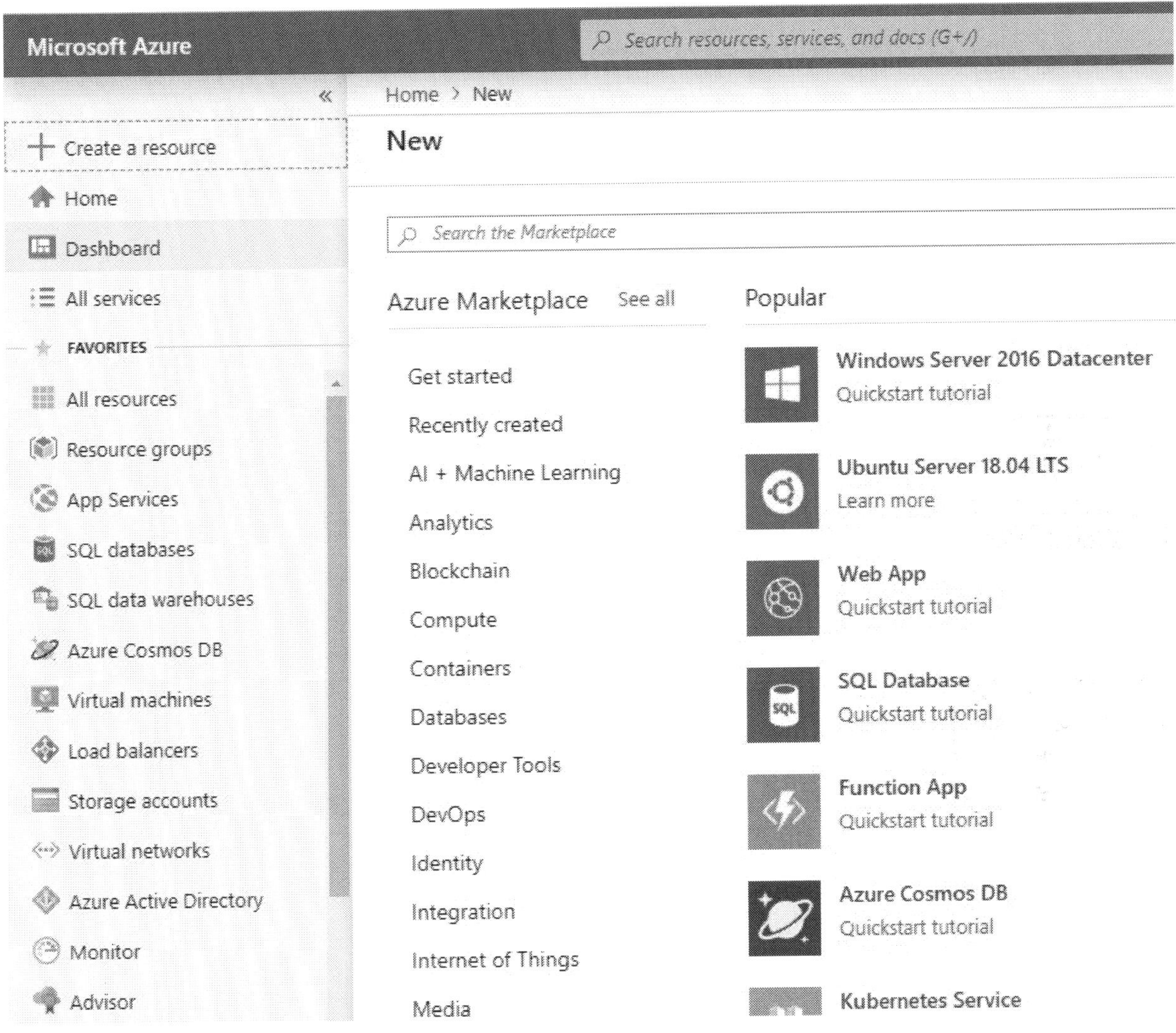

How to Create Resource: Option 2

Many times you will not find your required resource using option 1 (+ **Create a resource**). In this case you need to use option 2.

In Azure Portal Click **All Services** in left pane>All Service pane opens> Select category of your resource and then the resource itself.

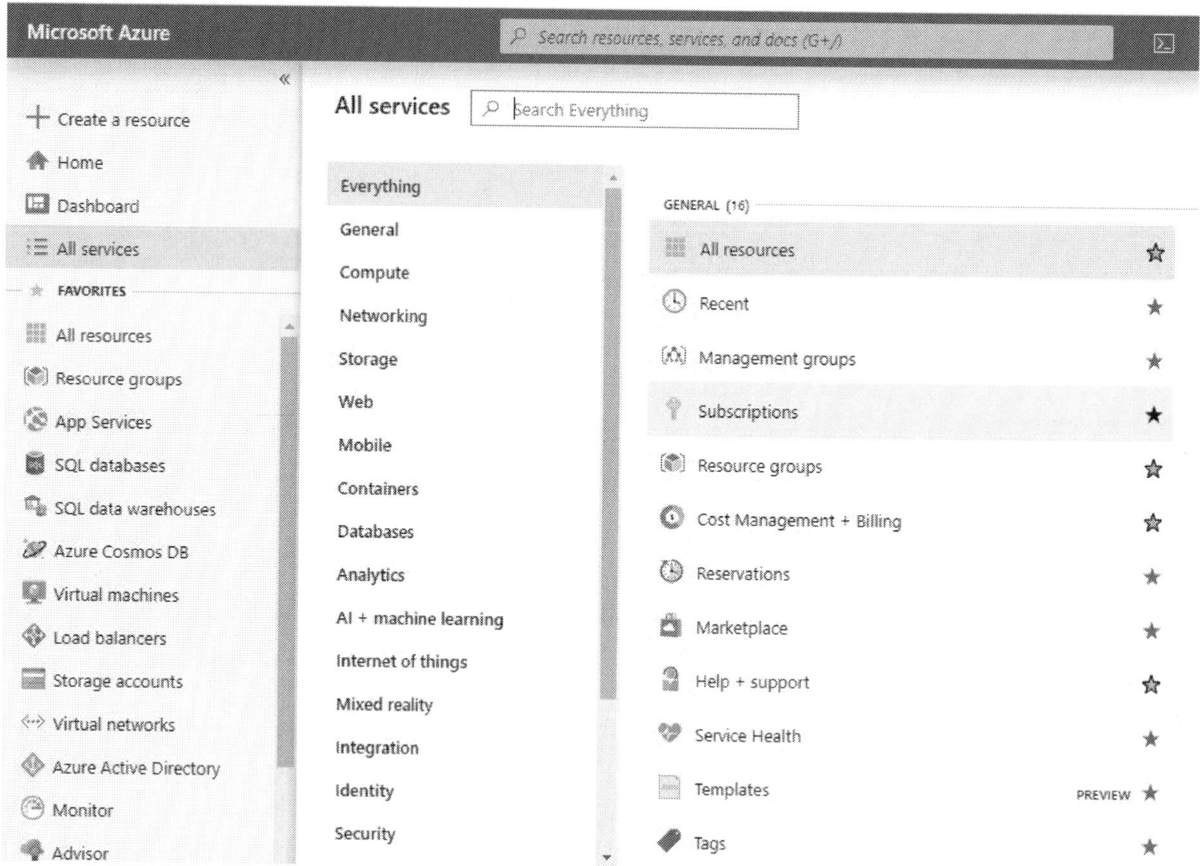

Note: I might have used option 1 to create a resource. There is a possibility that you may not find the resource with option 1. In that case you can use option 2 to create the resource.

Topologies

High Level View of Topology

We will create 4 Virtual Networks – VNETCloud, VNETOnPrem, VNETCloud2 & VNETCloud3 as shown below.

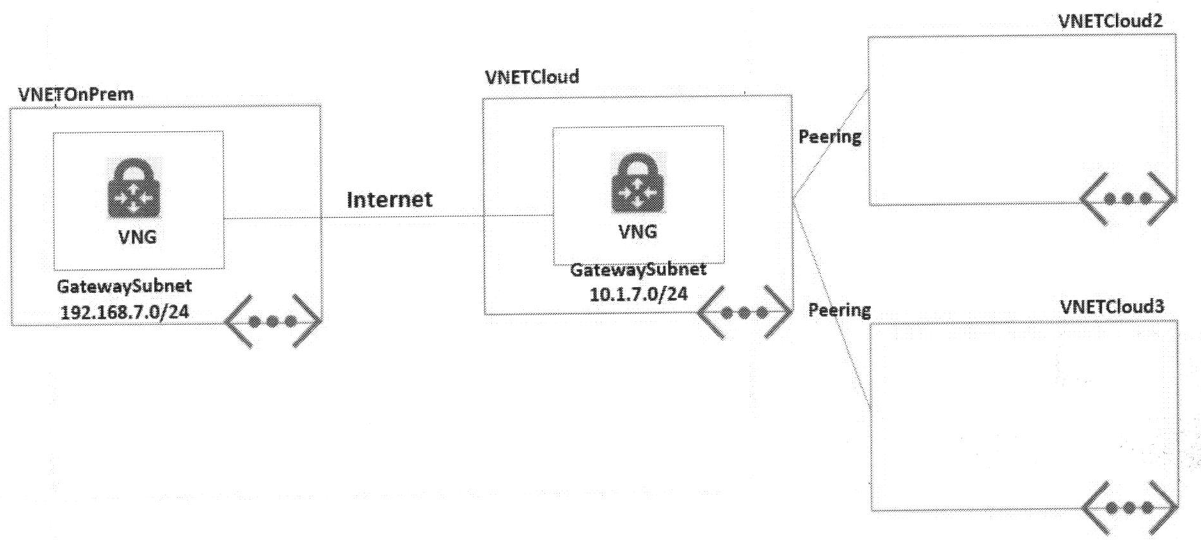

Virtual Network **VNETOnPrem** will represent on-premises Datacentre.

We will connect VNETCloud and VNETOnPrem using Virtual Network Gateway and S2S VPN over Internet connectivity.

We will connect VNETCloud to VNETCloud2 & VNETCloud3 using Virtual Network Peering. The peering connectivity will be over Azure Backbone Network.

VNETCloud Topology

Virtual Network VNETCloud will be our main Virtual Networks for all labs in all the Chapters.

We will create below Topology using Virtual Network VNETCloud. It will have Five Subnets – Web-Subnet, DB-Subnet, DMZ-Subnet, GatewaySubnet & AG-Subnet.

DB-Subnet, DMZ-Subnet and GatewaySubnet are not shown because of space constraint.

Students will create the topology as they progress through Chapter Labs.

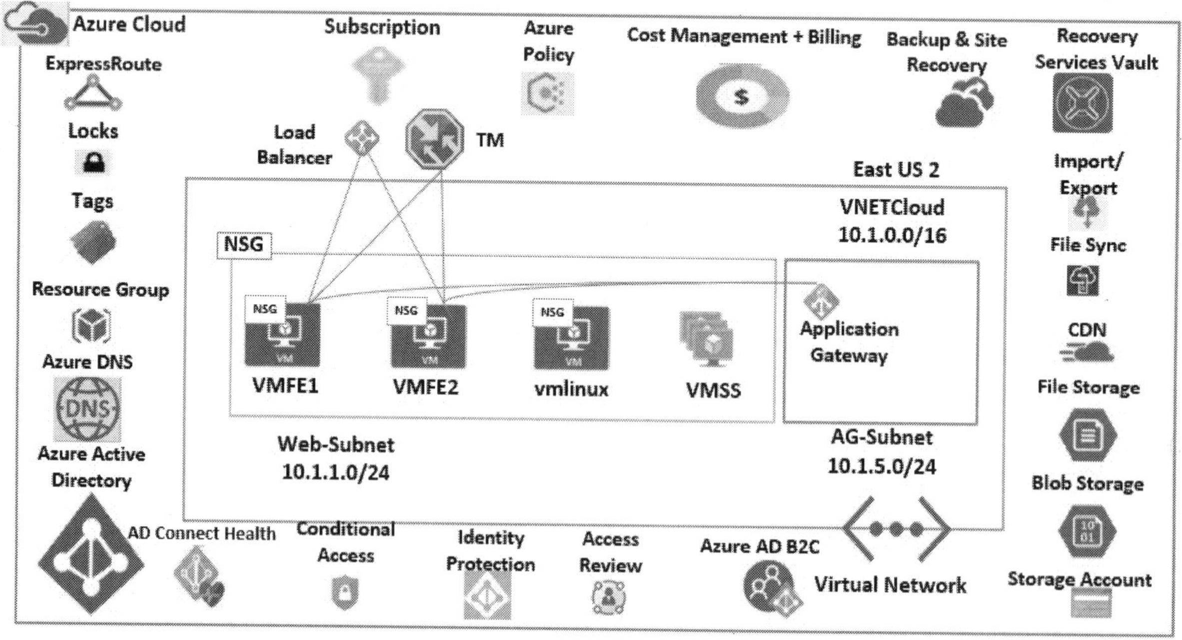

Most of the Resources in this topology were created in Resource Group RGCloud. Azure Portal was used to create resources in this topology.

VNETOnPrem Topology

<u>Virtual Network **VNETOnPrem** will represent on-premises Datacentre.</u>

We will create below Topology using Virtual Network VNETOnPrem. It will have two Subnets – OnPrem-Subnet and GatewaySubnet.

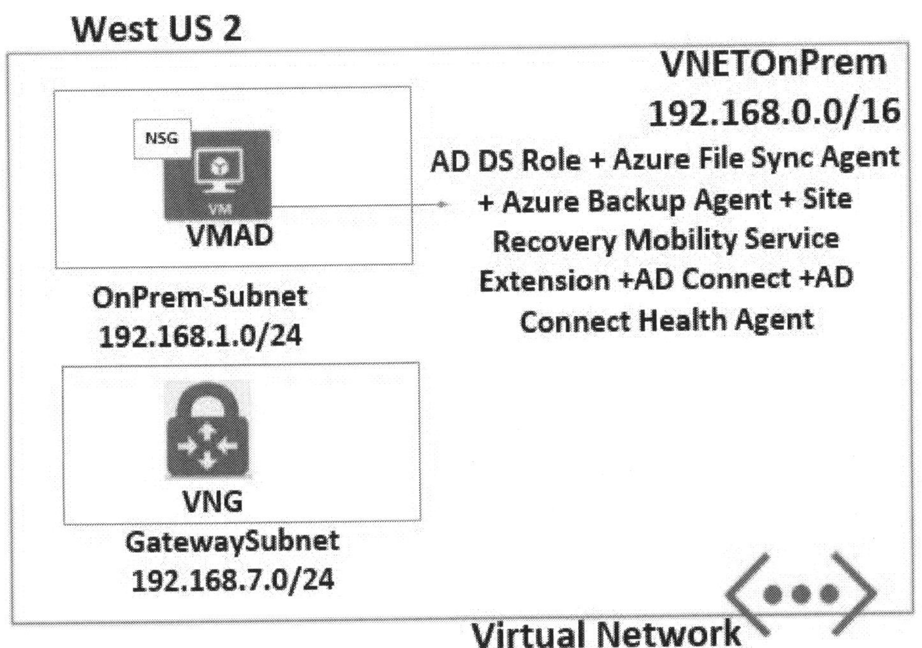

Virtual Machine VMAD will be created in Virtual Network VNETOnPrem. Following will be installed or enabled on Virtual Machine VMAD.

Active Directory Domain services (AD DS) role
Azure File Sync Agent
Azure Backup Agent
Azure Site Recovery (ASR) Mobility Service Extension
Azure AD Connect
AD Connect Health Agent

Resources in this topology were created in Resource Group RGOnPrem. Azure Portal was used to create resources in this topology.

Lab Exercises using Azure CLI and PowerShell

Labs in Chapter 21, 22, 23, 24 & 25 were done using Azure CLI and PowerShell. I used Azure CLI and Azure PowerShell Installed on my desktop.

Readers are requested to go through **Chapter 21 Installing Azure PowerShell Module & Azure CLI** before proceeding with labs using Azure CLI and PowerShell.

All Lab resources using Azure CLI were created in Resource Group HKCLI and Virtual Network VNETCLI.
All Lab resources using Azure PowerShell were created in Resource Group HKPS and Virtual Network VNETPS.

I did these labs separately from Lab exercises using Azure Portal. Readers can proceed as per their comfort factor with Azure CLI and PowerShell.

Chapter 1 Virtual Networks

This Chapter covers following Topic Lessons

- Virtual Networks
- Virtual Networks Pricing & Limits
- Public IP Addresses in Azure
- Private IP Addresses
- Public IP Addresses Pricing and Limits
- Network Security Groups
- NSG Limits
- Azure DNS
- Azure DNS for private domains
- Azure DNS Pricing
- Virtual Networks Peering
- Virtual Network Peering Pricing
- Gateway Transit and Remote Gateways
- Routing within VNET using System Route
- Routing within VNET using User Defined Route (UDR)
- Next Hop Options when adding Route in Route Table
- VNET Service Endpoints
- Bandwidth or Data Transfer Pricing

This Chapter covers following Lab Exercises

- Create Resource Group RGCloud
- Create Resource Group RGOnPrem
- Create Virtual Network VNETCloud
- Create additional Subnet (DB-Subnet 10.1.2.0/24)
- Create additional Subnet (DMZ-Subnet 10.1.3.0/24)
- Create Virtual Network representing On-Prem Network
- Create Virtual Network VNETCloud2
- Create Virtual Network VNETCloud3
- Create Dynamic Public IP
- Change Dynamic Public IP to Static IP
- Create NSG and add inbound http, RDP and SSH allow rule
- Associate Network Security Group (NSG) with Subnet
- Exploring IP Address Option in Network Security Group
- Exploring Tag Option in Network Security Group
- DNS Zone, DNS Records and Delegation to Azure DNS
- Peering between VNETs - VNETCloud & VNETCloud2

- Peering between VNETs - VNETCloud & VNETCloud3
- Routing Traffic between 2 Subnets to pass through another Subnet using UDR
- Setting up Virtual Network (VNET) Service Endpoints

This Chapter covers following Case Studies

- Design Virtual Network and Network Security Groups
- Workload Isolation with Hub and Spoke VNETs using VNET Peering
- Controlling Access to Database VM using NSG
- Access to Database VM using UDR
- Access to Azure SQL Database

Chapter Topology

In this chapter we will create 4 Virtual Networks – VNETCloud, VNETOnPrem, VNETCloud2 & VNETCloud3. VNETCloud will be our main Virtual Network for all labs in all the Chapters. In some labs we will also use VNETOnPrem.

In hhis Chapter we will create below Topology using Virtual Network VNETCloud. We will create 3 Subnets. We will add NSG, Azure DNS & Resource Group to the topology. Default Azure AD is created when you sign for Azure subscription.

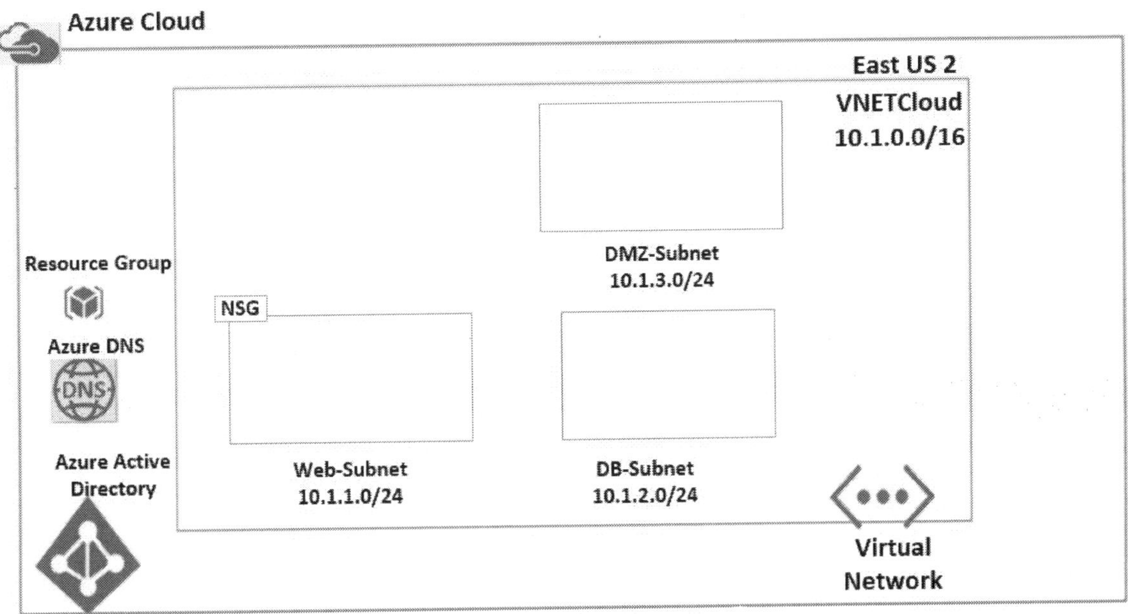

Figure below shows Topology for Virtual Network VNETOnPrem. We will rename default subnet as OnPrem-Subnet. There was lack of space in above figure so I am showing it separately.

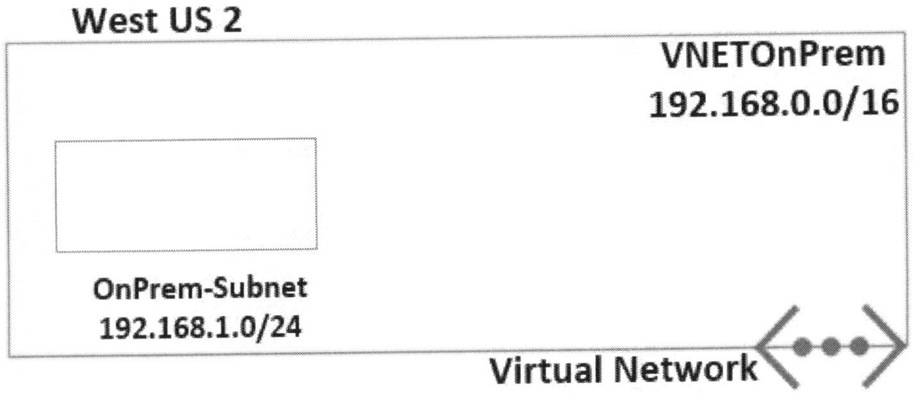

Following Topology will be used in VNET Peering Labs.

In Exercise 16 we will do peering between VNETCloud and VNETCloud2.
In Exercise 17 we will do peering between VNETCloud and VNETCloud3.

The peering connectivity will be over Azure Backbone Network.

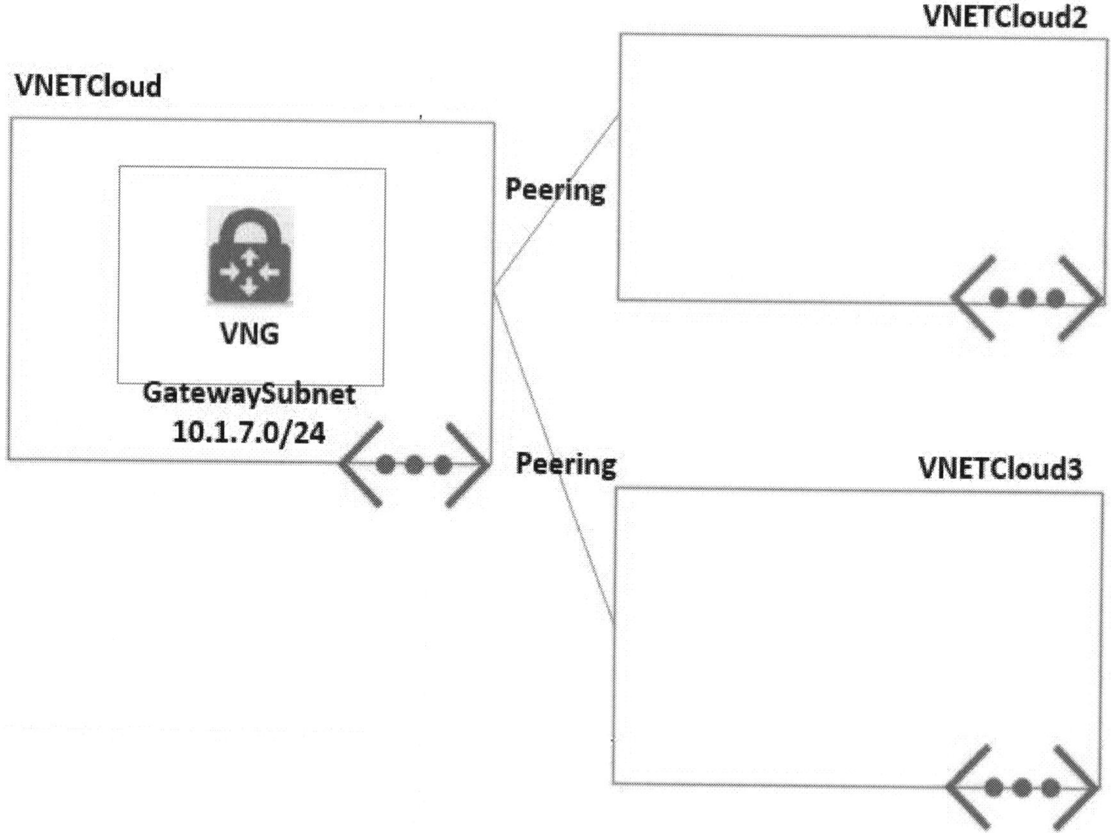

Virtual Networks (VNET)

An Azure virtual network (VNET) is Virtual Data Centre in the cloud. Virtual Network is further segmented into subnets. Access to the subnets can be controlled using Network Security groups. Virtual Machines are created in Subnets.

End customers create Virtual Networks. End customers define the IP address blocks, security policies, and route tables within this network.

Figure below shows virtual network KNET1 with 2 subnets – Web-Subnet and DB-Subnet. There are 3 virtual machines in these subnets.
End customer has defined Network address of 192.168.0.0/16 for virtual network KNET1, 192.168.1.0/24 for Web-Subnet and 192.168.2.0/24 for DB-Subnet.

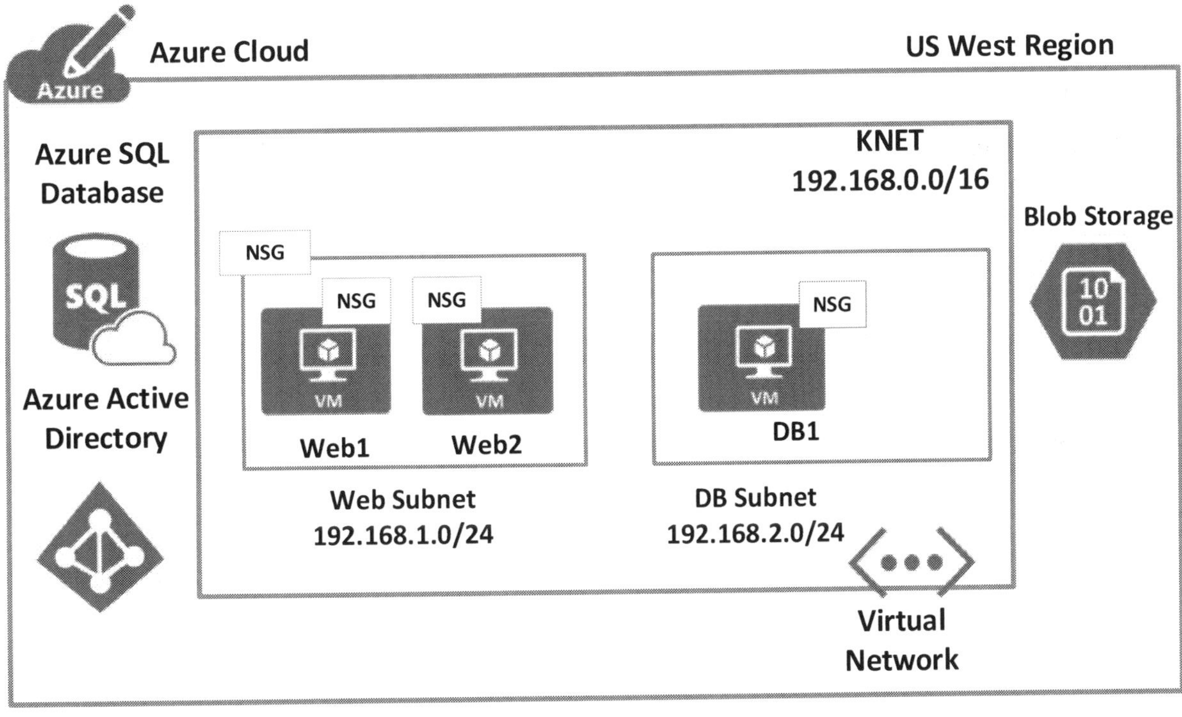

Virtual Network is created by the customer. Resources within Virtual Network are created and managed by end customers. Whereas Resources outside of VNET (Azure SQL, Azure AD etc) are Azure Managed Resources with Public IPs. Azure Managed Resources are not only accessed by VMs in VNET but are also accessed through internet.

Virtual Network Subnets

VNET is divided into subnets. Subnets are assigned IP addresses by Subnetting VNET network address space. Access to the subnet can be controlled through Network Security groups (NSG). User defined route (UDR) tables can also be assigned to subnets. Virtual Machines are created in Subnets.

Default Communication within and between Virtual Network Subnets

1. All VM to VM traffic within subnet or between subnets is allowed.
2. VM to internet traffic is allowed.
3. Azure Load balancer to VM is allowed.
4. Inbound internet to VM is blocked.

Note: Default rules can be overridden by new rules you create using NSG.

Private Address Range for Virtual Networks

You can use following class A, Class B and Class C address range for virtual networks.

10.0.0.0/8
172.16.0.0/12
192.168.0.0/16

Once the IP address range is decided, we can then divide this range into subnets. Virtual Machines NICs in the subnet are assigned private IP addresses via Azure DHCP from the subnet network address range.

There are 5 Reserved addresses within the subnet: Within a virtual network subnet, the protocol reserves the first and last IP addresses of a subnet: a host ID of all 0s is used for the network address, and a host ID of all 1s is used for broadcast. In addition, Azure reserves the first three IP addresses in each subnet (binary 01, 10, and 11 in the host ID portion of the IP address) for internal purposes.

Exercise 1: Create Resource Group RGCloud

1. In Azure Portal click Resource Groups in left pane> All Resource Groups pane opens> Click +Add> Create Resource Group blade opens>Enter RGCloud for name and Select East US 2 as location and click Review + Create (Not Shown)>Click Create (Not Shown).

Create a resource group

Basics   Tags   Review + Create

Resource group - A container that holds related resources for an Azure solution. The resource group can include all the resources for the solution, or only those resources that you want to manage as a group. You decide how you want to allocate resources to resource groups based on what makes the most sense for your organization. Learn more

PROJECT DETAILS

* Subscription: Pay-As-You-Go

* Resource group: RGCloud

RESOURCE DETAILS

* Region: East US 2

Figure below shows dashboard of Resource Group RGCloud.

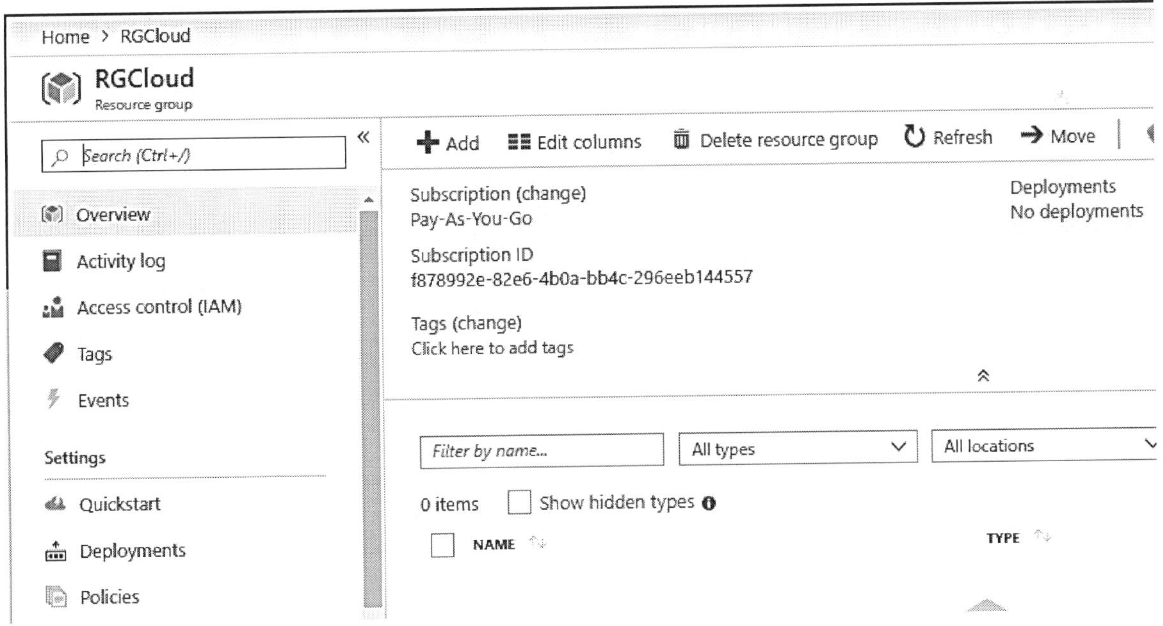

Note: Resource Groups will be discussed extensively in Chapter 15.

Exercise 2: Create Resource Group RGOnPrem

In Azure Portal click Resource Groups in left pane> All Resource Groups pane opens> Click +Add> Create Resource Group blade opens>Enter RGOnPrem for name and Select West US 2 as location and click Review + Create (Not Shown)>Click Create (Not Shown).

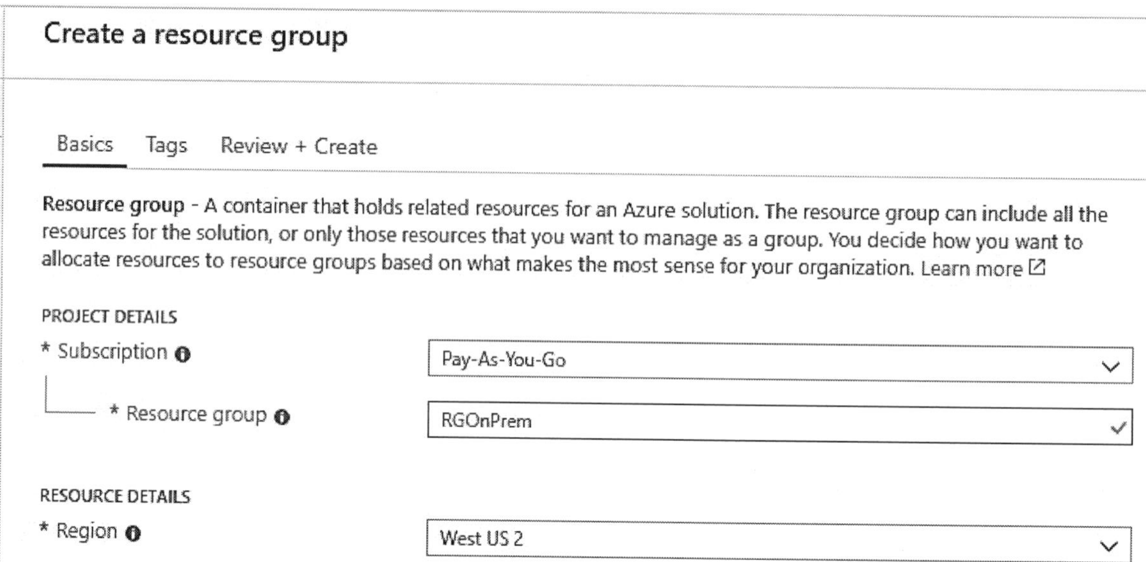

Figure below shows dashboard of Resource Group RGOnPrem.

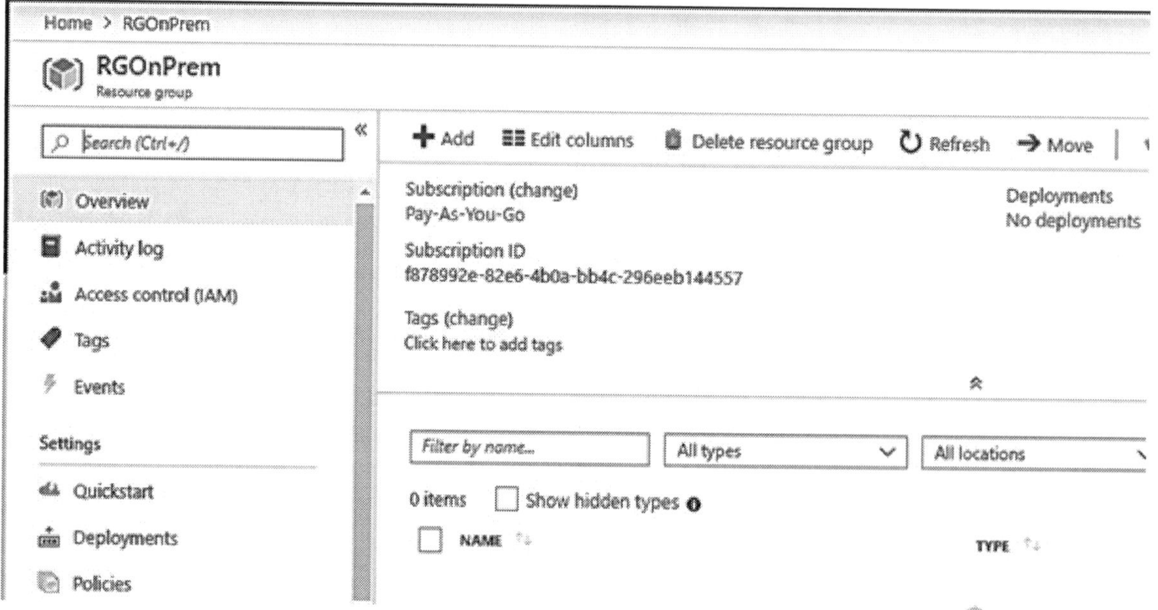

Note: Resource Groups will be discussed extensively in Chapter 15.

Exercise 3: Create Virtual Network VNETCloud

In this exercise we will create Virtual Network **VNETCloud** in Resource Group **RGCloud** (Created in Exercise 1) using 10.1.0.0/16 address space in **East US 2** Location. We will name Default Subnet as **Web-Subnet** with address 10.1.1.0/24.

1. In Azure Portal Click +Create a Resource in left pane> Networking> Virtual Networks> Create Virtual Network blade opens> Enter VNETCloud for name, Select RGCloud in Resource Group Box and Select East US 2 in location Box, Enter Web-Subnet in Subnet Name and click create.

Note: Rest select all values as default- DDoS Protection Basic, Service endpoints disabled and Firewall disabled. You need to scroll down to see these options.

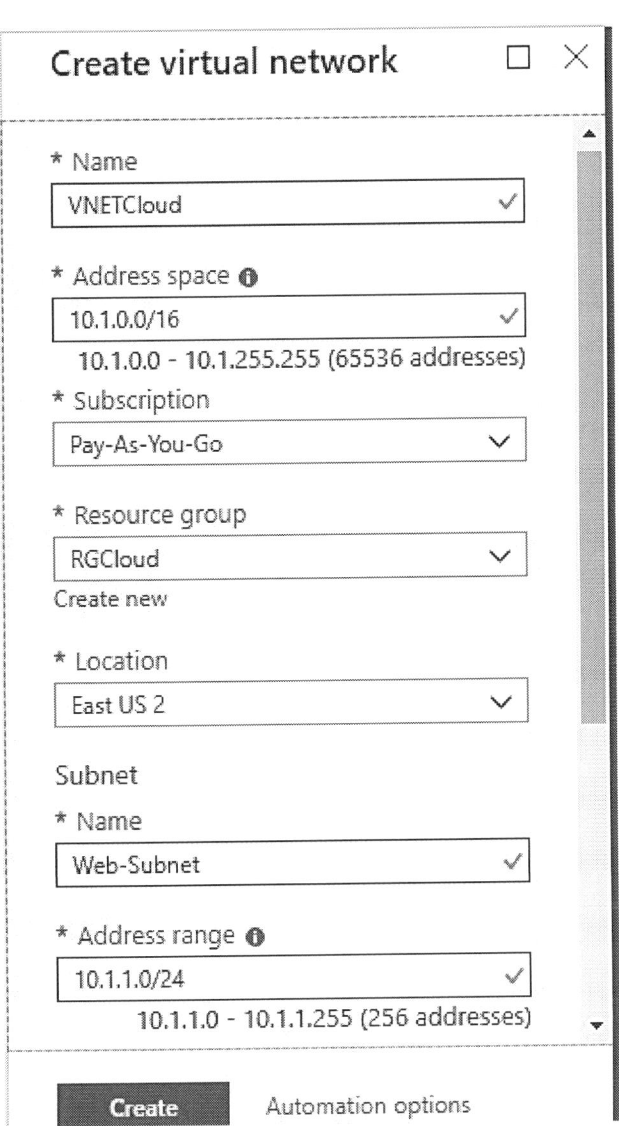

Figure below shows dashboard of Virtual Network VNETCloud.

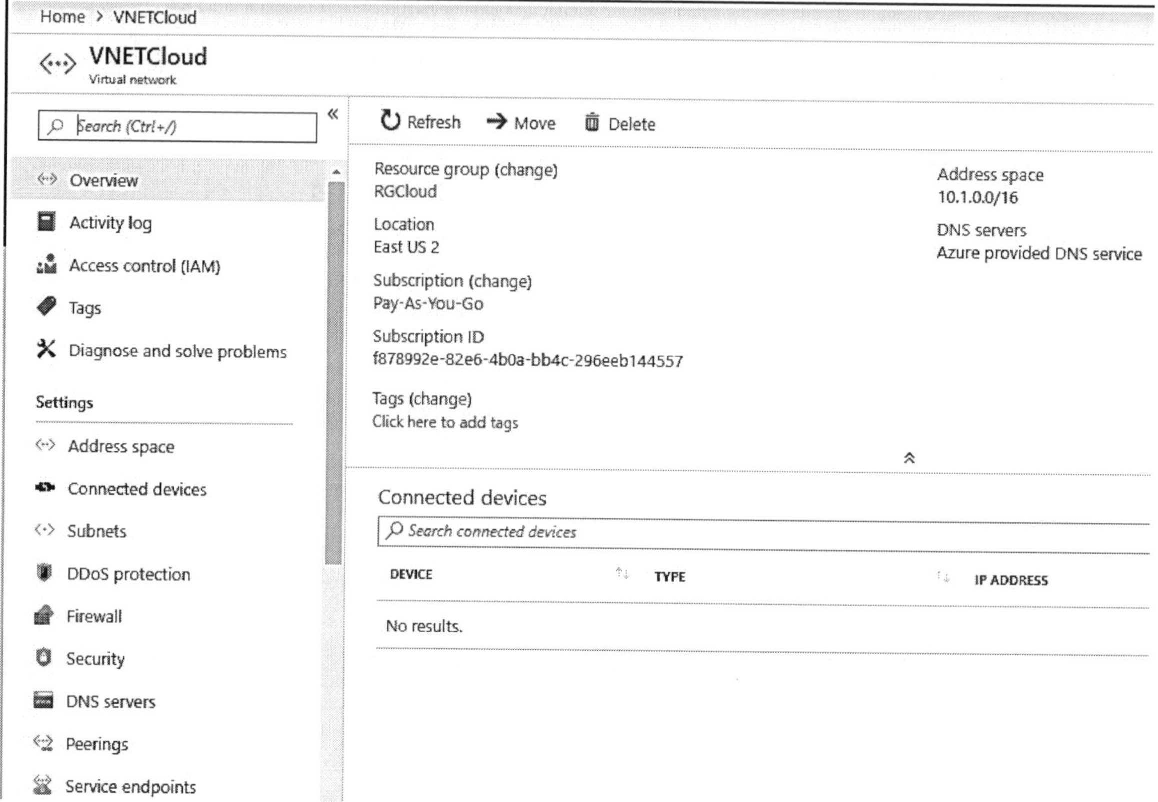

Exercise 4: Create additional Subnet (DB-Subnet 10.1.2.0/24)

1. Go to Virtual Network VNETCloud Dashboard> Click Subnets in left pane> Subnet blade opens. Web-Subnet was created during VNET creation time.

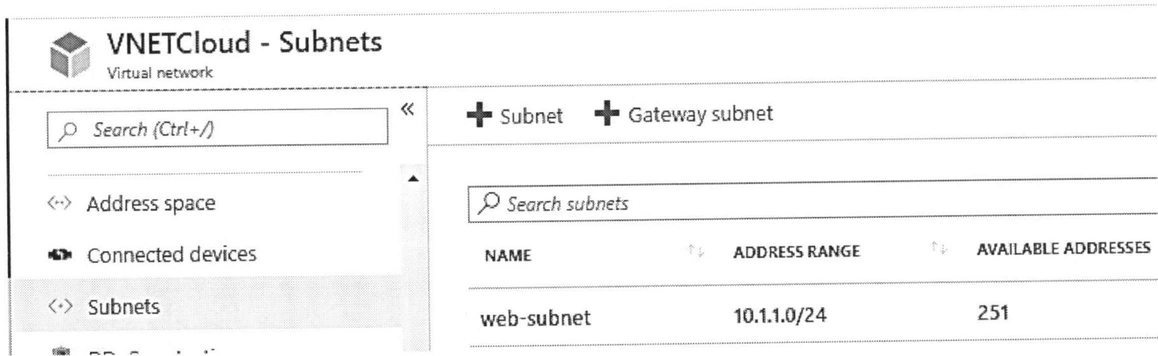

2. Click + Subnet>Add Subnet blade opens>Enter DB-Subnet in name and Address Range as 10.1.2.0/24. Select none for NSG and Route table, 0 for Service Endpoints and none for Subnet Delegation>Click Ok. NSG and Route Table will be discussed later in the chapter. Service Endpoints will be discussed in Chapter 5.

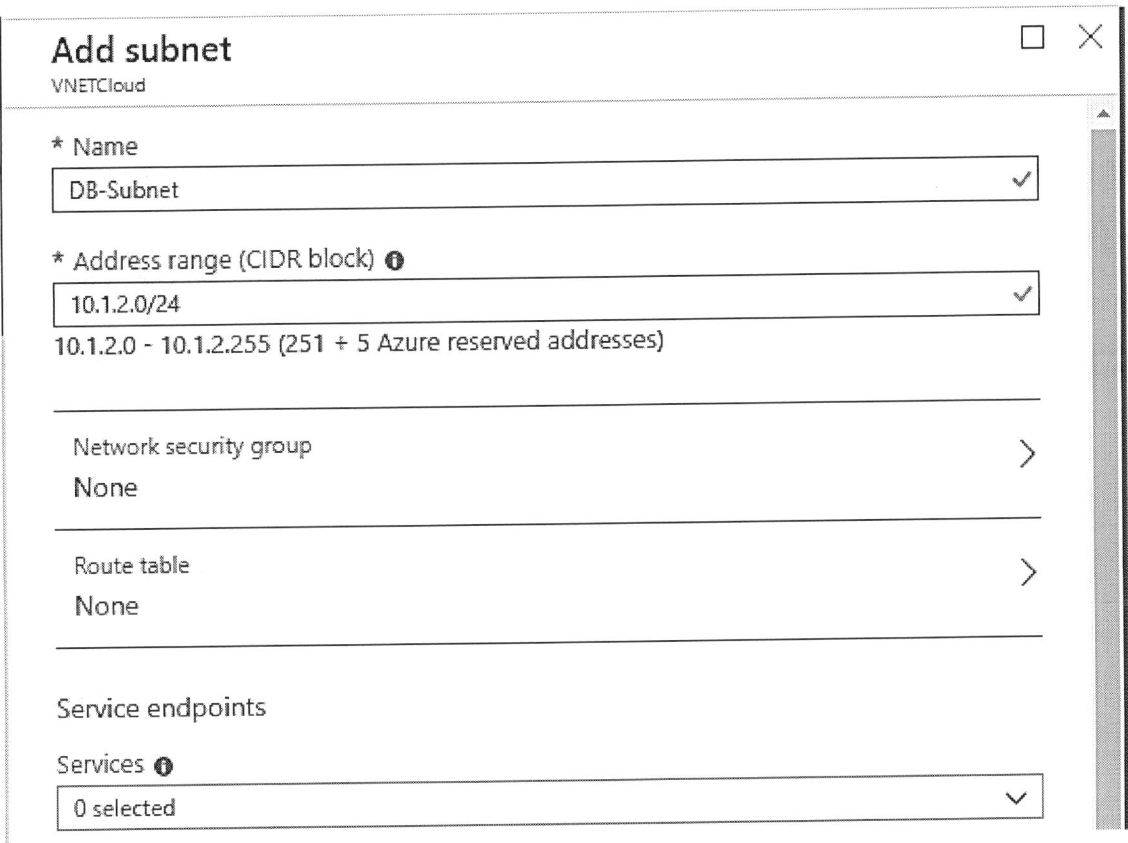

Exercise 5: Create additional Subnet (DMZ-Subnet 10.1.3.0/24)

1. In Virtual Network VNETCloud Dashboard Click Subnets in left pane> Subnet blade opens as shown below.

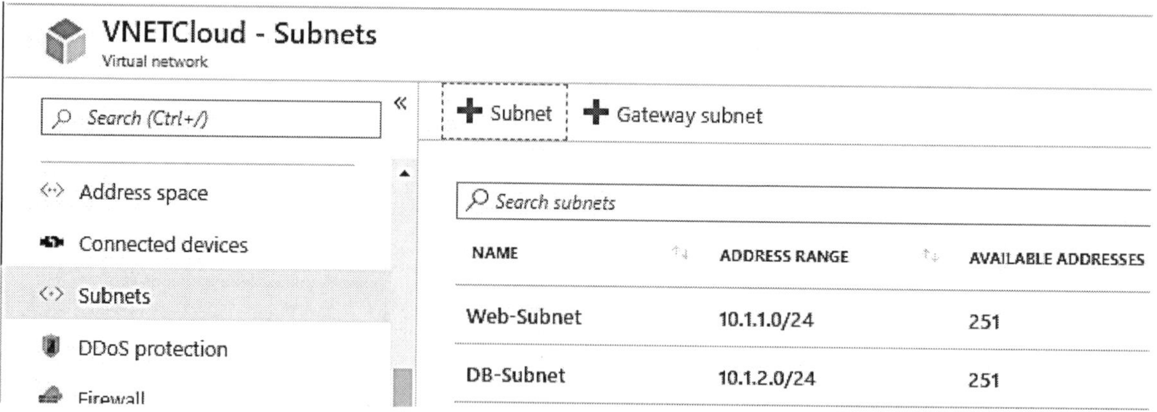

2. Click + Subnet>Add Subnet blade opens>Enter DMZ-Subnet in name and Address Range as 10.1.3.0/24. Select none for NSG, Route table & Subnet Delegation & 0 for Service Endpoints>Click Ok (Not Shown).

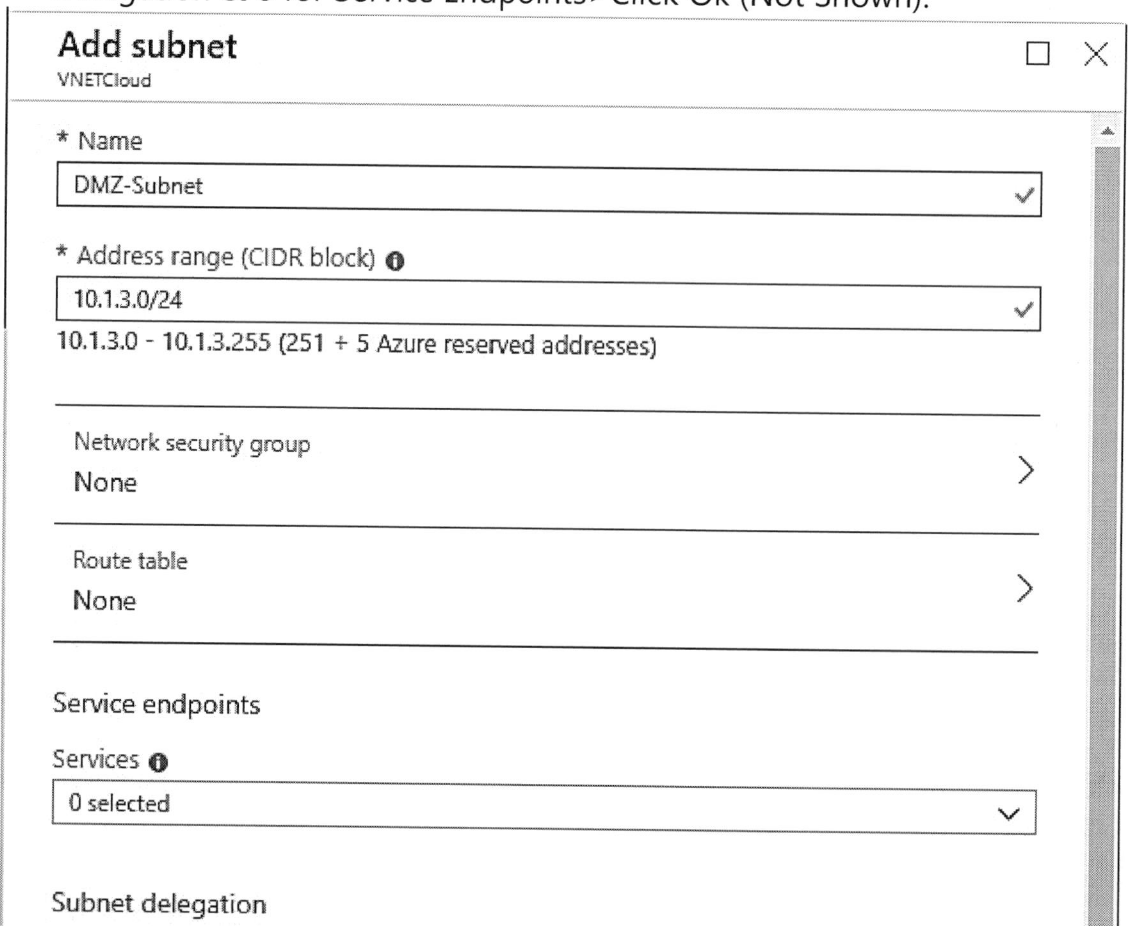

Exercise 6: Create Virtual Network representing On-Prem Network

In this exercise we will create Virtual Network **VNETOnPrem** in Resource Group **RGOnPrem** (Created in Exercise 2) using 192.168.0.0/16 address space in West US 2 Location. We will name Default Subnet as **OnPrem-Subnet** with address 192.168.1.0/24.
This Virtual Network will act as on-premises datacentre for our topology.

1. In Azure Portal Click +Create a Resource in left pane> Networking> Virtual Networks> Create Virtual Network blade opens> Enter **VNETOnPrem** for name, Select **RGOnPrem** in Resource Group Box and Select **West US 2** in location Box, Enter **OnPrem-Subnet** in Subnet Name and click create.

Note: Rest select all values as default.

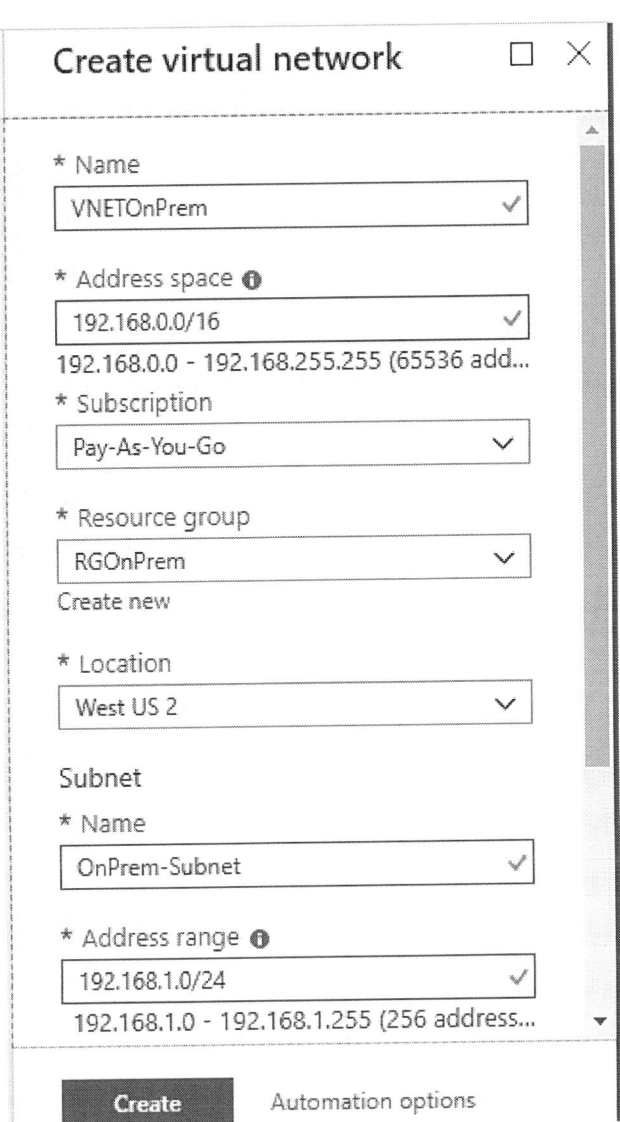

2. Figure below shows the Dashboard of Virtual Network VNETOnPrem.

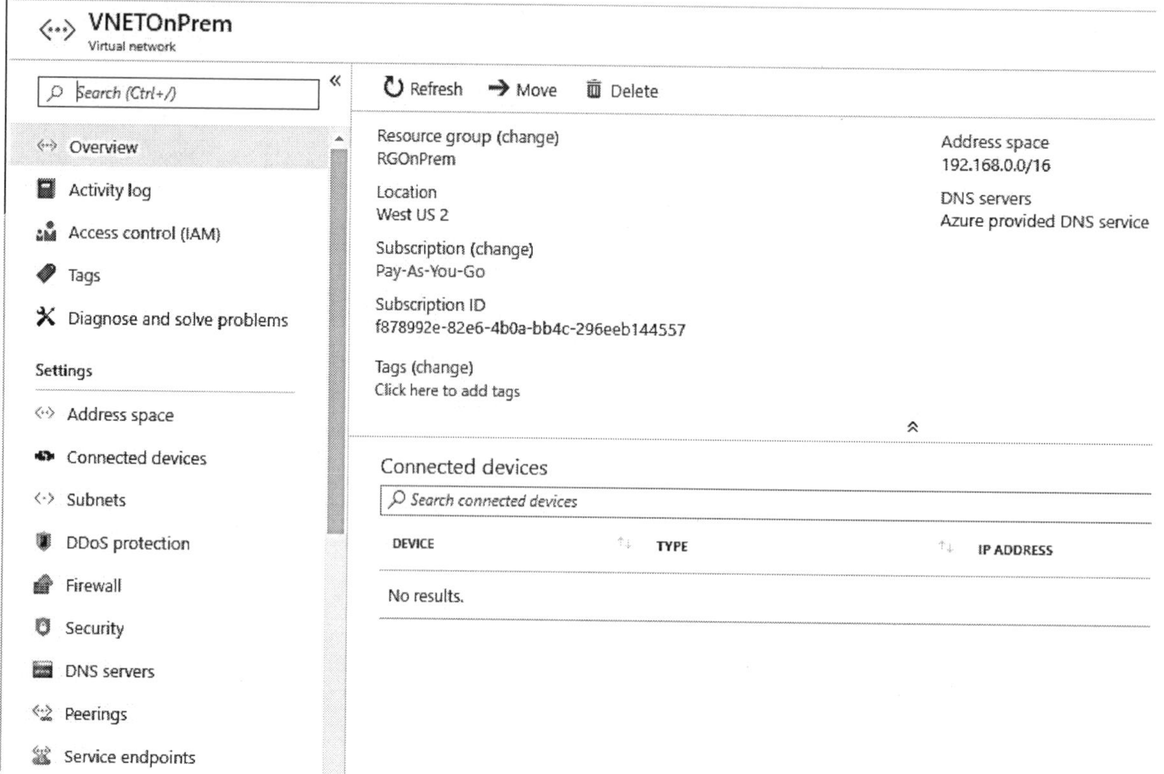

Exercise 7: Create Virtual Network VNETCloud2

In this exercise we will create Virtual Network **VNETCloud2** in Resource Group RGCloud using 10.7.0.0/16 address space. The Default Subnet Address will be changed to 10.7.1.0/24. **This Virtual Network will be used in Peering Lab Exercise 16.**

1. In Azure Portal Click +Create a Resource in left pane> Networking> Virtual Networks> Create Virtual Network blade opens> Enter VNETCloud2 for name, Select RGCloud in Resource Group Box and Select East US 2 in location Box and click create.

Note: Rest select all default values.

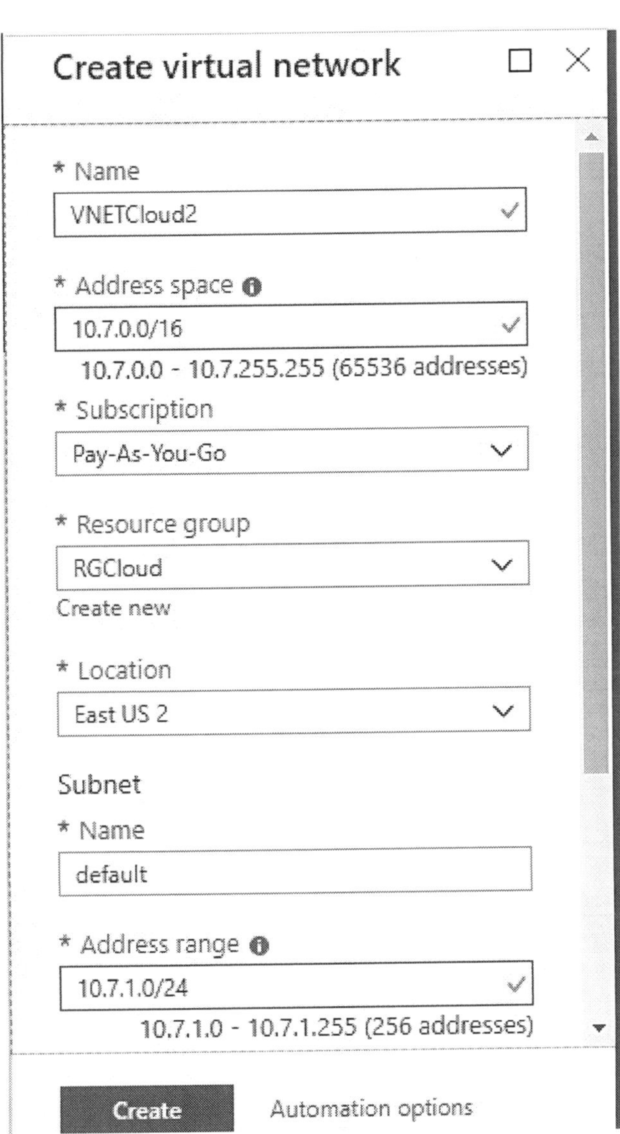

Exercise 8: Create Virtual Network VNETCloud3

In this exercise we will create Virtual Network **VNETCloud3** in Resource Group RGCloud using 10.8.0.0/16 address space. The Default Subnet Address will be changed to 10.8.1.0/24. **This Virtual Network will be used in Peering Lab Exercise 17.**

1. In Azure Portal Click +Create a Resource in left pane> Networking> Virtual Networks> Create Virtual Network blade opens> Enter VNETCloud2 for name, Select RGCloud in Resource Group Box and Select East US 2 in location Box and click create.

Note: Rest select all default values.

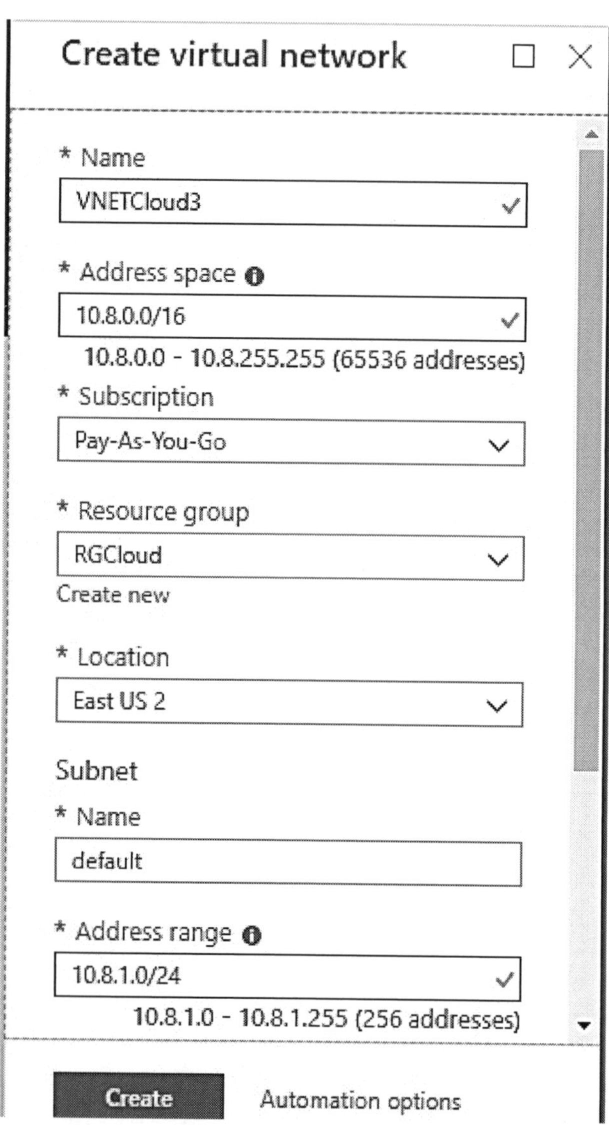

Virtual Networks Pricing & Limits

Virtual Network in Azure is free of charge.

Public IP addresses used on services inside a virtual network are charged. Virtual Machines & Network appliances such as VPN Gateway and Application Gateway that are run inside a virtual network are also charged.

The following limits apply for Virtual Network managed through Azure Resource Manager **per region per subscription.**

Resource	Default/Maximum
Virtual Networks	1000
Subnets per Virtual Network	3000
Virtual network peerings per virtual network	200
Private IP addresses per virtual network	65536

Note: Don't try to remember these limits.

Public IP Addresses in Azure

Public IP addresses allow Azure resources to communicate with Internet and to Azure public-facing services such as Azure Redis Cache, Azure Event Hubs, SQL databases, and Azure storage etc.

Public IP Address Allocation Methods

Dynamic Public IP: IP address is **not** allocated at the time of its creation. Instead, the Dynamic public IP address is allocated when you start or create the associated resource (like a VM or load balancer).
The IP address is released when you stop or delete the resource. This causes the IP address to change when you stop and start a resource.

Static Public IP: IP address for the associated resource remains the same when start or stop the resource.
In this case an IP address is assigned immediately. It is released only when you delete the resource or change its allocation method to *dynamic*.

You can associate a public IP address resource with following resources:

VMs | Internet-facing load balancers | VPN gateways | Application gateways

Azure Resource	Dynamic	Static
Virtual Machine	Yes	Yes
Internet-facing load balancers	Yes	Yes
VPN gateways	Yes	No
Application gateways	Yes	No

Static Public IP Use Case

Static Public IP addresses are often used for Web Servers that require SSL connections in which SSL certificate is linked to an IP address.

Types of Public IP Addresses (Basic & Standard)

Basic IP Address Features

1. Assigned with the static or dynamic allocation method.
2. Network security groups are recommended but optional for restricting inbound or outbound traffic.
3. Assigned to Azure resource such as network interfaces, VPN Gateways, Application Gateways, and Internet-facing load balancers.
4. Can be assigned to a specific zone. Not zone redundant.

Standard IP Address Features

1. Assigned with the static allocation method only.
2. Are secure by default and closed to inbound traffic. You must explicit whitelist allowed inbound traffic with a network security group.
3. Assigned to network interfaces or public standard load balancers.
4. Zone redundant by default.

Default DNS hostname resolution for Resources with Public IP

Resources with Public IP have Fully Qualified Domain Name in the format **resourcename.location.cloudapp.azure.com.**
For Example, if you create a public IP resource with **test** as a *resource name* in the **West US** Azure *location*, the fully qualified domain name (FQDN) **test.westus.cloudapp.azure.com** resolves to the public IP address of the resource.

DNS hostname resolution for Resources using Custom Domain options

If you want use your own domain name (Test.com) with Azure Resource with Public IP, you have 2 options depending upon IP Address allocation method.
Dynamic IP: Use cname record to point to Azure resource FQDN.
Static IP: You can either use A record name to point to Azure resource Public IP or use cname record to point Azure Resource FQDN.

Private IP Addresses

Private IP addresses allow Azure resources to communicate with other resources in a virtual network or an on-premises network through a VPN gateway or ExpressRoute circuit, without using an Internet-reachable IP address.

Private IP address is associated with following types of Azure resources:

1. VMs
2. Internal load balancers (ILBs)
3. Application gateways

Private IP Addresses are assigned from the subnet address range in which the resource is created. Private IP Address can be Static or Dynamic. Private IP Address is created during resource creation time.

Private Dynamic IP Address: Azure assigns the next available unassigned or unreserved IP address in the subnet's address range. Once assigned, dynamic IP addresses are only released if a network interface is deleted, assigned to a different subnet within the same virtual network, or the allocation method is changed to static, and a different IP address is specified.
Dynamic is the default allocation method.

Private Static IP Address: You select and assign any unassigned or unreserved IP address in the subnet's address range. Static addresses are only released if a network interface is deleted. Static Private IP Addresses are often used with DNS or Domain Controller VMs.

Internal DNS hostname resolution for virtual machines with Private IP using Azure Managed DNS Servers

When you create a virtual machine, a mapping for the hostname to its private IP address is added to the Azure-managed DNS servers by default.
These DNS servers provide name resolution for virtual machines that reside within the same virtual network. To resolve host names of virtual machines in different virtual networks, you must use a custom DNS server.

Exercise 9: Create Dynamic Public IP

In this Exercise we will create Dynamic Public IP in Resource Group RGCloud. Resource Group RGCloud was created in Exercise 1.

1. In Azure Portal Click **All Services** in left pane>Scroll down and Under Networking Click Public IP Addresses>All Public IP Addresses Dashboard opens>Click +Add>Create Public IP Address blade opens> Enter DPIPCloud in name box, Select Basic SKU, Select IP address as Dynamic, Give a unique DNS name dpipcloud, select RG RGCloud and Location EastUS2 > Click create.

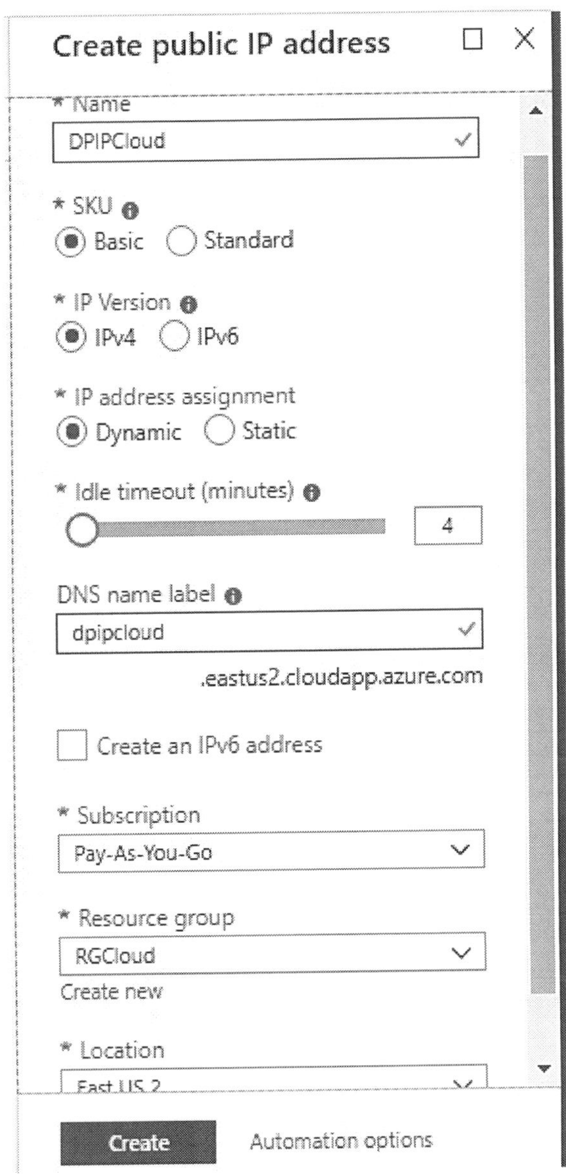

Note: You can create Public IP separately or create during Resource creation time. Figure below shows Dynamic Public IP "DPIPCloud" Dashboard.

Note that no address is assigned. Dynamic public IP address is allocated when you start or create the associated resource (like a VM or load balancer).

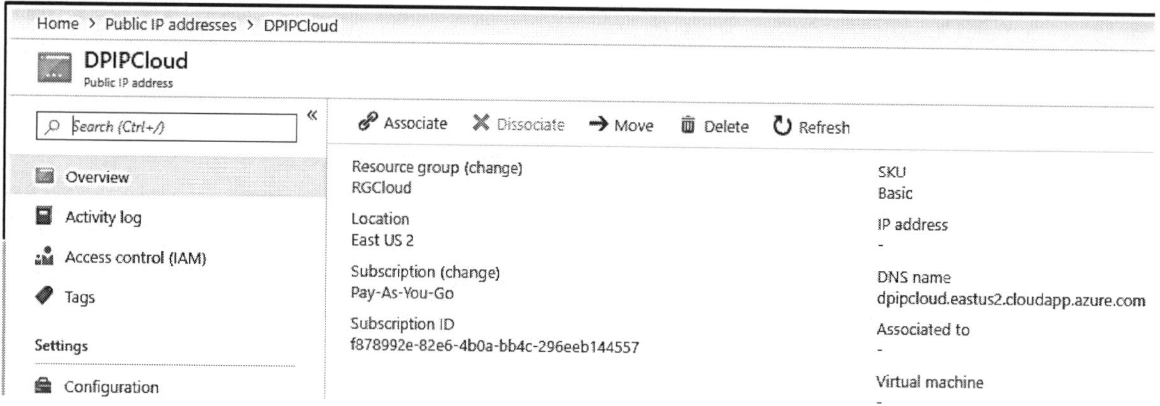

Exercise 10: Change Dynamic Public IP to Static IP

In Public IP "**DPIPPortal**" Dashboard Click Configuration in left pane>Select Static and click save.

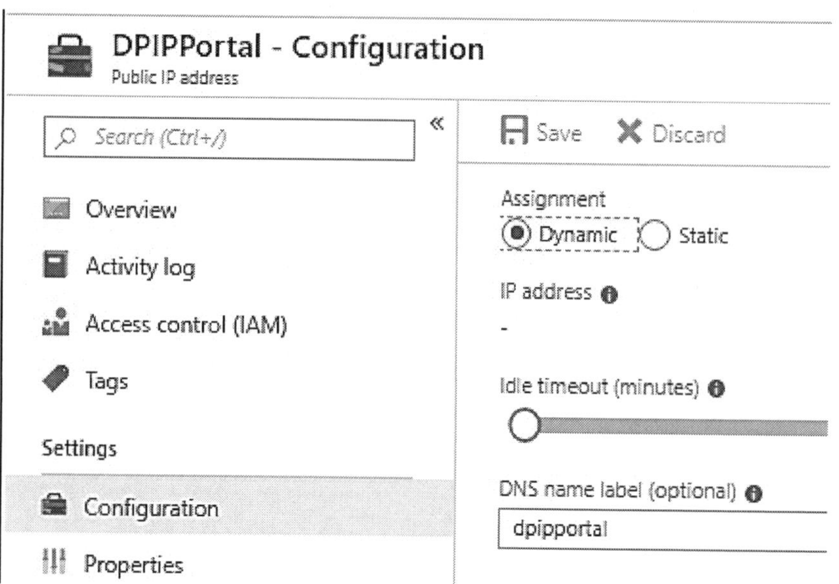

Public IP Addresses Pricing and Limits

The following limits apply for Public IP Addresses managed through Azure Resource Manager **per region per subscription.**

Resource	Default
Public IP addresses - dynamic	1,000 for Basic
Public IP addresses - static	1,000 for Basic
Public IP addresses - static	200 for Standard
Public IP prefix length	/28

Public IP Address Pricing

Type	Basic (ARM)	Standard (ARM)
Dynamic IP address	$0.004/hour	NA
Static IP address (reservation + usage)	First 5: $0.004/hour Additional: $0.008/hour	$0.005/hour
Public IP prefix	N/A	$0.006 per IP/hour

Note 1: Public IP prefix is a range of contiguous public IP addresses.
Note 2: Public IP prefixes are charged per IP per hour. As soon as a prefix is created, you are charged.

Network Security Groups

Network Security Group (NSG) is a Virtual Firewall. NSGs control **inbound** and **outbound** access to network interfaces (NICs) and subnets. Each NSG contains one or more rules specifying whether or not traffic is approved or denied based on source IP address, source port, destination IP address, destination port and protocol.

NSGs can be associated with subnets and network interfaces of Virtual Machines within that subnet. When a NSG is associated with a subnet, the ACL rules apply to all the VM instances in that subnet. In addition, traffic to an individual VM can be further restricted by associating a NSG directly to that VM NIC.

Figure below Shows VNET with 2 Subnets. Virtual Machine in Web-Subnet is protected by 2 Levels of NSG – NSG at Subnet level and NSG at Virtual Machine Network Interface level. Whereas Virtual Machine in DB-Subnet is protected by one level of NSG applied at Virtual Machine Network Interface Level.

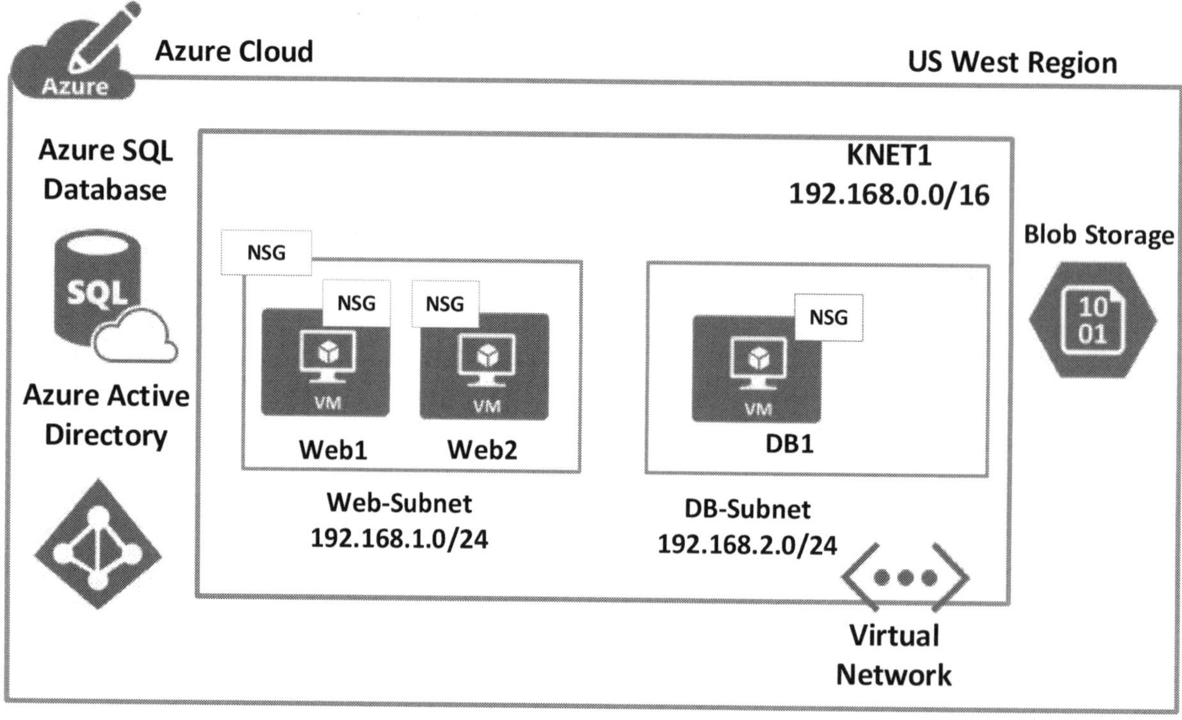

Default NSG rules

NSGs contain a set of default rules. The default rules cannot be deleted, but because they are assigned the lowest priority, they can be overridden by creating new rules with higher priority. **Higher the Number Lower the priority.**

Inbound default rules

Name	Priority	Source IP	Src Port	Dest IP	Dest Port	Protocol	Access
ALLOW VNET INBOUND	65000	VIRTUAL_NETWORK	*	VIRTUAL_NETWORK	*	*	Allow
ALLOW AZURE LOAD BALANCER INBOUND	65001	AZURE_LOADBALANCER	*	*	*	*	Allow
DENY ALL INBOUND	65500	*	*	*	*	*	Deny

Outbound default rules

Name	Priority	Source IP	Src Port	Dest IP	Dest Port	Protocol	Access
ALLOW VNET OUTBOUND	65000	VIRTUAL_NETWORK	*	VIRTUAL_NETWORK	*	*	Allow
ALLOW INTERNET OUTBOUND	65001	*	*	Internet	*	*	Allow
DENY ALL OUTBOUND	65500	*	*	*	*	*	Deny

- * Represent all addresses, Ports & Protocols.

We can infer following from the above default rules:

1. All VM to VM traffic within subnet or between subnets is allowed.
2. VM to internet traffic is allowed.
3. Azure Load balancer to VM is allowed.
4. Inbound internet to VM is blocked.
5. Default rules can be overridden by creating new rules with higher priority.

NSG Design Rules

1. By Default there is no NSG assigned to a subnet. But you have option of adding NSG during subnet creation or after subnet is created. To assign a NSG to a subnet you need to first create NSG.
2. Associating NSG to subnet is recommended and not compulsory.
3. You can apply only one NSG to a subnet or a VM NIC. But same NSG can be applied to multiple resources.
4. Deploy each tier of your workload into different subnet and then apply NSG to the subnets.
5. When implementing a subnet for a VPN gateway, or ExpressRoute circuit, do not apply an NSG to that subnet. If you do so, your cross-VNet or cross-premises connectivity will not work.
6. **Each NSG rules has a priority. Higher the priority number, lower the priority. You can override default NSG by creating new NSG rules with higher priority than default rules.**

Note: This topic is relevenat for both AZ-300 & AZ-301.

Service Tags for identification of category of IP Addresses in NSG Rules

Service tags are system-provided identifiers to address a category of IP addresses. Service tags are used in the source address prefix and destination address prefix properties of any NSG rule.

1. **VirtualNetwork**: This default tag denotes virtual network address space assigned to Azure Virtual Network.
2. **AzureLoadBalancer**: This default tag denotes Azure's Infrastructure load balancer. This will translate to an Azure datacenter IP where Azure's health probes originate.
3. **Internet**: This default tag denotes the IP address space that is outside the virtual network and reachable by public Internet. This range includes Azure owned public IP space as well.
4. **AzureTrafficManager**: This tag denotes the IP address space for the Azure Traffic Manager probe IPs.
5. **Storage**: This tag denotes the IP address space for the Azure Storage service. If you specify *Storage* for the value, traffic is allowed or denied to storage. If you only want to allow access to storage in a specific region, you can specify the region.
6. **Sql**: This tag denotes the address prefixes of the Azure SQL Database and Azure SQL Data Warehouse services. If you specify *Sql* for the value, traffic is allowed or denied to Sql.
7. **AzureCosmosDB** (Resource Manager only): This tag denotes the address prefixes of the Azure Cosmos Database service. If you specify AzureCosmosDB for the value, traffic is allowed or denied to AzureCosmosDB.
8. **AzureKeyVault** (Resource Manager only): This tag denotes the address prefixes of the Azure KeyVault service. If you specify *AzureKeyVault* for the value, traffic is allowed or denied to AzureKeyVault.

Effective NSG Permissions

NSG can be applied at Subnet or VM NIC level or both Subnet and VM NIC.

Let's take an example to check what's the effective traffic reaching Virtual Machine when NSG is applied at both Subnet and VM NIC level. We have 2 VMs (App-Prod & App-Test) created in App Subnet as shown in below figure.

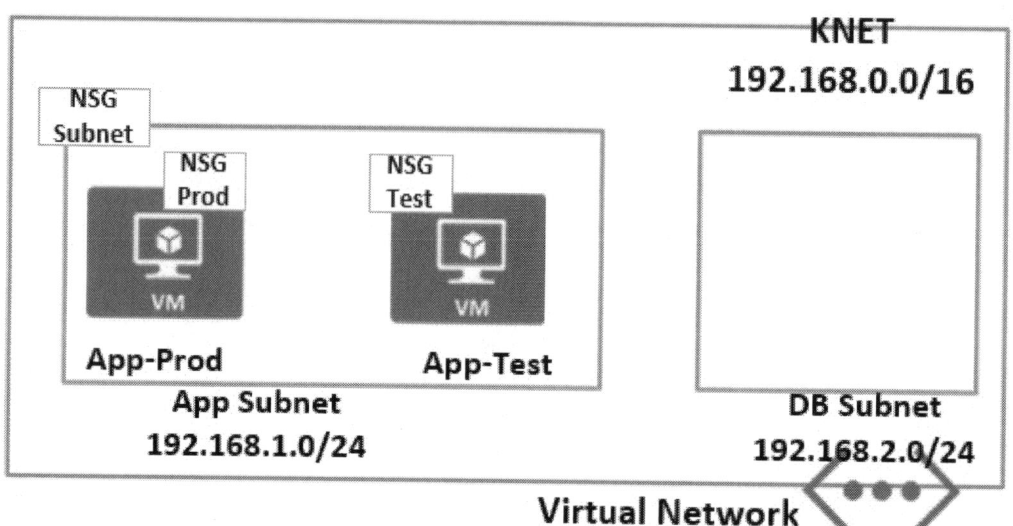

NSGSubnet has 3 inbound allow rules - http, https & RDP.
NSGProd has 2 inbound allow rules - https & RDP.
NSGTest has 2 inbound allow rules - http & RDP.

Effective traffic entering the subnet is http, https & RDP. NSGSubnet blocks any other traffic apart from http, https & RDP.

Effective traffic entering VM App-prod is https & RDP. NSGProd blocks http traffic.

Effective traffic entering VM App-Test is http & RDP. NSGTest blocks https traffic.

Exercise 11: Create NSG and add inbound http, RDP and SSH allow rule

In this Exercise we will create Network Security Group **NSGCloud** in resource group **RGCloud** and in **US East 2** Location. We will add inbound http, RDP & SSH allow rule in NSGCloud. This rule will allow http, RDP & SSH traffic to **Windows VM & Linux VM in Web-Subnet.** Windows and Linux VM will be created in compute chapter 2. In Next exercise we will associate this rule with Web-Subnet in Virtual Network VNETCloud.

1. In_Azure_Portal_Click + Create a resource>Networking>Network Security Group>Create Network Security Group opens> Enter a name, Select resource group RGCloud, Select Location East US 2 and Click create.

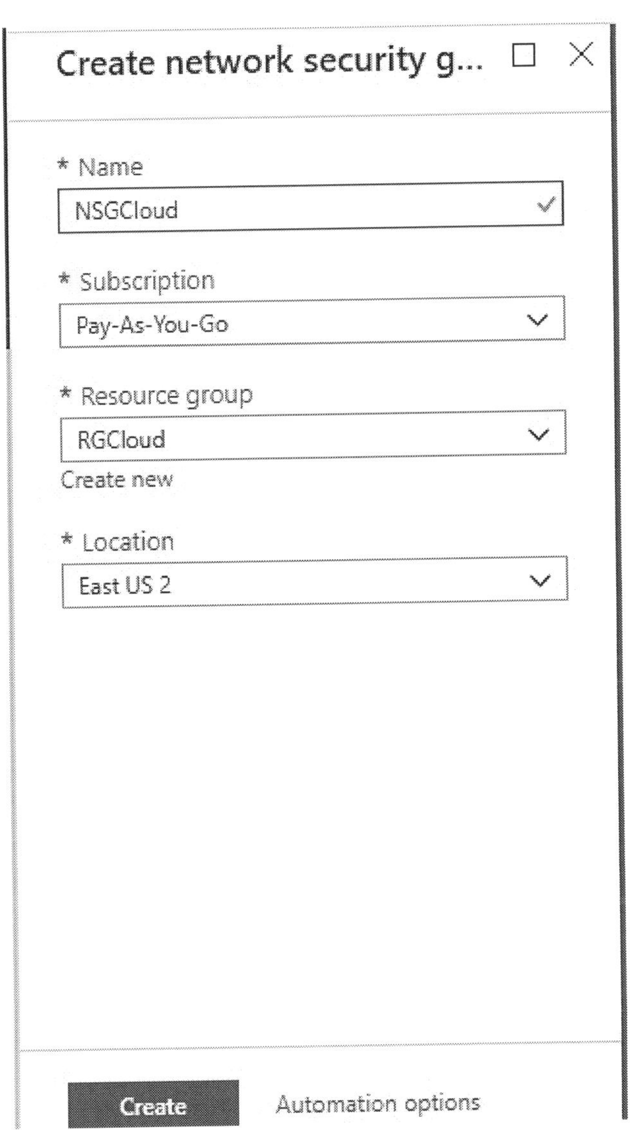

2. Figure below shows Network Security Group NSGCloud Dashboard with default inbound and outbound security rules.

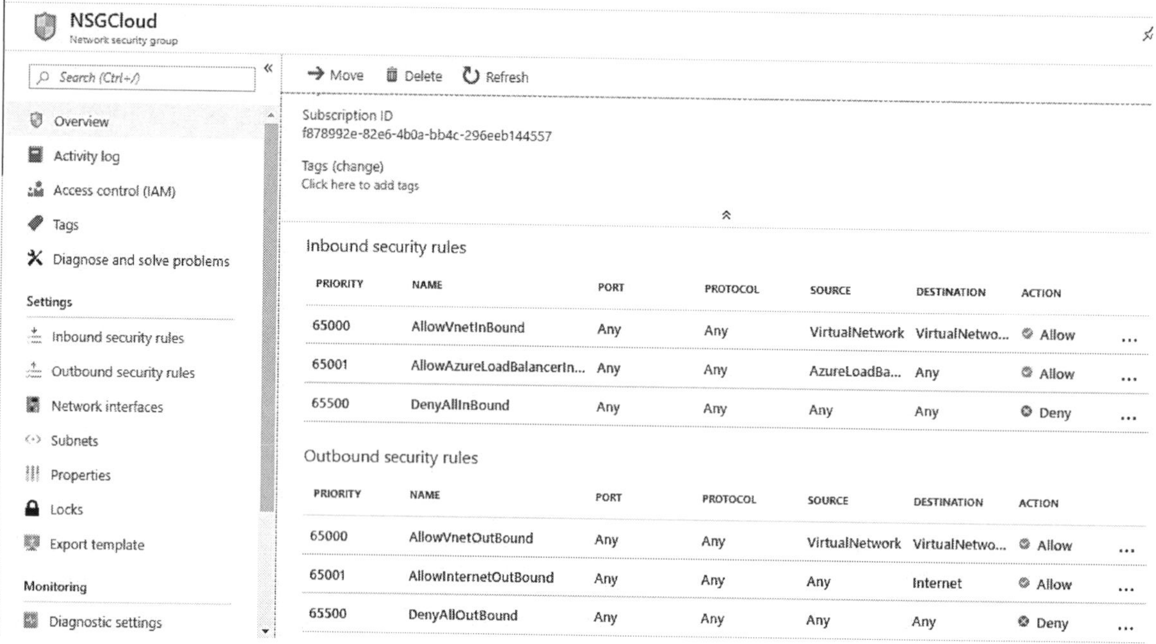

Note on Inbound Rules

Note 1: In inbound security rules, all inbound traffic is set to deny (Rule number 3) except for VNET to VNET and Azure Load Balancer to Any.

Note 2: Best Practice is to create a new inbound rule and allow traffic which is needed. Do not make this rule allow for all the traffic.

Note 3: Override Default inbound rule by creating new rule with higher priority or lower number than the default inbound rule.

Note 4: In next step we will allow inbound HTTP, RDP and SSH traffic to windows server VM and Linux VM in web-subnet. Windows Server VM and Linux VM will be created in compute chapter.

Note on Outbound Rules

Note 1: Internet outbound is allowed.
Note 2: Outbound VNET to VNET is allowed.

3. **Add inbound RDP rule**: In NSG dashboard click inbound security rules in left pane>In Right pane click +Add>Add inbound security rule blade opens> In Destination Port Ranges Enter RDP port number **3389** > Assign Priority of **100**>Give a name to the rule> Rest select all default values and click Add.

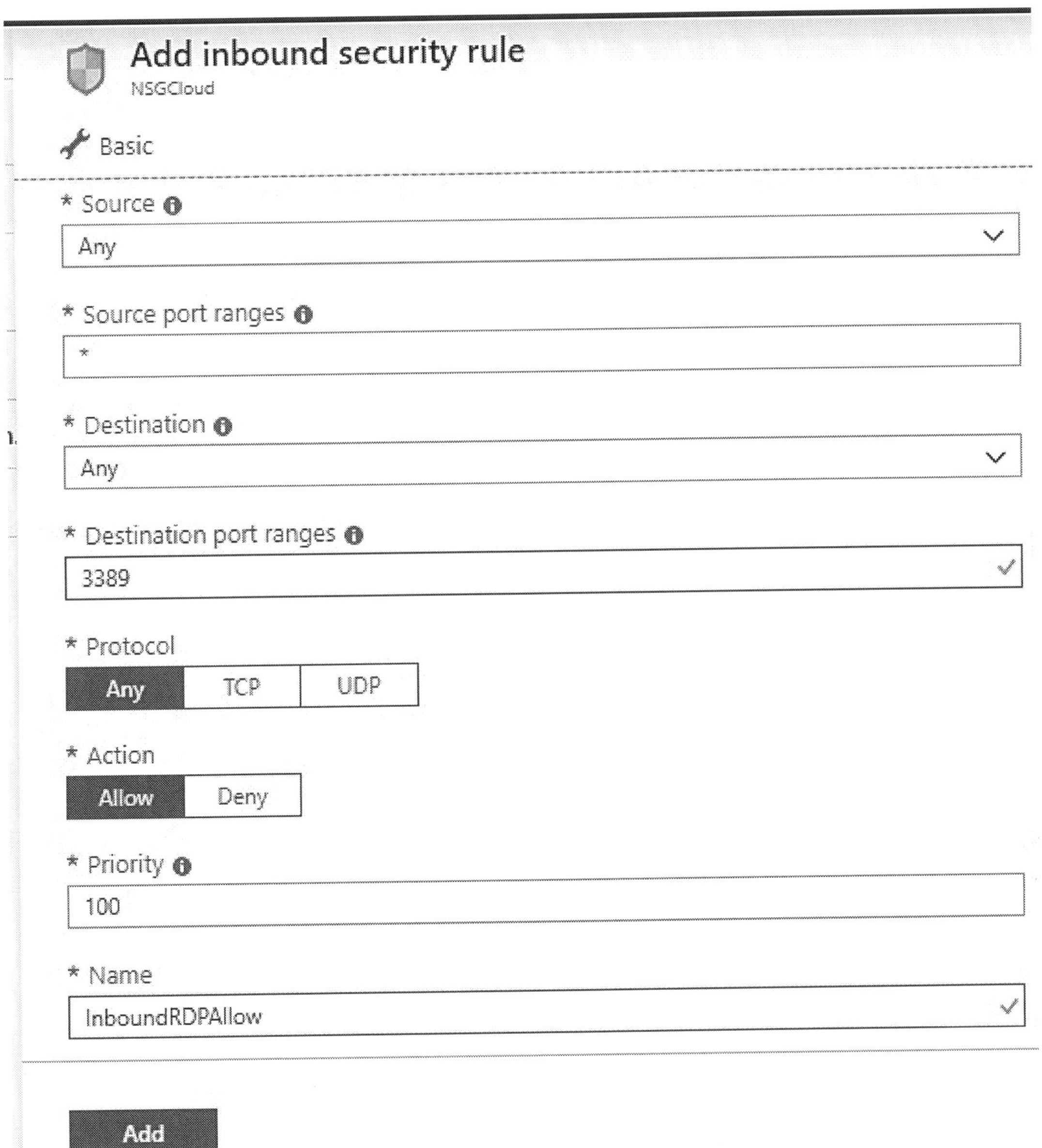

Note: Readers are advised to click the Source and destination drop boxes to see the options.

4. **Add inbound allow http rule**: Similarly add allow http rule. Enter http port **80** in destination port range> Assign Priority of **110**>Give a name to the rule> Rest select all default values and click Add.

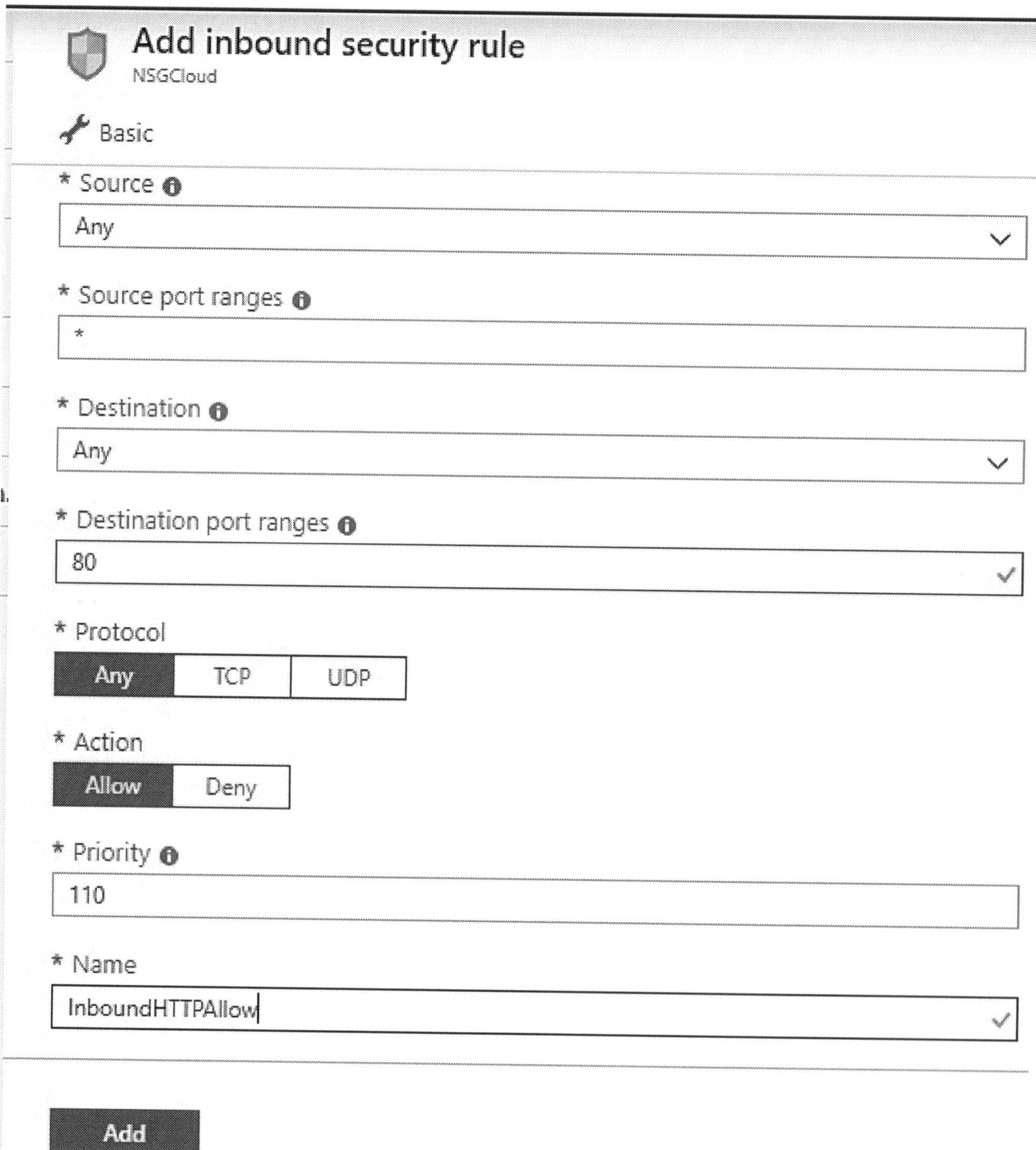

5. **Add inbound allow SSH rule**: Similarly add allow SSH rule. Enter SSH port **22** in destination port range> Assign Priority of **120**>Give a name to the rule> Rest select all default values and click Add.

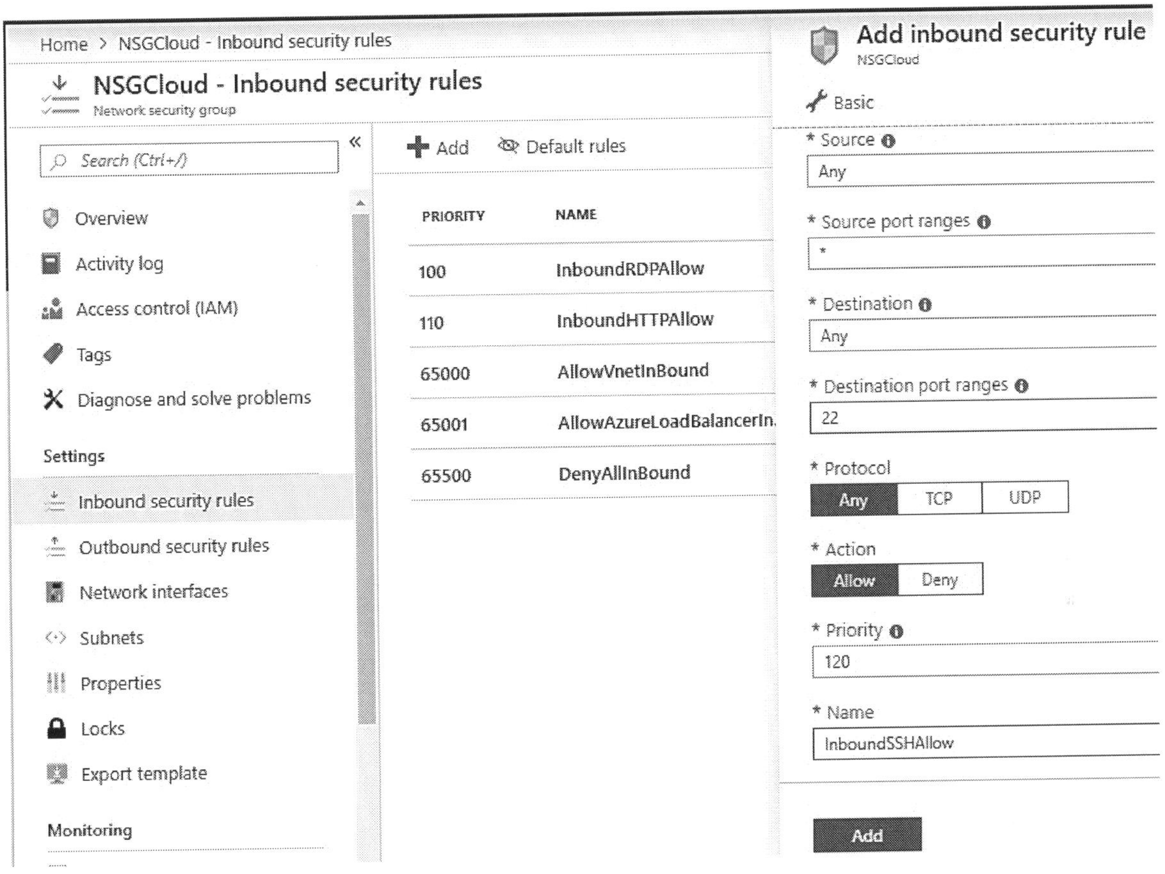

6. Figure below shows inbound rules with 3 new rules added.

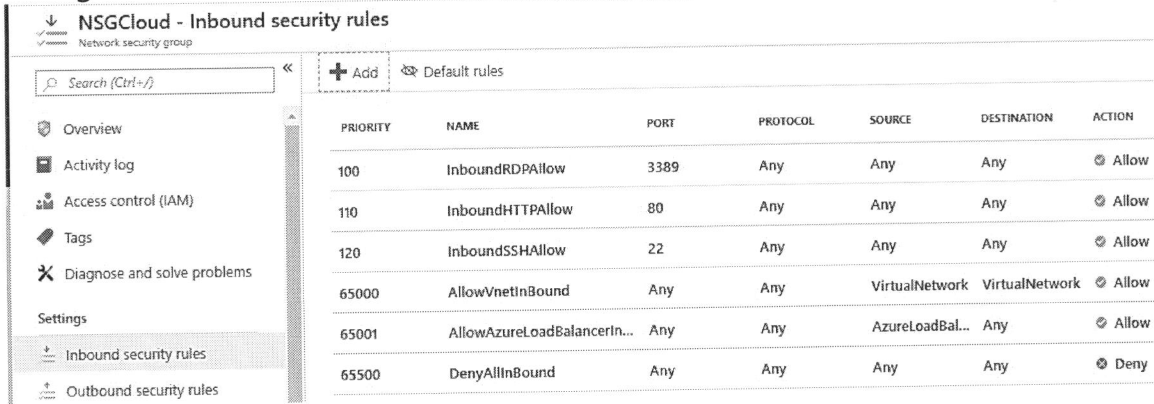

Note 1: You can edit the rule by clicking the rule in the right pane or delete the rule by clicking ellipsis ..(Not shown).
Note 2: You cannot edit or delete the default rules (65000, 65001 & 65500).

Exercise 12: Associate Network Security Group (NSG) with Subnet

In this exercise we will associate Network Security Group NSGCloud created in previous exercise with Web-Subnet in Virtual Network VNETCloud.

1. In NSG Dashboard click Subnets in left pane.

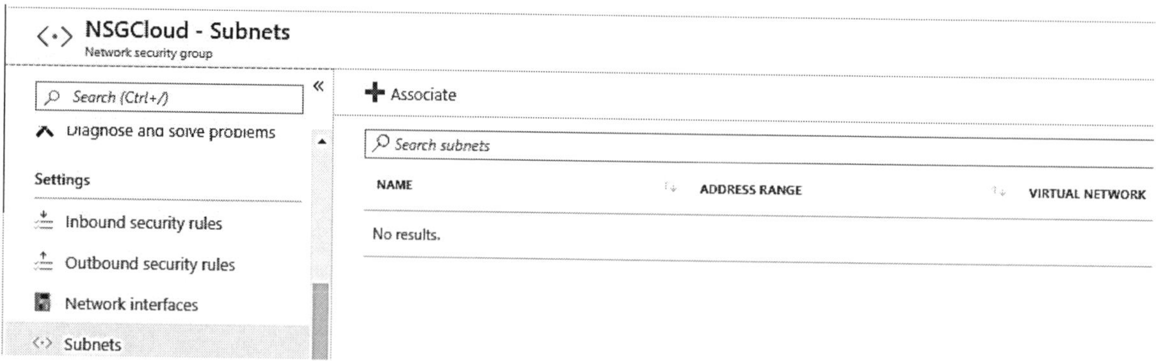

2. In right pane click +Associate > Associate Subnet blade opens> In Associate Subnet Blade select Virtual Network VNETCloud & Subnet Web-Subnet and click ok (Not Shown).

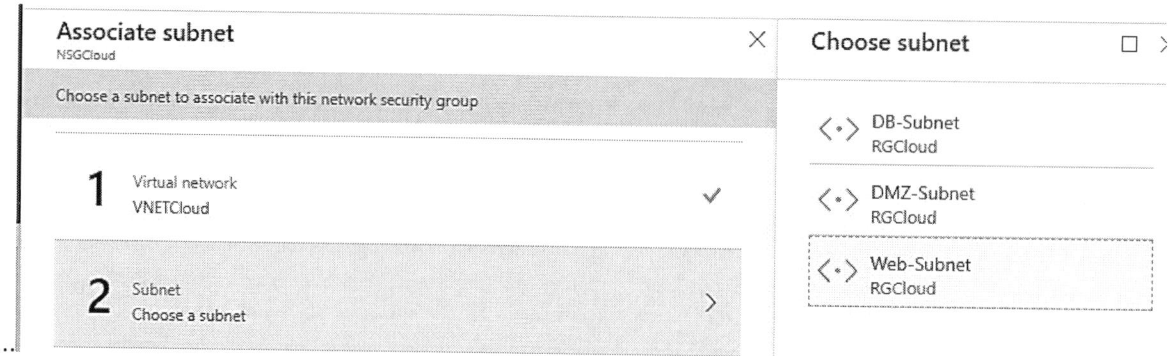

3. Figure below shows Web-Subnet in VNETCloud associated with NSG.

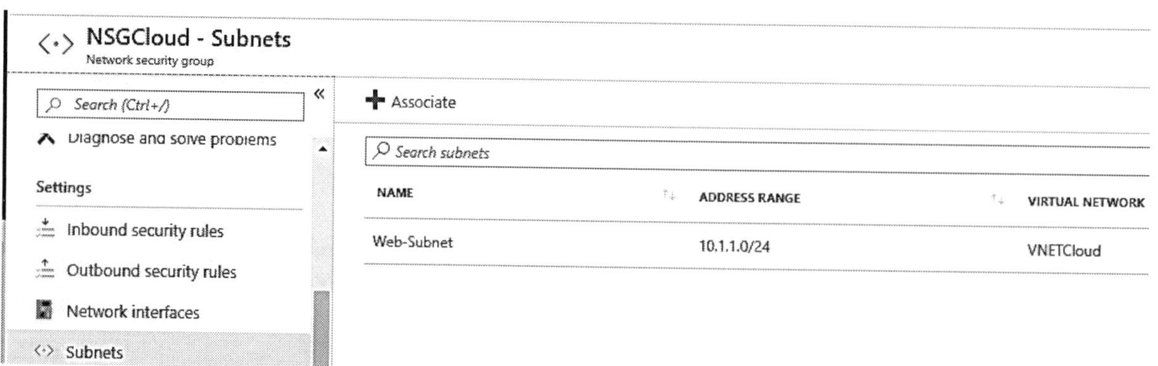

Exercise 13: Exploring IP Address Option in Network Security Group

Go to Network Security Group NSGCloud Dashboard>Click Inbound security rules or oubound security rules in left pane> In Right pane click +Add> Add Inbound security rules blade opens>In Source select IP Address> Here you can specify the IP Address as source.

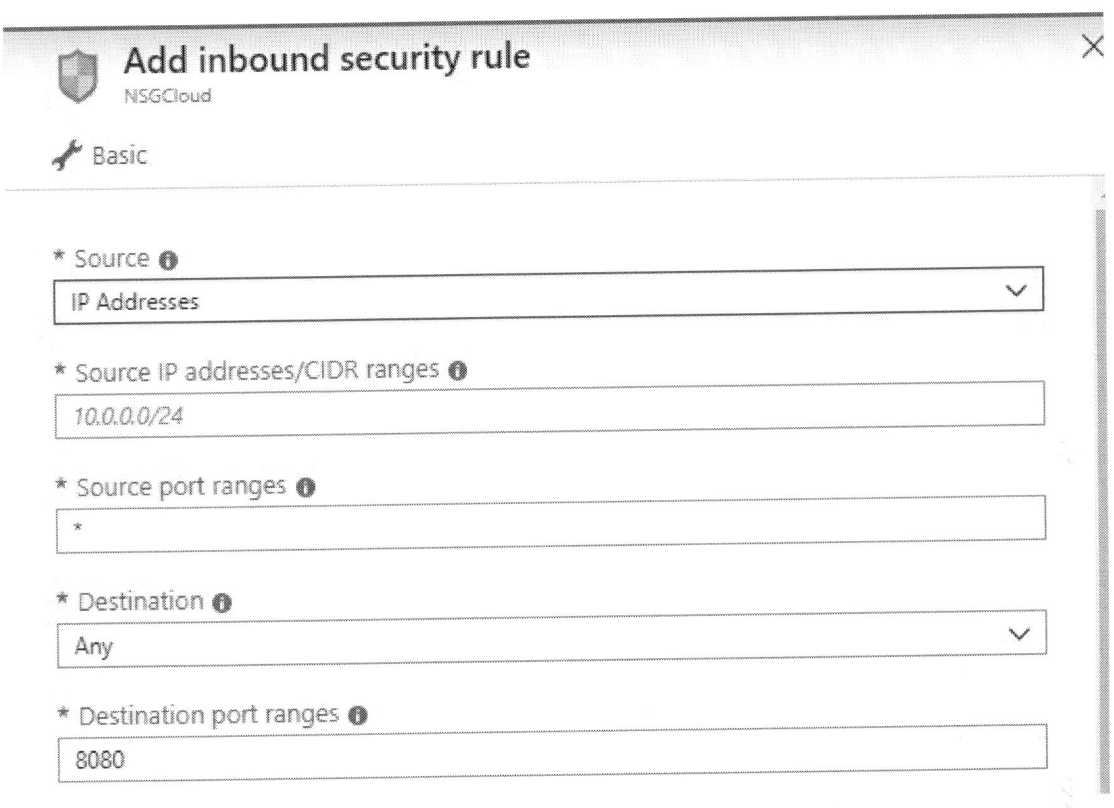

Similarly you can select IP address option in destination if required.

Same options are available with outbound security rules also.

Exercise 14: Exploring Tag Option in Network Security Group

Go to Network Security Group NSGCloud Dashboard>Click Inbound security rules in left pane> In Right pane click +Add> Add Inbound security rules blade opens>In Source select Service Tag> Here you can select options like Internet, Virtual Network and Load Balancer in Source.

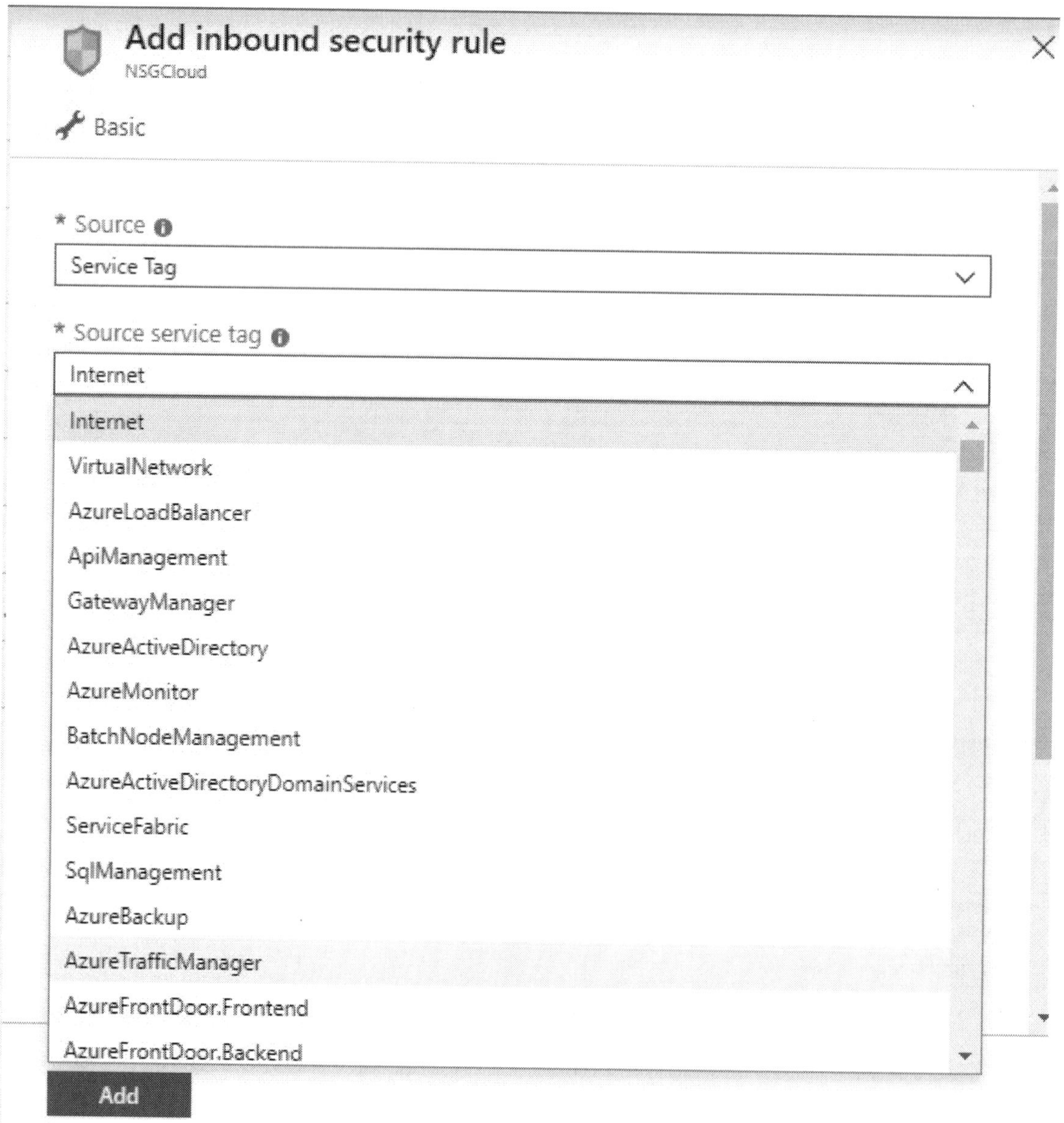

Similarly you can select Service Tag option in destination if required. Same options are available with outbound security rules also.

NSG Pricing & Limits

Network Security Group (NSG) in Azure is free of charge.

1. NSGs per region per subscription: 5000
2. NSG rules per NSG: 1000

Design Nugget: Number of NSGs you can associate to a subnet or NIC: 1
Design Nugget: You can associate same NSG to Multiple Subnets or/and NICs.

Name Resolution with Azure DNS

Before going into Azure DNS let's discuss about DNS. DNS or Domain Name System translates domain name to IP Address. The process of DNS resolution involves converting a hostname such as www.test.com into IP address such as 192.168.10.1. When a user wants to access www.test.com, a translation occurs between test.com and the IP address assigned to End user Server. This whole translation involves Global infrastructure of DNS Servers including top level name servers, root servers and Authoritative name server for that particular domain etc.

Azure DNS is a managed hosting service which provides Global infrastructure of name servers to translate Domain Name to IP Address. Azure DNS is a hosting service for DNS domains (Containing DNS Records of a Domain), providing name resolution using Microsoft Azure infrastructure.

Design Nugget: You can't use Azure DNS to buy a domain name.

Features and Benefits of Azure DNS

Availability: DNS domains in Azure DNS are hosted on Azure's global network of DNS name servers which can withstand Datacentre or a Region failure.
Performance: Azure DNS uses anycast networking so that each DNS query is answered by the closest DNS server available to user. This provides fast performance.
Ease of use: You can manage your DNS records using the same credentials, APIs, tools, and billing as your other Azure services. You can use Azure portal, Cli or PowerShell to manage Azure DNS.
Security: Azure DNS can be secured using RBAC & Resource locking. You can use Activity logs to monitor user actions and for troubleshooting.
DNS Record types: Azure DNS supports all common DNS record types including A, AAAA, CAA, CNAME, MX, NS, PTR, SOA, SRV, and TXT records.

Solution Components of Azure DNS

DNS Zones
DNS Records
Delegation to Azure DNS Name Servers from Domain Registrar of your domain.

Working in Brief

Using Azure DNS create DNS Zone. DNS Zone creates 4 Name Servers for Your Domain. In DNS Zone, you add DNS records (A, CNAME or MX) pointing to your resource. In domain registrar where you have registered you domain, add Azure DNS Name servers which will delegate DNS Name resolution to Azure DNS Name servers for your domain.

DNS Zones & Records

A DNS zone is used to host the DNS records for a particular domain. DNS record for your domain is created inside this DNS zone. For example, the domain 'contoso.com' may contain several DNS records, such as 'mail.contoso.com' (MX record for a mail server) and 'www.contoso.com' (A record for a web site).

DNS Records

DNS records are mapping files that tell the DNS server which IP address each domain is associated with, and how to handle requests sent to each domain. Each DNS record has a name and a type. Azure DNS supports all common DNS record types including A, AAAA, CAA, CNAME, MX, NS, PTR, SOA, SRV, and TXT.

A Record: An A record points a domain or subdomain to an IP address.
MX Record: A MX record specifies a mail server responsible for accepting email messages on behalf of a recipient's domain.
CNAME or Alias Record: A CNAME Record points one domain or subdomain to another domain. For Example when you create Azure VM it is assigned a domain name in the form pipportal.eastus2.cloudapp.azure.com. Using CNAME records you can use **www.test.com** to point to pipportal.eastus2.cloudapp.azure.com.
NS Record: NS record set contains the names of the Azure DNS name servers assigned to the zone. The NS record is set at the zone apex and is created automatically with each DNS zone, and is deleted automatically when the zone is deleted
SOA Record: A start of authority (SOA) record is information stored in a domain name system (DNS) zone about that zone and about other DNS records. Each zone contains a single SOA record. The SOA record stores information about the name of the server that supplied the data for the zone; the administrator of the zone; the current version of the data file; the number of seconds a secondary name server should wait before checking for updates; the number of seconds a secondary name server should wait before retrying a failed zone transfer; the maximum number of seconds that a secondary name server can use data before

it must either be refreshed or expire; and a default number of seconds for the time-to-live file on resource records.

Time to Live (TTL)

TTL specifies how long each record is cached by clients before being re-queried.

Exercise 15: DNS Zone, DNS Records and Delegation to Azure DNS

For this exercise we will use **mykloud.in** domain which is registered with Domain Registrar Go Daddy. We will Create DNS Zone and Add DNS A Record pointing to VM VMFE1 Public IP Address (137.116.68.235). We will then delegate DNS Resolution for myKloud.in domain to Azure DNS Name servers.

Note 1: Do this Exercise after you have done Exercise 25 in Chapter 4 where VM VMFE1 was deployed.

Step 1 Create DNS Zone

1. In Azure Portal Click All Services>Networking>DNS Zone>All DNS Zone blade opens>Click +ADD>Create DNS Zone blade opens as shown below>In Resource Group select RGCloud>In Name enter **mykloud.in**> Click Review + Create>After validation is passed click create.

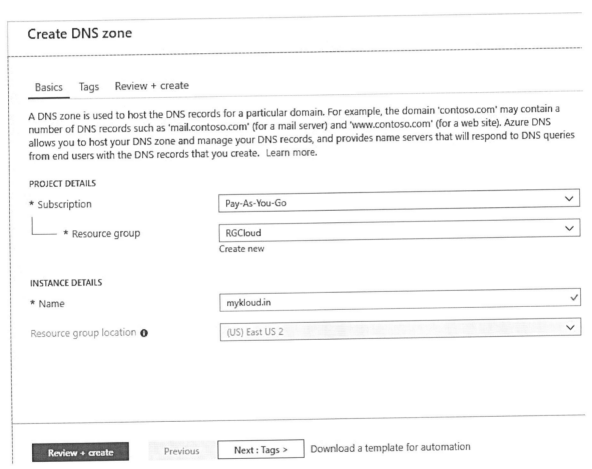

Create DNS zone

Basics Tags Review + create

A DNS zone is used to host the DNS records for a particular domain. For example, the domain 'contoso.com' may contain a number of DNS records such as 'mail.contoso.com' (for a mail server) and 'www.contoso.com' (for a web site). Azure DNS allows you to host your DNS zone and manage your DNS records, and provides name servers that will respond to DNS queries from end users with the DNS records that you create. Learn more.

PROJECT DETAILS

* Subscription: Pay-As-You-Go

* Resource group: RGCloud

Create new

INSTANCE DETAILS

* Name: mykloud.in

Resource group location: (US) East US 2

Review + create | Previous | Next : Tags > | Download a template for automation

2. Figure below shows DNS Zone Dashboard. There are 4 Name Servers- ns1, ns2, ns3 & ns4. The SOA is ns1.

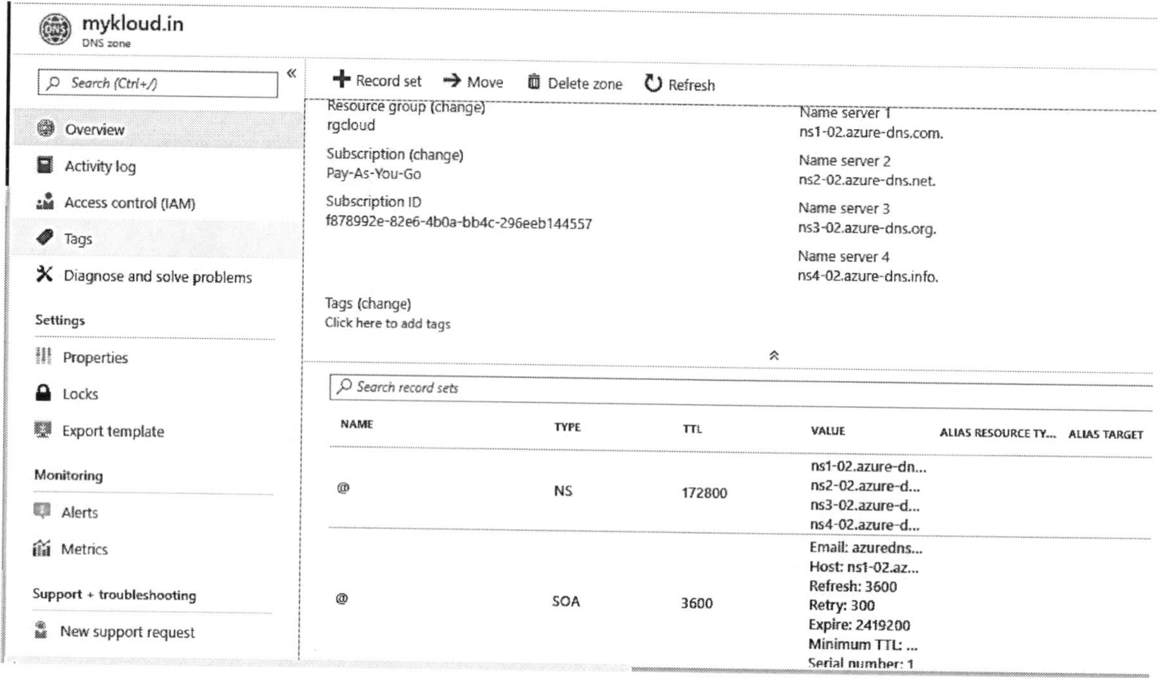

Step 2 Create DNS Records: In DNS Zone dashboard click +Record Set>Add Record Set Blade opens>In Name enter **www**>Select Record type A> In IP address enter 137.116.68.235 >Click Ok (Not Shown).

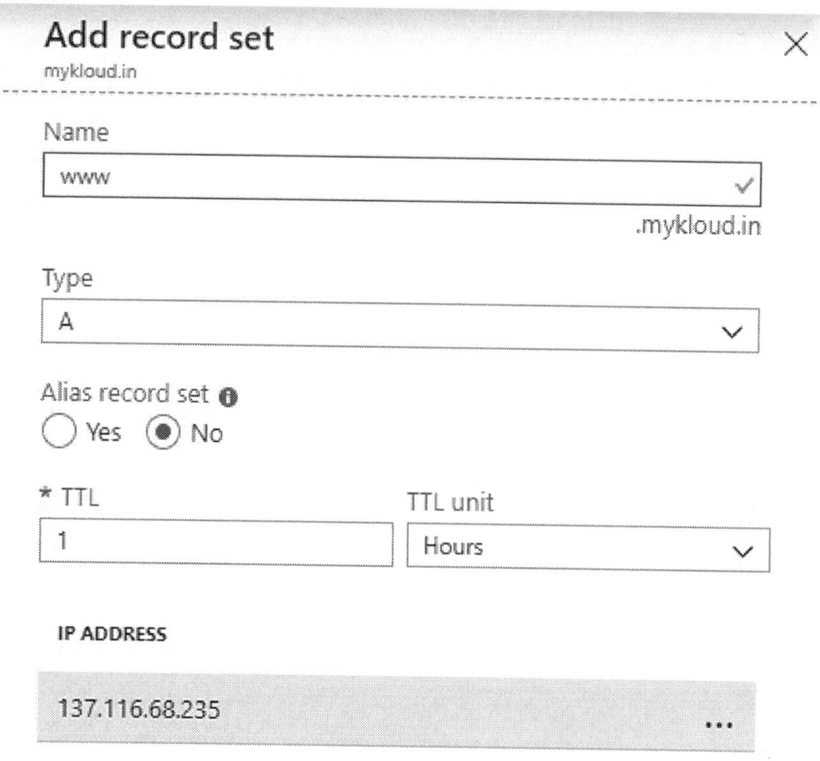

Step 3 Add Azure DNS Name Servers in Go Daddy Portal for delegation

1. Copy the Name servers from DNS Zone Dashboard.
2. Go to Go Daddy DNS Management page>Scroll down and you can see Name Servers for mykloud.in

Nameservers

Last updated 19-03-2019 11:39 AM

Using default nameservers **Change**

Nameserver
ns73.domaincontrol.com
ns74.domaincontrol.com

3. Click change>Select Custom from dropdown box>Click Add Name Server two Times to make space for 4 Name Servers>Add the Azure DNS Name Servers copied from DNS Zone dashboard>Click save> You can see Azure DNS Name servers in Go Daddy DNS Management responsible for domain mykloud.in

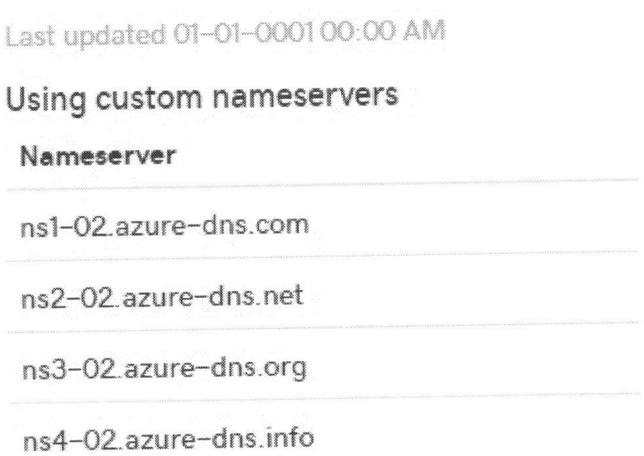

With this step Azure DNS servers become Authoritative Name Servers for domain mykloud.in

Step 4: Test the name resolution

1. From DNS zone dashboard copy the name of Azure DNS name server and run following nslookup command on your laptop command prompt.
   nslookup www.mykloud.in ns1-02.azure-dns.com

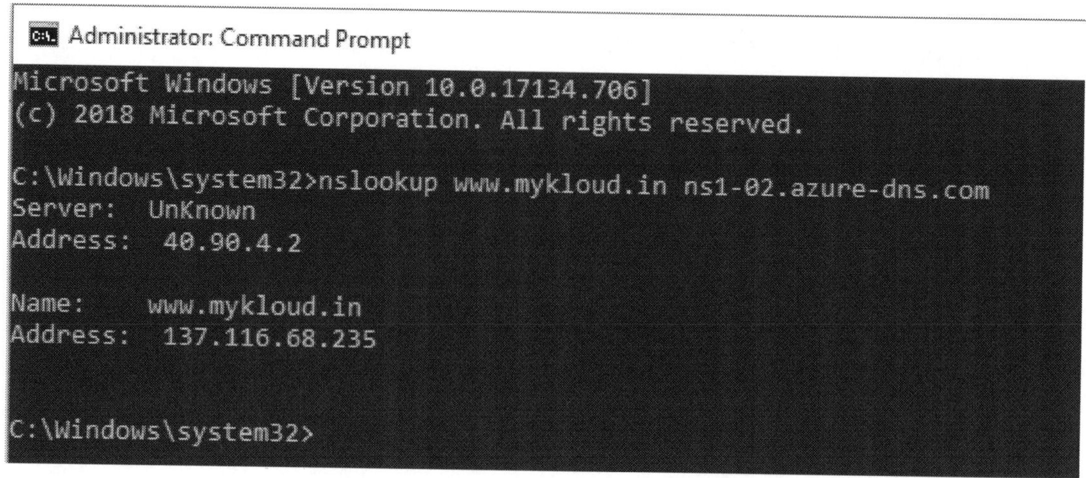

The domain name **www.mykloud.in** resolves to **137.116.68.235** which is the IP address of VM VMFE1. The result verifies that name resolution is working correctly using Azure DNS Name Servers.

2. Open Browser and enter www.mykloud.in. You can see the VM VMFE1 default website opens. Do this step after 5-10 Minutes as it takes time to propagate DNS changes.

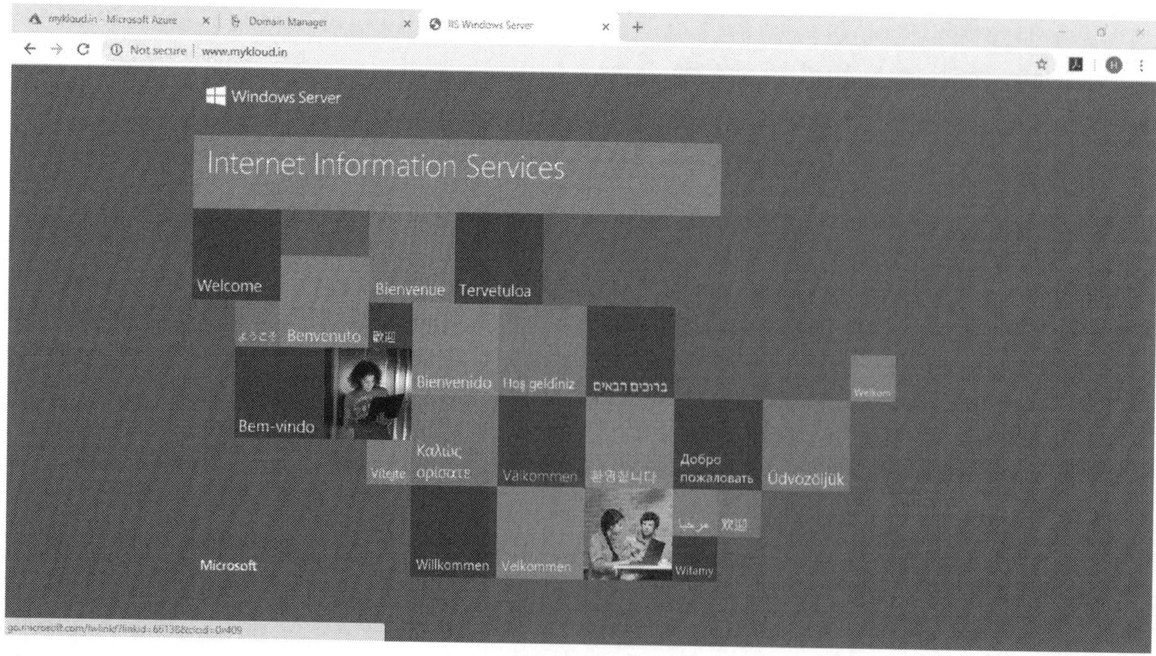

Azure DNS for private domains

Azure DNS also supports Domain Name Resolution (DNS) for Private Domains in Azure Virtual Network.

Azure DNS Private Zone feature resolves private domain names in a virtual network without needing to add a custom DNS solution. By Using Private DNS Zone you can assign Custom Private Domain names to Azure VMs instead of using Azure assigned DNS names such as **x.eastus2.cloudapp.azure.com**

Figure below shows Azure DNS providing Name resolution to Azure VMs which are assigned Custom Private Domain name such as x.contoso.local.

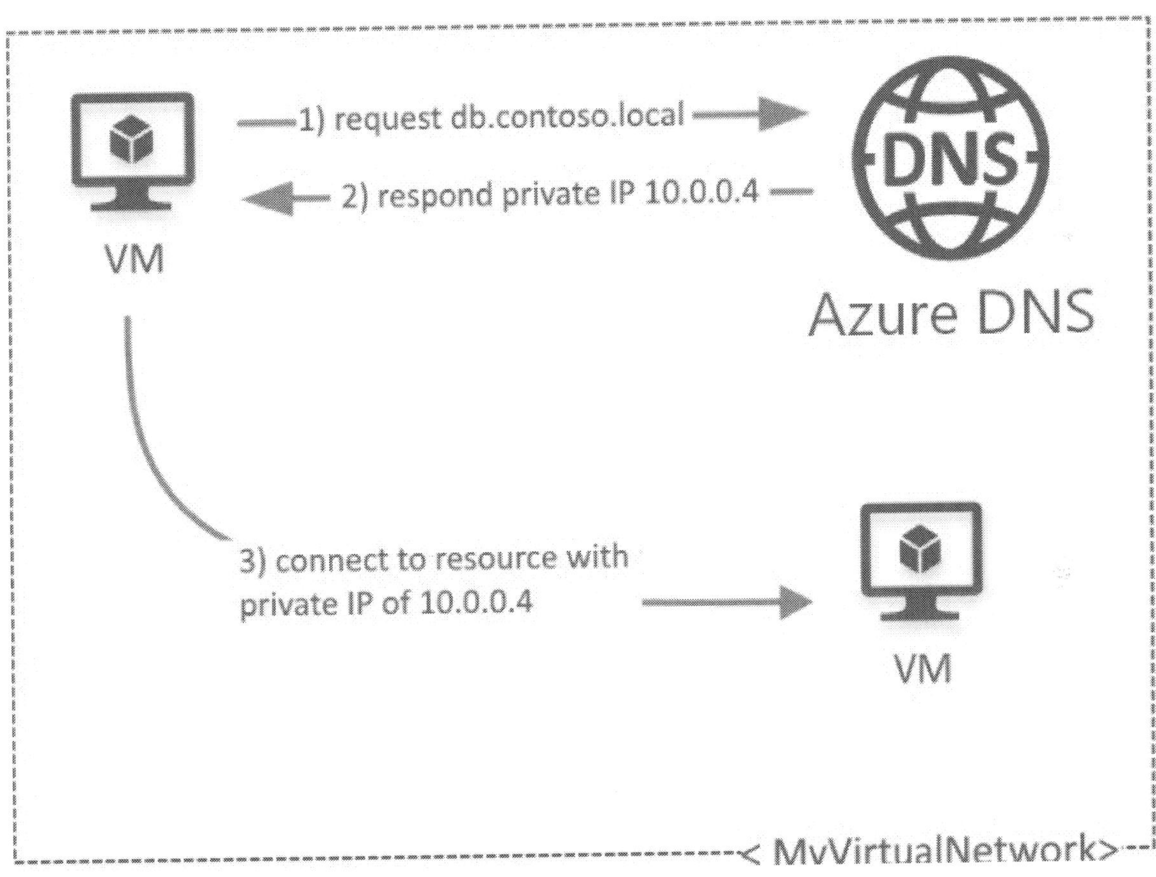

You can link virtual network to a DNS private zone as a **Registration Virtual Network** or as a **Resolution Virtual Network.** With a Registration virtual network, Azure will automatically register DNS records for the VMs. In case of Resolution Virtual Network you need to manually add DNS records into the zone for VMs. **Only one registration virtual network is allowed per private zone.** A Reverse DNS (PTR) query is scoped to the same virtual network.

Benefits of Azure DNS for Private Domains

1. **Removes the need for custom DNS solutions.**
2. **Supports all common DNS records types**. Azure DNS supports A, AAAA, CNAME, MX, PTR, SOA, SRV, and TXT records.
3. **Automatic hostname record management**. Along with hosting custom DNS records, Azure automatically maintains hostname records for the VMs in the specified virtual networks.
4. **Hostname resolution between virtual networks**. Unlike Azure-provided host names, private DNS zones can be shared between virtual networks. This capability simplifies cross-network and service-discovery scenarios.
5. **Split-horizon DNS support**. With Azure DNS, you can create Public and Private zones with the same name that resolve to different answers from within a virtual network and from the public internet. The following diagram depicts this scenario.

In this case we have created both Public and Private DNS Zone with same name contoso.com. When an internet client issues a DNS query to look up VNETA-VM1.contoso.com, Azure will return the Public IP record from the public zone. If the same DNS query is issued from another VM (for example: VNETA-VM2) in the same virtual network A, Azure will return the Private IP record from the private zone.

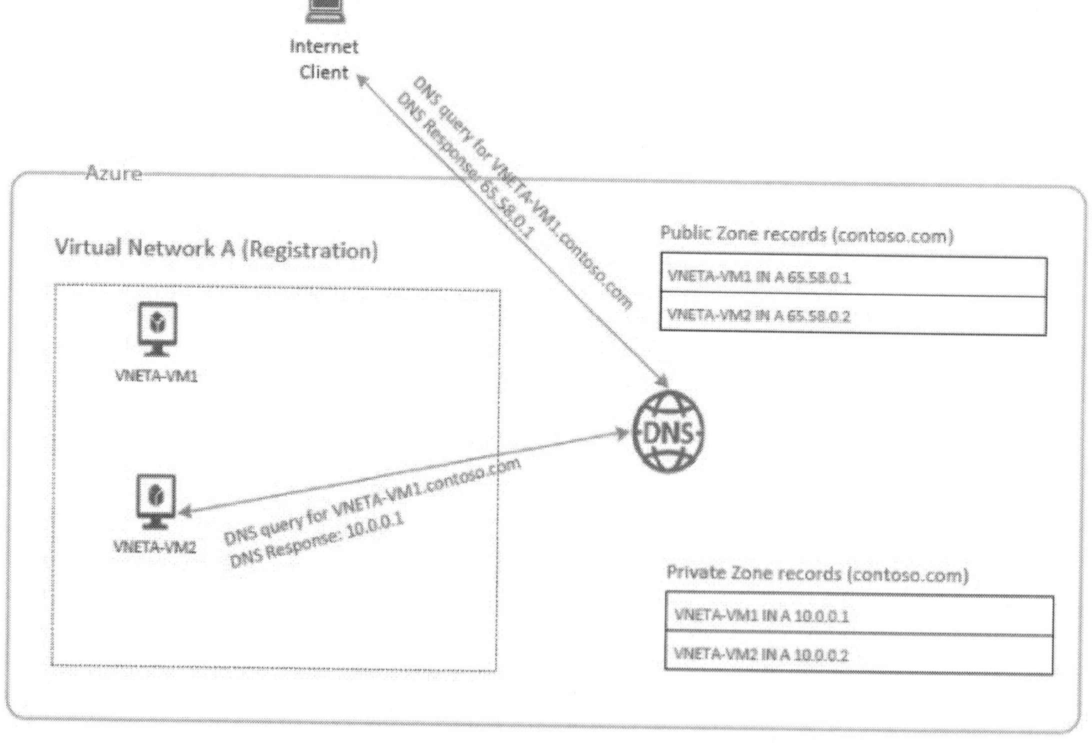

Creating Private DNS Zone using PowerShell

New-AzDnsZone -Name private.contoso.com -ResourceGroupName MyAzureResourceGroup -ZoneType Private -RegistrationVirtualNetworkId @($vnet.Id)

Note: In this case A records of VMs in Virtual Network will be automatically added to the Zone private.contoso.com as we have used Registration Virtual Network option. You also have the option to use ResolutionVirtualNetworkId.

You can add DNS records using Command **New-AzDnsRecordSet.**

Creating Private DNS Zone using Azure CLI

az network dns zone create -g MyAzureResourceGroup –n private.contoso.com --zone-type Private --registration-vnets myAzureVNet

Note: In this case A records of VMs in Virtual Network will be automatically to the Zone private.contoso.com as we have used registration-vnets option. You also have the option to use resolution-vnets.

You can add DNS records using Command **az network dns record-set.**

Azure DNS Private Zones Scenarios

Readers are requested to read some common Azure DNS Private Zones Scenarios at following link.

https://docs.microsoft.com/en-in/azure/dns/private-dns-scenarios

Design Nugget

You can link virtual network to a DNS private zone as a **Registration Virtual Network** or as a **Resolution Virtual Network.** With a Registration virtual network, Azure will automatically register DNS records for the VMs. In case of Resolution Virtual Network you need to manually add DNS records into the zone for VMs. **Only one registration virtual network is allowed per private zone.** A Reverse DNS (PTR) query is scoped to the same virtual network.

Azure DNS Pricing

Azure DNS billing is based on the number of DNS zones hosted in Azure and the number of DNS queries received.

DNS	Public Zones
First 25 hosted DNS zones	$0.50 per zone per month
Additional hosted DNS zones (over 25)	$0.10 per zone per month
First billion DNS queries/month	$0.40 per million
Additional DNS queries (over 1 billion)/month	$0.20 per million

Virtual Networks Peering

Virtual network (VNET) peering connects two VNETs in the same region or different region through the Azure backbone network. Once peered, the two VNETs appear as one for connectivity purposes. Virtual machines (VM) in the peered VNETs can communicate with each other directly by using private IP addresses.

You no longer have to configure Site-to-Site (S2S) VPN between Virtual Networks using Virtual Network gateway. The disadvantage of this option is that connectivity between VNET is over the internet backbone.

Figure Below shows VNET peering between 2 Virtual Networks (VNET1 & VNET2). VMs in both VNETs can now communicate with each other using their Private IPs.

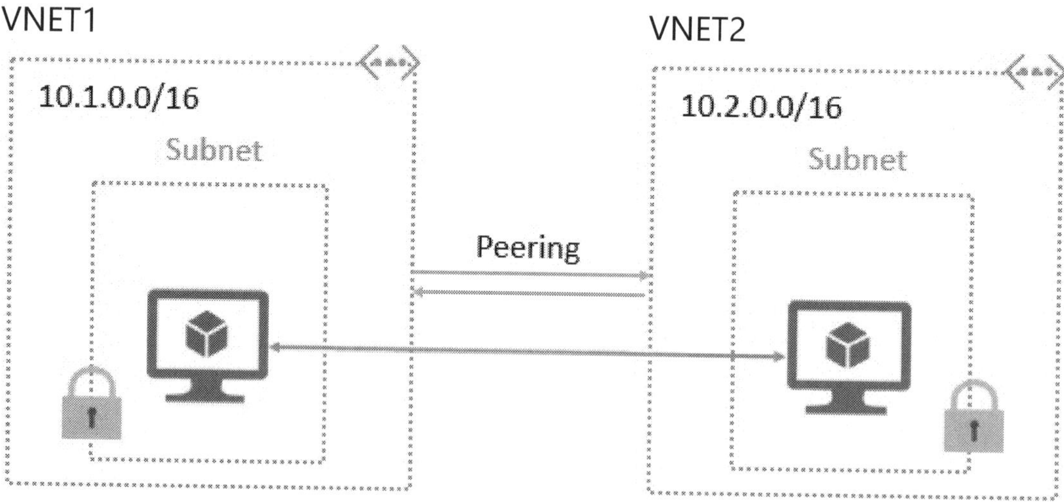

Advantages of VNET Peering

1. VNET-VNET connectivity happens over a low-latency, high-bandwidth connection instead of internet in the case S2S VPN.

2. You no longer have to configure Site-to-Site (S2S) VPN between Virtual Networks using Virtual Network gateway. This results in operational simplicity as Installing and Configuring VPN Gateway is a complex operation. Installation of VPN Gateway takes around 45 Minutes.

Pre-requisite for VNET-VNET Connectivity

1. The peered VNETs must have non-overlapping IP address spaces.

Features of VNET Peering

1. You can peer across VNETs in the same region or different regions.
2. You can globally peer across subscriptions.
3. Traffic across peered links is completely private and stays on the Microsoft Backbone Network.

Note 1: You pay for Data charges for inbound and outbound traffic.
Note 2: You pay more data charges for inbound and outbound traffic when VNETs are in different regions.

Gateway Transit and Remote Gateways

A Virtual Network can connect to on-premises Network even if it does not have its own Virtual Network Gateway. It can use the Gateway of Peered Network.

During Peering configuration you must Enable **Use Remote gateways** option in Virtual Network for Virtual Network to use Virtual Network Gateway of Peered Virtual Network.

During Peering configuration you must Enable **Allow Transit gateway** option in Virtual Network for Virtual Network to provide its Virtual Network Gateway to other Peered Virtual Networks.

Figure below shows VNETCloud and VNETOnPrem are connected through Virtual Network Gateway over Internet Connectivity. By enabling Use Remote Gateway option in VNETCloud2, VNETCloud2 can use Gateway of VNETCloud. You also need to enable Allow Gateway Transit on VNETCloud.

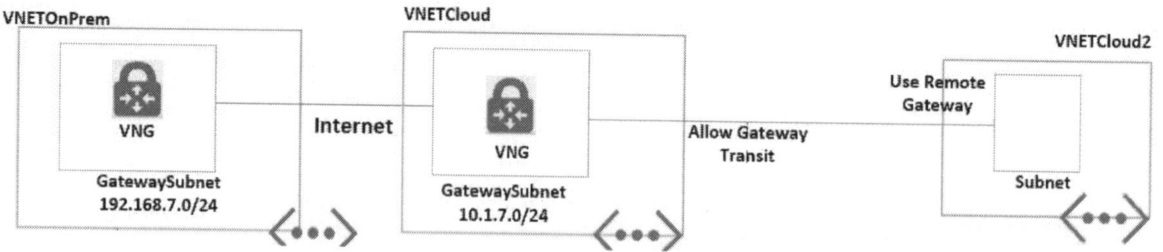

Note: Use Remote Gateway functionality requires Virtual Network Gateway (VNG) to be present in peered Network.

Exercise 16: Peering between VNETs - VNETCloud & VNETCloud2

In this exercise we will do peering between Virtual Networks VNETCloud & VNETCloud2. See the topology on Page 27.

1. Go to VNETCloud Dashboard>Click Peering in left pane> In Right Pane Click +Add > Add Peering blade opens > Enter a name>Select VNETCloud2 in Virtual Network> click ok (Not Shown).

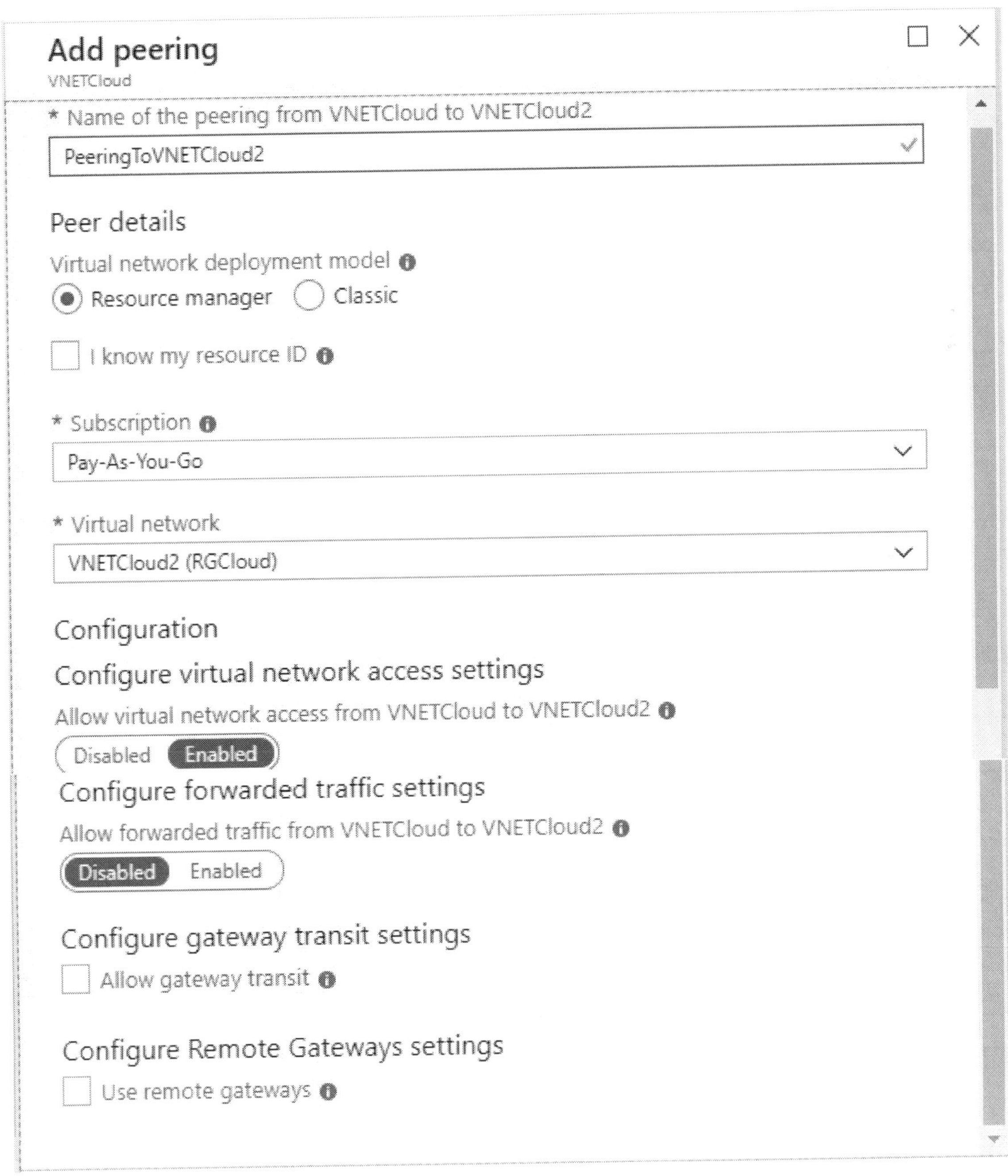

2. Go to VNETCloud2 Dashboard>Click Peering in left pane> In Right Pane Click +Add > Add Peering blade opens> Enter a name> Select VNETCloud in Virtual Network>click ok.

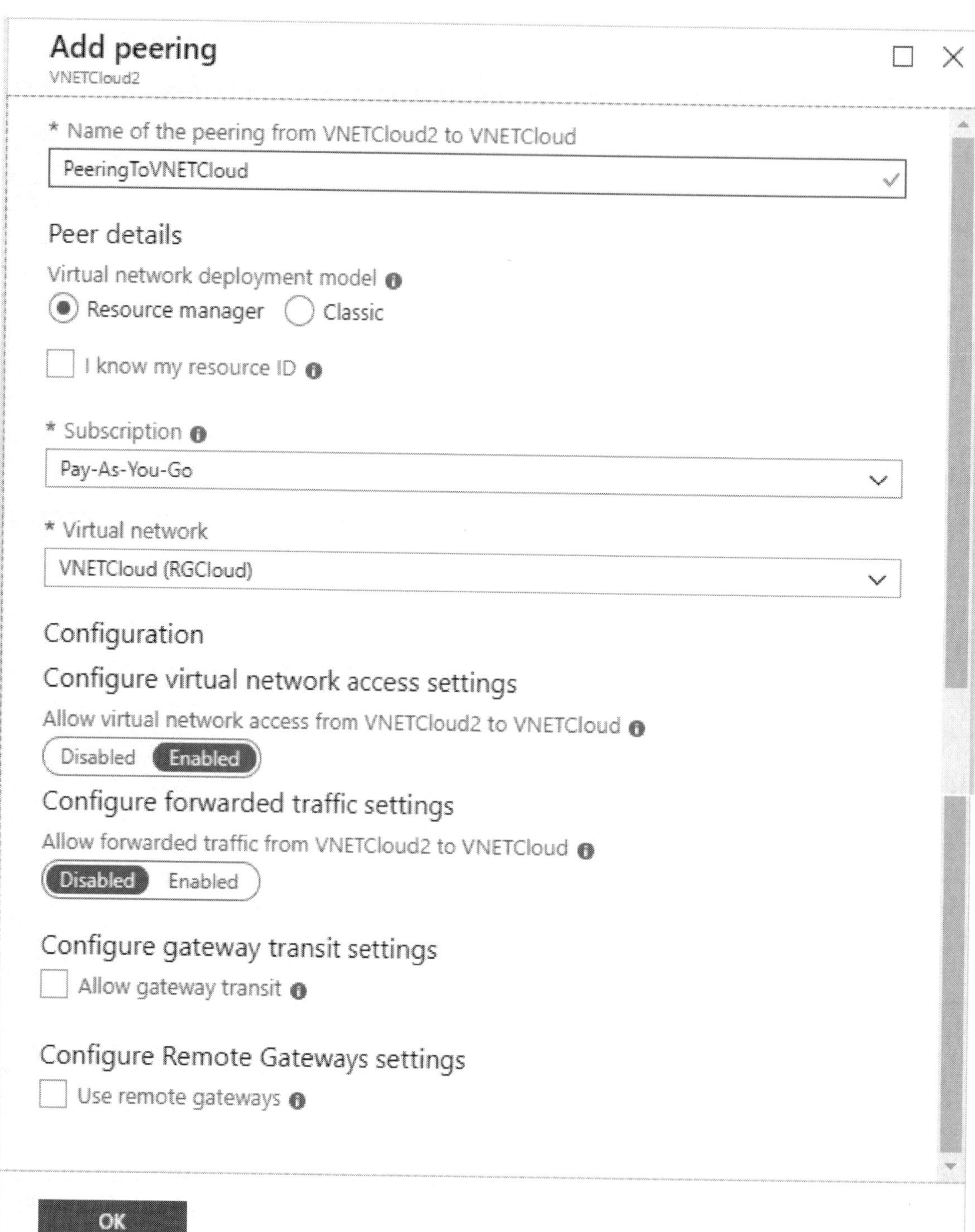

3. The 2 VNETs are now peered and connected. You can check the peering status by clicking peering in Virtual Network dashboard. Figure below shows VNETCloud Dashboard with Peering selected in left pane.

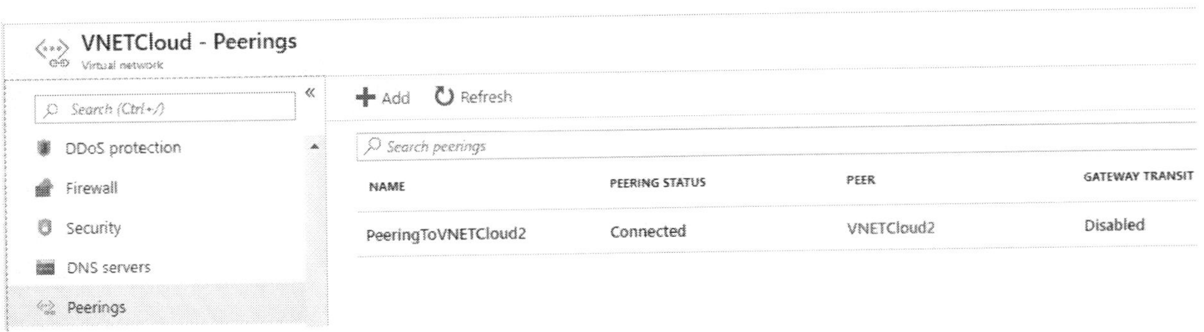

4. Figure below shows VNETCloud2 Dashboard with Peering selected in left pane.

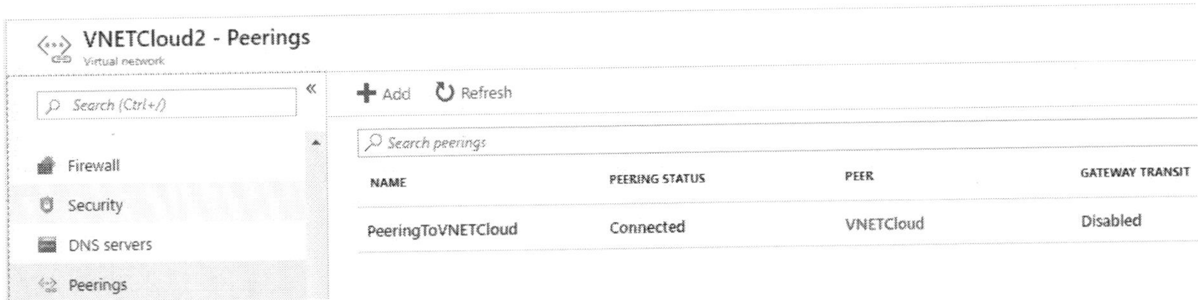

You can see in above configuration how easily VNET peering was done in just 2 steps. Secondly there was no complex configuration to be completed as we do in S2S VPN using Virtual Network gateway.

Exercise 17: Peering between VNETs - VNETCloud & VNETCloud3

In this exercise we will do peering between Virtual Networks VNETCloud & VNETCloud3. See the topology on Page 27.

1. Go to VNETCloud Dashboard>Click Peering in left pane> In Right Pane Click +Add > Add Peering blade opens >Enter a name> Select VNETCloud3 in Virtual Network> click ok (Not Shown).

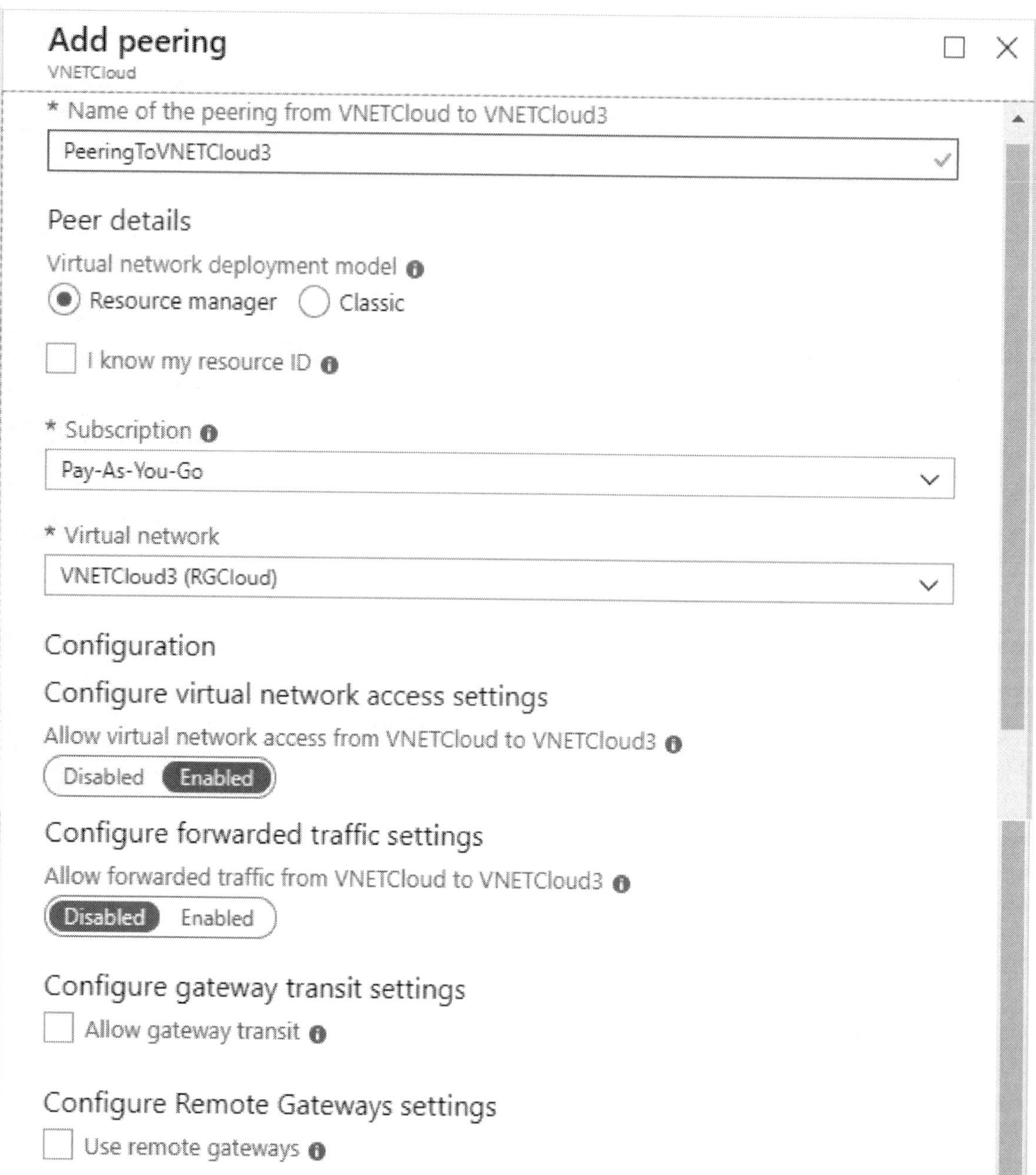

2. Go to VNETCloud3 Dashboard>Click Peering in left pane> In Right Pane Click +Add > Add Peering blade opens > Enter a name> Select VNETCloud in Virtual Network> click ok.

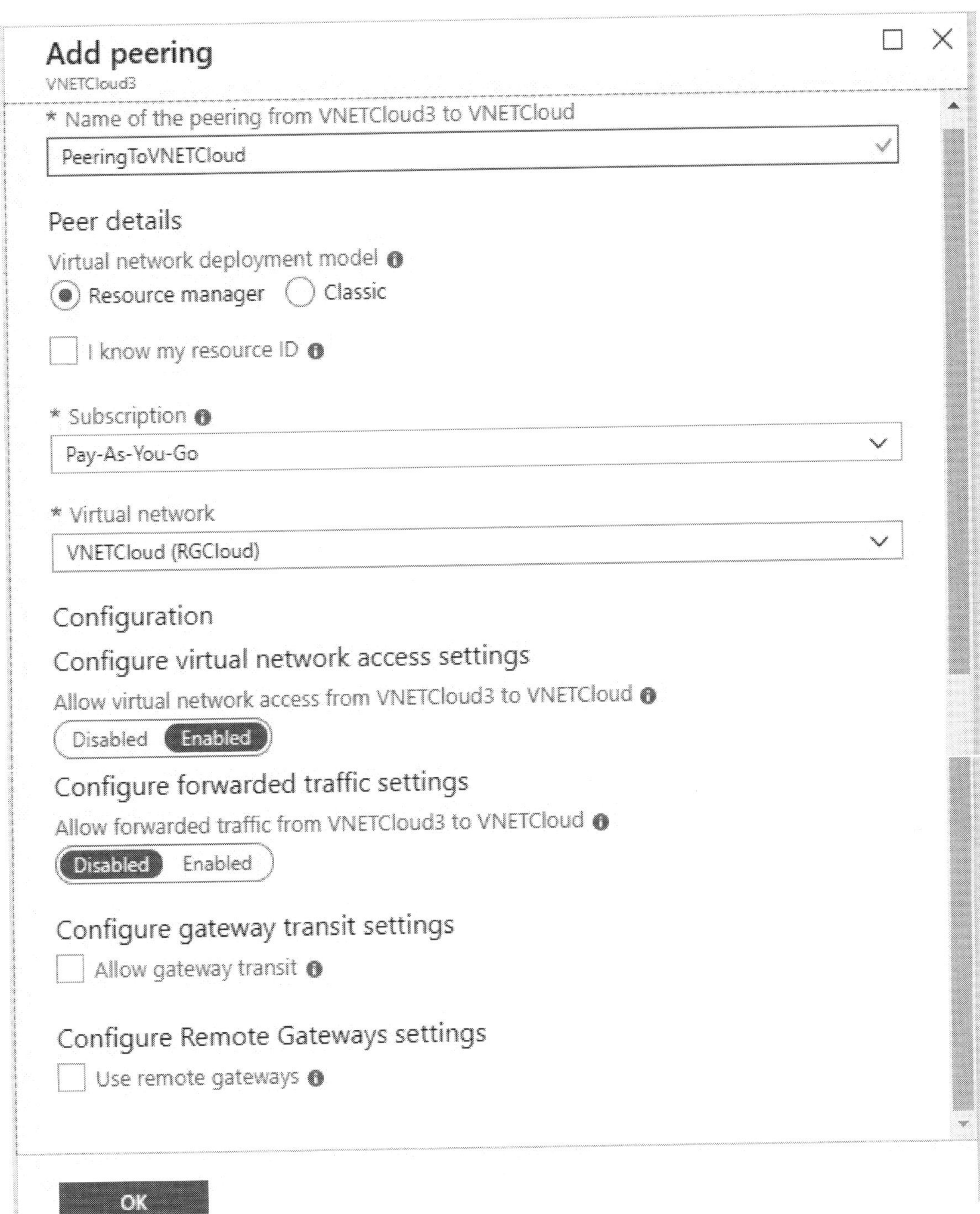

3. The 2 VNETs are now peered and connected. You can check the peering status by clicking peering in Virtual Network dashboard. Figure below shows VNETCloud Dashboard with Peering selected in left pane.

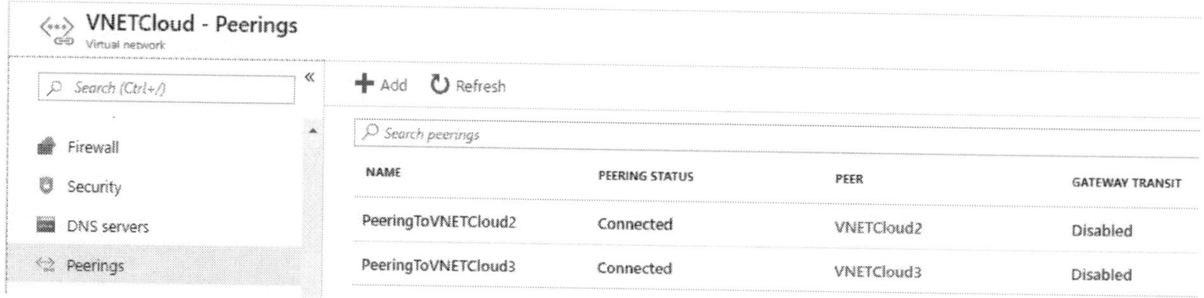

4. Figure below shows VNETCloud3 Dashboard with Peering selected in left pane.

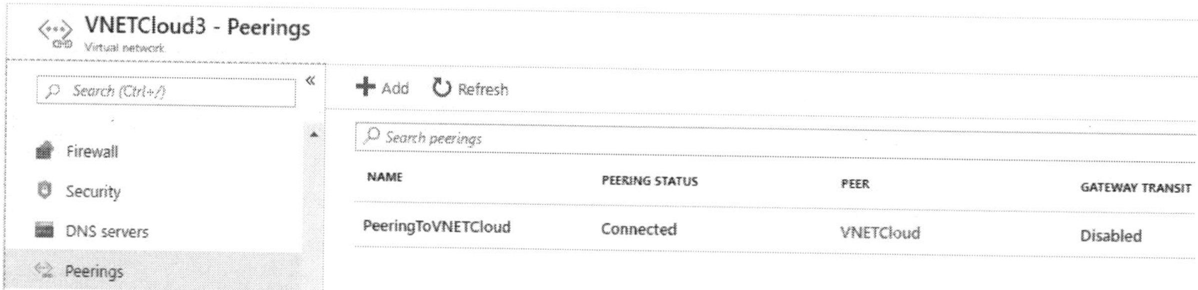

Virtual Network Peering Pricing

You pay for Data charges for inbound and outbound traffic.

VNET Peering within the same region

Inbound Data Transfer	$0.01 per GB
Outbound data transfer	$0.01 per GB

VNET Peering across regions

	Zone 1	**Zone 2**	**Zone 3**	**Zone 4**
Inbound Data Transfer	$0.035 per GB	$0.09 per GB	$0.16 per GB	$0.044 per GB
Outbound data transfer	$0.035 per GB	$0.09 per GB	$0.16 per GB	$0.044 per GB

From above you can infer that you pay more data charges for inbound and outbound traffic when VNETs are in different regions.

Routing within VNET using Default System Route

Azure automatically creates Default system routes and assigns the routes to each subnet in a virtual network. You can't create system routes, nor can you remove system routes, but you can override some system routes with Custom Routes which can be User Defined Routes (UDR) or BGP Routes or both.

For Example Virtual machines (VMs) in virtual networks can communicate with each other and to the public internet, automatically. You do not need to specify a gateway, even though the VMs are in different subnets.

This happens because every subnet created in a virtual network is automatically associated with a system routes that contains the following system route rules:

- **Local VNET Rule:** This rule is automatically created for every subnet in a virtual network. It specifies that there is a direct link between the VMs in the VNET and there is no intermediate next hop.
- **Internet Rule:** This rule handles all traffic destined to the public Internet (address prefix 0.0.0.0/0) and uses the infrastructure internet gateway as the next hop for all traffic destined to the Internet.
- **On-premises Rule:** This rule applies to all traffic destined to the on-premises address range and uses VPN gateway as the next hop destination.

Azure automatically creates the following default system routes for each subnet:

Source	Address Prefix	Next Hop Type
Default	Unique to the virtual network	Virtual network
Default	0.0.0.0/0	Internet
Default	10.0.0.0/8	None
Default	172.16.0.0/12	None
Default	192.168.0.0/16	None
Default	100.64.0.0/10	None

Traffic routed to the **None** next hop type is dropped, rather than routed outside the subnet. But for these Addresses (10.0.0.0/8, 172.16.0.0/12, 192.168.0.0/16, 100.64.0.0/10) Azure automatically changes the next hop type for the route from None to **Virtual network** (Local VNET Rule).

Optional Default System Routes

Azure creates default system routes for each subnet, and adds additional optional default routes to specific subnets, or every subnet, when you enable specific Azure capabilities.

Source	**Address Prefix**	**Next Hop Type**	**Subnet within VNET that route is added to**
Default	Unique to the virtual network	VNET peering	All
Virtual network gateway	Prefixes advertised from on-premises via BGP or configured in the local network gateway	Virtual Network Gateway	All
Default	Multiple	VirtualNetworkServiceEndpoint	Only the subnet a service endpoint is enabled for.

System routes control the flow of communication in the following scenarios:

- From within the same subnet.
- From a subnet to another within a VNET.
- From VMs to the Internet.
- From a VNET to another VNET through a VPN gateway.
- From a VNET to another VNET through VNET Peering.
- From a VNET to your on-premises network through a VPN gateway.
- From a Subnet to Azure Services through VirtualNetworkServiceEndpoint.

Figure Below shows Default System Route associated with Subnets.

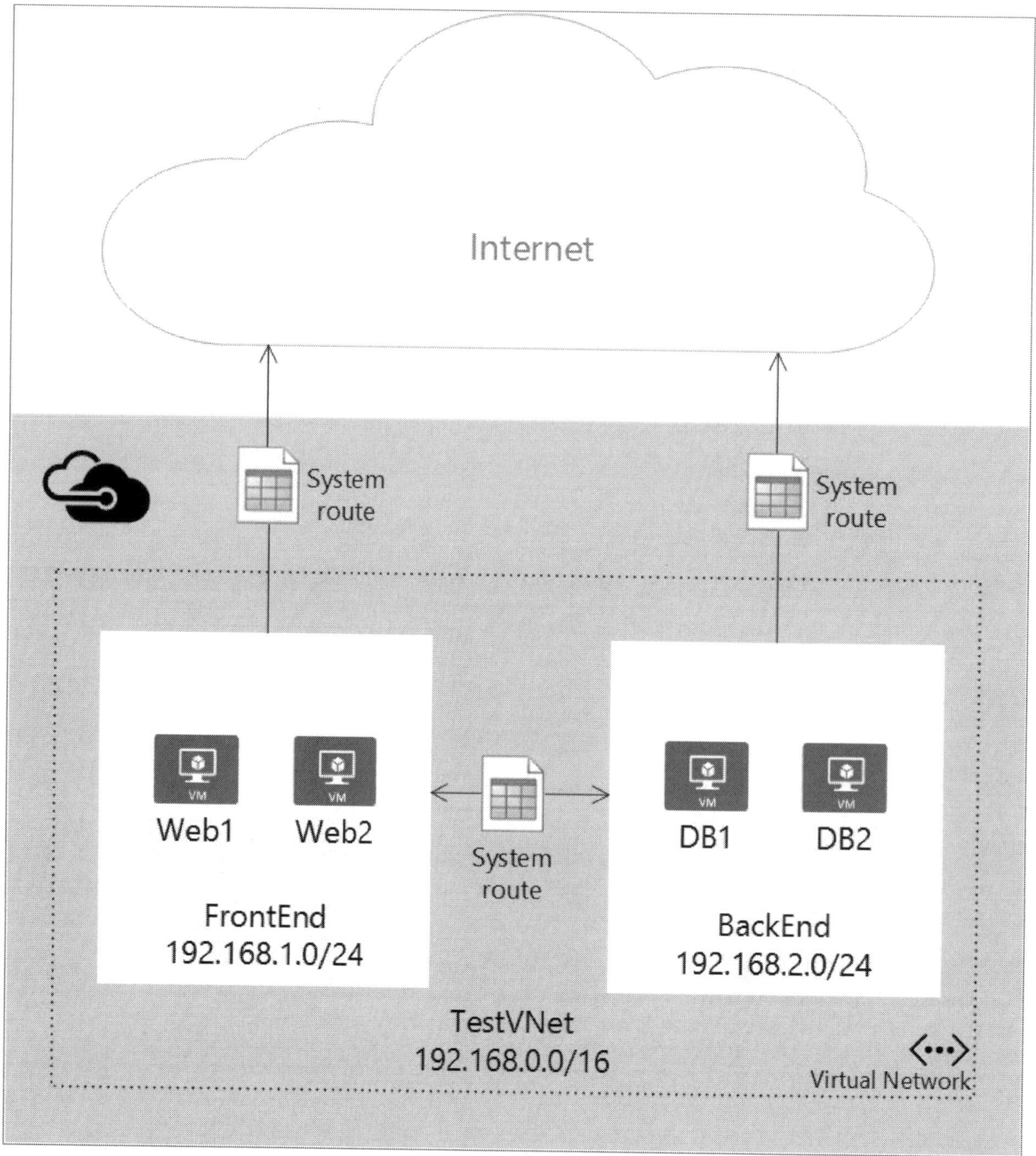

Routing within VNET using User Defined Route (UDR)

With user-defined routes you not only override Azure's default system routes but can also add additional routes to a subnet's route table.

With User Defined routes, Virtual Machine traffic in a Subnet goes through a **Network virtual appliance (NVA)** located in another subnet. This is done by creating Route table (Consisting User Defined Routes) and associating Route Table with the Subnets where traffic originates and terminates.

With UDR, NVA VM acts the gateway for other VMs in your virtual network.

In Figure below a Custom route table consisting of UDR is created and Associated with Web-Subnet and DB-Subnet. Traffic from Web-Subnet to DB-subnet and Vice versa goes through network virtual appliance (NVA) located in DMZ subnet **as UDR Route is preferred over Default System Route.**

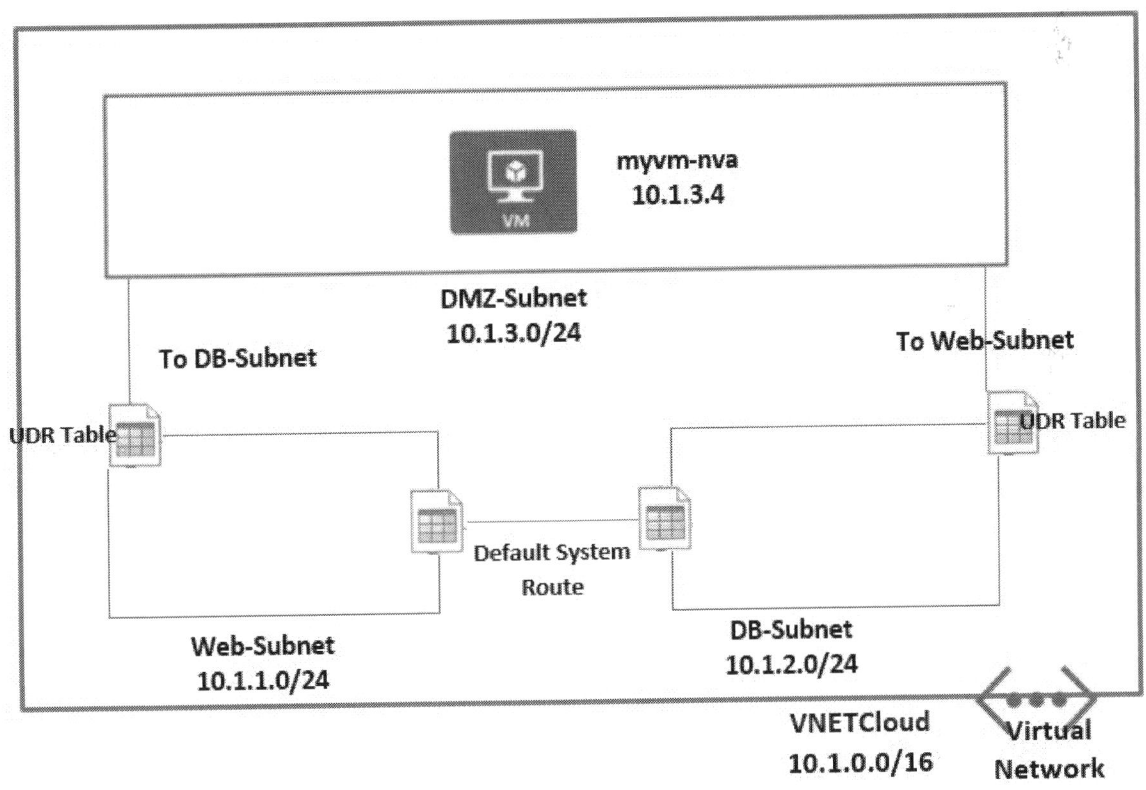

Network virtual appliance (NVA) VM: NVA VM is a Windows Server VM with Private IP and with IP forwarding enabled on Network Interface of the VM.

How Azure selects a route

Subnets rely on Default system routes until a route table is associated to the subnet. Once an association exists, routing is done based on Longest Prefix Match (LPM) among both user defined routes and system routes. If multiple routes contain the same address prefix, Azure selects the route type, based on the following priority:

1. User defined route.
2. BGP route (when ExpressRoute is used).
3. System route.

Route Table

A route table is a collection of individual routes used to decide where to forward packets based on the destination IP address. Route table is associated with Subnet. A route consists of the following:

Address prefix: The destination address in CIDR format.
Next hop type: Next hop type can be Virtual Network, Virtual Network gateway, Internet, virtual appliance (NVA) or none.
Next hop Address: It is the Address of the Virtual Appliance VM. Next hop values are only allowed in routes where the next hop type is *Virtual Appliance*.

IP Forwarding

To allow Virtual Machine (NVA) to receive traffic addressed to other destinations, enable IP Forwarding for the NVA VM.

Design Nugget UDR

Design Nugget 1: User defined routes are only applied to traffic leaving a subnet. You cannot create routes to specify how traffic comes into a subnet.
Design Nugget 2: The appliance you are forwarding traffic to cannot be in the same subnet where the traffic originates. Always create a separate subnet for your appliances.
Design Nugget 3: Each subnet can be associated with one or zero route table apart from system routes. But the same route table can be associated to one or more subnets. All VMs in a subnet use the route table associated to that subnet.

Exercise 18: Routing Traffic between 2 Subnets to pass through another Subnet using UDR (Refer this Lab Exercise for AZ-301 also)

For this Demonstration Exercise we will create user-defined routes to route traffic between Web-Subnet and DB-Subnet to pass-through a network virtual appliance located in DMZ-Subnet as shown in figure below. For this Demonstration lab we will use Virtual Network **VNETCloud** created in Exercise 3.

Note: Readers are requested to attempt this Exercise at the end of the book otherwise by mistake you can break the topology.

Pre-Req for this Exercise

Windows Server 2016 NVA VM (myvm-nva) is created in DMZ-Subnet with Private IP only. You can do this Exercise even If you have not created NVA VM. If you have not deployed NVA VM then just skip step 1.

Solution

Figure below shows the architecture of the solution.

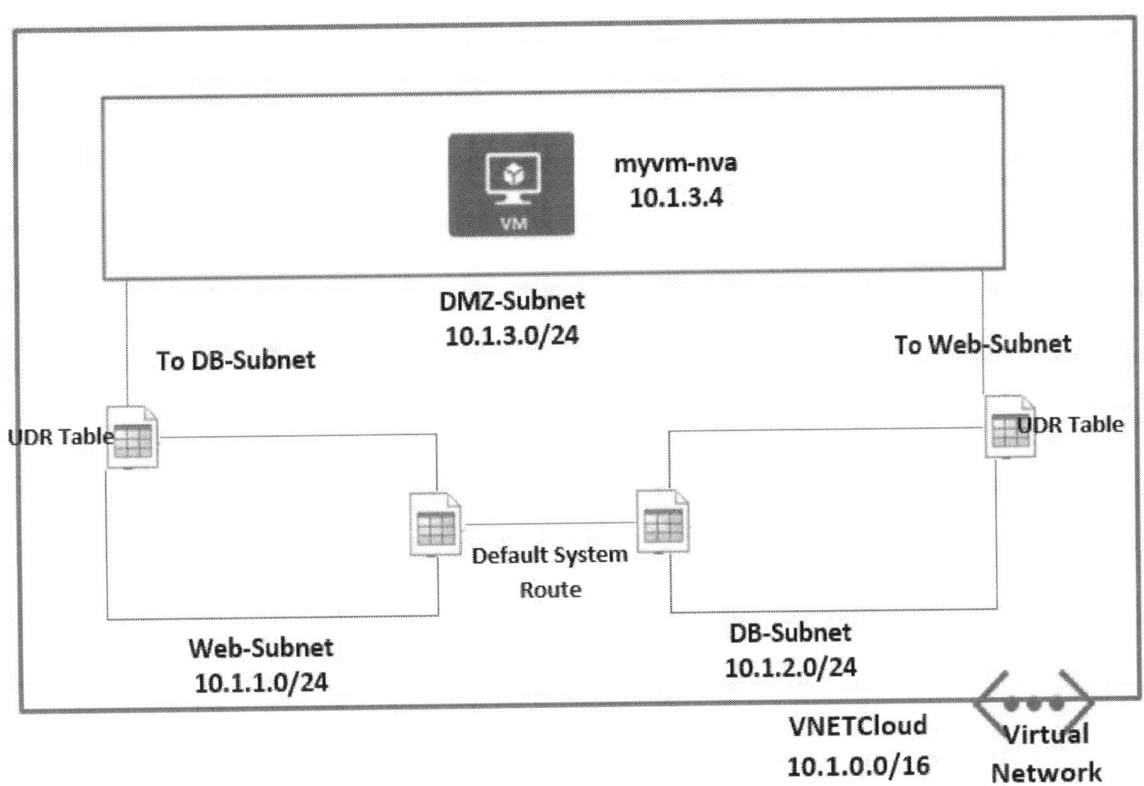

Step 1: To allow NVA Virtual Machine in DMZ subnet to receive traffic addressed to other destinations, enable IP Forwarding for the NVA VM.

Enable IP Forwarding in NVA Virtual Machine in DMZ subnet: Go to NVA VM Dashboard> Click Networking under settings> In Right pane click Private Network Interface attached to NVA VM>Network Interface Dashboard opens>Click IP Configuration in left Pane>In Right Pane Click Enabled.

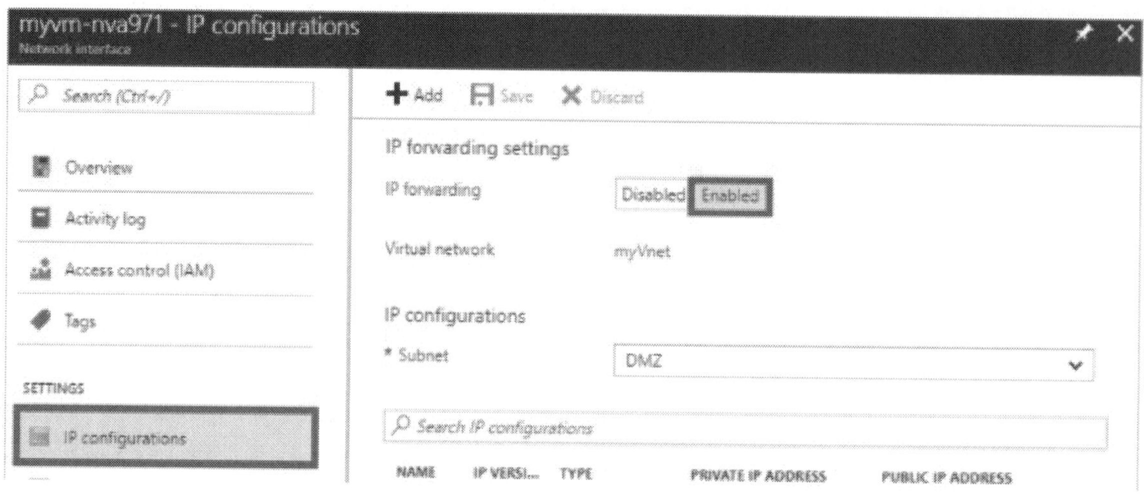

Step 2 Create Route Table (To be associated with Web-Subnet): In Azure Portal Click All services>Networking>click Route Tables> All Route Tables blade opens> Click + Add> Create Route Table Blade opens>Enter name ToDBSubnet, Select Resource Group RGCloud, Location East US 2 and click create (Not Shown).

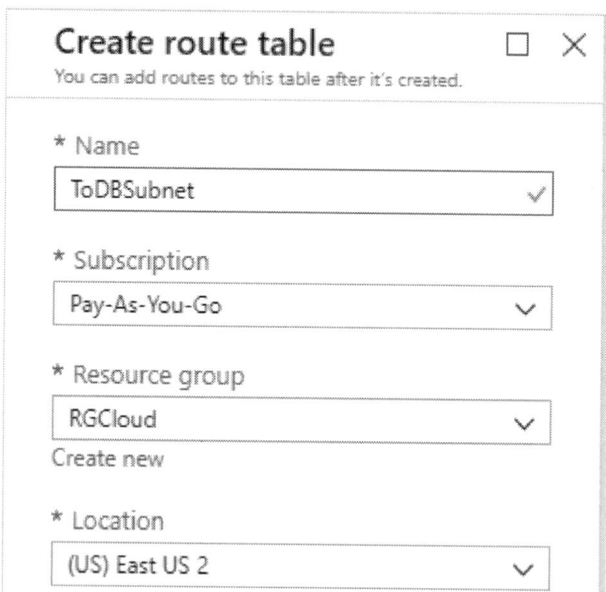

Figure below shows Dashboard of Route Table **ToDBSubnet.**

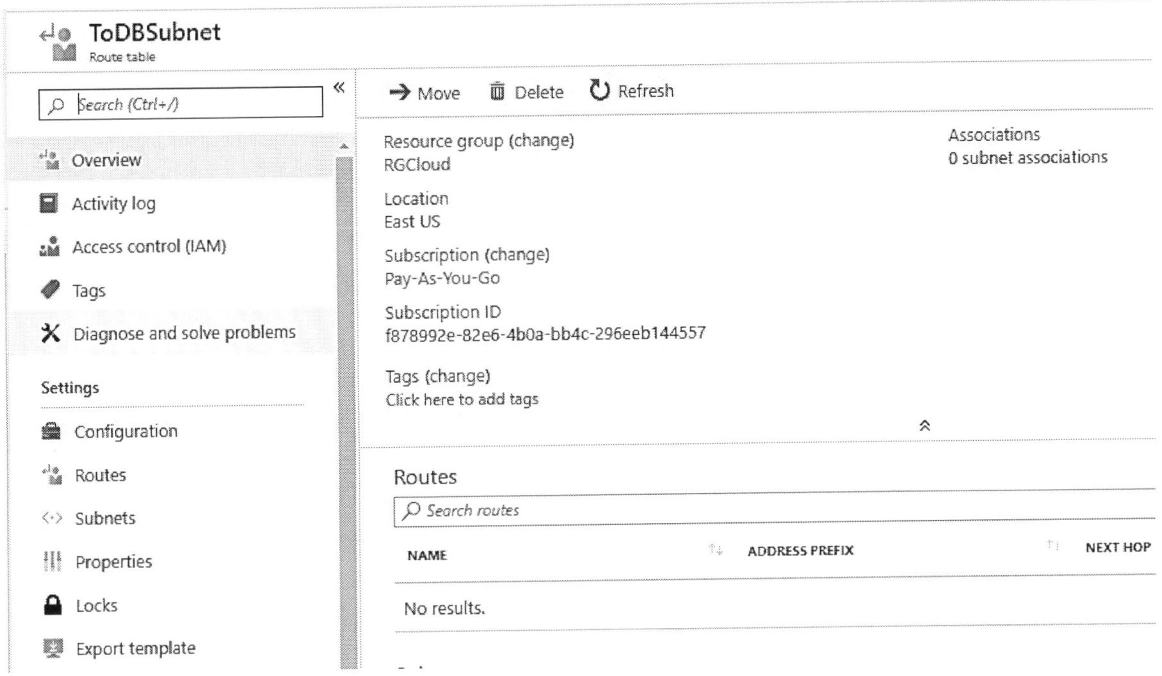

Step 3 Add a route in Route Table (ToDBSubnet): Go to ToDBSubnet Route table Dashboard> Click Routes in left Pane>Click +Add> Add Route Blade opens > Enter following information and click ok (Not Shown).

Route name: RouteToDBSubnet.

Address Prefix: Network Address of DB-Subnet 10.1.2.0/24.

Next Hop type: Select Virtual Appliance from Drop Down box.

Next Hop Address: IP Address of NVA VM (myvm-nva) 10.1.3.4.

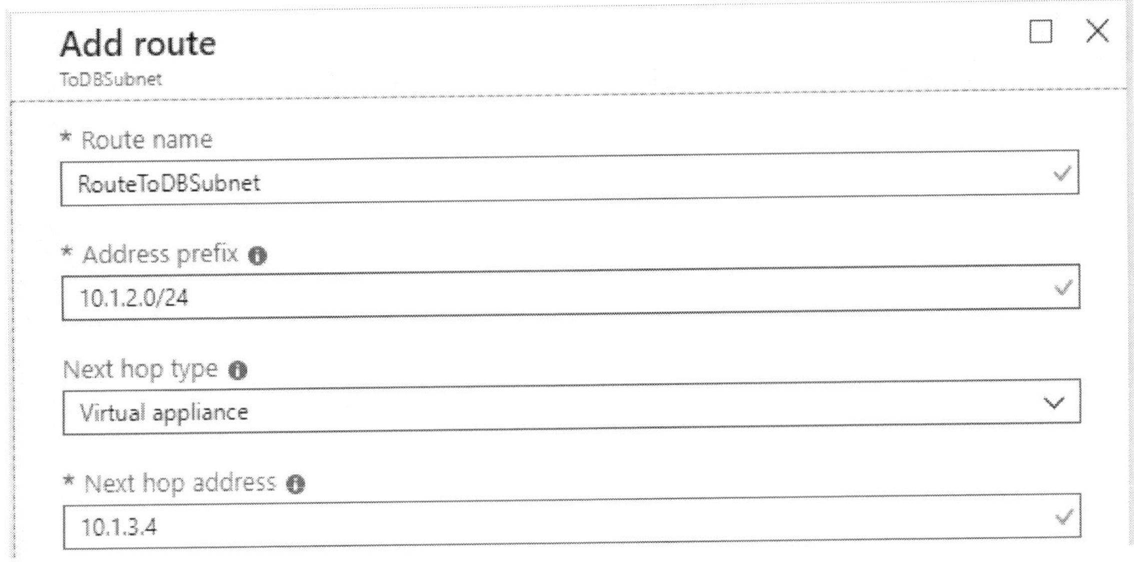

Step 4 Associate Route Table (ToDBSubnet) with Web-Subnet: Go to Route Table ToDBSubnet Dashboard>click Subnets in left pane>In Right pane click + Associate>Associate Subnet Blade opens>Click Virtual Network and select VNETCloud>Click Subnet and select Web-Subnet>Click Ok (Not Shown).

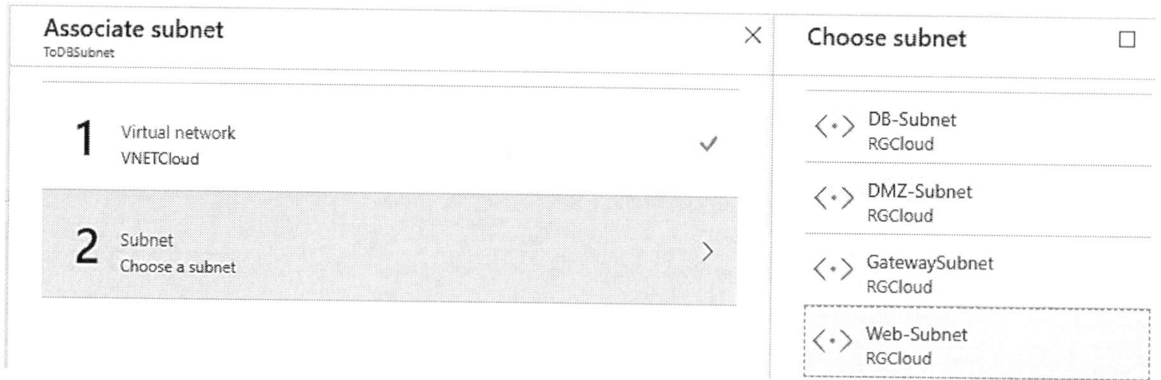

Figure below shows Route Table Dashboard. It has one Route and is associated with Web-Subnet.

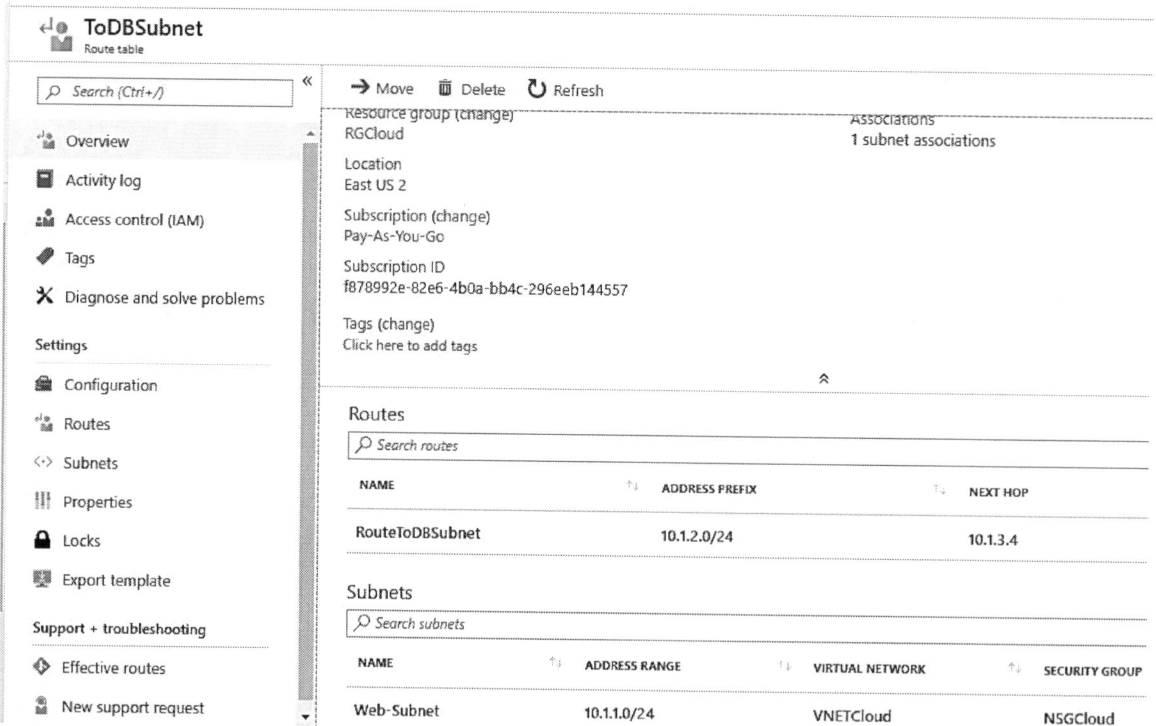

Step 5: **Create Route Table (To be associated with DB-Subnet)**:): In Azure Portal Click All services>Networking>click Route Tables> All Route Tables blade opens> Click + Add> Create Route Table Blade opens>Enter name ToWebSubnet, Select Resource Group RGCloud, Location East US 2 and click create (Not Shown).

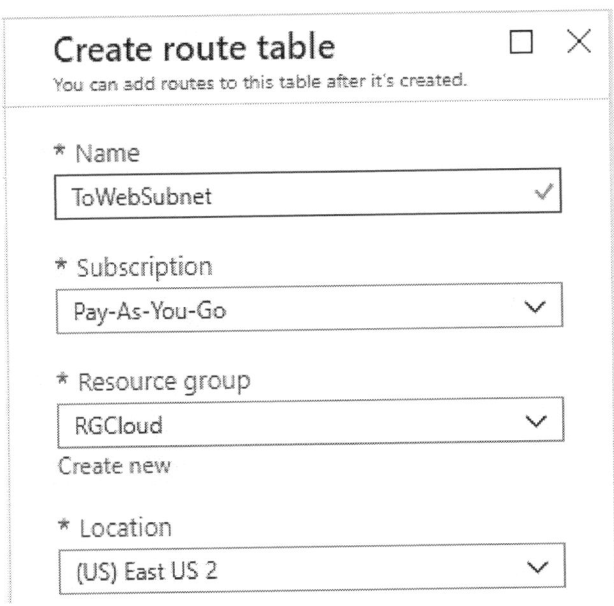

Step 6 Add a route in Route Table (ToWebSubnet): Go to ToWebSubnet Route table Dashboard> Click Routes in left Pane>Click +Add> Add Route Blade opens > Enter following information and click ok (Not Shown).
Route name: RouteToWebSubnet.
Address Prefix: Network Address of Web-Subnet 10.1.1.0/24.
Next Hop type: Select Virtual Appliance from Drop Down box.
Next Hop Address: IP Address of NVA VM (myvm-nva) 10.1.3.4.

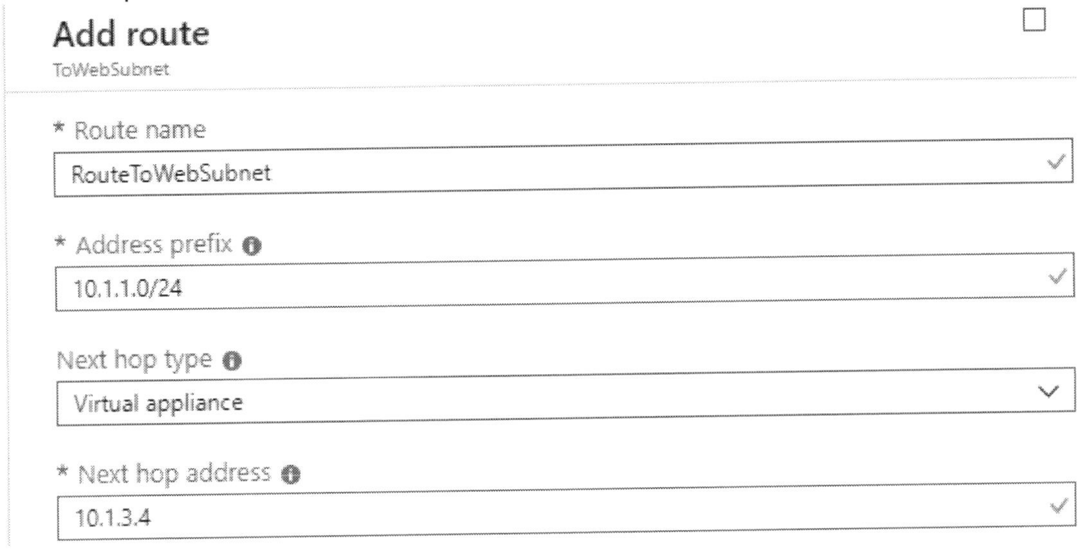

Step 7 Associate Route Table (ToWebSubnet) with DB-Subnet: Go to Route Table ToWebSubnet Dashboard>click Subnets in left pane>In Right pane click + Associate>Associate Subnet Blade opens>Click Virtual Network and select VNETCloud>Click Subnet and select DB-Subnet>Click Ok (Not Shown).

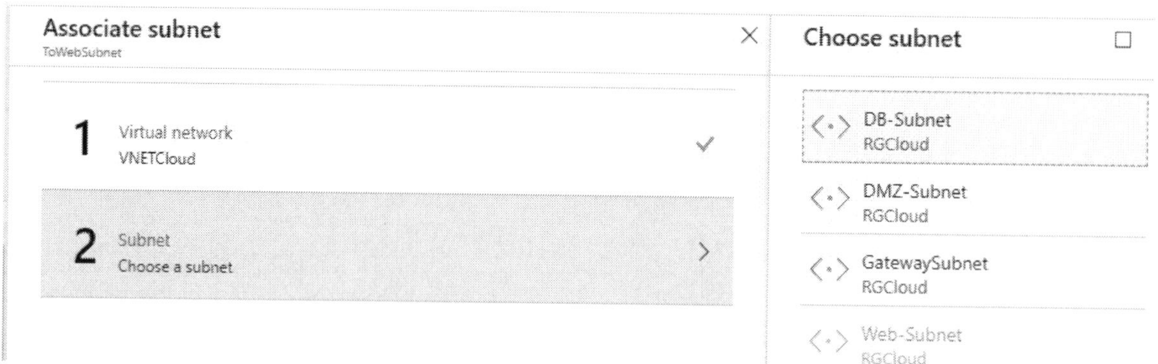

Figure below shows the Dashboard of Route Table ToWebSubnet. It has one Route and is associated with DB-Subnet.

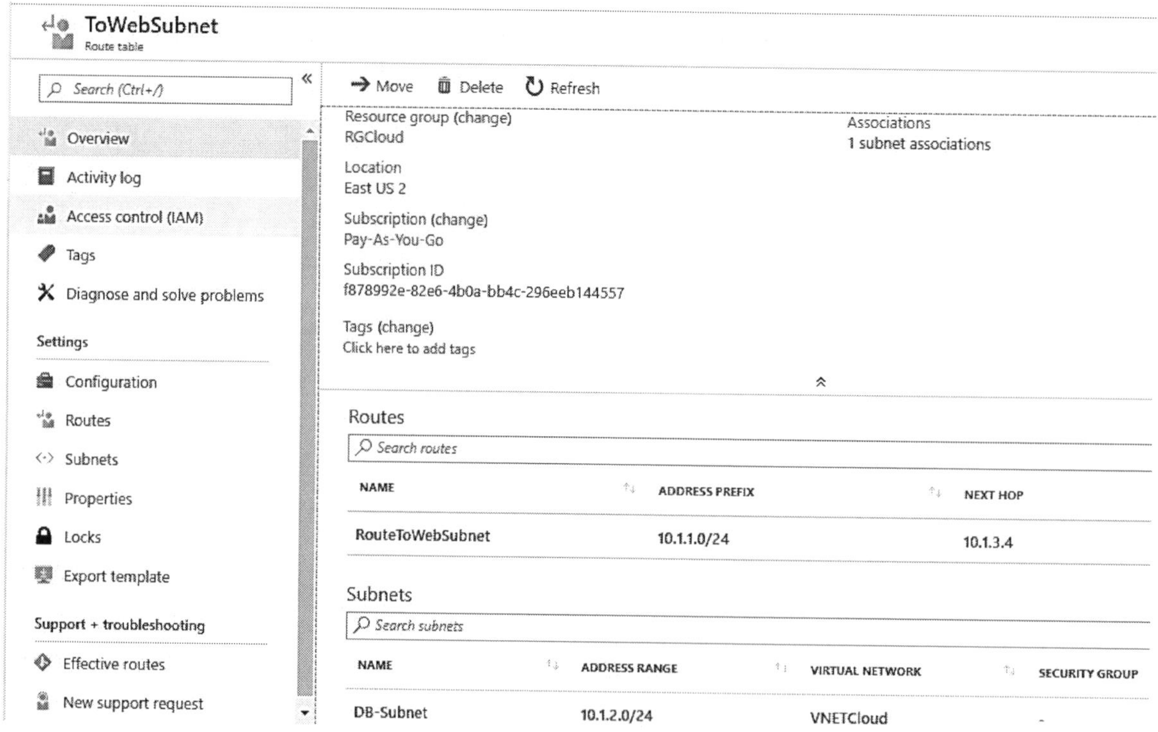

Result 1 of above actions: We have both default route and User defined Route associated with Web-Subnet & DB-Subnet.
Result 2 of above actions: Network traffic between Web-Subnet and DB- Subnets flows through the network virtual appliance (NVA). Though default system route specify that Traffic can flow directly between Web and DB subnet but Traffic flows through NVA **as UDR is preferred.**

Next Hop Options when adding Route in Route Table

You get following options in Next Hop type when adding route in Route Table.

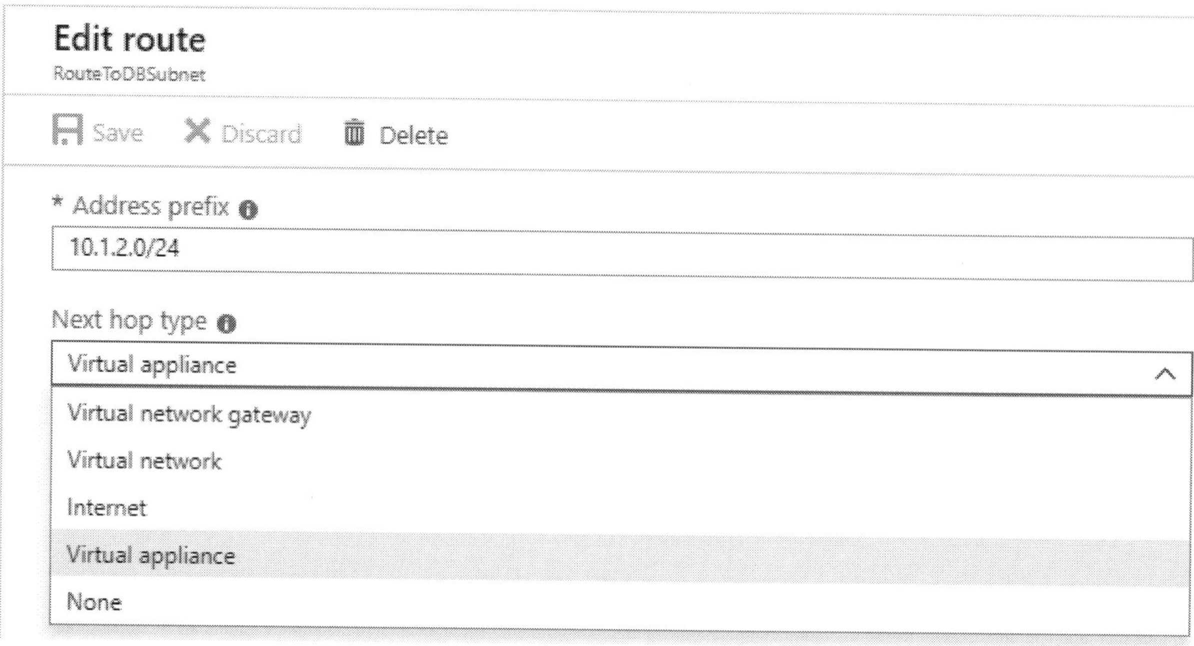

Virtual Network Gateway Option: This option is used when you want traffic destined for specific address prefixes routed to a virtual network gateway. The virtual network gateway must be of type VPN. For Example **Virtual Network Gateway Option** can be used if you want all traffic to Internet 0.0.0.0/0 should be routed to on-premises device that inspects the traffic and determines whether to forward or drop the traffic.

Internet: Specify when you want to explicitly route traffic destined to an address prefix to the Internet, or if you want traffic destined for Azure services with public IP addresses kept within the Azure backbone network.

Virtual Network: Specify when you want to override the default routing within a virtual network.

VNET Service Endpoints

Azure Managed Resources such as Azure Storage or Azure SQL Database can be accessed from outside Azure and by VMs in Virtual Network over internet connection.

With Azure Virtual Network Service Endpoints, traffic between Azure Virtual Network and Azure Managed Resources such as Storage Accounts remains on the Microsoft Azure backbone network and not on Public Internet. Virtual Network Endpoints feature is currently available for the following Azure services:

Azure Storage | Key Vault | Service Bus | Event Hub | App Service
Azure Cosmos DB | Azure SQL Data Warehouse | Azure SQL Database | Maria DB

Virtual Network Service Endpoint Architecture

Figure below shows the Architecture of VNET Service Endpoints. Resources in Virtual Network are accessing Azure Storage over Microsoft backbone network.

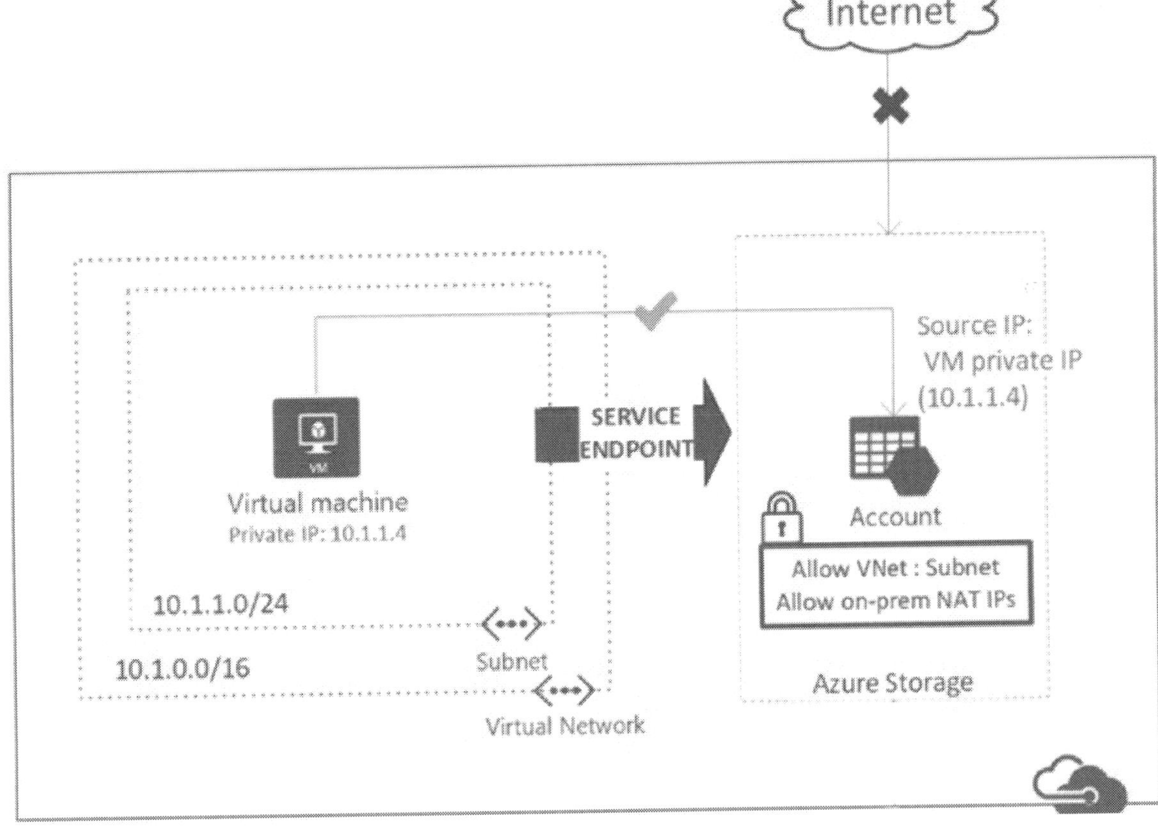

WORKING OF VNET SERVICE ENDPOINTS

Virtual Network Service Endpoints are created in Virtual Network and are attached to Subnets. They extend Azure Virtual Network private address space to Azure Managed services. You can also restrict Azure resources to only be accessed from your VNET and not via the Internet. You also have the option to allow access from internet or from particular IP range only.

WHY WE NEED AZURE VIRTUAL NETWORK ENDPOINTS

Azures Managed Resources such as Azure Storage and Azure SQL have Internet facing IP addresses. Because of **security and compliance** reasons many customers prefer that their Azure Managed Services not be exposed directly to the Internet.

Exercise 19: Setting up Virtual Network (VNET) Service Endpoints

In this Exercise we will create VNET Service Endpoints for Azure Storage Account sastdcloud. After setting up Service Endpoint and blocking access of Azure Storage Account from internet we will check whether we can still open HelloWorld.txt @ https://sastdcloud.blob.core.windows.net/hk410/HelloWorld.txt We will then access HelloWorld.txt using Internet Explorer from Azure VM VMF1 located in Web-Subnet in Virtual Network VNETCloud.

Note for the Readers: **Attempt this exercise after you have completed Exercise 69 in Chapter 8.** In Storage Account Chapter 8 we created Container hk410 and uploaded HelloWorld.txt with Anonymous access.

Step 1: Check whether you can access Hello World.txt from internet or not @ https://sastdcloud.blob.core.windows.net/hk410/HelloWorld.txt
HelloWorld opens from Internet.

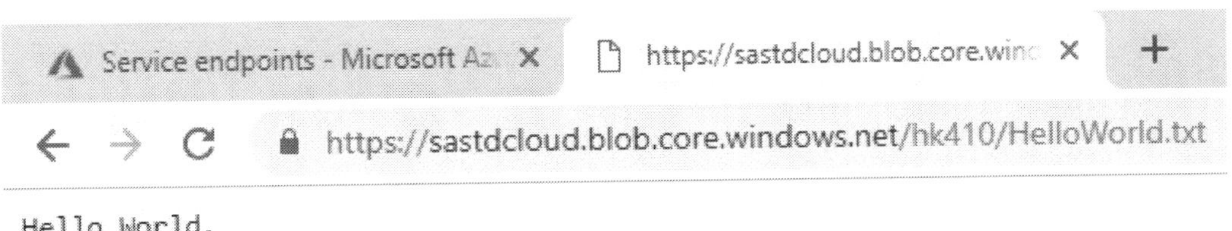

Step 2: Go the Virtual Network VNETCloud Dashboard> click Service endpoints in left pane> Click +Add> Add service endpoints blade opens> Select Storage from Service Dropdown box and Web-subnet from Subnets dropdown box>click Add (Not Shown).

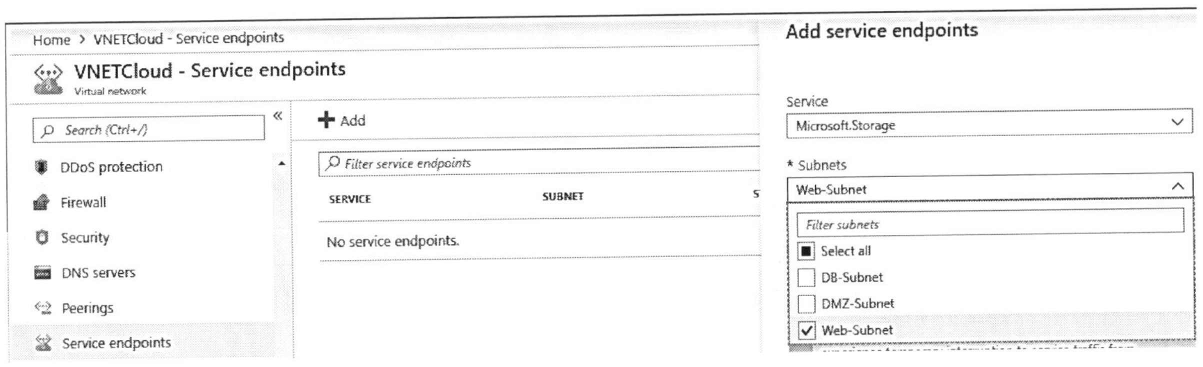

Note: Readers are requested to See service Endpoint options in service dropdown box.

Step 3: Go Storage Account sastdcloud dashboard>Click Firewalls and Virtual Networks in left pane>Click selected Networks Radio Button in right pane>click +Add Existing Virtual Network> Add Network blade opens>Select VNETCloud from Virtual Networks Dropdown box and Web-Subnet from Subnets dropdown box and click Add>click save.

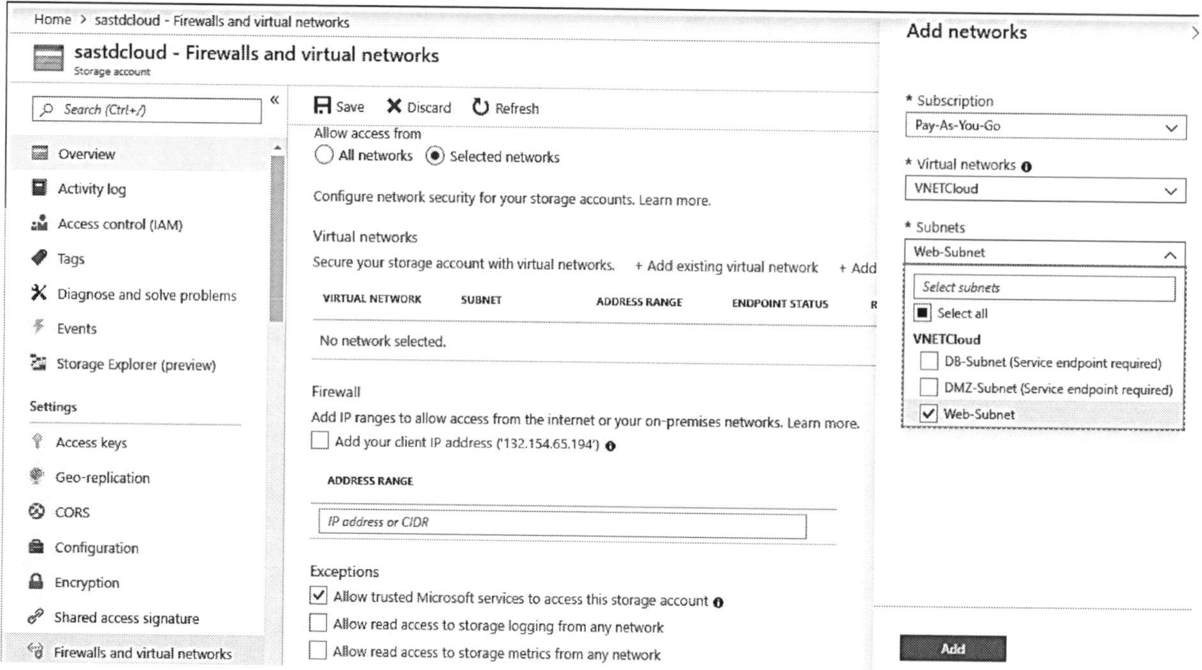

Note Firewall option: Here you can add IP address range which can access Azure storage from internet.

Step 4: Use Firefox to Check whether you can access Hello World.txt from internet or not @ https://sastdcloud.blob.core.windows.net/hk410/HelloWorld.txt
The figure below shows that we cannot access HelloWorld.txt.

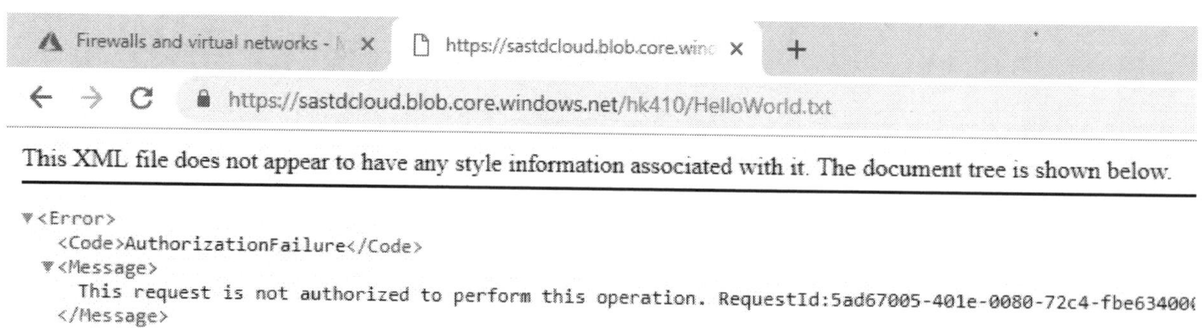

Step 5: RDP to Virtual Machine VMFE1>open internet explorer and log on Azure Portal @ https://portal.azure.com>Go to Storage Account sastdcloud Dashboard>In right pane Click Blobs>Click container hk410>Click Hello World.txt>Click download button at top>You get the option to open or save.

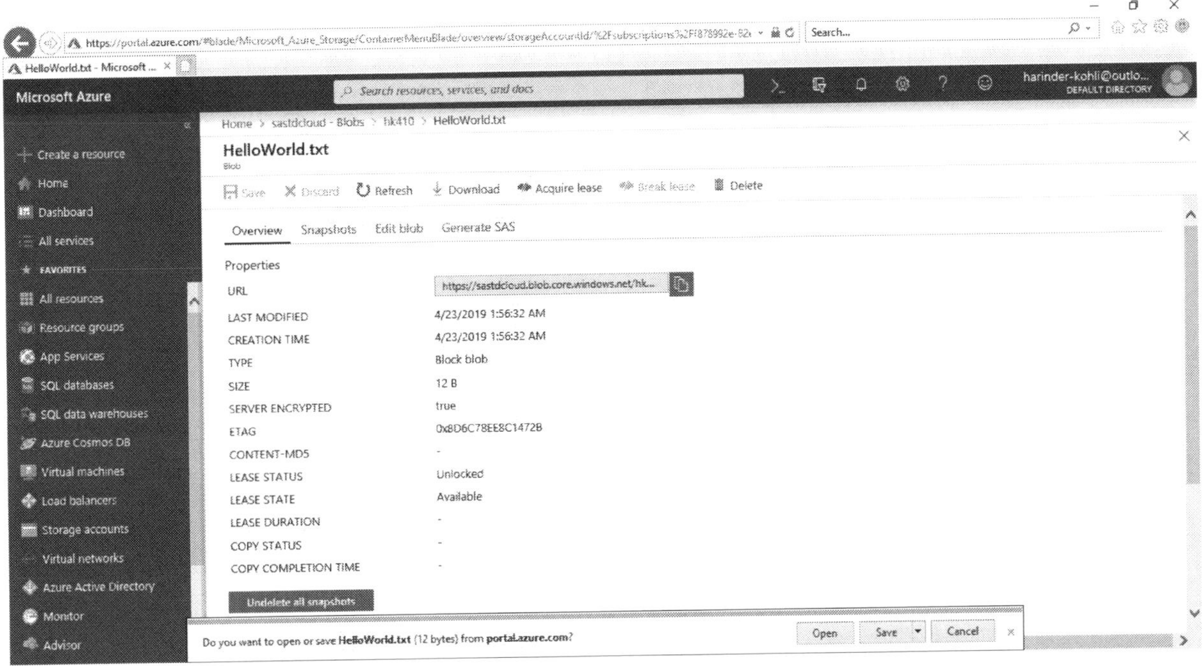

From above we infer that we cannot access HelloWorld.txt from internet but we can access from VM VMFE1 located in Web-Subnet using VNET Service Endpoints.

Note: Disable Internet Explorer Enhanced Security Configuration in Windows Server 2019 VM.

Step 6: Enable back Storage Account access from all Networks

In Storage Network sastdcloud Dashboard click Firewall and Virtual Networks in left pane>Select the radio button All Networks>Click save.

Note: We need access to Storage Account from internet for other exercises.

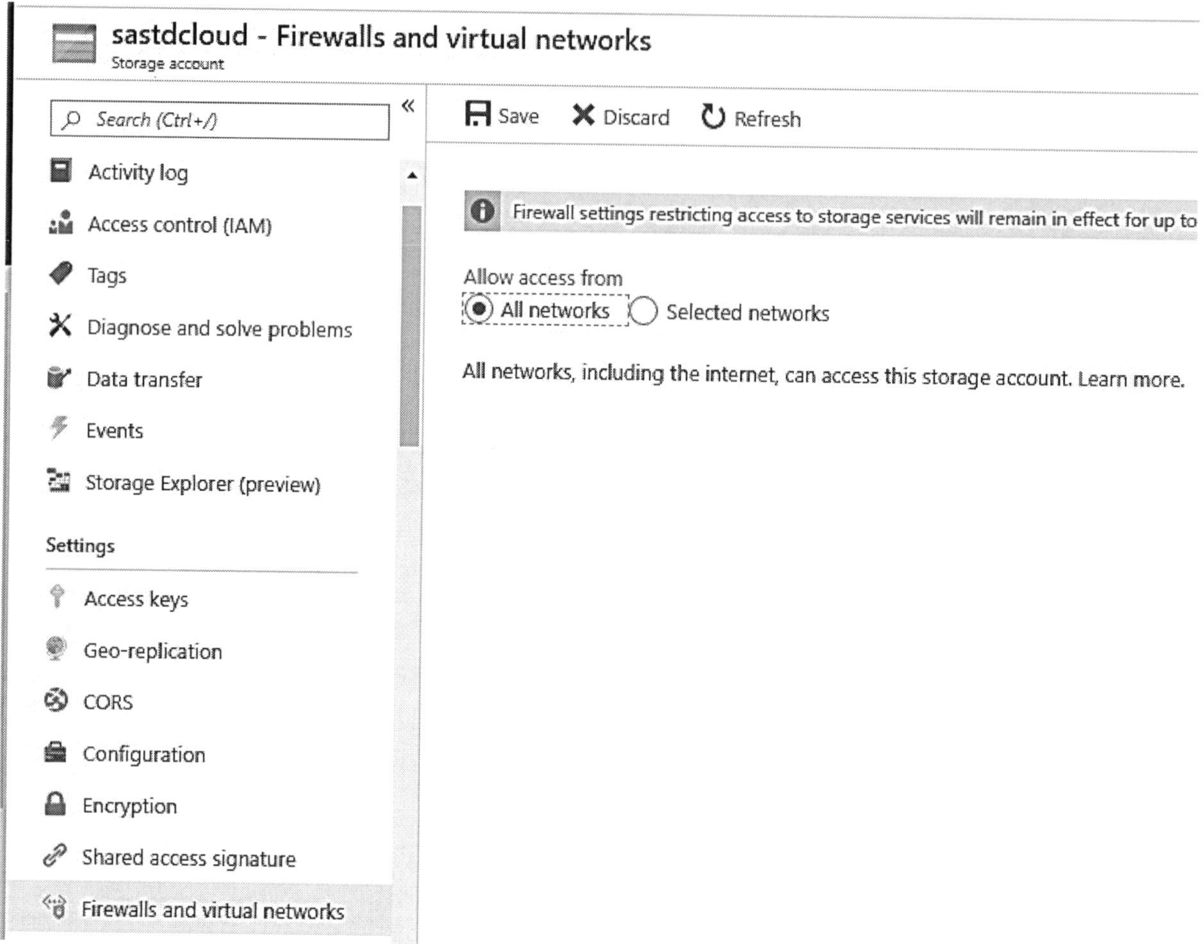

Case Study 1: Design Virtual Network and Network Security Groups

Design a virtual network (KNET) with 2 subnets (App & DB) using Class A address of 192.168.0.0/16. App subnet will have 2 application servers - Production Application Server (App-Prod) and Test Application Server (App-Test).

Design Network Security groups to satisfy following requirements:
Traffic allowed inside App Subnet is http, https & RDP.
Traffic allowed to Production Application Server (App-Prod) is https and RDP.
Traffic allowed to Test Application Server (App-Test) is http and RDP.

Solution

Subnet VNET network address space 192.168.0.0/16 into 192.168.1.0/24 and 192.168.2.0/24 and assign it to App and DB subnets respectively as shown below.

We will create 3 Network Security Groups – NSGSubnet, NSGProd & NSGTest.

- NSGSubnet will be associated with App Subnet and add 3 inbound allow rules - http, https & RDP.
- NSGProd will be associated with Network Interface of App-Prod Server and add 2 inbound allow rules - https & RDP.
- NSGTest will be associated with Network Interface of App-Test Server and add 2 inbound allow rules - http & RDP.

NSG Working: NSGSubnet will only allow inbound http, https and RDP traffic and will block any other traffic. NSGProd will allow https & RDP and will block http. NSGTest will allow http & RDP and will block https. From above you can infer that 2 levels of Firewalls (NSG) are Protecting Virtual Machines.

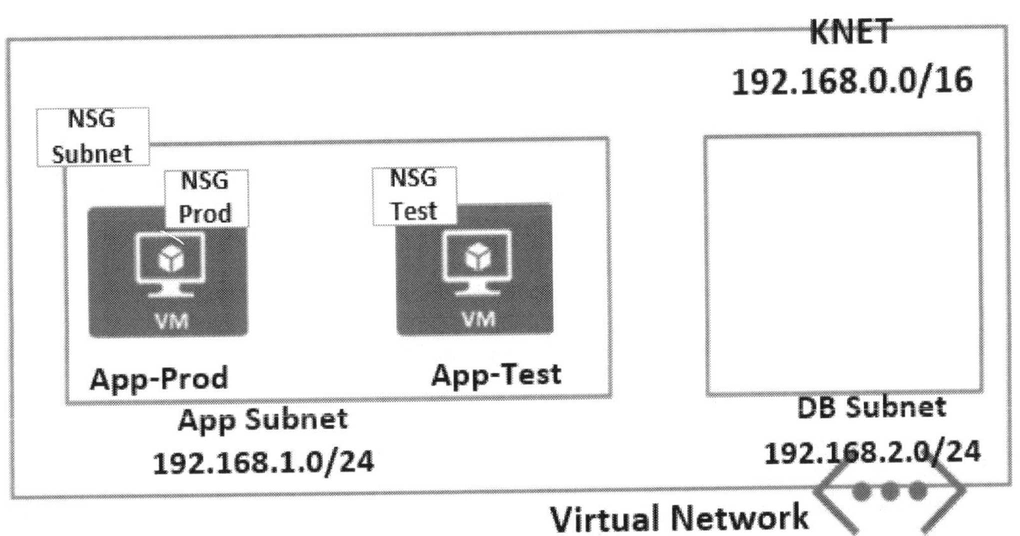

Case Study 2: Workload Isolation with Hub and Spoke VNETs using VNET Peering

Spoke VNETs will be used to isolate workloads such as Production & Dev & Test.

Hub VNET will run shared workloads such as DNS, AD DS & Security Appliances.

Spoke VNETs will peer with Hub VNET. Hub VNET will also provide hybrid connectivity to on-premises Data center over internet using Virtual Network Gateway. Using **Use Remote gateways** & **Allow Transit gateway options** Spoke VNETs will use the Virtual Network Gateway of Hub VNET to connect to on-premises Dara Center.

Hub VNET acts as a central point of connectivity for on-premises network and spoke VNETs.

Figure below shows Spoke 1 and Spoke 2 VNETs are peered with Hub VNET. Hub VNET is also connected to on-premises network using VPN Gateway.

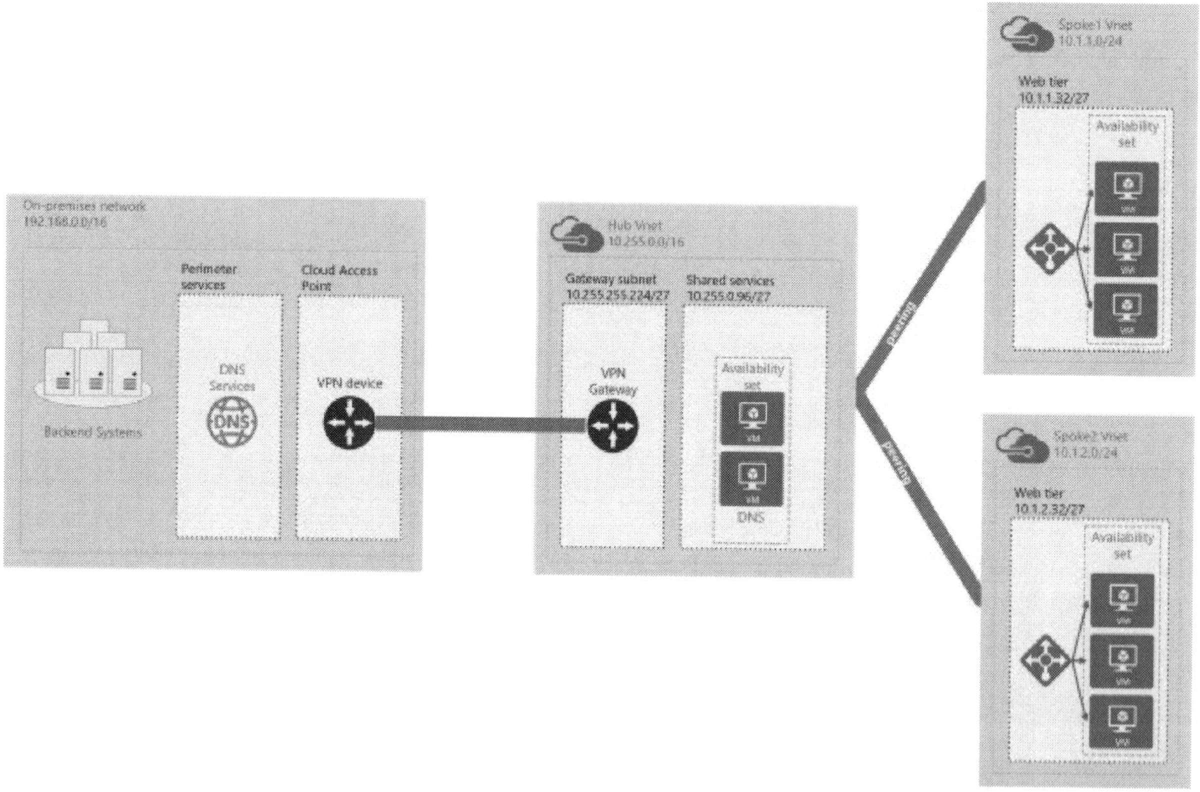

Spoke VNET to Spoke VNET Connectivity (Optional)

If Spoke to Spoke connectivity is required then User Defined Route (UDR) and Network Virtual Appliances (NVA) will be used.

UDR attached to Subnet in the Spoke VNET will forward traffic to NVA VM in Hub VNET. NVA VM will route traffic to other spoke VNET.

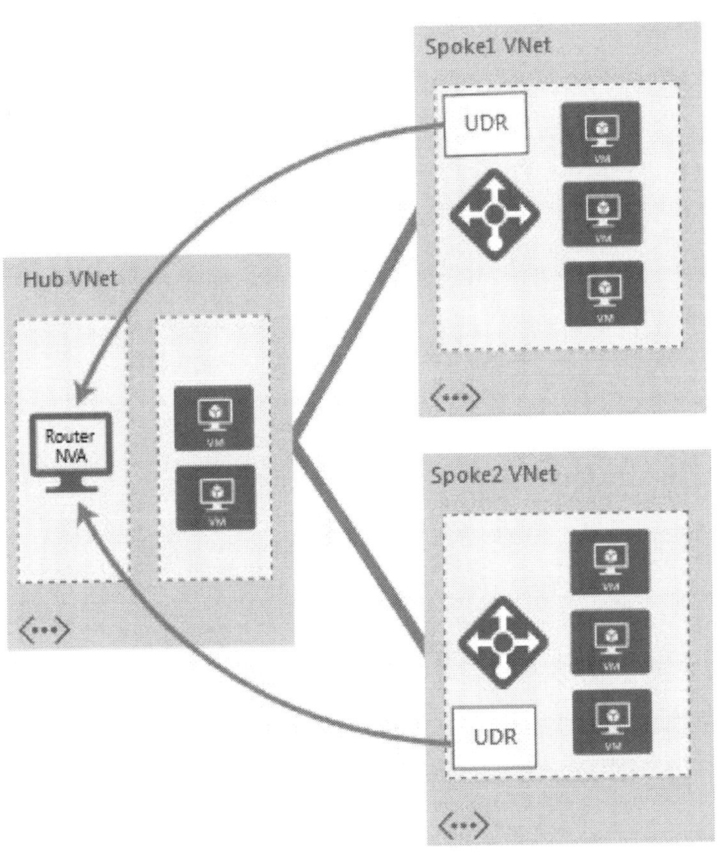

Enterprise use case for this architecture include following:

1. Workloads requiring isolation such as development, testing, and production, but require shared services such as DNS, IDS, NTP, or AD DS. Shared services are placed in the Hub VNET, while each environment is deployed to a spoke VNET to maintain isolation.
2. Enterprises that require central control over security aspects, such as a firewall in the hub as a DMZ, and segregated management for the workloads in each spoke.
3. Require secure Hybrid connectivity to on-premises Data Center.

Benefits of this Architecture include following:

1. **Cost savings** by centralizing services such as network virtual appliances (NVAs), Virtual Network Gateway and DNS servers in Hub VNET, that can be shared by multiple workloads in Spoke VNETs.

2. **Separation of operations** between central IT (SecOps, InfraOps) and workloads (DevOps). Central IT Managing Hub VNET and Application owners managing Spoke VNETs.

Case Study 3: Controlling Access to Database VM using NSG

A BFSI Company is running 2 Tier (App VM & Sql Server Database VM) Financial Application in Azure. App VM is running in **App** Subnet and Sql Server Database VM is running in **DB** Subnet. Subnet are in Virtual Network KNET.

Virtual Network KNET Address is 192.168.0.0/16.
App Subnet Address is 192.168.2.0/24.
DB Subnet Address is 192.168.3.0/24.

Network security Group (NSG) with default values is associated with App and DB Subnet. No NSG is associated with VM NICs.

Management and Configuration of Database VM will happen through Application VM. Which means somebody will log on App VM and from their they will log on to SQL Server VM. SQL Server Management Studio is also installed on APP VM.

Following Requirement has been given by the Application Team.

1. Database Inbound and Outbound access to Internet should be blocked.
2. Database can only be accessed by App VM.

.

Solution: Blocking Database VM outbound Internet access

By default inbound Internet is blocked and Outbound Internet access is allowed on Azure VM. To Block Outbound internet Access on Database VM we will add a **Outbound Security rule** on NSG associated with DB Subnet which will **Deny** internet access as shown below.

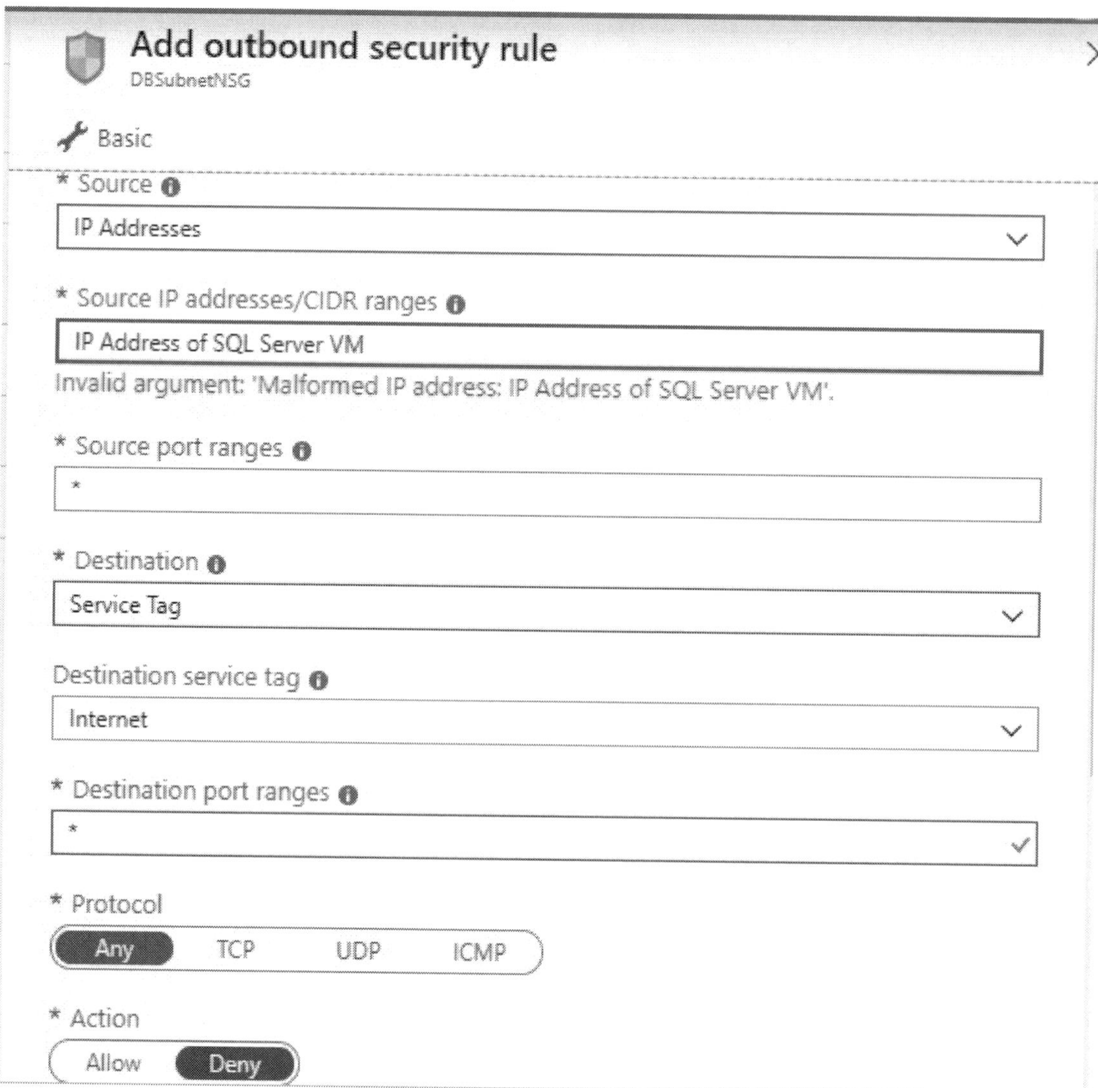

Block All Access to Database VM from all Sources

We will add **inbound security rule** on NSG associated with **DB Subnet** which will **block** Traffic from all sources to Database VM with **Priority 200** as shown below.

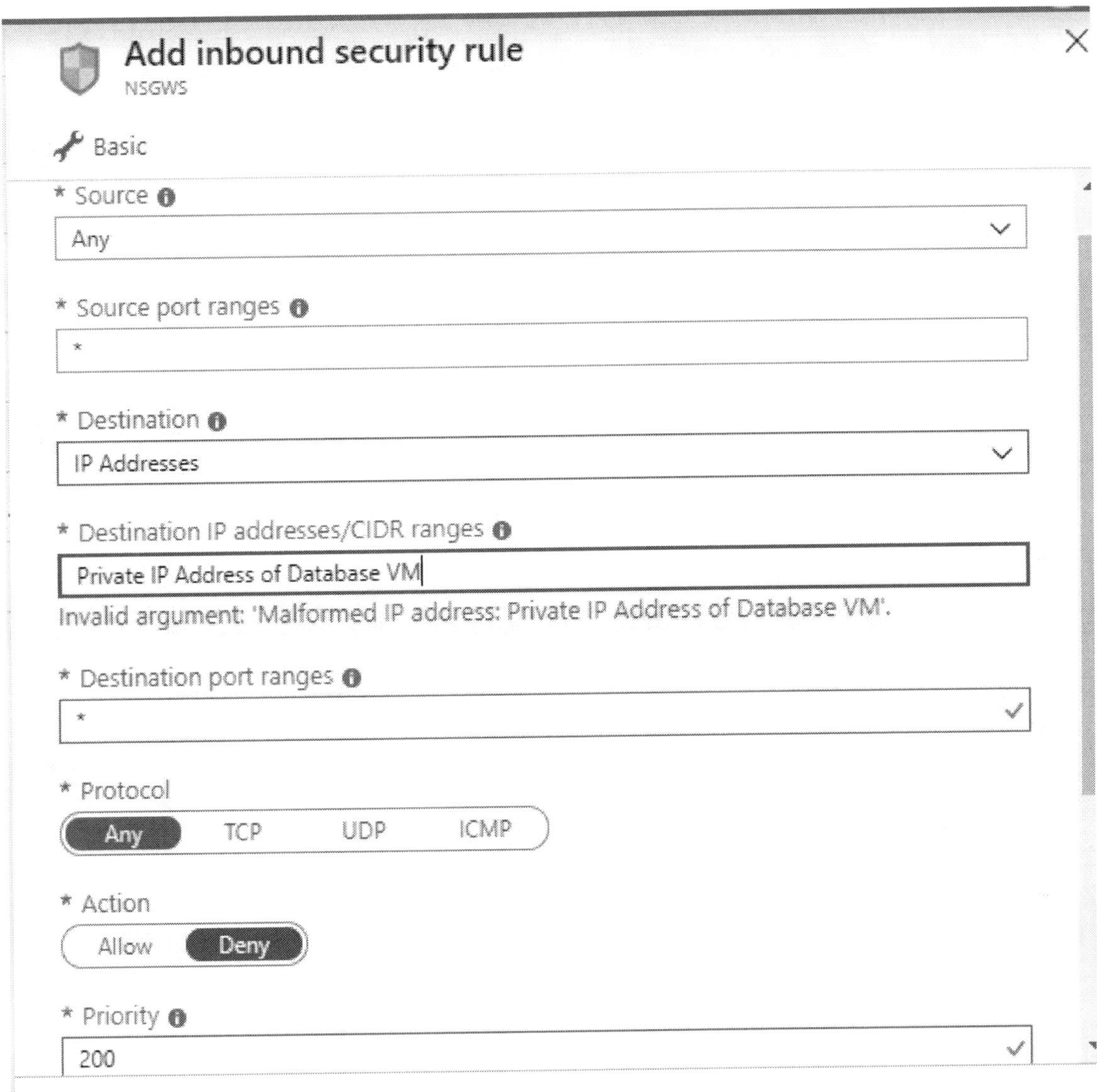

Allow Database access by App VM

We will add **inbound security rule** on NSG associated with DB Subnet which will **allow** Traffic only from App VM Private IP with **Priority 100** as shown below. This rule will Override Previous block rule as it has higher priority. Lower the Number higher the priority.

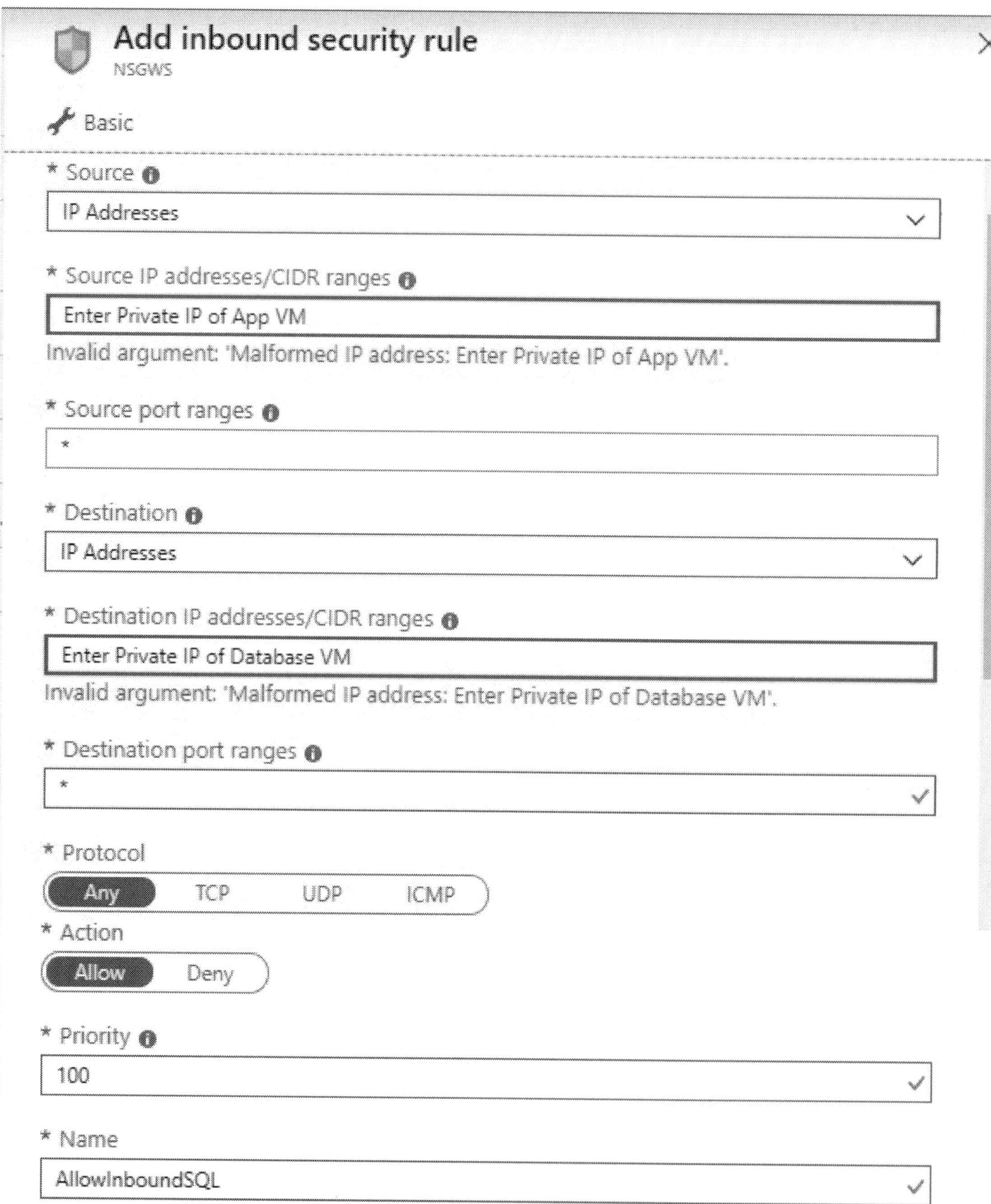

Case Study 4: Access to Database VM using UDR

A BFSI Company is running 2 Tier (App VM & Sql Server Database VM) Financial Application in Azure. App VM is running in **App** Subnet and Sql Server Database VM is running in **DB** Subnet. Subnet are in Virtual Network KNET.

Virtual Network KNET Address is 192.168.0.0/16.
App Subnet Address is 192.168.2.0/24.
DB Subnet Address is 192.168.3.0/24.

Network security Group with default values is associated with App and DB Subnet.

Following Requirement has been given by the company.

1. App VM Access to Database VM should be through Palo Alto Virtual Firewall.

App VM Access to Database VM through Palo Alto Virtual Firewall

We will create a new **DMZ** subnet with address 192.168 5.0 in Virtual Network KNET. We will install Palo Alto Virtual Firewall in DMZ Subnet. Lets assume the Private IP assigned to Firewall is 192.168.5.4. We will also enable IP forwarding on Palo Alto VM.

We will create a Route Table to be associated with App Subnet. We will add Route to this Route table with following values.

Address Prefix: Network Address of **DB** Subnet **192.168.3.0/24**.
Next Hop type: Select **Virtual Appliance** from Drop Down box.
Next Hop Address: Private IP Address of Palo Alto VM **192.168.5.4**.

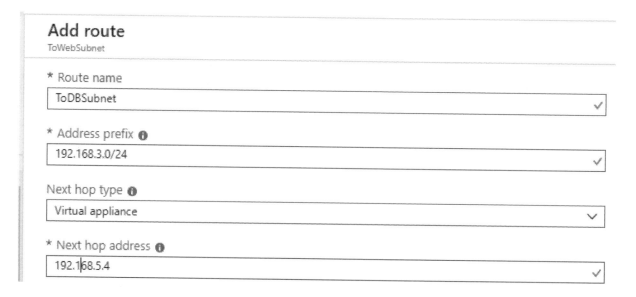

Though default system route specify that Traffic can flow directly between App and DB subnet but Traffic flows through Palo Alto VM **as UDR is preferred.**

Note 1: How to create Route Table and Add Route was shown in Exercise 18.
Note 2: How to enable IP Forwarding was shown in Exercise 18.

Case Study 5: Access to Azure SQL Database

A BFSI Company is running 2 Tier (App VM & Azure SQL Database) Financial Application in Azure. Azure SQL Database is Azure Managed Database Service. App VM is running in **On-Prem-Subnet** Subnet. **On-Prem-Subnet** is in Virtual Network **VNETOnPrem.**

Virtual Network **VNETOnPrem** Address is 192.168.0.0/16.
On-Prem-Subnet Subnet Address is 192.168.1.0/24.

Network security Group (NSG) with default values is associated with App. No NSG is associated with VM NICs.

Following Requirement has been given by the Application Team.

1. All Access of SQL Database should be through App Subnet in Virtual Network VNETOnPrem. The Traffic between App VM and Azure SQL Database should be on Microsoft Backbone Network and not on Public Internet.
2. Access to Azure SQL Database from Internet for Management purpose from specific Client IP is allowed.

Solution

We will use Virtual Network service Endpoint solution to allow access to Azure SQL Database only throught OnPrem-Subnet Subnet in Virtual Network VNETOnPrem. Using Virtual Network service Endpoint all Traffic between App VM and Azure SQL Database remains on Microsoft Backbone Network

To enable this solution we will use Firewall & Virtual Network option in Azure SQL Database Server Dashboard as shown below> We will click the link +Add existing Virtual Network to add the required Virtual Network & Subnet.

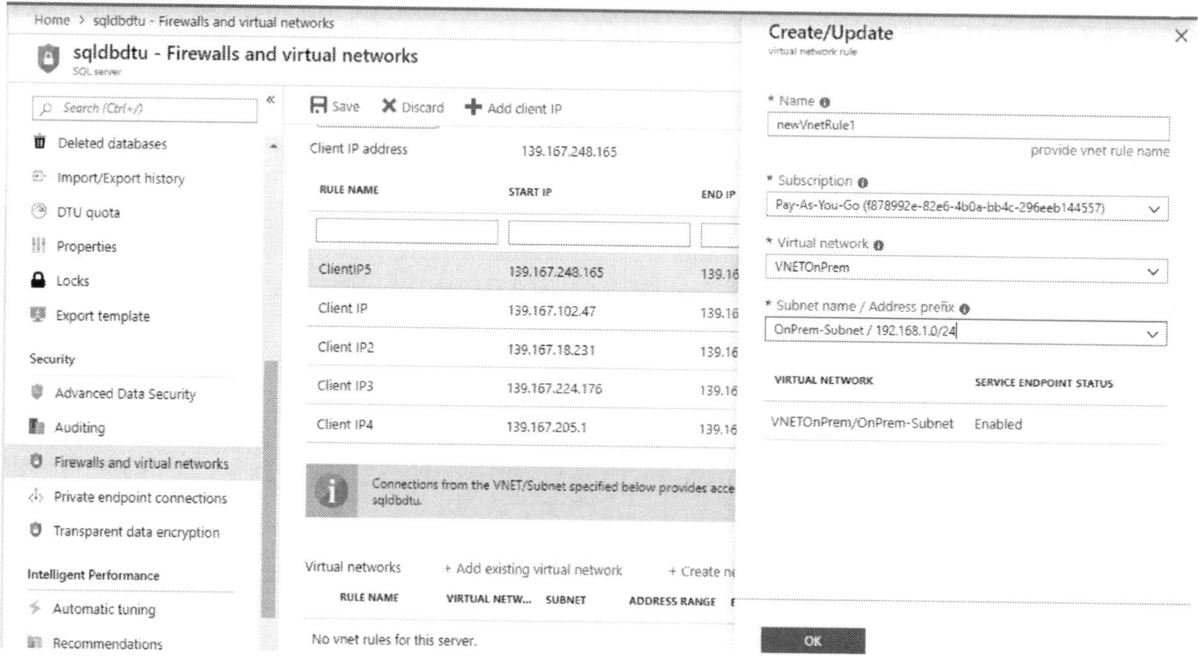

Make sure to Set the **Allow access to Azure services** control to Off in the above pane.

Bandwidth or Data Transfer Pricing

Bandwidth refers to data moving in and out of Azure data centers other than those explicitly covered by the Content Delivery Network or ExpressRoute pricing.

Inbound data transfers (data going into Azure data centers) is free.

Outbound Data Transfer (data going out of Azure data centers) is charged as shown below.

Outbound Data Transfer	Pricing
First 5 GB /Month	Free
5 GB - 10 TB /Month	$0.087 per GB
Next 40 TB (10 - 50 TB) /Month	$0.083 per GB
Next 100 TB (50 - 150 TB)/Month	$0.07 per GB
Next 350 TB (150 - 500 TB) /Month	$0.05 per GB
Over 500 TB / Month	Contact MS

Chapter 2 Virtual Network Hybrid Connectivity over Internet

This Chapter covers following Topic Lessons

- Virtual Network Hybrid Connectivity using Virtual Network Gateway
- VNET Hybrid Connectivity over Internet
- VPN Type
- VPN Gateway Editions
- VPN Gateway SKUs Use cases
- Site to Site VPN (S2S)
- Point to Site VPN (P2S)
- VPN Gateway Redundancy
- Border Gateway Protocol (BGP) with Azure VPN Gateways
- Forced Tunnelling

This Chapter covers following Lab Exercises

- Connecting Virtual Networks using S2S VPN
- Connecting Virtual Network to On-Premises VPN Device using S2S VPN

Chapter Topology

In this chapter we will add GatewaySubnet to Virtual Network VNETCloud. We will then create Virtual Network Gateway (VNG) in GatewaySubnet.

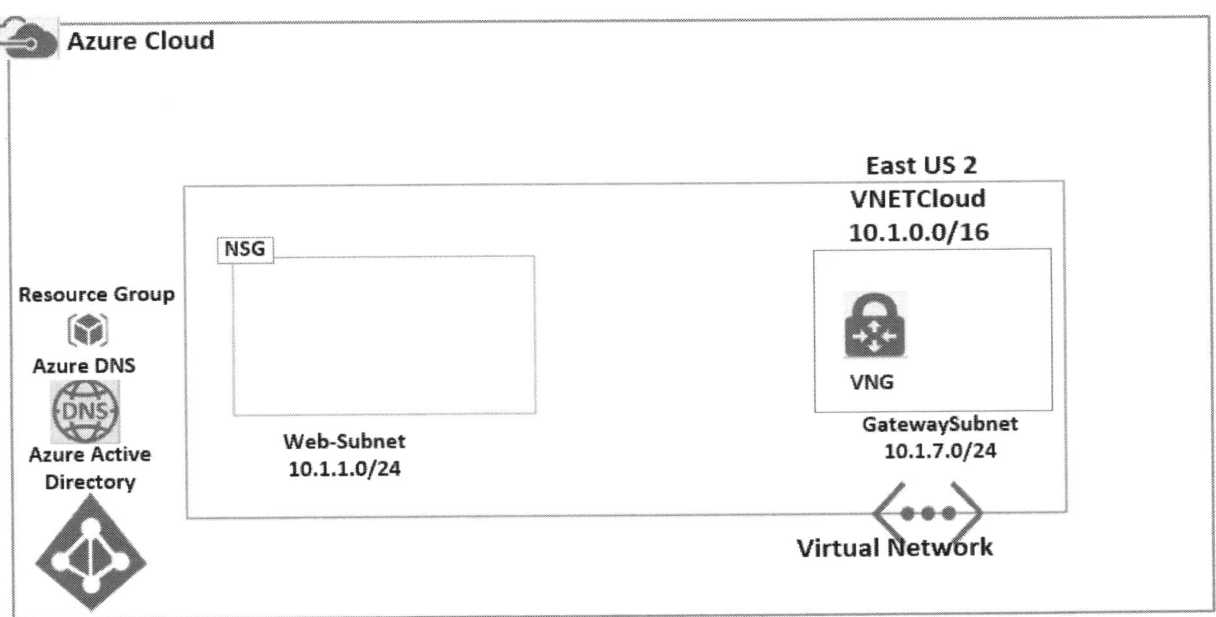

We will also add GatewaySubnet to Virtual Network VNETOnPrem. We will then create Virtual Network Gateway (VNG) in GatewaySubnet.

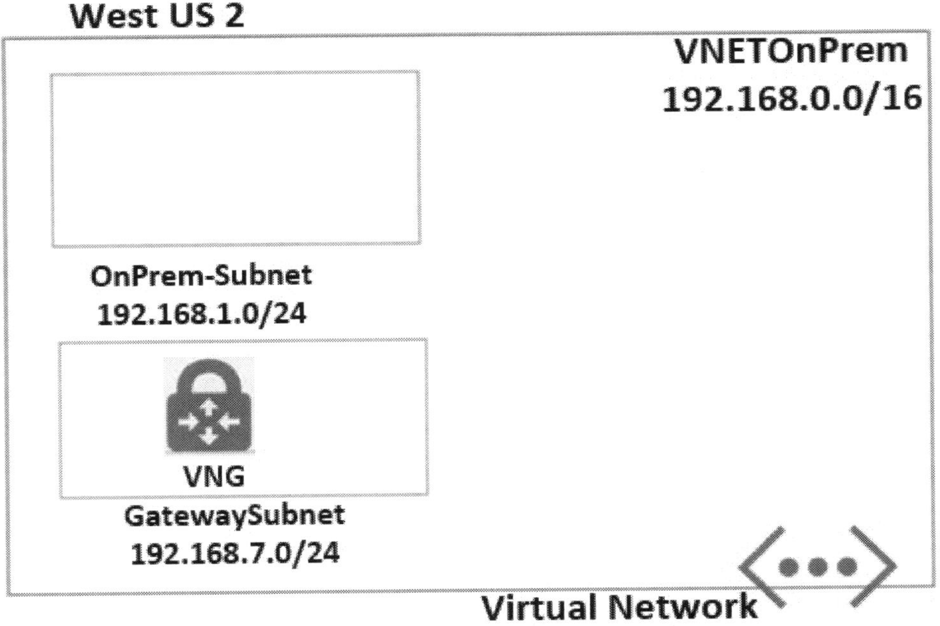

We will connect VNETCloud and VNETOnPrem using S2S VPN.

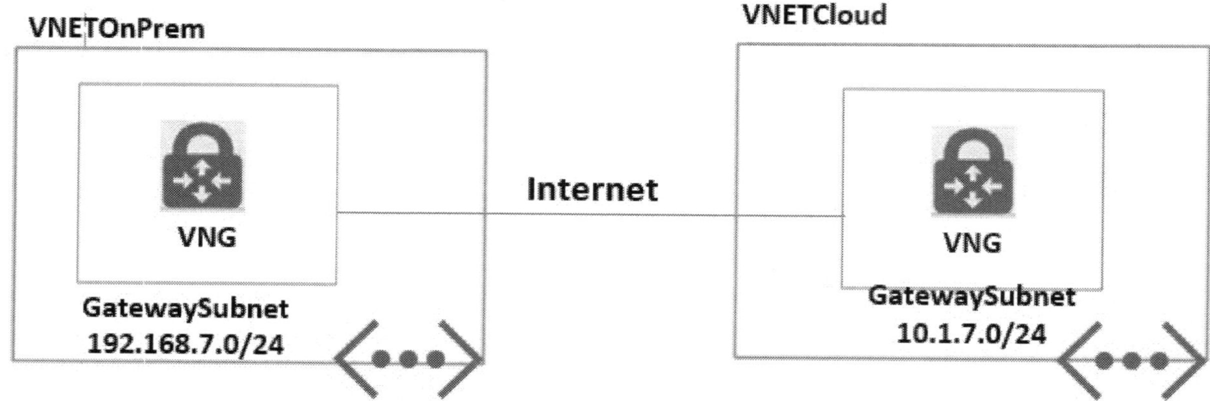

Virtual Network Hybrid Connectivity using Virtual Network Gateway

You can connect Virtual Network to on-premises Datacenter through virtual network gateway located in GatewaySubnet using either Internet VPN (P2S or S2S VPN) or ExpressRoute Private WAN connectivity.

For Internet VPN you deploy virtual network gateway of type VPN. For Private WAN connectivity you deploy virtual network gateway of type ExpressRoute.

Figure below shows Virtual Network Connected to on-premises Datacenter.

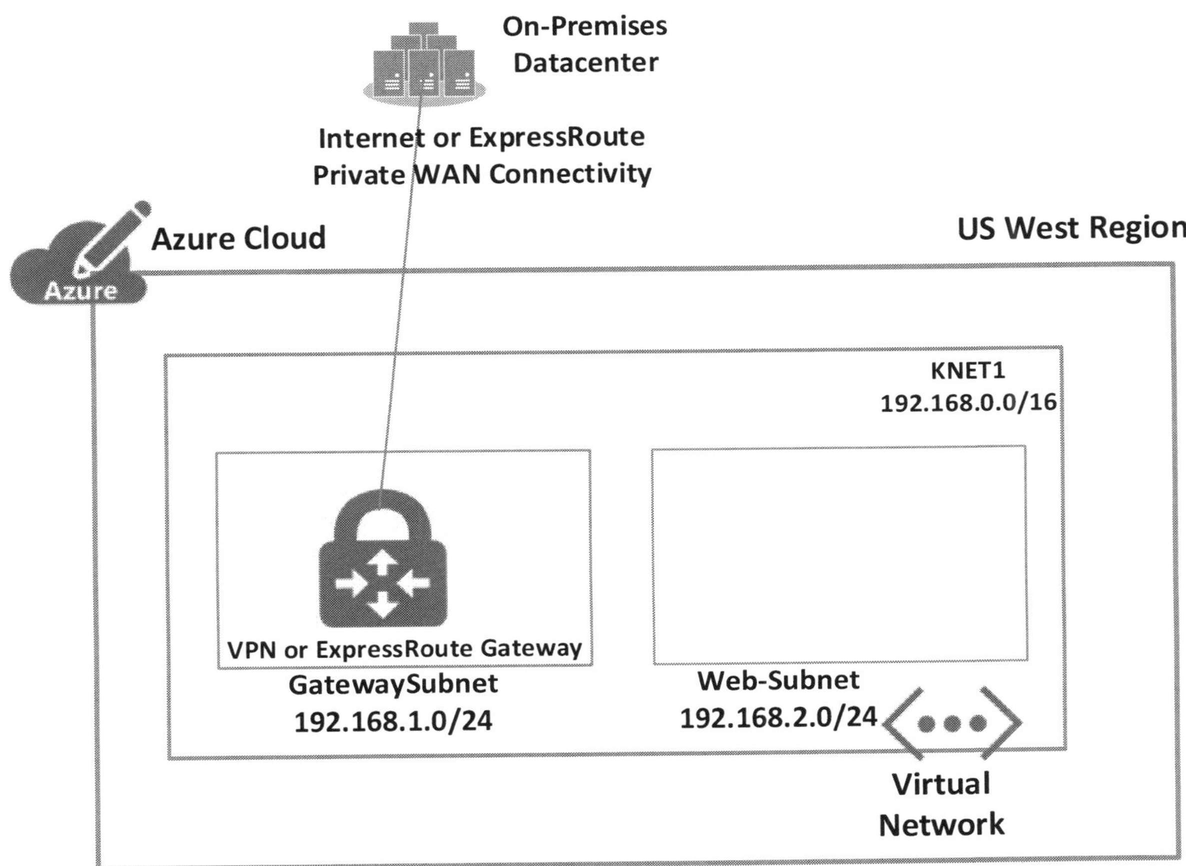

Every Azure VPN gateway consists of two instances in an active-standby or active-active configuration.

Note: ExpressRoute will be discussed in Chapter 13

VNET Hybrid Connectivity over Internet

You can connect Virtual Network (VNET) to your on-premises networks over public internet using Azure VPN Gateway. A VPN gateway is a type of virtual network gateway that sends encrypted traffic across a public connection. The connectivity uses the industry-standard protocols Internet Protocol Security (IPsec) and Internet Key Exchange (IKE).

VPN gateway connects VNET to on-premises network using Site to Site VPN (S2S) or Point to Site VPN (P2S). S2S VPN uses **VPN device** on-premises. P2S VPN uses **VPN client software** on client computers in on premises infrastructure.

VPN Gateway is created in GatewaySubnet. A GatewaySubnet is created in Azure Virtual Network (VNET).

Figure below shows Virtual Network Connected to on-premises Datacenter.

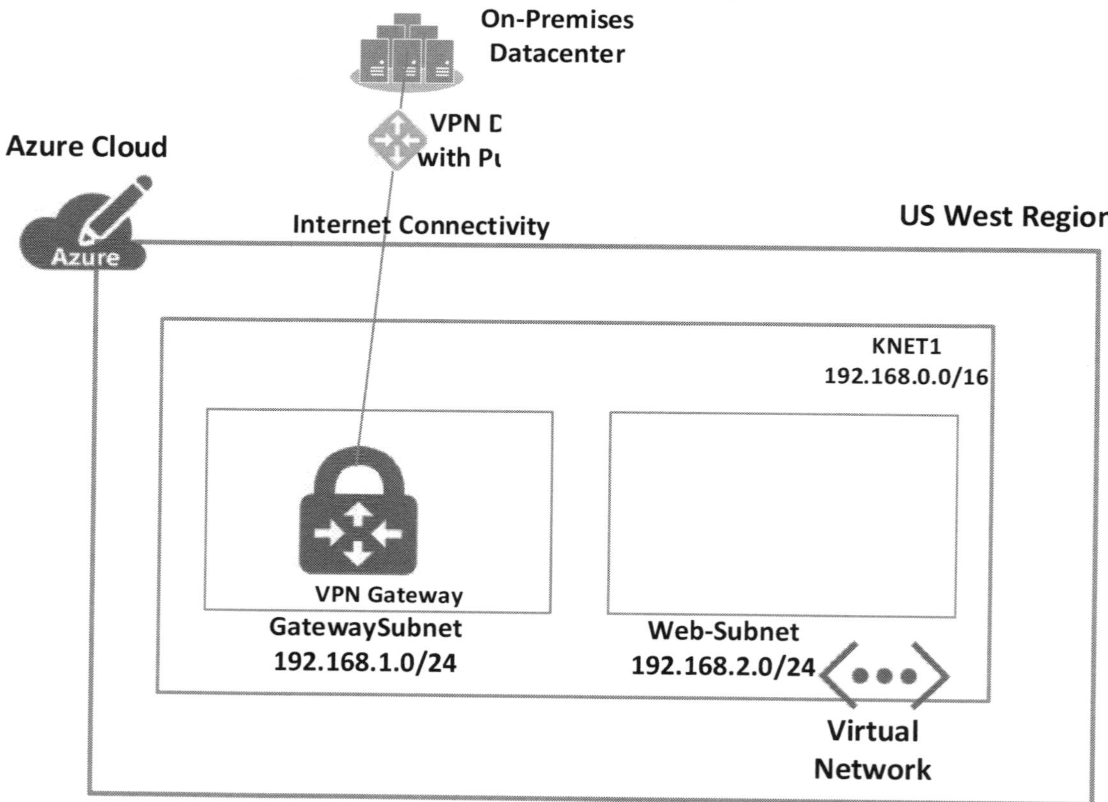

Every Azure VPN gateway consists of two instances in an active-standby configuration.

VPN Type

VPN gateway supports following 2 type of VPN. VPN Types are selected when you are creating Virtual Network gateway of type VPN.

PolicyBased: PolicyBased VPNs were previously called static routing gateways. Policy-based VPNs encrypt and direct packets through IPsec tunnels based on the IPsec policies configured with the combinations of address prefixes between your on-premises network and the Azure VNet.

1. PolicyBased VPNs can **only** be used on the Basic gateway SKU.
2. You can have only 1 tunnel when using a PolicyBased VPN.
3. You can only use PolicyBased VPNs for S2S connections.
4. PolicyBased VPN does not support Point to Site VPN (P2S).

RouteBased: RouteBased VPNs were previously called dynamic routing gateways. RouteBased VPNs use "routes" in the IP forwarding or routing table to direct packets into their corresponding tunnel interfaces. The tunnel interfaces then encrypt or decrypt the packets in and out of the tunnels.

Table below shows comparison between Route-Based and Policy Based VPN.

Features	Route-Based	Policy-Based
Point-to-Site (P2S)	Supported	Not Supported
Site-to-Site (S2S)	Supported	Supported
S2S VNet-to-VNet	Supported	Not Supported
S2S Multi-Site	Supported	Not Supported
S2S and ExpressRoute coexist	Supported	Not Supported
Max IPSec Tunnels	128	1
Authentication	Pre-shared key for S2S connectivity, Certificates for P2S connectivity	Pre-shared key
Gateway SKU	Basic, VpnGw1, VpnGw2, VpnGw3	Basic

VPN Gateway Editions

VPN gateway comes in following 4 Editions or SKUs.

Features	Basic Gateway	VpnGw1	VpnGw2	VpnGw3
Gateway throughput	100 Mbps	650 Mbps	1 Gbps	1.25 Gbps
Gateway max IPsec tunnels for Route Based VPN	10	30	30	30
Gateway max IPsec tunnels for Policy Based VPN	1	NA	NA	NA
Max P2S connections	128	128	128	128
Active-Active S2S VPN	No	Yes	Yes	Yes
BGP support	No	Yes	Yes	Yes
Route-Based VPN	Yes	Yes	Yes	Yes
Policy-Based VPN	Yes	No	No	No

VPN Gateway SKUs Use cases

Workloads	SKUs
Production & critical workloads	VpnGw1, VpnGw2, VpnGw3
Dev-test or proof of concept	Basic

Site to Site VPN (S2S)

A Site-to-Site (S2S) VPN gateway connects Virtual Network (VNET) to on premises infrastructure over IPsec/IKE VPN tunnel. This type of connection requires a VPN device located on-premises that has public IP address assigned to it and is not located behind a NAT.

Site to Site VPN can also be used to connect VNET to VNET.

Figure below shows VNET to on-premises connectivity. A VPN Device is required on-premises with Public IP (Not shown in below Figure).

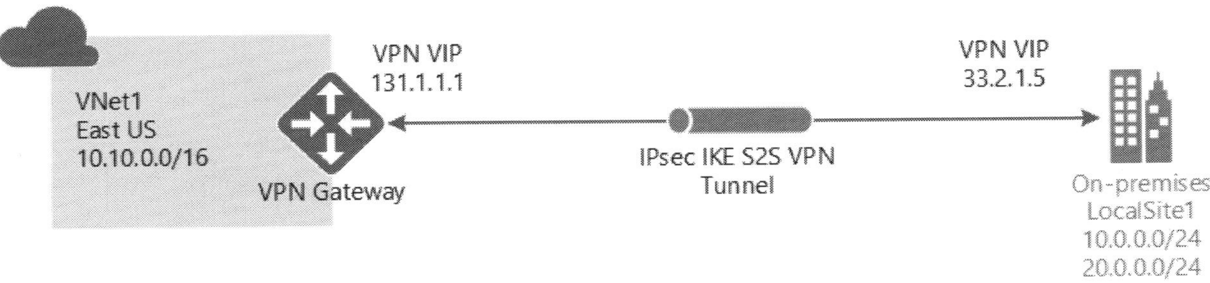

Figure below Shows VNET to on-premises Connectivity (Multisite).

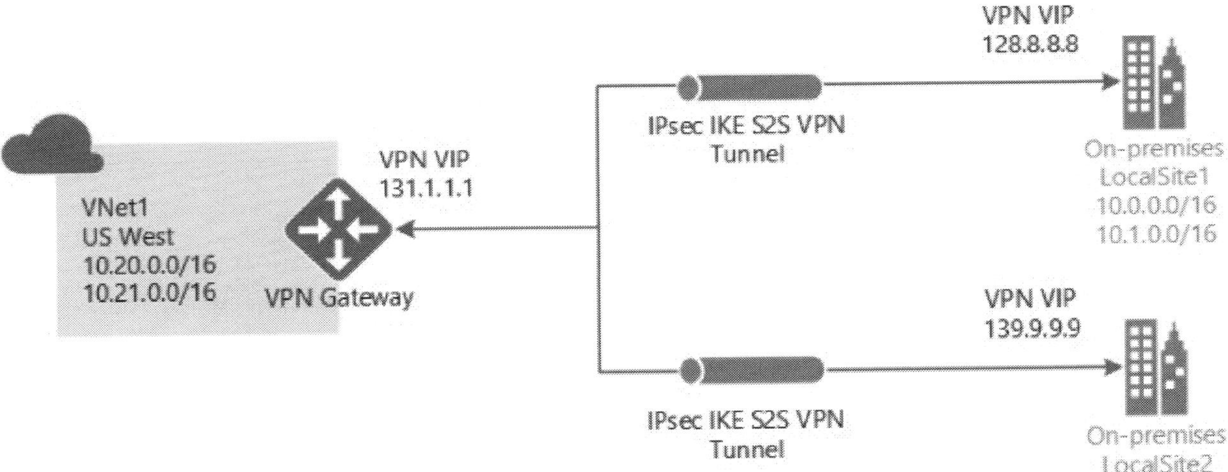

Figure below shows VNET to VNET connectivity.

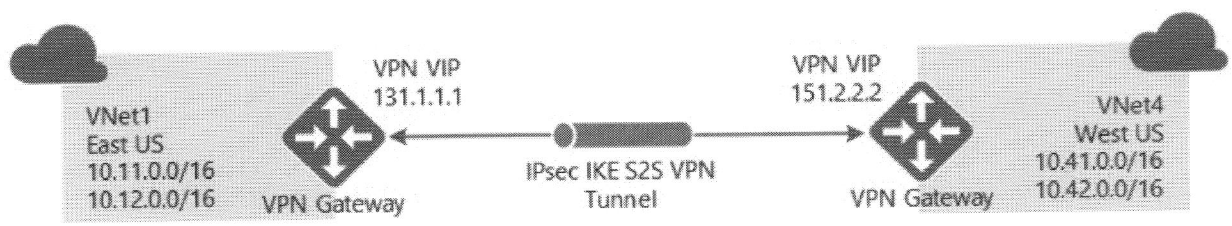

Design Nuggets for S2S VPN

a. VPN Gateway is created in GatewaySubnet (Not shown above).
b. By default VPN gateway consists of two instances in an active-standby configuration.
c. On-Premises require a VPN device with Public IP (Not shown above).
d. On premises addresses should not overlap with VNET addresses.
e. **S2S VPN only supports pre shared key as Authentication.**
f. **Public IP is dynamically assigned. Static IP is not supported for VPN Gateway.**
g. Do not assign Network Security Group (NSG) to GatewaySubnet.

Point to Site VPN (P2S)

A Point-to-Site (P2S) VPN gateway creates a secure connection between virtual network and on-premises using VPN client software installed on individual client computers. P2S is a VPN connection over SSTP (Secure Socket Tunneling Protocol). P2S connections do not require a VPN device or a public-facing IP address to work.

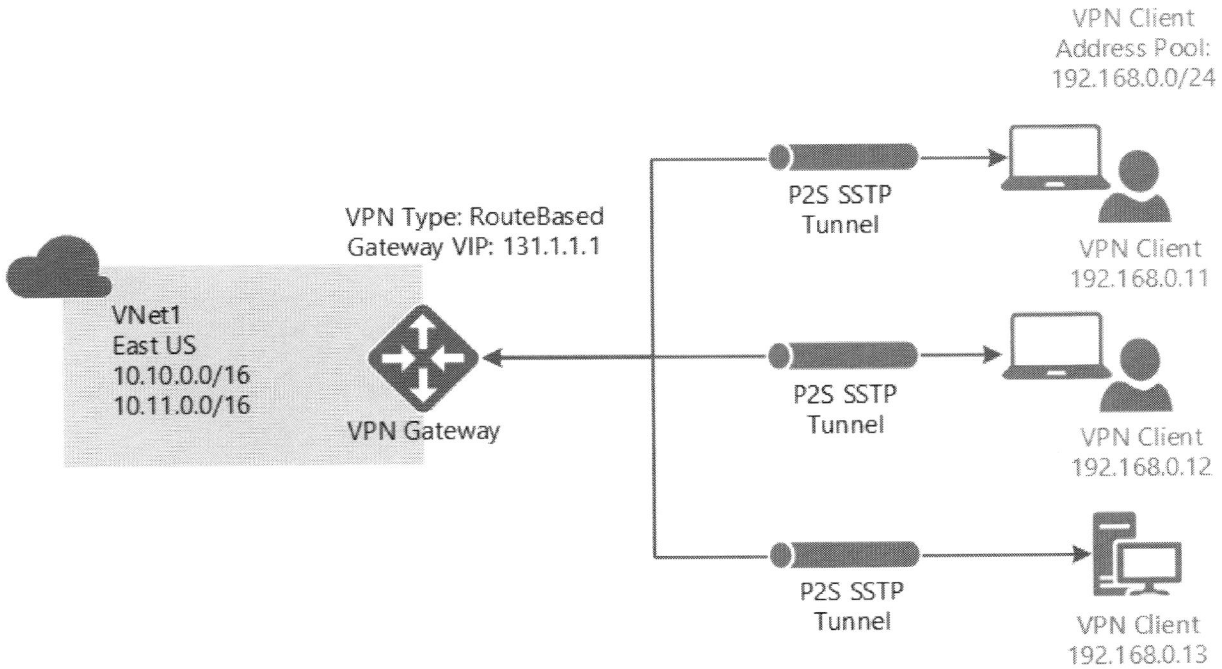

Design Nuggets P2S VPN

1. VPN Gateway is created in GatewaySubnet (Not shown above).
2. By default VPN gateway consists of two instances in an active-standby configuration.
3. On premises addresses should not overlap with VNET addresses.
4. **P2S VPN uses certificates as Authentication for client connections.**
5. **Public IP is dynamically assigned. Static IP is not supported for VPN Gateway.**
6. Do not assign Network Security Group (NSG) to GatewaySubnet.

Note: In Chapter 4, Part 2 Book we have P2S VPN Lab Exercise.

Exercise 20: Connecting Virtual Networks using S2S VPN

In this exercise we will Connect Virtual Networks VNETCloud & VNETOnPrem using S2S VPN. VNETCloud & VNETOnPrem were created in Exercise 3 and 6 respectively in Chapter 1.

Step 1 Create GatewaySubnet in Virtual Network VNETCloud

In Virtual Network VNETCloud Dashboard Click Subnets in left pane> Subnet blade opens as shown below.

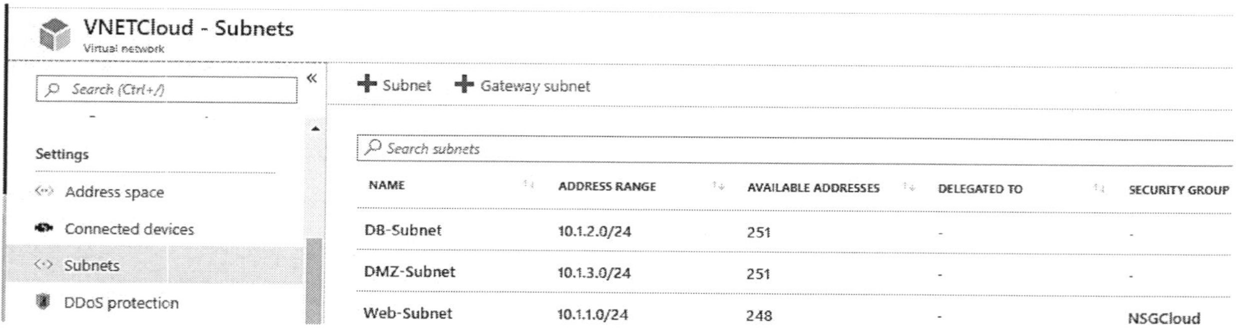

In right pane Click +GatewaySubnet> Add Subnet blade opens> In Address Range enter 10.1.7.0/24. Select none for Route table & Subnet Delegation & 0 for Service Endpoints>Click Ok (Not Shown).

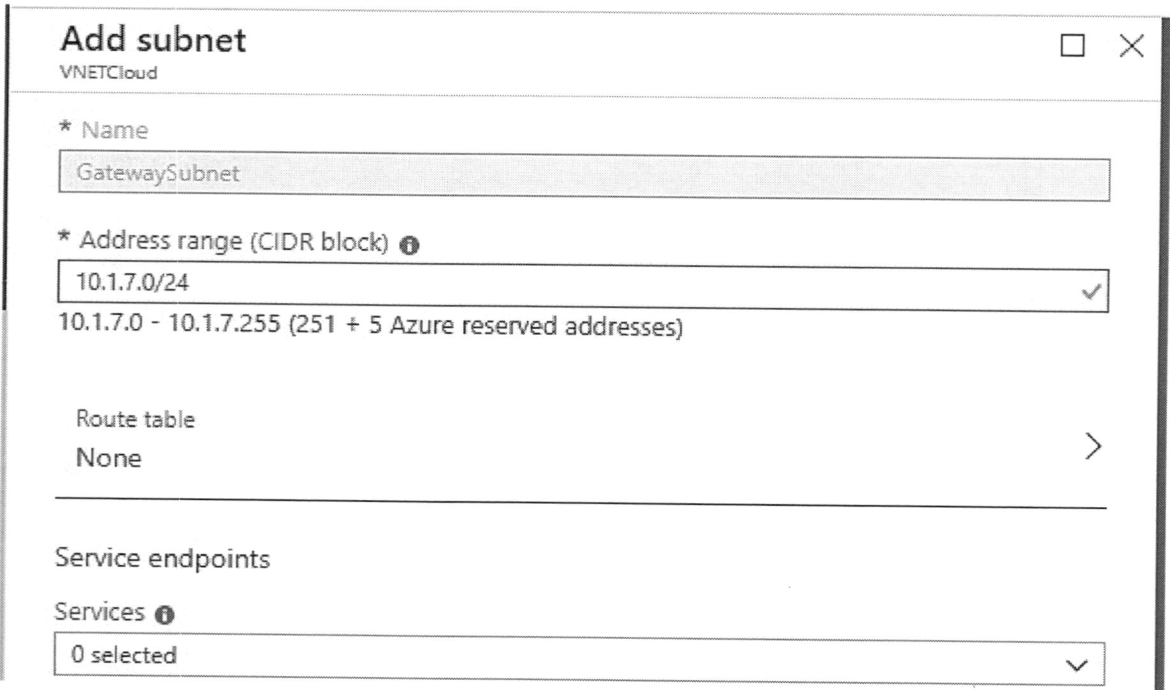

Step 2 Create Virtual Network Gateway in GatewaySubnet of VNETCloud

Click Create a resource>Networking>Virtual Network gateway> Create virtual network gateway blade opens>Enter a name, Select Location EAST US 2, Select gateway type as VPN, VPN type as route based, Select SKU VpnGw1, Select VNETCloud and Select Create new Public IP and enter a name> Make sure active-active mode and BGP option are disabled>Click Review +create (Not Shown)>After validation is passed click create.

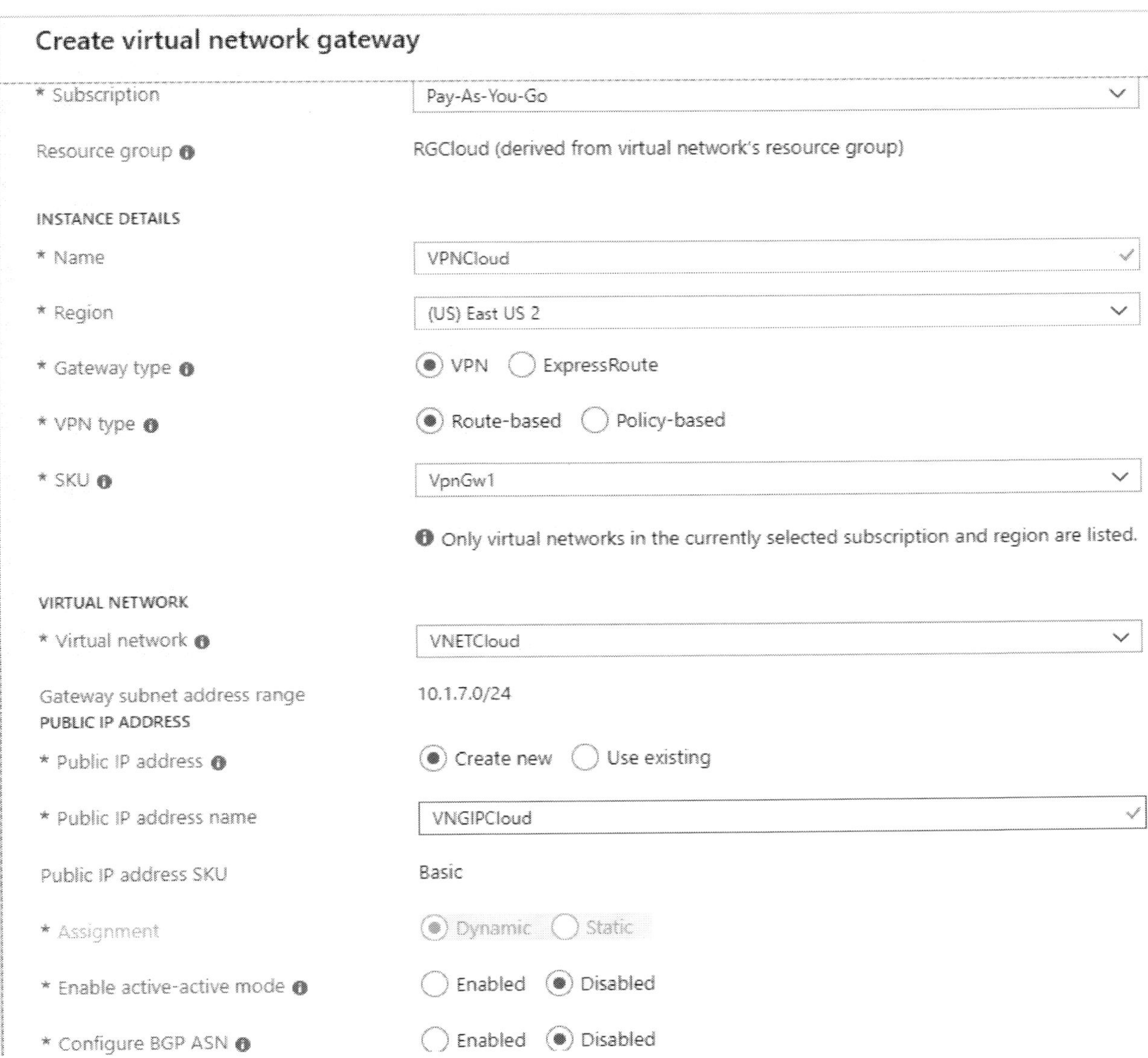

Figure below shows Dashboard of Virtual Network gateway VPNCloud.

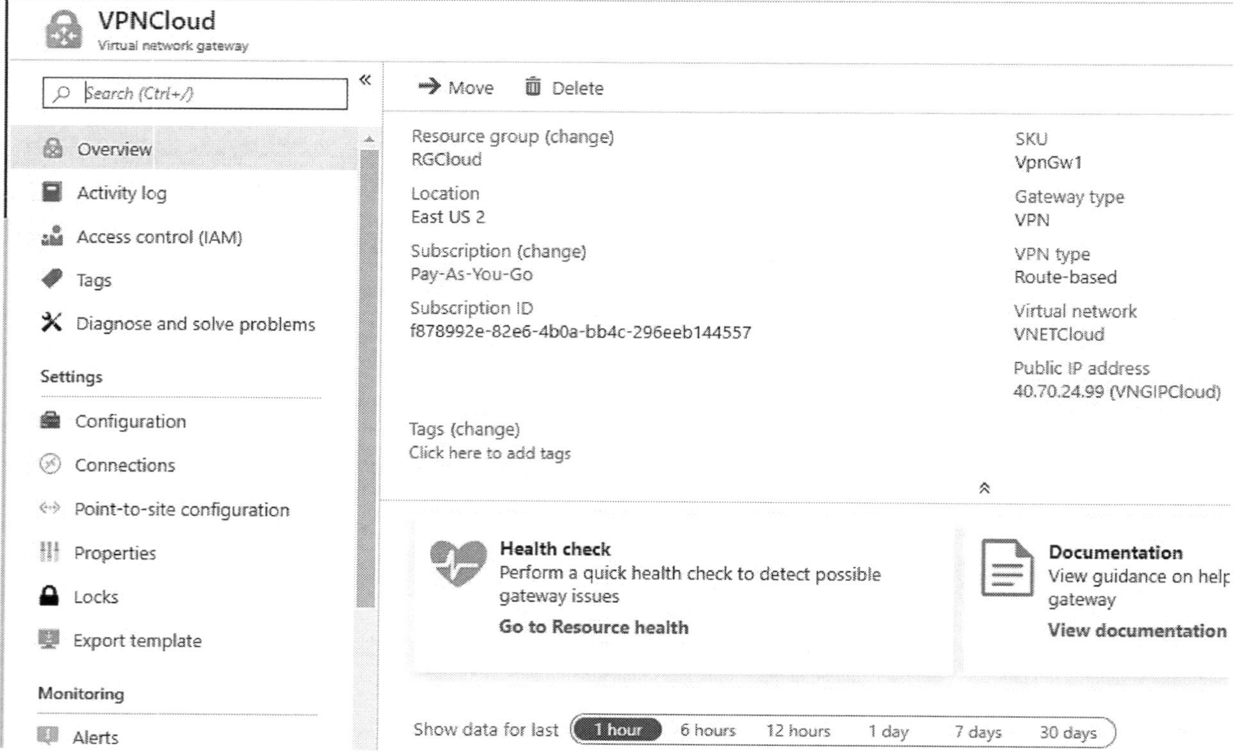

Step 3 Create GatewaySubnet in Virtual Network VNETOnPrem

In Virtual Network VNETCloudOnPrem Dashboard Click Subnets in left pane> Subnet blade opens as shown below.

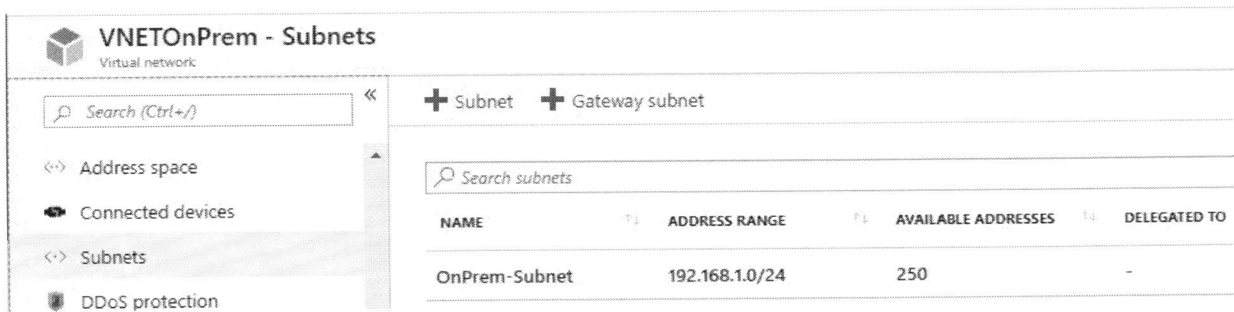

In right pane Click +GatewaySubnet> Add Subnet blade opens> In Address Range enter 192.168.7.0/24. Select none for Route table & Subnet Delegation & 0 for Service Endpoints>Click Ok (Not Shown).

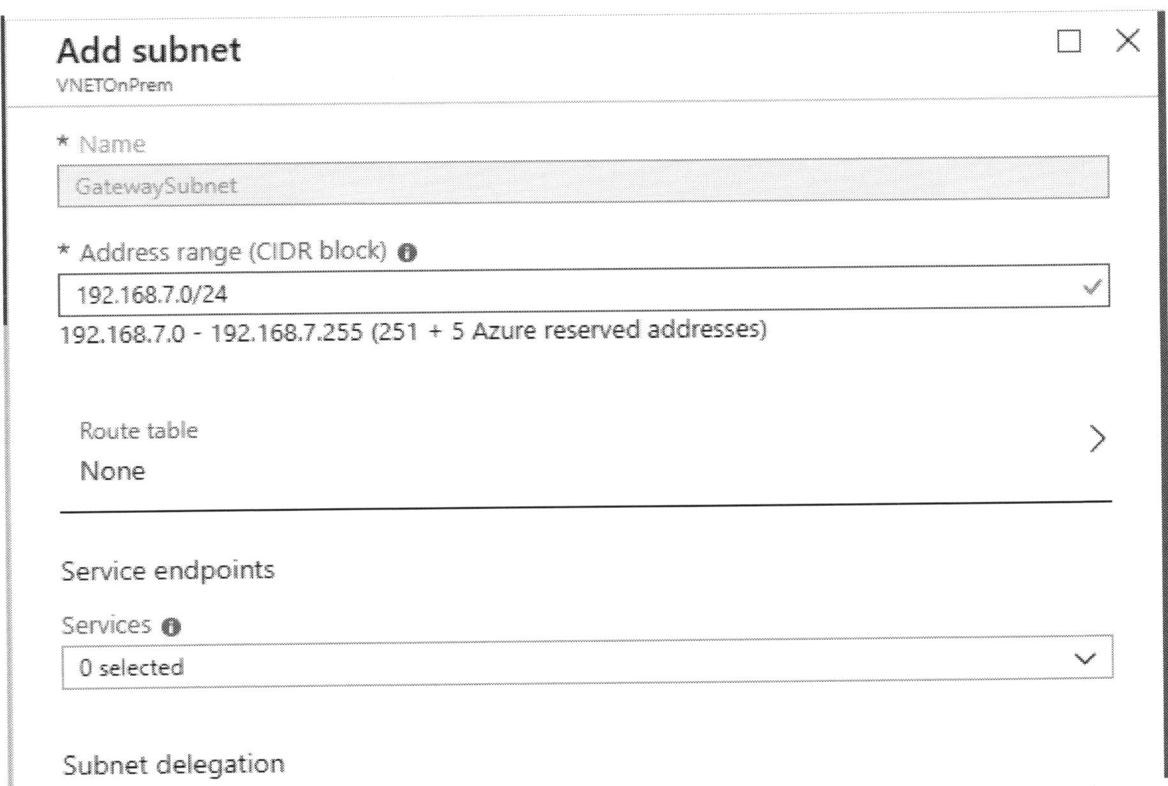

Step 4 Create Virtual Network Gateway in GatewaySubnet of VNETOnPrem

Click Create a resource>Networking>Virtual Network gateway> Create virtual network gateway blade opens>Enter a name, Select Location West US 2, Select gateway type as VPN, VPN type as route based, Select SKU VpnGw1, Select VNETOnPrem and Select Create new Public IP and enter a name> Make sure active- active mode and BGP option are disabled>Click Review +create (Not Shown)>After validation is passed click create.

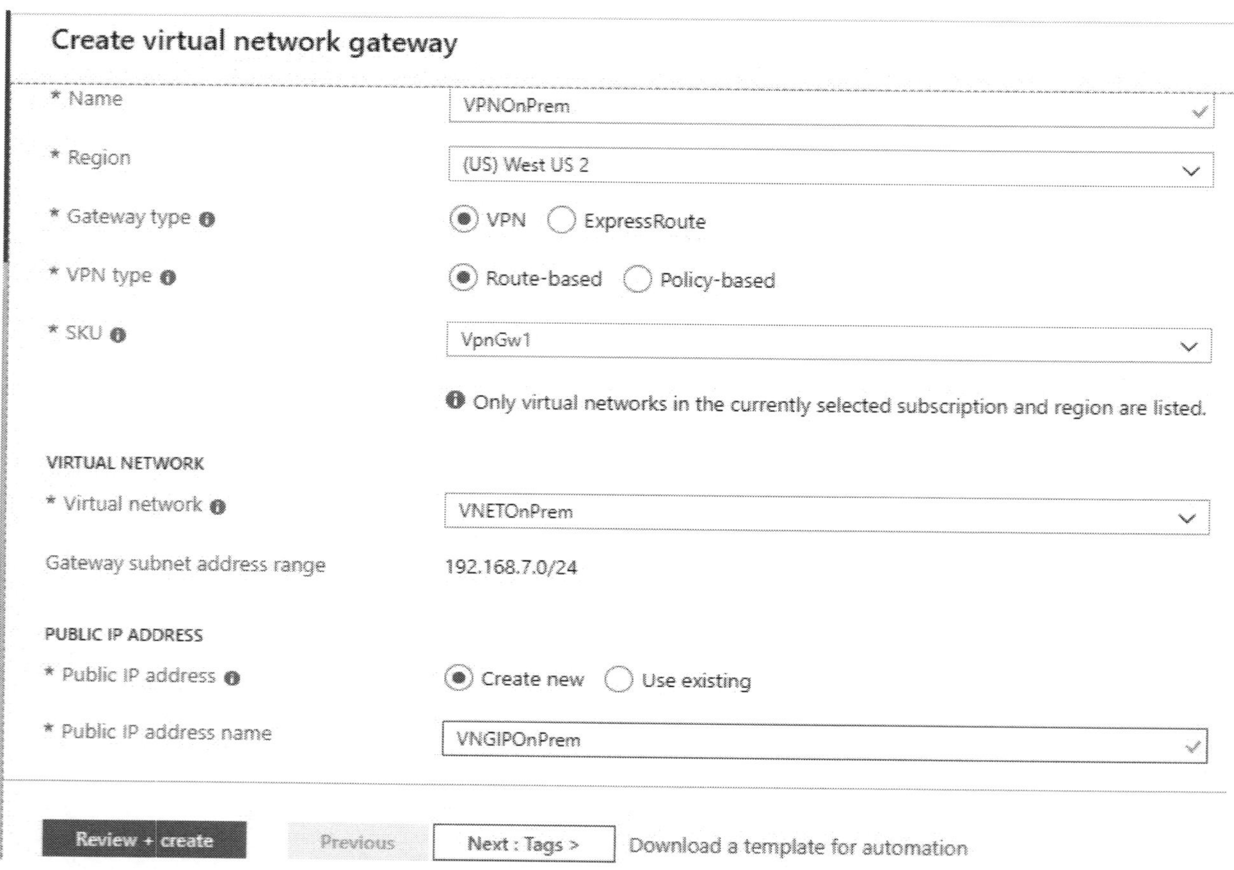

Figure below shows Dashboard of Virtual Network Gateway VPNOnPrem

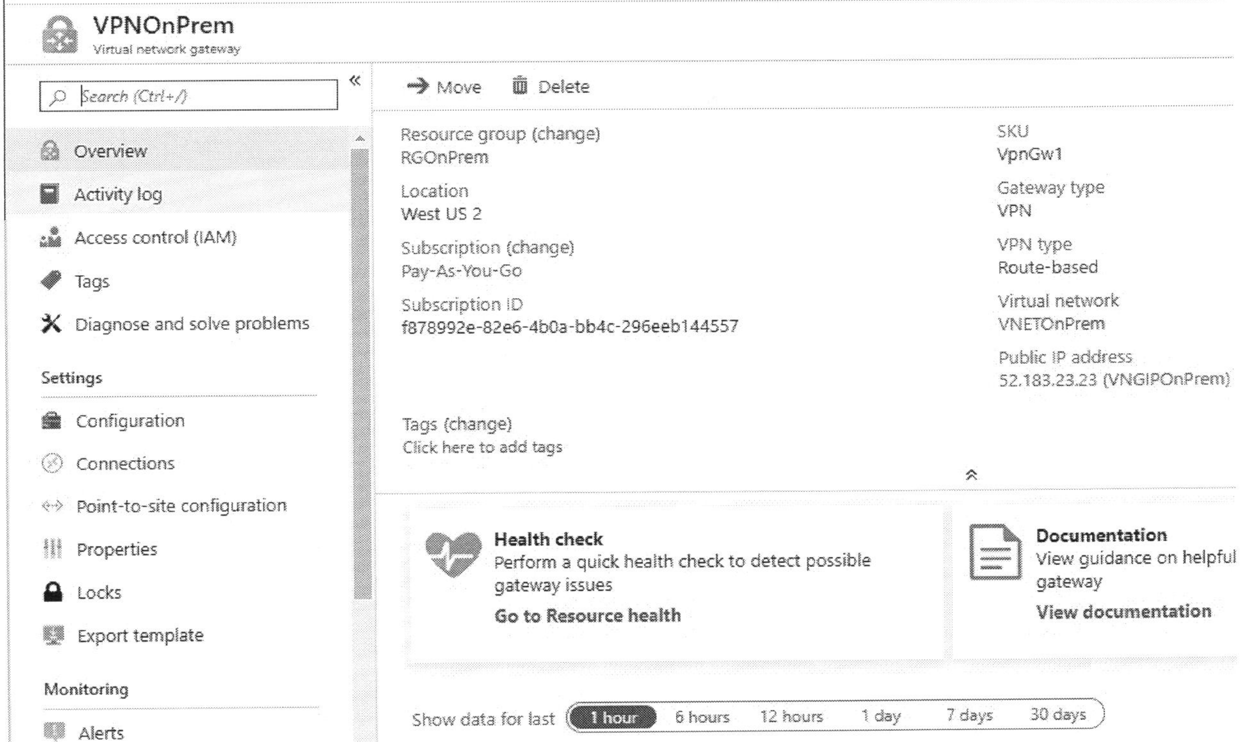

Step 3 Create Virtual Network VNETCloud Gateway Connection

Go to Virtual Network gateway VPNCloud Dashboard>Click Connections in left pane> In Right pane Click +Add> Add Connection Blade opens>Enter a name> In Connection type select VNet-to-VNet> First VNG should be VPNCloud, Second VNG should be VPNOnPrem, Enter a shared key 123xyz>Make sure Resource Group is RGCloud> Click Ok.
Note: Shared key must be same on both sides.

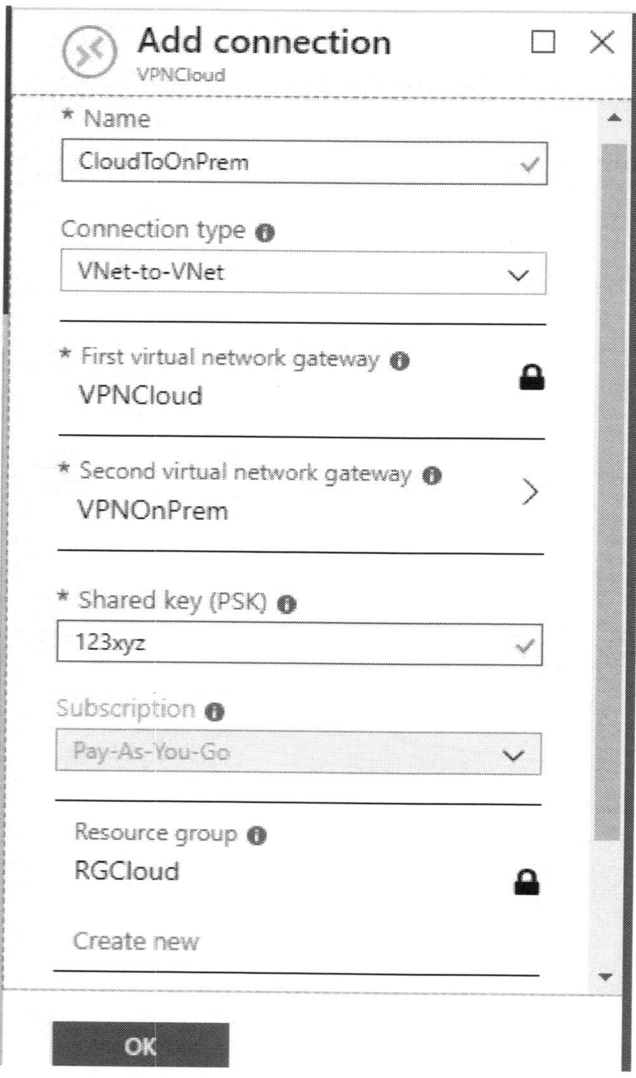

Step 4 Create Virtual Network VNETOnPrem Gateway Connection

Go to Virtual Network gateway VPNOnPrem Dashboard>Click Connections in left pane> In Right pane Click +Add> Add Connection Blade opens>Enter a name> In Connection type select VNet-to-VNet> First VNG should be VPNOnPrem, Second VNG should be VPNCloud, Enter a shared key 123xyz>Make sure Resource Group is RGOnPrem> Click Ok.
Note: Shared key must be same on both sides.

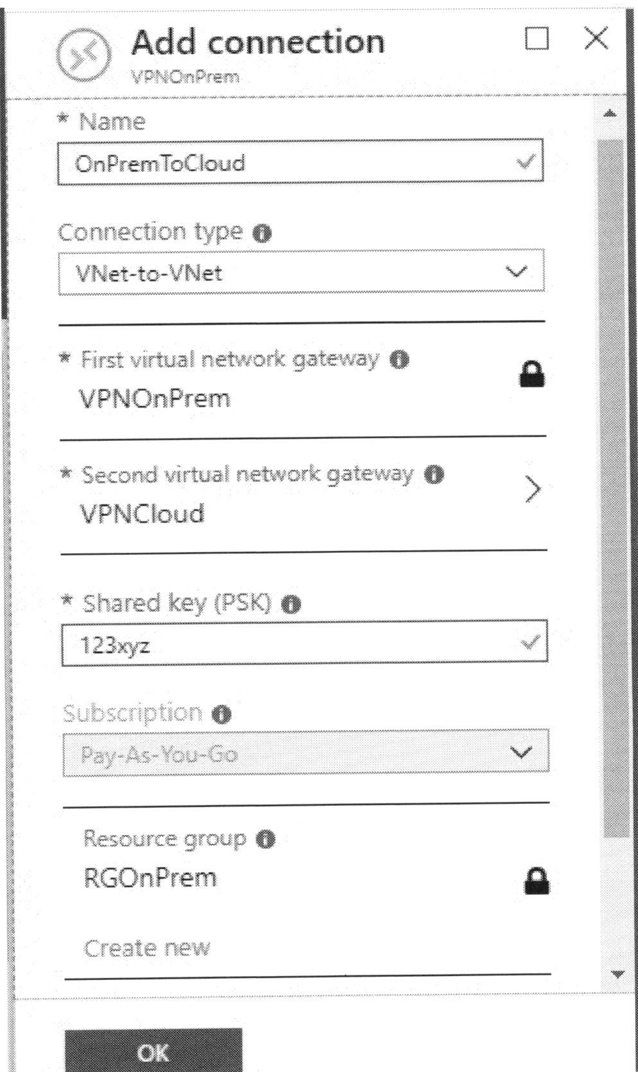

Step 5 Checking the Connections Created and flow of Data

Do this exercise after 5 minutes of previous exercise.

1. Go to either Virtual Network Gateway VPNCloud or VPNOnPrem Dashboard> Click Connections in left pane> It will show both the connection with status Connected. If not then wait till it shows. If required refresh the screen with F5.

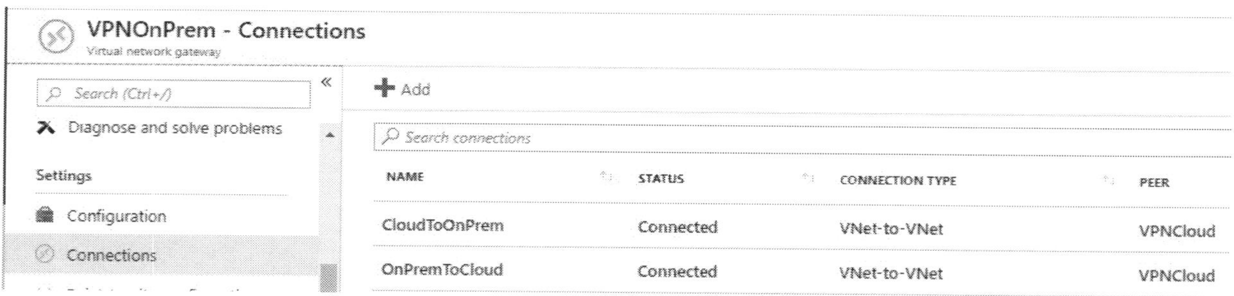

2. RDP to VM VMFE1> Open Command Prompt and Ping Private IP of VMAD. It was successful.

Administrator: Command Prompt

```
Microsoft Windows [Version 10.0.17763.437]
(c) 2018 Microsoft Corporation. All rights reserved.

C:\Users\AdminAccount>ping 192.168.1.4

Pinging 192.168.1.4 with 32 bytes of data:
Reply from 192.168.1.4: bytes=32 time=72ms TTL=128
Reply from 192.168.1.4: bytes=32 time=72ms TTL=128
Reply from 192.168.1.4: bytes=32 time=71ms TTL=128
Reply from 192.168.1.4: bytes=32 time=71ms TTL=128

Ping statistics for 192.168.1.4:
    Packets: Sent = 4, Received = 4, Lost = 0 (0% loss),
Approximate round trip times in milli-seconds:
    Minimum = 71ms, Maximum = 72ms, Average = 71ms
```

3. Click one of the connection. You can see Data in and Data Out.

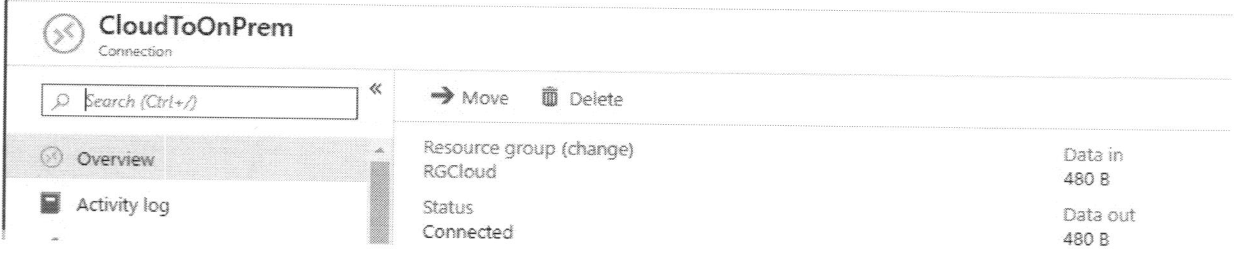

Exercise 21: Connecting VNET to On-Prem VPN Device using S2S VPN

This is a demonstration exercise to Connect Virtual Network VNETCloud to On-Prem VPN Device. We will use the Virtual Network Gateway VPNCloud created in Previous Exercise. **We will assume Public IP Assigned to On-Prem VPN device is 128.8.8.8.** We will assume Address range of On-Prem Network located behind public IP is 10.101.0.0/24. Virtual Network VNETCloud was created in Exercise 3.

Below is the topology for this Exercise.

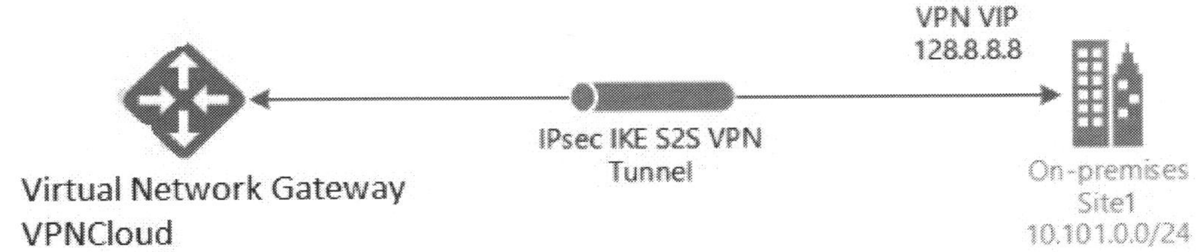

In this setup we add one more step, which is creating Local Network Gateway. Local network gateway refers to your on-premises location.

Following are the steps for this exercise.

1. Create GatewaySubnet (Already created in previous Exercise 20).
2. Create Virtual Network Gateway VPNCloud (created in previous Exercise 20).
3. Create Local Network Gateway
4. Configure On-Prem VPN Device
5. Create VPN Connection

Step 3: Create Local Network Gateway

Local network gateway refers to your on-premises location. We need to specify the IP address of the on-premises VPN device to which we will create a connection. We also need to specify the IP address prefixes. The address prefixes you specify are the prefixes located on your on-premises network.

Click Create a resource> In the search box, type Local network gateway, then press Enter to search. This will return a list of results. Click Local network gateway and then click the Create button to open the Create local network gateway Blade>Enter name>Enter Public IP of VPN Device and select IP Addresses of on-premises network >Select RG RGCloud>Click Create.

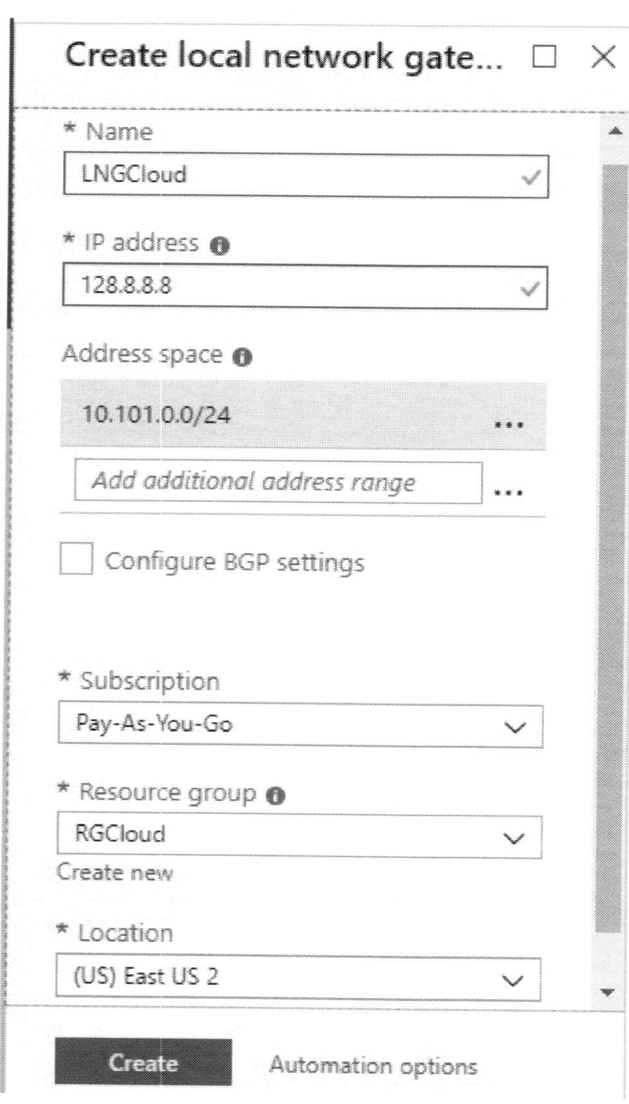

Figure below shows the dashboard of Local Network Gateway LNGCloud.

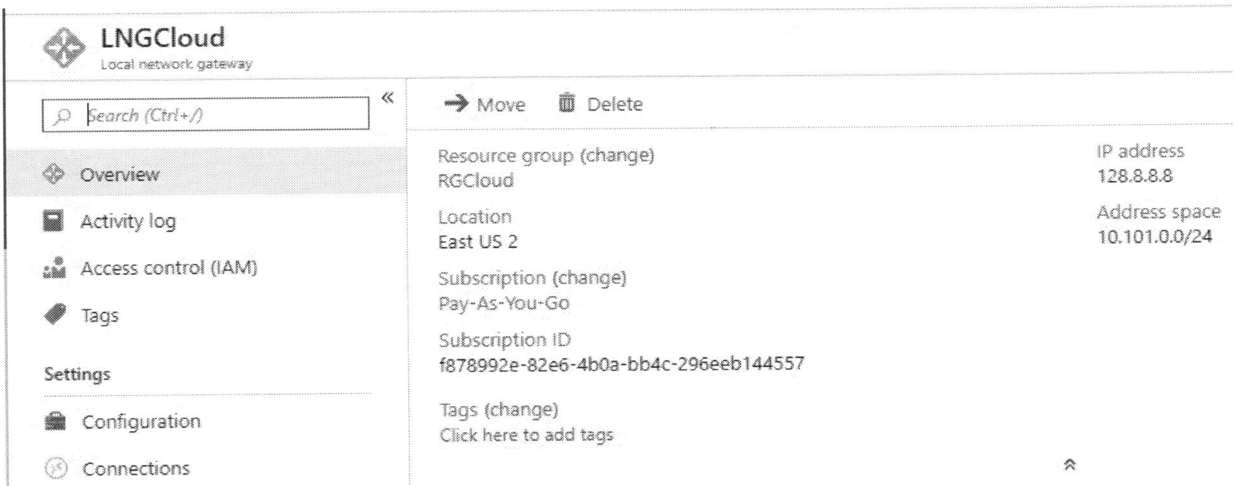

Step 4: Configure On-prem VPN Device with S2S VPN and shared key 123xyz.

Step 5 Create the VPN connection: Go to Local Network Gateway LNGCloud or Virtual Network Gateway VPNCloud Dashboard>Click Connections in left pane> Click +Add. Add Connection blade opens> Enter a name>In Virtual Gateway Select VPNCloud>In Local Network Gateway select LNGCloud>Enter Shared key 123xyz> Select Resource Groups RGCloud>Click OK (Not Shown).
Note: Shared key must be same on both sides.

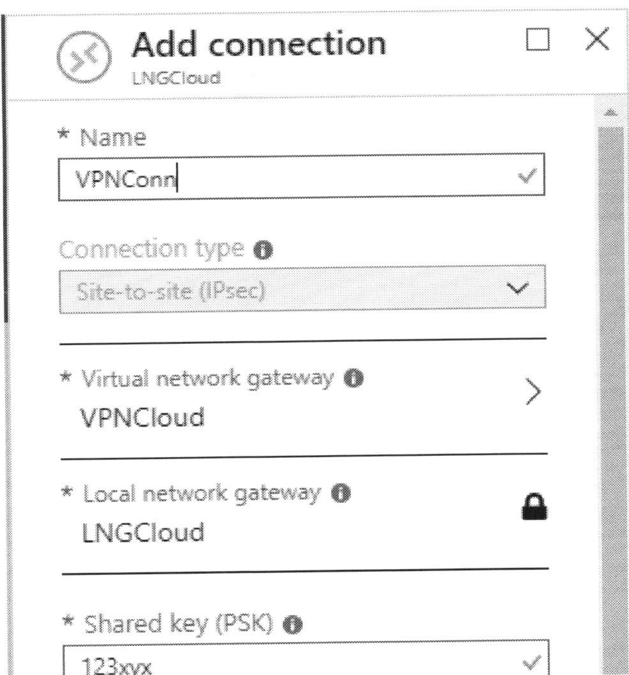

VPN Gateway Redundancy

Active-Passive Azure VPN gateway with Single VPN Device

Every Azure VPN gateway consists of two instances in an active-standby configuration. This is the default configuration.

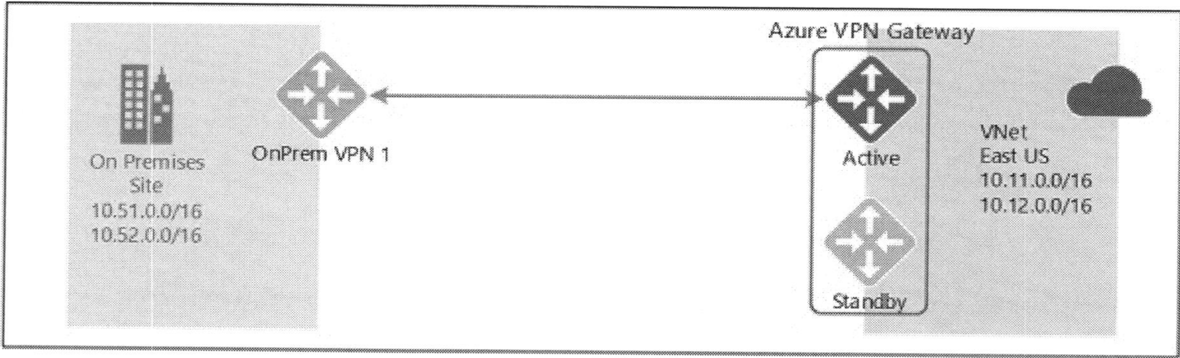

Active-Passive Azure VPN gateway with Dual VPN Device

This configuration provides multiple active tunnels from the same Azure VPN gateway to your on-premises devices in the same location.

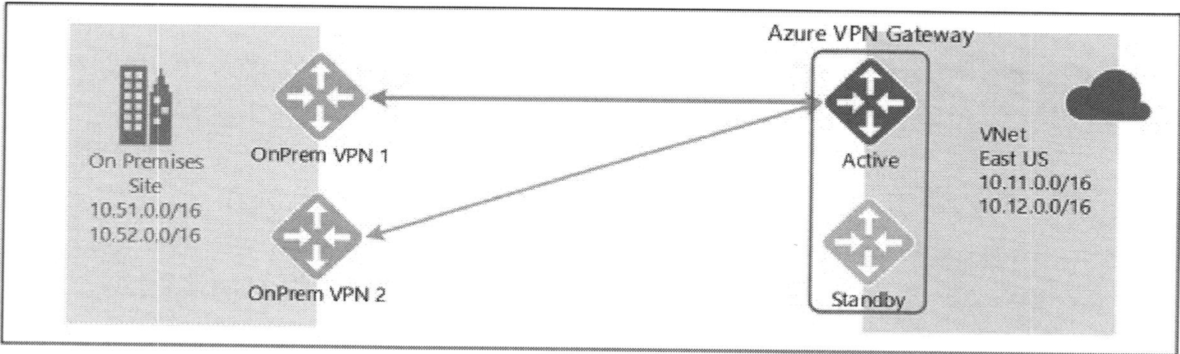

1. You need to create one local network gateway for each VPN device.
2. Each local network gateways corresponding to your VPN devices must have unique public IP addresses.
3. **BGP is required for this configuration**. Each local network gateway representing a VPN device must have a unique BGP peer IP address.

Active-Active Azure VPN gateway with Single VPN Device

In Active-Active Azure VPN gateway configuration, each Azure gateway instance will have a unique public IP address, and each will establish an IPsec/IKE S2S VPN tunnel to on-premises VPN device specified in local network gateway configuration. **Both VPN tunnels are part of the same connection.**

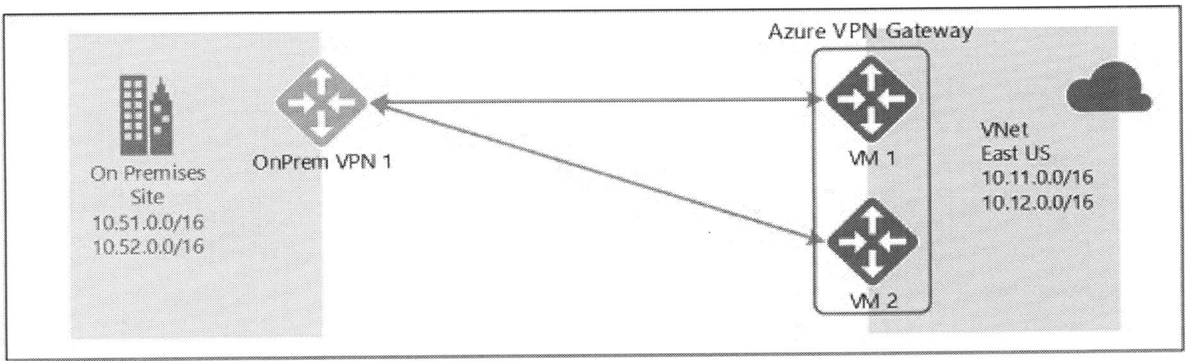

Active-Active Azure VPN gateway with Dual VPN Device

In this case both Azure VPN gateway and on premises VPN device are in active-active configuration. The result is a full mesh connectivity of 4 IPsec tunnels between your Azure virtual network and your on-premises network. **BGP is required to allow the two connections to the same on-premises network.**

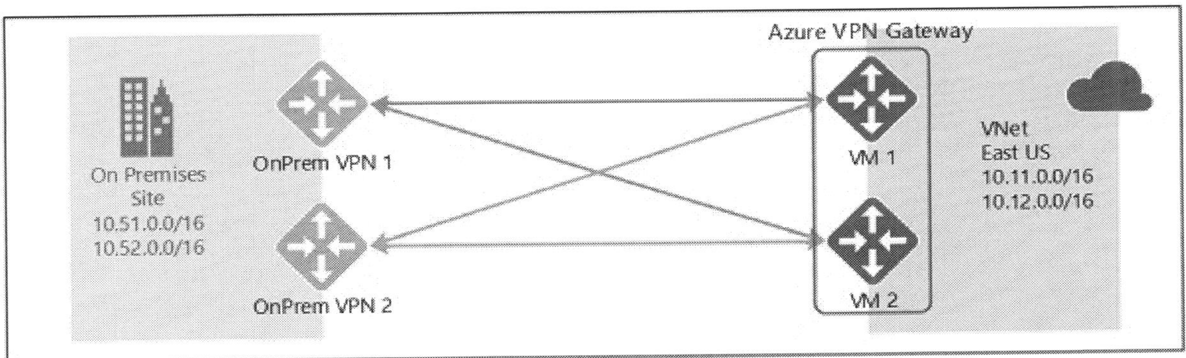

This topology will require two local network gateways and two connections to support the pair of on-premises VPN devices, and BGP is required to allow the two connections to the same on-premises network.

Border Gateway Protocol (BGP) with Azure VPN Gateways

BGP routing protocol is commonly used over Internet to exchange routing and reachability information between two or more networks.

In the context of Azure Virtual Network, BGP enables the Azure VPN Gateways and your on-premises VPN devices, called BGP peers or neighbours, to exchange "routes" that will inform both gateways on the availability and reachability for those prefixes to go through the gateways or routers involved.

BGP is an optional feature you can use with Azure Route-Based VPN gateways. Azure Route-Based VPN gateway supports both static routes (without BGP) *and* dynamic routing with BGP between your networks and Azure.

BGP Use case 1

BGP is required to support **multiple S2S VPN tunnels from the same Virtual Network Gateway.** This happens when you have Dual VPN devices on-premises.

Figure below shows multiple tunnels from same VPN gateway to on-premises VPN devices.

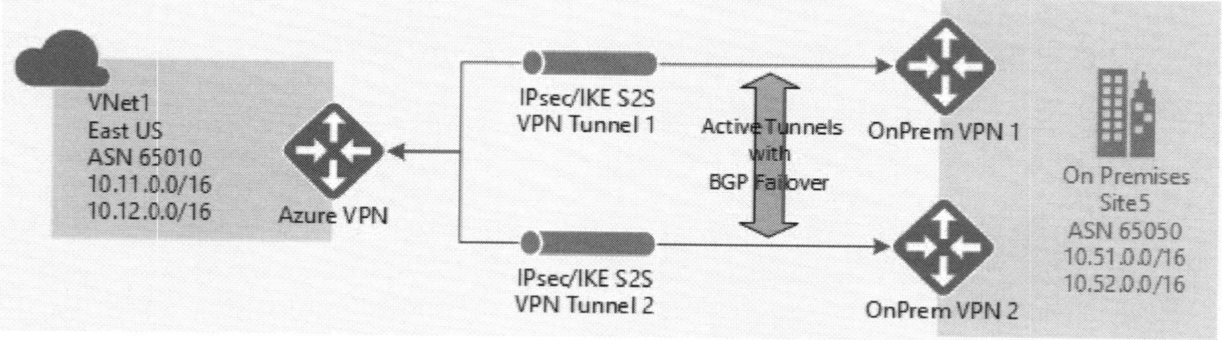

1. This configuration setup provides multiple tunnels (paths) between the two networks in an active-active configuration. If one of the tunnels is disconnected, the corresponding routes will be withdrawn via BGP and the traffic automatically shifts to the remaining tunnels.
2. Supports automatic and flexible prefix updates to BGP peer over the IPsec S2S VPN tunnel.

BGP Use case 2

BGP Supports **transit routing** between your on-premises networks and multiple Azure Virtual Networks.

BGP enables multiple gateways to learn and propagate prefixes from different networks, whether they are directly or indirectly connected. This can enable transit routing with Azure VPN gateways between your on-premises sites or across multiple Azure Virtual Networks.

The following diagram shows an example of a multi-hop topology with multiple paths that can transit traffic between the two on-premises networks through Azure VPN gateways within the Microsoft Networks.

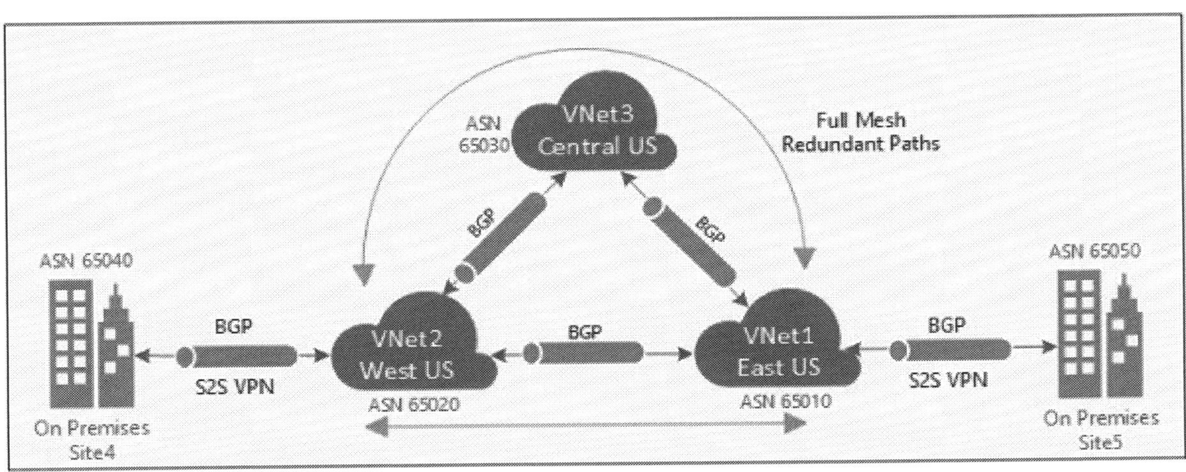

BGP Use case 3

With BGP you can control which on-premises network prefixes you want to advertise to Azure to allow your Azure Virtual Network to access.

With BGP you can advertise specified VNET Prefixes to on-premises VPN device.

BGP Design Nuggets

1. You cannot use same Autonomous System Numbers (ASN) for both on-premises VPN networks and Azure VNETs.
2. You cannot use ASN reserved by Azure and IANA.
3. You can use your own **public ASNs** or **private ASNs** for both your on-premises networks and Azure virtual networks.
4. BGP is supported on Azure **VpnGw1**, **VpnGw2** and **VpnGw3 VPN** Gateways. Basic Gateway is not supported.
5. BGP is supported on Route-Based VPN gateways only. There is no BGP support on Policy based VPN Gateways.
6. You can mix both BGP and non-BGP connections for the same Azure VPN gateway.

Using BGP

To use BGP you must either create VNG with BGP option or enable BGP option from VPN Gateway Dashboard as shown below.

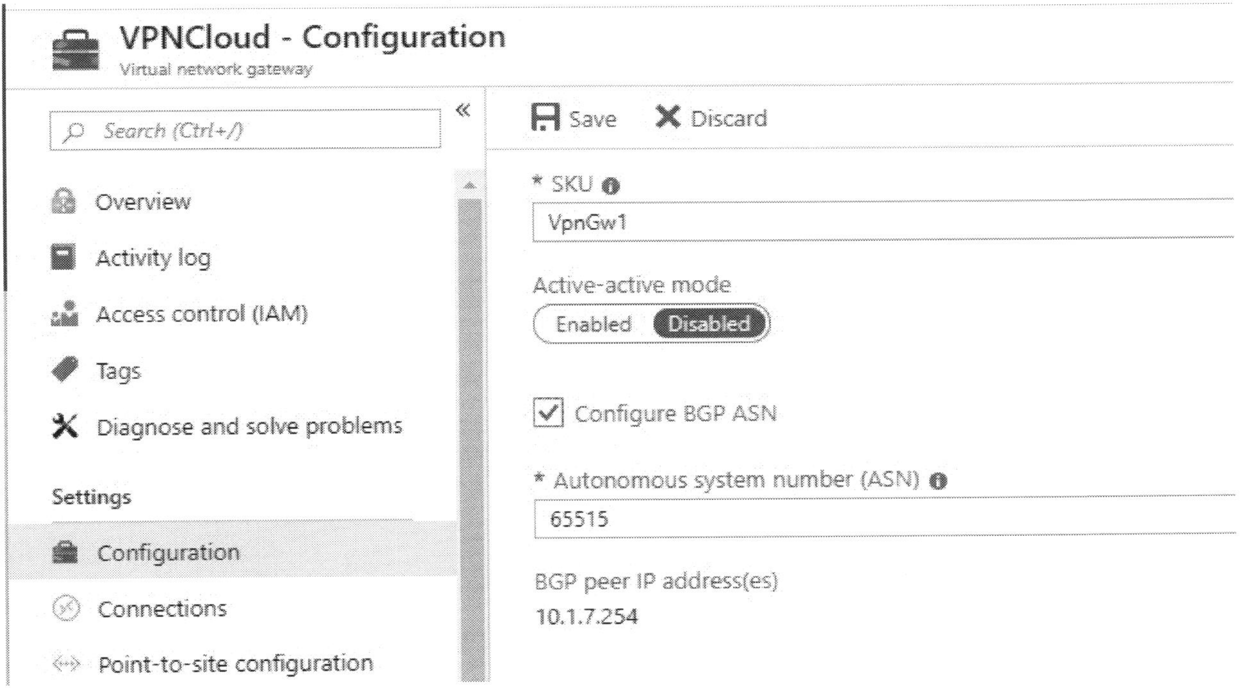

Forced Tunnelling

Forced tunnelling redirects all Internet-bound traffic back to your on-premises location via a Site-to-Site VPN tunnel for inspection and auditing. Without forced tunnelling, Internet-bound traffic from your VMs in Azure always traverses from Azure network infrastructure directly out to the Internet.

Forced tunnelling option allows you to inspect or audit the traffic. Unauthorized Internet access can potentially lead to information disclosure or other types of security breaches.

Figure below shows the Architecture of Forced Tunnelling Solution.

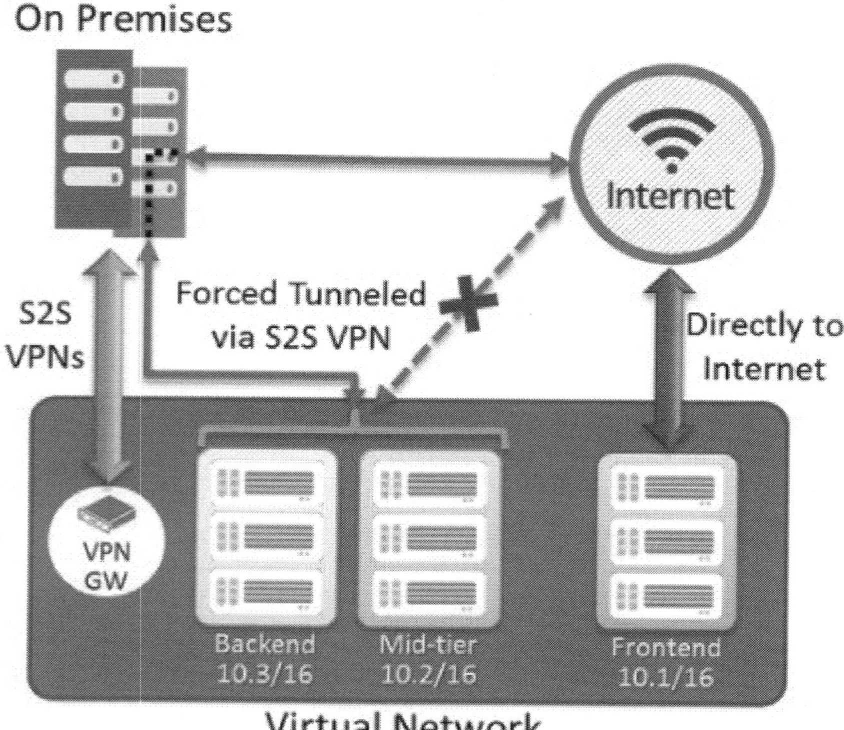

As seen in above figure the Mid-tier and Backend subnets are forced tunneled. Any outbound connections from these two subnets to the Internet are redirected back to an on-premises site via one of the S2S VPN tunnels.

Frontend subnet is not forced tunnelled. The workloads in the Frontend subnet can continue to accept and respond to customer requests from the Internet directly.

Forced Tunnelling Configuration

Forced tunnelling is configured using user-defined routes (UDR). You create a Route Table and add a route which forces internet bound traffic to Virtual Network Gateway in GatewaySubnet. The Route Table will be associated with Subnet whose internet traffic you want to Force Tunnel to on-premises.

Chapter 3 VNET Hybrid Connectivity with ExpressRoute

This Chapter covers following Topic Lessons

- Virtual Network Hybrid Connectivity using Virtual Network Gateway
- VNET Hybrid Connectivity over ExpressRoute connection
- Connecting Azure Virtual Network to On-Premises
- ExpressRoute Routing Domains
- ExpressRoute Connectivity Options (3 Options)
- ExpressRoute Connection Tiers
- ExpressRoute Gateway SKU
- ExpressRoute Bandwidth options
- ExpressRoute Health
- Comparing ExpressRoute and VPN
- Connecting Virtual Networks (VNET) to ExpressRoute circuit
- ExpressRoute Gateway Pricing
- ExpressRoute Connection Pricing
- ExpressRoute Direct

This Chapter covers following Lab Exercises

- Create Virtual Network Gateway of Type ExpressRoute
- Create ExpressRoute Circuit and Connect to VNETCloud

Chapter Topology

In this Chapter we will add ExpressRoute to the topology. We will create Virtual Network Gateway of type ExpressRoute in GatewaySubnet of Virtual Network VNETCloud. We will also Create ExpressRoute Circuit. Provisioning of Circuit will not be done as we don't have access to ExpressRoute Service Provider.

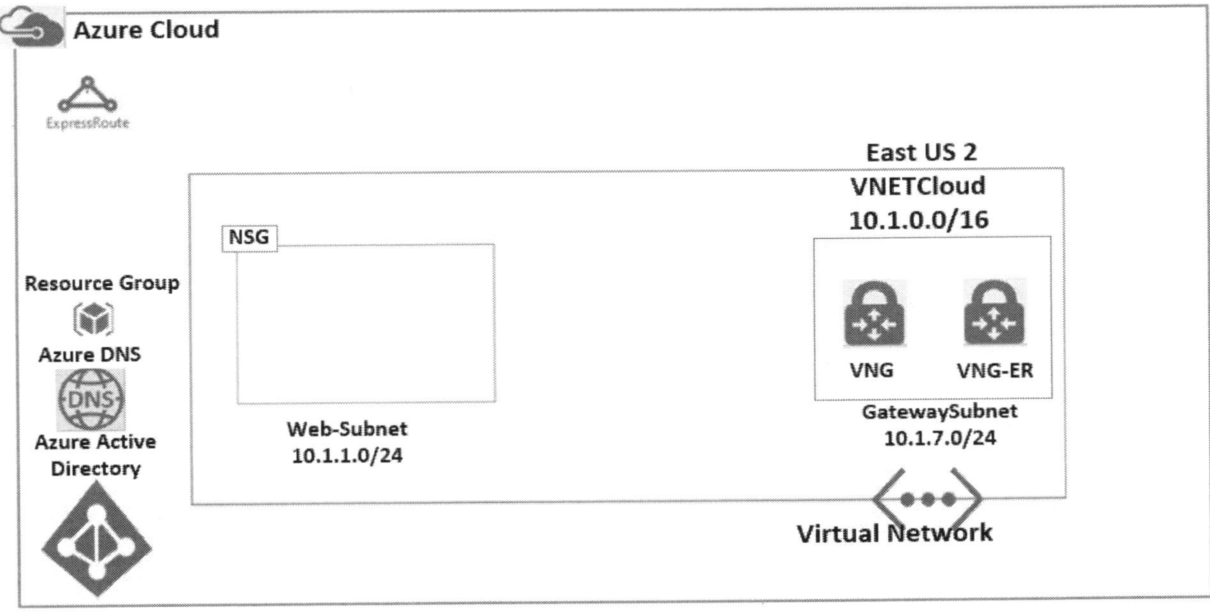

Virtual Network Hybrid Connectivity using Virtual Network Gateway

You can connect Virtual Network to on-premises Datacenter through virtual network gateway located in GatewaySubnet using either Internet VPN (P2S or S2S VPN) or ExpressRoute Private WAN connectivity.

For Internet VPN you deploy virtual network gateway of type VPN. For Private WAN connectivity you deploy virtual network gateway of type ExpressRoute.

Figure below shows Virtual Network Connected to on-premises Datacenter.

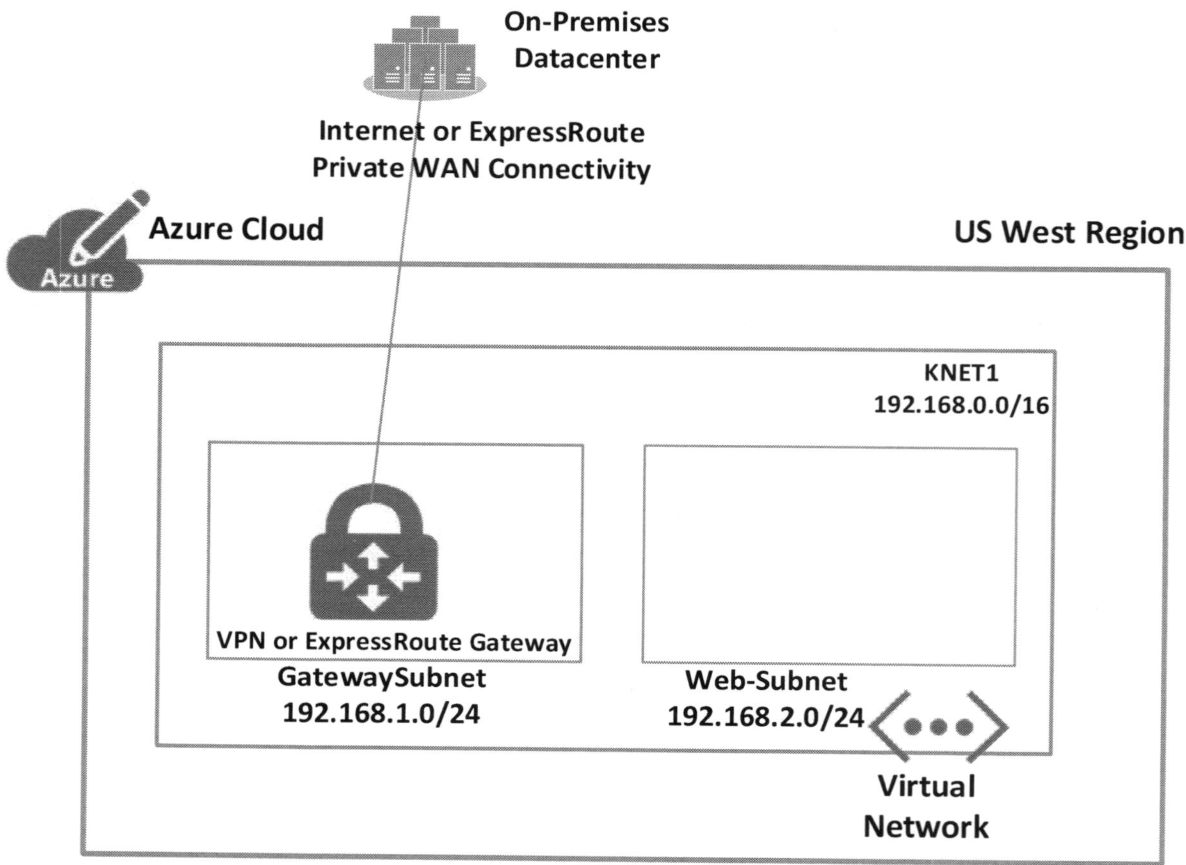

Every Azure VPN gateway consists of two instances in an active-standby or active-active configuration.

VNET Hybrid Connectivity over ExpressRoute connection

ExpressRoute is an Azure Managed service, which creates dedicated private connections between Microsoft Datacenters and on-premises infrastructure.

ExpressRoute connections don't go over the public internet. They offer more reliability, faster speeds, lower latencies and higher security than typical internet connections.

Azure ExpressRoute connects Virtual Network (VNET), Azure PaaS Services (Azure SQL, Azure Storage etc) and Microsoft Online Services (Dynamics 365 & Office 365) to your on-premises infrastructure.

ExpressRoute, connections to Azure are established at an Exchange provider facility. Each ExpressRoute circuit consists of two connections to two Microsoft Enterprise edge routers (MSEEs) from the connectivity provider.

Figure below shows ExpressRoute Circuit Dual Connection (Primary & Secondary) between Microsoft Edge Routers and Partner Service Provider. From Service Provider to Customer Network it can be dual or single connection.

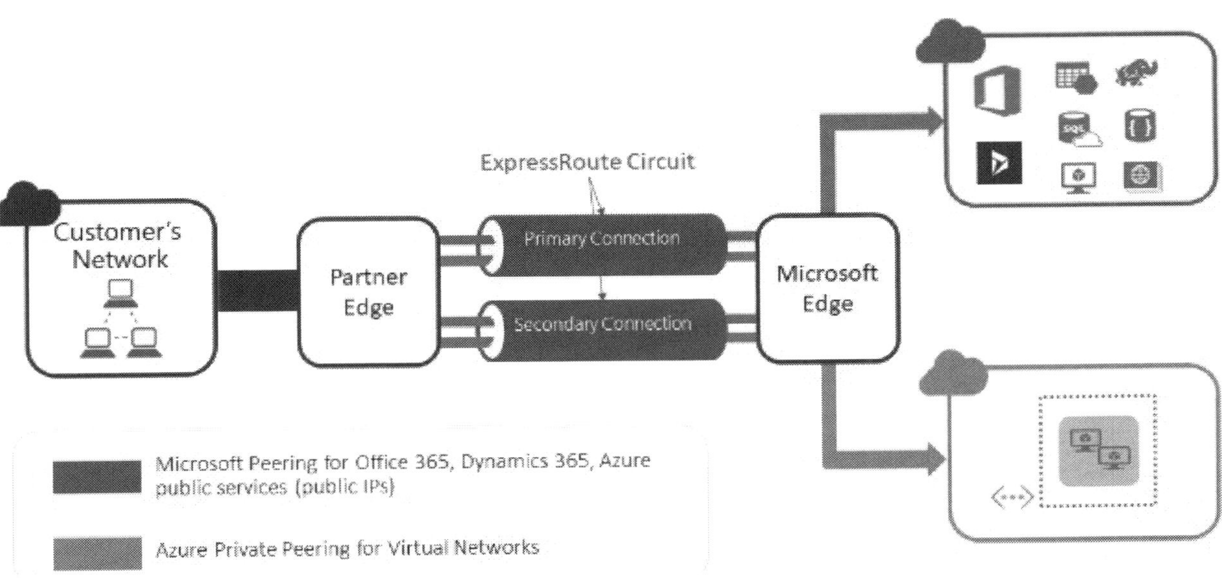

Connecting Azure Virtual Network to On-Premises

For Connecting Virtual Network (VNET) to on-premises infrastructure, ExpressRoute Gateway is created in GatewaySubnet. A GatewaySubnet is created in Azure Virtual Network (VNET).

ExpressRoute Private WAN connection connects ExpressRoute Gateway to On-Premises infrastructure.

Figure Below shows Virtual Network with ExpressRoute Gateway installed in Gateway Subnet. Virtual Network is connected to ExpressRoute Circuit at Azure Side. On-premises Infrastructure is connected to ExpressRoute Circuit at Service Provide end.

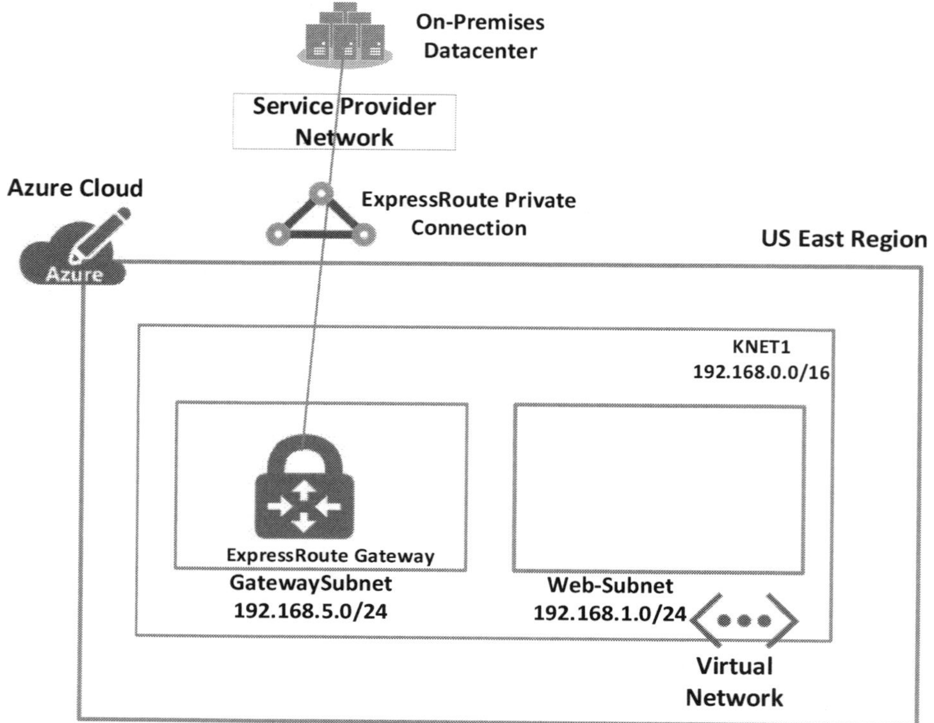

Note 1: Azure ExpressRoute Gateway consists of two instances.
Note 2: There is dual Connectivity from Microsoft to Service Provider edge.
Note 3: Connectivity from Customer Network to Service Provider can be single or dual.

ExpressRoute Routing Domains

An ExpressRoute circuit has multiple routing domains associated with it: Azure private and Microsoft. See Figure on page 155.

Private peering domain

On premises infrastructure connects with Azure virtual network (VNET) through the private peering domain. The private peering domain is an extension of your on premises network into Microsoft Azure Virtual Network. Private peering lets you connect to virtual machines directly on their private IP addresses.

Microsoft Peering

Connectivity to **Microsoft online services** (Office 365 services & Dynamics 365) and **Azure PaaS Services** will be through the Microsoft peering. Microsoft Peering enables bi-directional connectivity between your WAN and Microsoft cloud services through the Microsoft peering routing domain.

Note: Peering type is configured through ExpressRoute Circuit Dashboard.

ExpressRoute Connectivity Options (3 Options)

Layer 3 Connectivity: With ExpressRoute you can establish Layer 3 connectivity between your on-premises network and the Microsoft Cloud through a connectivity provider. For layer 3 Connectivity Microsoft uses BGP to exchange routes between your on-premises network, your instances in Azure, and Microsoft public addresses.

Layer 2 Connectivity: With ExpressRoute you can establish Layer 2 connectivity between your on-premises network and the Microsoft Cloud using Point to Point Ethernet links.

Integrating your IPVPN WAN: IPVPN providers (typically MPLS VPN) offer any-to-any connectivity between your branch offices and Datacenters. The Microsoft cloud can be interconnected to your WAN to make it look just like any other branch office as shown below.

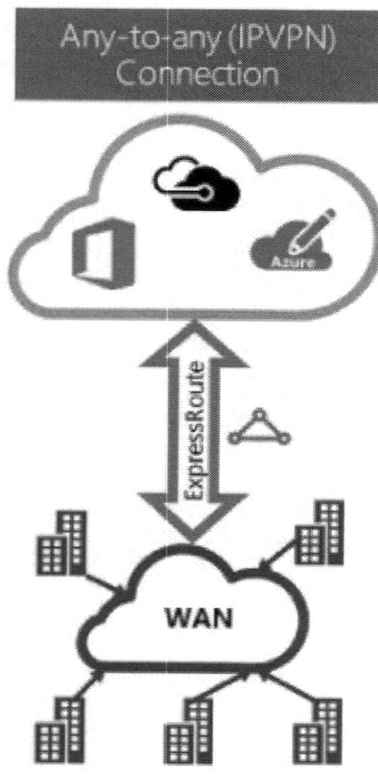

Connectivity Redundancy: Each ExpressRoute circuit consists of two connections to two Microsoft Enterprise edge routers (MSEEs) from the connectivity provider. Connectivity from Customer Network to Service Provider can be single or dual.

ExpressRoute Connection Tiers

ExpressRoute Connection Circuit comes in 2 Tiers: Standard & Premium Add on.

ExpressRoute Standard Connection

The ExpressRoute Standard Connection provides the following capabilities:

1. Up to 10 VNET Links per ExpressRoute circuit.
2. An ExpressRoute circuit created in any region will have access to resources across any other region in the same Geographic region. For Example a VNET created in US East can be accessed through ExpressRoute circuit provisoned in any region in United States only. This VNET in US east cannot be accessed by ExpressRoute Circuit provisioned in Europe.
3. Supports Private and Public Peering
4. Supports upto 4000 routes for Azure Public & Private Peering.

ExpressRoute Premium Connection

The ExpressRoute premium is an add-on over the ExpressRoute circuit. The ExpressRoute premium add-on provides the following capabilities:

1. Increased route limits for Azure public and Azure private peering from 4,000 routes to 10,000 routes.
2. An ExpressRoute circuit created in any region (excluding Azure China, Azure Germany and Azure Government cloud) will have access to resources across any other region in the world. For example, a virtual network created in West Europe can be accessed through an ExpressRoute circuit provisioned in Silicon Valley.
3. Increased number of VNet links per ExpressRoute circuit from 10 to a larger limit of 100 (depending on the bandwidth of the circuit).
4. Supports Private, Public Peering & Microsoft Peering.

ExpressRoute Gateway SKU

Standard
High Performance
Ultra High Performance

Comparison of aggregate throughput by gateway SKU.

SKU	ExpressRoute Gateway Throughput
Standard	1 Gbps
High Performance	2 Gbps
Ultra High Performance	10 Gbps

ExpressRoute Bandwidth options

ExpressRoute connection is available in multiple bandwidth options.

50 Mbps
100 Mbps
200 Mbps
500 Mbps
1 Gbps
2 Gbps
5 Gbps
10 Gbps

Dynamic scaling of bandwidth

You can increase the ExpressRoute circuit bandwidth (on a best effort basis) without having to tear down your connections.

ExpressRoute Health

ExpressRoute circuits may be monitored for availability, connectivity to VirtualNetworks and bandwidth utilization using Network Performance Monitor (NPM).

NPM monitors the health of Azure private peering and Microsoft peering.

ExpressRoute Service Providers

Microsoft has large Service Provider partner network which provide ExpressRoute Circuit across various locations in the world. Some of the Service Provider partners include AT&, Airtel, British Telecom, China Telecom, Comcast, Colt, Equinix, MTN, NTT Communications, Sify, Singtel, Tata Communications, Telenor, Vodafone & Verizon etc.

ExpressRoute System Integrators

Microsoft ExpressRoute System Integrator Partners provide ExpressRoute circuit integration services. These partners help in connecting on-premises Data center with Azure using ExpressRoute circuit. Some of the System Integrator Partners include Avande, Equinix, Bright Skies GmbH, Orange Networks & Presidio etc.

ExpressRoute Limits

ExpressRoute circuits per region per subscription for ARM	10
Maximum number of routes for Azure private peering with ExpressRoute standard	4000
Maximum number of routes for Azure private peering with ExpressRoute premium add-on	10000
Maximum number of routes for Azure public peering with ExpressRoute standard or Premium add-on	200
Maximum number of routes for Azure Microsoft peering with ExpressRoute standard or Premium add-on	200

Number of Virtual Networks per ExpressRoute circuit

Circuit Speed	ExpressRoute Standard	ExpressRoute Premium Add-on
50 Mbps	10	20
100 Mbps	10	25
1 Gbps	10	50
10 Gbps	10	100

Comparing ExpressRoute and VPN

	P2S VPN	S2S VPN	ExpressRoute
Bandwidth	100 Mbps, 650 Mbps, 1 Gbps & 1.25 Gbps	100 Mbps, 650 Mbps, 1 Gbps & 1.25 Gbps	5 Mbps, 100 Mbps 200 Mbps, 500 Mbps, 1 Gbps and 10 Gbps
Protocols Supported	Secure Sockets Tunneling Protocol (SSTP)	IPsec	Direct connection over VLANs
Routing	Static	policy—based (static routing) and route-based (Static or dynamic routing VPN)	BGP
use cases	Prototyping, dev / test / lab scenarios for cloud services and virtual machines	Dev / test / lab scenarios and small scale production workloads for cloud services and VMs	Enterprise-class and mission critical workloads, Backup, Azure as a DR site.

Connecting Virtual Networks (VNET) to ExpressRoute circuit

There are 6 steps to connecting Virtual Networks to ExpressRoute circuit. This assumes that VNET is already created. 7th Step is configured on-premises to connect on-prem Router to Service Provider ExpressRoute Circuit line.

1. Create GatewaySubnet in Virtual Network.
2. Create Virtual Network Gateway of type **ExpressRoute** in GatewaySubnet.
3. Create an ExpressRoute Circuit.
4. From ExpressRoute Circuit Dashboard copy the key and send to your Service Provider for provisioning the circuit.
5. After Circuit is Provisioned, Configure Routing (Private Peering) in ExpressRoute Dashboard.
6. From ExpressRoute Dashboard Link VNET to ExpressRoute Circuit.
7. Connect and configure on-premises Device to Service Provider ExpressRoute Circuit line. Use the same shared key which was specified during Peering Configuration on Azure Side.

Exercise 22: Create Virtual Network Gateway of Type ExpressRoute

In this exercise we will create VPN Gateway of Type **ExpressRoute** in GatewaySubnet in VNETCloud. VNETCloud was created in Exercise 3, Chapter 1. GatewaySubnet was created in VNETCloud in Exercise 20, Chapter 2.

1. Click Create a resource>Networking>Virtual Network gateway> Create virtual network gateway blade opens>Enter a name, Select Location EAST US 2, Select Gateway type as **ExpressRoute**, Select SKU Standard, Select Virtual Network VNETCloud and Select Create new Public IP and enter a name> Click Review +create (Not Shown)>After validation is passed click create.

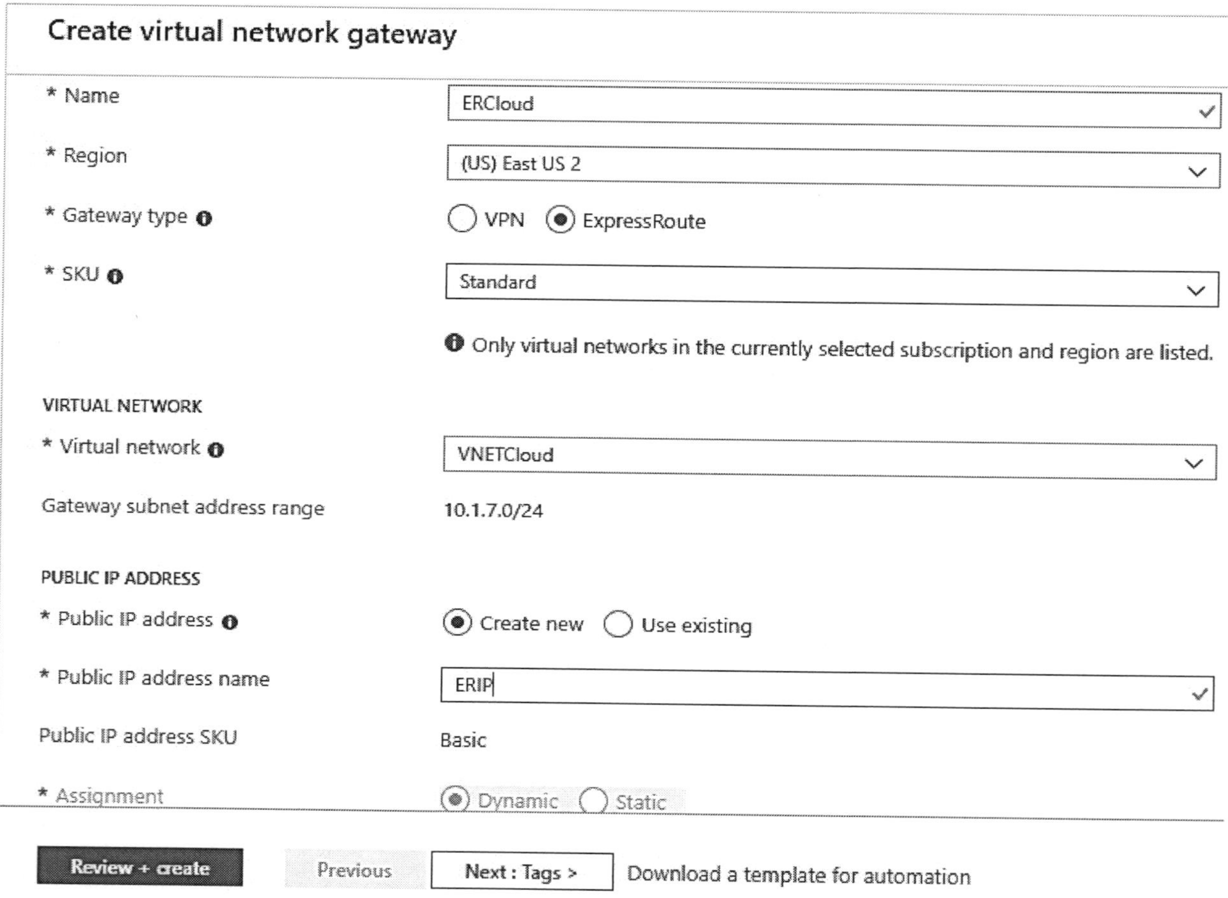

Figure below shows Dashboard of Virtual Network Gateway (Type ExpressRoute) ERCloud.

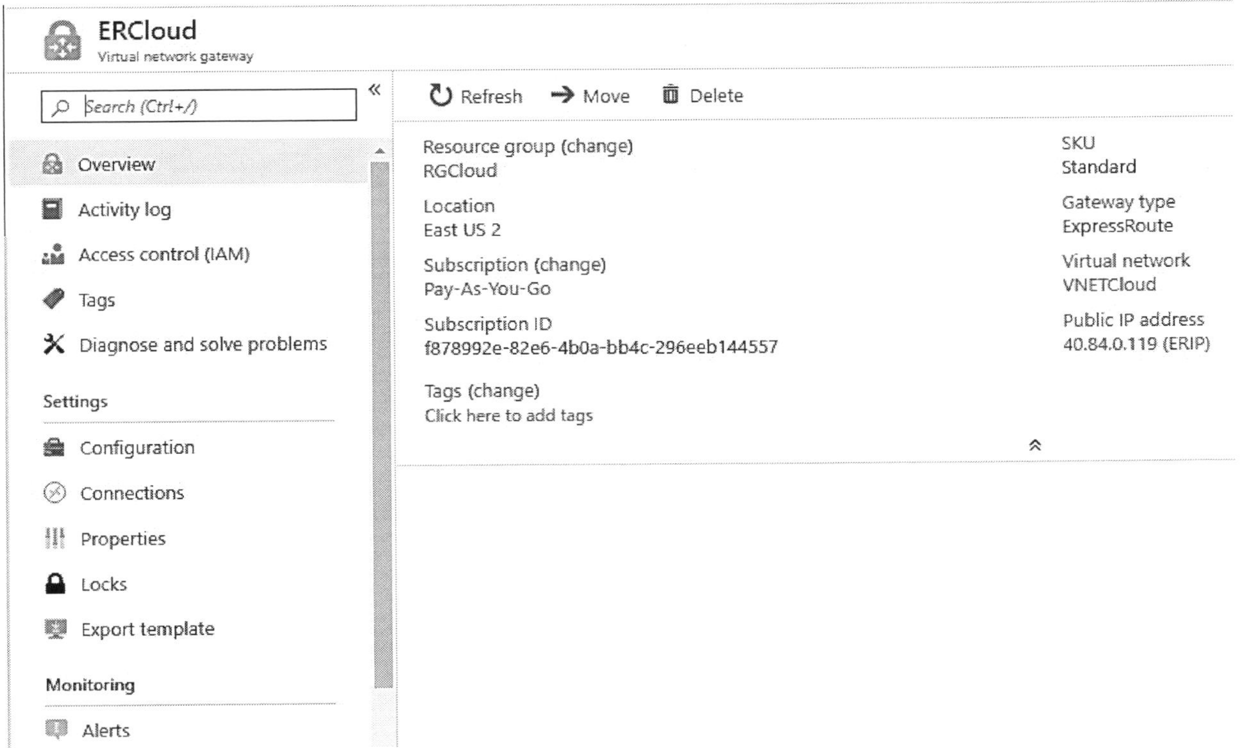

Exercise 23: Create ExpressRoute Circuit and Connect to VNETCloud

This is a demonstration Exercise. We will create ExpressRoute Circuit in Resource Group RGCloud and show how to connect it to Virtual Network VNETCloud. Provisioning of Circuit will not be shown as we don't have access to Service Provider. Resource Group RGCloud was created in Exercise 1, chapter 1.

1. Click Create a resource>Networking>ExpressRoute>Create ExpressRoute Circuit Blade opens>Enter a name>Select Provider AT&T, Select Peering location Washington DC, Bandwidth 50 Mbps, SKU Standard, Select Billing Model Metered> Select Resource Group RGCloud and Location East US 2> Click create.

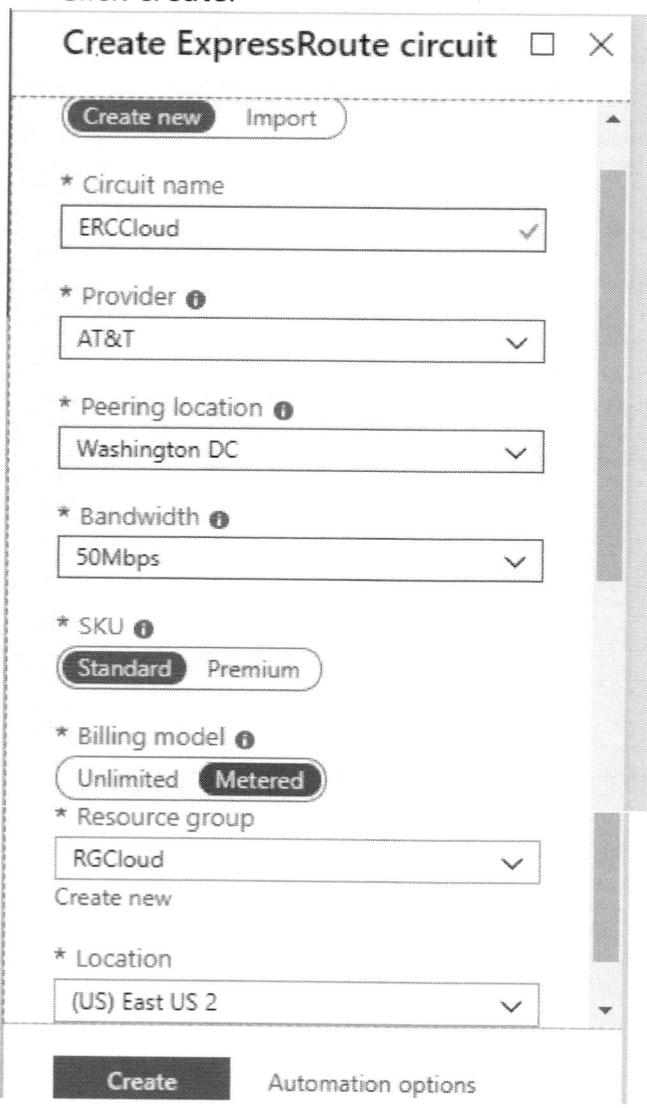

Figure below shows Dashboard of ExpressRoute Circuit ERCCloud. Note the Service Key in Right pane. It shows Provider Status as not enabled.

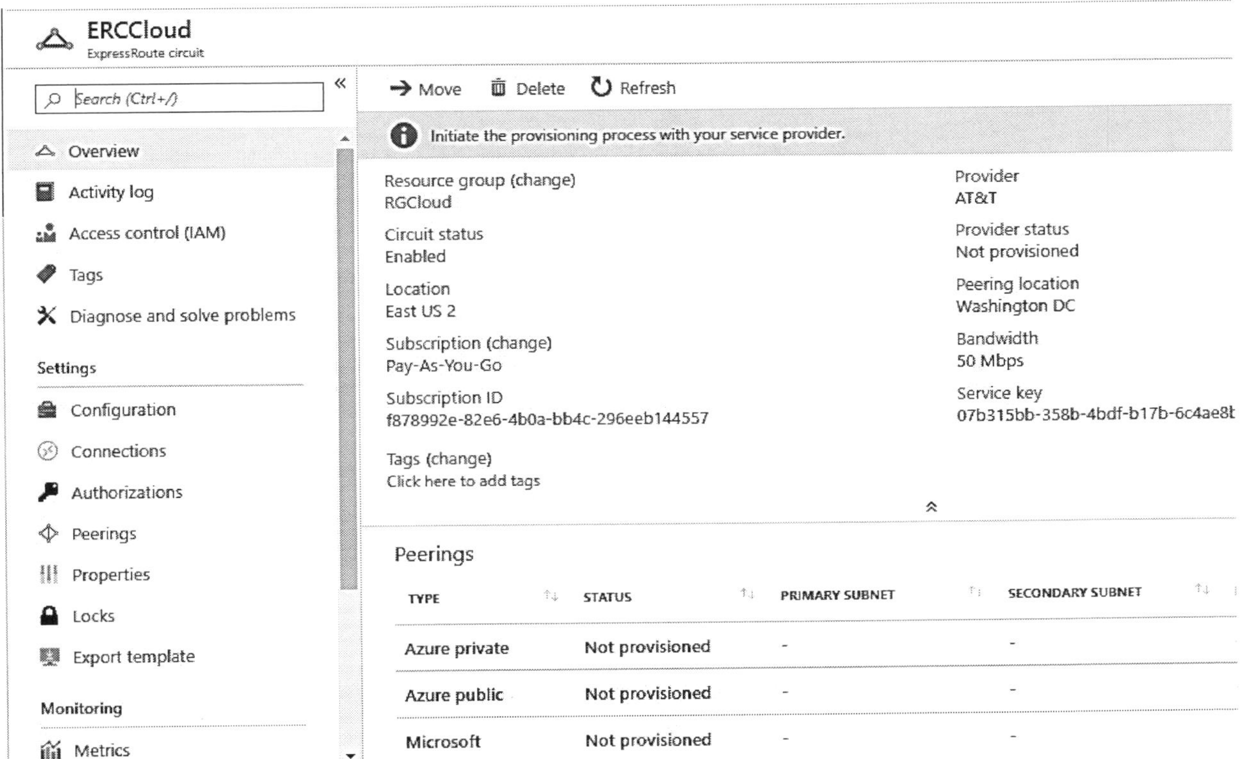

2. In Right pane Note down the Service Key and send it to your Service Provider for Provisioning of the Circuit. Go to Next step after ER Circuit is provisioned.

3. **Configure Routing (Private Peering) in ExpressRoute Dashboard.** In ExpressRoute Circuit Dashboard Click Peerings in left pane > Peering pane opens as shown below.

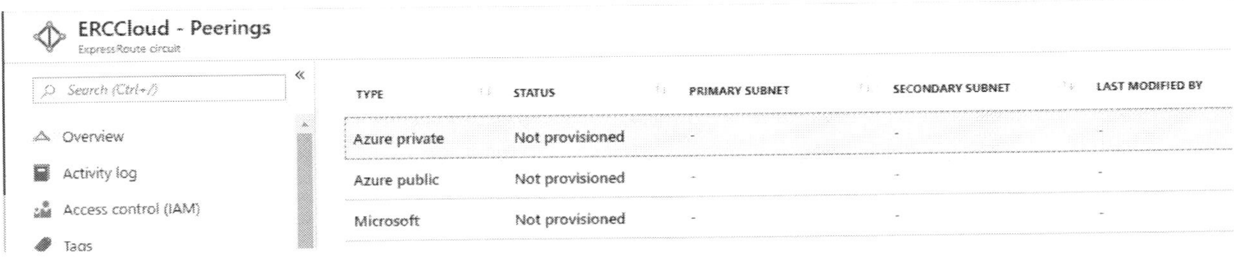

In right pane Click Azure Private>Private Peering blade opens as shown below. All options are greyed out as Circuit is not provisioned by the Service Provider. Here Primary/Secondary Subnet is /30 subnet of a **Public IP owned by you**. From this subnet you will assign the first useable IP address to your router. Microsoft uses the second useable IP for its router. Primary/Secondary Subnet refer to Primary/Secondary links. Specify VLAN & Public/private ASN for peering.

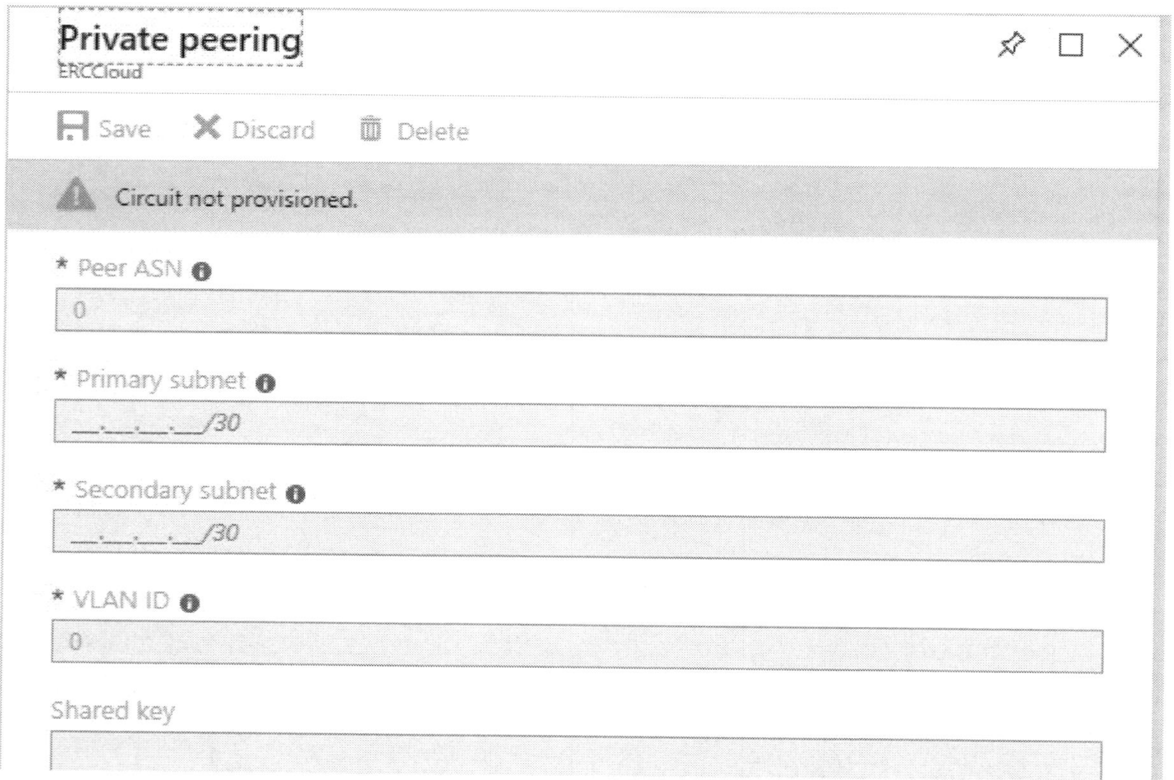

4. **Connect ExpressRoute Circuit to Virtual Network VNETCloud.** In ExpressRoute Circuit Dashboard Click Connections in left pane.

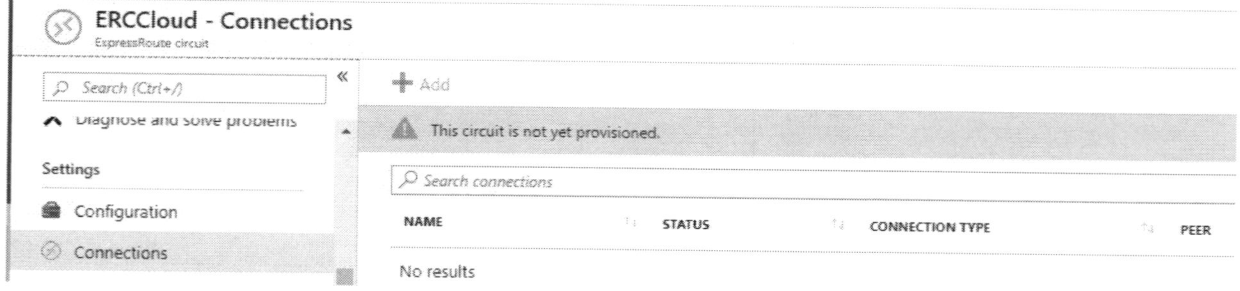

In Right pane you need to click +Add to open the Connection pane. **It is currently greyed out as ExpressRoute circuit is not provisioned.**

Click + Add to open Connection pane. **Here I am showing you connection pane from Azure Docs.** Here select your Virtual Network and ExpressRoute Circuit.

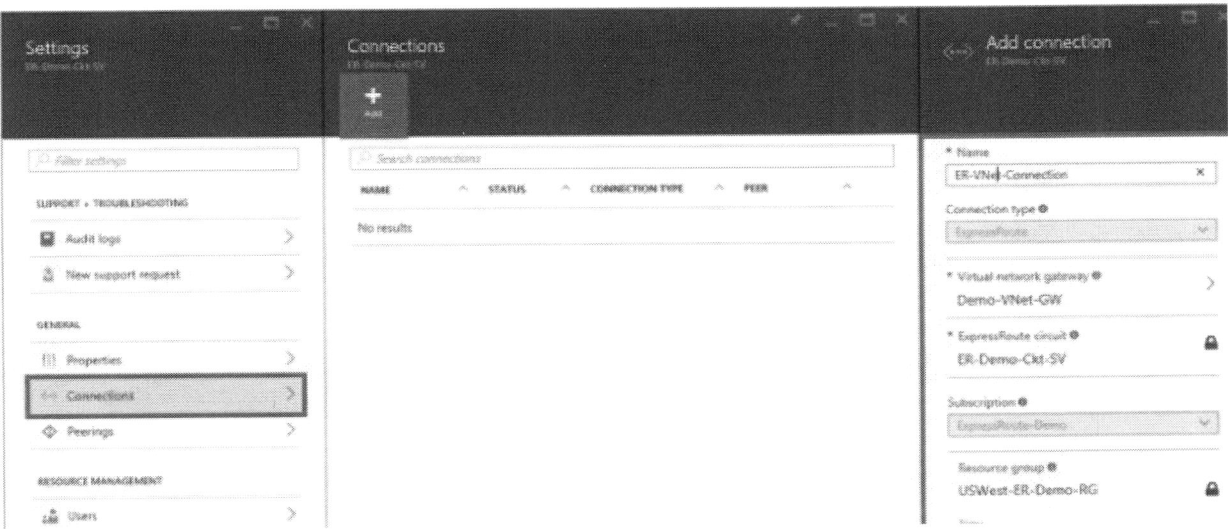

5. **Configure on-premises router** using the same shared key which was specified in Private Peering Configuration in step 3. Connect it to ER Circuit.
6. **Monitor ExpressRoute using Network Performance Monitor (NPM)**. In ExpressRoute Circuit Dashboard click Health using NPM>

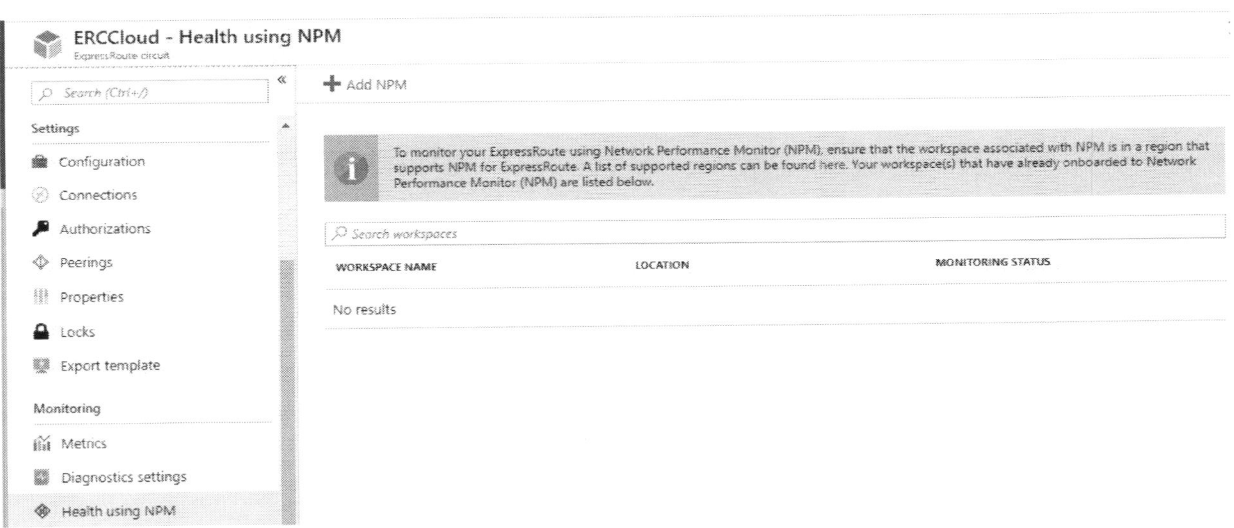

Note 1: Network Performance Monitor (NPM) will be discussed in Exam AZ-300 & AZ-301 Lab Study Guide Part 2.

Note 2: Delete VPN Gateway and ExpressRoute Circuit as we no longer require it.

ExpressRoute Gateway Pricing

ExpressRoute Gateway Type	Price
Standard ExpressRoute Gateway	$0.19/hour
High Performance ExpressRoute Gateway	$0.49/hour
Ultra Performance ExpressRoute Gateway	$1.87/hour

ExpressRoute Connection Pricing

ExpressRoute has 2 Pricing option – Metered Data Plan and Unlimited Data Plan.

Metered Data Plan

Metered Data Plan has 2 components – Fixed monthly port fee (High Availability dual ports) based on Bandwidth and outbound data charge. Figure below show ExpressRoute pricing for port speed of 50 Mbps and 100 Mbps only. Note - speed can go upto 10 Gbps.

Port Speed	Price/Month with Standard SKU	Price/Month with Premium add-on	Inbound Data Transfer	Outbound Transfer
50 Mbps	$55	$130	Unlimited	See note below
100 Mbps	$100	$200	Unlimited	See note below

Note 1 - Outbound data transfer is charged at a rate of $0.025 per GB for Zone 1, $0.05 per GB for Zone 2 and $0.14 per GB for Zone 3.

Unlimited Data Plan

With Unlimited Data Plan users are charged a single fixed monthly port fee (High Availability dual ports) based on Bandwidth. All inbound and outbound data transfer is free of charge. Figure below show ExpressRoute pricing for port speed of 50 Mbps and 100 Mbps only. Note - speed can go upto 10 Gbps.

Port Speed	Price/Month with Standard SKU	Price/Month with Premium add-on	Inbound Data Transfer	Outbound Transfer
50 Mbps	$300	$375	Unlimited	Unlimited
100 Mbps	$575	$675	Unlimited	Unlimited

ExpressRoute Direct (In Preview)

With ExpressRoute Direct, customers connect directly to Microsoft's network through a pair of 100Gbps ports to create 5Gbps, 10Gbps, 40Gbps and 100Gbps ExpressRoute Local, Standard and ExpressRoute Premium circuits.

ExpressRoute Direct contains both a monthly Port fee and, for ExpressRoute Premium circuits, a Premium Circuit fee. Outbound data transfer is applicable to Standard and Premium circuits and not applicable to Local circuits.

Chapter 4 Azure Compute

This Chapter covers following Topic Lessons

- Azure Virtual Machine
- Virtual Machines Series
- Low Priority VMs
- Azure Virtual Machine Storage
- Comparing Virtual Machine Disks
- Backup for Managed Disk
- DR for Managed Disk
- Virtual Machine Disk Storage Design Parameters
  Azure Virtual Machine Networking
- Virtual Machine Accelerated Networking (AN)
- Virtual Machine Security using Network Security Group (NSG)
- VM High Availability Options
- VM High Availability using Availability Set (AS)
- VM High Availability using Availability Zones
- Virtual Machine Snapshot
- Linux VM in Azure
- Customizing Linux VM with Cloud init
- Images
- Azure Virtual Machine Agent
- Virtual Machine Extensions
- Custom Script Extension
- Manage VM Sizes
- VM Auto-Shutdown
- Reset Password
- Redeploy VM
- VM Backup & Restore
- Moving Virtual Machines
- VM Alerts, Metrics & Diagnostic Settings
- VM Update, Inventory, Change & Configuration Management
- PowerShell DSC Extension
- ARM Template
- Virtual Machine Limits
- Virtual Machine Compute Pricing
- General Purpose Dv3 and DSv3 Series Pricing (PAYG)
- Dv3Pricing (PAYG, Reserved Instance & Reserved Instance+ Hybrid)
- How to Save on Virtual Machine Compute Pricing

- Virtual Machine Managed Pricing

This Chapter covers following Lab Exercises

- Create Availability Set (AS) using Azure Portal
- Create Windows Virtual Machine VMFE1
- Log on to Windows VM with RDP
- Install IIS
- Access Default IIS website on VM VMFE1
- Add Data Disk
- Initialize the Data Disk
- Create Snapshot of VM VMFE1 OS Hard Disk
- Create and Add Network Interface to VM VMFE1
- Create Windows Virtual Machine VMFE2
- Log on to Windows VM with RDP
- Install IIS
- Access Default IIS website on VM VMFE2
- Create Custom Website on VM VMFE2
- Access Custom IIS website on VM VMFE2
- Create Windows VM representing On-Premises AD DS
- Enable AD DS Role in Virtual Machine VMAD
- Create Linux VM
- Connecting to Linux VM
- Update Linux VM & Install NGINX Web Server
- Create Custom Image of Azure VM
- Deploy VM from Custom image
- Demonstrating various VM Extensions available
- Demonstrating Custom Script Extension using Azure Portal
- Resizing VM
- Virtual Machine Auto-Shutdown
- Reset Password
- Redeploy VM

This Chapter covers following Case Studies

- Designing Disk Solution
- Designing Disk and VM Soultion
- Design for IOPS and Throughtput/Bandwidth for your Application using Different I/O Sizes
- Choosing VM size and Designing IOPs
- Placement of Virtual Machines in Availability Set

Chapter Topology

In this chapter we will add Virtual Machines **VMFE1, VMFE2, and vmlinux** to the topology. These VMs will be created in Web-Subnet in Virtual Network VNETCloud.

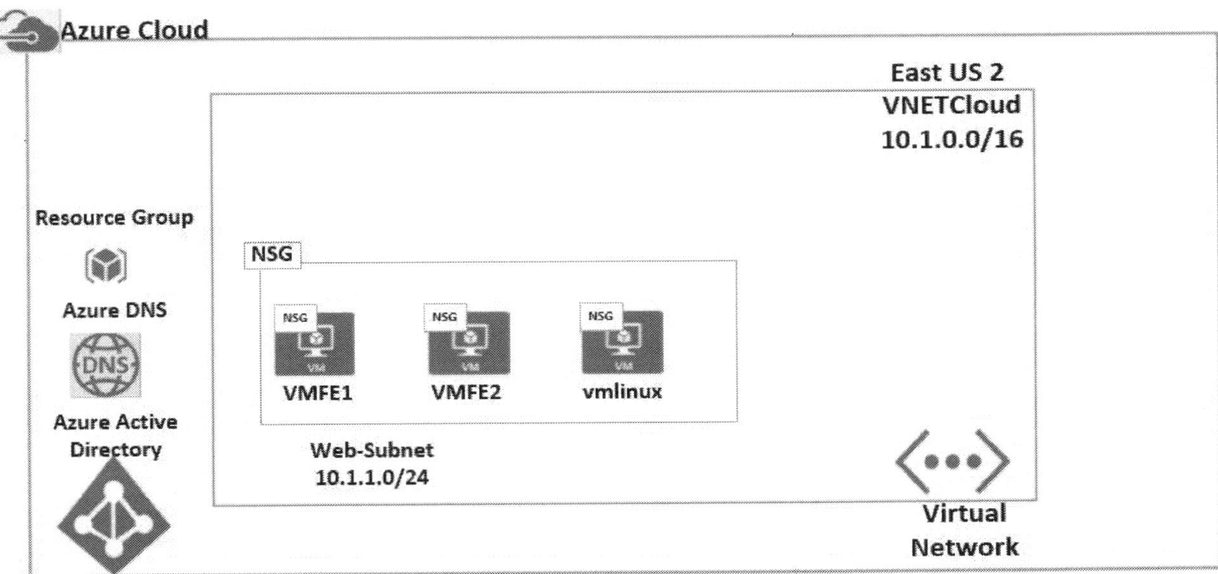

We will also add Virtual Machine **VMAD** in Virtual Network VNETOnPrem. We will then install Active Directory Domain Services (AD DS) role in VM **VMAD**.

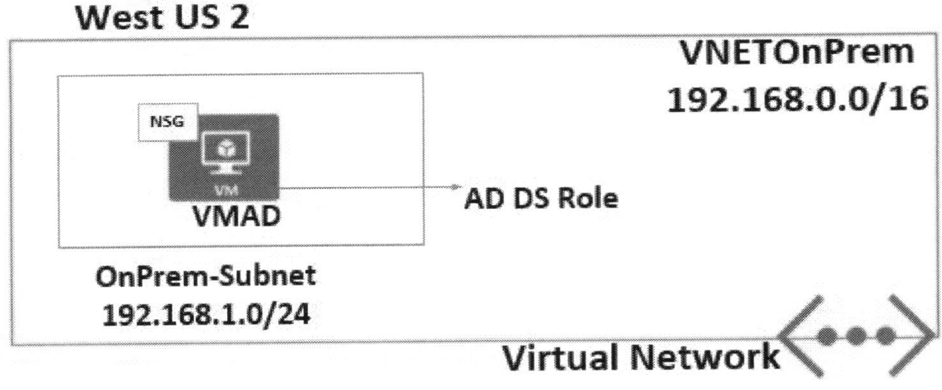

Note 1: This diagram is shown separately as there is space constrained in top diagram.
Note 2: I am not showing DB-Subnet, DMZ-Subnet & GatewaySubnet as they are no longer being used for the rest of the Chapters.

Azure Virtual Machine (VM)

Azure Virtual Machine is on-demand resizable computing resource in the cloud that can be used to host variety of applications. Azure Virtual Machine runs on a Hyper-V host which also runs other Virtual Machines.

You can scale up by using bigger size Virtual Machine or scale out using additional instance of the virtual machine and then Load Balancing them.

Azure VM can be Windows or Linux based.

Virtual Machine (VM) Sizes

Virtual Machines are available in various sizes and categorized under series. Under each series various virtual machine sizes are available with options for memory, CPU family, Number of CPU cores, Standard or Premium Storage, Number of Data Disks, Number of NIC's and Temporary Storage.

Various Virtual Machine Series are available either with Standard Storage or both Standard & Premium Storage.

Virtual Machines with standard storage are available under A-series, Av2-series, D-series, Dv2-series, Dv3, F-series, G-Series, H-series and N-series. These VMs use magnetic HDD to host a virtual machine disks (OS and Data Disk). Temporary storage is on SSD except for A series which are on magnetic HDD.

Virtual Machines with premium Storage are available under DS-series, DSv2-series, DSv3, ESv3, FS-series, GS-series etc. These VMs can use solid-state drives (SSDs) or HDD to host a virtual machine disks (OS and Data Disk) and also provide a local SSD disk cache. Temporary storage is on SSD.

Note: Virtual Machines with letter **s** in its size designation support both Standard Storage and Premium Storage.

Virtual Machines Series

Virtual Machines series in Azure can be categorized under General purpose, Compute optimized, Memory optimized, Storage Optimized, GPU and High Performance Compute.

Type	Series	Description
General purpose	DSv3, Dv3, DSv2, Dv2, DS, D, Av2, A0-4 Basic, A0-A7 Standard	Balanced CPU-to-memory ratio. Ideal for testing and development, General Purpose Production workloads, small to medium databases, and low to medium traffic web servers.
Compute optimized	Fs, F, Fv2 & FSv2	High CPU-to-memory ratio. Good for medium traffic web servers, network appliances, batch processes, and application servers.
Memory optimized	ESv3, Ev3, M, GS, G, DSv2, Dv2, DS & D	High memory-to-core ratio. Great for relational database servers, medium to large caches, and in-memory analytics.
Storage optimized	Ls	High disk throughput and IO. Ideal for Big Data, SQL, and NoSQL databases.
GPU	NC, NCv2, NCv3, NV & ND	Specialized virtual machines targeted for heavy graphic rendering and video editing. Available with single or multiple GPUs.
High performance compute	H, A8-11	High Performance Computing VMs are good for high performance & parallel computing workloads such as financial risk modeling, seismic and reservoir simulation, molecular modeling and genomic research.

Note 1: D, DS and A0-A7 Standard are being phased out.
Note 2: Virtual Machines with letter **s** in its size designation support both Standard Storage and Premium Storage.
Note 3: Dv2 & DSv2 machines are included in both General Purpose & Memory Optimized. General Purpose includes following sizes: D1v2, D2v2, D3v2, D4v2 and D5v2. Memory Optimised includes following: D11v2, D12v2, D13v2, D14v2 & D15v2.
Note 4: Microsoft recommends that to get the best performance for price, use the latest generation VMs where possible.

General Purpose Compute Series

General purpose VMs have Balanced CPU-to-memory ratio. **Example use cases include** test & development servers, General Purpose Production workloads, low traffic web servers, small to medium databases servers, servers for proof-of-concepts and code repositories.

A Series VMs are Entry-level Low Cost VMs. **Example use cases include development** and test servers, low traffic web servers, small to medium databases, servers for proof-of-concepts and code repositories.

B Series does not use full vCPU assigned to it but is allowed to burst up to 100% of the CPU (based on accumulated CPU credit) when your application requires the higher CPU performance. B-series VMs are low-cost option for workloads that do not require the use of the full CPU all the time, but occasionally will need to burst to finish some tasks more quickly. **Example use cases include** development and test servers, low-traffic web servers, small databases, micro services, servers for proof-of-concepts.

Dv2 & DSv2 series instances offer a combination of CPU, memory and disk for most production applications. They are based on the 2.4 GHz Intel Xeon E5-2673 v3 (Haswell) processor and can achieve 3.1 GHz with Turbo Boost.

Dv3 & DSv3 Series have Balanced CPU-to-memory configuration making them suitable for most production workloads. D Series VMs is hyper-threaded and is based on the 2.3 GHz Intel XEON E5-2673 v4 (Broadwell) processor and can achieve 3.5 GHz with Intel Turbo Boost.

In Dv3 and DSv3 VMs there is shift from physical cores to Virtual CPU. These latest series VMs allow nested virtualization when running Windows Server 2016.

E Series (Memory Optimised VM)

E Series VMS have High memory-to-CPU ratio. **Example use cases include** relational database servers, medium to large caches, and in-memory analytics.

F Series (Compute Optimised VM)

F Series VMs have High CPU-to-memory ratio. **Example use cases include** batch processing, web servers, analytics and gaming.

LS Series (Storage optimized)

The Ls-series VMs are storage optimized. These are ideal for applications requiring low latency, high throughput, and large local disk storage. The latest Lsv2-series features high throughput, low latency, directly mapped local NVMe storage. **Example use cases include** NoSQL databases such as Cassandra, MongoDB, Cloudera, and Redis. Data warehousing applications and large transactional databases are great use cases as well.

H Series (High Performance Computing VM)

The HC-series VMs are optimised for HPC applications driven by intensive computation. **Example use cases include** fluid dynamics, finite element analysis, seismic processing, reservoir simulation, risk analysis, EDA, rendering, Spark, weather modeling, quantum simulation, computational chemistry.

N Series (GPU enabled VM)

The N-series VMs have GPU capabilities. GPUs are ideal for compute and graphics-intensive workloads. **Example use cases include** simulation, deep learning, graphics rendering, video editing, gaming and remote visualisation.

M Series (Large memory optimised VM)

M-series are large memory optimised VMs. These VMs are ideal for in-memory workloads such as SAP HANA. **Example use cases include** SAP HANA, SAP S/4 HANA, SQL Hekaton and other large in-memory business critical workloads requiring massive parallel compute power.

G Series (Memory and storage optimised VM)

G-series VMs have two times more memory and four times more Solid State Drive storage (SSDs) than the General Purpose D-series. **Example use cases include** large SQL and NoSQL databases, ERP, SAP and data warehousing solutions.

Low Priority VMs

Low Priority VMs are available at lower cost than normal VMs and are allocated from surplus or spare Azure compute capacity.

The advantage of Low Priority VM is that it reduce the costs of running workloads or allow much more work to be performed at a greater scale for the same cost.

The disadvantage of Low Priority VM is that Azure can take back Low priority VMs when spare compute capacity decreases.

Low Priority VMs are currently available for Azure Batch and Virtual Machine Scale Set (VMSS).

Virtual Machine Storage

Storage for Virtual Machines is provided by Virtual Machine Disks. Azure Virtual Machine Disks (OS & Data) are stored in Page Blob and are accessed over the network.

You can also mount Azure File shares to Virtual Machine disks for additional Storage. File shares will be further discussed in Storage chapter.

Figure bellows shows Storage options for Azure Virtual Machines.

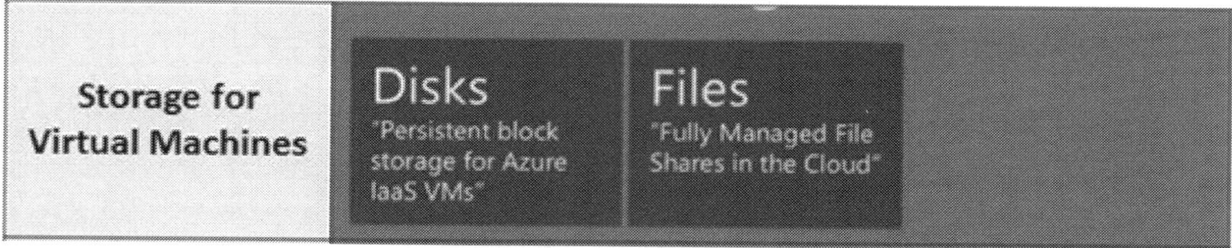

Figure below shows OS and Data Disks are stored in Azure Blob (Page) Storage and are accessed over the network. Temporary disk is located on the physical host where the virtual machine is running.

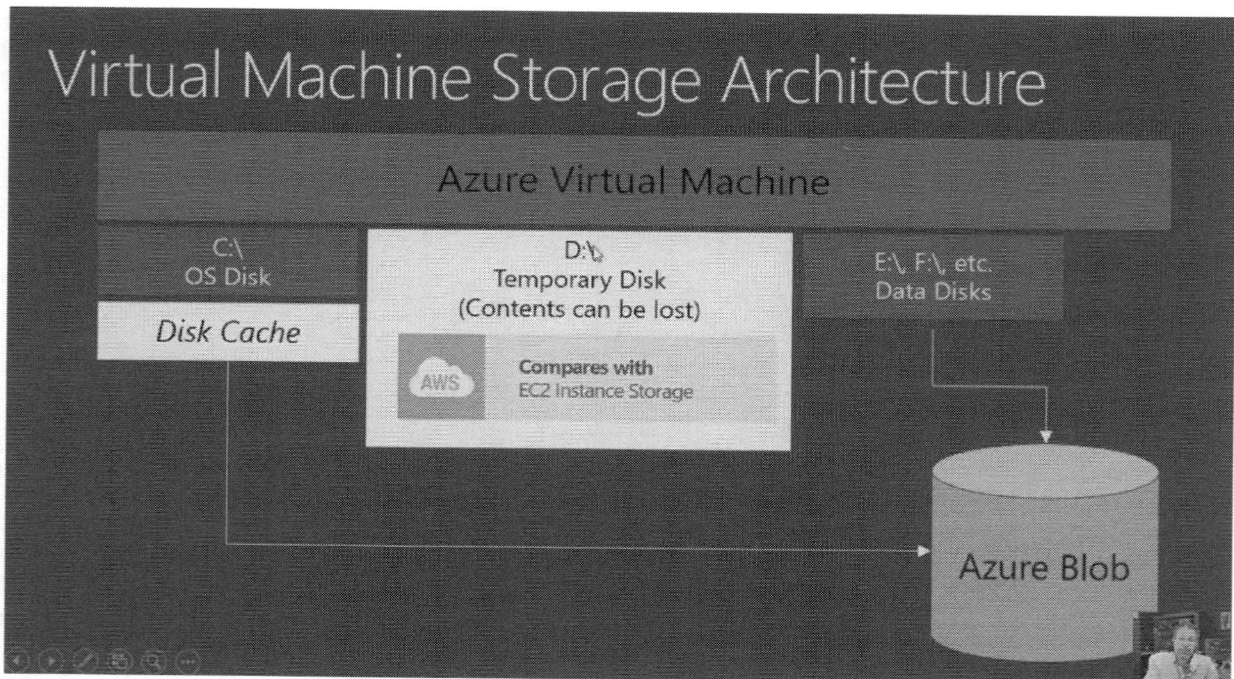

Virtual Machine Storage Disk Types

Azure Virtual Machine Disks are stored in Page Blob storage. Page Blob storage can use Standard Storage or Premium Storage. Standard Storage is backed by Magnetic HDD and Premium Storage is backed by SSD.

Azure Virtual Machines have minimum of 2 disks: OS Disk and Temporary Disk. You can also attach additional Data Disks. Number of Data Disks depend upon the series and the size of the VM chosen.

Virtual Machine Disks (OS and Data disk) are accessed over the network. Temporary disk is located on the physical host where the virtual machine is running. Virtual machines use virtual hard disks (VHDs) to store their operating system (OS) and data. Virtual Machine disks (VHDs) are stored in page blobs.

Operating System Disks

Every virtual machine has one **network attached** operating system disk and is **accessed over the network**. It's labelled as the C: drive. This disk has a maximum capacity of 4095 gigabytes (GB). Data is persisted in the event virtual machine is rebooted, started or stopped. It is registered as SATA Drive.

Temporary Disk

The temporary disk is automatically created on physical host where virtual machine is running. The temporary disk is labelled as the D: drive and it is used for storing page or swap files. Data is lost in the event virtual machine is rebooted or stopped. The size of the temporary disk is based on the size of the VM.

Data Disk

A data disk is a VHD that's network attached to a virtual machine to store application data and is **accessed over the network**. The size of the virtual machine determines how many data disks you can attach to it. Data is persisted in the event virtual machine is rebooted, started or stopped. Data disks are registered as SCSI drives and are labelled with a letter that you choose.

Managed and Unmanaged Disk

Azure Virtual Machine disk types (OS & Data Disk) can be Unmanaged or Managed.

Disks are associated with storage accounts. Maximum IOPS of storage account is 20000 IOPS. We have to make sure that IOPS of all disks in the storage account should not exceed 20000 IOPS otherwise throttling happens.

MS recommends that Managed Disk option to be used for all new VMs and convert previously created unmanaged disks to managed disks to take advantage of new features in managed disks.

Unmanaged Disks

With unmanaged disks we have to create and specify the storage account when we create unmanaged disk. We have to make sure that the combined IOPS of disks in the storage account do not exceed 20000 IOPS. We have to also plan number of storage accounts needed to accommodate our disks.

Managed Disks

Managed Disk option takes care of storage account creation and management and also ensures that users do not have to worry about 20000 IOPS limit in the storage account.

Managed Disks allow you to create up to 50,000 VM disks in a subscription.

When using availability set (AS) managed disk option ensures that disks of VMs in AS are isolated from each other to avoid SPOF.

The advantage of Managed Disk option is that it eliminates the operational overhead of planning, creating and managing Storage Accounts.

The disadvantage of Managed Disk option is that it only supports LRS for replication.

Note 1: Unmanaged or Managed OS Disk is chosen during VM creation.
Note 2: Managed Disk is important topic so please read it seriously.

Comparing Managed & Unmanaged Disks

	Managed Disks	**Unmanaged Disk**
Replication	**LRS**	**LRS, GRS & RA-GRS**
Pricing	Standard Storage: Per Disk Premium Storage: Per Disk	Standard Storage: Per GB Premium Storage: Per Disk
Storage Account Selection	Automatic	Manual
RBAC	Disk Level	Storage Account Level
Tags	Disk Level	Storage Account Level
Locks	Disk Level	Storage Account Level

Note 1: Managed disk & Unmanaged Premium Disk are charged for the Provisioned size.
Note 2: Unmanaged HDD is charged for the Storage used.
Note 3: Managed Disk only supports LRS for replication.
Note 4: Managed Disk option takes care of storage account creation and management. You need not create Storage Account for Managed Disk.

Virtual Machine Disk Performance Tiers

There are **Four** Performance tiers for virtual machine disk storage – **Standard Storage, Premium SSD Storage, Standard SSD Storage & Ultra SSD.** Virtual Machines disks are stored in Page Blobs. Page blobs can be created under General Purpose Standard Storage or General purpose premium Storage account.

Standard HDD Storage

With Standard Storage, OS and Data disks are stored in page blob backed by Magnetic HDD. You can use standard storage disks for Dev/Test scenarios and less critical workloads.

Standard Storage disks can be created in 2 ways – Unmanaged disks or Managed Disks. **With Unmanaged disk you need to create storage account. Whereas Managed Disk option takes care of storage account creation.**

Standard Unmanaged disk limits

VM Tier	**Standard Tier**
Max Disk size	4095 GB
Max 8 KB IOPS per disk	500
Max throughput per disk	60 MB/s

Standard Managed Disk Limits

Standard Managed Disk Type	S4	S6	S10	S20	S30	S40	S50
Disk Size (GB)	32	64	128	512	1024	2048	4095
Max IOPS per disk	500	500	500	500	500	500	500
Max throughput per disk	60 MB/s	60 MB/s	60 MB/s	60 MB/s	60 MB/s	60 MB/s	60 MB/s

MS has now released S60, S70 & S80 with 8, 16 and 32 TB respectively. Refer to end of the chapter for Pricing and information on P60, P70 & P80.

Premium SSD Storage

Premium Storage disks are backed by solid-state drives (SSDs). With Premium Storage, OS and Data disks are stored in page blob backed by SSD.

Azure Premium Storage delivers high-performance, low-latency disk support for virtual machines (VMs) with input/output (I/O)-intensive workloads. You can use Premium storage disks for I/O intensive and mission-critical production applications.

Requirements for Premium Storage

1. Premium Storage is supported in VMs with letter **s** in its size designation.
2. You can use Premium Storage disks only with VMs that are compatible with Premium Storage Disks. Premium Storage supports DS-series, DSv2-series, DSv3 Series, GS-series, Ls-series, and Fs-series, ESv3 VMs etc only.
3. You will require Premium storage account to create Premium Storage Disks. A premium storage account supports only locally redundant storage (LRS) as the replication option. Locally redundant storage keeps three copies of the data within a single region.

Features of Virtual Machines (DS-series, DSv2-series, DSv3, ESv3GS-series, Ls-series, and Fs-series, M etc) backed by Premium Storage

1. **Virtual Machine OS Disk:** Premium Storage VM can use either a premium or a standard operating system disk.
2. **Virtual Machine Data Disk:** Premium Storage VM can use both Premium and Standard Storage Disks.
3. **Cache:** VMs with Premium Storage have a unique caching capability for high levels of throughput and latency. The caching capability exceeds underlying premium storage disk performance. You can set the disk caching policy on premium storage disks to **ReadOnly**, **ReadWrite**, or **None**. The default disk caching policy is **Read Only** for all premium data disks and **ReadWrite** for operating system disks.

VM scale limits and performance: Premium Storage-supported VMs have scale limits and performance specifications for IOPS, bandwidth, and the number of disks that can be attached per VM.

For example, a STANDARD_DS1 VM has a dedicated bandwidth of 32 MB/s for premium storage disk traffic. A P10 premium storage disk can provide a bandwidth of 100 MB/s. If a P10 premium storage disk is attached to this VM, it can only go up to 32 MB/s. It cannot use the maximum 100 MB/s that the P10 disk can provide.

Premium Storage disk Sizes and limits (Unmanaged)

Premium storage disk type	P10	P20	P30	P40	P50
Disk Size (GB)	128	512	1024	2048	4095
Max Throughput per Disk	100 MB/s	150 MB/s	200 MB/s	250 MB/s	250 MB/s
Max IOPS per Disk	500 IOPS	2300 IOPS	5000 IOPS	7500 IOPS	7500 IOPS

Premium Storage Managed disk Sizes and limits

Premium storage disk type	P4	P6	P10	P20	P30	P40	P50
Disk Size (GB)	32	64	128	512	1024	2048	4095
Max Throughput per Disk	25 MB/s	50 MB/s	100 MB/s	150 MB/s	200 MB/s	250 MB/s	250 MB/s
Max IOPS per Disk	120 IOPS	240 IOPS	500 IOPS	2300 IOPS	5000 IOPS	7500 IOPS	7500 IOPS

Note 1: MS has now released Premium SSD Unmanaged Disk P60 with 8 TB.
Note 2: MS has now released Premium SSD Managed Disk P60, P70 & P80 with 8, 16 and 32 TB respectively.

Note: Refer to end end of the chapter for Pricing and information on P60, P70 & P80.

Standard SSD Managed Disk Storage

Standard SSD Storage disk is a low-cost SSD offering and are backed by solid-state drives (SSDs).

Standard SSD Managed Disks deliver lower latency compared to Standard HDDs, while improving reliability and scalability for your applications, and are available with all Azure VM sizes.

Standard SSD Managed Disks are optimized for test and entry-level production workloads requiring consistent latency. Standard SSD Managed Disks can also be used for big data workloads that require high throughput.

Standard SSD Storage comes in Managed Disk option only.

Standard SSD Managed Disks can be easily upgraded to Premium SSD Managed Disks for more demanding and latency-sensitive enterprise workloads.

Standard SSD Managed Storage disk Sizes and limits

	E10	**E15**	**E20**	**E30**	**E40**	**E50**	**E60**
Disk Size (GB)	128 GB	256 GB	512 GB	1 TB	2 TB	4 TB	8 TB
Max Throughput	60 MB/s	60 MB/s	60 MB/s	60 MB/s	60 MB/s	60 MB/s	300 MB/s
Max IOPS per Disk	500	500	500	500	500	500	1300

MS has now released Standard SSD Managed Disk E70 & E80 with 16 and 32 TB respectively. Refer to end end of the chapter for Pricing and information on P70 & P80.

Ultra SSD Managed Storage Disk

Ultra SSD Storage have very high **IOPS** and **throughput** compared to Premium SSD Storage. All VMs that support Premium SSD can leverage Ultra SSD Managed Disks.

Ultra SSD Managed Disks offer extremely scalable performance with **sub-millisecond latency**.

They are best suited for IO-intensive workloads such as SAP HANA, top tier databases (for example, SQL, Oracle), and other transaction-heavy workloads.

Ultra SSD Storage comes in Managed Disk option only.

Ultra SSD Managed Storage disk Sizes and limits

Disk Size (GiB)	4	8	16	32	64	128	256	512
IOPS Range	1200	2400	4800	9600	19200	38400	76800	160000
Throughput Range (MB/s)	300	600	1200	2000	2000	2000	2000	2000

Comparing Virtual Machine Disks

	Ultra disk	**Premium SSD**	**Standard SSD**	**Standard HDD**
Disk type	SSD	SSD	SSD	HDD
Scenario	IO-intensive workloads such as SAP HANA, top tier databases (for example, SQL, Oracle), and other transaction-heavy workloads.	Production and performance sensitive workloads.	Web servers, lightly used enterprise applications and dev/test.	Backup, non-critical, infrequent access.
Disk Size	65,536 (GiB)	32,767 GiB	32,767 GiB	32,767 GiB
Max throughput	2,000 MiB/s	900 MiB/s	750 MiB/s	500 MiB/s
Max IOPS	160,000	20,000	6,000	2,000

Backup for Managed Disk

Managed Disk only supports LRS for replication. You must take backup of Managed Disk to safeguard from Local or Regional disasters.

Some of the options for Managed Disk Backup are as follows:

1. Azure Backup
2. Snapshots of Managed Disk

Azure Backup for Managed Disk will be discussed in Azure Backup Chapter. Snapshots are discussed on Page 228.

DR for Managed Disk

DR for Managed Disk will be discussed in Azure Site Recovery Chapter.

Virtual Machine Disk Storage Design Parameters

IOPS

IOPS, or Input/output Operations Per Second is the number of requests that your application is sending to the storage disks in one second.

When you attach a premium storage disk to your VM, Azure provisions a guaranteed number of IOPS as per the disk specification. For example, a P50 disk provisions 7500 IOPS.

Example of Application requiring high IOPS is online retail website. Online retail website need to process many concurrent user requests immediately. The user requests are insert and update intensive database transactions, which the application must process quickly. Therefore applications require very high IOPS. You need to design your disk storage accordingly.

Throughput

Throughput or bandwidth is the amount of data that your application is sending to the storage disks in a specified interval.

If your application is performing input/output operations with large IO unit sizes, it requires high throughput.

Example of Application requiring high Throughput or bandwidth is Data Warehouse. Data Warehouse applications tend to issue scan intensive operations that access large portions of data at a time and commonly perform bulk operations Therefore Data Warehouse applications requires very high throughput.

Figure below shows relation between throughput and IOPS.

I/O Size

The IO size is the size of the input/output operation request generated by your application. The IO size has a significant impact on performance especially on the IOPS and Bandwidth that the application is able to achieve.

Smaller IO size gets higher IOPS. For example, 8 KB for an OLTP application. **Larger IO size gets higher Bandwidth/Throughput.** For example, 1024 KB for a data warehouse application.

Latency

Latency is the time it takes an application to receive a single request, send it to the storage disks and send the response to the client.

Premium Disks are designed to provide single-digit millisecond latencies for most IO operations. If you enable ReadOnly host caching on premium storage disks, you can get much lower read latency.

When you are optimizing your application to get higher IOPS and Throughput, it will affect the latency of your application. After tuning the application performance, always evaluate the latency of the application to avoid unexpected high latency behavior.

Disk Caching

VMs that use Azure Premium Storage have a multi-tier caching technology called BlobCache. BlobCache uses a combination of the Virtual Machine RAM and local SSD for caching.

With disk caching enabled on the Premium Storage disks, the VMs can achieve extremely high levels of performance that exceed the underlying disk performance.

Following are Default Cache settings for OS and Data disks.

Disk type	Default cache setting
OS disk	ReadWrite
Data disk	ReadOnly

Following are the recommended disk cache settings for data disks.

Disk caching setting	recommendation on when to use this setting
None	Configure host-cache as None for write-only and write-heavy disks.
ReadOnly	Configure host-cache as ReadOnly for read-only and read-write disks.
ReadWrite	Configure host-cache as ReadWrite only if your application properly handles writing cached data to persistent disks when needed.

Disk Stripping

When a VM is attached with several Data disks, the disks can be striped together to aggregate their IOPs, bandwidth, and storage capacity.

On Windows, you can use Storage Spaces to stripe disks together.
On Linux, use the MDADM utility to stripe disks together.

You must configure one column for each disk in a pool. For example, if there are 16 disks in a single stripe set; specify 16 columns in the NumberOfColumns parameter of the *New-VirtualDisk* PowerShell cmdlet. Otherwise, the overall performance of striped volume can be lower than expected, due to uneven distribution of traffic across the disks.

Queue Depth

The queue depth or queue length or queue size is the number of pending IO requests in the system. The value of queue depth determines how many IO operations your application can line up, which the storage disks will be processing.

Queue depth affects all the three application performance parameters including IOPS, throughput, and latency.

A high queue depth lines up more operations on the disk. Very high queue depth value also has its drawbacks. **If queue depth value is too high, the application will try to drive very high IOPS resulting in high application latencies.**

Formula shows the relationship between IOPS, latency, and queue depth.

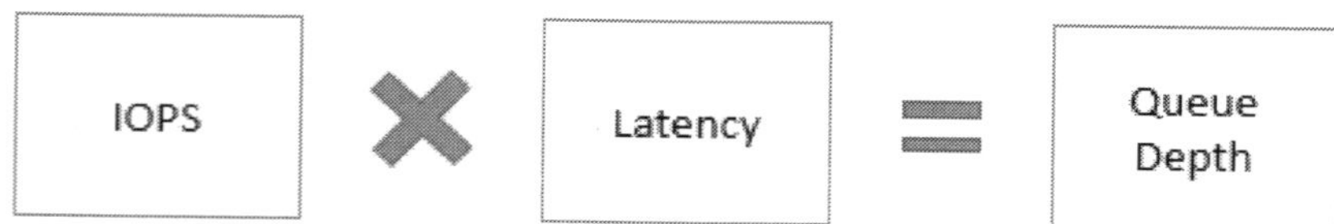

You should not configure Queue Depth to any high value, but to an optimal value, which can deliver enough IOPS for the application without affecting latencies. For example, if the application latency needs to be 1 millisecond, the Queue Depth required to achieve 5,000 IOPS is, QD = 5000 x 0.001 = 5.
Note: 1 Millisecond = 0.001 Seconds

Optimize IOPS, throughput, and latency

	IOPS	Throughput	Latency
Example Scenario	Enterprise OLTP application requiring very high transactions per second rate.	Enterprise Data warehousing application processing large amounts of data.	Near real-time applications requiring instant responses like online gaming.
Performance factors			
IO size	Smaller IO size yields higher IOPS.	Larger IO size to yields higher Throughput.	
VM size	Use a VM size that offers IOPS greater than your application requirement.	Use a VM size with throughput limit greater than your application requirement.	Use a VM size that offers scale limits greater than your application requirement.
Disk size	Use a disk size that offers IOPS greater than your application requirement.	Use a disk size with Throughput limit greater than your app requirement.	Use a disk size that offers scale limits greater than your app requirement.
VM and Disk Scale Limits	IOPS limit of the VM size chosen should be greater than total IOPS driven by premium storage disks attached to it.	Throughput limit of the VM size chosen should be greater than total Throughput driven by premium storage disks attached to it.	Scale limits of the VM size chosen must be greater than total scale limits of attached premium storage disks.
Disk Striping	Use multiple disks and stripe them together to get a combined higher IOPS and Throughput limit. The combined limit per VM should be higher than the combined limits of attached premium disks.		
Stripe Size	Smaller stripe size for random small IO pattern seen in OLTP applications. For example, use stripe size of 64 KB for SQL Server OLTP application.	Larger stripe size for sequential large IO pattern seen in Data Warehouse apps. For e.g use 256 KB stripe size for SQL Server Data warehouse apps	
Queue Depth	Larger Queue Depth yields higher IOPS.	Larger Queue Depth yields higher Throughput.	Smaller Queue Depth yields lower latencies.

Case Study 6: Designing Disk Solution

Your company has standardized on P30 Disk for their Virtual Machines. You have a OLTP application which requires 9000 IOPS. Design a solution for satisfying the requirement. Application IO Size will be 16 KB.

Solution

The maximum IOPS and Throughput/Bandwidth a P30 disk can achieve is 5000 IOPS and 200 MB per second respectively.

To get IOPS higher than the maximum value of a single premium storage disk, we will use multiple premium disks striped together. In this case we will stripe two P30 disks to get a combined IOPS of 10,000 IOPS which will satisfy Application IOPS requirement of 9000.

Make sure to use the P30 Disks with Virtual Machine which can support 9000 IOPS.

Case Study 7: Designing Disk and VM Soultion

Your company has standardized on P30 SSD Disk for their Virtual Machines. The Company has also standardized on Dsv3 Virtual Machines Series for running applications.

You have a I/O intensive OLTP application which requires 9000 IOPS.
The operations team has given D2sv3 Azure VM to implement the solution.

Design a solution for satisfying the above requirement.

Solution- Designing for IOPS

The maximum IOPS and Throughput/Bandwidth a P30 disk can achieve is 5000 IOPS and 200 MB per second respectively.

In this case we will stripe two P30 disks to get a combined IOPS of 10,000 IOPS which will satisfy Application IOPS requirement of 9000.

Solution- Designing for Azure VM

D2sv3 VM is limited to 3,200 IOPS. Consequently, the application performance will be constrained by the VM limit at 3,200 IOPS and there will be degraded performance. Table below Show various Dsv3 Sizes with Max IOPS.

Size	vCPU	Memory	Max NICs	Temp Storage SSD	Max Data Disks	Max IOPS/MBps Supported	Price/ hour
D2s v3	2	8	2	50 GB	4	3200/48	$0.188
D4s v3	4	16	2	100 GB	8	6400/96	$0.376
D8s v3	8	32	4	200 GB	16	12800/192	$0.752
D16s v3	16	64	8	400 GB	32	25600/384	$1.504
D32s v3	32	128	8	800 GB	32	51200/768	$3.008
D64s v3	64	256	8	1600 GB	32	80000/1200	$6.016

Instead of D2sv3 we will ask the operations team to provide D8sv3 VM to satisfy the Application requirement of 9000 IOPS.

Case Study 8: Design for IOPS and Throughtput/Bandwidth for your Application using Different I/O Sizes

Your application will be using P30 Managed disk. The maximum IOPS and Throughput/Bandwidth a P30 disk can achieve is 5000 IOPS and 200 MB per second respectively.

You Application can be OLTP or Data Warehousing. Depending upon the application requirements, Design Application IOPS and Throughtput/Bandwidth for various IO sizes.

Application Requirements can be Max IOPS, Max Throughput, Max Throughput + high IOPS and Max IOPS + high Throughput.

Solutions

Formula below shows relationship between IOPS and throughput.

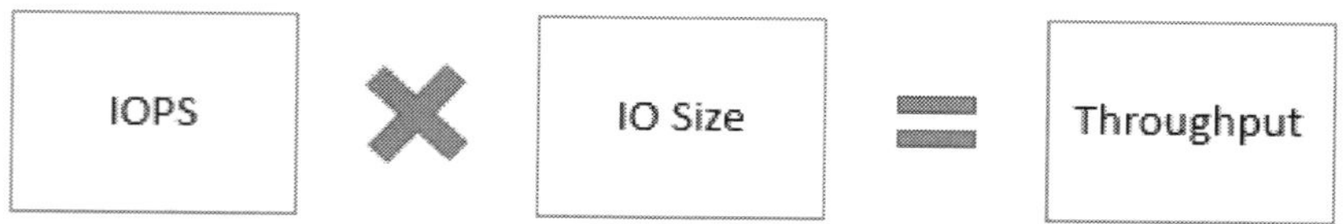

Depending upon the Application requirement, Table below summarizes the different IO sizes and their corresponding IOPS and Throughput for a P30 disk.

Application Requirement	**I/O size**	**IOPS**	**Throughput/Bandwidth**
Max IOPS	8 KB	5000	(8*5000/1024) = **40 MB Per Second**
Max Throughput	1024 KB	(200*1024/1024) = **200**	200 MB Per Second
Max Throughput + high IOPS	64 KB	(200*1024/64) = **3200**	200 MB Per Second
Max IOPS + high Throughput	32 KB	5000	(32*5000/1024) = **160 MB Per Second**

Case Study 9: Choosing VM size and Designing IOPs

A company is shifting test & Dev app to cloud. It's a 2 Tier application – Web/App & Database tier. Application & Database owner have specified following requirements for the Virtual Machines.

Feature	Application	Database
vCPU	8	4
Memory	16 GB	64 GB
IOPS	500	1200
Database Size		100 GB

They want to use latest Generation Dv3 VM. To save on cost they want use Unmamaged Magnetic HDD for storage. They want Database Data to be on separate Data Disks and not on OS Disk.
Suggest size and configuration for Dv3 VM for Application and Database server.

Solution

Following Sizes are available in Dv3 series.

Size	**vCPU**	**Memory**	**Max NICs**	**Temp Storage SSD**	**Max Data Disks**	**Max IOPS**	**Price/ hour**
D2 v3	2	8	2	50 GB	4	4X500	$0.188
D4 v3	4	16	2	100 GB	8	8X500	$0.376
D8 v3	8	32	4	200 GB	16	16X500	$0.752
D16 v3	16	64	8	400 GB	32	32X500	$1.504
D32 v3	32	128	8	800 GB	32	32X500	$3.008
D64 v3	64	256	8	1600 GB	32	32X500	$6.016

For App Server We will choose D8v3 to satisfy both vCPU and Memory Req.

For DB Server we will choose D16v3 to satisfy both vCPU and Memory Req.

We need to add 3 Data disks to Database instance to satisfy IOPS requirement of 1200. 3 Data Disks will give an IOPS of 1500 (3X500). Note 2 Data disks will give an IOPS of 1000 only. Data will be stripped across 3 Hard Disk to achieve the required IOPS.

Virtual Machine Networking

Azure Virtual Machines are created in Virtual Networks. An Azure virtual network (VNET) is Virtual Datacenter in the cloud. You can further segment virtual network (VNET) into subnets. Access to the subnets can be controlled using Network Security groups. You can define the IP address blocks, security policies, and route tables within this network.

In the below diagram you have Virtual Network KNET1 with network address 192.168.0.0/16 divided into two Subnets- Web-Subnet1 and DB-Subnet1 with network addresses 192.168.1.0/24 and 192.168.2.0/24 respectively.

These Network Addresses are defined by the user and not by Azure Cloud.

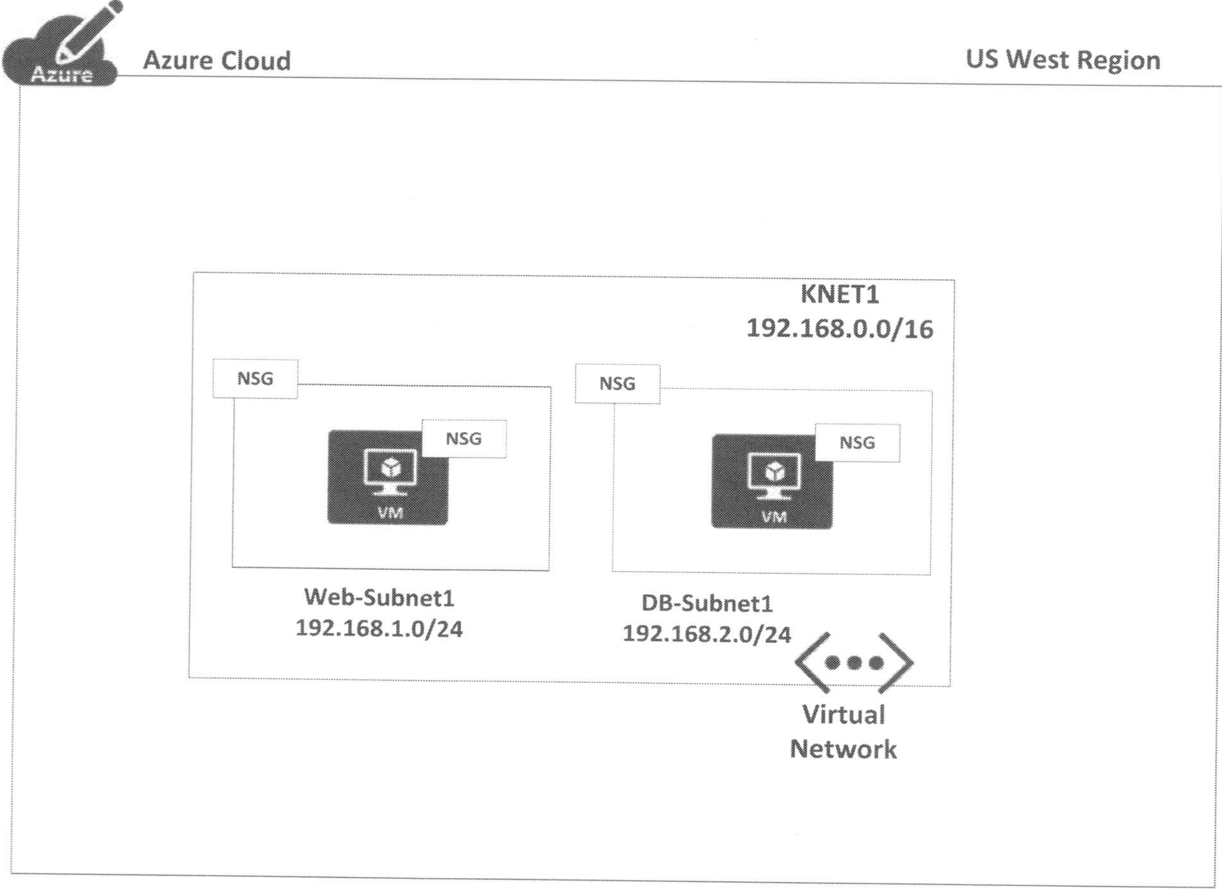

Azure Virtual Machines private address is derived from subnet address. In the above figure Virtual Machines in Web-Subnet1 will get **private address** of 192.168.1.x/24 and Virtual Machines in DB-Subnet1 will get private address of 192.168.2.x/24. Private IP Address is used for communication within a Virtual Network, your on-premises network and the Internet (with NAT).

You can use following class A, Class B and Class C address range for virtual networks.

10.0.0.0/8
172.16.0.0/12
192.168.0.0/16

Once the IP address range is decided, we can then divide this range into subnets. Azure Virtual Machines private address is derived from subnet address.

VM Private IP Address can be dynamic or Static. The default allocation is dynamic. You can assign static private IP address to VM from VM Subnet address range.

Virtual Machine Public address is assigned by Azure. Public Address can be Static or Dynamic. Dynamic Public IP will change every time you stop or reboot your Virtual Machine. To ensure the IP address for the VM remains the same, set the allocation method to static.
Public IP address is used for communication with internet and Public facing Azure resources which are not part of Virtual Network.

Virtual Machine Accelerated Networking (AN)

Accelerated Networking (AN) provides ultra-low network latency for Virtual Machine Network Traffic. AN provides up to 30Gbps in networking throughput.

With AN, Virtual Machine Networking Traffic bypasses Virtual switch on the host and directly connects to Host SmartNIC, reducing latency, jitter, and CPU utilization. All network policies that the virtual switch applies are now offloaded and applied in hardware.

With AN much of Azure's software-defined networking stack is moved into FPGA-based SmartNICs. Accelerated networking enables single root I/O virtualization (SR-IOV) to a VM, greatly improving its networking performance.
The SR-IOV allows different virtual machines (VMs) in a virtual environment to share a single PCI Express hardware interface.

Figure below shows communication between two VMs with and without accelerated networking.

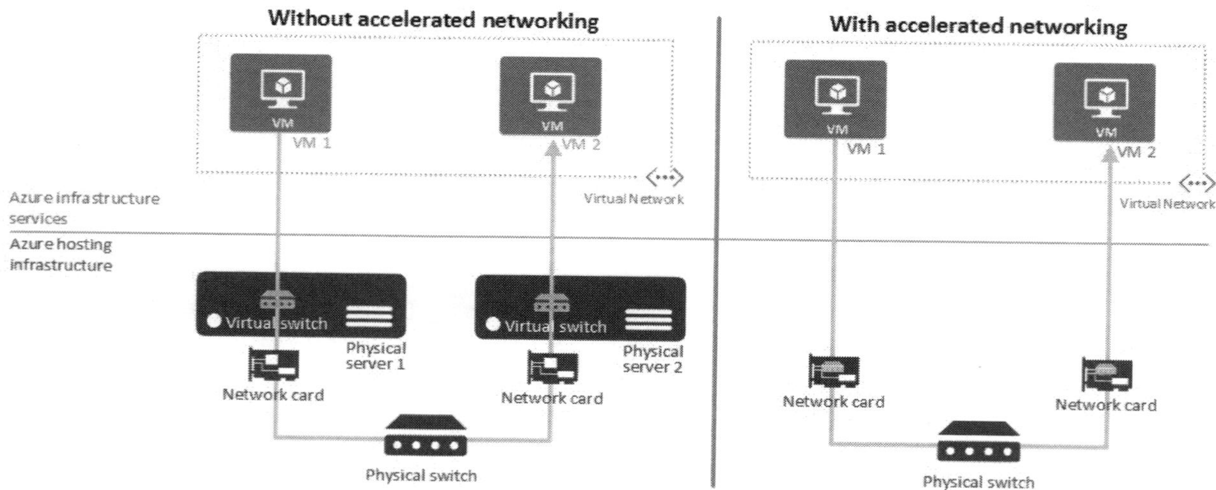

AN features has best results when enabled on VMs which are connected to same Virtual Network (VNET). When communicating across VNETs or connecting on-premises, this feature has minimal impact to overall latency.

Benefits of Accelerated Networking (AN)

Lower Latency / Higher packets per second (pps): Removing the virtual switch from the datapath removes the time packets spend in the host for policy processing and increases the number of packets that can be processed inside the VM.
Reduced jitter: Virtual switch processing depends on the amount of policy that needs to be applied and the workload of the CPU that is doing the processing. Offloading the policy enforcement to the hardware removes that variability by delivering packets directly to the VM, removing the host to VM communication and all software interrupts and context switches.
Decreased CPU utilization: Bypassing the virtual switch in the host leads to less CPU utilization for processing network traffic.

Operating System supported by Accelerated Networking

Windows	Linux
Windows Server 2016 Datacenter	Ubuntu 16.04
Windows Server 2012 R2 Datacenter	SLES 12 SP3
	RHEL 7.4
	CentOS 7.4
	CoreOS Linux
	Debian "Stretch" with backports kernel
	Oracle Linux 7.4

Supported VM instances

Accelerated Networking is supported on most general purpose and compute-optimized instance sizes with 2 or more vCPUs. These supported series are: D/DSv2 and F/Fs.

On instances that support hyperthreading, Accelerated Networking is supported on VM instances with 4 or more vCPUs. Supported series are: D/DSv3, E/ESv3, Fsv2, and Ms/Mms.

Virtual Machine Security using Network Security Group (NSG)

Network Security Group (NSG) acts as a Firewall. Network Security Group (NSG) contains a list of rules that allow or deny network traffic to VM NICs or subnets or both.

NSGs can be associated with subnets and/or individual VM NICs connected to a subnet. When an NSG is associated with a subnet, the rules apply to all the VMs in that subnet. In addition, traffic to an individual VM NIC can be restricted by associating an NSG directly to a VM NIC.

NSGs contain rules that specify whether the traffic is approved or denied. Each rule is based on a source IP address, a source port, a destination IP address, and a destination port. Based on whether the traffic matches this combination, it either is allowed or denied.

Figure below shows Web1 & Web2 VMs are protected by 2 levels of Firewall. One at VM NIC level and other at Subnet Level. Whereas DB1 VM is protected at VM NIC level only.

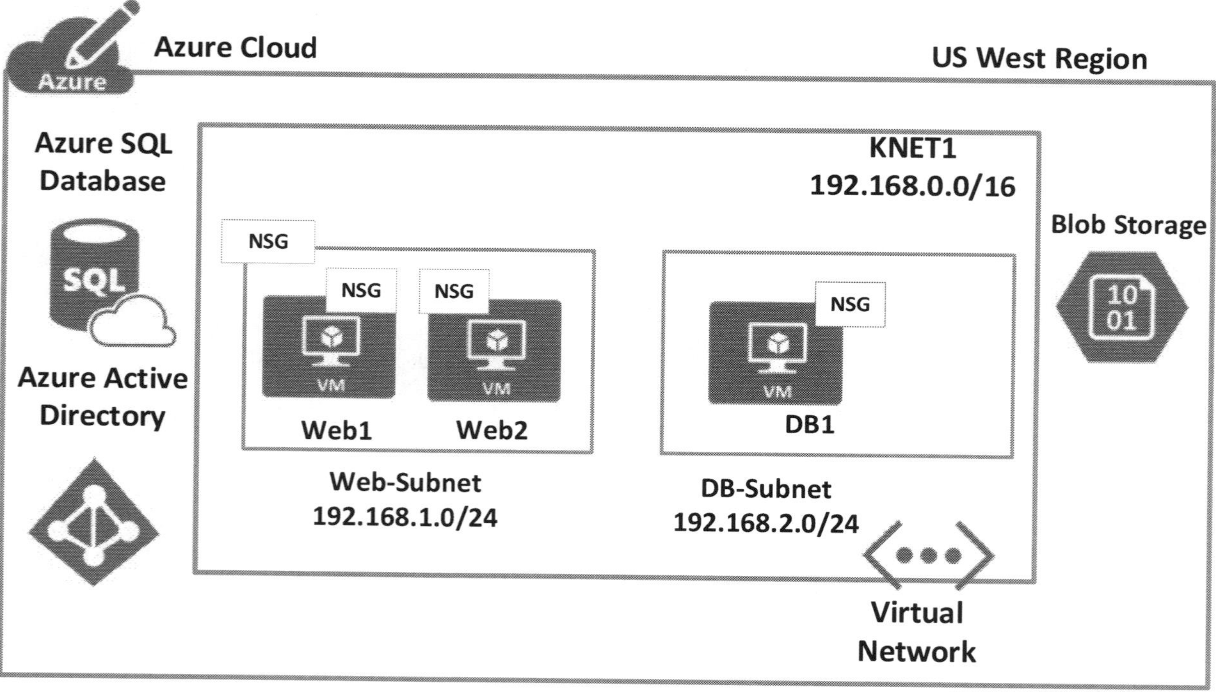

Note: NSG was discussed in Implementing Virtual Networks chapter.

VM High Availability Options

You can configure Virtual Machine High Availability either with Availability Set (AS) or with Availability Zones (AZ).

This is done during Virtual Machine creation. You can't do it afterwards. During VM creation you can choose AZ or AS under Availability options as shown below.

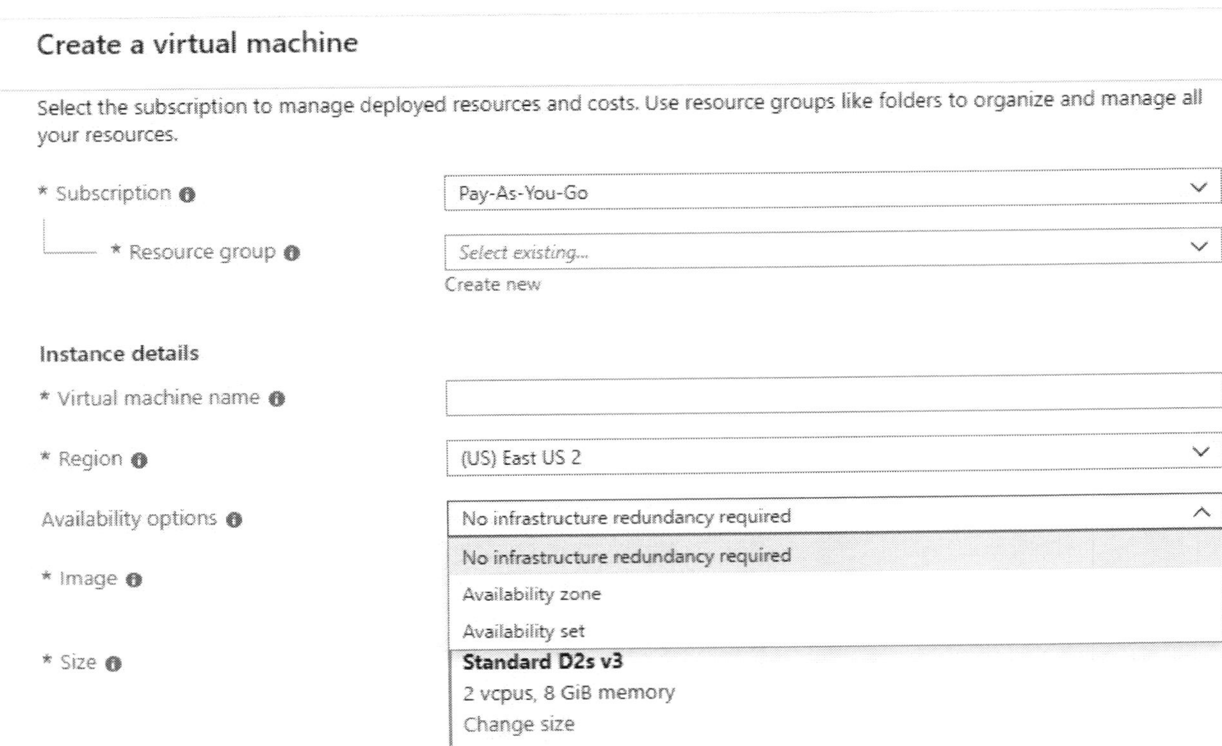

Note 1: To Provide VM High Availabilty using AS or AZ you must have minimum of 2 instances of VM.
Note 2: To provide application HA, VMs in AS or AZ must be combined with Load Balancer.
Note 3: To use Load Balancer with VMs, VMs must be in AS or AZ.

VM High Availability using Availability Set (AS)

Availability Set (AS) Provides high Availability against hardware failure in Azure Cloud by eliminating single point of failure. Availability Set (AS) in itself is not a full high availability solution. **To provide application HA, Availability Set (AS) has to be combined with Azure Load Balancer.**
Note: To Provide VM High Availabilty using AS you must have minimum of 2 instances of VM.

Before going into details of Availability Set, let's discuss why we need it in first place. Consider a scenario where there are 2 applications and each application is running 2 instances - Application A (VMA-1 & VMA-2) & Application B (VMB-1 & VMB-2). Application Instances are load balanced.

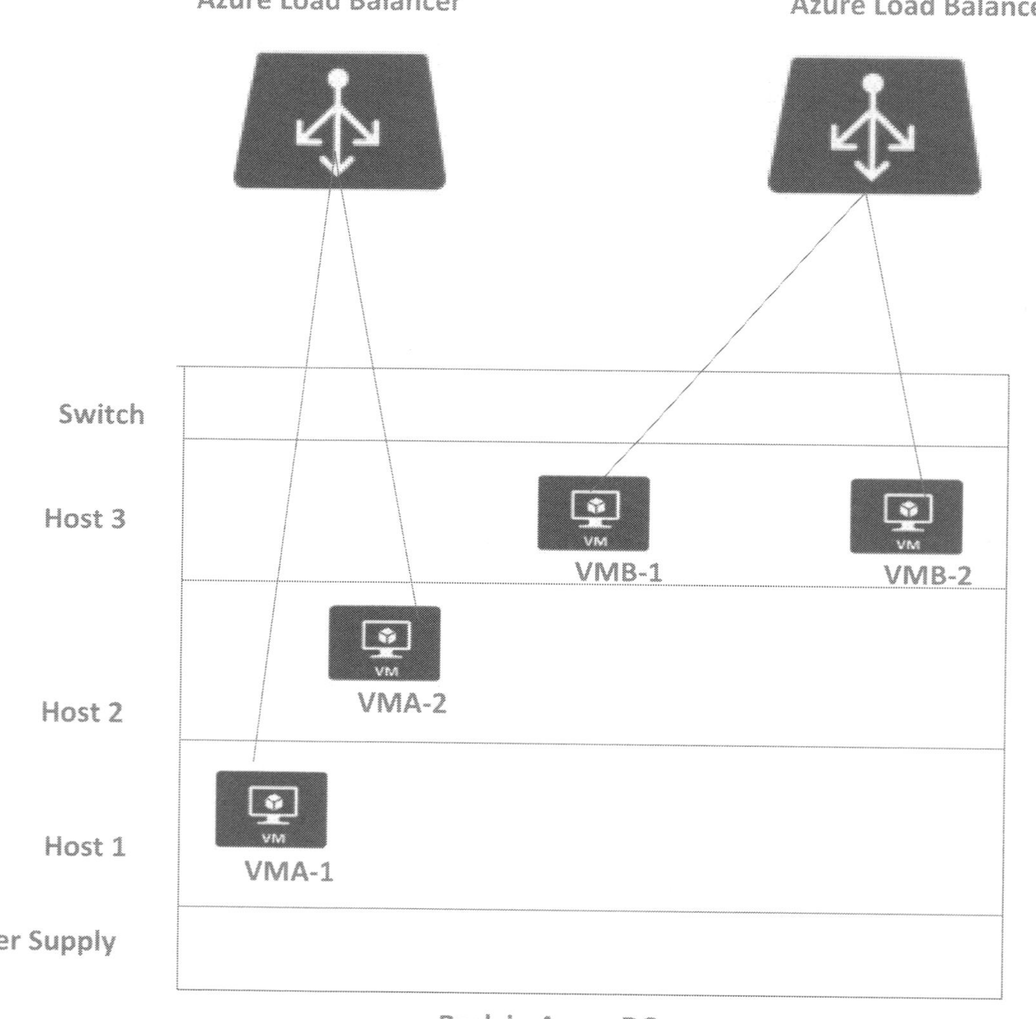

Application A has 2 single point of failure – Power Supply & TOR Switch.
Application B has 3 single point of failure - Host, Power Supply & TOR Switch.

With Availability Set we can eliminate above single point of failures.
By creating an **Availability Set** and adding virtual machines to the Availability Set, Azure will ensure that the virtual machines in the set get distributed across the physical hosts, Network switch & Rack that run them in such a way that a hardware failure will not bring down all the machines in the set.
Each virtual machine in the Availability Set is assigned an update domain and a fault domain by Azure.

An **Update Domain (UD)** is used to determine the sets of virtual machines and the underlying hardware that can be rebooted together. **For each Availability Set created, five Update Domains will be created by default, but can be changed. You can configure Maximum of 20 Update Domains.** When Microsoft is updating physical host it will reboot only one update domains at a time.

Fault domains (FD) define the group of virtual machines that share a common power source and network switch. **For each Availability Set, two Fault Domains will be created by default, but can be changed. You can configure Maximum of 3 Fault Domains.**

Design Nuggets

1. Update Domains helps with Planned Maintenance events like host reboot by Azure.
2. Fault Domain helps with unplanned Maintenance events like hardware (TOR Switch or Rack Power Supply) failure.
3. Configure each application tier into separate availability sets.
4. Assign different storage accounts to virtual machines in the availability set. If there is an outage in the storage account it will not affect all the virtual machines in the set.
5. Use Azure Load Balancer to distribute traffic to virtual machines in the Availability Set. If there is a Hardware failure (Host, TOR Switch, Rack Power Supply) then it will not affect traffic to other virtual machines in the Availability Set.
6. **To Provide VM High Availabilty using AS you must have minimum 2 instances of VM.**

VM High Availability using Availability Zones (AZ)

Azure Availability Zone protects your applications and data from Complete Location breakdown or Datacenter wide outage which affects the entire Azure Data Center. **You create VMs in different Availability Zones. To provide application HA, Availability Zones has to be combined with Azure Standard Load Balancer.**

With Azure Availability Zones (AZ), **Azure Region will have 3 or more physically separate Data Centre's within Metro distance connected by High Speed Fibre Optic cables.** This distance can be 500M, 1 KM, 5 KM or 10 KM etc. The important point here is that Availability Zones (AZ) will not be sharing any infrastructure like Networking, Grid Power Supply and Cooling etc. The figure below shows three Availability Zones in a Region connected by High speed Fibre Optic Cables. These AZs are separate Azure Data Centers.

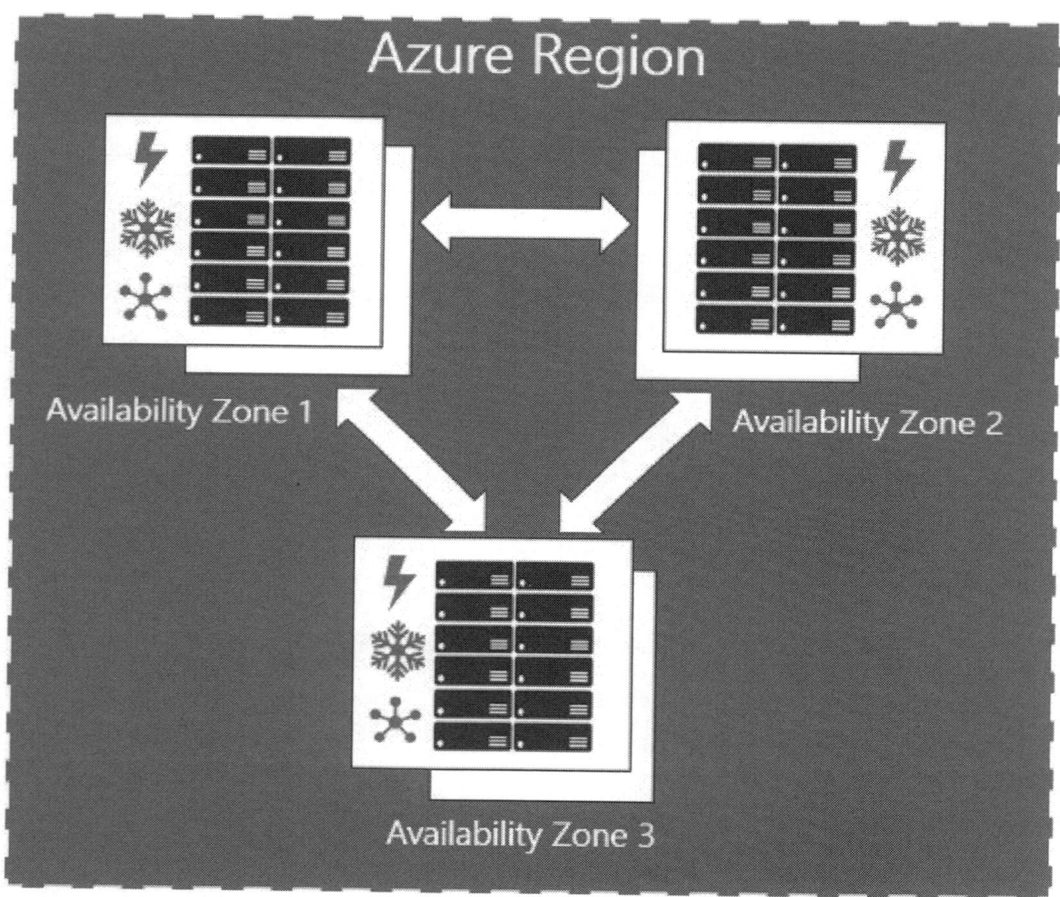

Note: To Provide VM High Availabilty using AZ you must have minimum of 2 instances of VM.

Azure services that support Availability Zones fall into two categories:
Zonal services – you pin the resource to a specific zone (for example, virtual machines, managed disks, IP addresses).
Zone-redundant services – platform replicates automatically across zones (for example, zone-redundant storage, SQL Database).

STEP BY STEP PROVIDING HIGH AVAILABILITY TO LOAD BALANCED WEB 1, WEB2 & WEB3 VIRTUAL SERVERS USING AZURE AVAILABILITY ZONES

1. Virtual Network & Subnet created will span Availability Zone 1 (AZ1), Availability Zone 2 (AZ2) and Availability Zone 3 (AZ3) in the region.
2. Create Web1 VM with Managed disk in Subnet1 in AZ1.
3. Create Web2 VM with Managed disk in Subnet1 in AZ2.
4. Create Web3 VM with Managed disk in Subnet1 in AZ3.
5. Use Azure Standard Load Balancer (Zone Redundant) with Standard IP (Zone Redundant) to Load Balance Traffic to Web1, Web2 & Web3 Virtual Server.

Figure below shows Azure Standard Load Balancer providing cross-zone Load Balancing to 3 VMs located in AZ1, AZ2 and AZ3 respectively.

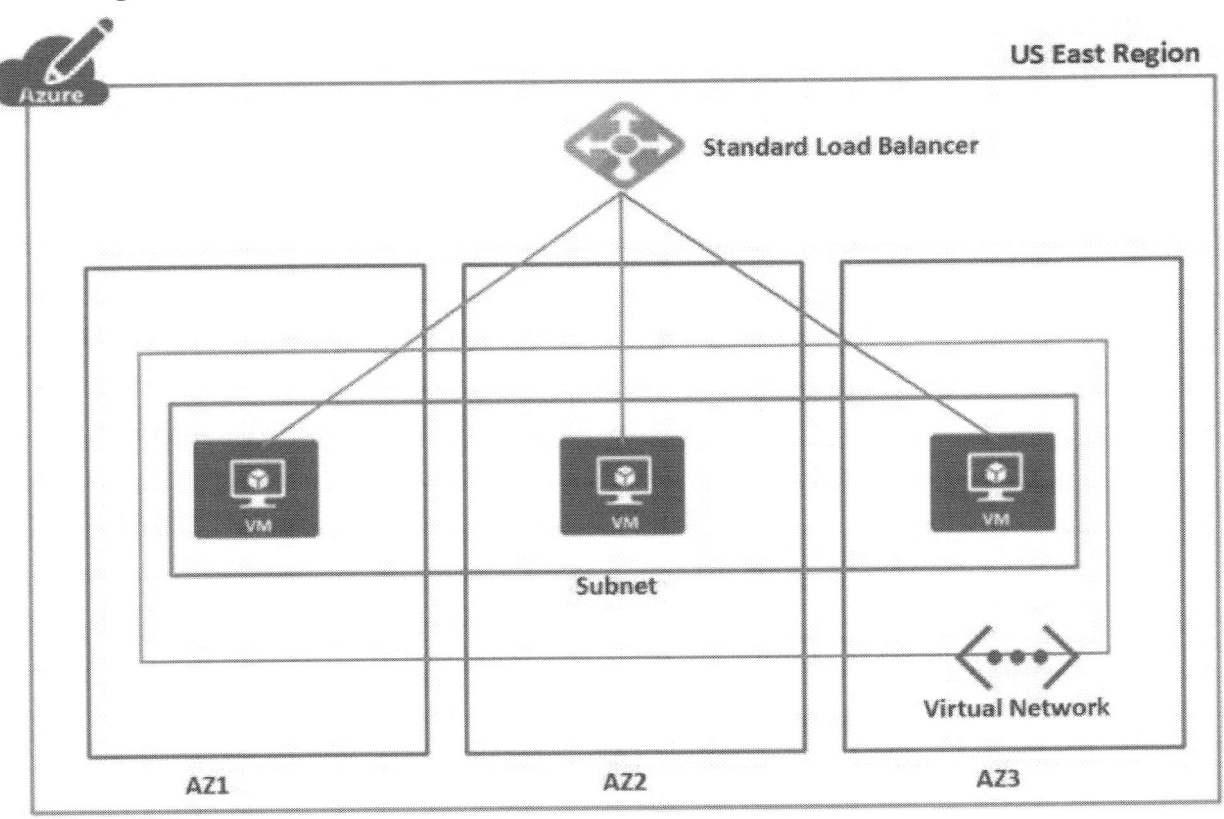

Azure Services that support Availability Zones

Azure Availability Zones preview supports following Azure Services:

Windows Virtual Machine
Linux Virtual Machine
Zonal Virtual Machine Scale Sets
Managed Disks
Load Balancer
Public IP address
Zone-redundant storage
SQL Database

Important Note: Availability Zones (AZ) are currently in Preview in many regions. AZ is not currently part of AZ 300 Exam topics. AZ can be asked AZ-301 Design Exam.

Case Study 10: Placement of Virtual Machines in Availability Set

Consider a scenario where we have 5 Virtual Machines in Availability Set with 3 Update Domains (UD) and 2 Fault Domains (FD) are configured. Show the possible placement of Virtual Machines.

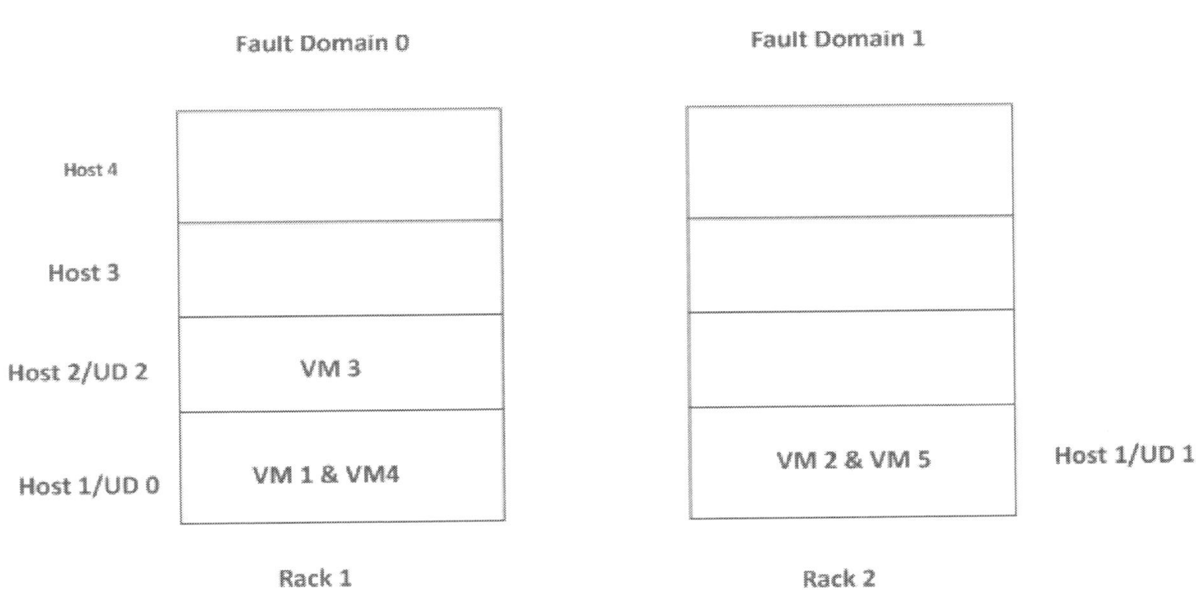

AS is configured with 2 Fault Domains which means VMs will be spread across 2 racks. AS is configured with 3 Update Domains which means VMs will be placed across 3 hosts.

VM1, VM2 & VM3 will be placed in UD 0, UD 1 and UD 2 respectively. VM4 will be placed in UD 0 and VM5 will be placed in UD1.

VM1, VM3 & VM4 will share FD 0 and VM2 & VM5 will share FD 1.

In case of host failure, maximum of 2 VMs out of 5 VMs will be affected. In case of Rack Failure (PS/TOR Switch) maximum of 3 VMs out of 5 VMs will be affected.

Exercise 24: Create Availability Set (AS) using Azure Portal

1. In Azure Portal click **All Services** in left pane>Under Compute section Click Availability Sets> Availability Sets Dashboard opens>Click +Add>Create Availability Set Blade opens>Enter **ASCloud** in name box, Select **RGCloud** in Resource Group, Select **East US 2** in location and rest select all defaults and click create. (Resource GroupRGCloud was created in Exercise 1, Chapter 1)

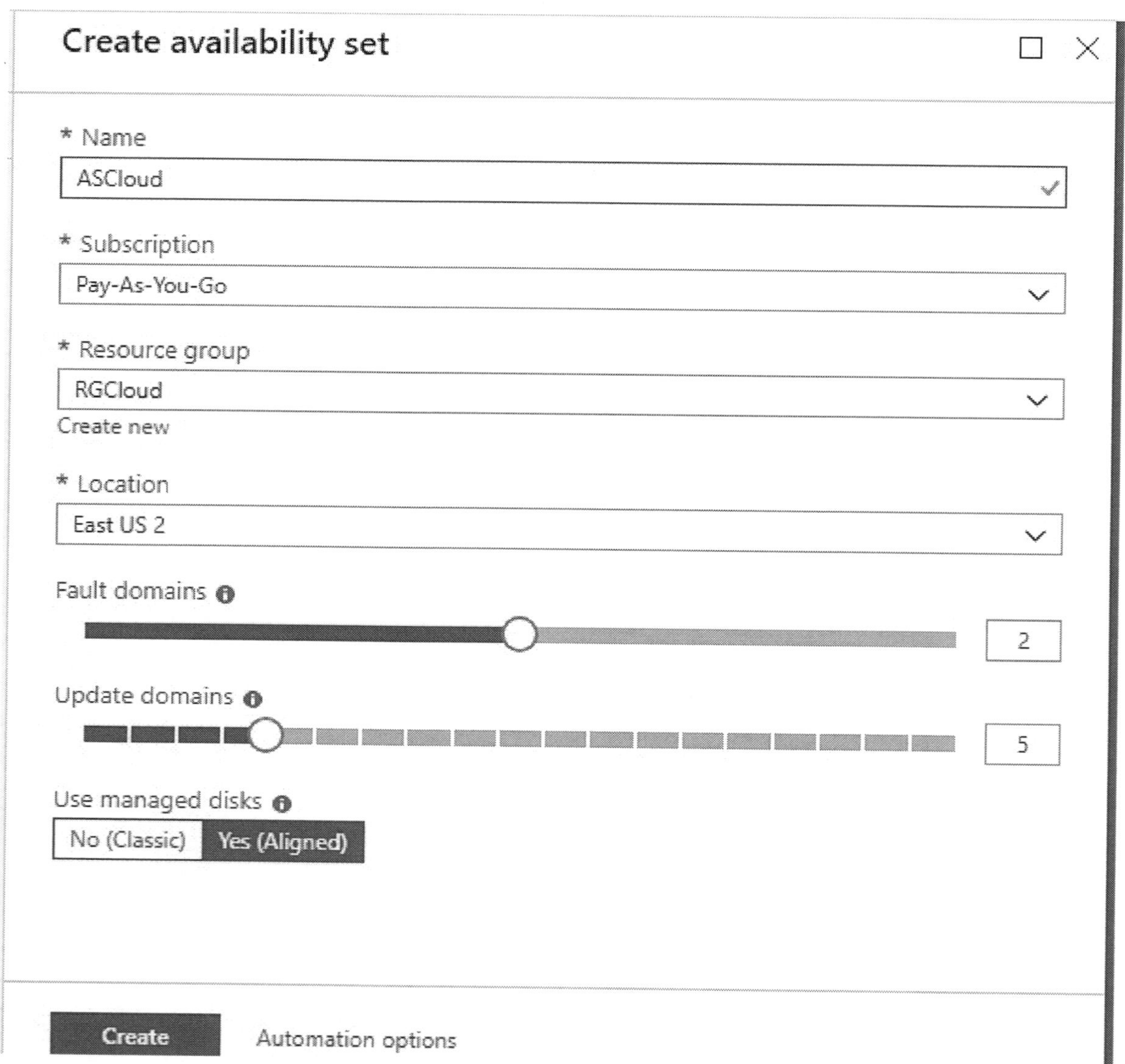

Note 1: AS is off use when you are using 2 or more VMs in the set. Single VM in an AS does not provide any benefit.
Note 2: Secondly to Add VMs to Load Balancer, VMs must be in Availability Set.

Exercise 25: Create Windows Virtual Machine VMFE1

In this exercise we will create Windows Server 2019 VM VMFE1 in Web-Subnet of Virtual Network **VNETCloud** created in Exercise 3 and in Resource Group **RGCloud** created in Exercise 1. We will use **Managed disk option**, select **AS** created in Exercise 24 and will use **System created Dynamic Public IP**. We will convert Dynamic IP to Static IP in Step 9.

1. In Azure Portal Click Create a Resource> Compute> Virtual Machine> Create Virtual Machine Blade opens>Select Resource Group RGCloud, Enter VM name, Select East US 2 in region, Select Availability Set in Availability option and Select ASCloud, In Image Dropdown box Select Windows Server 2019 Datacenter, Enter Administrator Account name and password> Select none for inbound port option. We will select under networking >Click Next: Disks (Not Shown).

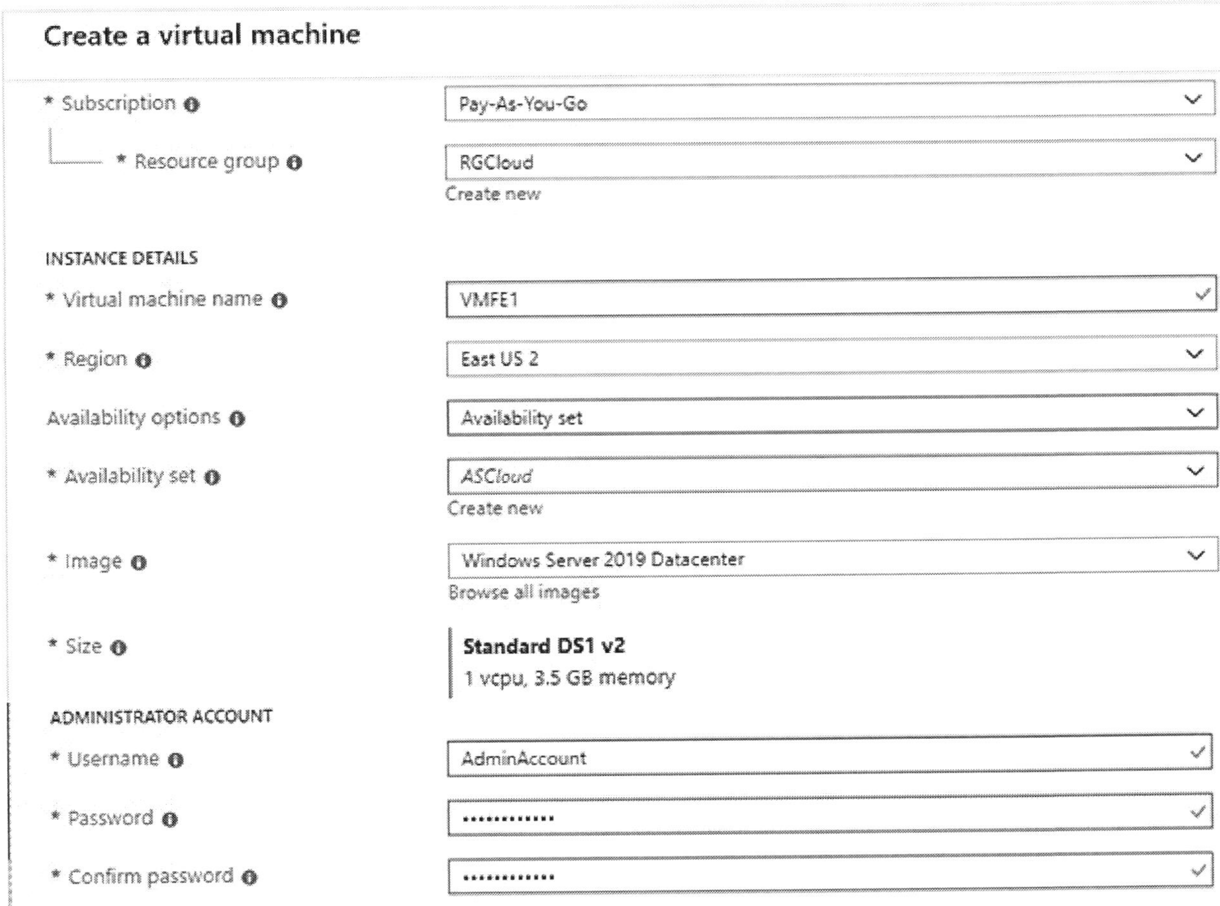

2. Disk Screen opens>Select your HDD Option>Click Advanced and select yes for managed disk (default option) and click Next: Networking.

Create a virtual machine

DISK OPTIONS

* OS disk type: Standard HDD

The selected VM size supports premium disks. We recommend Premium SSD for high IOPS workloads. Virtual machines with Premium SSD disks qualify for the 99.9% connectivity SLA.

Enable Ultra SSD compatibility (Preview): Yes / No (selected)

Ultra SSD compatibility is not available for this VM size and location.

DATA DISKS

You can add and configure additional data disks for your virtual machine or attach existing disks. This VM also comes with a temporary disk.

LUN	NAME	SIZE (GIB)	DISK TYPE	HOST CACHING

Create and attach a new disk   Attach an existing disk

ADVANCED

Use managed disks: No / Yes (selected)

Review + create   Previous   Next : Networking >

3. Networking Screen opens> Select VNETCloud and Web-Subnet from dropdown boxes> Select Basic in NSG>select Allow selected ports and select RDP, HTTP and HTTPS> Select off for AN>Click Next: Management.

* Virtual network: VNETCloud
Create new

* Subnet: Web-Subnet (10.1.1.0/24)
Manage subnet configuration

Public IP: (new) VMFE1-ip
Create new

NIC network security group: None / Basic (selected) / Advanced

The selected subnet 'Web-Subnet (10.1.1.0/24)' is already associated to a network

* Public inbound ports

- [x] HTTP (80)
- [ ] HTTPS (443)
- [ ] SSH (22)
- [x] RDP (3389)

* Select inbound ports: HTTP, RDP

4. Management Screen opens>Select No for Security Center and off for Monitoring, Identity and Auto-Shutdown. Click Next: Advanced.
   Note: Readers can enable some options according to their requirement.

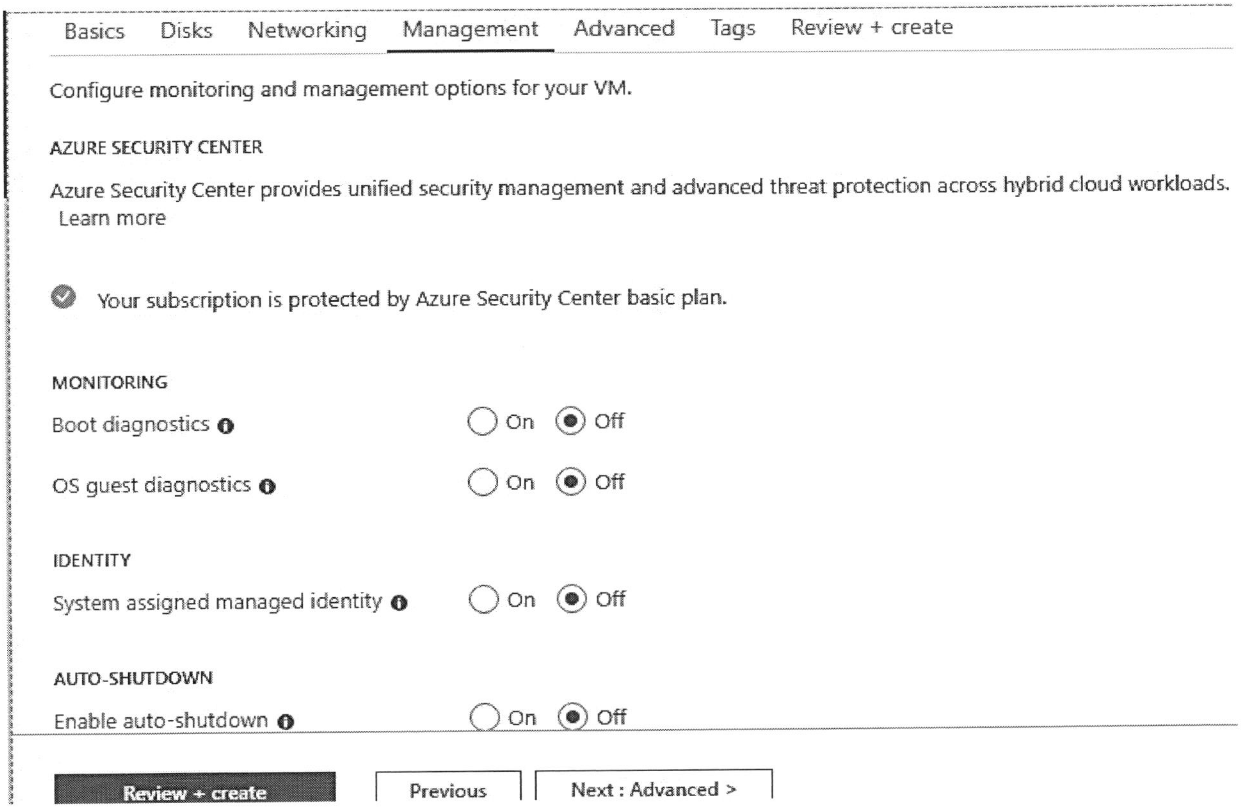

Basics Disks Networking Management Advanced Tags Review + create

Configure monitoring and management options for your VM.

AZURE SECURITY CENTER

Azure Security Center provides unified security management and advanced threat protection across hybrid cloud workloads. Learn more

Your subscription is protected by Azure Security Center basic plan.

MONITORING

Boot diagnostics — On / Off

OS guest diagnostics — On / Off

IDENTITY

System assigned managed identity — On / Off

AUTO-SHUTDOWN

Enable auto-shutdown — On / Off

Review + create | Previous | Next : Advanced >

5. Select all default values in Advanced>Click Next:Tags

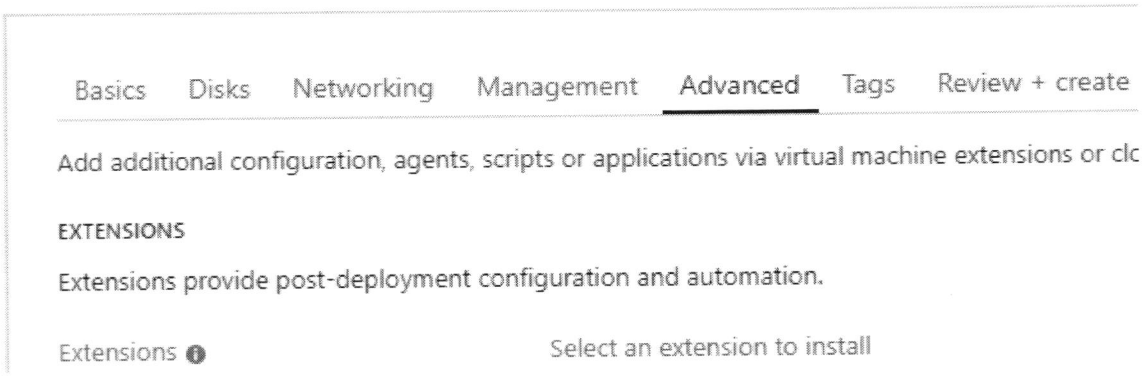

Basics Disks Networking Management Advanced Tags Review + create

Add additional configuration, agents, scripts or applications via virtual machine extensions or clc

EXTENSIONS

Extensions provide post-deployment configuration and automation.

Extensions — Select an extension to install

6. Select all default values in Tags>Click Review +Create.

7. In Review+Create Screen click create after validation is passed.

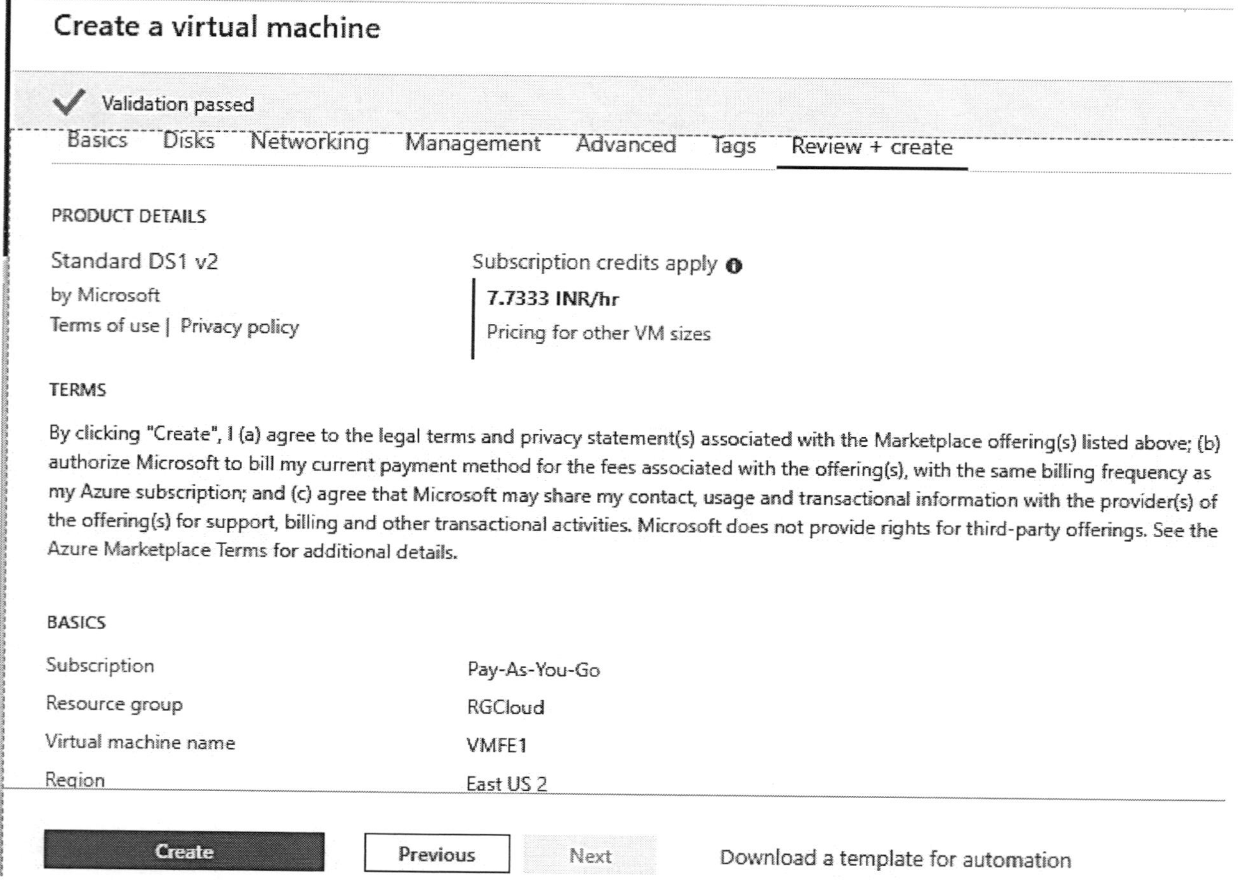

Note 1: In disk screen if you select no for use managed disk option then you need to specify the storage account or use a system created storage account.

Note 2: In Network Security Group under Networking you have the option to select advanced. With advanced option you can assign pre-created NSG. Exercise 11 in Chapter 1 shows how to create NSG.

8. Figure below shows the dashboard of VMFE1 Virtual Machine.

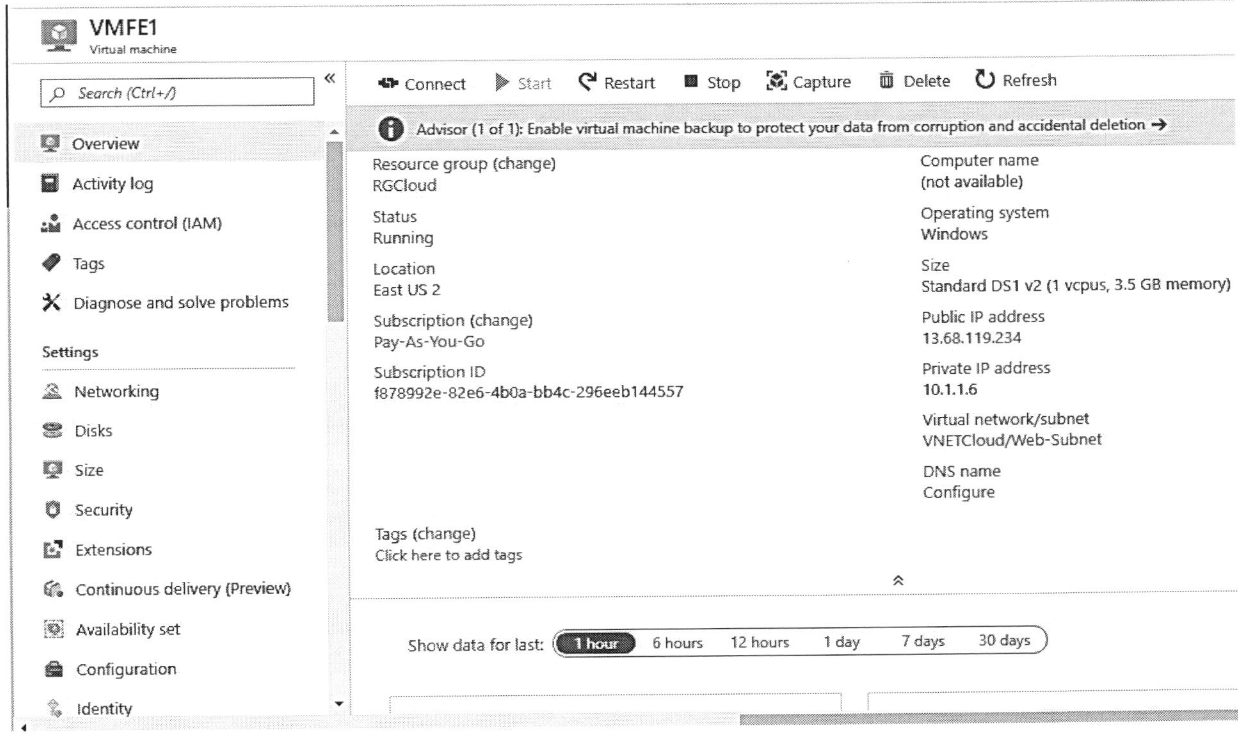

9. In right pane Click Configure under DNS Name>Public IP Address pane opens> Under DNS name enter **vmfe1**> Select **Static** Radio Box>Click **save** and close the Pubic IP pane.

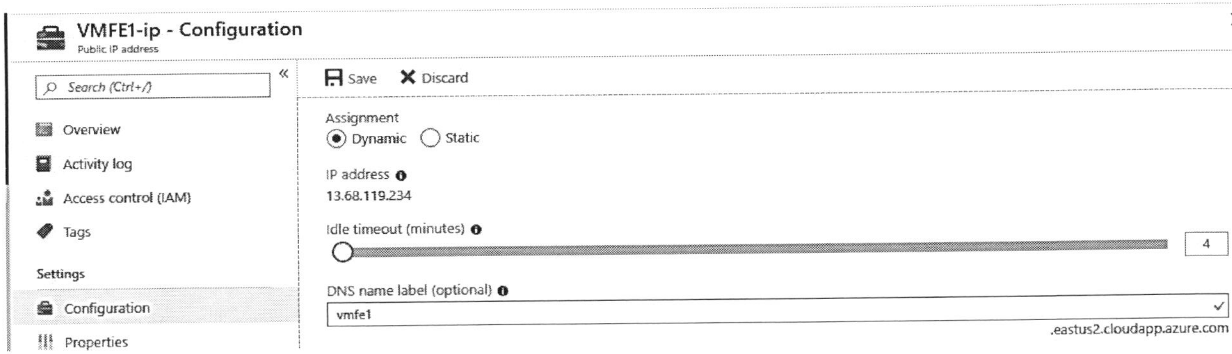

10. Click Refresh in VMFE1 dashboard and you can see the DNS name of VMFE1 under DNS name.

Note: Make sure to select Static in above figure.

Exercise 26: Log on to Windows VM VMFE1 with RDP

1. From the VM VMFE1 dashboard click **connect** in top pane and download the RDP file based on DNS name on your desktop. Close the Connect option.

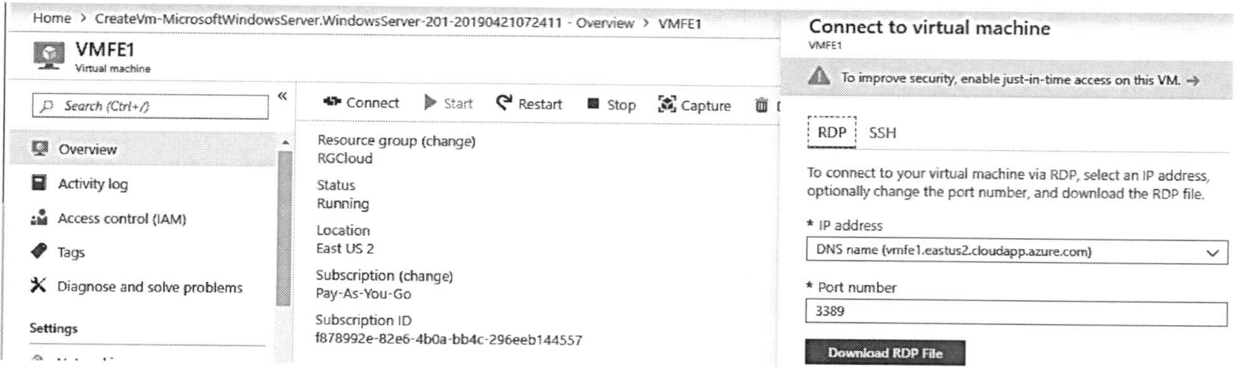

2. Click the downloaded RDP file on your desktop>Click Connect>Credential box for connecting to VM will Pop up on your desktop. Enter the admin name and password you entered during VM creation and click ok.

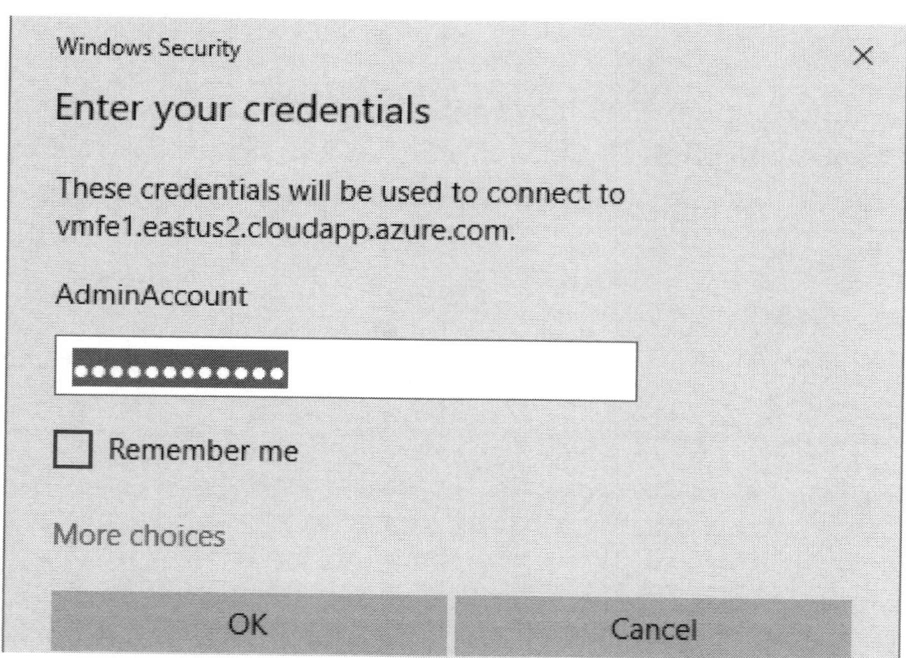

3. Figure below shows the screen of Windows VM VMFE1 with Server Manager open.

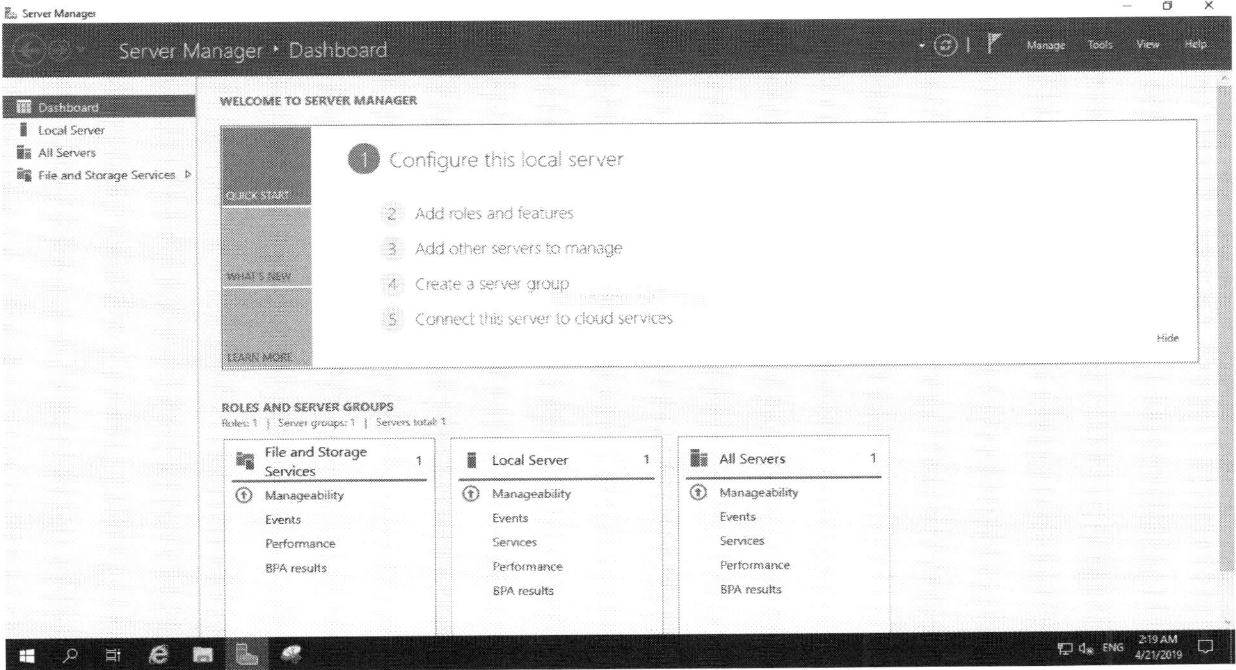

Note the **Add roles and feature** link. In next exercise we will use this link to Install IIS.

Exercise 27: Install IIS

1. Connect to VM VMFE1 using RDP.
2. Open server Manager> Click add roles and features link>Add Roles and Feature Wizard opens as shown below. Click Next.

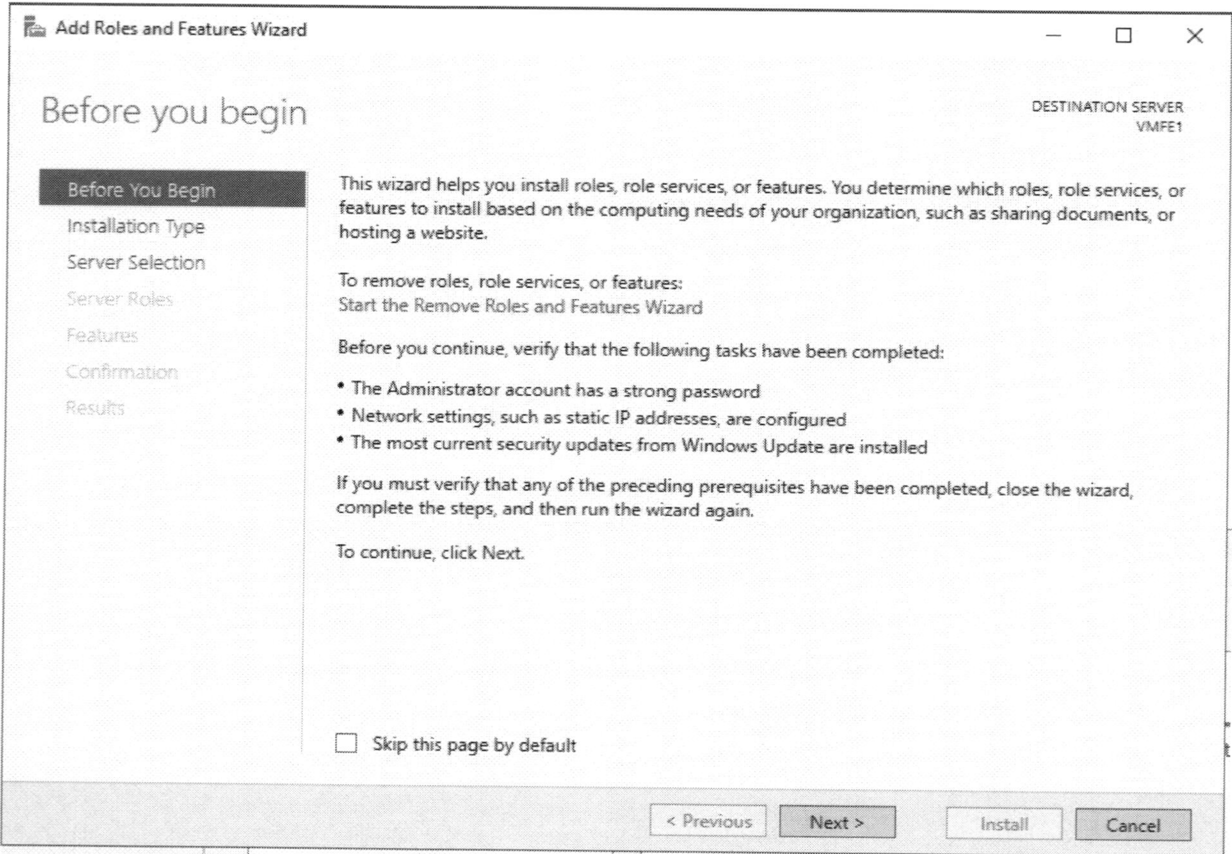

3. In the Add Roles and Features Wizard, on the Installation Type page, choose **Role-based or feature-based installation**, and then click Next.
4. Select VMFE1 VM from the server pool and click Next.
5. On the Server Roles page, select Web Server (IIS).
6. In the pop-up about adding features needed for IIS, make sure that Include management tools is selected and then click Add Features. When the pop-up closes, click Next in the wizard.
7. next, next, next, next.
8. Install.
9. It will take around 1 minute to install the IIS. After Installation is complete click close.

Exercise 28: Access Default IIS website on VMFE1

1. Go to VM VMFE1 dashboard. Note down DNS name.
2. Open a browser and type: http://vmfe1.eastus2.cloudapp.azure.com.

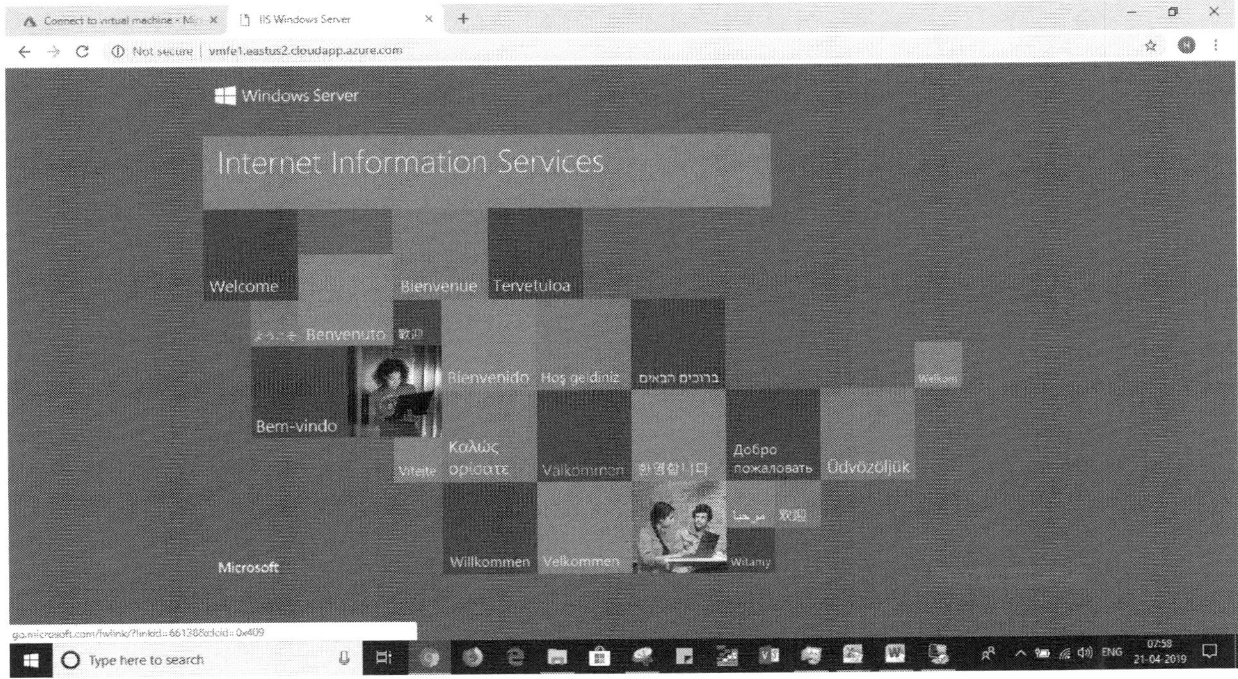

Exercise 29: Add Data Disk

1. Go to VMFE1 VM dashboard> Click Disks in left pane.

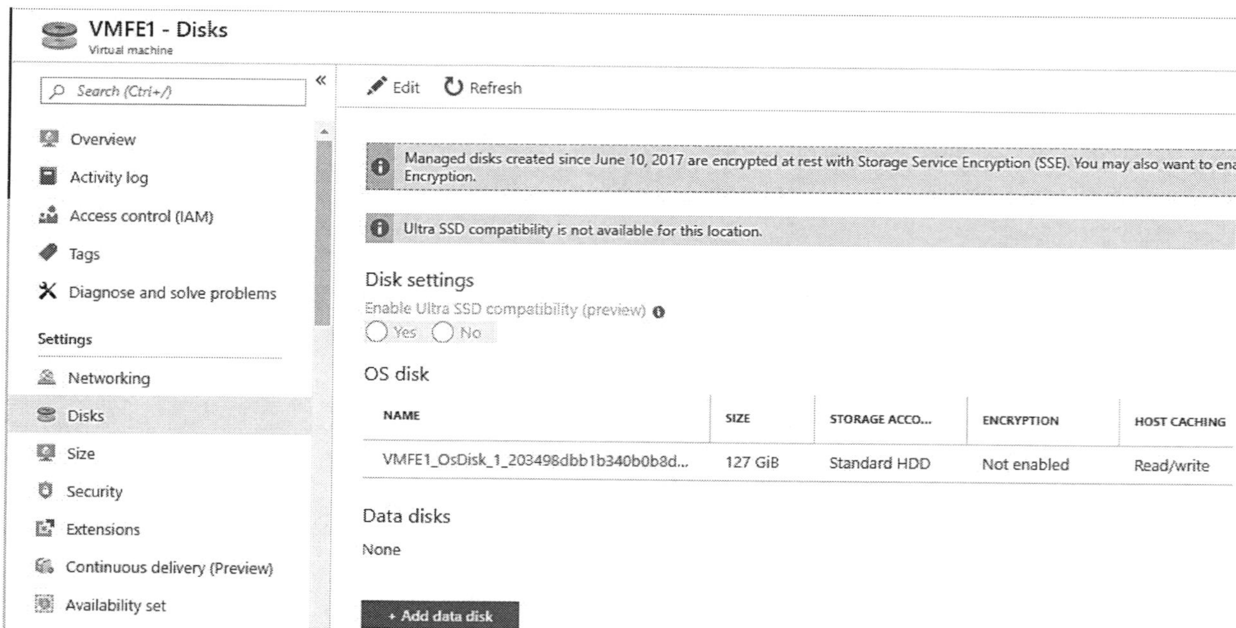

2. Click +Add data disk> Add disk pane opens under Data disks>Enter 1 as LUN value> Select **create disk** under Name Dialog Box.

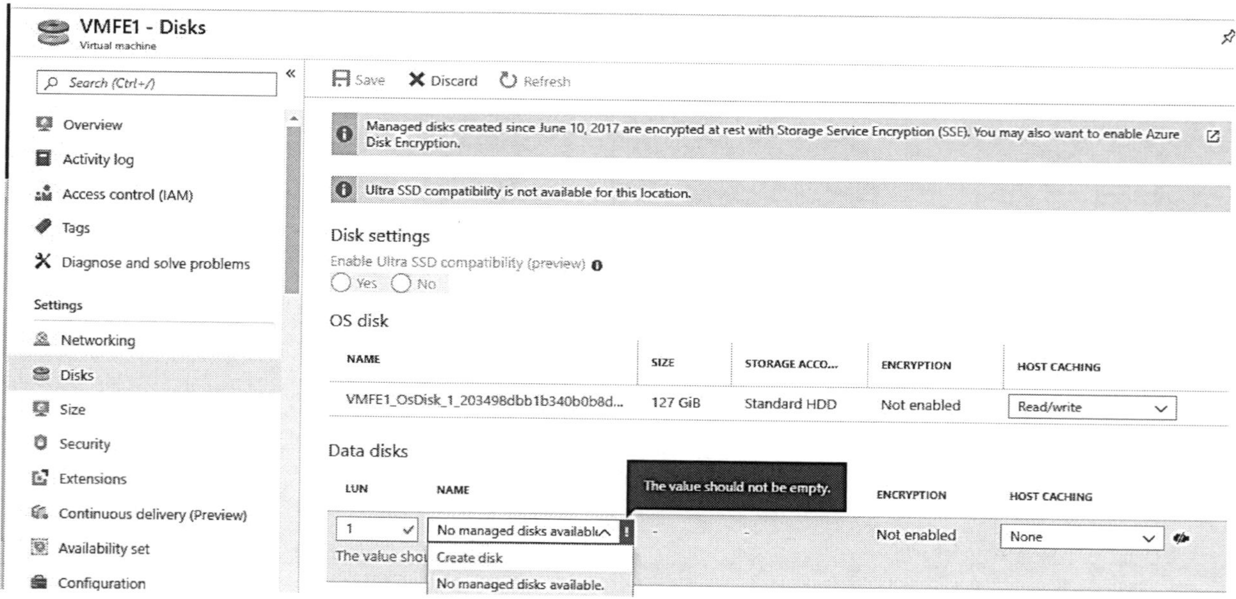

3. When you select create disk under name dialog box> Create Managed Disk Blade opens> Enter name, Resource group as RGCloud and select Account Type and enter size as per your requirement>Click create (Not Shown).

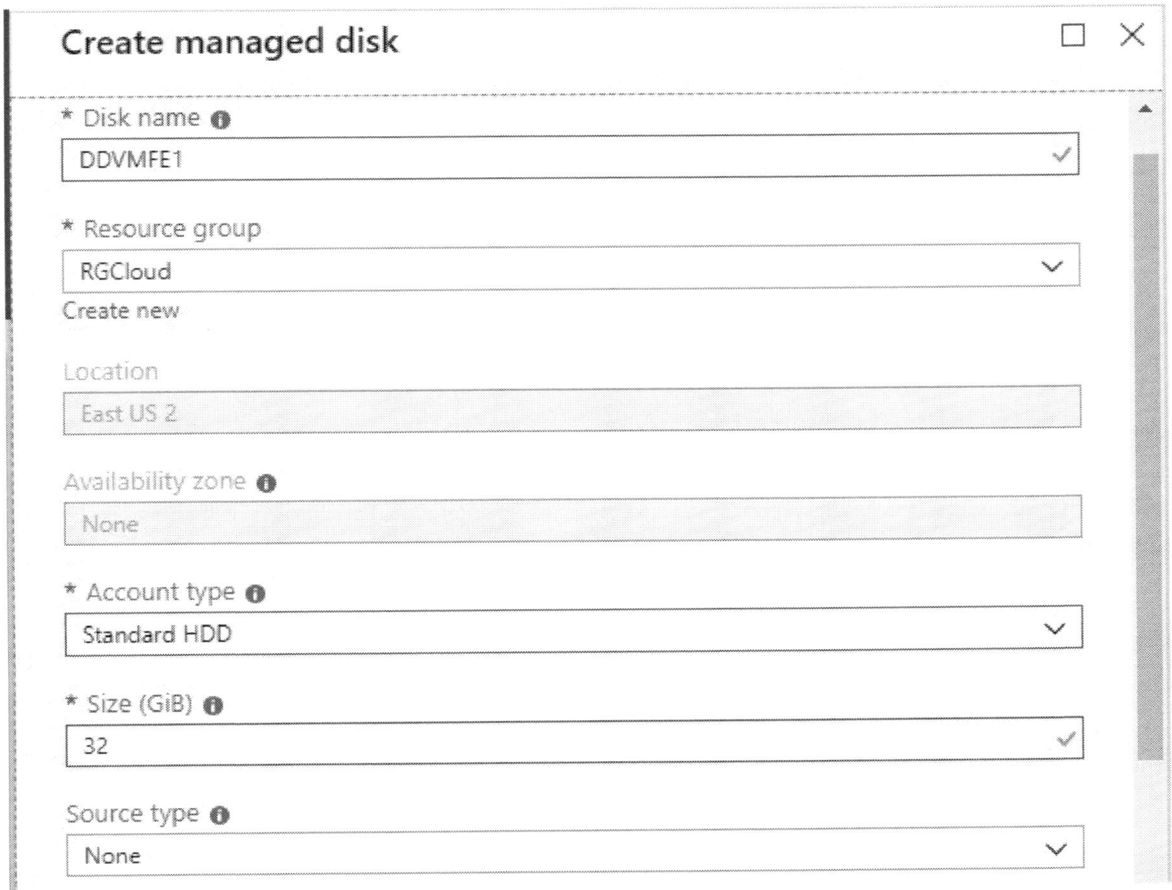

4. Click save in Disk Dashboard. You can see disk added.

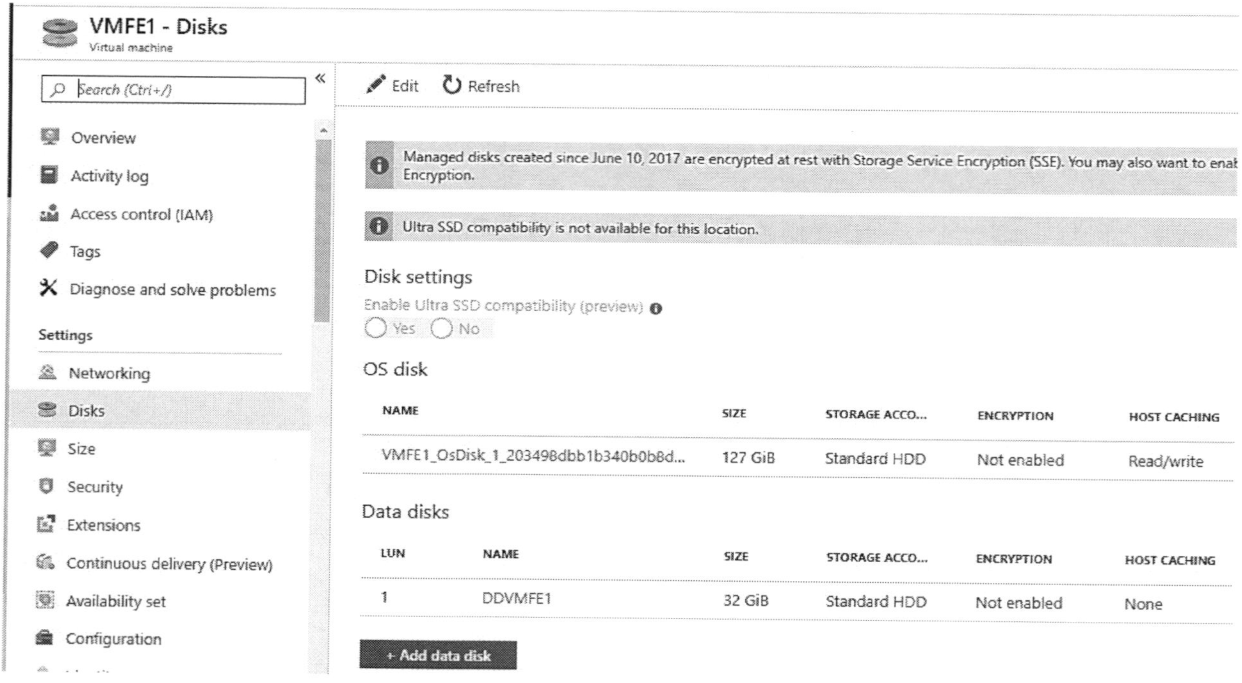

Exercise 30: Initialize the Data Disk

1. Connect to VMFE1 using RDP.
2. Open Server Manager. In the left pane> click File and Storage Services.
3. Click Disks. The Disks section lists the disks. The Disk 0 is the operating system Disk. Disk 1 is the temporary disk. Disk 2 is the Data Disk. The Data disk you just added will list the Partition as Unknown.

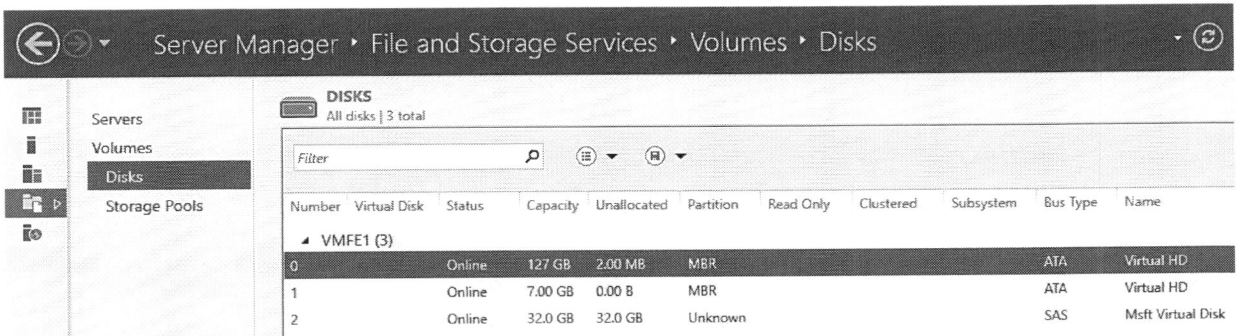

4. The Data disk you just added will list the Partition as Unknown. Right-click the data disk and select Initialize. Once complete, the Partition will be listed as GPT.

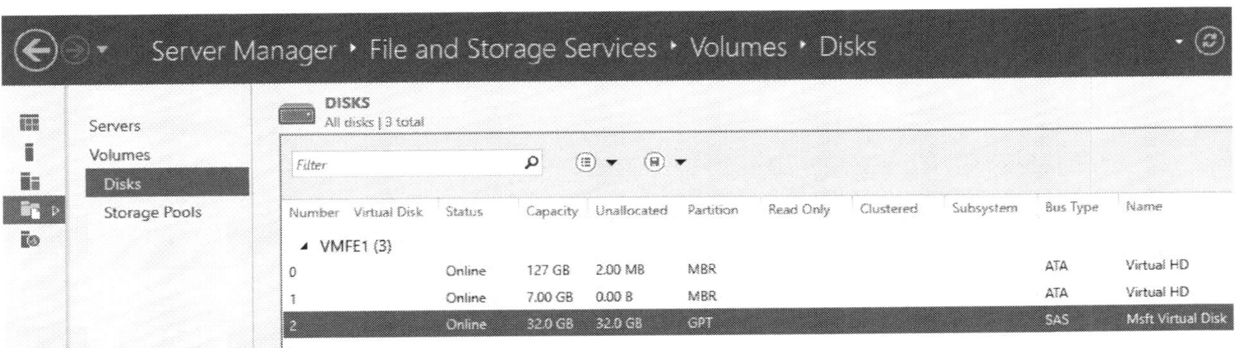

Virtual Machine Snapshot

A snapshot is a full, read-only copy of a VM virtual hard drive (VHD). You can take a snapshot of an OS or data disk VHD to use as a backup, or to troubleshoot virtual machine (VM) issues.

Exercise 31: Create Snapshot of VM VMFE1 OS Hard Disk

1. Go to VMFE1 Dashboard>Click Disks in left pane> In Right pane under OS Disk click the Disk VMFE1_OsDisk_1_xxx>OS Disk Dashboard opens.

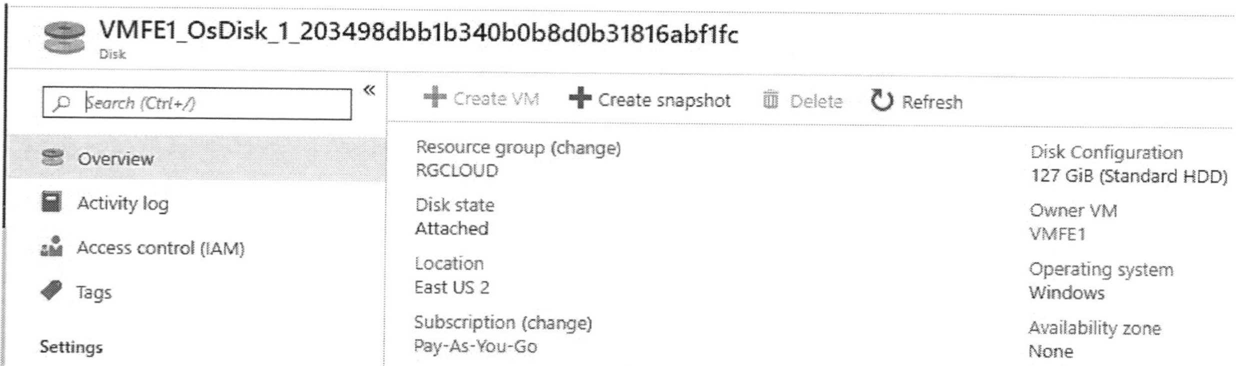

2. Click +Create Snapshot> Create snapshot blade opens> Give a name, Select Resource group RGCloud and select Account type as Standard HDD and click create (Not Shown).

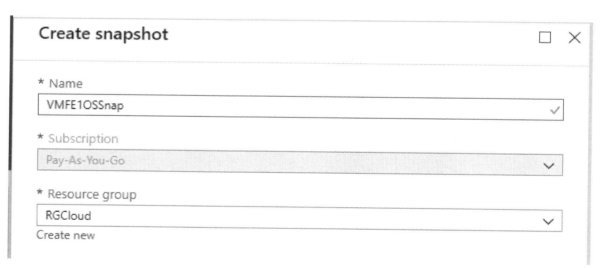

3. Figure below dashboard of the snapshot.

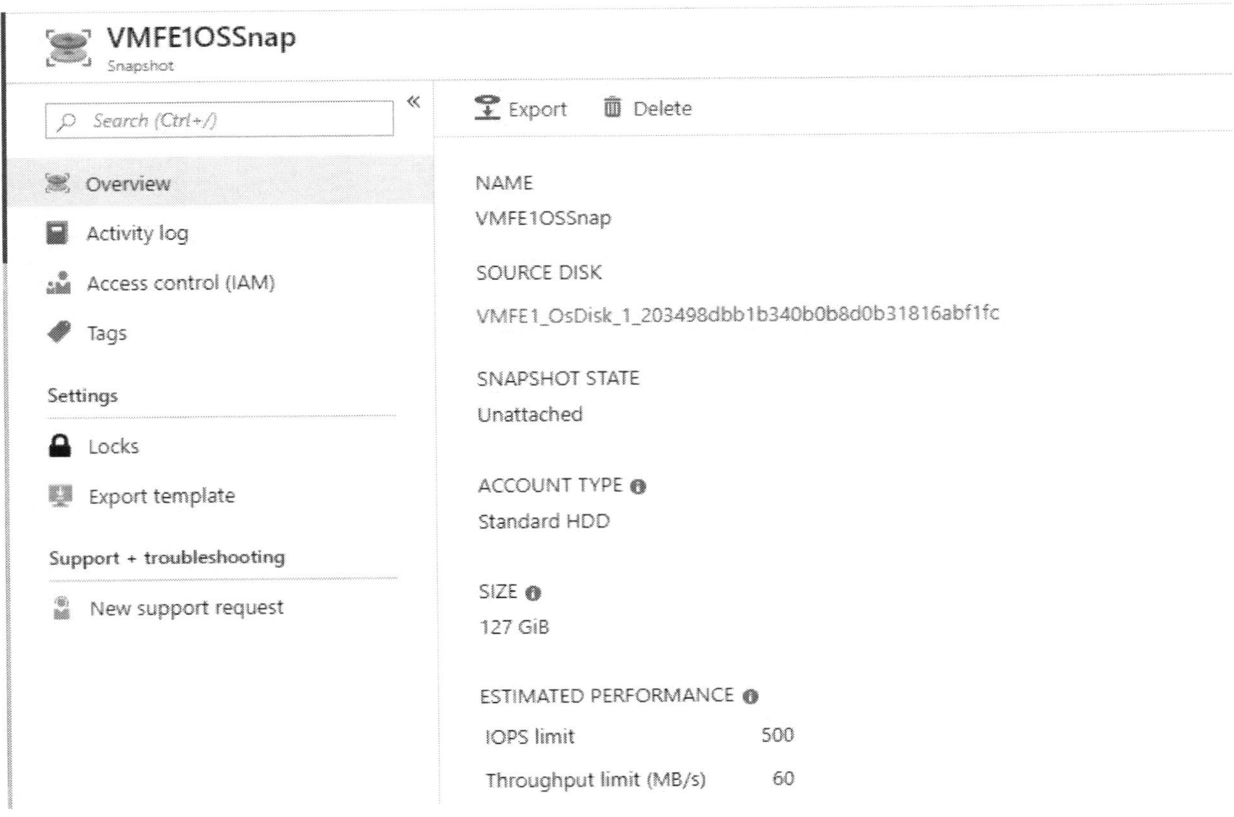

4. Delete the snapshot as it is no longer required.

Exercise 32: Create and Add Network Interface to VM VMFE1

1. In VM VMFE1 dashboard click Networking in left pane> Click Attach network Interface in right pane>You are provided with 2 options - either create a new interface or select an existing interface from drop down box.

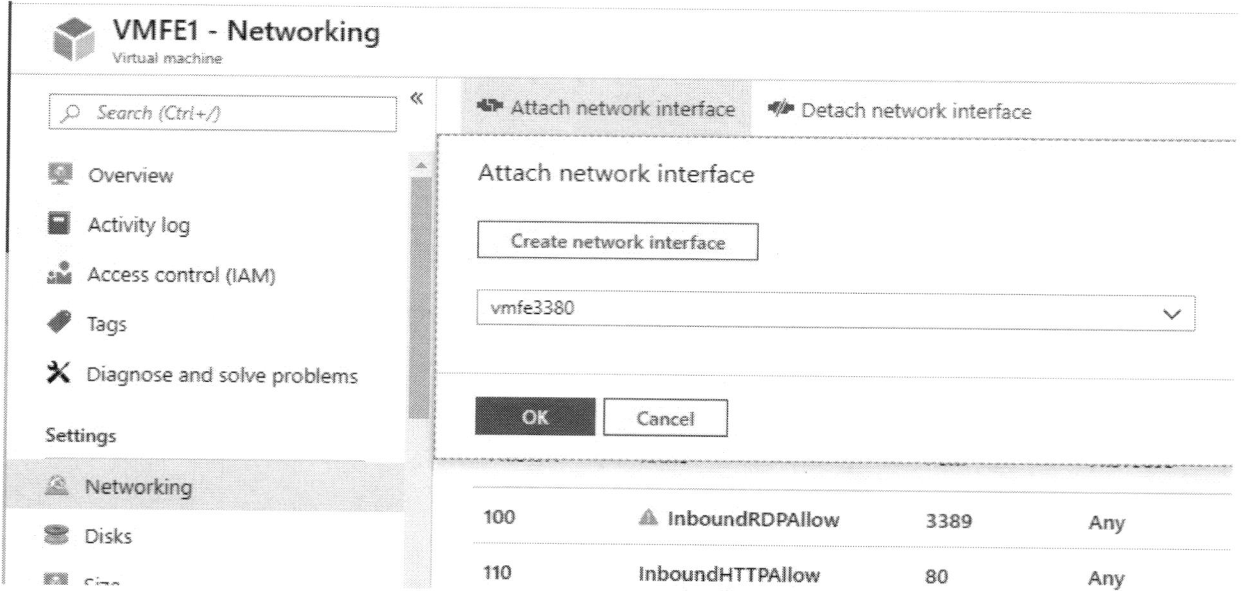

2. In this exercise we will create a network interface. Click Create network interface> Create network interface blade opens>Enter a name, Select Web-Subnet and Resource Group RGCloud>Click create.

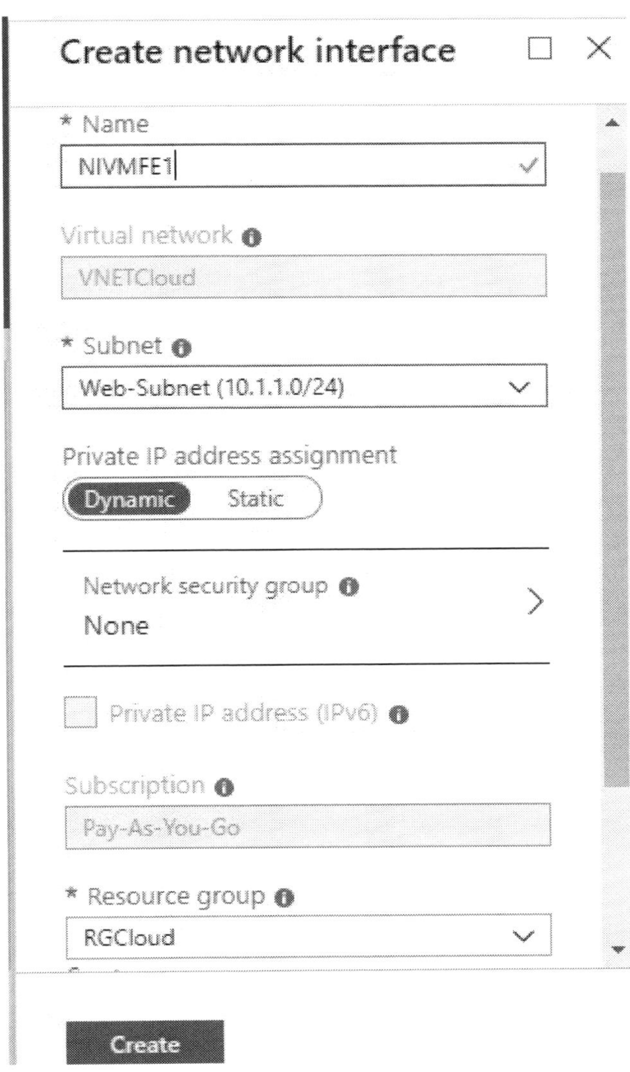

3. Go Virtual Network VNETCloud Dashboard and you can see the Network Interface NIVMFE1 attached to Web-Subnet.

Exercise 33: Create Windows Virtual Machine VMFE2

In this exercise we will create Windows Server 2019 VM in Virtual Network **VNETCloud** and in Resource Group **RGCloud**. We will use **Managed disk option**, select **AS** created in Exercise 24 and will use **System created Dynamic Public IP**.

1. In Azure Portal Click Create a Resource> Compute> Virtual Machine> Create Virtual Machine Blade opens>Select Resource Group RGCloud, Enter VM name, Select East US 2 in region, Select Availability Set in Availability option and Select ASCloud, In Image Dropdown box Select Windows Server 2019 Datacenter, Enter Administrator Account name and password> Select none for inbound port option. We will select under networking >Click Next: Disks (Not Shown).

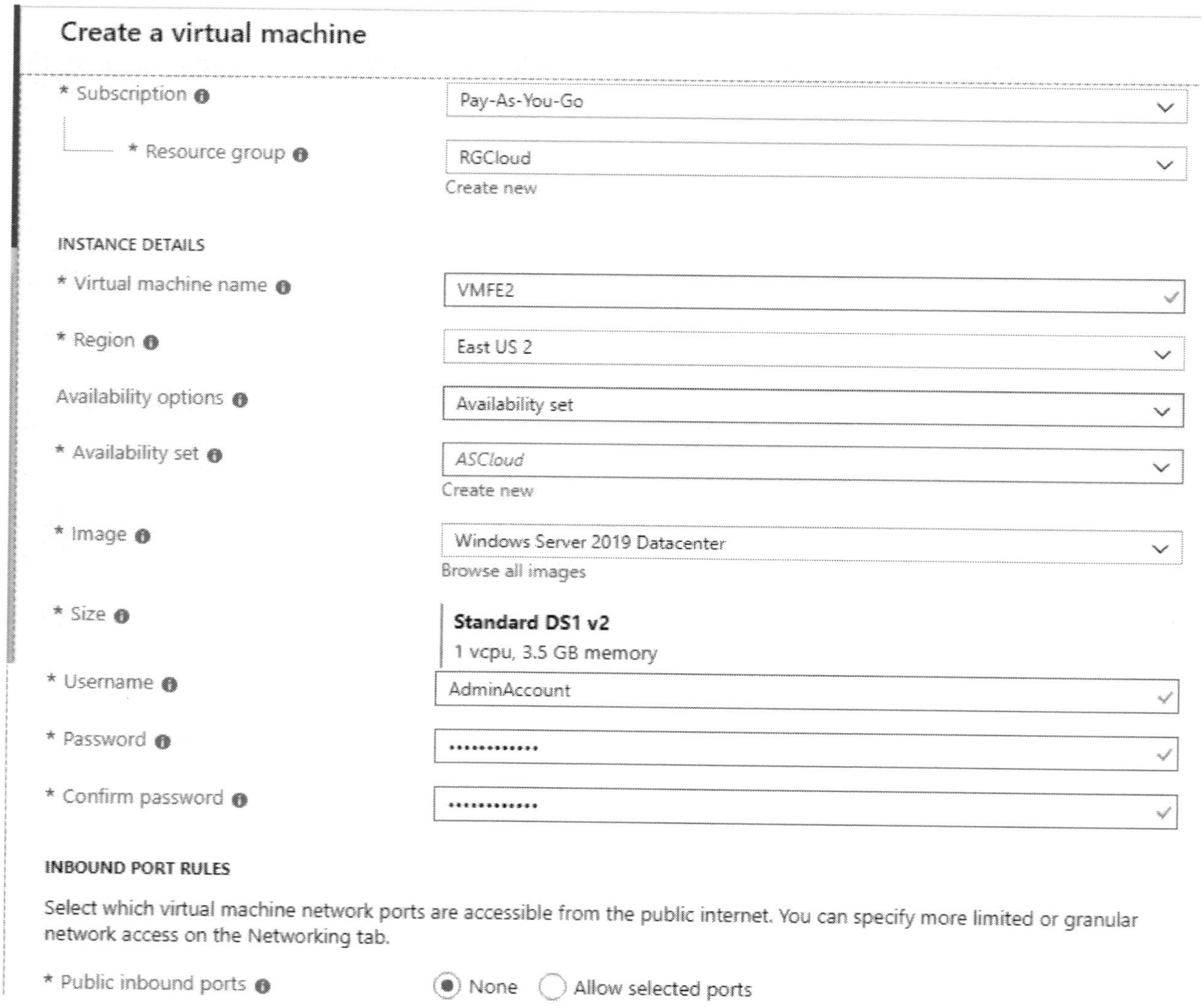

Create a virtual machine

* Subscription: Pay-As-You-Go
* Resource group: RGCloud
Create new

INSTANCE DETAILS

* Virtual machine name: VMFE2
* Region: East US 2
Availability options: Availability set
* Availability set: ASCloud
Create new
* Image: Windows Server 2019 Datacenter
Browse all images
* Size: Standard DS1 v2
1 vcpu, 3.5 GB memory
* Username: AdminAccount
* Password: ••••••••••••
* Confirm password: ••••••••••••

INBOUND PORT RULES

Select which virtual machine network ports are accessible from the public internet. You can specify more limited or granular network access on the Networking tab.

* Public inbound ports: (•) None ( ) Allow selected ports

4. Disk Screen opens>Select your HDD Option>Click advanced and make sure yes is selected for managed disk (not Shown) and click Next: Networking.

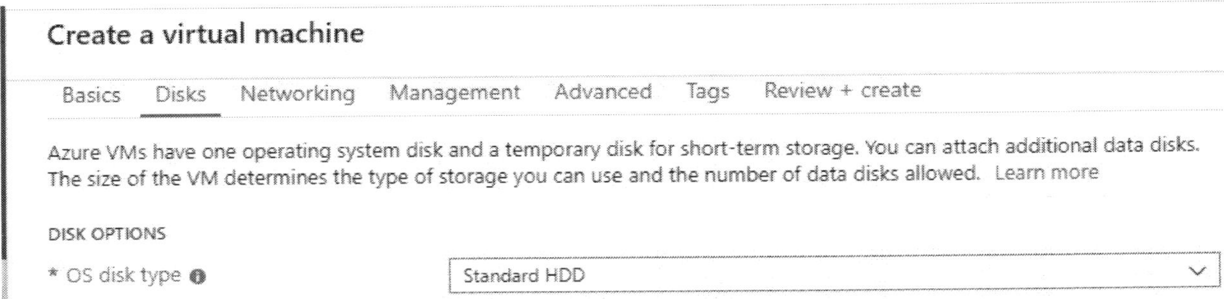

5. Networking Screen opens> Select **VNETCloud**, **Web-Subnet** from dropdown boxes>Use System created IP> Select Basic in NSG>In Public Inbound ports select allow selected ports> In Select Inbound ports select RDP and HTTP> Select off for AN> Click Next: Management.

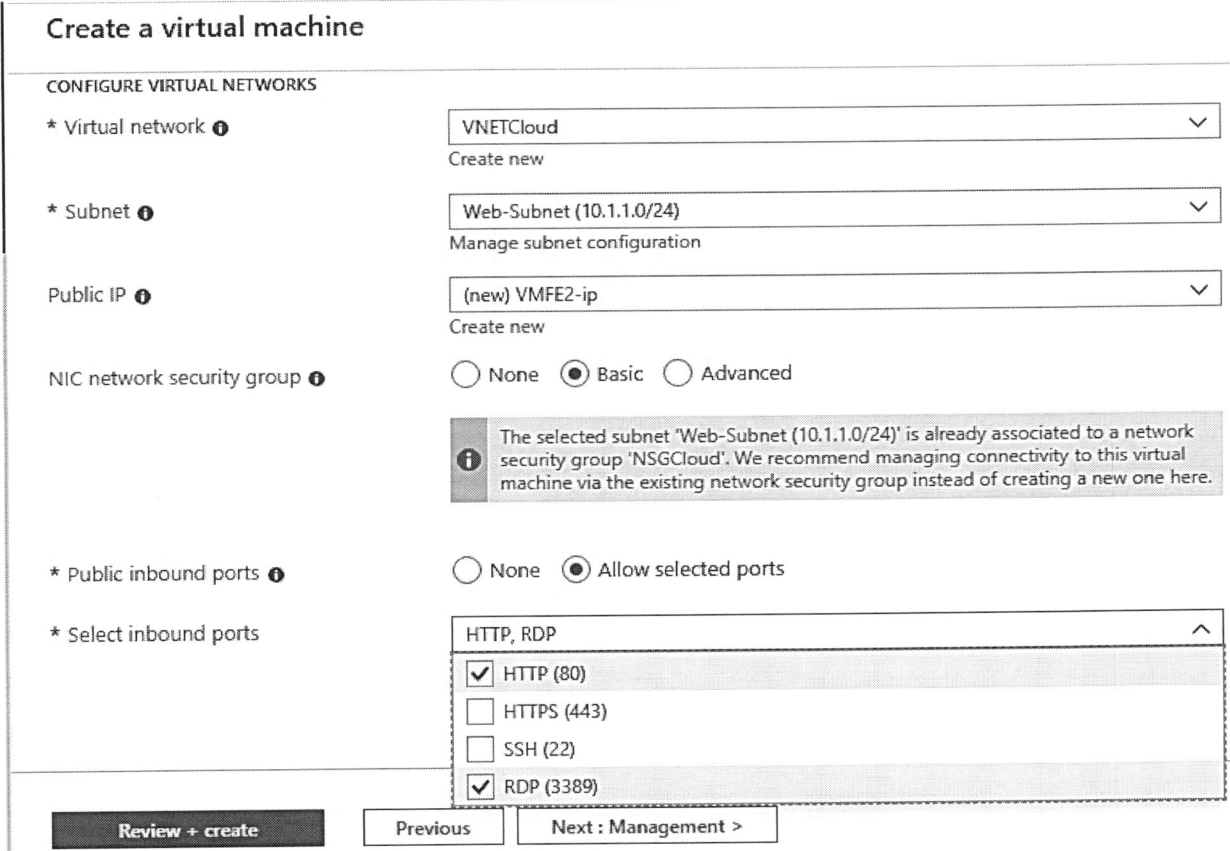

6. Management Screen opens>Select No for Security Center and off for Monitoring, Identity and Auto-Shutdown. Click Next: Advanced.
   Note: Readers can enable some options according to their requirement.

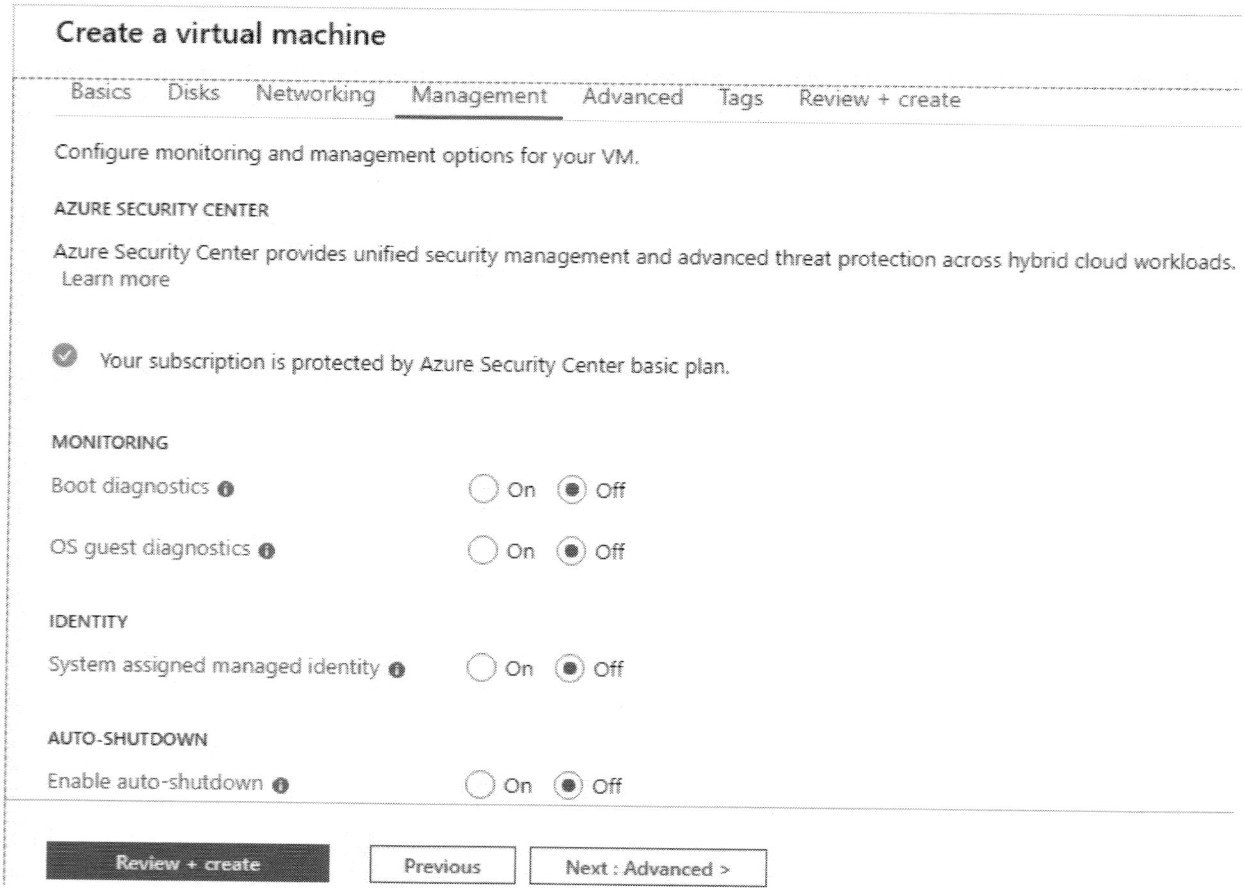

7. Select all default values in Advanced Screen>Click Next: Tags.

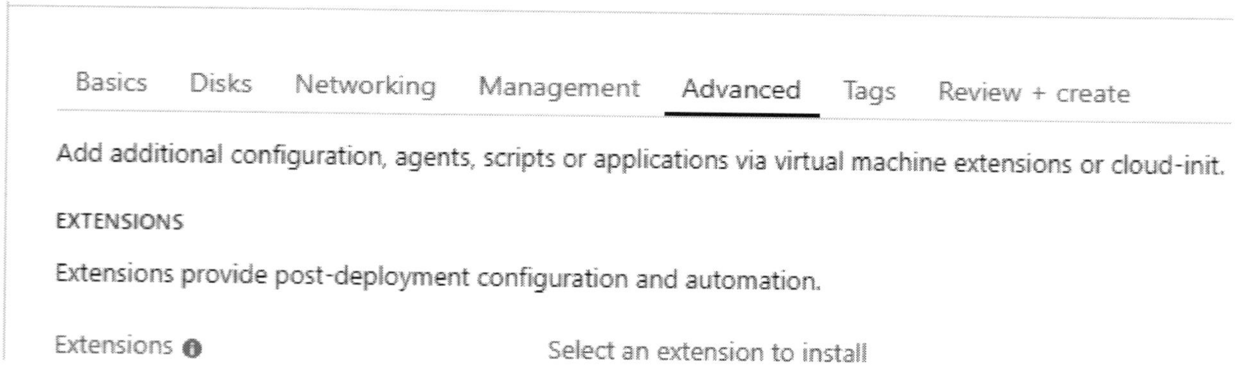

8. Select all default values in Tags>Click Review +Create.

9. In Review+Create Screen click create after validation is passed.

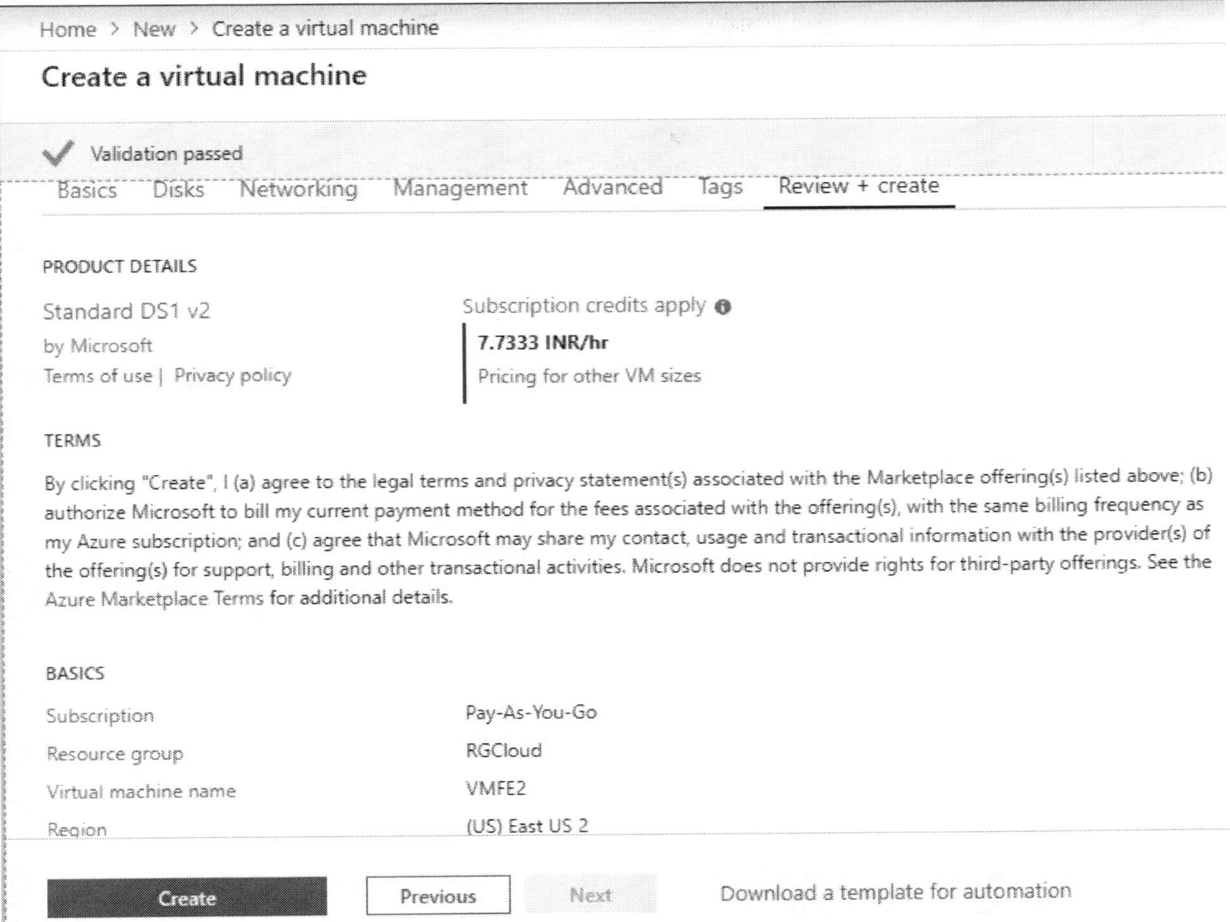

Note 1: In disk screen if you select no for use managed disk option then you need to specify the storage account or use a system created storage account.

Note 2: In Network Security Group under Networking you have the option to select advanced. With advanced option you can assign pre-created NSG. Exercise 11 shows how to create NSG.

Note 3: Virtual Network VNETCloud and Resource RGCloud were created in Exercise 1 & 3 respectively in Chapter 1.

10. Figure below shows the dashboard of VM VMFE2.

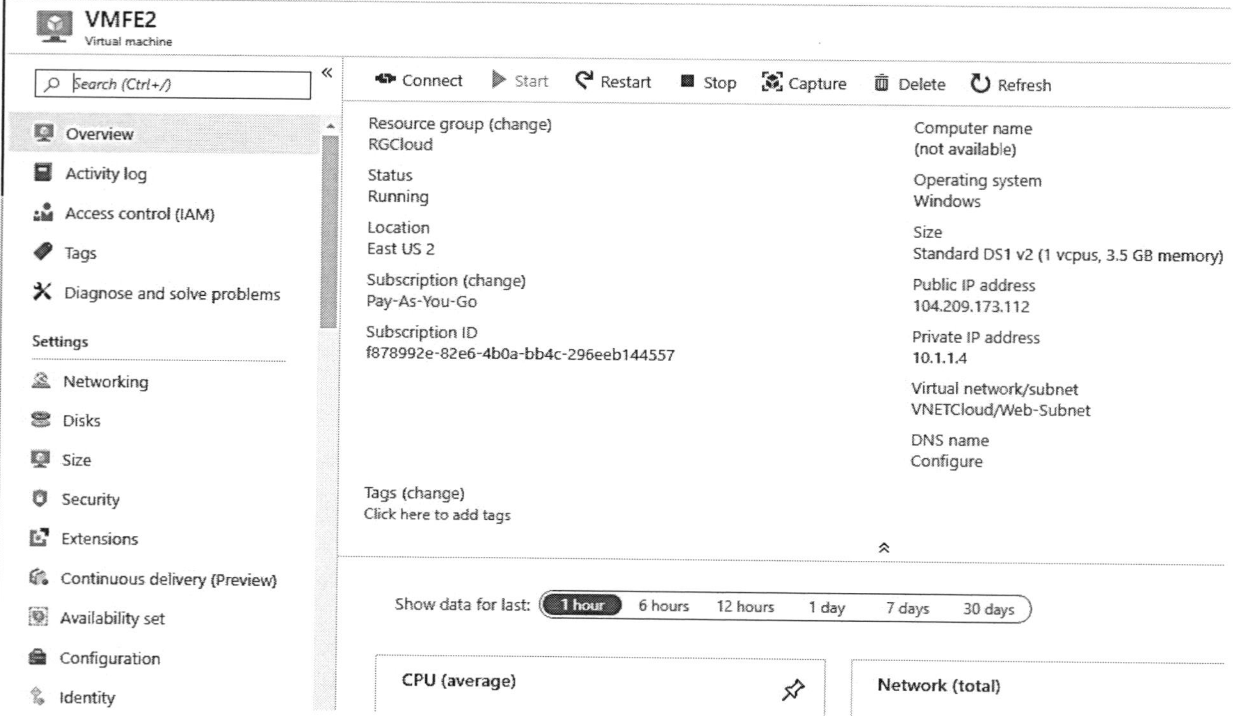

11. In right pane Click Configure under DNS Name>Public IP Address pane opens> **Under Assignment Select Static**> Under DNS name enter **vmfe2**> Click **save** and close the Pubic IP pane.

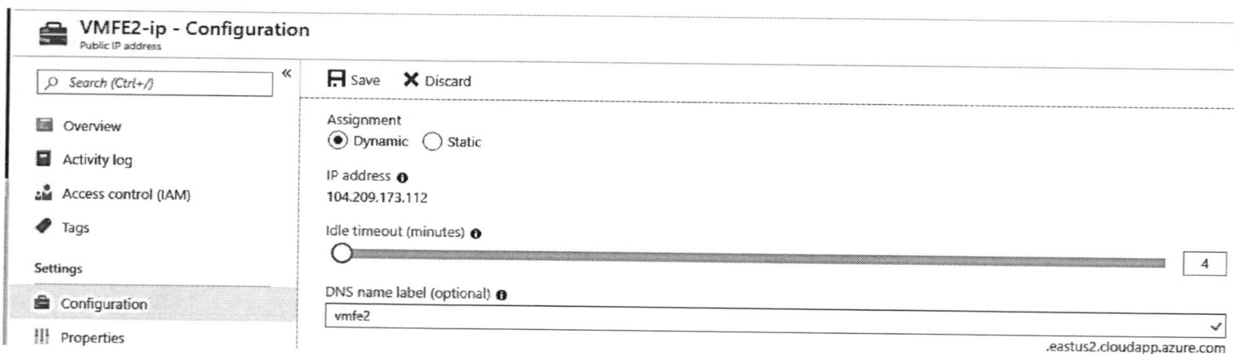

Exercise 34: Log on to Windows VM with RDP

1. From the VM VMFE2 dashboard click **connect** in top pane and download the RDP file on your desktop. Close the Connect Box.

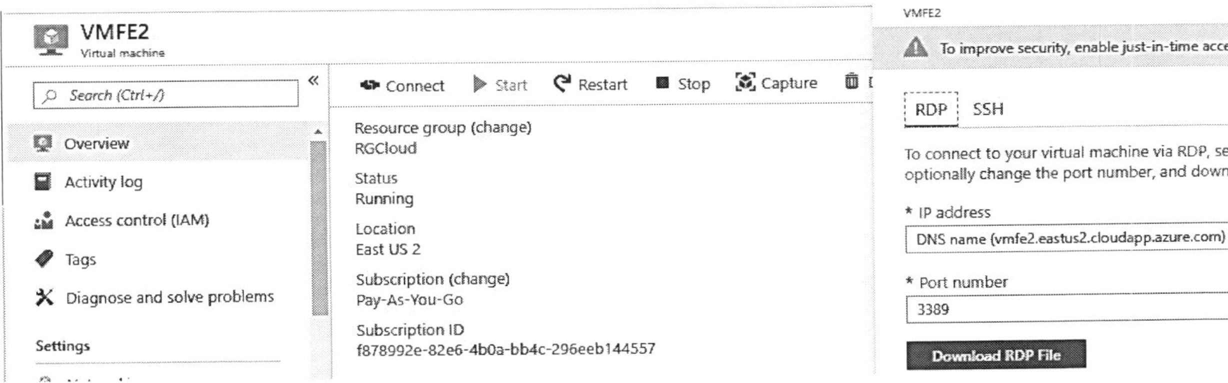

4. Click the downloaded RDP file on your desktop>Click Connect>Credential box for connecting to VM will Pop up on your desktop. Enter the admin name and password you entered during VM creation and click ok.

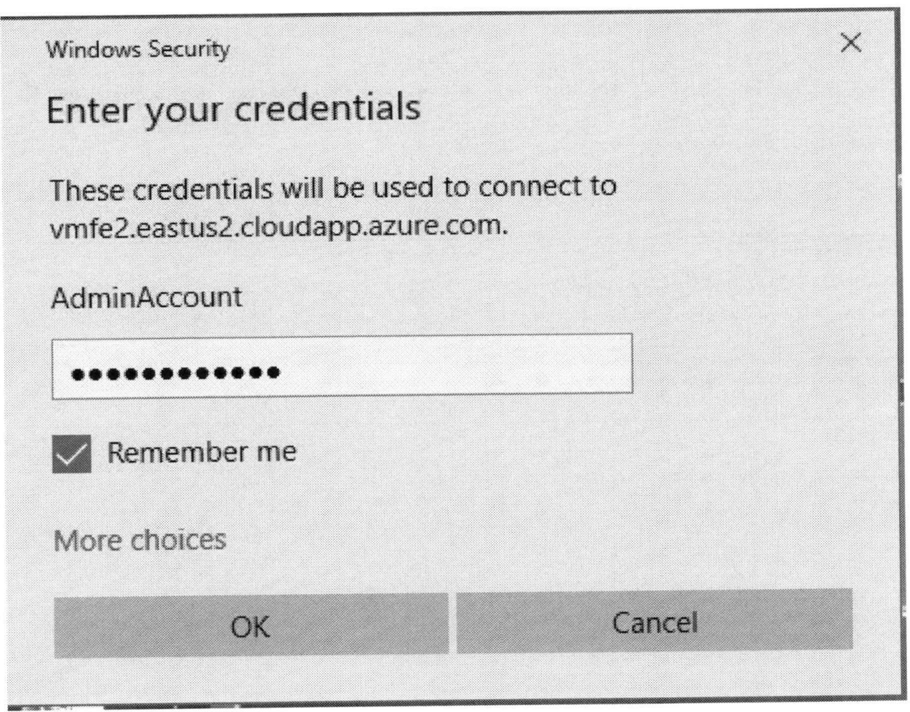

5. Figure below shows the screen of VM VMFE2 with Server Manager open.

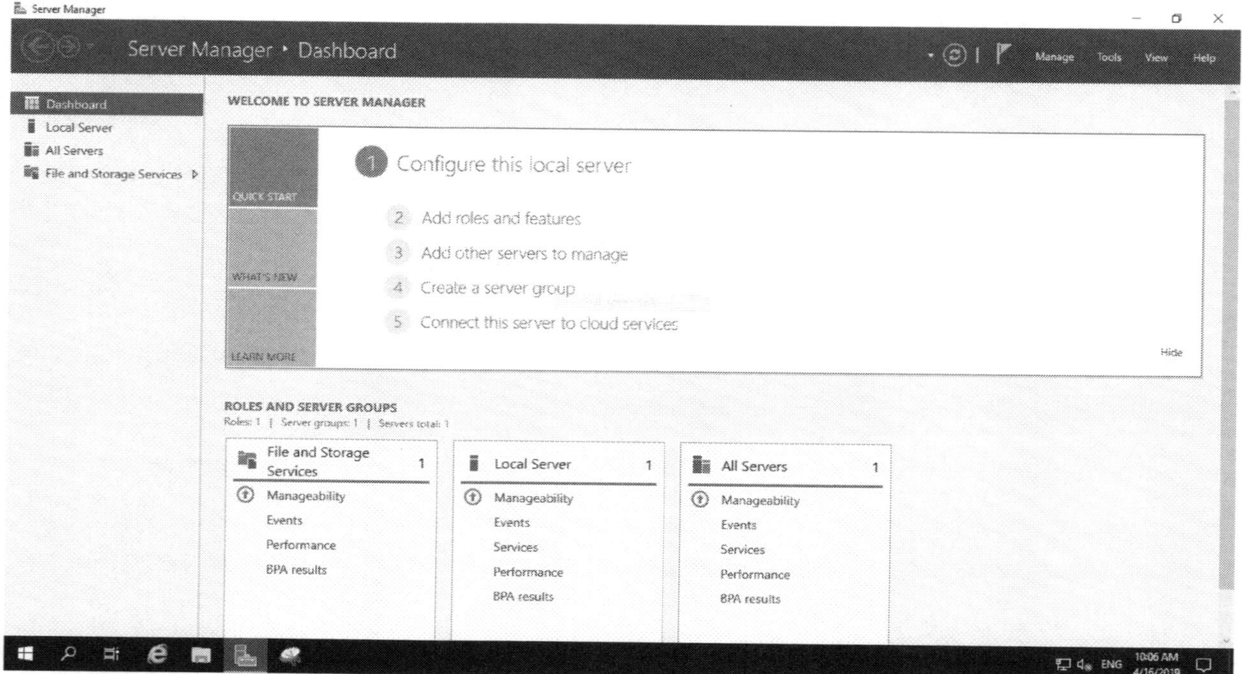

Note the **Add roles and feature link**. In next exercise we will use this link to Install IIS.

Exercise 35: Install IIS

1. Connect to VMFE2 using RDP.
2. Open server Manager> Click add roles and features>Next.

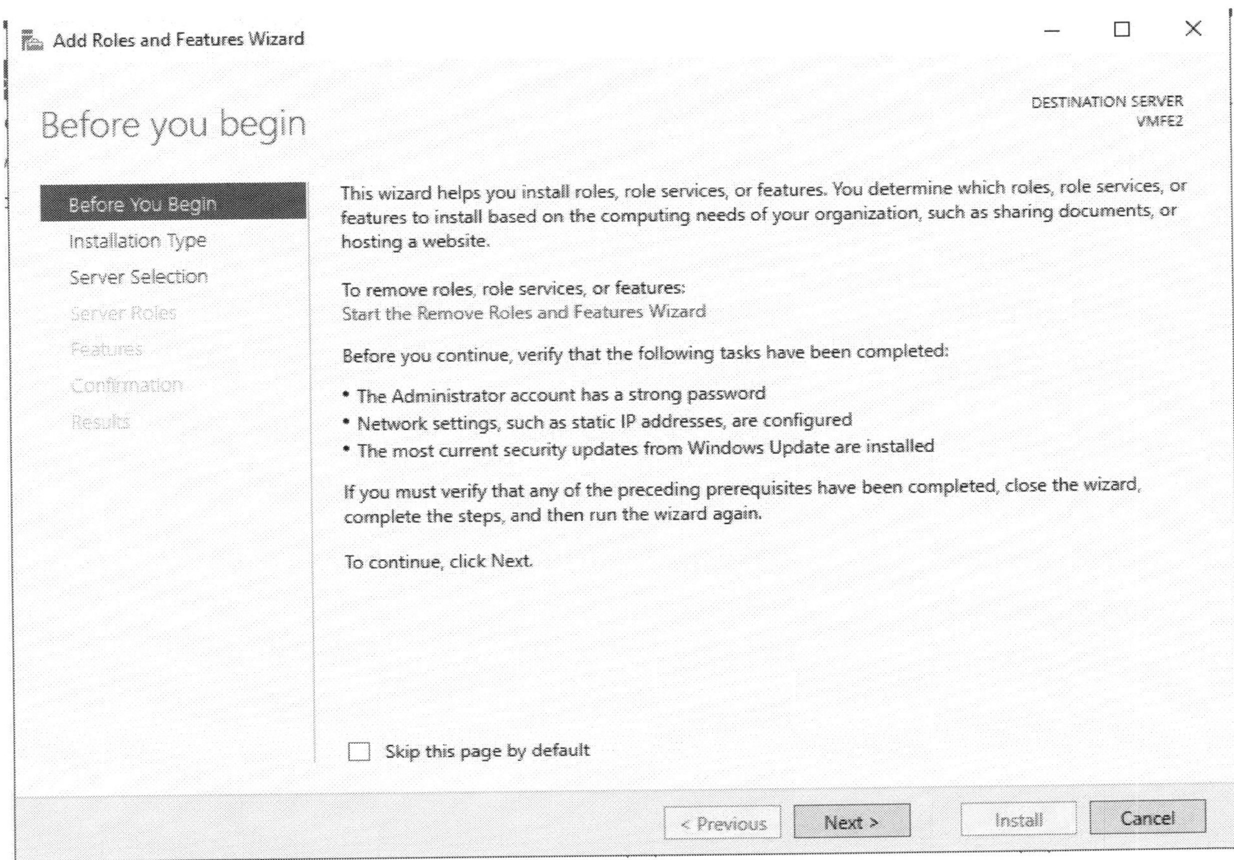

3. In the Add Roles and Features Wizard, on the Installation Type page, choose Role-based or feature-based installation, and then click Next.
4. Select VMFE2 from the server pool and click Next.
5. On the Server Roles page, select Web Server (IIS).
6. In the pop-up about adding features needed for IIS, make sure that Include management tools is selected and then click Add Features. When the pop-up closes, click Next in the wizard.
7. next, next, next, next.
8. Install.
9. It will take around 1 minute to install the IIS. After Installation is complete click close.

Exercise 36: Access Default IIS website on VMFE2

1. Go to VMFE2 dashboard. Note down VM IP address or DNS name.
2. Open a browser and type: http:// vmfe2.eastus2.cloudapp.azure.com.

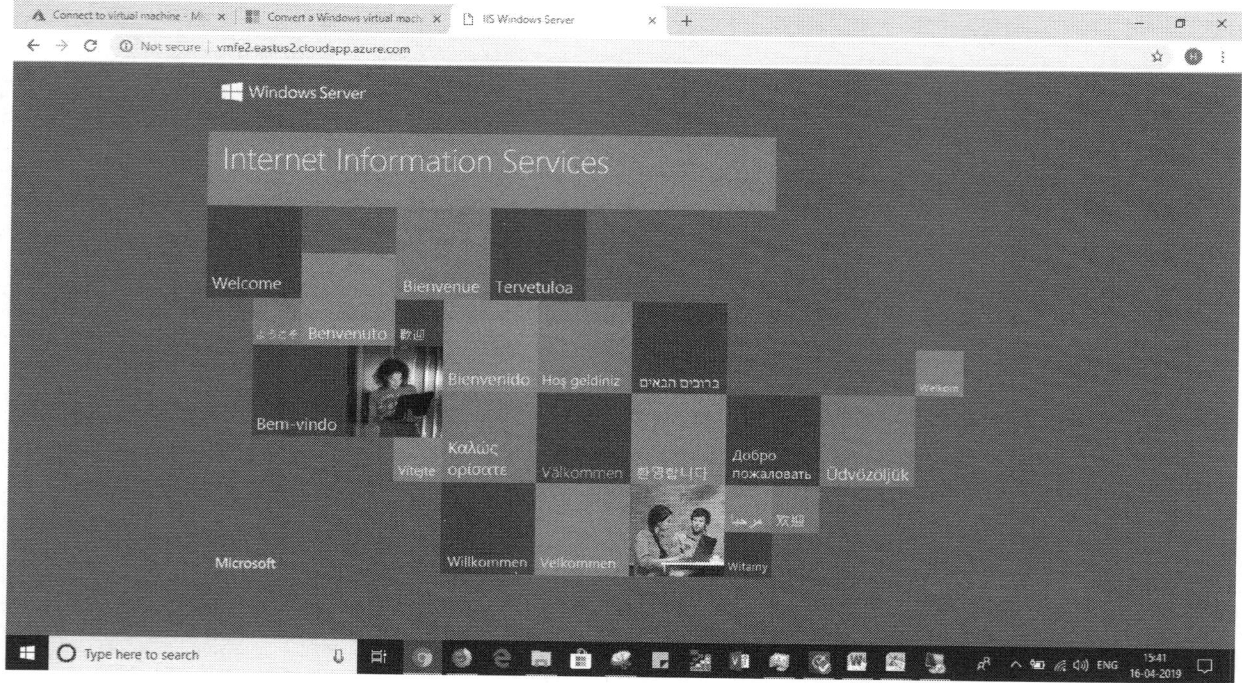

Exercise 37: Create Custom Website on VM VMFE2 (optional)

1. RDP to Windows VM VMFE2> Right click on Desktop>Click New>Click Text Document>Notepad opens> Enter following in the Notepad.

```
<!DOCTYPE html>
<html>
<head>
<title>AZ-103 Study & Lab Guide</title>
<meta charset="utf-8">
</head>
<body>
<h1>Exam AZ-103 Study & Lab Guide</h1>
<p> Author: Harinder Kohli </p>
</body>
</html>
```

2. Save the file as index.html. Save the file in C:\InetPub\wwwroot folder.

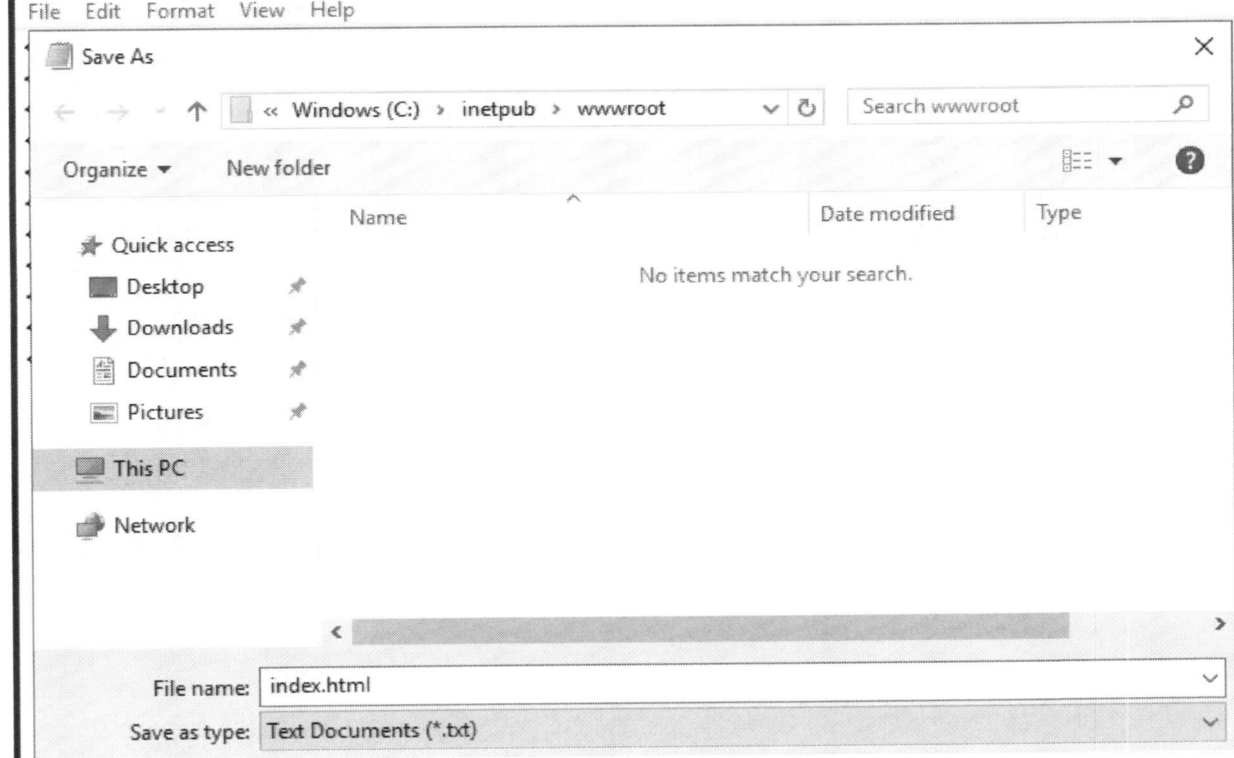

Note: The link to download Custom code is given in next page.

Exercise 38: Access Custom IIS website on VM VMFE2

1. Go to VM VMFE2 dashboard. Note down VMFE2 DNS name.
2. Open a browser and type: http://vmfe2.eastus2.cloudapp.azure.com>Custom IIS website opens as shown below.

Exam AZ-103 Study & Lab Guide

Author: Harinder Kohli

Note 1: Exercise 27 & 28 are optional. The reason we are adding custom code to VMFE2 is that in Load balancing we can test that both VMs are being accessed.

Note 2: Download the Website custom code from Box.com at following link.
https://app.box.com/s/5pisg4mjiji27ucx1fdwj4fexbbrc3kj

Exercise 39: Create Windows VM representing On-Premises AD DS

In this exercise we will create Windows Server 2016 VM **OnPremAD** in Virtual Network **VNETOnPrem**, Resource Group **RGOnPrem** and Location **West US 2**. Resource group RGOnPrem and Virtual Network VNETOnPrem were created in Exercise 2 & 6 Respectively in Chapter 1. This VM will represent on-premises Active Directory Domain Services (AD DS).

1. In Azure Portal Click Create a Resource> Compute> Virtual Machine>Create Virtual Machine pane opens>Select Resource Group **RGOnPrem**>Select Region **West US 2**>In image Dropdown box select **Windows Server 2016 Datacenter**, Enter Username and password>Select none in public inbound ports>Click Next:Disks (Not shown).

Create a virtual machine

* Subscription: Pay-As-You-Go
* Resource group: RGOnPrem
Create new

INSTANCE DETAILS

* Virtual machine name: VMAD
* Region: (US) West US 2
Availability options: No infrastructure redundancy required
* Image: Windows Server 2016 Datacenter
Browse all images
* Size: **Standard DS1 v2**
1 vcpu, 3.5 GB memory
Change size

ADMINISTRATOR ACCOUNT

* Username: AdminAccount
* Confirm password: ••••••••••••

INBOUND PORT RULES

Select which virtual machine network ports are accessible from the public internet. You can specify more limited or granular network access on the Networking tab.

* Public inbound ports: (•) None ( ) Allow selected ports

2. Disk Screen opens>Select your HDD Option>Click advanced and make sure yes is selected for managed disk (not Shown) and click Next: Networking.

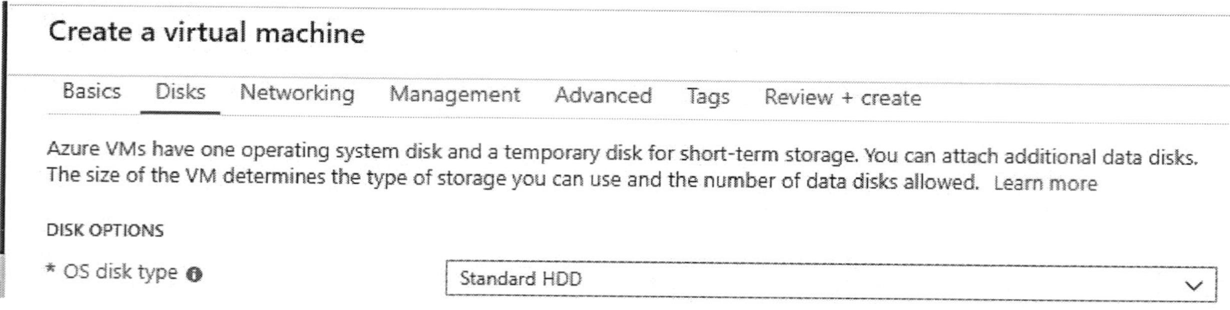

3. Networking Screen opens> Select **VNETOnPrem** and **OnPrem-Subnet** from dropdown boxes>Use System created IP> Select Basic in NSG>In Public Inbound ports select allow selected ports> In Select Inbound ports select RDP and HTTP> Select off for AN> Click Next: Management.

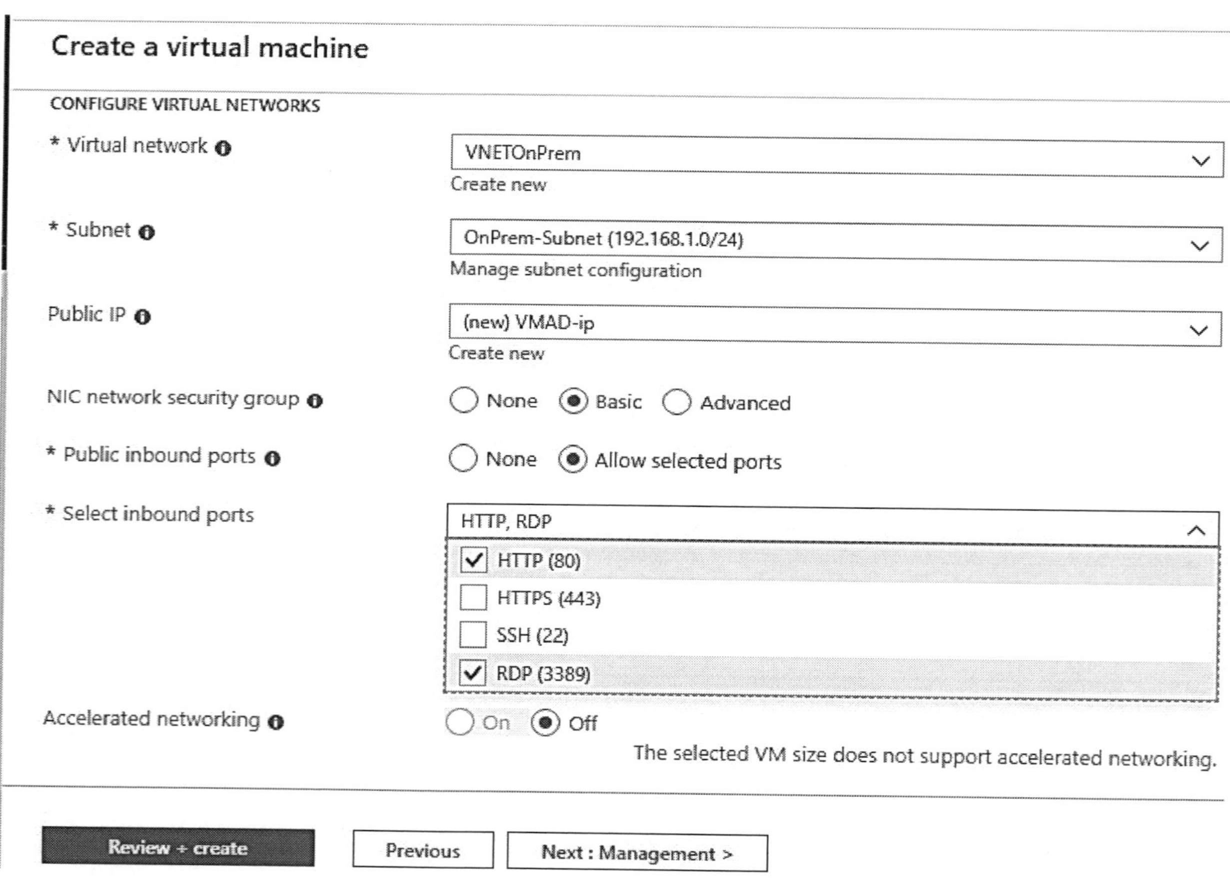

4. Management Screen opens>Select No for Security Center and off for Monitoring, Identity and Auto-Shutdown. Click Next: Advanced.
   Note: Readers can enable some options according to their requirement.

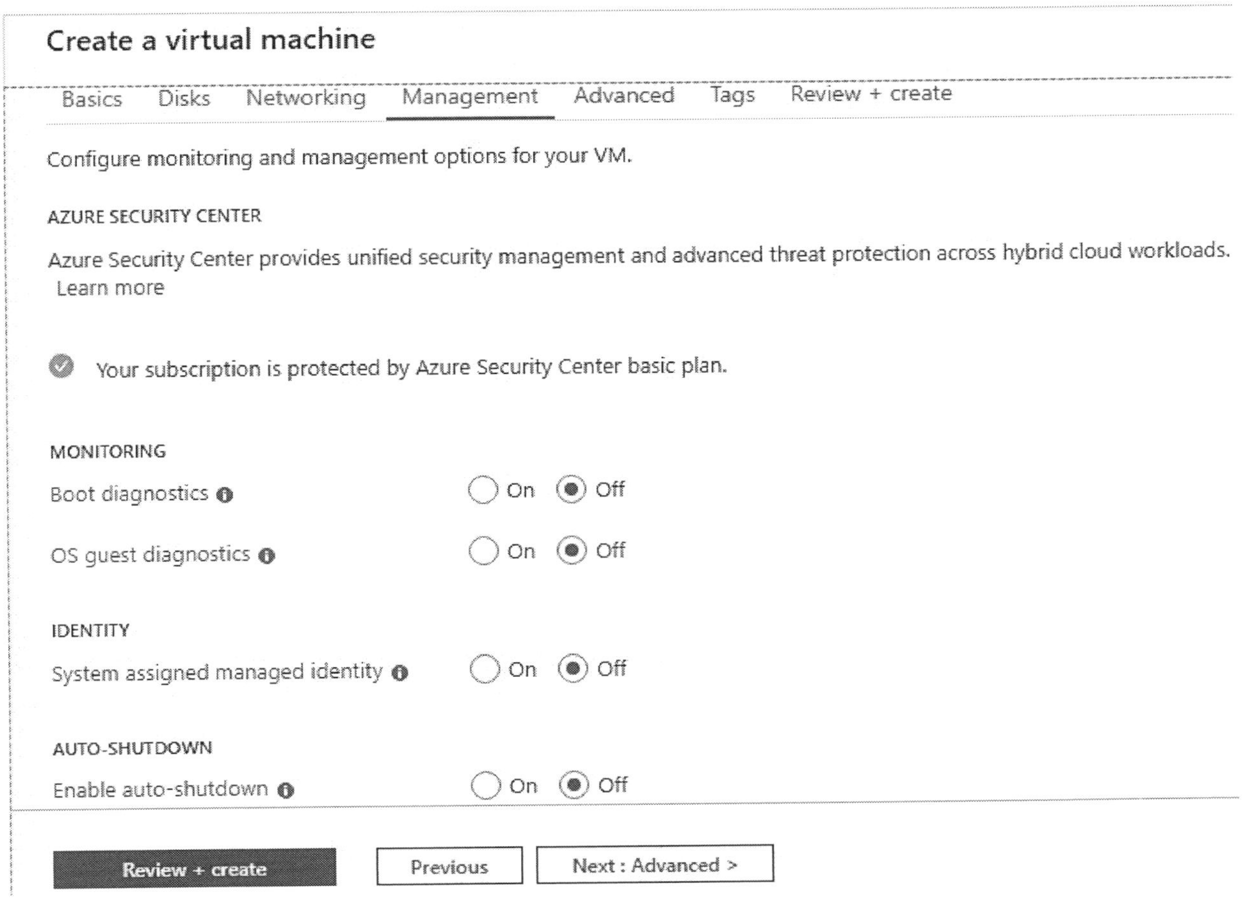

Create a virtual machine

Basics Disks Networking Management Advanced Tags Review + create

Configure monitoring and management options for your VM.

AZURE SECURITY CENTER

Azure Security Center provides unified security management and advanced threat protection across hybrid cloud workloads. Learn more

Your subscription is protected by Azure Security Center basic plan.

MONITORING

Boot diagnostics — On / Off (Off selected)

OS guest diagnostics — On / Off (Off selected)

IDENTITY

System assigned managed identity — On / Off (Off selected)

AUTO-SHUTDOWN

Enable auto-shutdown — On / Off (Off selected)

Review + create | Previous | Next : Advanced >

5. Select all default values in Advanced Screen>Click Next: Tags.

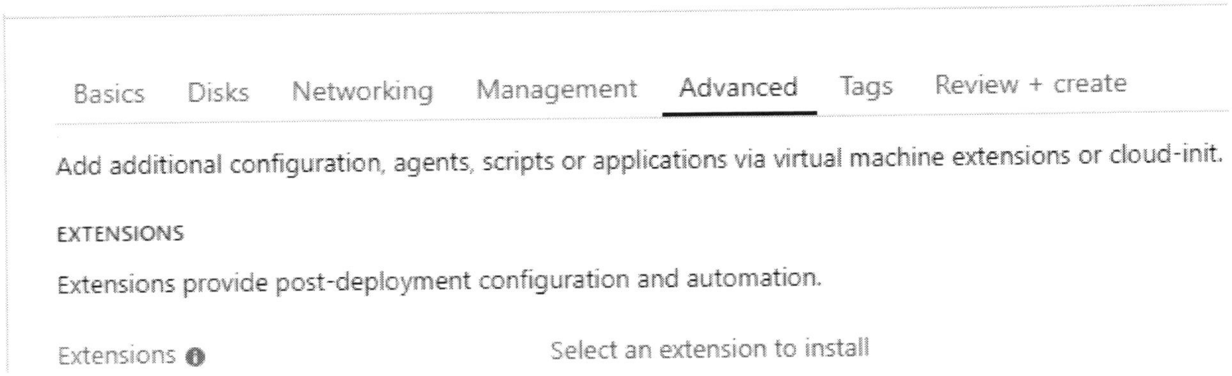

Basics Disks Networking Management Advanced Tags Review + create

Add additional configuration, agents, scripts or applications via virtual machine extensions or cloud-init.

EXTENSIONS

Extensions provide post-deployment configuration and automation.

Extensions — Select an extension to install

6. Select all default values in Tags>Click Review +Create.

7. In Review+create Screen click create after validation is passed.

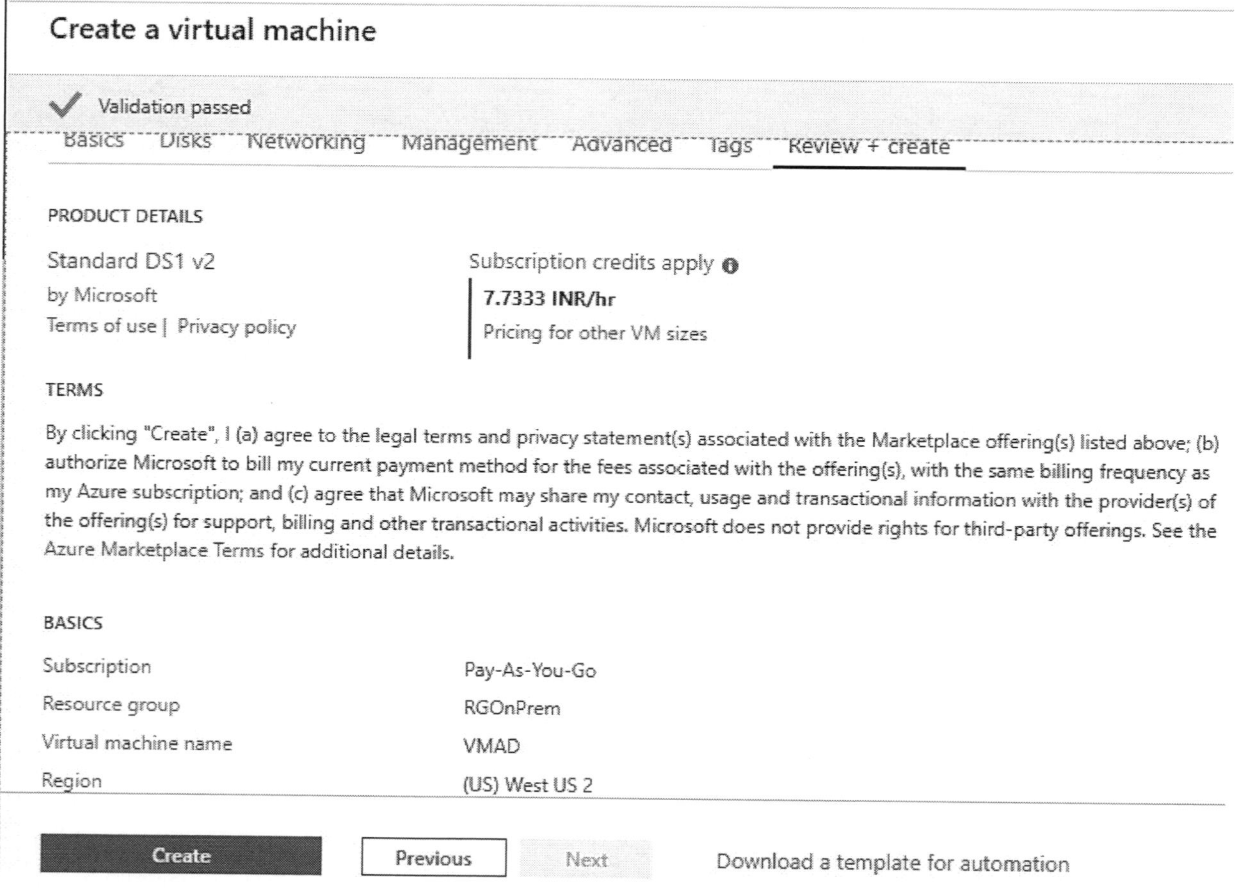

Note 1: In disk screen if you select no for use managed disk option then you need to specify the storage account or use a system created storage account.

Note 2: In Network Security Group under Networking you have the option to select advanced. With advanced option you can assign pre-created NSG. Exercise 11 shows how to create NSG.

8. Figure below shows VM VMAD dashboard.

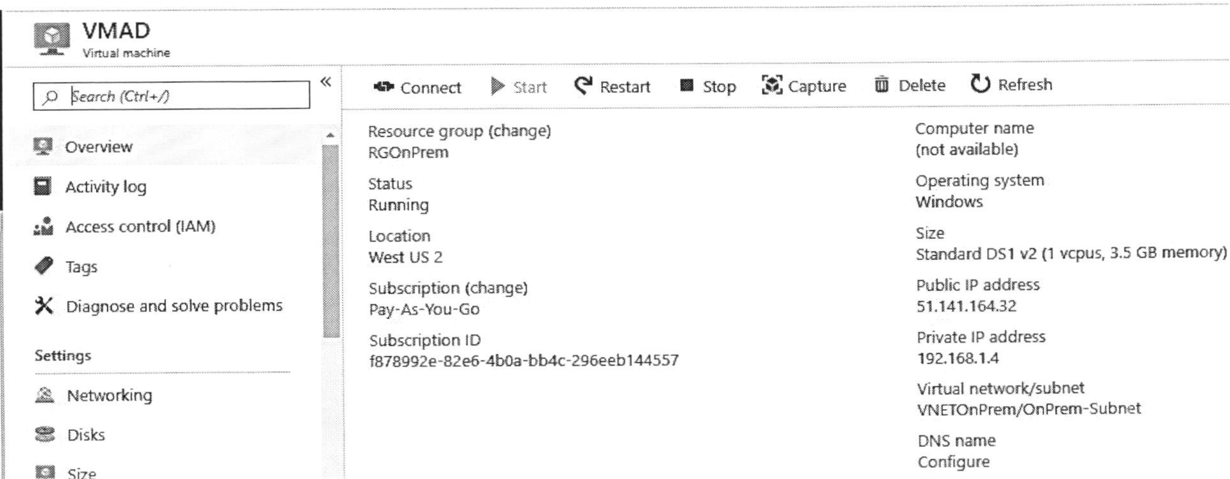

In right pane Click Configure under DNS Name>Public IP Address pane opens> Under DNS name enter **vmad**> Click **save** and close the Pubic IP pane.

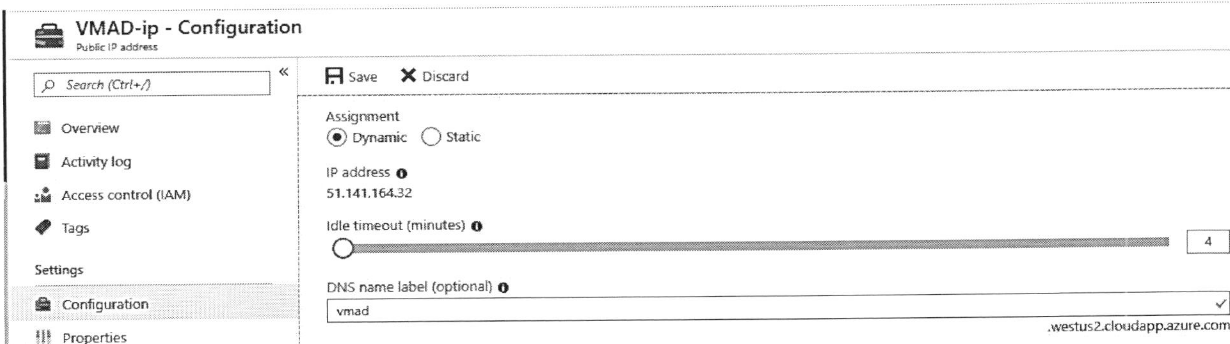

9. From Virtual Machine VMAD dashboard click connect and download RDP File based on DNS Address.

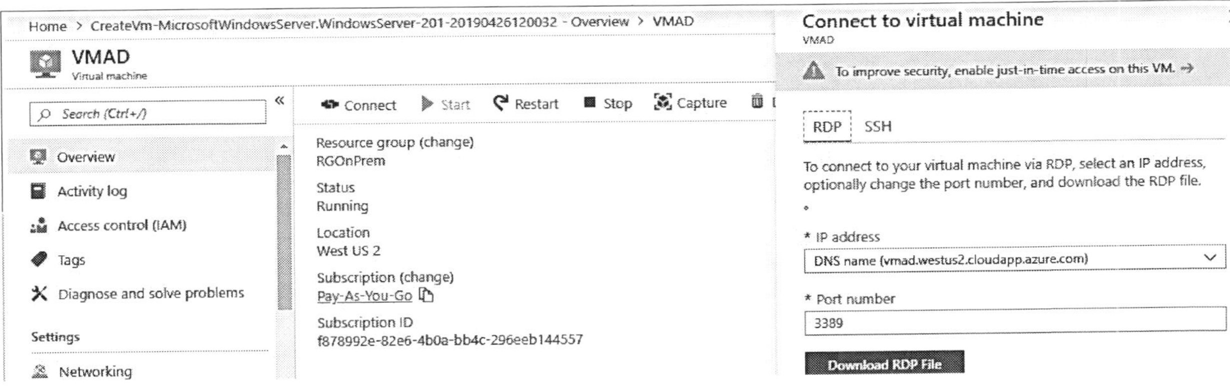

Exercise 40: Enable AD DS Role in Virtual Machine VMAD

In this exercise we will enable Active Directory Domain services (AD DS) role in Virtual Machine OnPremAD created in previous Exercise.

1. RDP to VMAD using username and password you entered during VM creation.
2. Open server Manager> Click add roles and features>Next.
3. In the Add Roles and Features Wizard, on the Installation Type page, choose Role-based or feature-based installation, and then click Next.
4. Select OnPremAD VM from the server pool and click Next.
5. On the Server Roles page, select Active Directory Domain Services.
6. In the pop-up about adding features, make sure that Include management tools is selected and then click Add Features. When the pop-up closes, click Next in the wizard.

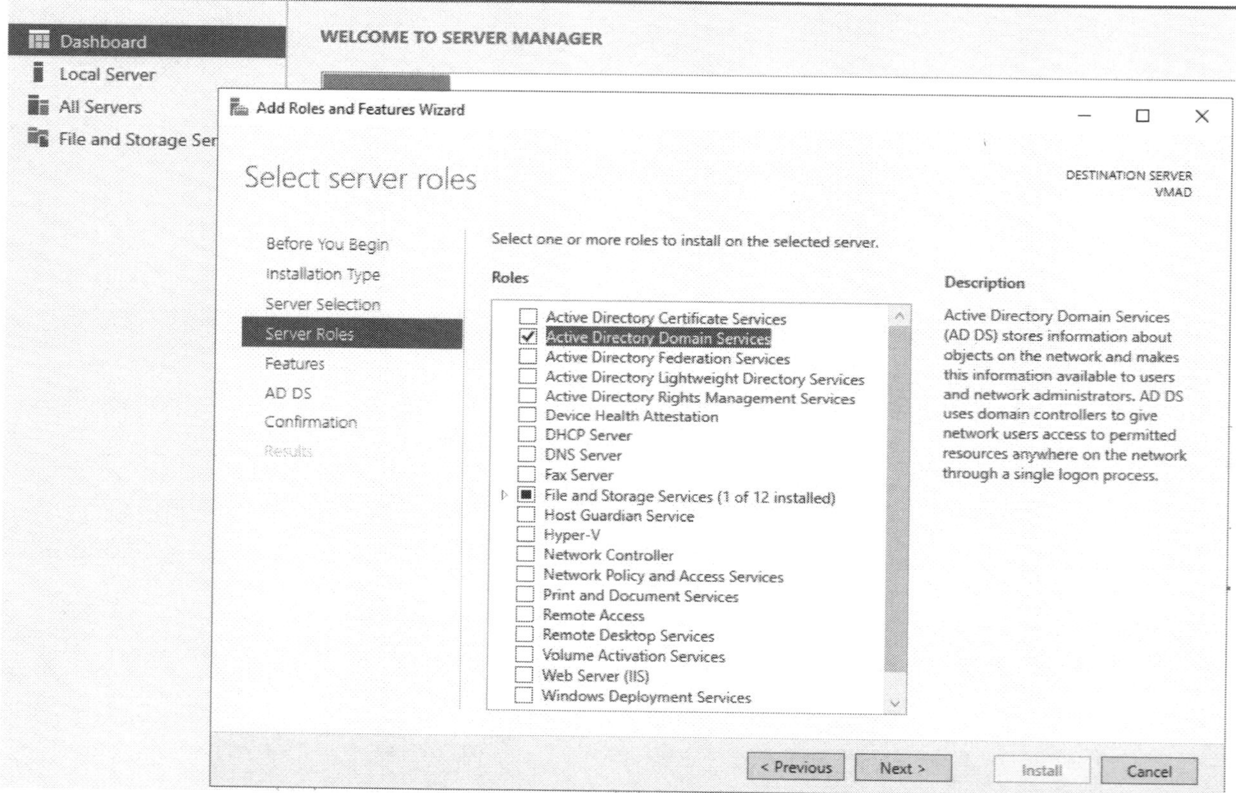

7. Next, Next. In the Confirmation select checkbox for Restart and click Install.
8. It will take around 2-3 minute to install the AD DS. After Installation is complete click close.

9. In the Server Manager click the Flag icon with Yellow triangle> dropdown box opens. In the dropdown box click the link **Promote this server to a domain controller.**

10. Active Directory Domain Services Configuration wizard opens>Select Add a New Forest> Enter a Domain name. I entered **AZX0X.local**>Click Next.

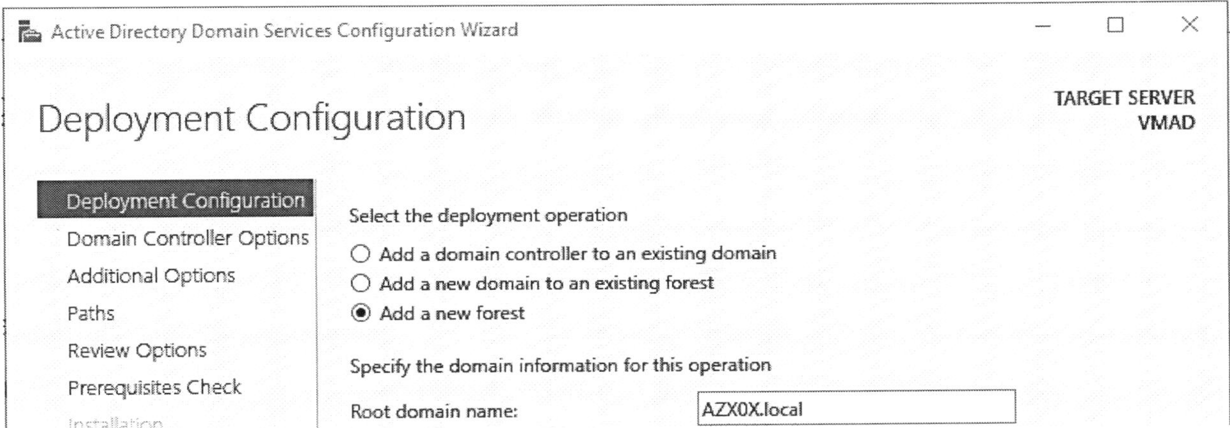

11. In Domain Controller options Enter the Directory Services Restore mode password >Click next 4 or 5 times.
12. In Prerequisites Check click Install. After Installation Server will automatically restart and RDP windows will close automatically.
13. After 3-4 Minutes RDP to windows VM again. You can see AD DS role.

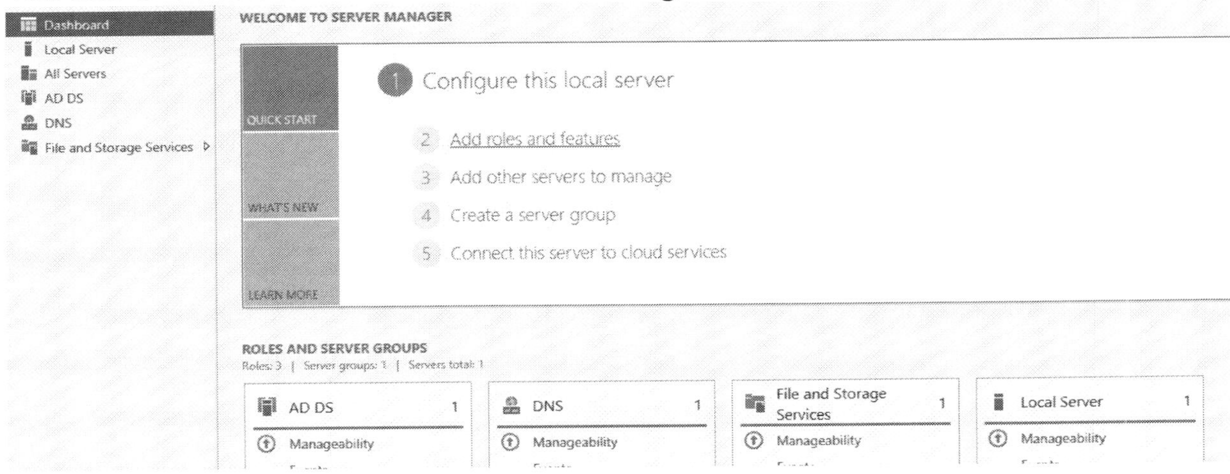

14. **Install Azure PowerShell Module**. Open PowerShell in VM OnPremAD>Change directory to WINDOWS\system32 and run following commands.
Install-Module -Name AzureRM
Import-Module -Name AzureRM

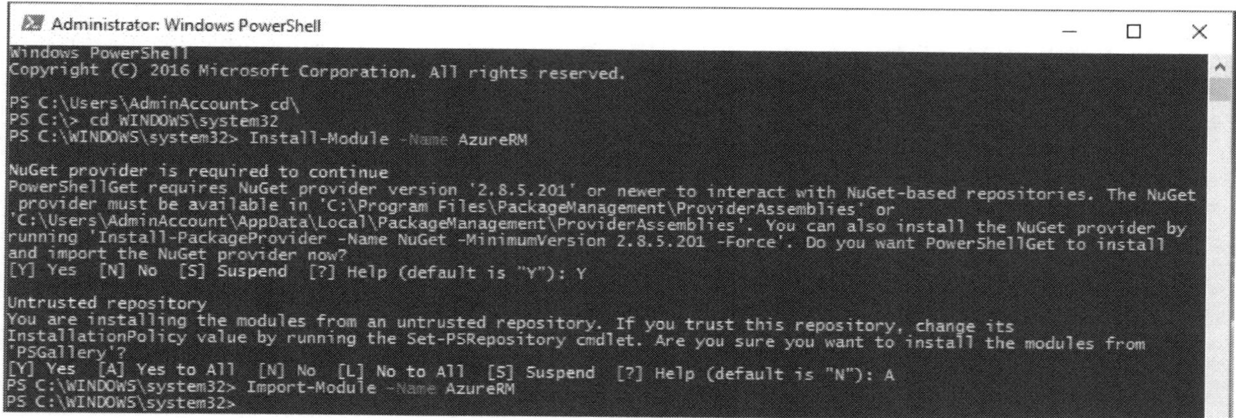

15. **Change Dynamic IP to Static IP.** In VM VMAD dashboard click the IP Address link under Public IP Address in right pane>IP Address dashboard opens> click configuration in left pane>Select Radio Button for Static and click save> **In VM dashboard click restart.**

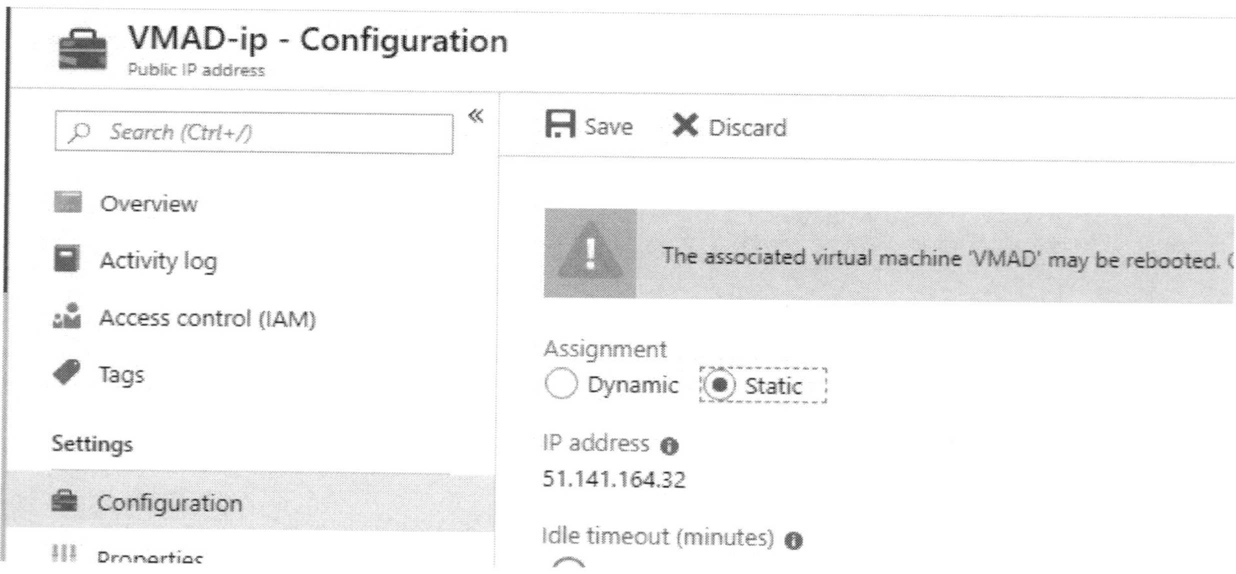

Note: Go to VM dashboard and click Stop in Right pane. This VM will be used in Azure File Sync and Azure AD Connect Labs. If we don't stop it will continuously incur charges and might finish the credit in case you are using trial account.

Linux VM in Azure

Linux is fully supported in Azure with images available from multiple vendors including Red Hat, Suse, Ubuntu, Debian, Free BSD and CoreOS etc.

Connecting to Linux VM

You can connect and log on to Linux VM with **SSH Keys** or **Password.**

Passwords over SSH connections are vulnerable to brute-force attacks or guessing of passwords.

MS recommends connecting to a Linux VM using a public-private key-pair known as SSH keys. Azure currently supports SSH protocol 2 (SSH-2) RSA public-private key pairs with a minimum length of 2048 bits.

The **public key** is placed on your Azure Linux VM.
The **private key** is place on your local system and is used by an SSH client to verify your identity when you connect to your Linux VM. Do not share the private key.

You can generate Public-Private key pair on your windows system using ssh-keygen command or a GUI tool like PuTTYgen.

For the next lab we will be using password option.

Exercise 41: Create Linux VM

In this exercise we will create Ubuntu Server VM in **Web-Subnet** of Virtual Network VNETCloud and in Resource Group RGCloud. We will use **Unmanaged disk option** using Storage Account **sastdcloud.** Attempt this Disk Exercise after you have completed Exercise 69 in Storage Accounts chapter 8.

1. In Azure Portal Click Create a Resource>Compute> Virtual Machine> Create VM Blade opens>Select Resource Group RGCloud, Region East US 2, In Image box select Ubuntu server 18.04 LTS, Enter Username and Password and select none for inbound ports.

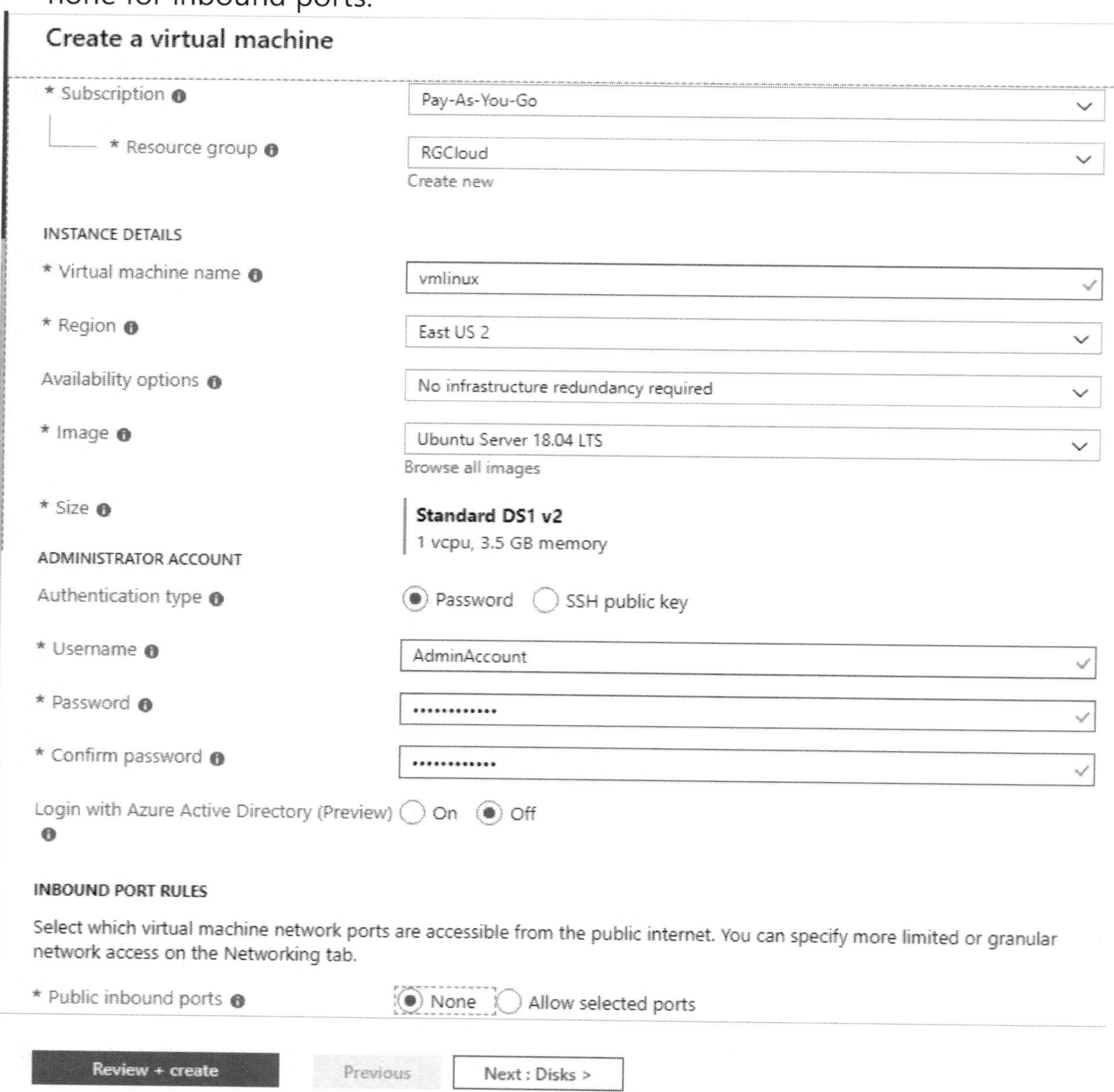

2. Click Next:Disks in bottom pane or Disks in Top pane> Disk pane opens>Select Standard HDD>Click Advanced and select No for Managed disk option>Select Storage Account sastdcloud.

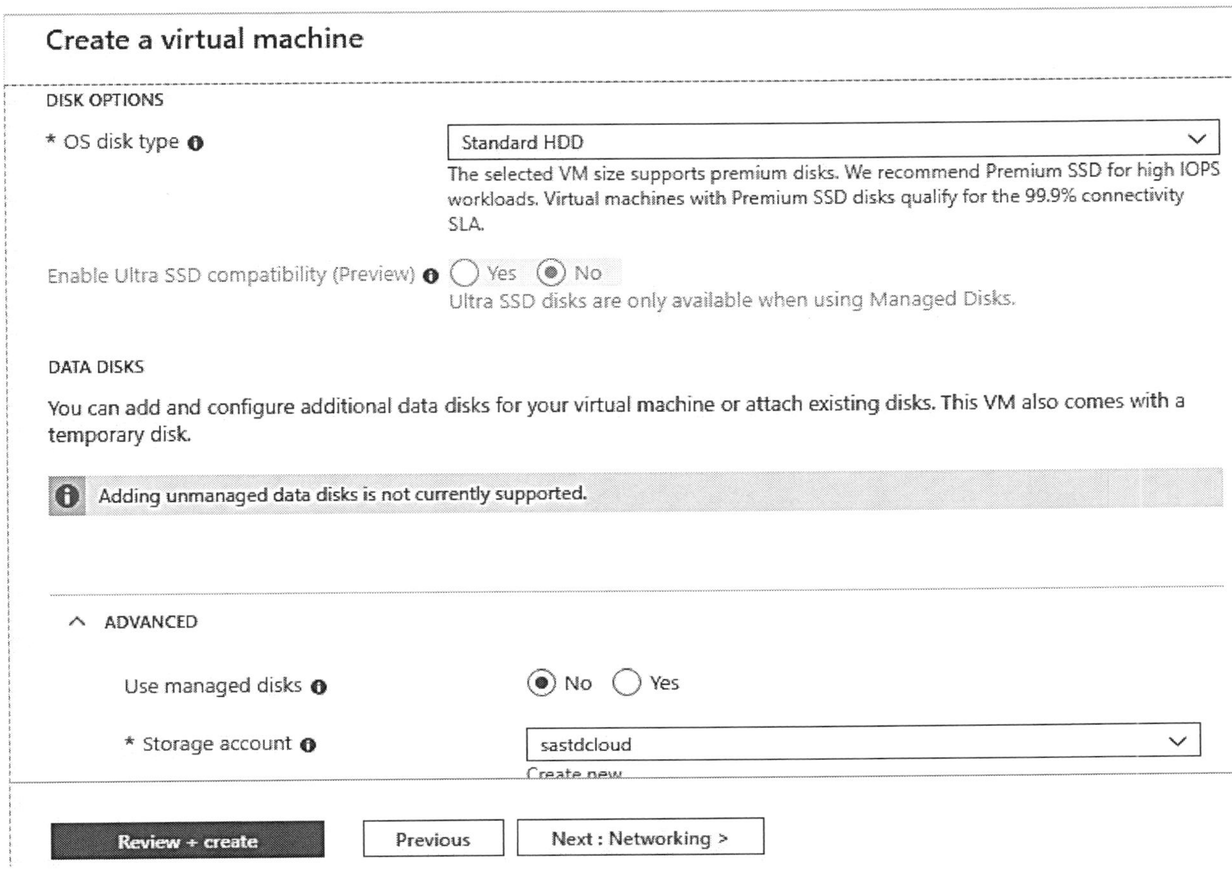

Note: Resource Group RGCloud and Virtual Network VNETCloud were created in Exercise 1 & 3 Respectively in Chapter 1.

3. Click Next:Networking>Networking pane opens> Select VNETPortal and **Web-Subnet** from drop down box>Dynamic Public is automatically created>Select Basic for NSG>Select Allow Selected Ports and select HTTP and SSH.

Create a virtual machine

CONFIGURE VIRTUAL NETWORKS

* Virtual network: VNETCloud (Create new)

* Subnet: Web-Subnet (10.1.1.0/24) (Manage subnet configuration)

Public IP: (new) vmlinux-ip (Create new)

NIC network security group: None / Basic / Advanced

The selected subnet 'Web-Subnet (10.1.1.0/24)' is already associated to a network security group 'NSGCloud'. We recommend managing connectivity to this virtual machine via the existing network security group instead of creating a new one here.

* Public inbound ports: None / Allow selected ports

* Select inbound ports: HTTP, SSH

HTTP (80)
HTTPS (443)
SSH (22)
RDP (3389)

Review + create | Previous | Next : Management >

4. Click Review + Create> After Validation is passed Click create.

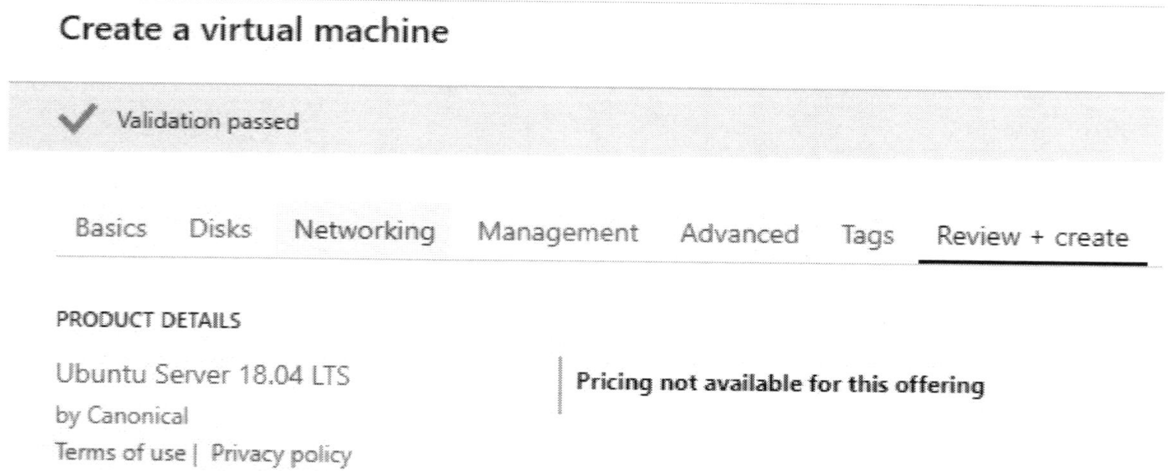

5. Figure below dashboard of Ubuntu VM.

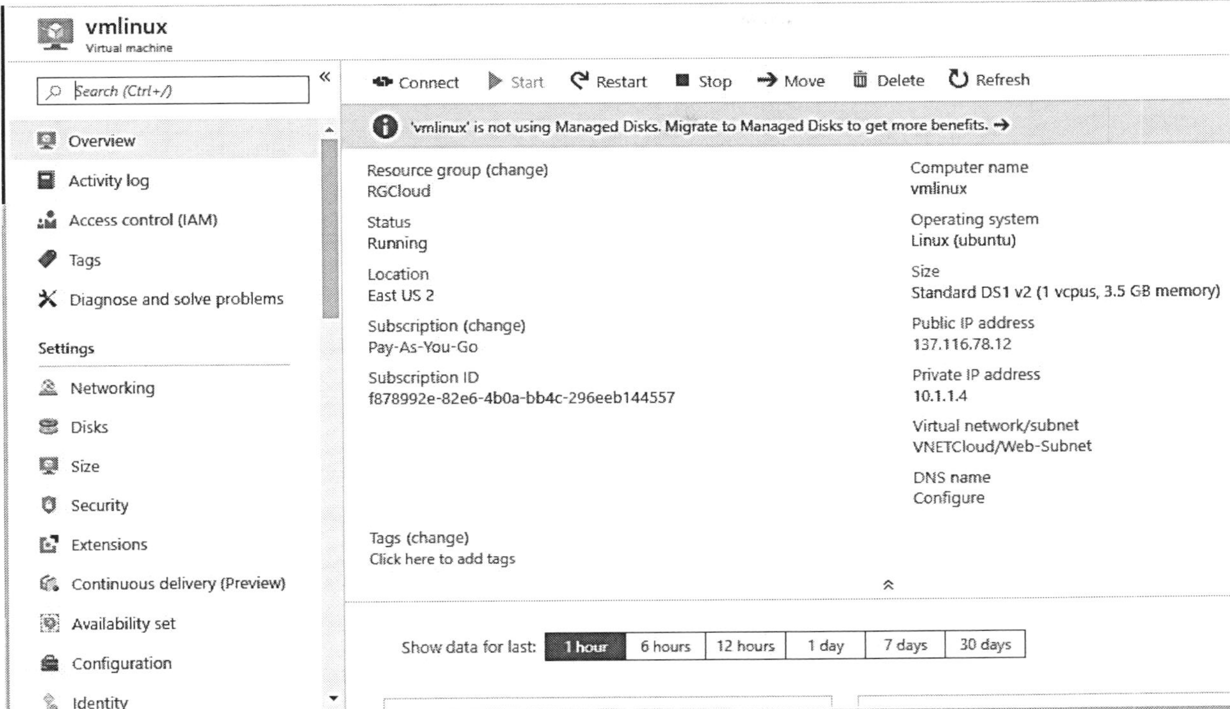

6. **Configure DNS name.** Click Configure in Right pane under DNS>Public IP Address pane opens> Enter a name. In this case I entered **vmlinuxcloud**>click save. Close the Public IP Pane. In VM dashboard click refresh and you can see DNS name of VM.

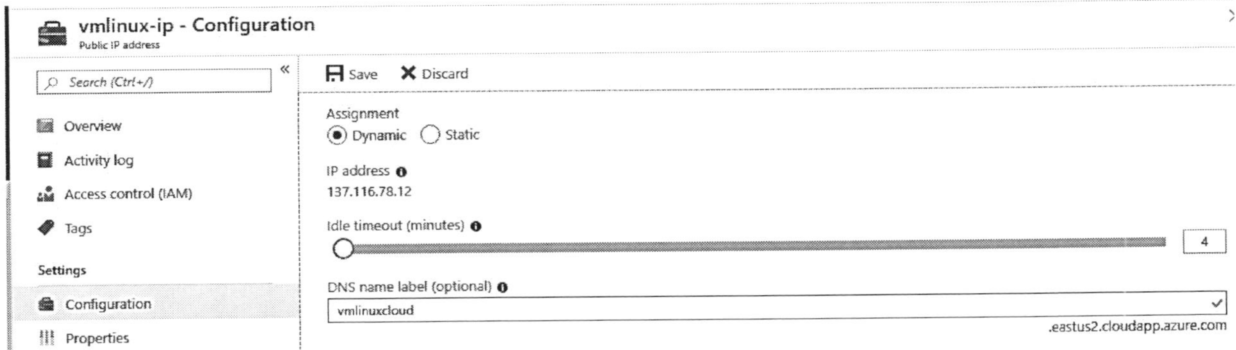

Exercise 42: Connecting to Linux VM

For this exercise I downloaded and installed Putty client.

1. Open putty Client and enter Linux VM IP or DNS name and select SSH.

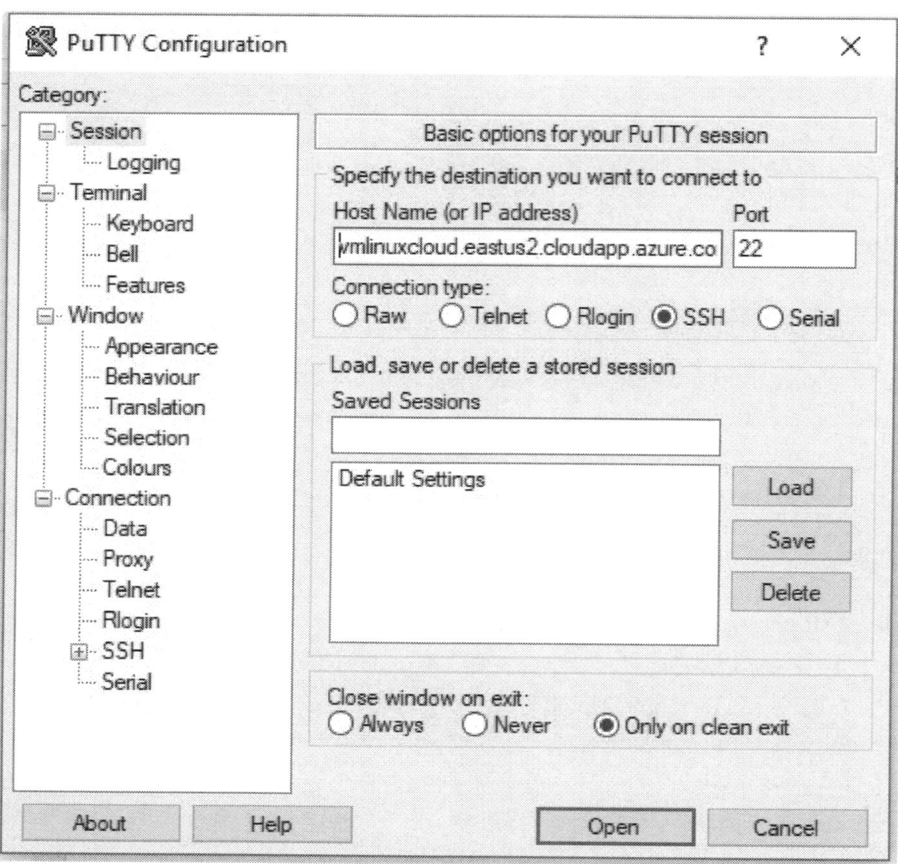

2. Click open and Putty client connects to Linux VM> Enter Username and password you entered during VM creation>Press Enter> You are now connected to Linux VM.

AdminAccount@vmlinux: ~

```
login as: AdminAccount
AdminAccount@vmlinuxcloud.eastus2.cloudapp.azure.com's password:
Welcome to Ubuntu 18.04.2 LTS (GNU/Linux 4.18.0-1014-azure x86_64)

 * Documentation:  https://help.ubuntu.com
 * Management:     https://landscape.canonical.com
 * Support:        https://ubuntu.com/advantage

  System information as of Tue Apr 23 12:15:21 UTC 2019
```

Exercise 43: Update Linux VM & Install NGINX Web Server

1. **Elevate Permission to root user**> sudo su.

```
root@vmlinux: /home/AdminAccount
AdminAccount@vmlinux:~$ sudo su
root@vmlinux:/home/AdminAccount# clear
root@vmlinux:/home/AdminAccount#
```

2. **Update Ubuntu Linux Machine**> apt-get –y update.

```
root@vmlinux: /home/AdminAccount
root@vmlinux:/home/AdminAccount# apt-get -y update
Hit:1 http://azure.archive.ubuntu.com/ubuntu bionic InRelease
Get:2 http://azure.archive.ubuntu.com/ubuntu bionic-updates InRelease [88.7 kB]
Get:3 http://azure.archive.ubuntu.com/ubuntu bionic-backports InRelease [74.6 kB
]
Get:4 http://security.ubuntu.com/ubuntu bionic-security InRelease [88.7 kB]
Get:5 http://azure.archive.ubuntu.com/ubuntu bionic-updates/main amd64 Packages
[580 kB]
Get:6 http://azure.archive.ubuntu.com/ubuntu bionic-updates/main Translation-en
[214 kB]
Get:7 http://azure.archive.ubuntu.com/ubuntu bionic-updates/universe amd64 Packa
ges [861 kB]
Get:8 http://azure.archive.ubuntu.com/ubuntu bionic-updates/universe Translation
```

3. **Install Nginx Web Server**> apt-get –y install nginx

```
root@vmlinux: /home/AdminAccount
root@vmlinux:/home/AdminAccount# apt-get -y install nginx
Reading package lists... Done
Building dependency tree
Reading state information... Done
The following additional packages will be installed:
  fontconfig-config fonts-dejavu-core libfontconfig1 libgd3 libjbig0
  libjpeg-turbo8 libjpeg8 libnginx-mod-http-geoip
  libnginx-mod-http-image-filter libnginx-mod-http-xslt-filter
  libnginx-mod-mail libnginx-mod-stream libtiff5 libwebp6 libxpm4 nginx-common
  nginx-core
```

Note: We also used clear command to clear the screen. This is optional.

4. **Access the default NGINX Website**> open browser and enter VM IP address or DNS name> Default website opens.

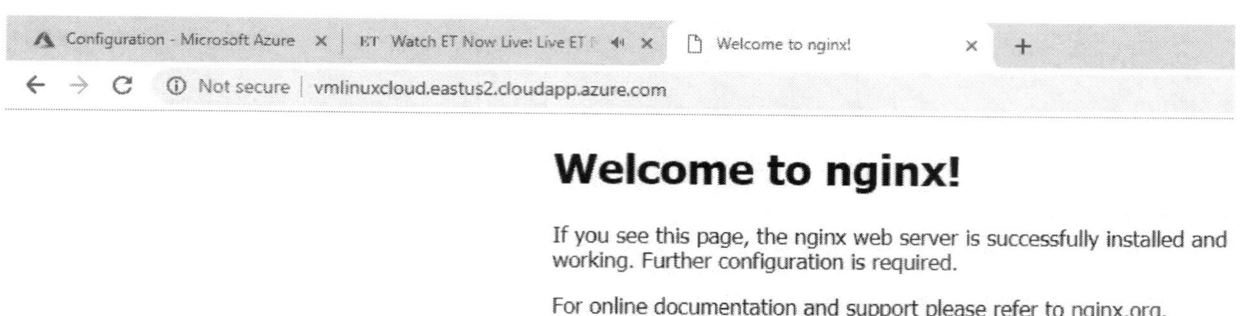

5. Delete VM by clicking Delete in VM Dashboard.
6. Click All Resources in Azure Portal and **Delete Public IP and Network Interface** of Linux VM.
7. Linux VM **OS disk** was not visible in All Resources. I deleted OS disk using Azure Storage Explorer.

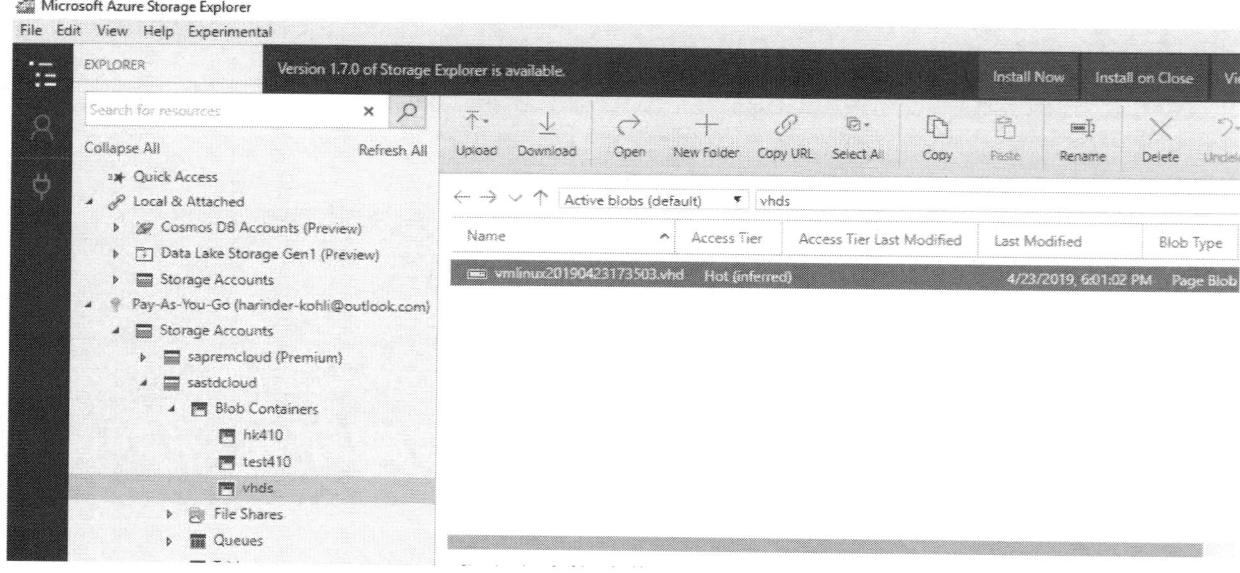

Note: To know more about Azure Storage Explorer refer to Chapter 5.

Customizing Linux VM with Cloud init

Cloud init is a widely used approach to customize a Linux VM as it boots for the first time. You can use cloud-init to install packages and write files or to configure users and security.

Because cloud-init is called during the initial boot process, there are no additional steps or required agents to apply your configuration.

Cloud init is deployed using Advanced Tab during Linux VM creation using Azure Portal a shown below.

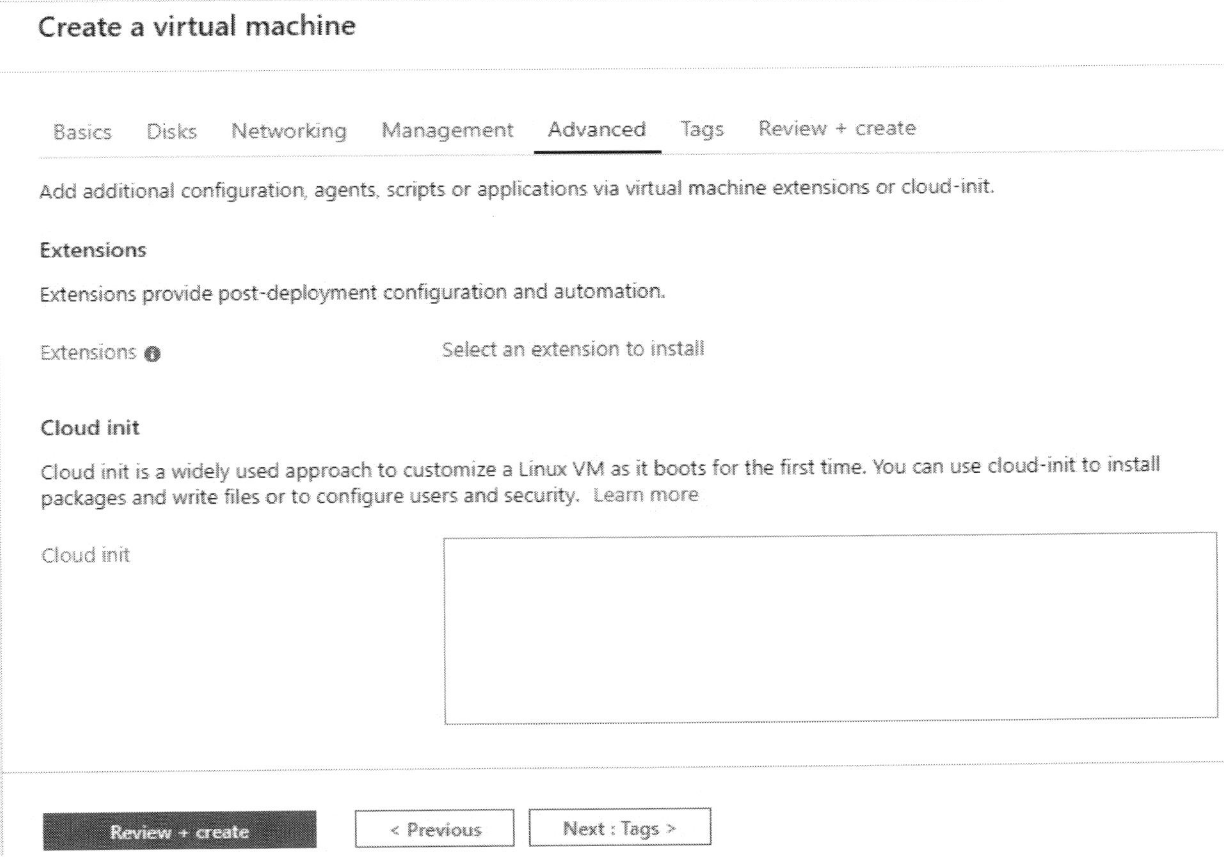
Create a virtual machine
Basics
Disks
Networking
Management
Advanced
Tags
Review + create
Add additional configuration, agents, scripts or applications via virtual machine extensions or cloud-init.
Extensions
Extensions provide post-deployment configuration and automation.
Extensions
Select an extension to install
Cloud init
Cloud init is a widely used approach to customize a Linux VM as it boots for the first time. You can use cloud-init to install packages and write files or to configure users and security. Learn more
Cloud init
Review + create
< Previous
Next : Tags >

Cloud init can also be deployed when you are creating linux VM using Azure CLI.

Images

Images are VHD files that contains syspreped version of Windows VM. Sysprep removes all your personal account and security information, and then prepares the machine to be used as an image. Image contains all the information necessary for creating a VM.

Why Custom Image

Many Organization's have a requirement that their VMs should have certain dot net version or IIS Server installed or a Monitoring Agent installed. Instead of installing feature in each VM, just install the required feature in one VM and create image of the VM. Then deploy your VMs with the image.

Custom Image Advantages

Custom image reduces the administrative overhead of deploying VMs.

Custom Image Deployment Process

To create a custom image start by installing required features in the Virtual Machine, Sysprep the VM and thirdly create image from the Syspreped VM.

Exercise 44: Create Custom Image of Azure VM (VMFE3)

In this Exercise we will first create Windows server 2019 Datacenter VM **VMFE3**. We will then install IIS and Access default website. We will then create image from this VM. This image will be used to deploy Windows Server VM in next exercise and will also be used to deploy VM Scale Set (VMSS) in Chapter 7.

Step 1 Deploy Windows Server 2019 Datacenter VM VMFE3 and Install IIS in Web-Subnet in Virtual Network VNETCloud, Resource Group RGCloud and in Region East US 2> **Follow the exact procedure shown in exercise 25, 26, 27 & 28.** Figure below shows the dashboard of VM VMFE3.

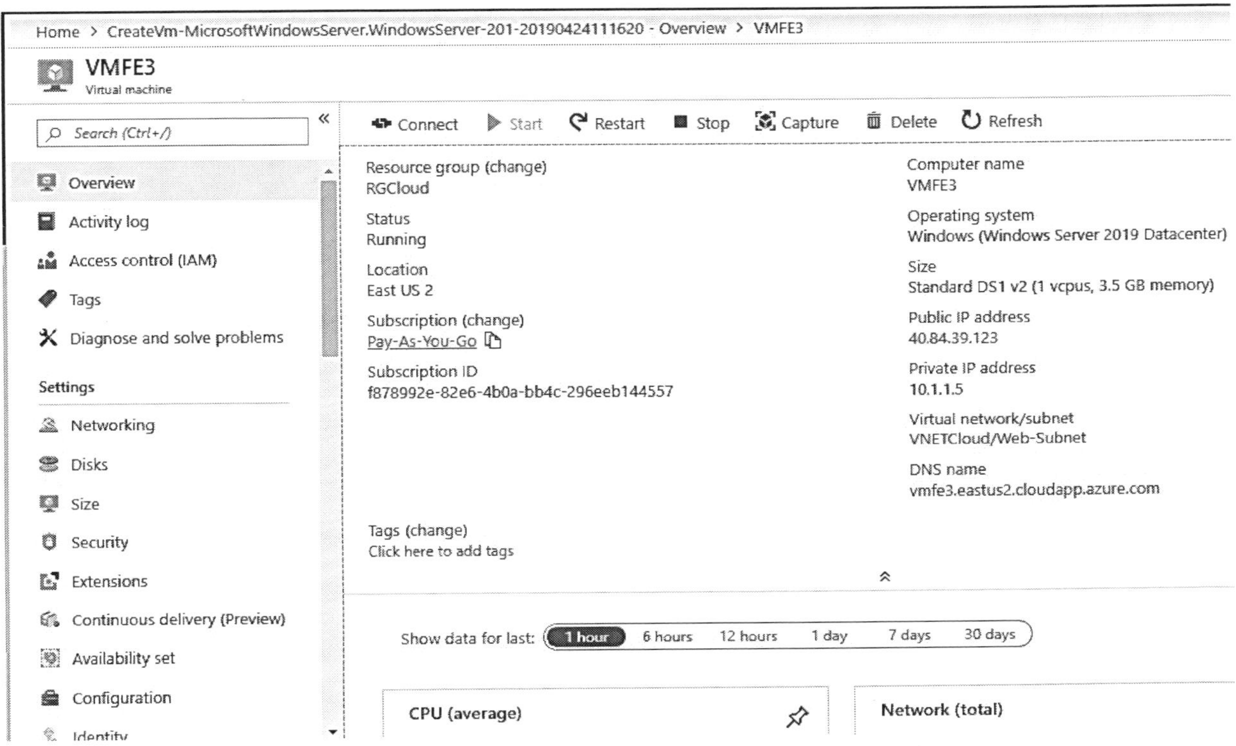

Note: Resource Group RGCloud & Virtual Network VNETCloud were created In Exercise 1& 3 respectively in Chapter 1.

Step 2: **Generalize the Windows VM VMFE3 using Sysprep**.

Sysprep removes all your personal account and security information, and then prepares the machine to be used as an image.

1. RDP to VMFE3>open Command Prompt and enter following command to change directory> **cd %windir%/system32/sysprep**

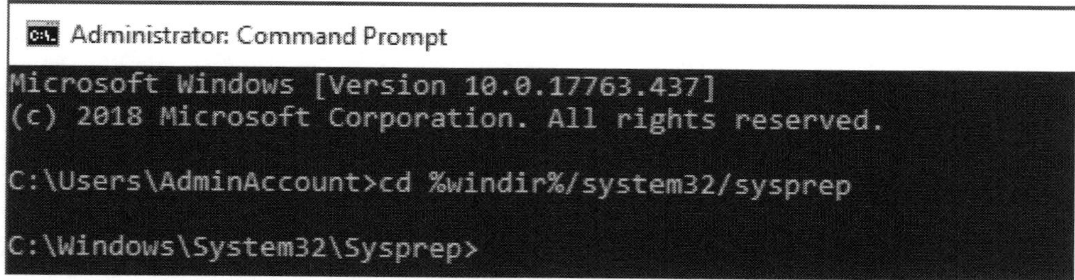

2. **Run sysprep.exe**> System Preparation Tool Box opens>In the System Preparation Tool dialog box, select Enter System Out-of-Box Experience (OOBE) and **select the Generalize check box** and For Shutdown Options select Shutdown and click OK.

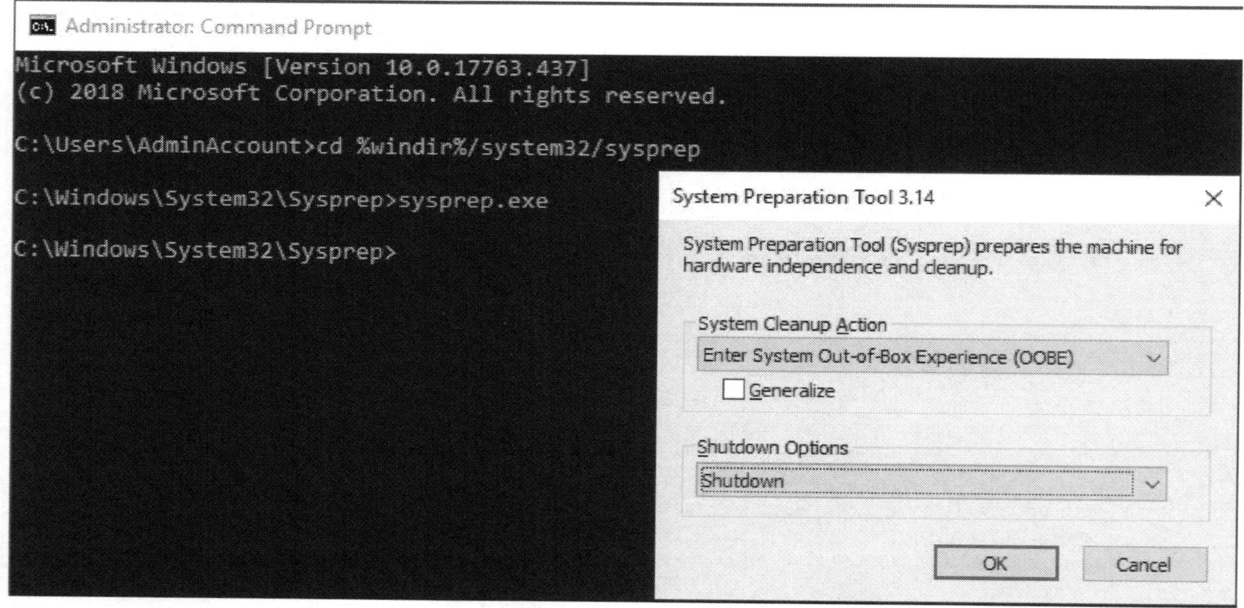

3. After Sysprep operation is complete RDP automatically closes.

Note: You can capture image of VM only when it is in stop state.

Step 5: Capture the image from the VM VMFE3 Dashboard

Go to VM VMFE3 dashboard which was syspreped in step 4>Click capture in top pane>Create image Dailog box opens as shown below> Select Resource group RGCloud, Check **Automatically delete this VM**> click create. It will take couple of minutes to complete the image creation process.

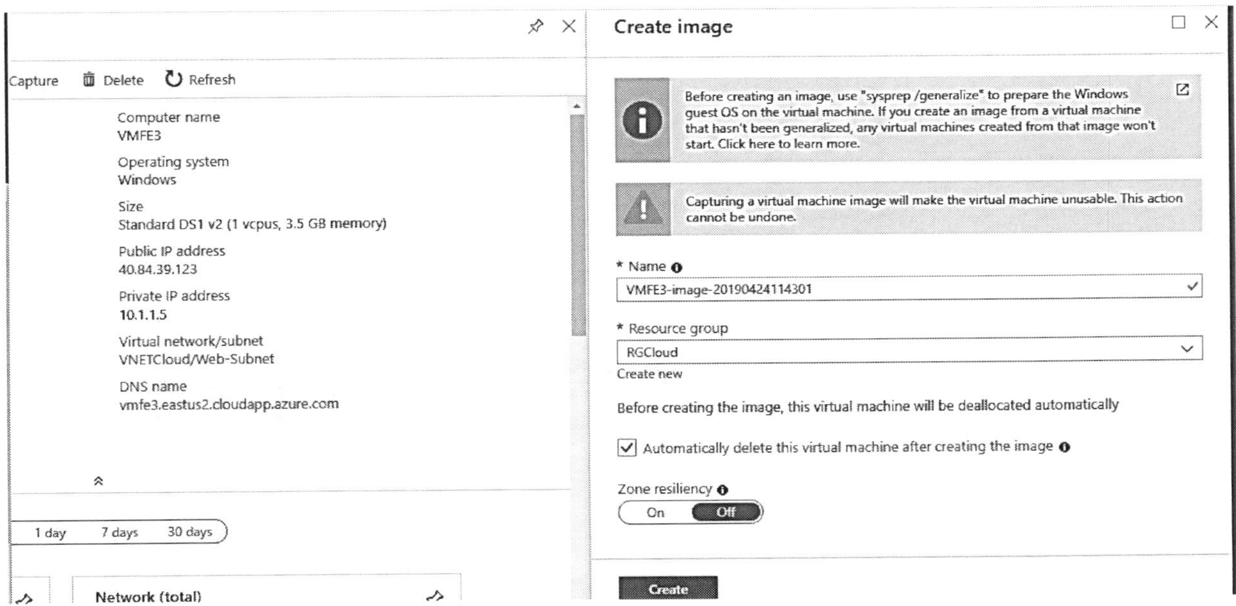

Step 4: Check the image In Azure Portal

In Azure Portal click All Services in left pane> Under Compute option scroll down and Click images> All Images dashboard opens with the image created.

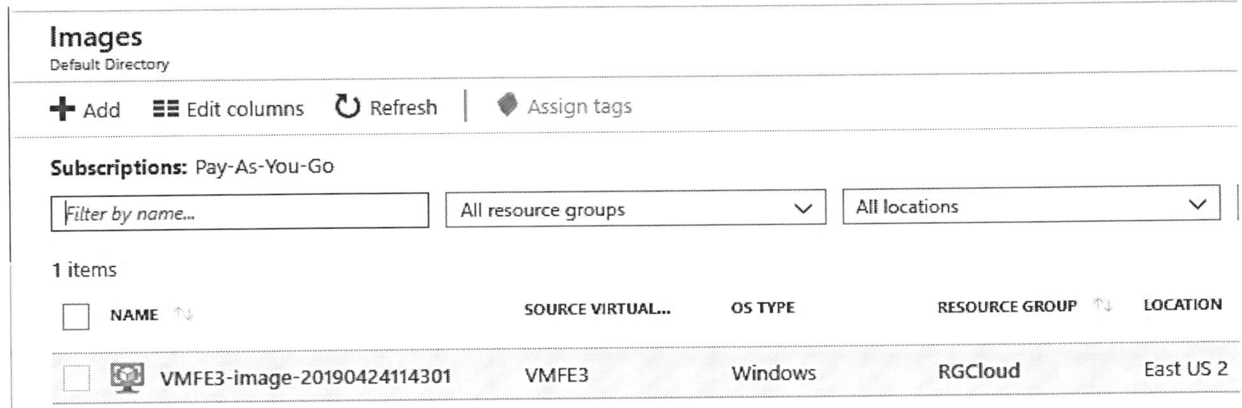

Note 1: we will use this image to deploy a VM in next exercise.
Note 2: We will use this image to deploy VM Scale Set (VMSS) in Chapter 7.

Exercise 45: Deploy VM from Custom image created in Exercise 44

1. In Azure Portal click All Services in left pane> Under Compute option Click images> Al Images pane opens >Click the image VMFE3-image-xxx >Image Dashboard opens.

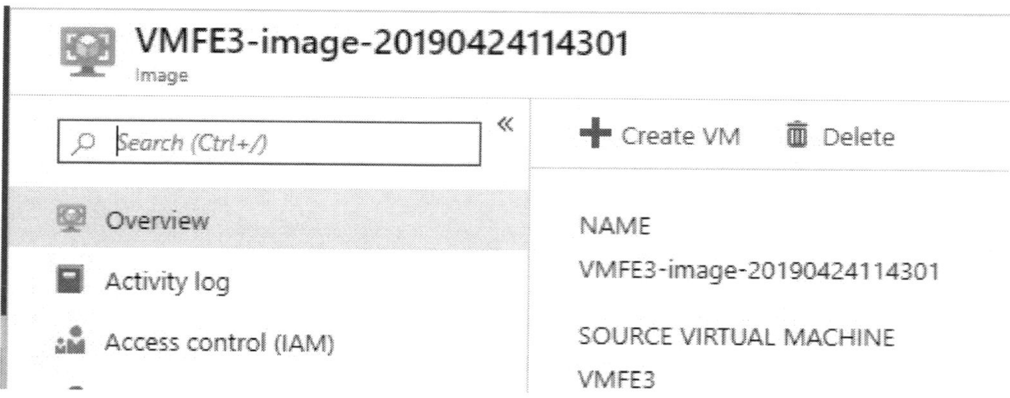

2. In the image Dashboard>Click Create VM>Create Virtual Machine dialog box opens>Enter information as per your requirement.

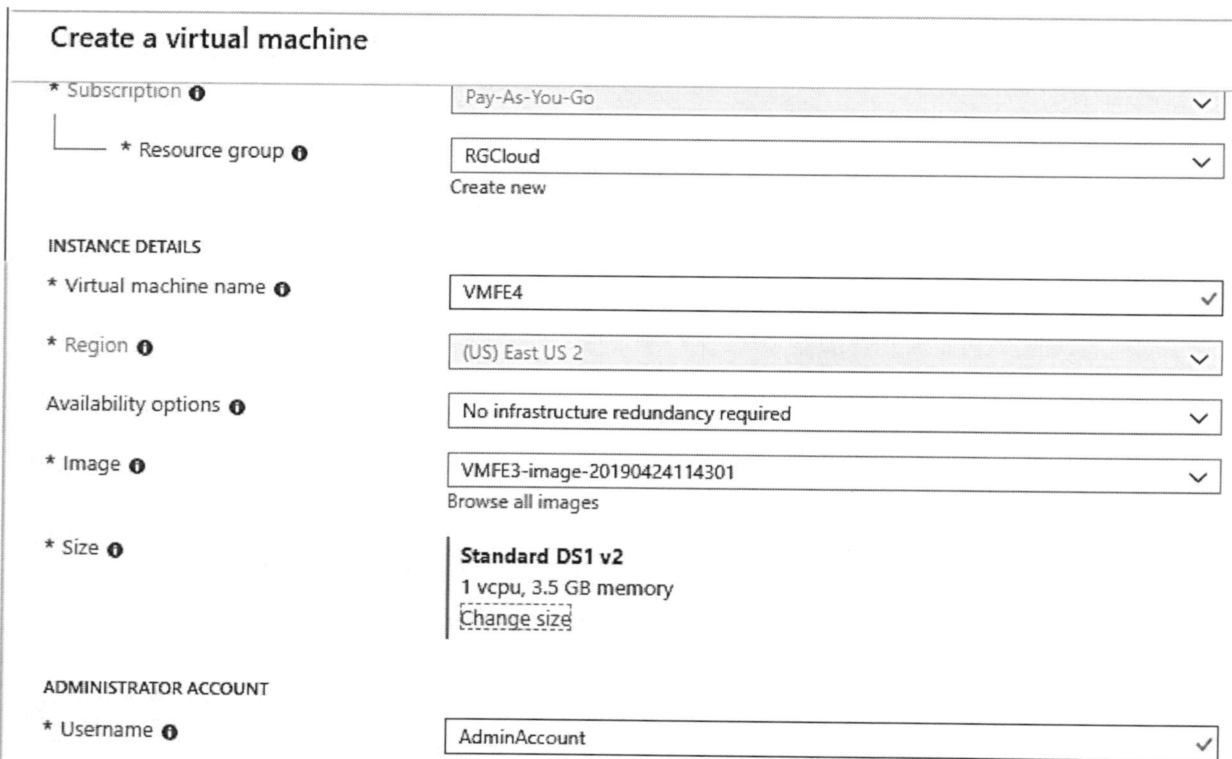

Rest steps are same as shown in exercise 25. After VM is created, access the default website. Delete the VM, IP Address, OS disk after the exercise.

Azure Virtual Machine Agent

The Microsoft Azure Virtual Machine Agent (VM Agent) is a secure, lightweight process that manages virtual machine (VM) interaction with the Azure Fabric Controller. The Primary role of Azure VM Agent is to enable and execute Azure virtual machine extensions.

VM Extensions enable post-deployment configuration of VM, such as installing and configuring software. VM extensions also enable recovery features such as resetting the administrative password of a VM. Without the Azure VM Agent, VM extensions cannot be run.

Installing the VM Agent

The Azure VM Agent is installed by default on any Windows VM deployed from an Azure Marketplace image.

Manual Installation of VM Agent: Manual installation is required when you deploy a Virtual Machine with a custom VM image. The Windows VM agent can be manually installed with a Windows installer package. Download the Windows installer package from go.microsoft.com/fwlink/?LinkID=394789

Checking for VM Agent using "Get-AzureRmVM" PowerShell Command

```
Get-AzureRmVM -ResourceGroupName myrg -Name myVM

OSProfile                  :
  ComputerName             : myVM
  AdminUsername            : myUserName
  WindowsConfiguration     :
    ProvisionVMAgent       : True
    EnableAutomaticUpdates : True
```

To get properties of all VMs running in resource group use following command:
Get-AzureRmVM -ResourceGroupName myrg

To get properties of all VMs running in Subscription use following command:
Get-AzureRmVM

Manually Checking for VM Agent

Log on to Azure VM and open Task Manager and click details tab. Look for a process name **WindowsAzureGuestAgent.exe**. The presence of this process indicates that the VM agent is installed.

Figure below shows Task Manager of VM VMFE1. It shows **WindowsAzureGuestAgent.exe**.

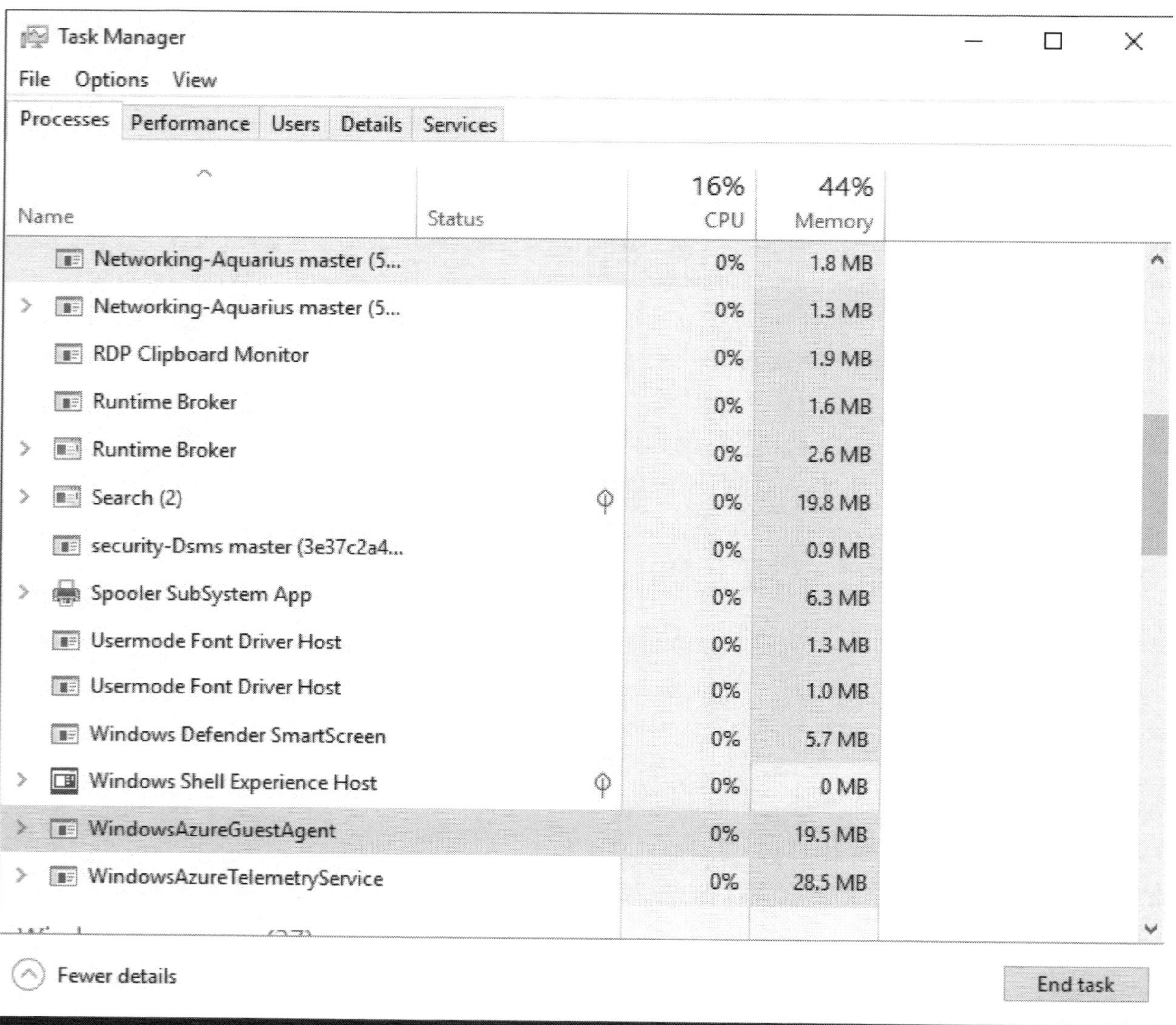

Virtual Machine Extensions

Azure virtual machine (VM) extensions are small applications that provide post-deployment configuration and automation tasks on Azure VMs. For example, if a virtual machine requires software installation, anti-virus protection, or to run a script inside of it, a VM extension can be used.

Types of Virtual Machines Extensions

1. VM Extensions provided by Microsoft. Example of VM Extension provided by Microsoft include Microsoft Monitoring Agent VM extension for monitoring VMs.
2. Third Party VM Extensions provided by companies like Symantec, Qualys, Rapid7 & HPE etc. Examples of third part VM Extensions include VM vulnerability tool from Qualys, Rapid7, HPE or Anti Virus products from Symantec & TrendMicro etc.
3. Custom Script Extensions written by customers themselves.

Note: Extensions can be added to Azure Virtual Machine during installation time or post installation.

Exercise 46: Demonstrating various VM Extensions available

Go to VM VMFE1 dashboard>Click Extension in left pane>In Right pane click + Add> Add Extension blade opens> click an Extension. In this case I clicked Symantec Agent for Cloud workload Protection Extension> In Right pane agent opens.

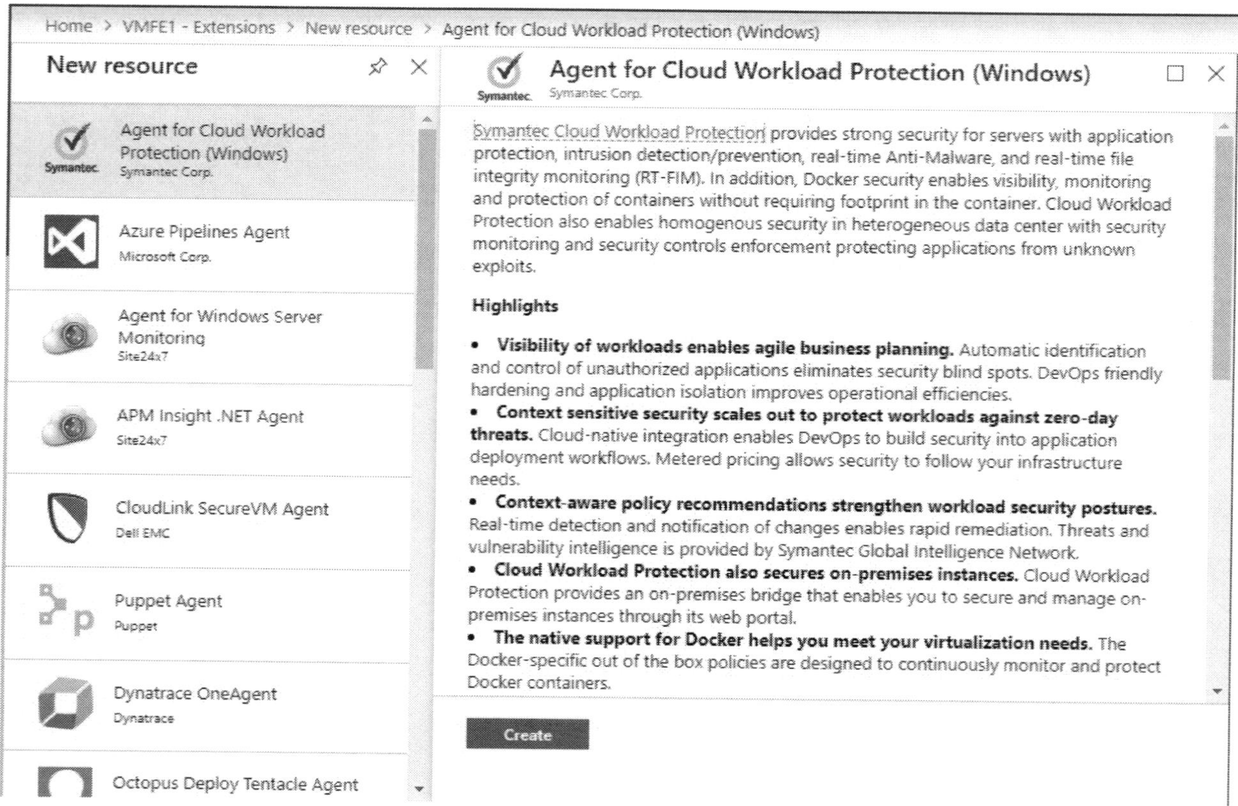

Readers are advised to scroll down the left pane to see the various extension available.

Custom Script Extension

Custom Script Extension is a tool that can be used to automatically launch and execute VM customization tasks. Custom Scripts are written by customers themselves.

The Custom Script Extension downloads and executes scripts on Azure Virtual Machines. Scripts can be downloaded from Azure storage or GitHub, or provided to the Azure portal at extension run time.

Custom Script Extension extension is useful for post deployment configuration, software installation, or any other VM configuration/management task.

Custom Script Installation Methods

Azure Templates
Azure CLI using **az vm extension set** command.
Azure PowerShell using **Set-AzureRmVMExtension** command.
Azure Portal

Exercise 47: Demonstrating Custom Script Extension using Azure Portal

1. Go to VM VMFE1 dashboard>Click Extension in left pane>In Right pane click + Add> Add Extension blade opens>Scroll down and Select Custom Script Extension> Custom Script Extension blade opens in right pane.

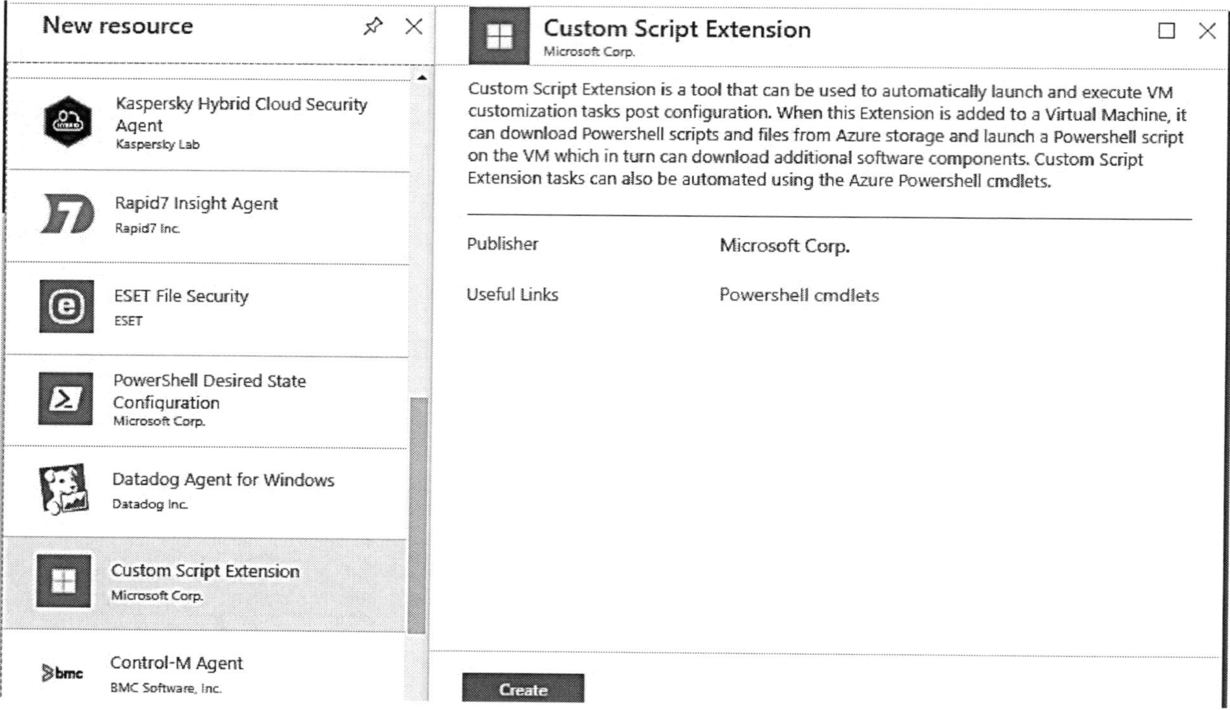

2. In right pane click create> Install Extension Blade opens>Click folder icon and upload file for executing on VM wvmportal.

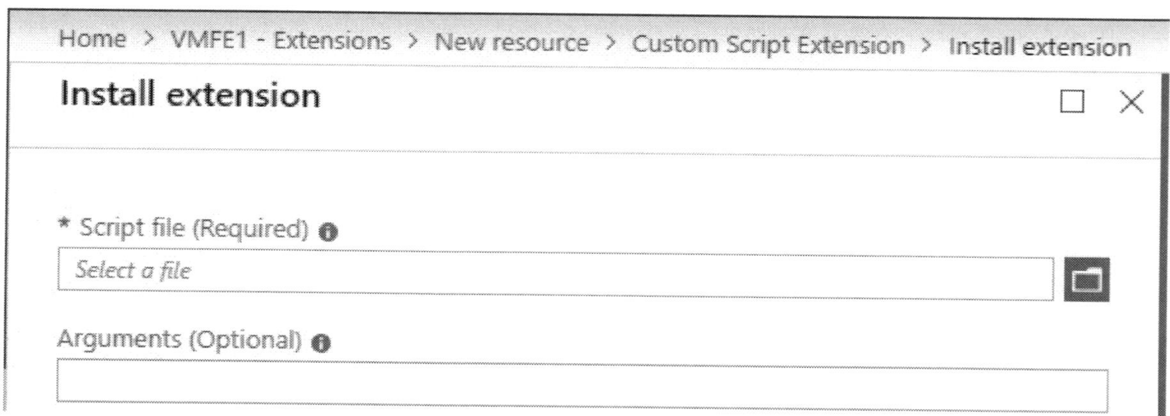

Manage VM Sizes

You can resize Azure VM to give it more/less CPU cores and RAM.

You can resize VM within same series to a larger VM or a smaller VM.
You can resize VM between different series (From D series to E Series). In this case resizing depends upon whether resize is to same hardware or different hardware families.

The typical impact to resizing a VM is a restart which can take up to five minutes for the resizing operation to complete.
If you are resizing VM's onto new hardware which is in an Availability Set (AS), then all the VMs need to be powered off for the resizing operation to begin.
If you are resizing to a VM onto new hardware (e.g. change in chipset), then the VM will need to be powered off first before the resize operation can begin.

Exercise 48: Resizing VM

In this exercise we will just show how to resize a VM but will not implement it.

1. Go to VM VMFE1 Dashboard>Click Size in left pane>Select size of new VM and click Resize.

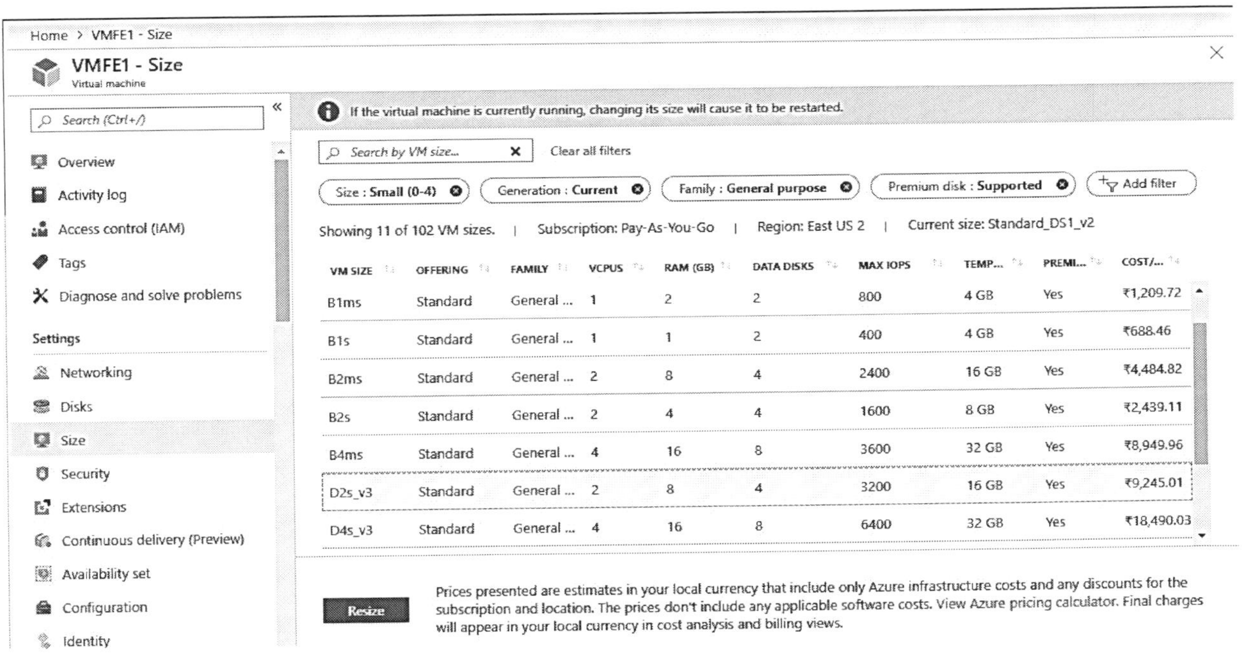

VM Auto-Shutdown

With VM Auto-Shutdown feature you can control VM cost.
Let's say that you don't require VMs to operate after office hours (After 5.30 PM).
You can enable VM Auto shutdown to shut down VM @ 5.30 PM.
This feature will not enable auto start-up. You need to start-up the VM manually.
Note: Auto Start-up & Auto-Stop VMs will be discussed in Azure Automation chapter.

Exercise 49: Virtual Machine Auto-Shutdown

Go to VM VMFE1 Dashboard>Click Auto-Shutdown in left pane>In Right pane click On to enable Auto-Shutdown> Enter the Required time as per your requirement>Click save.

If you require notification when VM is about to be shutdown you can enable Notification by clicking Yes under send notification. You have 2 options for notification – Webhook URL and Email.

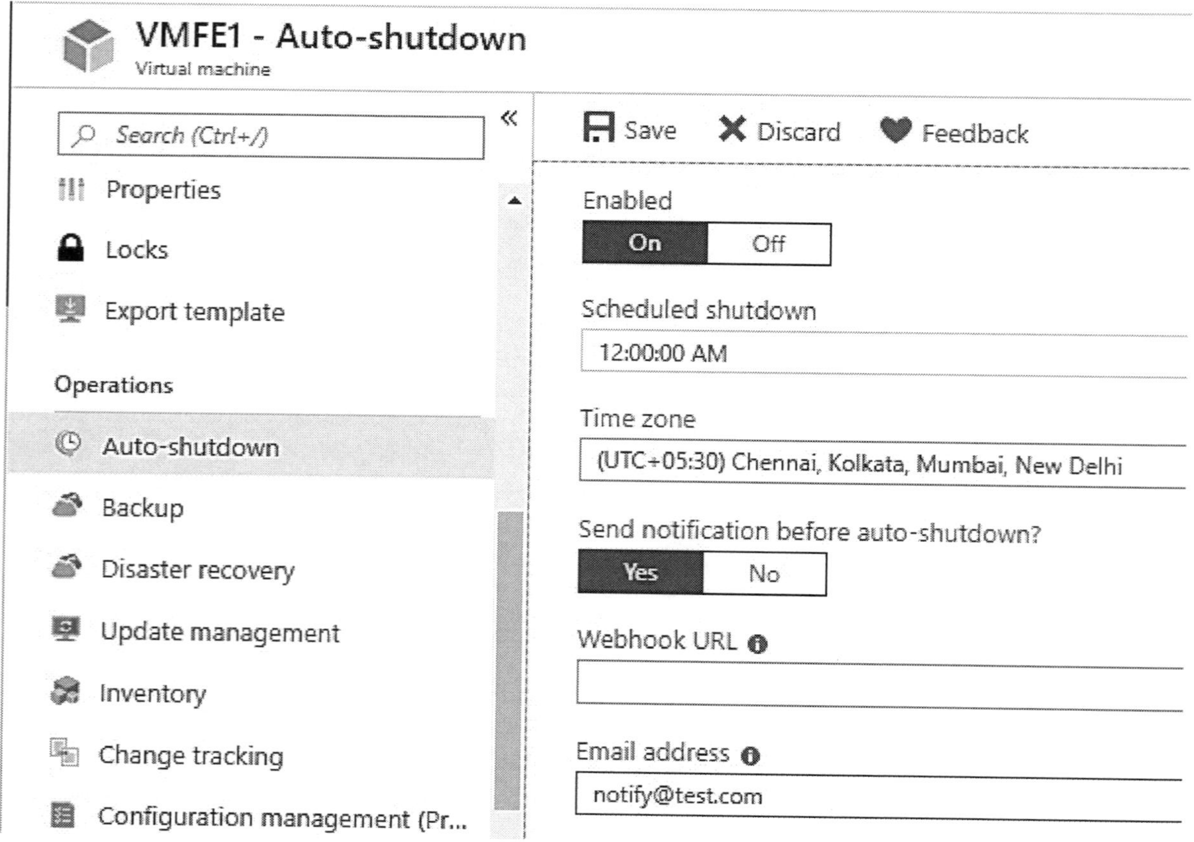

Reset Password

If you have forgotten the administrator password of Azure Virtual machine you can reset it from Azure Portal.

Exercise 50: Reset Password

Go to VM VMFE1 Dashboard> Click Reset Password in left pane>In right pane select reset password button, enter username, password and click update.

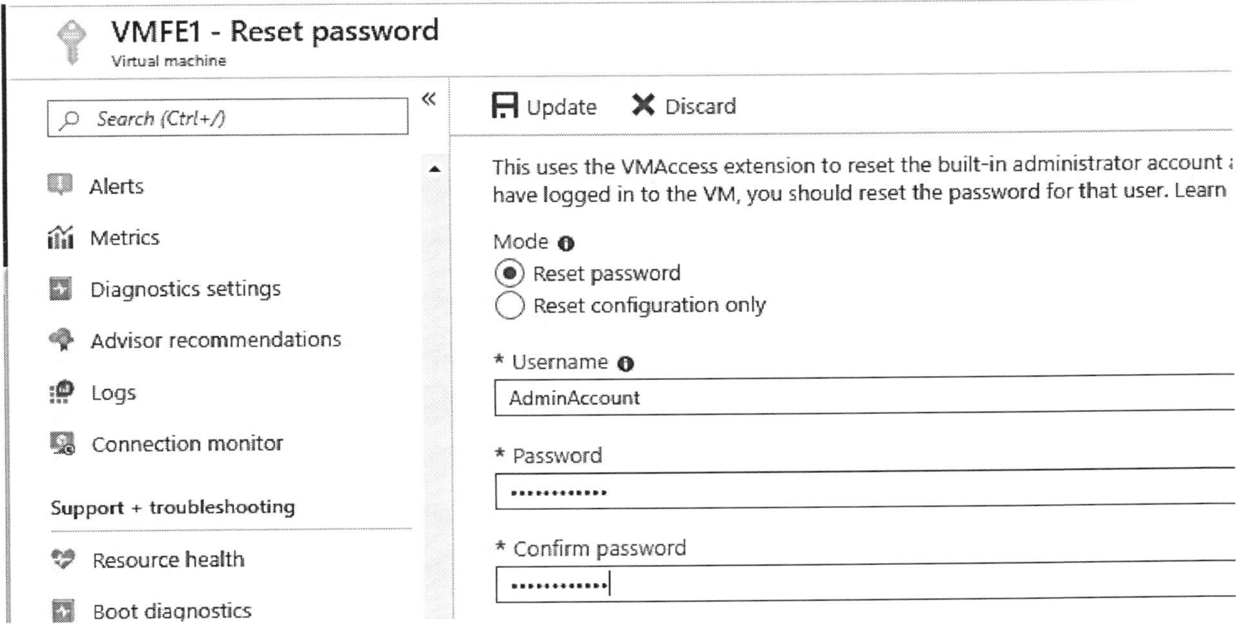

Redeploy VM

With Redeploy options you can migrate Azure VM to a new Azure host. During redeployment VM will be restarted and you will lose any data on the temporary drive. While the redeployment is in progress, the VM will be unavailable.

Exercise 51: Redeploy VM

Go to VM VMFE1 dashboard> Click Redeploy in left pane>In right pane click Redeploy. Your VM will be migrated to new host.

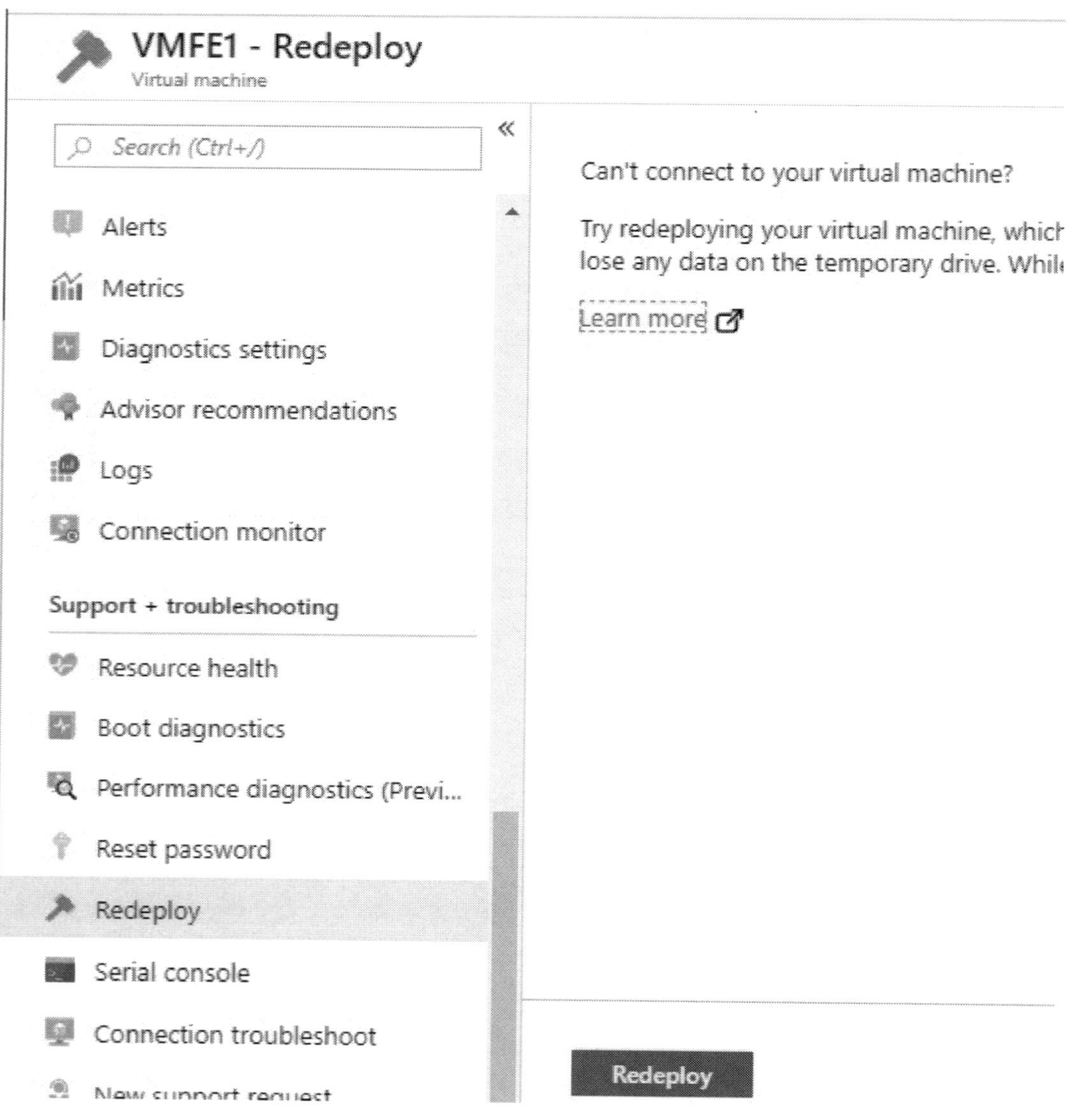

VM Backup & Restore

Chapter 10 Implement Azure Backup.

Moving Virtual Machines

Chapter 19 Azure Resource Groups, Tags and Locks.

VM Alerts, Metrics & Diagnostic Settings

Chapter 9 Analyzing & Monitoring Azure Resources in AZ-300 & AZ-301 Study & Lab Guide Part 2.

VM Update, Inventory, Change & Configuration Management

Chapter 11 Azure Automation in AZ-300 & AZ-301 Study & Lab Guide Part 2.

PowerShell DSC Extension

Chapter 11 Azure Automation in AZ-300 & AZ-301 Study & Lab Guide Part 2.

ARM Template

Chapter 12 Azure Resource Manager (ARM) Template in AZ-300 & AZ-301 Study & Lab Guide Part 2.

Virtual Machine Limits

Resource	Default Limit	Max Limit
VMs per subscription	25000 Per Region	25000 Per Region
VM total cores per subscription	20/Region	Contact Support
VM per series (Dv2, F, etc.) cores per subscription	20/Region	Contact Support
Virtual machines per Availability Set (AS)	**200**	**200**

Design Nugget: If you want to get the best performance for your VMs, you should limit the number of data disks to 2 disks per vCPU.
Note 1: Virtual Machines with letter **s** in its size designation support both Standard Storage and Premium Storage.
Note 2: MS recommends the latest generation VMs be used where possible.

Virtual Machine Compute Pricing

Virtual Machine Compute pricing includes cost of compute instance, Operating System & Temporary Storage on the host. OS Disk Storage and Data Disk Storage cost is separate. IP addressing Cost is separate.

Payment options for Virtual Machines

Pay as you go (PAYG): Pay for compute capacity by the second, with no long-term commitment or upfront payments. Increase or decrease compute capacity on demand. Start or stop at any time and only pay for what you use.

Reserved Virtual Machine Instances: An Azure Reserved Virtual Machine Instance is an advanced purchase of a Virtual Machine for **one** or **three** years in a specified region. The commitment is made up front, and in return, you get between (20% - 65%) price savings compared to pay as you go pricing. Reserved VM Instances are flexible and can easily be exchanged or returned. **You get Maximum price saving when you purchase 3 years reserved instance of M Series VM.**

Pay as you go	Reserved Virtual Machine Instances
Users who prefer the low cost and flexibility of Azure Virtual Machines.	Applications with steady-state usage.
Applications with short-term, spiky, or unpredictable workloads that cannot be interrupted.	Customers who want budget predictability.
Applications being developed or tested on Azure Virtual Machines for the first time.	Customers who can commit to using a Virtual Machine over a one or three-year term to reduce computing costs.

Azure Hybrid Benefit

PAYG and Reserved Virtual Machine payment options can be combined with Azure Hybrid Benefit for additional saving. Use your on-premises Windows Server licenses with Software Assurance to cover the cost of the OS (on up to two virtual machines!), while you just pay for base compute costs. **You can save upto 80% when Azure Hybrid Benefit is combined with 3 Years Reserved Instance.**

Important Points

Note 1: All Pricing for Azure VMs shown in following pages are with Windows OS.
Note 2: I am just showing Pricing for Dv3 and DSv3 VMs only.
Note 3: Please refer to Virtual Machine Series at the start of the chapter. This topic is very important from AZ-301 point of view.
Note 4: MS recommends the latest generation VMs be used.

General Purpose Dv3 and DSv3 Series Pricing (PAYG)

Dv3 and DSv3 are latest generation of Virtual Machines which offer hyper threading technology. In Dv3 and DSv3 VMs there is shift from physical cores to Virtual CPU. These latest series VMs allow nested virtualization when running Windows Server 2016.

The new Hyper-Threaded VM sizes will be priced up to 28% lower than the previous Dv2 sizes.

Dv3 VM sizes offer a good balance of memory to vCPU performance, with up to 64 vCPU's and 256GB of RAM.

Dsv3-series sizes are based on the 2.3 GHz Intel XEON E5-2673 **v4 (Broadwell) processor** and can achieve 3.5GHz with Intel Turbo Boost Technology 2.0.

Dv3 Series

Size	vCPU	Memory	Max NICs	Temp Storage SSD	Max Data Disks	Max IOPS	Price/ hour
D2 v3	2	8	2	50 GB	4	4X500	$0.188
D4 v3	4	16	2	100 GB	8	8X500	$0.376
D8 v3	8	32	4	200 GB	16	16X500	$0.752
D16 v3	16	64	8	400 GB	32	32X500	$1.504
D32 v3	32	128	8	800 GB	32	32X500	$3.008
D64 v3	64	256	8	1600 GB	32	32X500	$6.016

DSv3 Series (Premium SSD Support)

Size	vCPU	Memory	Max NICs	Temp Storage SSD	Max Data Disks	Max IOPS/MBps Supported	Price/ hour
D2s v3	2	8	2	50 GB	4	3200/48	$0.188
D4s v3	4	16	2	100 GB	8	6400/96	$0.376
D8s v3	8	32	4	200 GB	16	12800/192	$0.752
D16s v3	16	64	8	400 GB	32	25600/384	$1.504
D32s v3	32	128	8	800 GB	32	51200/768	$3.008
D64s v3	64	256	8	1600 GB	32	80000/1200	$6.016

Dv3Pricing (PAYG, Reserved Instance & Reserved Instance+ Hybrid)

Dv3 Series Sizes

Size	Price/ hour	ONE YEAR RESERVED/HOUR (% SAVINGS)	THREE YEAR RESERVED/HOUR (% SAVINGS)	3 YEAR RESERVED WITH AZURE HYBRID BENEFIT (% SAVINGS)
D2 v3	$0.188	$0.1492 (~21%)	$0.1289 (~31%)	$0.0369 (~80%)
D4 v3	$0.376	$0.2985 (~21%)	$0.2578 (~31%)	$0.0738 (~80%)
D8 v3	$0.752	$0.597 (~21%)	$0.5154 (~31%)	$0.1474 (~80%)
D16 v3	$1.504	$1.1940 (~21%)	$1.0308 (~31%)	$0.2948 (~80%)
D32 v3	$3.008	$2.3880 (~21%)	$2.0616 (~31%)	$0.5896 (~80%)
D64 v3	$6.016	$4.7760(~21%)	$4.1232 (~31%)	$1.1792 (~80%)

DSv3 Series (Premium SSD Support)

Size	Price/ hour	ONE YEAR RESERVED/HOUR (% SAVINGS)	THREE YEAR RESERVED (% SAVINGS)	3 YEAR RESERVED WITH AZURE HYBRID BENEFIT (% SAVINGS)
D2s v3	$0.188	$0.1492 (~21%)	$0.1289 (~31%)	$0.0369 (~80%)
D4s v3	$0.376	$0.2985 (~21%)	$0.2578 (~31%)	$0.0738 (~80%)
D8s v3	$0.752	$0.597 (~21%)	$0.5154 (~31%)	$0.1474 (~80%)
D16s v3	$1.504	$1.1940 (~21%)	$1.0308 (~31%)	$0.2948 (~80%)
D32s v3	$3.008	$2.3880 (~21%)	$2.0616 (~31%)	$0.5896 (~80%)
D64s v3	$6.016	$4.7760(~21%)	$4.1232 (~31%)	$1.1792 (~80%)

Note: Figure in bracket shows percentage saving with respect to Pay as you go (PAYG) model.

How to Save on Virtual Machine Compute Cost

You can save Virtual Machine Compute Cost in following ways:

1. Combine Pay as you go (PAYG) with Azure Hybrid Benefit.
2. Use 1 Year Reserved Instance.
3. Use 3 Year Reserved Instance.
4. Combine 1 Year Reserved Instance with Azure Hybrid Benefit.
5. Combine 3 Year Reserved Instance with Azure Hybrid Benefit.
6. Use Low Priority VMs.

Azure Hybrid Benefit

PAYG and Reserved Instance can be combined with Azure Hybrid Benefit for additional saving. Use your on-premises Windows Server licenses with Software Assurance to cover the cost of the OS (on up to two virtual machines!), while you just pay for base compute costs. **You can save upto 80% when Azure Hybrid Benefit is combined with 3 Years Reserved Instance.**

Reserved Virtual Machine Instances

An Azure Reserved Virtual Machine Instance is an advanced purchase of a Virtual Machine for **one** or **three** years in a specified region. The commitment is made up front, and in return, you get between (20% -65%) price savings compared to pay as you go pricing.

Low Priority VMs

Low Priority VMs are available at lower cost than normal VMs and are allocated from surplus or spare Azure compute capacity.

The advantage of Low Priority VM is that it reduce the costs of running workloads or allow much more work to be performed at a greater scale for the same cost. The disadvantage of Low Priority VM is that Azure can take back Low priority VMs when spare compute capacity decreases.

Low Priority VMs are currently available for Azure Batch and Virtual Machine Scale Set (VMSS).

Virtual Machine Disk Pricing

Note 1: Managed disk is charged for the Provisioned size where as Unmanaged Disk is charged for the Storage used.
Note 2: Managed Disk only supports LRS for replication.
Note 3: Managed Disk option takes care of storage account creation and management. You need not create Storage Account for Managed Disk.

Premium SSD Managed Disk Pricing

Premium SSD Managed Disks are high performance Solid State Drive (SSD) based Storage designed to support I/O intensive workloads with significantly high throughput and low latency.

Virtual Machines with letter **s** in its size designation support Premium Storage. Premium SSD Managed Disks are supported by DS-series, DSv2-series, FS-series, and GS-series VM sizes which are specifically targeted for Premium SSD Managed Disks.

Total Cost of Premium Disk depends upon following 2 factors:

1. Premium SSD Managed Disk Cost.
2. Number of outbound data transfers.

	Disk Size	**Price/Month**	**IOP/Disk**	**THROUGHPUT/DISK**
P4	32 GB	$4.81	120	25 MB/second
P6	64 GB	$9.29	240	50 MB/second
P10	128 GB	$17.92	500	100 MB/second
P15	256 GB	$34.56	1100	125 MB/second
P20	512 GB	$66.56	2300	150 MB/second
P30	1 TB	$122.88	5000	200 MB/second
P40	2 TB	$235.52	7500	250 MB/second
P50	4 TB	$450.56	7500	250 MB/second
P60	8 TB	$860.16	16000	500 MB/second
P70	16 TB	$1,638.40	18000	750 MB/second
P80	32 TB	$3,276.80	20000	900 MB/second

Standard SSD Managed Disk Pricing

Standard SSD Managed Disk is a low-cost SSD offering that are optimized for test and entry-level production workloads requiring consistent latency. Standard SSD Managed Disks deliver lower latency compared to Standard HDDs, while improving reliability and scalability for your applications, and are **available with all Azure VM sizes.**

Total Cost of Standard SSD Disk depends upon following 3 factors:

1. Premium SSD Managed Disk Cost.
2. Number of outbound data transfers.
3. Number of transactions.

	Disk Size	**Price/Month**	**IOP/Disk**	**THROUGHPUT/DISK**
E4	32 GB	$2.40	120	25 MB/second
E6	64 GB	$4.80	240	50 MB/second
E10	128 GB	$9.60	500	60 MB/second
E15	256 GB	$19.20	500	60 MB/second
E20	512 GB	$38.40	500	60 MB/second
E30	1 TB	$76.80	500	60 MB/second
E40	2 TB	$153.60	500	60 MB/second
E50	4 TB	$307.20	500	60 MB/second
E60	8 TB	$614.40	2000	400 MB/second
E70	16 TB	$1,228.80	4000	600 MB/second
E80	32 TB	$2,457.60	6000	750 MB/second

Standard HDD Managed Disk Pricing

Standard HDD Managed Disks use Hard Disk Drive (HDD) based Storage media. They are best suited for dev/test and other infrequent access workloads that are less sensitive to performance variability.

Total Cost of Standard HDD depends upon following 3 factors:

1. Managed Disk Cost.
2. Number of outbound data transfers.
3. Number of transactions.

	Disk Size	Price/Month	IOP/Disk	THROUGHPUT/DISK
S4	32 GB	$1.54	500	60 MB/second
S6	64 GB	$3.01	500	60 MB/second
S10	128 GB	$5.89	500	60 MB/second
S15	256 GB	$11.33	500	60 MB/second
S20	512 GB	$21.76	500	60 MB/second
S30	1 TB	$40.96	500	60 MB/second
S40	2 TB	$77.83	500	60 MB/second
S50	4 TB	$143.36	500	60 MB/second
S60	8 TB	$262.14	1300	300 MB/second
S70	16 TB	$524.29	2000	500 MB/second
S80	32 TB	$1,048.58	2000	550 MB/second

Ultra SSD Managed Disk Pricing

Ultra Disk is high performance Solid State Drive (SSD) with configurable performance attributes that provides the lowest latency and consistent high IOPS/throughput. Ultra Disk offers unprecedented and extremely scalable performance with sub-millisecond latency. As a customer you can start small on IOPS and throughput and adjust your performance as your workload becomes more IO intensive.

They are best suited for IO-intensive workloads such as SAP HANA, top tier databases (for example, SQL, Oracle), and other transaction-heavy workloads.

Total Cost of Ultra SSD depends upon following 3 factors:

Provisioned Size.
Provisioned IOPS.
Provisioned Throughput.

Ultra disk is billed accordingly on an hourly basis. For example, if you provisioned a 200 GiB Ultra Disk, with 20,000 IOPS and 1,000 MB/second and deleted it after 20 hours, it will map to the disk size offer of 256 GiB and you'll be billed for the 256 GiB, 20,000 IOPS and 1,000 MB/second for 20 hours. This is regardless of the amount of actual data and number of IOs written to the disk.

Ultra Disk GA pricing will be effective starting October 1, 2019.

Disk Size (GiB)	4	8	16	32	64	128	256	512
IOPS Range	1200	2400	4800	9600	19200	38400	76800	160000
Throughput Range (MB/s)	300	600	1200	2000	2000	2000	2000	2000

Premium SSD Unmanaged Disk Pricing

Premium SSD Unmanaged Disks are high performance Solid State Drive (SSD) based Storage designed to support I/O intensive workloads with significantly high throughput and low latency.

Premium SSD Unmanaged Disks require Storage Account.

Virtual Machines with letter **s** in its size designation support Premium Storage.

Total Cost of Premium Disk depends upon following 2 factors:

1. Premium SSD Managed Disk Cost.
2. Number of outbound data transfers.

	Disk Size	Price/Month	IOP/Disk	THROUGHPUT/DISK
P10	128 GB	$17.92	500	100 MB/second
P20	512 GB	$66.56	2300	150 MB/second
P30	1 TB	$122.88	5000	200 MB/second
P40	2 TB	$235.52	7500	250 MB/second
P50	4 TB	$450.56	7500	250 MB/second
P60	8 TB	$860.16	7500	250 MB/second

Note 1: Pricing of Premium SSD Managed and Unmanaged Disks are same.
Note 2: Specs of Premium SSD Managed and Unmanaged Disks are same except for P60. Managed P60 has IOPS of 16000 & Throughput of 500 MB/second whereas Unmanaged P60 has IOPS of 7500 & Throughput of 250 MB/second. This is according to Azure Docs.

Standard HDD Unmanaged Disk Pricing

Standard HDD Managed Disks use Hard Disk Drive (HDD) based Storage media. They are best suited for dev/test and other infrequent access workloads that are less sensitive to performance variability.

Standard HDD Unmanaged Disk requires Storage Account.

Total Cost of Standard HDD Unmanaged Disk depends upon following 4 factors:

1. Ammount of Storage Used.
2. Operations prices for Page Blobs used as Unmanaged Disks. Any type of operation against against Unmanaged Disks is counted as a transaction including reads, writes, and deletes.
3. Data transfer prices ocured due to replication
4. Outbound data transfers cost.

LRS	GRS	RA-GRS
$0.045 per GB	$0.06 per GB	$0.075 per GB

There is a charge $0.00036 per 10,000 transactions for Standard Page Blobs attached to VM and used as Unmanaged Disks. Any type of operation against against Unmanaged Disks is counted as a transaction including reads, writes, and deletes.

Design Nugget: The largest page blob size that Azure supports is 8 TiB (8,191 GiB). **The maximum page blob size when attached to a VM as data or operating system disks is 4 TiB (4,095 GiB).**

Chapter 5 Azure Load Balancer

This Chapter covers following Topic Lessons

- Load Balancers in Azure
- Comparing Different Types of Azure Load Balancers
- Azure Load Balancer
- Internet or Public Facing Load Balancer
- Internal load Balancer
- Azure Load Balancer Types
- Additional Features in Standard Load Balancer
- Traffic Distribution Mode for Azure Load Balancer
- Load Balancer Health Probes
- Idle timeout settings for Azure Basic Load Balancer
- Outbound connections of Load Balanced VMs
- Port Forwarding in Azure Load Balancer
- Azure Basic Load Balancer Pricing
- Azure Standard Load Balancer Pricing

This Chapter covers following Lab Exercises

- Create Internet facing Azure Load Balancer
- Create Backend Address Pool and Add Endpoints (VMs)
- Create Health Probe
- Create Load Balancer Rule
- Access the Websites on Load Balanced VMs

Chapter Topology

In this chapter we will add Azure Load Balancer to the topology. Virtual Machine **VMFE1 and VMFE2** will be added as an endpoint to the Azure Load Balancer. We will then access default website on VMFE1 and Custom Website on VMFE2 using public IP of the Azure Load Balancers.

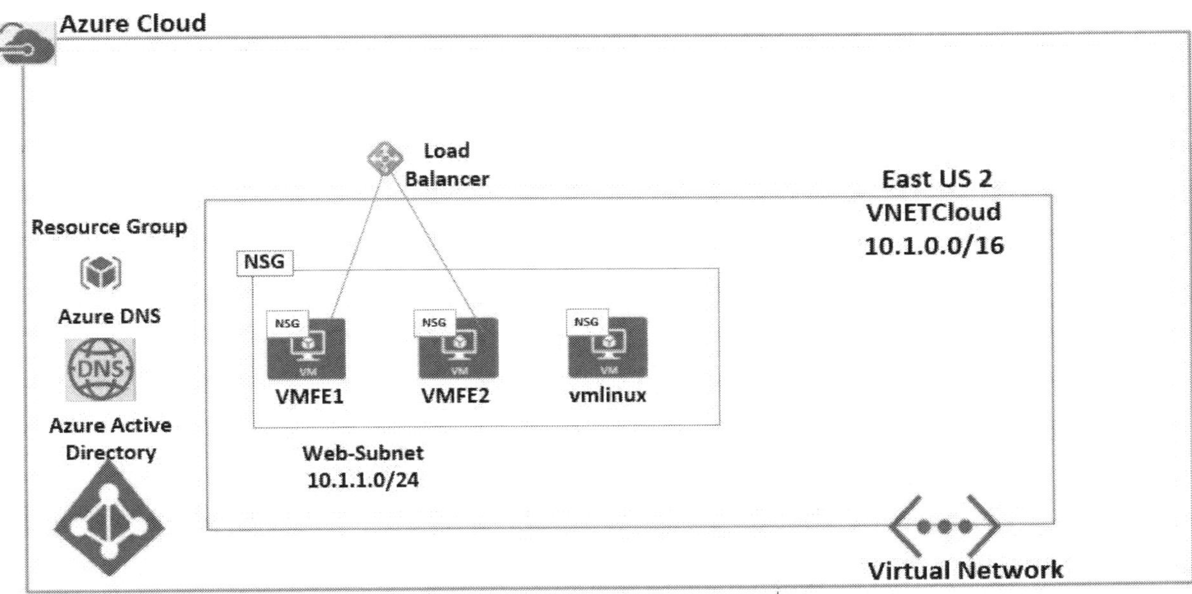

Note: Virtual Machines VMFE1 & VMFE2 were created in Exercise 25 & Exercise 33 respectively in Chapter 4.

Load Balancers in Azure

Load balancing distributes traffic across multiple computing resources.

Microsoft Azure offers three types of load Balancers: Azure Load Balancer, Application Gateway & Traffic Manager.

Azure Load Balancer is a Layer 4 (TCP, UDP) load balancer that distributes incoming traffic among healthy instances defined in a load-balanced set.

Application Gateway works at the application layer (Layer 7). Application Gateway deals with web traffic only (HTTP/HTTPS/WebSocket). It acts as a reverse-proxy service, terminating the client connection and forwarding requests to back-end endpoints.

Traffic Manager works at the DNS level. It uses DNS responses to direct end-user traffic to globally distributed endpoints. Clients then connect to those endpoints directly.

Comparing Different Types of Azure Load Balancers

Feature	Load Balancer	Application Gateway	Traffic Manager
Working	Transport level (Layer 4)	Application level (Layer 7)	DNS level
Application protocols supported	Any	HTTP, HTTPS, and WebSockets	Any (An HTTP endpoint is required for endpoint monitoring)
Endpoints	Azure VMs and Cloud Services role instances	Any Azure internal IP address, public internet IP address, Azure VM, or Azure Cloud Service	Azure VMs, Cloud Services, Azure Web Apps, and external endpoints
Configuration Modes	Can be used for both Internet facing and internal (VNET) applications	Can be used for both Internet facing and internal (VNET) applications	Only supports Internet-facing applications
Endpoint Monitoring	Supported via probes	Supported via probes	Supported via HTTP/HTTPS GET

Azure Load Balancer

Azure Load Balancer is a managed Layer 4 (TCP, UDP) load balancer that distributes incoming traffic among healthy instances of services defined in a load-balanced set.

Azure Load Balancer Types: Basic & Standard.

Azure Load Balancer can be configured as Internet/Public Facing Load Balancer or Internal Load Balancer.

Internet or Public Facing Load Balancer

Internet or Public Facing Load Balancer distributes incoming Internet traffic to virtual machines. Figure below show shows internet traffic being distributed between Virtual Machines. LB has public IP and DNS name.

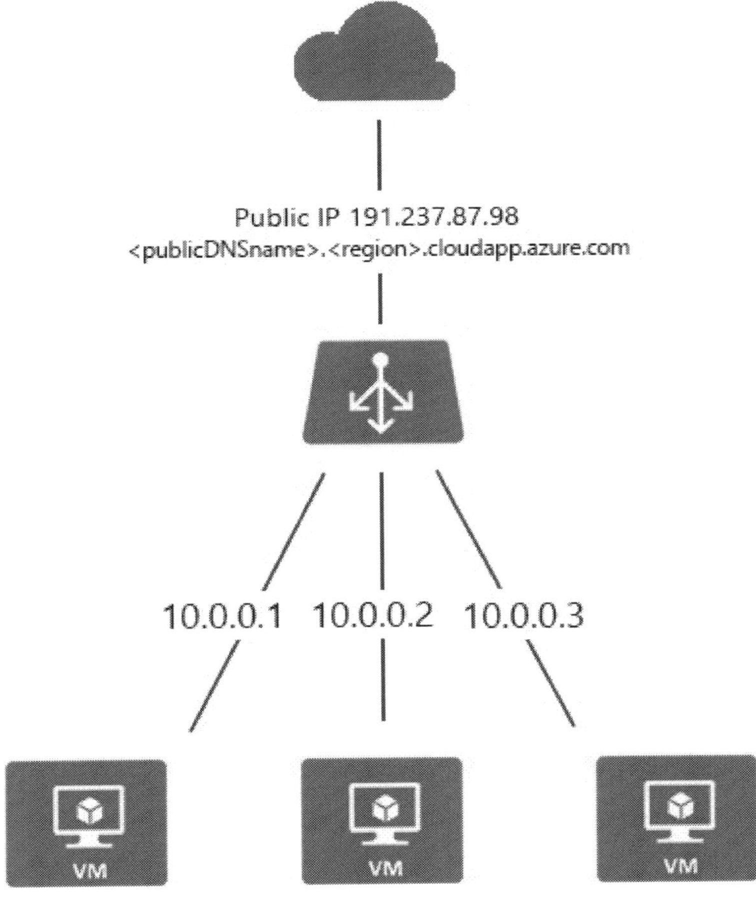

Internal load Balancer

In Multi-Tier applications, Internal Load Balancer distributes traffic coming from Internet/Web tier to virtual Machines which are in back-end tiers and are not Internet-facing.

Internal Load Balancers can also distribute traffic coming from application tier which is not internet facing to Database tier which is also not internet facing.

An internal load balancer is configured in a virtual network.

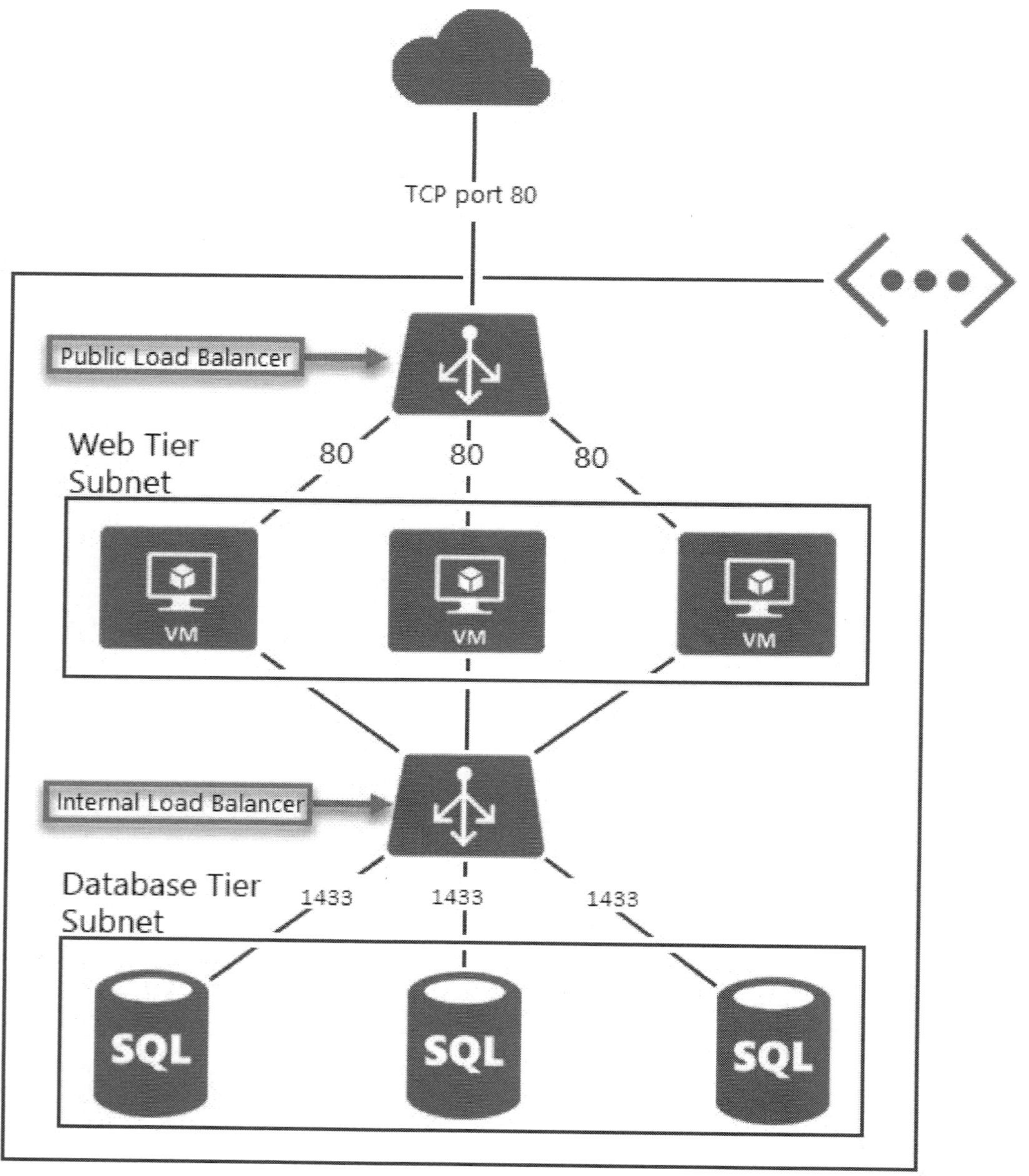

Important Point: Internal Load Balancer can also direct traffic to on-premises VM which are connected to Azure through VPN gateway.

An internal Load Balancer enables the following types of load balancing:

1. **Within a virtual network**: Load balancing from VMs in the virtual network to a set of VMs that reside within the same virtual network.
2. **For a cross-premises virtual network**: Load balancing from on-premises computers to a set of VMs that reside within the same virtual network.
3. **For multi-tier applications**: Load balancing for internet-facing multi-tier applications where the backend tiers are not internet-facing. The backend tiers require traffic load-balancing from the internet-facing tier (see the figure in previous page).

Azure Load Balancer Types

Azure Load Balancer comes in 2 types: **Basic & Standard**. Basic Load Balancer is free of charge whereas Standard Load Balancer is charged.

Standard includes all the functionality of Basic Load Balancer and provides additional functionalities.

Azure Load Balancer Standard and Public IP Standard together enable you to provide additional capabilities such as multi-zone architectures, Low latency, high throughput, and scalability for millions of flows for all TCP and UDP applications.

Additional Features in Standard Load Balancer

Enterprise scale: With Standard Load Balance you can design Virtual Data Center which can support up to 1000 Virtual Machine instances.

Cross-zone load balancing: With Standard Load Balancer you can load balance Virtual Machines in backend pool spread across Availability Zones. Note that Availability Zones are also in Preview.

Resilient virtual IPs (VIP): A single front-end IP address assigned to Standard Load Balancer is automatically zone-redundant. Zone-redundancy in Azure does not require multiple IP addresses and DNS records.

Improved Monitoring: Standard Load Balancer is integrated with Azure Monitor (Preview) which provides new metrics for improved monitoring. Monitor your data from front-end to VM, endpoint health probes, for TCP connection attempts, and to outbound connections. New Metrics include VIP Availability, DIP Availability, SYN Packets, SNAT connections, Byte counters and Packets counters.

New SNAT: Load Balancer Standard provides outbound connections for VMs using new port-masquerading Source Network Address Translation (SNAT) model that provides greater resiliency and scale. When outbound connections are used with a zone-redundant front-end, the connections are also zone-redundant and SNAT port allocations survive zone failure.

Traffic Distribution Mode for Azure Load Balancer

Traffic Distribution mode determines how Load Balancer will distribute client traffic to load balanced set.

Traffic Distribution mode is selected in Load Balancing Rules.

Hash-based distribution mode

It uses 5 tuple hash of source IP, source port, destination IP, destination port, protocol type to map client traffic to available load balanced servers.

It provides stickiness only within a transport session. Packets in the same session will be directed to the same datacenter IP (DIP) instance behind the load balanced endpoint.

When the client starts a new session from the same source IP, the source port changes and causes the traffic to go to a different DIP endpoint.

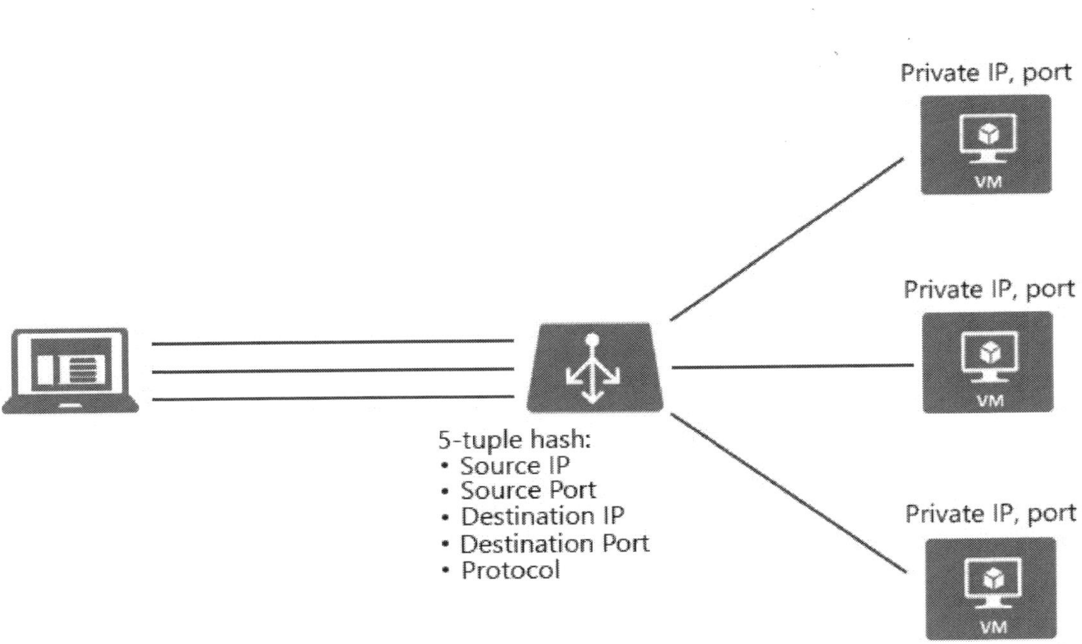

Source IP affinity distribution mode

Source IP Affinity also known as session affinity or client IP affinity use a 2-tuple (Source IP, Destination IP) or 3-tuple (Source IP, Destination IP, Protocol) to map traffic to the available servers.

By using Source IP affinity, connection initiated from the same client IP goes to the same datacenter IP (DIP) instance.

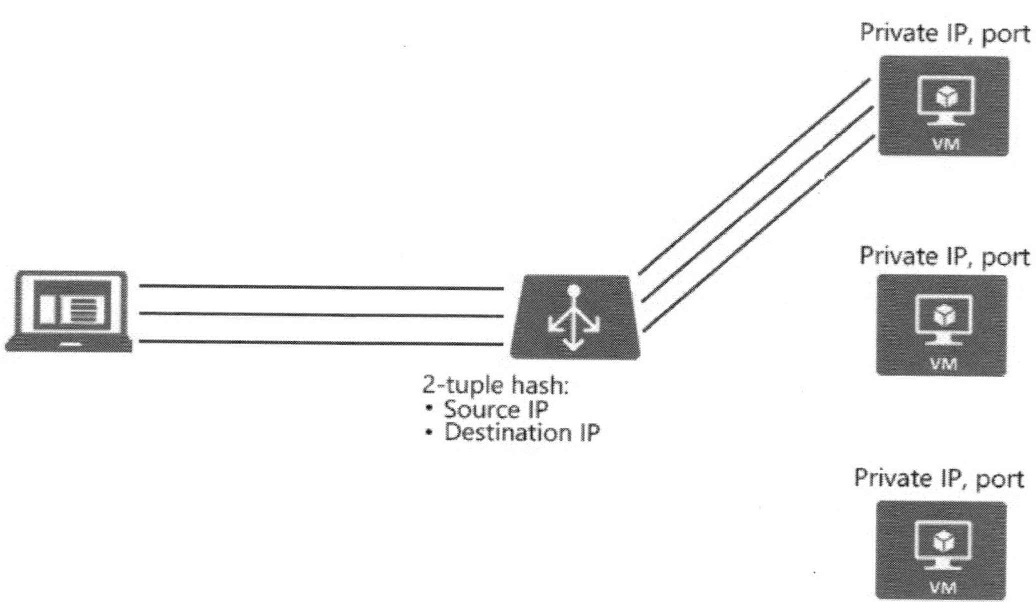

Source IP Affinity distribution method provides session affinity based on Client IP address.

Source IP Affinity distribution method can result in uneven traffic distribution if clients are coming behind a proxy.

Load Balancer Health Probes

Load Balancer uses health probes to determine the health of instances in the backend pool.

When a probe fails to respond, the Load Balancer stops sending new connections to the unhealthy instances. Existing connections are not affected, and they continue until the application terminates the flow, an idle timeout occurs, or the VM is shut down.

Health Probes timeout and interval values

Timeout and interval values are used to determine whether an instance is marked as up or down.

Interval: Interval is the number of seconds between probe attempts.
Unhealthy threshold: This value is the number of consecutive probe failures that occur before a VM is considered unhealthy.

Timeout and interval values are specified when you create Health Probes.

Health Probe Types

Azure Load Balance supports 3 probes types depending on the Load Balancer type.

	Standard Load Balancer	Basic Load Balancer
Probe Types	TCP, HTTP & HTTPS	TCP & HTTP

TCP Probe

TCP probes initiate a connection by performing a three-way open TCP handshake with the defined port.

The minimum probe interval is 5 seconds and the minimum number of unhealthy responses is 2. You can change these values when you are creating Health Probes.

TCP probe Failure

1. The TCP listener on the instance doesn't respond at all during the timeout period. A probe is marked down based on the number of failed probe requests, which were configured to go unanswered before marking down the probe.
2. The probe receives a TCP reset from the instance.

HTTP/HTTPS Probe

HTTP and HTTPS probes build on the TCP probe and issue an HTTP GET request with the specified path. HTTPS probe is same as HTTP probe with the addition of a Transport Layer Security (TLS, formerly known as SSL) wrapper.

HTTP / HTTPS probes can also be used if you want to implement your own logic to remove instances from load balancer rotation. For example, you might decide to remove an instance if it's above 90% CPU and return a non-200 HTTP status.

The health probe is marked up when the instance responds with an HTTP status 200 within the timeout period.

HTTP / HTTPS probe fails when:

1. Probe endpoint returns an HTTP response code other than 200 (for example, 403, 404, or 500). This will mark down the health probe immediately.
2. Probe endpoint doesn't respond at all during the 31-second timeout period. Multiple probe requests might go unanswered before the probe gets marked as not running and until the sum of all timeout intervals has been reached.
3. Probe endpoint closes the connection via a TCP reset.

Idle timeout settings for Azure Basic Load Balancer

In its default configuration, Azure Load Balancer has an idle timeout setting of 4 minutes. If a period of inactivity is longer than the timeout value, there's no guarantee that the TCP or HTTP session is maintained between the client and your cloud service.

A common practice is to use a TCP keep-alive so that the connection is active for a longer period. With keep-alive enabled, packets are sent during periods of inactivity on the connection. These keep-alive packets ensure that the idle timeout value is never reached and the connection is maintained for a long period.

Idle timeout is configured in Load Balancing Rules. TCP Timeout is configured on Virtual Machine Public IP.

Outbound connections of Load Balanced VMs

Load-balanced VM with no Instance Level Public IP address: Azure translates the private source IP address of the outbound flow to the public IP address of the public Load Balancer frontend.

Azure uses Source Network Address Translation (SNAT) to perform this function. Ephemeral ports of the Load Balancer's public IP address are used to distinguish individual flows originated by the VM. SNAT dynamically allocates ephemeral ports when outbound flows are created.

Load-balanced VM with Instance Level Public IP address (ILPIP): When an ILPIP is used, Source Network Address Translation (SNAT) is not used. The VM uses the ILPIP for all outbound flows.

Port Forwarding in Azure Load Balancer

With Port forwarding you can connect to virtual machines (VMs) in an Azure virtual network by using an Azure Load Balancer public IP address and port number.

This option is commonly used to connect to Azure VMs when Azure VMs have private IP assigned only.

Port Forwarding is enabled by Creating Load Balancer **Inbound Nat Rules** which forward traffic from a specific port of the front-end IP address to a specific port of a back-end VM.

Steps to creating Internet or Public facing Azure Basic Load Balancer

1. Create Load Balancer with **Public** option.
2. Create backend address pool and add end points (VMs) to it.
3. Create a probe for monitoring end points (VMs).
4. Create Load Balancing rules (add backend address pool & probe created in step 2 and step 3 respectively and choose session persistence method)

Steps to creating Internal Azure Basic Load Balancer

1. Create Load Balancer with **internal** option.
2. Create backend address pool and add end points to it.
3. Create a probe for monitoring end points
4. Create Load Balancing rules (add backend address pool & health probe created in step 2 and step 3 respectively and choose session persistence method).

Exercise 52: Create Internet facing Azure Load Balancer

In this Exercise we will create Basic Azure Load Balancer in Resource Group **RGCloud** and in region **East US 2**. Resource Group RGCloud was created in Exercise 1, Chapter 1.

In Azure Portal Click +Create a Resource> Networking> Load Balancer>Create Load Balancer Blade opens>Select Resource Group RGCloud, Enter a name, For Location select East US 2, For type Select Public and for SKU select Basic> For IP address select Create new and enter a name and select Dynamic> Click review + Create> After validation is passed click create.

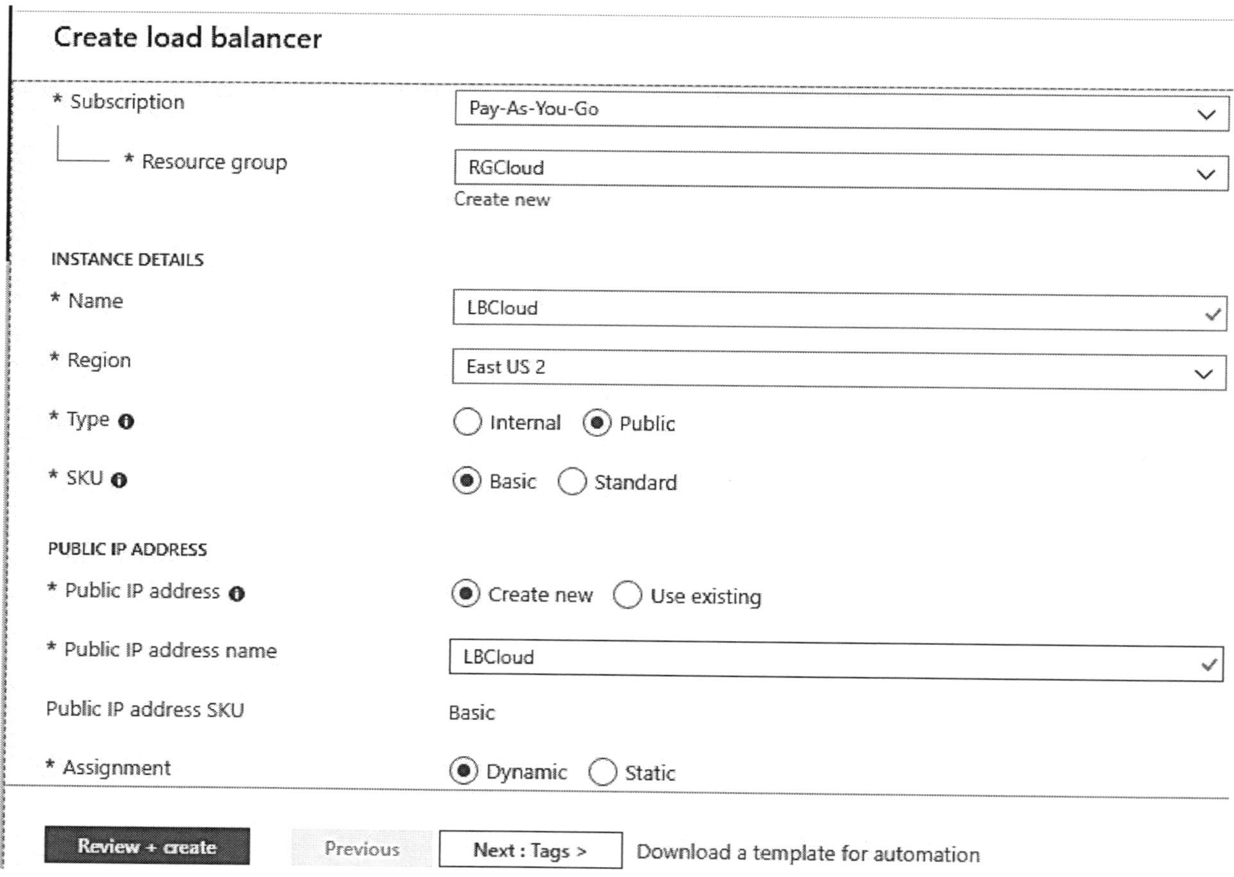

Note: We have chosen IP Address as Dynamic to save on Azure Credits.

Figure below shows the Dashboard of Load Balancer.

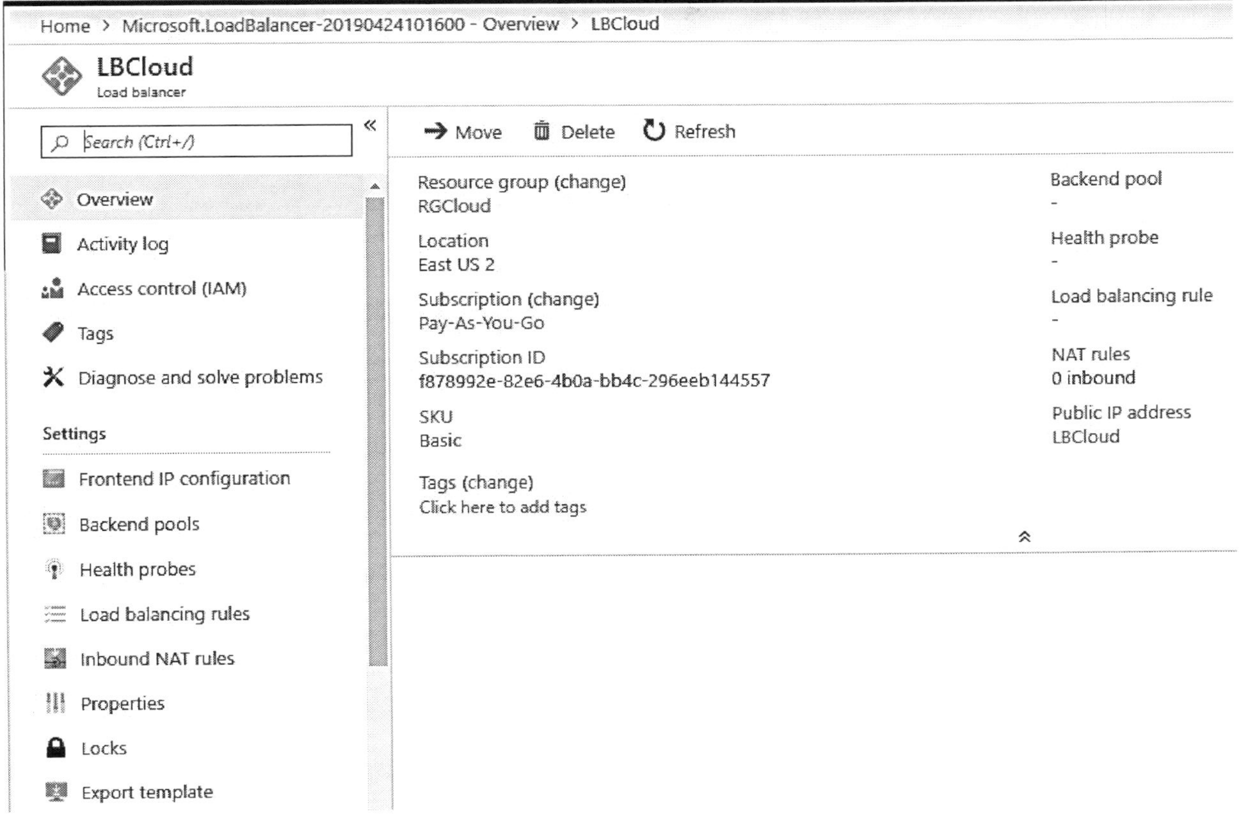

Exercise 53: Create Backend Address Pool and Add Endpoints (VMs)

Backend Address pool will include VMs (VMFE1 & VMFE2) which are to be load balanced. VMFE1 has default website and VMFE2 has Custom website. VMFE1 & VMFE2 were created in Exercise 25 & Exercise 33 in Chapter 4.

Click Backend pools in left pane of Load Balancer Dashboard> Click +Add> Add Backend pool Blade opens> Give a name> Select Availability Set from Drop Down box> In Availability Set Select ASCloud> Add Virtual Machine VMFE1 and VMFE2 by clicking +Add a target Network IP configuration>Click OK.

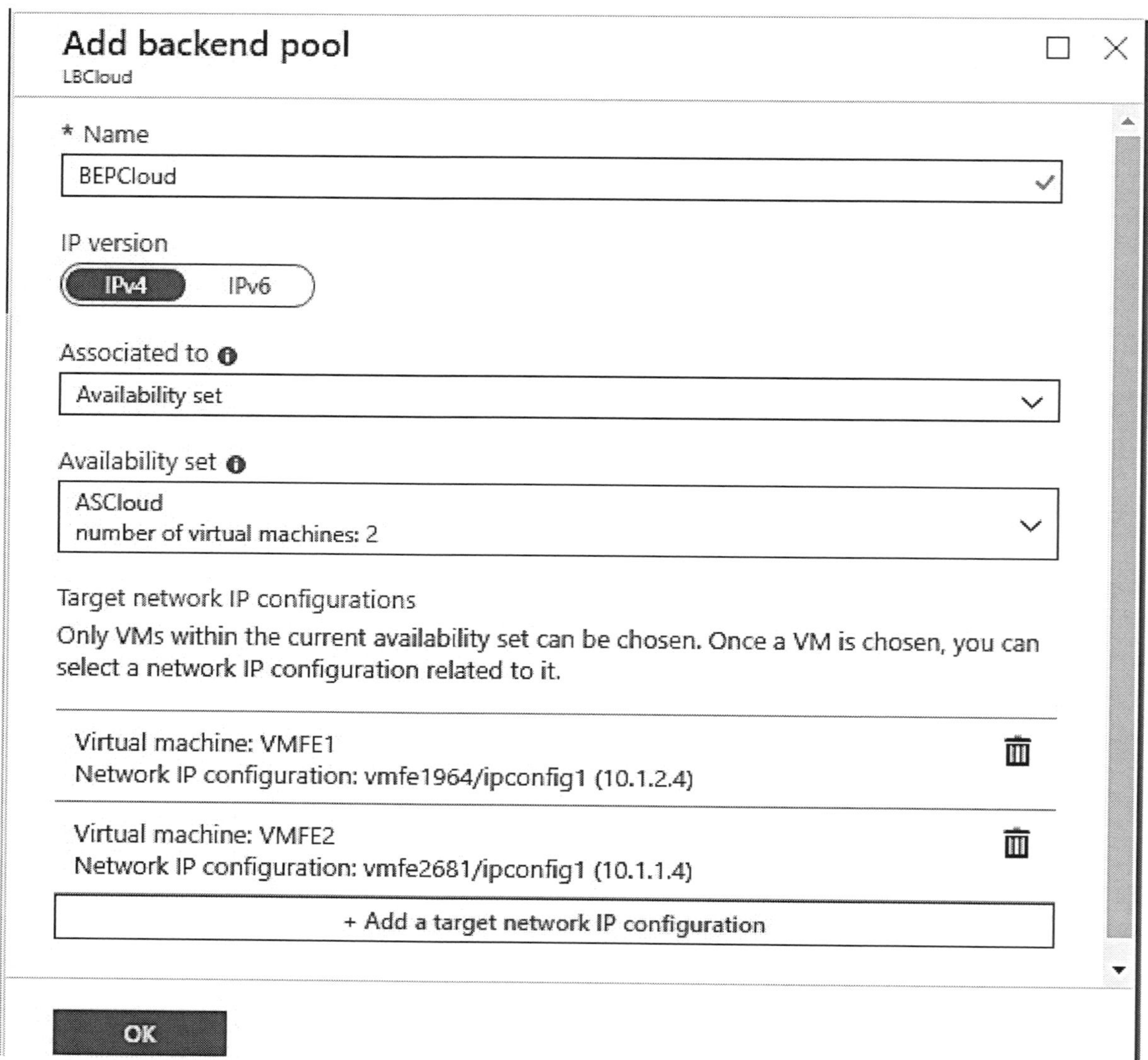

It will take 2-3 minutes to add both VMs to Backend pool. Proceed to next step after both VMs are added to the backend pool.

Exercise 54: Create Health Probe

Health probes are used to check availability of virtual machines instances in the back-end address pool. When a probe fails to respond, Load Balancer stops sending new connections to the unhealthy instance. Probe behavior depends on:

1. The number of successful probes that allow an instance to be labeled as up.
2. The number of failed probes that cause an instance to be labeled as down.
3. The timeout and frequency value set in SuccessFailCount determine whether an instance is confirmed to be running or not running.

Go to Load Balancer Dashboard>Click Health Probes in left Pane>+Add>Add health Probe blade opens>Enter a name>Select HTTP in Protocol>Click Ok.

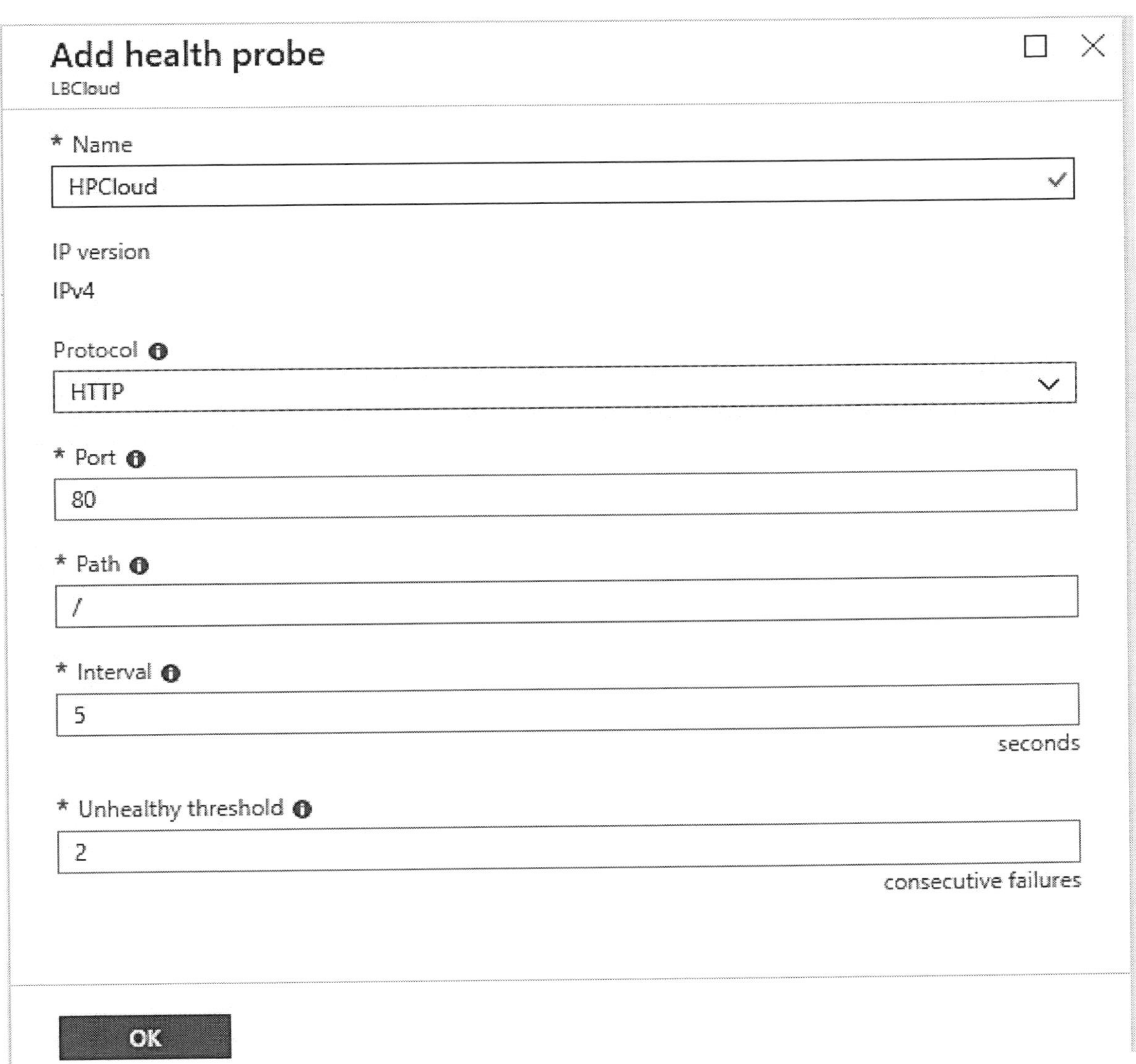

Exercise 55: Create Load Balancer Rule

Load Balancer rule defines how traffic is distributed to the VMs. You define the front-end IP configuration for the incoming traffic and the back-end IP pool to receive the traffic, along with the required source and destination port, Health probe, session persistence and TCP idle timeout.

Go to Load Balancer Dashboard and Click Load Balancing Rules in left Pane> +Add> Add load Balancing Rule blade opens>Enter a name>Select Backend Pool and health Probe creates in previous exercise>Rest Select all default values>Ok.

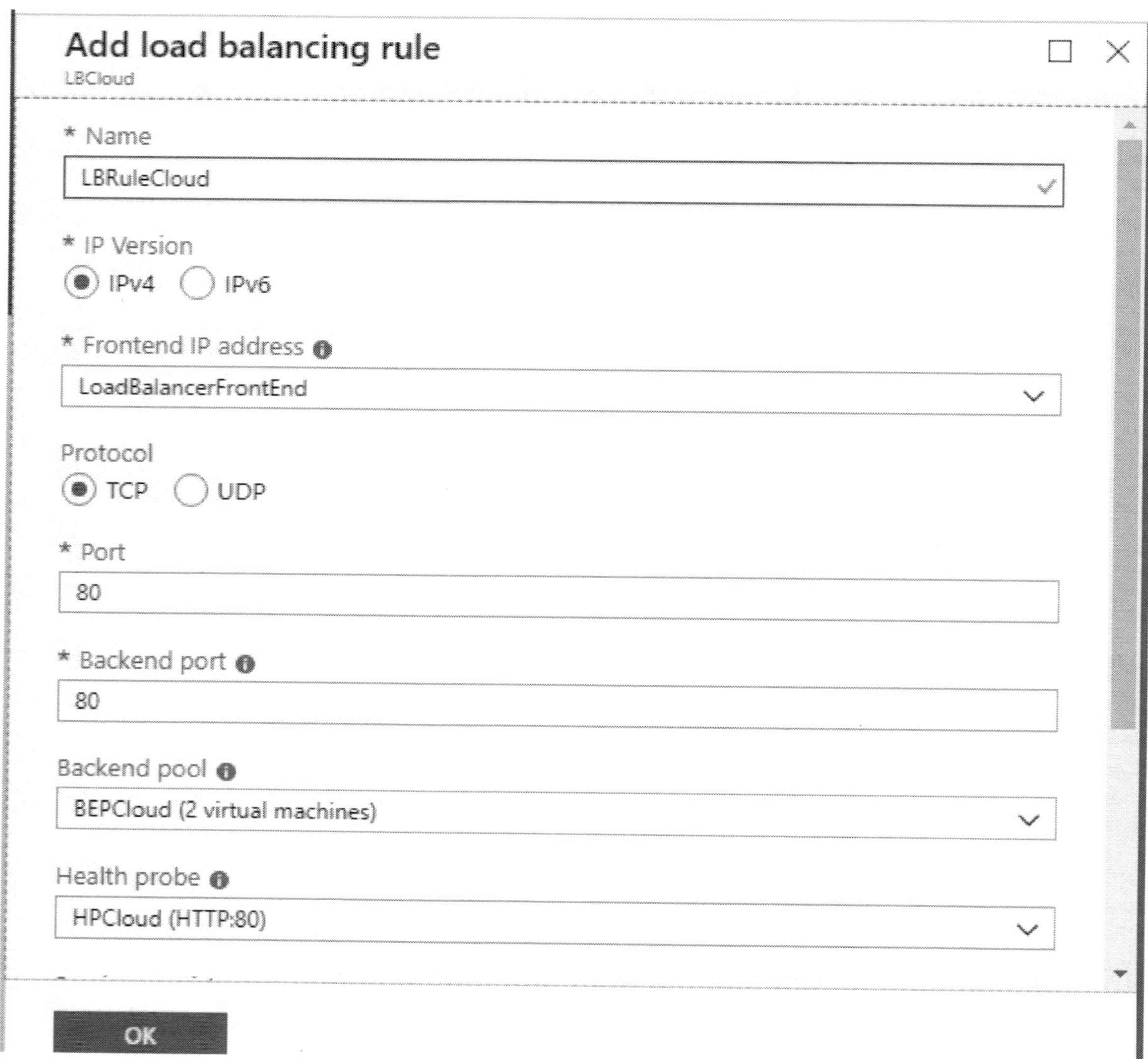

Note: There is Session Persistence and idle Timeout setting are also there which is not shown in above figure. You just need to scroll down.

Exercise 56: Access the Websites on Load Balanced VMs

1. Go to Load Balancer Dashboard>From right pane copy the Public IP Address (104.208.234.10)> Open a browser and http:// 104.208.234.10> Custom website on VMFE2 opens.

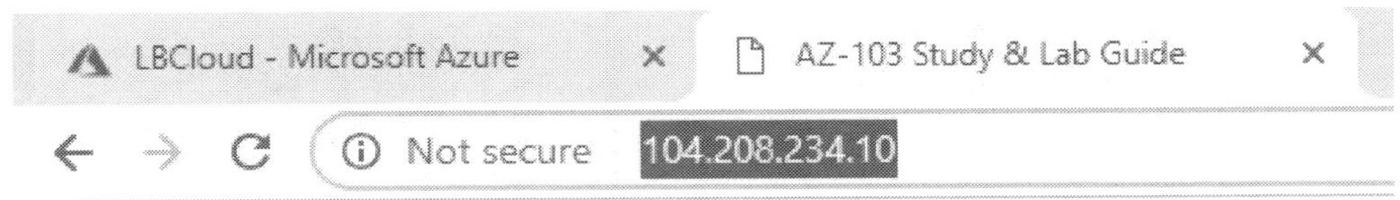

Exam AZ-103 Study & Lab Guide

Author: Harinder Kohli

2. Pres f5 couple of times to refresh the browser> Default Website of VMFE1 opens as shown below.

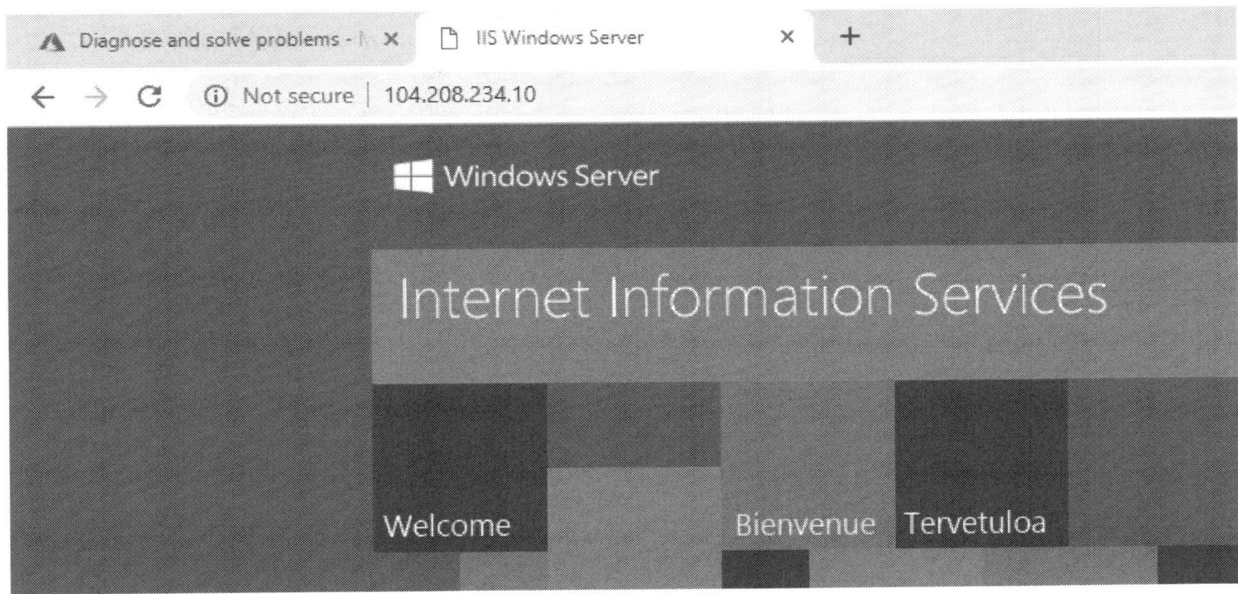

Note: In Load Balancing rule we had chosen Session Persistence as none.

Azure Basic Load Balancer Pricing

Azure Basic Load Balancer is free of charge.

Azure Standard Load Balancer Pricing

The pricing for standard Load Balancer will be based on the number of rules configured (load balancer rules and NAT rules) and data processed for inbound originated flows.

Note: IP Address assigned to Load Balancer is chargeable.

Load Balancer rules: (free during preview period)
First five rules—$0.025/hour
Additional rules—$0.01/rule/hour

NAT Rules: (free during preview period)
NAT rules are free.

Data processed: (free during preview period)
$0.005 per GB

Chapter 6 Azure Application Gateway & Traffic Manager

Note: AZ-300 Exam syllabus does not mentions Traffic Manager. But For Exam AZ-301 Traffic Manager is an important component for Designing & Implementing Multi-Region High Availablility Solutions. You can Skip Traffic Manager for AZ-300 Exam. **But my suggestion is that you go through Traffic Manager even for AZ-300 also.**

- Application Gateway
- Application Gateway Configuration Options
- Application Gateway Use cases
- Application Gateway Editions
- Application Gateway Features
- Web Application Firewall (WAF)
- Application Layer Persistence using Cookie-based session affinity
- Endpoint health monitoring with Probes
- SSL Termination
- End to End SSL with Application Gateway
- Listeners
- URL-based content routing
- Multiple site hosting
- Application Gateway Design Nuggets
- Application Gateway Pricing
- Traffic Manager
- Traffic Manager Routing Methods
- Traffic Manager Pricing

This Chapter Covers following Lab Exercises

- Create Dedicated Subnet for Application Gateway
- Create Application Gateway and add VMFE1 & VMFE2
- Explore Dashboard of Application Gateway
- ADD VMs VMFE1 and VMFE2 to Default Backend pool
- Test the Load Balancing
- Enabling HTTPS
- Listeners
- Create & Implement Traffic Manager in 2 Steps

This Chapter covers following Case Studies

- Load Balancing e-commerce server
- Highly Available Multisite Website

Chapter Topology

In this chapter we will add **AG-Subnet**, **Application Gateway (AG)** & **Traffic Manager (TM)** and to the topology. Virtual Machine **VMFE1 and VMFE2** will be added as an endpoint to the Azure Application Gateway & Traffic Manager. We will then access default website on VMFE1 and Custom Website on VMFE2 using public IP of the Azure Application Gateway & Traffic Manager.

Note: Application Gateway will be created in AG-Subnet

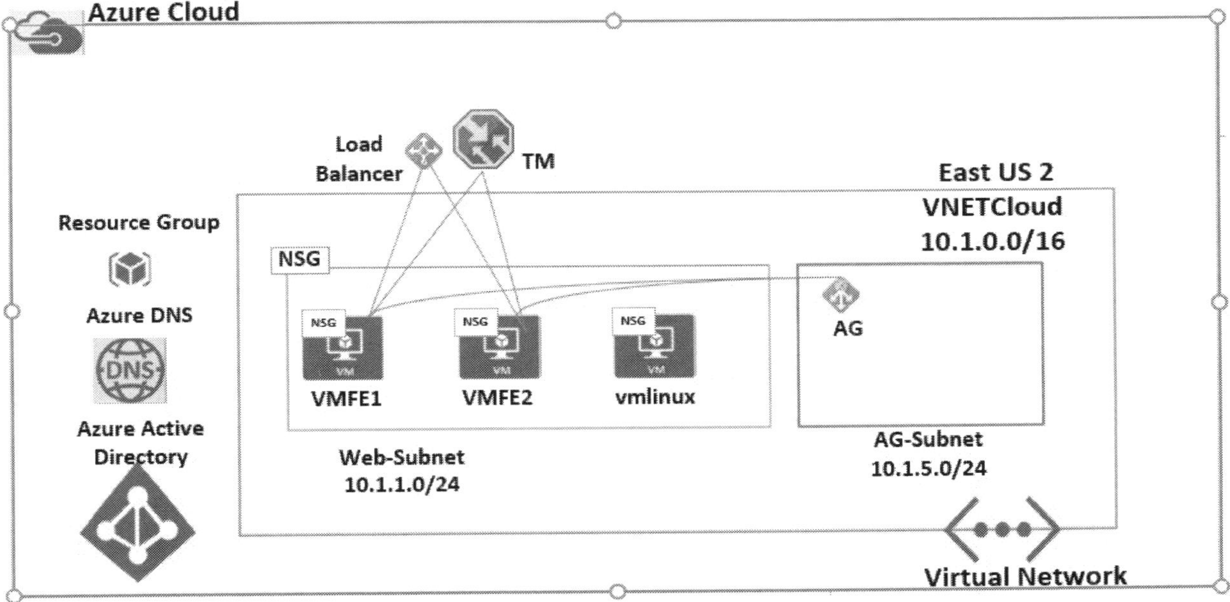

Application Gateway

Azure Application Gateway is an Azure managed layer-7 load balancer.

Application Gateway deals with **web traffic only (HTTP/HTTPS/WebSocket).**

Application Gateway is highly available and scalable service, which is fully managed by Azure.

Figure below shows Application Gateway is load Balancing HTTP traffic to Azure VMs.

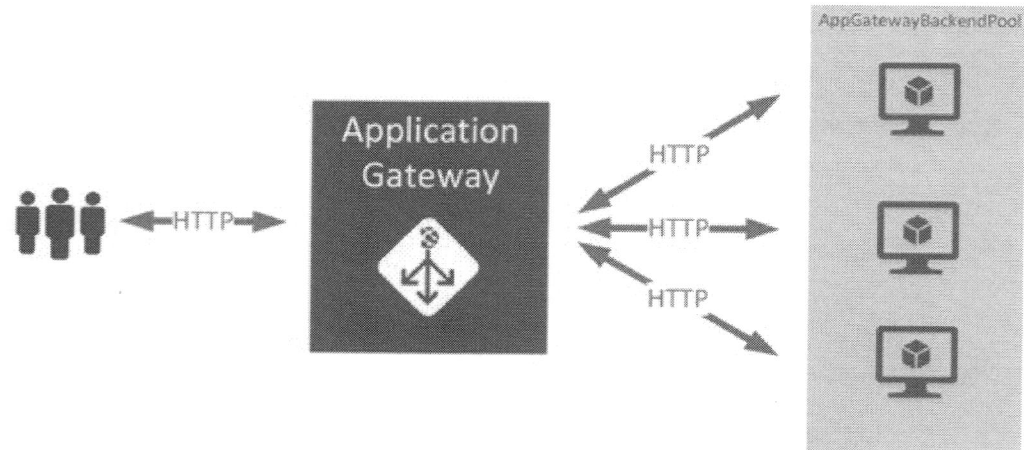

Application Gateway Configuration Options

Application Gateway can be configured as **Public facing** or as **internal/private** load balancer.

Application Gateway is deployed in **dedicated subnet** in your virtual network. The subnet used for application gateway cannot contain any other types of resources. Only resources that are allowed in the subnet are other application gateways.

Application Gateway is deployed either in **Standard SKU Mode** or in **WAF Mode**. In WAF mode, Web application firewall (WAF) is also deployed with Application Gateway to provide centralized protection to your web applications from common exploits and vulnerabilities. SKU mode is chosen when you are creating Application Gateway instance.

Application Gateway Use cases

1. Application Gateway deals with **web traffic only (HTTP/HTTPS/WebSocket).**
2. **Application Gateway is used in cases where application layer session persistence is required.**
3. To improve performance of web applications by freeing web server farms from SSL termination overhead.
4. Applications that support websocket traffic.
5. Protecting web applications from common web-based attacks like SQL injection, cross-site scripting attacks, and session hijacks.

Application Gateway Editions

Application Gateway comes in two SKUs. A Standard SKU and a Web Application Firewall (WAF) SKU. SKU mode is chosen when you are creating Application Gateway instance.

Application Gateway Standard SKU is currently offered in three sizes: Small, Medium & Large.

Application Gateway WAF SKU is currently offered in two sizes: Medium & Large.

Note: In WAF mode, Web application firewall (WAF) is also deployed with Application Gateway to provide centralized protection to your web applications from common exploits and vulnerabilities. SKU mode is chosen when you are creating Application Gateway instance.

Application Gateway Features

1. **HTTP/HTTPS load balancing** - Load balancing is done at Layer 7 and is used for HTTP or HTTPS traffic only.

2. **Cookie-based session affinity** - This feature keeps a user session on the same back-end server. By using gateway managed cookies, the Application Gateway is able to direct subsequent traffic from a user session to the same back-end for processing.

3. **Secure Sockets Layer (SSL) offload** - By terminating the SSL connection at the Application Gateway and forwarding the request to server unencrypted, the web server is unburdened by the decryption. Application Gateway re-encrypts the response before sending it back to the client. This feature is useful in scenarios where the back-end is located in the same secured virtual network as the Application Gateway in Azure.

4. **URL-based content routing** - This feature provides the capability to use different back-end servers for different traffic. Traffic for a folder on the web server or for a CDN could be routed to a different back-end, reducing unneeded load on backends that don't serve specific content.

5. **Multi-site routing** - Application gateway consolidate up to 20 websites on a single application gateway.

6. **Websocket support** - Application Gateway provides native support for Websocket.

7. **Web Application Firewall** - The web application firewall (WAF) in Azure Application Gateway protects web applications from common web-based attacks like SQL injection, cross-site scripting attacks, and session hijacks.

8. **Integration with Azure Services**: Application Gateway can be integrated with Azure Traffic Manager to support multi-region redirection & failover. Application Gateway is also integrated with Azure Load Balancer to support scale-out and high-availability for Internet-facing and internal-only web front ends.

Web Application Firewall (WAF)

Web application firewall (WAF) is a feature of Application Gateway that provides centralized protection to web applications from common exploits and vulnerabilities. **With Application Gateway WAF SKU, WAF (web application firewall) is directly integrated into the ADC offering.**

Web application firewall is based on rules from the Open Web Application Security Project (OWASP) core rule sets.

The OWASP Core Rule Set (CRS) is a set of generic attack detection rules. The CRS protects web applications from a wide range of attacks, including SQL Injection, Cross Site Scripting, Locale File Inclusion, etc.

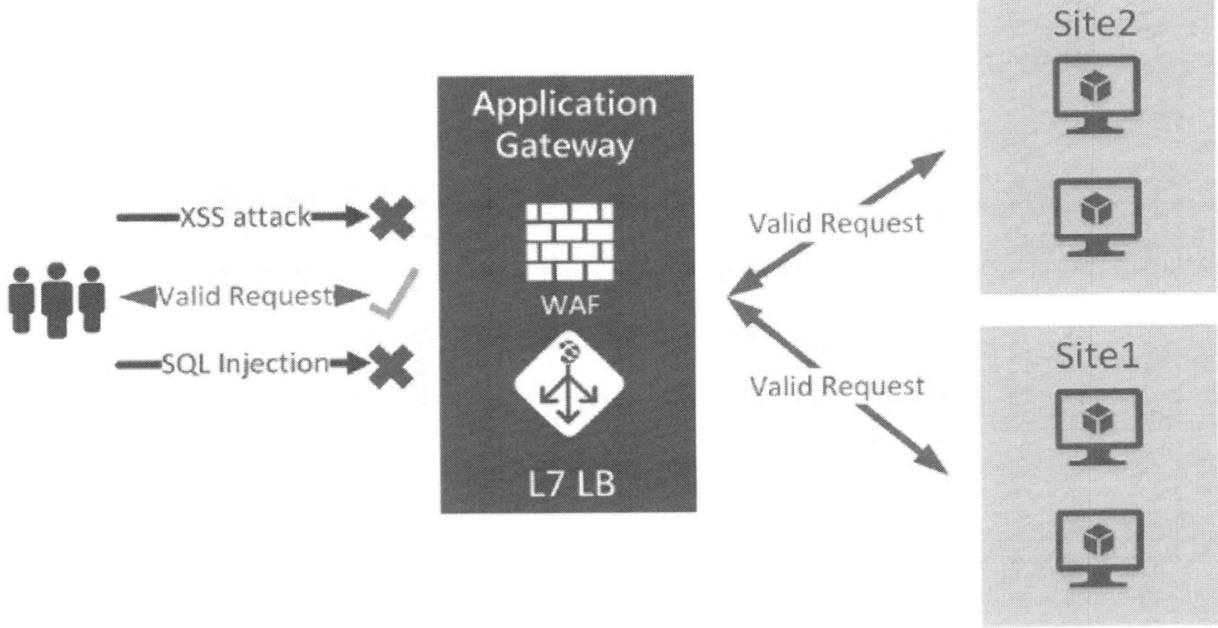

Benefits of Web Application Firewall (Good Design Point)

A WAF solution reacts to a security threat faster by patching a known vulnerability at a central location versus securing each of individual web applications.
Protect multiple web applications at the same time behind an application gateway. Application gateway supports hosting up to 20 websites behind a single gateway that could all be protected against web attacks with WAF.

Application Layer Persistence using Cookie-based session affinity

Cookie-based session affinity keeps a user session on the same back-end server by using Application Gateway managed cookies.

With cookie based session affinity even if client IP address is changed it is still directed to the same backend server. This feature is important in cases such as e-commerce web sites where user must be directed to same backend server even if user IP address is changed.

Cookies are small pieces of information that are sent in response from the web server to the client. **Cookies are used for storing client state.**
Cookies are stored on client's computer. They have a lifespan and are destroyed by the client browser at the end of that lifespan.

Note: This topic is very relevant for AZ-301 Exam.

Endpoint health monitoring with Probes

Azure Application Gateway automatically monitors the health of the back-end instances through basic or custom health probes. Health probes, ensures that only healthy hosts respond to traffic.

Application Gateway automatically removes any resource considered unhealthy from the pool. Application Gateway continues to monitor the unhealthy instances and adds them back to the healthy back-end pool once they become available and respond to health probes.

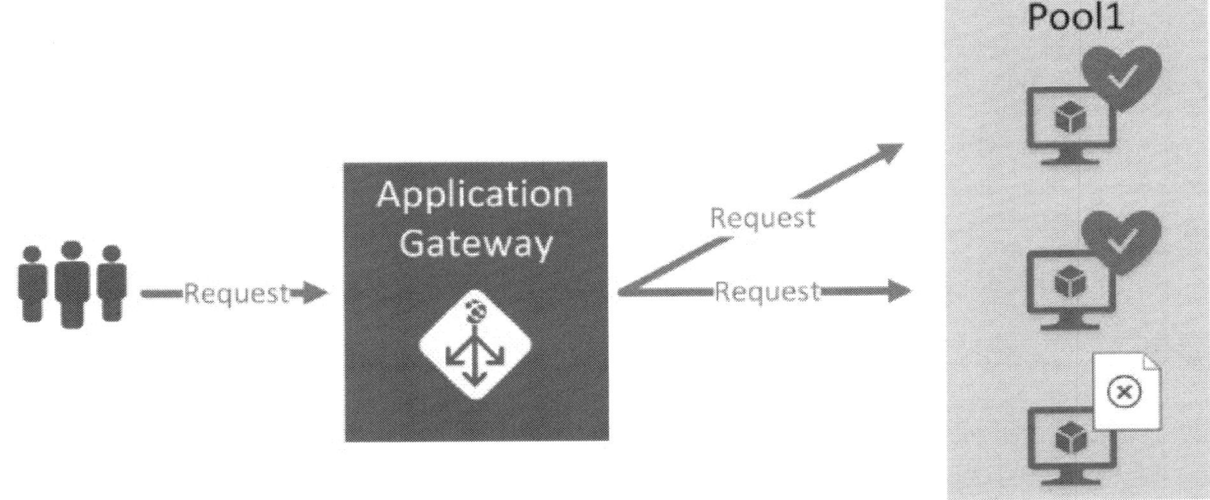

Default Health Probe: An application gateway automatically configures a default health probe when you create Backend pool and add instances to the pool. Default Health probe monitors endpoint by making an HTTP/HTTPS request to the IP addresses configured for the back-end pool.

Probe Property	Value	Description
Interval	30	Probe interval in seconds
Time-out	30	Probe time-out in seconds
Unhealthy threshold	3	Probe retry count. The back-end server is marked down after the consecutive probe failure count reaches the unhealthy threshold.

Design Nugget: You cannot change Default Health probe values.

Custom Health Probe

Custom probes are useful for applications that have a specific health check page or for applications that do not provide a successful response on the default web application.

You can create Custom Health Probe using Application Gateway Dashboard as shown below.
Click Health Probes in left pane> Click + Add> Add Health Probe blade opens as shown below.

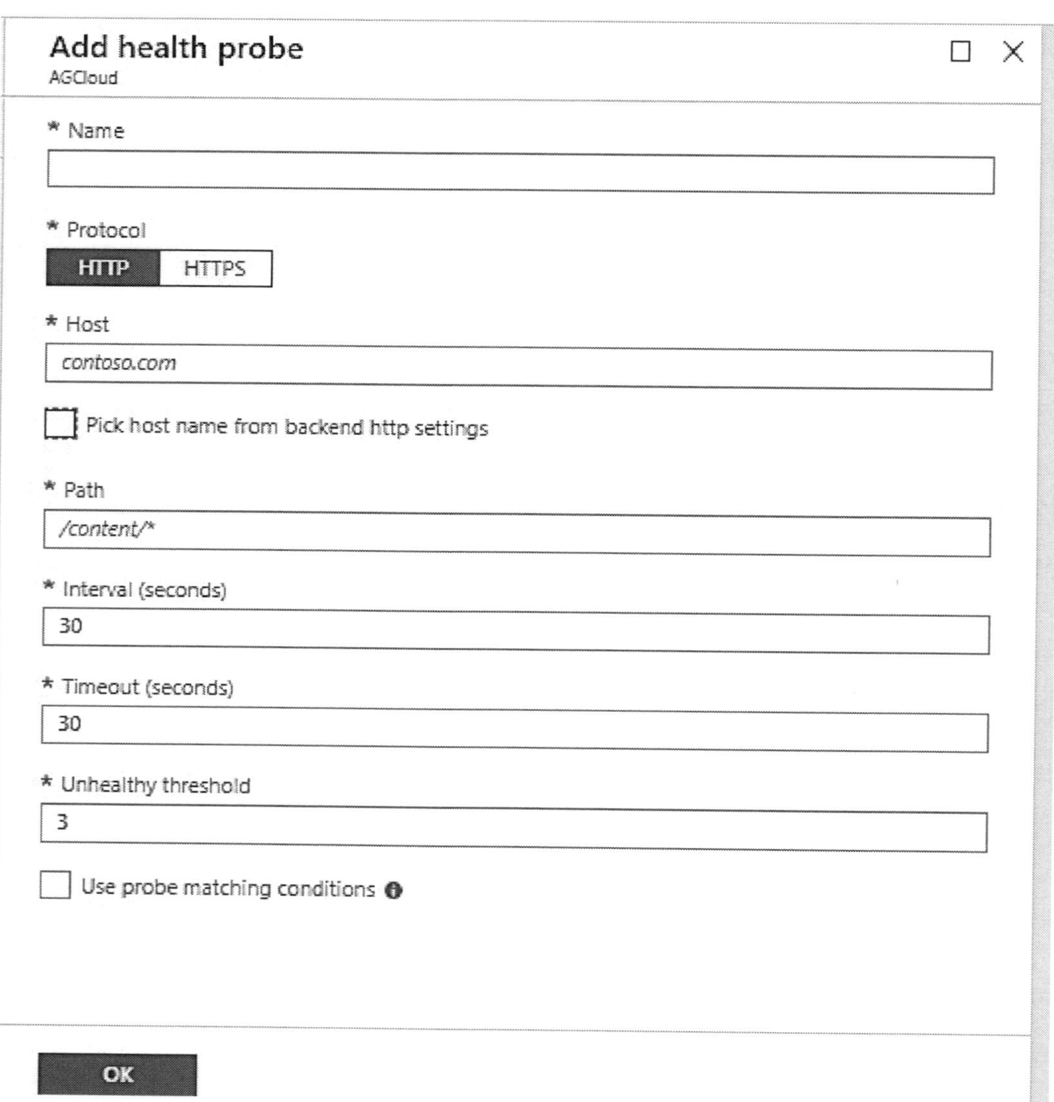

Exercise 57: Create Dedicated Subnet for Application Gateway

Application Gateway is deployed in **dedicated subnet** in your virtual network. The subnet used for application gateway cannot contain any other types of resources. Only resources that are allowed in the subnet are other application gateways.

In this Exercise we will create **AG-Subnet** in Virtual Network VNETCloud with address space 10.1.5.0/24. Virtual Network VNETCloud was created in Exercise 3, Chapter 1.

1. Go to VNETCloud Dashboard> Click Subnets in left pane>All Subnet pane opens as shown below.

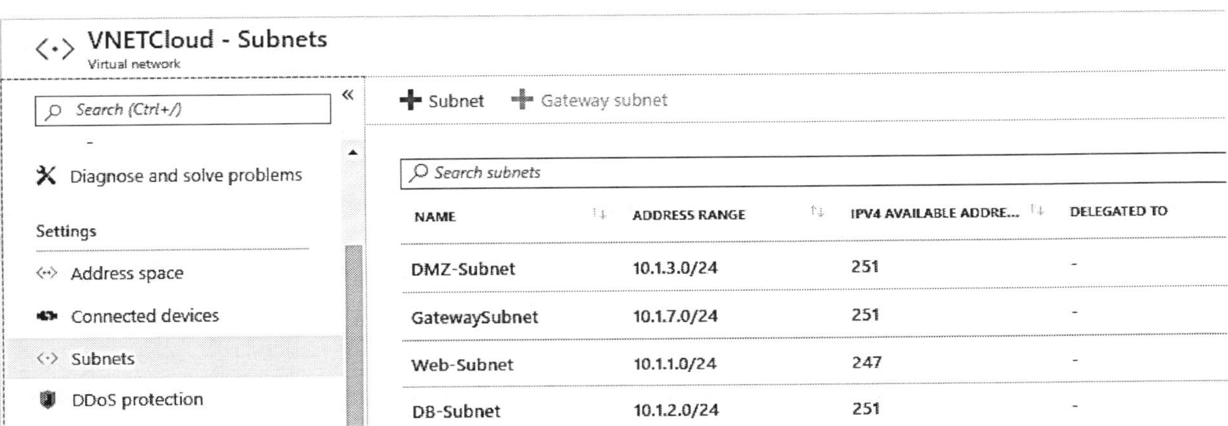

2. Click +Subnet>Add Subnet blade opens> Enter name>In Address range enter 10.1.5.0/24>Rest Select all default values>Click OK (Not shown).

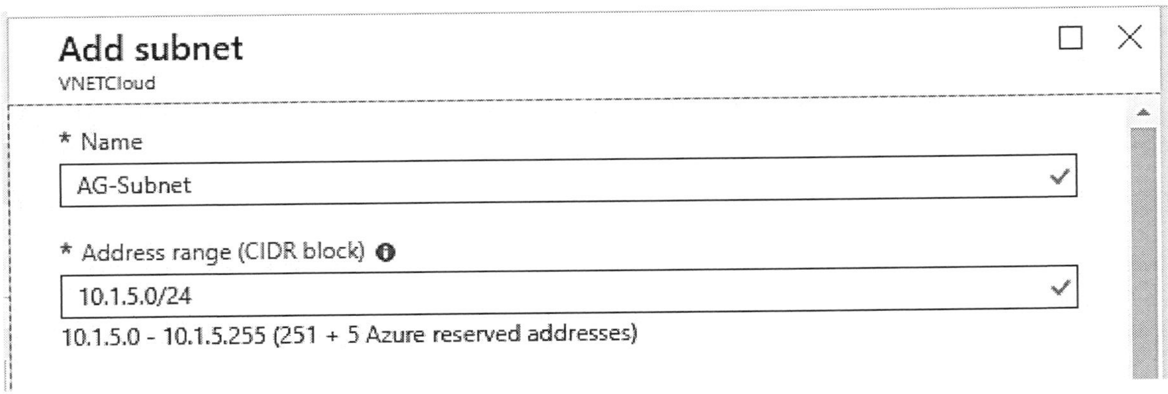

Exercise 58: Create Application Gateway

In this Exercise we will create Standard Application Gateway in Subnet **AG-Subnet** and in Resource Group **RGCloud** and in region **East US 2**. AG-Subnet was created in Virtual Network **VNETCloud** in previous Exercise.

Step 1: In Azure portal click +Create a resource> Networking> Application Gateway> Create Application Gateway Blade open>Enter a name, Choose Standard Tier, SKU size Small, Resource Group RGCloud>Click OK.

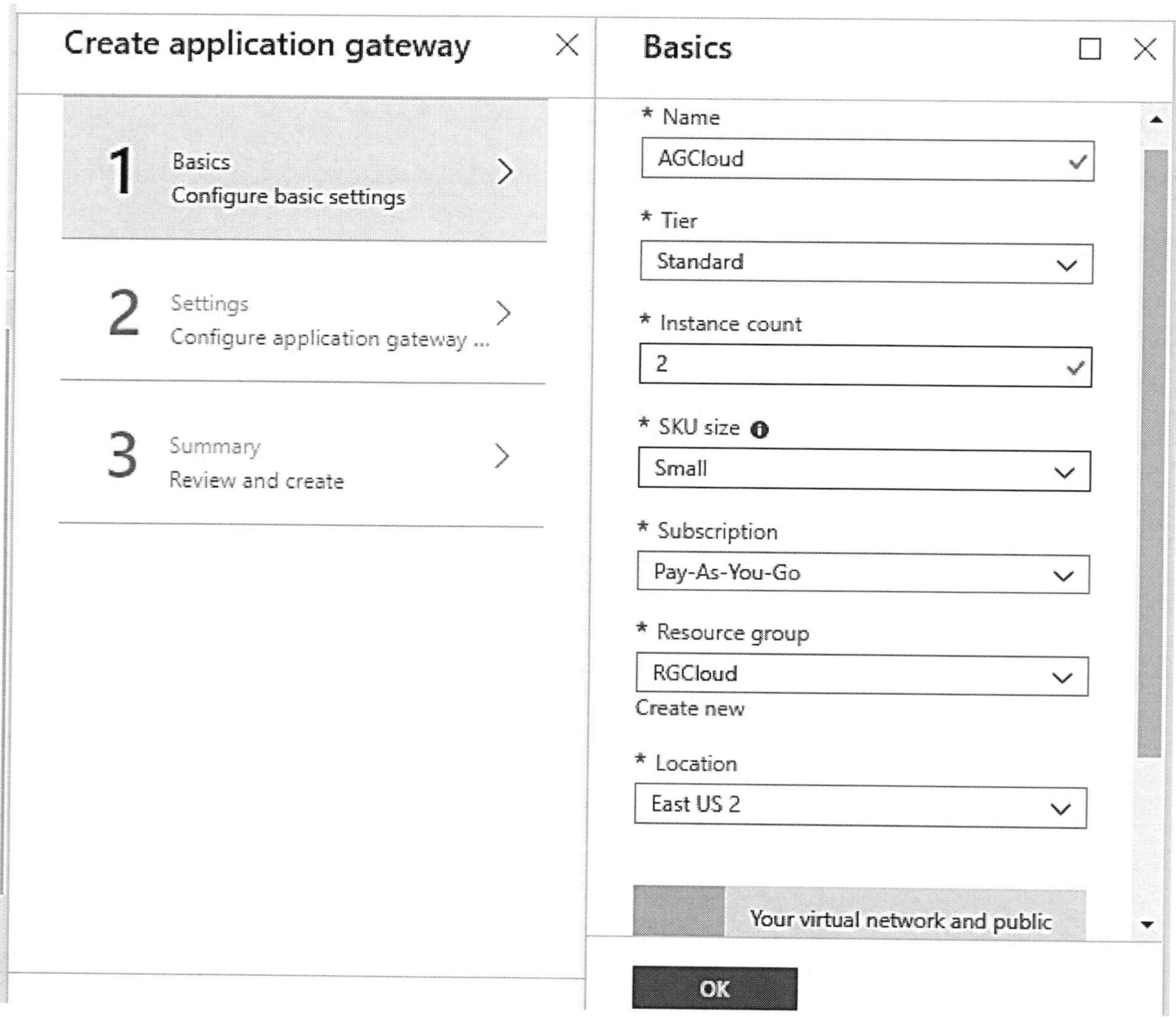

Step 2: Setting Pane opens>Select Virtual Network VNETCloud>Subnet AG-Subnet>IP Address Public>For DNS name enter agcloud> Rest Select all default values. For Listener Configuration (Not shown) we selected default value HTTP>Click Ok>Summary pane opens. Click OK to create Application Gateway.

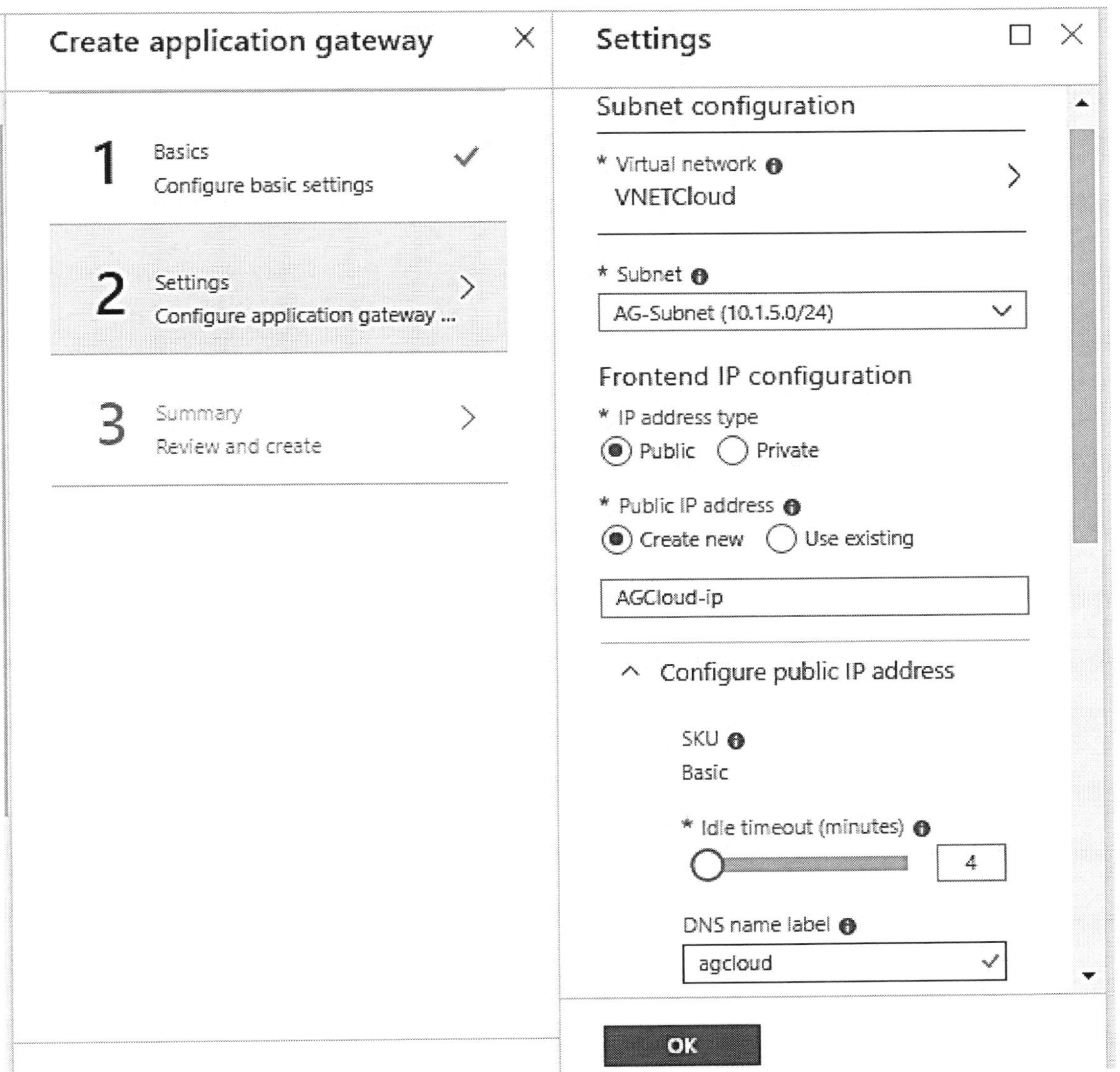

Exercise 59: Explore Dashboard of Application Gateway

Figure below shows Dashboard of Application Gateway AGCloud.

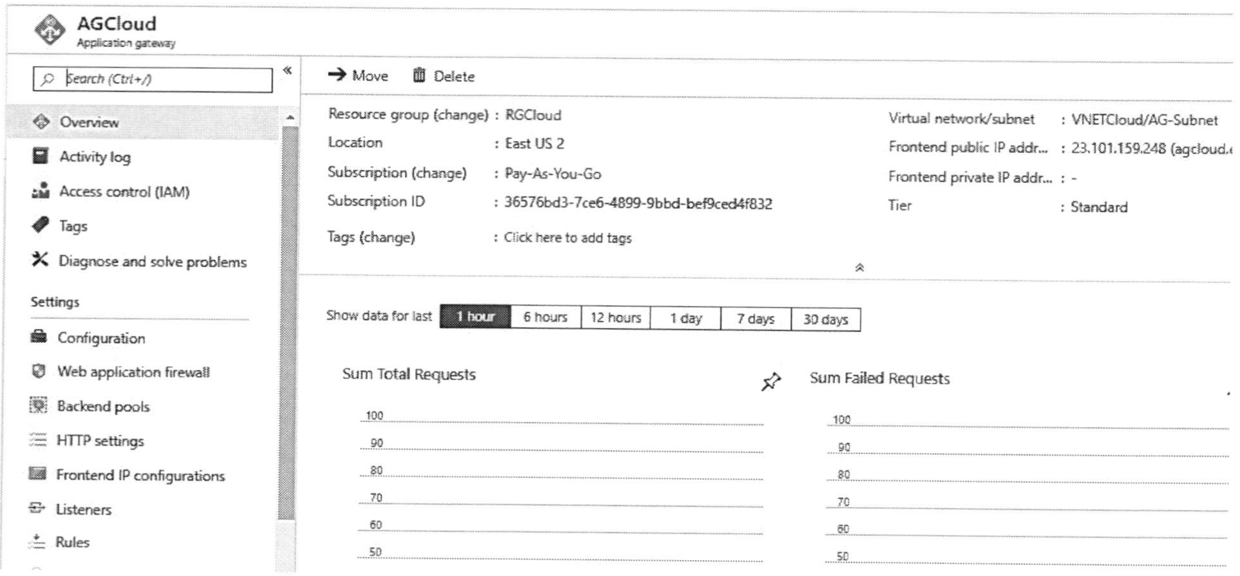

Click on **Configuration** in left pane> Here you can change the Tier from Standard to WAF, SKU from small to medium or large and Application Gateway Instance count.

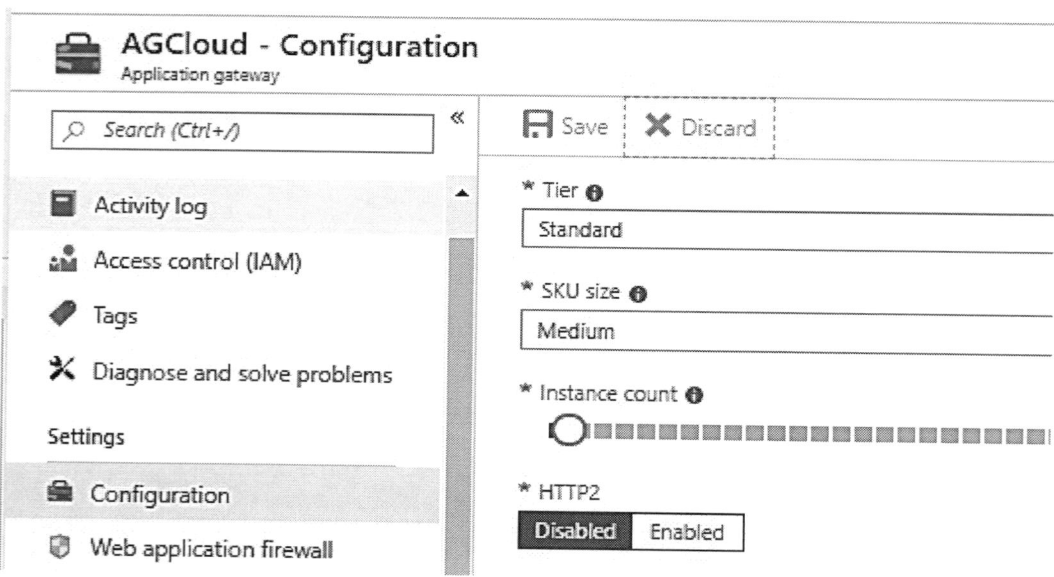

Click on **Backend pools** in left pane>In right pane you can see a default Backend pool is created by system. Please note that VMs to be load balanced are added to Backend pool

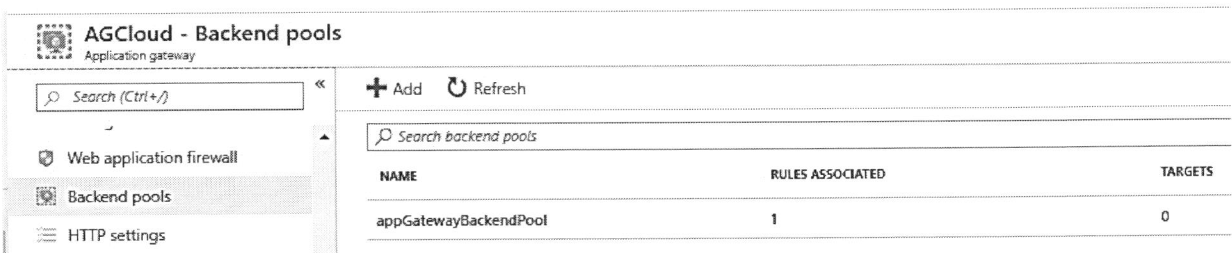

Click on **Web application Firewall**. Currently Web Application firewall is disabled. Here you can enable the Firewall.

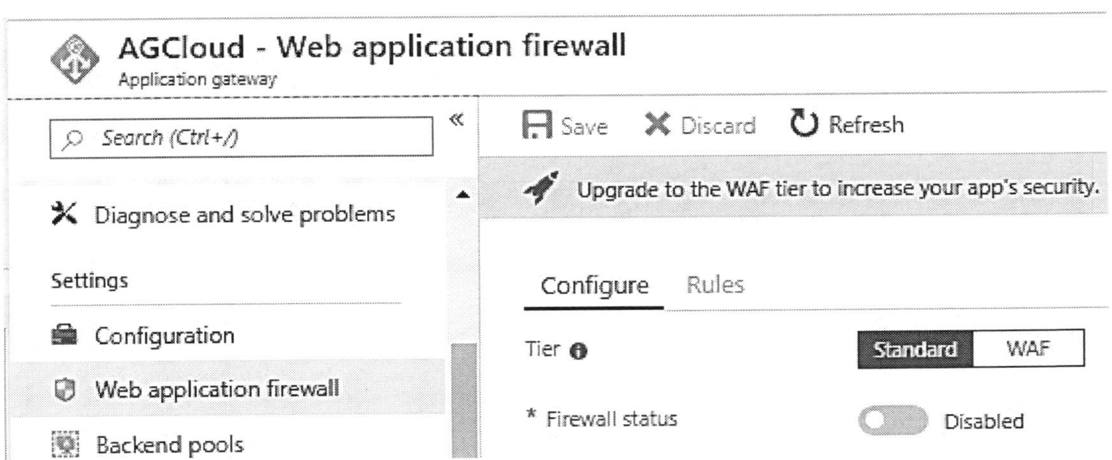

Click on Http settings to enable client HTTPS traffic access to Application Gateway from browser.

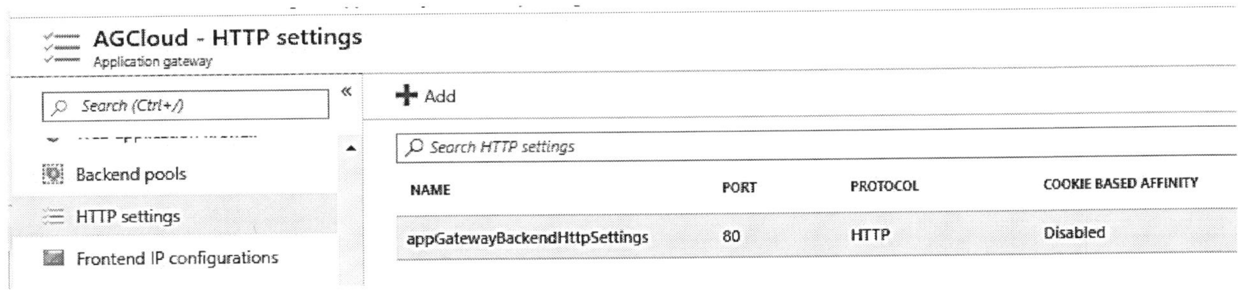

Click on Frontend IP Configurations. It shows the Frontend IP of the AG and listener associated with it.

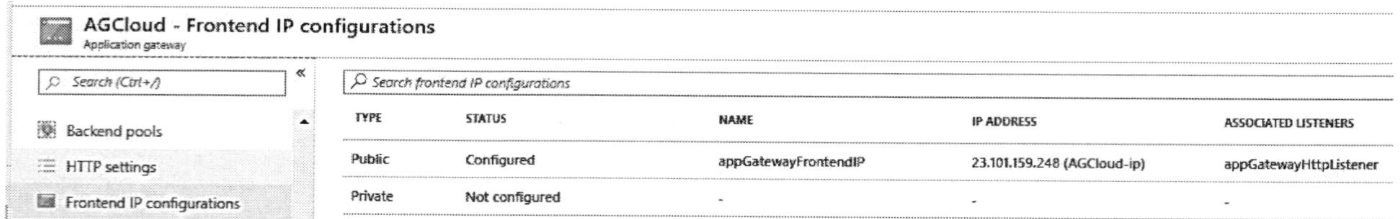

Exercise 60: ADD VMs VMFE1 and VMFE2 to Default Backend pool

In this we will add VMs (VMFE1 and VMFE2) to be load balanced to the Application Gateway Default Backend pool. VMFE1 has default website and VMFE2 has Custom website.

1. In Application Gateway AGCloud Dashboard click Backend pools in left pane>In right pane click the default pool appGatewayBackendPool>Edit Backend Pool blade opens>Under Target select Virtual Machines>Then from drop down boxes select VMFE1 and VMFE2 and their Network Interfaces as shown below>Click save in top.

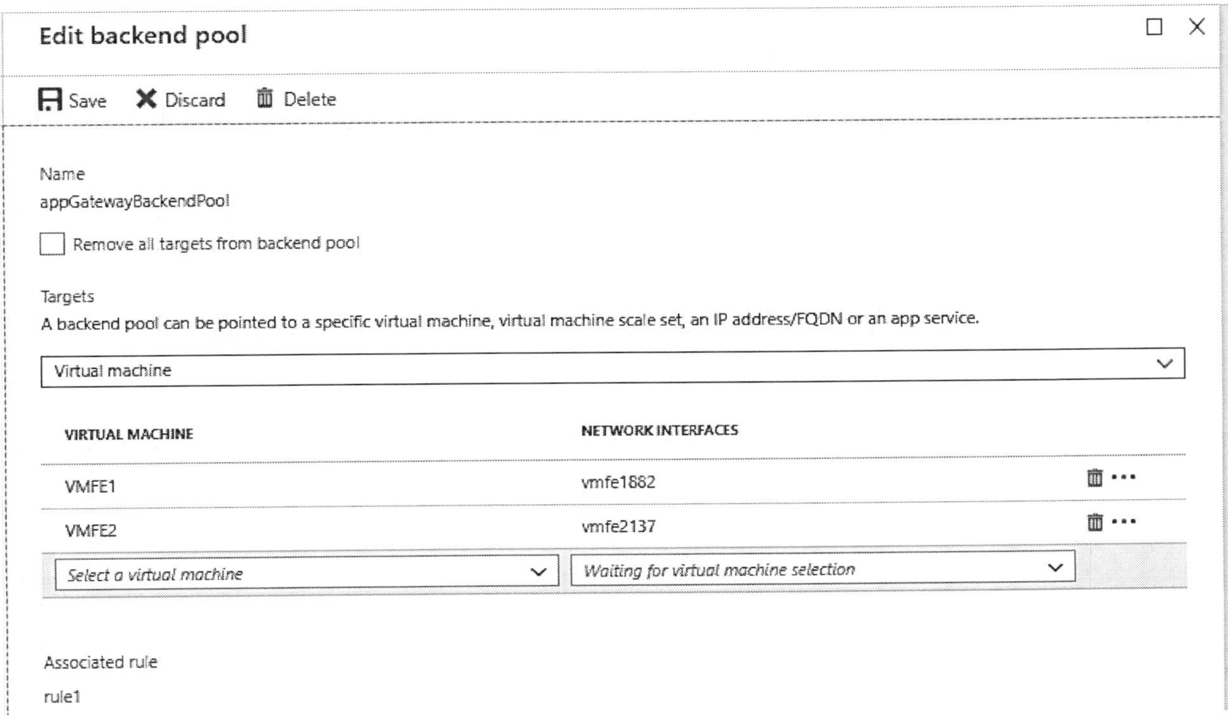

Figure below shows that 2 VMs are added to backend pool.

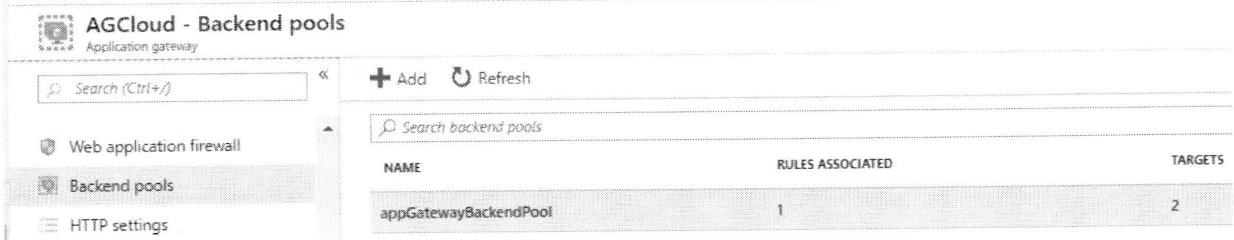

Exercise 61: Test the Load Balancing

1. Go to Application Gateway Dashboard>From right pane copy the Public IP Address (23.101.159.248)> Open a browser and http:// 23.101.159.248> Custom website on VMFE2 opens.

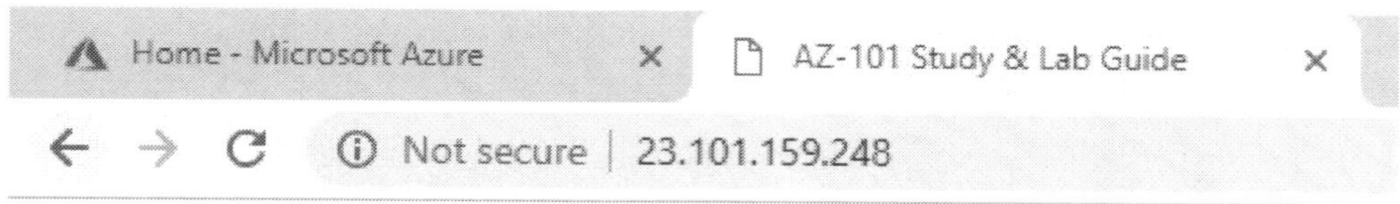

Exam AZ-103 Study & Lab Guide

Author: Harinder Kohli

2. Do F5 couple of times and you can see the Default website on VMFE1.

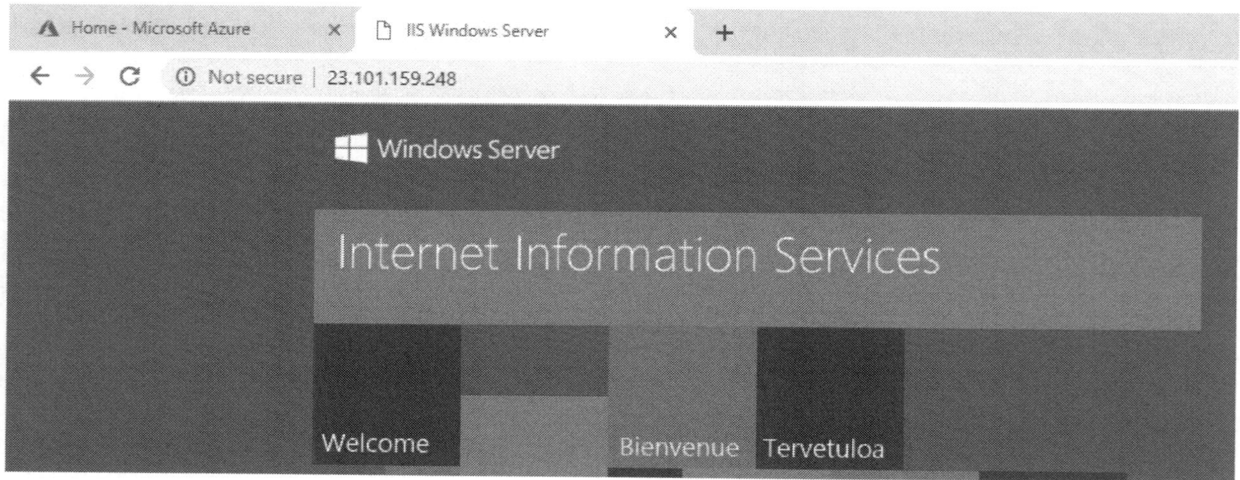

Note 1: Backend pools can be composed of NICs, virtual machine scale sets, public IPs, internal IPs, and fully qualified domain names (FQDN). Members of backend pools can be across clusters, data centers, or outside of Azure as long as they have IP connectivity.

Note: Application gateway automatically configures a default health probe.

3. **Health of Backend Pool Virtual Machines:** You can check the health of VMs in Backend pool using Backend Health tab.

In AG dashboard click Backend health tab in left pane>In right pane you can see that both VMs in the pool are healthy.

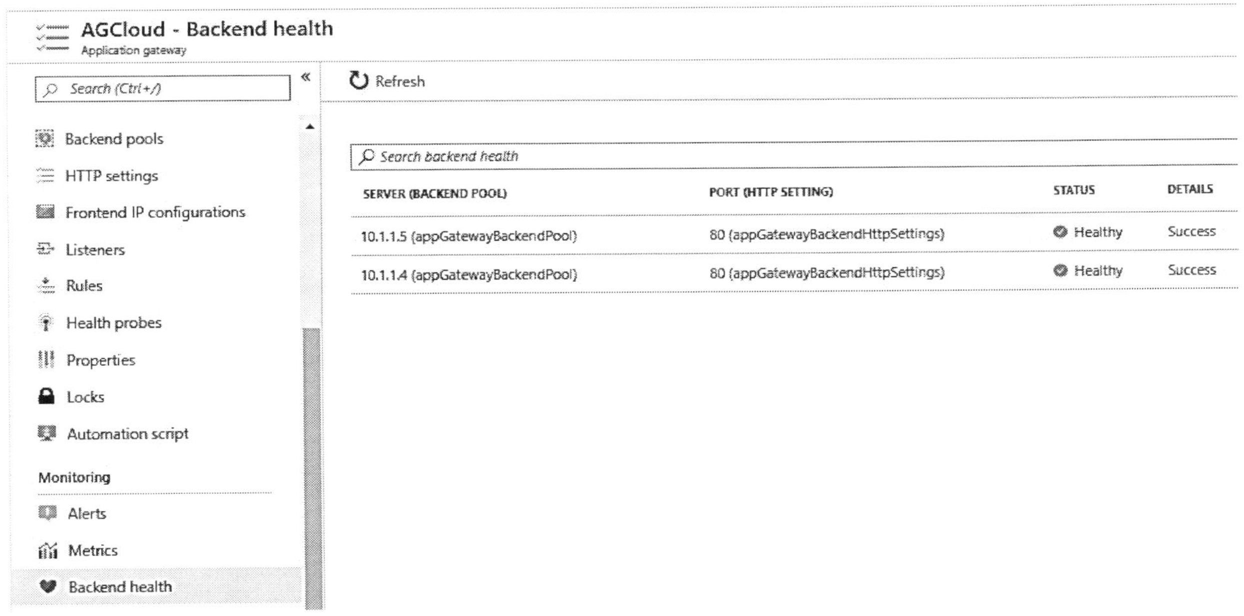

SSL Termination

With SSL termination, client HTTPS traffic is terminated at Application Gateway and traffic from Application Gateway to backend servers is send unencrypted. Application Gateway re-encrypts the response before sending it back to the client.

The advantage of this option is that you can use Azure Application Gateway to centralize SSL certificate management and reduce encryption and decryption overhead from a back-end server farm.

To enable SSL Termination you need to create Application Gateway with the Certificate or add certificate after creation. You can use a Self-signed Certificate or use Certificate from Certification Authority (Public or Private).

Demonstration Exercise 62: Enabling HTTPS

1. Go to AG AGCloud Dashboard>Click HTTP settings in left pane> In right pane click the appGatewayBackendHttpSettings> appGatewayBackendHttpSettings blade opens>Under Protocol click HTTPS and upload Certificate.

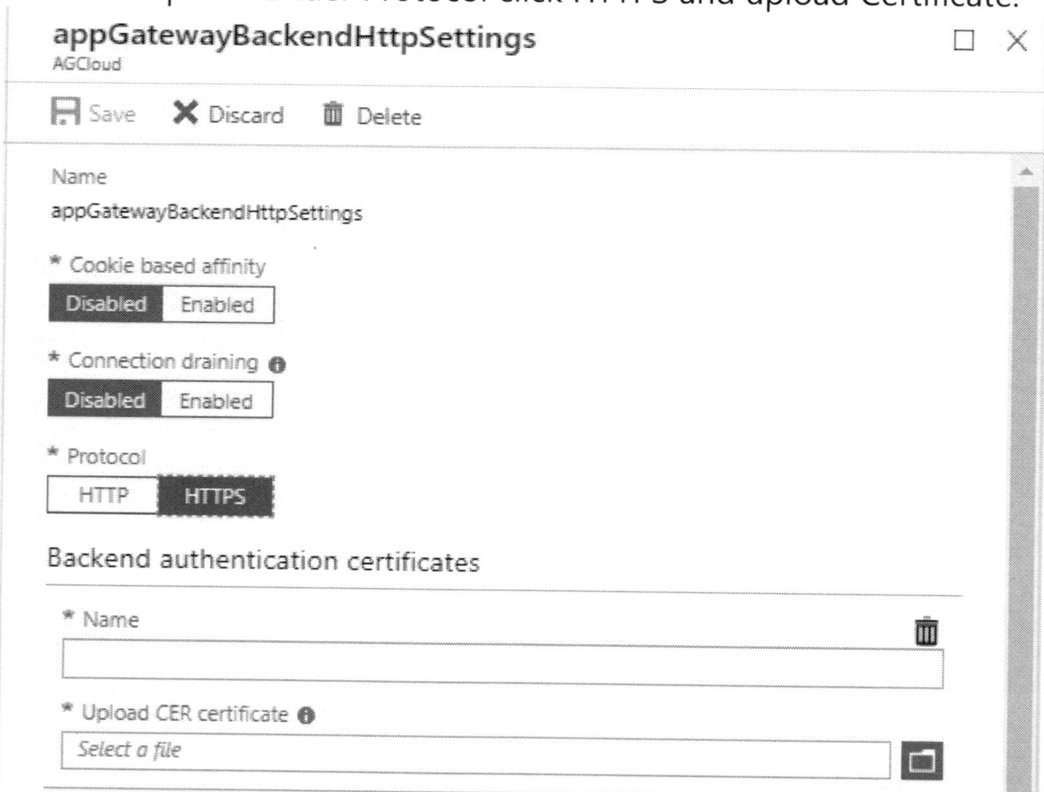

End to End SSL with Application Gateway

With SSL termination enabled, HTTPS traffic is terminated at Application Gateway and traffic from Application Gateway to backend servers is unencrypted.

In certain scenarios unencrypted communication to servers is not allowed because of security or compliance requirements or the application may only accept a secure connection. **End to end SSL allows you to securely transmit sensitive data from Application Gateway to the backend encrypted.**

End to end SSL Working

When configured with end to end SSL, application gateway terminates the SSL sessions at the gateway and decrypts user traffic. Application gateway then initiates a new SSL connection to the backend server and re-encrypts data using public key of backend server's certificate. End to end SSL is enabled by setting protocol setting in **BackendHTTPSettings** to HTTPS, which is then applied to a backend pool. Each backend server in the backend pool with end to end SSL enabled must be configured with a certificate to allow secure communication.

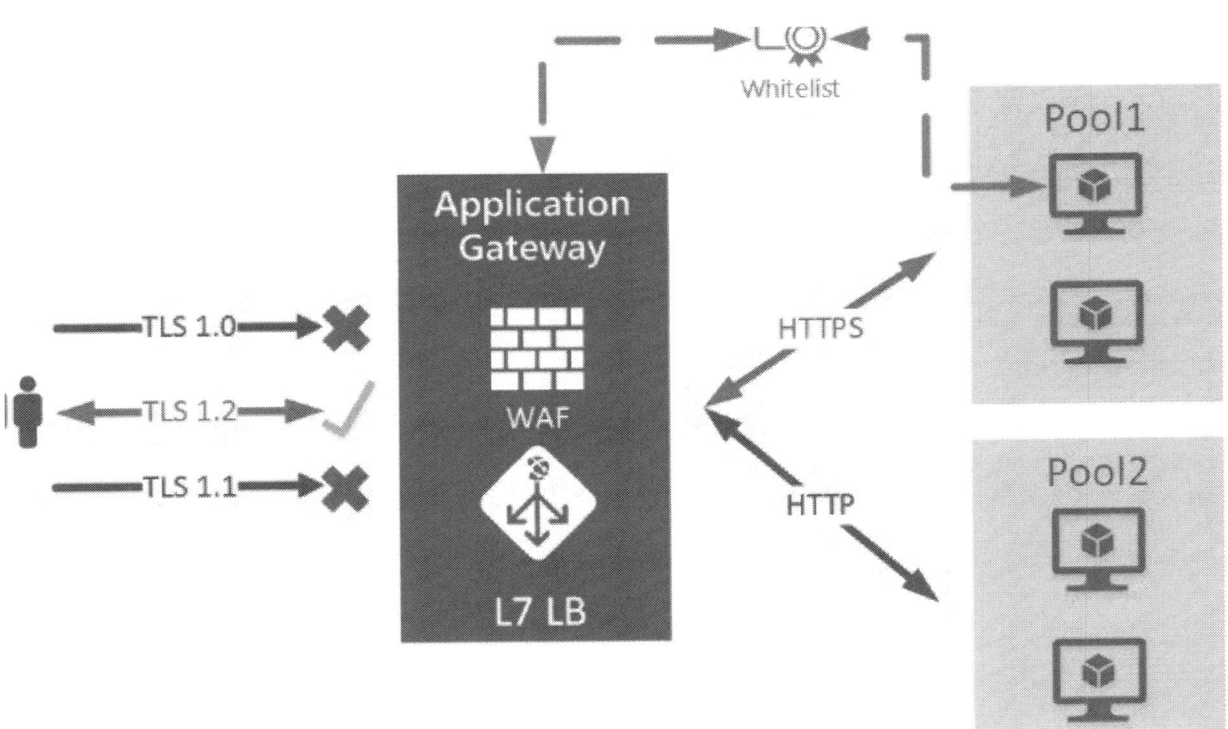

End to end SSL and whitelisting of certificates

Application gateway only communicates with known backend instances that have whitelisted their certificate with the application gateway. To enable whitelisting of certificates, you must upload the public key of backend server certificates to the application gateway (not the root certificate). Only connections to known and whitelisted backends are then allowed.

Listeners

Listeners are used by application gateway to route traffic to appropriate backend pool. There are 2 types of listeners - **Basic Listener & Multi-site Listener.**

Multi-site Listener is used for multiple site hosting. For each Backend in multiple site hosting you need to create Listener of type Multisite.

Demonstration Exercise 63: Listeners

Go to AG AGCloud Dashboard>Click Listeners in left pane> In right pane you can see a default Listener> From here you can create additional Basic or Multi-site Listeners.

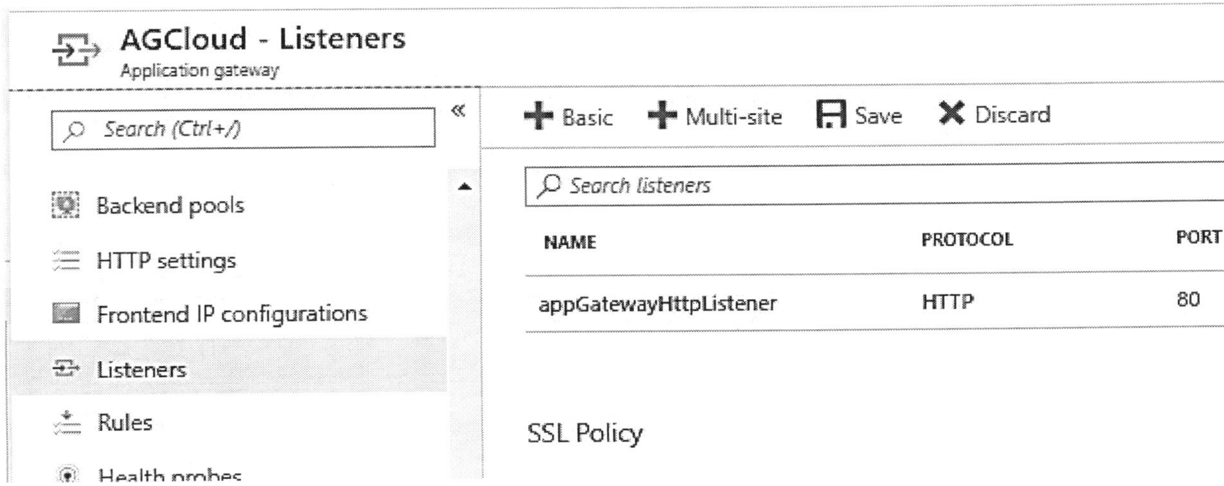

URL-based content routing

This feature provides the capability to use different back-end servers for different traffic. URL Traffic for a folder on the web server or URL traffic for Images could be routed to a different back-end, reducing unneeded load on backend that don't serve specific content.

Path Based Routing allows you to route traffic to back-end server pools based on URL Paths of the request.

In the Figure below, Application Gateway is serving traffic for contoso.com from three back-end server pools: VideoServerPool, ImageServerPool, and AppGatewayBackendPool (Not shown below). AppGatewayBackendPool is automatically created with application gateway.

Requests for http://contoso.com/video/* are routed to VideoServerPool, and http://contoso.com/images/* are routed to ImageServerPool. AppGatewayBackendPool is selected if none of the path patterns match.

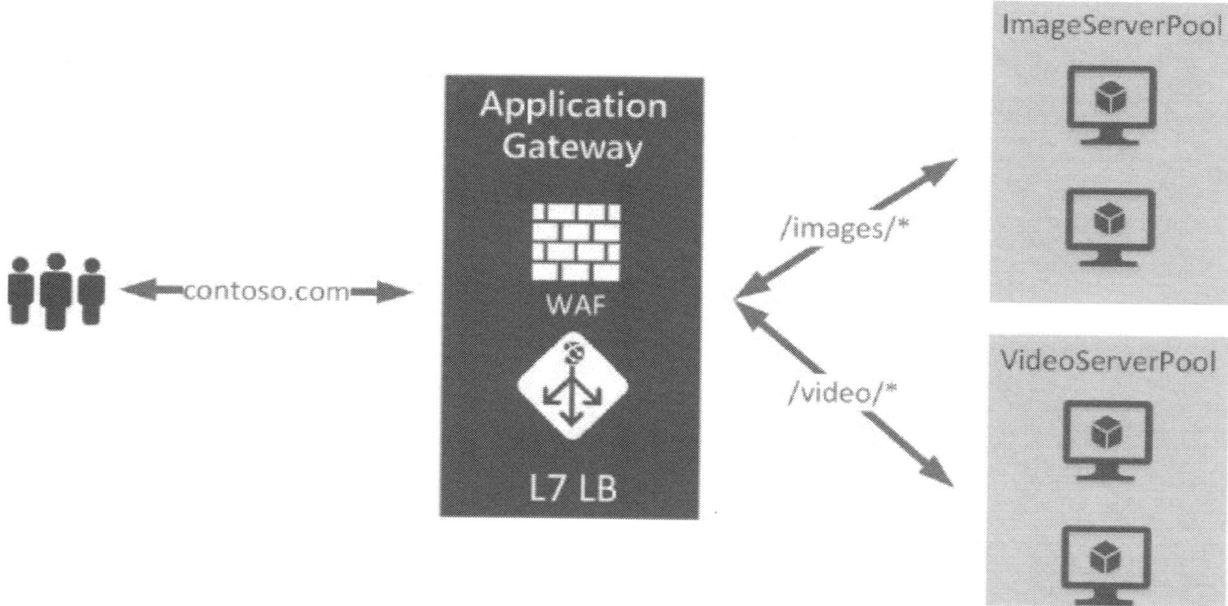

Configuring Path based Routing for above Example

1. Create Application Gateway.
2. Create backend Pools (ImageServerPool & VideoServerPool) and add instances. Note a default backend pool is created with application gateway.
3. Create Basic listener with name **mybackendlistener**.
4. **Create Path Based Routing Rules**. In Application Gateway Dashboard click Rules in left pane>In right Click +Path-based>Add path-based rule blade opens>Enter following and click ok.

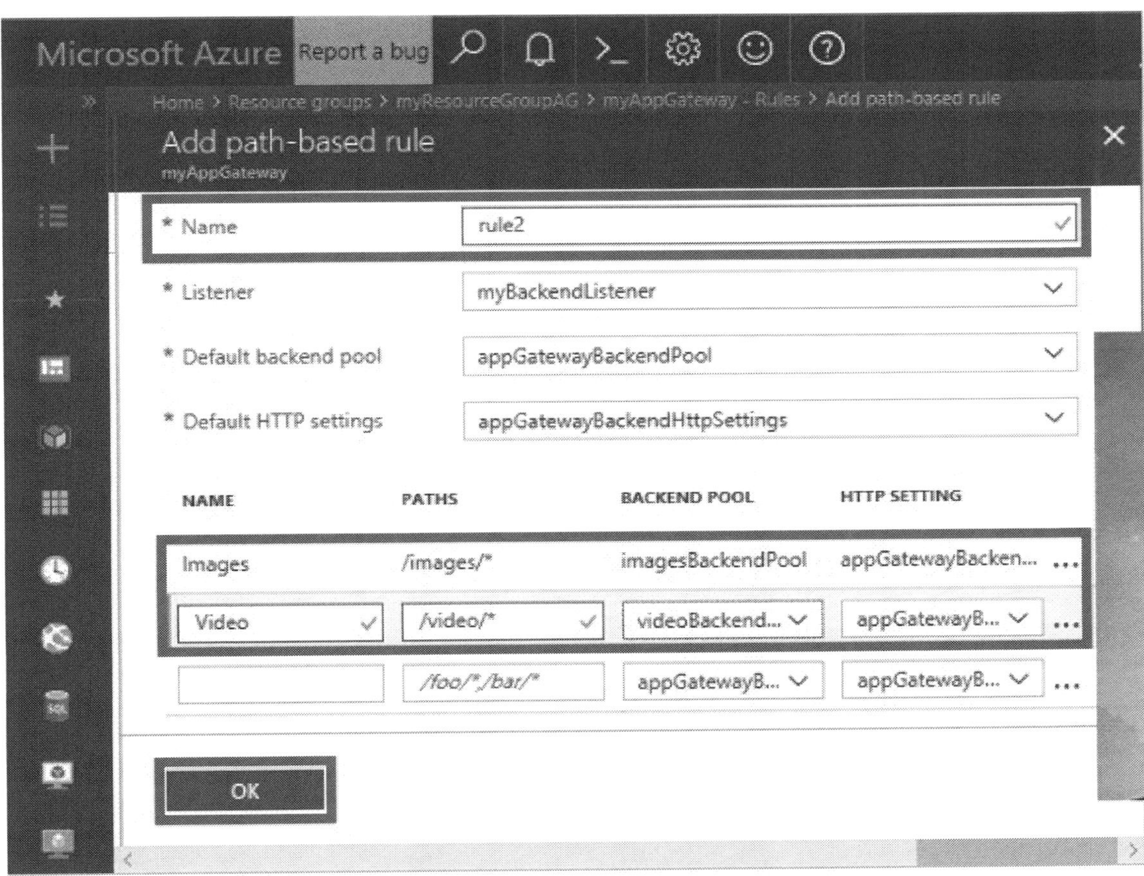

Multiple site hosting

Multiple site hosting feature allows you to configure up to 20 websites to one application gateway. Each website can be directed to its own backend pool.

Multiple Site Hosting Working

Application Gateway uses httplisteners to direct traffic to right backend. For each Backend you need to create Listener of type Multisite.

Application Gateway relies on HTTP 1.1 host headers to host more than one website on the same public IP address and port. This is the preferred mechanism for enabling multiple site hosting on the same infrastructure.

In the following example, application gateway is serving traffic for contoso.com and fabrikam.com from two back-end server pools called ContosoServerPool and FabrikamServerPool.

Requests for http://contoso.com are routed to ContosoServerPool, and http://fabrikam.com are routed to FabrikamServerPool.

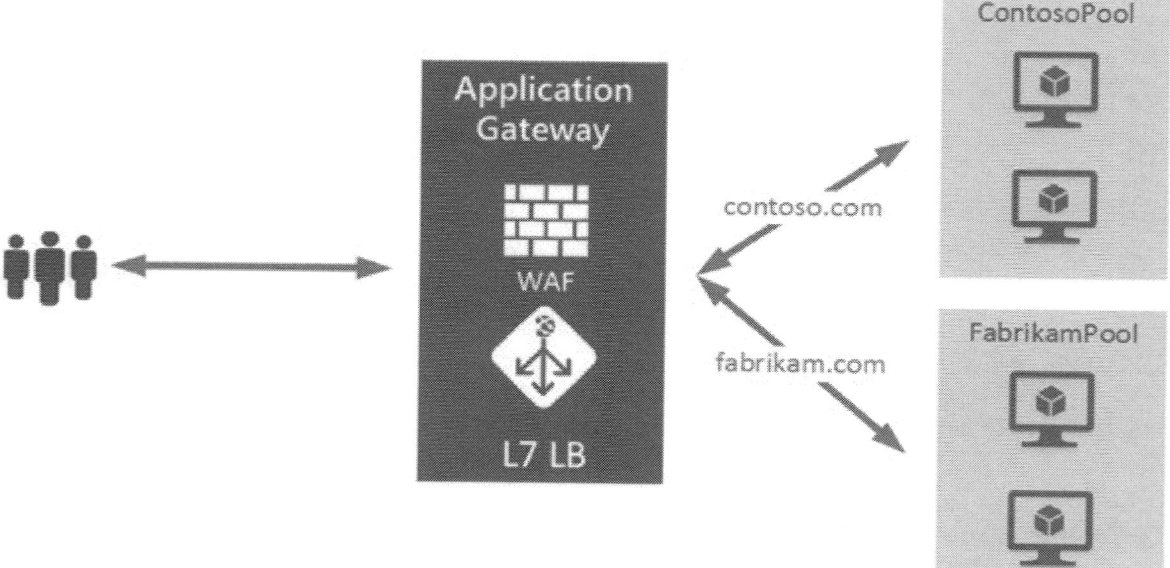

The sites hosted on application gateway can also support SSL offload with Server Name Indication (SNI) TLS extension.

Configuring Multiple Site hosting for above Example

1. Create Application Gateway.
2. Create backend Pools (ContosoPool & FabrikamPool) and add instances.
3. Create first Multi-site listener with name *contosoListener*.
4. Create second Multi-site listener with name *fabrikamListener*.
5. **Create first Basic Rules**. In Application Gateway Dashboard click Rules in left pane>Basic>Add basic rule blade opens>Enter following and click ok.
   Name: contosorule
   Select Listener: contosoListener
   Select Backend pool: contosopool

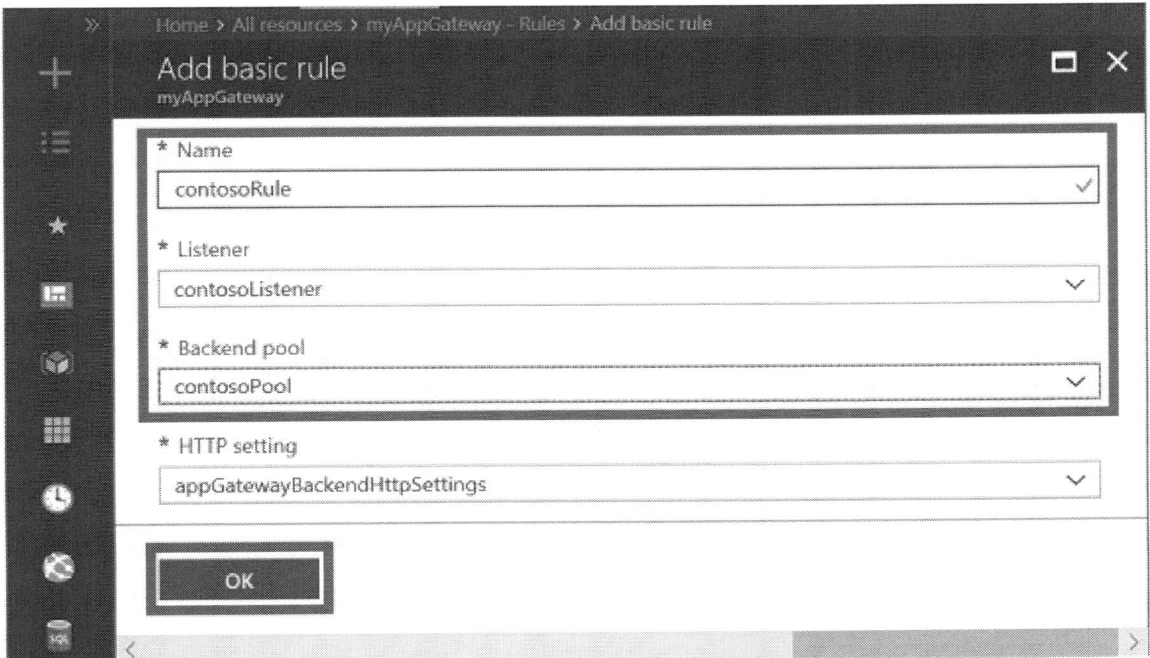

6. **Create second Basic Rules**. In Application Gateway Dashboard click Rules in left pane>Basic>Add basic rule blade opens>Enter Following:
   Name: fabrikamrule
   Select Listener: fabrikamlistener
   Select Backend pool: fabrikampool

Application Gateway Design Nuggets

1. Application Gateway is configured inside a virtual network in its own dedicated subnet. The subnet created or used for application gateway cannot contain any other types of resources. Only resources that are allowed in the subnet are other application gateways.
2. **Application Gateway does not support static public IP**. The VIP can change if the gateway is stopped and started by the customer. The DNS associated with Application Gateway does not change over the lifecycle of the gateway. Use a CNAME alias and point it to the DNS address of the Application Gateway.
3. Application Gateway can talk to instances outside of the virtual network that it is in as long as there is IP connectivity. If you plan to use internal IPs as backend pool members, then it requires VNET Peering or VPN Gateway.
4. A default backend pool is automatically created with the application gateway.
5. An application gateway automatically configures a default health probe when you create Backend pool and add instances to the pool.

Note: Application Gateway support for Static IP is now in Preview.

Application Gateway Pricing

Application Gateway Pricing consists of 2 components.

1. Amount of time that the gateway is provisioned and available
2. Amount of data processed by the Application Gateways.

Application Gateway Type	APPLICATION GATEWAY	WAF APPLICATION GATEWAY
Small	$0.025 per gateway-hour	NA
Medium	$0.07 per gateway-hour	$0.126 per gateway-hour
Large	$0.32 per gateway-hour	$0.448 per gateway-hour

DATA PROCESSING	Small	Medium	Large
First 10 TB/month	$0.008 per GB	Free	Free
Next 30 TB	$0.008 per GB	$0.007 per GB	Free
Over 40 TB/month	$0.008 per GB	$0.007 per GB	$0.0035 per GB

Traffic Manager

Traffic Manager works at the DNS level. It uses Public DNS responses to direct end-user traffic to globally distributed endpoints. Clients then connect to those endpoints directly. Traffic Manager does not see the traffic passing between the client and the service.

An endpoint is any Internet-facing service hosted inside or outside of Azure with public DNS name. Endpoints can be in different Data centers or in different regions.

Endpoints supported by Traffic Manager include Azure VMs, Web Apps, Cloud Services and Non Azure Endpoints. Traffic Manager also supports Azure Load Balancers and Application Gateway as Endpoints.

Traffic Manager Working.

Traffic Manager uses the Domain Name System (DNS) to direct client requests to the most appropriate endpoint based on a traffic-routing method and the health of the endpoints. Figure below shows the working of Traffic Manager.

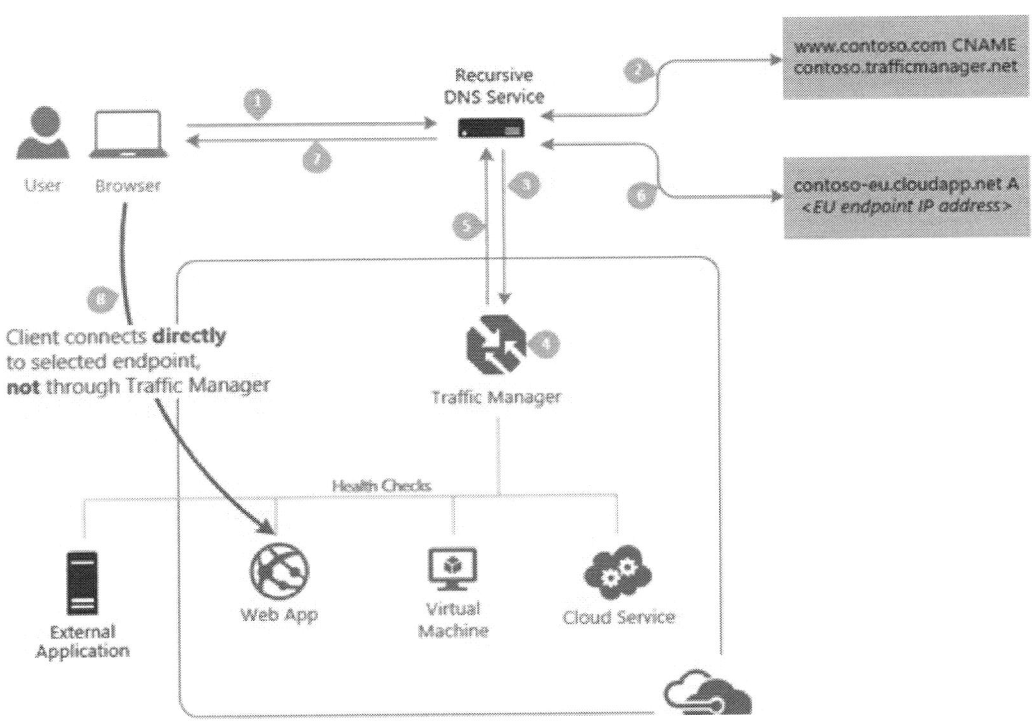

Traffic Manager Working (Continued from Previous Page)

Azure Traffic Manager distributes traffic across application endpoints. An endpoint is any Internet-facing service hosted inside or outside of Azure.

Traffic Manager does two things:

1. Distribution of traffic according to one of several traffic-routing methods.
2. Continuous monitoring of endpoint health and automatic failover when endpoints fail

When a client attempts to connect to a service, Traffic Manager first resolve's the DNS name of the service to an IP address. The client then connects to that IP address directly to access the service.

The most important point to understand is that Traffic Manager works at the DNS level. Traffic Manager uses DNS to direct clients to specific service endpoints based on the rules of the traffic-routing method. **Clients connect to the selected endpoint directly**. Traffic Manager does not see the traffic passing between the client and the service.

Traffic Manager Routing Methods

Azure Traffic Manager supports **six** traffic-routing methods to determine how to route network traffic to the various service endpoints.

Priority
Weighted
Performance
Geographic
Multivalue
Subnet

Priority: With Priority you use a primary service endpoint for all traffic, and provide backups in case the primary endpoints are unavailable.

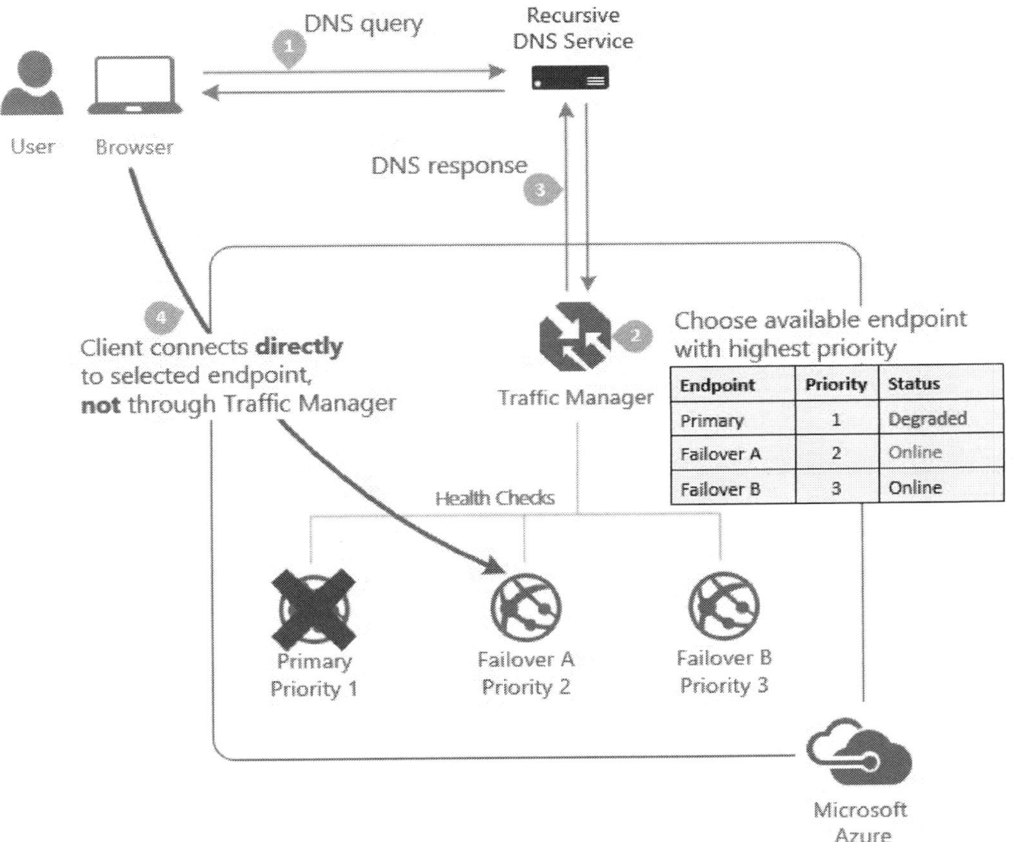

Weighted: Weighted traffic routing method distributes traffic across a set of endpoints, either evenly or according to weights defined.

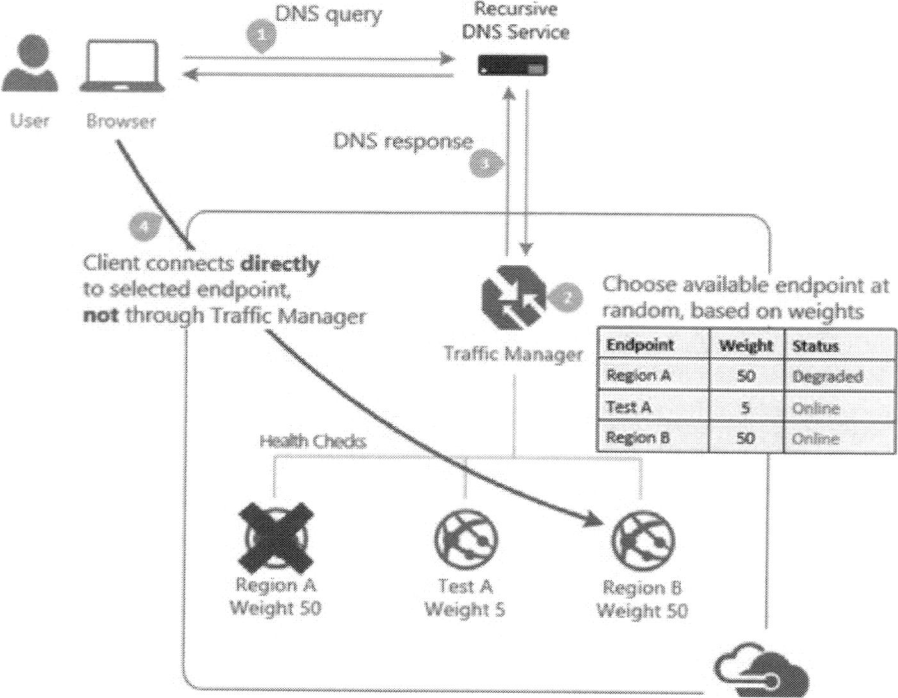

Performance: With Performance routing method users connect to the endpoint which offers lowest network latency.

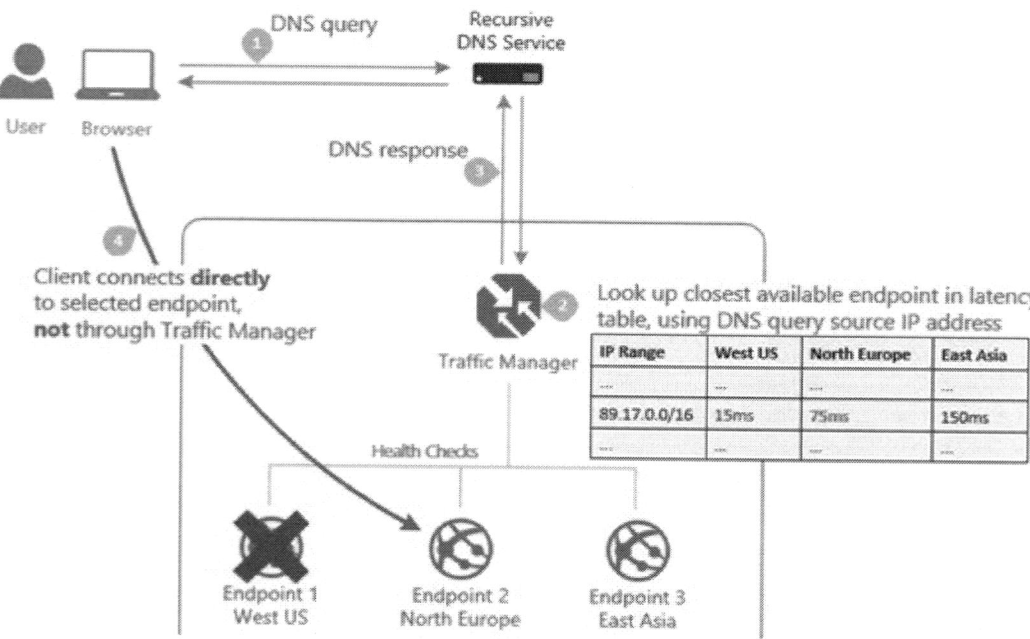

Geographic: With Geographic routing method users are directed to specific endpoints (Azure, External or Nested) based on which geographic location their DNS query originates from.

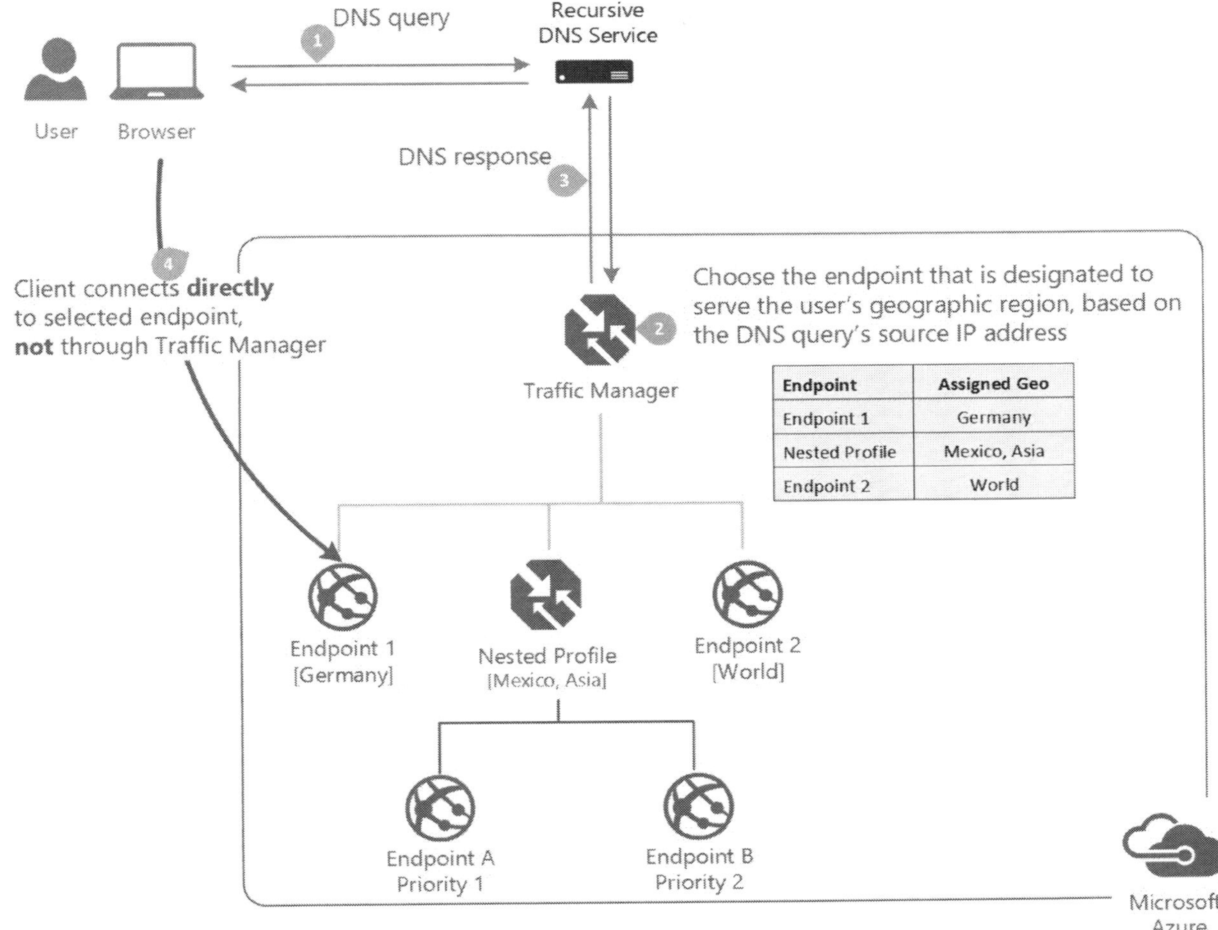

Subnet: The Subnet traffic-routing method allows you to map a set of end user IP address ranges to specific endpoints in a profile. After that, if Traffic Manager receives a DNS query for that profile, it will inspect the source IP address of that request (in most cases this will be the outgoing IP address of the DNS resolver used by the caller), determine which endpoint it is mapped to and will return that endpoint in the query response.

Use case for Subnet traffic-routing method

Subnet routing allows you to differentiate the experience you deliver for specific sets of users identified by the source IP of their DNS requests IP address. An example would be showing different content if users are connecting to a website from your corporate HQ. Another example would be restricting users from certain ISPs to only access endpoints that support only IPv4 connections if those ISPs have sub-par performance when IPv6 is used.

Multivalue: The Multivalue traffic-routing method allows you to get multiple healthy endpoints in a single DNS query response. MultiValue routing method works only if all the endpoints of type 'External' and are specified as IPv4 or IPv6 addresses.

Use case for Multivalue traffic-routing method

1. This is applicable for availability of sensitive applications that want to minimize the downtime.
2. Another use for MultiValue routing method is if an endpoint is "dual-homed" to both IPv4 and IPv6 addresses and you want to give the caller both options to choose from when it initiates a connection to the endpoint.

Exercise 64: Create & Implement Traffic Manager in 2 Steps

Note: For this Exercise we are using VMFE1 and VMFE2 as endpoints. Virtual Machines VMFE1 and VMFE2 were created in Exercise 25 & 33 in Chapter 4.

Step 1 Creating TM Profile: In Azure Portal Click **All Services**>Networking>Traffic Manager Profile> Click +Add> Create Traffic Manager profile blade opens> Enter name, for Routing Method select weighted or as per your requirement and for Resource Group Select RGCloud> click create. Resource Group Select RGCloud was created in Exercise 1, Chapter 1.

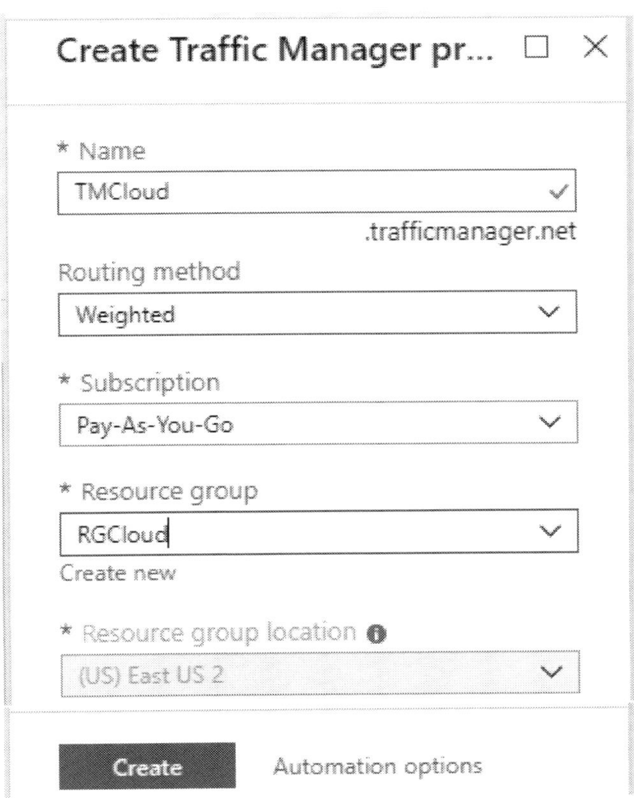

Figure Below shows Traffic Manager Dashboard.

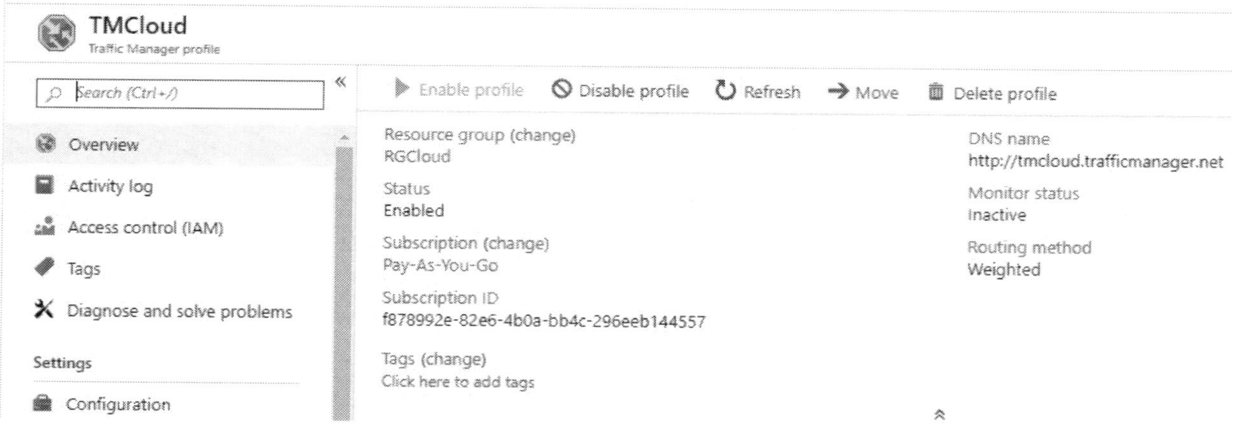

Add Endpoints (VMFE1 & VMFE2) in Traffic Manager Profile: In Traffic Manager dashboard click endpoints in left pane>In Right pane click +Add>Add endpoint blade opens>In type select Azure Endpoint> Enter a name> Target Resource type select Public IP Address> In Target Resource Select VMFE1 IP>Select Default value of weight as 1>Click OK (Not Shown).

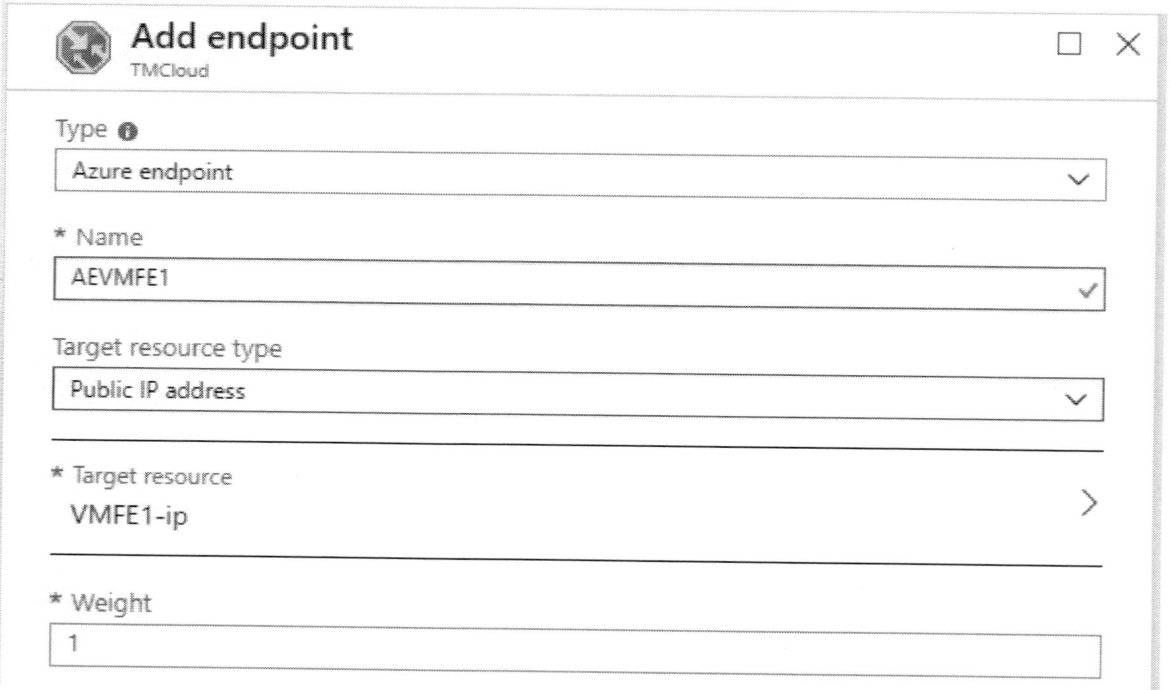

Repeat the above step for VMFE2.

Step 2b Access website on VMFE & VMFE2 using DNS name of Traffic Manager: Go to TM Profile Dashboard and note down DNS name of Traffic Manager Profile which in this case is http://tmcloud.trafficmanager.net

Open a browser and http://tmcloud.trafficmanager.net. Default Website of VMFE1 opens as shown below.

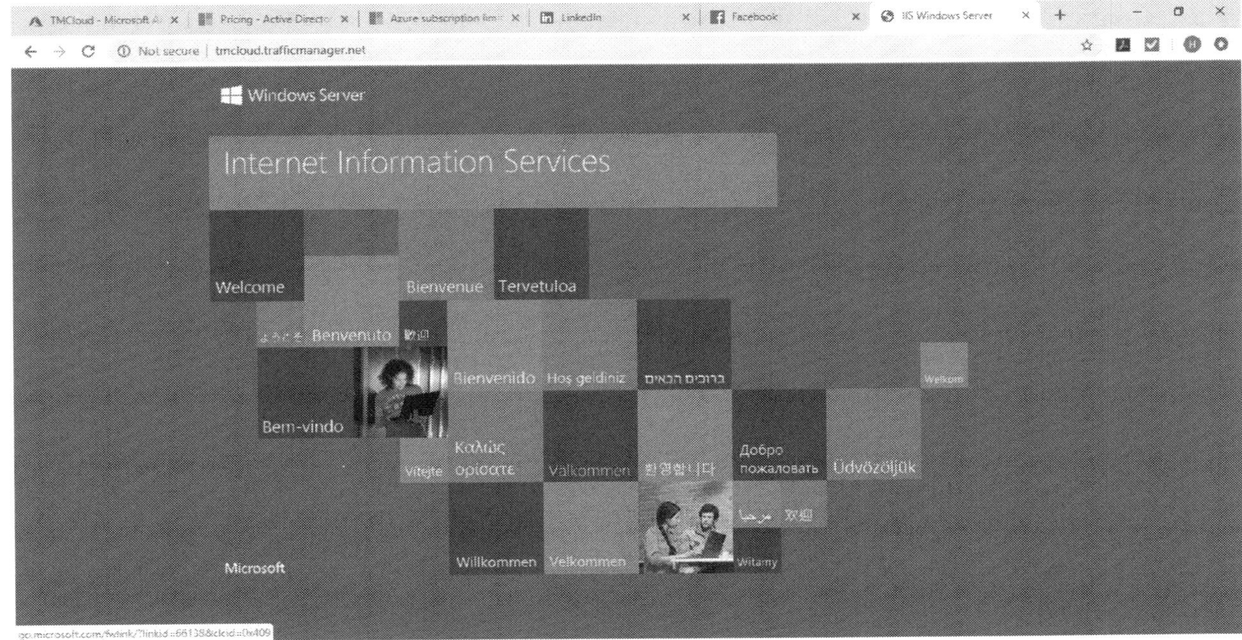

Traffic Manager Pricing

Traffic Manager Pricing consists of 2 components.

1. Number of DNS queries received
2. Health check charge for each monitored endpoint.

Pricing Details	Pricing
First 1 billion DNS queries / month	$0.54 per million queries
Over 1 billion DNS queries / month	$0.375 per million queries
Health Checks (Azure)	$0.36 per Azure endpoint / month
Health Checks (External)	$0.54 per External endpoint / month

Case Study 11: Load Balancing e-commerce server

You are connected to e-commerce website through a wired broadband connection. This internet connection goes down during your purchase cycle. You now re-connect to e-commerce website by connecting your computer to internet using mobile phone as hot spot.

Which Load Balancer you will use to load balance e-com application – layer 4 Azure Load Balancer or Layer 7 Azure Application Gateway so that client session reconnect to same e-com application server.

Note: Both layer 4 and layer 7 load balancer support session Persistence.

Solution

We will use Azure Application Gateway to load balance e-com application.

If e-commerce website is load balanced with Application gateway you will be re-directed to the same backend server because of cookies stored in client computers irrespective of which internet connection you use.

If e-commerce website is load balanced with azure layer 4 load balancer configured with client IP affinity, you will not know which e-com server you will be re-directed as in this case client IP has changed. If client IP was not changed then client will be re-directed to same e-com application.

Case Study 12: Highly Available Multisite Website

An IT giant located in Pala Alto, California does business with customers and partners located across the world.

There existing website on a single server is located in Palo Alto and is heavily accessed. End users (Customers and Partners) are complaining about slow performance of the website.

They want to give best experience to customers and partners visiting there website. They have short listed 3 locations for their website. Palo Alto serving North America and South America region, Germany serving EMEA region and Singapore serving APAC region including Australia and New Zealand.

There requirement is that each region should have highly available website and should be accessed by the users of that region only. Load Balancing solution in each region must support cookie based session affinity, SSL termination & URL based content routing.

Suggest a solution which satisfies above requirement.

Solution

We will use combination of Traffic Manager and Application Gateway to satisfy the customer requirement.

Each region will have multiple servers hosting the website to provide highly available website.

Application gateway in each region will provide round robin distribution of incoming traffic to the servers hosting the website. Application Gateway will also provide SSL termination, cookie based session affinity and URL based content routing.

Traffic Manager will provide DNS based Load Balancing and will route the user request to the Application Gateway in the respective region using Geographic routing method.

Figure below shows the Architecture of the solution.

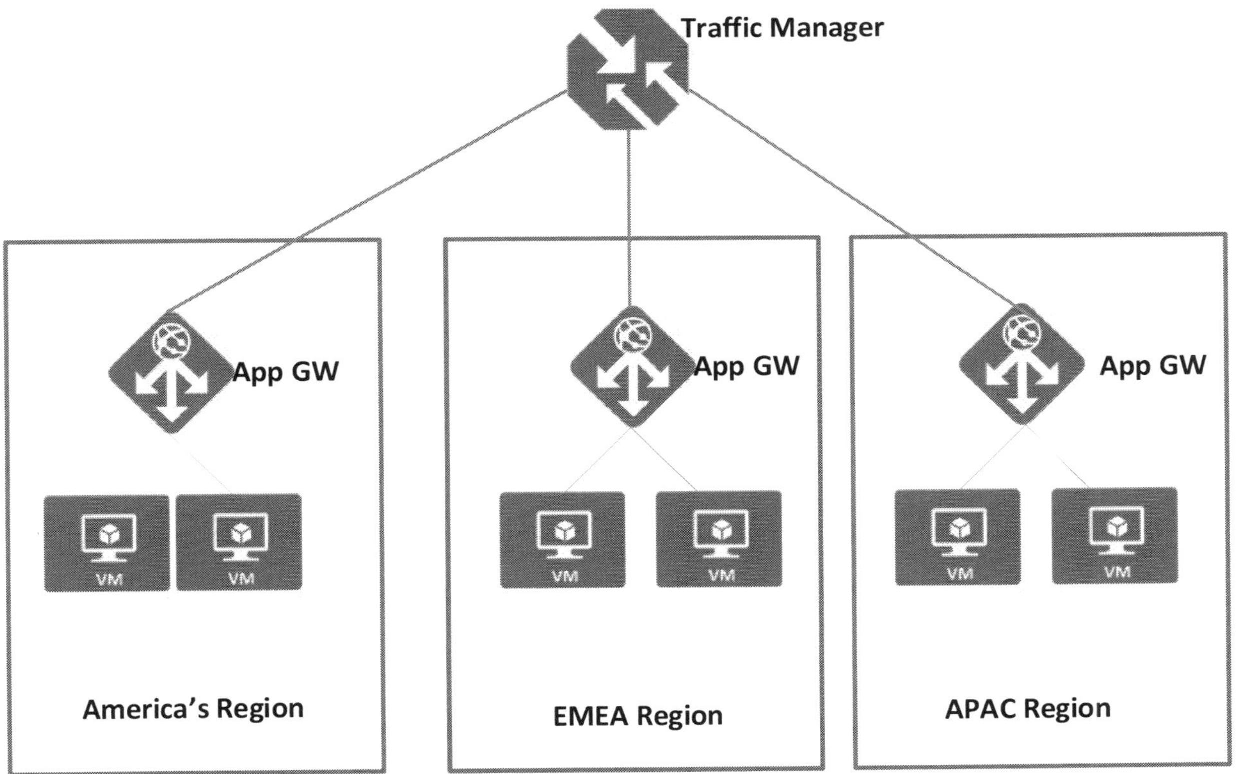

Chapter 7 Deploy Virtual Machines Scale Sets (VMSS)

This Chapter covers following Topic Lessons

- Virtual Machine Scale Set (VMSS)
- Virtual Machine Scale Set (VMSS) Architecture
- Autoscaling with VMSS
- Virtual Machine Scale Set (VMSS) Maximums
- Design Nuggets

This Chapter covers following Lab Exercises

- Deploying VMSS
- Connecting to Instances in VMSS
- Register Resource Provider Microsoft.Insight
- Enabling Autoscaling

This Chapter covers following Case Studies

Design Compute Solution for Image Processing Application

Chapter Topology

In this chapter we will add Virtual Machines Scale Set (VMSS) to the topology. VMSS will be created in Web-Subnet of Virtual Network VNETCloud.

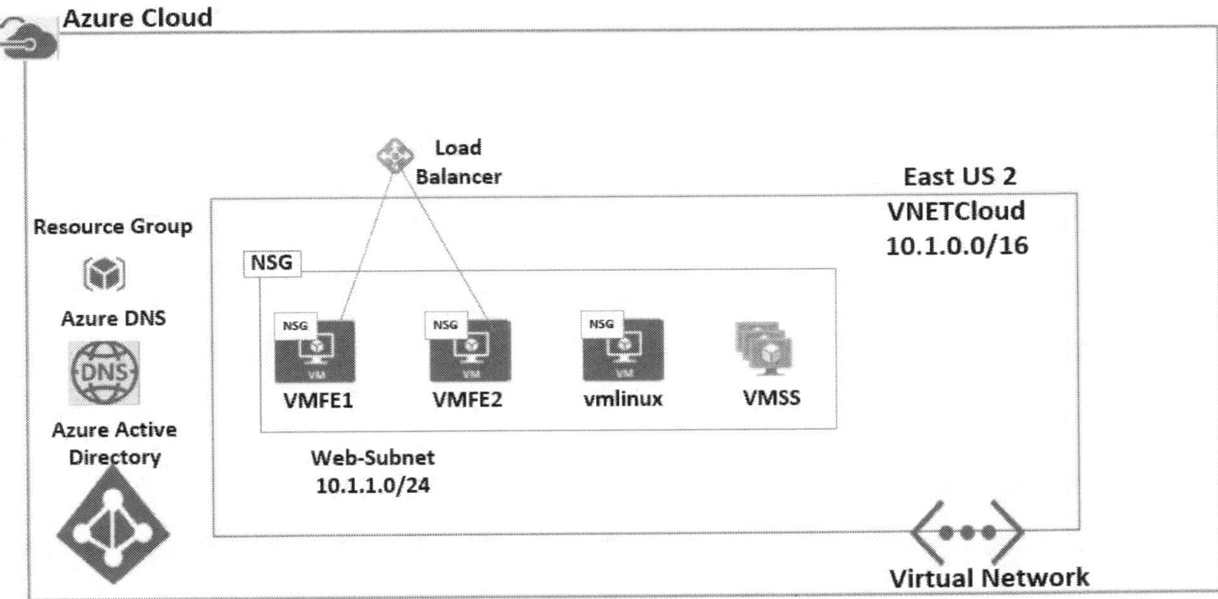

Note 1: I am no longer showing Subnets (DB-Subnet, DMZ, GatewaySubnet & AG-Subnet) in VNET Cloud because of Lack of space and also they are no longer required.

Virtual Machine Scale Sets (VMSS)

Virtual Machine Scale Sets creates scalable & high available Virtual Machine infrastructure by deploying and managing identical VMs as a set in a single Subnet of Virtual Network. An Azure Load Balancer or Azure Application Gateway is also deployed along with set of identical VMs.

Scale sets provide high availability to your applications, and allow you to centrally manage, configure, and update a large number of VMs. With virtual machine scale sets, you can build large-scale services for areas such as compute, big data, and container workloads.

VMs in the scale set are managed as a unit. All VMs in the scale set are identical and are either Windows VM or Linux VMs. All VMs are of same size and series.

VMSS supports Azure Windows and Linux images and Custom images.

Optionally by enabling Autoscaling on VMSS, Virtual Machines instances in the set can be added or removed automatically.

Features of Virtual Machine Scale Sets

Identical VMs deployed as a set.
Easy to create and manage multiple VMs.
Provides high availability and application resiliency.
Allows your application to automatically scale as resource demand changes.
Works at large-scale.

VM-specific features not available in Scale Set

1. You can snapshot an individual VM but not a VM in a scale set.
2. You can capture an image from an individual VM but not from a VM in a scale set.
3. You can migrate an individual VM from native disks to managed disks, but you cannot do this for VMs in a scale set.

Virtual Machine Scale Set (VMSS) Architecture

Virtual Machine Scale Set (VMSS) deploys set of Identical VMs in a single subnet of a Virtual Network. Figure below shows Architecture of Virtual Machine Scale Set (VMSS) deployed in single subnet with Single Placement group.

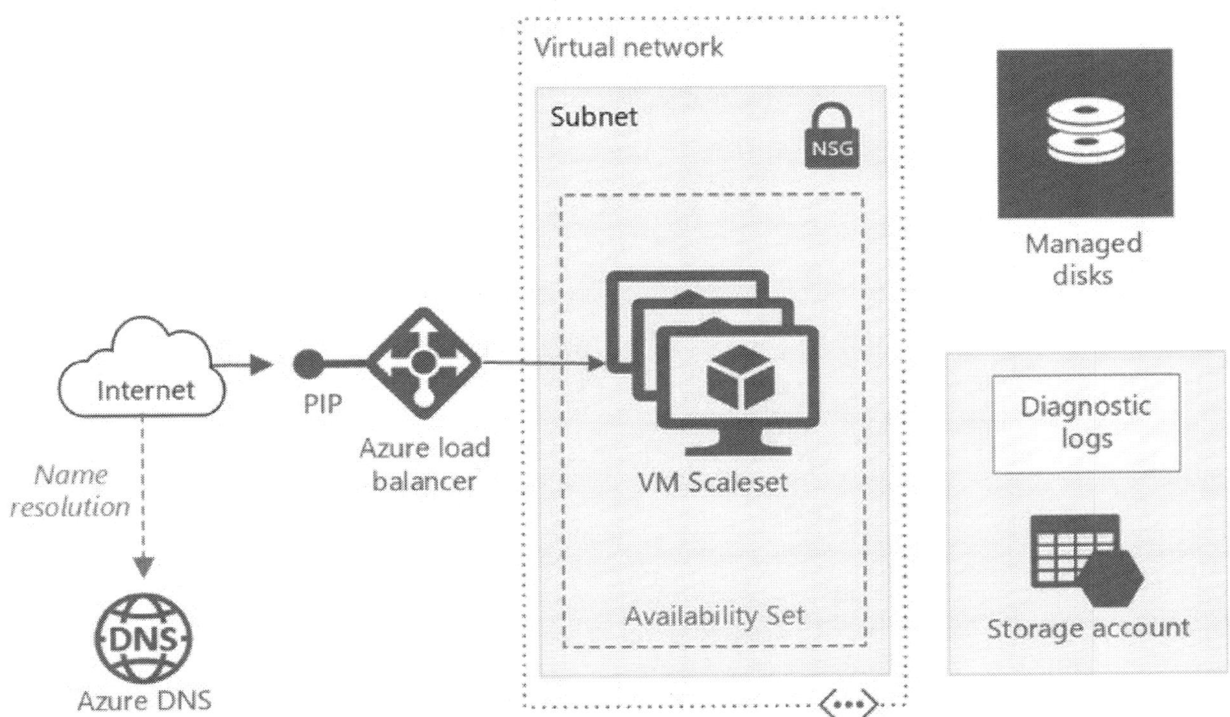

Set of identical VMs are deployed in the Single Subnet of Virtual Network.
You can select Existing or create new Virtual Network with **Single Subnet** during VM Scale set deployment.
Azure Load Balancer or Application Gateway with Public IP is created during VMSS deployment.
Placement group is availability set with five fault domains and five update domains and support up to 100 VMs. Placement group is automatically created by VMSS. Additional Placement groups will be automatically created by VMSS if you are deploying more than 100 instances.
Storage: VMSS can use managed disks or unmanaged disks for Virtual Machine storage. Managed disks are required to create more than 100 Virtual Machines. Unmanaged disks are limited to 100 VMs and single Placement Group.

Autoscaling with VMSS

With Autoscaling, Virtual Machines can be added (scale-out) or removed (scale-in) automatically from Virtual Machine Scale Set (VMSS) based on rules configured for metrics (CPU utilization, Memory utilization, Storage Queue etc.).

During Autoscaling the application continues to run without interruption as new resources are provisioned. When the provisioning process is complete, the solution is deployed on these additional resources. If demand drops, the additional resources can be shut down cleanly and de-allocated automatically.

How to Enable Autoscaling in VMSS

You can enable Autoscaling during VMSS creation or after the creation from VMSS dashboard or Azure Monitor Dashboard. If enabled during VMSS creation then only CPU metrics can be used for Autoscaling. Autoscaling can be based on schedule or on metric condition. **Metrics can be derived locally from VMSS or externally from Azure Resources such Service Bus, Storage Queue etc.**

Autoscaling Metrics

Autoscaling is enabled by configuring rules on Metrics or on Schedule. VMSS supports following types of metrics for configuring Autoscaling rules:

Host level Metrics: Host level metrics such as % CPU Utilization, Disk Read/write, Network in/out traffic at Network interface etc are emitted by Virtual Machines by default.
Guest OS level Metrics: You need to enable Guest OS diagnostics to use OS level metrics. OS level metrics are Operating system performance counters. Performance metrics are collected from inside of each VM instance and are streamed to an Azure storage account. VMSS can configure Autoscaling rules based on Guest OS level metrics,.
Application Insights: Application insights provide performance data for application running on VM.
Azure Resources: Azure resources such as Azure Storage queue can be used as a metric for configuring Autoscaling rules. For Example you can configure Autoscaling rule which scale-out by 2 instances when Storage Queue length is greater than 5.

Autoscaling Working

When threshold for a metric is reached scale-out or scale-in happens. For Example a rule configured for CPU utilization states that if CPU utilization crosses 80% then scale-out by 2 instances and if CPU utilization drops below 30% then scale-in by one instance.

All thresholds are calculated at an instances level (Average of all instances in VMSS). For example scale- out by 2 instance when average CPU > 80%, means scale-out happens when the average CPU across all instances is greater than 80%.

Note About VMSS Exercise

1. We will use Image Created in Exercise 44, Chapter 4 for deploying VMSS. If you have not done image exercise you can choose any Windows image.
2. We will create VMSS in Web-Subnet in Virtual Network VNETCloud and in Resource Group RGCloud. Resource Group RGCloud & Virtual Network VNETCloud were created in Exercise 1 & 3 respectively in Chapter 1.

Exercise 65: Deploying VMSS

In Azure Portal click +Create a Resource> In search box type virtual machine scale set and click enter>In the result click Virtual Machine Scale set>Click create>Create Virtual Machine Scale set blade opens>Enter a name> For OS disk image click Browse all images>Select an image blade opens>Click My Items>**Select the image created in Exercise 44, Chapter 4**> Select RGCloud>Enter username and password (Not Shown)>Autoscale Disabled >Select Load Balancer and enter name for IP & Domain>Select VNETCloud and Web-Subnet>create.

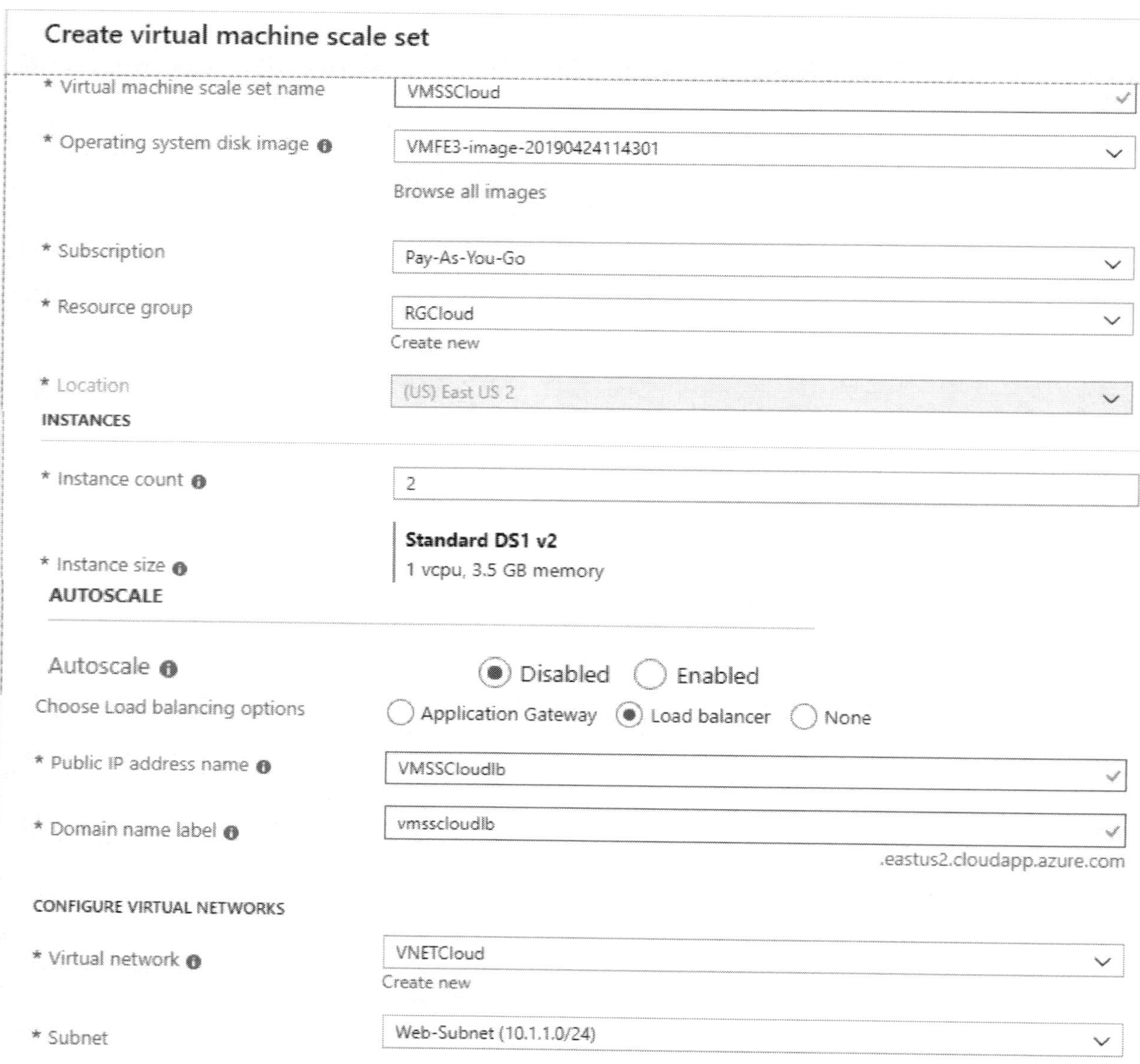

Note: If you have not done image exercise you can choose any Windows image.

Figure below shows the Dashboard of VMSS

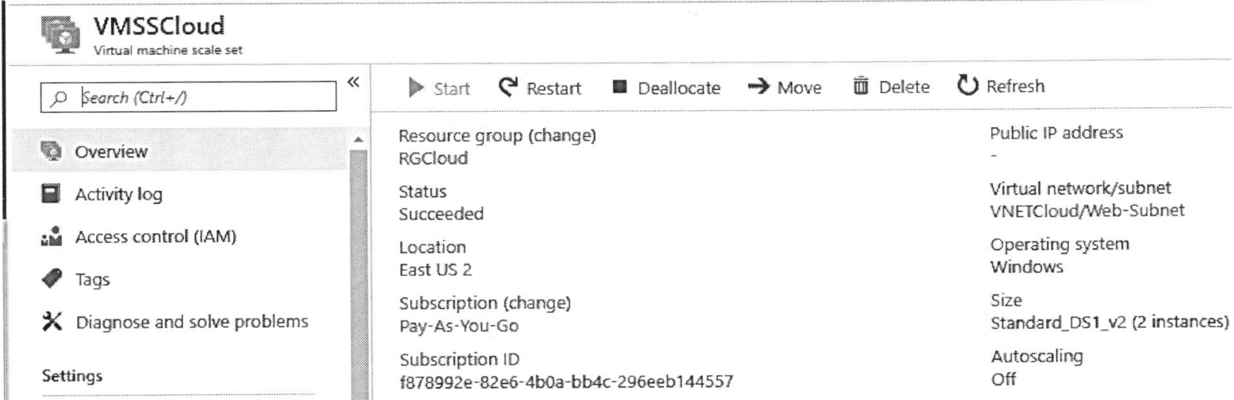

VMSS Dashboard is not showing public IP of the Load balancer. To Know public IP of Load Balancer Click All Resources in left pane>Select RGCloud in Resource Group and in type select Load Balancer> You can see Load Balancer vmsscloudlb.

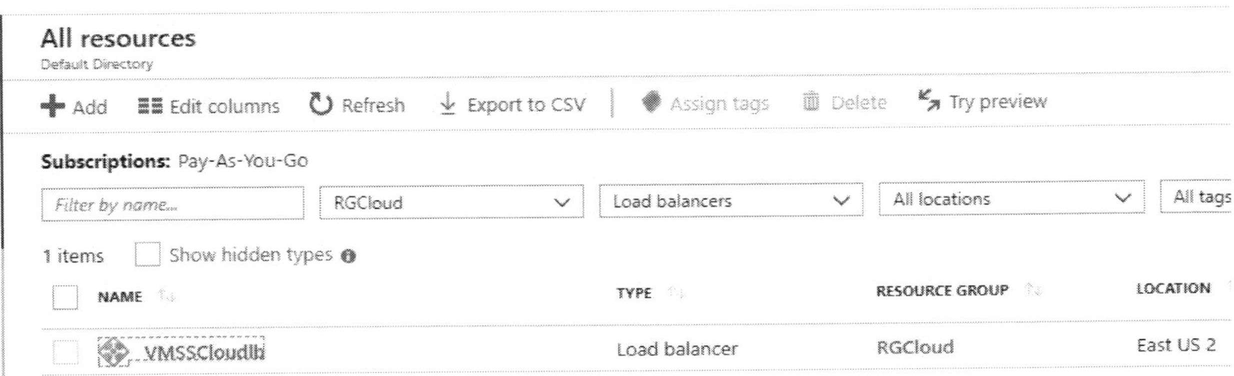

Click VMSSCloudlb to open the dashboard. Note down the IP Address.

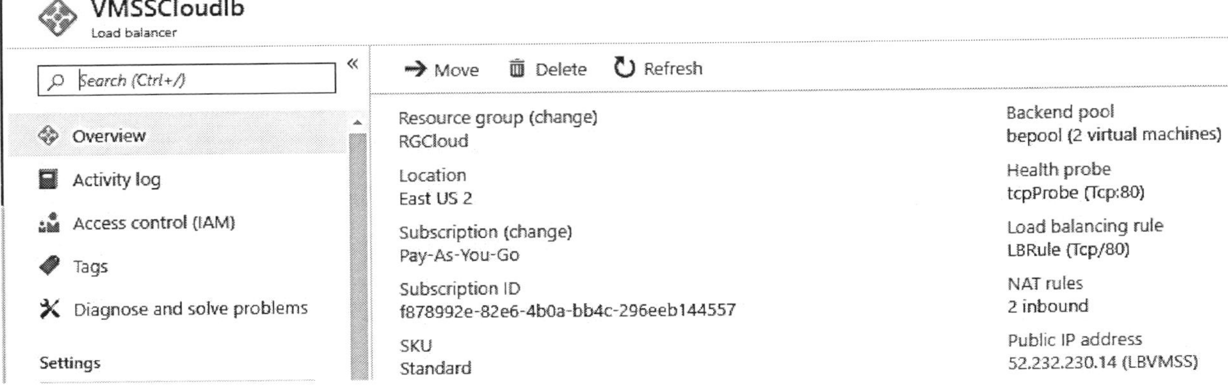

In a browser enter Load Balancer Public IP(52.232.230.14) shown in VMSSCloudlb dashboard. Default website opens.

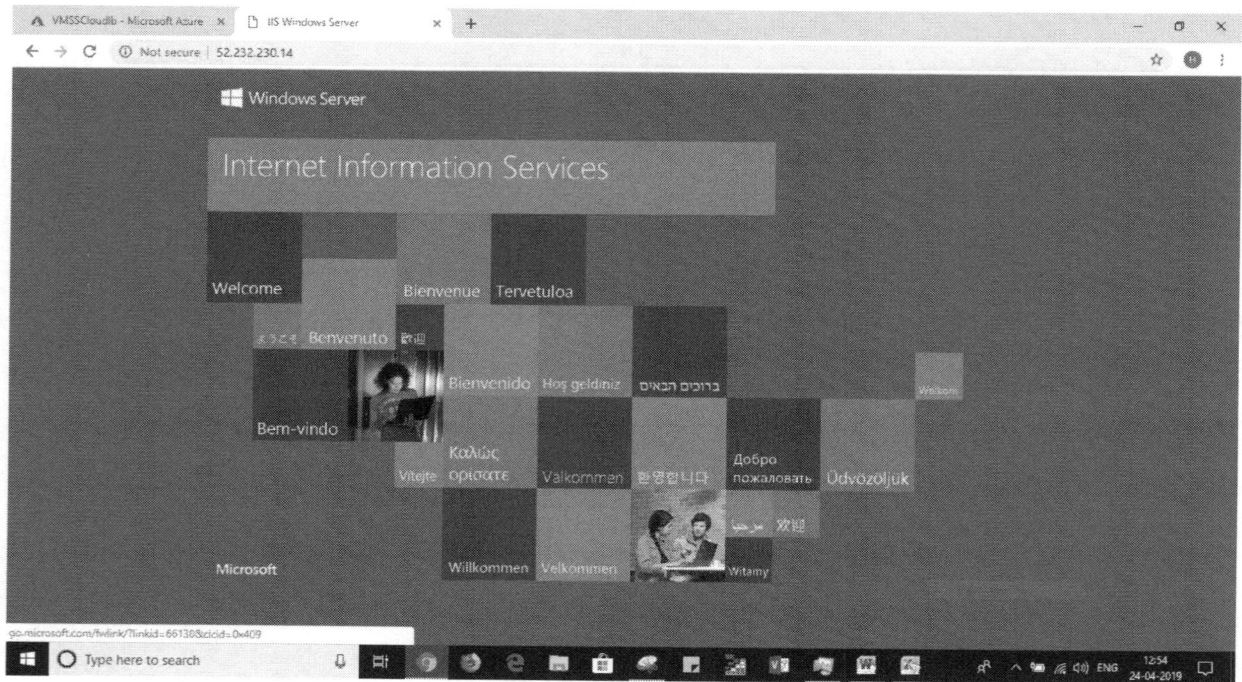

Note: Using Custom Image is the best way to deploy VMSS. Create a VM and Install Applications, add Disks or NIC etc. Create Image of it. In this way you need not go and install apps on individual Instances.

Exercise 66: Connecting to Instances in VMSS

When you create a scale set in the portal, a load balancer is created. Based on Public IP of Load Balancer, Network Address Translation (NAT) rules are used to distribute traffic to the scale set instances.

1. Click All Resources in left pane>Select RGCloud in Resource Group and in type select Load Balancer> You can see Load Balancer VMSSCloudlb. Alternatively in All Resources just scroll down and select vmsscloudlb.

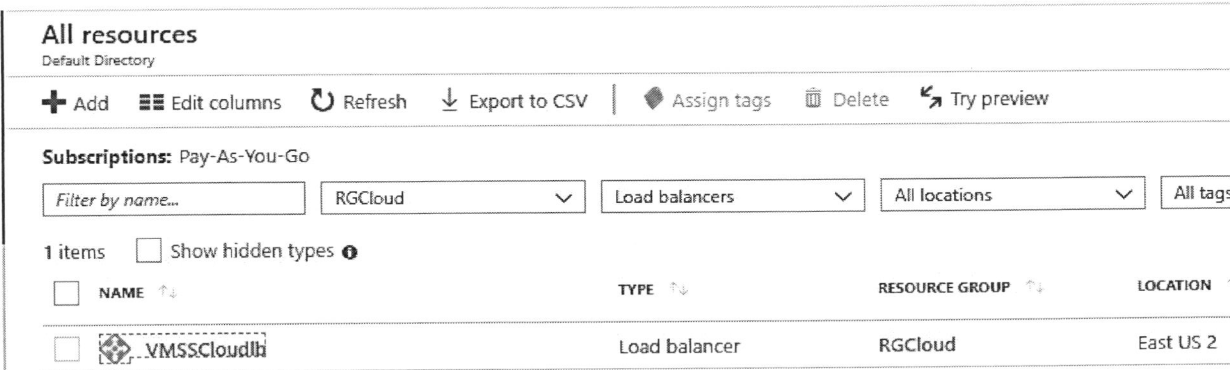

2. Click Load Balancer **VMSSCloudlb** in All Resources pane>Load Balancer dashboard opens>Click Inbound NAT Rules in left pane> In right pane you can see Instances IP address which is same for both instances but TCP Port for Instances are 50000 & 50001 respectively.

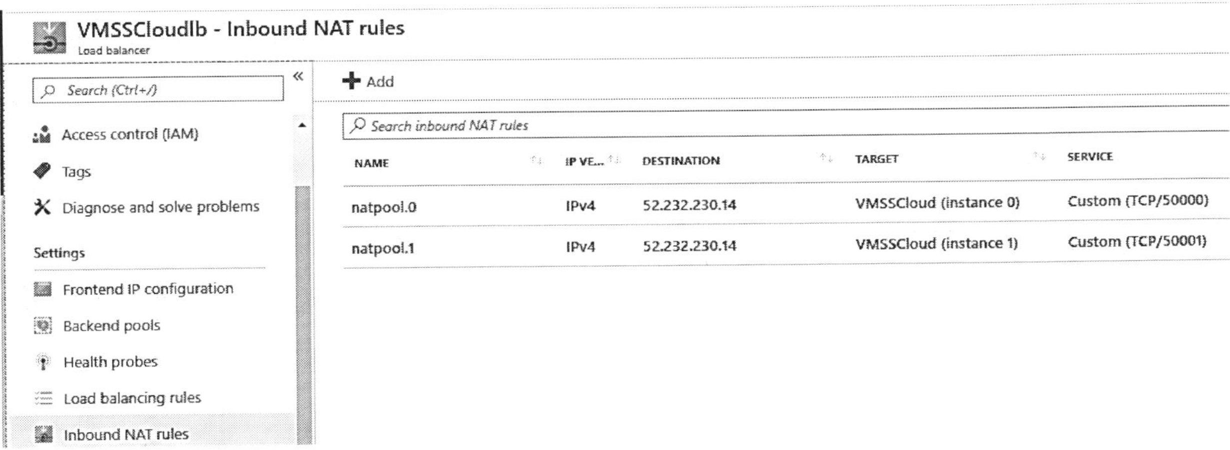

3. To connect to Instances using RDP use IP address appended with TCP Port.
   For Instance 1 connect to RDP using 52.232.230.14:50000
   For Instance 2 connect to RDP using 52.232.230.14:50001

4. Open RDP Application on your PC and enter 52.232.230.14:50000 and click Connect> Enter username and password you entered during VMSS creation.

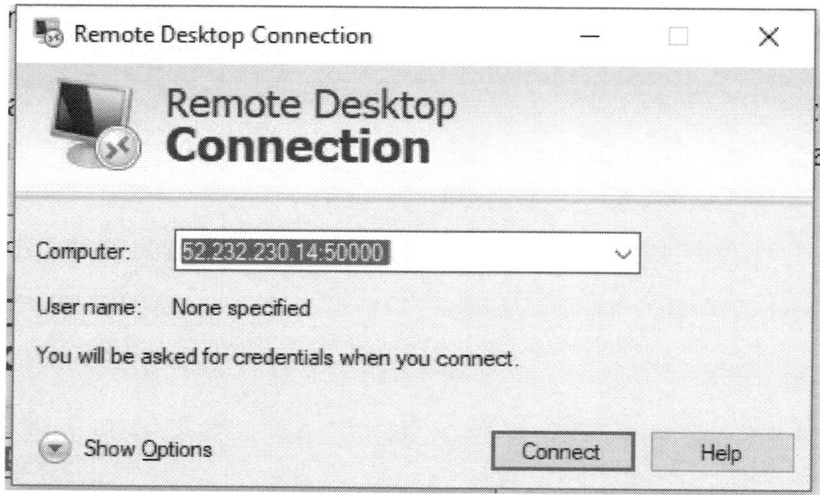

5. RDP session is opened for Instance 1. Server Manager is already opened.

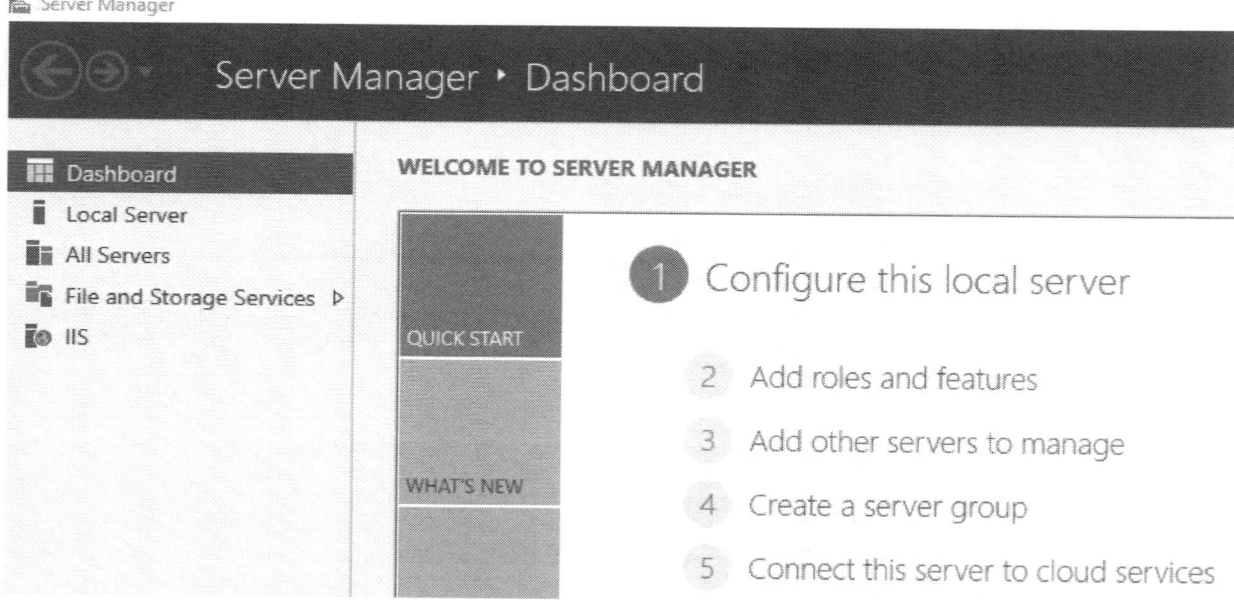

Exercise 67: Register Resource Provider Microsoft.Insight

This is required for Autoscaling exercise otherwise Autoscaling will give error. This error happens if you are using a resource provider that you haven't previously used in your subscription.

In Azure Portal Click Cost Management + Billing in left pane> Cost Management + Billing Dashboard opens. Click Subscription in left pane>In right pane click your subscription>Subscription Dashboard opens. In left pane under settings click Resource Providers> In right pane scroll and select microsoft.insights.

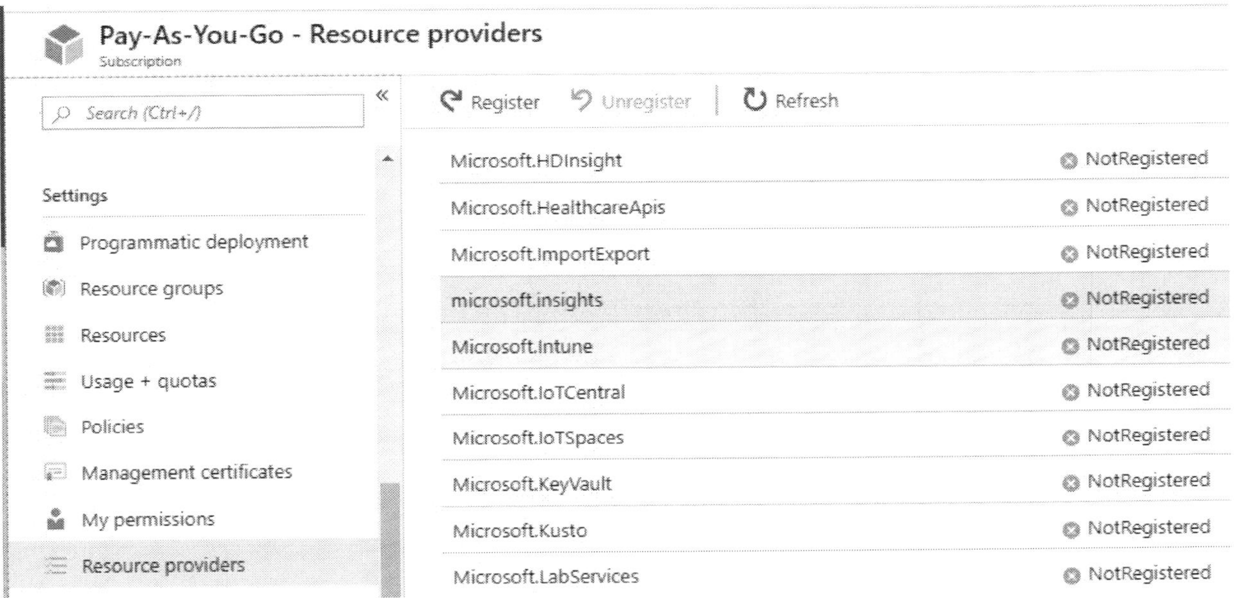

Make sure microsoft.insights is selected>Click Register in Top>After 1-2 minutes it will get registered. Press refresh if required.

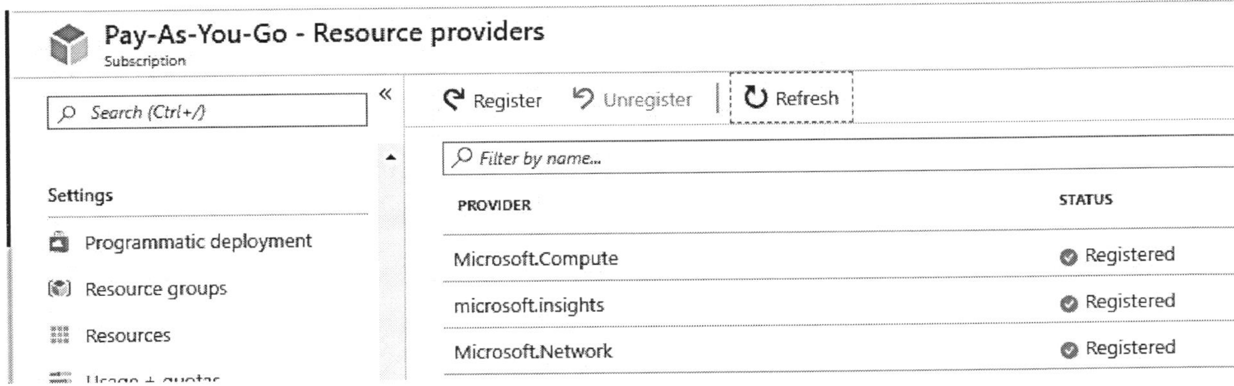

Exercise 68: Enabling Autoscaling

1. Click Scaling in VMSS dashboard>Scaling blade opens in right pane.

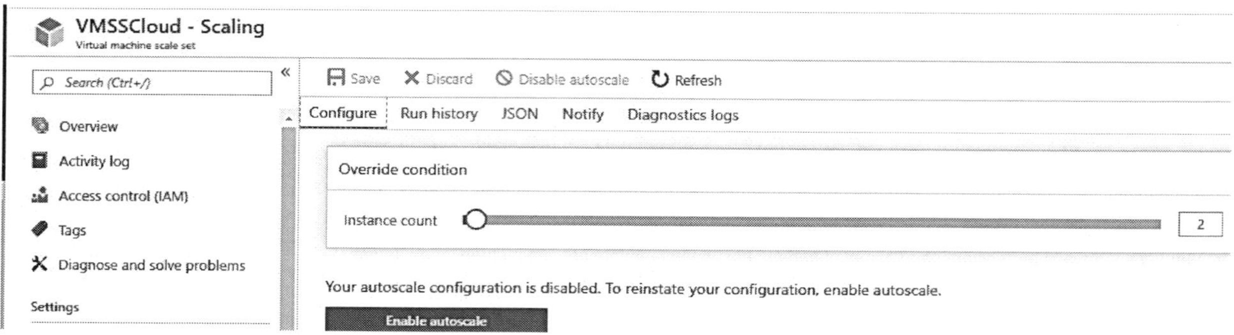

2. Click Enable Autoscale in right pane> Scale Condition Blade opens> we will edit the default scale condition Rule>Enter a name>In Instance limits Enter 4 in Maximum.
   Note + **Add a Rule Link**. We will use this to create Scale out and Scale in Rule.

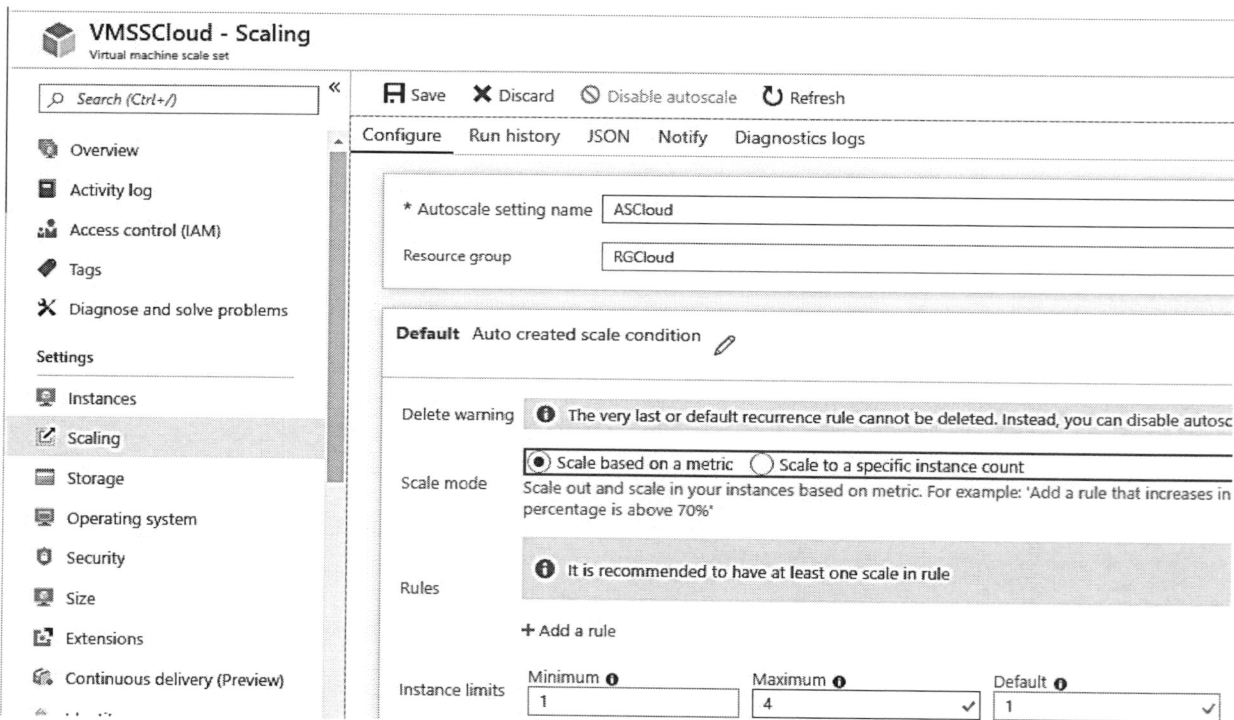

3. **Create Scale Out Rule**: In Scale condition pane Click + Add a rule >Scale rule opens in right pane. Note the metrics sources. Metric Sources can be from VMSS or External Sources such as Storage queue or Service Bus Queue etc. For Metric we will select % CPU> In operation Box select **Increase count by**> Rest select all default values and click Add

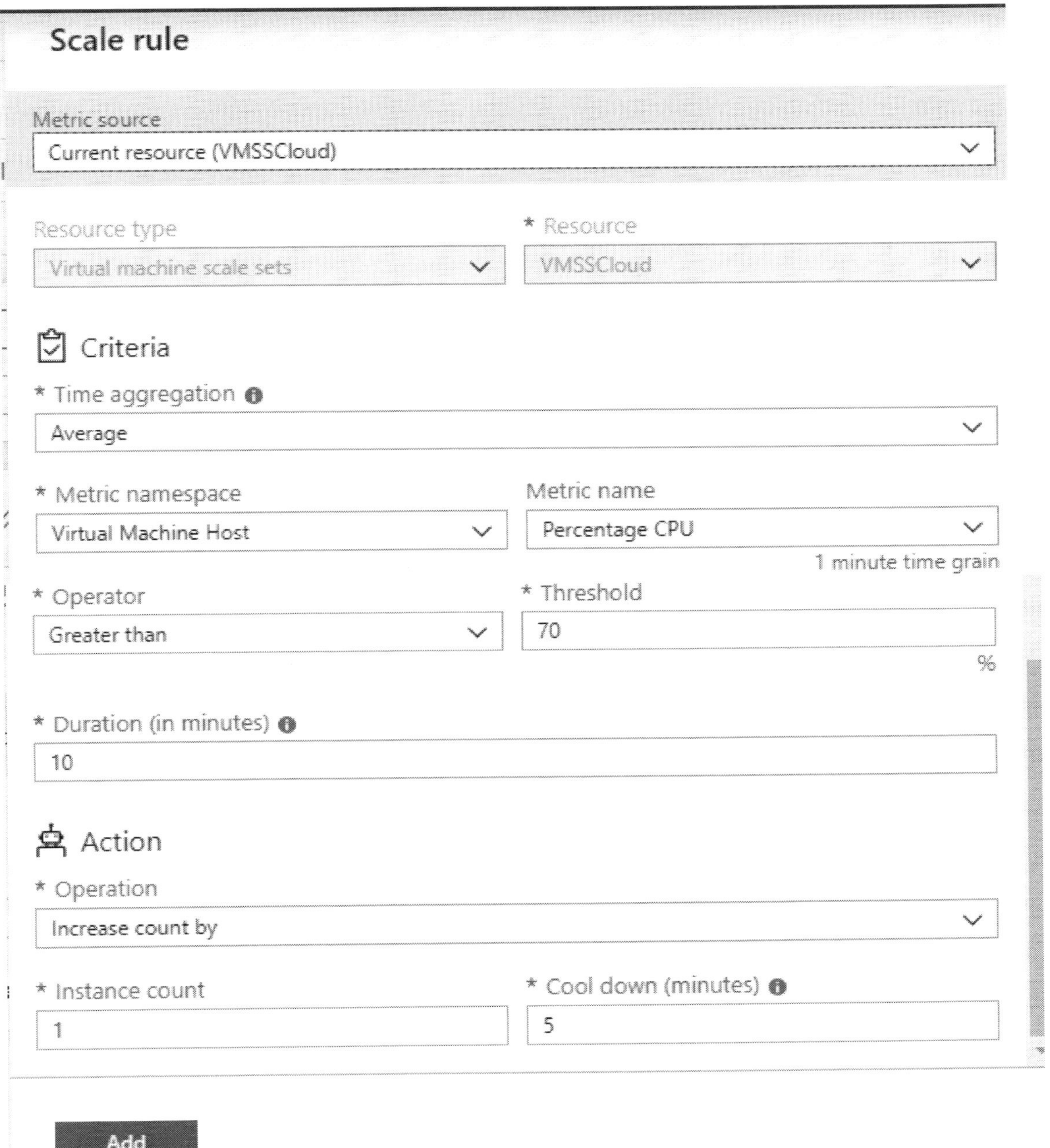

4. **Create Scale in Rule**: In Scale condition pane Click + Add a rule >Scale rule opens in right pane. For Metric we will select % CPU>Select **less than** in operator> Select 30% in Threshold> In operation Box select **decrease count by**>Rest select all default values and click Add> **click Save.**

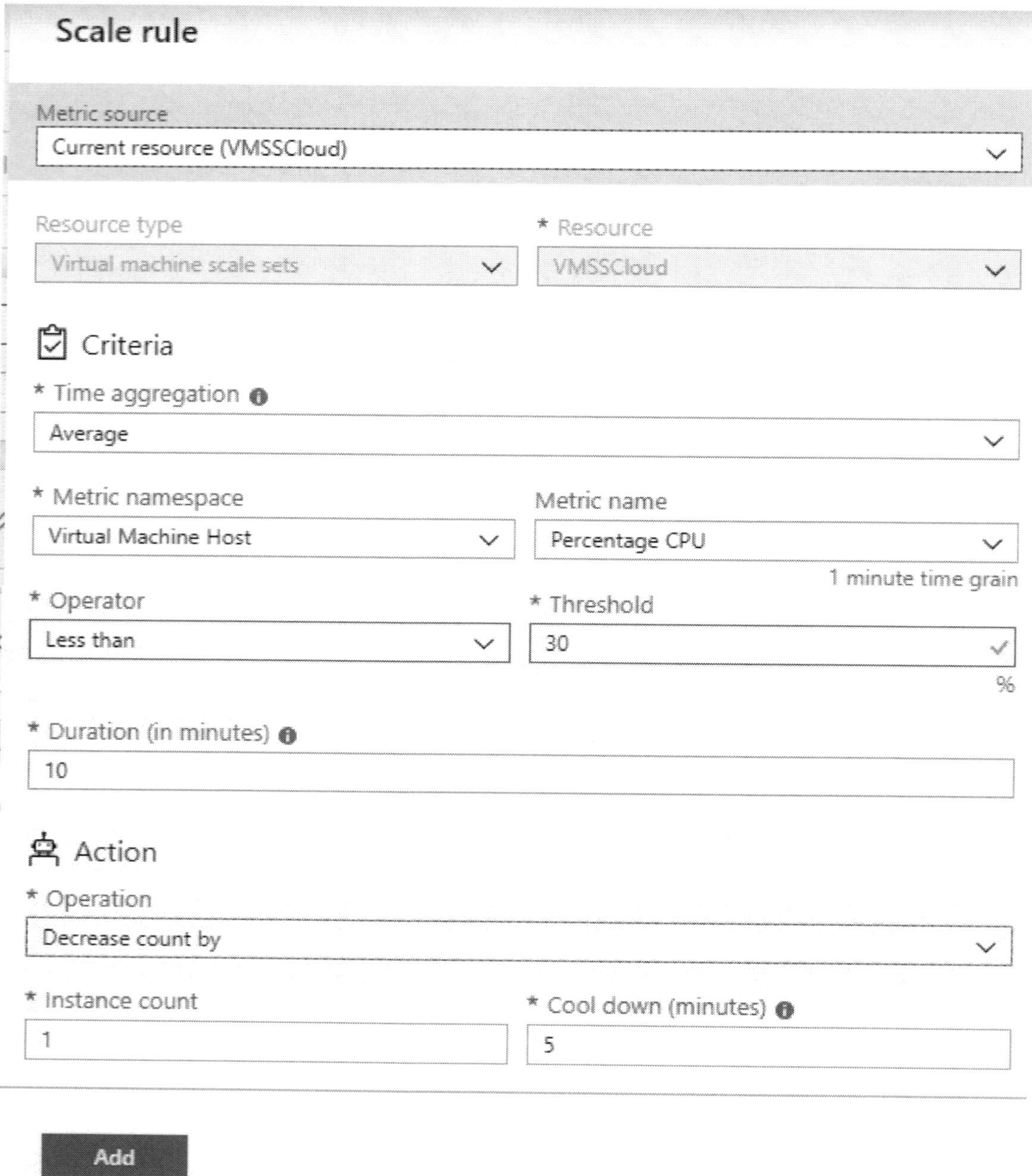

5. In scaling pane you can see the Scale in and scale out rules created. Make sure to click save so that Autoscaling rules are saved.

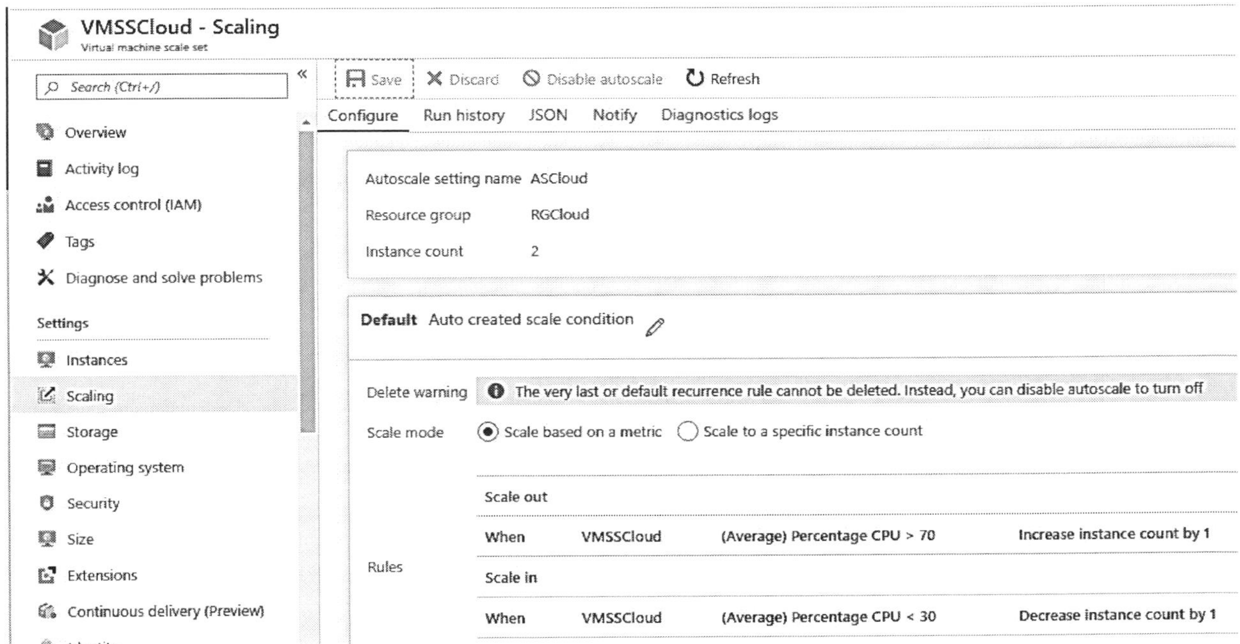

Note: Delete the VMSS, Load Balancers & Public IP as we longer need it.

Virtual Machine Scale Set (VMSS) Maximums

1. Maximum Number of VMs in a scale set when using Azure Platform images is 1000.
2. Maximum Number of VMs in a scale set when using Custom VM images is 600.
3. To have more than 100 VMs in the scale set you need to use Managed Disks for VM storage.
4. A scale set configured with unmanaged disks for VM storage is limited to 100 VMs.

Design Nuggets

Design Nugget: If Multiple Rules are configured then *scale-out* happens if any rule is met and *scale-in* happens when all rules are met.
Design Nuggets: You can only attach data disks to a scale set that has been created with Azure Managed Disks.
Design Nuggets: If you are not using managed disks, we recommend no more than 20 VMs per storage account with overprovisioning enabled and no more than 40 VMs with overprovisioning disabled.

Case Study 13: Design Compute Solution for Image Processing Application

A company wants to run image processing application in Azure. Application running in Azure VM will process images uploaded to Azure Blob Storage.

The Application team has given following requirements:

1. Users will be upload images to Container in Azure Blob Storage.
2. Azure VMs will process Uploaded images.
3. The Processed image will be stored in another Container in Blob Storage.
4. When average of % CPU utilization reaches 75% or above over 5 minutes interval then additional 2 instances of Azure VM should be automatically created to Process the image.
5. When average of % CPU reaches 30% or below over 5 minutes interval then the VM instances should decreased by 2 automatically.
6. The Solution should be Highly Available & Scalable.
7. The Maximum Instances should be 6. The minimum Instances should be 2. Default Instances should be 4.

Design Compute solution which meets above requirements.

Note 1: Application Team will provide Image from which you will create Azure VM instance for Virtual Machine Scale Set (VMSS). The image will have pre-installed application which will process user images uploaded to Azure Blob Storage.
Note 2: It will be Application Teams responsibility to connect Application to Azure Blob Storage.

Solution

Requirement 4 & 5 mentions automatic creation and deletion of VMs based on a % CPU Metric.
Requirement 6 mentions Highly Available & Scalable Solution.

We will use Virtual Machine Scale Set (VMSS) Solution. VMSS is both highly available and scalable solution. By enabling Autoscaling on Virtual Machine Scale Set (VMSS), VMs can be added (scale-out) or removed (scale-in) automatically from Virtual Machine Scale Set (VMSS) based on rules configured for metrics (CPU utilization, Memory utilization, Queue Storage etc.).

We will create VMSS with 4 VM Instances using image provided by Application team.

We will enable Autoscaling on VMSS using % CPU Utilization Metric.

We will create **Scale-out Rule** with a threshold of 70% and above for % CPU Metric and with an Action of increasing 2 Instances if the threshold of 70% and above is reached.

We will create **Scale-in Rule** with a threshhold of 30% and below for % CPU Metric and with an Action of decreasing 2 Instances if the threshold of 30% or below is reached.

Chapter 8 Storage Accounts

This Chapter covers following Topic Lessons

- Storage Accounts
- Storage Account Types
- Azure Storage Account Replication
- Storage Account endpoints
- Object Endpoints
- Network Access to Storage Account using VNET Service Endpoints
- Azure Storage Explorer
- Options to Connect to Azure Storage using Storage Explorer
- Download Storage Explorer
- Accessing Azure Storage Accounts using Azure Account Credentials
- Accessing Azure Storage Account using Storage Account Access Keys
- Accessing Storage Account using Shared Access Signature
- Accessing Storage Account using Azure Active Directory (Preview)

This Chapter covers following Lab Exercises

- Create GPv2 Standard Storage Account
- Create GPv2 Premium Storage Account
- Demonstrating Storage Account sastdcloud functionalities
- Demonstrating Storage Account Security
- Connect to Azure Storage using Azure Account Credentials
- Get Storage Account sastdcloud Access Keys
- Connect to Storage Account sastdcloud using Access key
- Generate Shared Access Signature of Storage Account
- Connect to Storage Account using Shared Access Signature

Chapter Topology

In this chapter we will add Azure Storage Account to the topology. We will create two Storage Accounts - GPv2 Standard Storage Account & GPv2 Premium Storage Account.

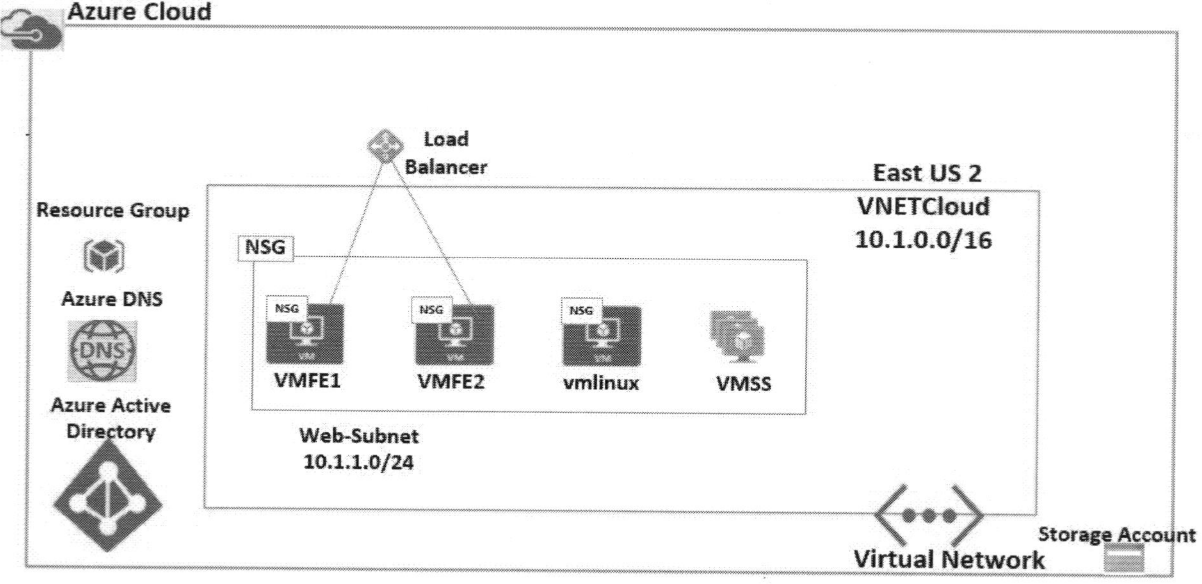

Storage Accounts

An Azure storage account provides a unique namespace to store and access your Azure Storage data objects.

Azure Storage (Blob, Table, Queue and Files) is created under Storage Accounts. Storage Account is prerequisite for creating Azure Storage.

The image below shows the dashboard of General Purpose Storage Account. From here you will create Blob, File, table or Queue Storage.

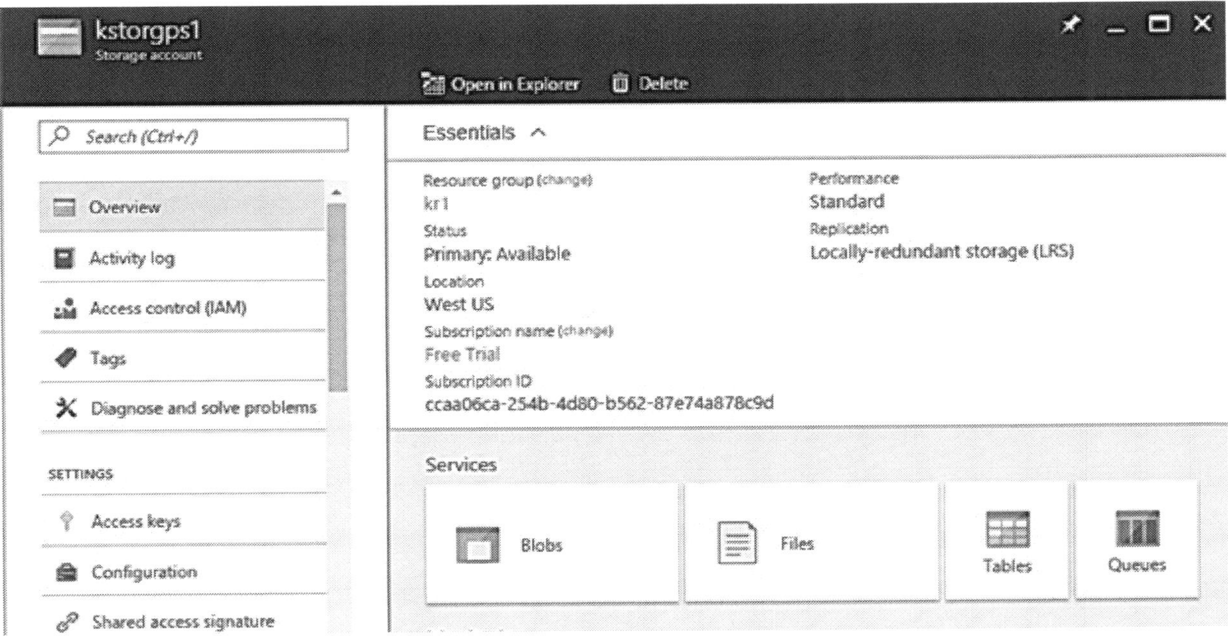

Figure below shows components of Blob, Table, Queue and File Storage.

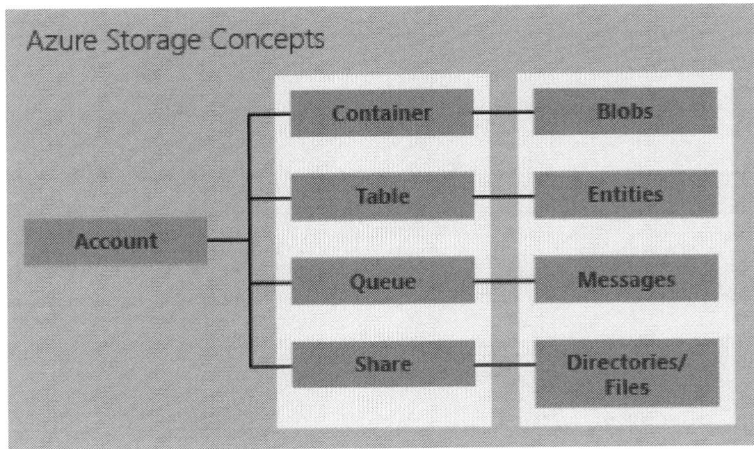

Storage Account Types

There are three types of storage accounts - General-purpose v2 (GPv2) Storage Account, General-purpose v1 (GPv1) Storage Account & Blob Storage Account.

General-purpose v2 (GPv2) Storage Account

General-purpose v2 (GPv2) storage accounts support storage services including blobs, files, queues, and tables. It supports all latest features for storage services.

For block blobs in a GPv2 storage account, you can choose between hot and cool storage tiers at the account level, or hot, cool, and archive tiers at the blob level.

General-purpose v1 (GPv1) Storage Account

General-purpose v1 (GPv1) storage account supports storage services including blobs, files, queues, and tables. It does not support latest features for storage services. It does not support blob storage tiering.

Blob Storage Account

Blob Storage accounts are specialized for storing blob data and support choosing an access tier – Hot or cool at account level.
Blob storage accounts support only block and append blobs and not page blobs.

Storage Account Performance Tiers

1. A **standard storage performance tier** allows you to create Blobs, Tables, Queues, Files and Azure virtual machine disks.
   It is backed by magnetic disk HDD.
   Supports GPv1, GPv2 and Blob Storage Account.

2. A **premium storage performance tier** allows you to create Blobs and Azure virtual machine disks.
   It is backed by SSD.
   Supports GPv1 & GPv2 Storage Account. Supports LRS replication only.

   Note: Premier storage performance tier now also supports and Azure File Storage (Preview). It is in Preview as of writing.

Comparing Storage Accounts

Description	GPv2	GPv1	Blob Storage Account
Storage Type Supported	Blob, File, Table and Queue	Blob, File, Table and Queue	Blob (block and append blob)
Types of Blob supported	page, block and append blob	page, block and append blob	block and append blob
Disk Type	HDD & SSD	HDD & SSD	HDD
Replication Options (Standard Storage	LRS, ZRS, GRS and RA-GRS	LRS, GRS and RA-GRS	LRS, GRS, RA-GRS
Replication Options (Premium Storage)	LRS	LRS	NA
Can be used for Virtual Machine Disks	Yes through page blobs	Yes through page blobs	No
Blob Storage Tiering	Yes	No	Yes
Use Case	It has wide and large use cases including VM disk.	It has wide and large use cases including VM disk.	Object Storage and Archiving

Note: MS now recommends Managed disks for Azure VMs. Managed Disks obviates the need to have storage account. Managed disks only support LRS for replication.

Azure Storage Account Replication

The data in the Microsoft Azure storage account is always replicated to ensure high availability. Replication copies data, either within the same Data Centre, or to a second Data Centre, depending on the replication option chosen. Azure Storage Accounts offer 4 Replication options – LRS, ZRS, GRS, RA-GRS.

Comparing Storage Account Replication Options

Features	LRS	ZRS	GRS	RA-GRS
Data is replicated across multiple datacenters.	No	Yes	Yes	Yes
Data can be read from a secondary location as well as the primary location.	No	No	No	Yes
Data Availability if Node becomes unavailable within Data Center	Yes	Yes	Yes	Yes
Data Availability if Data Center goes down	No	Yes	Yes	Yes
Data Availability if there is Region wide outage	No	No	Yes	Yes
SLA	11 9's	12 9's	16 9's	16 9's
Storage Account Supported	GPv1, GPv2, Blob	GPv2	GPv1, GPv2, Blob	GPv1, GPv2, Blob

Locally redundant storage (LRS)

Locally redundant storage (LRS) replicates your data three times in a datacenter in the region in which you created your storage account. A write request returns successfully only once it has been written to all three replicas. The three replicas each reside in separate fault domains and upgrade domains within one storage scale unit.

LRS is the lowest cost option. LRS can protect your data from underlying storage node failure but not from Data Centre wide outage.

Use Case for Locally Redundant Storage

LRS can be used in cases where applications are restricted to replicating data only within a country due to data governance requirements.

Storage Accounts Supported: GPv2, GPv1 and Blob Storage Account.

Zone-redundant storage (ZRS)

ZRS replicates your data synchronously across three availability zones. ZRS enables customers to read and write data even if a single zone is unavailable or unrecoverable. Inserts and updates to data are made synchronously and are strongly consistent.

ZRS provides durability for storage objects of at least 99.9999999999% (12 9's) over a given year. Consider ZRS for scenarios like transactional applications where downtime is not acceptable.

ZRS provides higher durability than LRS. Data stored in ZRS is durable even if the primary Datacentre is unavailable or unrecoverable.

ZRS will not protect your data against a regional disaster where multiple zones are permanently affected. For protection against regional disasters, Microsoft recommends using Geo-redundant storage (GRS): Cross-regional replication for Azure Storage.

Storage Accounts Supported: GPv2.

Geo Redundant Storage (GRS)

Geo-redundant storage (GRS) replicates your data to a secondary region that is hundreds of miles away from the primary region.

With GRS, data is first replicated 3 times within the primary region and then asynchronously replicated to the secondary region, where it is also replicated three times.
With GRS, data is durable even in the case of a complete regional outage or a disaster in which the primary region is not recoverable.

When you create a storage account, you select the primary region for the account. The secondary region is determined based on the primary region, and cannot be changed.

Storage Accounts Supported: GPv2, GPv1 and Blob Storage Account.

Read-access geo-redundant storage (RA-GRS)

Read-access geo-redundant storage (RA-GRS) not only replicates your data to a secondary region but also provides read-only access to the data in the secondary location.

With RA-GRS, data is first replicated 3 times within the primary region and then asynchronously replicated to the secondary region, where it is also replicated three times.

With RA-GRS, data is durable even in the case of a complete regional outage or a disaster in which the primary region is not recoverable.

When you create a storage account, you select the primary region for the account. The secondary region is determined based on the primary region, and cannot be changed.

Storage Accounts Supported: GPv2, GPv1 and Blob Storage Account.

Additional Replication Options

Following replication options are now in preview. Since they are in preview they will not be asked Exams. We will not discuss them here.

Geo-zone-redundant storage (GZRS)
Read-access geo-zone-redundant storage (RA-GZRS)

Storage Account endpoints

Every object that you store in Azure Storage has a unique URL address. The storage account name forms the subdomain of that address. The combination of subdomain and domain name, which is specific to each service, forms an *endpoint* for your storage account.

For example, if your storage account is named *mystorageaccount*, then the **default endpoints for your storage account** are:

Blob service: http://*mystorageaccount*.blob.core.windows.net
Table service: http://*mystorageaccount*.table.core.windows.net
Queue service: http://*mystorageaccount*.queue.core.windows.net
File service: http://mystorageaccount.file.core.windows.net

Object Endpoints

The URL for accessing an object in a storage account is built by appending the object's location in the storage account to the endpoint. For example, a blob address might have this format:
http://mystorageaccount.blob.core.windows.net/mycontainer/myblob.

You can also configure a custom domain name to use with your storage account.

Storage Account Design Nuggets

1. Storage Account name must be unique within Azure.
2. Read-access geo-redundant storage (RA-GRS) is the default replication option when you create a storage account.

Exercise 69: Create GPv2 Standard Storage Account

In this exercise we will create Standard GPv2 Storage Account with name **sastdcloud** in resource group **RGCloud** and in location US East 2. Resource Group RGCloud was created in Exercise 1, Chapter 1.

1. In Azure Portal Click +Create a Resource in left pane> Storage> Storage Accounts> Create Storage Account Blade opens> Select Resource Group **RGCloud**> Give a unique name to storage Account **sastdCloud**> Select location East US 2>Performance standard>Account Type as GPv2>Replication RA-GRS> Access Tier Hot> Rest keep as default> Click Next: Advanced

Create storage account

* Subscription: Pay-As-You-Go
* Resource group: RGCloud
Create new

INSTANCE DETAILS

The default deployment model is Resource Manager, which supports the latest Azure features. You may choose to deploy using the classic deployment model instead. Choose classic deployment model

* Storage account name: sastdcloud
* Location: East US 2
Performance: (•) Standard ( ) Premium
Account kind: StorageV2 (general purpose v2)
Replication: Read-access geo-redundant storage (RA-GRS)
Access tier (default): ( ) Cool (•) Hot

Review + create | Previous | Next : Advanced >

Note 1: Storage Account name has to be unique within Azure.
Note 2: You can choose between Standard or premium (SSD) performance Tier.
Note 3: Note Access Tier option. This is not available with GPv1 Account.

2. In Advanced screen just go through options. Keep everything at default and click Review +create.

Create storage account

Basics Advanced Tags Review + create

SECURITY

Secure transfer required — Disabled / Enabled (selected)

VIRTUAL NETWORKS

Allow access from — All networks (selected) / Selected network

All networks will be able to access this storage account. Learn more

DATA PROTECTION

Blob soft delete — Disabled (selected) / Enabled

DATA LAKE STORAGE GEN2

Hierarchical namespace — Disabled (selected) / Enabled

Review + create | Previous | Next : Tags >

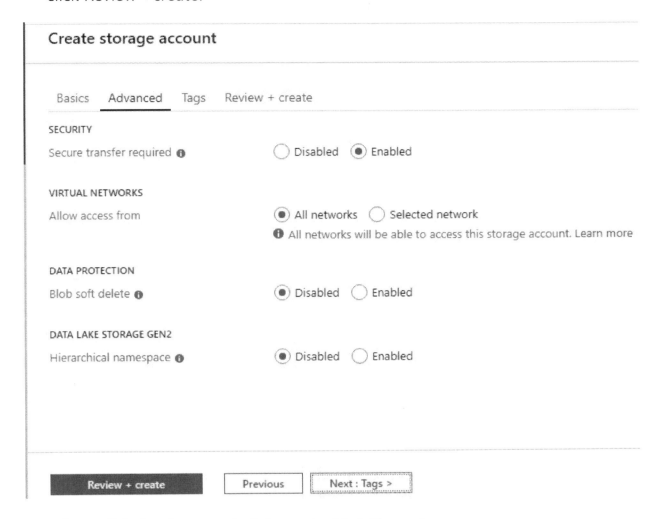

3. After validation is passed click create (Not Shown).

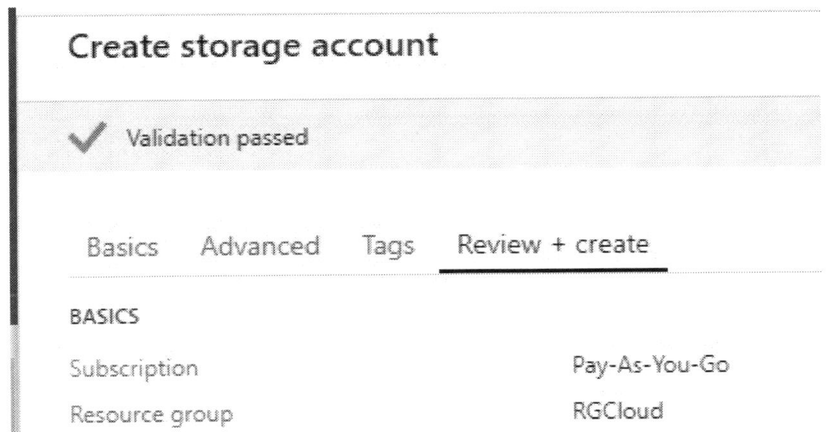

4. Figure below shows the dashboard of Storage Account. From here you can create Blob, file, table or queue Storage.

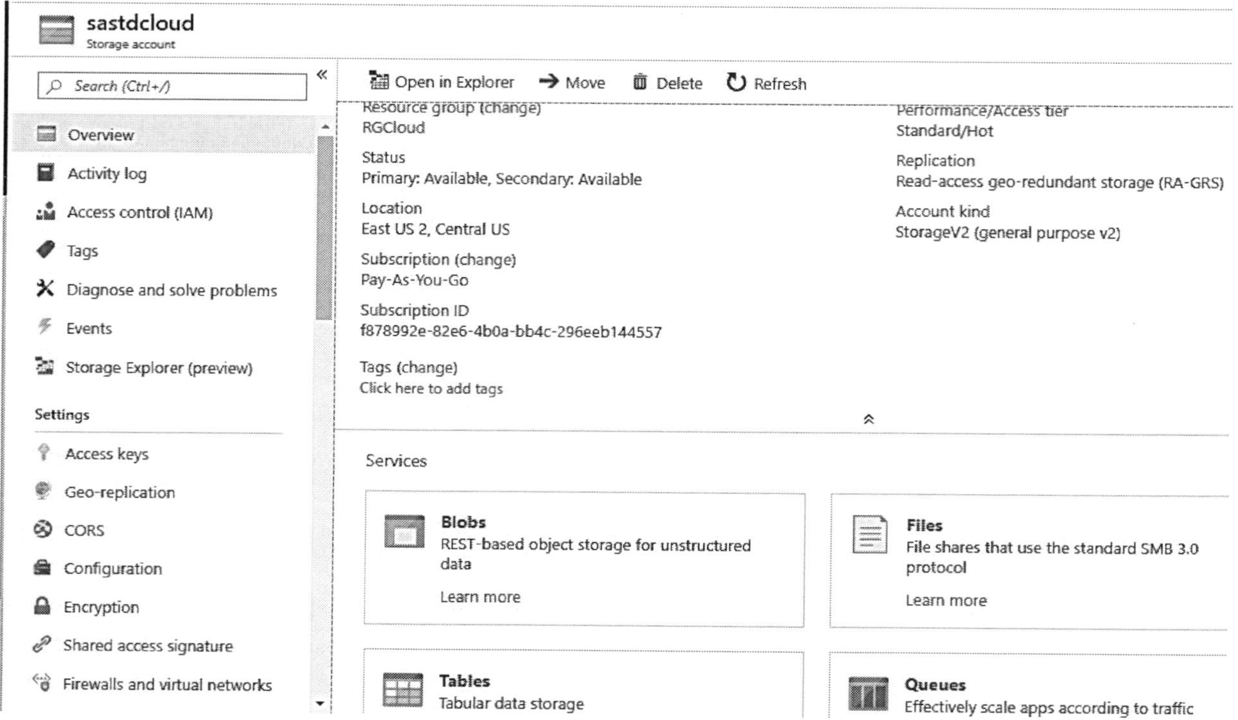

Exercise 70: Create GPv2 Premium Storage Account

In this exercise we will create Premium GPv2 Storage Account with name **sapremcloud** in resource group **RGCloud** and in location US East 2. Resource Group RGCloud was created in Exercise 1, chapter 1.

1. In Azure Portal Click Storage Accounts in left pane> Storage Accounts Dashboard opens> Click + Add> Create Storage Account Blade opens> Select Resource Group **RGCloud**> Give a unique name to storage Account **sapremcloud**> Select location East US 2>Performance Premium>Account Type as GPv2>Replication LRS> Rest keep as default> Click Review +create>After Validation is passed click create.

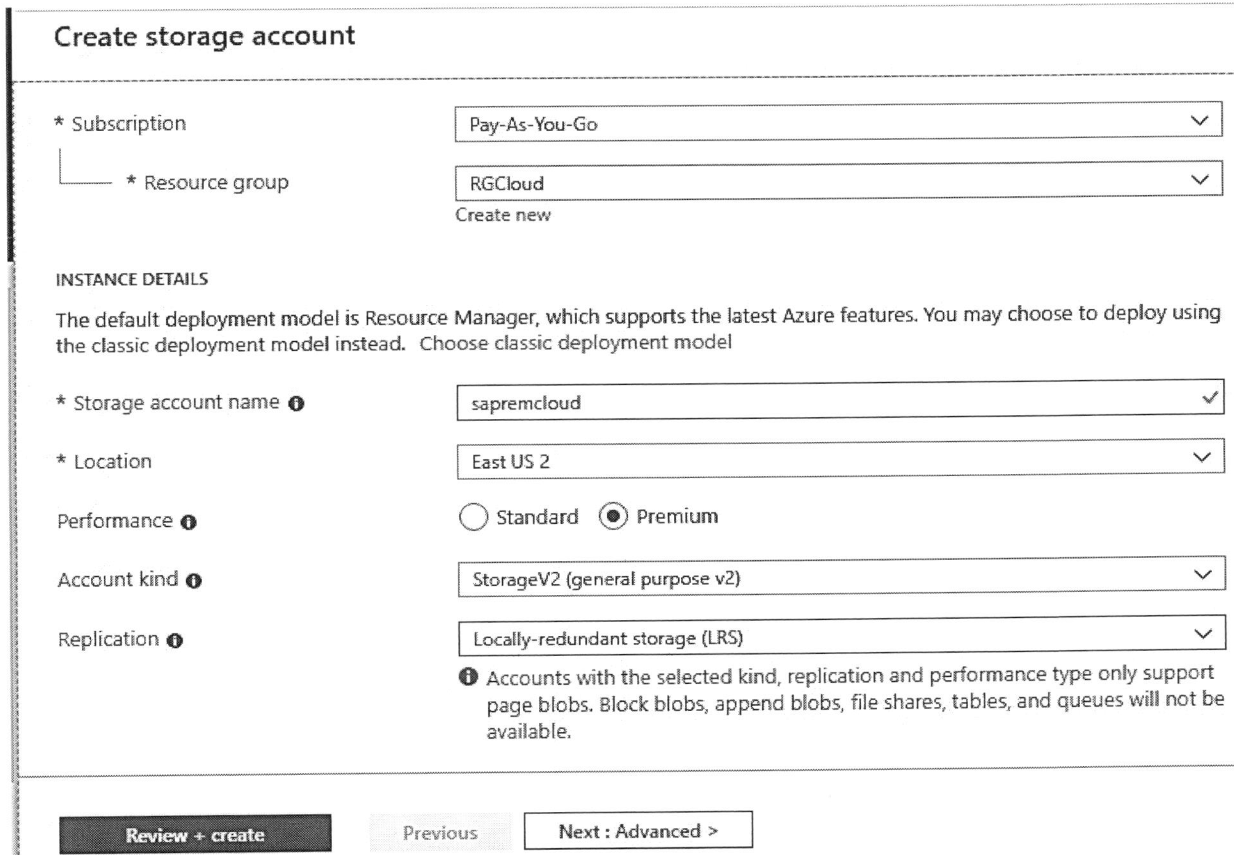

Note: Premium Storage Supports only LRS Replication.

2. Figure below shows the dashboard of Storage Account **sapremcloud.**

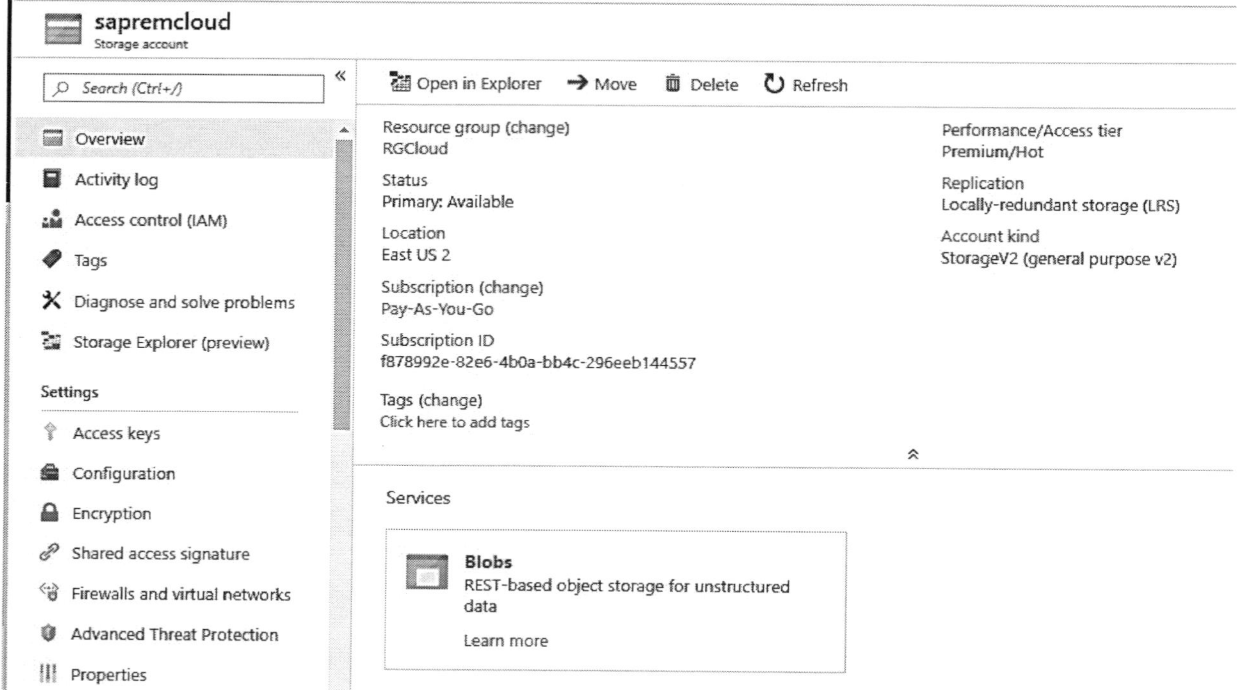

With Premium Account only Page Blob Storage option is there.

Note: Premier storage performance tier now also supports and Azure File Storage (Preview). It is in Preview as of writing.

Exercise 71: Demonstrating Storage Account sastdcloud functionalities

1. Figure below shows dashboard of GPv2 Storage Account **sastdcloud**. From here you can create Blob, file, table or queue Storage. Storage Account sastdcloud was created in Exercise 69 in this chapter.

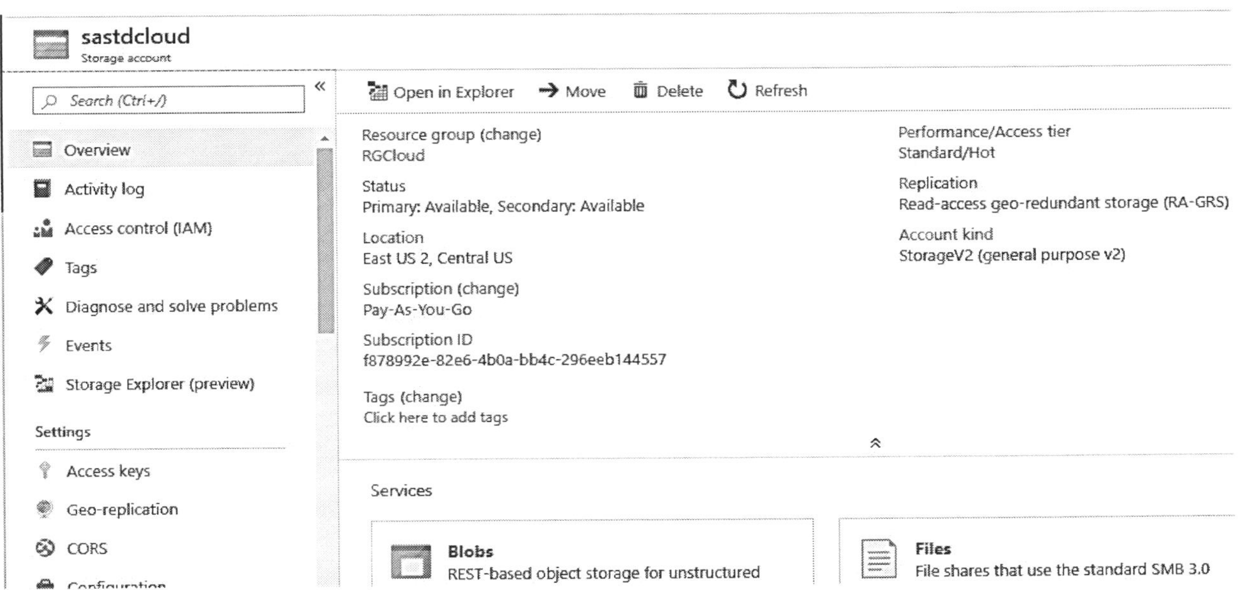

2. **Change configuration of storage account**: Click configuration in left pane. From here you can change Access tier and **Replication option**.

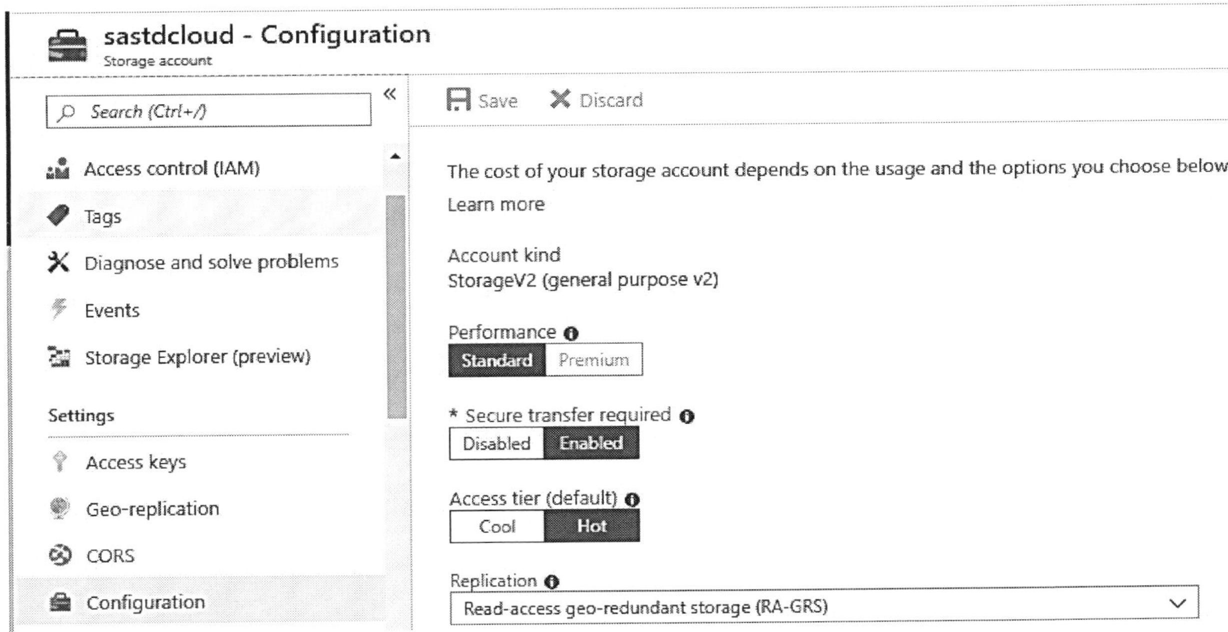

Exercise 72: Demonstrating Storage Account Security

Storage Account Security with RBAC: By default owner can access the Storage Account. You can delegate the Storage Account administration using Role Based Access control (RBAC). You can assign role of an owner, contributor, reader, Backup operator etc depending upon your requirement.
Note: RBAC will be extensively discussed in Chapter 17.

Go to sastdcloud Dashboard>Click Access Control (IAM) in left pane>+ Add Role assignment>Add role assignment blade opens> Select the role and the user.

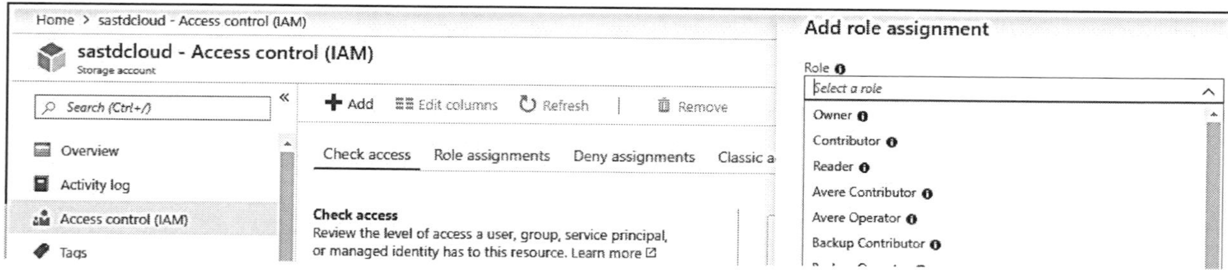

Storage Account Security with Storage Service Encryption (SSE): By default SSE protects your data at Rest using MS managed keys. You can use your own to keys to encryption storage data.
Click encryption in left pane> check box use your own key and select Key vault and key.

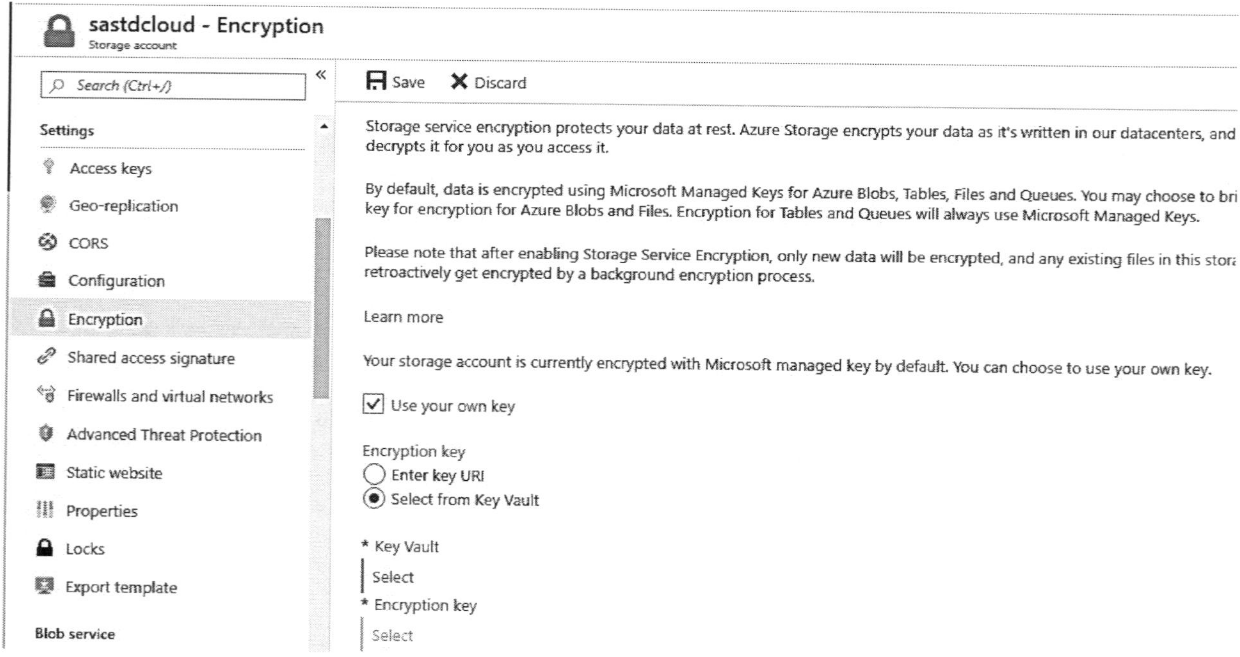

Storage Account Security using Azure Virtual Network Service Endpoints: By default owner can access storage account from internet. This is a security loophole. Using **Firewall and Virtual Network** option you can limit access to Storage account from Virtual Network only. You also have the option of allowing Storage account access from internet from particular IP address only.

Click Firewall and Virtual Networks in left pane>Click Add existing Virtual Network>Select your Virtual Network.

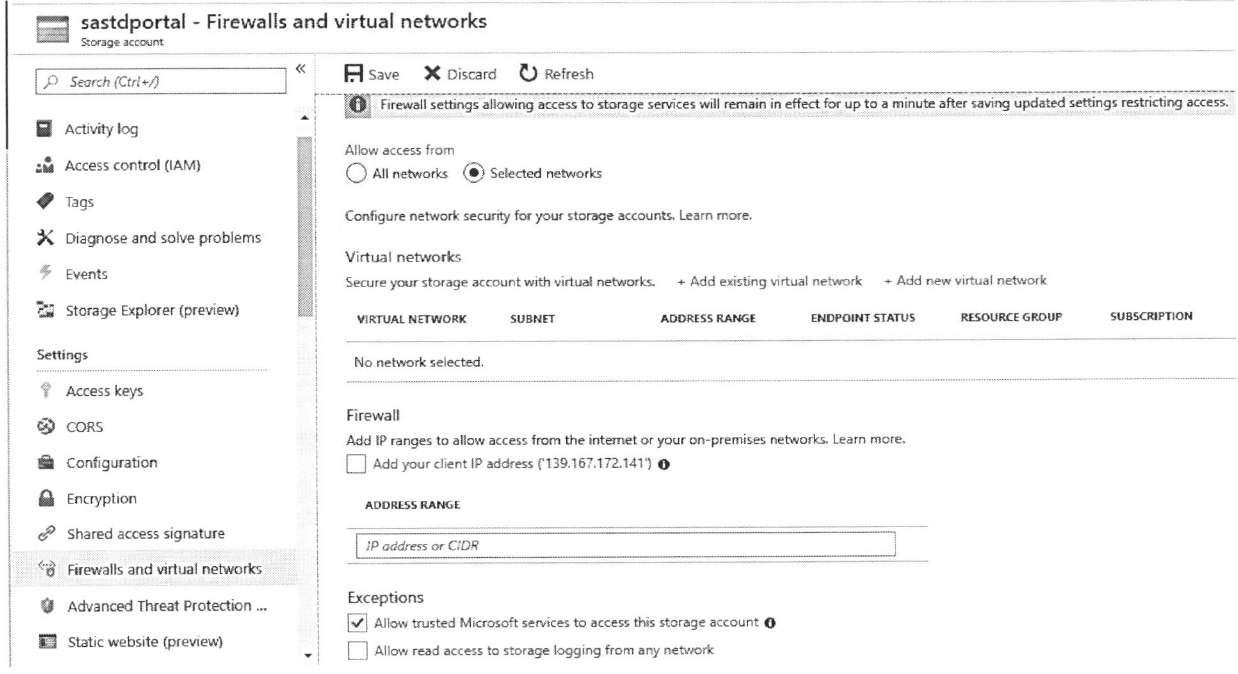

Network Access to Storage Account using VNET Service Endpoints

Azure Managed Resources such as Azure Storage or Azure SQL Database can be accessed from outside Azure and by VMs in Virtual Network over internet connection.

With Azure Virtual Network Service Endpoints, traffic between Azure Virtual Network and Azure Managed Resources such as Storage Accounts remains on the Microsoft Azure backbone network and not on Public Internet.

Note: Refer to Chapter 1 Virtual Networks for Protecting Storage Accounts using Azure Virtual Network Service Endpoints.

Azure Storage Explorer

Microsoft Azure Storage Explorer is a standalone app (available on Windows, Mac & Linux) that allows you to easily work with Azure Storage data.

Using Storage Explorer you can Upload, download and manage blobs, files, queues, tables and Cosmos DB entities. Storage Explorer also provides easy access to manage your virtual machine disks.

Figure below shows Dashboard of Storage Explorer Application running on Windows Desktop.

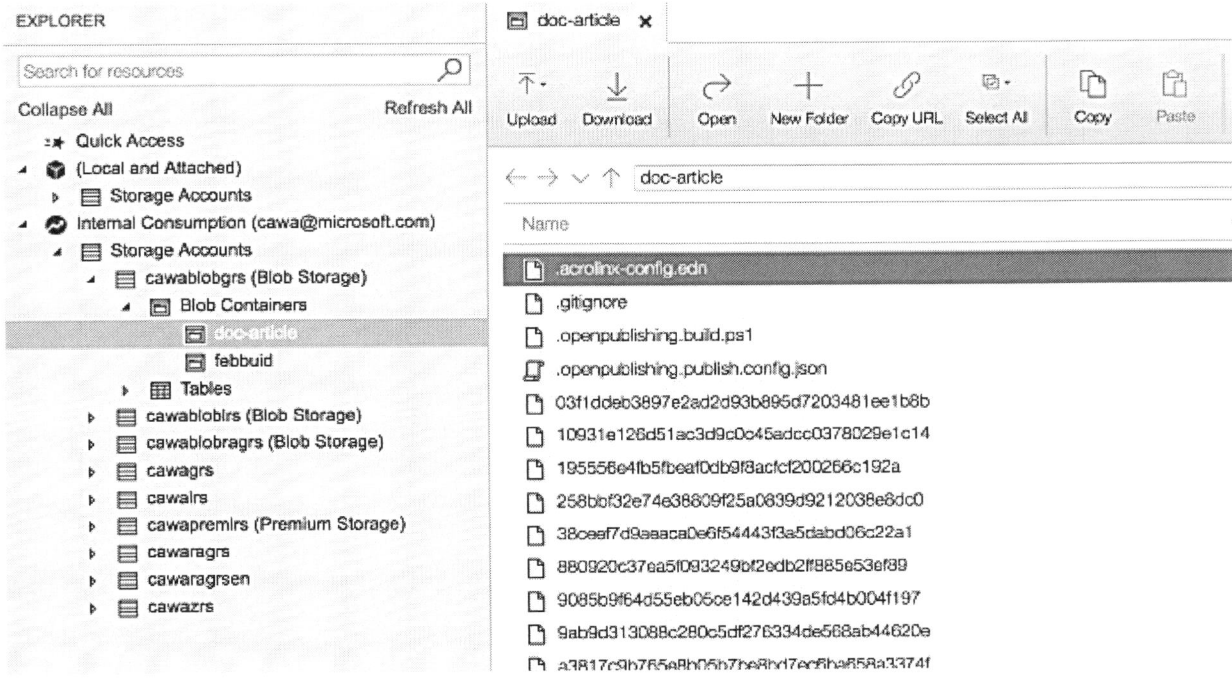

Options to Connect to Azure Storage using Storage Explorer

Azure Account Subscription credentials
Storage Account Name and Key
Use a Shared Access Signature URI
Use a Connection String

Download & Install Storage Explorer

https://go.microsoft.com/fwlink/?LinkId=708343&clcid=0x4009

Accessing Azure Storage Accounts using Azure Account Credentials

By using Azure Subscription Account credentials with Azure Storage Explorer you get full access to **all Storage Accounts** in Azure Subscription.

Exercise 73: Connect to Azure Storage using Azure Account Credentials

1. Open Storage Explorer app on your desktop>In left pane **right click** Storage Accounts and click connect to Azure Storage> A dialog Box will pop and will show 5 options to connect to Azure Storage.

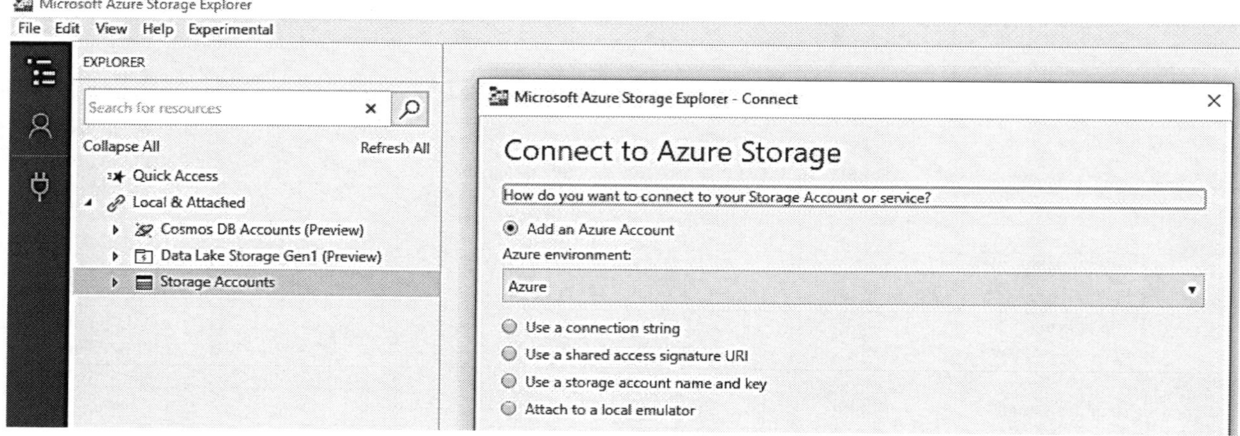

2. Select Add an Azure Account radio Button and click sign in box at the bottom of the Pop up dialog box>Sign-in to your account Blade will pop up. Enter your account credentials>click apply in Storage Explorer Dashboard. You can see all your storage Accounts (Created in Ex 54 & 55) in your subscription.

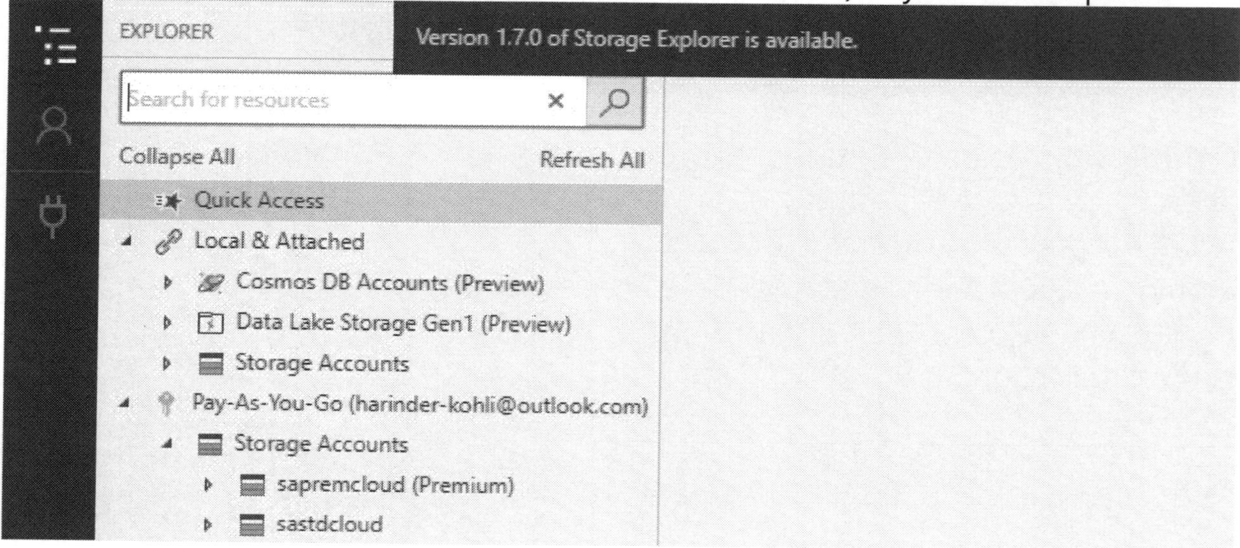

3. Enlarge the Storage Accounts and you can see the options available under each Storage Account. Storage Account sapremcloud has only Blob Storage option as it is was created with Premium Performance Tier (SSD) whereas Storage Account sastdportal has Blob, File, table and Queue option as it was created with Standard Storage Performance tier (HDD).

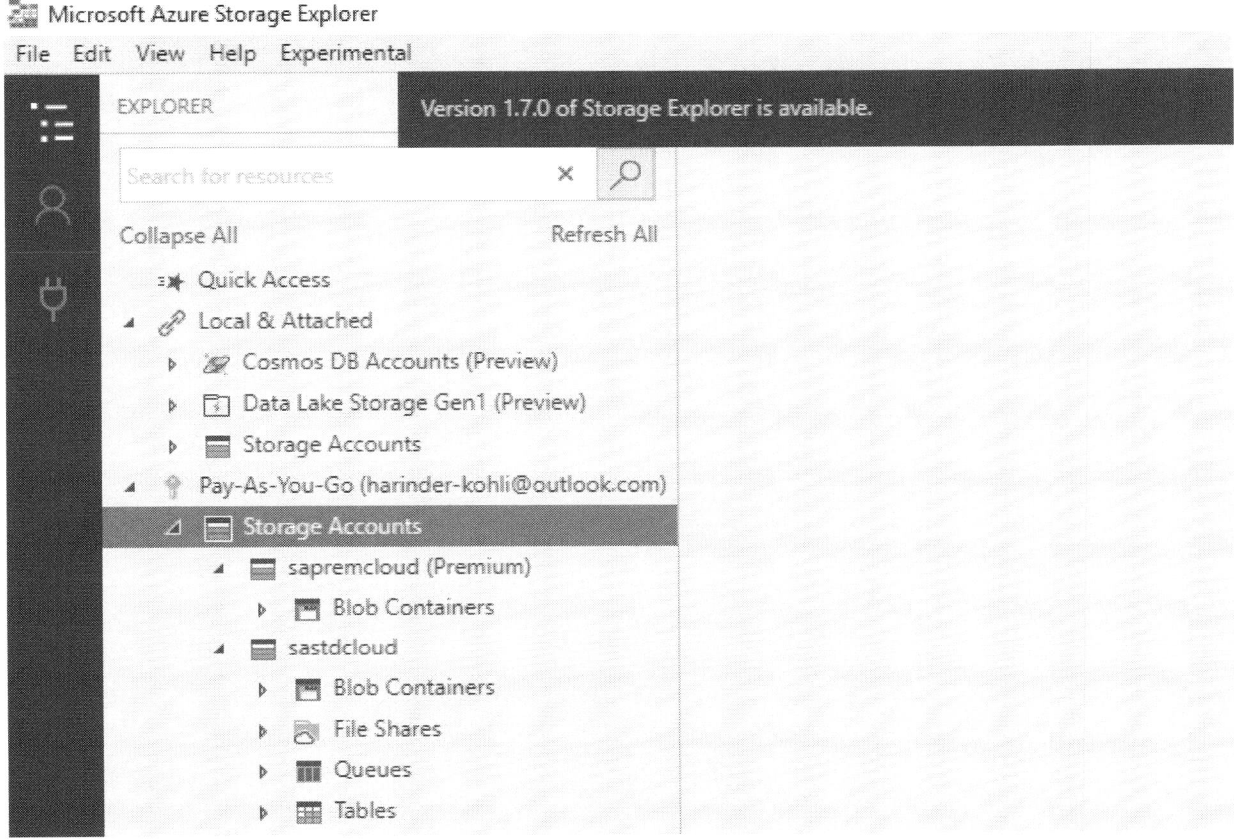

Note: Readers are advised to go through all the options here. Just Right click Blob Container and you can create a container. In next chapter we will show how to create a container and upload a file using Storage Explorer.

Accessing Azure Storage Account using Storage Account Access Keys

Using Azure Storage Explorer with Storage Account Access keys you get full access to that **particular** Storage Account only.

Anybody having access to Storage account key will have unlimited access to storage account.
Be careful not give account key to anybody as this will give them full access control to Storage Account.

Exercise 74: Get Storage Account sastdcloud Access Keys

1. In Azure Portal go to Storage Account sastdcloud dashboard>Click Access Keys in left pane> Copy Key 1 and paste in Notepad. We will use this to connect to storage Account using Storage Explorer.

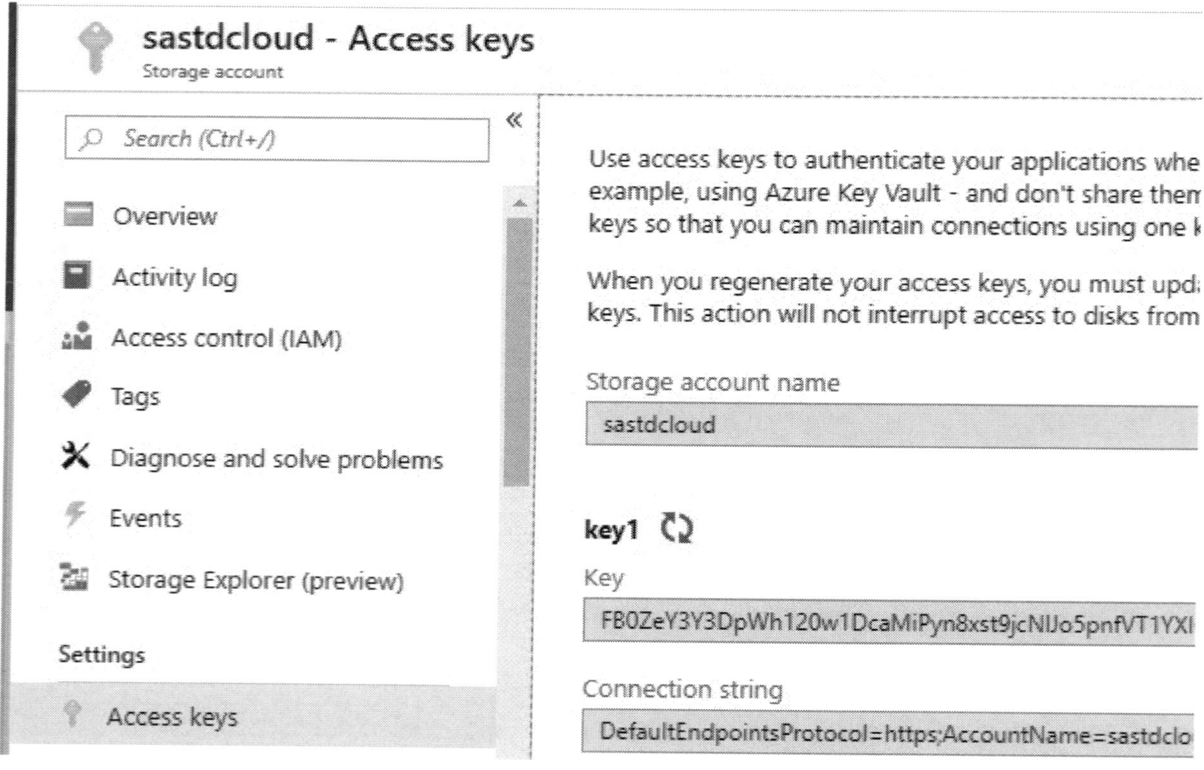

Exercise 75: Connect to Storage Account sastdcloud using Access key

1. **In Storage Explorer Dashboard right click Storage Accounts** and click connect to Azure Storage> A dialog Box will pop and will show 5 options to connect to Azure Storage>Select use a Storage account name and key radio button.

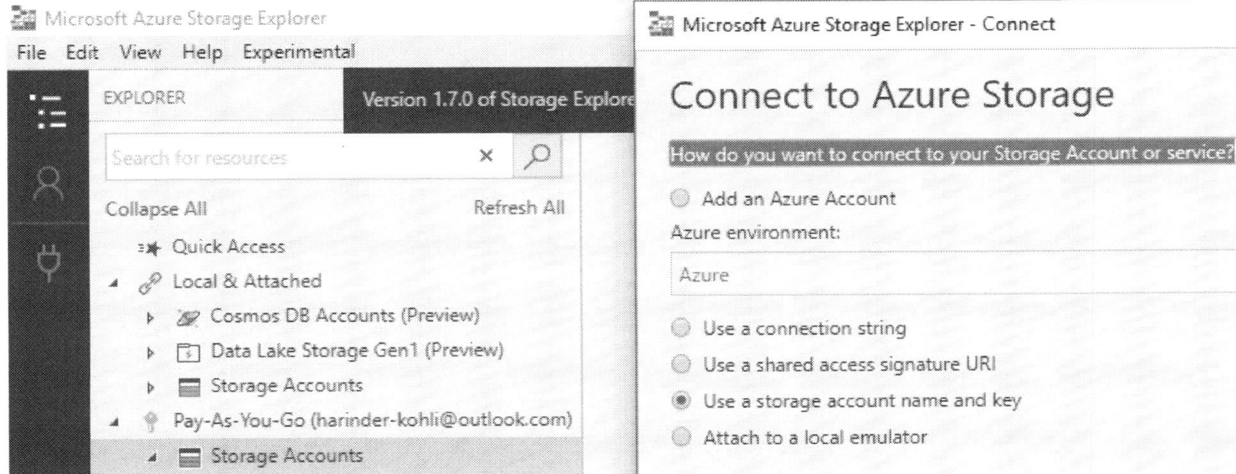

2. Select use a Storage account name and key radio button and click next button at bottom of the dialog box>Connect with Name and Key dialog box will pop up>Give a display name, enter Storage Account name sastdcloud in Account name and paste the key you copied previous exercise and click next.

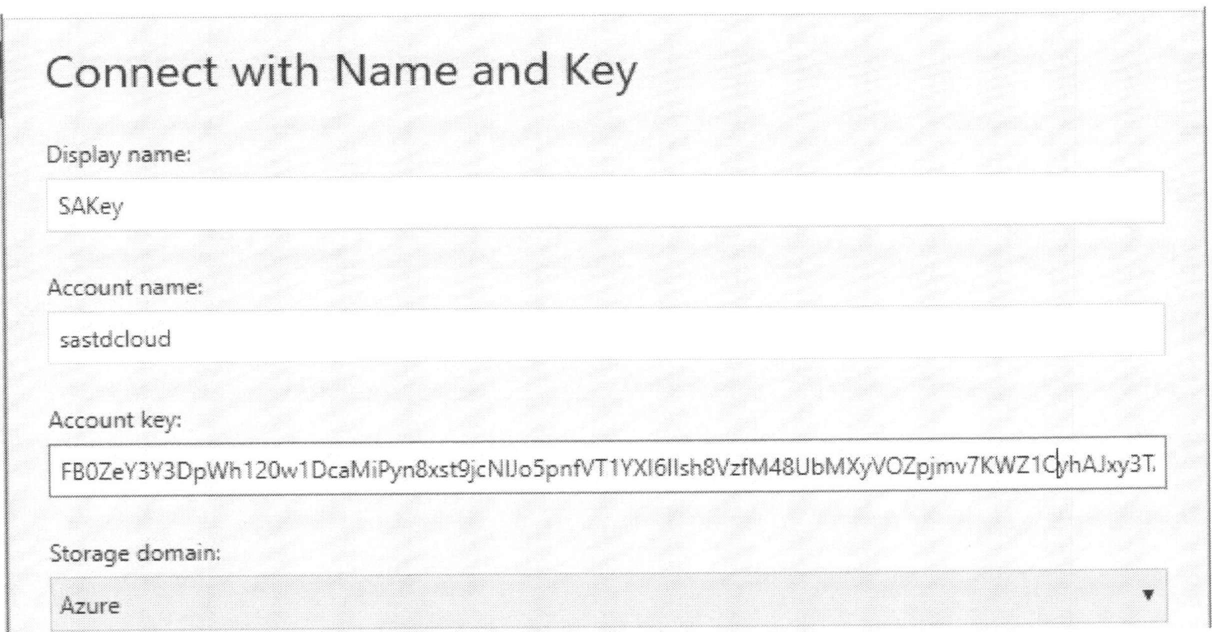

3. Connection summary box will pop up>Click connect.

4. In Explorer Dashboard you can see SAKey. This name was given for storage Account sastdcloud in step 2. Expand Test-sastd and it will show all the 4 options-Blob, File, Queues and tables.

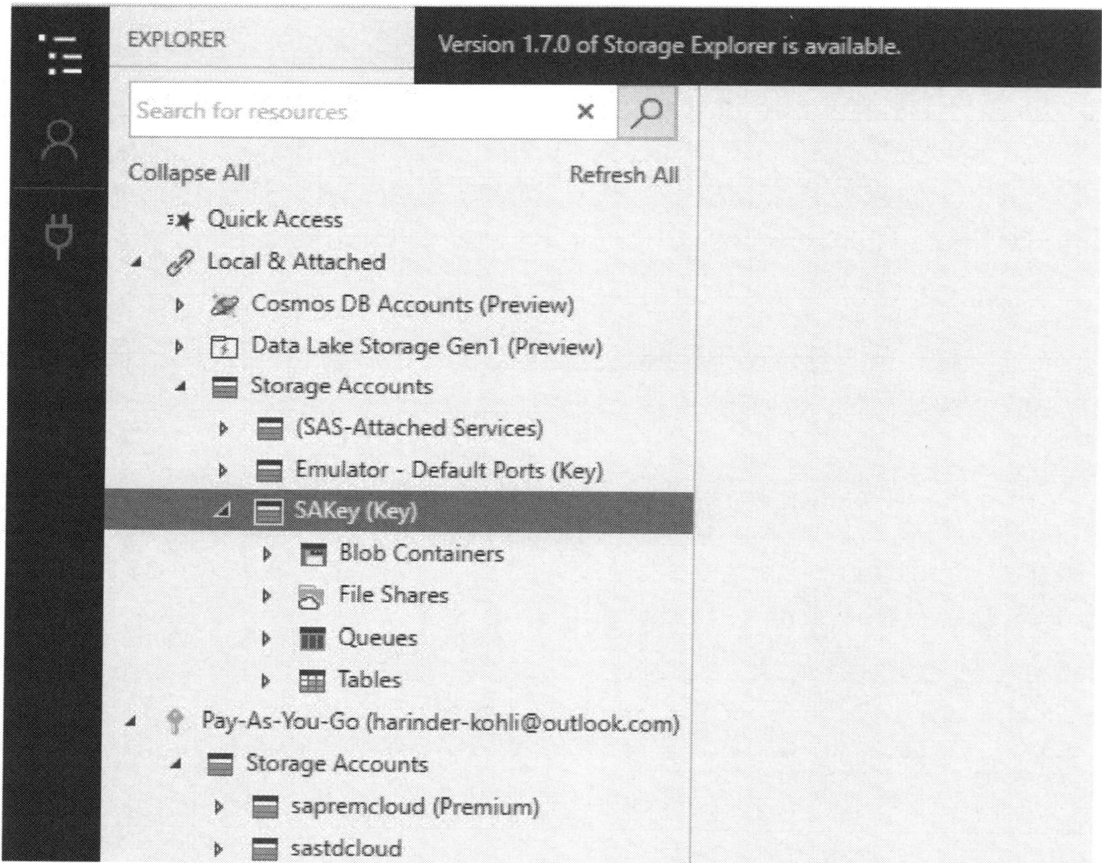

Accessing Storage Account using Shared Access Signature

Anybody having access to Storage account key will have unlimited access to storage account.

Shared access signature (SAS), provide delegated access to a resource in your storage account, without having to share your account access keys. SAS is a secure way to share your storage resources without compromising your account keys.

A shared access signature is a token that encapsulates all of the information needed to authorize a request to Azure Storage on the URL. You can specify the storage resource, the permissions granted, and the interval over which the permissions are valid as part of the shared access signature.

You can provide a shared access signature to clients who should not be trusted with your storage account key but whom you wish to delegate access to certain storage account resources. By distributing a shared access signature URI to these clients, you grant them access to a resource for a specified period of time.

SAS granular control features

1. You can specify interval over which the SAS is valid, including the start time and the expiry time.
2. You can specify permissions granted by the SAS. For example, a SAS on a blob might grant a user read and write permissions to that blob, but not delete permissions.
3. An optional IP address or range of IP addresses from which Azure Storage will accept the SAS
4. The protocol over which Azure Storage will accept the SAS. You can use this optional parameter to restrict access to clients using HTTPS.

Types of shared access signatures (SAS)

Service SAS delegates access to particular storage services: the Blob, Queue, Table, or File service.

An **Account-level SAS** can delegate access to multiple storage services (i.e. blob, file, queue, table).

Exercise 76: Generate Shared Access Signature of Storage Account

In this exercise we will generate Shared Access Signature (SAS) for Storage Account sastdcloud (Created in Exercise 69) for Blob service only.

1. In Azure Portal go to Storage Account sastdcloud dashboard>Click Shared Access Signature in left pane>In right pane under allowed service Select **Blob** only and rest select all default values>Click generate SAS and Connection String Box.

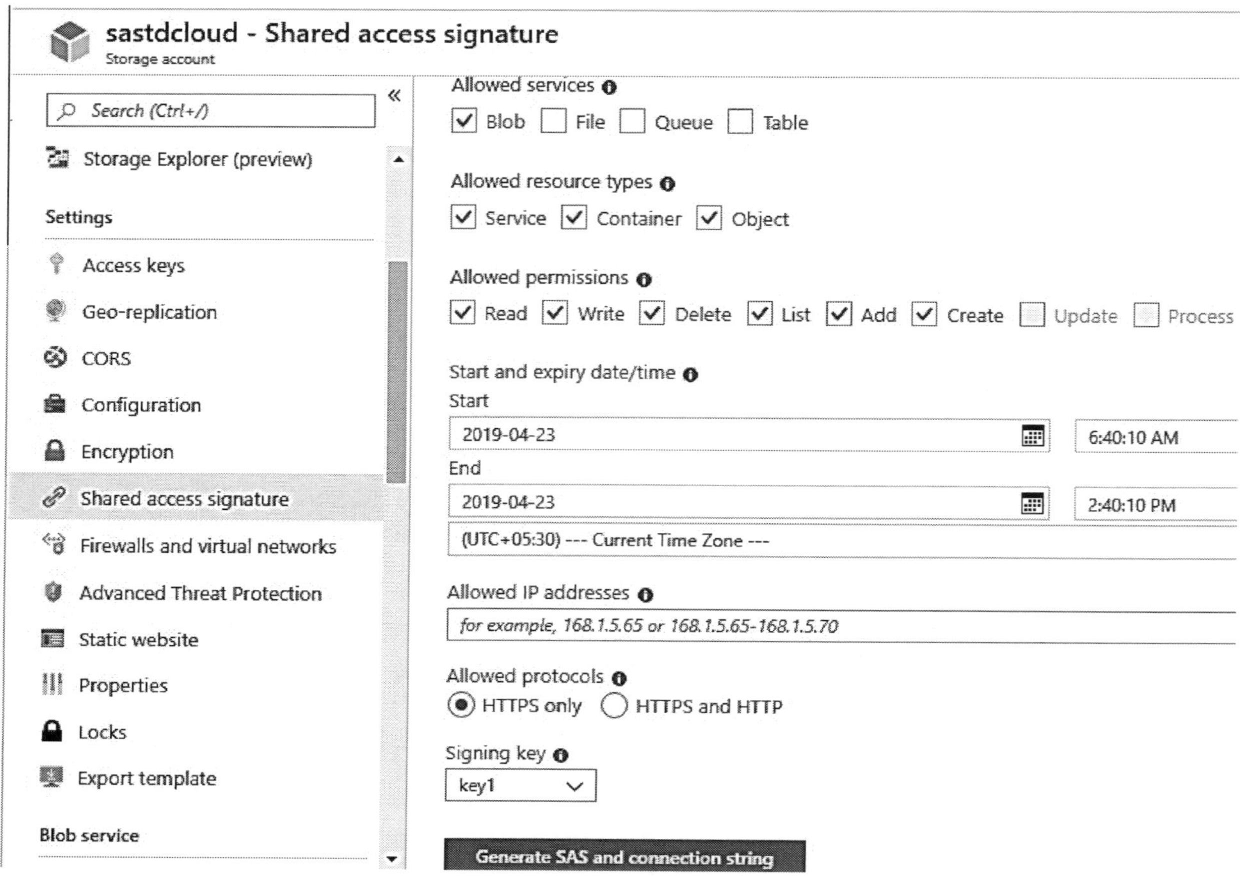

2. SAS will be generated and will be shown in bottom of the screen. Copy the Blob Service SAS URL.

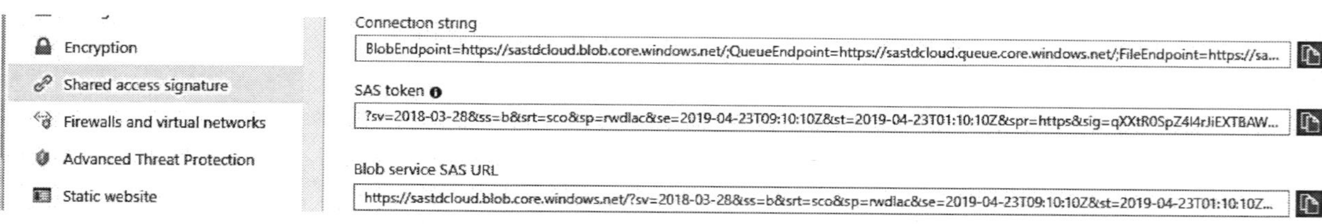

Exercise 77: Connect to Storage Account using Shared Access Signature

1. In Storage Explorer Dashboard right click Storage Accounts and click connect to Azure Storage> A dialog Box will pop and will show 5 options to connect to Azure Storage>Select use a Shared Access Signature URI radio button.

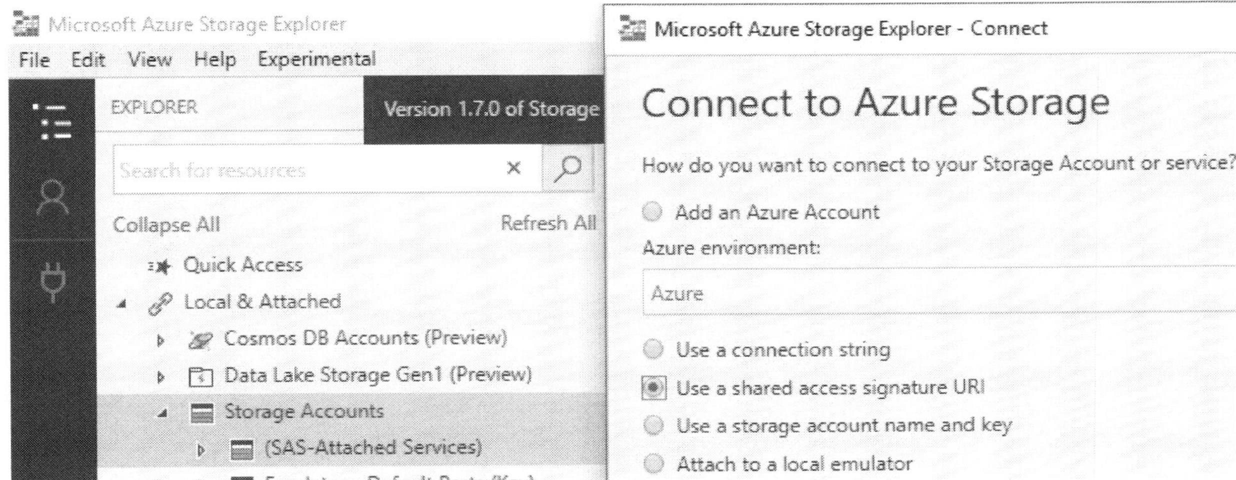

2. Select use a shared access signature URL and Click next> Attach with SAS URI Blade opens>Enter a Display name >Enter URL which was generated in previous exercise and click Next>In summary box click connect.

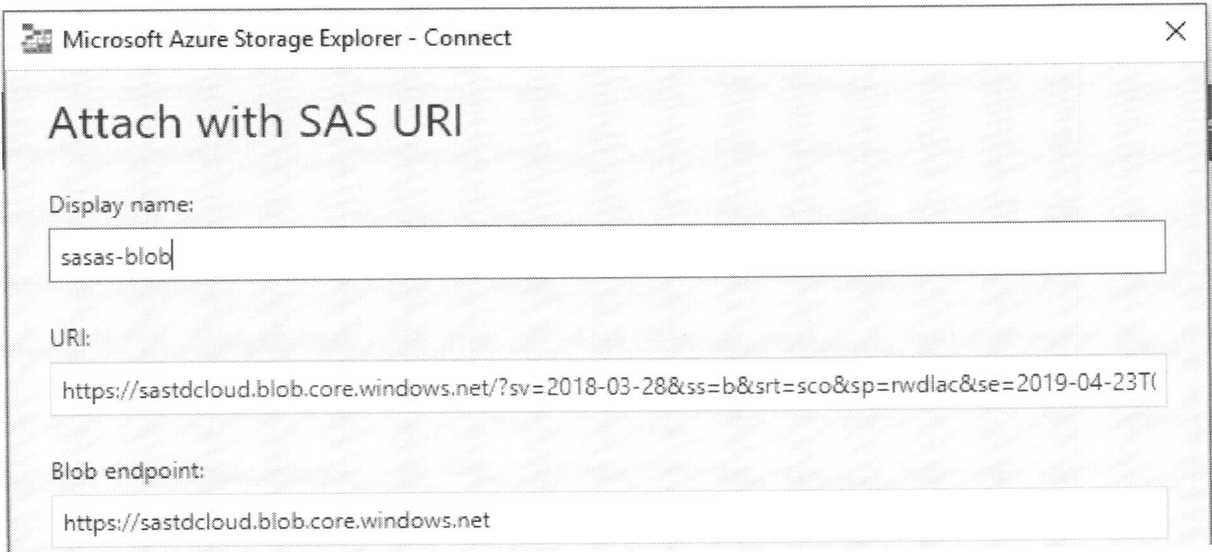

3. In Storage Explorer dashboard you can see sasa-blob under Storage Account. We only have access to Blob Service as we have generated SAS for Blob service in previous exercise.

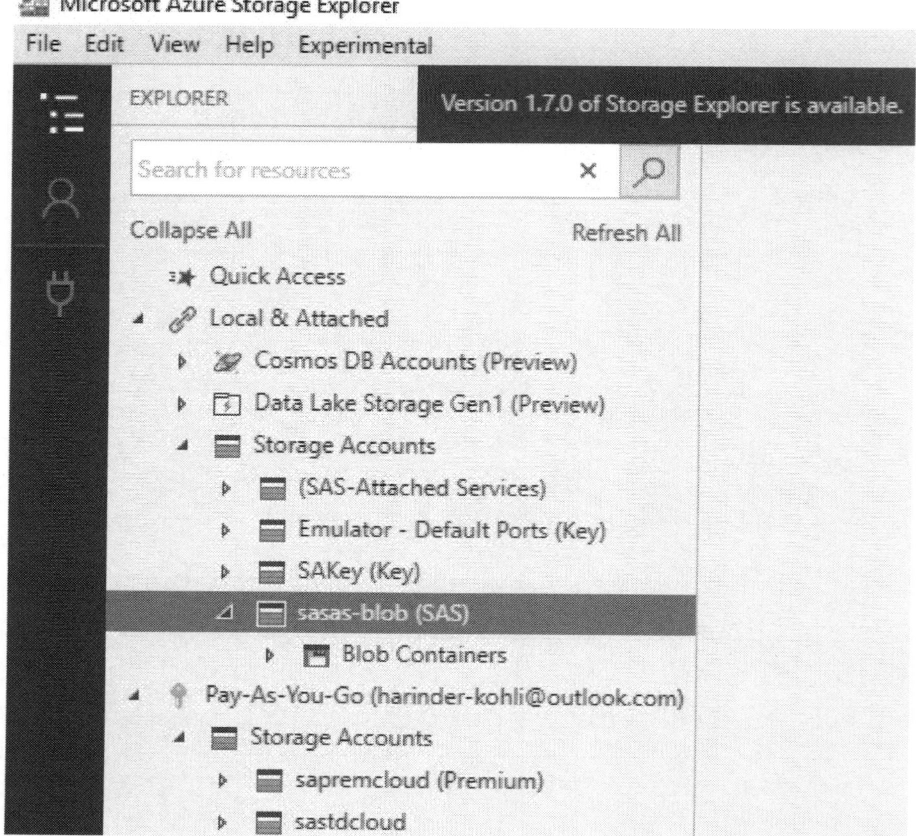

Inference from Previous Exercises

Accessing Azure Storage Accounts using Azure Account Credentials shows all the Storage Accounts created in the Subscription as we used Azure Subscription credentials for Connection.
Accessing Azure Storage Account using Storage Account Access Keys shows only one Storage Account sastdcloud with all four services (Blob, File, Queue and Table) listed. This connection used the Storage Account sastdcloud Access key.
Accessing Storage Account using Shared Access Signature showed only one Storage Account sastdcloud with Blob service listed. Shared access signature was generated for Storage Account sastdcloud blob service only.

Similarly you can connect your application to Azure Storage by adding Shared Access Signature (SAS) or Storage Account key in your application code.

Accessing Storage Account using Azure Active Directory (Preview)

You can use Azure Active Directory (Azure AD) credentials to authenticate a user, group, or other identity for access to blob and queue data (preview). If authentication of an identity is successful, then Azure AD returns a token to use in authorizing the request to Azure Blob storage or Queue storage.

Note: Currently this feature is in preview and is not part of the exam and is not being discussed further.

Chapter 9 Azure Storage

Note: AZ-300 Exam syllabus does not mention's Storage Topics. But For Exam AZ-301 Storage Topics are very important component for Designing & Implementing Storage Solutions. **You can Skip this Chapter for AZ-300 Exam. But my suggestion is that you go through this Chapter even for AZ-300 also.**

This Chapter covers following Topic Lessons

- Azure Storage Introduction
- Blob Storage
- Data Compliance in Azure Cloud with Immutable Blob Storage
- Blob Storage Pricing using GPv2 Storage Account (4 Components)
- Premium Blob Storage Pricing using GPv2 Storage Account
- Azure File Storage
- File Storage Pricing using General Purpose v2 Account
- Azure File Sync
- Azure Import/Export service
- Export from Azure
- Import to Azure
- Azure Import/Export Pricing
- Azure Data Box
- StorSimple
- Content Delivery Networks (CDN)

This Chapter covers following Lab Exercises

- Create Blob Storage Container and upload a File
- Blob Storage Tiering
- Create Blob Storage Container using Storage Explorer
- Applying Time Based Tetention Policy
- Creating and Mount File Share
- Deploying Azure File Sync in 4 Steps
- Demonstrating Export Job Creation
- Demonstrating Data Box Order through Azure Portal
- Implementing Azure CDN using Azure Portal
- Enabling or Disabling Compression
- Changing Optimization type
- Changing Caching Rules
- Allow or Block CDN in Specific Countries

Chapter Topology

In this chapter we will add Blob Storage, File Storage, Azure File Sync service, CDN & Import/Export Job to the Topology. We also demonstrate how to create Azure Data Box Ordering.

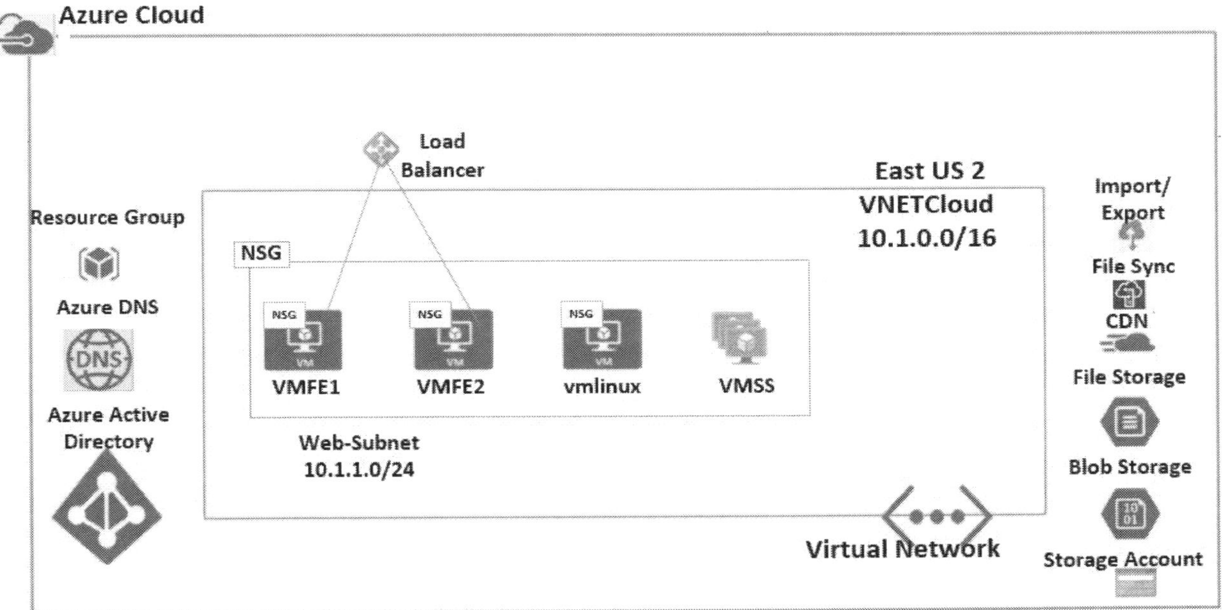

We will install Azure File Sync Agent on VM OnPremAD.

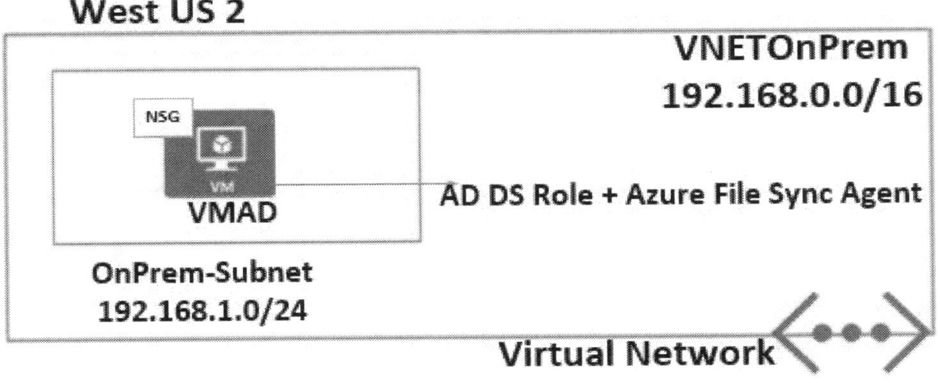

This diagram is shown separately as there is space constrained in top diagram.

Azure Storage Introduction

Azure Storage is the Managed cloud storage solution. Azure Storage is highly available and massively scalable. Azure provides five types of storage - Blob, Table, Queue, Files and Virtual Machine Disk storage (Page Blobs).

Azure Blobs: A massively scalable object store for unstructured data.
Azure Files: Managed file shares for cloud or on-premises deployments. File Storage provides shared storage for Azure/on-premises VMs using SMB protocol.
Azure Queues: A messaging store for reliable messaging between application components.
Azure Tables: A NoSQL store for schemaless storage of structured data.

Figure Below shows five types of Azure Storage Services.

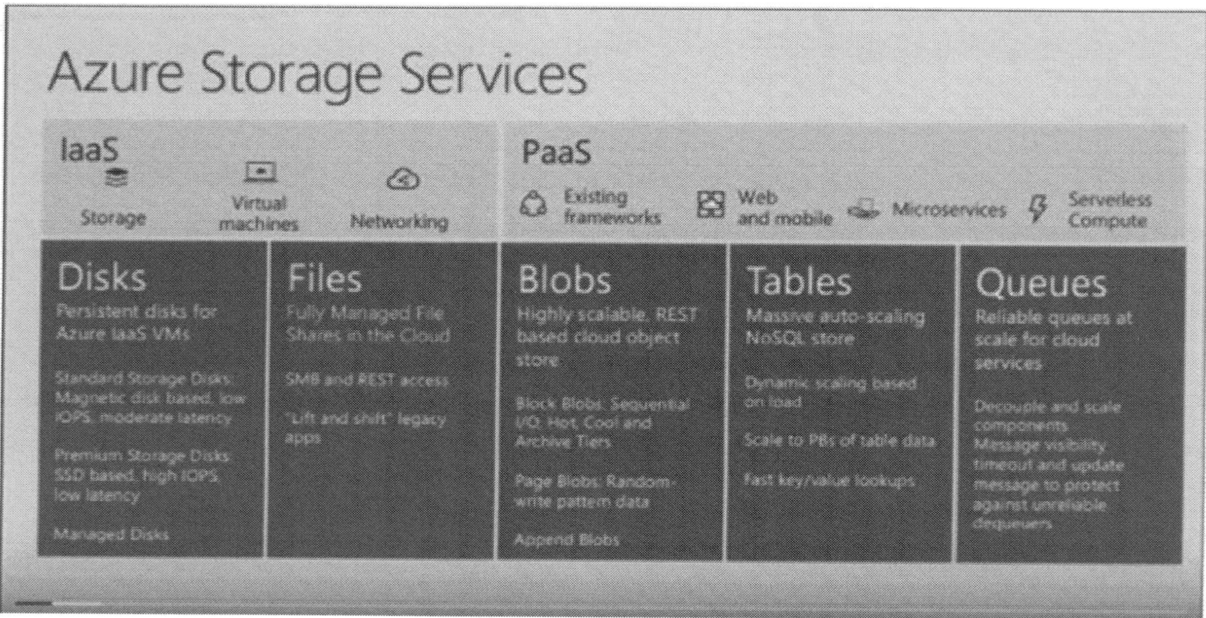

Comparing Different Azure Storage Services types

Azure Storage	Data Type
Blob	Unstructured
Table	Structured
Queue	Messaging
File	Shared Storage

Feature of Azure Storage

Durable and highly available: Redundancy ensures that your data is safe in the event of transient hardware failures. You can also opt to replicate data across datacenters or geographical regions for additional protection from local catastrophe or natural disaster. Data replicated in this way remains highly available in the event of an unexpected outage.

Secure: All data written to Azure Storage is encrypted by the service. Azure Storage provides you with fine-grained control over who has access to your data.

Scalable: Azure Storage is designed to be massively scalable to meet the data storage and performance needs of today's applications.

Managed: Microsoft Azure handles maintenance and any critical problems for you.

Accessible: Data in Azure Storage is accessible from anywhere in the world over HTTP or HTTPS. Microsoft provides SDKs for Azure Storage in a variety of languages -- .NET, Java, Node.js, Python, PHP, Ruby, Go, and others -- as well as a mature REST API. Azure Storage supports scription in Azure PowerShell or Azure CLI. And the Azure portal and Azure Storage Explorer offer easy visual solutions for working with your data.

Blob Storage

Azure Blob storage stores unstructured data in the cloud as objects/blobs. Azure Blob storage is massively scalable, highly redundant and secure **object storage** with a **URL/http based access** which allows it to be accessed within Azure or outside the Azure. Though Azure objects are regionally scoped you can access them from anywhere in the world.

Azure Blob Storage is a **Managed Service** that stores large amount of unstructured data in the cloud as objects/blobs. Blob storage can store any type of text or binary data, such as a document, media file, or application installer that can be accessed anywhere in the world via http or https.

Blob storage is also referred to as object storage.

Blobs are basically files like those that you store on your computer. They can be pictures, Excel files, HTML files, virtual hard disks (VHDs), log files & database backups etc. Blobs are stored in containers, which are similar to folders. Containers are created under Storage account.

You can access Blob storage from anywhere in the world using URLs, the REST interface, or one of the Azure SDK storage client libraries. Storage client libraries are available for multiple languages, including Node.js, Java, PHP, Ruby, Python, and .NET.

You can create Blob Storage using 3 ways – General Purpose Storage Account v1, General Purpose Storage Account v2 or Blob storage Account.

Common Use cases for Blob Object Storage

For users with large amounts of unstructured object data to store in the cloud, Blob storage offers a cost-effective and scalable solution. You can use Blob storage to store content such as:

- Serving images or documents directly to a browser.
- Storing files for distributed access.
- Streaming video and audio.
- Storing data for backup and restore, disaster recovery, and archiving.

Blob Storage Service Components

Blob Service contains 3 components.

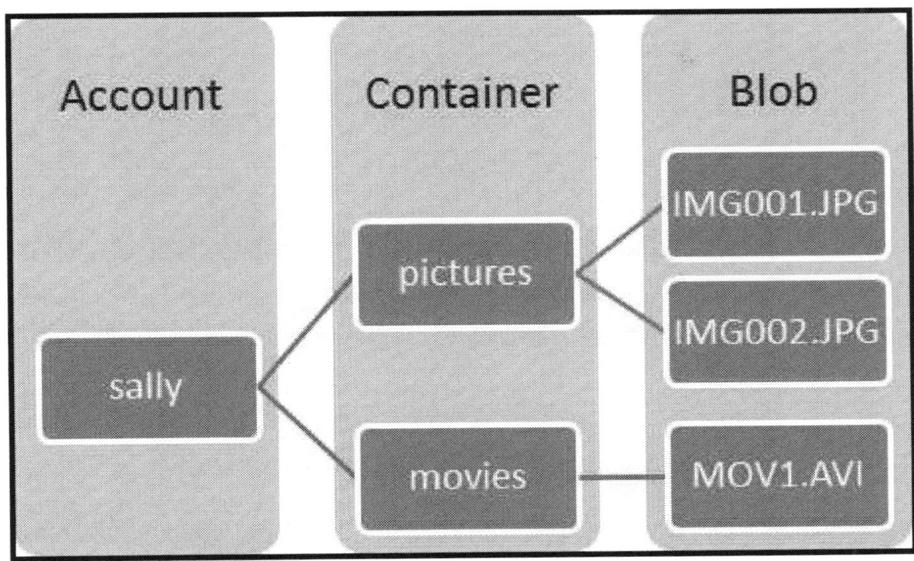

Storage Account

All access to Azure Storage is done through a storage account. This storage account can be a **General-purpose v1 & v2** or a **Blob storage account** which is specialized for storing objects/blobs.

Containers

Container is like a folder which store Blob Files. Container provides a grouping of a set of blobs. All blobs must be in a container. An account can contain an unlimited number of containers. A container can store an unlimited number of blobs. Container name must be lowercase.

Blob

A file of any type and size.

Azure Storage offers three types of blobs: block, page and append blobs.
Blob Storage tiering is available with GPv2 Account and Blob Storage Account.

Types of Blob Storage in Azure Cloud

Blob storage offers three types of blobs – Block Blobs, Page Blobs and Append Blobs.

Block blobs are optimized for storing cloud objects, streaming content and and are a good choice for storing documents, media files, backups etc. It is backed by HDD.

Append blobs are similar to block blobs, but are optimized for append operations. An append blob can be updated only by adding a new block to the end. Append blobs are a good choice for scenarios such as logging, where new data needs to be written only to the end of the blob. It is backed by magnetic HDD.

Page blobs are used for storing virtual machine disks (OS and Data Disks). Page Blob can use both HDD and SSD. Page Blob was covered in compute chapter. Page blobs can be up to 8 TB in size and are more efficient for frequent read/write operations.

Comparing 3 types of Blob Storage

Description	Block Blob	Append Blob	Page Blob
Storage Account Supported	General purpose v1 & v2 and Blob Storage Account	General purpose v1 & v2 and Blob Storage Account	General purpose – v1 & v2
Disk Type	**HDD**	**HDD**	**HDD & SSD**
Managed Disk Option	No	No	Yes
Can be used for Virtual Machine Disks	No	No	Yes
Use case	documents, media files, backups	logging	Virtual Machine Disks

In this chapter we will focus only on Block blobs and Append bobs as we already have covered Page Blobs in Azure Compute Chapter.

Azure Blob Storage Tiering: Hot, Cool & Archive Storage tiers

Azure Blob Storage tiering is available with General Purpose v2 Account and Blob Storage Account. General Purpose v1 Account does not offers Blob Storage Tiering. Microsoft Recommends using GPv2 instead of Blob Storage accounts for tiering.

General Purpose v2 Account & Blob storage accounts expose the **Access Tier** attribute, which allows you to specify the storage tier as **Hot** or **Cool**. **The Archive tier** is only available at the blob level and not at the storage account level.

Hot Storage Tier

The Azure hot storage tier is optimized for storing data that is frequently accessed at lower access cost but at higher storage cost.

Cool Storage Tier

The Azure cool storage tier is optimized for storing data that is infrequently accessed at lower storage cost but at higher access cost.

Archive Storage Tier

Archive storage_tier is optimized for storing data that is rarely accessed and has the lowest storage cost and highest data retrieval costs compared to hot and cool storage. The archive tier can only be applied at the blob level.

Blob rehydration (Important Concept)

Data is offline in Archive Storage Tier. To read data in archive storage, you must first change the tier of the blob to hot or cool. This process is known as rehydration and can take up to 15 hours to complete.

If there is a change in the usage pattern of your data, you can also switch between these storage tiers at any time.

Data in hot storage tier has slightly higher availability (99.9%) than cool storage tier (99%). Availability is not applicable for Archive tier as data is offline.

Hot Tier use case

1. Data that is in active use or expected to be accessed frequently.
2. Data that is staged for processing and eventual migration to the cool storage tier.

Cold Tier Use case

1. Short-term backup and disaster recovery datasets.
2. Older media content not viewed frequently anymore but is expected to be available immediately when accessed.
3. Large data sets that need to be stored cost effectively while more data is being gathered for future processing.

Archive Tier Use case

1. Long-term backup, archival, and disaster recovery datasets.
2. Original (raw) data that must be preserved, even after it has been processed into final usable form.
3. Compliance and archival data that needs to be stored for a long time and is hardly ever accessed. (For example, Security camera footage, old X-Rays/MRIs for healthcare organizations, audio recordings, and transcripts of customer calls for financial services).

Comparison of the storage tiers

Features	Hot Storage Tier	Cool Storage Tier	Archive Tier
Availability	99.9%	99%	NA
Availability (RA-GRS reads)	99.99%	99.9%	NA
Usage charges	Higher storage costs, lower access and transaction costs	Lower storage costs, higher access and transaction costs	lowest storage cost and highest retrieval costs
Minimum Storage Duration	NA	30 days (GPv2 only)	180 days
Latency	Milliseconds	Milliseconds	<15 Hrs

Options to make blob data available to users

Private access: Owner of the Storage Account can access the Blob Data.
Anonymous access: You can make a container or its blobs publicly available for anonymous access.
Shared access signatures: Shared access signature (SAS), provide delegated access to a resource in your storage account, with permissions that you specify and for an interval that you specify without having to share your account access keys.

Anonymous read access to containers and blobs

By default, a container and any blobs within it may be accessed only by the owner of the storage account (Public Access level: Private). To give anonymous users read permissions to a container and its blobs, you can set the container & Blob permissions to allow full public access.

Container (anonymous read access for containers and blobs): Container and blob data can be read via anonymous request. Clients can enumerate blobs within the container via anonymous request, but cannot enumerate containers within the storage account.
Blob (anonymous read access for blobs only): Blob data within this container can be read via anonymous request, but container data is not available. Clients cannot enumerate blobs within the container via anonymous request.

Http access to Blob data using DNS names

By default the blob data in your storage account is accessible only to storage account owner because of Default **Private (no anonymous access)** Policy. Authenticating requests against Blob storage requires the account access key.

Using DNS names you can http access Blob endpoint if anonymous access is configured.

https://mystorageaccount.blob.core.windows.net/mycontainer/myblob

Here mystorageaccount is storage account name, mycontainer is container name and myblob is uploaded file name.

Controlling access to blob data using Shared access signatures (SAS)

Anybody having access to Storage account key will have unlimited access to storage account.

Shared access signature (SAS), provide delegated access to a resource in your storage account, without having to share your account access keys. SAS is a secure way to share your storage resources without compromising your account keys.

A shared access signature (SAS) is a URI that grants restricted access rights to Azure Storage resources. You can provide a shared access signature to clients who should not be trusted with your storage account key but whom you wish to delegate access to certain storage account resources. By distributing a shared access signature URI to these clients, you grant them access to a resource for a specified period of time.

SAS granular control features

1. The interval over which the SAS is valid, including the start time and the expiry time.
2. The permissions granted by the SAS. For example, a SAS on a blob might grant a user read and write permissions to that blob, but not delete permissions.
3. An optional IP address or range of IP addresses from which Azure Storage will accept the SAS.
4. The protocol over which Azure Storage will accept the SAS. You can use this optional parameter to restrict access to clients using HTTPS.

Types of shared access signatures (SAS)

Service SAS delegates access to a resource in just one of the storage services: the Blob, Queue, Table, or File service.

Account-level SAS can delegate access to multiple storage services (i.e. blob, file, queue, table).

Note: Exercise 76 & 77 in Chapter 8 shows how to create SAS and use it.

Exercise 78: Create Blob Storage Container and upload a File

In this exercise we will create Blob Storage Container hk410 in Storage Account sastdcloud and in resource group RGCloud. Upload a file to the Blob Container hk410 and access it over internet. Change the permission to private and then access the file over internet. Resource group RGCloud was Created in Exercise 1, Chapter 1. Storage Account sastdcloud was Created in Exercise 69, Chapter 8.

1. Go to Storage Account sastdcloud Dashboard > Click Blobs under services>Blob Dashboard opens> In Right pane click +container>Create New Container blade opens>Enter name **hk410** and select access level **Blob** and click ok.

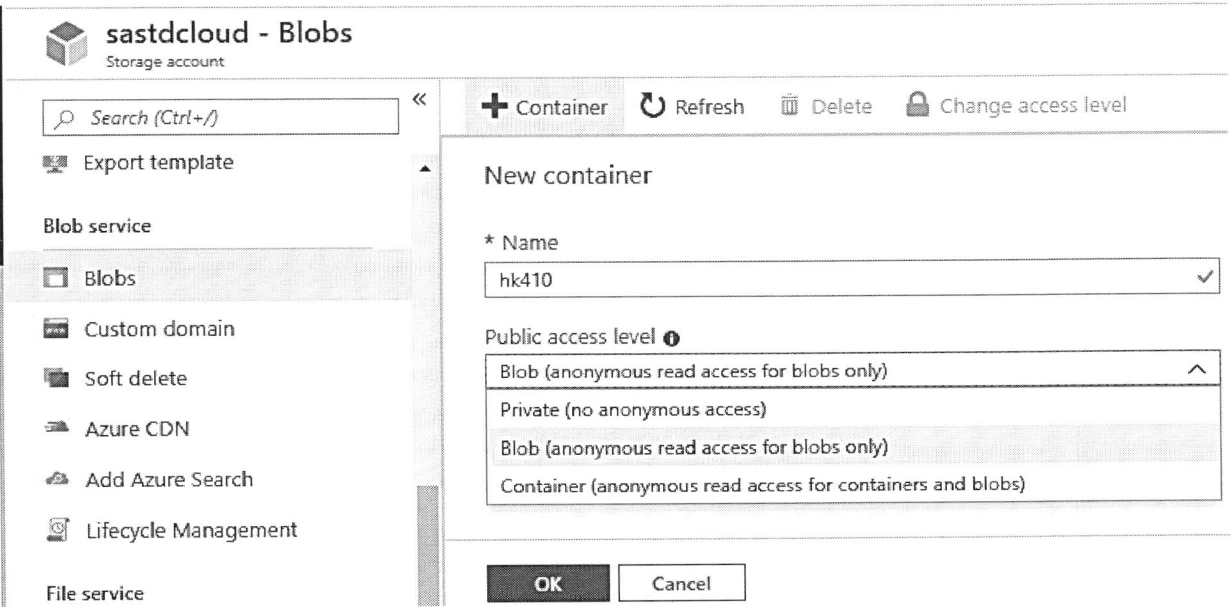

2. Container is created as shown below.

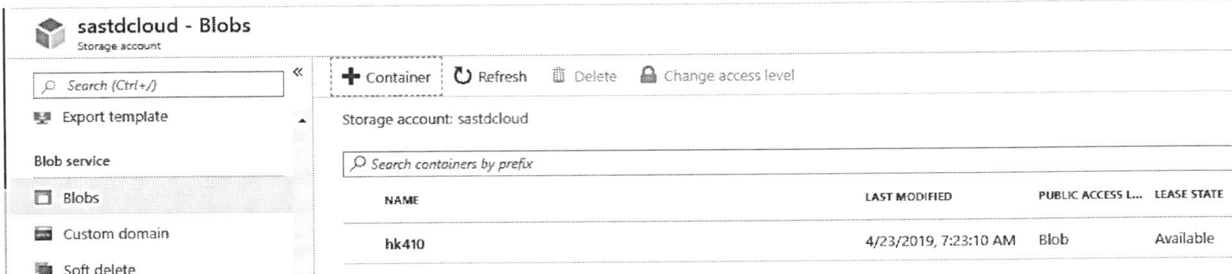

3. **Upload a file from your desktop**. I have created a helloworld.txt file on my desktop. I also added Hello World as content in the file. Click the container hk410>Container hk410 dashboard opens>click upload>Upload blob blade opens>Click file button to upload HelloWorld.txt file from desktop>Rest keep all values as default>Click upload>Close the Upload pane.

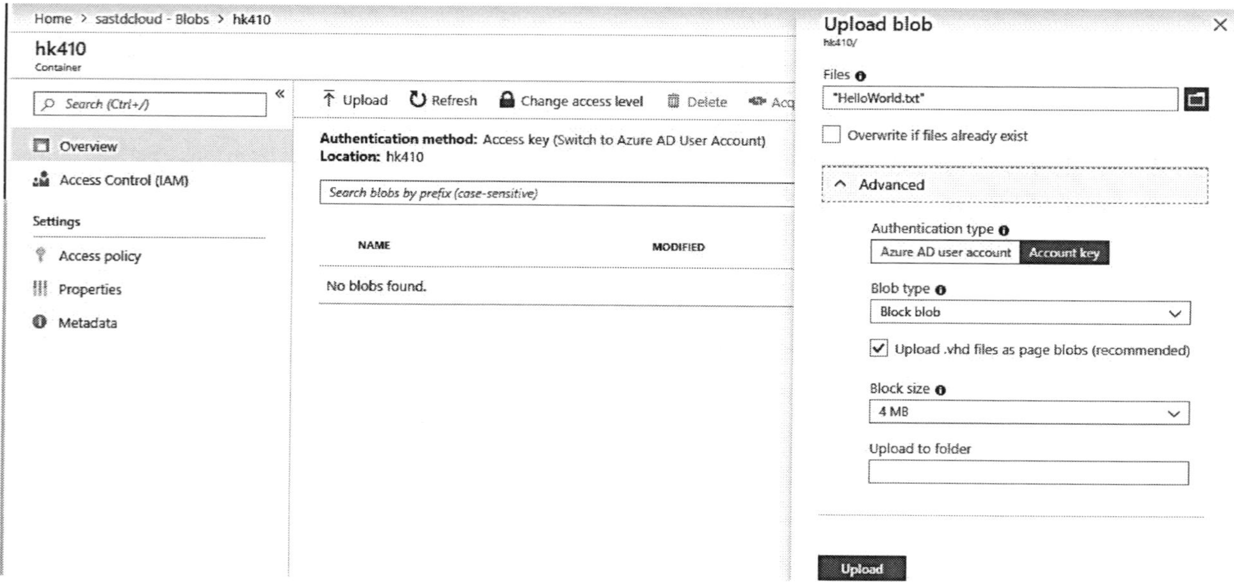

4. File is uploaded as shown below. I also clicked ... in extreme right to see the option available.

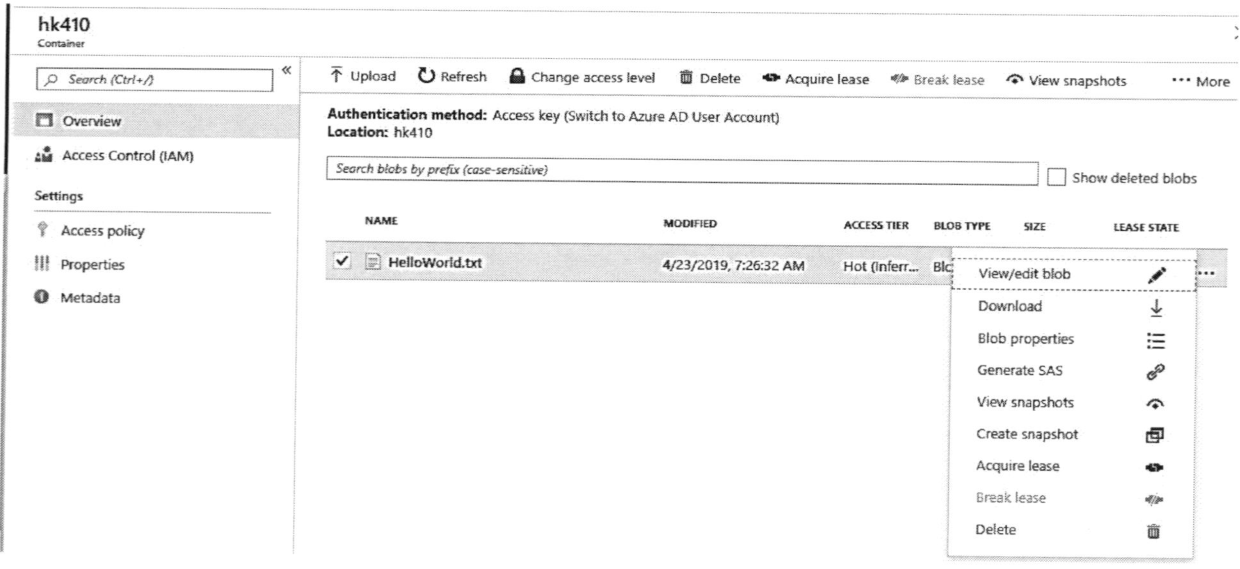

5. Double click HelloWorld.Txt in Container pane>Blob Dashboard opens>Copy the URL of the file.

6. Open a browser and paste the URL copied in step 5. We were able to open the file as we had chosen Blob anonymous read permission.

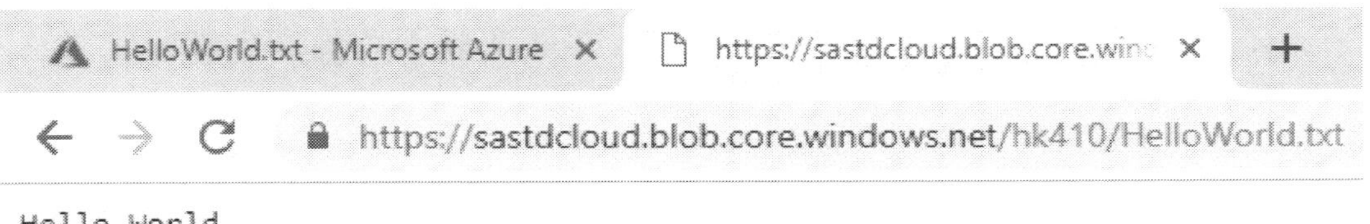

7. **Change the permission to private**. In Blob dashboard select container hk410 and click Change Access Level>Change Access Level blade opens>Select private from drop down box and click **ok.**

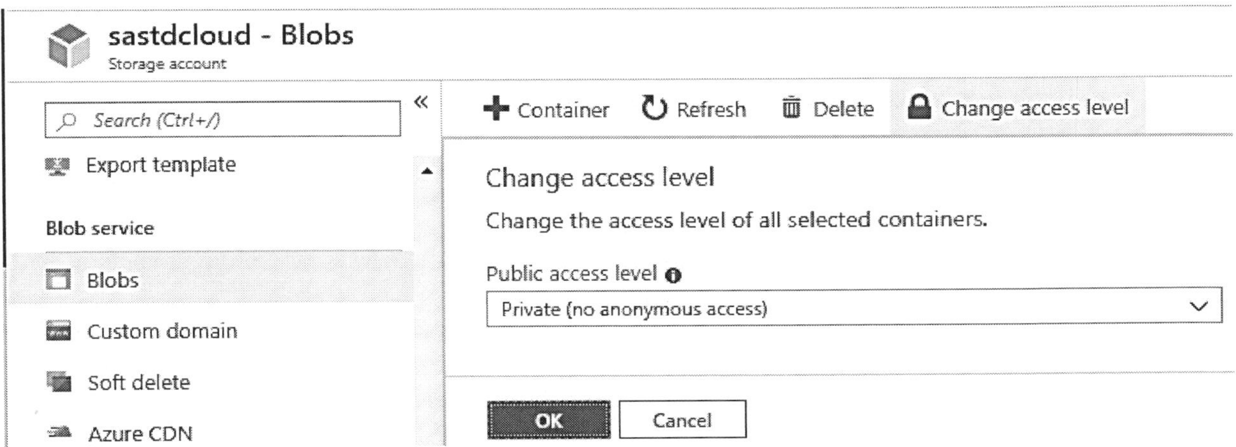

8. Open a browser and paste the URL copied in step 5. We were not able to open the file as we had chosen Private (no anonymous access) permission.

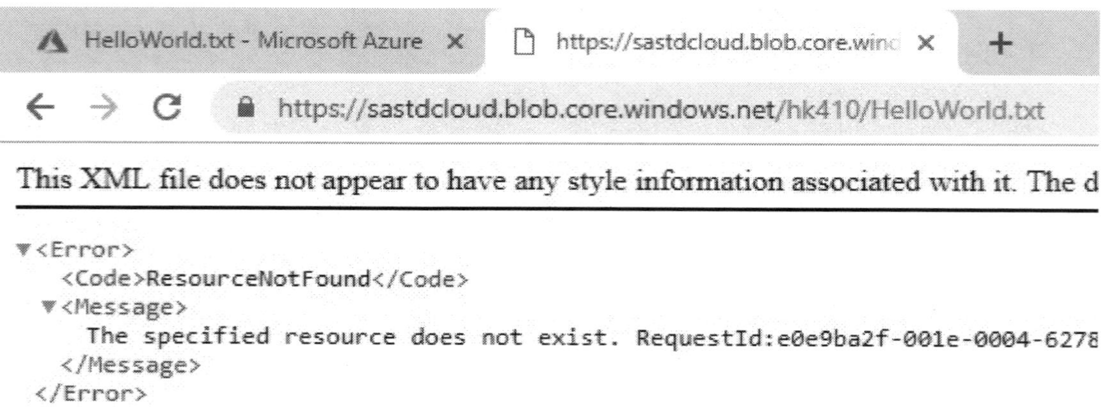

9. **Change the permission back to Blob** as we need it for other exercises. In Blob dashboard select container hk410 and click Change Access Level>Change Access Level blade opens>Select Blob from drop down box and click **ok.**

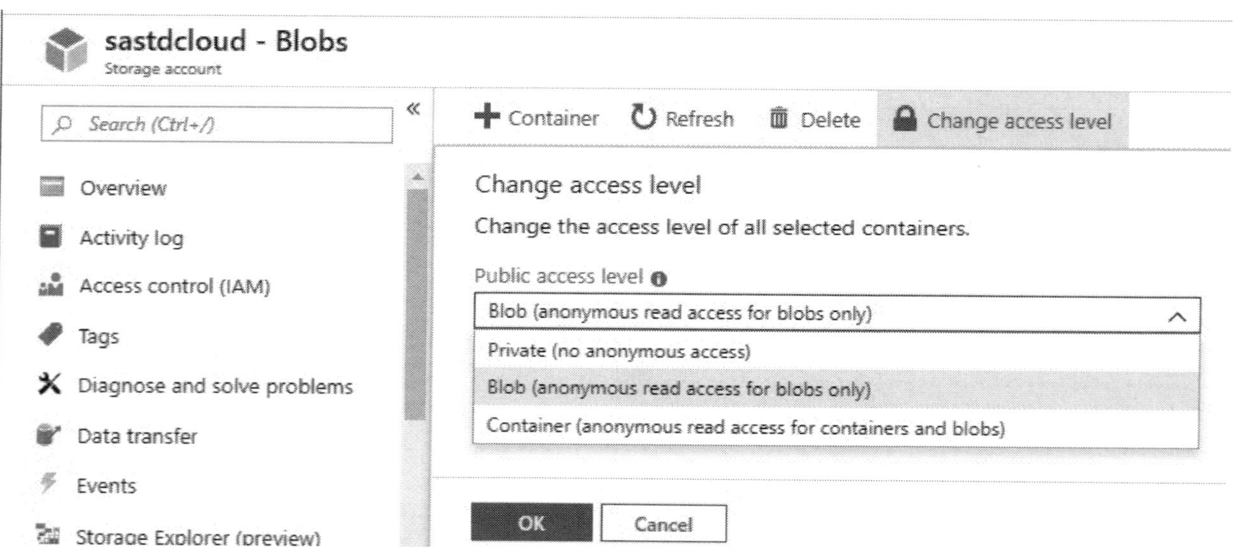

Exercise 79: Blob Storage Tiering

In this exercise we will just demonstrate how to move Blob Object HelloWorld.txt from Hot Access tier to Cool or Archive Tier using Azure Portal. We will not actually move it.

1. Go to Blob Container hk410 dashboard>Click the HelloWorld.txt in right pane>Blob Properties pane open>Scroll down and under Access tier select cool or Archive tier.

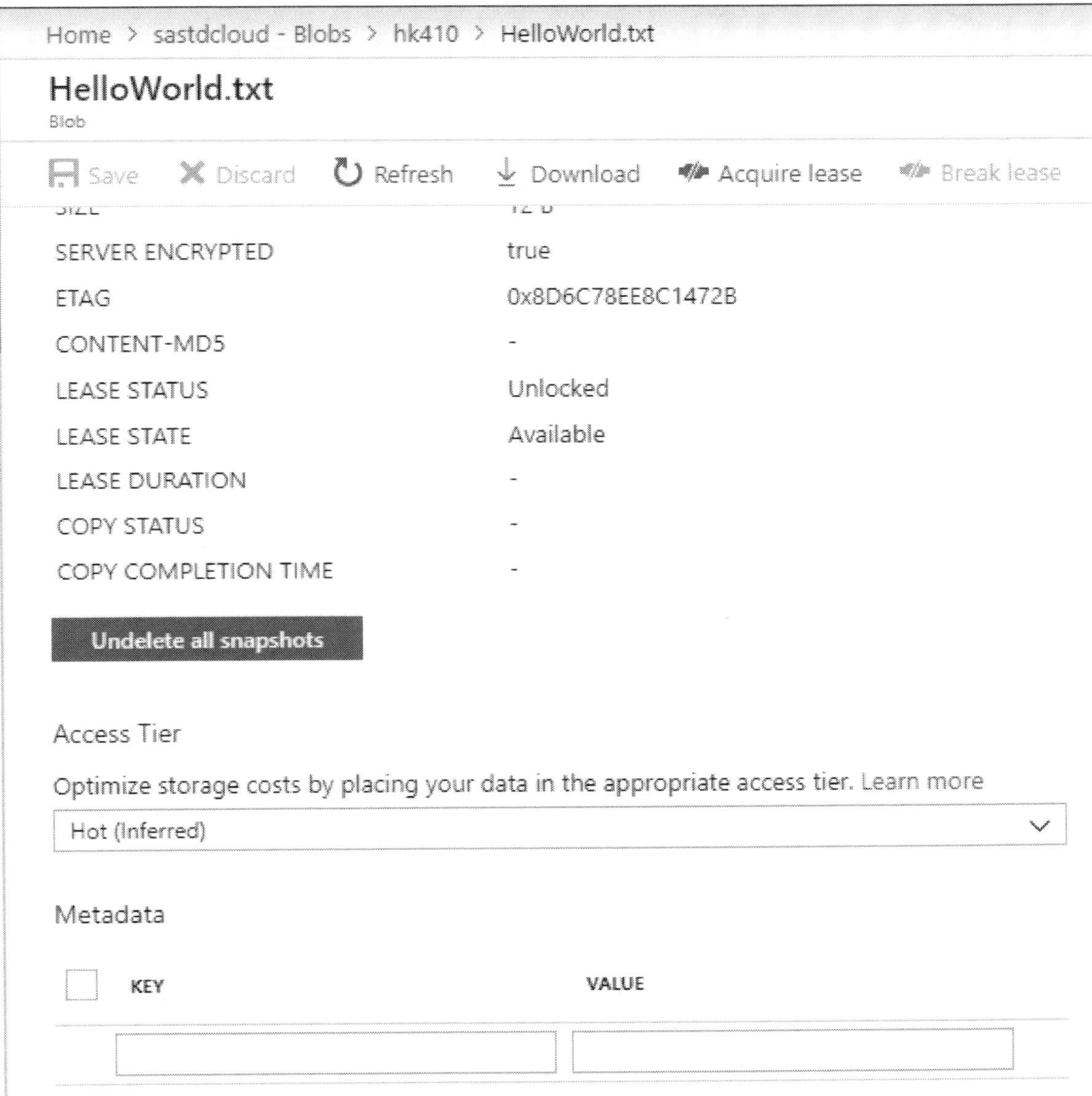

Exercise 80: Create Blob Storage Container using Storage Explorer

In this exercise we will create Blob Storage Container **test410** in Storage Account sastdcloud (Created in Exercise 69, chapter 8). We will then upload a text file HelloWorld.txt to the Blob Container.

1. In Storage Explorer Dashboard enlarge Storage Account sastdcloud under Pay you go subscription.

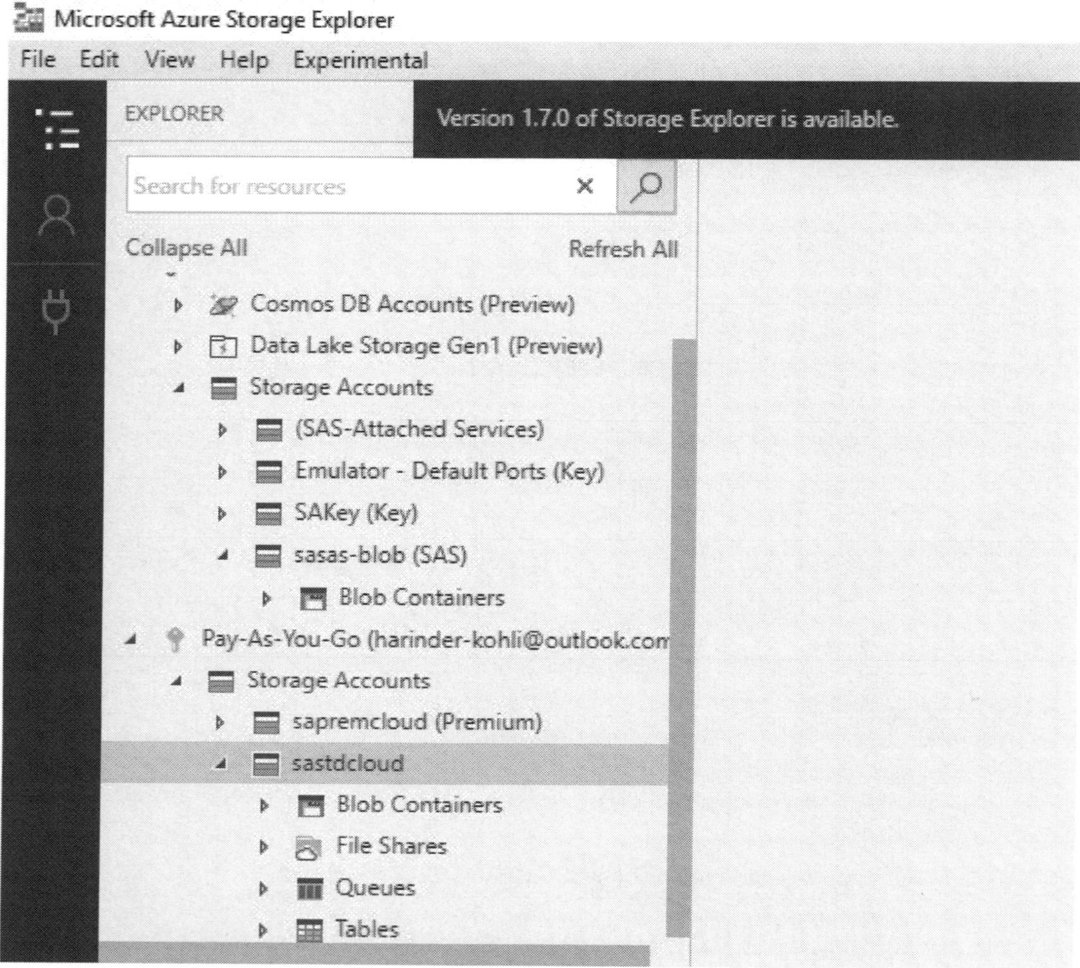

2. Right click Blob Containers under sastdcloud>Dailog Box opens. Click create Blob container> In dialog box type test410 and press enter. Container test410 is created as shown below with Private no anonymous access. You can also see container hk410 created in exercise 64.

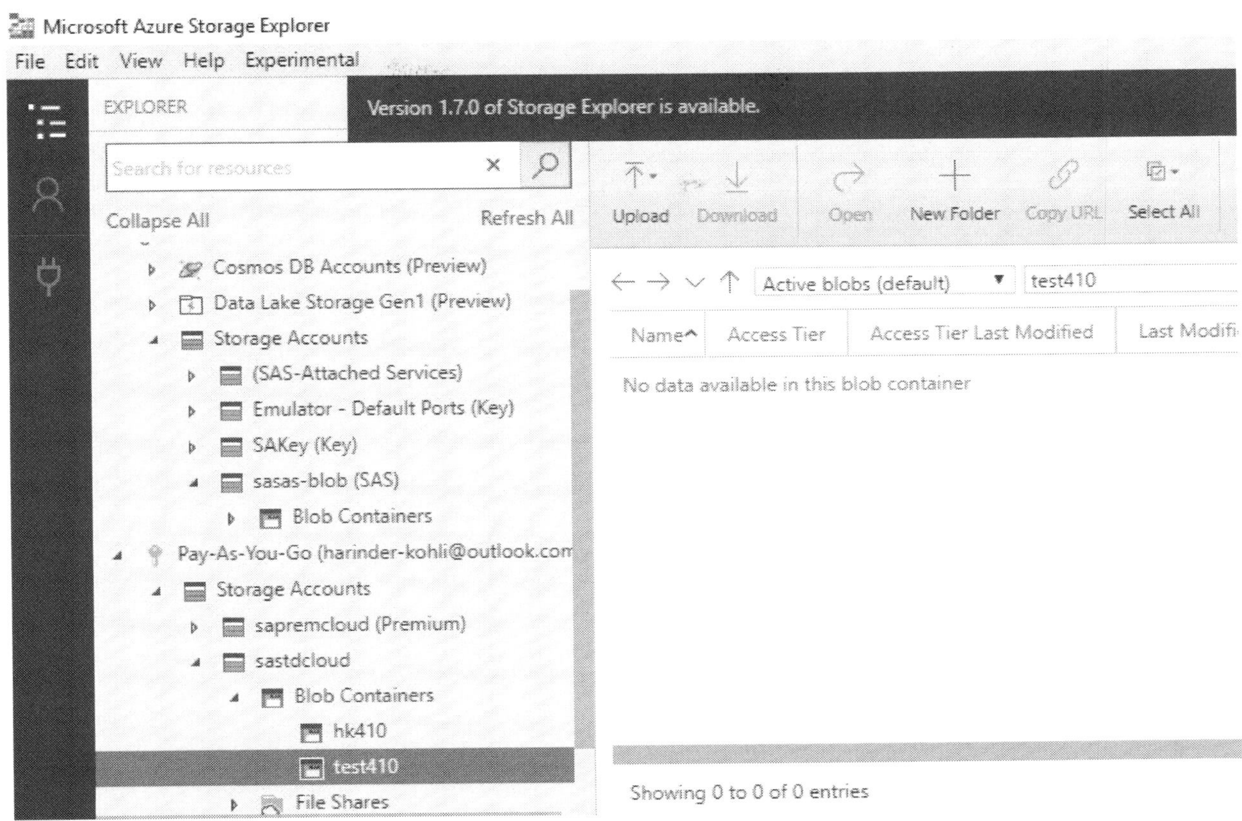

3. Create HelloWorld.txt file with contents Hello World on your desktop. Click upload in right pane and select upload files>Upload File Blade opens>Click ... and select HelloWorld.txt from your desktop>Click upload.

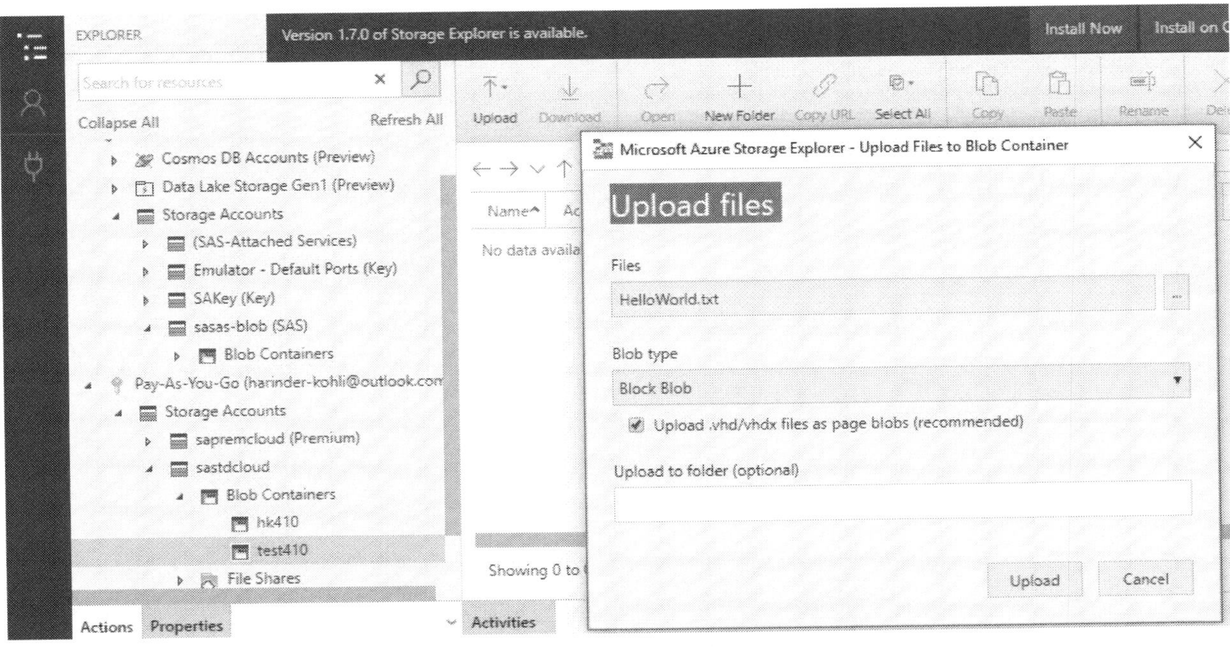

4. Figure below shows HelloWorld.txt file uploaded.

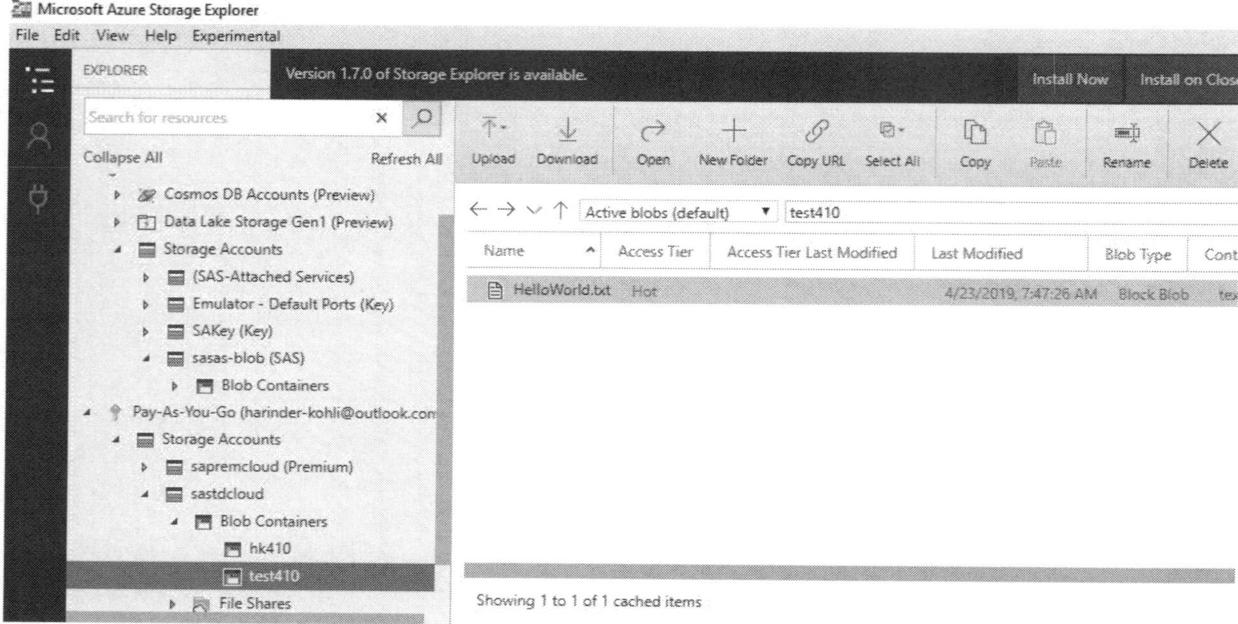

5. You can change the Public Access level by right clicking container test410 and click Set Public Access level>Public Access level blade opens. You can change access level as per your requirement.

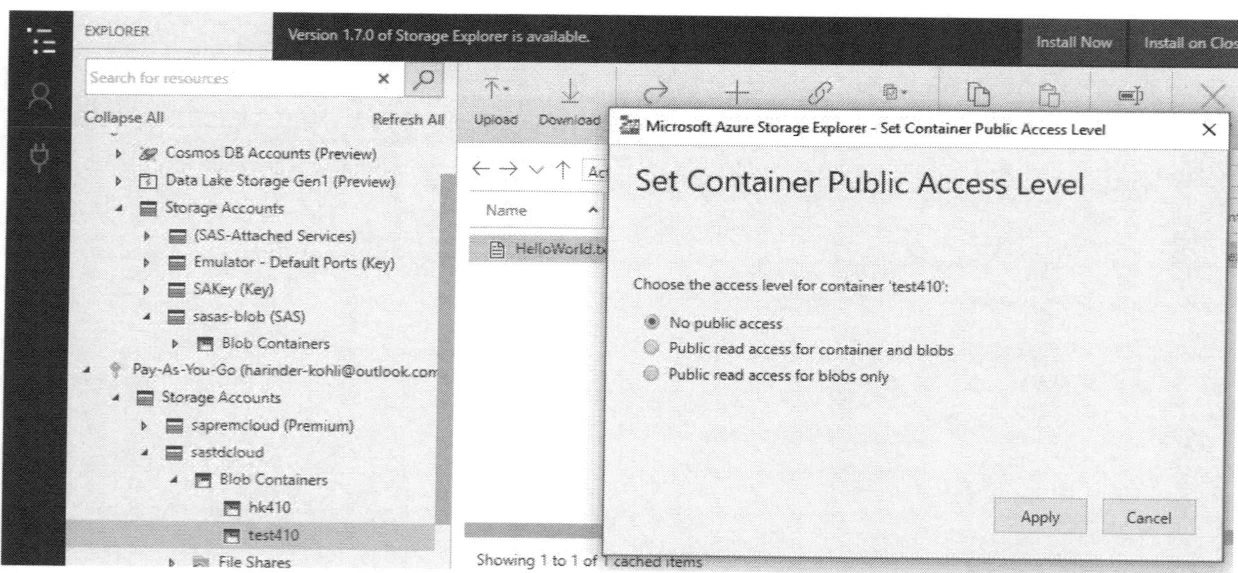

Data Compliance in Azure Cloud with Immutable Blob Storage

Many BFSI companies are not moving data to cloud because of regulatory compliance issues.

BFSI organizations are required to retain business-related communications in a Write-Once-Read-Many (WORM) or immutable state that ensures they are non-erasable and non-modifiable for a specific retention interval by regulators such as Securities and Exchange Commission (SEC), Commodity Futures Trading Commission (CFTC), Financial Industry Regulatory Authority (FINRA), Investment Industry Regulatory Organization of Canada (IIROC), Financial Conduct Authority (FCA) and many more in different countries.

IMMUTABLE STORAGE FOR AZURE BLOB (OBJECT) STORAGE

Immutable storage for Azure Blob (object) storage enables users to store business-critical data in a WORM (write once, read many) state. This state makes the data non-erasable and non-modifiable for a user-specified interval. Blobs can be created and read, but not modified or deleted, for the duration of the retention interval.

Immutable storage for Azure Blob (object) storage helps financial institutions and related industries to not only store data securely but also helps in Regulatory Compliance.

WORM (WRITE ONCE, READ MANY) POLICY TYPES

Immutable storage for Azure Blob storage supports two types of WORM or immutable policies: time-based retention and legal holds.

Time Based Retention: With time-based retention policy all blobs in the container will stay in the immutable state for the duration of the *effective* retention period.

Legal Hold: With legal hold policy all blobs in the container will stay in the immutable state until the legal hold is cleared.

IMMUTABLE STORAGE FOR AZURE BLOB USE CASES

Regulatory compliance: Immutable storage for Azure Blob storage helps organizations address SEC 17a-4(f), CFTC 1.31(d), FINRA, and other regulations.

Secure document retention: Blob storage ensures that data can't be modified or deleted by any user, including users with account administrative privileges.

Legal hold: Immutable storage for Azure Blob storage enables users to store sensitive information that's critical to litigation or a criminal investigation in a tamper-proof state for the desired duration.

STORAGE ACCOUNT REQUIREMENT FOR IMMUTABLE BLOB STORAGE

Blob Container must be created in GPv2 or Blob Storage Account.

Note: This topic is very relevant for AZ-301 Exam.

Exercise 81: Applying Time Based Retention Policy

In this exercise we will apply Time based retention policy on newly created Blob Container in Storage Account sastdcloud. Storage Account sastdcloud was created in Exercise 69, Chapter 8.

1. **Create Blob Container.** Go to Storage Account **sastdcloud** Dashboard > Click Blobs under services>Blob Dashboard opens> In Right pane click +container>Create New Container blade opens>Enter name **dk410** and select access level **Private** and click ok.

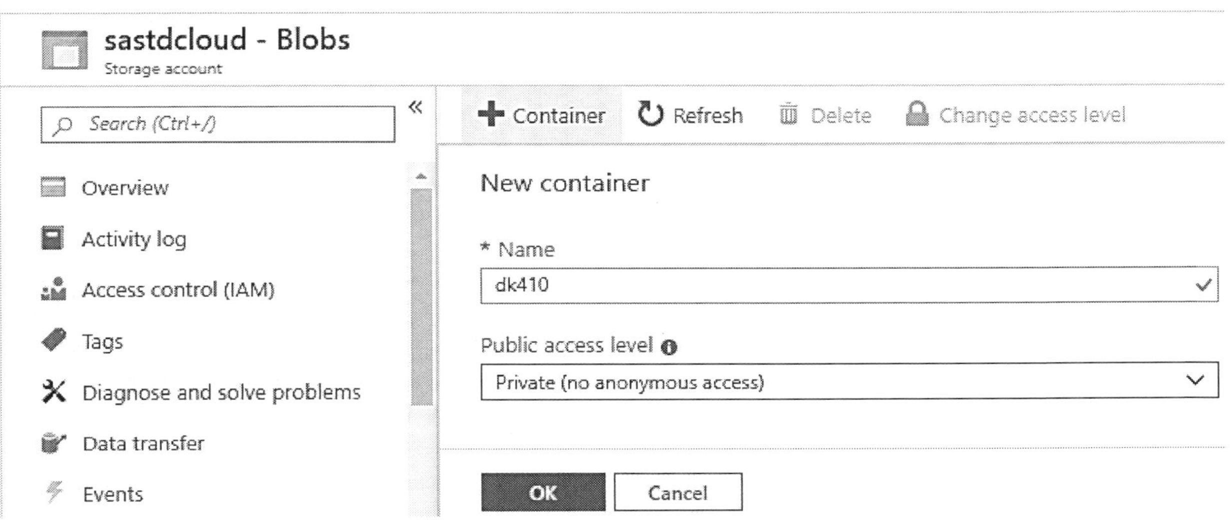

2. Figure below shows dashboard of newly created container dk410.

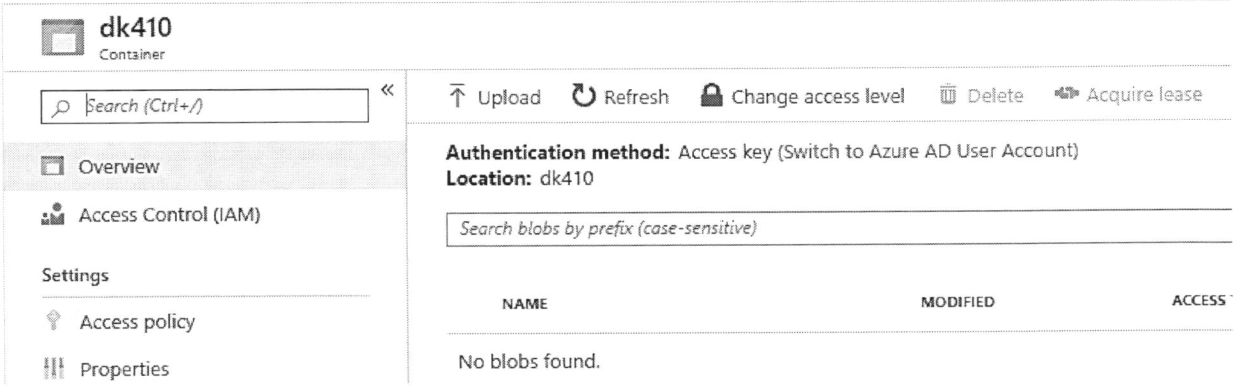

3. In container dk410 dashboard click Access policy in left pane>Access Policy pane opens.

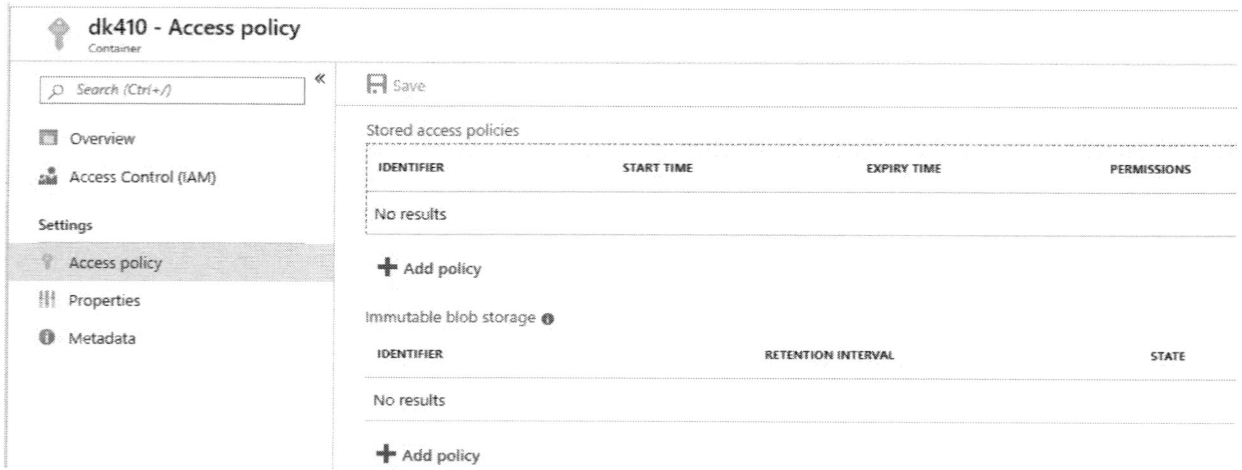

4. Under Immutable Blob storage Click + Add policy>Immutable Blob Storage Pane open in right side> In dropdown box in right pane select Policy type as Time-based retention> In set retention period enter number of days as per your requirement and click ok. I entered 1 days.

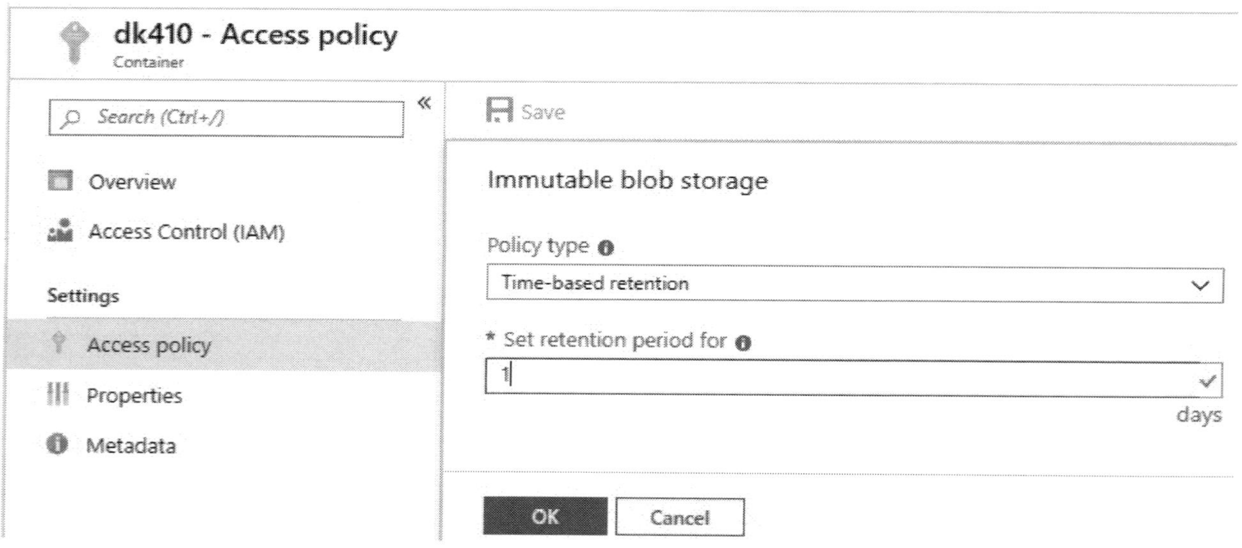

5. Figure below shows newly created Policy. The initial state of the policy is unlocked. You make changes to the policy before you lock it. Locking is essential for compliance with regulations such as SEC 17a-4.

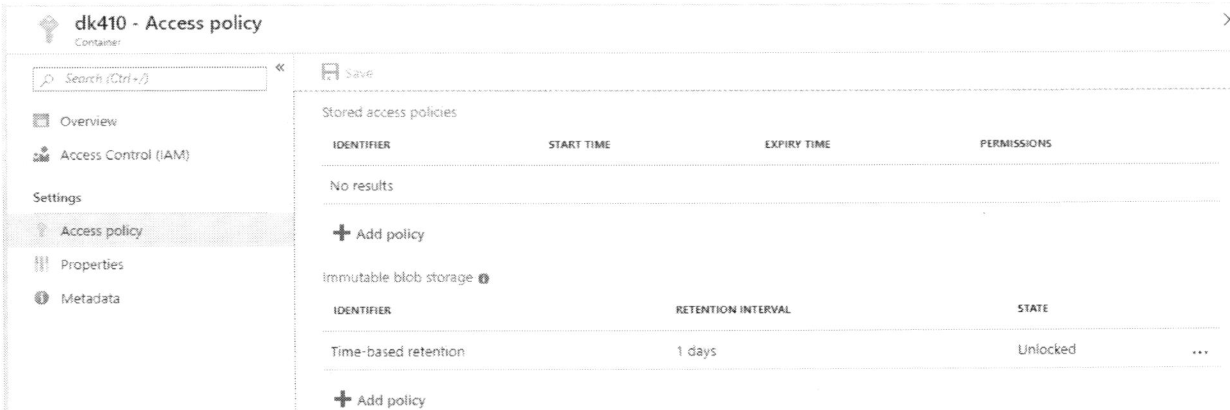

6. To lock the policy, click the ellipsis (...) in right pane, and in the drop down menu select lock policy>A Box pops up. Enter yes> Click ok.

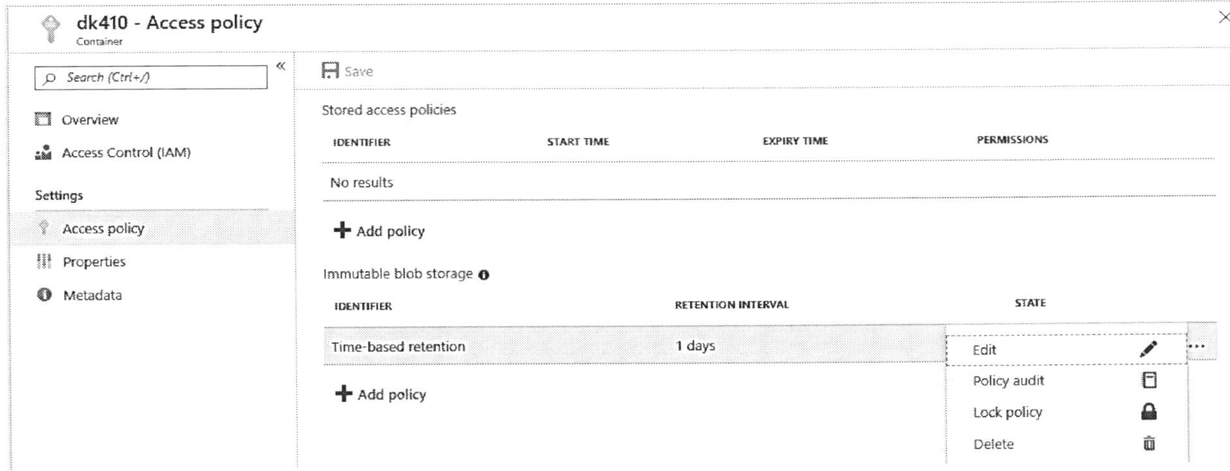

7. The policy state now appears as locked as shown below. After the policy is locked, it can't be deleted, and only extensions of the retention interval will be allowed.

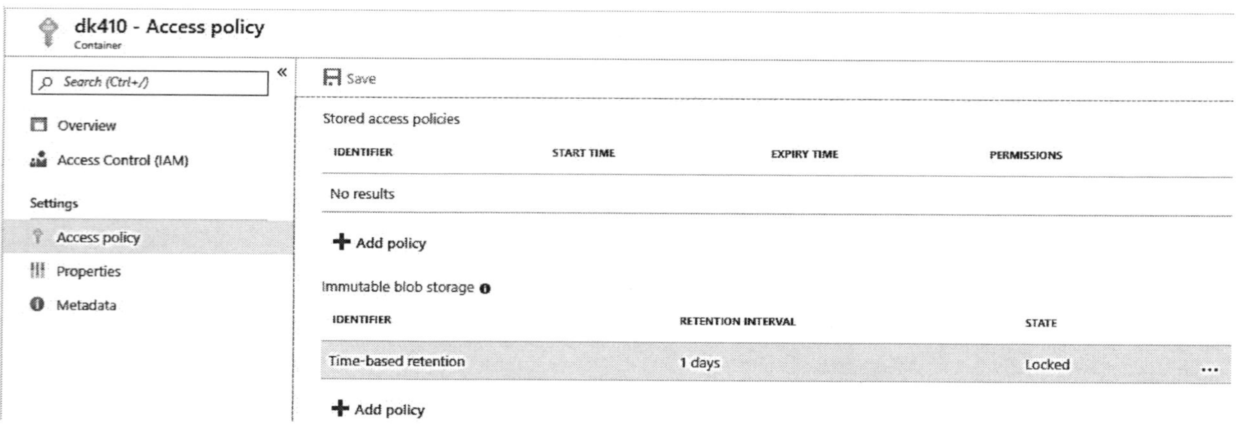

PRICING

Immutable data is priced in the same way as mutable data and there is no additional charge for using this feature.

As you can see from the above that Immutable storage for Azure Blob storage helps address Data regulations such as SEC 17a-4(f), CFTC 1.31(d), FINRA and other regulations. Enabling Immutable storage does not requires massive administrative and cost overhead.

Blob Storage Pricing using GPv2 Storage Account (4 Components)

1. Cost of storing data in Blobs.
2. Operation Prices
3. Geo-Replication Data Transfer charge (Applicable only for GRS & GRS-RA)
4. Cool & Archive Early Deletion

Storage Charges for RA-GRS (LRS, ZRS & GRS prices are not shown)

	Hot	**Cool**	**Archive**
First 50 terabyte (TB) / month	$0.046 per GB	$0.025 per GB	$0.00299 per GB
Next 450 TB / Month	$0.0442 per GB	$0.025 per GB	$0.00299 per GB
Over 500 TB / Month	$0.0424 per GB	$0.025 per GB	$0.00299 per GB

Operation Prices RA-GRS

	Hot	**Cool**	**Archive**
Write Operations* (per 10,000)	$0.10	$0.20	$0.20
List and Create Container Operations (per 10,000)	$0.10	$0.10	$0.10
Read Operations** (per 10,000)	$0.004	$0.01	$5
Other Operations (per 10,000), except Delete, which is free	$0.004	$0.004	$0.004
Data Retrieval (per GB)	Free	$0.01	$0.02
Data Write (per GB)	Free	Free	Free

Note: Storage Charges are high but Access charges are lower in Hot Tier.

Geo-Replication Data Transfer charge

LRS OR ZRS	GRS OR RA-GRS
NA	$0.02

Cool and Archive early deletion pricing (GPv2)

Any blob that is moved to Cool or Archive tier is subject to an Archive early deletion period of 180 days and Cool early deletion period of 30 days. For example, if a blob is moved to Archive and then deleted or moved to the Hot tier after 45 days, the customer is charged an early deletion fee equivalent to 135 (180 minus 45) days of storing that blob in Archive.

Premium Blob Storage Pricing using GPv2 Storage Account

Premium blob storage is only available for Locally Redundant Storage (LRS). Premium blob storage has following Pricing components.

Storage Charges

	Premium
First 50 terabyte (TB) / month	$0.15 per GB
Next 450 TB / Month	$0.15 per GB
Over 500 TB / Month	$0.15 per GB

Operation Prices

	Premium
Write Operations* (per 10,000)	$0.0175
List and Create Container Operations (per 10,000)	$0.05
Read Operations** (per 10,000)	$0.0014
Other Operations (per 10,000), except Delete, which is free	$0.0014
Data Retrieval (per GB)	Free
Data Write (per GB)	Free

File Storage

Azure Files Storage offers fully managed file shares in the cloud that are accessible via the industry standard Server Message Block (SMB 3.0) protocol (also known as Common Internet File System or CIFS).
Azure File shares can be mounted concurrently by cloud or on-premises deployments of Windows, Mac OS, and Linux instances.

Figure below shows Multiple Virtual Machines accessing Azure File share.

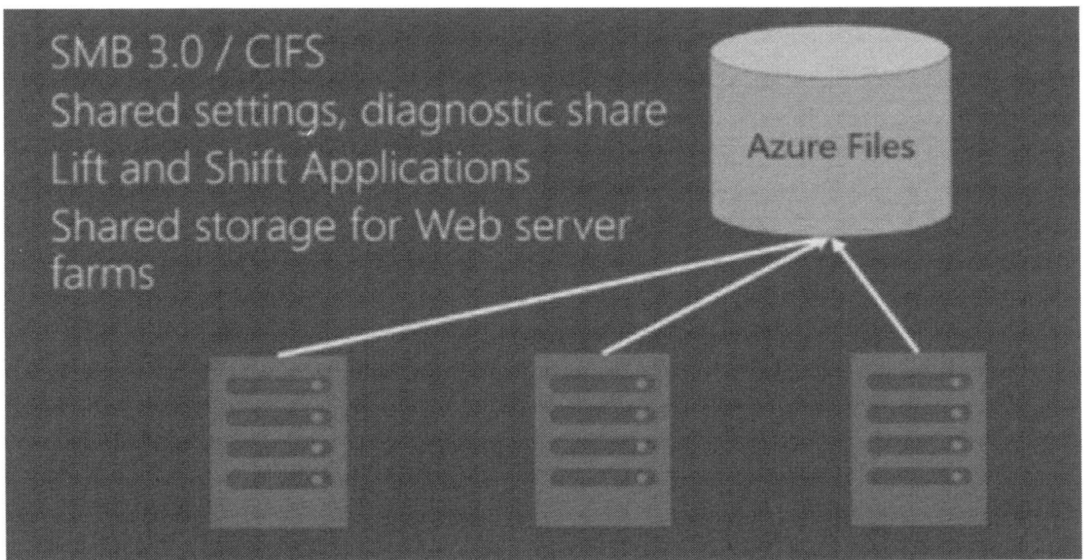

Azure File share Use case

1. Azure Files can be used to completely replace or supplement traditional on-premises file servers or NAS devices.
2. Developers can leverage their existing code and skills to migrate existing applications that rely on file shares to Azure quickly and without costly rewrites.
3. An Azure File share is a convenient place for cloud applications to write their logs, metrics, and crash dumps.
4. When developers or administrators are working on VMs in the cloud, they often need a set of tools or utilities. Copying such utilities and tools to each VM can be a time consuming exercise. By mounting an Azure File share locally on the VMs, a developer and administrator can quickly access their tools and utilities, no copying required.

File Service Architecture and components

Figure below shows the architecture of File share. File share is mounted as a drive on Virtual Machine and is accessed over the network.

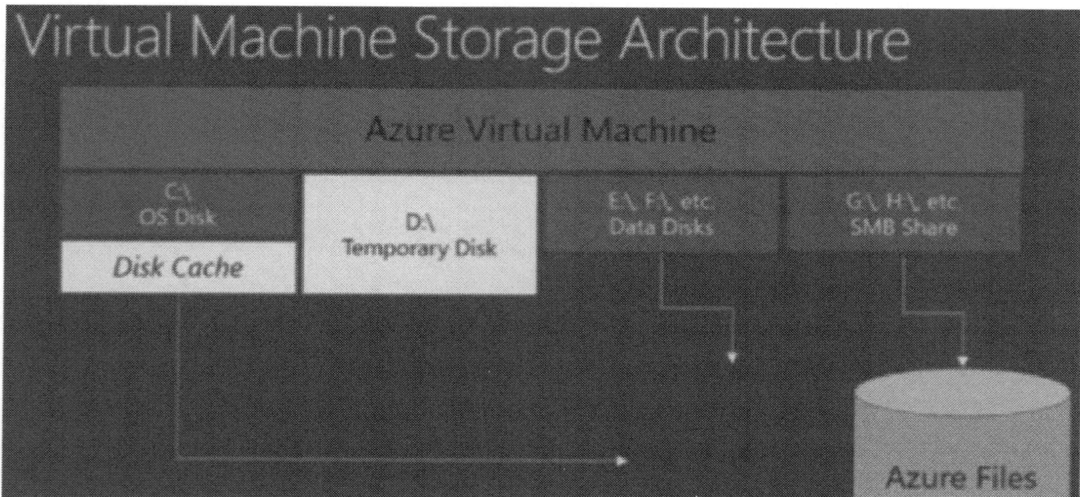

File Service contains 3 components: Storage Account, File Shares and Files.

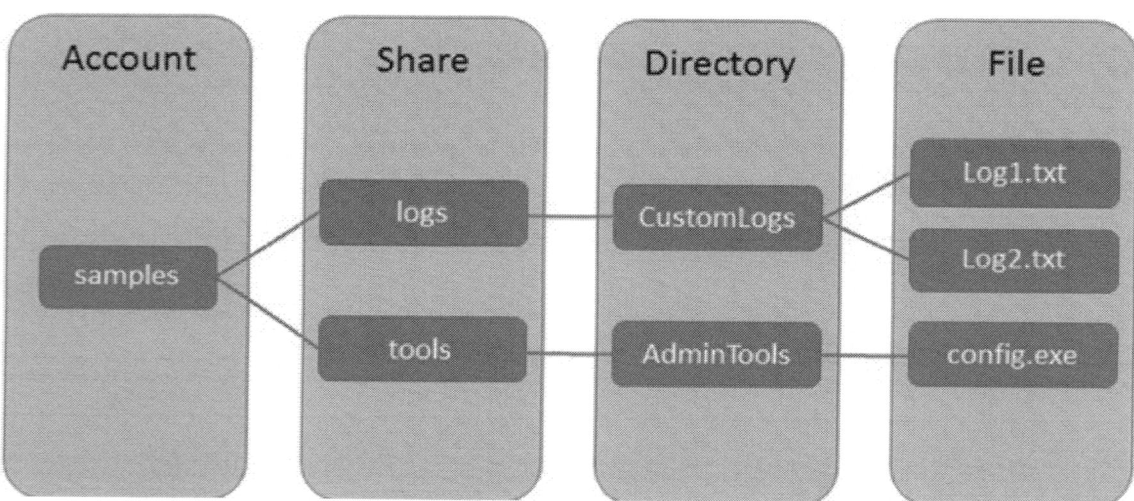

Storage Account: This storage account can be a General-purpose v1 or v2 storage account. It supports only Standard Storage for File service.
Share: Share stores the files. Azure File shares can be mounted and accessed concurrently by cloud or on-premises deployments of Windows, Linux, and macOS. A share can store an unlimited number of files.
Directory: Directory is optional. Directory is like a folder for files.
File: A file of any type with max size of 1 TB.

Exercise 82: Create and Mount File Share

In this Exercise we will create File Share fsaz103 and mount it to Windows VM VMFE1. Creating and Mounting File share is a 2 step process:

1. Create File Share in Storage Acount sastdcloud and upload a file. Storage Acount sastdcloud was created in Ex 69, Chapter 8.
2. Mount the File share on a Server instance in cloud or on-Prem. In this Exercise we will mount file share on windows VM VMFE1 created in Ex 25, Chapter 4.

Creating File Share

1. Go to Storage Account sastdcloud Dashboard.

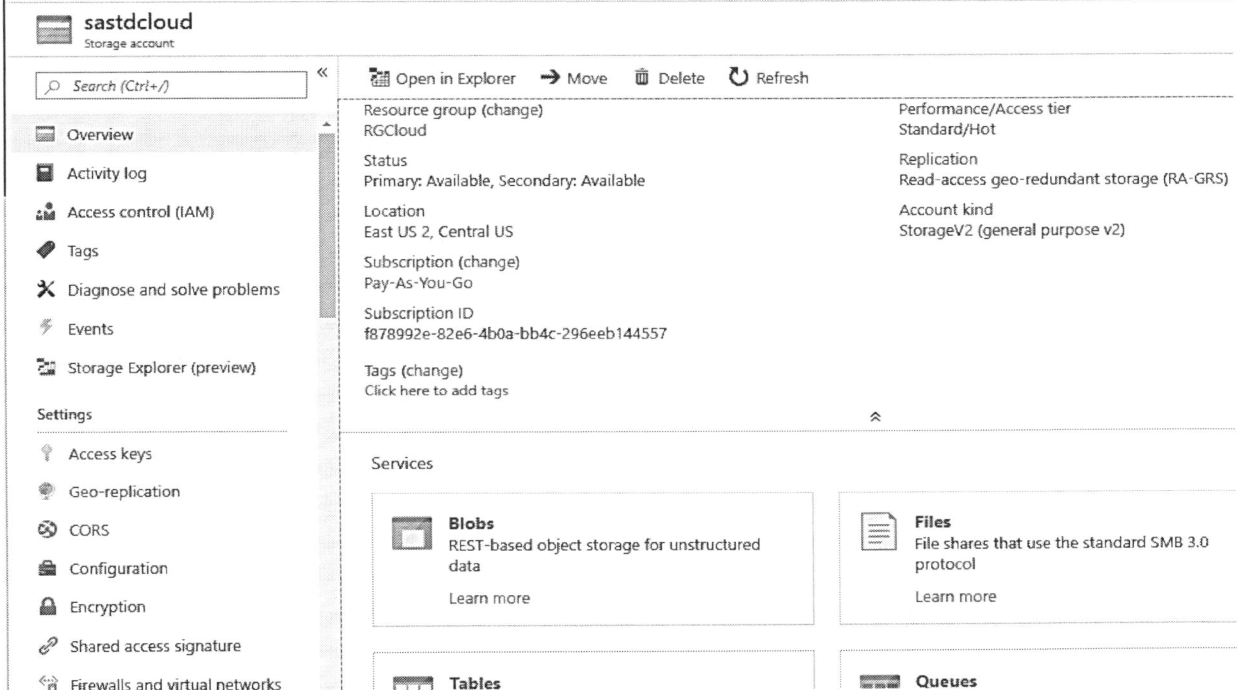

2. Click Files in right pane>File dashboard opens>Click + File share> Create File share blade opens>Enter name **fsaz103** and 1 GB in Quota and click create.

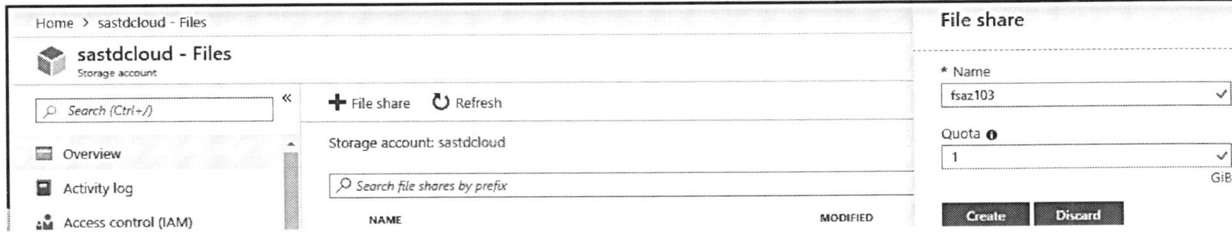

3. Click File share fsaz103 in File service pane> File share fsaz103 dashboard opens. Click upload in right pane> Upload File Blade open> Upload a file from your desktop and click upload. After file is uploaded close the upload blade.

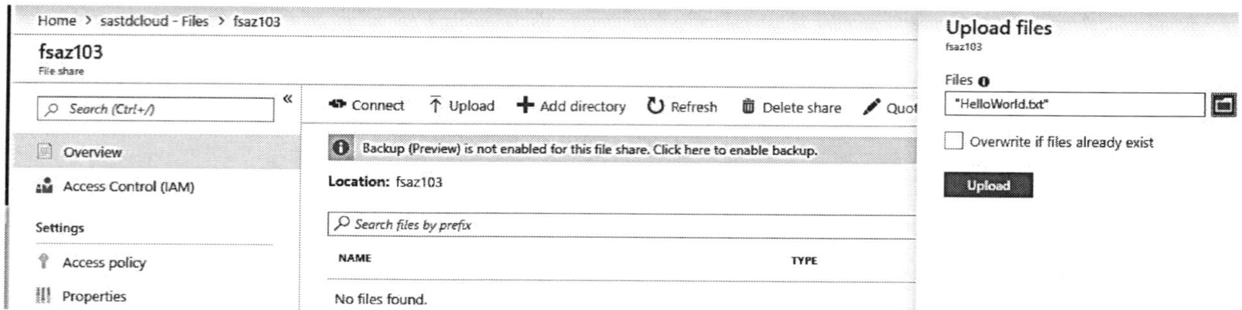

4. In File share fsaz103 dashboard Click Connect in right pane>Connect Blade opens. In connect pane go to second rectangular box and scroll down. Copy command appended to net use Z:
   In this case it is **\\sastdcloud.file.core.windows.net\fsaz103**

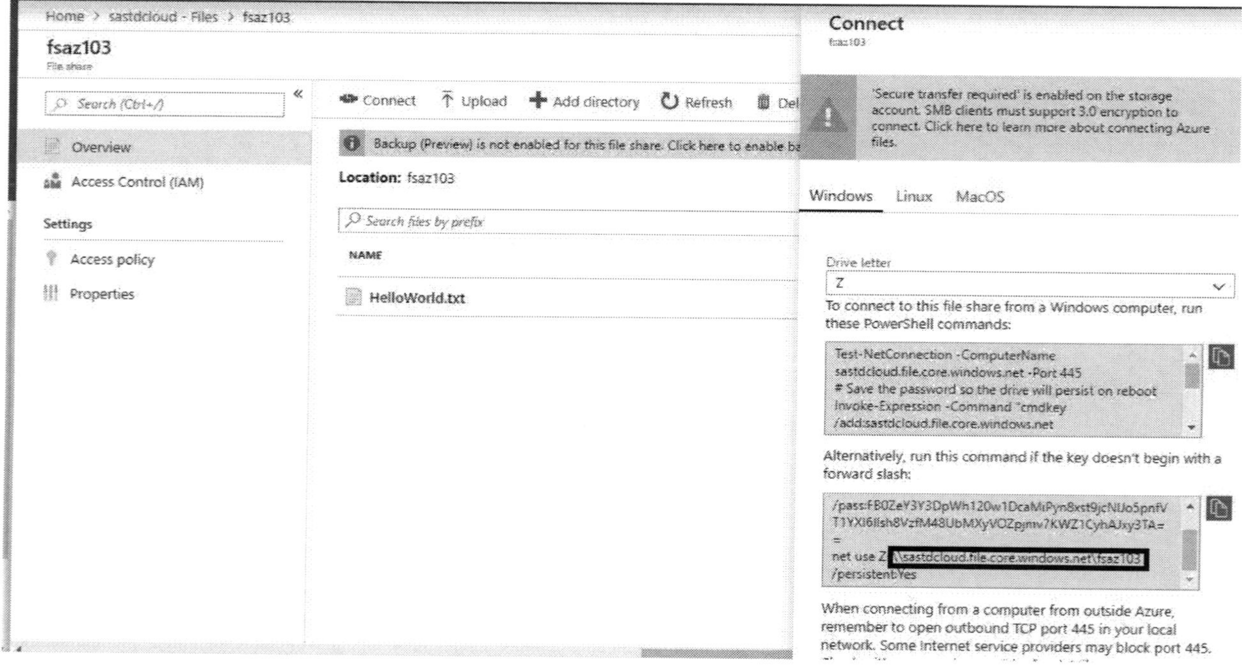

Also read the explanation under the box which says: **When connecting from a computer from outside Azure, remember to open outbound TCP port 445 in your local network.** In our case we are connecting from VMFE1 inside Azure.

5. Go to Storage Account Dashboard sastdcloud Dashboard>Click Access keys in left pane> In right pane copy key1.

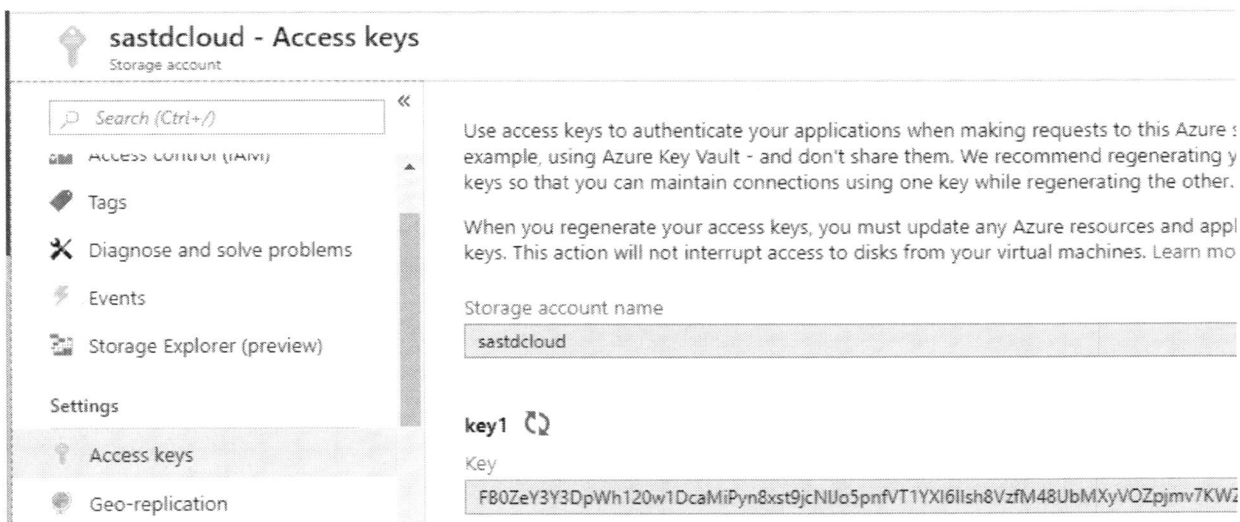

6. Connect to Azure VM VMFE1 using RDP> Open File Explorer and click **This PC** in left pane.

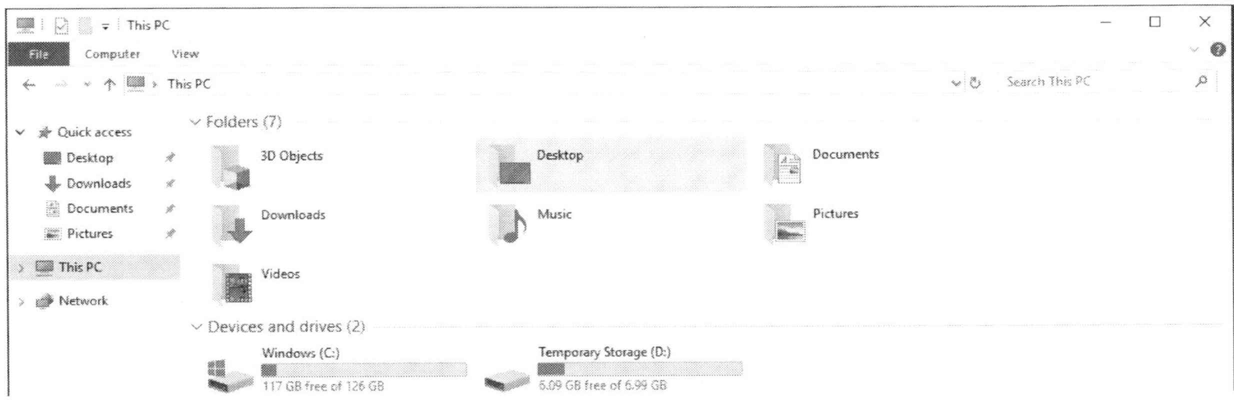

7. Click ˅ icon in right side and it opens ribbon items. Note the Map network drive option.

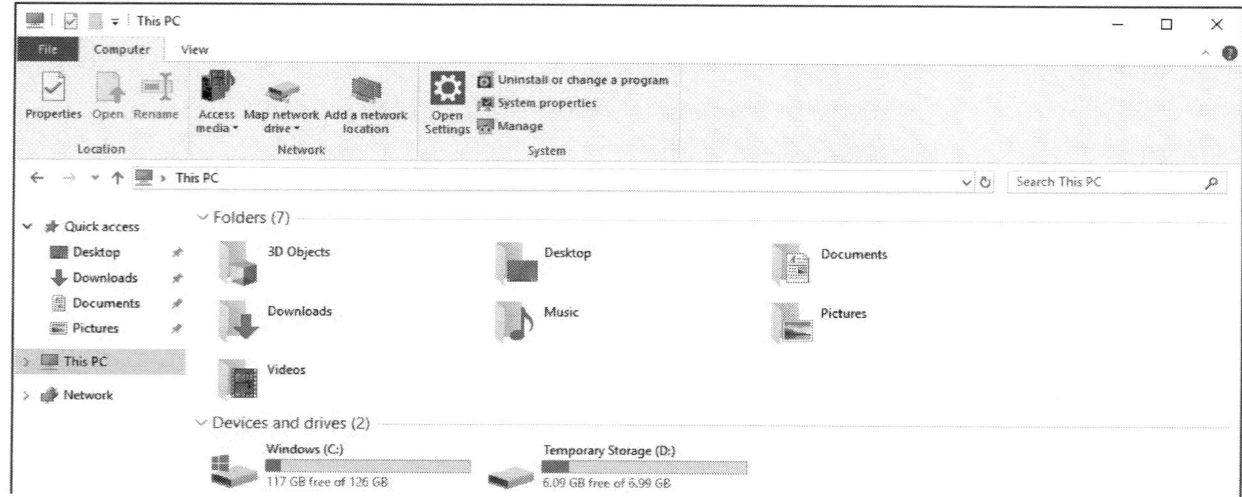

8. Click Map Network Drive>Map Network drive>In Folder enter command copied in step 4: **sastdcloud.file.core.windows.net\fsaz103**> Click Finish.

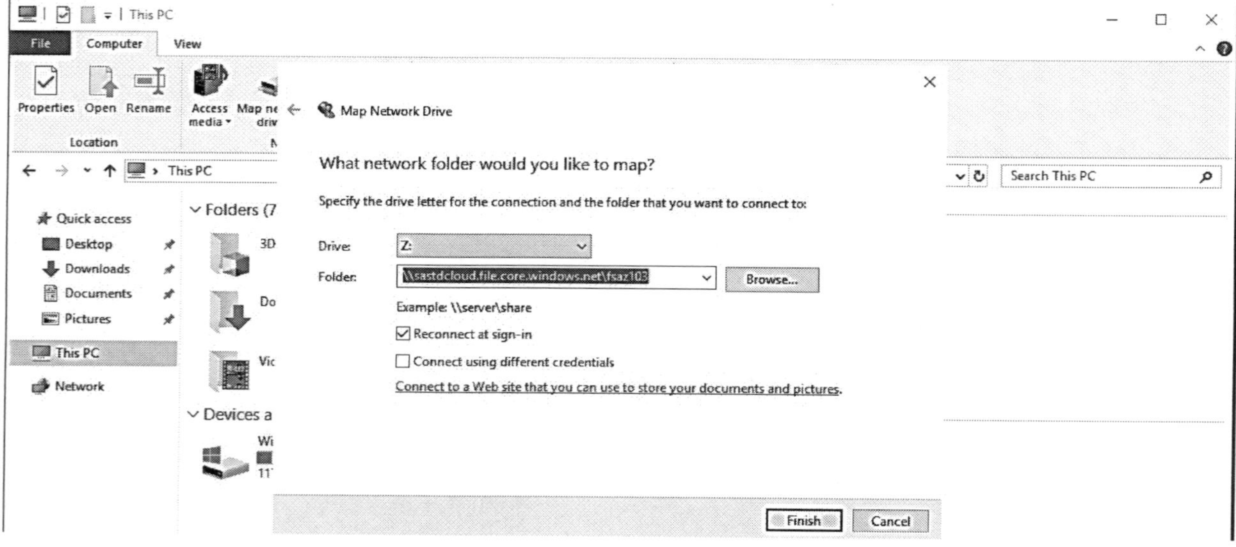

9. Enter Credential dialog box opens>In Username enter Storage Account name (sastdcloud) prepended with Azure\>In password enter Storage Account Key>Ok.

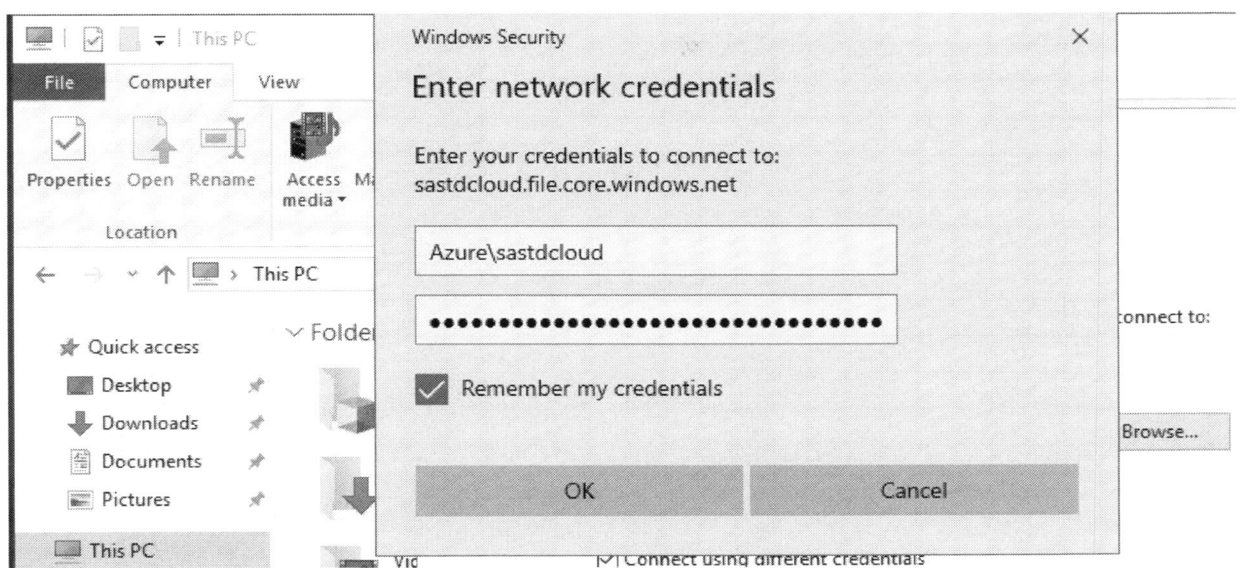

10. After VMFE1 connects you can see File share fsaz103 mounted to VMFE1.

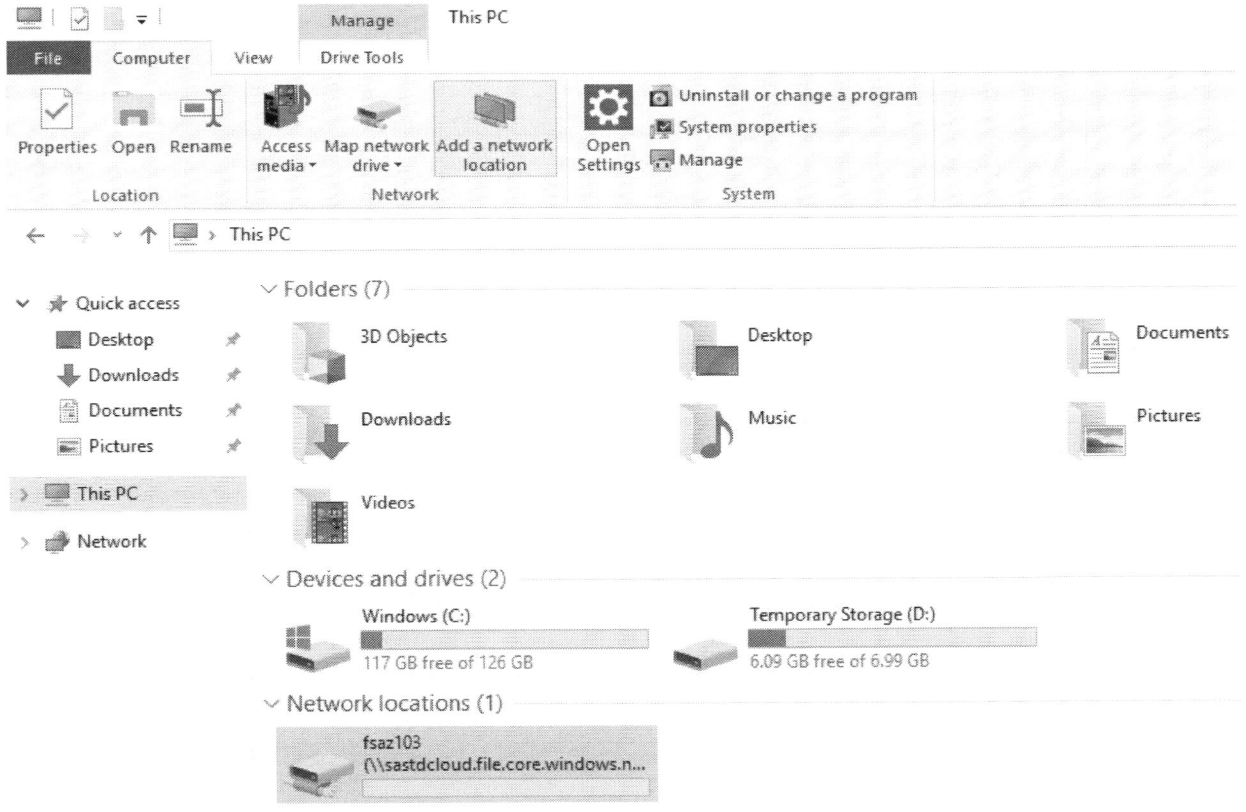

11. Click on File share fsaz103 and you can see HelloWorld.txt file.

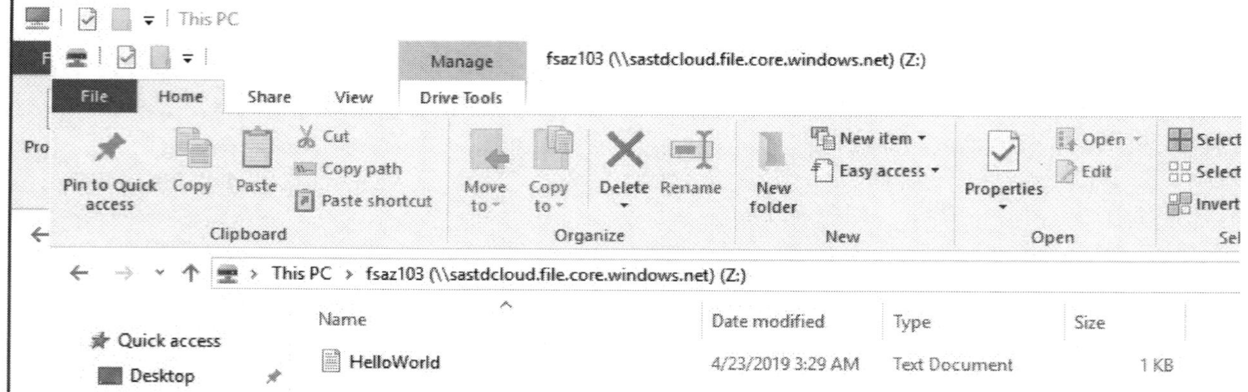

File Storage Pricing using General Purpose v2 Account

Standard Storage Pricing

Pricing is based on the Storage used.

LRS	ZRS	GRS
$0.06/GB/Month	$0.075/GB/Month	$0.10/GB/Month

Premium Storage Pricing

Premium storage is billed on provisioned Storage in GB. You just pay price per GiB for the Storage Provisioned with no transaction fees.

LRS
$0.24 per provisioned GiB

Operation & Data Transfer Pricing for Standard Storage

Access Prices are transaction for both SMB and REST operations against your Azure File share. These are the costs for operations, such as enumerating a directory or reading a file, against the data you store on an Azure File share.

	LRS	GRS
Put, Create Container Operations (per 10,000)	$0.015	$0.03
List Operations (per 10,000)	$0.015	$0.015
All other operations except Delete, which is free (per 10,000)	$0.0015	$0.0015
Geo-Replication Data Transfer (per GB)	NA	$0.02

Azure File Sync Service

Azure File Sync enables synchronization or replication of file data between on-premises file servers and Azure Files shares while maintaining local access to your data. It's a 2 way synchronization.

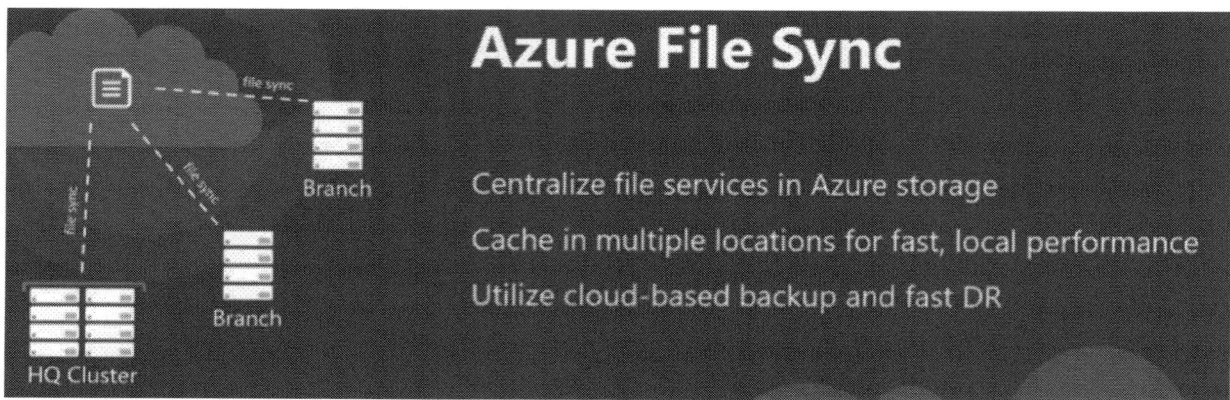

Benefits of Azure File Sync

1. By synchronizing on-premises File share data to Azure Share you can eliminate on-premises Backup and DR requirement. This reduces both cost and administrative overhead of managing Backup and DR.
2. With *Azure File Sync* you have the option to eliminate on-premises file server. User and On-premises application servers can access data in Azure File share.
3. With *Azure File Sync,* Branch office can access Head Office File share data in Azure File shares without requiring any complex set up to integrate Branch and HO File servers.

Azure File Sync Cloud Tiering Option

Cloud tiering is an optional feature of Azure File Sync in which infrequently used or accessed files greater than 64 KiB in size are moved or tiered to Azure File shares.

When a user opens a tiered file, Azure File Sync seamlessly recalls the file data from Azure Files without the user needing to know that the file is not stored locally on the system.

Components of Azure File Sync Solution

Azure Storage Sync Service

On-Premises Windows Server also known as Registered Server.

Azure File Sync Agent: Azure File Sync agent is installed on on-premises server which enables Windows Server to be synced with an Azure file share.

Server Endpoint: A server endpoint represents a specific location on a Windows or registered server, such as a folder on a server volume. Multiple server endpoints can exist on the same volume if their namespaces do not overlap (for example F:\sync1 and F:\sync2). You can configure cloud tiering policies individually for each server endpoint.

Cloud Endpoint: A cloud endpoint is an Azure file share. Azure file share can be a member of only one sync group. A cloud endpoint is a pointer to an Azure file share. All server endpoints will sync with a cloud endpoint, making the cloud endpoint the hub.

Sync Group: Sync Group has one cloud endpoint, which represents an Azure File share, and one or more server endpoints, which represents a path on a Windows Server. Endpoints within a sync group are kept in sync with each other.

Cloud tiering (optional): Cloud tiering is an optional feature of Azure File Sync in which infrequently used or accessed files greater than 64 KiB in size can be tiered to Azure Files. When a file is tiered, the Azure File Sync file system filter (StorageSync.sys) replaces the file locally with a pointer, or reparse point. The reparse point represents a URL to the file in Azure Files. A tiered file has the "offline" attribute set in NTFS so third-party applications can identify tiered files. When a user opens a tiered file, Azure File Sync seamlessly recalls the file data from Azure Files without the user needing to know that the file is not stored locally on the system.

Design Nugget: Storage Sync service should be in same region and Resource Group as Storage Account. The File Share should be in same Storage Account.

Exercise 83: Deploying Azure File Sync in 4 Steps

1. Using File sync we will synchronize files in Registered Server with File Share fsaz103. For Registered Server Use VM VMAD created in Ex 39, Chapter 4.
2. Use File Share fsaz103 created in this Chapter Exercise 82.
3. Use Storage Account sastdcloud created in Exercise 69, Chapter 8.
4. Use Resource Group RGCloud created in Exercise 1, chapter 1.

Step 1: Create File Sync Service

1. In Azure Portal Click create a Resource>Storage>Azure File Sync>Deploy Storage sync blade opens>Enter a name> Select **RGCloud** in Resource Group > Click create (Not Shown).

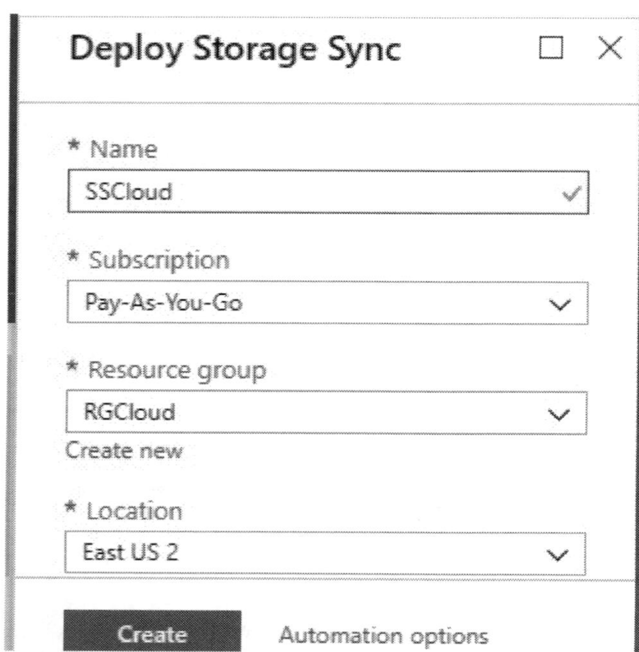

2. Figure below shows dashboard of Storage Sync Service.

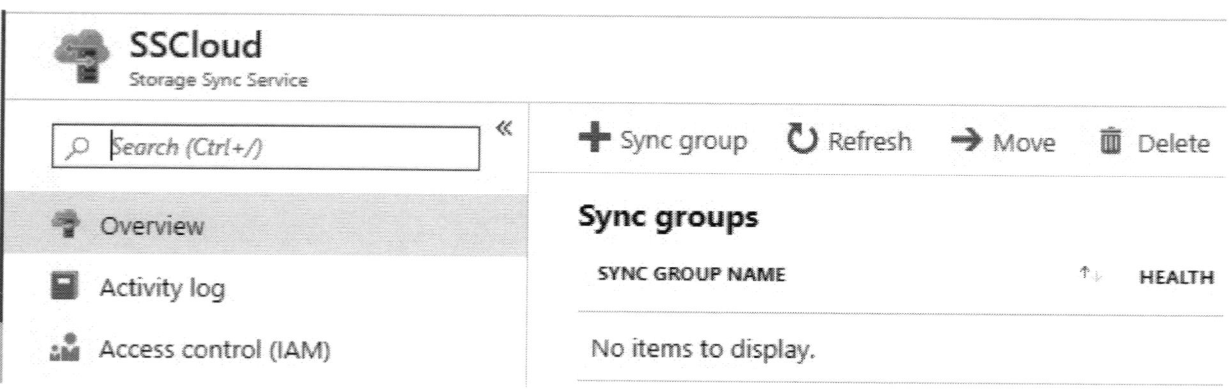

Step 2: Download, Install & Register Azure File Sync Agent on VM VMAD

1. RDP to Windows VM VMAD.
2. Open Internet explorer and Download Azure File Sync Agent for Windows Server 2016 from following link. Disable enhanced IE security settings. https://www.microsoft.com/en-us/download/details.aspx?id=57159
3. Click on Agent file to start the Installation. After Installation is complete Server Registration screen opens automatically.

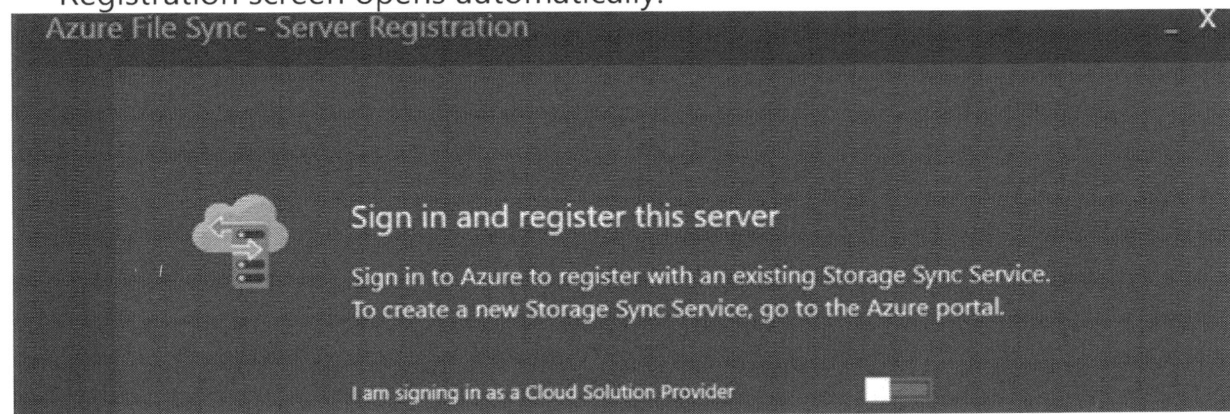

4. Click sign in and authentication box pops up> Enter your MS Account used for Subscription registration and following screen opens>Select your Subscription and Resource Group **RGCloud** and Storage Sync Service created in step 1.

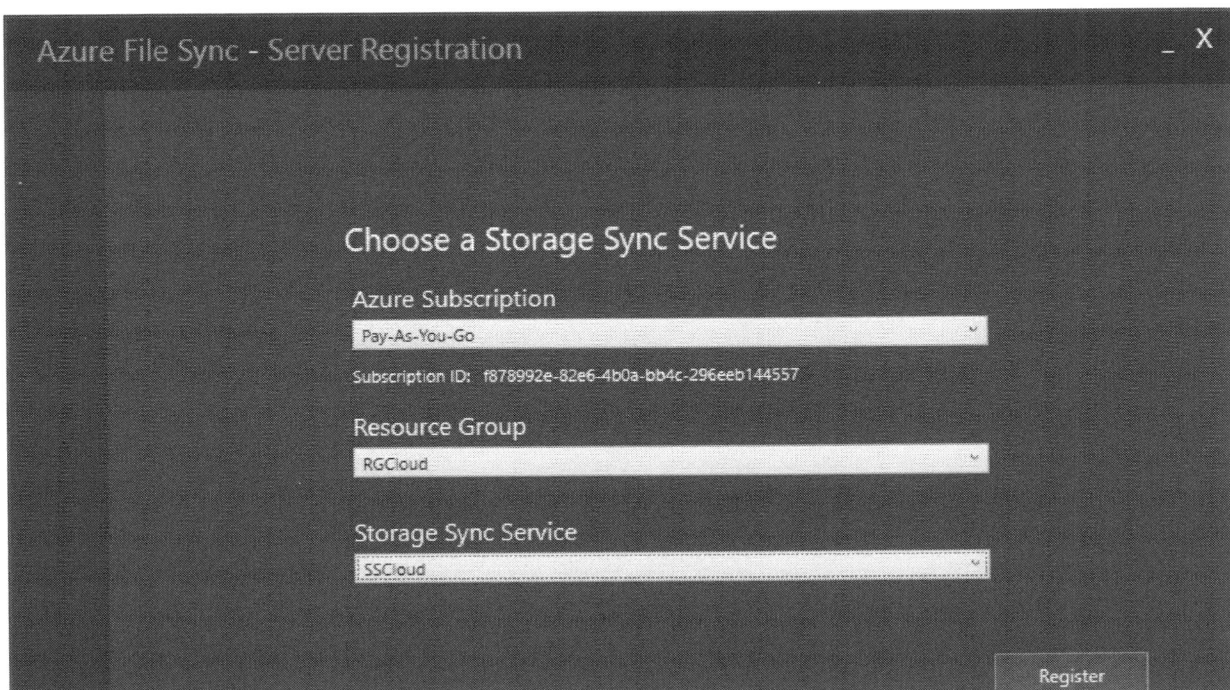

5. Click Register and authentication box pops up>Enter your Microsoft Account used for Subscription registration and password>Registration successful message pops up.

6. Go the Go Storage sync Service SSPortal created in step 1 Dashboard>Click Registered Servers in left pane>In right pane you can see VMAD is registered and is online.

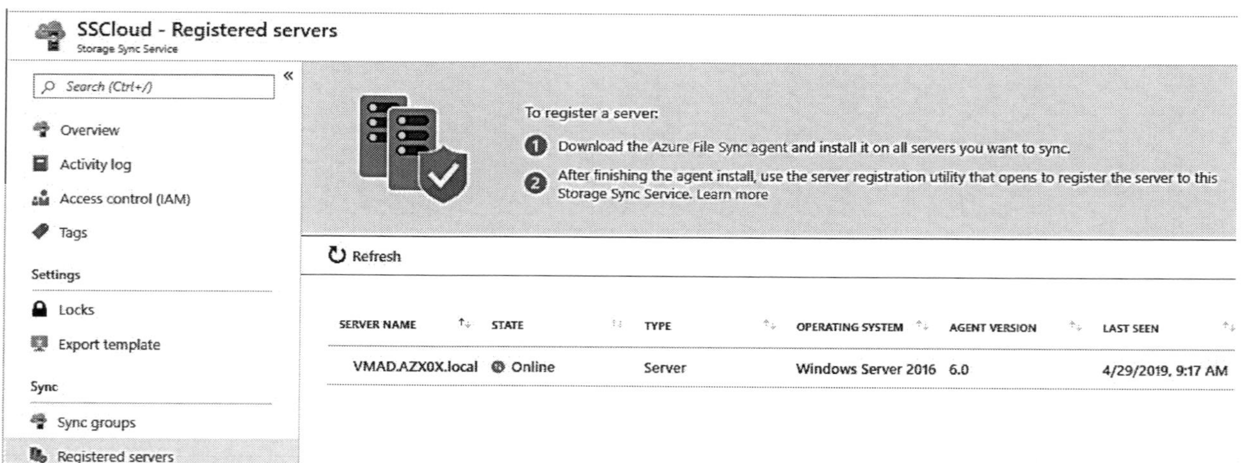

7. In Registered server VM OnPremAD I created a Folder **Public** under C Drive. In Public folder I created 2 text files – Test1 and Test2.

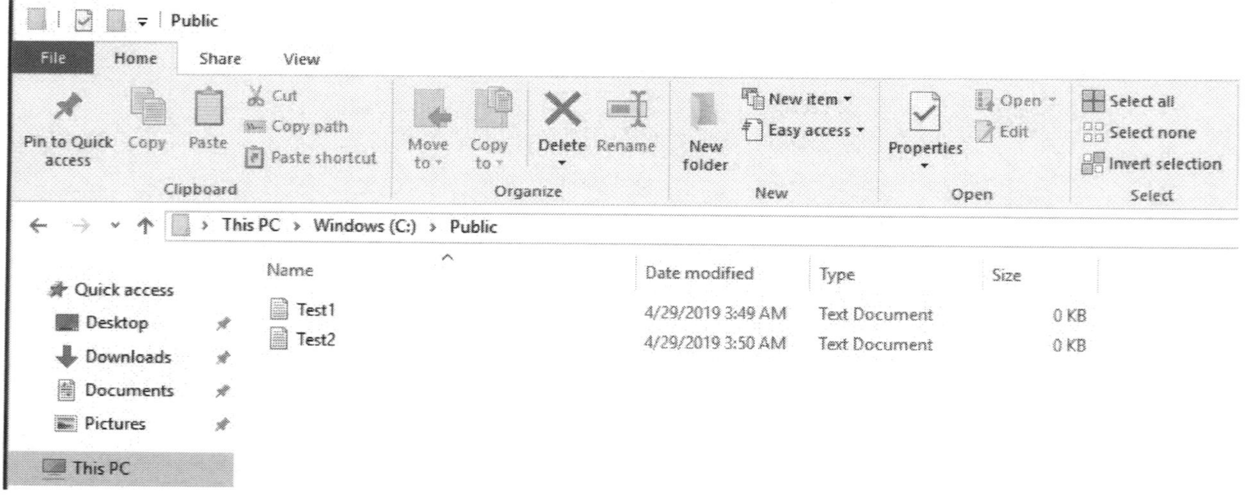

Step 3: Create a Sync group and add File share

In this we will add Storage Account sastdcloud and File Share fsaz103. Storage Account sastdcloud was created in exercise 54, Chapter 5 and File share fsaz103 was created in exercise 67 in this Chapter.

1. Go Storage sync Service SScloud created in step 1 Dashboard>Click sync group in left pane>In Right pane click +Sync Group>Create Sync group blade opens> Enter a name>Select Storage account sastdcloud created in exercise 54 and file share fsaz103 created in Exercise 67>click create.

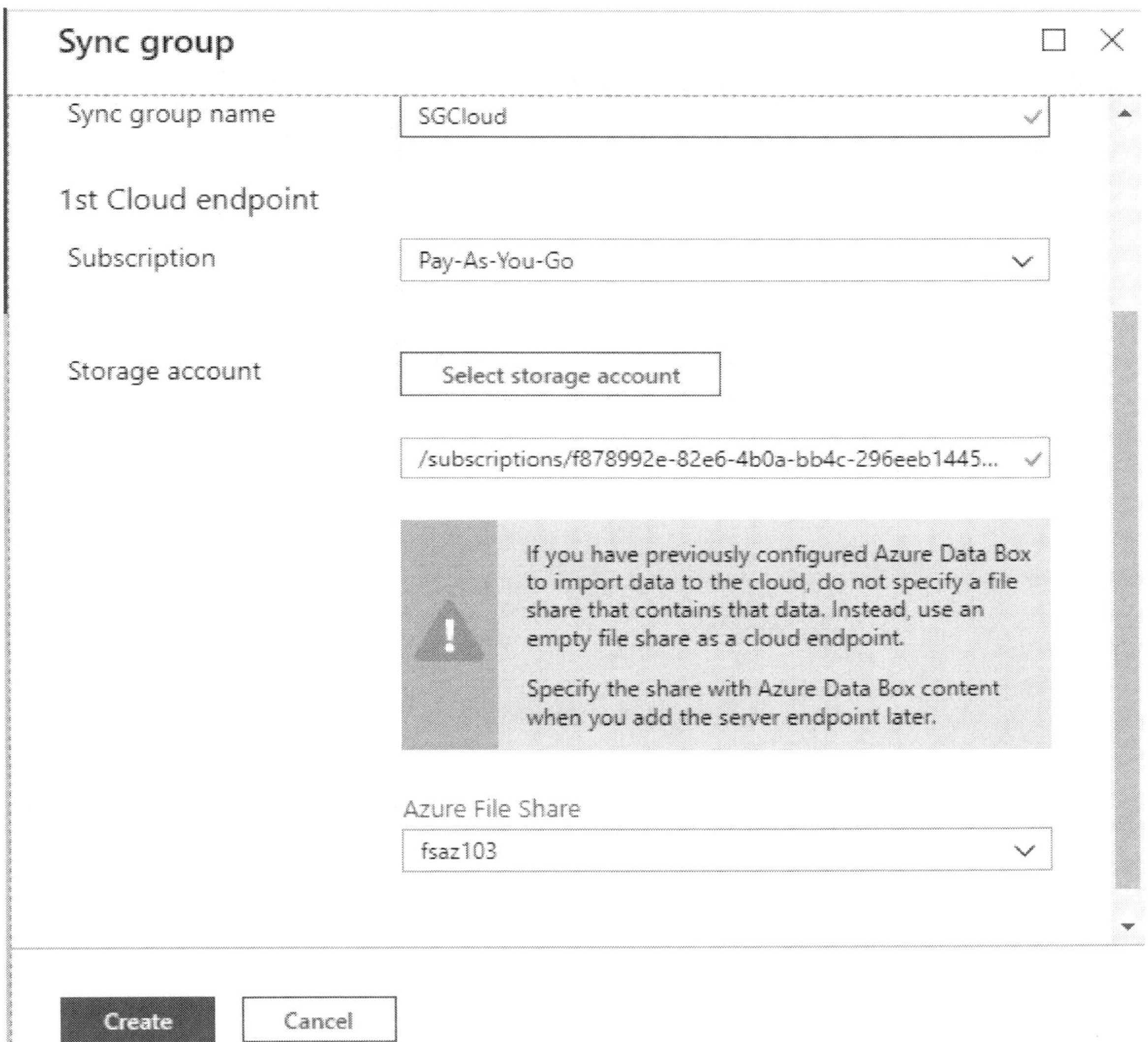

Step 4: Add Server Endpoint (Registered Server) to the sync Group

In this we will add VM VMAD on which we installed Azure File sync agent in step 2 to sync group. In Step 2 we also registered the VM with Storage sync service. VM VMAD was created in Chapter 2, Exercise 32.

1. Go Storage sync Service SSPortal created in step 1 Dashboard>You can see the sync group created in previous step.

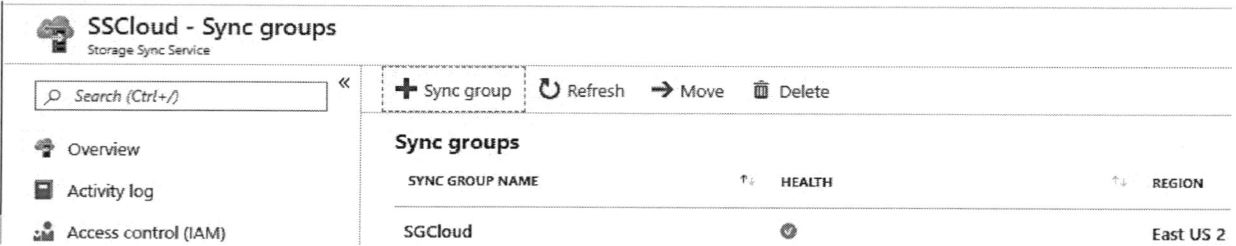

2. In right pane click the sync group SGCloud>Sync group pane opens>Click Add Server Endpoint>Add Server Endpoint blade opens>Select your registered server from drop down box> In path enter **C:\Public.** Public folder was created in Step 2>Click Enabled in Cloud Tiering> Click Create.

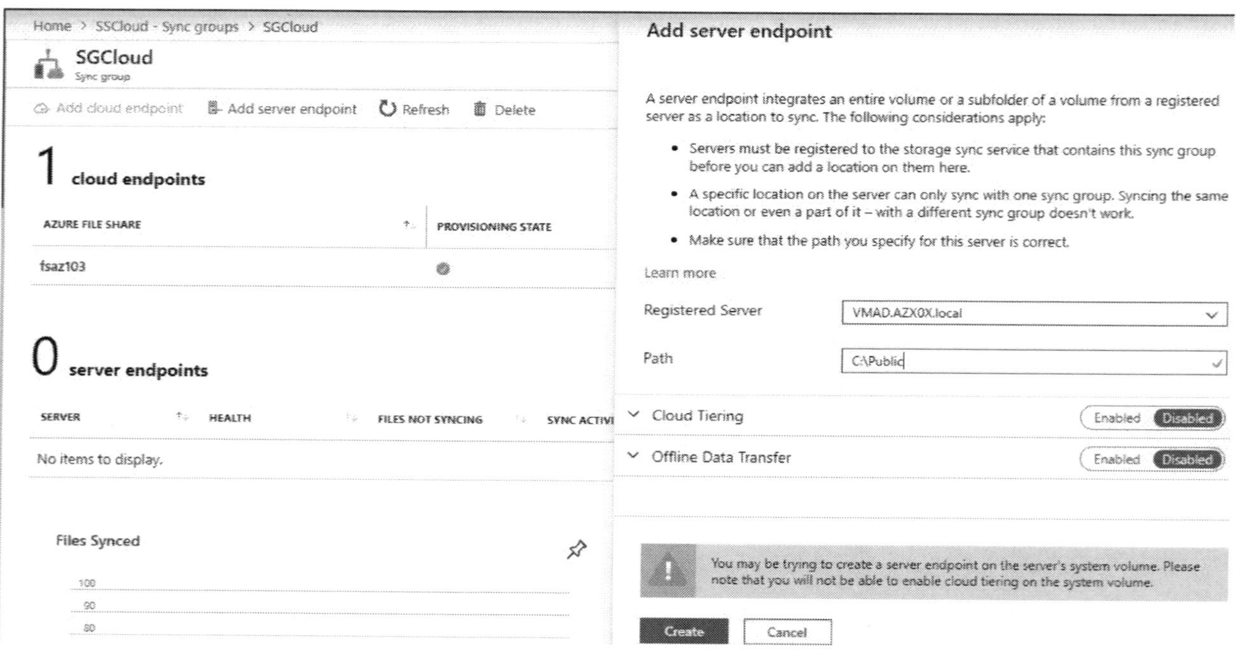

3. Sync Group pane now shows both Cloud Endpoint and Server endpoint. **It will take 5-10 minutes for health status of Server Endpoint to get updated.**

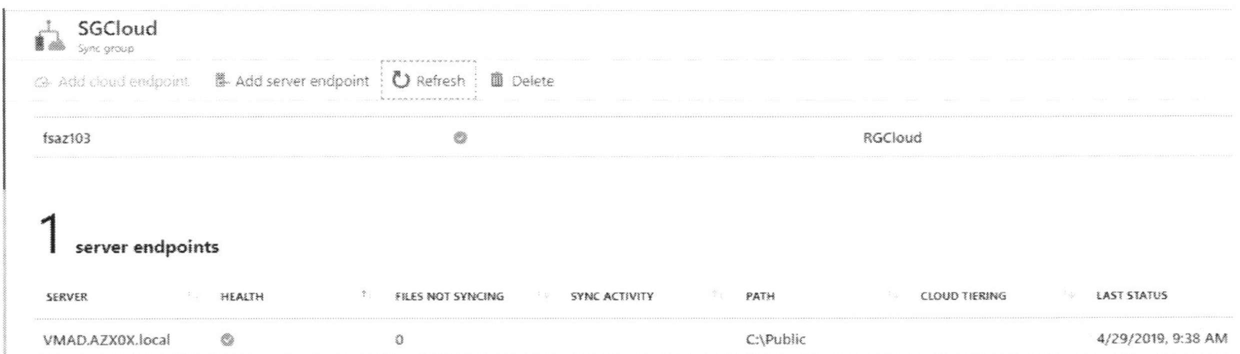

Step 5: Check whether Files from Public folder in Registered Server are synchronized to File share and vice versa or not.

1. In Azure Portal go to Storage Account sastscloud dashboard>Click Files in Right pane>Click the File share fsaz103>File share pane opens> You can see text files from Public Folder in Registered Server VMAD are synchronized to File Share fsaz103.

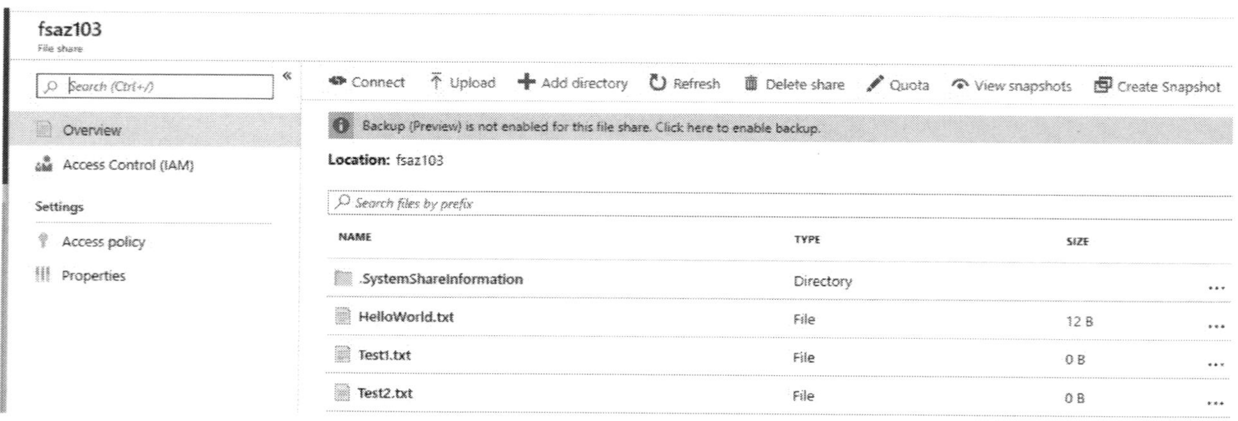

2. Go to Public Folder in registered server. HelloWorld from File share is synchronized to Public folder in Registered server.

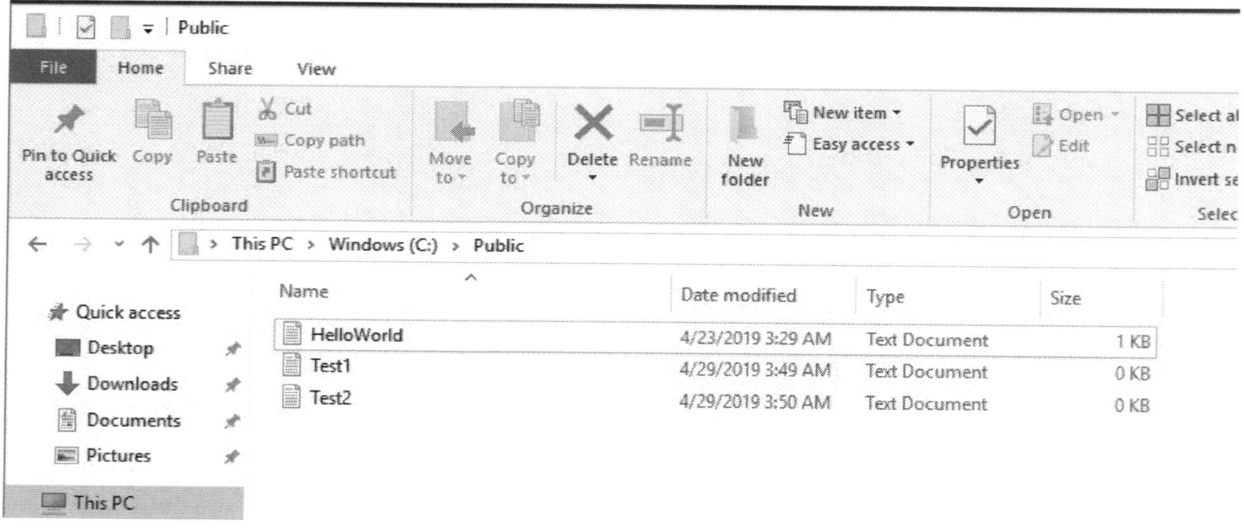

Note: After the exercise is completed stop the VM VMAD. We will now require this VM in Azure AD Connect lab.

Azure Import/Export service

Azure Import/Export service is used to securely **import/export** large amounts of data to Azure storage.

Azure Import service is used to import data to Azure Blob storage and Azure Files by shipping disk drives to an Azure Datacentre.
Azure Export service is used to export data from Azure Blob storage to disk drives and ship to your on-premises sites.

Important Point: In Azure Import/Export Service, Customer provides the Disks. Where as in Azure Data Box scenario the Disks are provided by Microsoft.

Azure Import/Export use cases

Consider using Azure Import/Export service when uploading or downloading data over the network is too slow, or getting additional network bandwidth is cost-prohibitive. Use this service in the following scenarios:

1. **Data migration to the cloud**: Move large amounts of data to Azure quickly and cost effectively.
2. **Content distribution**: Quickly send data to your customer sites.
3. **Backup**: Take backups of your on-premises data to store in Azure Storage.
4. **Data recovery**: Recover large amount of data stored in storage and have it delivered to your on-premises location.

Import/Export Service components

1. **Import/Export service**: This service available in Azure portal helps the user create and track data import (upload) and export (download) jobs.
2. **WAImportExport tool**: This is a command-line tool that does the following:
   Prepares your disk drives that are shipped for import.
   Facilitates copying your data to the drive.
   Encrypts the data on the drive with BitLocker.
   Generates the drive journal files used during import creation.
   Helps identify numbers of drives needed for export jobs.
3. **Disk Drives**: You can ship Solid-state drives (SSDs) or Hard disk drives (HDDs) to the Azure Datacentre. When creating an import job, you ship disk drives containing your data. When creating an export job, you ship empty drives.

Export from Azure Job

Azure Export service is used to transfer data from Azure Blob storage to disk drives and ship to your on-premises sites. When creating an export job, you ship empty drives to the Azure Datacentre. You can ship up to 10 disk drives per job.

Export Job Working in brief

1. Determine the data to be exported, number of drives you need, source blobs or container paths of your data in Blob storage.
2. Create an export job in your source storage account in Azure portal.
3. Specify source blobs or container paths for the data to be exported.
4. Provide the return address and carrier account number for shipping the drives back.
5. Ship the disk drives to the shipping address provided during job creation.
6. Update the delivery tracking number in the export job and submit the export job.
7. The drives are received and processed at the Azure Datacentre.
8. The drives are encrypted with BitLocker and the keys are available via the Azure portal.
9. The drives are shipped using your carrier account to the return address provided in the export job.

Export Job Flow

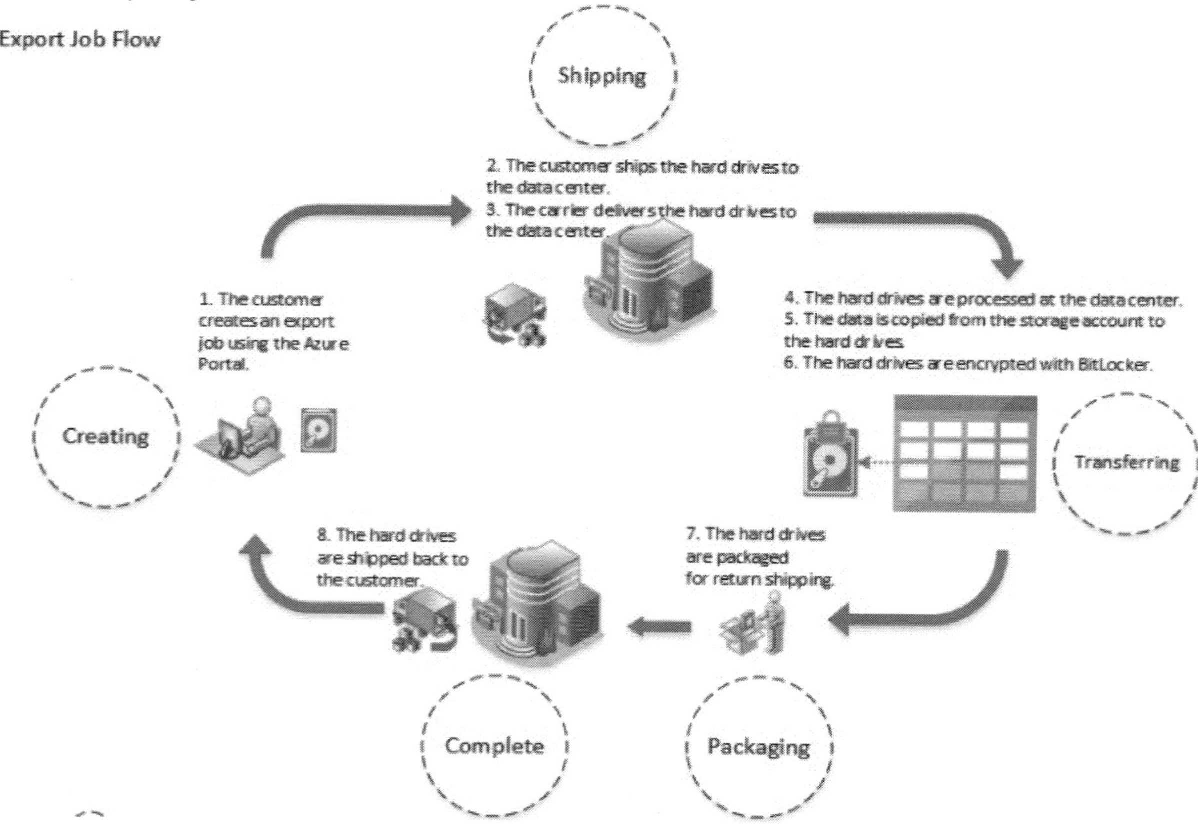

Import from Azure Job

Azure Import service is used to securely import large amounts of data to Azure Blob storage and Azure Files by shipping disk drives containing your data to an Azure Datacentre.

Import Job Working in brief

1. Determine data to be imported, number of drives you need, destination blob location for your data in Azure storage.
2. Use the WAImportExport tool to copy data to disk drives. Encrypt the disk drives with BitLocker.
3. Create an import job in your target storage account in Azure portal. Upload the drive journal files.
4. Provide the return address and carrier account number for shipping the drives back.
5. Ship the disk drives to the shipping address provided during job creation.
6. Update the delivery tracking number in the import details and submit the import job.
7. The drives are received and processed at the Azure Datacentre.
8. The drives are shipped using your carrier account to the return address provided in the import job. Figure below shows import job flow.

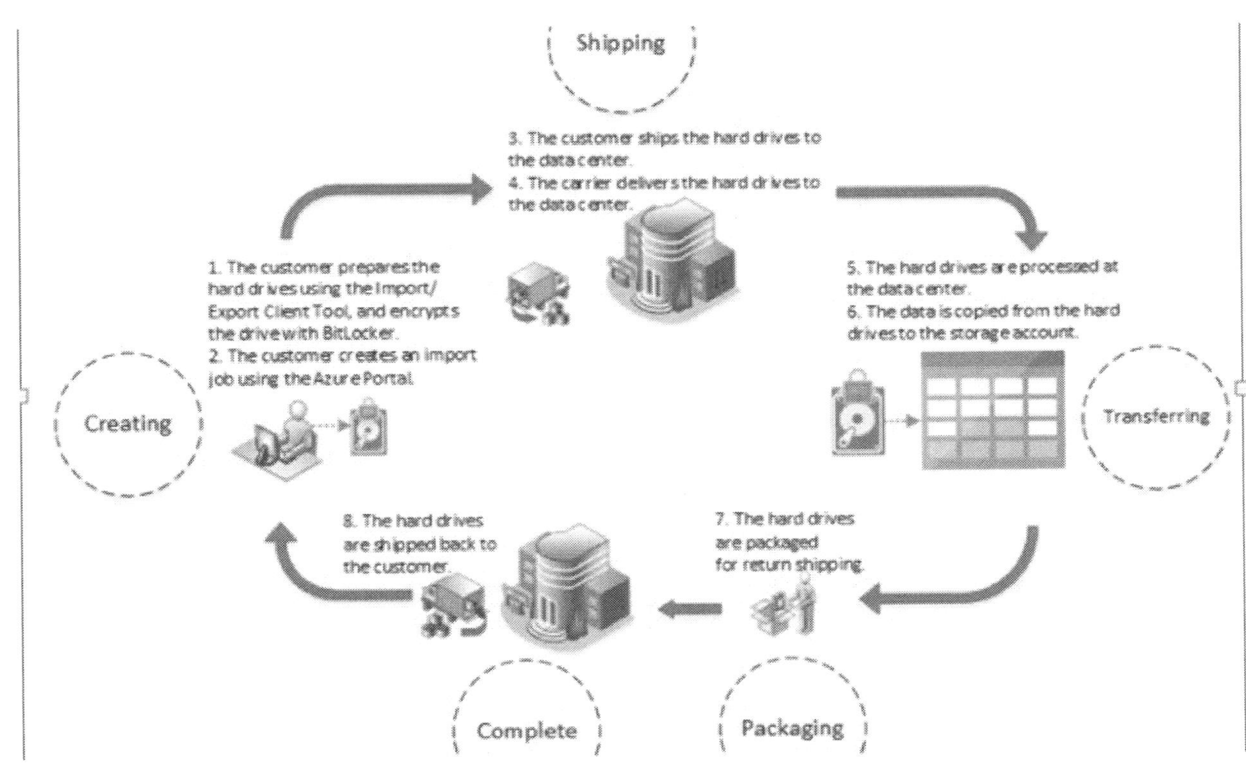

Exercise 84: Demonstrating Export Job Creation

In this exercise we will demonstrate how to create export job in Resource group RGCloud. We will export Blob file HelloWorld.txt. In this Chapter Exercise 78, Helloworld.txt file was uploaded in container hk410 which is in Storage account sastdcloud.

1. Click All Services in left pane>In Right pane All service blade opens>Scroll down to Storage section. Note the Import/Export Jobs option.

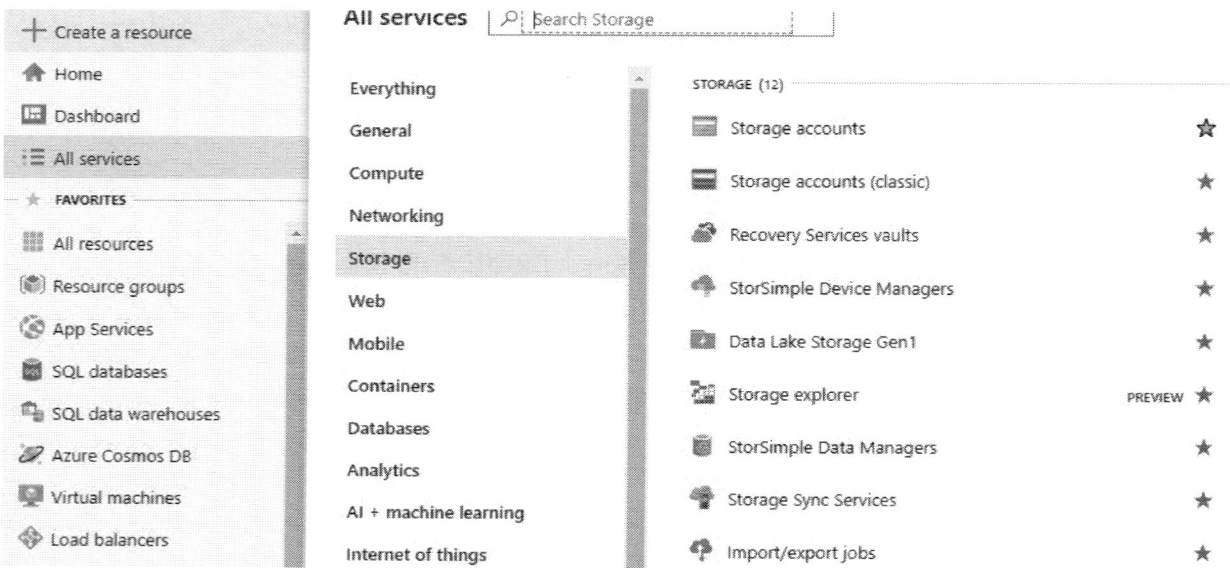

2. Click import/export jobs in storage section>Import/Export Jobs pane opens>click +Add>Create import/export job blade opens>Select export, enter a name and select RGCloud as resource group and click ok (Not Shown).

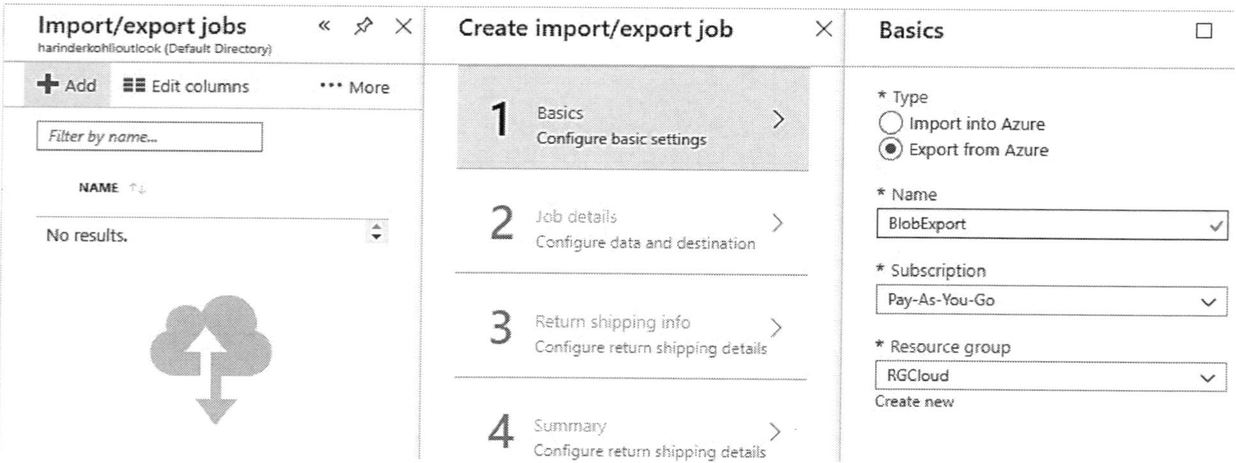

3. In Job detail pane select Storage Account sastdcloud> Click Ok (Not Shown).

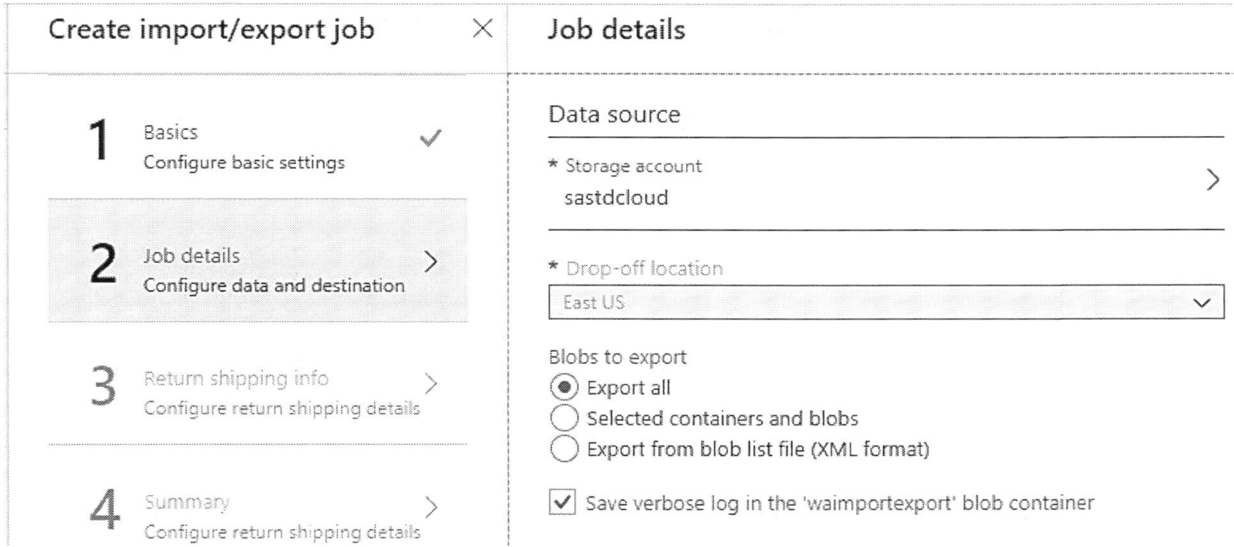

4. In return shipping information select your carrier, enter carrier account number (I entered Dummy num) and return address and click Ok (Not Shown).

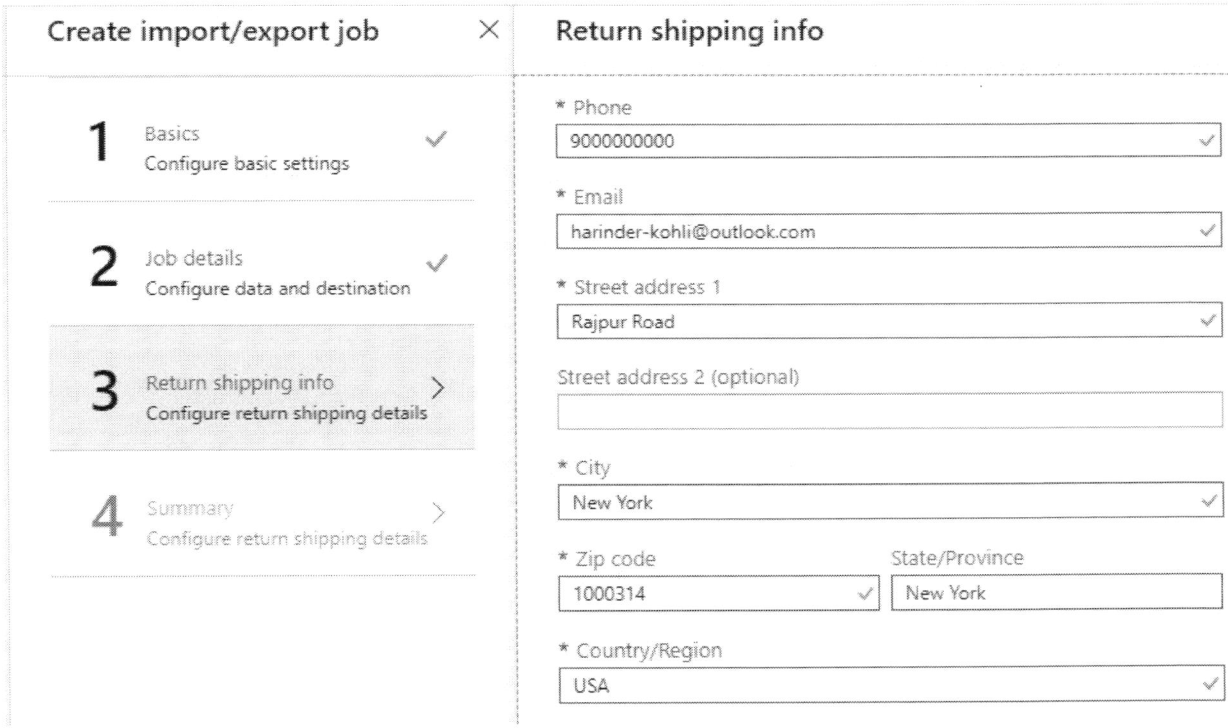

5. Summary pane will show you Export Job summary and MS Azure Datacenter address where you will ship your drives>Click Ok.

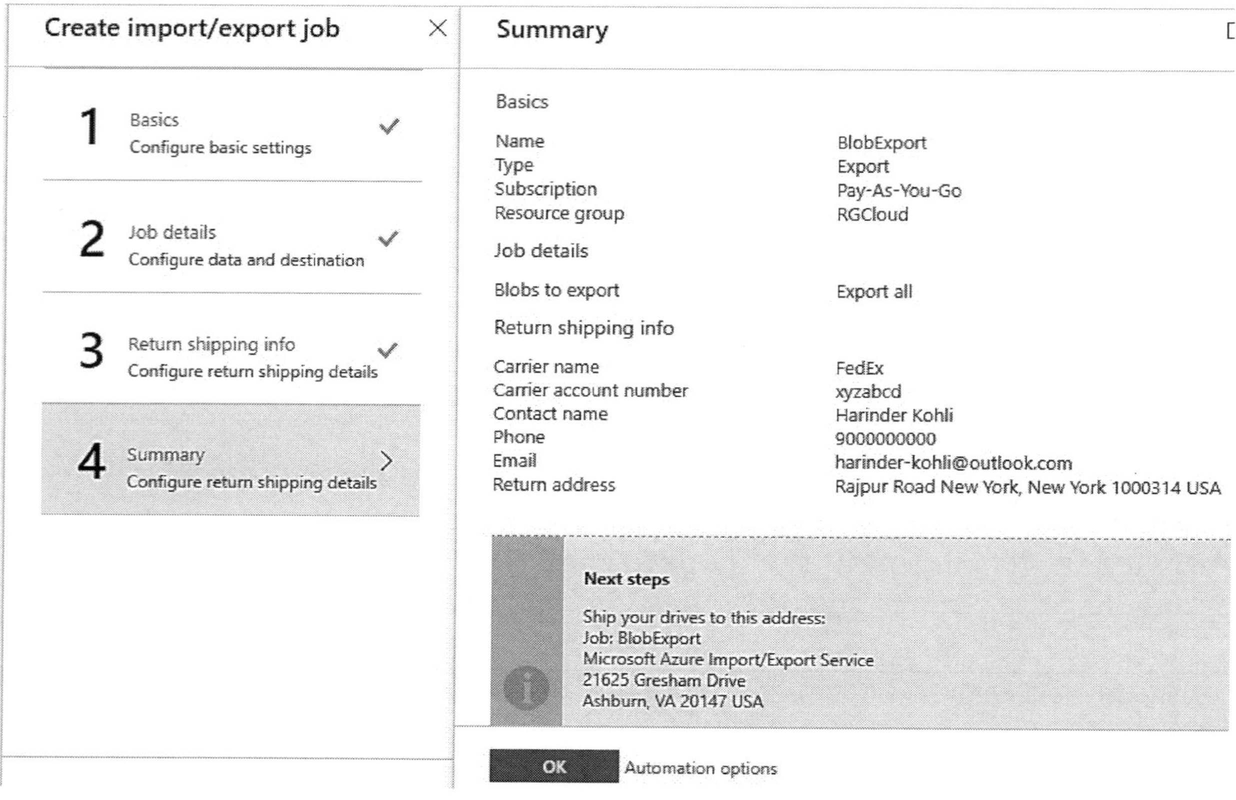

6. In All Import/Export job pane you can see the job listed.

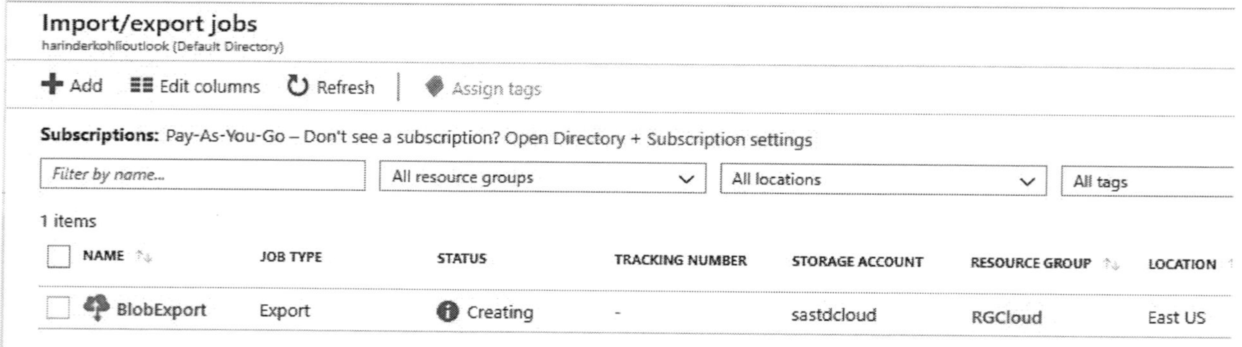

7. Ship the disk drives to Microsoft Azure Datacenter using the address provided in summary pane (Step 5).

8. In Export job **Blobexport** dashboard update that drives are shipped. Some information is missing in the dashboard as I have not provided proper carrier account number.

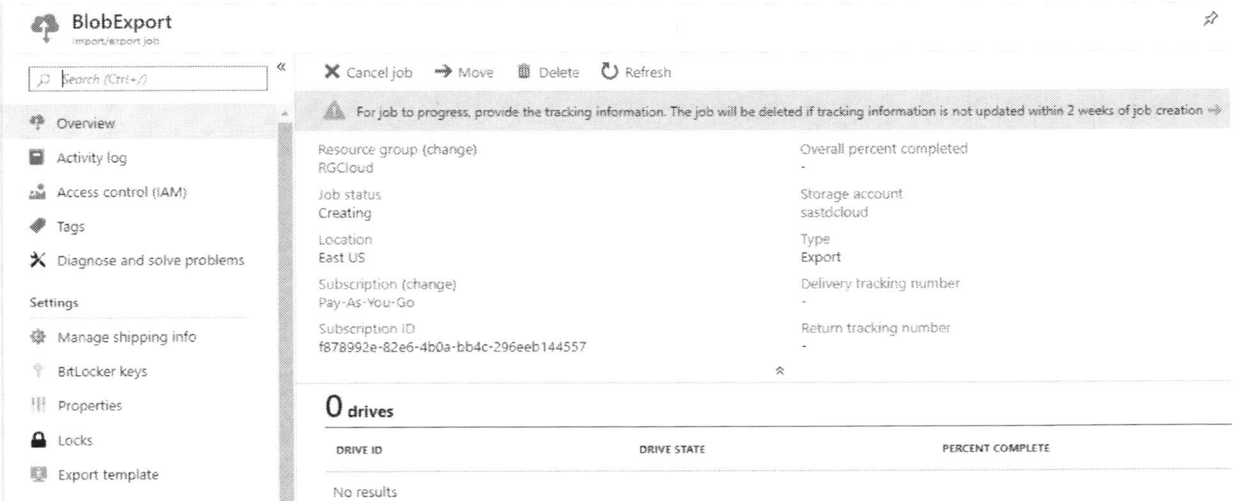

9. Once MS receives disk it will update the information in the dashboard. The disks are then shipped to you and the tracking number for the shipment is available on the portal.

10. You will receive the disk in encrypted format. You need to get the BitLocker keys to unlock the drives. Go to the export job dashboard and click BitLocker keys in left pane and copy the keys to unlock the drives.

Azure Import/Export Pricing

Device handling: $80 flat fee per storage device handled. No data transfer charge between the device and Azure Storage within the same datacenter.

Return shipping of devices: The customer's carrier account will be charged for any return shipping charges incurred.

Azure Data Box

Azure Data Box transfers on-premises data to Azure Cloud.

Azure Data Box is a Secure, Tamper proof and Ruggedised appliance as shown below. It is provided by Microsoft. Where as in Import/Export service, disks are provided by the customer.

Azure Data Box is used to transfer large amount of data which otherwise would have taken days, months or years to transfer using Internet or ExpressRoute connection.

Each storage device has a maximum usable storage capacity of 80 TB. Data Box can store a maximum of 500 million files.

Ordering, Setup & Working

Data Box is ordered to through Azure Portal.

Connect the Data Box to your existing Network. Assign an IP directly or through DHCP (Default). To access Web UI of Data box, connect a laptop to management port of Data Box and https://192.168.100.10. Sign in using the password generated from the Azure portal.

Load your data onto the Data Box using standard NAS protocols (SMB/CIFS). Your data is automatically protected using 256-AES encryption. The Data Box is returned to the Azure Data Centre to be uploaded to Azure. After data is uploaded the device is securely erased.

The entire process is tracked end-to-end by the Data Box service in the Azure portal.

Figure below shows the setup of Azure Data Box setup.

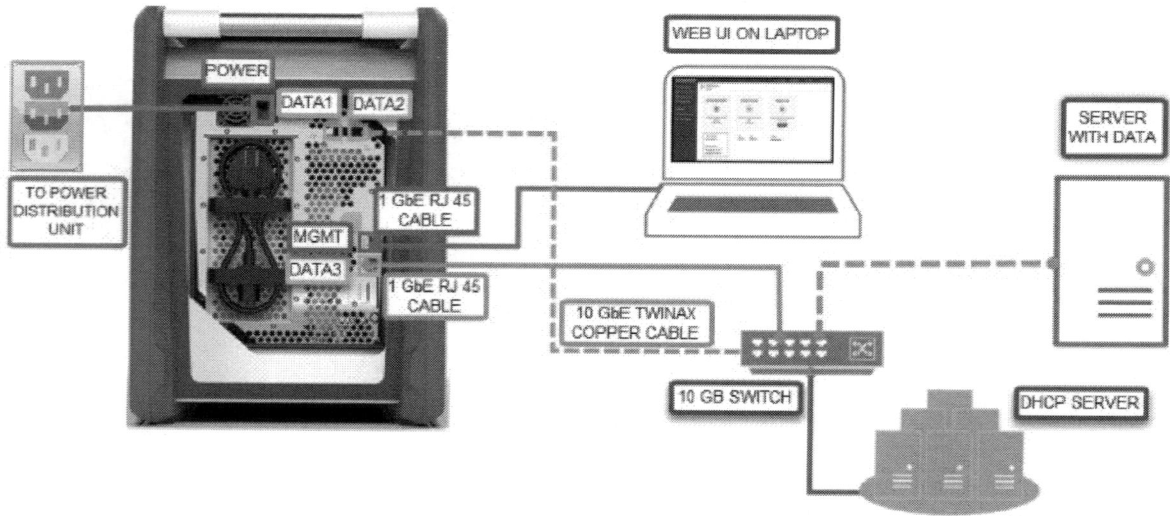

Azure Data Box Use Cases

Data Box is ideally suited to transfer data sizes larger than 40 TBs in scenarios with no to limited network connectivity. The data movement can be one-time, periodic, or an initial bulk data transfer followed by periodic transfers.

One time migration - when large amount of on-premises data is moved to Azure.

Initial bulk transfer - when an initial bulk transfer is done using Data Box followed by incremental transfers over the network. For example, backup solutions can use Data Box to move initial large backup to Azure. Once complete, the incremental data is transferred via network to Azure storage.

Periodic uploads - when large amount of data is generated periodically and needs to be moved to Azure. For example in energy exploration, where video content is generated on oil rigs and windmill farms.

Exercise 85: Demonstrating Data Box Order through Azure Portal

In Azure Portal click + Create a Resource>Storage>Azure Data Box>Select Your Azure Data Box Blade opens>Select your subscription>Transfer type>Source Country and Destination Azure region>Click Apply>Data Box options open> Select as per your requirement.

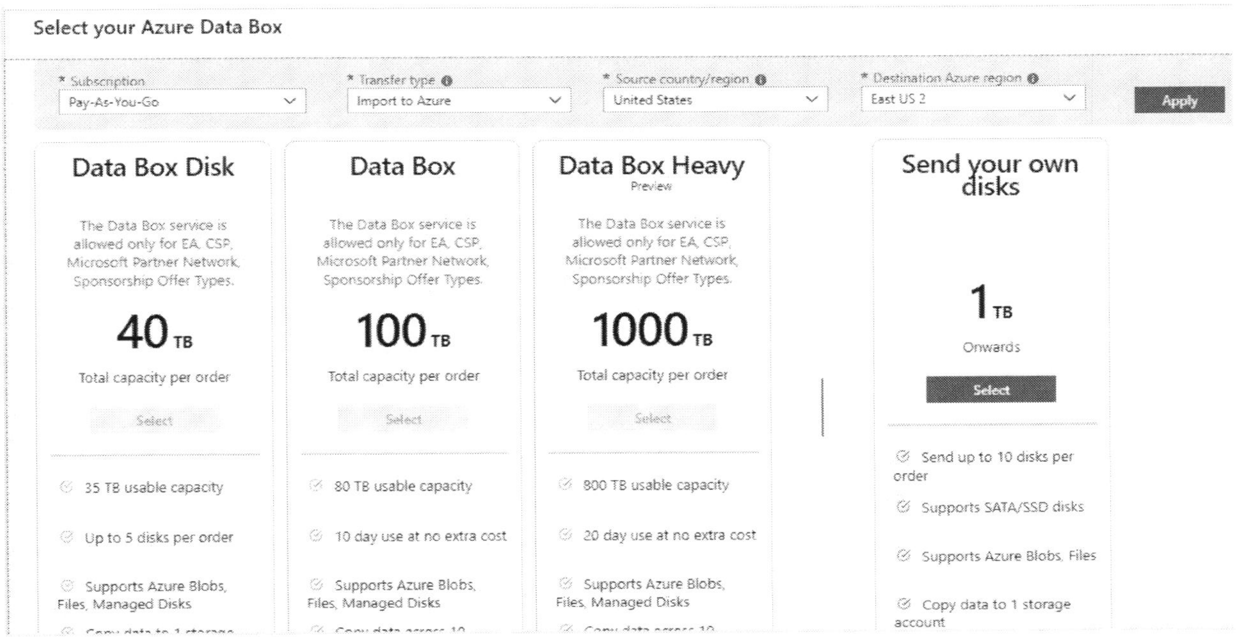

Note: To Order Data Box you require Enterprise Agreement (EA), CSP or Microsoft Partner Network option.

StorSimple

Azure StorSimple is a Hybrid storage solution that stores highly active and less frequently used data locally and moves archival data or inactive data into cloud.

StorSimple offers hybrid management solution wherein you can use StorSimple Device Manager service running in the Azure portal to manage data stored on multiple StorSimple devices and Cloud Storage

Microsoft Offers StorSimple Storage Solution in following Formats:

StorSimple 8000 Series Physical Arrays (8100 & 8600)
StorSimple 8000 Series Cloud Appliance for Azure Cloud
StorSimple on-premises Virtual Appliance - 1200

StorSimple 8000 Series Array

StorSimple 8000 series Physical array is iSCSI SAN Storage Array that has certain amount of Local Storage (SSD & HDD) and can leverage Azure Cloud Storage.

More frequently used data is stored in SSD, less frequently used data is stored in HDD and rarely used is used Data in Azure Storage. The reorganizing of data happens automatically using algorithms built in StorSimple.

Figure below shows the Architecture of the Hybrid Storage Solution using StorSimple 8000 series physical array.

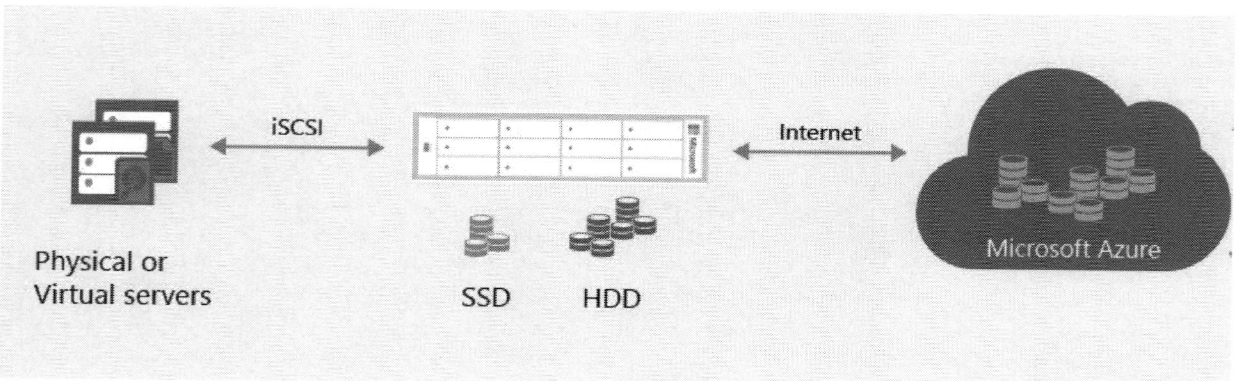

Working of 8000 Series Physical Array

Microsoft Azure StorSimple uses the following software technologies to provide quick access to data and to reduce storage consumption:

Automatic storage tiering
Thin provisioning
Deduplication and compression

Data sent to StorSimple is initially stored in the SSD tier of the hybrid storage array. When it approaches a threshold of fullness, the least recently accessed data will be deduplicated, compressed and then pushed to the HDD tier. When the HDD tier approaches a threshold for fullness, the least recently accessed data will be encrypted, using AES-256 bit encryption, and pushed to the cloud.

Figure below shows working of 8000 Series Physical Storage Appliance.

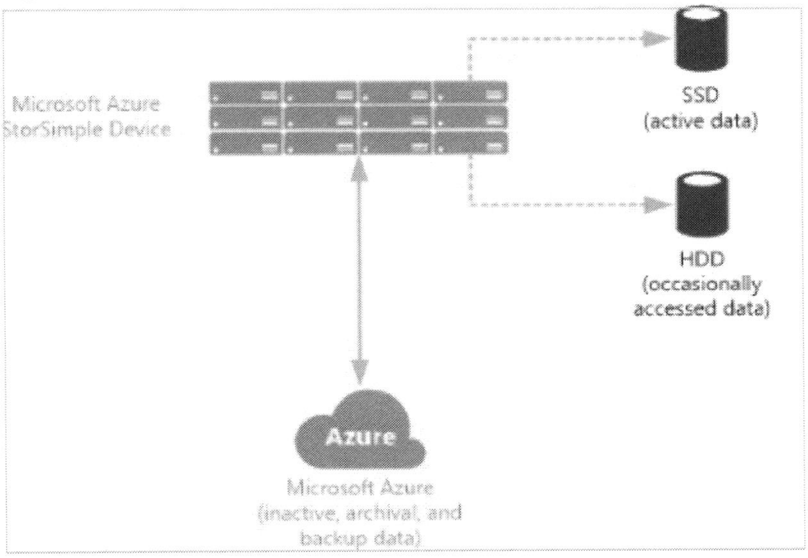

To enable quick access, StorSimple stores very active data (hot data) on SSDs in the StorSimple device. It stores data that is used occasionally (warm data) on HDDs in the device or on servers at the datacenter. It moves inactive data, backup data, and data retained for archival or compliance purposes to the cloud. The reorganizing of data happens automatically using algorithms built in StorSimple.

Pinned Volume: You can specify storage volume as locally pinned in which case the data remains on the local device and is not tiered to the cloud.

Comparing 8100 and 8600 Appliance

StorSimple Physical Array is dual controller array with only one controller active at any point in time. If the active controller fails, the second controller becomes active automatically. It comes with 6 Network interfaces.

	8100	8600
Number of HDDs	8	19
Number of SSDs	4	5
Single HDD capacity	4 TB	4 TB
Single SSD Capacity	400 GB	800 GB
Usable HDD capacity	14 TB	36 TB
Usable SSD capacity	800 GB	2 TB
Total usable capacity (Locally)	15 TB	38 TB
Maximum solution capacity (including cloud)	200 TB	500 TB

StorSimple Cloud Appliance

StorSimple cloud appliance replicates the architecture and capabilities of the 8000 series physical hybrid storage array. The StorSimple Cloud runs on a single node in an Azure virtual machine.

The StorSimple Cloud Appliance is available in two models: the 8010 device & 8020 device. The 8010 device has a maximum capacity of 30 TB and uses Azure Standard Storage (HDD). The 8020 device has a maximum capacity of 64 TB and uses Azure Premium Storage (SSD).

StorSimple on-premises Virtual Appliance – 1200

StorSimple on-premises Virtual Appliance – 1200 is a hybrid storage solution that uses both local storage and cloud storage.

The Virtual Array 1200 is a single-node virtual appliance that can run on Hyper-V or VMware hypervisor. The virtual Array can be configured as iSCSI target or File Server.

The Virtual Array is available in one model. The Virtual Array has a maximum capacity of 6.4 TB on the device (with an underlying storage requirement of 8 TB) and 64 TB including cloud storage.

The virtual array is particularly well-suited for remote office/branch office scenarios.

Figure below shows Architecture of Hybrid storage using Virtual array. It uses heat mapping to determine what data should be tiered in or out

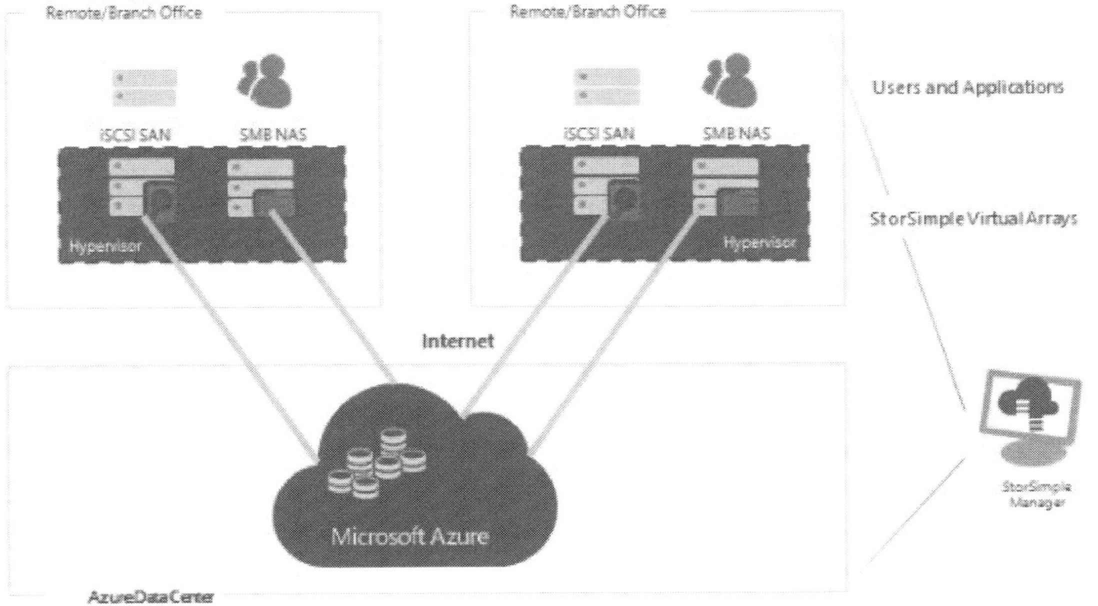

You Configure Virtual array 1200 using Local Web user interface. You can manage the Virtual Array using StorSimple Device Manager Service running in Azure cloud.

StorSimple Device Manager Service

StorSimple Device Manager Service runs in Azure cloud and manages StorSimple device (Physical or Virtual) or StorSimple Cloud Appliance from a single web interface. You can use the StorSimple Device Manager service to create and manage services, view and manage devices, view alerts, manage volumes, shares and view and manage backup policies and the backup catalog.

StorSimple Snapshot Manager – an MMC snap-in that uses volume groups and the Windows Volume Shadow Copy Service to generate application-consistent backups. In addition, you can use StorSimple Snapshot Manager to create backup schedules and clone or restore volumes.

Figure below shows StorSimple Device Manager Service running in Azure cloud managing StorSimple Physical array running on –premises and StorSimple Cloud Appliances. Not shown in the figure is StorSimple Virtual Array 1200.

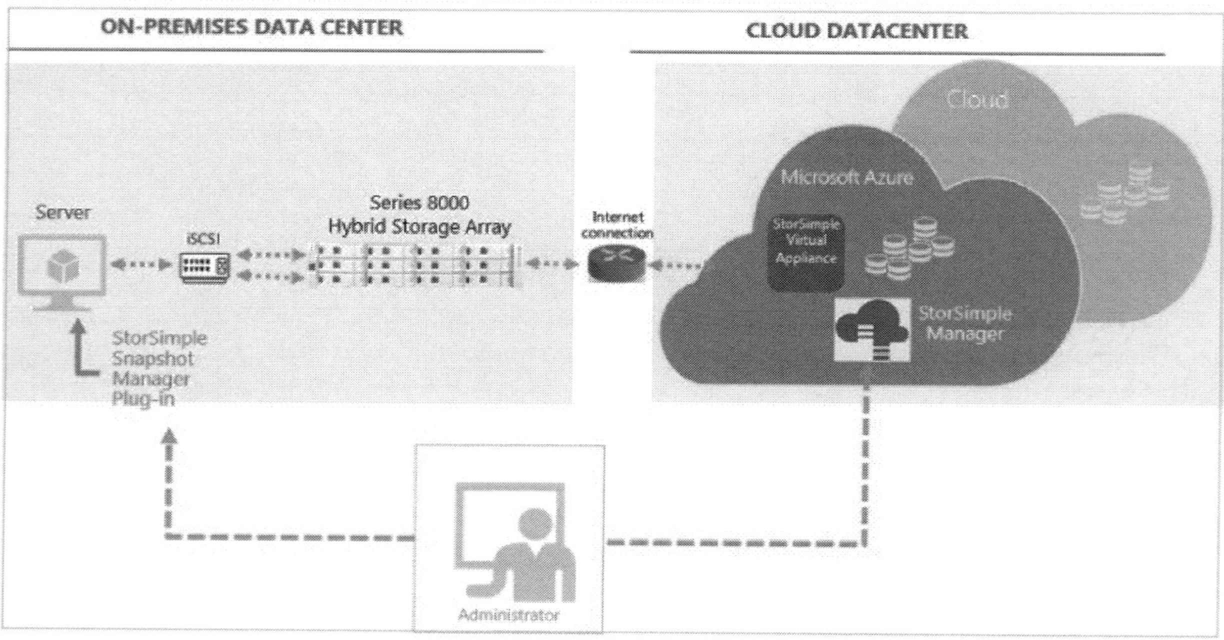

StorSimple Data Manager

The StorSimple Data Manager allows you to seamlessly access StorSimple data in the cloud. This service provides APIs to extract data from StorSimple and present it to other Azure services in formats that can be readily consumed. The formats supported initially are Azure blobs, Azure Files and Azure Media Services assets.

This enables you to use data stored on StorSimple 8000 series devices with Azure Media Services, Azure HDInsight, Azure Machine Learning and Azure Search.

Figure below shows working of StorSimple Data Manager.

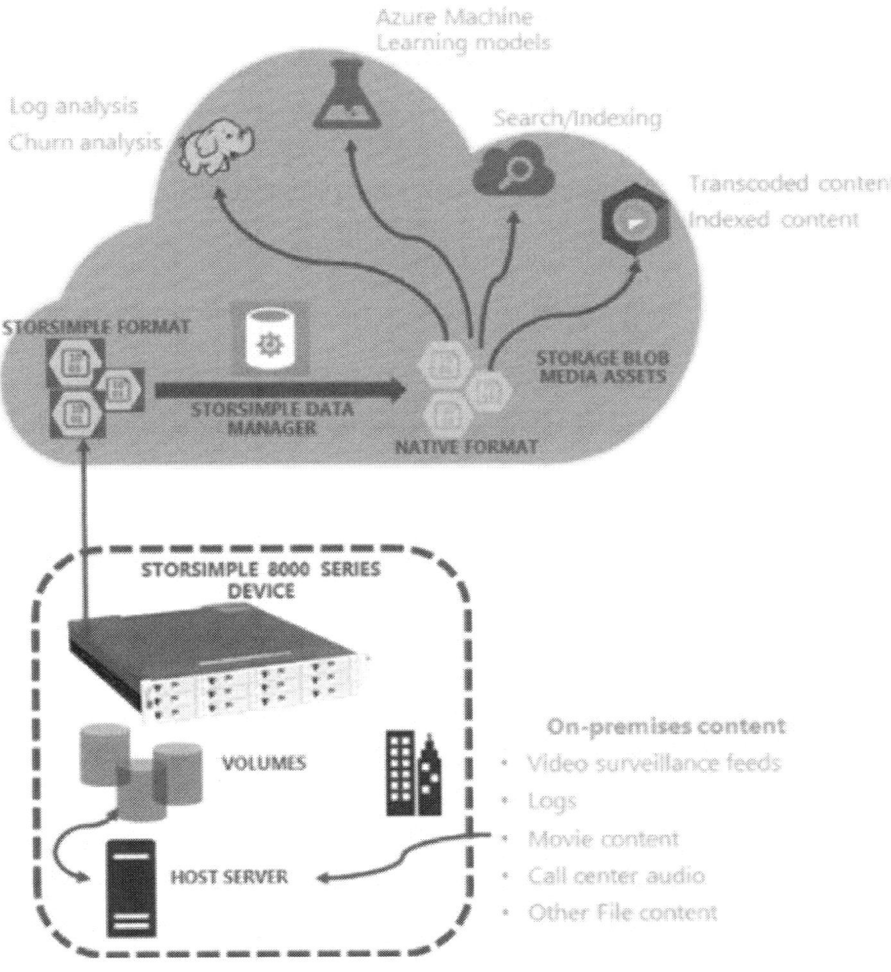

StorSimple Pricing

Model	Daily Rate	Monthly Rate
Physical appliance—8100	$43.84	$1,359.04
Physical appliance—8600	$63.01	$1,953.31
Cloud array 8010 or 8020	$4.11	$127.41
Virtual appliance—1200	$4.11	$127.41

StorSimple Data Manager Pricing

StorSimple Data Manager Pricing is based on the number of data transformation jobs run and how much data is transformed.

Data Transformation (per Job)	$1.50
Data Transformation (per GB)	$0.005

Azure Content Delivery Networks (CDN)

A content delivery network (CDN) is a distributed network of servers that deliver web content to users faster than the origin server. The Azure Content Delivery Network (CDN) caches web content from origin server at strategically placed locations to provide maximum throughput for delivering content to users.

Figure below shows Cached image being delivered to users by CDN server which is faster than the origin server.

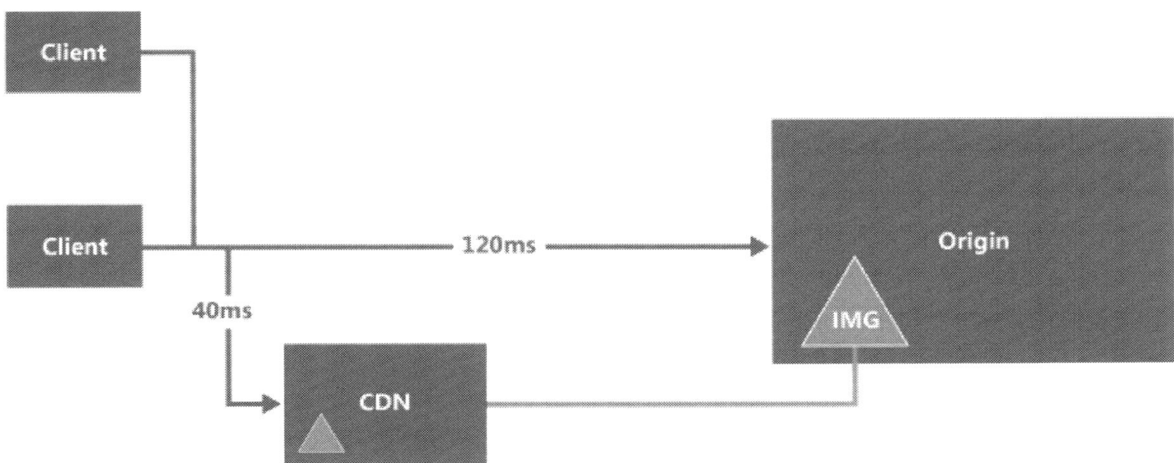

Use Cases

1. Azure CDNs are typically used to deliver static content such as images, style sheets, documents, client-side scripts, and HTML pages.
2. Streaming Video benefits from the low latency offered by CDN servers. Additionally Microsoft Azure Media Services (AMS) integrates with Azure CDN to deliver content directly to the CDN for further distribution.

Benefits of Azure CDN

1. CDN provides lower latency and faster delivery of content to users.
2. CDNs help to reduce load on a web application, because the application does not have to service requests for the content that is hosted in the CDN.
3. CDN helps to cope with peaks and surges in demand without requiring the application to scale, avoiding the consequent increased running costs.
4. Improved experience for users, especially those located far from the datacentre hosting the application.

Azure CDN Working

Figure below shows the working of Content Delivery Networks.

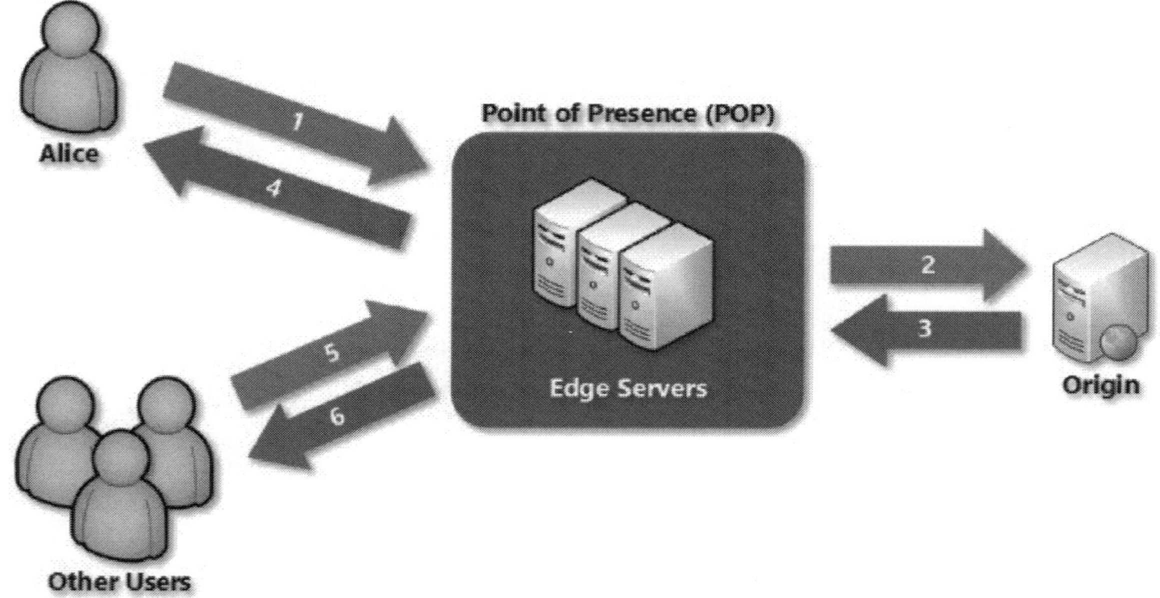

1. User Alice requests a file using URL **(<*endpoint name*>.azureedge.net**) in a browser. DNS routes the request to the CDN edge server Point-of-Presence (POP) location that is geographically closest to the user.

2. If the edge servers in the POP has file in their cache, it returns the file to the user Alice.
3. If the edge servers in the POP do not have the file in their cache, the edge server requests the file from the origin server. The origin server returns the file to the edge server, including optional HTTP headers describing the file's Time-to-Live (TTL). The edge server caches the file and returns the file to the user Alice. The file remains cached on the edge server until the TTL expires. If the origin didn't specify a TTL, the default TTL is seven days.

4. Additional users who request same file as user Alice and are geographically closest to the same POP will be get the file from Cache of the edge server instead of the origin server.

5. The above process results in a faster, more responsive user experience.

Azure CDN Architecture

Azure CDN Architecture consists of Origin Server, CDN Profile and CDN endpoints.

Origin Server

Origin server holds the web content which is cached by CDN Endpoints geographically closest to the user based on caching policy configured in CDN endpoint.

Origin Server type can be one of the following:

Storage
Web App
Cloud Service
Publically Accessible Web Server

CDN Profile

A CDN profile is a collection of CDN endpoints with the same pricing tier. CDN pricing is applied at the CDN profile level. Therefore, to use a mix of Azure CDN pricing tiers, you must create multiple CDN profiles.

CDN Endpoints

CDN Endpoint caches the web content from the origin server. It delivers cached content to end users faster than the origin server and is located geographically closest to the user. CDN Endpoints are distributed across the world.

The CDN Endpoint is exposed using the URL format ***<endpoint name>*.azureedge.net** by default, but custom domains can also be used.

A CDN Endpoint is an entity within a CDN Profile containing configuration information regarding caching behaviour and origin Server. Every CDN endpoint represents a specific configuration of content deliver behaviour and access.

Azure CDN Tiers

Azure CDN comes in Standard and Premium tiers. Azure CDN Standard Tier comes from Microsoft, Akamai and Verizon. Azure Premium Tier is from Verizon. Table below shows comparison between Standard and Premium Tiers.

	Standard MS	Standard Akamai	Standard Verizon	Premium Verizon
Performance Features and Optimizations				
Dynamic Site Acceleration (DSA)		✓	✓	✓
DSA - Adaptive Image Compression		✓		
DSA - Object Prefetch		✓		
Video streaming optimization	Note 1	✓	Note 1	Note 1
Large file optimization	Note 1	✓	Note 1	Note 1
Global Server Load balancing (GSLB)	✓	✓	✓	✓
Fast purge	✓	✓	✓	✓
Asset pre-loading			✓	✓
Cache/header settings (caching rules)		✓	✓	
Cache/header settings (rules engine)		✓		✓
Query string caching	✓	✓	✓	✓
IPv4/IPv6 dual-stack	✓	✓	✓	✓
HTTP/2 support	✓	✓	✓	✓
Security				
HTTPS support with CDN endpoint	✓	✓	✓	✓
Custom domain HTTPS	✓		✓	✓
Custom domain name support	✓	✓	✓	✓
Geo-filtering	✓	✓	✓	✓
Token authentication				✓
DDOS protection	✓	✓	✓	✓
Analytics and Reporting				
Azure diagnostic logs	✓	✓	✓	✓
Core reports from Verizon			✓	✓
Custom reports from Verizon				✓
Advanced HTTP reports				✓
Real-time stats				✓
Edge node performance				✓

Note 1: MS and Verizon support delivering large files and media directly via the general web delivery optimization.

Dynamic Site Acceleration (DSA) or Acceleration Data Transfer

Dynamic Site Acceleration (DSA), accelerates web content that is not cacheable such as shopping carts, search results, and other dynamic content.

Traditional CDN mainly uses caching to improve website and download performance. DSA accelerates delivery of dynamic content by optimising routing and networking between requester and content origin.

DSA configuration option can be selected during endpoint creation.

DSA Optimization Techniques

DSA speeds up delivery of dynamic assets using the following techniques:

Route optimization chooses the most optimal and the fastest path to the origin server.

TCP Optimizations: TCP connections take several requests back and forth in a handshake to establish a new connection. This results in delay in setting up the network connection.
Azure CDN solves this problem by optimizing in following three areas:
Eliminating slow start
Leveraging persistent connections
Tuning TCP packet parameters (Akamai only)

Object Prefetch (Akamai only): *Prefetch* is a technique to retrieve images and scripts embedded in the HTML page while the HTML is served to the browser, and before the browser even makes these object requests. When the client makes the requests for the linked assets, the CDN edge server already has the requested objects and can serve them immediately without a round trip to the origin.

Adaptive Image Compression (Akamai only): End users experience slower network speeds from time to time. In these scenarios, it is more beneficial for the user to receive smaller images in their webpage more quickly rather than waiting a long time for full resolution images. This feature automatically monitors network quality, and employs standard JPEG compression methods when network speeds are slower to improve delivery time.

Exercise 86: Implementing Azure CDN using Azure Portal

Implementing Azure CDN is a 2 step process – Create CDN profile and Add CDN endpoints to the profile.

In this exercise CDN Profile will be created in Resource Group RGCloud. We will add VM VMFE1 to CDN endpoint. CDN endpoint will cache default website on VM VMFE1. Resource Group RGCloud was created in Exercise 1, Chapter 1. VM VMFE1 was created in Exercise 25, Chapter 4.

Create CDN Profile: In Azure portal click create a resource>Web > CDN> Create CDN profile blade opens>Enter name, select resource group as RGCloud, select pricing tier and click create. We have the option to add CDN endpoint but we will add later.

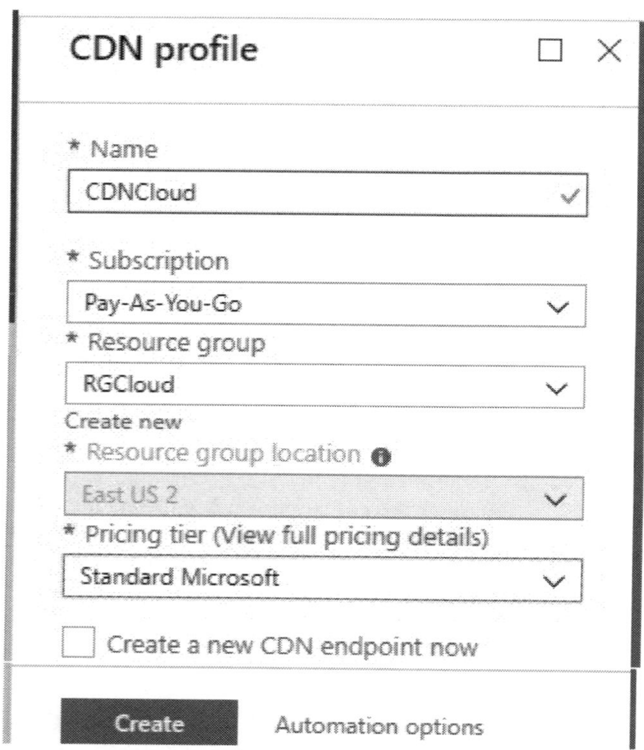

Note: In Next step readers are advised to see options available in **optimized for** Dropdown box.

Fig below shows CDN Profile Dashboard.

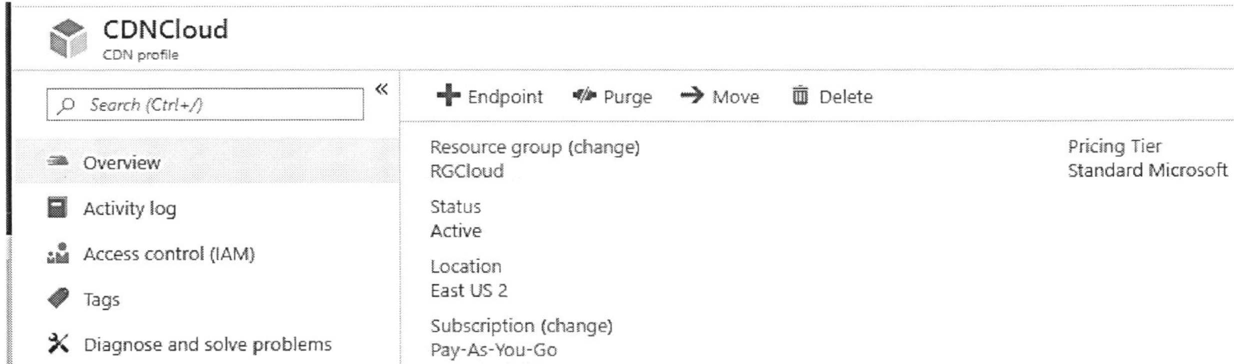

ADD CDN Endpoint: In CDN Profile dashboard click +Endpoint>Add an Endpoint Blade opens>Enter a name, Select Custom origin and in Origin hostname enter Public IP of VM VMFE1>Select HTTP as protocol>Click Add.

Figure below dashboard of CDN Endpoint vmfe1.

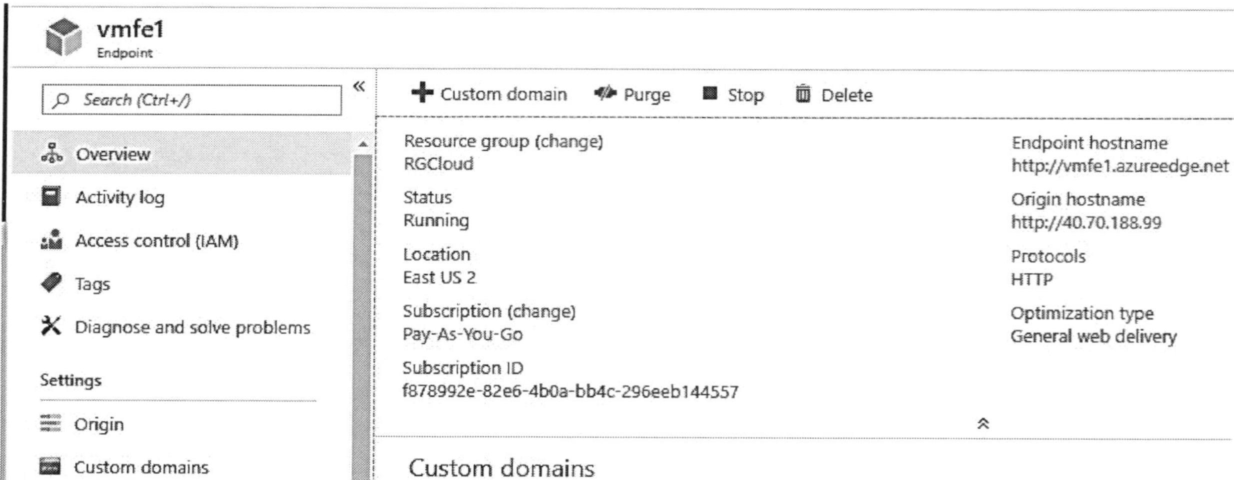

Access default website of VMFE1 VM using CDN endpoint address: From CDN Endpoint Dashboard copy the Endpoint address- http://vmfe1.azureedge.net. Open a browser and paste the CDN Endpoint address. The default website opens.

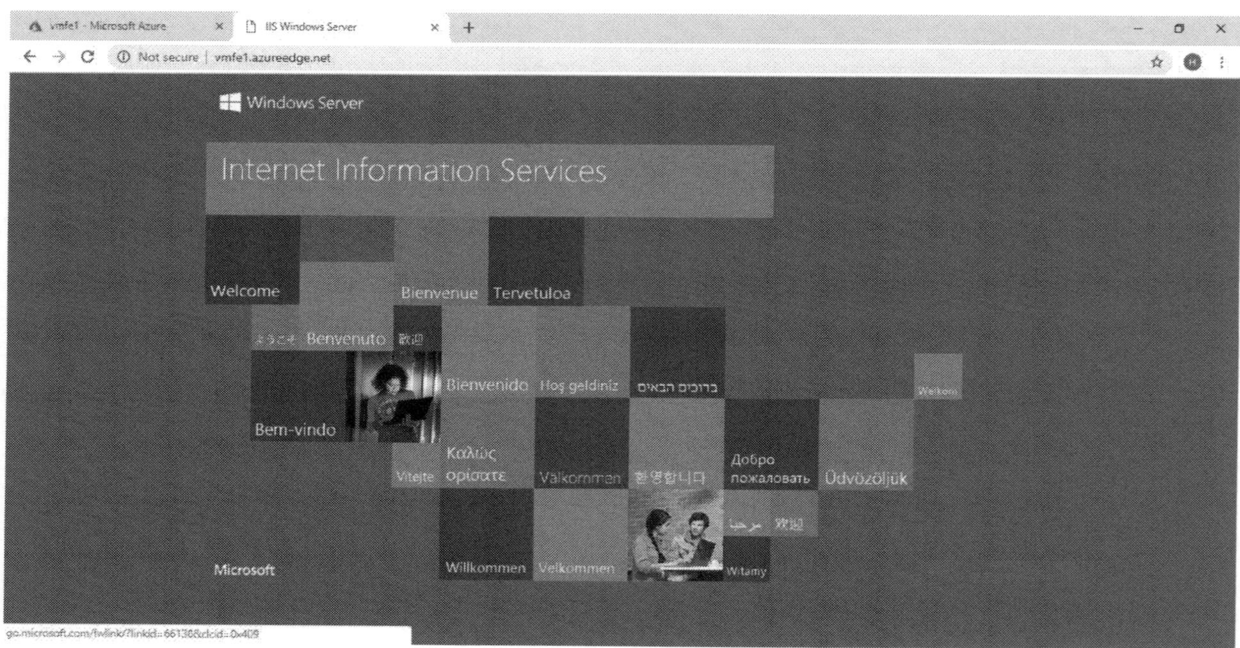

Virtual Machine VMFE1 default site is located in US East 2 region. I am accessing the default site from India. The CDN endpoint in Indian region will cache the default website. Next access of the website will happen through CDN endpoint.

CDN Endpoint Compression Functionality

Compression is used to reduce the bandwidth used to deliver and receive an object. By enabling compression directly on the CDN edge servers, CDN compresses the files and serves them to end users.

Compression is enabled by default.

Note that files are only compressed on the fly by the CDN if it is served from CDN cache. Compressed by the origin can still be delivered compressed to the client without being cached.

Exercise 87: Enabling or Disabling Compression

In CDN Endpoint Dashboard Click Compression in left pane> Compression pane opens>Click On or Off to Enable or Disable Compression.

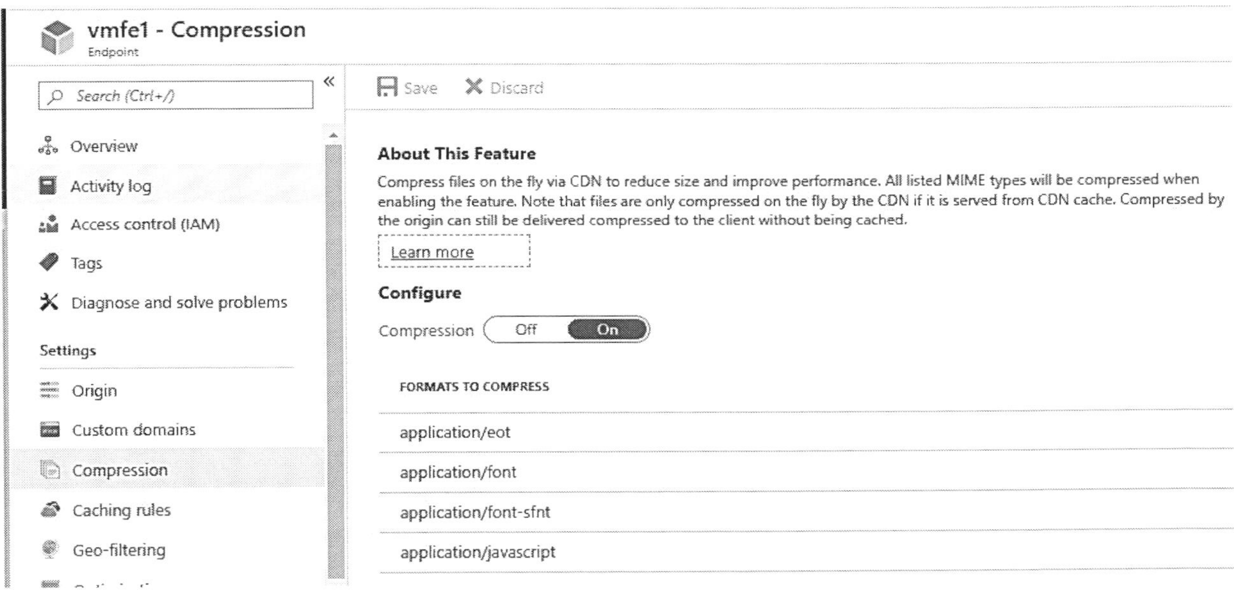

CDN Endpoint Optimization Functionality

Azure Content Delivery Network (CDN) can optimize the delivery experience based on the type of content you have. The content can be a website, a live stream, a video, or a large file for download. When you create a CDN endpoint, you specify optimization type. Your choice determines which optimization is applied to the content delivered from the CDN endpoint.

Optimization Types

General Web Delivery: It is designed for general web content optimization, such as webpages and web applications. This optimization also can be used for file and video downloads.

General media streaming: It is designed for live streaming and video-on-demand streaming. Media streaming is time-sensitive, because packets that arrive late on the client can cause a degraded viewing experience. Media streaming optimization reduces the latency of media content delivery and provides a smooth streaming experience for users.

Video-on-demand Streaming: Video-on-demand media streaming optimization improves video-on-demand streaming content. It reduces the latency of media content delivery and provides a smooth streaming experience for users.

Large File Download: This optimizes large file download (Files larger than 10 MB). If your average files sizes are consistently larger than 10 MB, it might be more efficient to create a separate endpoint for large files.

Dynamic site acceleration (DSA): DSA use optimization techniques such as route, network and TCP optimization to improve the latency and performance of dynamic content or non-cacheable content.

Note: Azure CDN Standard from Microsoft**,** Azure CDN Standard from Verizon, and Azure CDN Premium from Verizon, use the general web delivery optimization type to deliver general streaming media content, Video-on-demand media streaming and large File download.

Azure CDN optimization supported by various providers

Optimization	MS	Verizon	Akamai
General web Delivery	✓	✓	✓
General media streaming			✓
Video-on-demand media streaming			✓
Large file download (larger than 10 MB)			✓
Dynamic site acceleration		✓	✓

Important Note: MS & Verizon support Media Streaming, Video on demand streaming and large file download using the general web delivery optimization.

Exercise 88: Changing Optimization type

Go to CDN endpoint Dashboard>Click Optimization in left pane> Select optimized type from the drop down box>Click Save.

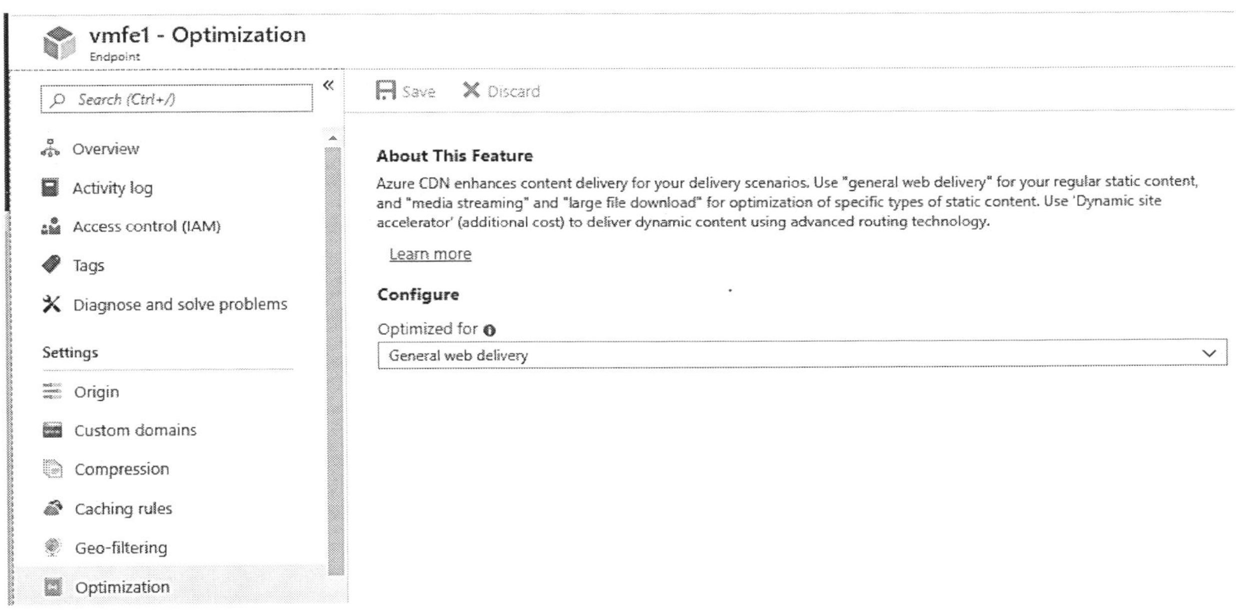

CDN Endpoint Caching Rules Functionality

Caching Rules Control how CDN caches your content including deciding caching duration and how unique query strings are handled.

Default Caching behaviour

The following table describes the default caching behaviour for the Azure CDN products and their optimizations.

	MS	Verizon	Verizon DSA	Akamai	Akamai DSA	Akamai Large File Download	Akamai VOD Streaming
Honor Origin	Yes	Yes	No	Yes	No	Yes	Yes
Cache Duration	2	7	None	7	None	1 day	1 Year

Honor origin: Specifies whether to honor the supported cache-directive headers if they exist in the HTTP response from the origin server.
CDN cache duration: Specifies the amount of time for which a resource is cached on the Azure CDN. If **Honor origin** is Yes and the HTTP response from the origin server includes the cache-directive header Expires or Cache-Control: max-age, Azure CDN uses the duration value specified by the header instead.

Control Azure CDN Caching behaviour with Query Strings

Before going into Caching behaviour with query Strings lets discuss what is Query String.

In a web request with a query string, the query string is that portion of the request that occurs after a question mark (?). A query string can contain one or more key-value pairs, in which the field name and its value are separated by an equals sign (=). Each key-value pair is separated by an ampersand (&). For example, http://www.contoso.com/content.mov?field1=value1&field2=value2.

With Azure Content Delivery Network (CDN), you can control how files are cached for a web request that contains a query string. Following Three query string modes are available:

Ignore query strings: This is default mode. In this mode, the CDN point-of-presence (POP) node passes the query strings from the requestor to the origin server on the first request and caches the asset. All subsequent requests for the asset that are served from the POP, until the cached asset expires.

Bypass caching for query strings: In this mode requests with query strings are not cached at the CDN POP node. The POP node retrieves the asset directly from the origin server and passes it to the requestor with each request.

Cache every unique URL: In this mode, each request with a unique URL, including the query string, is treated as a unique asset with its own cache.

You can Change query string caching settings for standard CDN profiles from Caching rules options in CDN Endpoint Dashboard.

Exercise 89: Demonstrating Changing Caching Rules

In CDN Endpoint Dashboard click Caching Rules in left pane> In right pane select the Query String caching option from Drop down box>Click save.

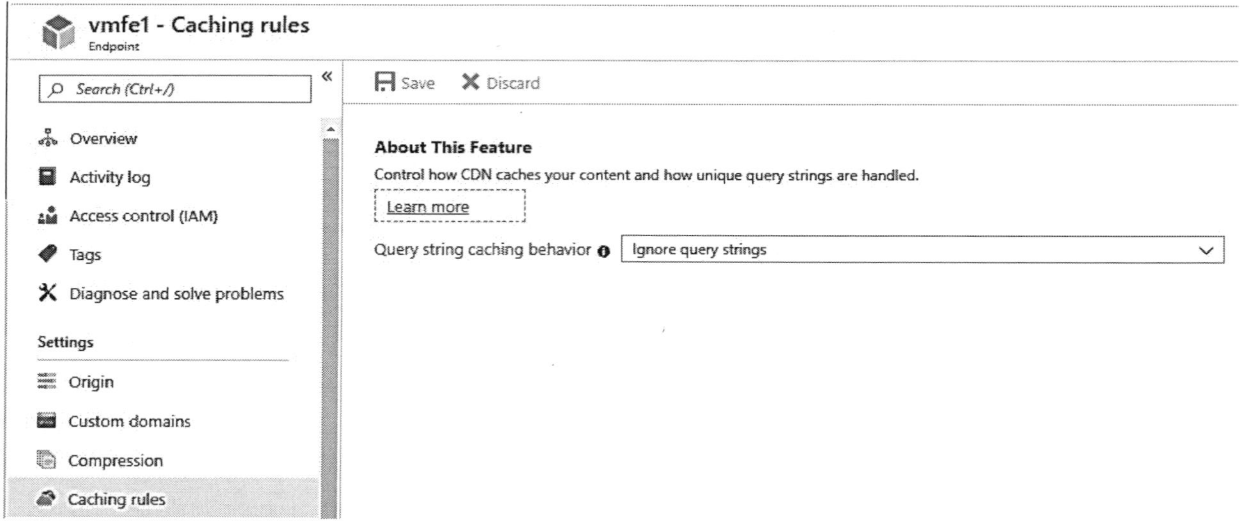

Geo-Filtering

By creating geo-filtering rules you can **block** or **allow** CDN content in the selected countries.

Exercise 90: Demonstrating Allow or Block CDN in Specific Countries

In CDN Endpoint Dashboard click Geo-Filtering in left pane> In right pane select an action (Allow or Block) from Dropdown box and select the countries on which action will applicable>Click save.

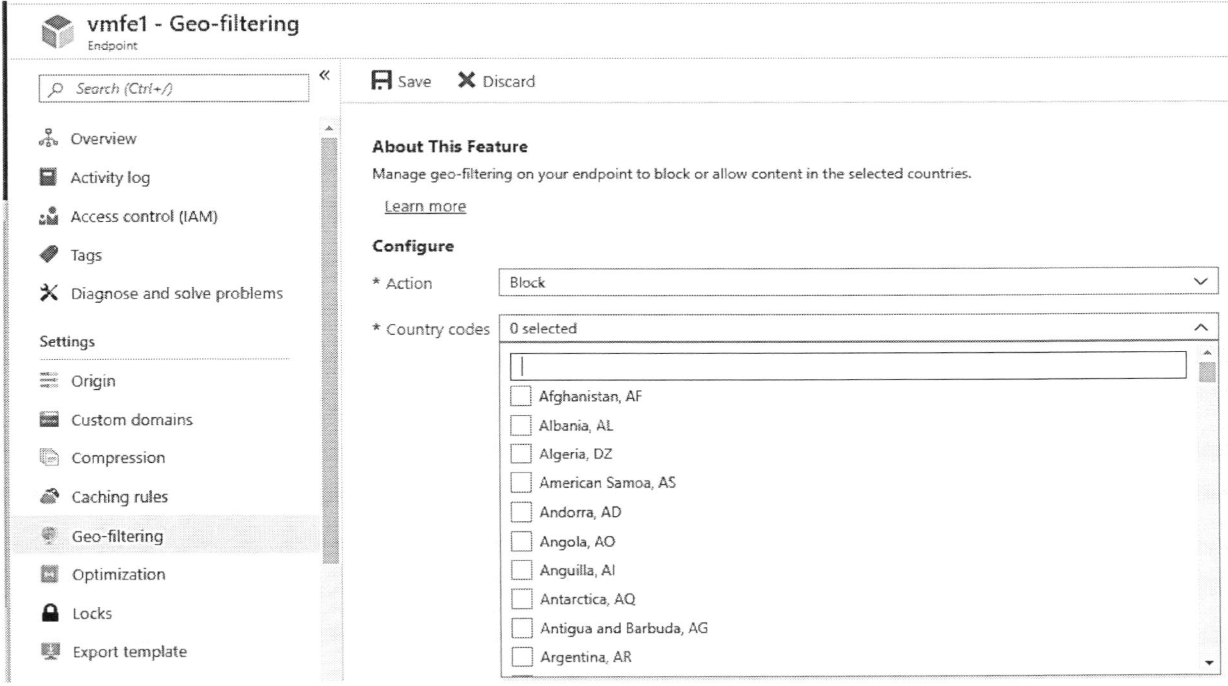

Azure CDN Pricing

Table below shows **Outbound Data Transfer Standard pricing** from Verizon (S1), Akamai (S2), and Microsoft (S3).

OUTBOUND DATA TRANSFERS[1]	ZONE 1 [2]	ZONE 2 [2]	ZONE 3 [2]	ZONE 4 [2]	ZONE 5 [2]
First 10 TB /Month	$0.081 per GB	$0.129 per GB	$0.233 per GB	$0.13 per GB	$0.158 per GB
Next 40 TB (10–50 TB)/Month	$0.075 per GB	$0.121 per GB	$0.186 per GB	$0.126 per GB	$0.121 per GB
Next 100 TB (50–150 TB)/Month	$0.056 per GB	$0.112 per GB	$0.168 per GB	$0.112 per GB	$0.102 per GB
Next 350 TB (150–500 TB)/Month	$0.037 per GB	$0.093 per GB	$0.149 per GB	$0.093 per GB	$0.093 per GB
Next 500 TB (500–1,000 TB)/Month	$0.028 per GB	$0.075 per GB	$0.13 per GB	$0.088 per GB	Contact us
Next 4,000 TB (1,000–5,000 TB)/Month	$0.023 per GB	$0.065 per GB	$0.121 per GB	$0.084 per GB	Contact us
Over 5,000 TB/Month	Contact us	Contact us	Contact us	Contact us	Contact us

Table below shows **Outbound Data Transfer Premium Pricing** from from Verizon (S1).

OUTBOUND DATA TRANSFERS[1]	ZONE 1 [2]	ZONE 2 [2]	ZONE 3 [2]	ZONE 4 [2]	ZONE 5 [2]
First 10 TB /Month	$0.158 per GB	$0.233 per GB	$0.466 per GB	$0.261 per GB	$0.317 per GB
Next 40 TB (10–50 TB)/Month	$0.14 per GB	$0.205 per GB	$0.396 per GB	$0.224 per GB	$0.27 per GB
Next 100 TB (50–150 TB)/Month	$0.121 per GB	$0.177 per GB	$0.335 per GB	$0.186 per GB	$0.228 per GB
Next 350 TB (150–500 TB)/Month	$0.102 per GB	$0.149 per GB	$0.279 per GB	$0.158 per GB	$0.196 per GB
Next 500 TB (500–1,000 TB)/Month	$0.093 per GB	$0.13 per GB	$0.242 per GB	$0.135 per GB	Contact us
Next 4,000 TB (1,000–5,000 TB)/Month	$0.084 per GB	$0.112 per GB	$0.21 per GB	$0.116 per GB	Contact us
Over 5,000 TB/Month	Contact us	Contact us	Contact us	Contact us	Contact us

Acceleration Data Transfer Pricing

Acceleration Data Transfers, also called Dynamic Site Acceleration (DSA), accelerates web content that is not cacheable such as shopping carts, search results, and other dynamic content.

OUTBOUND DATA TRANSFERS[1]	ALL ZONES
First 50 TB /Month	$0.177 per GB
Next 100 TB (50–150 TB)/Month	$0.158 per GB
Next 350 TB (150–500 TB)/Month	$0.14 per GB
Next 500 TB (500–1,000 TB)/Month	$0.121 per GB
Over 1,000 TB/Month	Contact us

- Zone 1—North America, Europe, Middle East and Africa
- Zone 2—Asia Pacific (including Japan)
- Zone 3—South America
- Zone 4—Australia
- Zone 5—India

Chapter 10 Implement Azure Backup

This Chapter covers following

- Azure Backup
- Recovery services Vault
- Backup scenarios with Azure Backup
- Architecture of Azure Backup using Azure Backup Agent
- Architecture of Azure Backup using System Center Data Protection Manager
- Architecture of Azure Backup using Azure Backup Server
- Azure IaaS VM Level Backup
- Azure IaaS VM File & Folder level Backup
- Backup Reports
- Azure Backup Pricing

This Chapter Covers following Lab Exercises

- Create Recovery Services Vault
- Azure VM-level backup
- Restoring Azure VM-level backup
- Create Custom Backup Policy
- Associating Custom Policy with VM VMFE1 Backup Job
- Backup Files & Folder using Azure Backup Agent

This Chapter covers following Case Studies

Backup of Azure VM with Managed Disk
Backup of Folder in Azure VM

Chapter Topology

In this chapter we will add Recovery Services Vault & Azure Backup to the Topology. We will backup System State of VM VMFE1 using Backup option in VMFE1 dashboard. This will Install Azure Backup Extension on VMFE1.

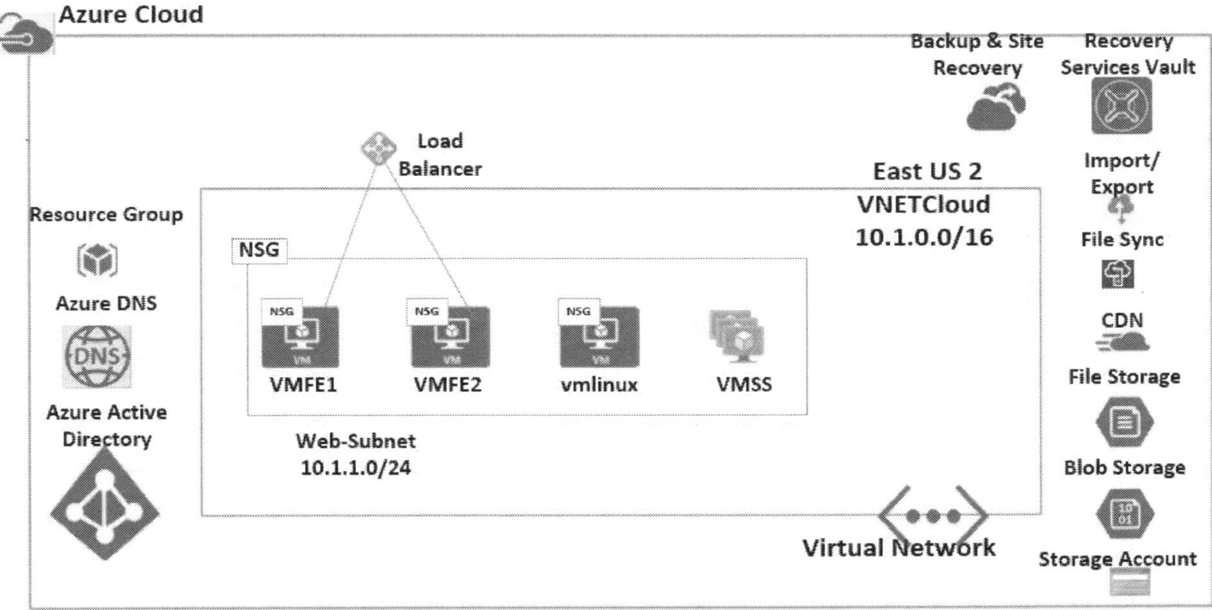

We will also install Azure Backup Agent (Mars) in VM VMAD. This will backup files and folders on VMAD to Recovery Services Vault,

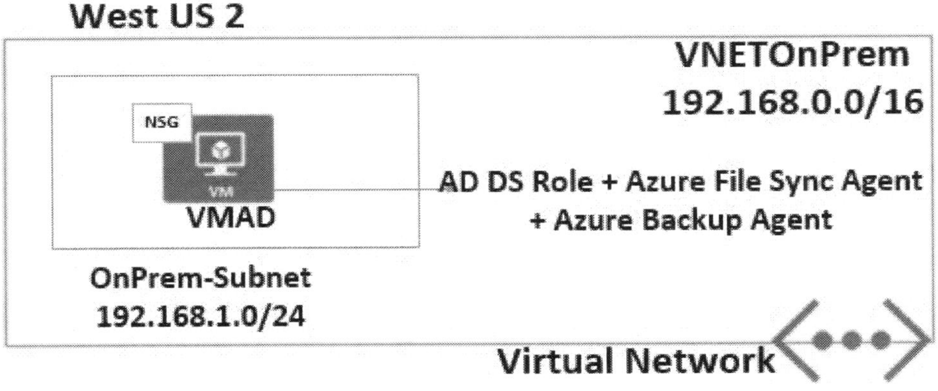

Azure Backup

Azure Backup is Backup as a service (BaaS) which you can use to backup and restore your data in Azure cloud.
You can backup both on Premises workloads and Azure workloads.
Azure Backups are stored in Recovery Services Vault.
Advantage of Azure backup is that we don't have to set up Backup infrastructure.

Feature of Azure Backup

1. No backup infrastructure to setup. It uses pay-as-you-use model.
2. Azure Backup manages backup storage scalability and high availability. Azure Recovery Services Vault offers unlimited Storage. For high availability, Azure Backup offers two types of replication: locally redundant storage and geo-redundant storage.
3. Azure Backup supports incremental backup. Incremental backup transfers changes made since the last full backup.
4. Data is encrypted for secure transmission between on-premises and Azure Cloud. The backup data is stored in the Recovery Services vault in encrypted form.
5. Backups are compressed to reduce the required storage space in Vault.
6. Azure Backup provides application-consistent backups for Microsoft Workloads, which ensured additional fixes are not needed to restore the data. Restoring application consistent data reduces the restoration time, allowing you to quickly return to a running state. This option is only available when we use either System Center DPM or Azure Backup server.

Recovery Services Vault

A Recovery Services Vault is a storage entity in Azure that houses backup data.

You can use Recovery Services vaults to hold backup data for on-premises workload and for various Azure services such as IaaS VMs (Linux or Windows) and Azure SQL databases.

Azure Backup offers two types of replication: locally redundant storage (LRS) and geo-redundant storage (GRS). GRS option ensures that backups are replicated to a different Azure region for safeguarding from regional disasters as shown below.

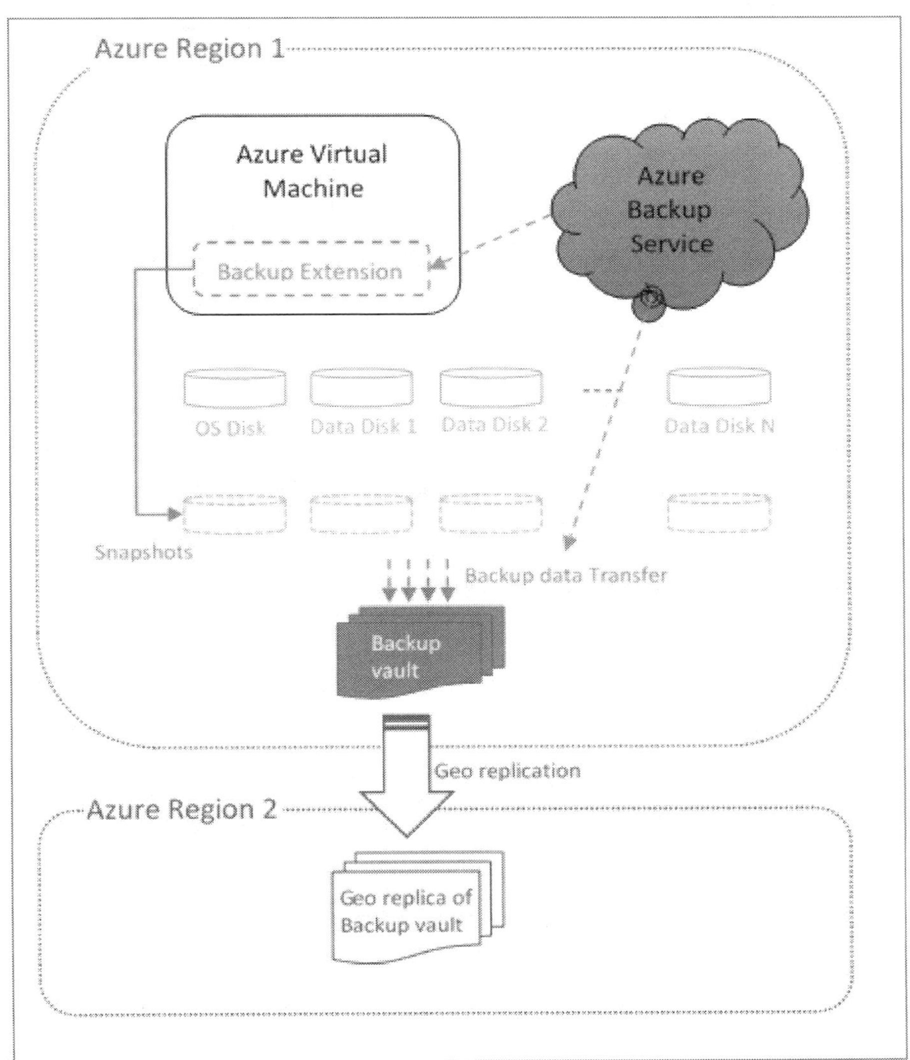
Azure Region 1
Azure Virtual Machine
Azure Backup Service
Backup Extension
OS Disk
Data Disk 1
Data Disk 2
Data Disk N
Snapshots
Backup data Transfer
Backup vault
Geo replication
Azure Region 2
Geo replica of Backup vault

Backup scenarios with Azure Backup

Azure Backup provides 4 options to Backup on-premises and Cloud workloads – Azure Backup Agent, System Center DPM Server, Azure Backup Server and Azure IaaS VM Backup.

Table below shows comparison of Azure Backup options.

Backup Option	Features	Deployment	Target Storage
Azure Backup Agent	Backs up Files and Folders on Windows Server and VMs. No Linux support. No backup server required.	On-premises and Cloud	RSV
System Center DPM	Backs up Files, folders, Volumes, VMs & Application aware backup (SQL, Exchange). Other features include Restore granuality and Linux support. Cannot back up Oracle workload.	On-premises and Cloud	RSV, Local Disk on DPM server and Tape (on-site only)
Azure Backup Server	Backs up Files, folders, Volumes, VMs & Application aware backup (SQL, Exchange). Restore granuality and Linux support. Cannot back up Oracle workload. Requires live Azure subscription. No support for tape backup. Does not require a System Center license	On-premises and Cloud	RSV, Local Disk on Azure Backup Server
Azure IaaS VM Backup	Backup Integrated in VM dashboard. Backs up VMs and Disks. No specific agent installation required. Fabric-level backup with no backup infrastructure needed	Cloud only	RSV

RSV: Recovery Services Vault

Architecture of Azure Backup using Azure Backup Agent (Mars)

Azure Backup agent backs up Windows server or Windows VM to Recovery Services Vault in Azure. Azure Backup Agent option can be used to backup both on-premises and cloud workloads.

Backup to Azure requires following components.
Recovery services Vault.
Azure Backup Agent.

Azure Backup Agent can backup following workloads

Files & Folders: Azure Backup agent backs up files and folders on Window server or Windows VM to Recovery Services Vault.

Windows System State

Backup Location

Backs up data to Recovery Services Vault in Azure. There is no option to backup Data locally.

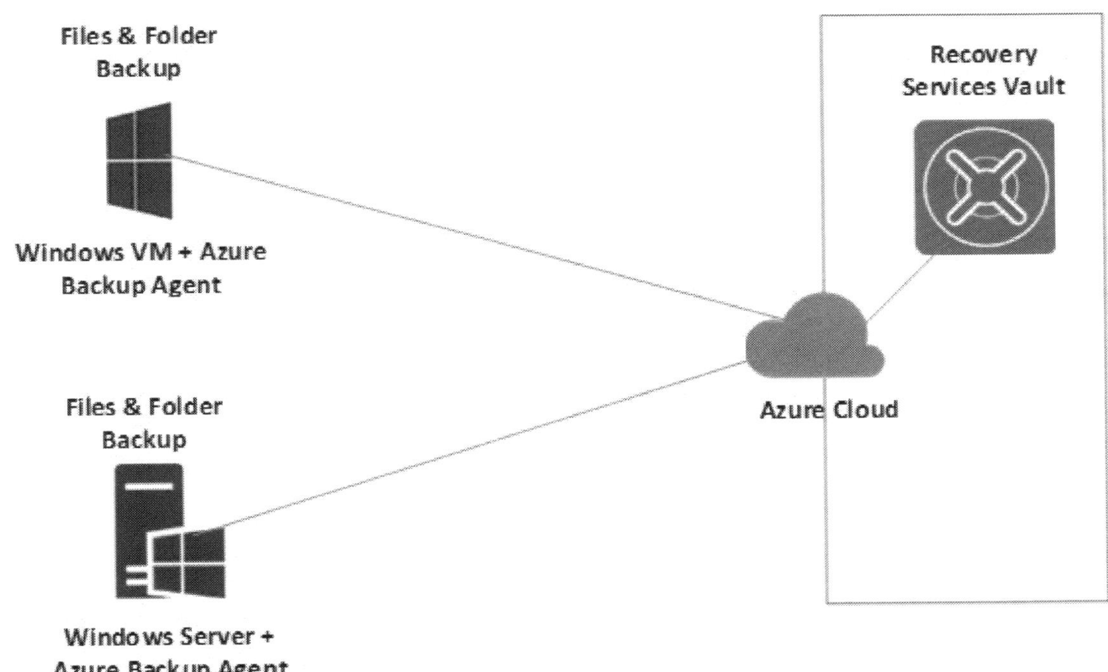

Installing & Working of Azure Backup Agent

1. Create Recovery Services vault.
2. Download Backup Agent and Vault Credentials to the on Premises server by configuring the Backup goal in Recovery services vault dashboard.
3. Install Azure Backup Agent on the on Premises Server and register the server with Recovery Services vault using Vault credentials.
4. Schedule the backup by opening Azure backup agent in the on premises server and configuring the backup policy.

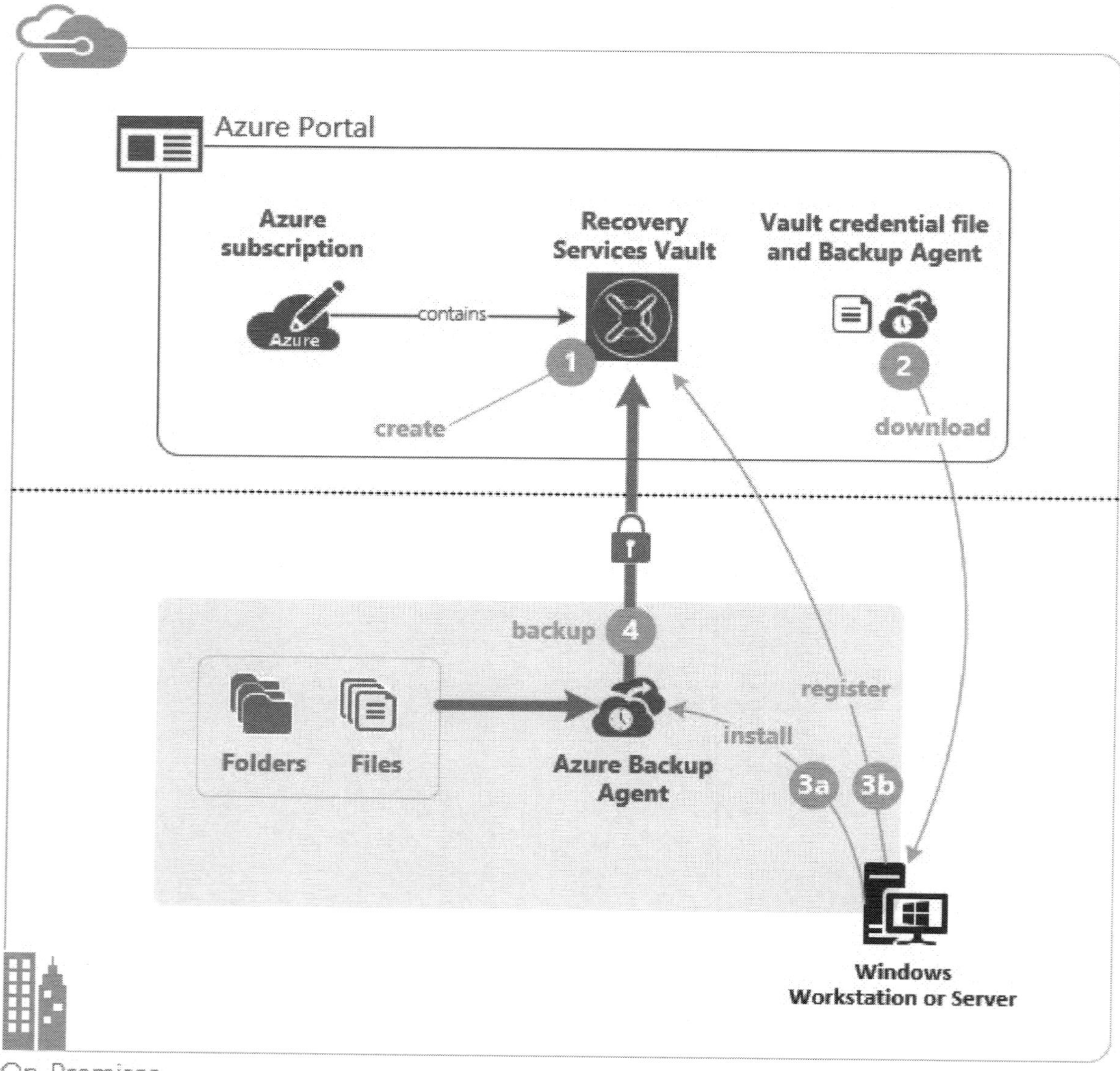

Architecture of Azure Backup using System Center DPM

Azure Backup using System Center Data Protection Manager (DPM) option not only backs up workload to Azure Recovery Service Vault but backup is also available locally on disk as well as on tape. This option can be used to backup both on-premises and cloud workloads.

Backup to Azure requires following components

Recovery Services Vault.
System Center Data Protection Manager (DPM).
Azure backup agent to be installed on DPM Server.
DPM Agents to be installed on Protected Servers.

In this case Backup agent will be installed on DPM server.

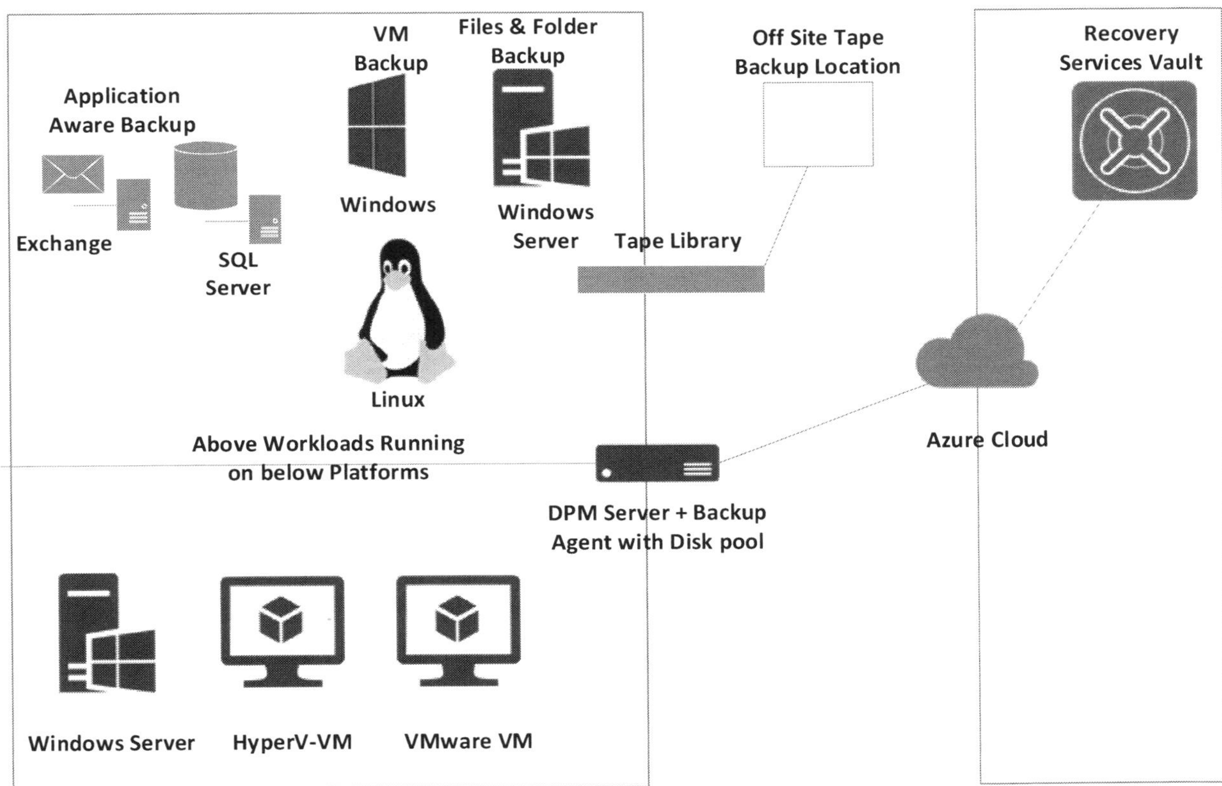

DPM can backup following workloads

Application-aware backup: Application-aware back up of Microsoft workloads, including SQL Server, Exchange, and SharePoint.

File backup: Back up files, folders and volumes for computers running Windows server and Windows client operating systems.

System backup: Back up system state or run full, bare-metal backups of physical computers running Windows server or Windows client operating systems.

Hyper-V backup: Back up Hyper-V virtual machines (VM) running Windows or Linux. You can back up an entire VM, or run application-aware backups of Microsoft workloads on Hyper-V VMs running Windows.

VMware VMs backup

DPM Backup Workload Locations

Disk: For short-term storage DPM backs up data to disk pools.

Azure Recovery Services Vault: For both short-term and long-term storage off-premises, DPM data stored in disk pools can be backed up to the Azure Recovery Services Vault using the Azure Backup service.

Tape: For long-term storage you can back up data to tape, which can then be stored offsite. This option is only available for on-premises workload.

Advantages of DPM backup

Backup is also available locally.
Linux VM backup.
Application Aware Backup.
Tape Backup option.

Architecture of Azure Backup using Azure Backup Server

This option is same as DPM option except for following 2 differences.

1. Tape option is not there with Azure backup server.
2. You don't have to pay license for Azure Backup server.

Backup to Azure requires following components

1. Recovery services Vault
2. Azure Backup Server
3. DPM Agents to be installed on Protected Servers.

In this case backup agent comes Pre-installed on Azure Backup Server.

Rest everything is same as discussed in Data protection Server in previous section.

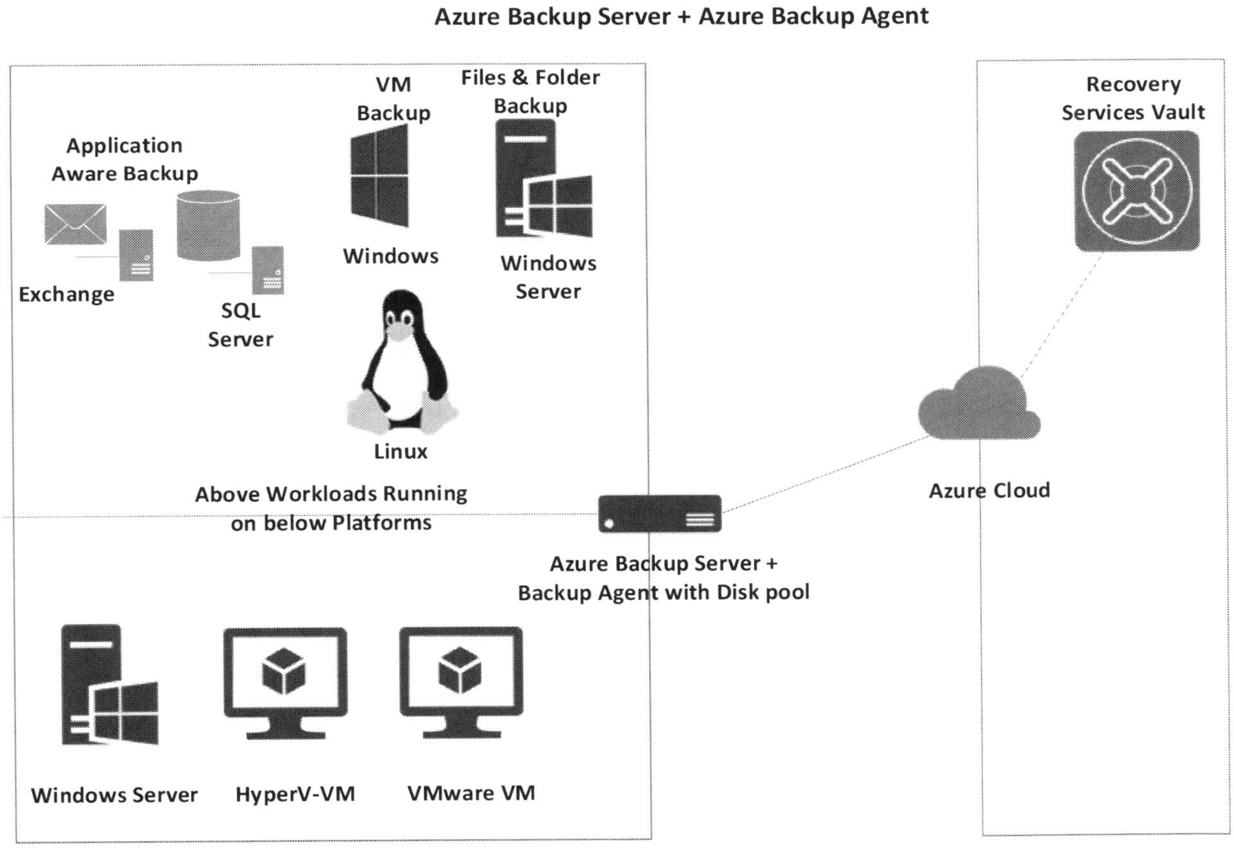

Azure Backup Server + Azure Backup Agent

VM Backup
Files & Folder Backup
Recovery Services Vault
Application Aware Backup
Exchange
SQL Server
Windows
Windows Server
Linux
Above Workloads Running on below Platforms
Azure Cloud
Azure Backup Server + Backup Agent with Disk pool
Windows Server
HyperV-VM
VMware VM

Azure IaaS VM Level Backup

Azure IaaS VM Backup provides Native backups for Windows/Linux. This option can be used to backup Azure VMs only. The benefit of this option is that Backup option is built in VM dashboard.

Backup to Azure requires following components

1. Recovery services Vault.
2. Azure backup agent extension is automatically enabled when backup is enabled in the VM.

Azure IaaS VM Backup can backup following workloads

Full Azure Windows/Linux VM backup.
VM Disk Backups (Using Powershell).

Backup Location

Backs up data to Recovery Services Vault in Azure.

Azure IaaS VM Backup Working

The Backup service uses the *VMSnapshot*extension to backup workloads. The Backup service coordinates with the Volume Shadow Copy Service (VSS) to get a consistent snapshot of the virtual machine's disks. Once the Azure Backup service takes the snapshot, the data is transferred to the vault.

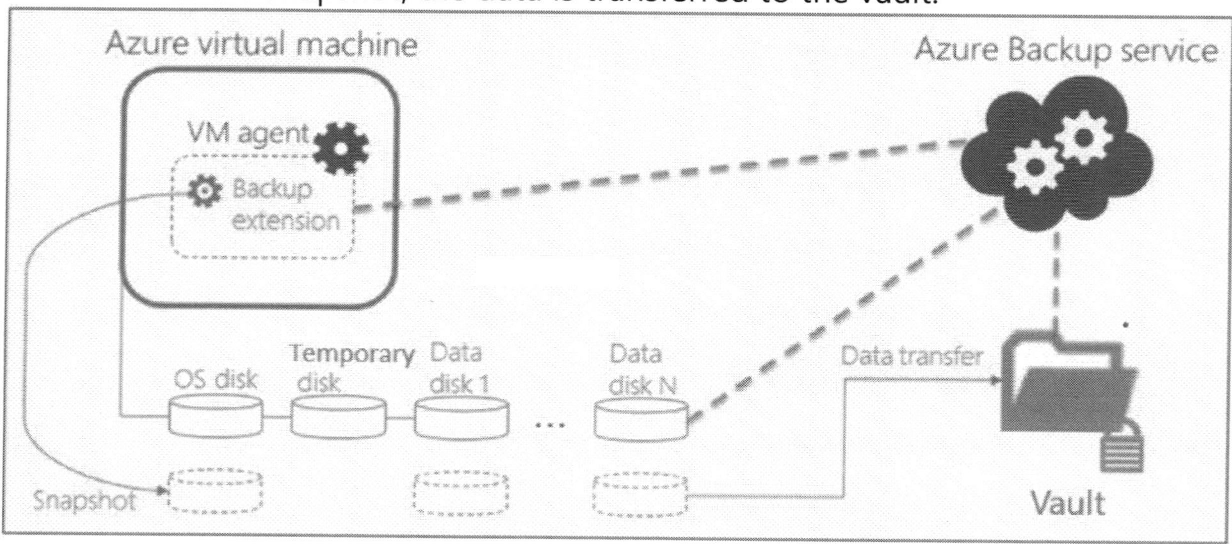

Azure IaaS VM File & Folder level Backup

If you want to backup Azure VM files & folders than you need to use Azure Backup Agent (Mars).

Refer to page 483 for Architecture and working of Azure Backup Agent (Mars).

Exercise 96 shows Azure VM level Backup of Files & Folder using Azure Backup Agent.

About Next Exercises

We will create Recovery Services Vault in Resource Group RGCloud. Resource Group RGCloud was created in Exercise 1, Chapter 1.

We will take Backup of VMFE1 system state using Backup option in VMFE1 dashboard. VM VMFE1 was created in Exercise 25, Chapter 4.

Exercise 91: Create Recovery Services Vault

1. In Azure Portal click create a resource> Storage> Backup and Site Recovery> Create Recovery Services Vault Blade opens> Enter a name, select RGCloud in Resource Group, select region East US 2 and click create (Not Shown).

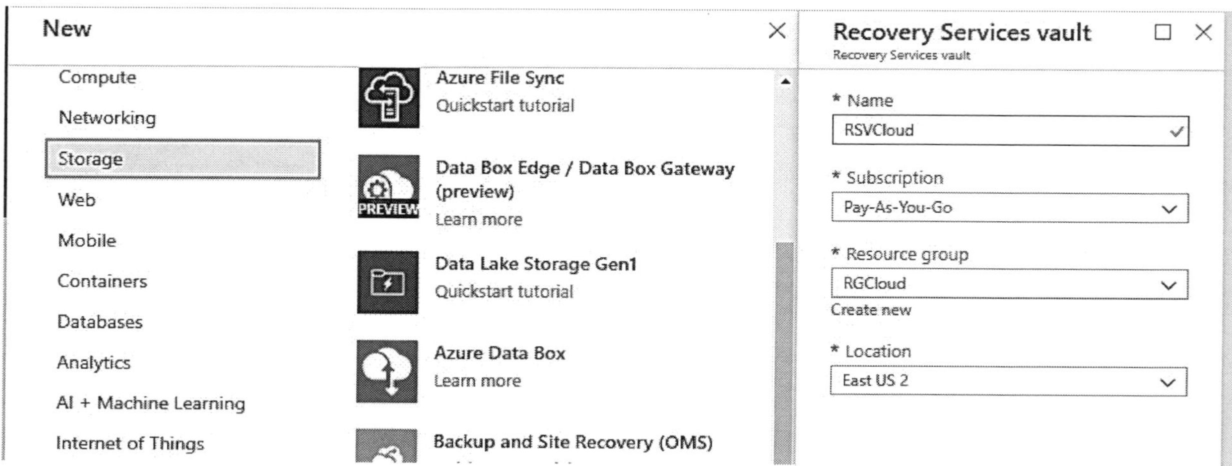

2. Figure below shows Dashboard of Recovery Services Vault.

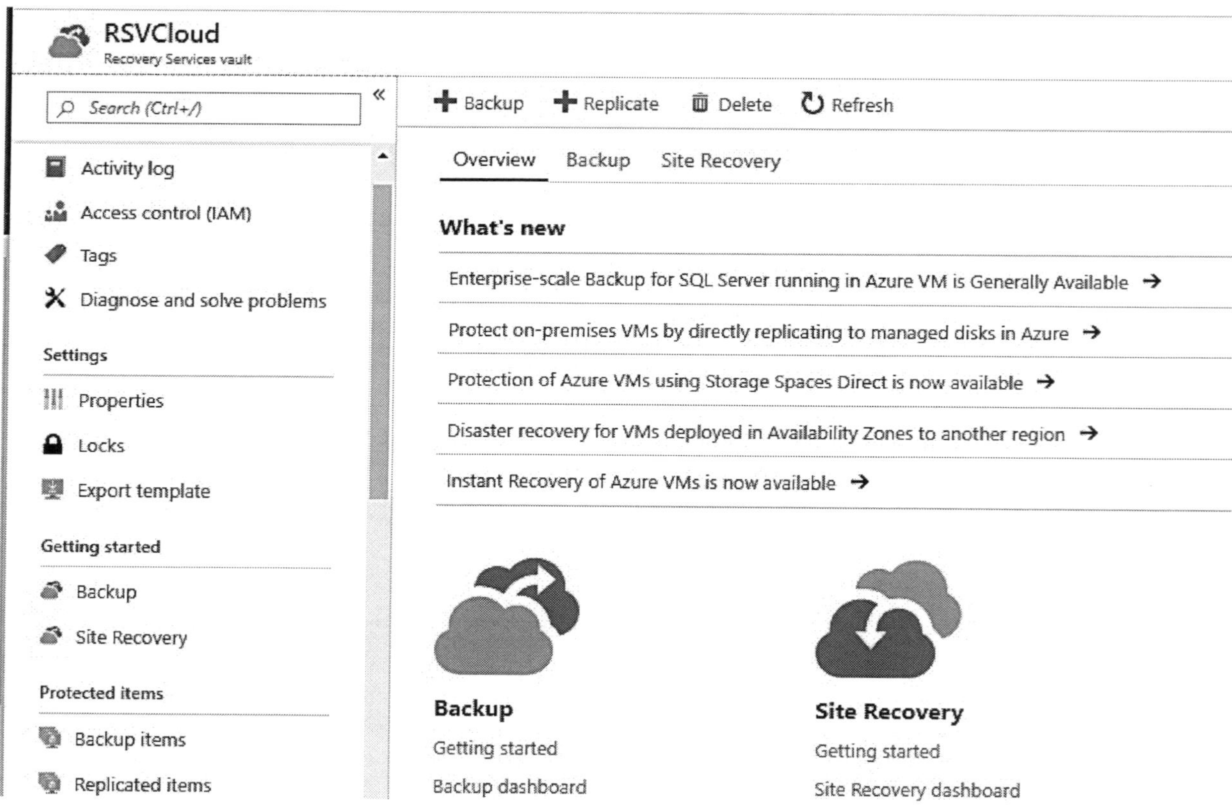

Exercise 92: Azure VM-level backup

1. In Azure Portal go to VM VMFE1 dashboard.

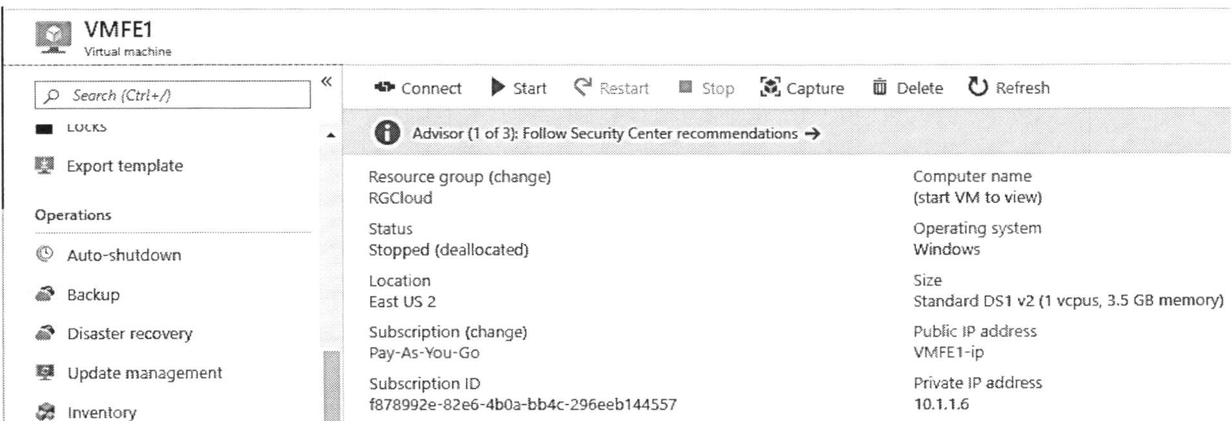

2. In left pane scroll down and Click Backup in left pane>Enable Backup blade opens> In right pane Select RSV created in Ex 76 and click enable backup.

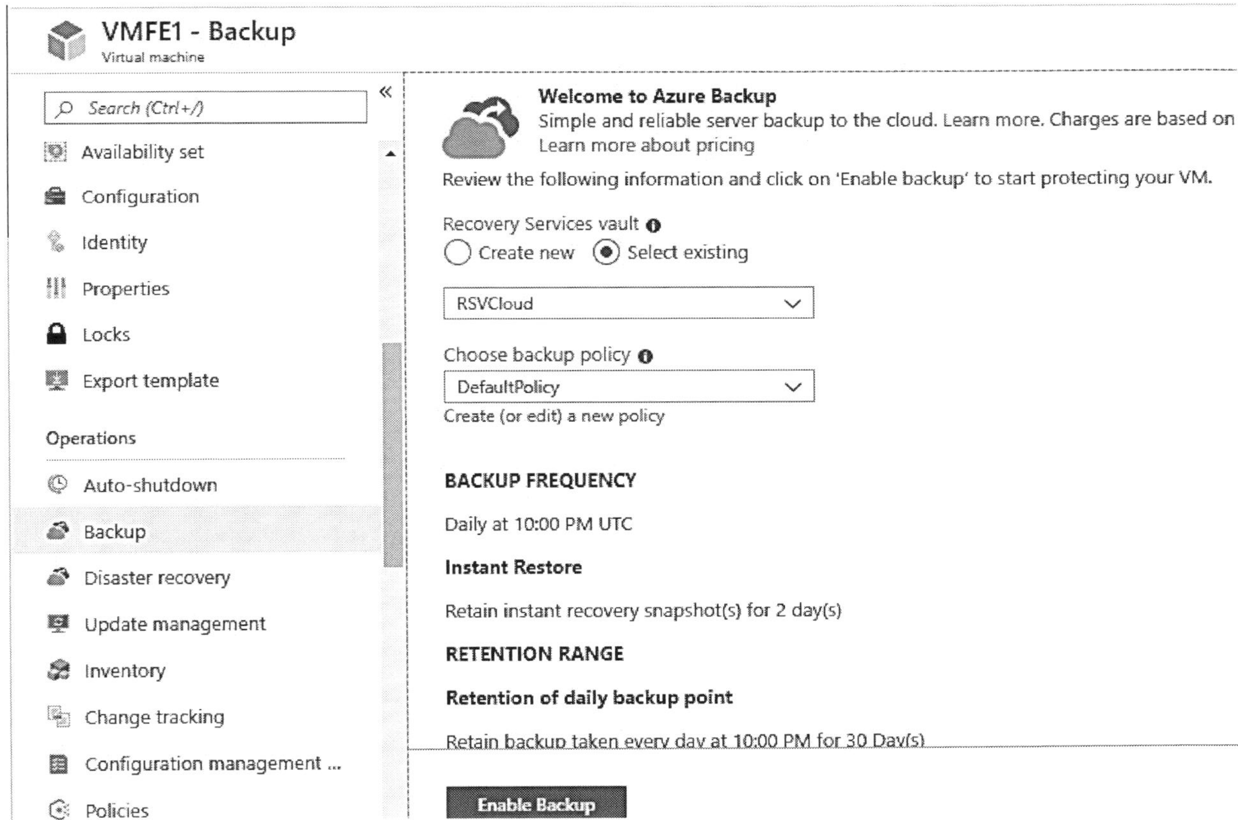

3. The default policy is to take Backup at 10 PM. Figure below shows the Backup status. It shows initial backup pending. This first backup job creates a full recovery point. Each backup job after this initial backup creates incremental recovery points. Incremental recovery points are storage and time-efficient, as they only transfer changes made since the last backup.

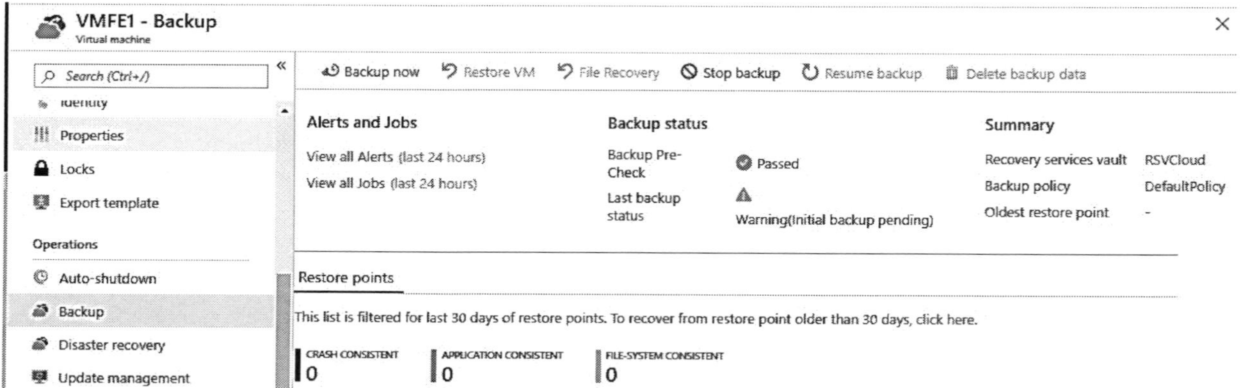

4. To start Backup instead of waiting for default policy to kick in Click Backup now in top right pane>Backup Now Blade opens.

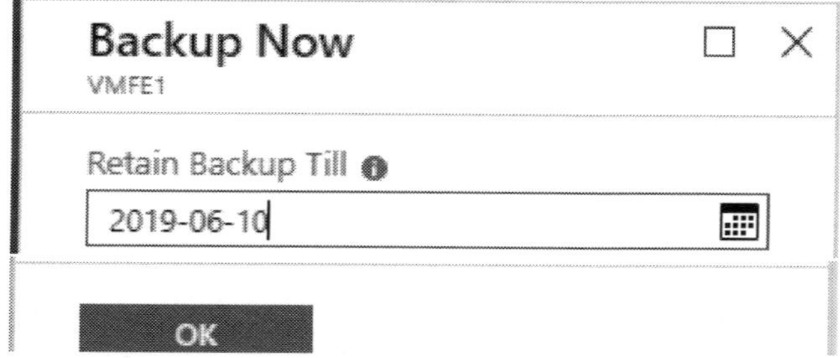

5. Click OK to start Backup now. You can monitor the Progress by Clicking **View all Jobs** in Right pane as shown in top figure. It shows backup job in progress.

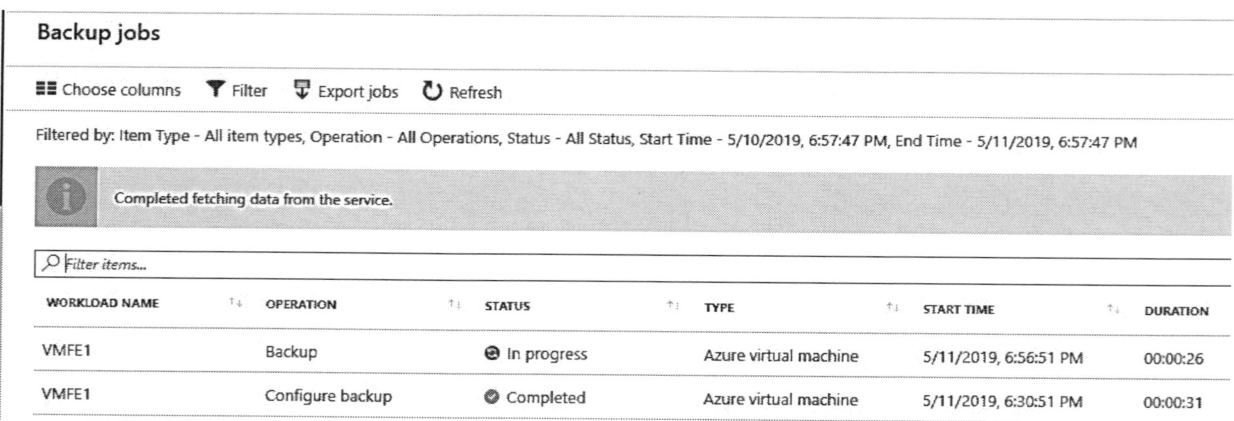

6. Just keep refreshing the backup job pane. You can see initial backup job completed. It took 1.15 hours to complete.

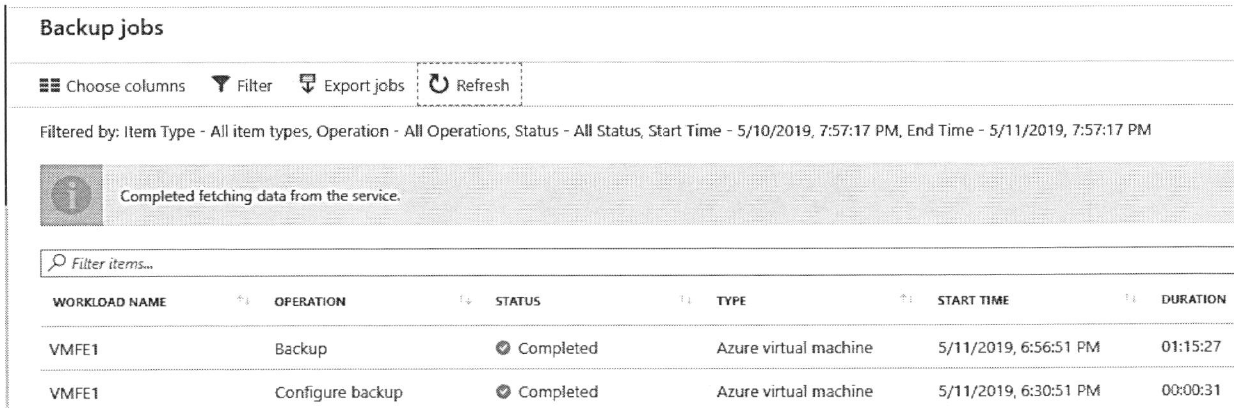

7. You can also track progress of backup in Recovery Services Vault. Click Backup items in Recovery Services vault. It will show Backup for Various Types.

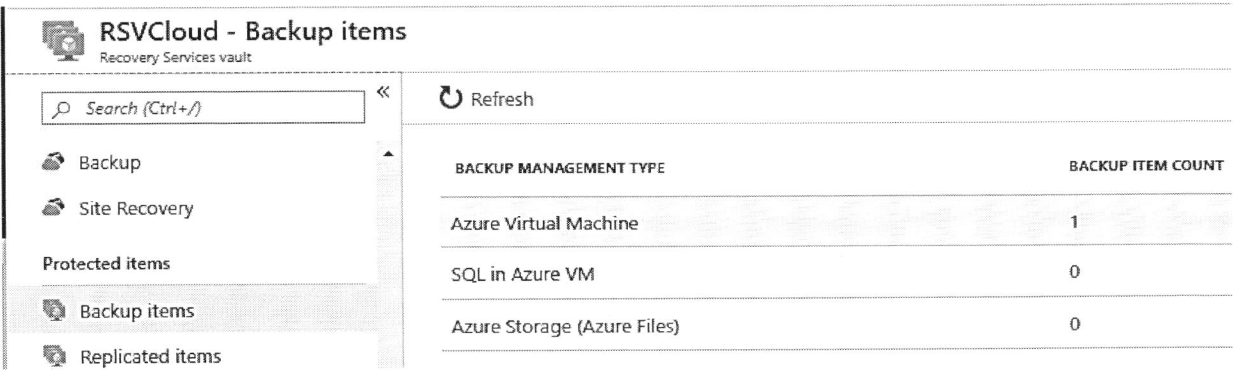

Click on Azure Virtual Machine and you can see backup Items for Azure VM.

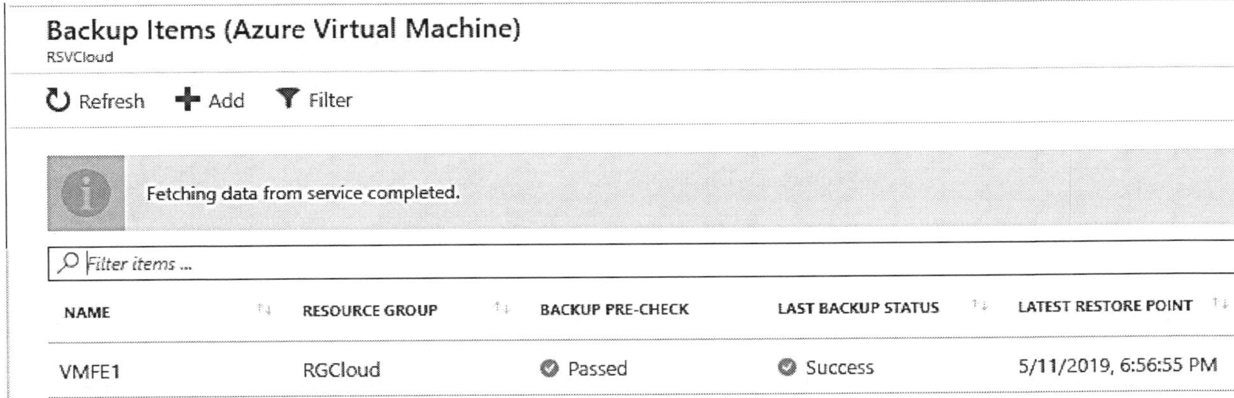

Exercise 93: Restoring Azure VM-level backup

In this exercise we will just demonstrate Restoration operation. We will show options for creating new VM from backup and replacing Disks of existing VM with Restore point disks.

1. Click Backup in VMFE1 Dashboard> Backup Pane opens. In right pane you can see option for Restore VM and File Recovery.

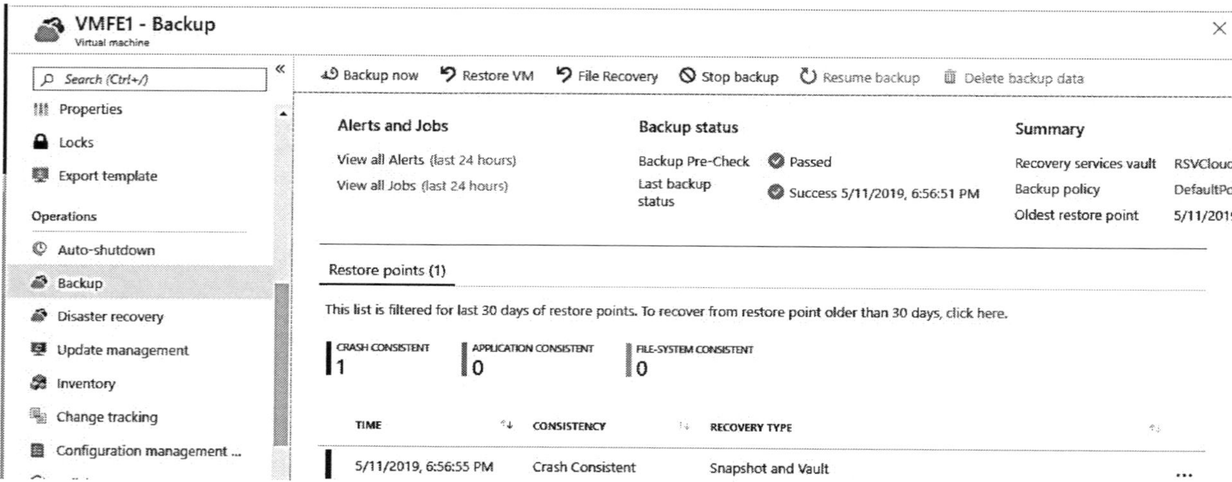

2. Click Restore VM in Right pane>Select your restore point>Click OK (Not Shown).

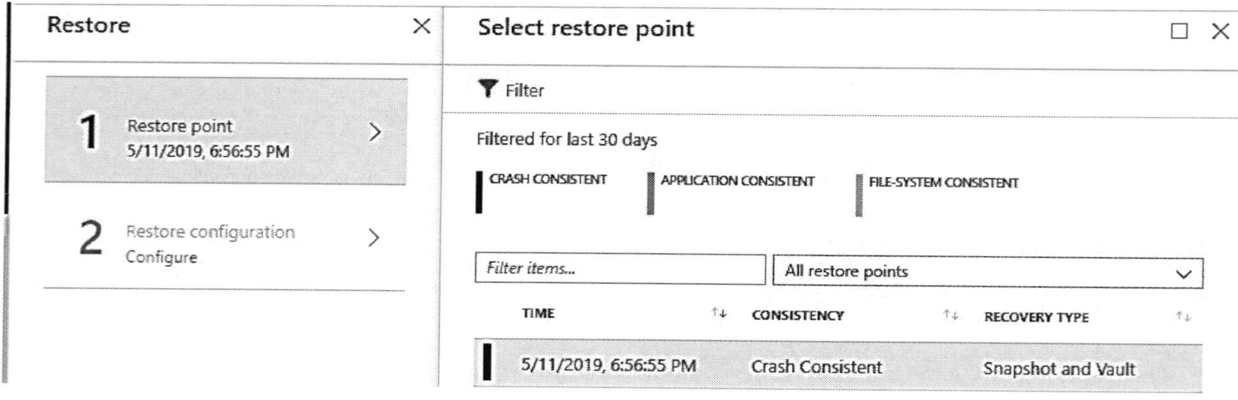

3. Restore Configuration pane. Here you have 2 options to Restore. Option 1 shown below is to create a new VM with the backup.

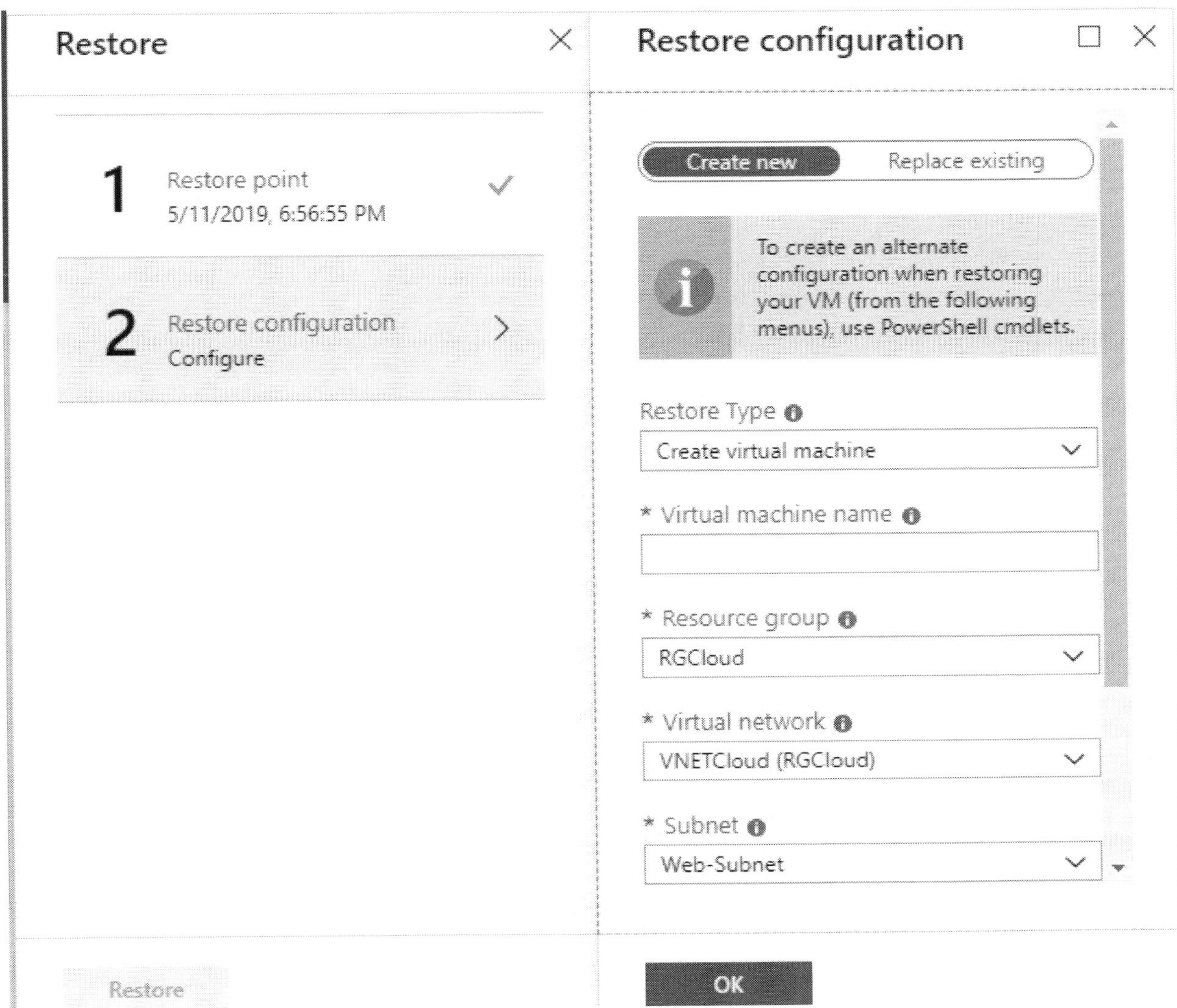

4. Second option in Restore Configuration pane is to replace disks in existing VM with disks from Restore points.

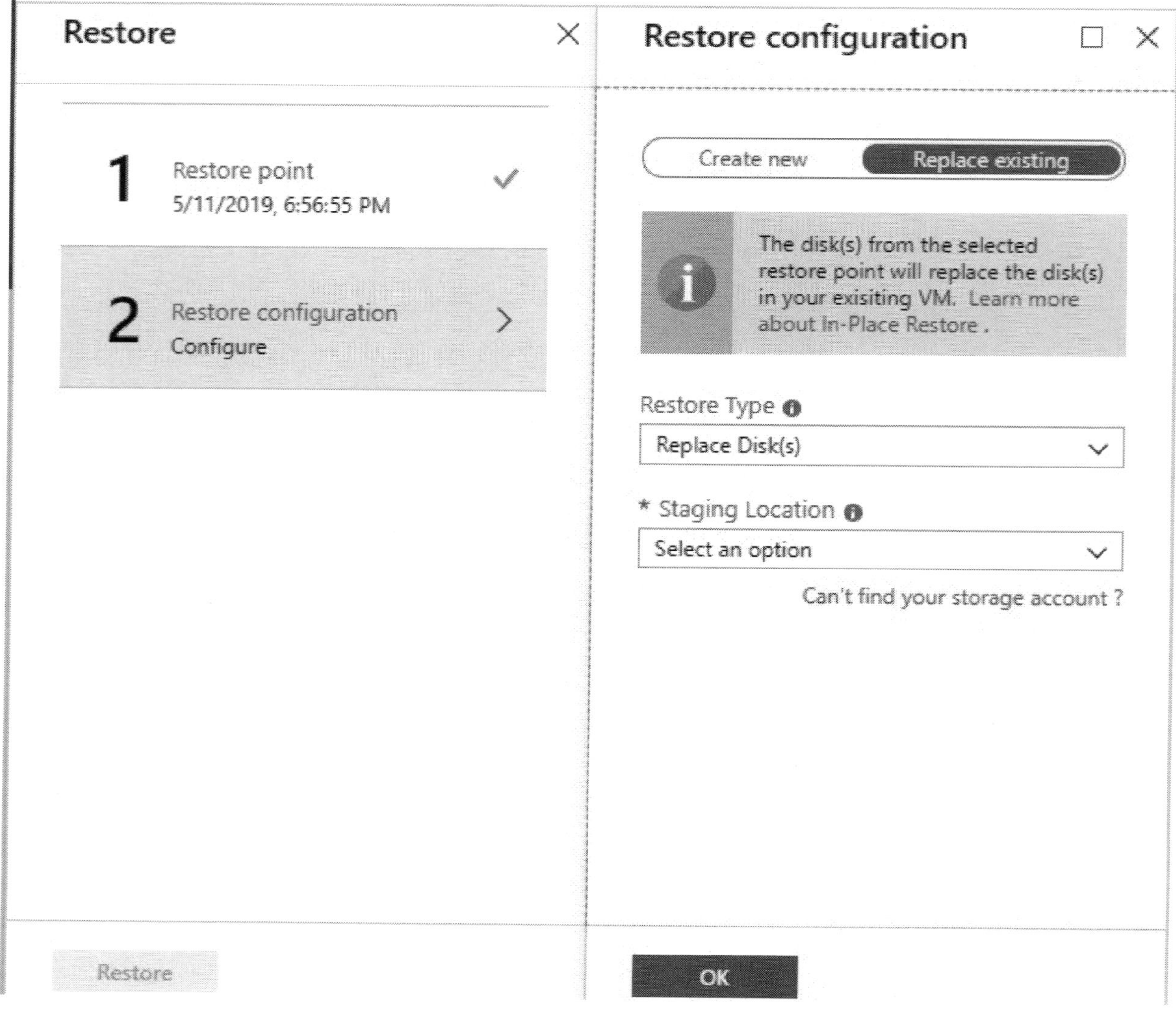

As an exercise for the readers use option 1 to create a new VM.

Virtual Machine Backup Policy

A backup policy defines a matrix of when the data snapshots are taken, and how long those snapshots are retained. When defining a policy for backing up a VM, you can trigger a backup job *once a day or weekly.*
A **default back policy** is applied when you create Backup job. With Default Policy backup is taken at 2.30 PM and Backup is retained for 30 days.
You can create a **Custom Policy** according to your requirements. Custom policy can be created during backup job creation time or afterwards.

Exercise 94: Create Custom Backup Policy

1. Go Recovery Service Vault rsvportal dashboard>Click Backup Polices in left pane>Backup policy blade opens in Right Pane.

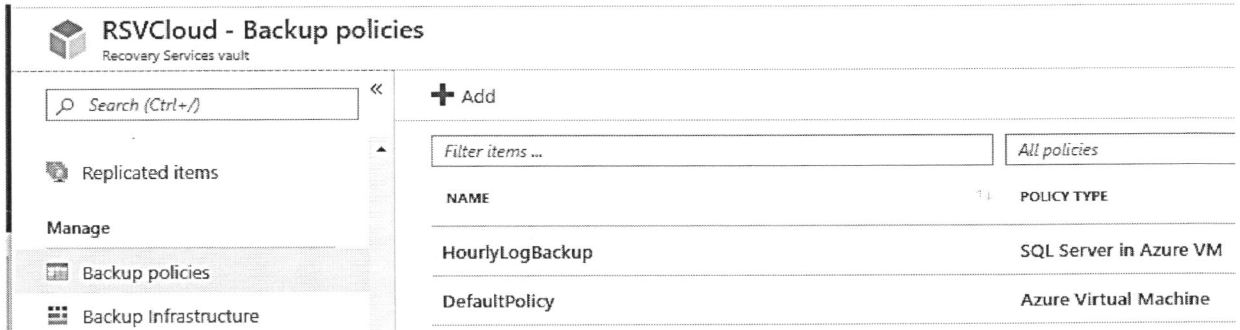

2. In Right pane Click +Add> Click Azure Virtual Machine>Create Policy blade opens> give a name and select Backup Frequency (Daily or weekly) and select retention of snapshots (daily, weekly, Monthly and Yearly). Selecting Weekly, Monthly and Yearly is optional>Click create.

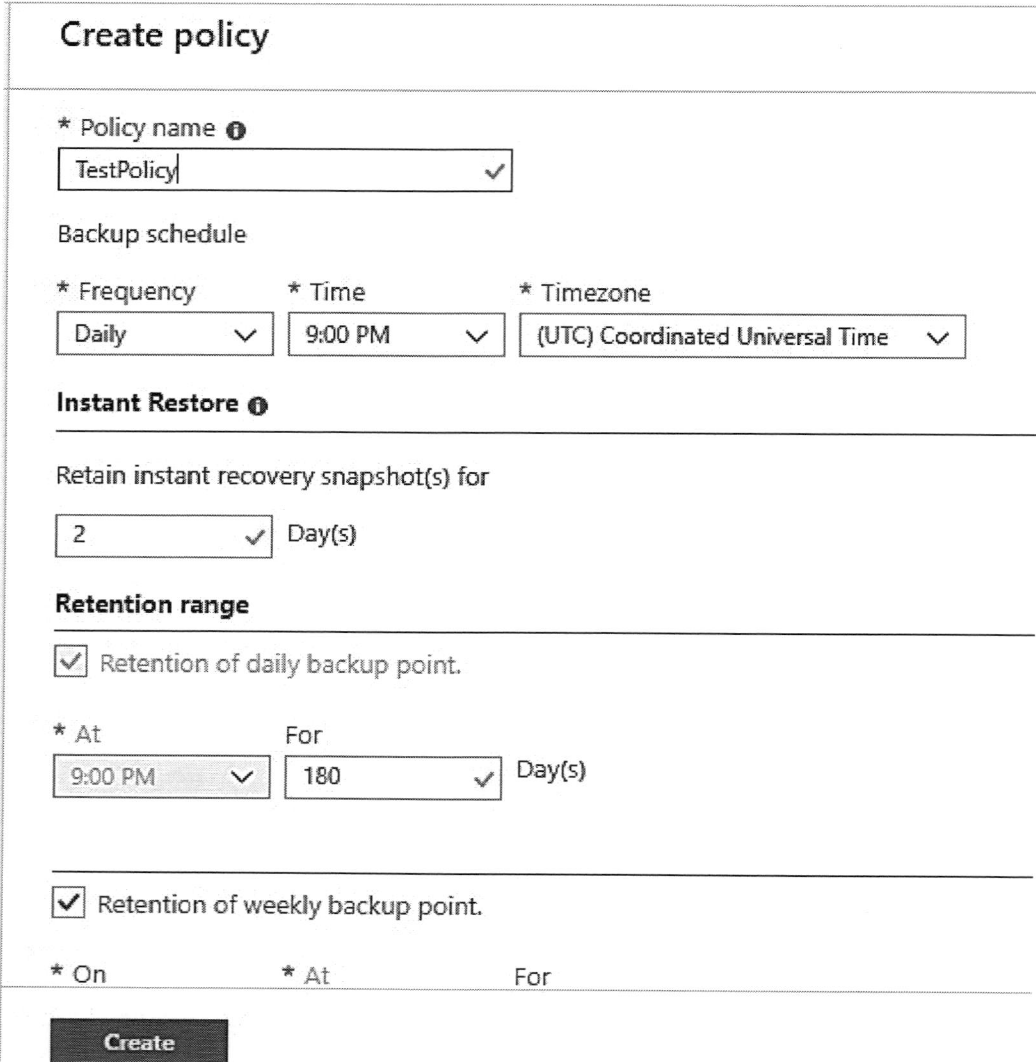

3. Figure below shows TestPolicy created Successfully.

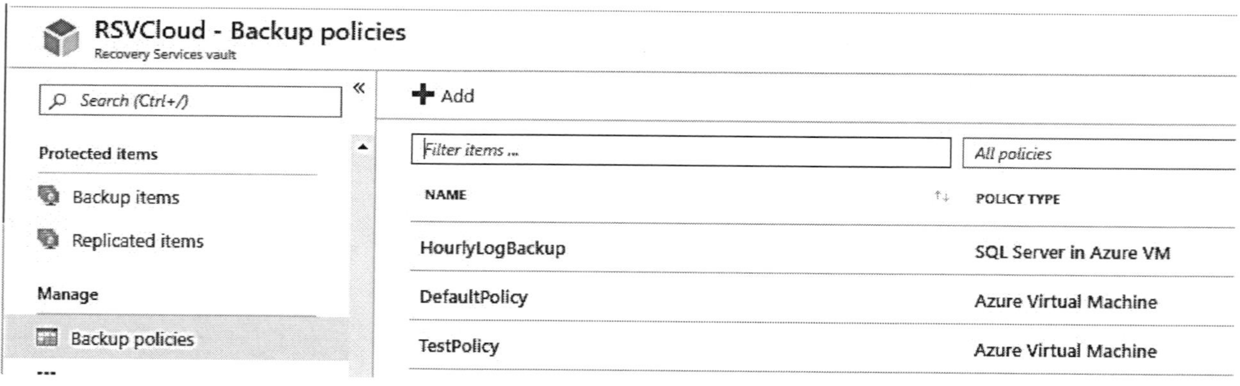

Exercise 95: Associating Custom Policy with VM VMFE1 Backup Job

In this exercise we will associate Custom Policy created in previous exercise with VM VMFE1 Backup job.

1. In Azure Portal go to VMFE1 dashboard> Click Backup in left pane. In right pane you can see a default backup policy is associated with Backup.

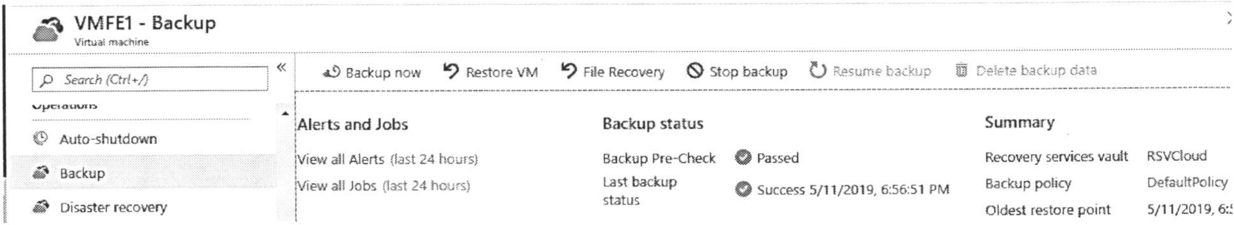

2. Click DefaultPolicy in right pane>Backup Policy blade opens>Choose TestPolicy from the dropdown box>Click save.

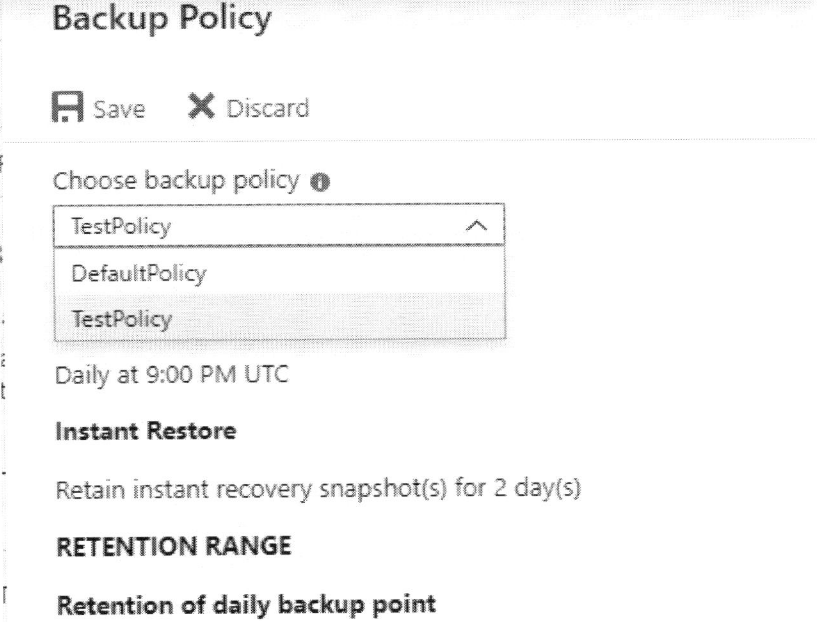

3. You can see in right pane that TestPolicy is applied to backup job.

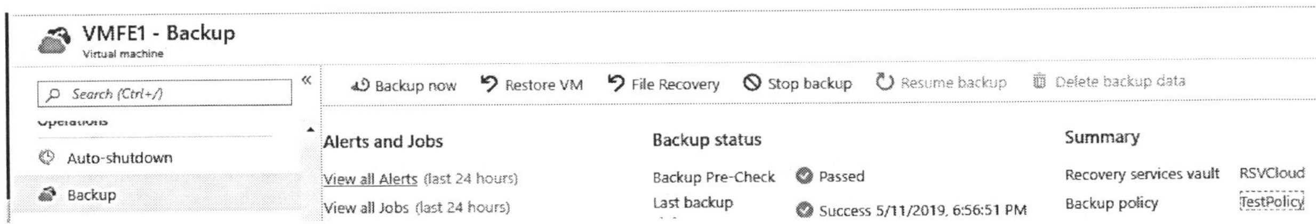

Exercise 96: Backup Files & Folder using Azure Backup Agent

In this exercise we will backup Files & Folders of Azure VM **VMAD** using Azure Backup Agent option. Azure VM VMAD was created in Exercise 39, Chapter 4.

1. RDP into VM VMAD. Create a folder name test on the VMAD C Drive. Create an empty text file HelloWorld.txt in the test folder.
2. In VMAD Open internet explorer and log on to Azure portal> Go to Recovery Services Vault Dashboard>Click Backup in left pane>Select **on-premises** and select **Files and Folder**.

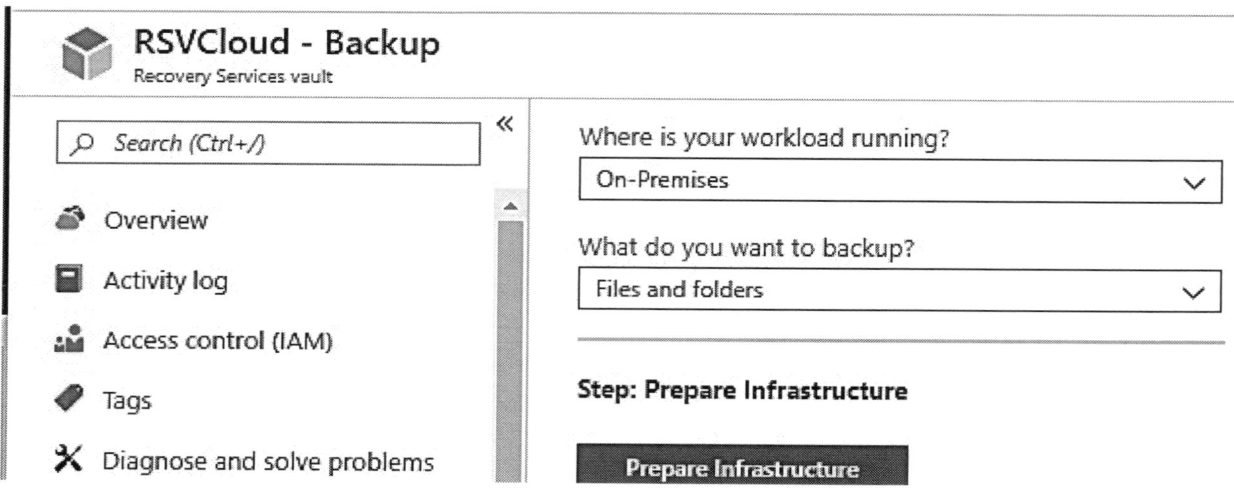

3. Click Prepare Infrastructure>Prepare Infrastructure Blade opens.

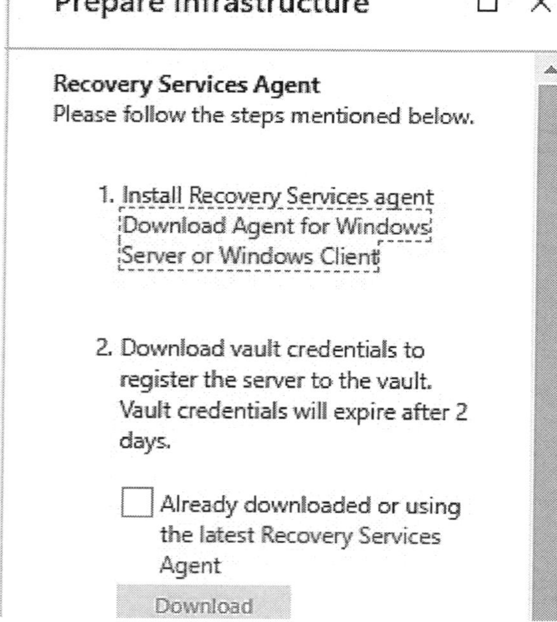

4. Click Download Agent for Windows Server and download the exe file.

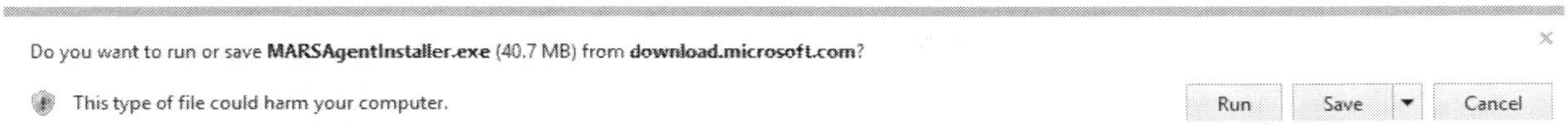

Do you want to run or save **MARSAgentInstaller.exe** (40.7 MB) from **download.microsoft.com**?

This type of file could harm your computer.

Run | Save | Cancel

5. Check mark the Vault credential and click download.

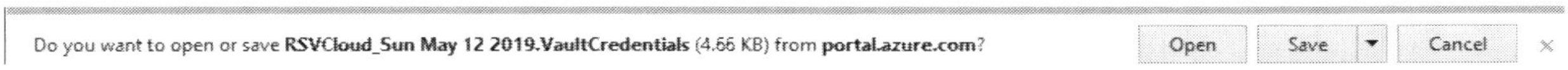

Do you want to open or save **RSVCloud_Sun May 12 2019.VaultCredentials** (4.66 KB) from **portal.azure.com**?

Open | Save | Cancel

6. On the VMAD VM double click MARSAgentInstaller.exe and start installation of the agent. At the end of installation click Proceed to Registration to register your on VMAD to Recovery Services Vault>Click Browse and upload Vault credential file downloaded in step 5.

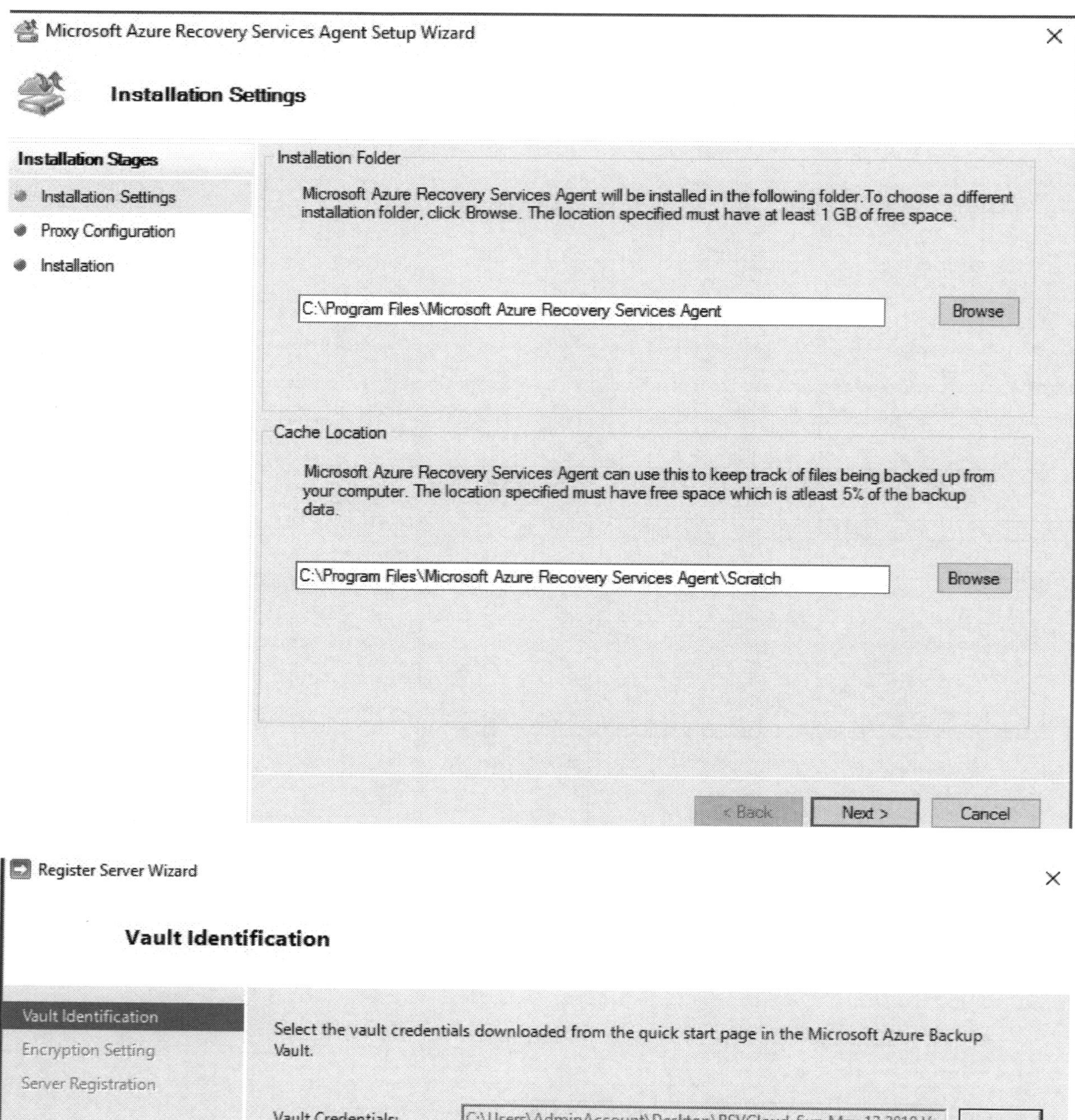

7. In Encryption setting enter a passphrase or generate passphrase and specify the location to save passphrase. I specified C:\>Click finish.

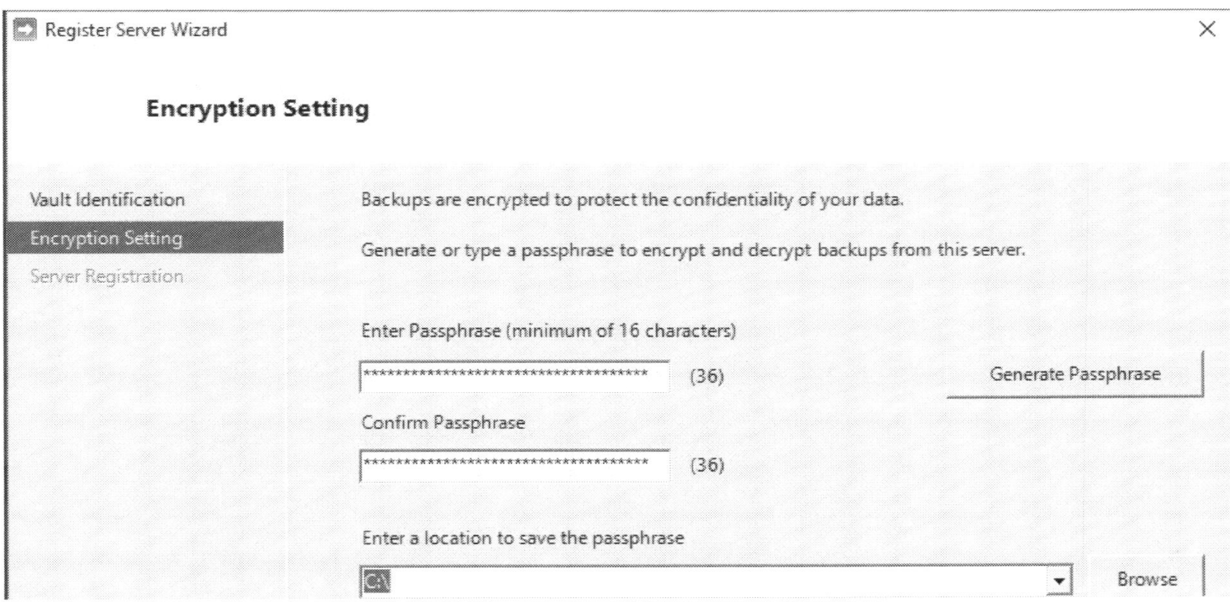

8. Microsoft Azure Backup Agent is installed and an icon shows on the desktop. 3rd icon from top.

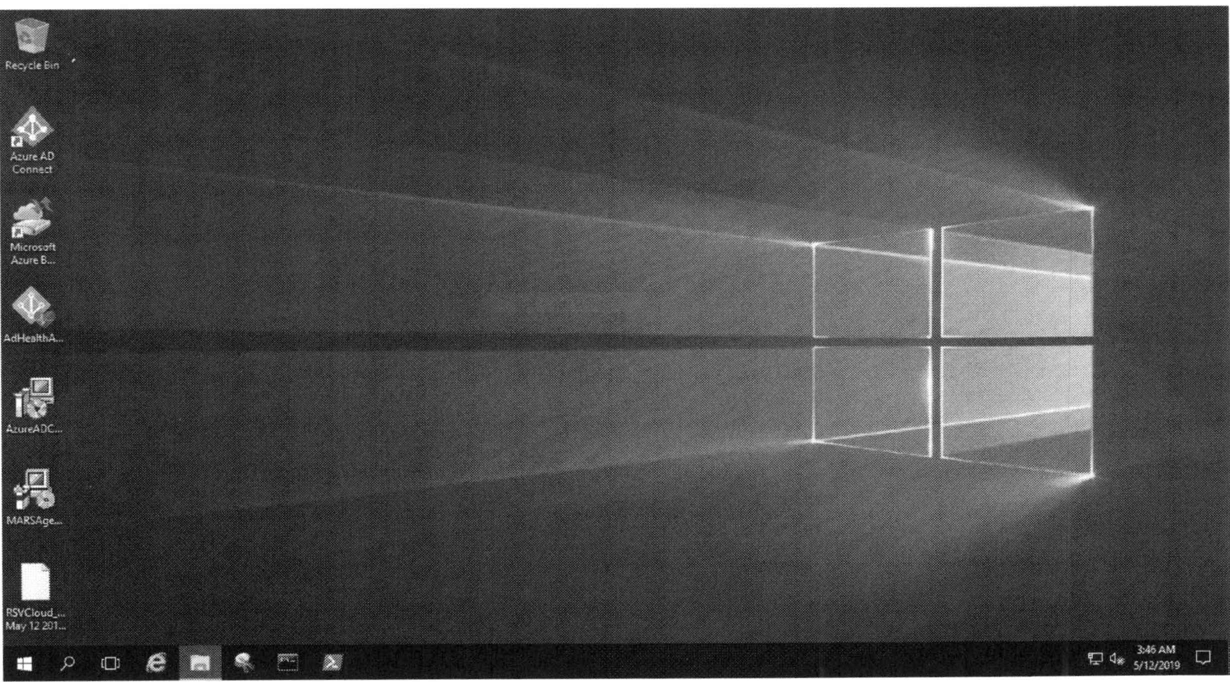

9. **Create a Backup Schedule & Select Backup items**. Open the Microsoft Azure Backup agent in VMAD>Click Action> Click schedule backup> Schedule Backup Wizard opens>Click Next> In Select Items to backup click Add items and select test folder created in step 2 and click ok> and for rest select all default values by clicking next> Click Finish>Click close.

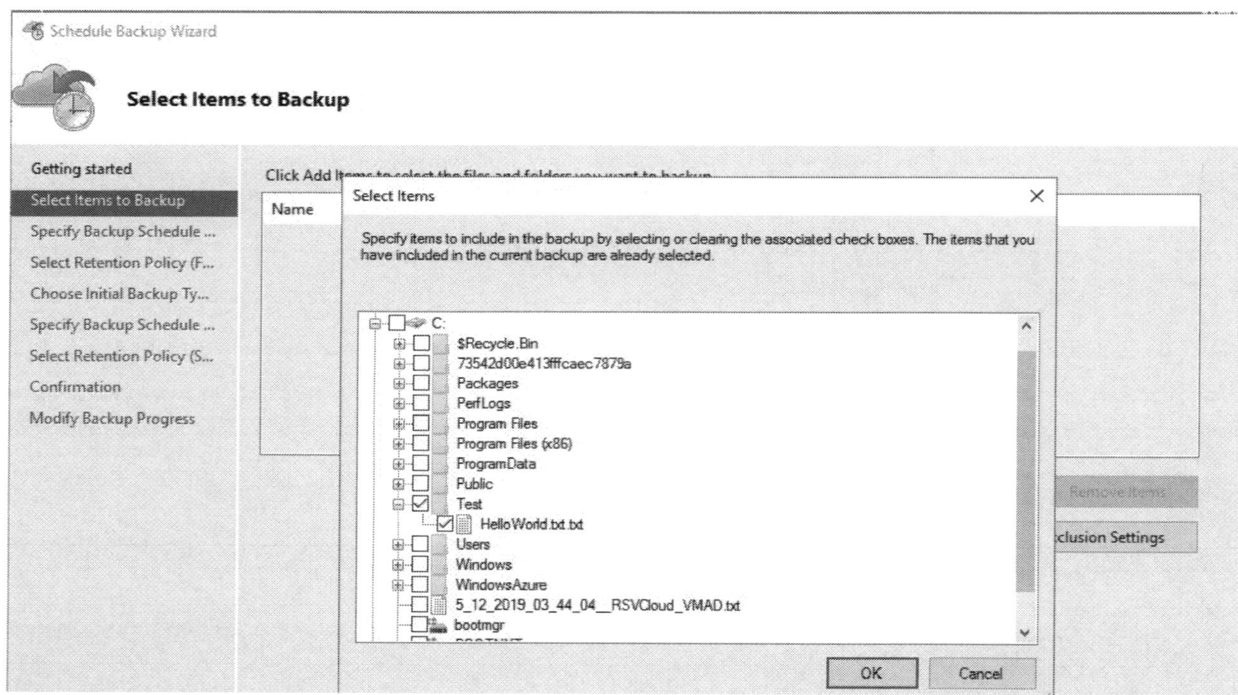

10. **To back up files and folders for the first time immediately** >open Microsoft Azure Backup Agent>Action>Backup now>Select Files & Folder and click next>On confirmation page click back up (Not Shown)> Monitor the progress in agent console> Click close when backup is completed.

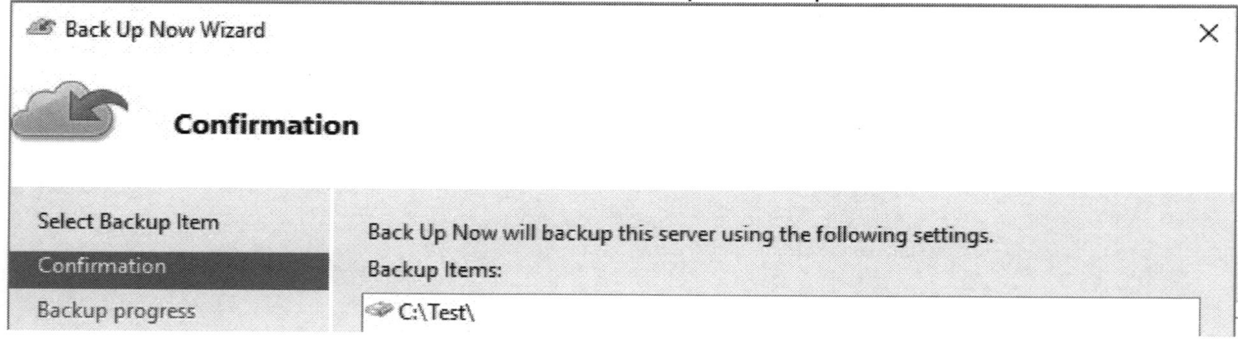

11. Once the backup is completed go the Recovery Services Vault RSVCloud Dashboard> Click Backup Items in left pane> Here you can see Backup Item Count against Azure Backup Agent.

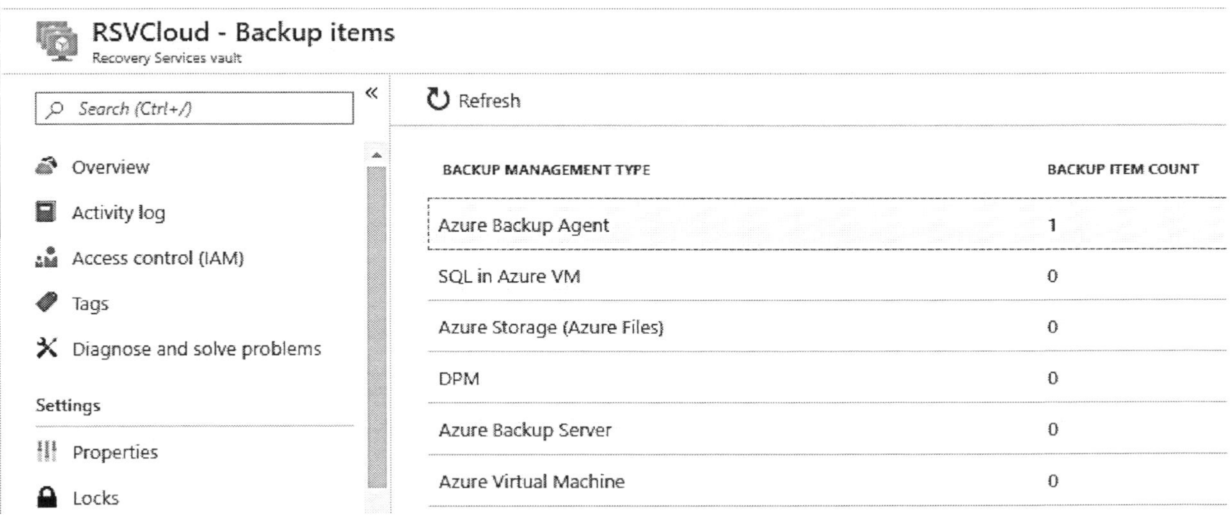

12. Click Azure Backup Agent and and Backup Items pane opens and you can see the backup is complete.

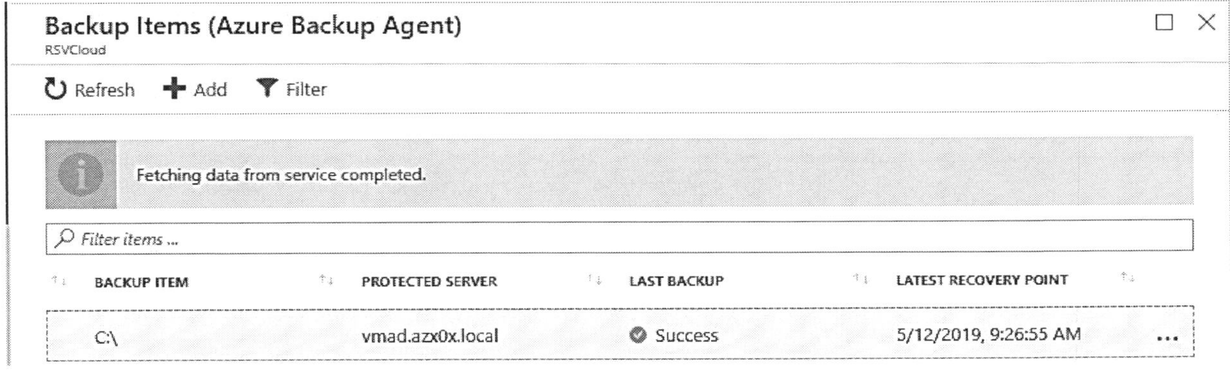

Backup Reports

Azure Backup reports are supported for Azure virtual machine backup and Azure Recovery Services Backup Agent option.

Requirement for Creating Backup Reports

Azure Storage Account: Storage account is used to store reports-related data.
Power BI account: Power BI account is used to view, customize and create reports by using the Power BI portal.

Create Backup Reports

In Recovery Services Vault Dashboard click Backup Reports in left pane> Backup Report pane opens. Enable diagnostic settings and select logs according to your requirement. You have the option to view reports Graphically in Power BI.

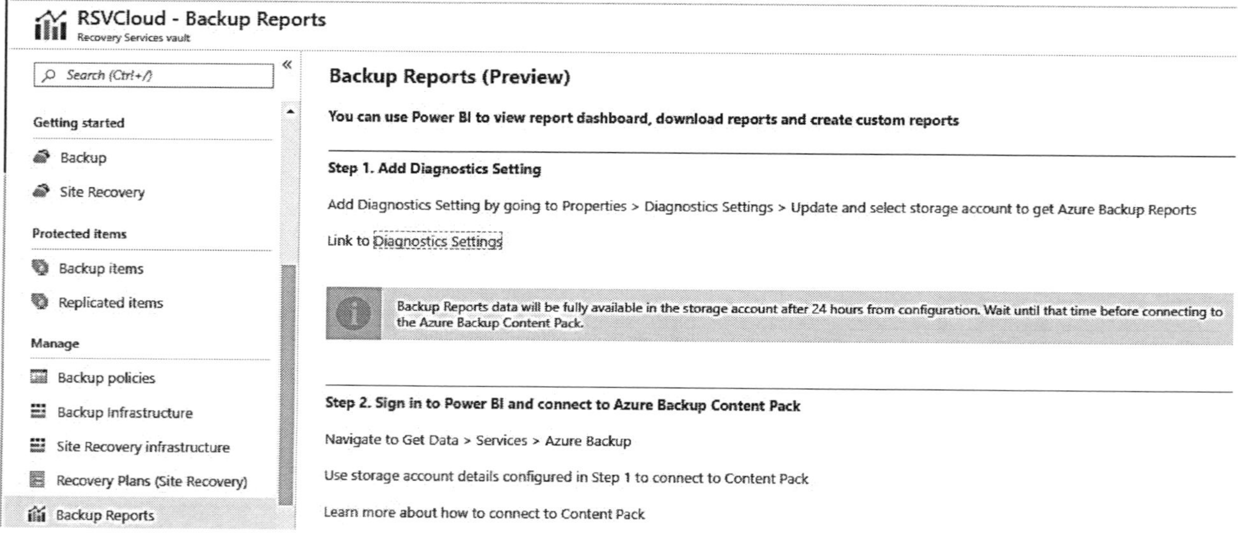

Azure Backup Pricing

Azure Backup pricing consist of 2 factors.

1. Size of the backed-up data of an instance.
2. Azure Storage consumed.

SIZE OF EACH INSTANCE	AZURE BACKUP PRICE PER MONTH
Instance < or = 50 GB	$5 + storage consumed
Instance is > 50 but < or = 500 GB	$10 + storage consumed
Instance > 500 GB	$10 for each 500 GB increment + storage consumed

Backup Storage Pricing

Azure Backup uses Block Blob storage for backing up your instances. You have the option to choose between locally redundant storage (LRS) or geo-redundant storage (GRS) for Recovery Services Vault.

LRS	GRS
$0.0224 per GB	$0.0448 per GB

Case Study 14: Backup of Azure VM with Managed Disk

You have an Azure VM with Managed Disk. Managed Disk are replicated locally with LRS Replication option.

Application team has given following requirements:

1. Application team wants periodic Backup to be taken to safeguard from VM level or DataCenter wide outage.

2. They also want that backup should be replicated to different region for safeguarding from regional disasters.

Suggest a solution to satisfy above requirements.

Solution

We will use Azure Backup Solution using VM level Backup. VM level Backup is integrated in Azure VM Dashboard.

Following will be implemented as part of the solution:

1. We will create Recovery Service Vault with Geo-Redundant option. This will ensure that Backup is replicated to different region.
   Note: Geo-Redundant Option is the default option when you create Recovery Service Vault.

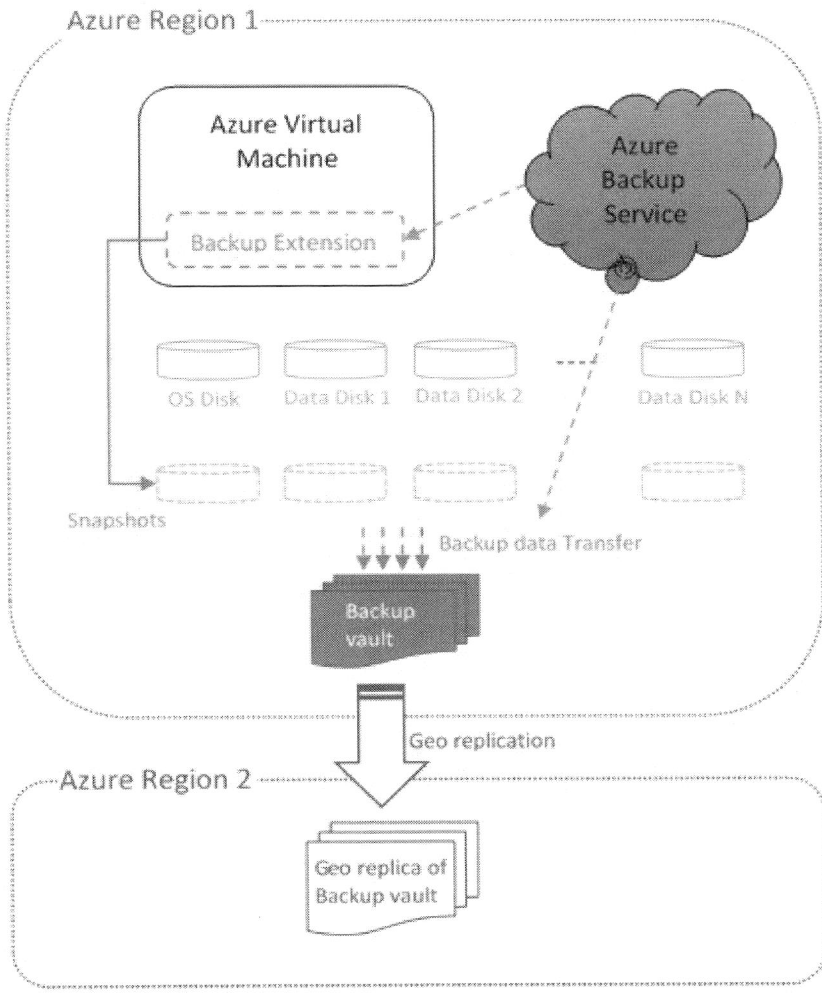

2. We will use Backup option in VM dashboard to Create the Backup.

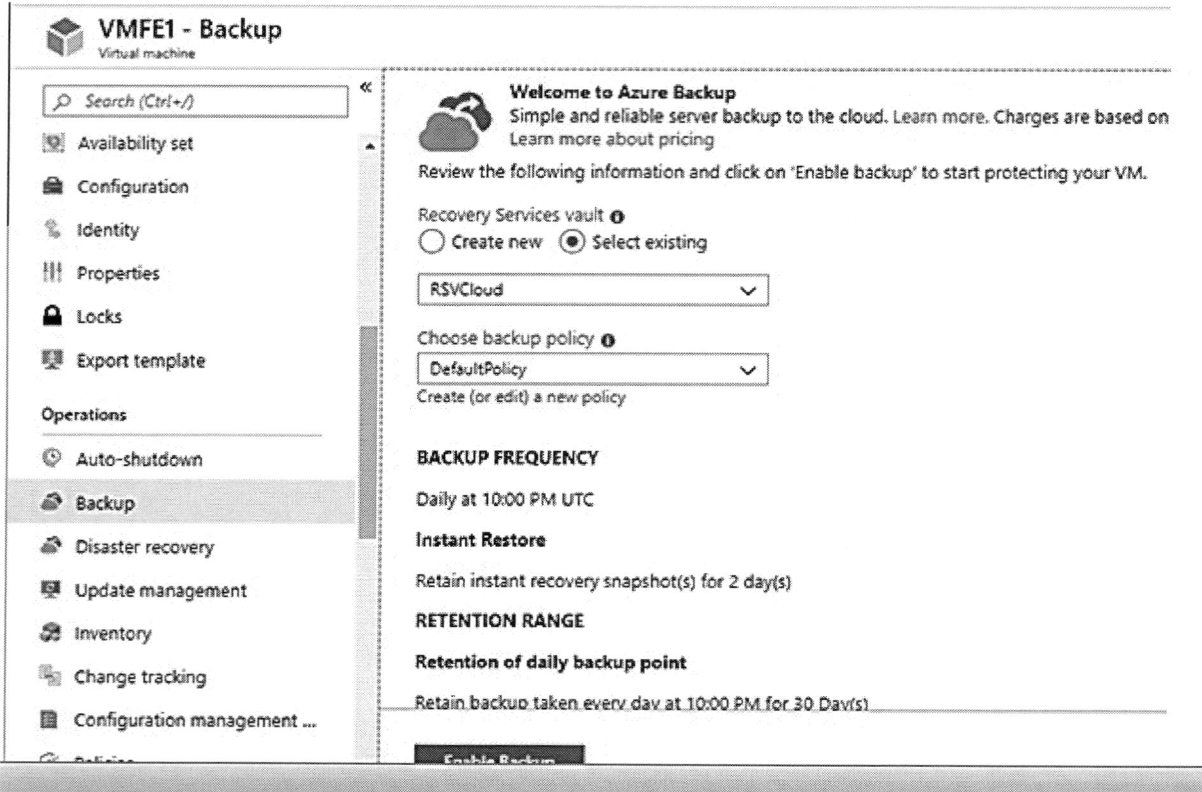

Important Note: MS recommends that Recovery Services Vault (RSV) should be created in a different region than the source VM. In above case RSV is in the same region as source VM but we have chosen Geo-Redundant Storage option with RSV which replicated Backup to another region.

Case Study 15: Backup of Azure VM with Managed Disk

You have an Azure VM with Managed Disk. Managed Disk are replicated locally with LRS Replication option.

Application team has given following requirements:

1. Application team wants periodic Backup to be taken to safeguard from VM level or DataCenter wide outage or regional outage.
2. They also want that backup of VM should be in different region.
3. To save on cost they want to use locally redundant storage (LRS) with recovery services vault.

Suggest a solution to satisfy above requirements.

Solution

We will use Azure Backup Solution using VM level Backup. VM level Backup is integrated in Azure VM Dashboard.

Following will be implemented as part of the solution:

1. We will create Recovery Service Vault with Geo-Redundant option which is default option in Region which is different from source VM.
2. From Recovery Service Vault dashboard we will change the Backup configuration from Geo-Redundant to Locally- Redundant.
3. We will then use Backup option in VM dashboard to Create the Backup.

Note: Paired Region concept will be discussed in next Chapter and Chapter 20.

Case Study 16: Backup of Folder in Azure VM

You have an Azure Windows VM which has important Files stored in a Folder. Folder is created under C drive. Azure VM has Managed Disk

Application team has given following requirements:

1. Application team wants daily Backup of folder.

2. They also want that backup should be replicated to different region for safeguarding from regional disasters.

Suggest a solution to satisfy above requirements.

Solution

We will use **Azure Backup Agent (Mars) option** to take backup of folder in Azure Windows VM.

Following will be implemented as part of the solution:

1. We will create Recovery Service Vault with Geo-Redundant option. This will ensure that Backup is replicated to different region.
2. Using Recovery Services Vault Dashboard we will download and Install Azure Backup Agent on Azure Windows VM.
3. We will open **Azure Backup Agent (Mars)** in the Azure Windows VM to configure the Backup Process to backup folder on Azure Windows VM.

Chapter 11 Azure Site Recovery (ASR)

This Chapter covers following

- Azure Site Recovery
- Replication scenarios with Azure Site Recovery
- Disaster Recovery Site option with Azure Site Recovery
- Architecture for Disaster Recovery to Azure
- Architecture for Disaster Recovery to Secondary Data Center
- RPO & RTO
- Replication Architecture of Azure VMs in Azure Cloud to Azure Cloud
- Replication Architecture of VMware VMs or Physical Servers to Azure
- Replication Architecture of Hyper-V VMs Managed by VMM to Azure
- Replication Architecture of Hyper-V VMs to Azure
- Replication Architecture of Hyper-V VMs Managed by VMM to Secondary Datacenter
- Azure Site Recovery Pricing

This Chapter Covers following Lab Exercises to build below topology

- Enabling Disaster Recovery for Azure VM using Azure Site Recovery
- Demonstration of Failover of VM VMAD

This Chapter covers following Case Studies

- DR for Azure VM

Chapter Topology

In this chapter we will add ASR to the topology which is part of Backup and Site Recovery.

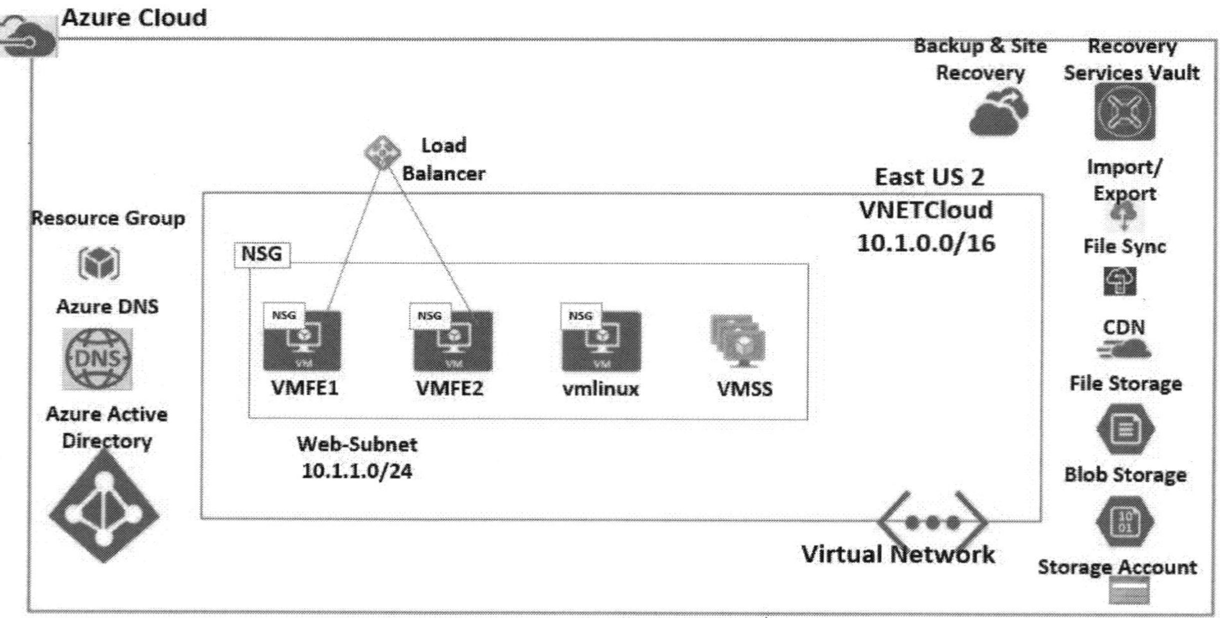

We will replicate VM VMAD in West US 2 region to East US 2 region using ASR. Site Recovery Mobility Service Extension will get installed on VM VMAD when replication is enabled on VMAD.

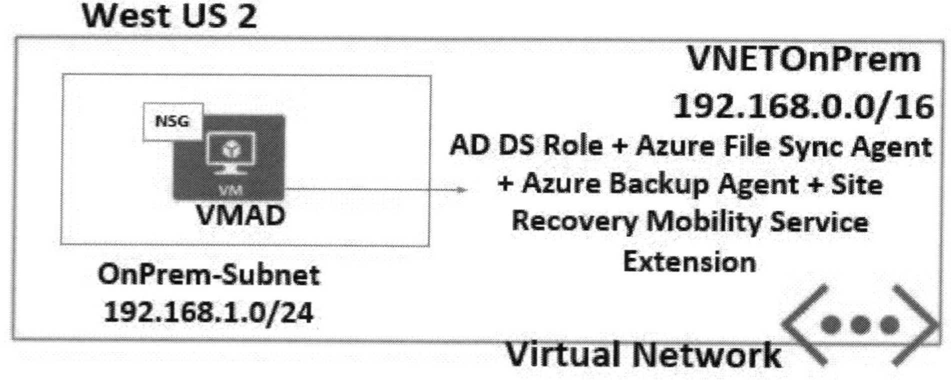

Azure Site Recovery

Azure Site Recovery provides Disaster Recovery as a Service (DRaaS).

Azure Site Recovery is an Azure Managed service that orchestrates and replicates Azure VMs and on-premises physical servers and virtual machines to the Azure cloud or to a secondary datacenter.

When outages occur in your primary location, you fail over to the secondary location to keep apps and workloads available. You fail back to your primary location when it returns to normal operations.

You can replicate Azure VMs in one Azure region to another Azure region.

You can replicate on-premises VMware VMs, Hyper-V VMs, Windows and Linux physical servers to Azure cloud or to a secondary datacenter.

Azure Recovery Services contribute to your BCDR strategy. The Azure Backup service keeps your data safe and recoverable. Site Recovery replicates, fails over, and recovers workloads when failure occurs.

Replication scenarios with Azure Site Recovery

Replicating Azure VMs in one region to another region in Azure Cloud: You can replicate Azure VMs from one Azure region to another Azure region.
Replicating on-premises VMs and Physical servers to Azure Cloud: You can replicate on-premises VMware VMs, Hyper-V VMs, Hyper-V VMs managed by SC VMM, Windows and Linux physical servers to Azure cloud.
Replicating to Secondary Data Center: You can replicate on-premises VMware VMs, Hyper-V VMs managed by VMM, Windows and Linux physical servers to Secondary Data Center. Note in this case we cannot replicate Hyper-V VMs to secondary Data Center.

Disaster Recovery Site option with Azure Site Recovery

1. Azure Cloud
2. Secondary Data Center (Non applicable for Azure VMs)

Architecture for Disaster Recovery to Azure

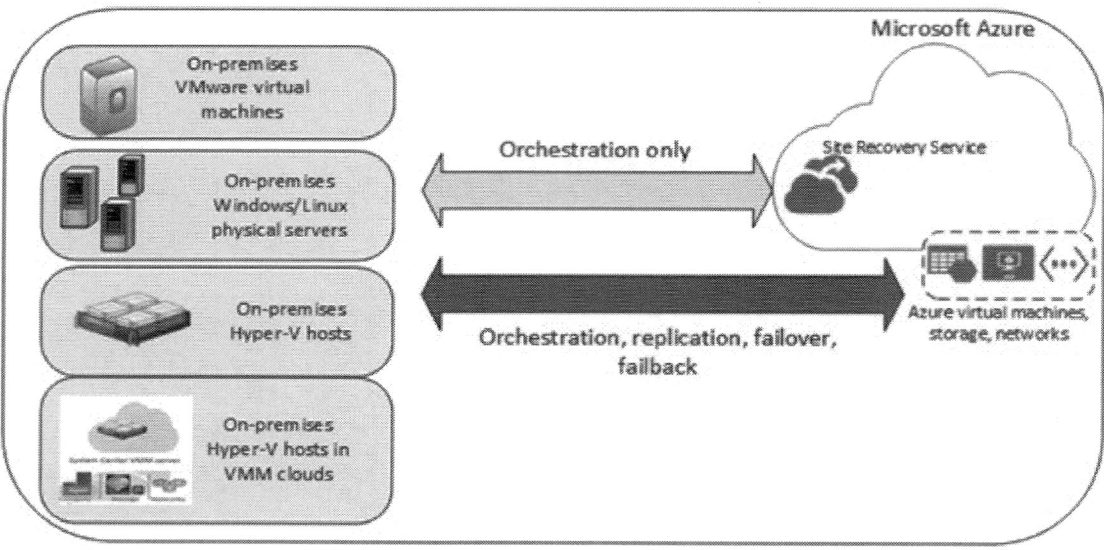

ON-PREMISES DATACENTER TO AZURE

Architecture for Disaster Recovery to Secondary Data Center

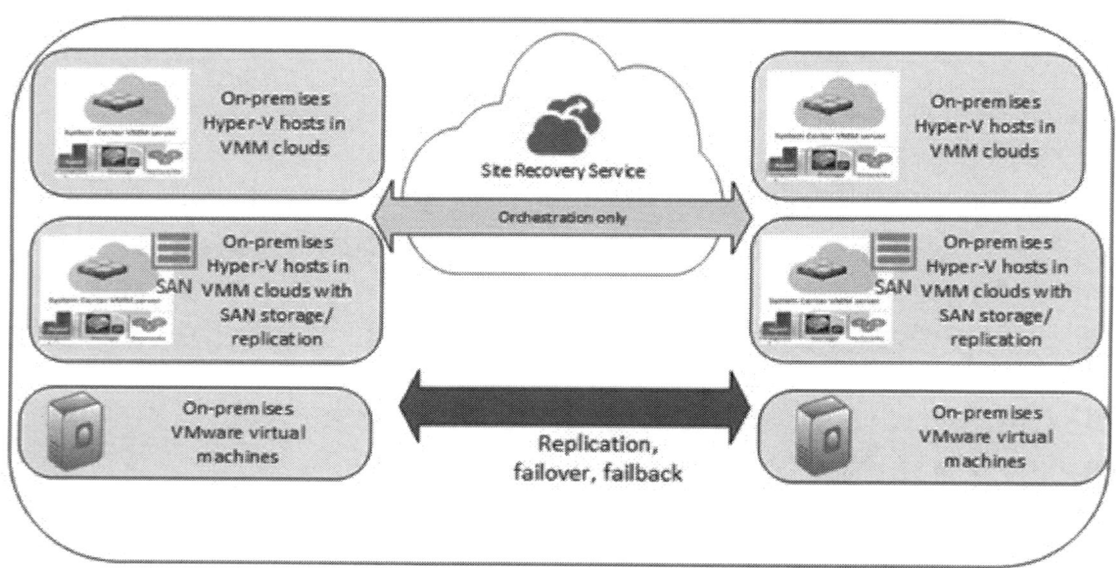

ON-PREMISES DATACENTER TO ON-PREMISES DATACENTER

RPO & RTO

Recovery Point Objective (RPO) and Recovery Time Objective (RTO) are two of the most important parameters of a disaster recovery or data protection plan.

Recovery Point Objective (RPO)

Recovery point objectives refer to amount of data that can be lost before significant harm to the business occurs. The objective is expressed as a time measurement from the loss event to the most recent backup.

For Example if you have a 4 hour RPO for an application then you will have a maximum 4 hour gap between backup and data loss. Lets further clarify it. You have taken backup of Data at 3 PM. Next backup is at 7 PM. If the disaster Strikes between 3 PM and 7 PM then Maximun Data loss you will have will be between 0-4 hours depending upon the time of disaster. If disaster happens at 4 PM then you will have 1 hour of Data Loss. If disaster happens at 6 PM then you will have 3 hours of Data loss. If disaster happens just before 7 PM then you will have 4 hours of Data loss.

Depending upon your application and business pripority you need define RPO for your application. The less the RPO time more expensive will be the solution.

RPO can range from hours (24 to 12, to 8, to 4), Minutes and down to near-zero seconds.

For 8 Hour RPO you can use Backup solution.
For 2 Hour RPO you can use Snapshot replication.
For near zero second RPO you can use continuous replication.

If you application require near zero second RPO and RTO then you need to use continuous replication (For Data) and Server Failover Service such as Load Balancer or Clustering (For Application switchover to another server).

Recovery Time Objective (RTO)

The Recovery Time Objective (RTO) is the duration of time within which application must be restored in working condition after a disaster. RTO is not just recovery of Application. RTO accounts for the steps IT must take to restore the application and its data for use by end users.

For near zero second RTO you can use Server Failover Service such as Load Balancer or Clustering (For Application switchover to another server).

For 4 Hour RTO you can do re installation of application on bare metal server or on Virtual Machine.

If you application require near zero second RPO and RTO then you need to use continuous replication (For Data) and Server Failover Service such as Load Balancer or Clustering (For Application switchover to another server).

Replication Architecture of VMware VMs or Physical Servers to Azure

Replicate VMs located on-premises VMware hosts managed by vCenter to Azure Storage. vCenter is not compulsory but it is recommended.

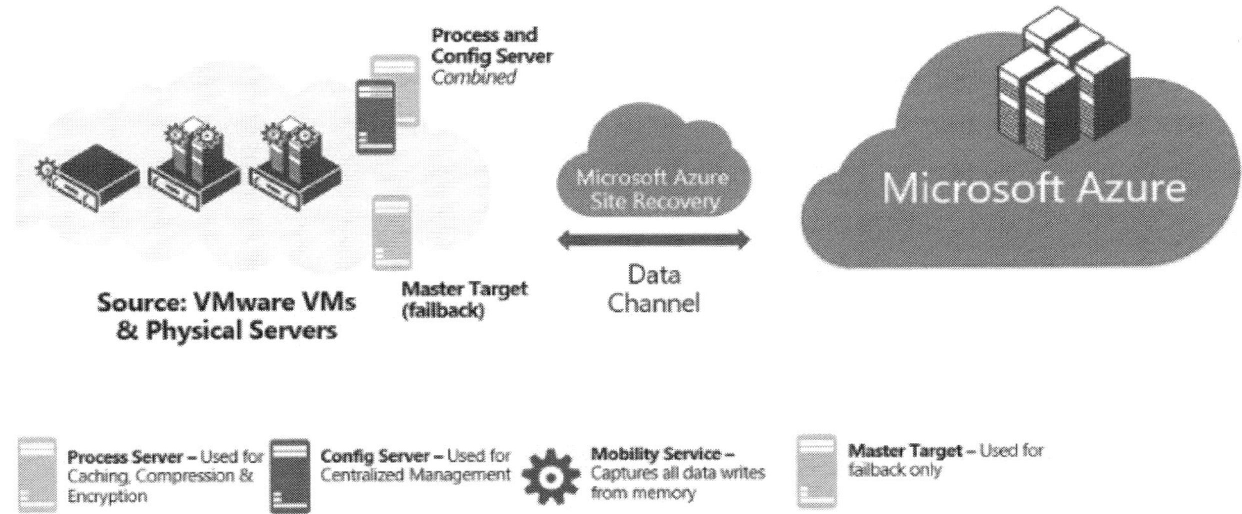

Requirements on Azure Side

1. **Storage Account:** You need an Azure storage account to store replicated data. Azure VMs are created from Replicated data when failover occurs.
2. **Virtual Network:** You need an Azure virtual network that Azure VMs will connect to when they're created at failover.
3. **Recovery Services Vault.**

Requirements on-premises side

1. **Configuration Server**: Coordinates communications between on-premises and Azure and manages data replication.
2. **Process server**: It receives replication data from VMware Virtual Machines or Physical Servers and optimizes it with caching, compression, and encryption and sends it to Azure Storage. Installed by default on the configuration server.
3. **Master target server**: It handles replication data during failback from Azure. For large deployments, you can add an additional, separate master target server for failback. Installed by default on the configuration server.
4. **Mobilty Service**: Mobility Service captures all data writes on VMware virtual machine and Physical Server and sends it to Process Server. Mobility Service is installed on each VMware VM and Physical Server that you replicate.

5. **VMware Virtual Machines with Mobility service Installed.**
6. **VMware ESXi Hosts and vCenter Server**: Requires vSphere 6.5, 6.0, or 5.5 and vCenter Server 6.5, 6.0, or 5.5.

Replication Process

VMware Virtual Machines replicate in accordance with the replication policy configured. Initial copy of the VM data is replicated to Azure Storage.

After initial replication finishes, replication of delta changes to Azure Storage begins.

1. VMware Machines send replication data to the process server using the Mobility service agent running on the VM.
2. The process server receives data from source machines, optimizes and encrypts it, and sends it to Azure Storage.
3. The configuration server orchestrates replication management with Azure.

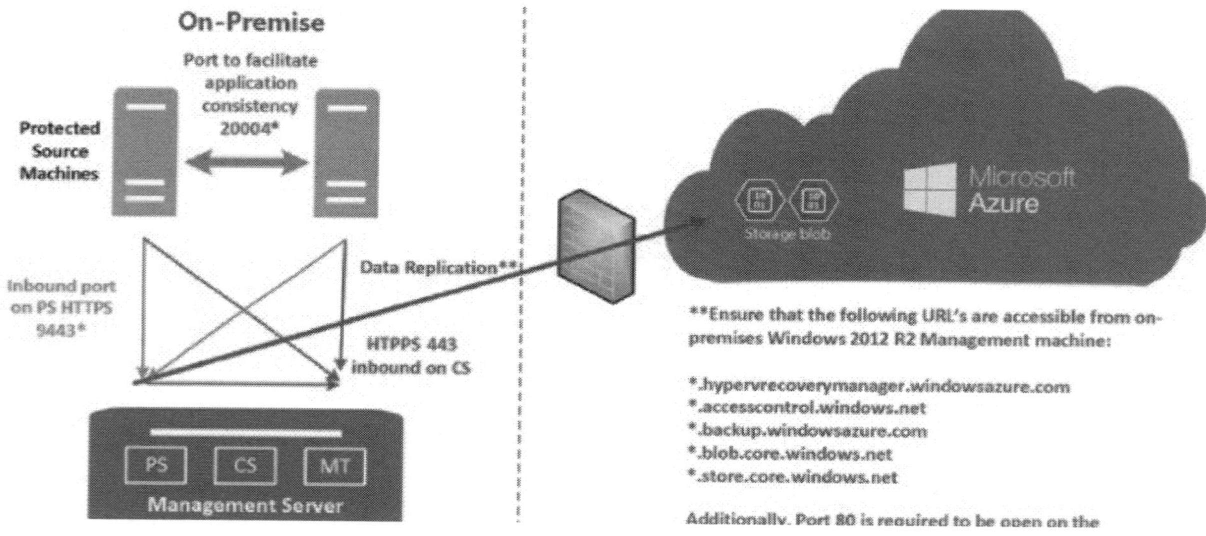

Testing Failover process

After replication is set up and you can run a disaster recovery drill (test failover) to check that everything's working as expected.

1. When you run a failover, Azure VMs are created from replicated data in Azure storage.
2. VMs are created in Virtual Network which was specified in Prepared Infrastructure –Target option.
3. You can fail over a single machine or use recovery plans to fail over multiple VMs.

Replication Architecture of Hyper-V VMs Managed by VMM to Azure

You can Replicate VMs located on-premises Hyper-V hosts managed by System Center Virtual Machine Manager (SC VMM) to Azure Storage. You can replicate Hyper-V VMs running any guest operating system supported by Hyper-V and Azure.

Figure below shows the Replication Architecture of Hyper-V VMs Managed by System Center VMM.

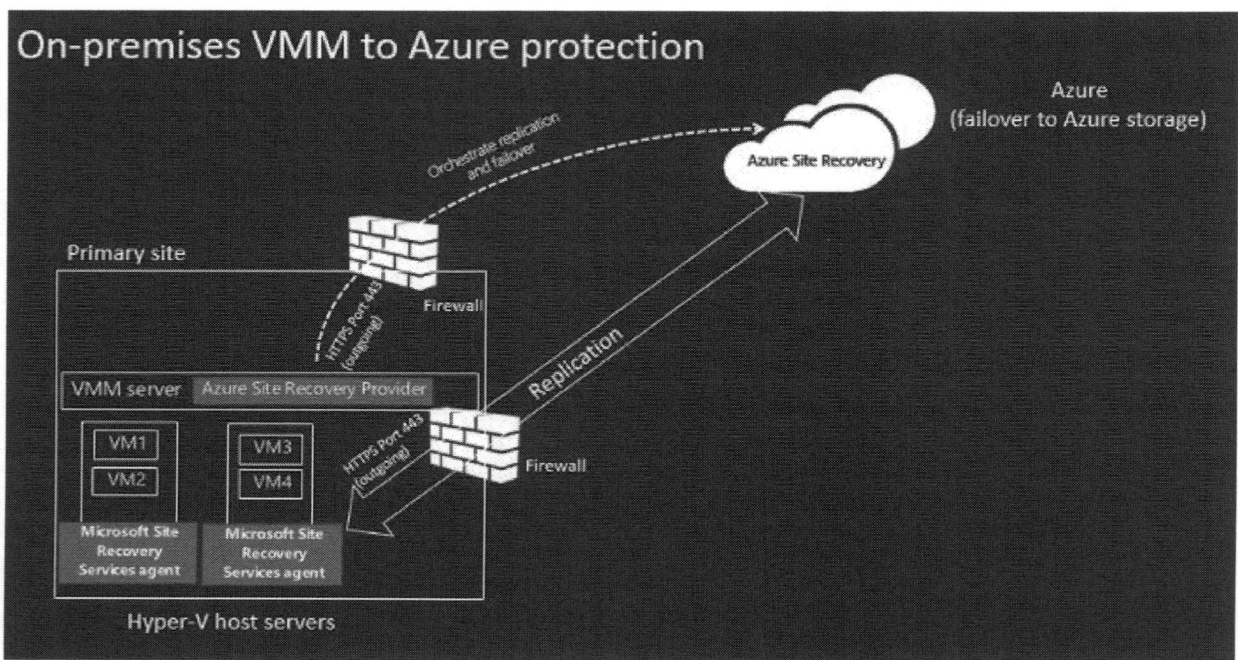

Requirements on Azure Side

1. **Storage Account:** You need an Azure storage account to store replicated data. Azure VMs are created from Replicated data when failover occurs.
2. **Virtual Network**: You need an Azure virtual network that Azure VMs will connect to when they're created at failover.
3. **Recovery Services Vault.**

Requirements on-premises side

1. **SC VMM**: You need one or more on-premises VMM servers running System Center VMM 2012 R2 with Azure Site Recovery Provider Installed.
2. **Hyper-V host**: You need one or more Windows Server 2016 or Windows Server 2012 R2 Hyper-V host server. During Site Recovery deployment you'll install the Microsoft Azure Recovery Services agent on the host.
3. **Azure Site Recovery Provider (Installed on VMM)**: The Provider coordinates and orchestrates replication with the Site Recovery service over the internet.
4. **Azure Recovery Service Agent (Installed on Hyper-V host)**: The agent handles data replication data over HTTPS 443. Communications from both the Provider and the agent are secure and encrypted. Replicated data in Azure storage is also encrypted.

Replication Process

Virtual Machines replicate in accordance with the replication policy configured. Initial copy of the VM Hard disk is replicated to Azure Storage.

After initial replication finishes, replication of delta changes in VM to Azure Storage begins.

1. When initial replication is triggered, a Hyper-V VM snapshot is taken.
2. Azure Recovery Service Agent replicates Virtual hard disks of the VM one by one, until they're all copied to Azure.
3. When the initial replication finishes, the VM snapshot is deleted.
4. After the initial replication, delta replication begins, in accordance with the replication policy.
5. Azure Site Recovery Provider (Installed on VMM) orchestrates replication management with Azure.

Failover and failback process

You can run a planned or unplanned failover from on-premises Hyper-V VMs to Azure. If you run a planned failover, then source VMs are shut down to ensure no data loss. Run an unplanned failover if your primary site isn't accessible.

1. You can fail over a single machine, or create recovery plans, to orchestrate failover of multiple machines.
2. You run a failover. After the first stage of failover completes, you should be able to see the created replica VMs in Azure. You can assign a public IP address to the VM if required.
3. You then commit the failover, to start accessing the workload from the replica Azure VM.

Replication Architecture of Hyper-V VMs to Azure

You can Replicate VMs located on-premises Hyper-V hosts to Azure Storage. You can replicate Hyper-V VMs running any guest operating system supported by Hyper-V and Azure.

Figure below shows the Replication Architecture of Hyper-V VMs to Azure Cloud.

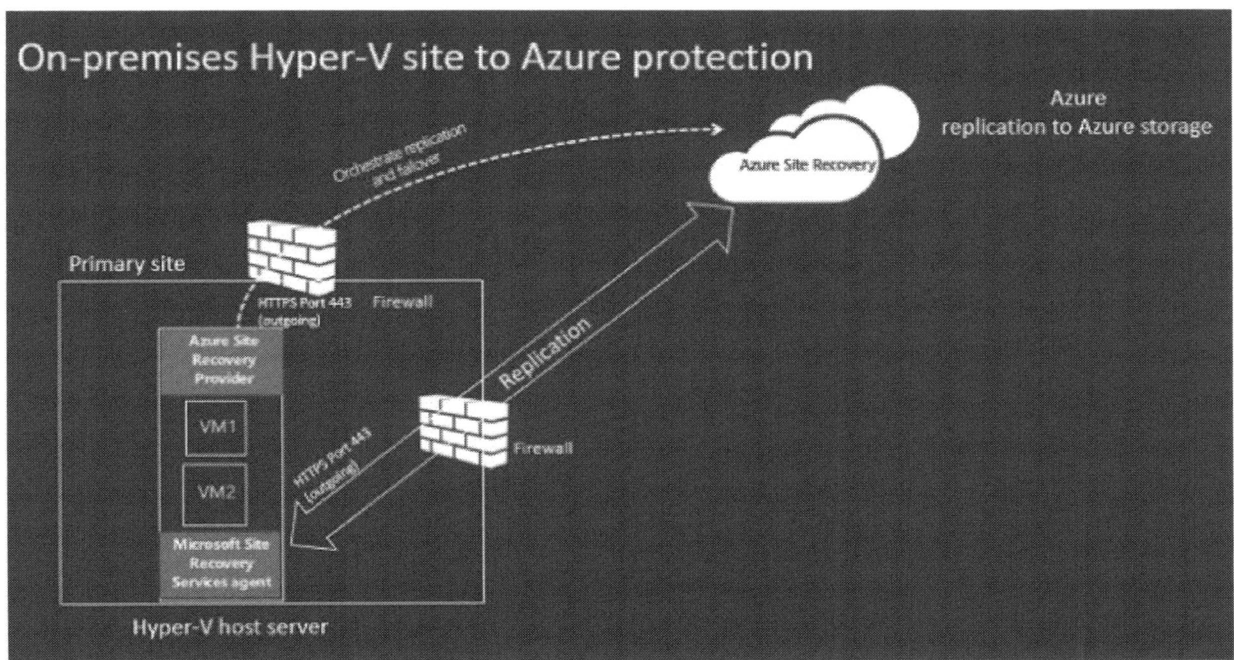

Requirements on Azure Side

1. Storage Account: You need an Azure storage account to store replicated data. Azure VMs are created from Replicated data when failover occurs.
2. Virtual Network: You need an Azure virtual network that Azure VMs will connect to when they're created at failover.
3. Recovery Services Vault.

Requirements on-premises side

1. **Hyper-V host**: You need one or more Windows Server 2016 or Windows Server 2012 R2 Hyper-V host server. Azure Recovery Services agent and Azure Site Recovery Provider will be installed on Hyper-V host.
2. **Azure Site Recovery Provider (Installed on Hyper-V host)**: The Provider coordinates and orchestrates replication with the Site Recovery service over the internet.

3. **Azure Recovery Service Agent (Installed on Hyper-V host)**: The agent handles data replication data over HTTPS 443. Communications from both the Provider and the agent are secure and encrypted. Replicated data in Azure storage is also encrypted.

Replication Process

Virtual Machines replicate in accordance with the replication policy configured. Initial copy of the VM Hard disk is replicated to Azure Storage.

After initial replication finishes, replication of delta changes in VM to Azure Storage begins.

1. When initial replication is triggered, a Hyper-V VM snapshot is taken.
2. Azure Recovery Service Agent replicates Virtual hard disks of the VM one by one, until they're all copied to Azure.
3. When the initial replication finishes, the VM snapshot is deleted.
4. After the initial replication, delta replication begins, in accordance with the replication policy.
5. Azure Site Recovery Provider (Installed on Hyper-V host) orchestrates replication management with Azure.

Failover and failback process

You can run a planned or unplanned failover from on-premises Hyper-V VMs to Azure. If you run a planned failover, then source VMs are shut down to ensure no data loss. Run an unplanned failover if your primary site isn't accessible.

1. You can fail over a single machine, or create recovery plans, to orchestrate failover of multiple machines.
2. You run a failover. After the first stage of failover completes, you should be able to see the created replica VMs in Azure. You can assign a public IP address to the VM if required.
3. You then commit the failover, to start accessing the workload from the replica Azure VM.

Replication Architecture of Hyper-V VMs Managed by SC VMM to Secondary Data Center

You can Replicate VMs located on-premises Hyper-V hosts managed by System Center Virtual Machine Manager (SC VMM) to secondary data center.

Figure below shows the Replication Architecture of Hyper-V VMs managed by VMM to Secondary Data Center.

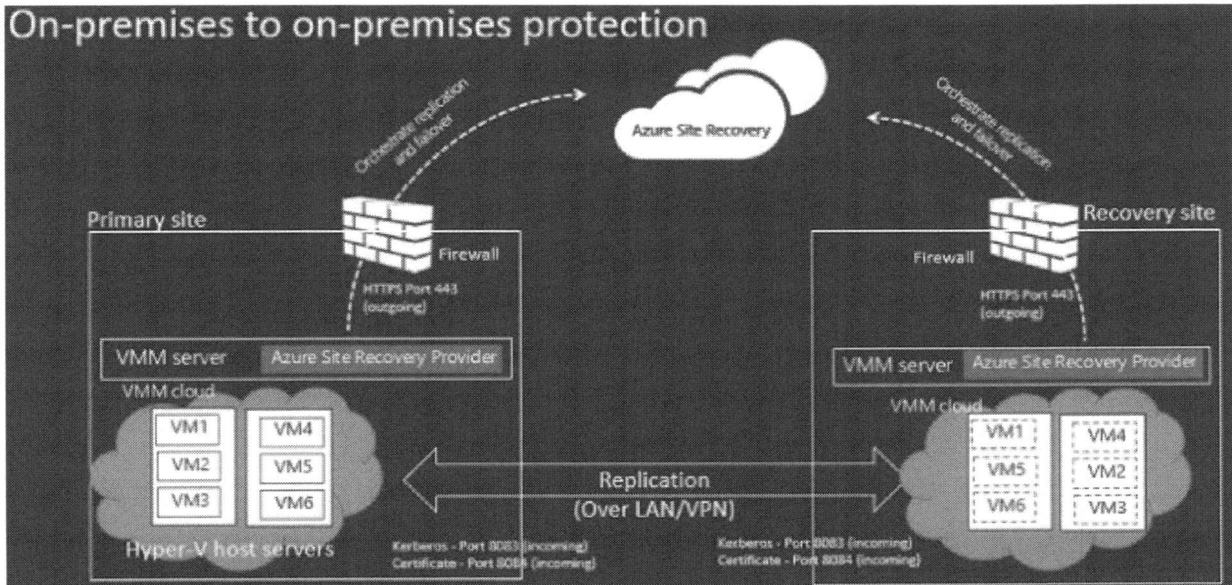

Requirements on Azure Side

1. Recovery Services Vault.

Requirements on-premises side

1. **VMM Server**: You need VMM server in both primary and secondary location.
2. **Hyper-V host**: You need one or more Hyper-V host server (Windows Server 2016 or 2012 R2) in both primary and secondary Datacenter. Azure Site Recovery Provider will be installed on Hyper-V host.
3. **Azure Site Recovery Provider (Installed on VMM Server)**: The Provider coordinates and orchestrates replication with the Site Recovery service over the internet.

Replication Architecture of Azure VMs in Azure Cloud to Azure Cloud

You can replicate Azure VMs from one Azure region to another Azure region using Azure Site Recovery. Biggest advantage of this option is that ASR is integrated in the VM dashboard.
Figure below shows Azure to Azure replication architecture.

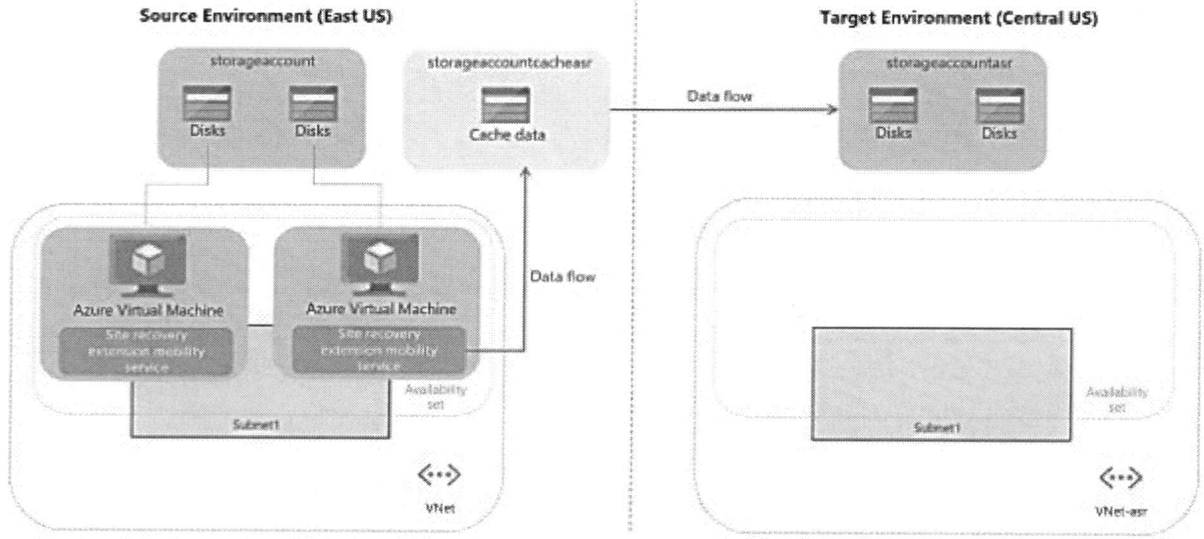

Requirements on Source Side

1. **Cache storage accounts:** Before source VM changes are replicated to a target storage account, they are tracked and sent to the cache storage account in source location.
2. **Site Recovery extension Mobility service**: Mobility Service captures all data writes on VM disks and transfers it to Cache Storage Account.

Requirements on Target Side

Target resource group: The resource group to which Source VMs are replicated.
Target virtual network: The virtual network in which replicated VMs are located after failover. A network mapping is created between source and target virtual networks, and vice versa.
Target storage accounts: Storage accounts in the target location to which the data is replicated.
Target availability sets: Availability sets in which the replicated VMs are located after failover.

Replication Process

The Site Recovery Mobility service extension is automatically installed on the VM when you enable replication for an Azure VM.

1. The extension registers the VM with Site Recovery.
2. **Continuous replication** begins for the VM. Disk writes are immediately transferred to the cache storage account in the source location.
3. Site Recovery processes the data in the cache, and sends it to the target Storage Account or to the replica managed disks.
4. After the data is processed, crash-consistent recovery points are generated every five minutes. App-consistent recovery points are generated according to the setting specified in the replication policy.

Failover process

When you initiate a failover, the VMs are created in the target resource group, target virtual network, target subnet, and in the target availability set. During a failover, you can use any recovery point.

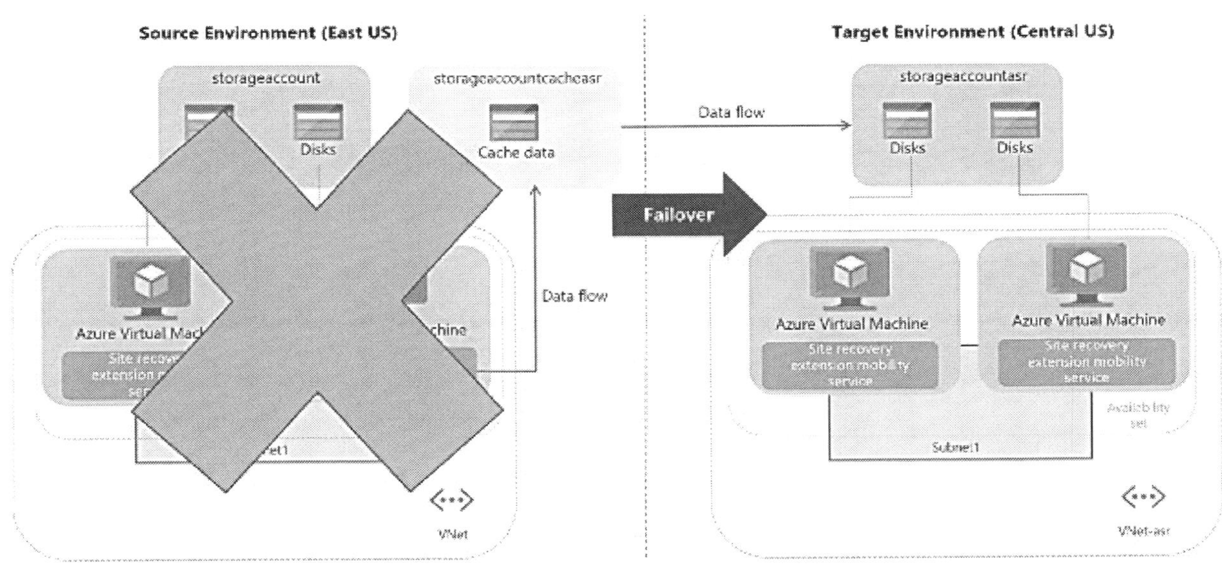

Exercise 97: Enabling Disaster Recovery (DR) for Azure VM using ASR

In this exercise we will enable DR for VMAD in West US 2 Location to East US 2. Azure VM VMAD was created in Exercise 39, Chapter 4.

1. In Azure Portal go to VM VMAD dashboard>click Disaster Recovery in left pane> Configure Disaster Recovery blade opens>For Target Region select region as per your requirement. Here I selected East US 2.

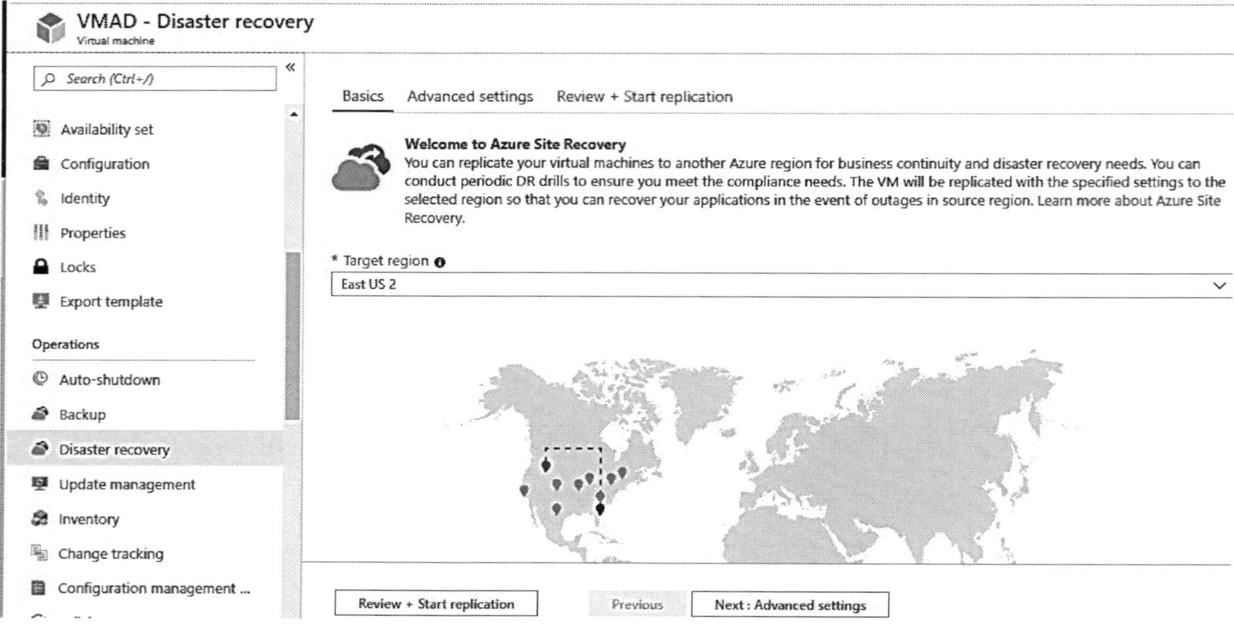

2. Click Next: Advanced settings> Here you can either select system created Resource Group and Virtual Network or Select Pre Created RG and VNET. I selected System Created Resource Group and Virtual Network> I selected System Created Cache Storage Account >In Replication Settings I selected Recovery Service Vault RSVCloud. RSVCloud was created in Exercise 76, Chapter 7> Select default values for Extension settings.

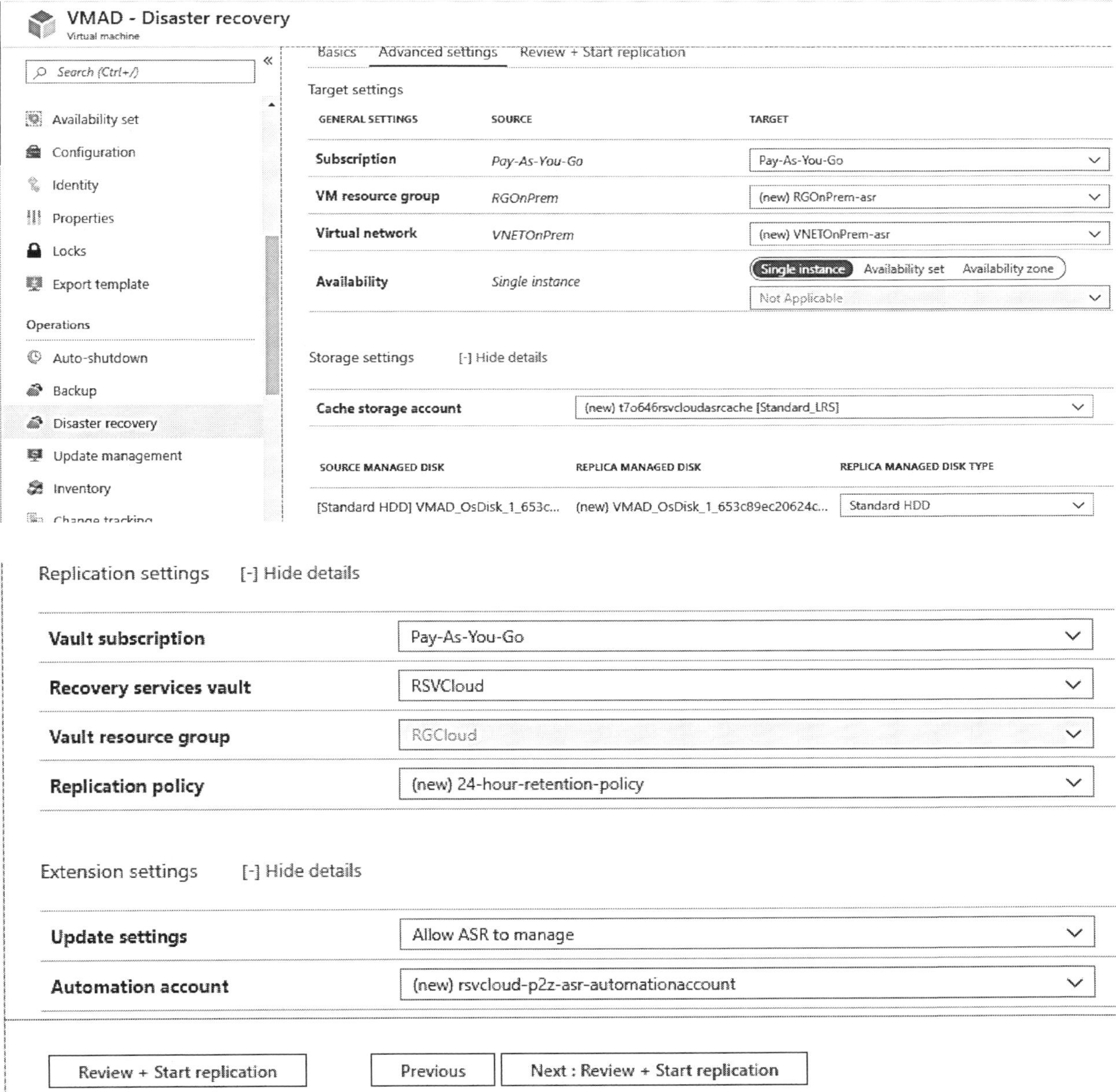

3. Click Next: Review + Start replication. Review the settings and click Start Replication. Deployment starts in the target region. First System created resources are created in target region and then replication starts for VMAD to target region.

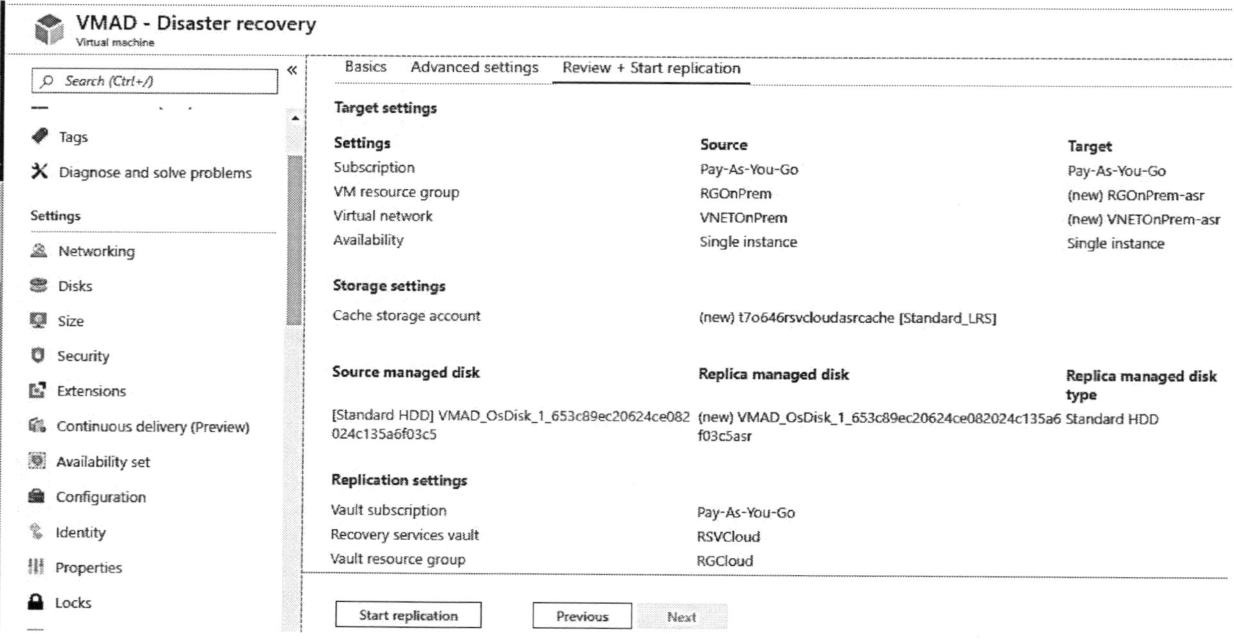

4. Go to Recovery Services Vault dashboard and click replicated items. You can see Replication status as protected. I did this step after 45 minutes.

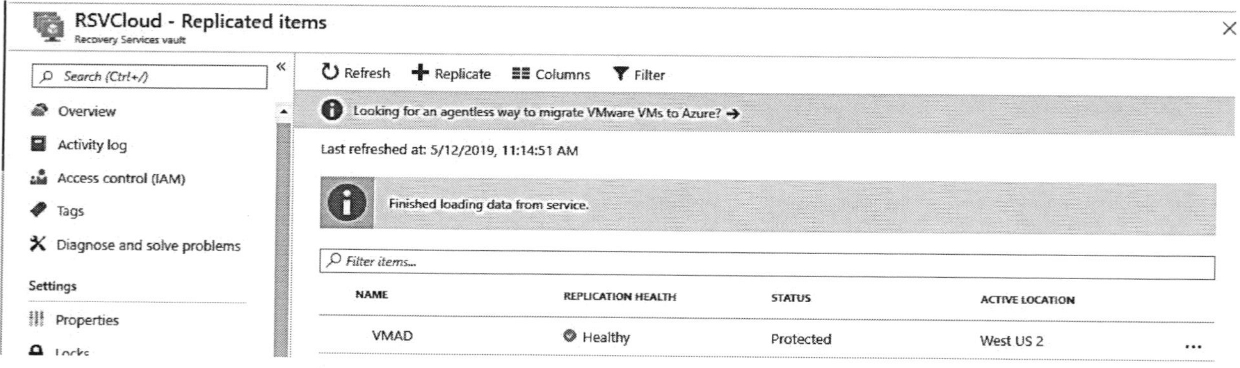

5. Go to System Created Resource Group RGOnPrem-asr Dashboard. You can see VMAD OS disk and System created Virtual Network in East US 2 location.

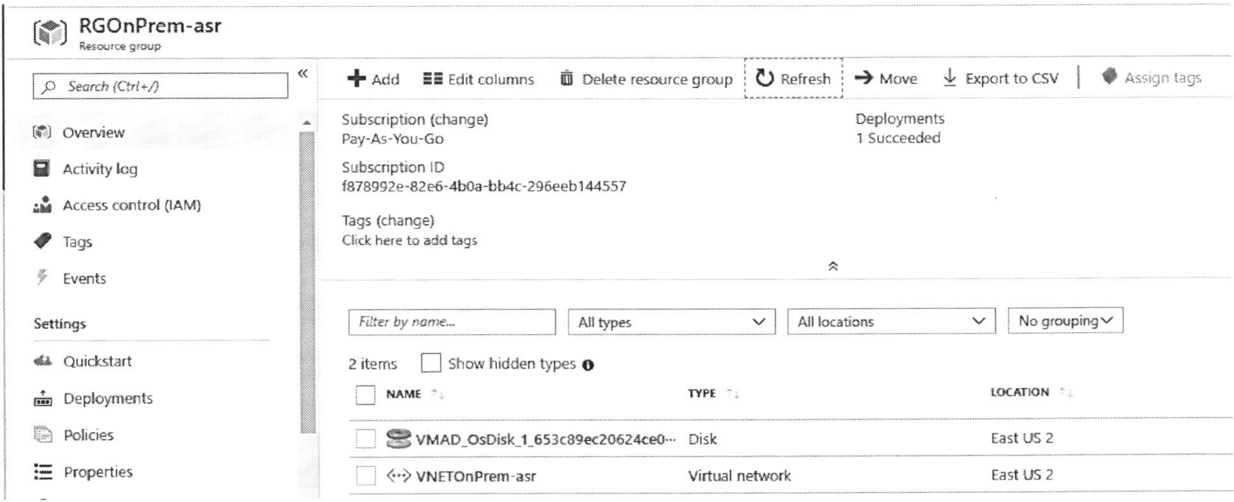

Exercise 98: Demonstration of Failover of VM VMAD

To Failover single VM or Multiple VMs individually you can go to Replicated Items in Recovery Services Vault dashboard.

To Failover Multiple VMs together you need create Recovery Plans where you can specify order of failover. You can Create Recovery Plans in Recovery Services Vault Dashboard by clicking Recovery Plans in left pane.

1. In Recovery Services Vault RSVCloud click Replicated Items in left pane.

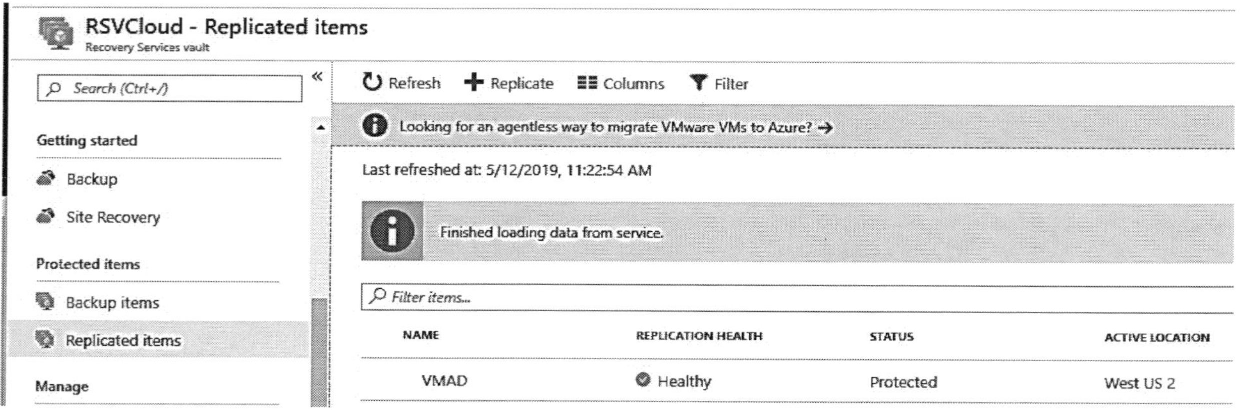

2. In Right pane click Item VMAD>Replicated Item Dashboard opens> From here you can failover VM or Test Failover.

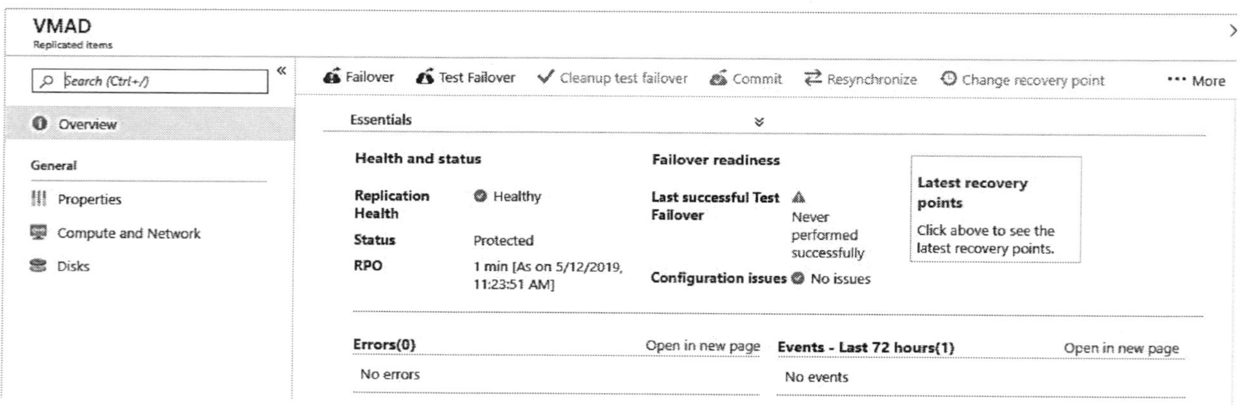

Note 1: Note the Compute and Network in left pane in above Figure. Using this you can customize networking configuration of Target VM.

Note: Disable the replication after the above exercise.

Customize networking configurations of the target Azure VM

With Azure Site Recovery, while configuring for disaster recovery for your virtual machines, you can also provide the input for corresponding network resources in the target, which will be honored at the time of failover. This takes away the complexities of having to deal with scripts or manual steps and reduces the RTO significantly. The service is also intelligent enough to allow selection of only those target resources that comply with the target virtual machine that will be created, thereby reducing the points of failover.

The following key resource configurations can be provided for the failover VM while replicating Azure VMs.

Internal Load Balancer
Public IP
Network Security Group both for the subnet and for the NIC

Customize failover networking configurations

In Recovery Services Vault Click Replicated Items>Select your VM which is being replicated> Click on **Compute and Network** and **Edit**. You can see the NIC configuration settings of Source and Target.

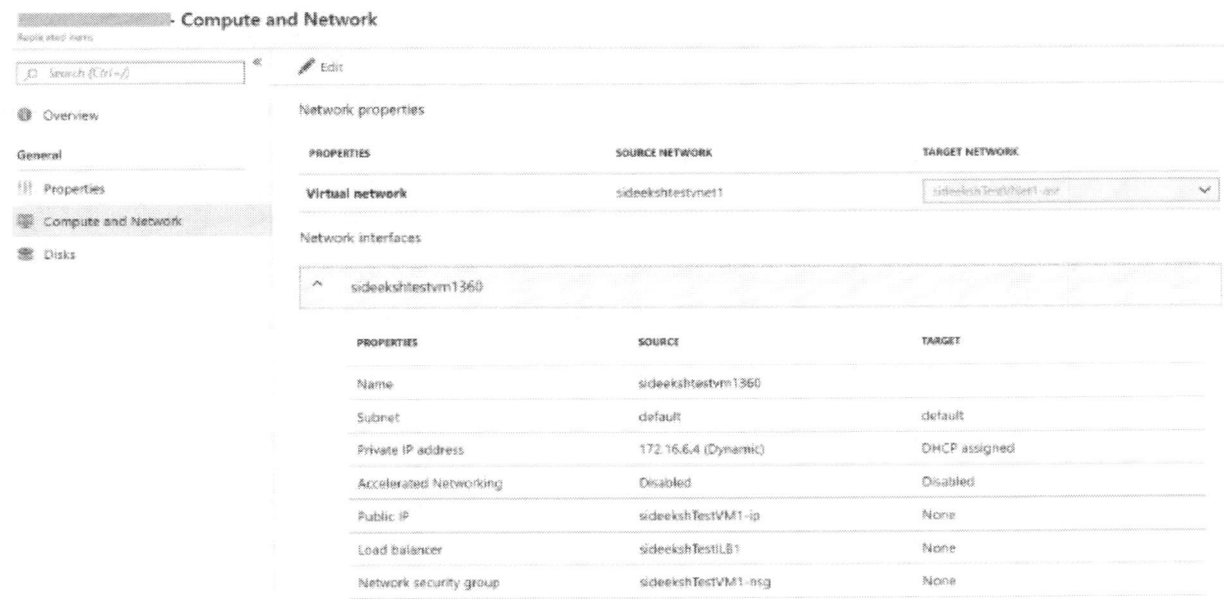

Click **Edit** near the NIC you want to configure. In the next blade that opens up, select the corresponding pre-created resources in the target.

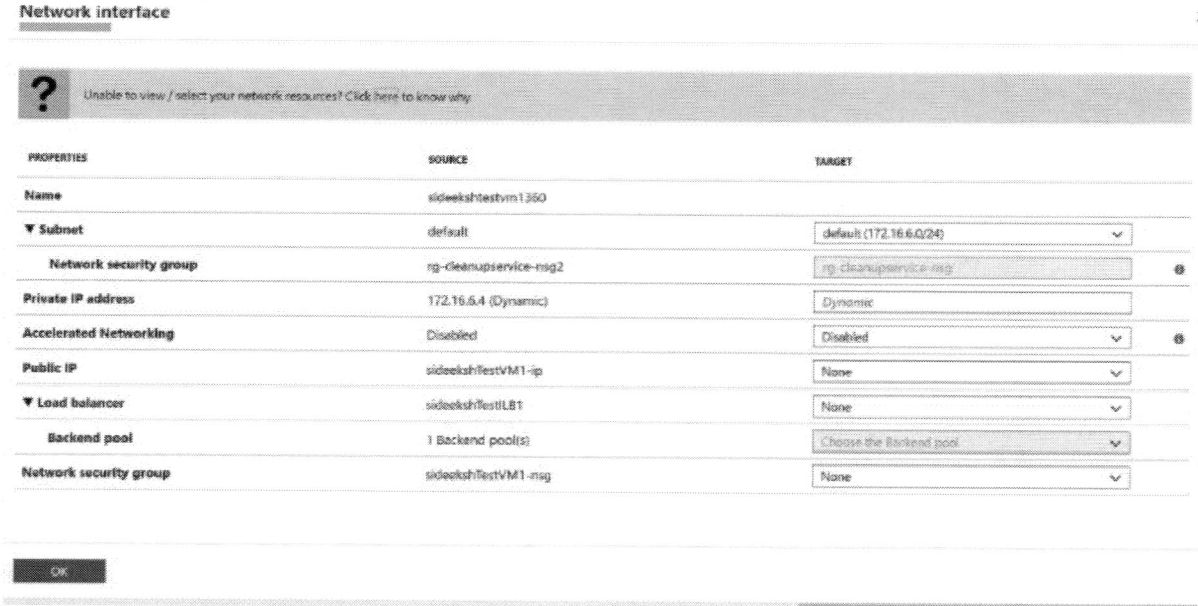

Important Note: I have taken above slides from Azure Docs as I had deleted the ASR configuration of Exercise 97 & 98.

Azure Site Recovery Pricing

Azure Site Recovery is billed based on number of instances protected.

	PRICE FOR FIRST 31 DAYS	PRICE AFTER 31 DAYS
Azure Site Recovery to customer owned sites	Free	$16/month/instance
Azure Site Recovery to Azure	Free	$25/month/instance

If you are replicating VMs to Azure, then you also will be charged for consumed storage and storage transactions.

If a failover occurred and protected VMs in Azure become active, then you also will be charged for consumed Compute resources.

Case Study 17: DR for Azure VM

You have a Azure VM with Managed Disk running in East US 2 Location. Managed Disk only supports LRS for replication.

Application team wants DR plan for Azure VM in the event of Datacenter wide outage or Regional outage.

Following requirement has been given by the application team.

1. In the event of disaster they want target Azure VM should be created in a different region than that of source VM.
2. They have specified a RTO and RPO of 15 minutes and 5 minutes respectively for the source Azure VM.

Suggest a solution which satisfies above requitement.

Solution

Requirement 2 specifies RTO and RPO of 15 minutes and 5 minutes respectively for Azure VM.

To achieve specified RTO and RPO we need to use continuous replication for Azure VM.

Azure Site Recovery for Azure VM uses Continous replication. With Continous replication Disk writes are immediately transferred to the cache storage account in the source location. Azure Site Recovery processes the data in the cache and sends it to the replica managed disks in the target location.

We will use Central US location as our DR site for Azure VM. This region is paired with East US 2 Location. Azure never applies updates to paired regions simultaneously. In the event of an outage affecting multiple regions, at least one region in each pair will be prioritized for recovery.

We will also create Target Virtual Network in Central US location.

Design Nuggets for Data Protection and Disaster Recovery Plans

1. For 8 Hour RPO you can use Backup solution.
2. For 2 Hour RPO you can use Snapshot replication.
3. For near zero second RPO you can use continuous replication.
4. If you application require near zero second RPO and RTO then you need to use continuous replication (For Data) and Server Failover Service such as Load Balancer or Clustering (For Application switchover to another server).
5. Microsoft recommends configuring business continuity disaster recovery (BCDR) across regional pairs or paired regions to benefit from Azure's isolation and availability policies.

Note: Paired Regions will be discussed in Chapter 20.

Chapter 12 Azure AD

This Chapter covers following Topic Lessons

- Azure AD Introduction
- Default Azure AD Domain
- Azure AD Basic & Premium License upgrade options
- Azure AD Users
- Azure AD Groups
- Custom Domains
- Self Service Password Reset (SSPR)
- Device Management in Azure AD
- Azure AD Join
- Enterprise State Roaming
- Managing Multiple Azure AD Directory Tenant

This Chapter covers following Lab Exercises

- Exploring Dashboard of Default Azure AD
- Activating Premium P2 Free Trial Licenses
- Create User (User1 with Global Administrator Role)
- Create User (User2 with Limited Administrator Role)
- Create User (User3 with Directory Role User)
- Exploring Dashboard of User
- Checking User3 Access level
- Create Group and add users manually
- Assigning Azure AD Premium P2 License to Users
- Add Custom Domain
- Create TXT record in Domain Name Registrar
- Verify the Custom Domain in Azure AD
- Change Azure AD Login names to custom domain for User2
- Enabling SSPR for Cloud Users
- Setup SSPR Authentications for User3
- Test SSPR for User3
- Checking Device Settings for Azure AD Users
- Joining Windows 10 PC to Azure AD using Azure AD Join
- Log on to Windows 10 PC with User2
- Enabling Enterprise State Roaming for Users

- Creating New Azure AD Tenant
- Associating Azure AD Tenant with the Subscription

Chapter Topology

In this chapter we will configure Default Azure AD Tenant. We will also create a new Azure AD Tenant.

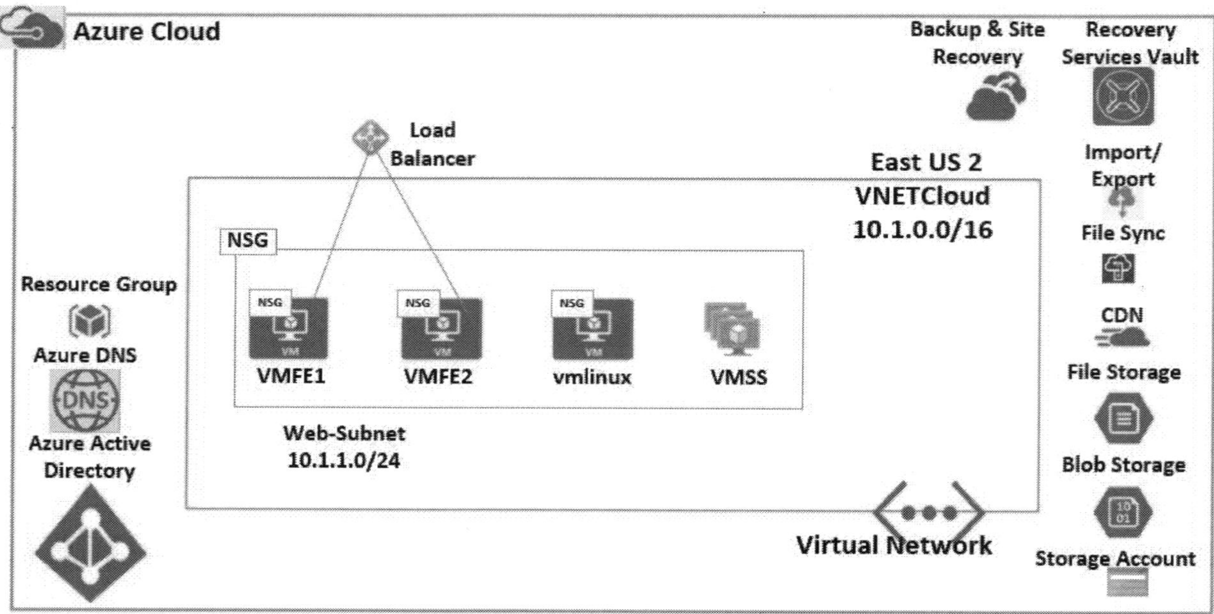

Azure AD Introduction

Microsoft Azure Active Directory (Azure AD) is a Multi-tenant cloud-based directory & identity management solution that combines core directory services, application access management, and identity protection into a single solution.

Azure AD also provides enterprise service's such as multifactor authentication service, a centralized application access panel for SaaS applications, an application proxy by which you can setup remote access for your on premises applications as well as Graph API that you can use to directly interact with Azure AD objects.

One of the Advantage of Azure AD is that application developers can easily integrate identity management in their application without writing complex code.

Azure AD can also act as SAML Identity provider. It Provides identity and authentication services to application using SAML, WS-Federation and OpenID connect protocols.

Azure Active Directory editions

Azure AD is offered in 4 Tiers: Free, Basic, Premium P1 and Premium P2.

Azure Active Directory Free edition can manage users and groups, synchronize with on-premises directories, get single sign-on across Azure, Office 365, and thousands of popular SaaS applications.

Azure AD Basic edition adds features such as group-based access management, self-service password reset for cloud applications, and Azure Active Directory Application Proxy.

Azure Active Directory Premium P1 edition add enterprise class features such as enhanced monitoring & security reporting, Multi-Factor Authentication (MFA), and secure access for your mobile workforce.

Azure Active Directory Premium P2 edition adds Identity Protection and Privileged Identity Management features.

Comparing Azure AD Editions (Important Topic for AZ-301)

Features	Free	Basic	Premium (P1 & P2)
Directory Objects	50000	No Limit	No Limit
User/Group Management	√	√	√
Single sign-on (SSO)	10 apps/user	10 apps/user	No limit
Self-Service Password Change for cloud users	√	√	√
AD Connect	√	√	√
Security/Usage Reports	3 Basic Reports	3 Basic Reports	Advanced Reports
Multi Factor Authentication for Administrator Roles	√	√	√
Group based access Management		√	√
Self Service password reset for cloud users		√	√
Logon page customization		√	√
SLA 99.9%		√	√
Multi Factor Authentication		√	√
Advanced Self Service Group and app management including Dynamic Groups			√
Self Service Password reset with on premises write back			√
Azure AD Join (MDM & Enterprise State Roaming)			√
Microsoft Identity Manager user CAL + MIM Server			√
Azure AD Connect Health			√
Application Proxy			√
Conditional Access			√
Identity Protection			Premium P2
Privileged Identity Management			Premium P2
Access Reviews			Premium P2
Pricing	**Free**	**Included with O365**	**P1- $6 user/month** **P2- $9 user/month**

Important Note Regarding Basic License: Basic license is being retired. Basic license has been renamed as Office 365 App Edition. This comes bundled with Office 365.

Azure AD Identity Management Features

- **Connect on-premises Active Directory with Azure AD:** In today's scenario, Organizations have large number of on-premises Active Directory users. Using Azure AD connect synchronize on-premises directory objects (users and groups) with Azure AD. This makes users more productive by providing a **common identity** for accessing resources regardless of location. Users and organizations can then use **single sign on (SSO)** to access both on-premises resources and Azure cloud services.

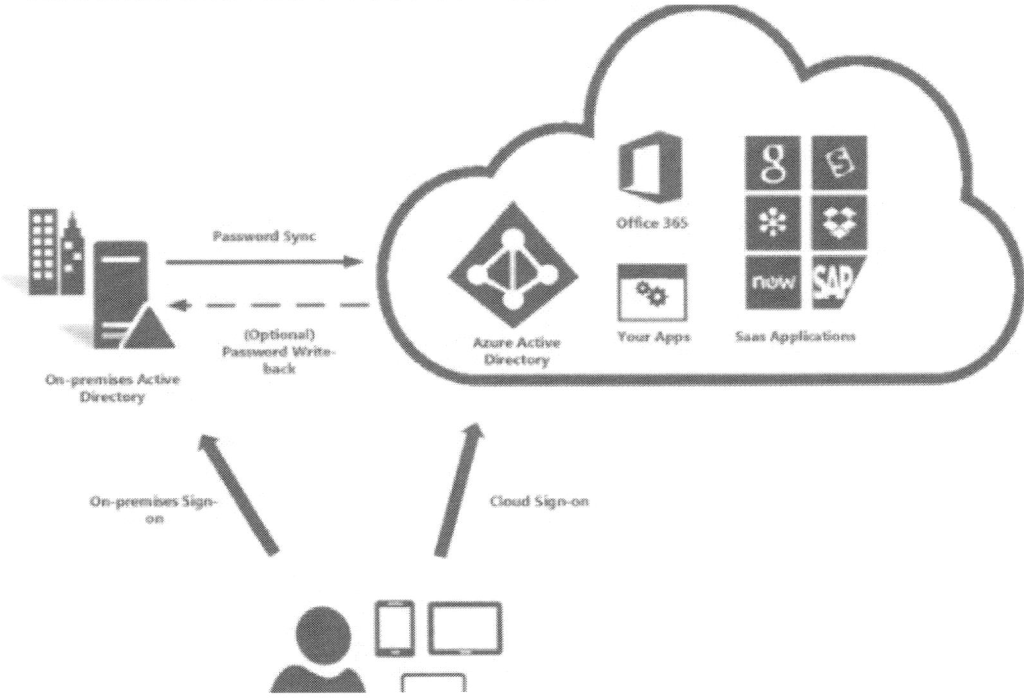

- **Manage and control access to corporate resources:** Enable application access security by using **Multi-Factor Authentication** for both on-premises and cloud applications.
- **Save on Help Desk Cost** with self-service password reset **(SSPR).**
- **Protecting Administrative Accounts:** Using Azure AD **Privileged Identity** Management you can restrict and monitor administrators and their access to resources and provide just-in-time access when needed.
- Provide **secure remote access** to on-premises application using Application Proxy without configuring VPN.

Default Azure AD Domain

A Default Azure AD Free Edition is automatically created with the subscription. You can upgrade Default Free edition to Premium Edition.

Domain name of the default Azure AD is in the following format: <System generated Name>.onmicrosoft.com

System generated Name is based on the name and mail id used to create the subscription. You can check default Azure AD by going to Azure AD Dashboard and click Azure Active Directory in left pane.

Figure below shows dashboard of default Azure AD Tenant **harinderkohlioutlook.onmicrosoft.com** which I am using for this book.

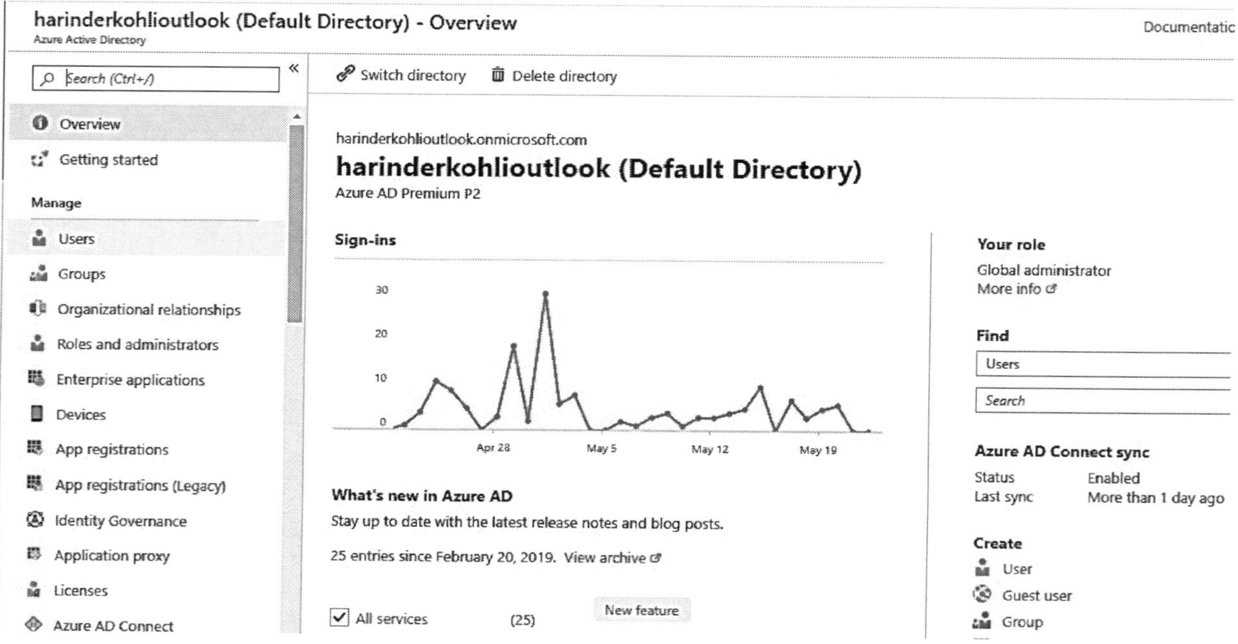

Note 1: User name should be in email format with a verified domain. Verified domain can be default domain or custom Domain. User login name for the above domain will be xyzxyz@harinderkohlioutlook.onmicrosoft.com
Note 2: You can assign custom Domain to your Default Azure AD. For example you can assign test.com. User login names will then be xyzxyz@test.com

Exercise 99: Exploring Dashboard of Default Azure AD

Login to Azure Portal @ https://portal.azure.com> Click Azure Active Directory in left Pane> Default Azure AD Tenant Dashboard Opens.

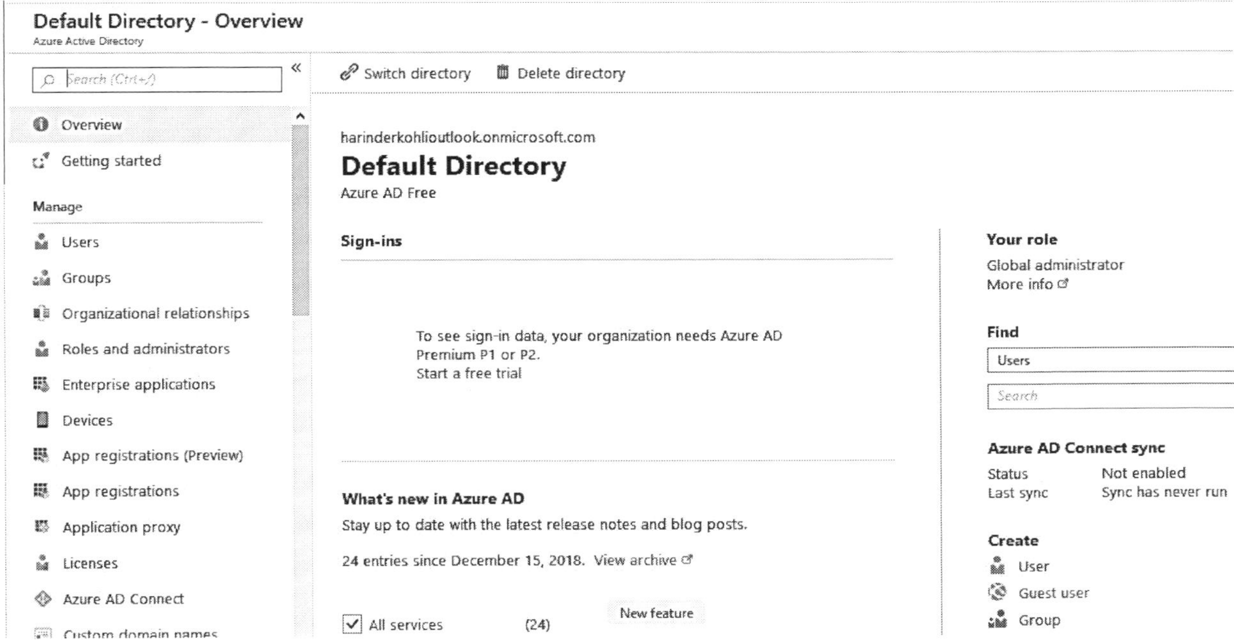

With **Users and Groups** option you can create user and Groups and Add users to groups.

With **Enterprise application** option you can provide single sign-on to SaaS and custom application.

With **Licenses** option you can assign Basic or Premium licenses to Users.

With **Custom domain Name** option you can assign custom Domain Names to Default Azure AD.

With **Application Proxy** option you can provide secure remote access to on-premises application.

With **AD Connect** option you can synchronize on-premises users to Azure AD.

Azure AD Basic & Premium License upgrade options

The Basic and Premium editions Licenses are available for purchase through following options:

1. Microsoft Enterprise Agreement.
2. Open Volume License Program.
3. Cloud Solution Providers.
4. Online using credit card (Azure Subscribers only).
5. Premium P2 Free Trial licenses.

After you have purchased license through one of the above method the licenses will then be available in Azure Portal after activation. You can then assign these licenses to Azure users or groups.

Exercise 100: Activating Premium P2 Free Trial Licenses

In Azure Portal you get 2 options to activate Premium P2 Free Trial Licenses.

One option is Enterprise Mobility + Security E5 option which includes Azure Active Directory Premium P2, Microsoft Intune and Azure Rights Management Trial Licenses for 250 users for 90 days.

Second Option is Azure AD Premium P2 trial licenses for 100 users for 30 days.

1. Go to Default Azure AD dashboard> In the middle pane click start a free trial> Activate Blade opens> For this book I selected Azure AD Premium P2 license>Click Free trial Under Azure AD Premium P2>Activate Premium P2 trial blade opens> Click Activate> Close the activate pane.

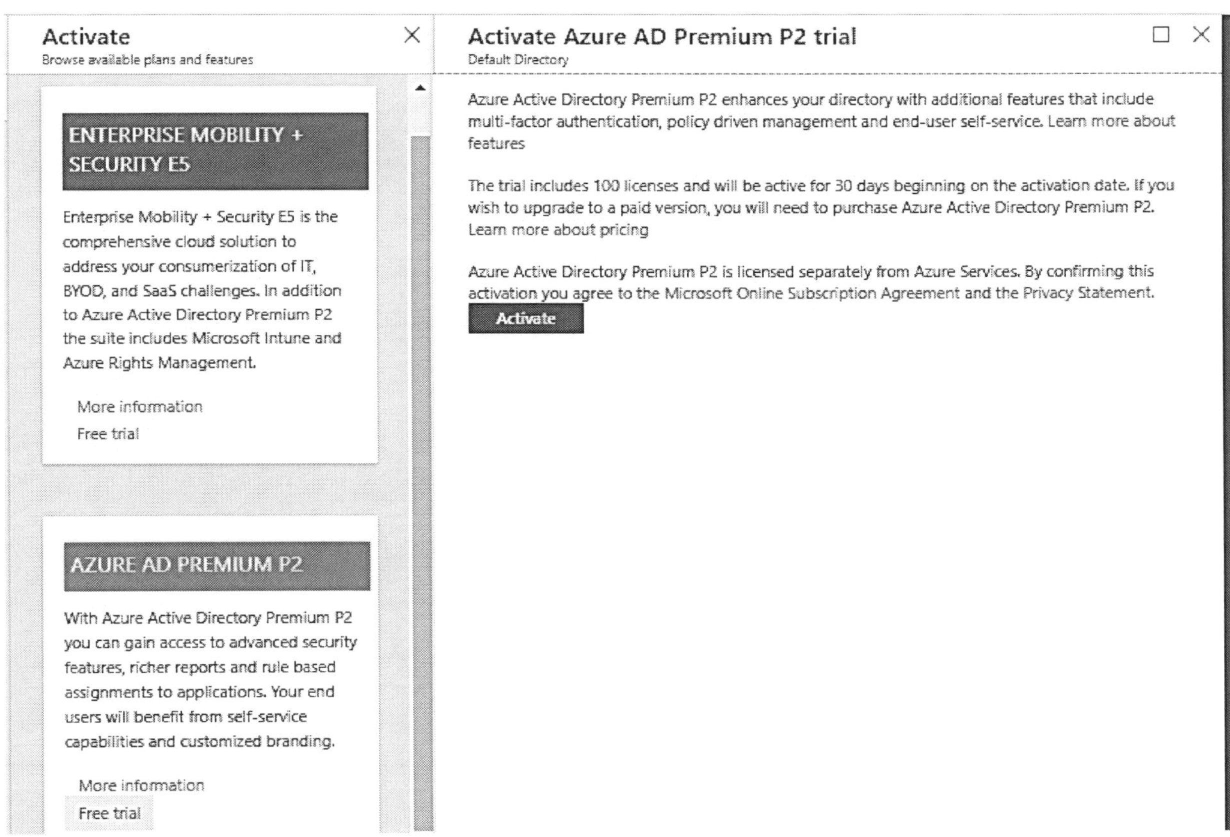

2. Refresh your Azure AD Dashboard using F5 keyboard button couple of times> It will take few minutes to show Azure AD Premium P2 option on Azure AD Dashboard.

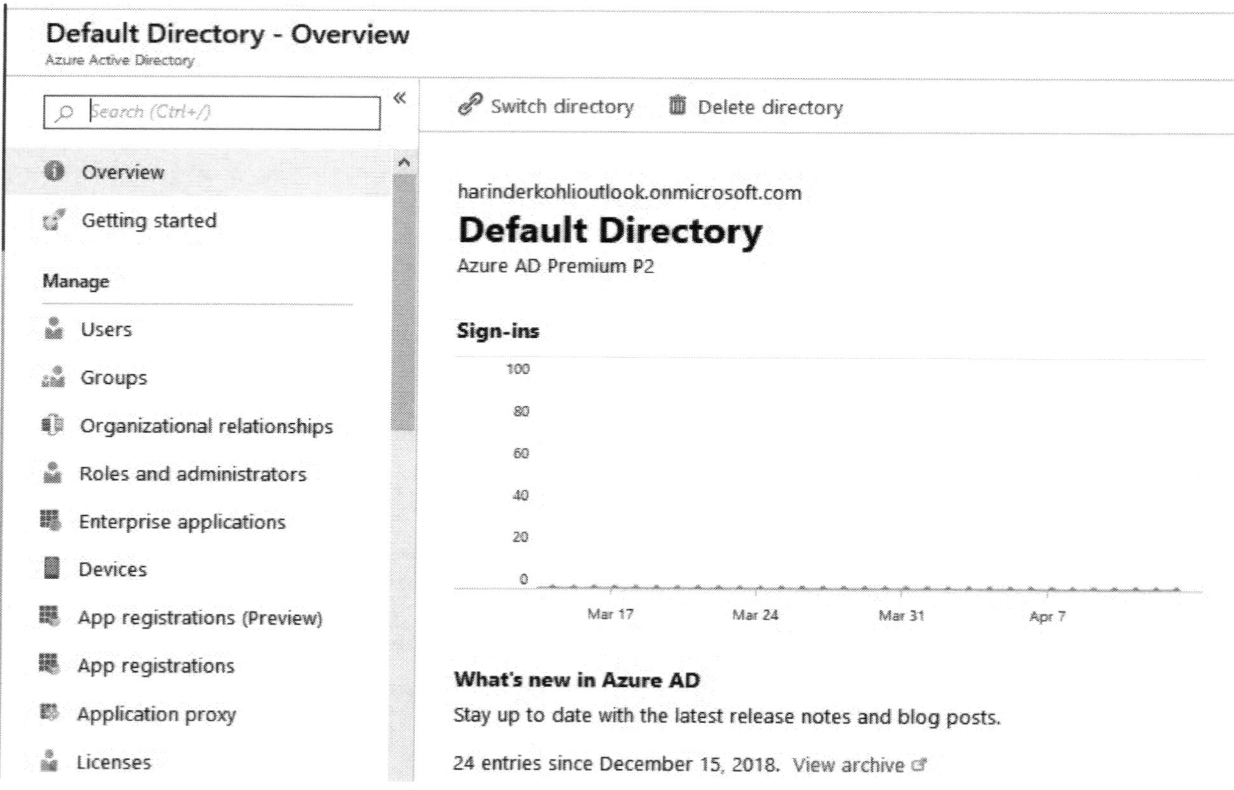

3. Click licenses in left pane> You can see 100 licenses. None of the license is assigned.

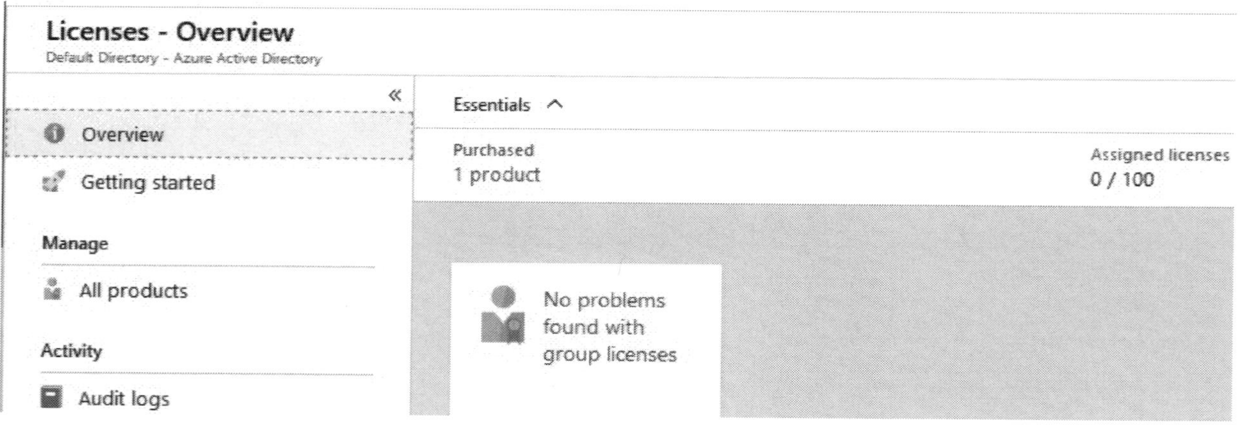

Azure AD Users

User name in Azure AD should be in email format with a verified domain. Verified domain can be default domain or custom Domain.

Directory Role for User

User is assigned Directory role during user creation time. A user can be assigned one of the following 3 directory roles:

User: User can login to Azure portal but cannot create, manage or view a resource. For a user to create, view or manage a resource in Azure Portal it needs to be assigned permissions Using Role based Access Control (RBAC).
Global Administrator: The Global administrators have full control over all **directory** (Azure AD) resources.
Limited Administrator: Limited administrator role has full access to particular Azure AD feature. Following Limited Administrative roles are available in Azure.

Billing Administrator	Exchange Service Administrator	Password Administrator / Helpdesk Administrator
Compliance Administrator	Global Administrator / Company Administrator	Power BI Service Administrator
Conditional Access Administrator	Guest Inviter	Privileged Role Administrator
Dynamics 365 service administrator	Information Protection Administrator	Security Administrator
Device Administrators	Intune Service Administrator	Service Support Administrator
Directory Readers	Mailbox Administrator	SharePoint Service Administrator
Directory Synchronization Accounts	Skype for Business / Lync Service Administrator	
Directory Writers	User Account Administrator	

Note: You can change user Directory role from Azure AD Dashboard.

Azure AD Password Policies for Cloud Users

The following table describes the available password policy settings that can be applied to user accounts that are created and managed in Azure AD:

<table>
<tr><td>Characters Allowed</td><td>A – Z, a – z, 0 – 9, @ # $ % ^ & * - _ ! + = [ ] { } | \ : ' , . ? / ` ~ " ( ) ;</td></tr>
<tr><td>Password restrictions</td><td>A minimum of 8 characters and a maximum of 16 characters.
Strong passwords only: Requires three out of four of the following:
• Lowercase characters.
• Uppercase characters.
• Numbers (0-9).
• Symbols</td></tr>
<tr><td>Password expiry duration</td><td>• Default value: 90 days.
• The value is configurable by using the `Set-MsolPasswordPolicy` cmdlet from the Azure Active Directory Module for Windows PowerShell.</td></tr>
<tr><td>Password expiry notification</td><td>• Default value: 14 days (before password expires).
• The value is configurable by using the `Set-MsolPasswordPolicy` cmdlet.</td></tr>
<tr><td>Password expiry</td><td>• Default value: false days (indicates that password expiry is enabled).
• The value can be configured for individual user accounts by using the `Set-MsolUser` cmdlet.</td></tr>
<tr><td>Password change history</td><td>The last password can't be used again when the user changes a password.</td></tr>
<tr><td>Password reset history</td><td>The last password can be used again when the user resets a forgotten password.</td></tr>
<tr><td>Account lockout</td><td>After 10 unsuccessful sign-in attempts with the wrong password, the user is locked out for one minute. Further incorrect sign-in attempts lock out the user for increasing durations of time.</td></tr>
</table>

Exercise 101: Create User (User1 with Global Administrator Role)

1. In Azure AD Dashboard>Click Users in left pane> All Users blade open>+New User> Add user blade opens> Enter name **User1** and User name as user1@harinderkohlioutlook.onmicrosoft.com>Assign Directory role of Global Administrator to user1> Click Ok>Click Show Password>Click create.

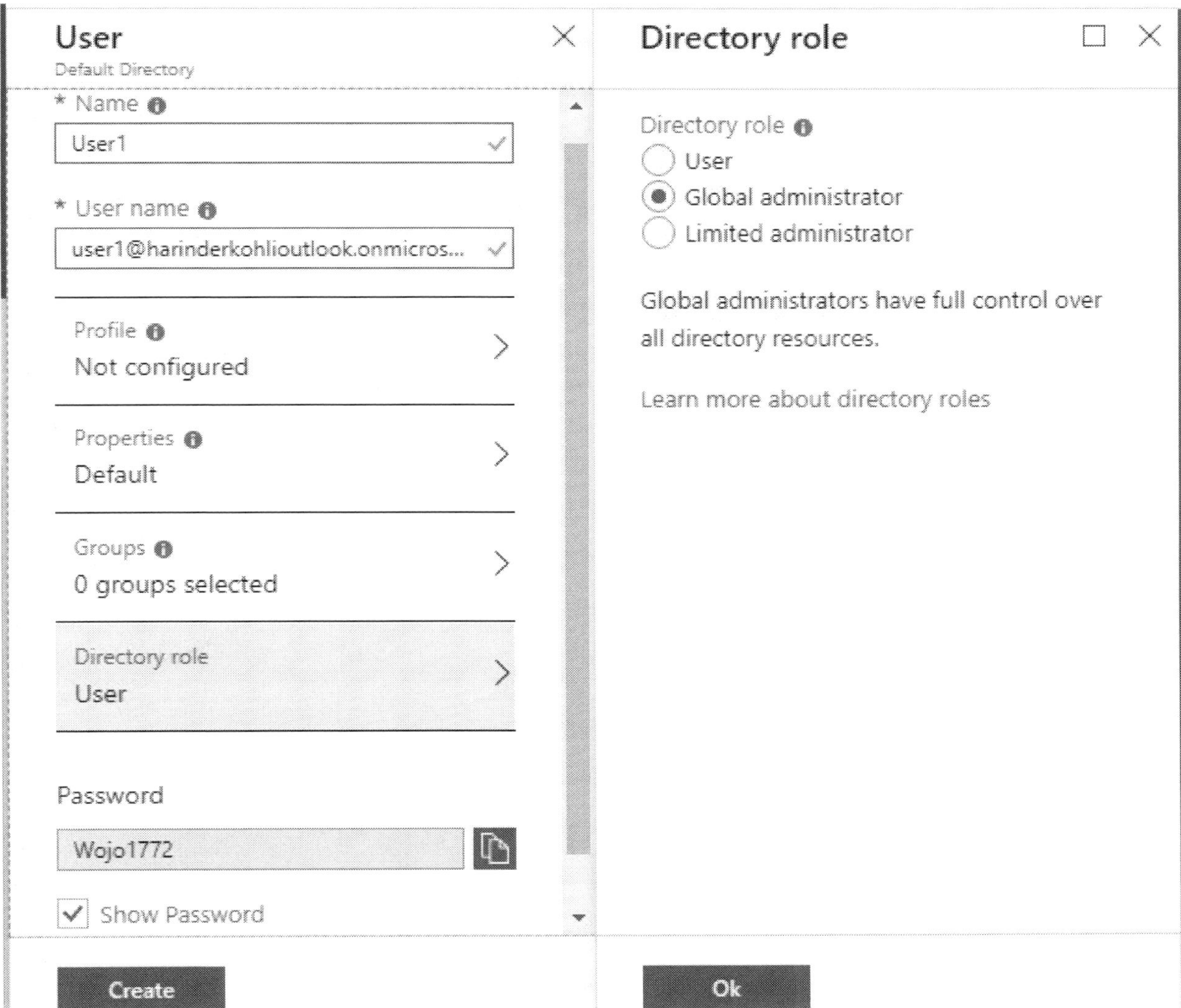

2. Note down the system generated Password>Open firefox and https://portal azure.com and Log on with User1 Credentials and change the password> Logout from Azure Portal. **Please do this step.**

Exercise 102: Create User (User2 with Limited Administrator Role)

1. In Azure AD Dashboard>Click Users in left pane> All Users blade open>+New User> Add user blade opens> Enter name **User2** and User name as user2@harinderkohlioutlook.onmicrosoft.com>Assign Directory role of Limited Administrator to user2 and Choose Billing Administrator Role> Click Ok>Click Show Password>Click create.

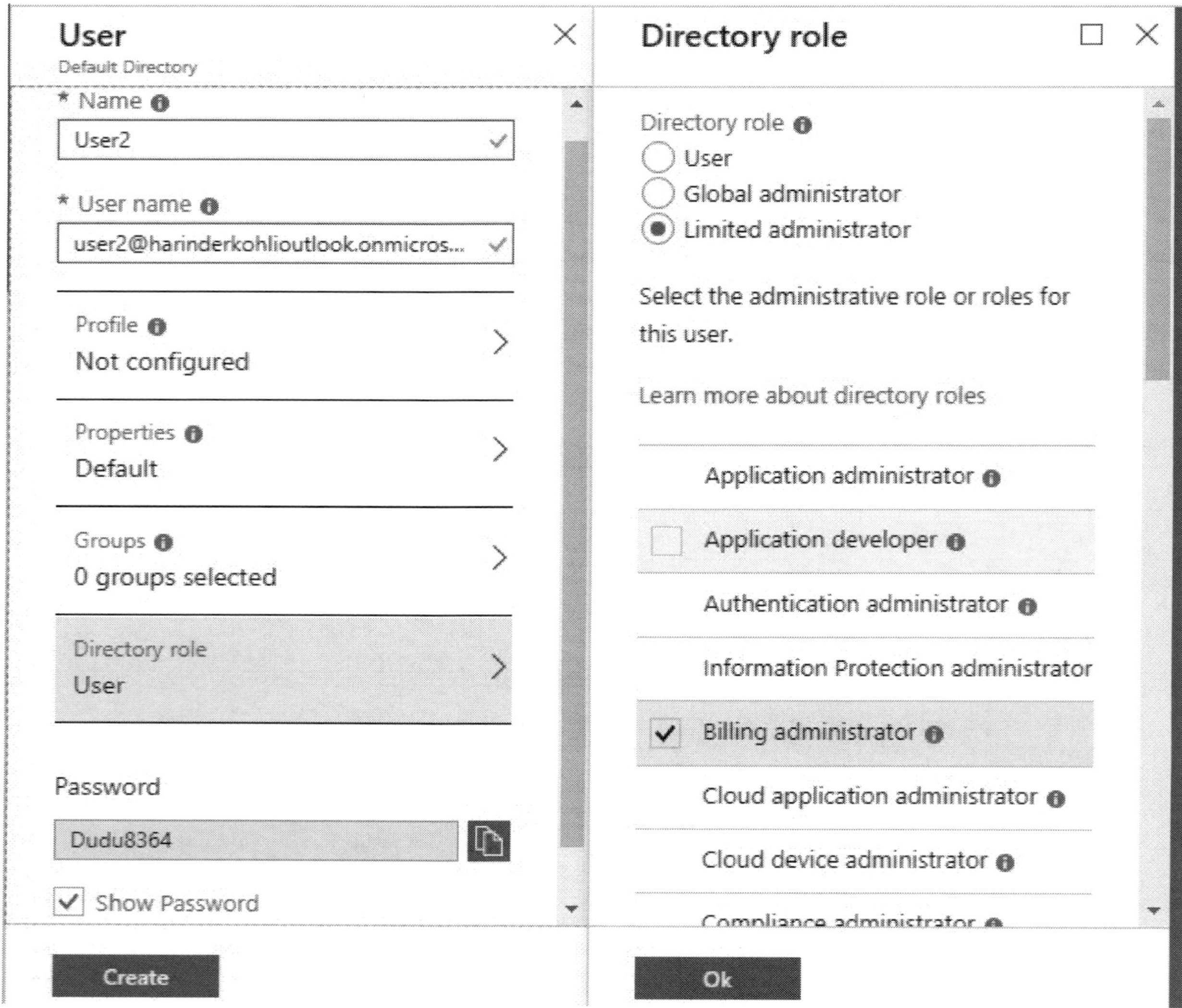

2. Note down the system generated Password. Open firefox and https://portal azure.com and Log on with User2 Credentials and change the password.

Exercise 103: Create User (User3 with Directory Role User)

1. In Azure AD Dashboard>Click Users in left pane> All Users blade open>+New User> Add user blade opens> Enter name **User3** and User name as user3@harinderkohlioutlook.onmicrosoft.com>Assign Directory role of User to user3> Click Ok>Click Show Password>Click create.

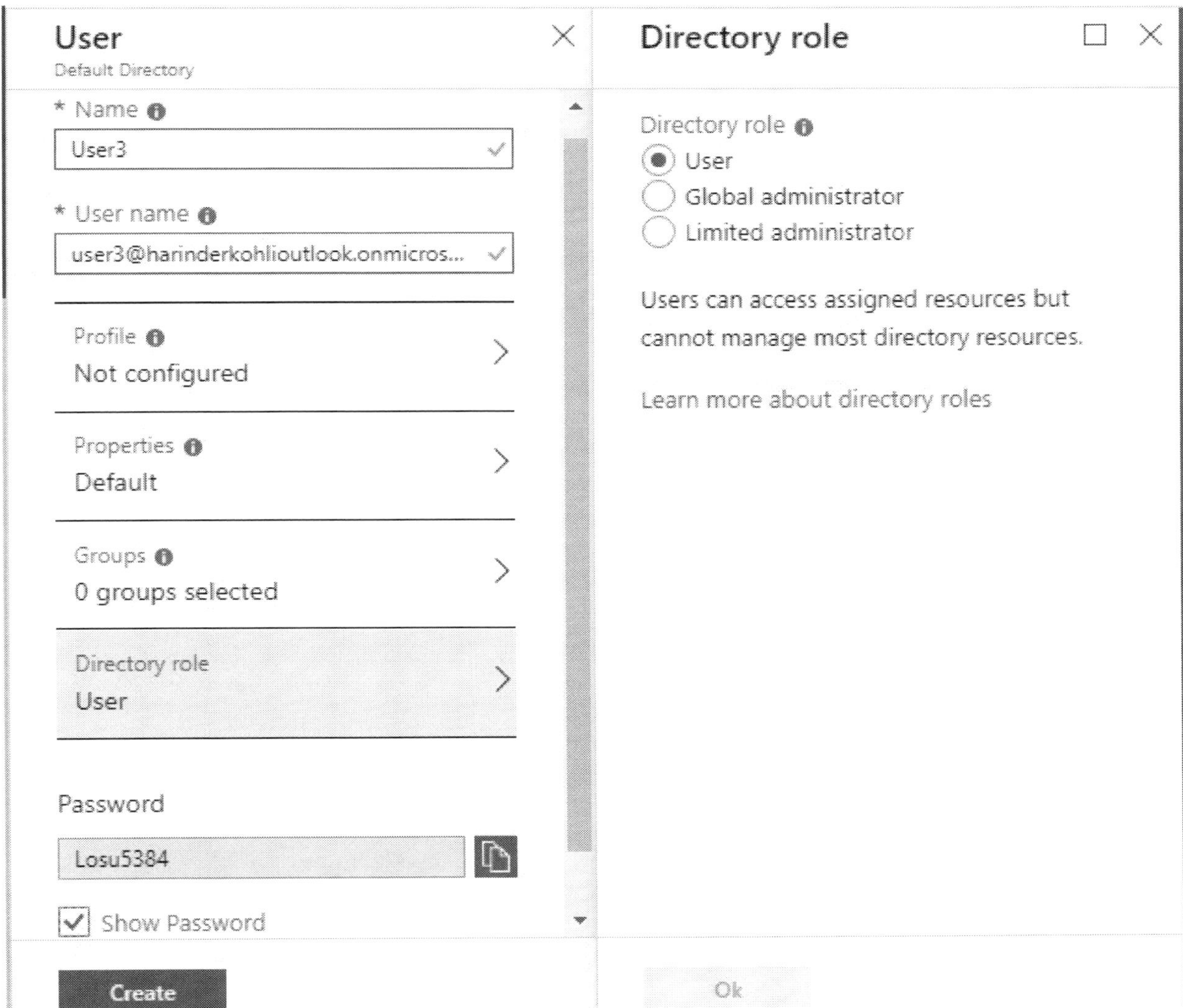

2. Note down the system generated Password. Open firefox and https://portal azure.com and Log on with User3 Credentials and change the password.

Exercise 104: Exploring Dashboard of User

1. In Azure AD Dashboard>Click Users in left pane>All Users blade open> Dashboard shows Subscription administrator (Harinder Kohli) and 3 users (User1, User2 & User3) we created in previous exercises.

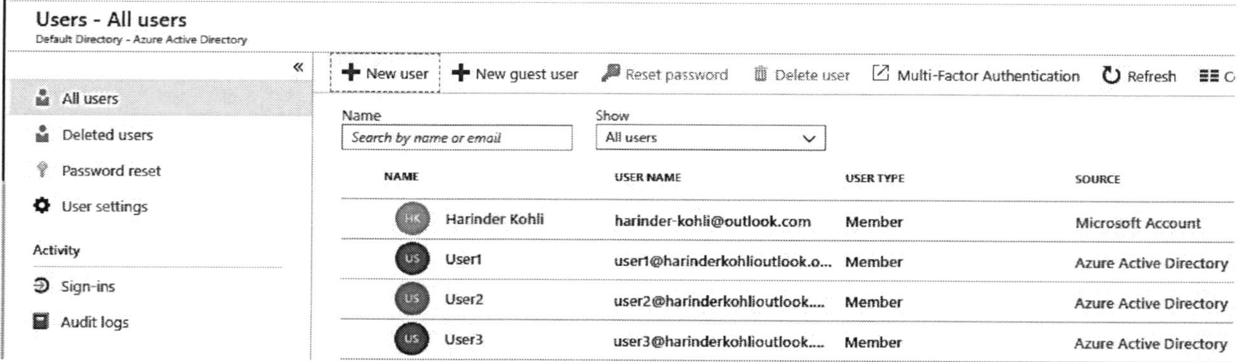

2. Select User3>user3 blade opens>From here you can assign Azure AD license, Change Directory role, Reset Password or delete the User etc.

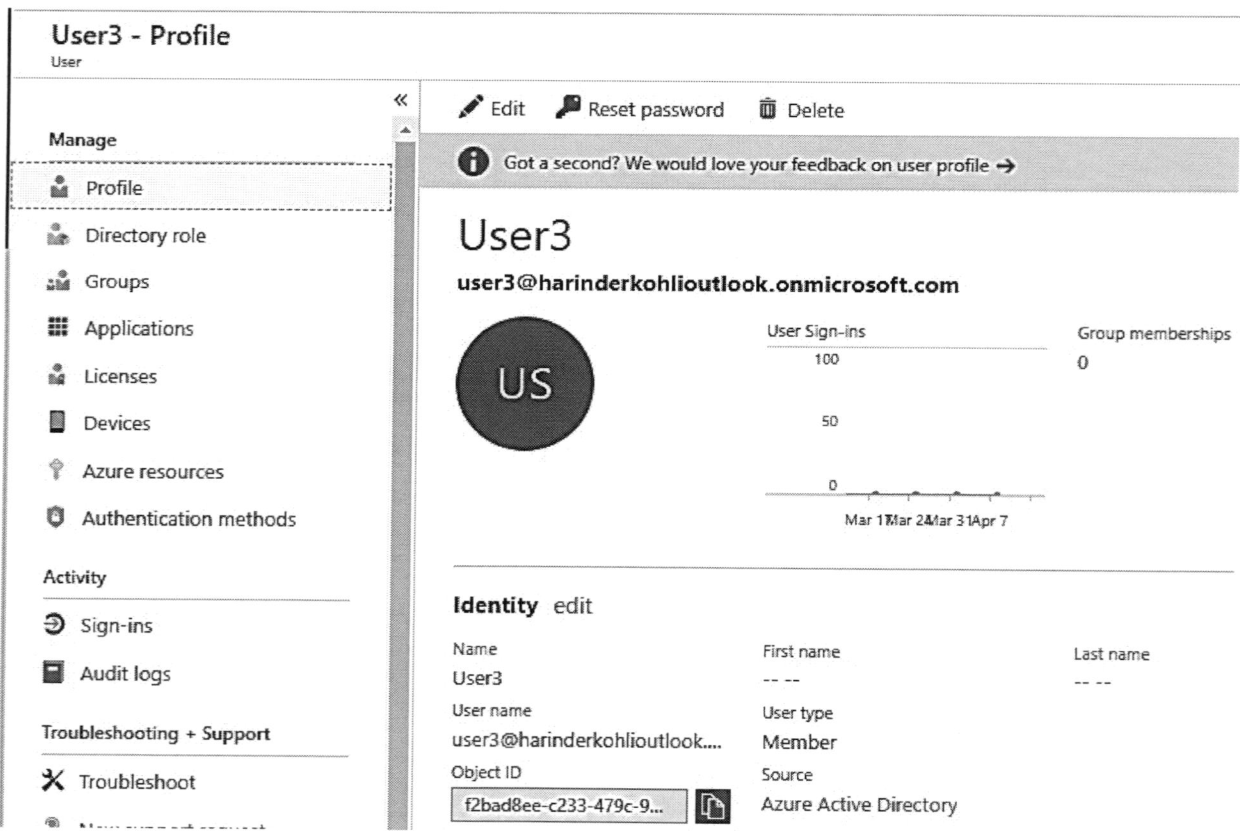

Exercise 105: Checking User3 Access level

In this exercise we will check User3 Access level in Azure Portal.

Log on to Azure portal @ https://portal.azure.com with User3 Credentials (user3@harinderkohlioutlook.onmicrosoft.com) and password. You can see there are no resources to display for User3 and user has no access to resources and User cannot create any resources.

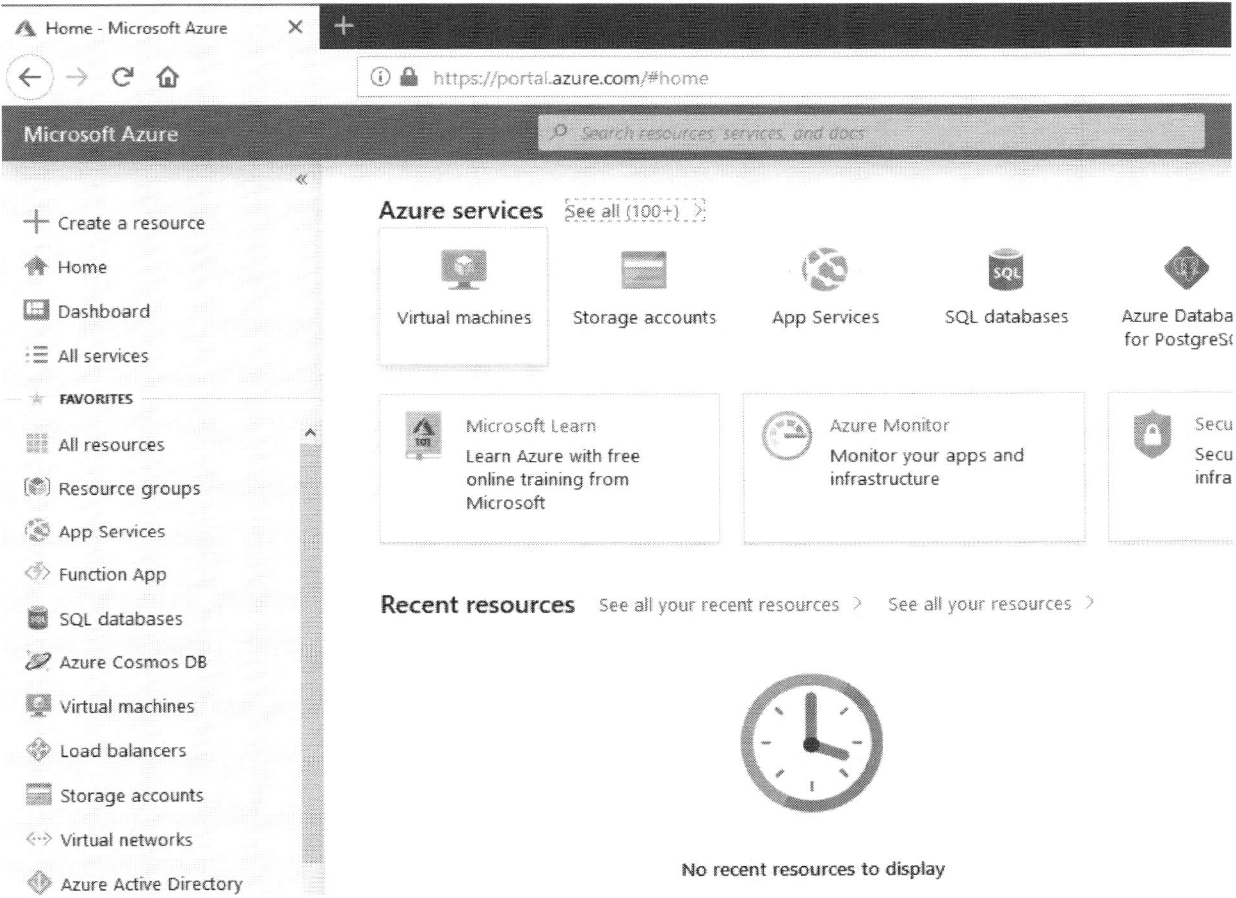

Note: In Chapter 17 Directory Role and RBAC we will discuss how we can assign Administrative permissions and Roles to Users.

Azure AD Groups

Group is a collection of users. The advantage of group is that it lowers administrative overhead of managing users. For Example instead of assigning Azure AD Basic or premium licenses to individual users, assign to group.

Adding users to group: Users can be added to group by manual selection or by using dynamic membership rules. Adding users by Dynamic rules requires an Azure AD Premium P1 or P2 license for each user member added.

Creating Group and Adding members manually: In Azure AD Dashboard>Click Users and Groups >All Groups>+ New Group> Add Group Blade opens>Select **Membership type assigned.**

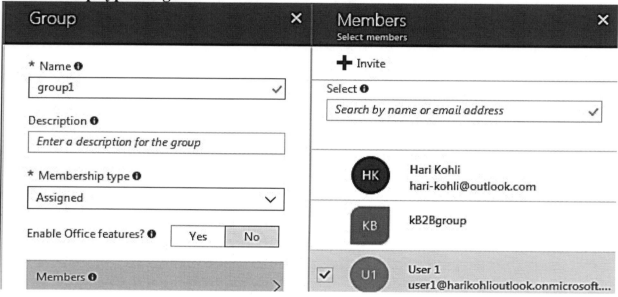

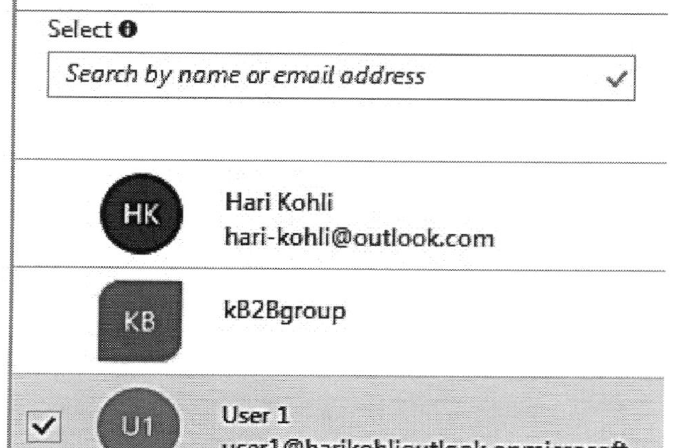

Adding members by Dynamic rules: Select **membership type Dynamic user**.

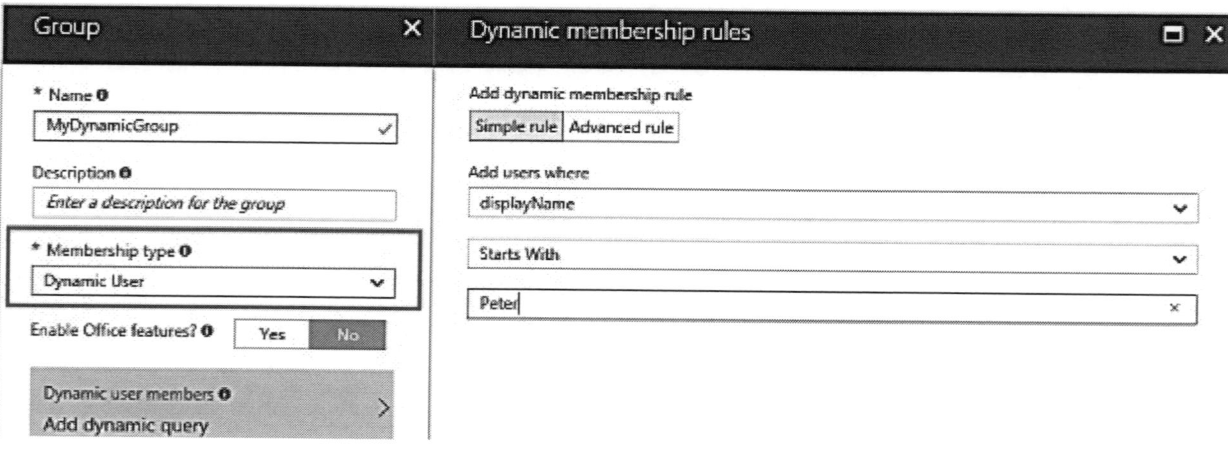

Exercise 106: Create Group and add users manually

In this exercise we will create Group AZ-103 and add 4 users (Harinder Kohli, User1, User2 and User3) to the group.

1. In Azure AD Dashboard>Click Groups >All Groups Blade open>Click + New Group> Add Group Blade opens>Select Group type as Security>For name I entered AZ-103>Select Membership type assigned>In Members Select Harinder Kohli, User1, User2 and User3 and click select and then create. **Note:** You need to scroll the right pane to see the Users- Harinder Kohli, User1, User2, User3. If you don't see your User then enter name of User in search pane, click enter and then select the User in the pane.

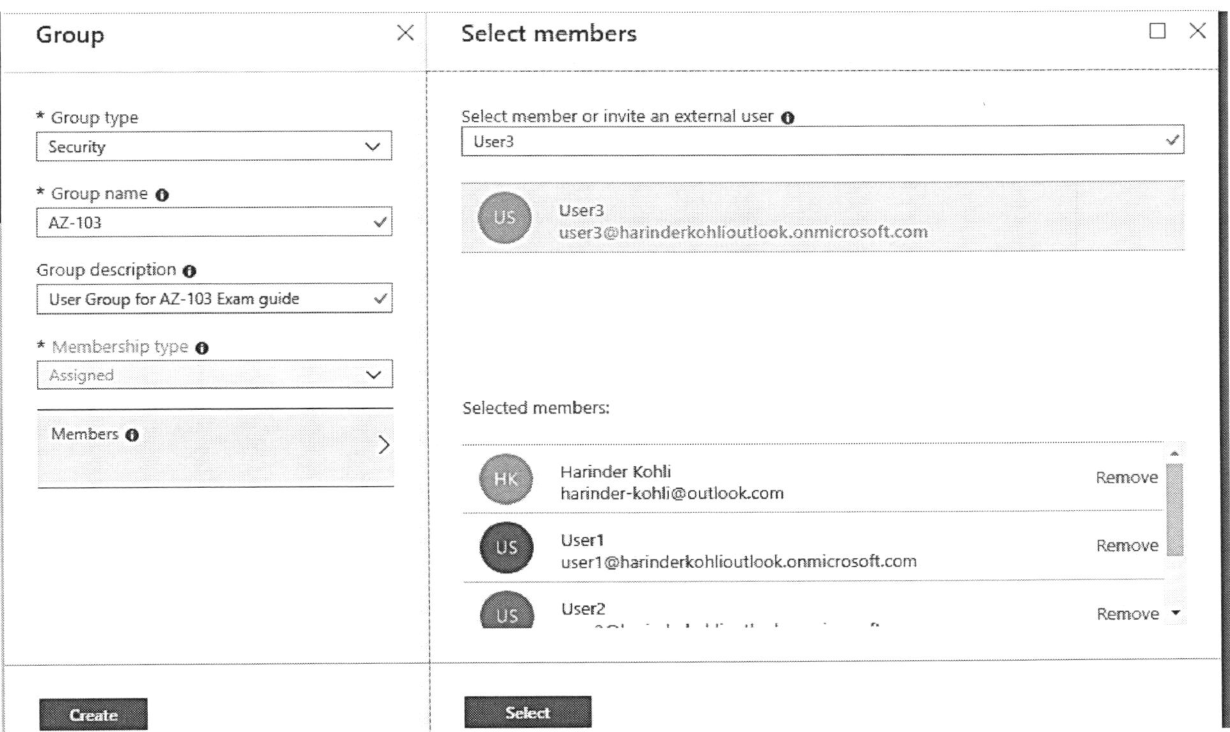

2. Figure below shows AZ-103 Group.

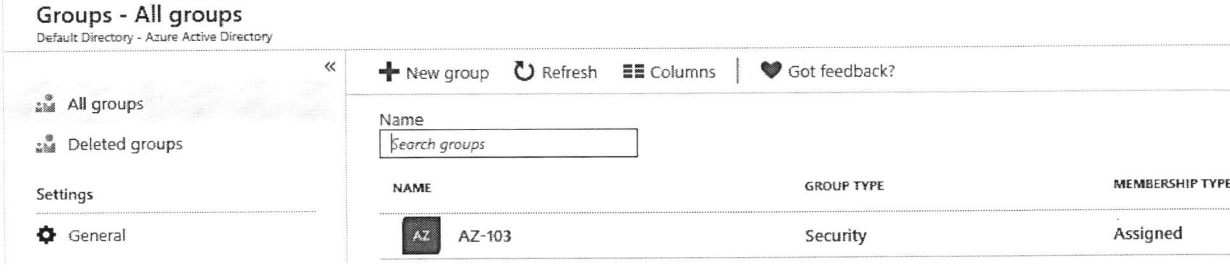

3. Click on AZ-103 Group and AZ-103 group dashboard opens.

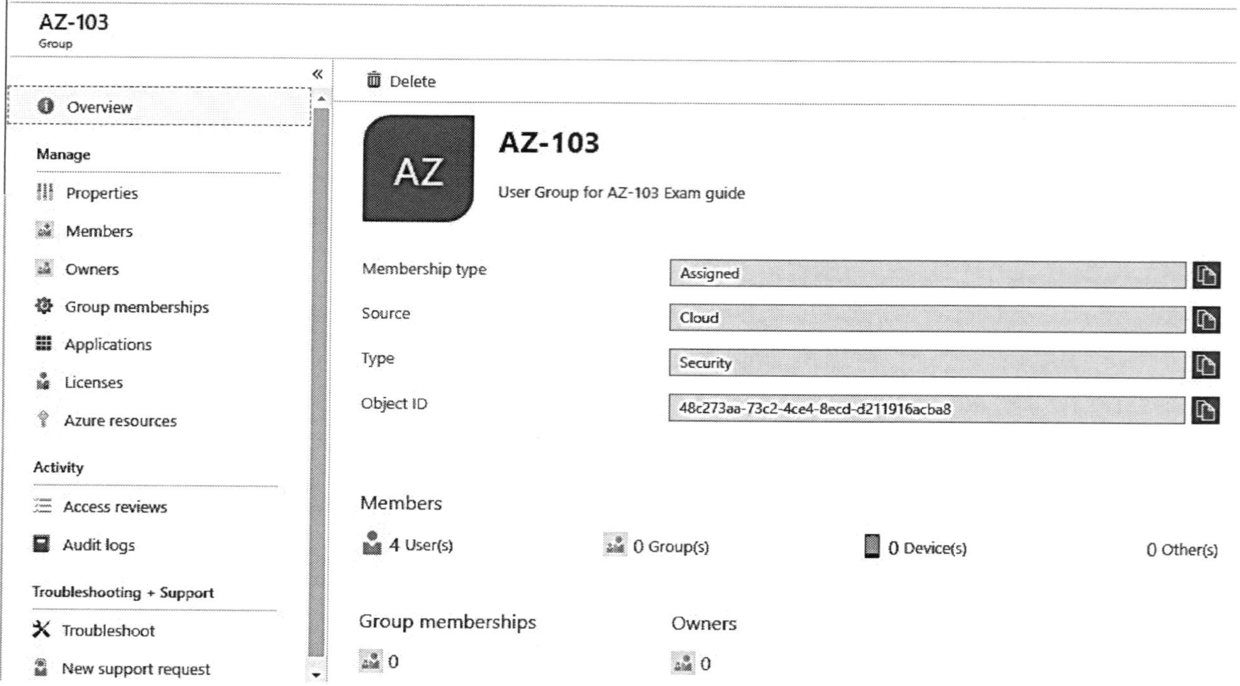

Note the **Licenses** option in left pane. We will use this option to assign Azure AD Premium P2 License to AZ-103 Group.

Exercise 107: Assigning Azure AD Premium P2 License to Users

In this exercise we will assign Premium P2 license to users. Instead of assigning Licenses to users individually we will assign to AZ-103 group created in previous exercise.

1. In Azure AD Dashboard>Click Groups in left pane>All Groups Blade open>Click AZ-103 Group Created in previous exercise>AZ-103 Group dashboard opens>Click licenses in left pane> License blade opens.

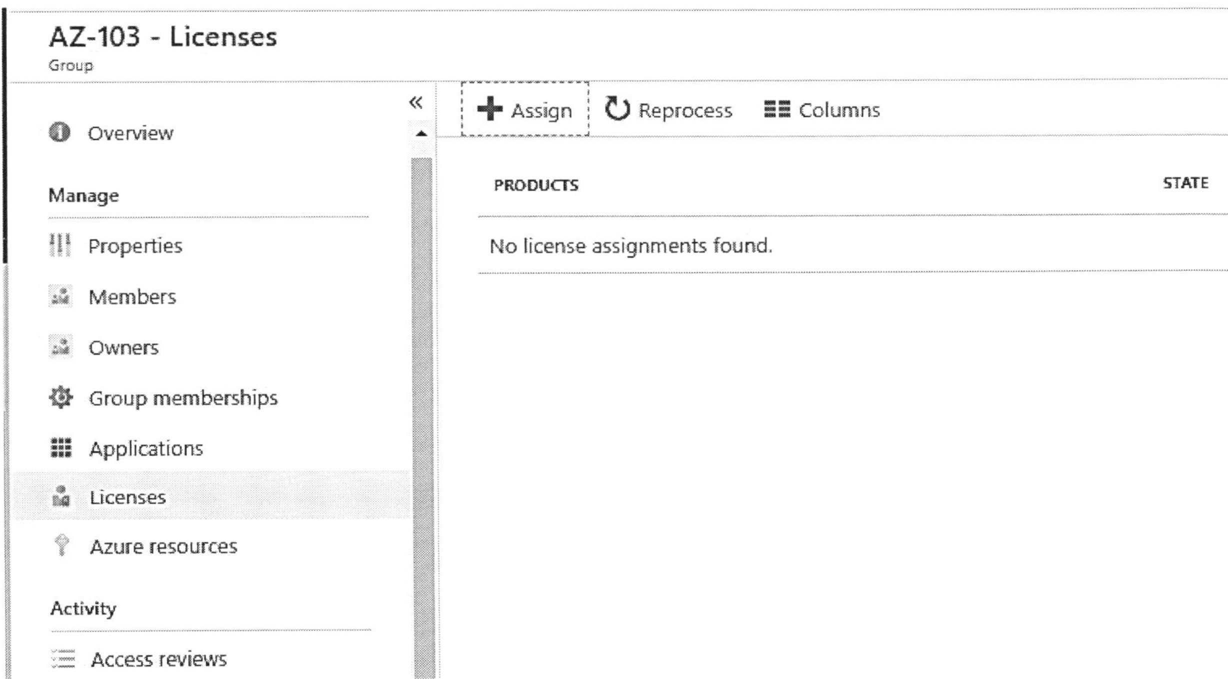

2. Click + Assign>Assign License blade opens>Click Products>In Right pane select Premium P2 >Click select (Not shown)> Click Assign (Not shown).

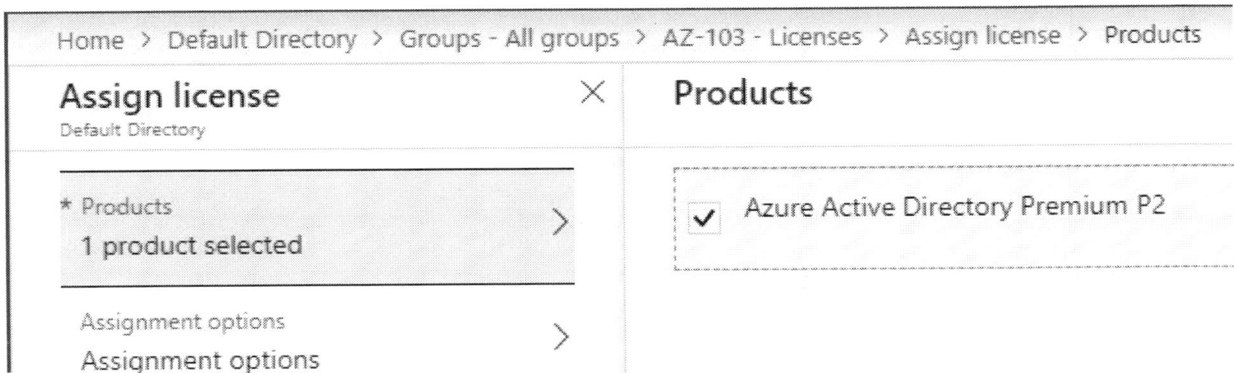

3. In AZ group license blade refresh the screen with F5 couple of times and you can see the licenses. It takes 3-4 min for licenses to get updated in Azure AD license blade.

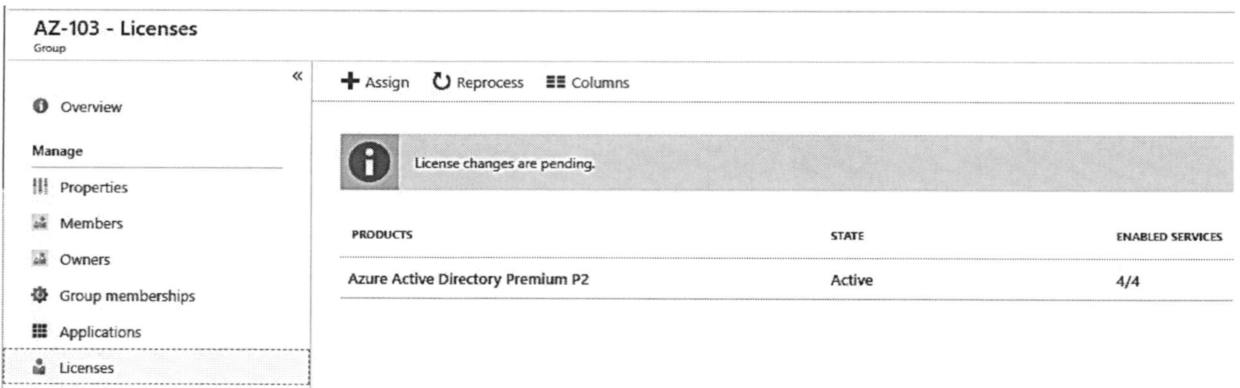

Note 1: When I tried to assign licenses to individual users it gave error. It wants Location to be specified in User Profile for license to be assigned on User basis.
Note 2: If you want to assign license per user then make sure to specify location in User profile.

Create Bulk Users using CSV files and PowerShell

You can create Bulk users by importing a list of users from CSV files which then will create corresponding users in Azure Active Directory.

Step by Step Creating Bulk Users

1. Make sure Azure AD PowerShell Module is installed on your desktop.
2. Create CSV file with required user updates.
3. Create PowerShell script (*.ps1) for User Creation. This script will refer to CSV file on your system.
   Alternatively you can download and edit sample PS script from link shown below.
   https://gallery.technet.microsoft.com/scriptcenter/Update-Active-Directory-cd5c5513/file/168800/1/UpdateUsersCsv.ps1
4. Run the PowerShell script (*.ps1) which was created in step 3 with required new user information.

Add Custom Domains

Every Azure AD directory comes with an initial domain name in the form of <System generated Name>.onmicrosoft.com. System generated Name is based on the name and mail id used to create the subscription.

It would be difficult for users to remember the format of Default Azure AD domain name. Adding custom domain names to Azure AD allows you to assign user names in the format such as hari@fabrikam.com instead of hari@<System generated Name>.onmicrosoft.com.

Pre-Requisite for Adding Custom domain

You own a domain name and have sign-in rights to update DNS records with the Domain Name Registrar.

Note about Adding Custom Domain lab Exercise

In next page we will add Custom Domain mykloud.in to Azure AD Tenant.

I did this exercise at the end of the Book. I suggest that readers should also do this exercise at end of the book as it might create problems in succeeding exercises.

Readers are requested to Exercise 92- 95 at the end of the book.

Exercise 108: Add Custom Domain

In this exercise we will add Domain **mykloud.in**. Recall that in Chapter 1, Ex 13 we delegated administration of mykloud.in domain to Azure DNS from Registrar Go Daddy.

Step 1: Add domain mykloud.in to Azure AD
In Azure AD dashboard click Custom domain names in left pane>In right pane click + Add Custom Domain> Add Custom Domain pane opens>Enter domain name mykloud.in and click Add Domain (Not shown).

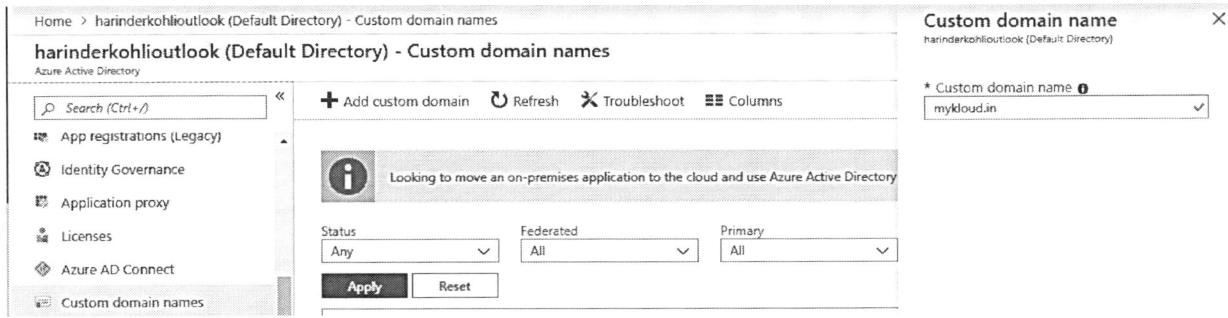

Step 2: Copy TXT Record Information from Custom Domain name pane.
Click Custom Domain created >Copy TXT Record information.

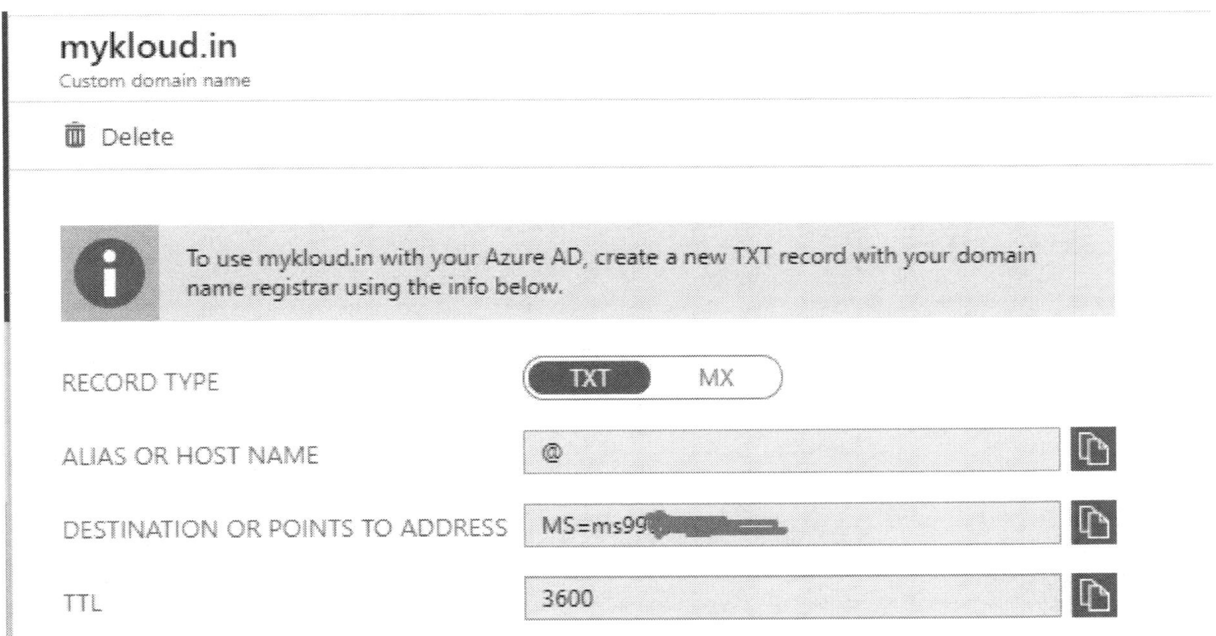

Exercise 109: Create TXT record in Domain Name Registrar

Recall that in Chapter 1, Ex 13 we delegated administration of mykloud.in domain to Azure DNS from Registrar Go Daddy. In Azure DNS we will create TXT record with TXT record information copied from previous Exercise.

1. In Azure Portal Click All Services in left pane> In Right pane under Networking click DNS Zones>DNS Zones pane opens>Click DNS Zone mykloud.in> DNS Zone dashboard opens as shown below.

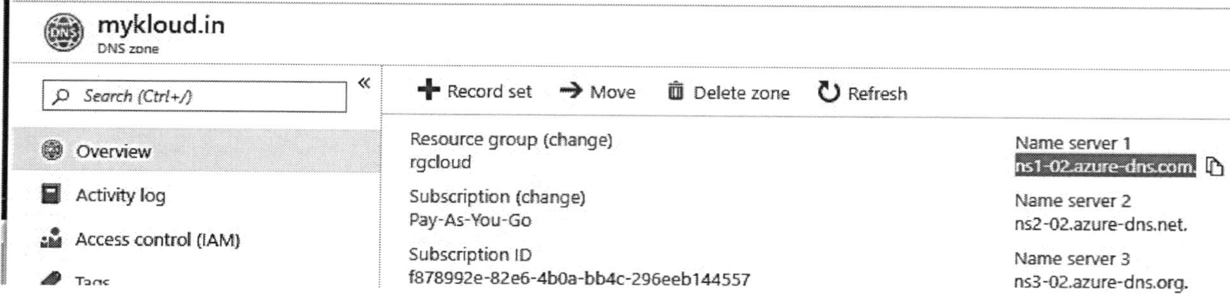

2. Click + Record Set in right pane> Add Record set blade opens>In name enter @>Select TXT from Dropdown box>In Value enter destination or point copied from step 2> Click OK (Not shown).

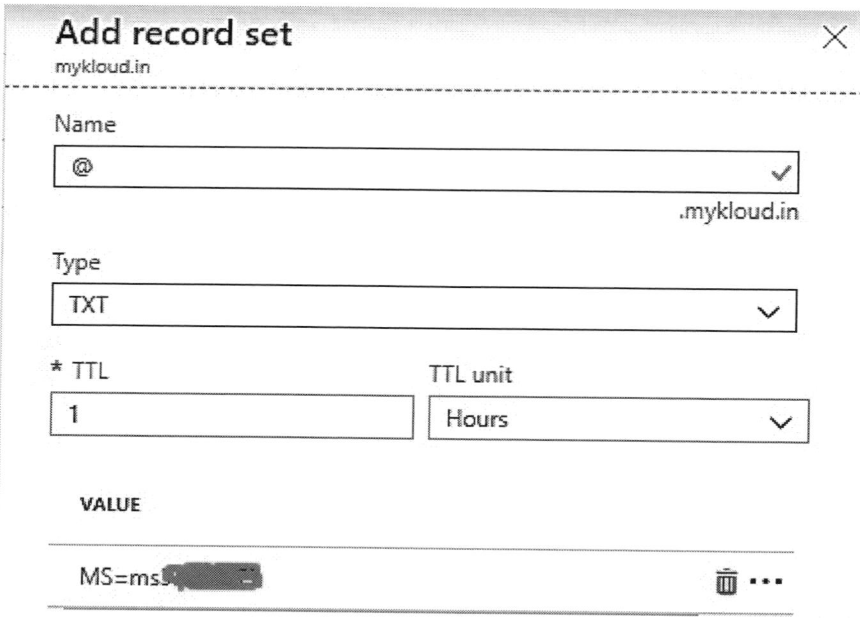

3. Txt Record is created and you can see in DNS Zone Dashboard.

Exercise 110: Verify the Custom Domain in Azure AD

In Azure AD dashboard click Custom domain names in left pane>In Right pane click the custom domain mykloud.in>Custom Domain pane opens>Click verify.

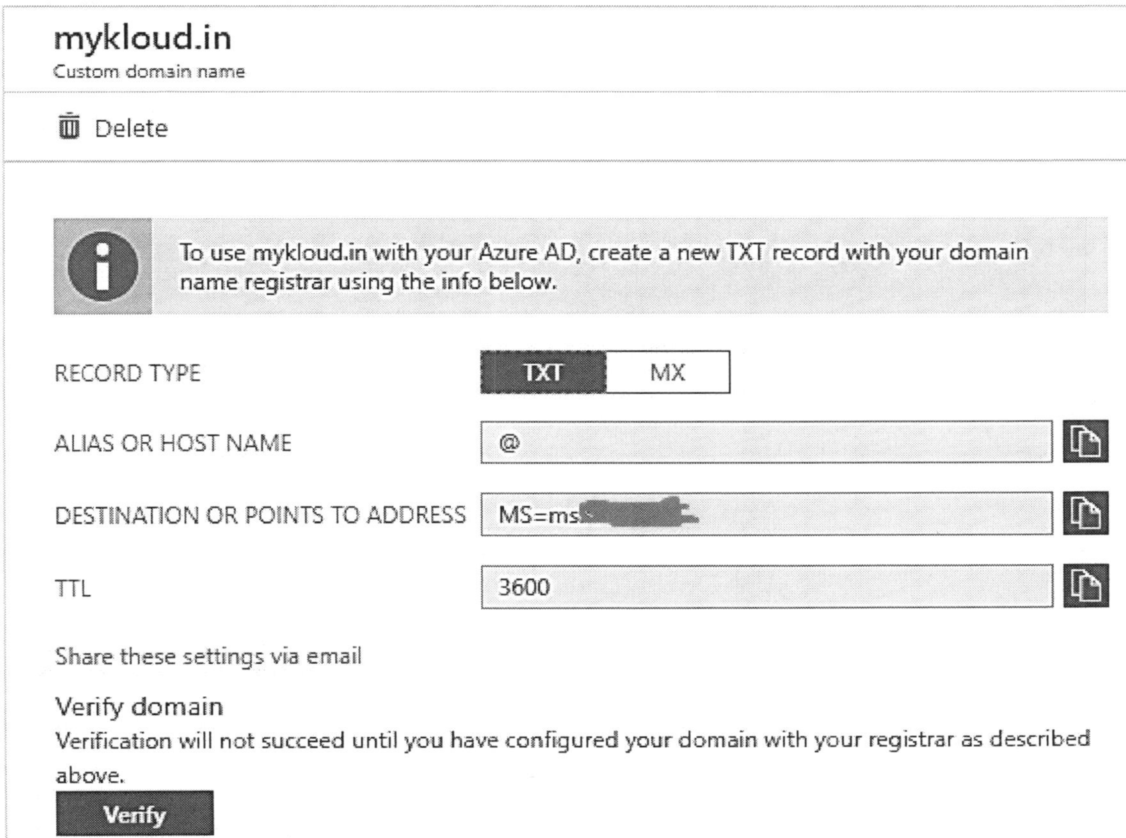

New pane opens and it shows verification is successful or you will get notification that verification is successful.

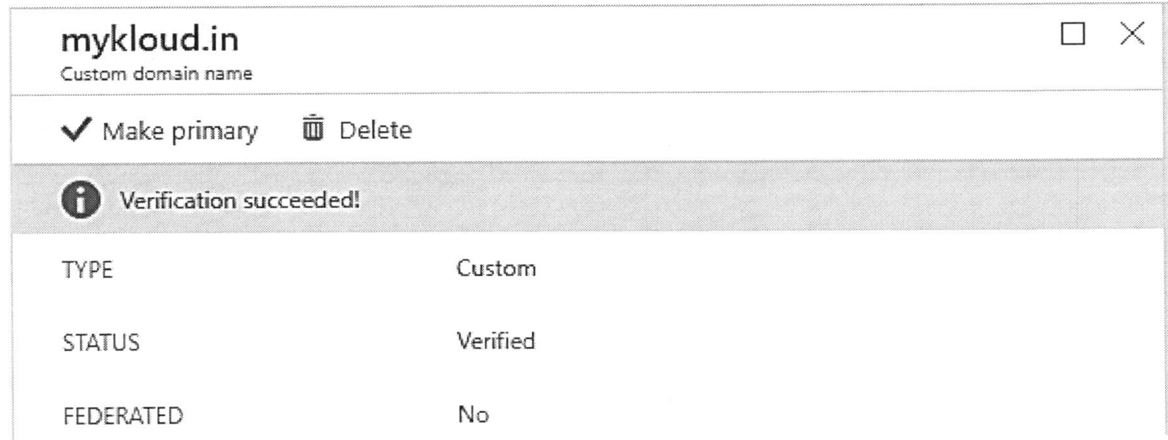

Exercise 111: Change Azure AD Login names to custom domain for User2

1. In Azure AD dashboard click Users in left pane>All Users pane opens>Click User2>User2 Profile opens>Click Edit> In user name box change user2@harinderkohlioutlook.onmicrosoft.com to user2@mykloud.in> Click save.

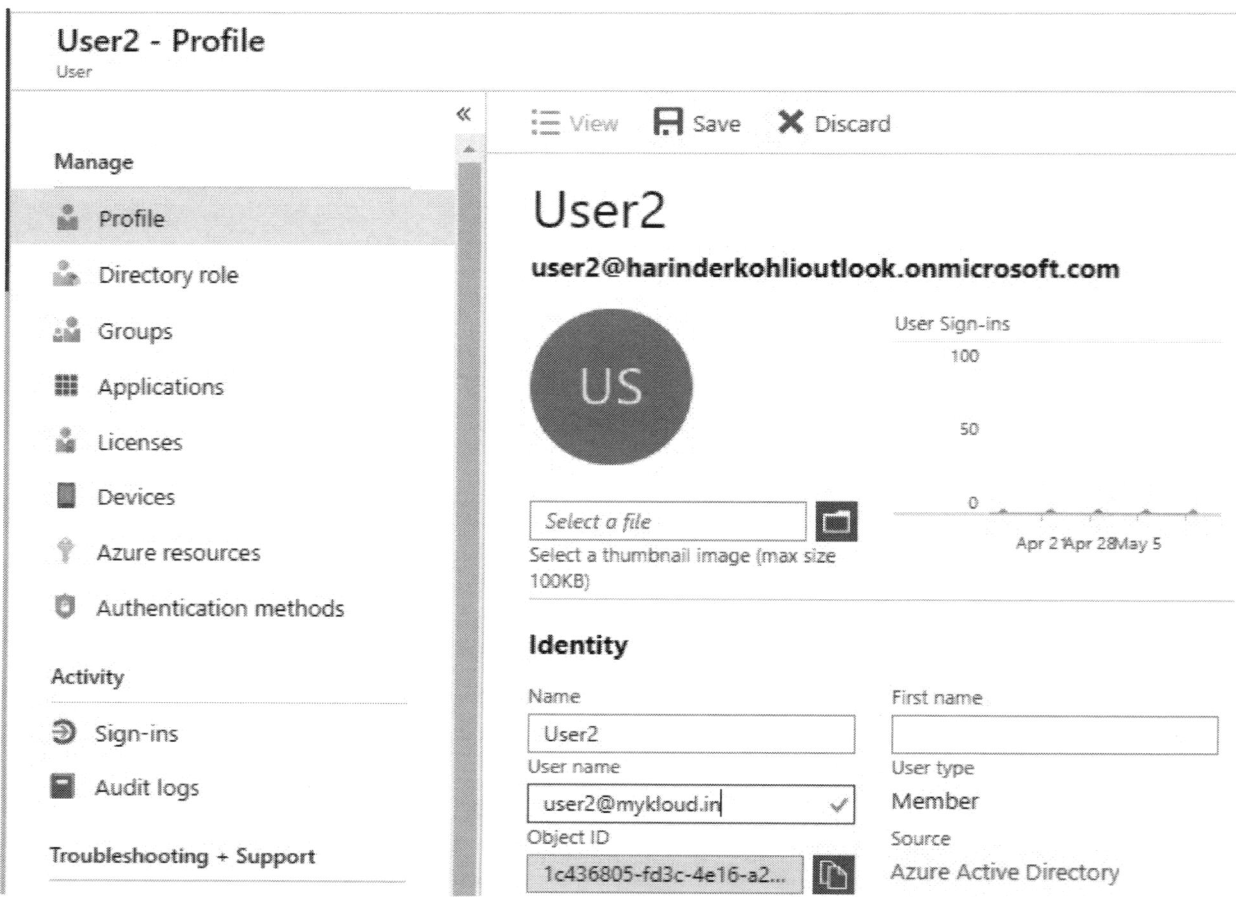

1. Open Firefox Browser and log on to Azure portal with user2@mykloud.in> Login was successful. In top right you can see user2@mykloud.in.

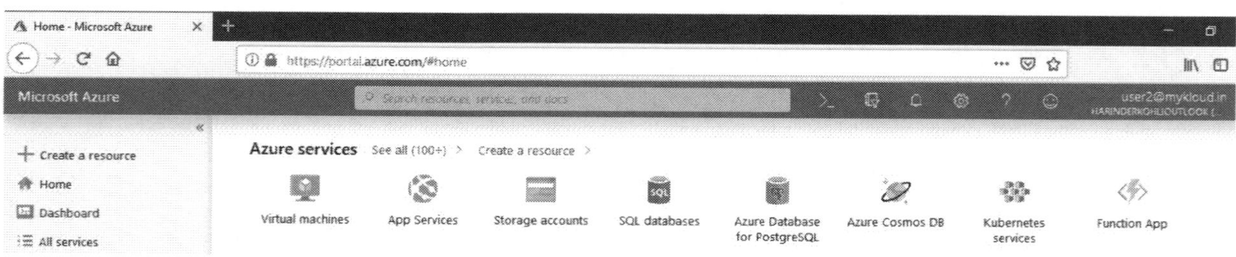

Self Service Password Reset (SSPR)

SSPR options allows users to change, reset and unlock there Azure AD login passwords.

SSPR option free's the helpdesk of password service queries and allow them to concentrate on more pressing issues. Helpdesk is an expensive resource. With SSPR option you can reduce the helpdesk cost.

Azure AD license Requirement for SSPC and SSPR

Self-Service Password Reset for cloud users: Requires AD Basic or Premium P1 or Premium P2 editions.
Self-Service Password Reset/Change/Unlock with on-premises writeback for hybrid users: Requires AD Premium P1 or Premium P2 editions.

Number of authentication methods required

This option determines the minimum number of the available authentication methods a user must go through to reset or unlock their password. **It can be set to either one or two.**

Authentication methods available for Self-Service Password Reset

If SSPR is enabled, you must select at least one or two of the following options for the authentication methods.

Mobile app notification (preview)
Mobile app code (preview)
Email
Mobile phone
Office phone
Security questions

Figure below shows Authentication methods available for password reset.

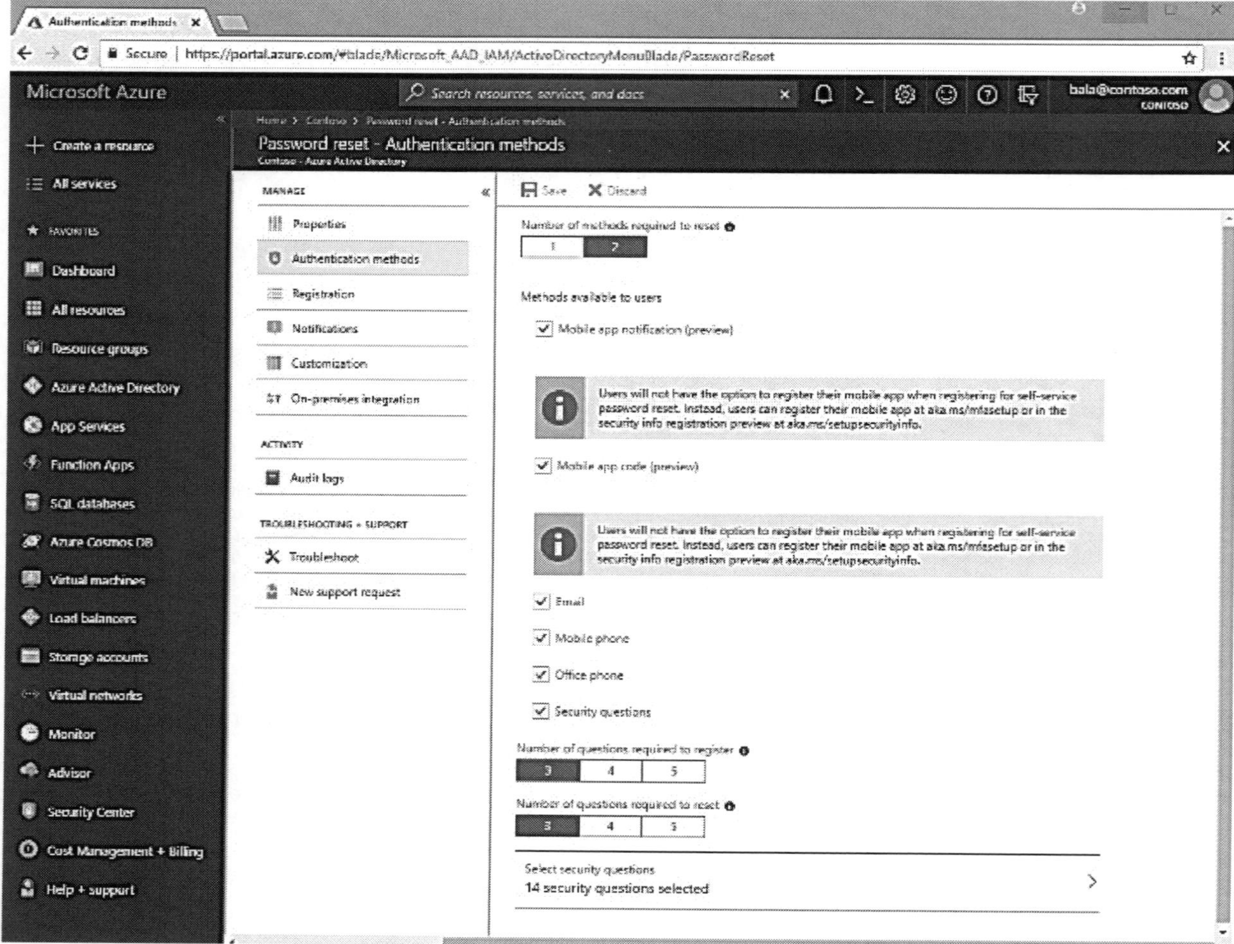

Exercise 112: Enabling SSPR for Cloud Users

1. In Azure AD Dashboard Click Password reset in left pane>Password Reset Blade opens> select either **Selected** or **All.** For this exercise I selected **All**> Click **save**.

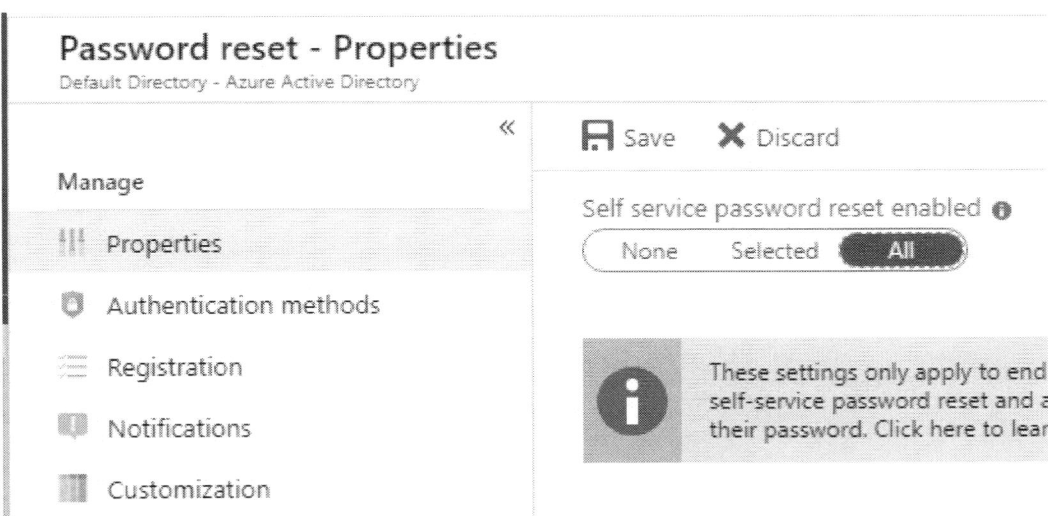

2. In Password reset blade click Authentication Methods>Select **1** and select **Mobile Phone** and click **save.**

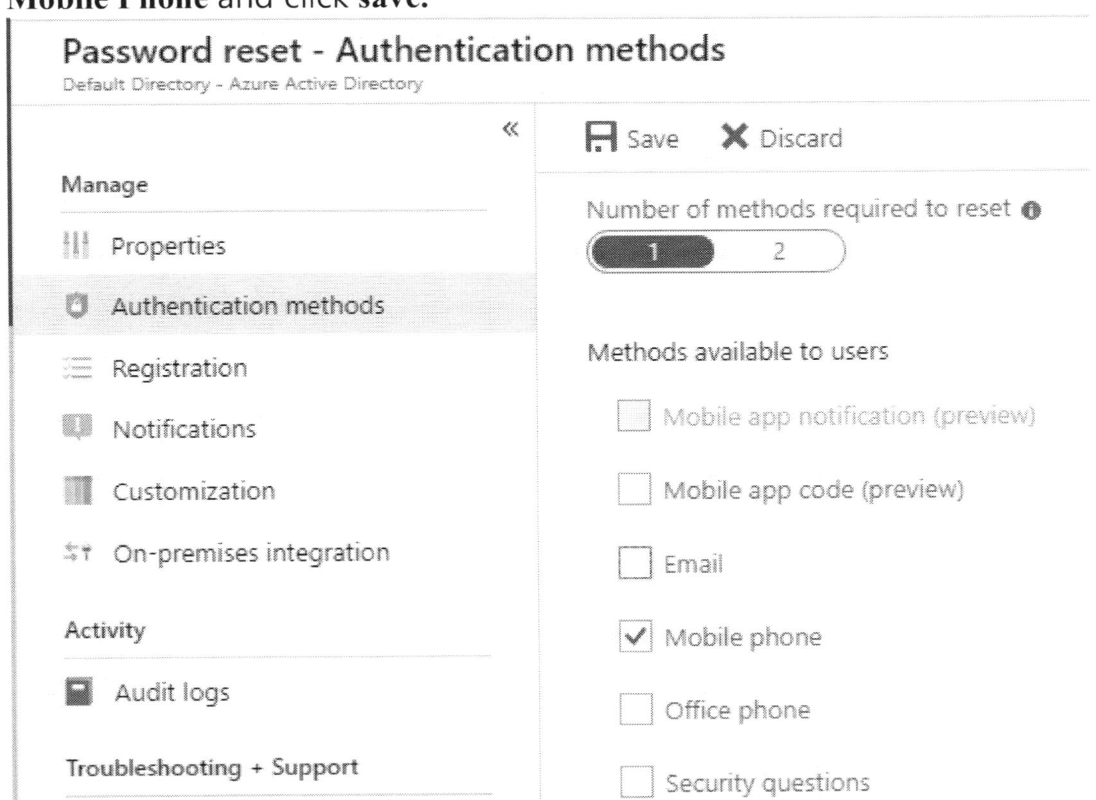

3. In Password reset blade click Registration> Select Yes. Note that save option is not highlighted as Yes is default option. You have the option change the number of days.

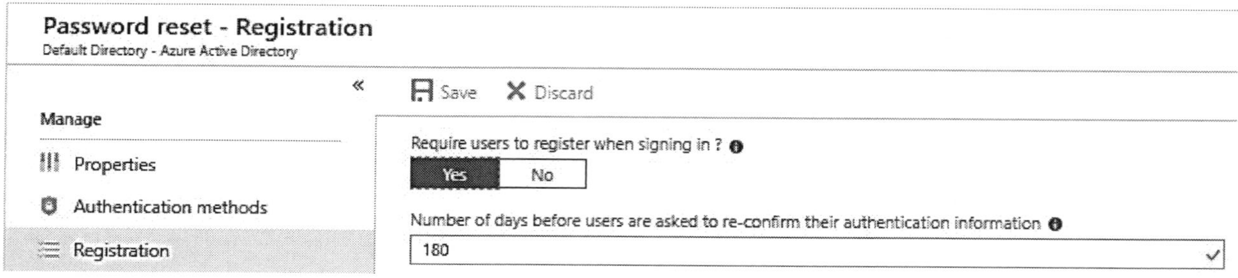

Note 1: After these steps are enabled whenever users log in, they will be asked to update their Mobile Number.
Note 2: If we selected No option, than it this case Administrator has to update Mobile Number in User Profile dashboard.

Exercise 113: Setup SSPR Authentications for User3

Open a different Browser than what is used for Administrator. I am using Chrome for Administrator. I will use **Firefox** for users.

1. Open Firefox and log on with user3@harinderkohlioutlook.onmicrosoft.com > System will ask to update your Authentication Phone number.
2. **Note**: Admin can also update phone from User Profile dashboard.

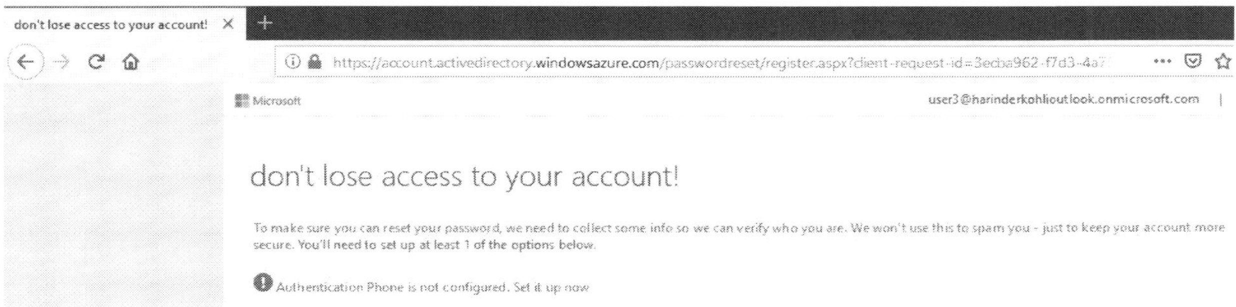

3. Click the link **set it up now** in browser to update User3 Phone number> Select your country and enter your mobile number and click text me>enter the verification code sent to your mobile>Click verify.
4. After you have updated click Finish to close the page.

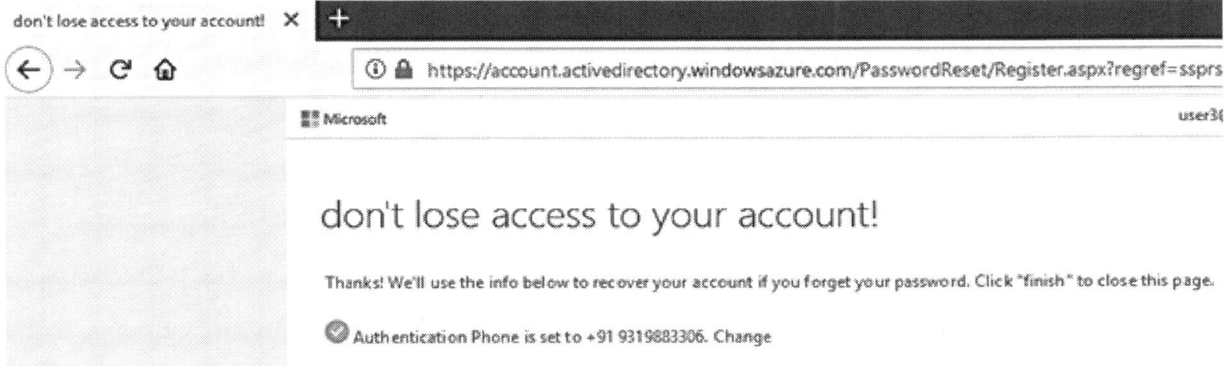

5. Log out of User3 account.

Exercise 114: Test SSPR for User3

1. In Firefox open https://portal.azure.com and enter username but don't enter password. user3@harinderkohli543hotmail.onmicrosoft.com
2. In browser windows click Forgot my password>Get back into your account pane opens> enter User3 user-id and capcha and click next.

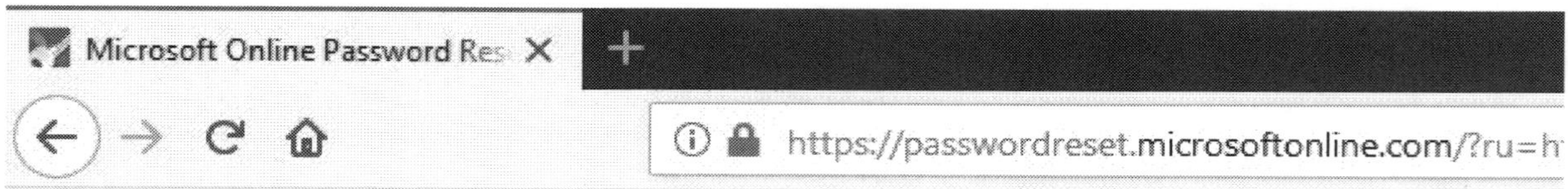

Microsoft

Get back into your account

Who are you?

To recover your account, begin by entering your user ID and the characters in the picture or audio below.

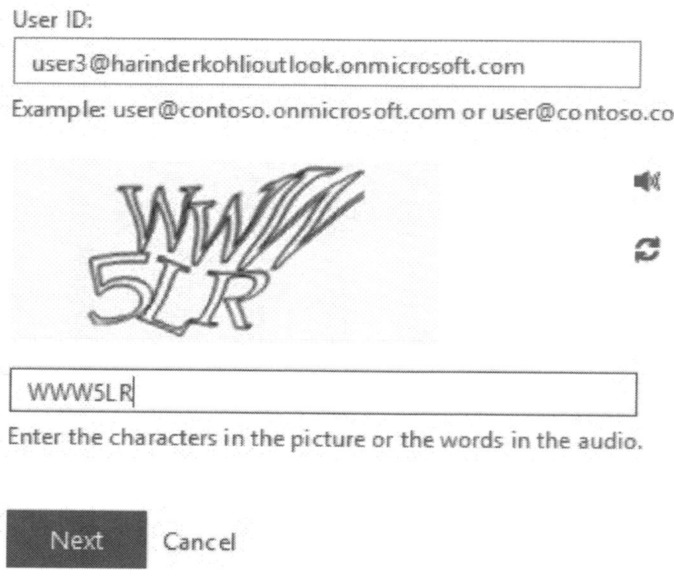

3. Enter Your Mobile Number and click text.

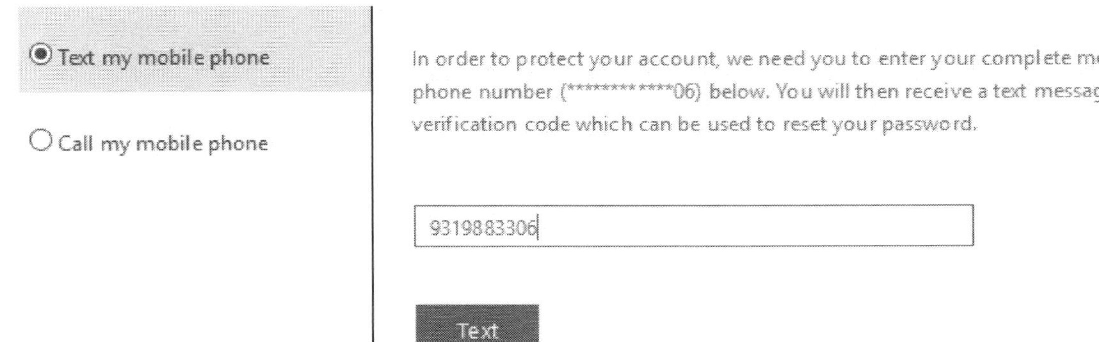

4. Enter Verification code sent to your number and click next.

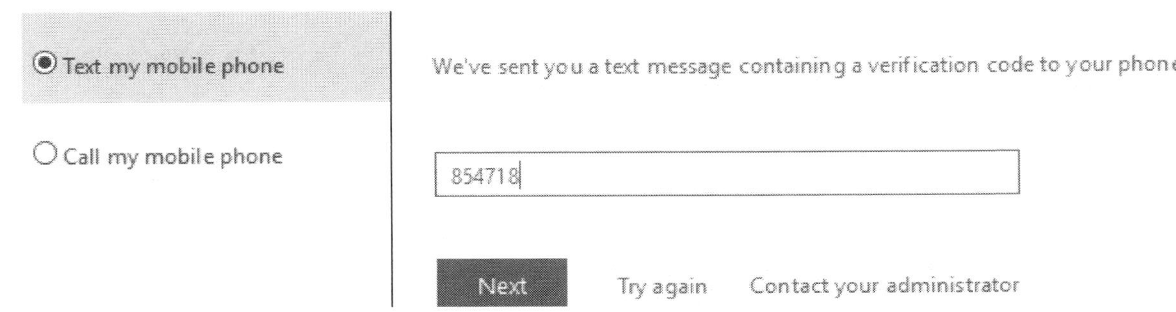

5. Password change pane opens> Enter your new password and click finish.

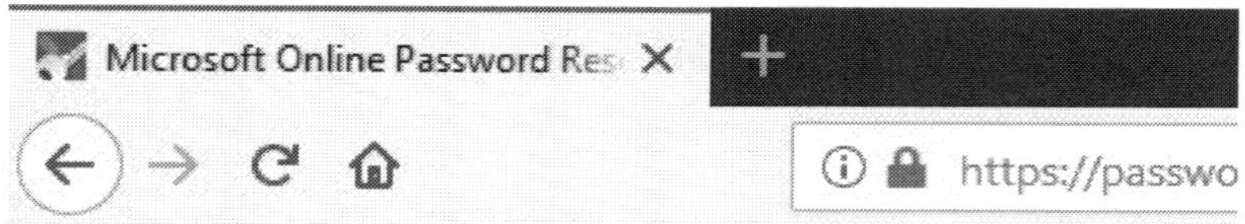

Microsoft

Get back into your account

verification step 1 ✓ > **choose a new password**

* Enter new password:

●●●●●●●●●●●●●

strong

* Confirm new password:

●●●●●●●●●●●●●

Finish Cancel

6. You can now log on with your new password.

You can see from above that User3 Reset its password without involving helpdesk.

Exercise 115: Disabling Self Service Password Reset (SSPR)

1. In Azure AD Dashboard Click Password reset in left pane>Password Reset Blade opens> select **none**>Click **save**.

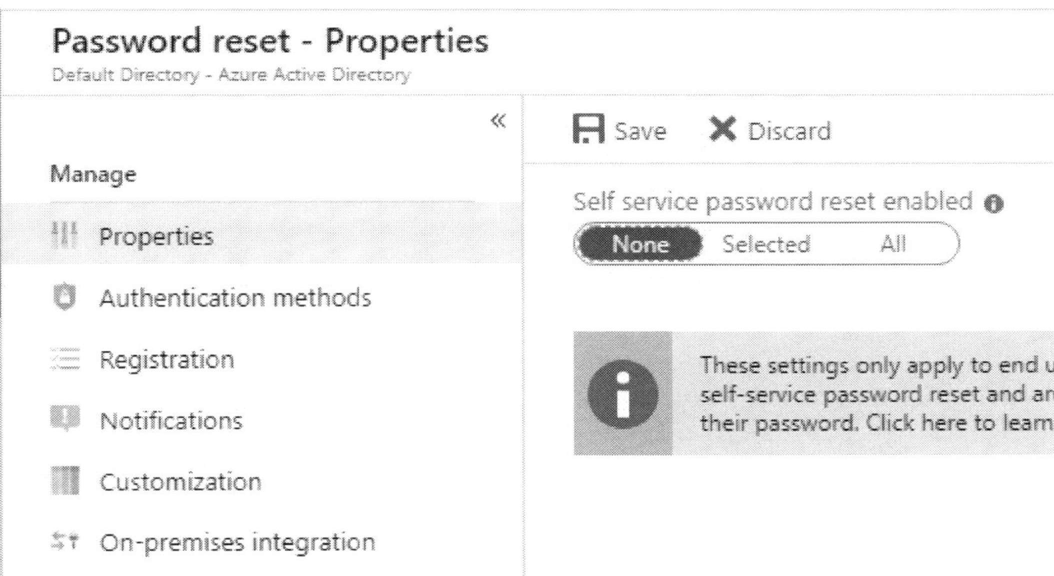

Device Management in Azure AD

In Today's scenario users are accessing corporate applications not only from on-premises but also from home using corporate owned or personal devices.

In Security paranoid world IT administrators want to make sure that devices accessing corporate resources meet their standards for security and compliance.

Device management using Azure AD is foundation for device-based conditional access. With device-based conditional access, you can ensure that access to resources in your environment is only possible with trusted devices.

To manage devices using Azure AD you have 2 options:
1. Registering
2. Joining (AD Join or Hybrid AD Join).

In this Chapter we will focus on Azure AD Join only.

Azure AD Join

With Azure AD Join you join Windows 10 (Professional or Enterprise) computer to Azure AD using user's Azure AD identity. Joining the Device to Azure AD enables you to manage device identity. With Azure AD Join you sign-in to a device using an organizational work or school account instead of a personal account.

Azure AD Join is intended for organizations that are cloud-first / cloud-only. These are typically small- and medium-sized businesses that do not have an on-premises Windows Server Active Directory infrastructure.

Benefits of Azure AD Join

1. With Azure AD Join you can separate the personal and official work on Windows 10 Computer as you get separate screen for official work when you logon with your Azure AD Identity.
2. With Azure AD Join you can provide Single-Sign-On (SSO) to Azure managed SaaS apps and services.
3. With Azure AD Join you can restrict access to apps from devices that meet compliance policy.
4. Enterprise compliant roaming of user settings across joined devices. Users don't need to connect a Microsoft account (for example, Hotmail) to see settings across devices.

5. Access to Windows Store for Business using an Azure AD account. Your users can choose from an inventory of applications pre-selected by the organization.
6. Windows Hello support for secure and convenient access to work resources.
7. Seamless access to on-premises resources when the device has line of sight to the on-premises domain controller.

Exercise 116: Checking Device Settings for Azure AD Users

By default all users can AD Join Devices to Azure AD.

In Azure AD Dashboard Click **Devices** in left pane>Devices pane opens>Click Device Settings in left pane> In right pane you can see All Users can join devices to Azure AD (First Row).

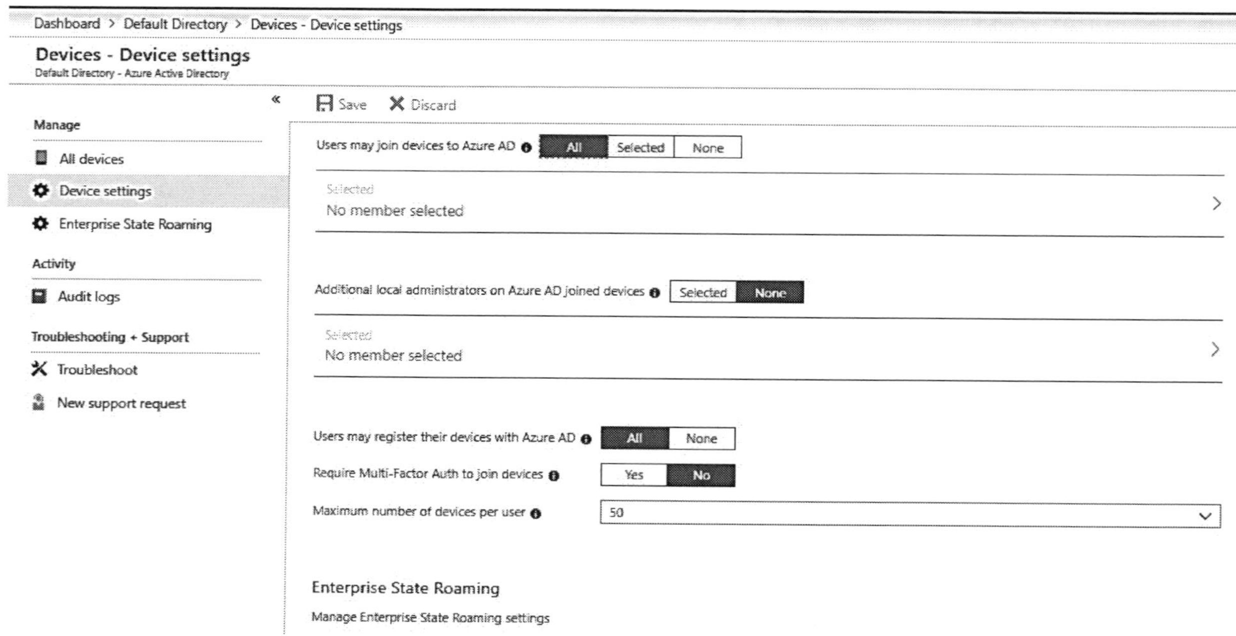

Word of Caution for Next Exercise: I joined my Windows 10 device to Azure AD using AD Join and User2 Credentials. It worked perfectly well. But after a recent Windows update a serious problem arose. I logged in using User2 credentials. When I logged out of system I could not get any option to log on my local desktop with my Local user account. It took me 4-5 hours of R&D to get back to my local desktop.

<u>I would suggest avoid this Exercise.</u>

Exercise 117: Joining Windows 10 PC to Azure AD using Azure AD Join

1. On your Windows 10 Pro Laptop>Click start>Settings Icon>Accounts>Access Work or School>+Connect> In bottom click join this device to Azure Active Directory> In Sign-in page enter User-id of User2 and click next.

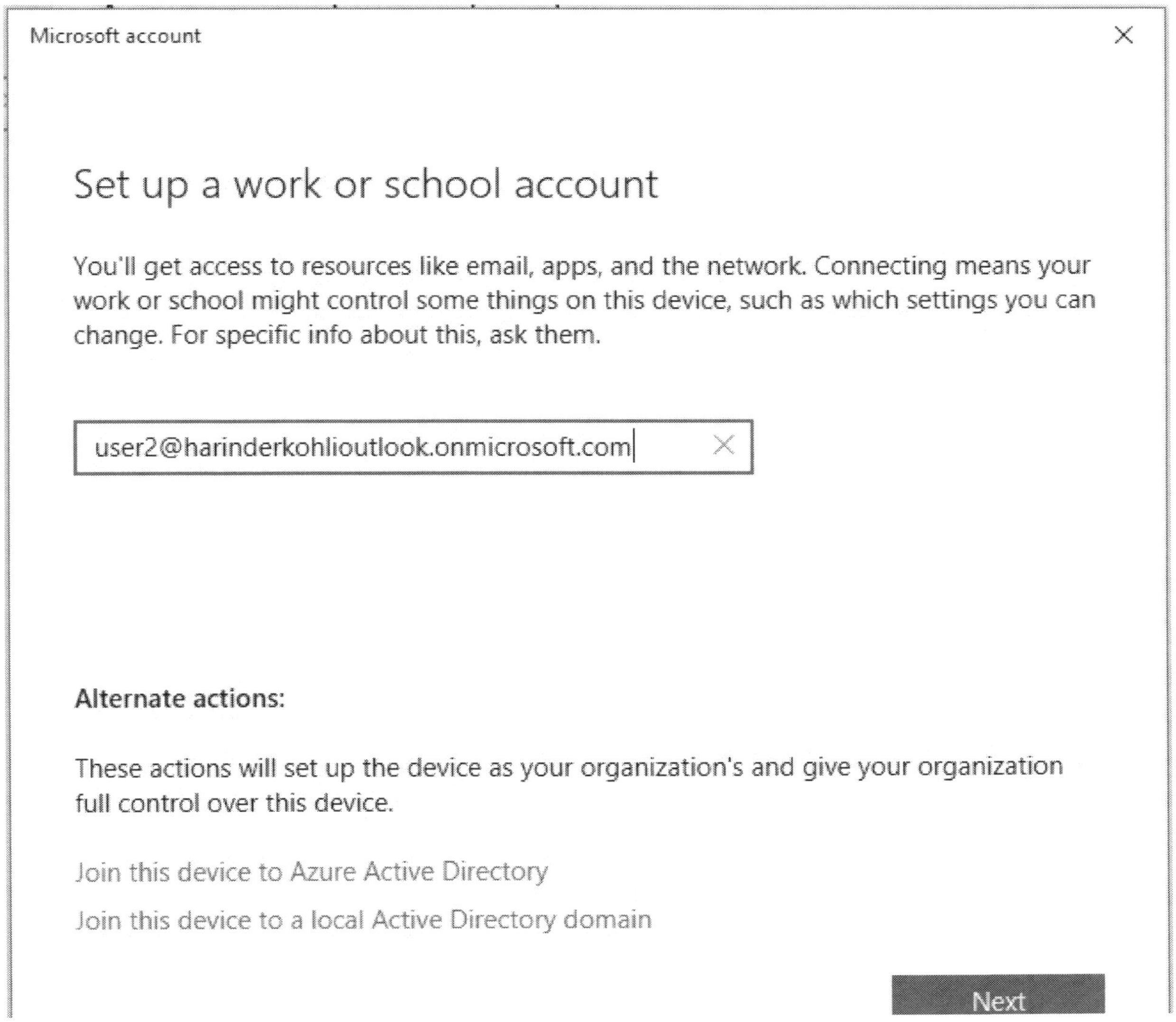

Microsoft account

Set up a work or school account

You'll get access to resources like email, apps, and the network. Connecting means your work or school might control some things on this device, such as which settings you can change. For specific info about this, ask them.

user2@harinderkohlioutlook.onmicrosoft.com

Alternate actions:

These actions will set up the device as your organization's and give your organization full control over this device.

Join this device to Azure Active Directory

Join this device to a local Active Directory domain

Next

2. Enter your password and click sign-in

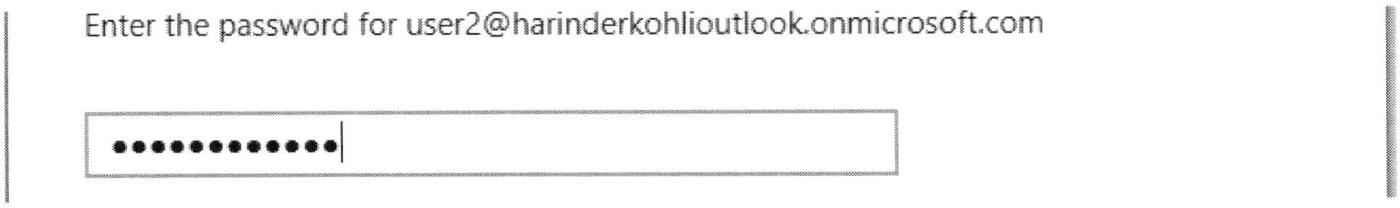

Enter the password for user2@harinderkohlioutlook.onmicrosoft.com

•••••••••••••

3. After Sign-in you get following message>Click Done (not Shown).

You're all set!

This device is connected to Default Directory.

When you're ready to use this new account, select the Start button, select your current account picture, and then select **'Switch account'**. Sign in using your **user2@harinderkohli543hotmail.onmicrosoft.com** email and password.

4. Setting Pane now shows User2 Connected to Default AD>Close the Pane.

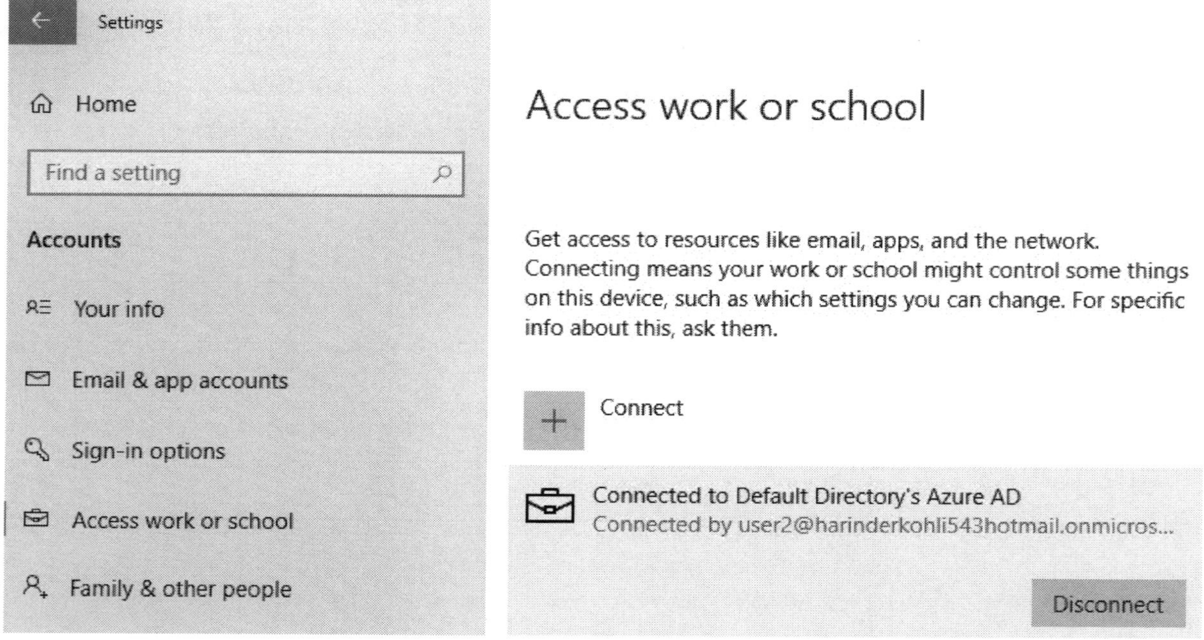

5. Devices Blade now shows Windows 10 AD Joined.

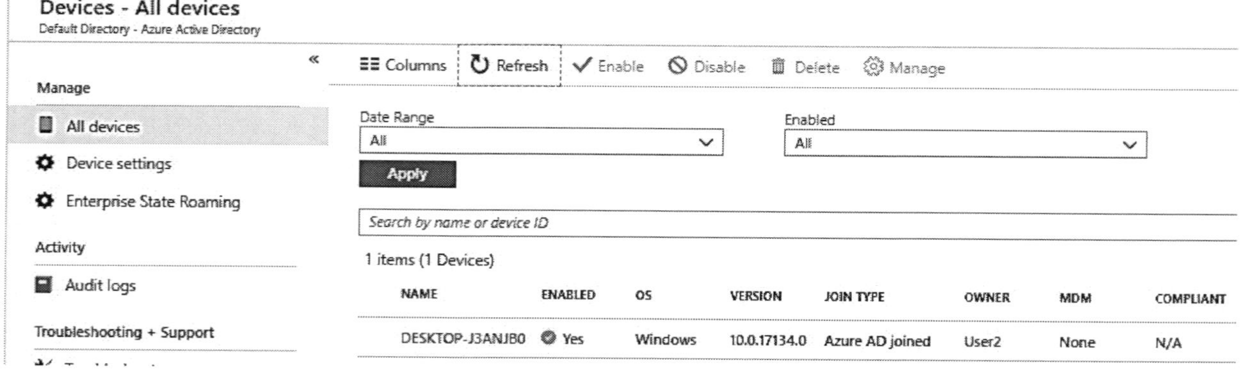

Exercise 118: Log on to Windows 10 PC with User2

1. On your Windows 10 laptop Logout of your personal account.
2. Log on with User2-id - user2@harinderkohlioutlook.onmicrosoft.com.
3. System will ask you verify your account. Use Text message for verifying the account.
4. System will ask you to generate a Pin.
5. You are now logged on to the system.

The laptop screen will now show your work account with no files or folders from your personal Account.

If you are logging from multiple devices then you can sync settings and app data from work account using Enterprise State Roaming

Enterprise State Roaming

With Enterprise State Roaming Users can sync settings and app data across devices.
By default users are not enabled for Enterprise State Roaming. You can enable Enterprise State Roaming for all the users or for Selected Users.

Exercise 119: Enabling Enterprise State Roaming for Users

1. In Azure AD Dashboard Click **Devices** in left pane>Devices pane opens>Click Enterprise State Roaming in left pane> ESR pane opens.

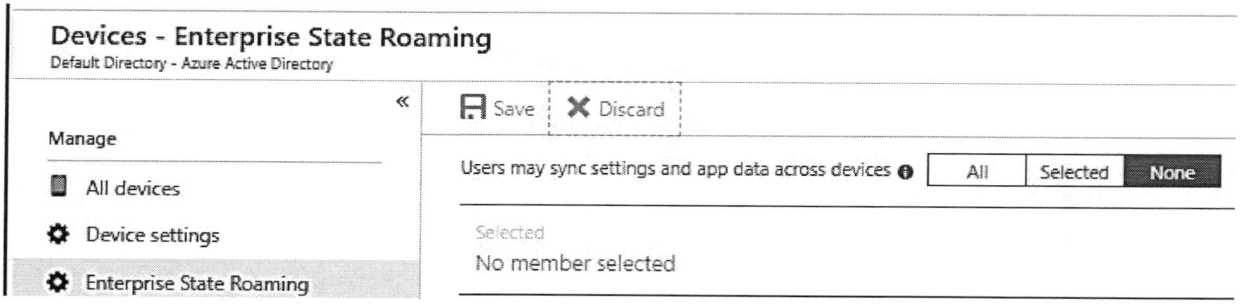

2. In Right Pane you can select **Selected** or **All.** For this exercise we will select All. >Click save.

Enterprise State Roaming data

Enterprise State Roaming data is hosted in one or more Azure regions that best align with the country/region value set in the Azure Active Directory instance.

Data synced to the Microsoft cloud using Enterprise State Roaming is retained until it is manually deleted or until the data in question is determined to be stale.

Managing Multiple Azure AD Directory Tenant

A Subscription can be associated with a Single Azure AD Tenant only. But Azure AD tenant can be associated with Multiple Subscriptions.

Instead of Default Azure AD Tenant you can associate a New Azure AD Tenant with the Subscription.

Exercise 120: Creating New Azure AD Tenant

2. In Azure Portal Click +Create a Resource in left pane> Identity> Azure Active Directory> Create Azure Active Directory blade opens> Enter a name, **aadncloud** for initial Domain name and select Country and click create.

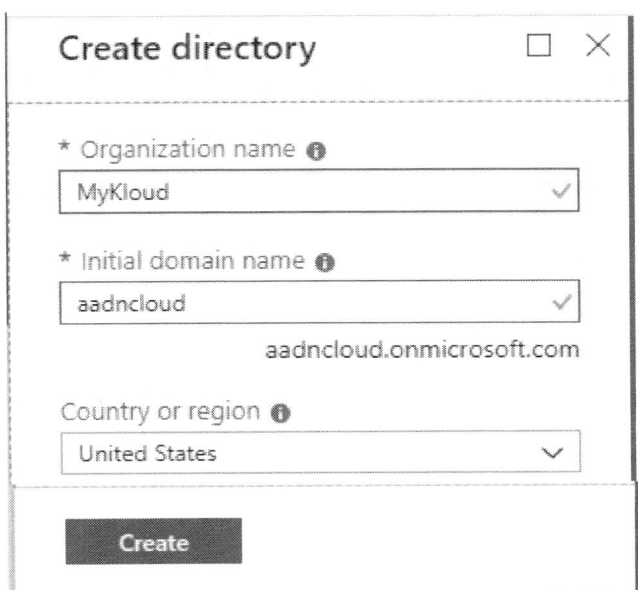

Exercise 121: Associating Azure AD Tenant with the Subscription

In this exercise we will just demonstrate how to associate our subscription with AD tenant created in previous Exercise. Actual association will not happen as we have to do more exercises with default AD tenant.

1. In Azure Portal Click **Cost Management** + **Billing** in left pane> Cost Management + Billing Dashboard opens>Click Subscriptions in left pane> In right pane click your subscription>Subscription Dashboard opens> You can see Subscription is associated with Default Azure AD Tenant.

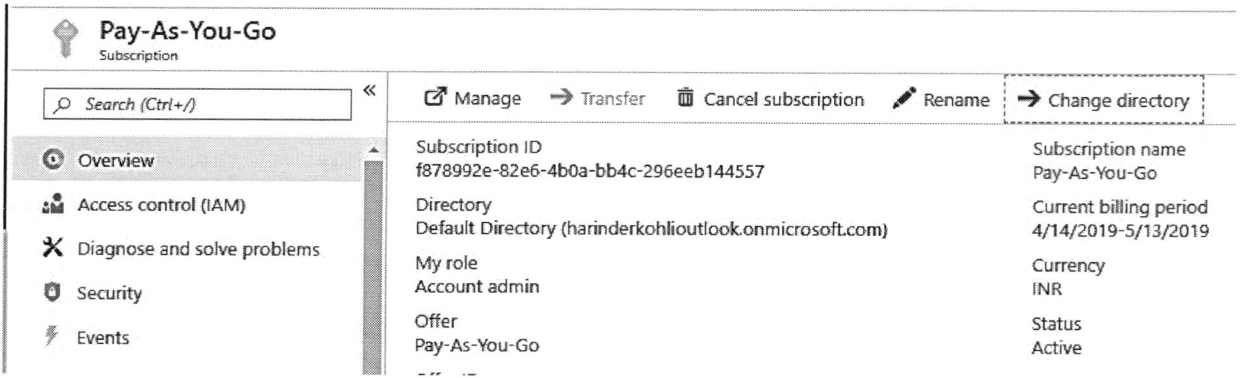

2. Click Change Directory in Right pane>Change Directory Blade opens>From Dropdown Box Select MyKloud Azure AD Tenant created in Previous Exercise. Don't proceed further as we need to more exercises with Default Tenant. Close the Change Directory Blade.

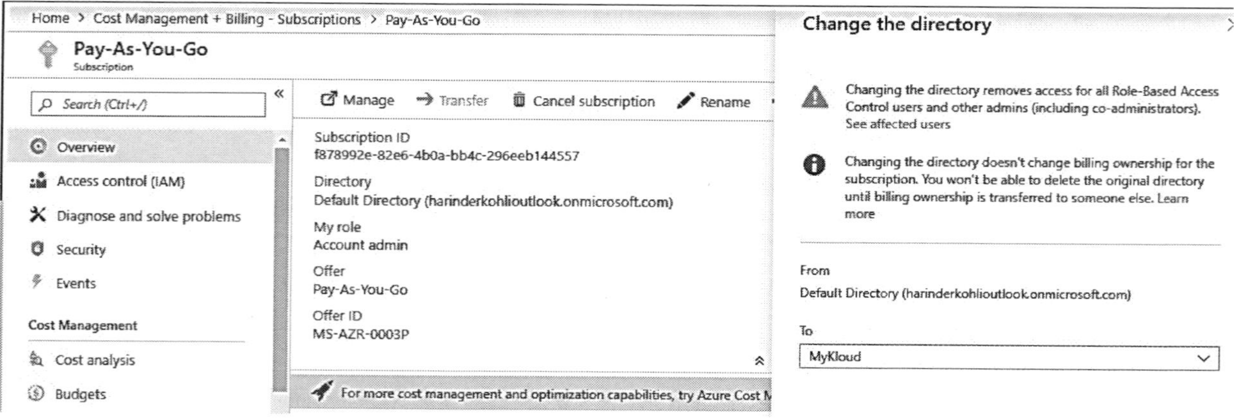

Chapter 13 Implementing Azure AD Hybrid Identities

This Chapter covers following Topic Lessons

- Azure AD Hybrid Identity options with AD Connect
- Components of AD Connect
- Requirements for deploying AD Connect Server
- Seamless Single Sign-on
- Password Writeback
- AD Connect with Federation with ADFS option
- IDFIX Tool

This Chapter covers following Lab Exercises

- Install AD Connect with Password Hash Synchronisation
- Check Users Test1 & Test2 synchronization to Azure AD
- Check AD Connect options
- AD Connect Health

Chapter Topology

In this chapter we will add **AD Connect** and **AD Connect health Agent** to the topology. They will be installed on VM VMAD. AD Connect will synchronize on-premises users in Active Directory Domain Services (AD DS) to Default Azure AD Tenant. **AD Connect health Agent** will monitor health of On-premises Active Directory (AD DS). AD DS role was installed on VM VMAD in Compute Chapter.

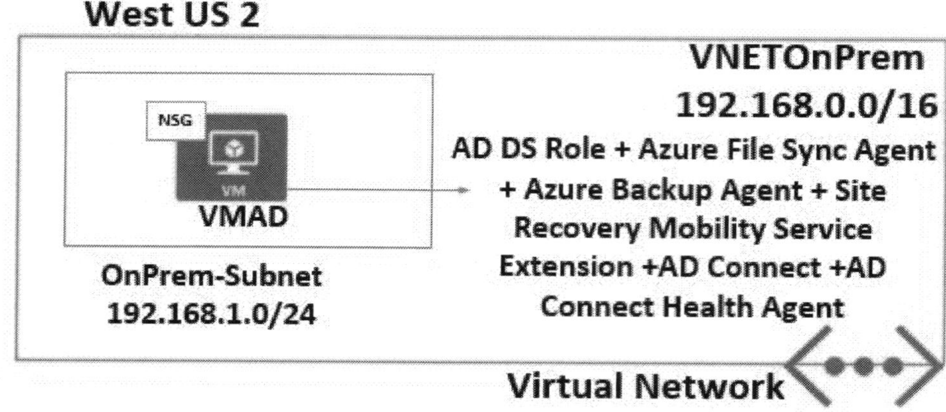

Users in on-premises AD DS (VMAD) will be synchronized to Default Azure AD Tenant.

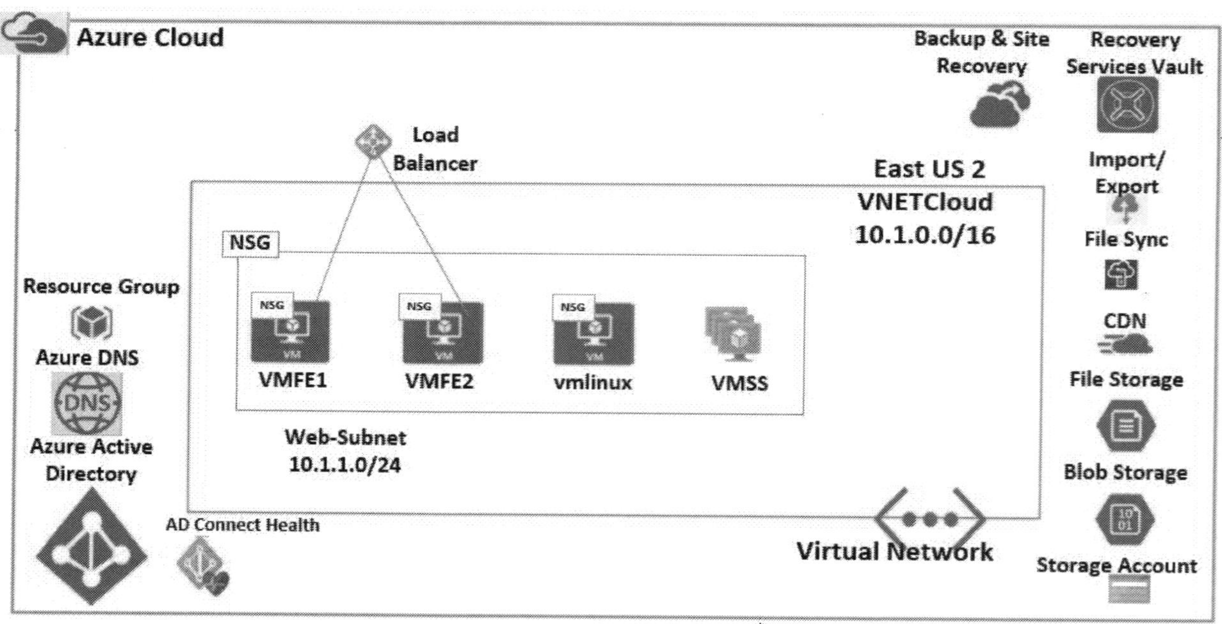

Azure AD Hybrid Identity options with AD Connect

Azure AD Connect integrates on-premises directories with Azure Active Directory. AD Connect synchronizes on-premises users in Active Directory Domain Services (AD DS) or any other compatible Directory Services to Azure Active Directory.

The **advantage** of AD Connect is that Users can access cloud and on-premises resources with the single identity. Another advantage is that we don't have to manually create user in Azure Active Directory as they synced from on-premises AD. Third advantage is that by enabling single sign-on, users who are logged on to on-premises can access cloud resources without logging to Azure.

You need to just manage your on-premises AD and all changes are synchronized with Azure AD.

AD Connect is usually installed on-premises with a service component in Azure. Figure below shows Architecture of AD Connect.

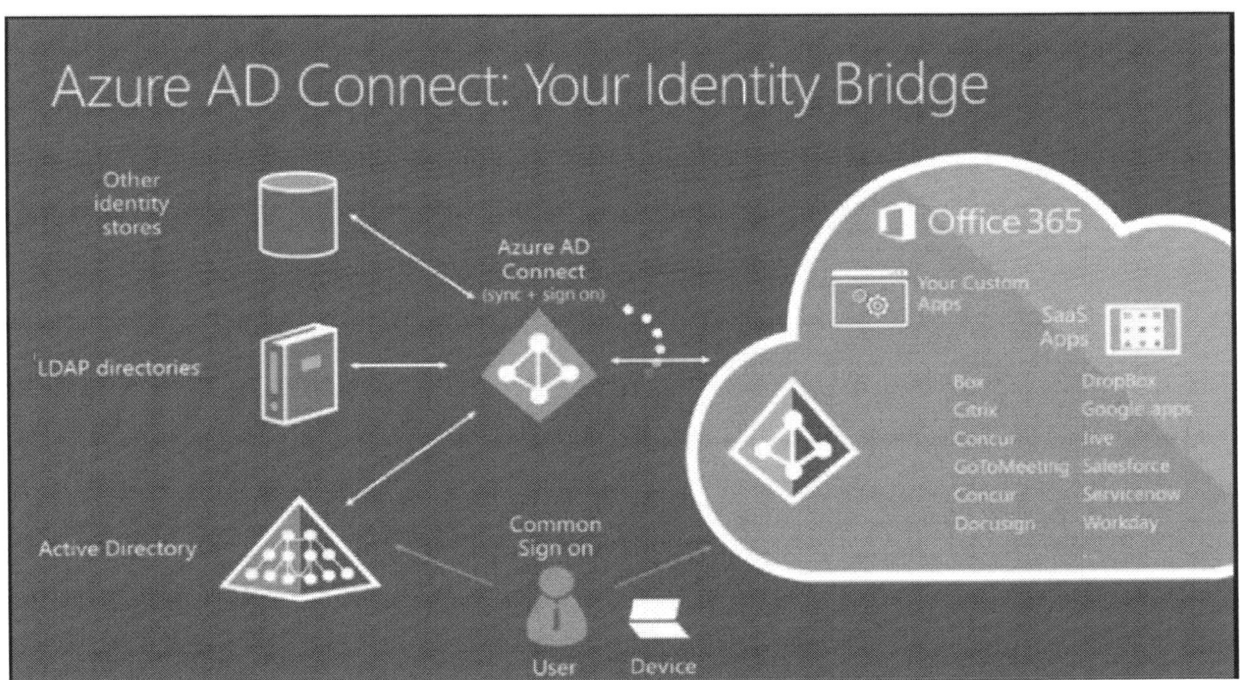

Following 5 identity options are available with Azure AD when used in conjunction with AD Connect. Figure below shows various Identity options available.

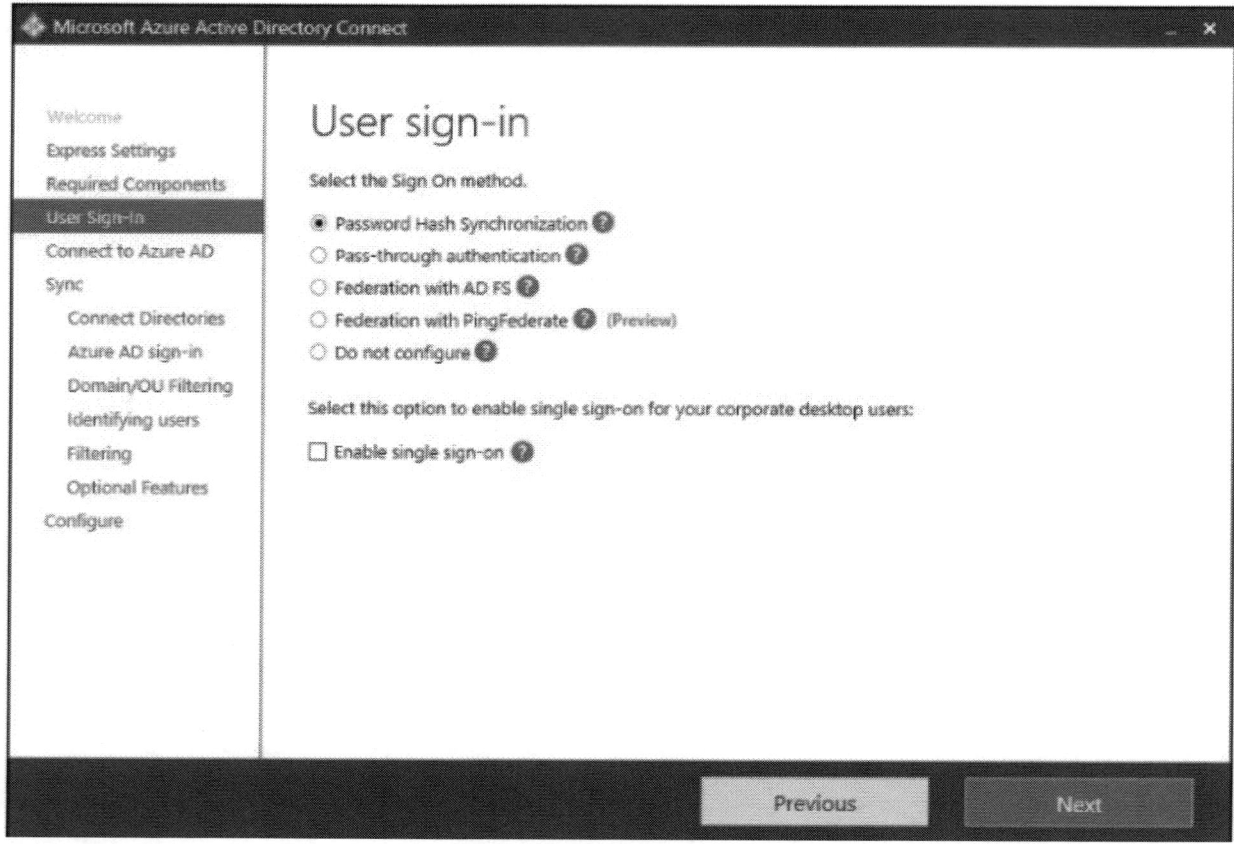

Synced Identity or Password Hash Synchronization: Identity is maintained both in cloud and on-premises. Authentication happens in cloud.

AD Connect installed on-premises with password synchronization option, synchronizes users and password hash of on-premises Active Directory users to Azure AD.

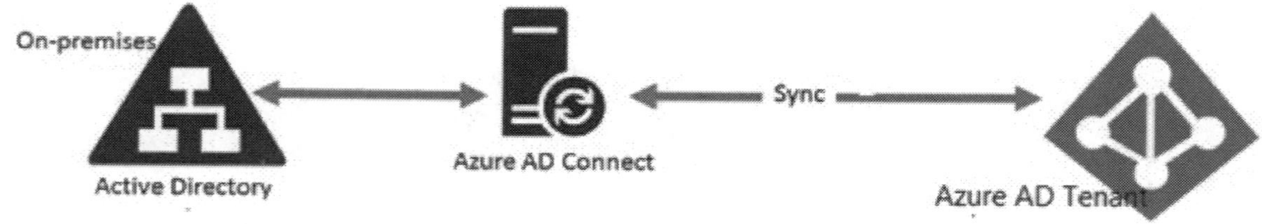

One advantage of this option is that you can enable single sign-on during AD Connect Installation without requiring any complex hardware setup.

Requires Azure AD Subscription, AD Connect Installed on-premises and on-premises AD DS.

Pass-through Authentication Option: Identity is maintained in both cloud and on-premises. Authentication happen on-premises with Active Directory.

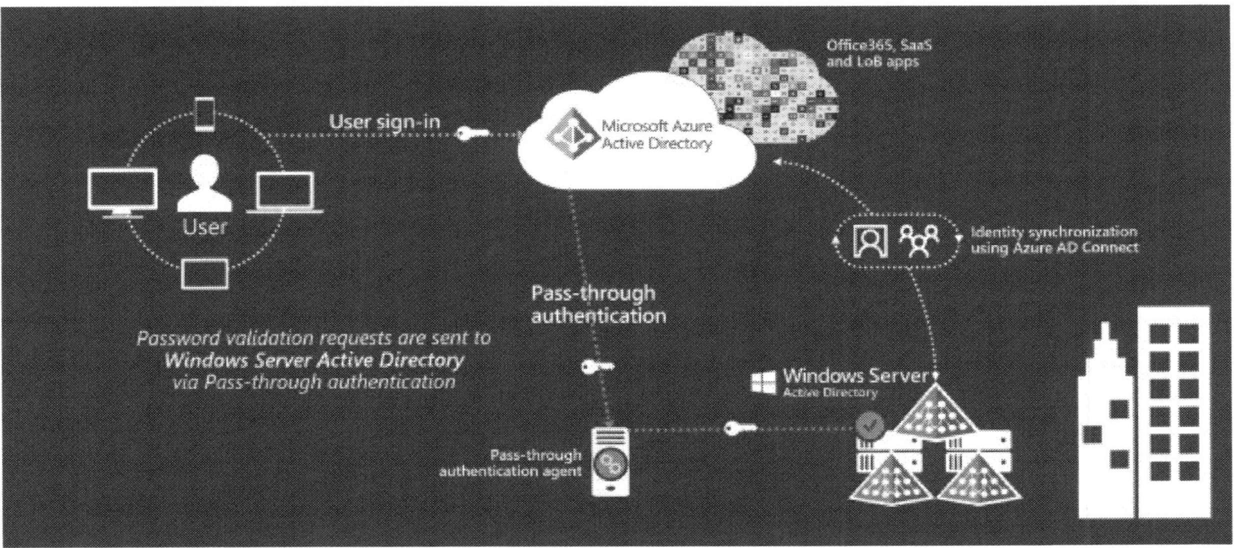

AD Connect installed on-premises with Pass-through Authentication Option, Synchronizes on premises Active Directory users to Azure AD. In this case Password Hash of users are not Synchronized.

A Pass through agent is installed on-premises on a windows server. The agent listens for and responds to password validation requests only. It receives encrypted password from Azure AD. It Decrypts it and validates it against Local Active Directory. The communication between Azure AD and Pass through agent is over Azure Service Bus. Azure SQL Database in cloud is used to holds information about metadata and encryption keys of Authentication Agents.

The advantage of this option is that there is no need for complex on-premises deployments or network configuration as in the case of ADFS. Second advantage is that you can enable seamless single sign-on during AD Connect Installation.

Requires Azure AD Subscription, AD Connect installed on-premises, Pass through agent installed on-premises, Azure SQL Database, Azure Service Bus and on-premises Active Directory.

Federated Identity with ADFS: Identity is maintained in both cloud and on-premises. User Authentication happen on-premises by Active Directory Federation Services (ADFS) server against local Active Directory.

AD Connect installed on-premises with Federation with ADFS option, Synchronizes on premises Active Directory users to Azure AD. In this case Password Hash of users are not Synchronized.

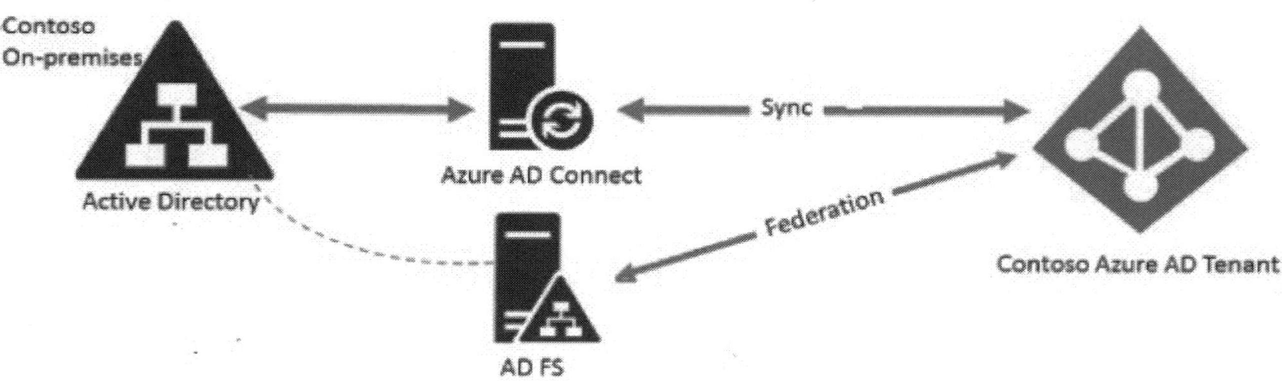

Active Directory Federation Services (ADFS) server installed on-premises and ADFS component in AD Connect, federate the 2 directories which results in one-way trust with Azure AD **Trusting** on-premises ADFS. User Login happens in cloud but user authentication is redirected to on-premises ADFS.

Requires Azure AD Subscription, AD Connect Installed on-premises, on-premises Active Directory Domain Services (AD DS) and on-premises Active Directory Federation services (AD FS).

ADFS option is used by organizations to address complex deployments such as enforcement of on-premises AD sign-in policy, Single Sign-on (SSO) and smart card or 3rd party MFA.

Federated Identity with PingFederate: Identity is maintained in both cloud and on-premises. User Authentication happen on-premises by PingFederate Instance against local Active Directory or any other LDAP Server.

AD Connect installed on-premises with Federation with PingFederate option, Synchronizes on premises users to Azure AD. In this case Password Hash of users are not Synchronized.

Requires Azure AD Subscription, AD Connect Installed on-premises, on-premises Active Directory and on-premises PingFederate Instance.

Federated Identity with 3rd Party Identity Manager: Identity is maintained in both cloud and on-premises. User Authentication happen on-premises by 3rd party identity manager server against local Active Directory.

3rd Party Identity Manager can be from Okta, Big-IP Access Policy Manager & IBM Tivoli Federated Identity Manager etc.

Requires Azure AD Subscription, AD Connect installed on-premises, on-premises Active Directory and on-premises 3rd Party Identity Manager.

Important Note: In this case Federation between 3rd party identity manager and Azure AD requires integration to be provided by 3rd party identity manager.

Components of AD Connect

Azure Active Directory Connect is made up of **three components**: the **synchronization services**, the optional **Active Directory Federation Services (ADFS)** component and the monitoring component named **Azure AD Connect Health**.

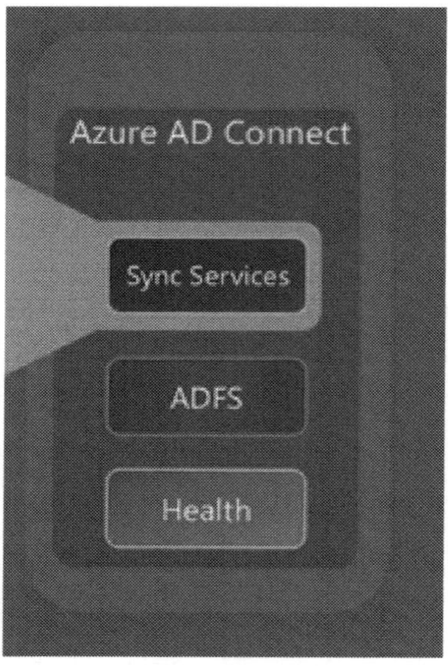

Synchronization Service

It synchronizes identity data between your on-premises Active Directory and Azure AD. The synchronization feature of Azure AD Connect has two components.

1. The on-premises component Azure AD Connect sync, also called sync engine.
2. The service residing in Azure AD also known as Azure AD Connect sync service.

Synchronization service copies usernames and password hash from on-premises active directory to Azure AD tenant. This allows users to authenticate against Azure AD using there on-premises credentials.

Note: We will not discuss ADFS here as we have already covered it in previuos section and we also cover it in next sections.

AD Connect Health

Azure AD Connect Health helps you monitor and gain insight into your on-premises identity infrastructure and the synchronization services.

AD Connect Health Monitors - Active Directory Federation Servers (AD FS), Azure AD Connect servers (Sync Engine), Active Directory Domain Controllers (AD DS).

Azure Connect Health requires Azure AD Premium edition. You also require an agent on each of your on-premises identity servers.

Figure below shows Azure AD Connect Health portal which is used to view alerts, performance monitoring, usage analytics, and other information for your identity Infrastructure.

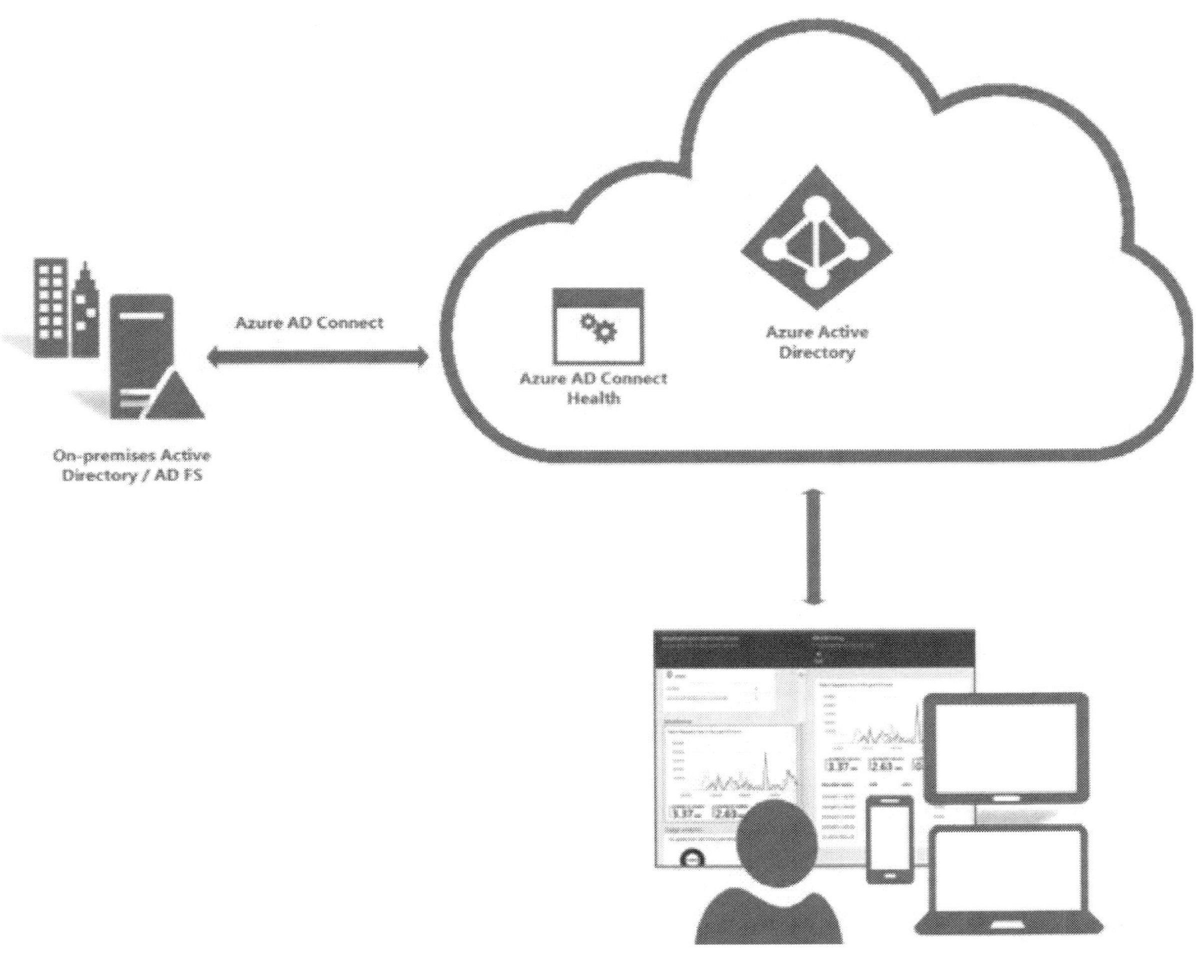

The AD Connect Health Portal URL is at https://aka.ms/aadconnecthealth. On the Portal you can see the identity services which are being monitored and the severity level of the services. You can drill down on the service further by clicking one of the tiles. Figure bellows AD Connect Health Portal dashboard showing monitoring of ADFS, AD Connect & AD DS.

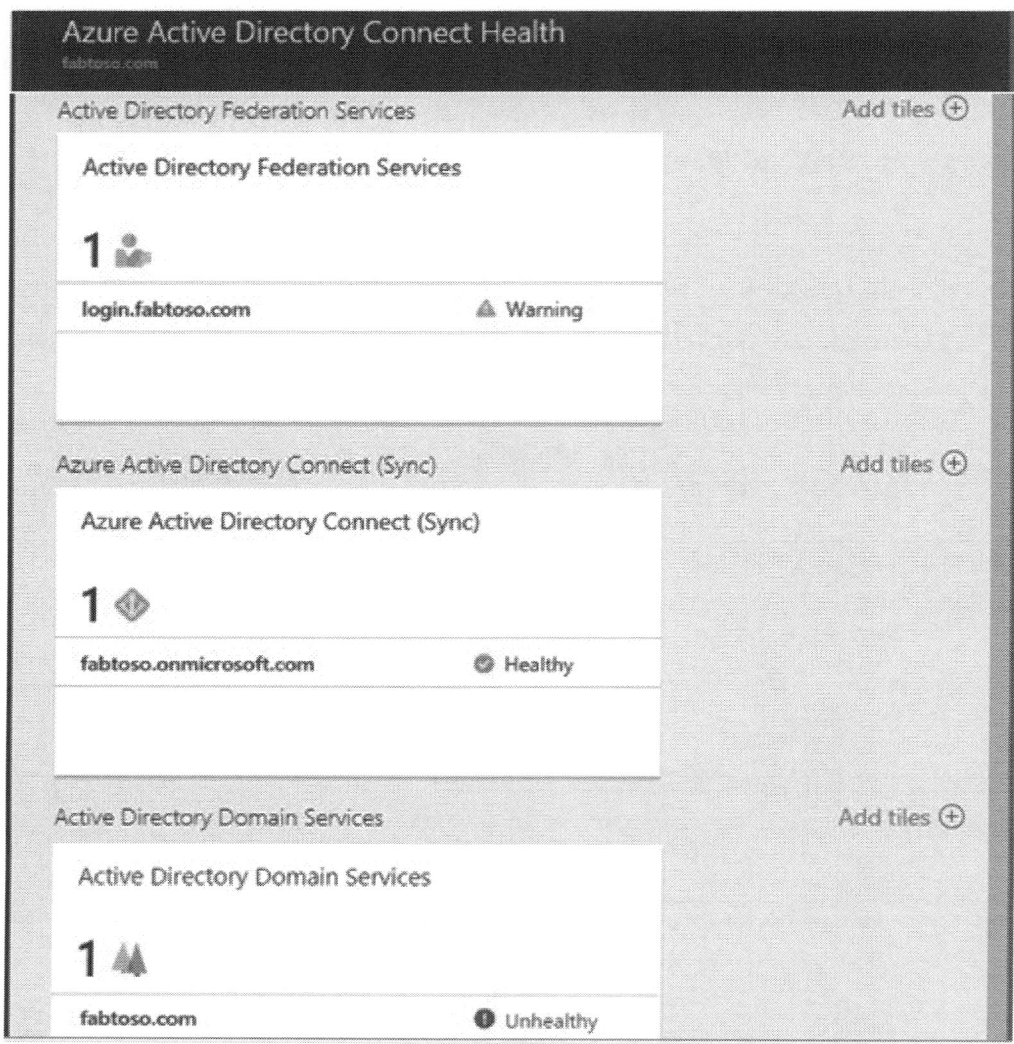

Requirements for deploying AD Connect Server

Hardware Requirement for AD Connect Server

CPU: Dual Core 1.6 GHz or Higher.
Memory: 4GB or Higher (Depends on number of objects in Active Directory).
HDD: 70 GB to 500 GB (Depends on number of objects in Active Directory).
Table below shows Database, Memory and HDD requirement for AD Connect based on number of objects in Active Directory. CPU Requirement remains same.

Number of objects in AD	Database	Memory	HDD
Upto 50000	SQL Server Express or SQL Server	4 GB	70 GB
50,000–100,000	SQL Server Express or SQL Server	16 GB	100 GB
100,000–300,000	SQL Server	32 GB	300 GB
300,000–600,000	SQL Server	32 GB	450 GB
More than 600,000	SQL Server	32 GB	500 GB

Software Requirements for AD Connect Server

Operating System: Recommended is to install on windows Server 2008 R2 SP1 Standard or higher version. The Azure AD Connect server must have .NET Framework 4.5.1 or later and Microsoft PowerShell 3.0 or later installed.
Database: SQL Server Express or SQL Server. By default a SQL Server 2012 Express is installed that enables you to manage approximately 100,000 objects. To manage more than 100000 objects you need SQL Server 2008 onwards.
Note 1: Certain feature like group managed service account require Windows server 2012.

DNS Requirement (Important Concept)

The Azure AD Connect server needs DNS resolution for both intranet and internet.

Exercise 122: Install AD Connect with Pass Hash Synchronisation

In this Lab we will install AD connect with Password Hash Synchronisation option on VM VMAD. VM VMAD was created in Exercise 39, Chapter 4. VM VMAD was configured with AD DS role in Exercise 40, Chapter 4.

We will use User1 to connect to Azure AD during AD Connect Installation. User1 was created in Exercise 101, Chapter 12. AD connect will synchronise on-premises users to Azure AD Tenant. You cannot use Subscription user with MS Hotmail Account.

Create 2 Users (Test1 & Test 2) in AD DS to be synced with Azure AD Tenant

1. RDP to VM VMAD.
2. Open Active Directory Users and Computers>Click on domain AZX0X.local> Right Click Users>New>User>Create User pane opens. Create 2 Users -Test1 & Test2.

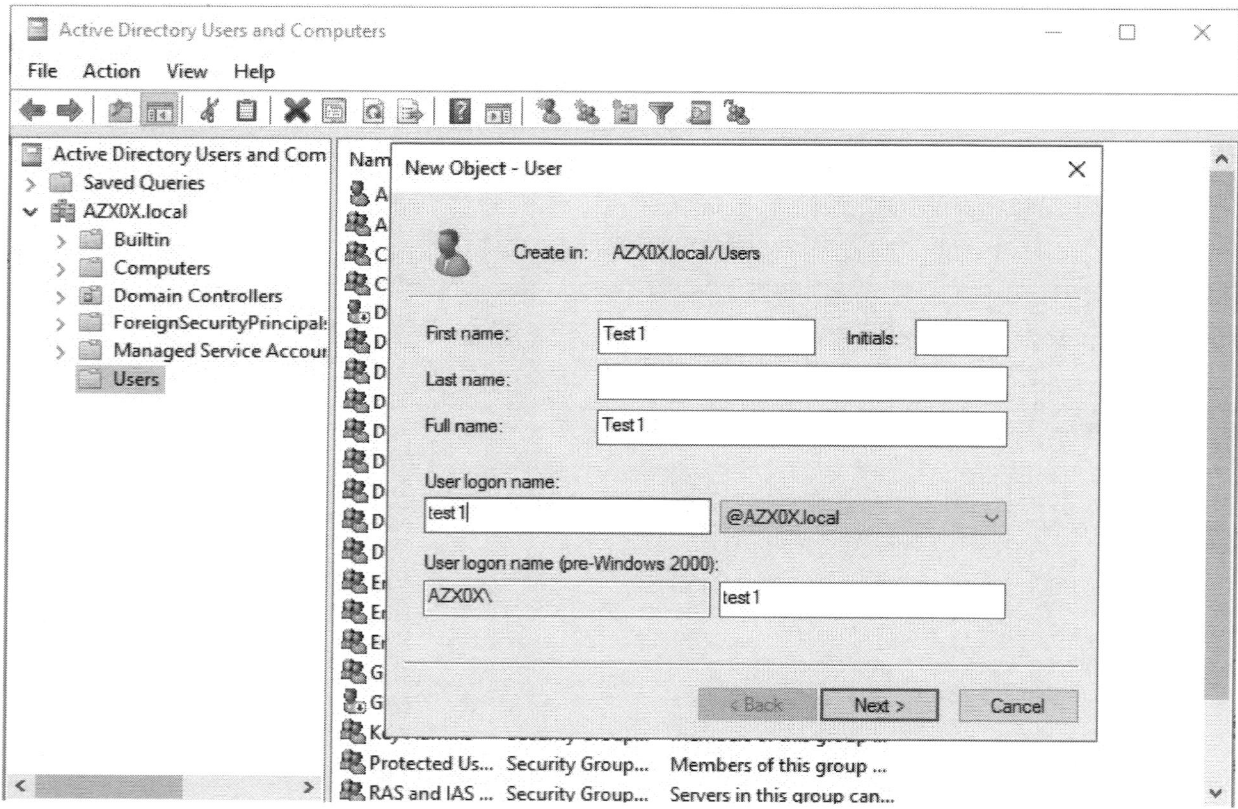

3. Close Active Directory Users and Computers.

Download and Install AD Connect

1. RDP to VM VMAD.
2. Open Internet Explorer and log on to https://portal.azure.com with **User1** Credentials user1@harinderkohlioutlook.onmicrosoft.com.
3. Click Azure Active Directory in left pane>In Azure AD Dashboard click AD Connect in left pane>In right pane Click Download Azure AD Connect>New Browser windows opens> click download to download AD Connect.

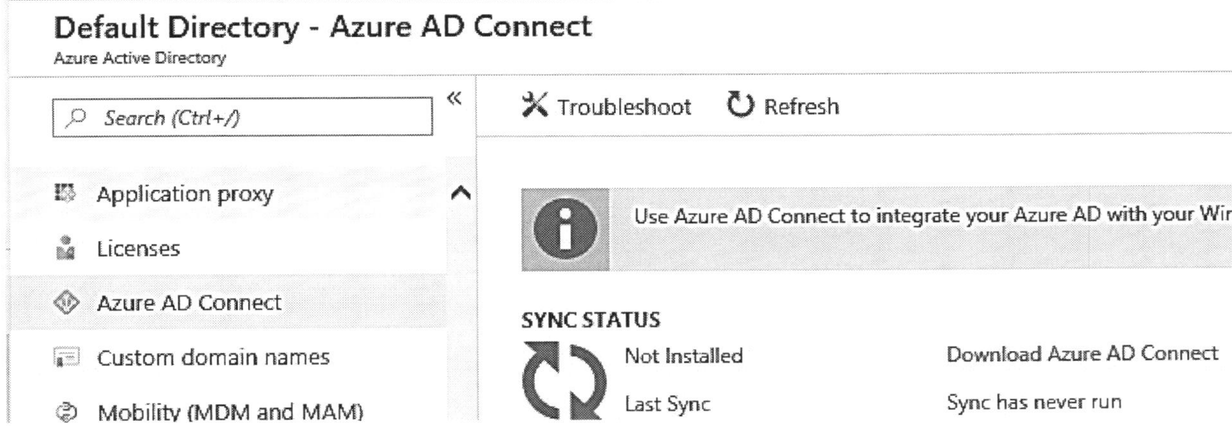

4. On VMAD Click the AD Connect downloaded file to start the installation>AD Connect Installation wizard opens>Select License terms check box>Click Continue (Not shown).

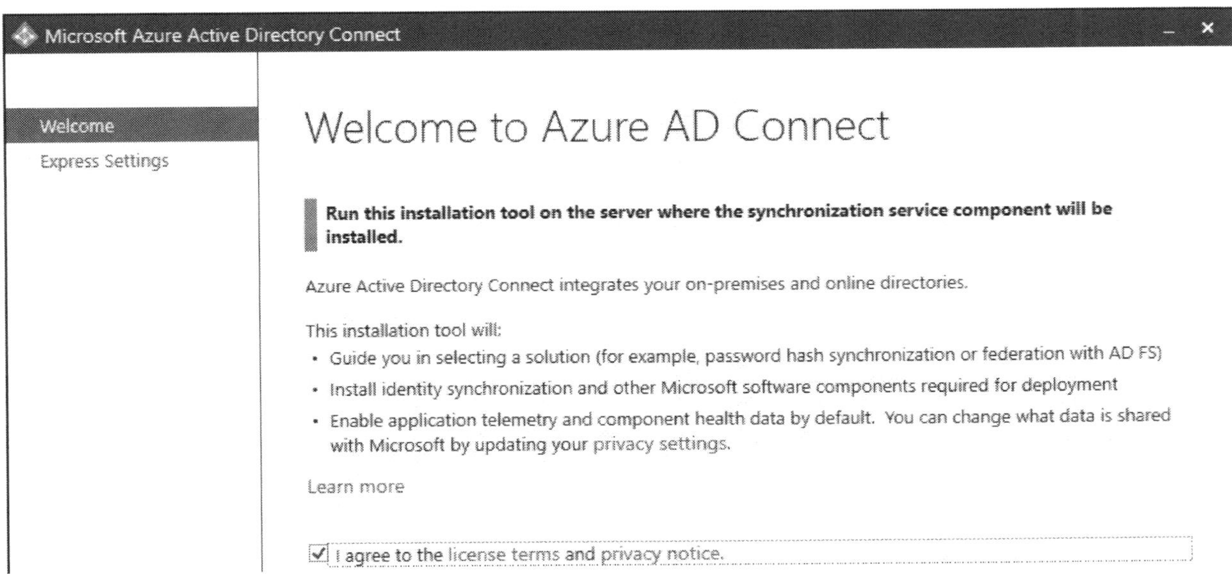

4. Express Setting Installation option opens> Click Customize in bottom.

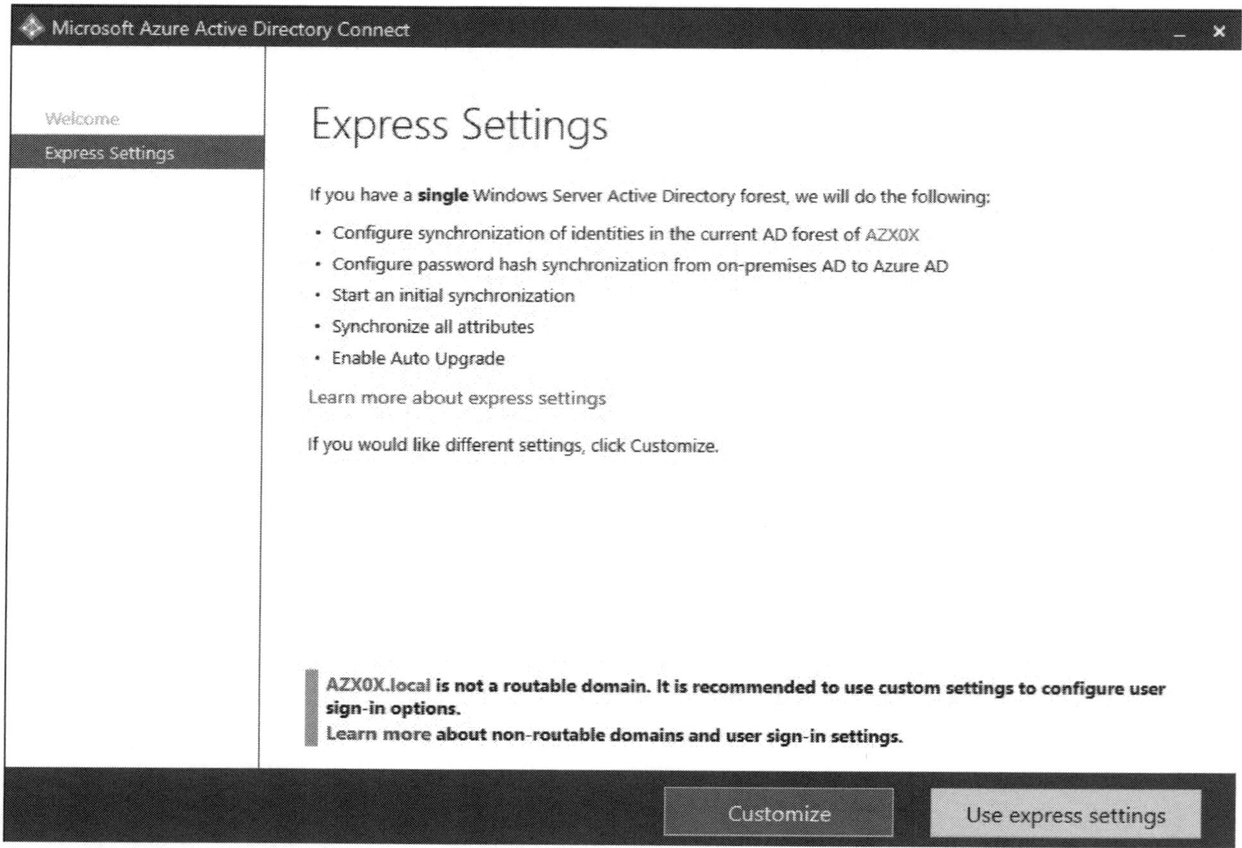

5. Install Required Components pane opens>Click Install in Bottom right (Not shown)> Installation starts. (Don't select any components here).

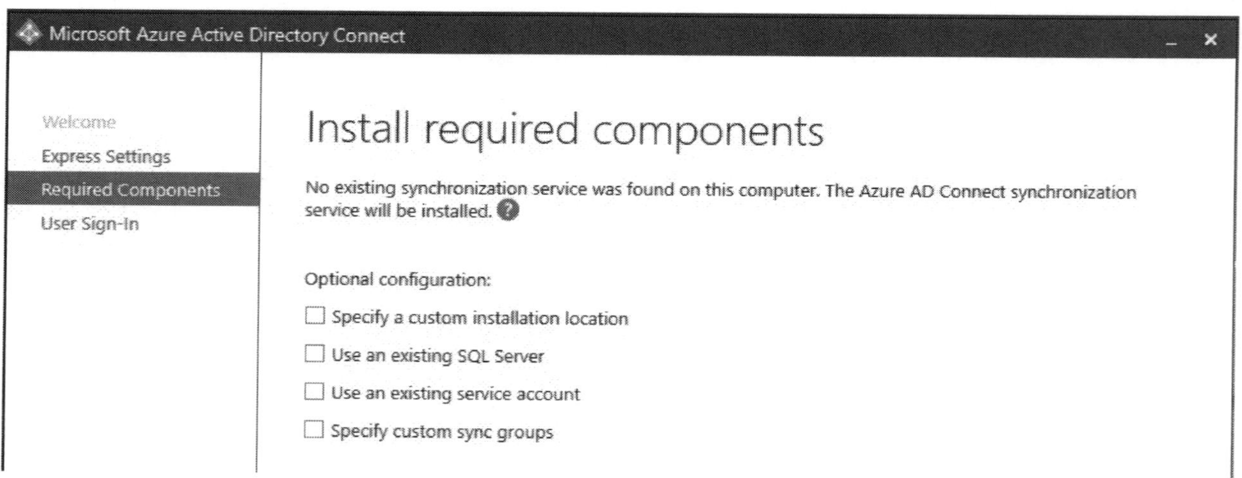

6. User Sign-in pane opens>Select Password Hash-Synchronization>Click next.

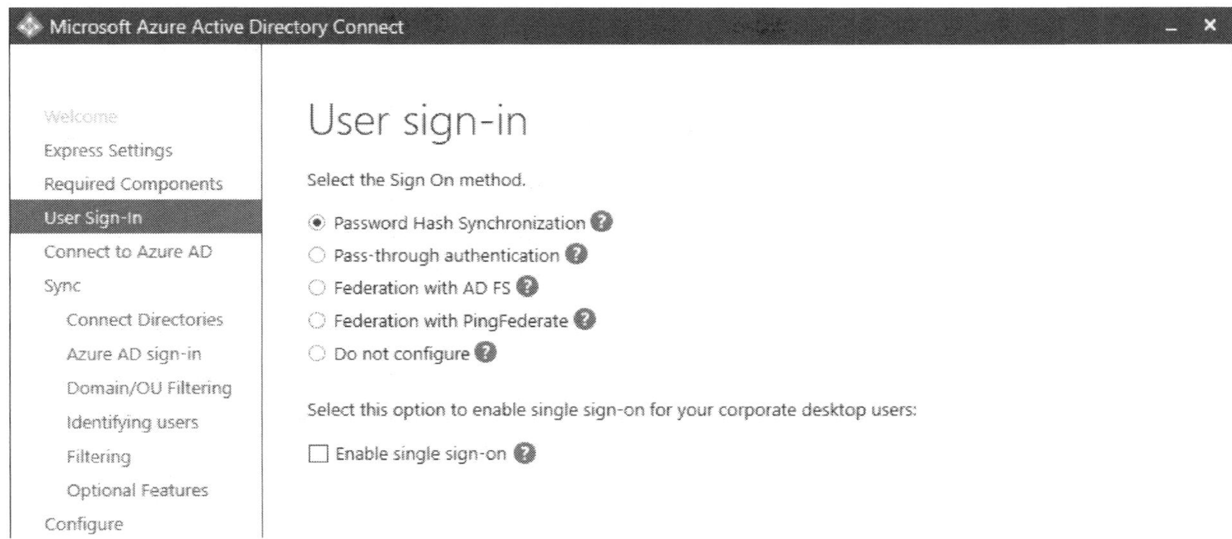

Note: There is Enable single sign-on check box. This enables seamless single sign-on for domain users. If you are logged on to on-premises Domain controller then you can log on to Azure AD without signing again.

7. In Connect to Azure AD pane Enter **User1** Credential and password>click next.

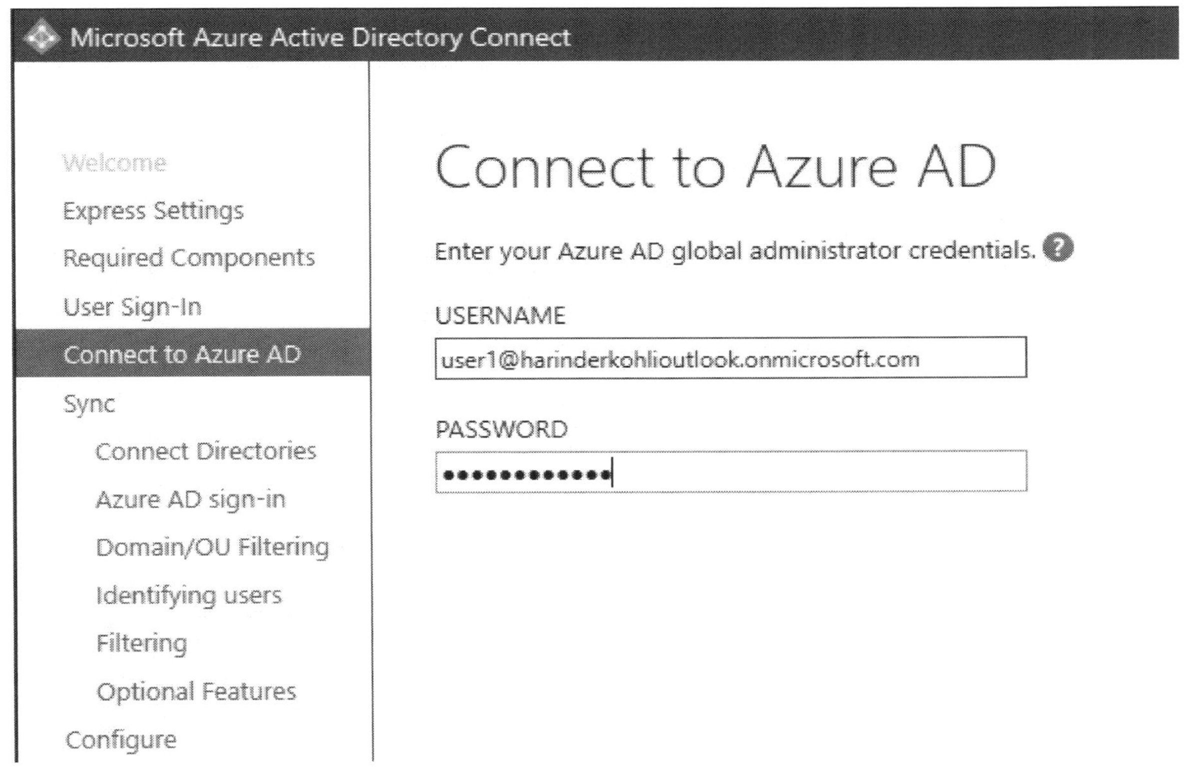

8. Connect Directories pane select Active directory and enter domain name AZX0X.local. This domain was configured in Chapter 2, Exercise 32.

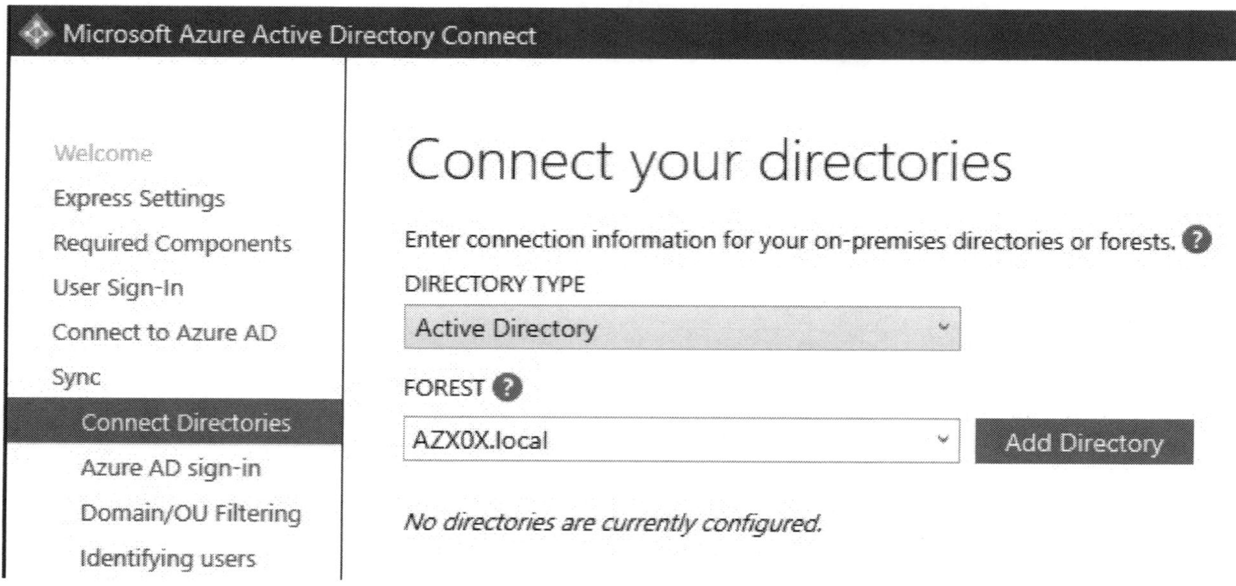

9. Click Add Directory>AD Forest Account pane pops up>Enter Administrator credentials in the format **AZX0X.local\AdminAccount**>Enter password>Click Ok>Click Next.

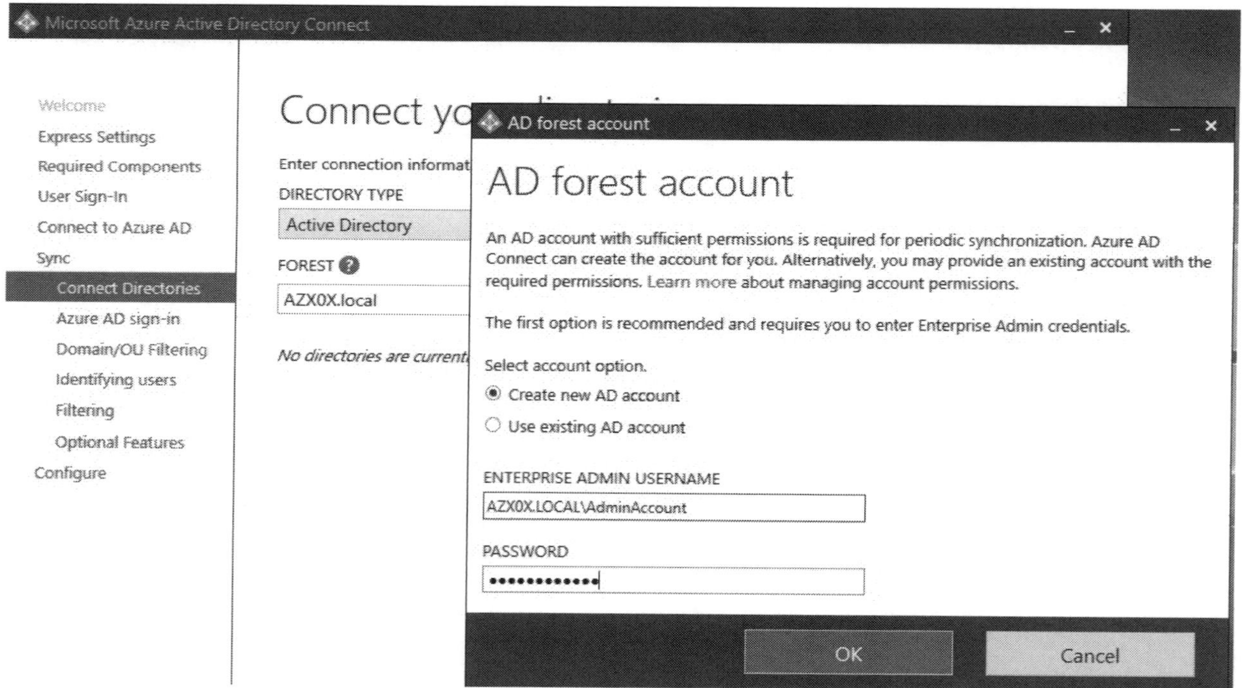

Note: AdminAccount is administrator which was created during VM installation.

10. In Azure AD sign-in pane>check mark Continue without matching all UPN suffixes to verified domains>Click Next.

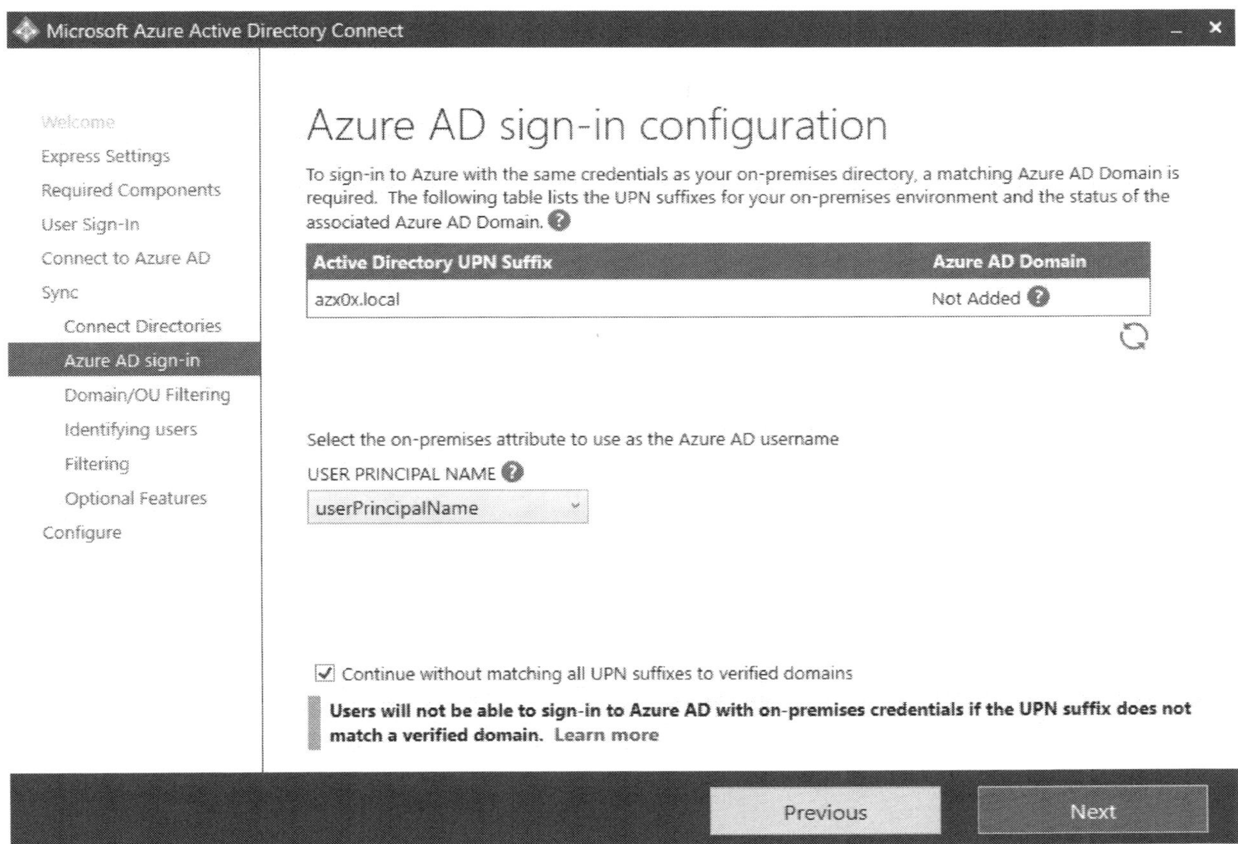

11. In Domain and OU Filtering pane>Select Sync all domains and OUs> Click Next. This allows you to select specific OUs or all OUs.

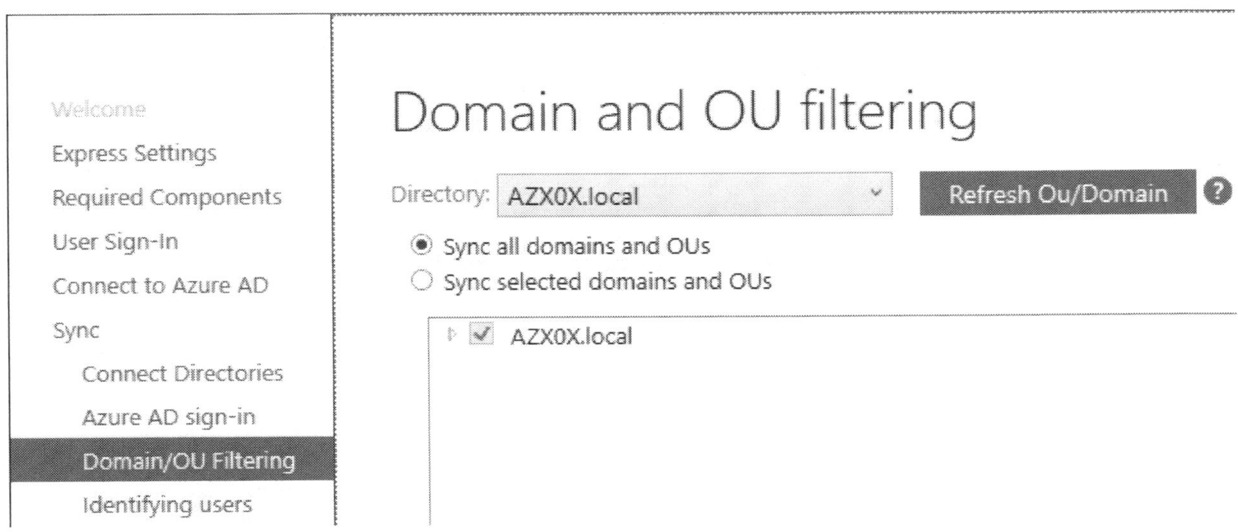

12. In identifying Users pane select the default values>Click next.

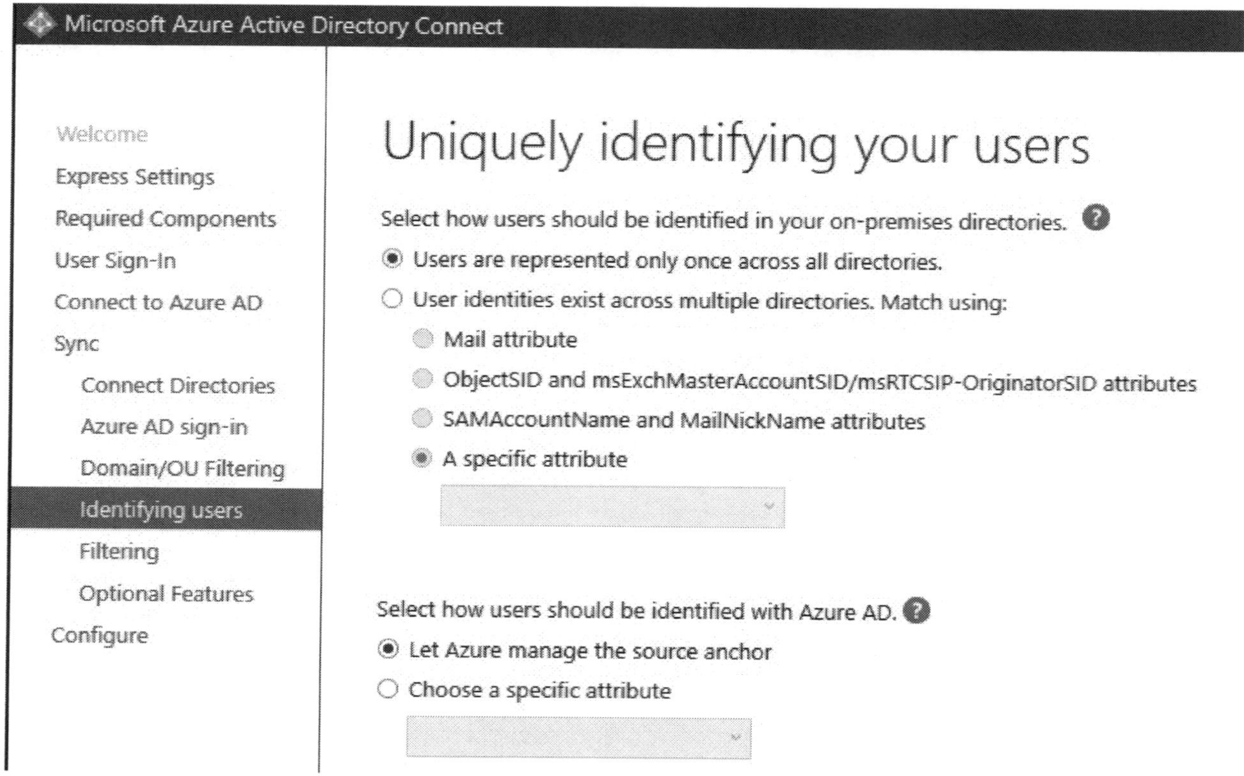

13. In Filtering pane select the default and click next.

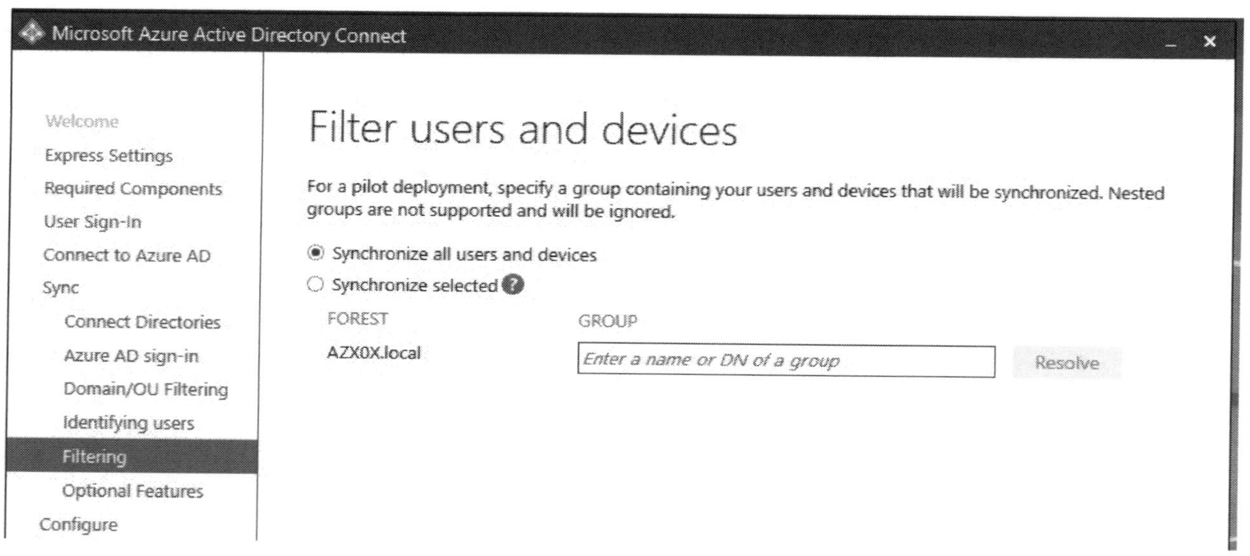

14. In optional make sure default option Password Hash Synchronization is selected and click next.

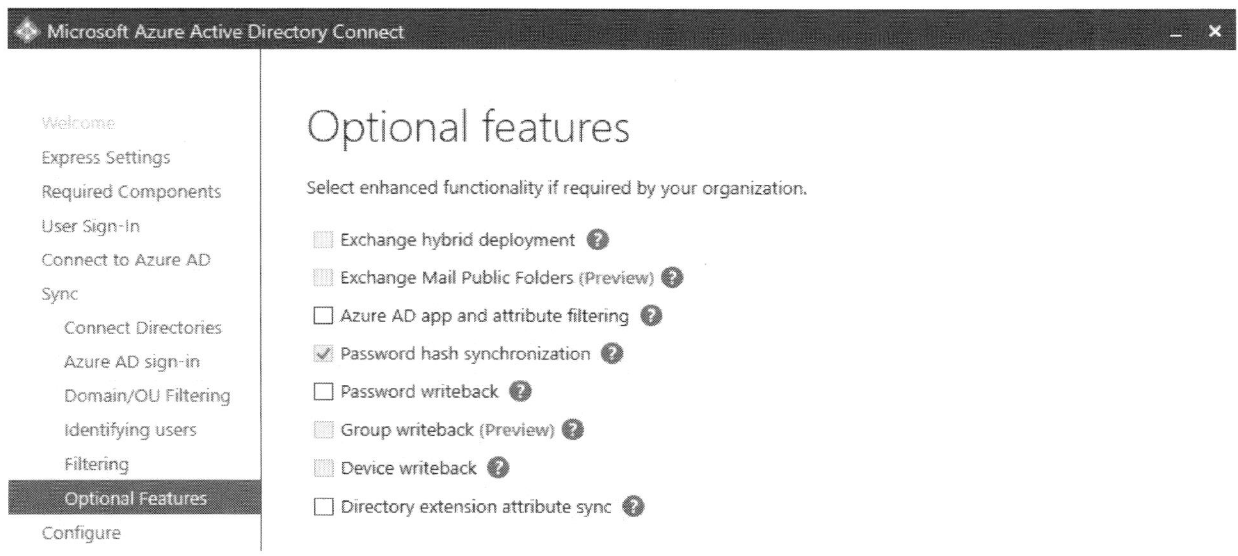

Note: Note the password Write Back Option. We will discuss it in next section.

15. In Configure select the default option and click install.

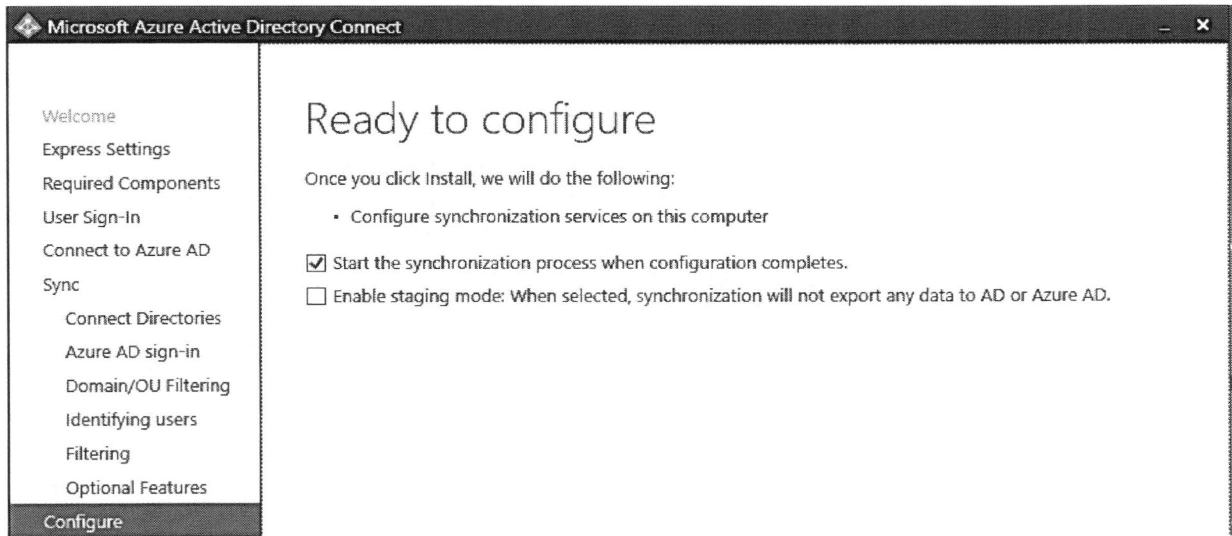

16. After Configuration Process gets complete click exit to close the Azure AD Connect Installation wizard.

17. In Windows VM OnPremAD logout User1 and close RDP session.

Exercise123: Check Users Test1 & Test2 synchronization to Azure AD

In Azure AD Portal Click Azure Active Directory in left pane>Azure AD Dashboard opens>Click Users in left pane>User Dashboard opens> You can see Test1 and Test2 users are synchronized to Azure AD and the source is Windows Server AD. User-id have become test1@harinderkohlioutlook.onmicrosoft.com.

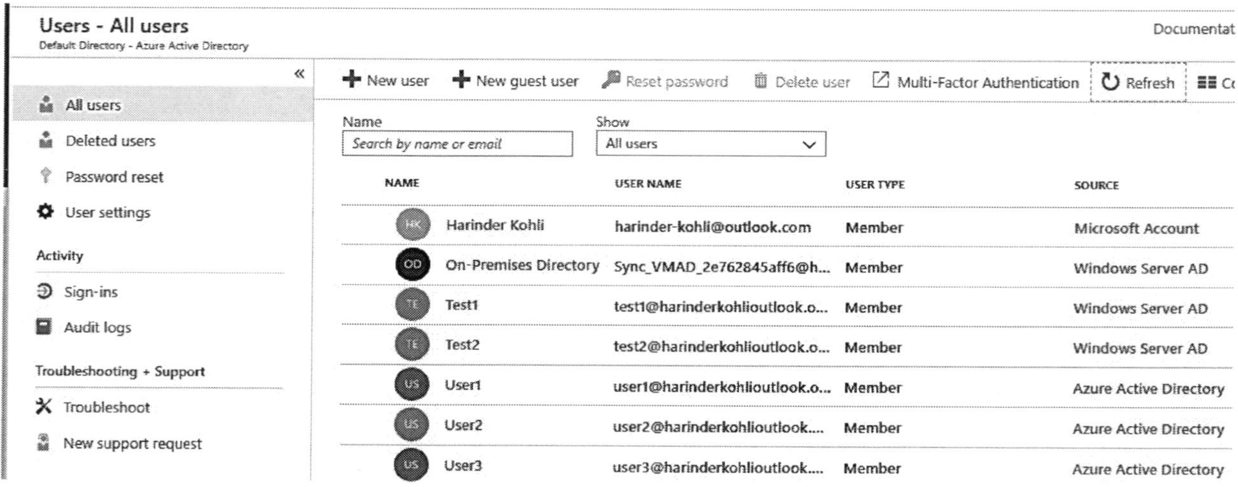

Open Firefox and log on to portal.azure.com with Test1 Credentials-
test1@harinderkohlioutlook.onmicrosoft.com

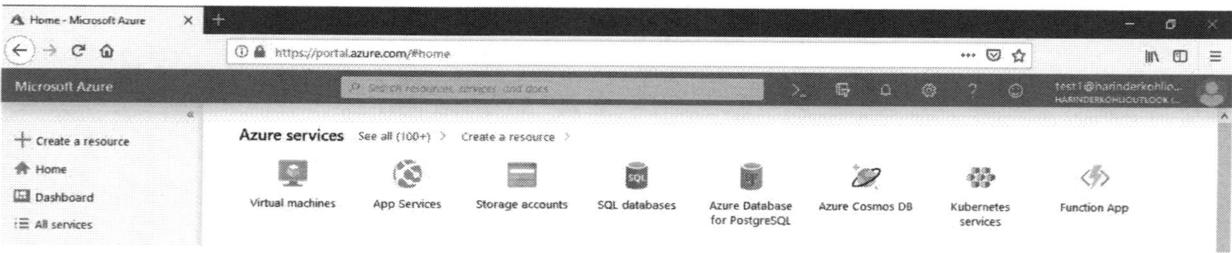

In right side on top you can see user test1.

Exercise 124: Check AD Connect options

In this exercise we will check options available to Operate and configure AD connect after Installation of AD Connect.

1. RDP to windows VM VMAD> click Start icon>Under AD Connect you can see following 4 applications installed.
   AD Connect.
   Synchronization Rules Editor.
   Synchronization Service.
   Synchronization Service Webservice Connector Config.

2. Click on AD connect icon on desktop which was installed in Previous exercise>AD Connect welcome screen opens>Click Configure> You can see various task available for configuration.

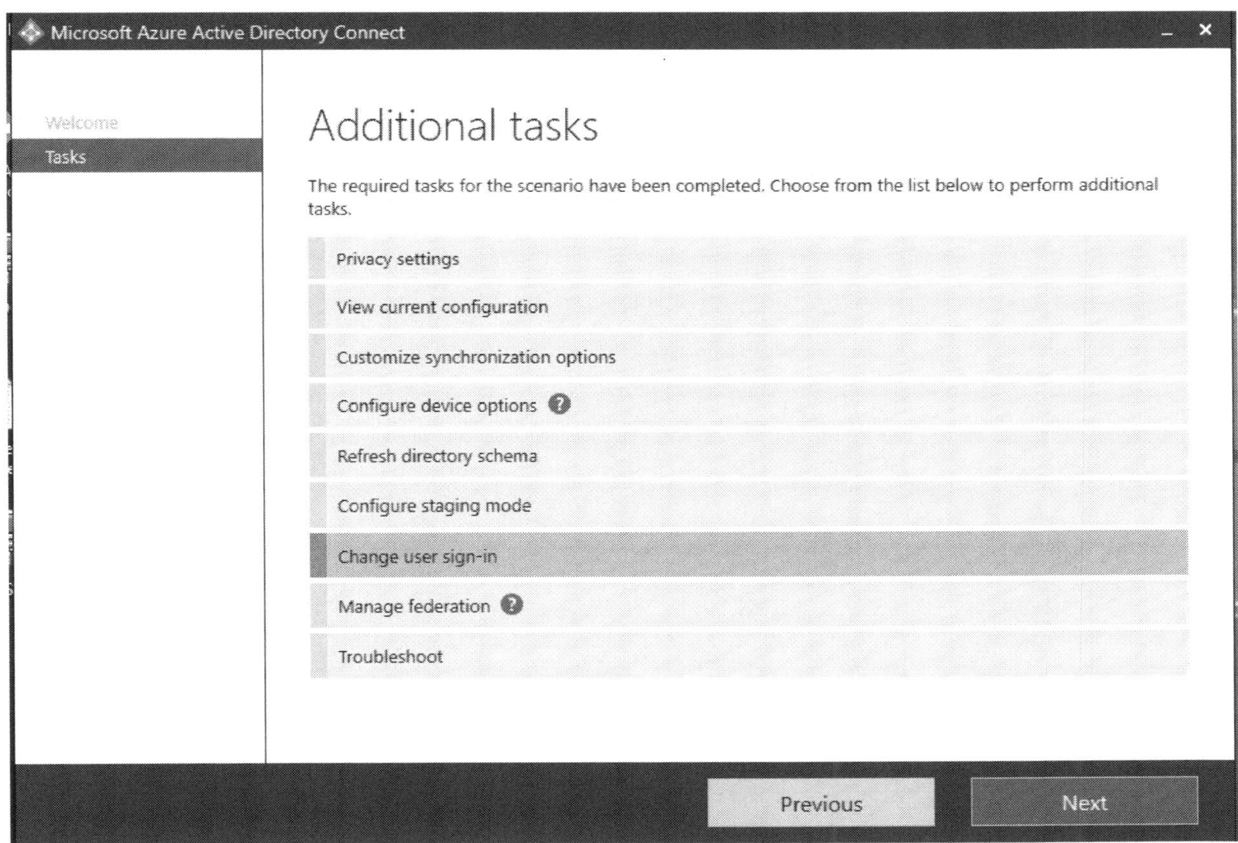

Note 1: Readers are advised to go through all tasks by selecting a task and clicking Next.

3. On VM OnPremAD click Start icon>Under AD Connect Click Synchronization Service> Synchronization Service Manager opens.

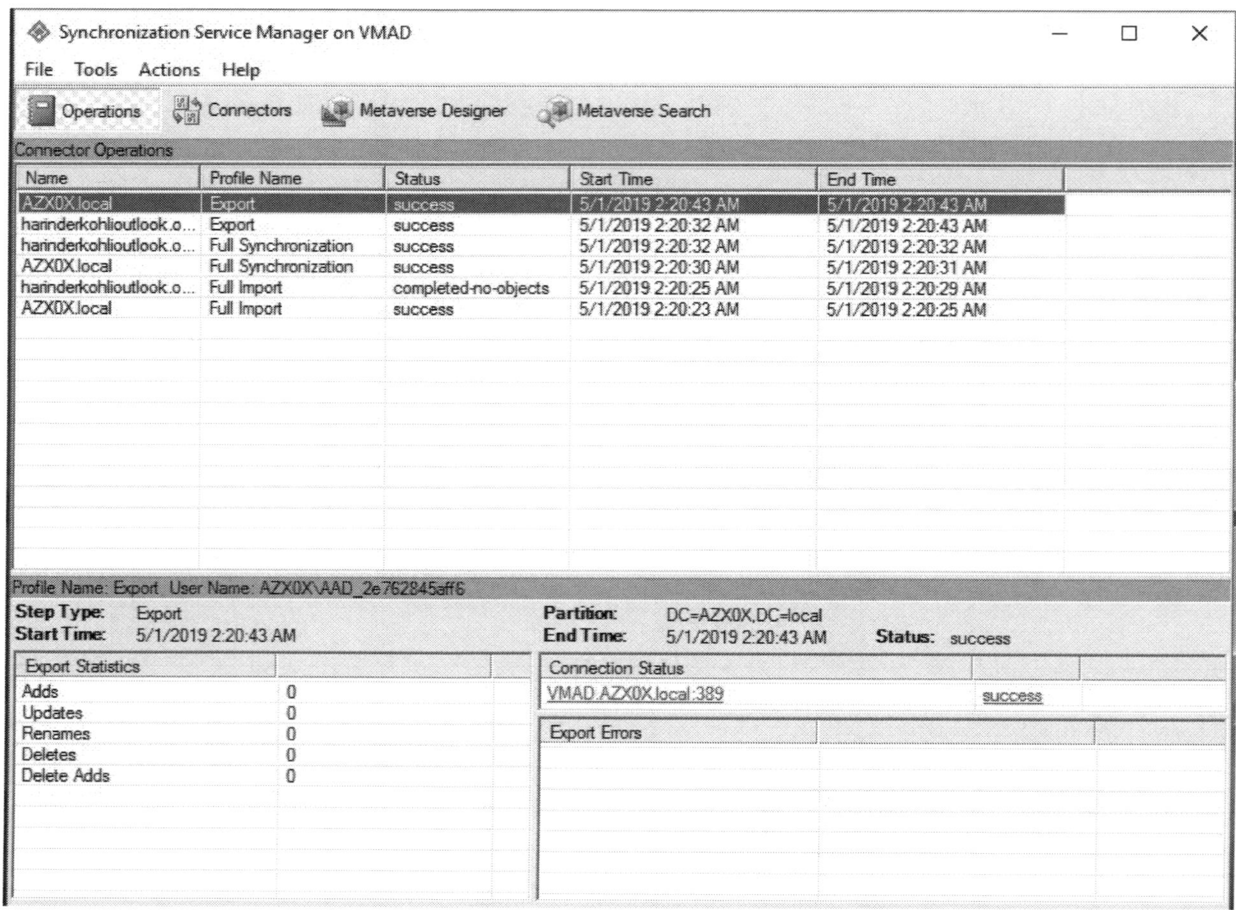

Readers are advised to click connectors tab and check the options available.

Exercise 125: AD Connect Health

In this exercise we will monitor Sync services and Active Directory Domain Services (AD DS) running on VM VMAD. To Monitor AD DS we will download and install AD Connect Health agent on VM VMAD.

Accessing AD Connect Health Dashboard

1. Open Browser and go to the AD Connect Health Portal URL at https://aka.ms/aadconnecthealth or Go to Azure Active Directory Dashboard >Click Azure AD Connect in left pane>Click Azure AD Connect Health in Right pane under Health and Analytics> Azure AD Connect Health pane opens.

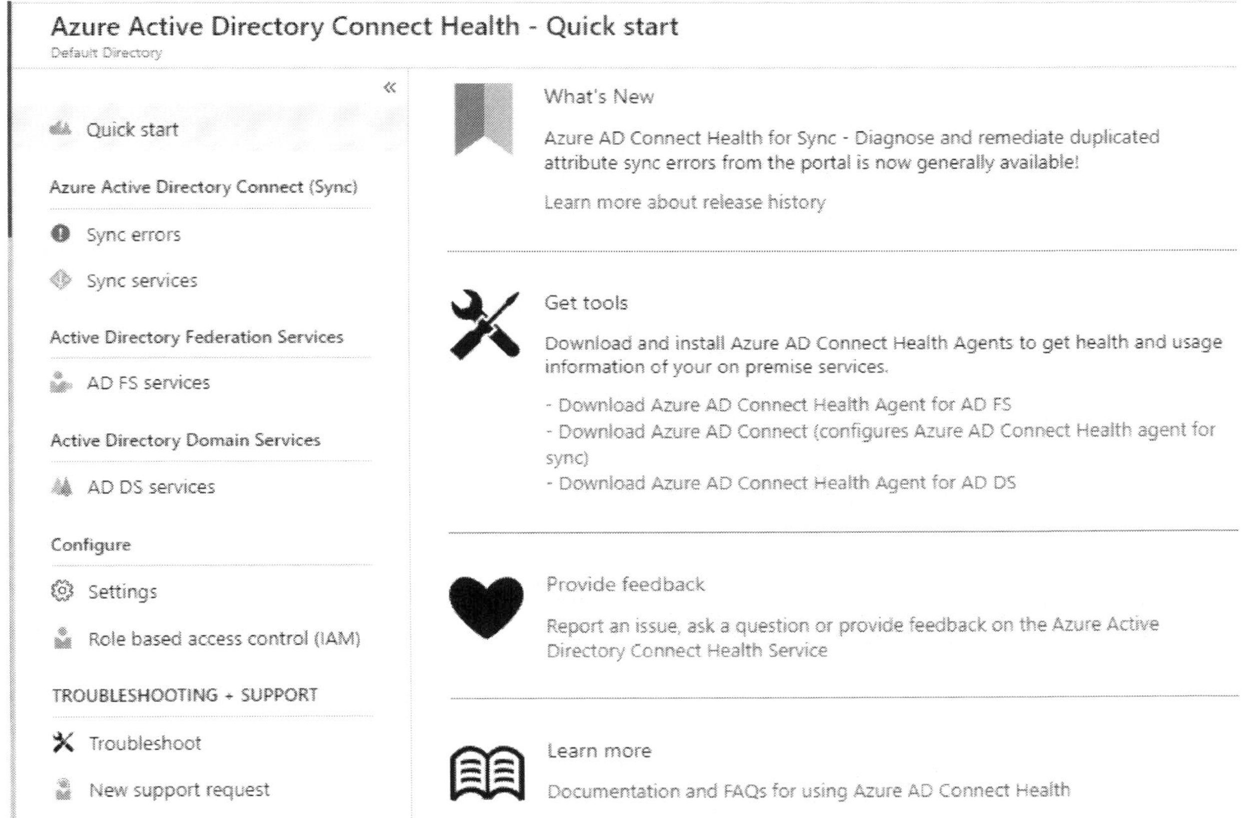

Note 1: In left pane you can see 3 Services which can be monitored – Sync Service, Active Directory Federation Services and Active Directory Domain Services.
Note 2: From right pane you can download AD Connect Health Agents.

Download and Install Agent for AD DS on VM VMAD

1. RDP to VM VMAD> Open Browser and log on to AD Connect Health Portal URL at https://aka.ms/aadconnecthealth
2. In Right pane Click Download Azure AD Connect Health Agents AD DS>New Browser window opens>Click download and save exe file on desktop.

3. Click exe file downloaded>Run>Install>After Setup is complete>Click Configure now>Some PowerShell scripts are automatically run and Sign in to your account box opens>Enter **User1 Credentials** and click next>enter password and click sign in.

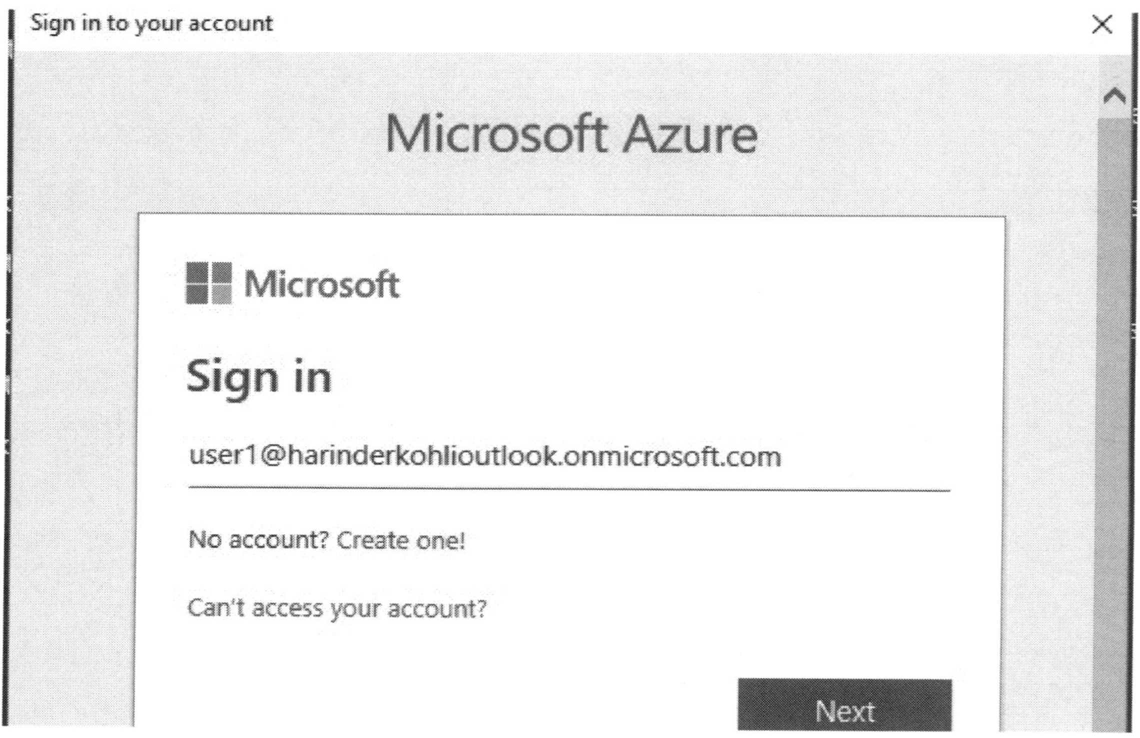

Agent registration completed successfully as shown.

```
2019-05-01 02:42:42.498 Agent registration completed successfully.

Detailed log file created in temporary directory:
C:\Users\AdminAccount\AppData\Local\Temp\2\AdHealthAddsAgentConfiguration.20

PS C:\Users\AdminAccount\Desktop>
```

Monitoring Active Directory Domain Services

1. Go to Azure AD Connect Health Dashboard> Click AD DS Services in left pane> In Right pane you can see that Domain Controller is Healthy.

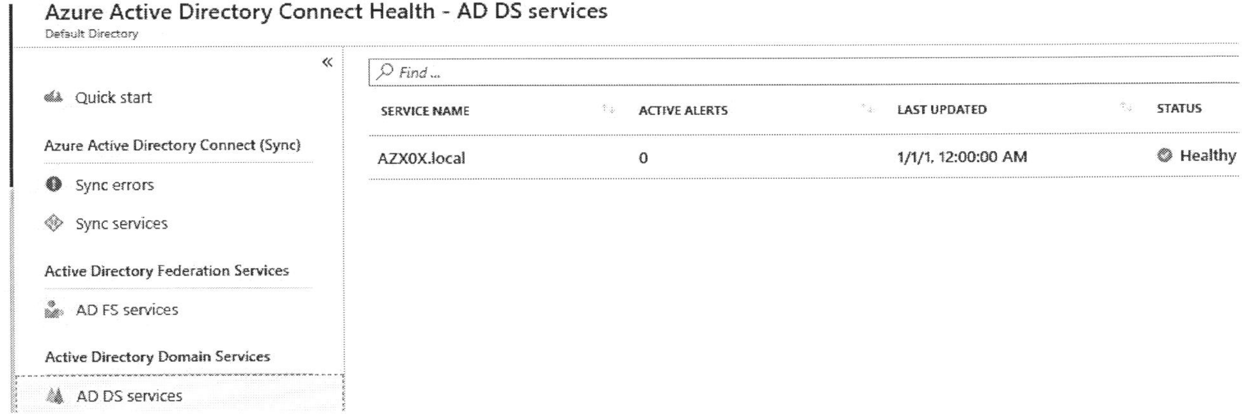

2. In Right pane click the domain name>Domain pane open>Scroll down to see more options.

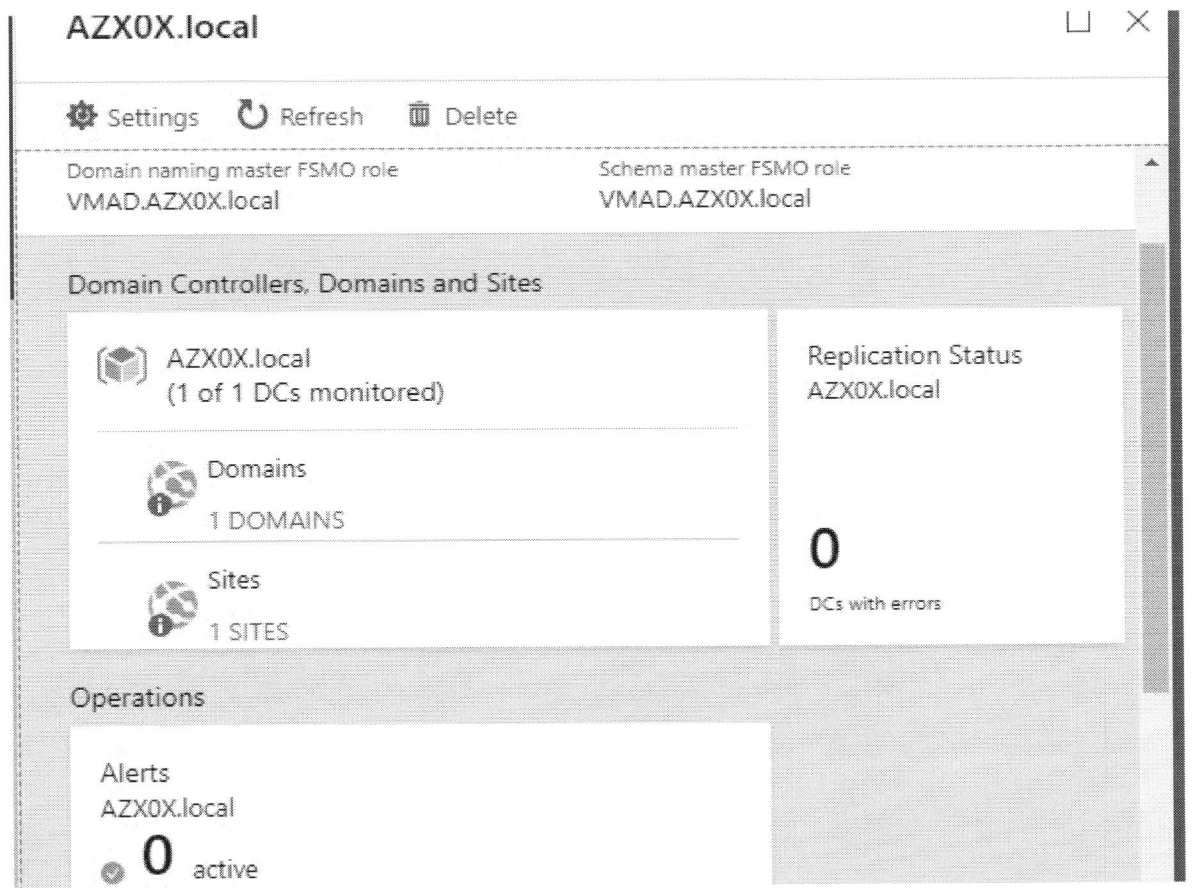

Monitoring Sync Services

1. Go to Azure AD Connect Health Dashboard> Click Sync Services in left pane> In Right pane you can see that sync status is Healthy.

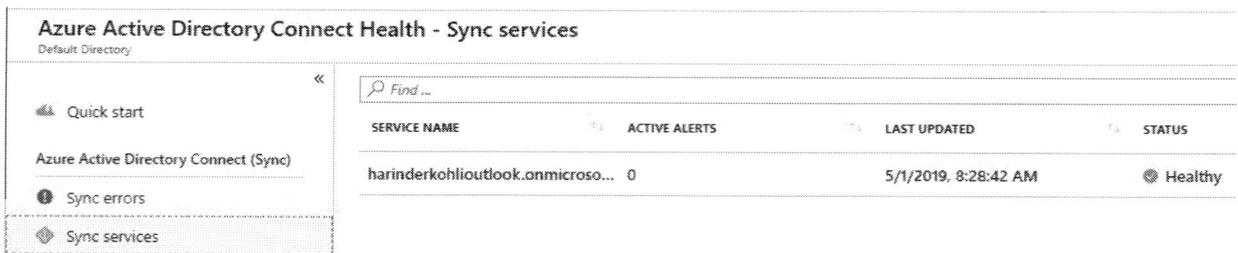

2. In Right pane click the sync service>Sync service pane open>Scroll down to see more options.

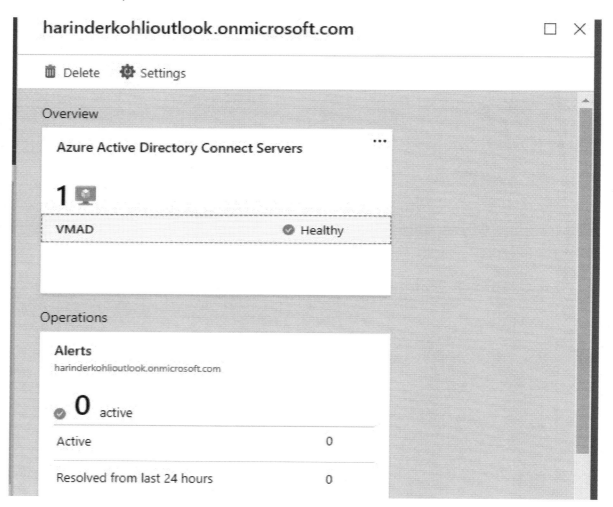

harinderkohlioutlook.onmicrosoft.com

Delete Settings

Overview

Azure Active Directory Connect Servers

1

VMAD Healthy

Operations

Alerts

harinderkohlioutlook.onmicrosoft.com

0 active

Active 0

Resolved from last 24 hours 0

Seamless Single Sign-on

Note: Seamless single sign-on option is only available for Password Hash Synchronization option and Pass-through Authentication option. It is not applicable for Federation with ADFS option.

With seamless single sign-on users who are already logged on to their corporate network on domain-joined machines can sign on to Azure AD without entering there on-premises password again.

The advantage of this feature is that it can be enabled without creating any complex on-premises deployments and network configuration as in the case of Federation with ADFS.

Enabling Seamless Single sign-on Step 1

Seamless Single sign-on is enabled during installation of AD Connect with either Password Hash Synchronization option or Pass-through Authentication option as shown in figure below. You to need to just check the Enable single sign-on box.

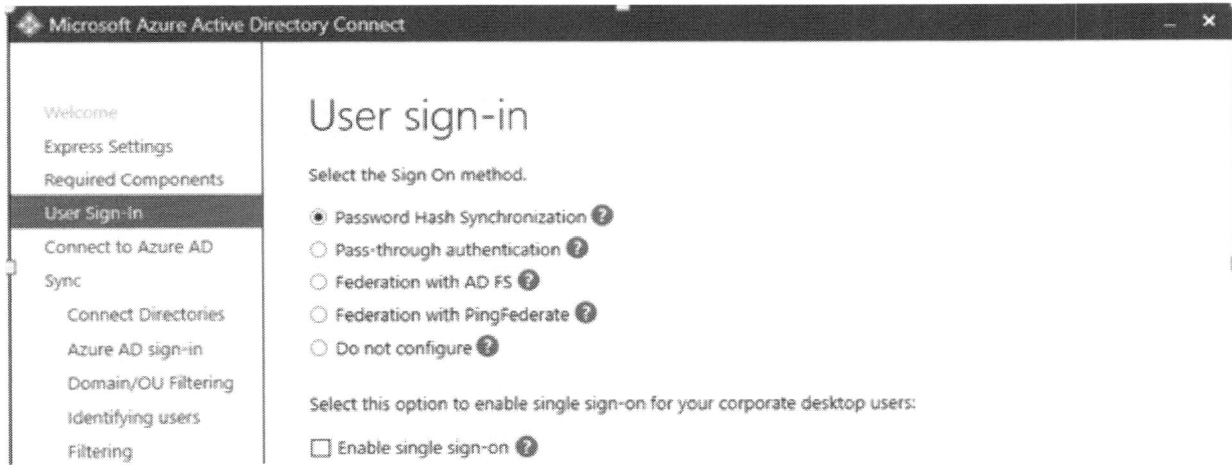

Enabling Seamless Single sign-on Step 2 - Configure the Intranet Zone for client machines

To ensure that the client sign-ins automatically in the intranet zone you need to ensure that two URLs are part of the intranet zone. This ensures that the domain joined computer automatically sends a Kerberos ticket to Azure AD when it is connected to the corporate network.
Create or Edit existing Group Policy which applies to all synchronized users.

1. Open the Group Policy Management tool on Domain Controller Machine.
2. Edit the Default Domain Group policy that will be applied to all users.
3. Navigate to **User Configuration\Administrative Templates\Windows Components\Internet Explorer\Internet Control Panel\Security Page** and select **Site to Zone Assignment List** as shown below.
4. Enable the policy, and enter the following item in the dialog box.

Value: https://autologon.microsoftazuread-sso.com
Data: 1

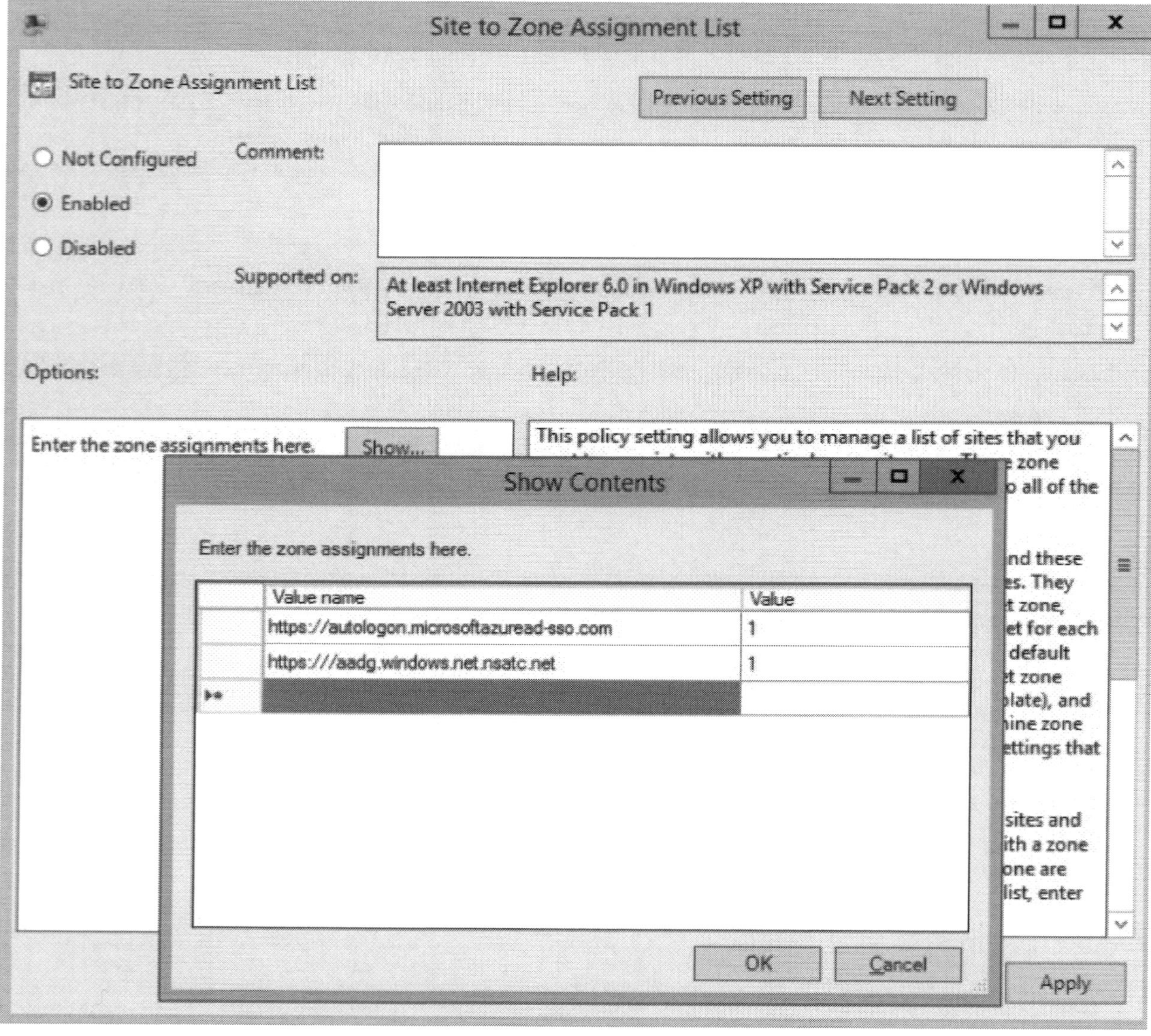

Key Features of Seamless Single sign-on

1. Users are automatically signed into both on-premises and cloud-based applications.
2. Works with Password Hash Synchronization or Pass-through Authentication option only.
3. Register Domain joined non-Windows 10 devices with Azure AD to **enable device based conditional access.** This capability needs you to install version 2.1 or later of the workplace-join client. Version 2.1 has added support for Azure Active Directory Seamless Single Sign On (https://aka.ms/hybrid/sso).

Note: For Windows 10, the recommendation is to use Azure AD Join for the optimal single sign-on experience with Azure AD.

Figure below shows using seamless single sign-on users logged on to domain joined machines can access Azure AD application without entering there passwords.

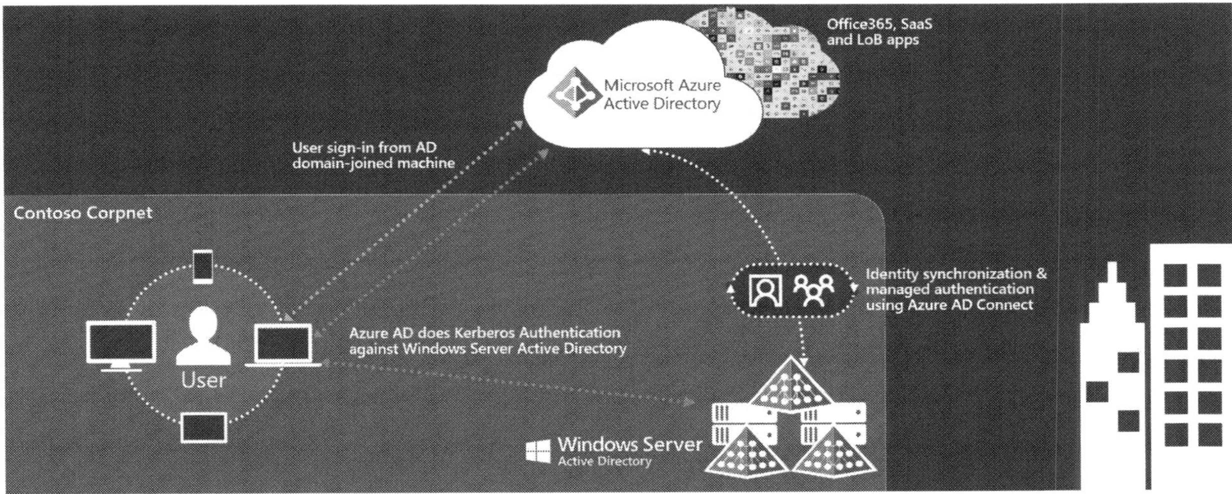

Password Writeback

Password Writeback is a feature enabled with Azure AD Connect that allows password changes in the cloud to be written back to an existing on-premises directory in real time.

This feature can be enabled during AD Connect Installation.

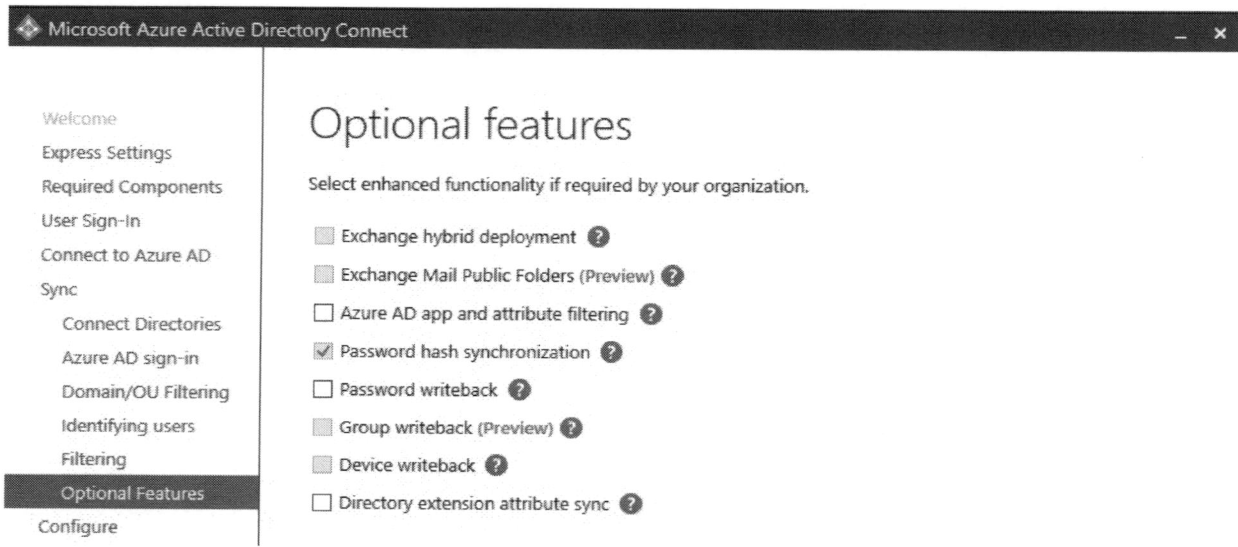

Password writeback is supported in following options only:

1. Active Directory Federation Services
2. Password hash synchronization
3. Pass-through authentication

License Requirement for Password Writeback option

Self-Service Password Reset/Change/Unlock with on-premises Writeback is a premium feature of Azure AD and requires Azure AD Premium P1 or Azure AD Premium P2 licenses.

AD Connect with Federation with ADFS option

Federation is a collection of domains that have established trust for shared access to a set of resources. Trust can be one way or 2 way. Trust with ADFS option includes authentication and authorization. This results that all user authentication occurs on-premises. This method allows administrators to implement more rigorous levels of access control including implementing on-premises password policies. This method also enables Single sign-on.

In ADFS, identity federation is established between two organizations by establishing trust between two security realms. A federation server on one side (Account side) authenticates the users against Active Directory Domain Services and then issues a token containing a series of claims about user. On the other side, resource side another federation server validates the token and issues another for the local servers to accept the claimed identity. This allows a system to provide controlled Access to its resources to a user that belongs to another security realm without requiring the user to authenticate directly to the system and without the two systems sharing a database of user identities or passwords.

Trust can be one-way or two-way trust. In one-way trust, trusted organization authenticates and issues claim based token to user of trusted organization who are connecting to trusting organization for resource access. In this way trusting organization need not maintain the identity infrastructure.

Note: Federation option is only available with ADFS and Ping Federate. ADFS or Ping Federate are option is chosen during AD Connect installation.

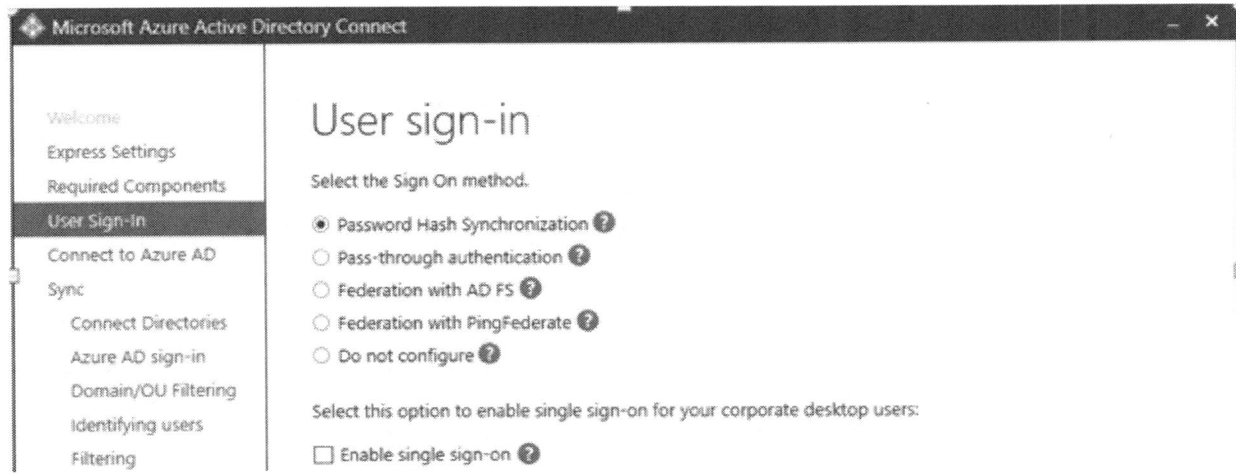

AD Connect installed on-premises with Federation with ADFS option, Synchronizes on premises Active Directory users to Azure AD. In this case Password Hash of users are not Synchronized.

Active Directory Federation Services (ADFS) server installed on-premises and ADFS component in AD Connect, federate the 2 directories which results in one-way trust with Azure AD **Trusting** on-premises ADFS. User Login happens in cloud but user authentication is redirected to on-premises ADFS.

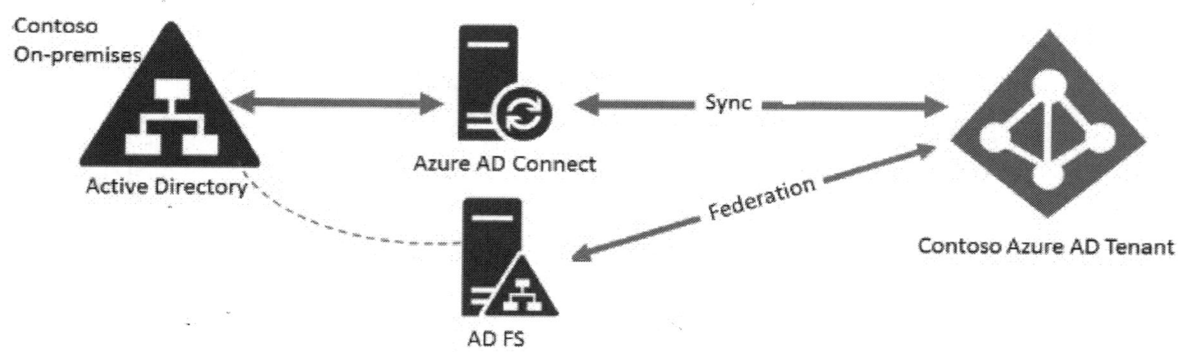

Federation can be used to configure a hybrid environment using an on-premises AD infrastructure. This can be used by organizations to address complex deployments, such as enforcement of on-premises AD sign-in policy, SSO and smart card or 3rd party MFA.

Single sign-on with ADFS

ADFS also enables single sign-on. Users who are already logged on to their corporate network can sign on to Azure AD without entering there on-premises password again.

Figure below show users accessing Corporate resources and Azure AD from within or outside the Corporate Headquaters using a single identity. Single sign-on is also enabled.

Note 1: Web Application proxy server is required when users are accessing from outside the Company premises.

Note 2: AD connect is not shown in the figure but is always required.

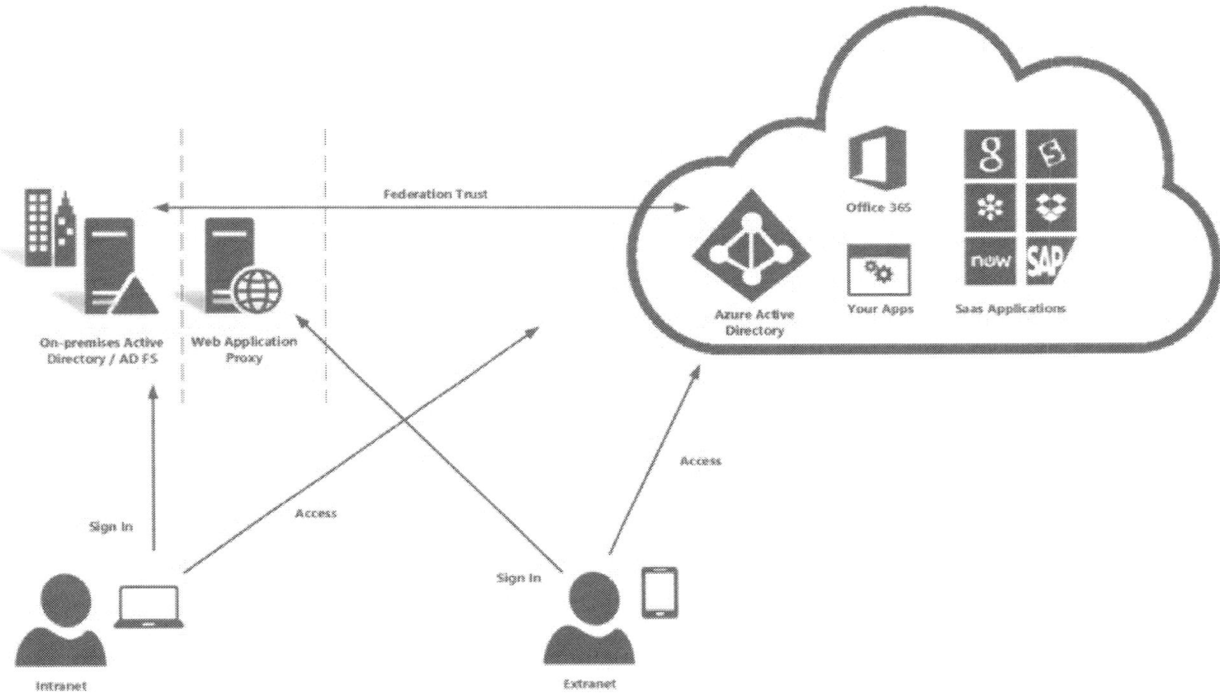

Installation of AD Connect with ADFS Option

Pre-Requisite

1. Azure AD Tenant.
2. On-premises Active Directory Domain Services (AD DS).
3. On-premises ADFS Server or ADFS Server farm. ADFS server requires SSL certificate. ADFS server also requires DNS records for the AD FS federation service name (for example adfs.test.com) for both the intranet (your internal DNS server) and the extranet (public DNS through your domain registrar). For the intranet DNS record, ensure that you use A records and not CNAME records.
4. On-Premises ADFS Web Application Proxy Server (Required only if users are accessing resources from outside the corporate HQ). ADFS Web Application Proxy Server requires SSL certificate.

AD Connect Installation

You need to install AD connect with Federation with AD FS option. The Azure AD Connect server needs DNS resolution for both intranet and internet.

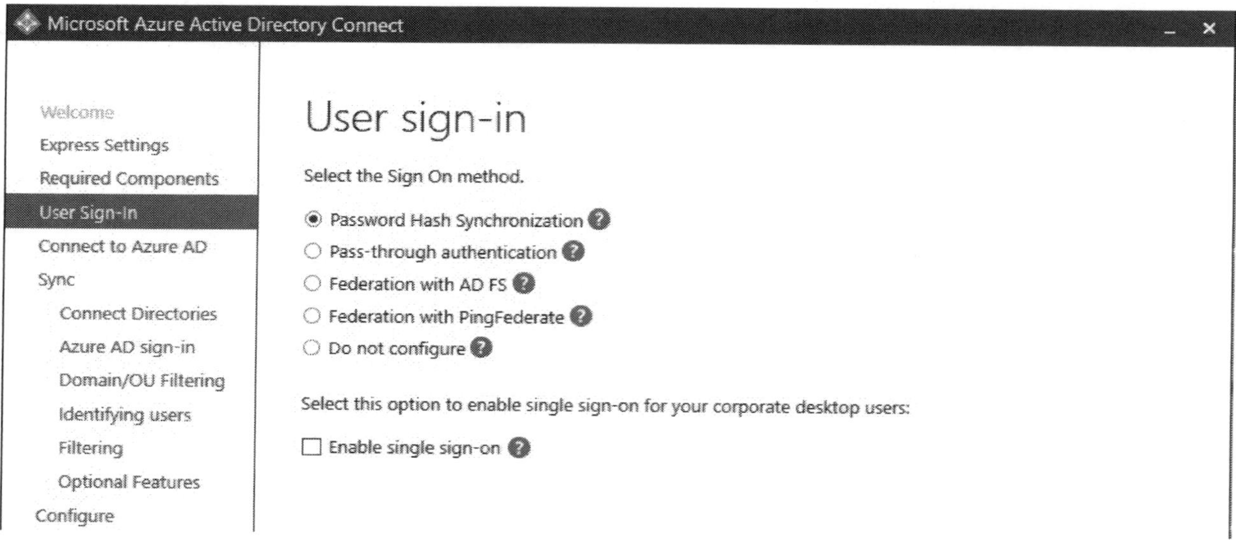

IDFIX tool

Azure AD requires that User Attributes are in specific format. Successful directory synchronization between AD DS and Azure AD requires that your AD DS attributes are properly prepared.

IdFix is used to perform **discovery** and **remediation** of identity objects and their attributes in an on-premises Active Directory Domain Services (AD DS) environment in preparation for migration to Azure AD using AD Connect.

The purpose of IdFix is to reduce the time involved in remediating the Active Directory errors reported by Azure AD Connect.

Download IDFIX Tool

https://www.microsoft.com/en-us/download/details.aspx?id=36832

Installation Requirement

Windows 7, Windows 10 or Windows Server 2008R2 and above.
Net 4.0 must running on the workstation running the IDFIX application.

Chapter 14 Azure Multi Factor Authentication

This Chapter covers following Topic Lessons

- Azure Multi Factor Authentication
- Versions of Azure Multi-Factor Authentication
- Comparison between versions of Azure Multi-Factor Authentication
- Azure Multi-Factor Authentication license options
- Enabling Azure MFA options
- MFA Service Settings
- MFA Verification Options
- App Passwords
- Trusted IPs
- Remember Multi-Factor Authentication
- Fraud Alert
- Block/Unblock Users
- Account Lockout
- One-time Bypass option

This Chapter covers following Lab Exercises

- Enabling MFA for User1
- Test MFA for User1
- Accessing MFA Service Settings
- Enable and disable verification methods
- Allow users to create app passwords
- Enabling Trusted IPs
- Enabling Remember Multi-Factor
- Enabling Fraud Alert
- Enabling Block/Unblock
- Enabling Account Lockout
- Demonstrating One-time Bypass

Chapter Topology

In this Chapter we will enable MFA for Azure AD Users.

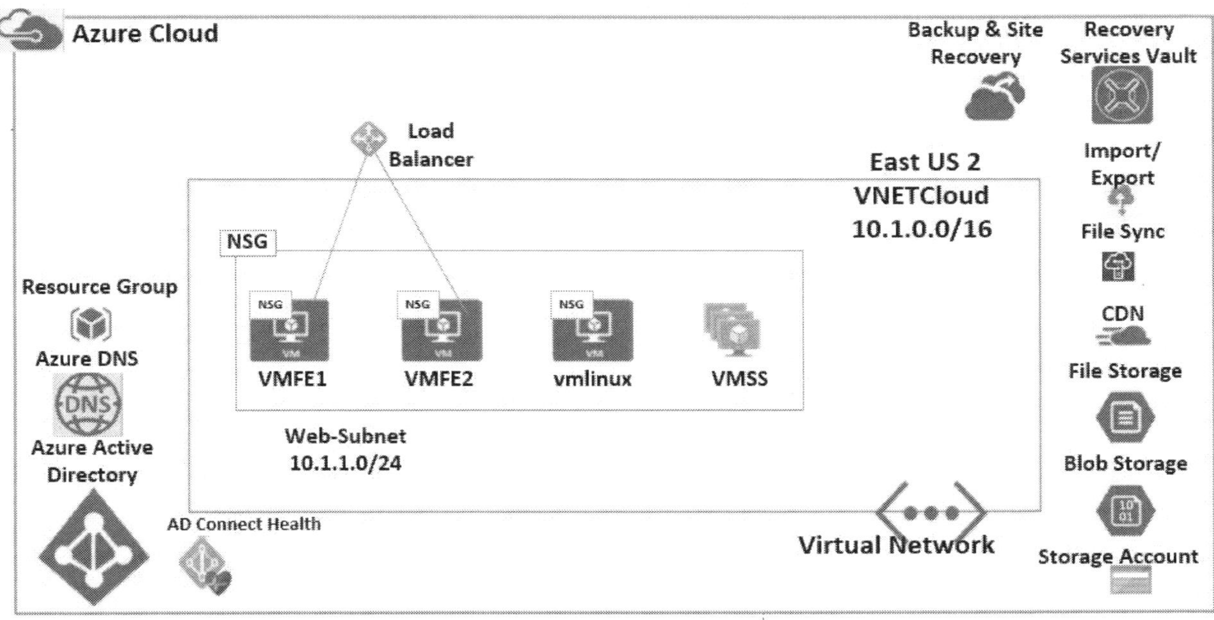

Azure Multi Factor Authentication

Multifactor authentication (**MFA**) is a security system that requires more than one method of authentication apart from username/password.

Azure multifactor authentication (MFA) provides a second level of security when signing into cloud-based or on-premises applications apart from user password. When enabled, Azure MFA can be configured to verify a user's identity using a call to a mobile or landline phone, a text message, a mobile app notification, Mobile app verification code or 3rd party OATH tokens.

Azure Multi-Factor Authentication is available as a service in cloud or as MFA Server to be installed on-premises.

Use Case

It can be used both on-premises and in the cloud to add security for accessing Microsoft online services, Azure Active Directory-connected SaaS applications, line of business applications and remote access applications.

Versions of Azure Multi-Factor Authentication

1. **Multi-Factor Authentication for Office 365**: This version works exclusively with Office 365 applications and is managed from the Office 365 portal. So administrators can now help secure their Office 365 resources by using multi-factor authentication. This version comes with an Office 365 subscription.

2. **Multi-Factor Authentication for Azure Administrators**: The same subset of Multi-Factor Authentication capabilities for Office 365 will be **available at no cost** to all Azure administrators. Users assigned with Directory role of Azure AD Global Administrator can enable two-step verification at no additional cost.

3. **Azure Multi-Factor Authentication:** Azure Multi-Factor Authentication offers the richest set of capabilities. It provides additional configuration options via the Azure Management portal, advanced reporting, and support for a range of on-premises and cloud applications. Azure Multi-Factor Authentication comes as part of Azure Active Directory Premium and Enterprise Mobility Suite.

Comparison between versions of Azure Multi-Factor Authentication

Feature	Multi-Factor Authentication for Office 365	Multi-Factor Authentication for Azure Administrators	Azure Multi-Factor Authentication
Protect admin accounts with MFA	√	√	√
Mobile app as a second factor	√	√	√
Phone call as a second factor	√	√	√
SMS as a second factor	√	√	√
App passwords for clients that don't support MFA	√	√	√
Admin control over verification methods	√	√	√
PIN mode			√
Fraud alert			√
MFA Reports			√
One-Time Bypass			√
Custom greetings for phone calls			√
Custom caller ID for phone calls			√
Trusted IPs			√
Remember MFA for trusted devices			√
MFA SDK			√
MFA for on-premises applications			√

Comparison between Azure Multi-Factor Authentication in the cloud and Multi-Factor Authentication Server

Features	MFA Cloud	MFA Server
Mobile app notification as a second factor	√	√
Phone call as a second factor	√	√
One-way SMS as second factor	√	√
Two-way SMS as second factor	√	√
Hardware Tokens as second factor		√
PIN mode		√
Fraud alert	√	√
MFA Reports	√	√
One-Time Bypass		√
Custom greetings for phone calls	√	√
Customizable caller ID for phone calls	√	√
Trusted IPs	√	√
Remember MFA for trusted devices	√	
Conditional access	√	√
Cache		√

Azure Multi-Factor Authentication license options

Azure MFA requires Users to have Azure AD Premium P1 or P2 License.

1. Use Azure Active Directory Premium edition as they include Azure MFA Licenses.
2. Use Enterprise Mobility + Security suite as they include Azure MFA licenses.
3. Microsoft Enterprise agreement option.
4. Purchase online Azure Premium P1 or P2 Licenses.
5. Create an Azure Multi-Factor Authentication Provider within an Azure subscription. Azure MFA Providers are Azure resources that are billed against your Enterprise Agreement, Azure monetary commitment, or credit card. There are two usage models available – per user and per authentication. With this option Azure AD Free and Basic Edition users can also use MFA. **This option is now deprecated as of September 2018.**

Enabling Azure MFA options

Azure MFA can be enabled in 3 ways for the users.

1. **Licenses:** If you have licenses (Azure AD Premium P1/P2 or EMS Suite License) then enable MFA per user.
2. **Enable Azure MFA with Conditional Access Policy:** This method uses the Azure AD Conditional Access Policy to enable MFA for Users defined in the policy. This method requires Azure Active Directory P2 licensing.
3. **Enable Azure MFA with Azure AD Identity Protection:** This method uses the Azure AD Identity Protection to enable MFA for Users defined in the Identity Protection Policy. This method requires Azure Active Directory P2 licensing.

Note: You can also enable MFA for Users with Directory Role of Global Administrator free of cost. This MFA is known as MFA for Azure Administrators.

Exercise 126: Enabling MFA for User1

In this Exercise we will enable MFA for User1 using Mobile Number as second Authentication. Mobile Number can be either added by Administrator in User Profile or User must specify Mobile number during MFA Authentication. Azure AD User1 was created in Exercise 101, Chapter 12.

1. In Azure AD Dashboard>Click Users in left pane>All User Blade open.

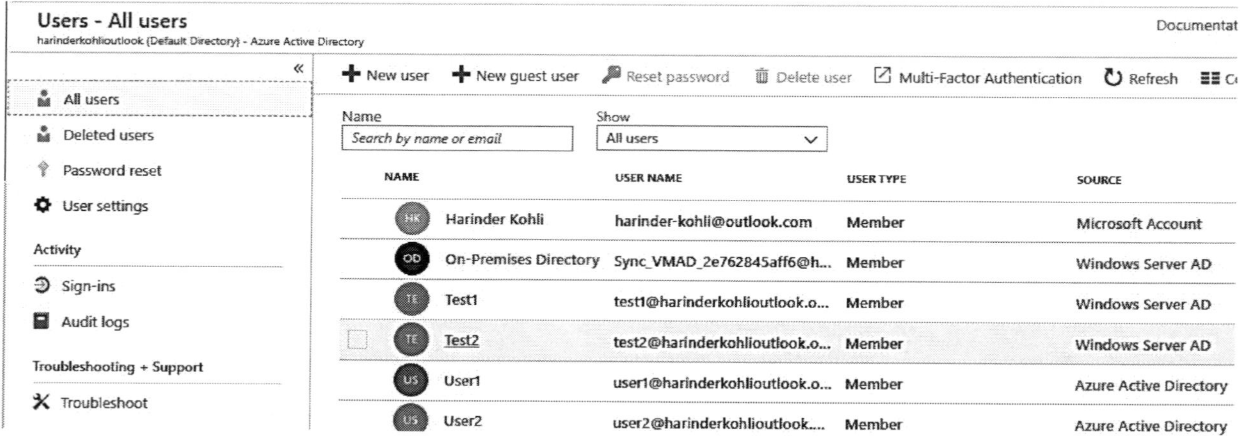

2. Click **Multi-Factor Authentication** in Top Right> A new Browser tab opens as shown below with users option>click User1> You can see option to enable MFA and Manage user settings for User1. Note the **service settings** tab in Top.

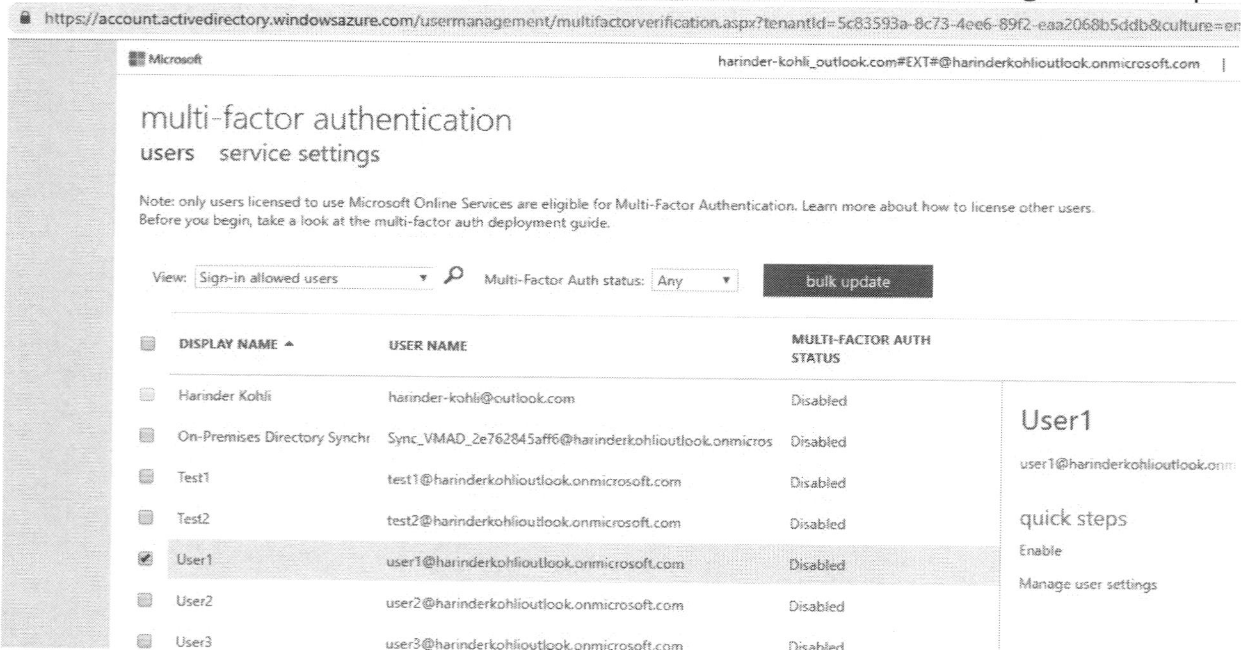

3. Click Manage User Settings> A box pops up> We will let it remain at default settings>Click Cancel.

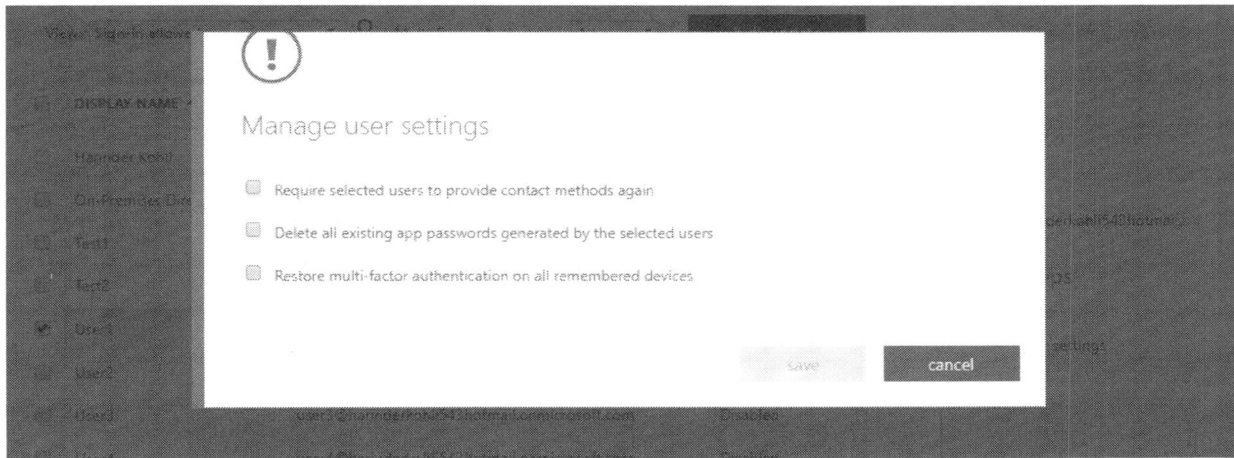

4. Click enable in right pane>Enabling multi-factor auth box pops up> Click enable multi-factor auth> Click close.

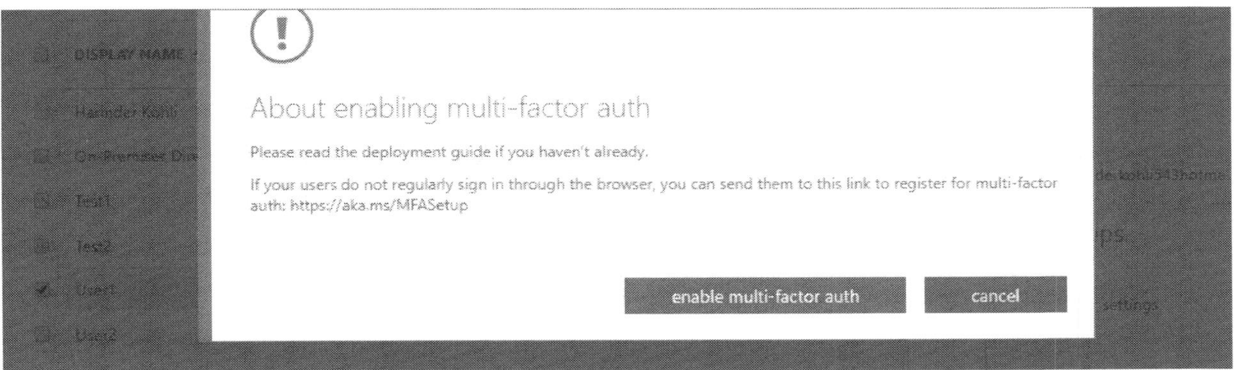

5. You can now see MFA is enabled for User1.

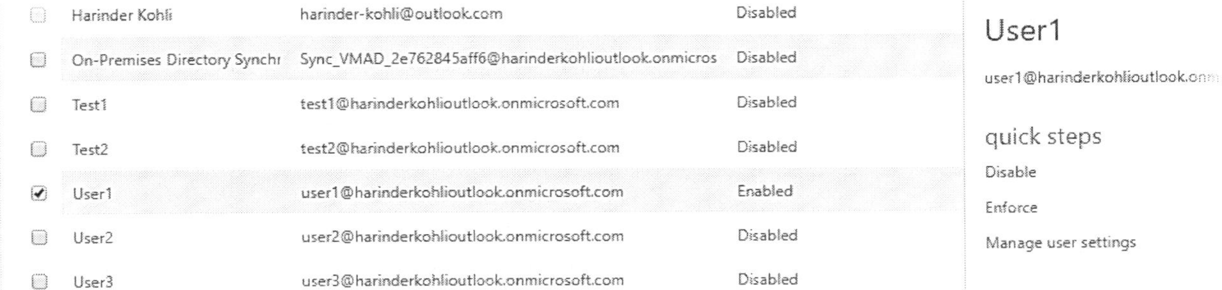

Exercise 127: Test MFA for User1

1. Open Firefox Browser and enter https://portal.azure.com and Log on with User1 credentials: **user1@harinderkohlioutlook.onmicrosoft.com**.
1. After you enter the password for User1>A dialog Box will pop in browser asking for more information required>Click Next> Additional Security Verification screen will open> Select **Authentication Phone** from Dropdown box>Select Your **Location**. In my case I selected India>Enter Your **Mobile Number**> In Method Select **Send me a code by text message**>Click Next. **Note:** Users are requested to see Authentication options in Dropdown box.

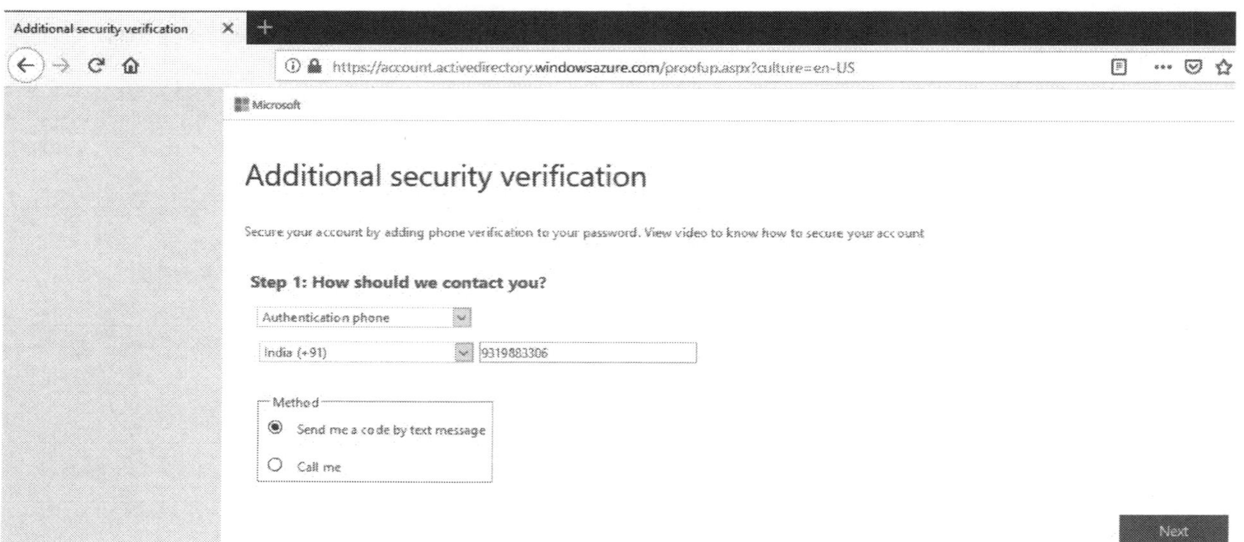

2. Click next and enter verification code sent to your mobile and click Verify.

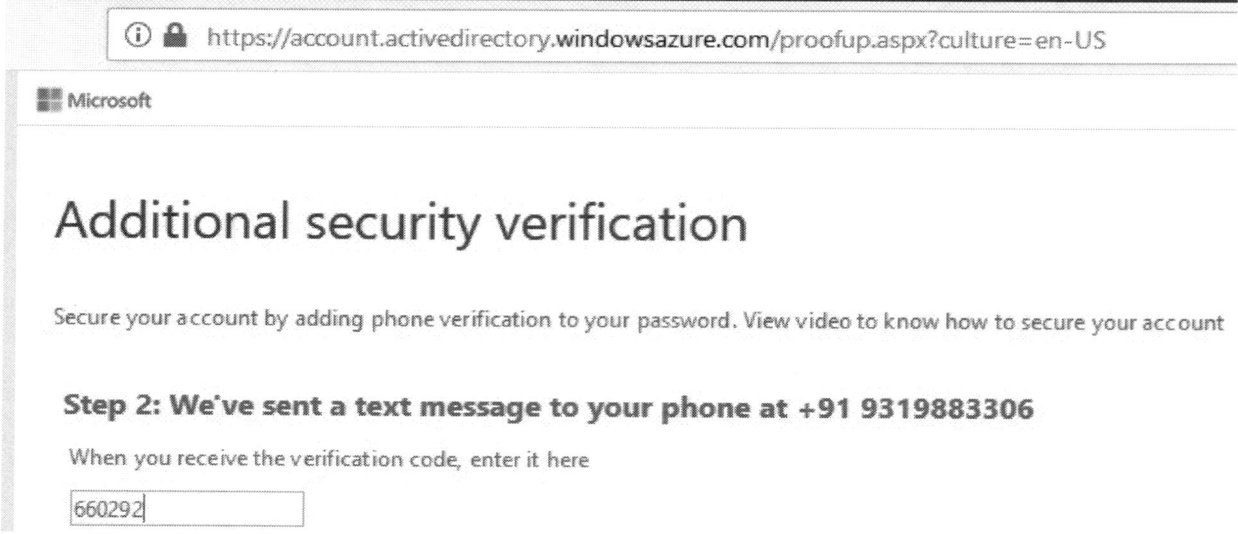

3. Additional Security Verification screen opens. This is basically for generating passwords for non-browser based applications which can't use phone for account verification> Click Done and you are logged on to Azure Portal.

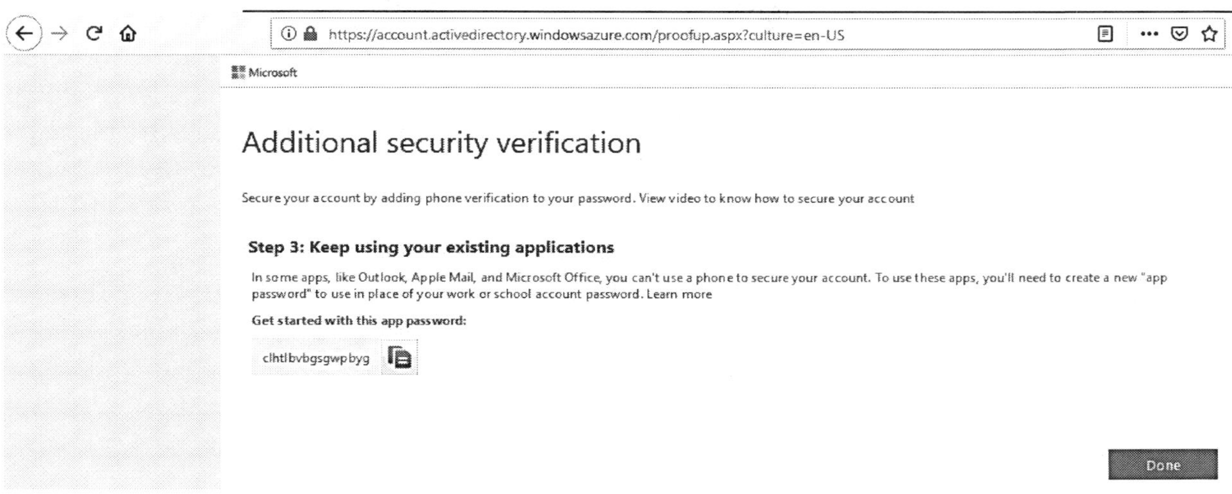

Note: Screens in step 2, 3 and 4 comes during first log only. In Subsequent log-on's you are asked to enter verification code sent to your mobile.

MFA Service Settings

With MFA Service setting you can configure **Verification options, setting for app passwords, Skip MFA for trusted IPs,** and **remember multi-factor authentication** option.

Exercise 128: Accessing MFA Service Settings

In Azure AD Dashboard Click Users in left pane>All User Blade open> Click **Multi-Factor Authentication** in Top Right> A new Browser tab opens as shown below with users option>Click service settings in Top> Service setting options open.

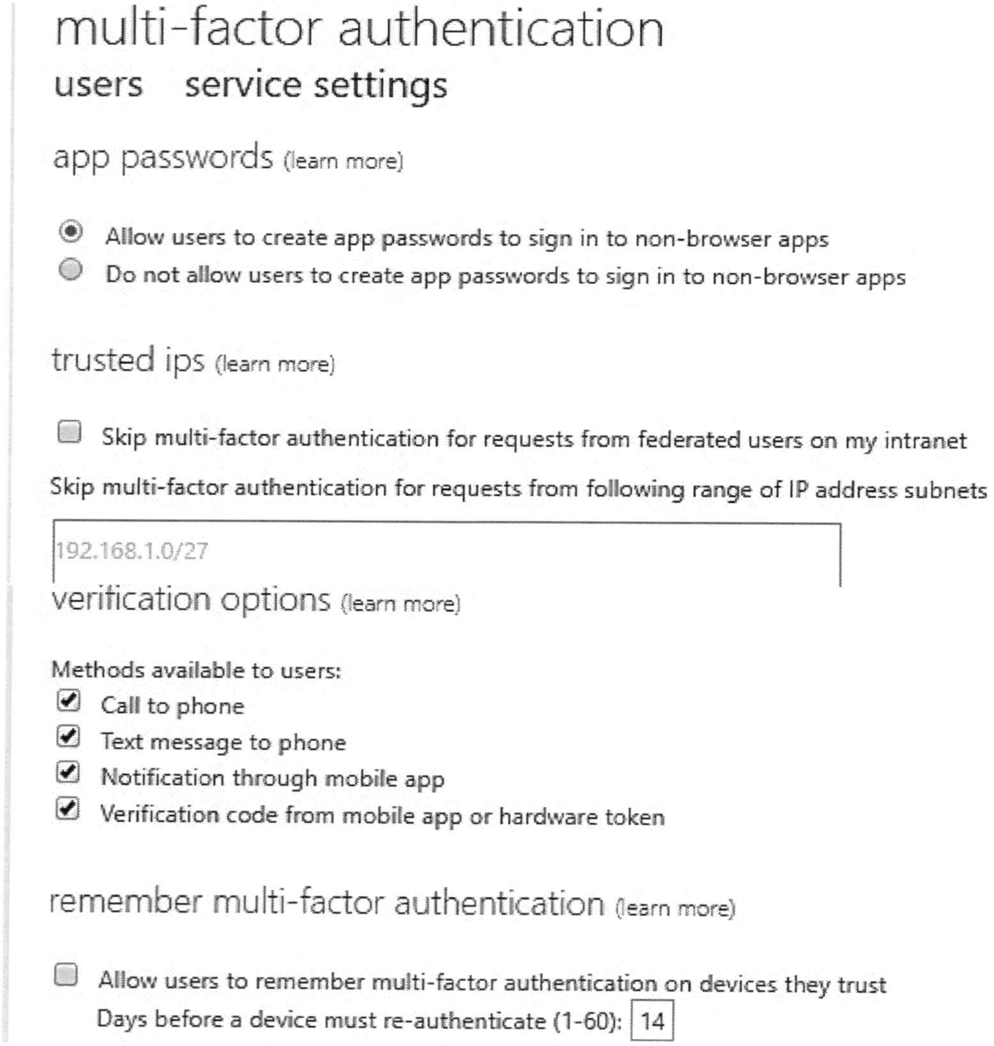

multi-factor authentication

users service settings

app passwords (learn more)

- (selected) Allow users to create app passwords to sign in to non-browser apps
- (not selected) Do not allow users to create app passwords to sign in to non-browser apps

trusted ips (learn more)

- [ ] Skip multi-factor authentication for requests from federated users on my intranet

Skip multi-factor authentication for requests from following range of IP address subnets

192.168.1.0/27

verification options (learn more)

Methods available to users:

- [x] Call to phone
- [x] Text message to phone
- [x] Notification through mobile app
- [x] Verification code from mobile app or hardware token

remember multi-factor authentication (learn more)

- [ ] Allow users to remember multi-factor authentication on devices they trust

Days before a device must re-authenticate (1-60): 14

MFA Verification Options

There are Four verification methods that are available for users. When your users enroll their accounts for Azure Multi-Factor Authentication, they choose their preferred verification method from the options that you have enabled.

Method	Description
Call to phone	Places an automated voice call. The user answers the call and presses # in the phone keypad to authenticate.
Text message to phone	Sends a text message that contains a verification code.
Notification through mobile app	Sends a push notification to Microsoft Authenticator app installed on your phone. The user views the notification and selects **Verify** to complete verification. The Microsoft Authenticator app is available for Windows Phone, Android, and iOS.
Verification code from mobile app or hardware token	The Microsoft Authenticator app generates a new OATH verification code every 30 seconds. The user enters the verification code into the sign-in interface. The Microsoft Authenticator app is available for Windows Phone, Android, and iOS.

Microsoft Authenticator app for Android
https://play.google.com/store/apps/details?id=com.azure.authenticator

Microsoft Authenticator app for iOS
https://itunes.apple.com/app/id983156458

Exercise 129: Enable and disable verification methods

In Azure AD Dashboard Click Users in left pane>All User Blade open> Click **Multi-Factor Authentication** in Top Right> A new Browser tab opens >Click Service Setting in Top> You can see the 4 option under verifications options>Select your options and click save (Not Shown).

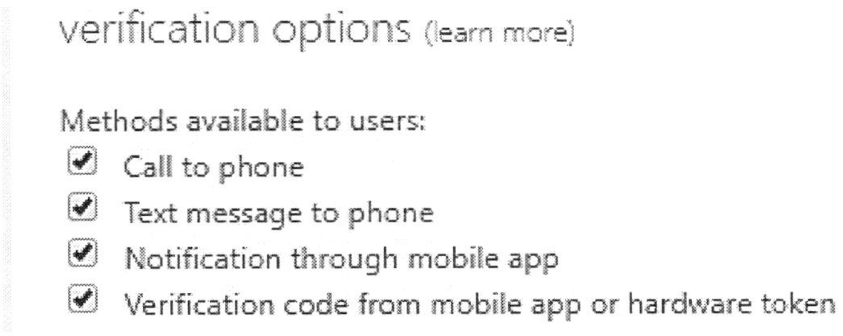

verification options (learn more)

Methods available to users:

- [x] Call to phone
- [x] Text message to phone
- [x] Notification through mobile app
- [x] Verification code from mobile app or hardware token

App Passwords

Some applications, like Office 2010 or earlier and Apple Mail before iOS 11, don't support two-step verification. The apps aren't configured to accept a second verification. To use these applications, take advantage of the *app passwords* feature. You can use an app password in place of your traditional password to allow an app to bypass two-step verification and continue working.

Enable app password option in MFA Service setting to allow users to create app passwords.

Exercise 130: Allow users to create app passwords

In Azure AD Dashboard Click Users in left pane>All User Blade open> Click **Multi-Factor Authentication** in Top Right> A new Browser tab opens >Click Service Setting in Top>Select Radio button Allow users to create app passwords to sign in to non-browser apps.

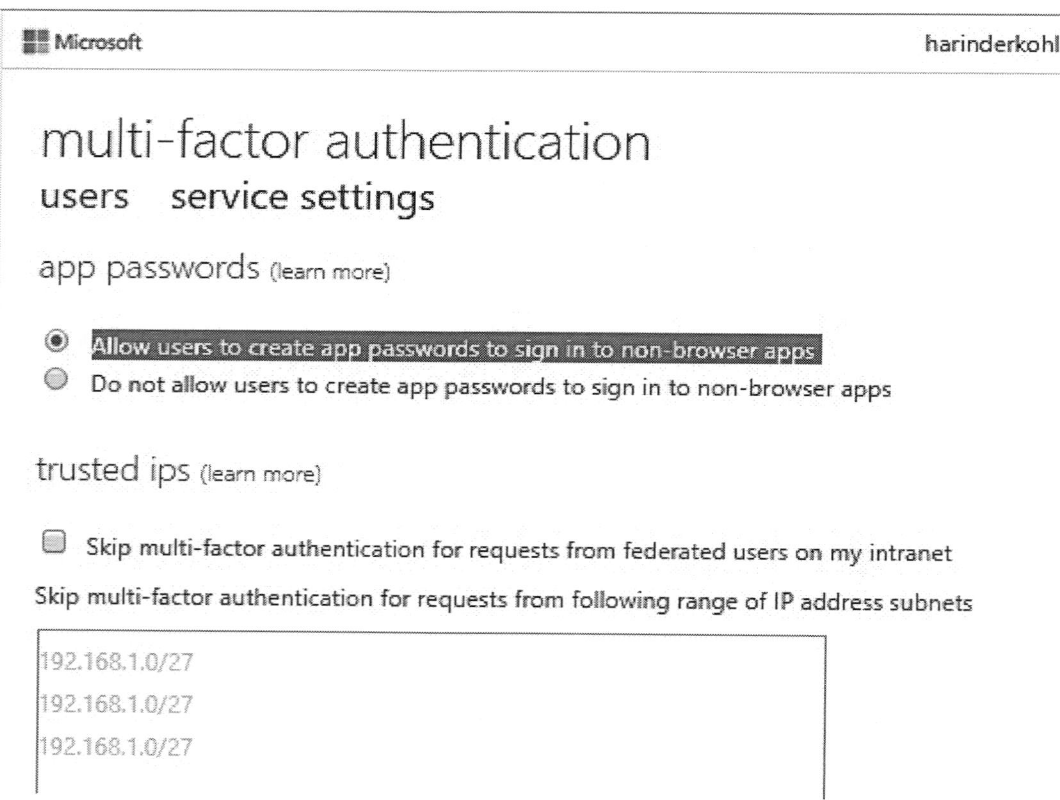

Trusted IPs

Trusted IPs feature bypasses two-step verification for users who sign in from the company intranet.

In Trusted IPs you have the option to bypasses two-step verification for Federated Users.

Note: When the Trusted IPs feature is enabled, two-step verification is *not* required for browser flows. App passwords are *not* required for older rich client applications, provided that the user hasn't created an app password. After an app password is in use, the password remains required.

Exercise 131: Enabling Trusted IPs

In Azure AD Dashboard Click Users in left pane>All User Blade open> Click **Multi-Factor Authentication** in Top Right> A new Browser tab opens >Click Service Setting in Top>Under Trusted IPs Enter the ranges of IP Addresses in the Box> Click save (Not Shown).

multi-factor authentication

users service settings

app passwords (learn more)

- (selected) Allow users to create app passwords to sign in to non-browser apps
- Do not allow users to create app passwords to sign in to non-browser apps

trusted ips (learn more)

- [ ] Skip multi-factor authentication for requests from federated users on my intranet

Skip multi-factor authentication for requests from following range of IP address subnets

192.168.1.0/27

Note: The option to bypass MFA for Federated Users.

Remember Multi-Factor Authentication

Remember Multi-Factor Authentication feature remembers the device from which user has logged. Users can then bypass subsequent MFA verifications for a specified number of days, after they've successfully signed-in to a device by using Multi-Factor Authentication.

Exercise 132: Enabling Remember Multi-Factor

In Azure AD Dashboard Click Users in left pane>All User Blade open> Click **Multi-Factor Authentication** in Top Right> A new Browser tab opens >Click Service Setting in Top> Under remember multi-factor authentication Select the check Box and enter number of days for which Users can bypass MFA verifications>click save.

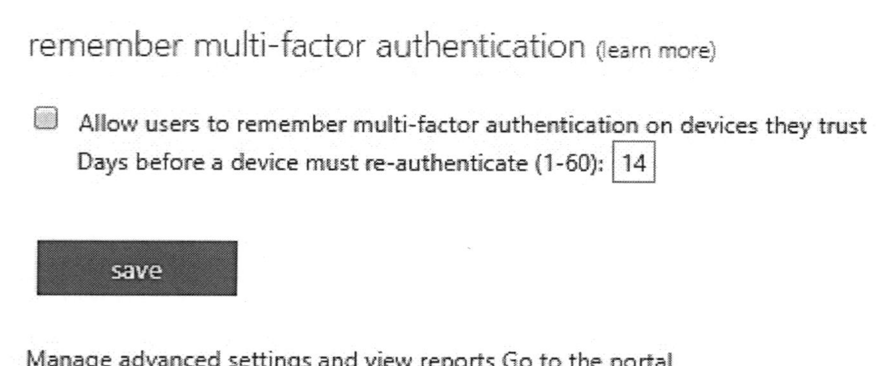

Fraud Alert

Fraud Alert feature Allows users to report fraud if they receive a two-step verification request that they didn't initiate.

Exercise 133: Enabling Fraud Alert

In Azure AD Dashboard Scroll down and click MFA in left pane>MFA Dashboard opens>Click Fraud Alert in left pane> In right pane select On under allow users to submit Fraud Details> Enter a code to report fraud during initial Greeting. If you don't enter then 0 is Fraud code> Click save.

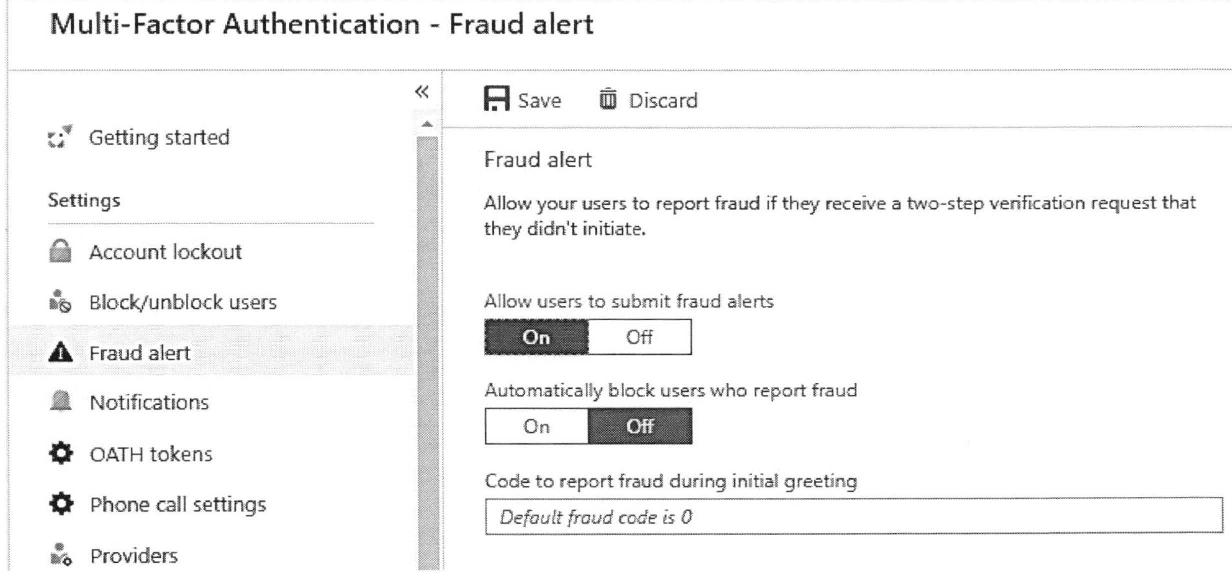

Block/Unblock Users

Block and unblock feature prevents users from receiving authentication requests. Any authentication attempts for blocked users are automatically denied. Users remain blocked for 90 days from the time that they are blocked.

Exercise 134: Enabling Block/Unblock

In Azure AD Dashboard Scroll down and click MFA in left pane>MFA Dashboard opens>Click Block/Unblock users in left pane> In right pane Click + Add>Block a User blade opens> Enter user log in credentials in email format such as **user1@harinderkohlioutlook.onmicrosoft.com**>Enter a reason> Click OK (Not shown).

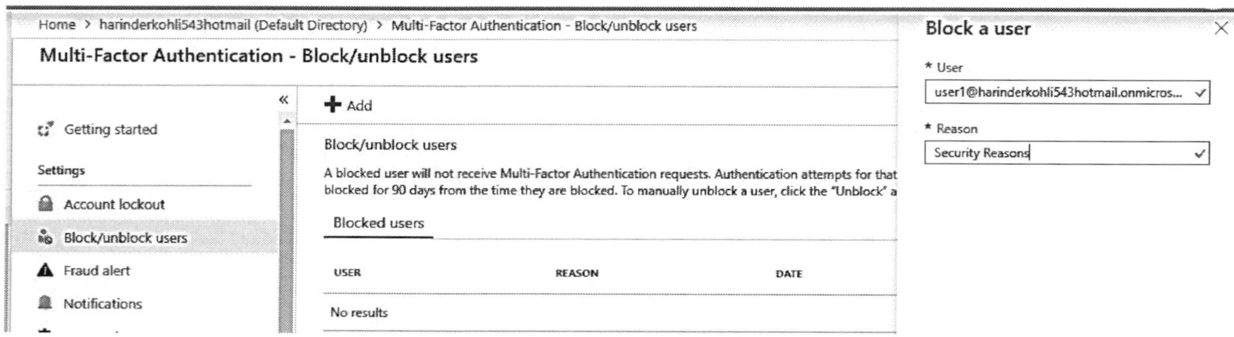

Figure below shows User1 is blocked from receiving MFA authentication request.

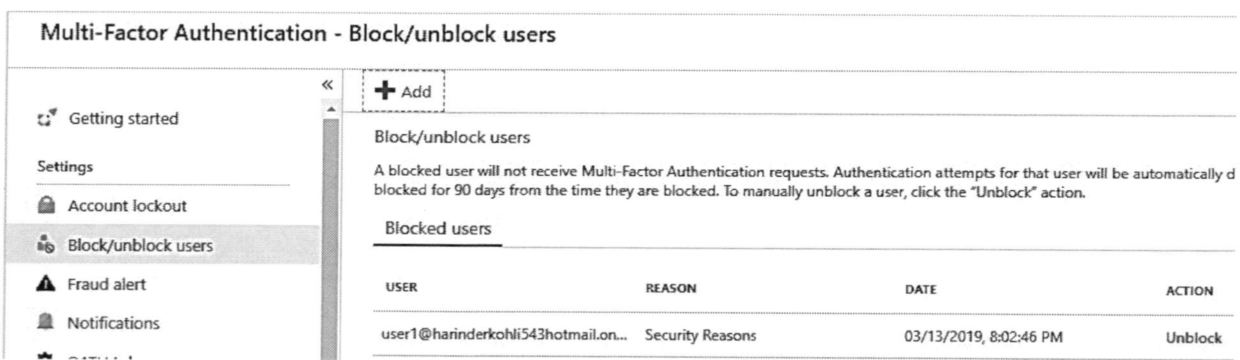

Note 1: I accessed Azure portal (https://portal.azure.com) and logged with User1 credentials and entered password but did not received MFA code.
Note 2: Unblock the user User1 as we require it for more exercises.

Account Lockout

Account Lockout option temporarily lock accounts in the multi-factor authentication service if there are too many denied authentication attempts in a row. This feature only applies to users who enter a PIN to authenticate.

Exercise 135: Enabling Account Lockout

In Azure AD Dashboard Scroll down and click MFA in left pane>MFA Dashboard opens>Click Account lockout in left pane> In right pane enter options for Account Lockout>Click save.

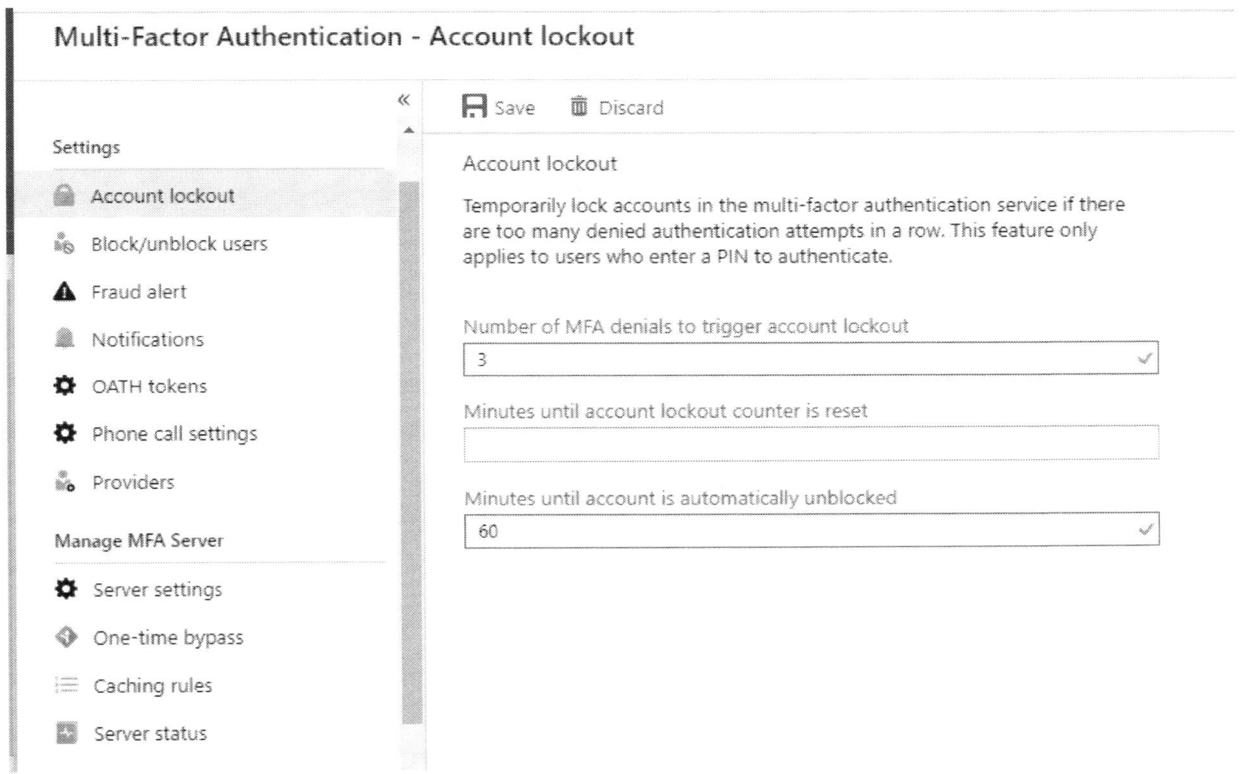

One-time Bypass option

One-time Bypass feature allow a user to authenticate without performing two-step verification for a limited time.

Important Note: This feature is only available with MFA Server only. This feature is not available for Cloud MFA.

Exercise 136: Demonstrating One-time Bypass

In Azure AD Dashboard Scroll down and click MFA in left pane>MFA Dashboard opens>Scroll down and under MFA Server click one-time bypass.

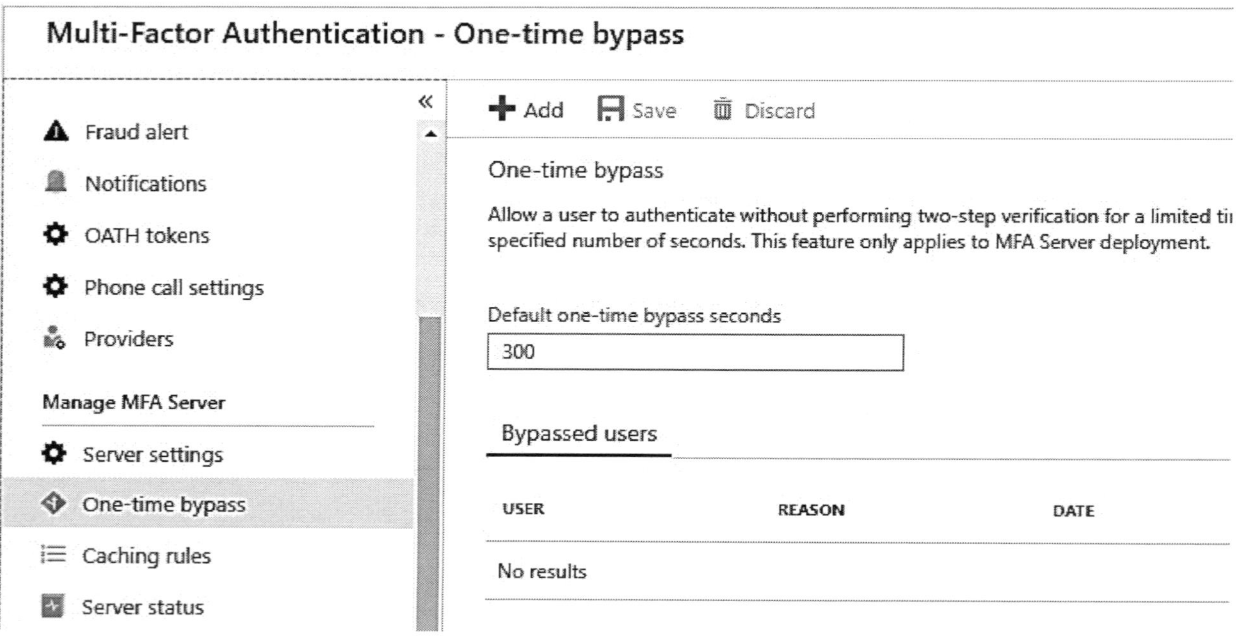

Chapter 15 Azure AD Premium Features

This Chapter covers following Topic Lessons

Conditional Access in Azure AD
Azure Active Directory Identity Protection
Azure AD Access Reviews
Azure AD Privileged Identity Management
What you can do with Privileged Identity Management
Just in time administrator access with Eligible Admin
Roles managed in PIM
Requirements to Enable Privileged Identity Management
Azure AD Application Proxy

This Chapter covers following Lab Exercises

- Create Conditional Access Policy
- Testing CA Policy from Location outside India
- Testing the CA Policy from Location in India
- Testing the Conditional Access Policy using What If option
- Simulate suspicious locations using TOR Browser
- Enabling Azure Active Directory Identity Protection
- Accessing Azure AD Identity Protection Dashboard
- Demonstrating Resetting Compromised User Password
- Investigating Risk Events
- Investigating Vulnerabilities
- Implementing Sign-in Risk Conditional Access Policy
- Create Access Review for Azure AD Group

This Chapter covers following Case Studies

- Secure Remote Access to on-premises Application

Chapter Topology

In this Chapter we will configure Premium P1 and P2 Features of Azure AD including Conditional Access, Identity Protection & Access Review.

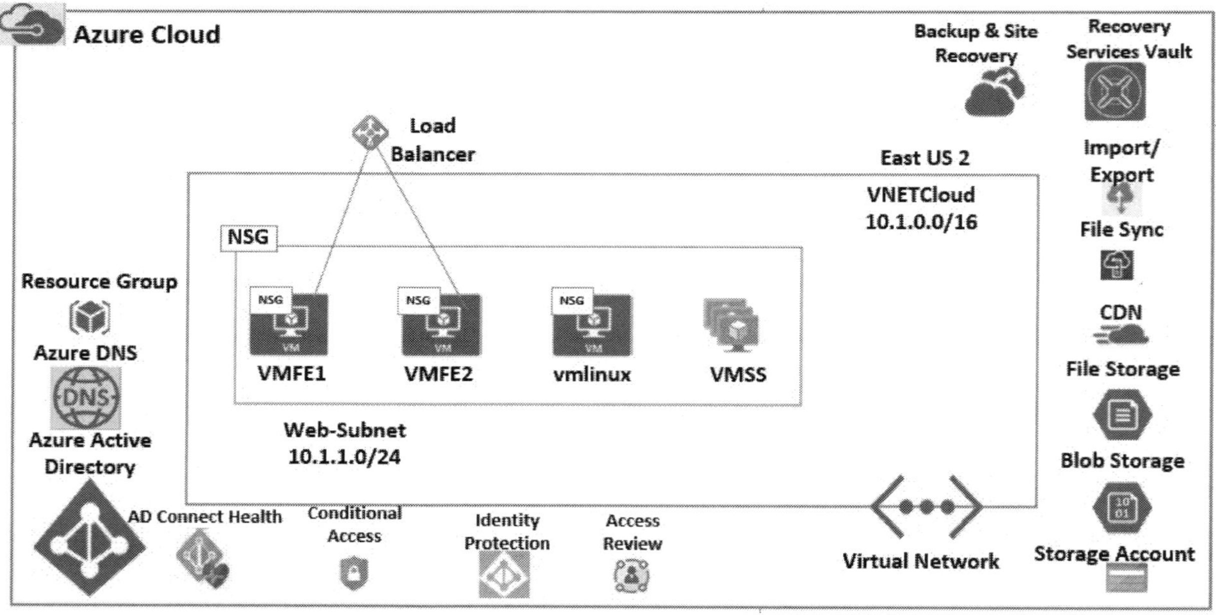

Conditional Access in Azure AD

Azure Conditional Access is a feature of the Azure AD Premium P2 edition.

Before going into Conditional Access in Azure AD let's discuss why we need it in first place. In today's Cloud and Mobile era users are accessing corporate applications & services not only from on-premises but also from home or anywhere in world using corporate owned or personal devices.

Corporate IT Administrators are faced with two opposing goals:

1. Empower the end users to be productive wherever and whenever.
2. Protect the corporate assets.

With Conditional Access you can balance both the above goals.

<u>**Conditional access** is a capability of Azure Active Directory that enables you to enforce controls on the access to apps based on specific conditions.</u>

With **controls**, you can either **block access** or **allow access with additional requirements.** The implementation of conditional access is based on policies.

Figure below shows that up to **6 conditions** can be applied before access to cloud apps is allowed or blocked.

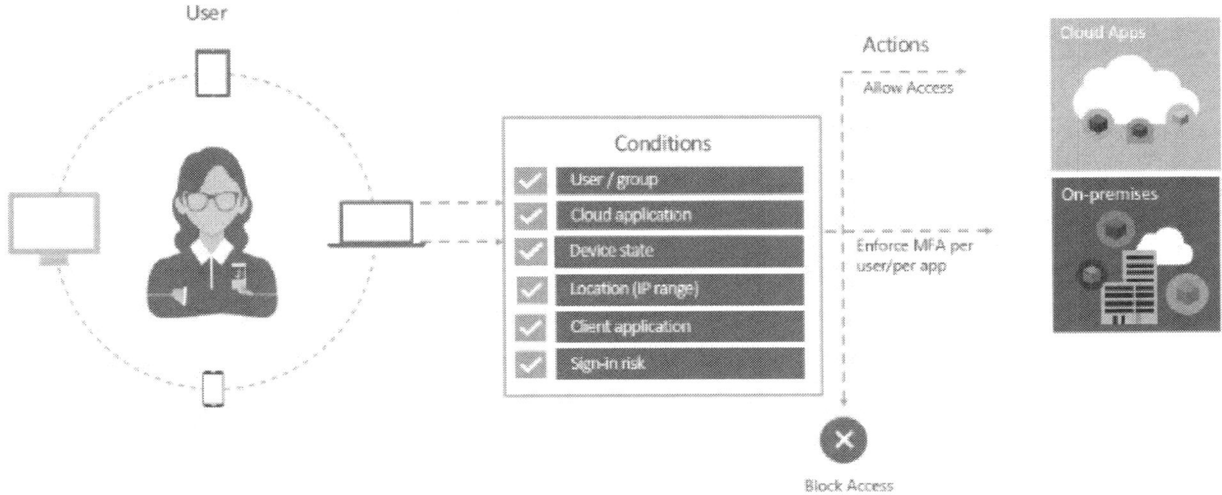

Conditional Access Policy

The combination of a condition statement with controls represents a conditional access policy. Figure below shows components of conditional access policy.

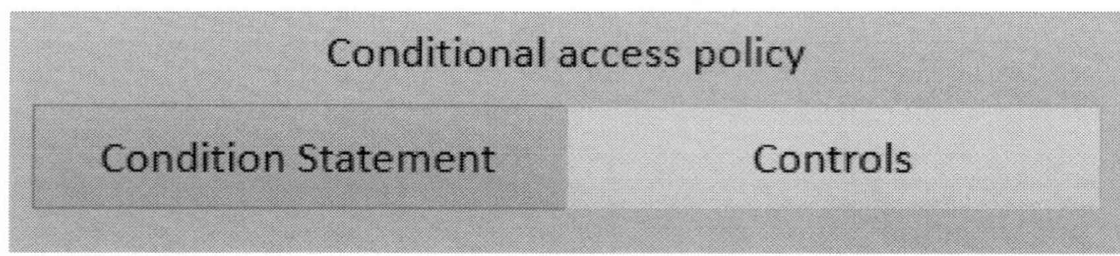

Based on the result of condition statement, controls are applied.

Condition Statements

In a conditional access policy, **condition statements are criteria that need to be met for your controls to be applied.**

You can include the **following 7 criteria's** into your condition statement:

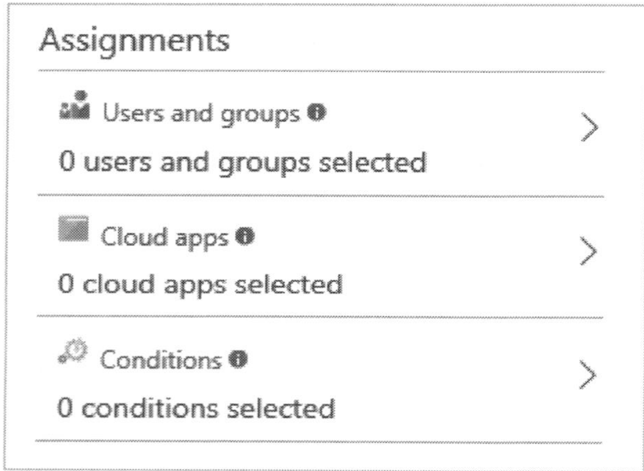

1. **Users & Groups:** In conditional access policy, you need to select the users or groups your policy applies to.

2. **Cloud Application:** In conditional access policy, you need to select the cloud application your policy applies to.

Conditions: In conditional access policy, you can define 5 conditions:

Sign-in risk | Device platforms | Locations | Client application | Device State

3. **Sign-in risk:** Sign-in risk level is used as a condition in a conditional access policy.

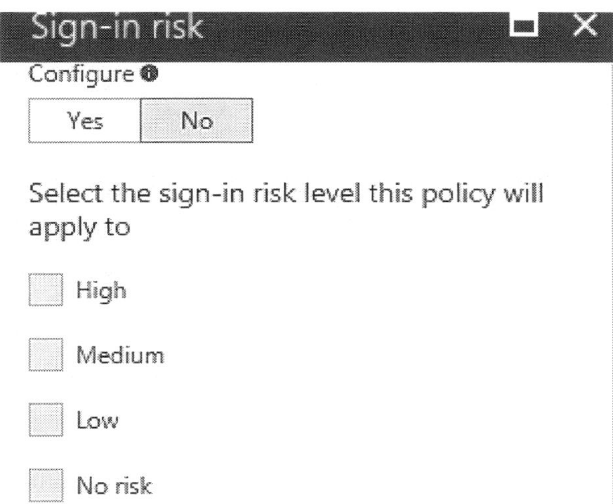

4. **Device Platform:** In a conditional access policy, you can configure the device platform condition to tie the policy to the operating system on a client. Azure AD conditional access supports the following device platforms:

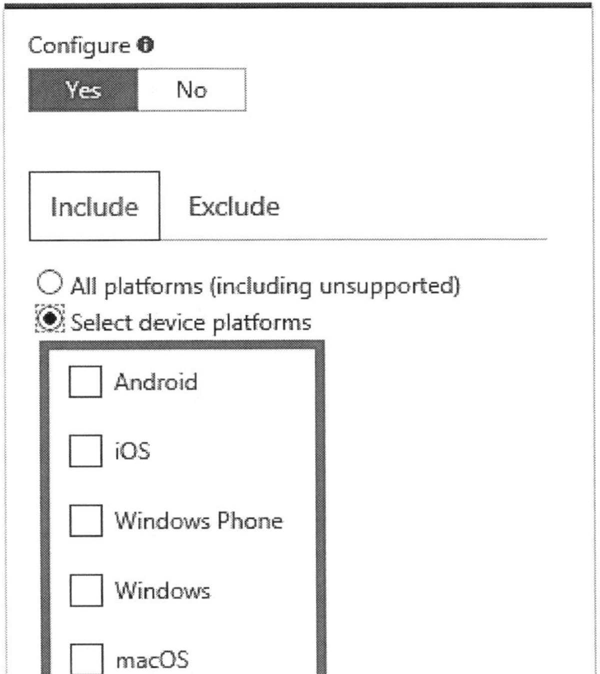

5. **Location:** In a conditional access policy, you can define conditions that are based on where a connection attempt was initiated from. The entries in the locations list are either **named locations** or **MFA trusted IPs**.

Named locations is a feature of Azure Active Directory that allows you to define labels for the locations connection attempts were made from. To define a location, you can either configure an IP address ranges or you select a country / region.
MFA trusted IPs is a feature of multi-factor authentication that enables you to define trusted IP address ranges representing your organization's local intranet. When you configure a location condition, Trusted IPs enables you to distinguish between connections made from your organization's network and all other locations.

6. **Client Apps:** The client apps condition allows you to apply a policy based on Client application type – Browser, Mobile apps or Desktop client.

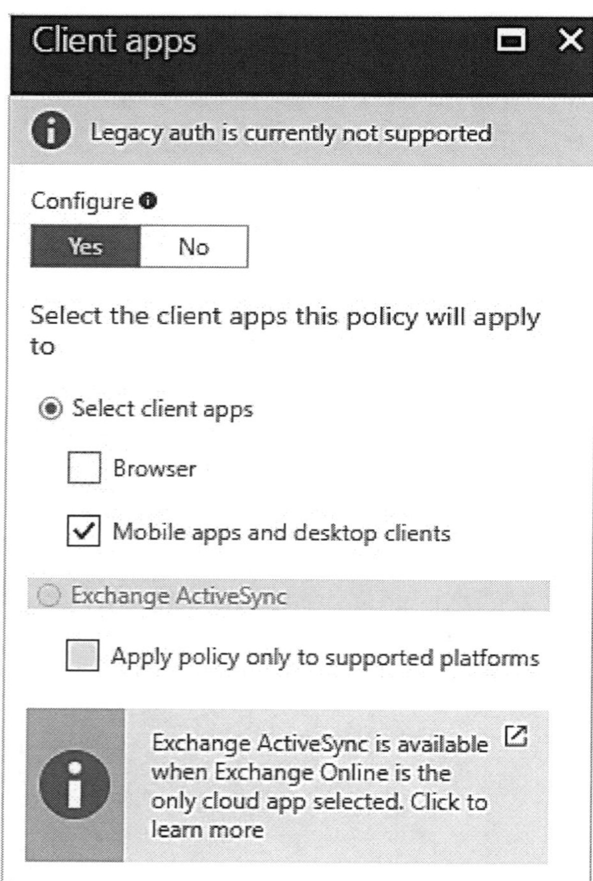

Controls

In a conditional access policy, controls define what it is that should happen when a condition statement has been satisfied.
With controls, you can either **block access** or **allow access with additional requirements**. When you configure a policy that allows access, you need to select at least one requirement.

There are two types of controls: Grant Control and Session Control.

Grant Control: With Grant controls, you can either **Block access** or **Grant access with additional requirements.** Azure AD enables you to configure the following if you choose Grant Access.

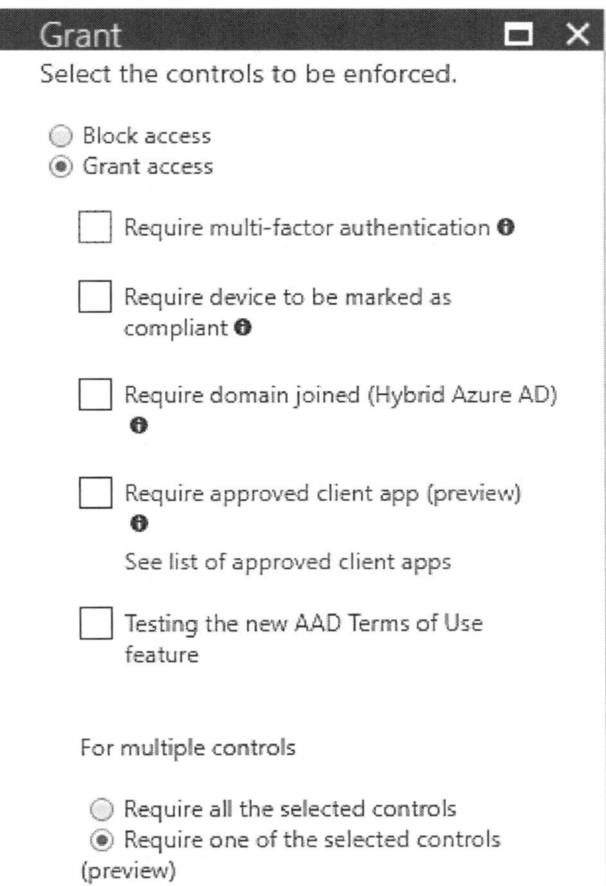

Session Control: Session controls enable limiting experience within a cloud app. The session controls are enforced by cloud apps and rely on additional information provided by Azure AD to the app about the session.

Exercise 137: Create Conditional Access (CA) Policy

In this exercise we will create Conditional Access Policy which will allow User3 to access Cloud app **Microsoft Azure Management or Azure Portal** only if User3 is accessing the Cloud app from India. User3 was created in Ex 103, Chapter 12.

1. In Azure AD Dashboard Click **Conditional Access** in left pane> Conditional Access Blade opens>Click Named Location in left pane.

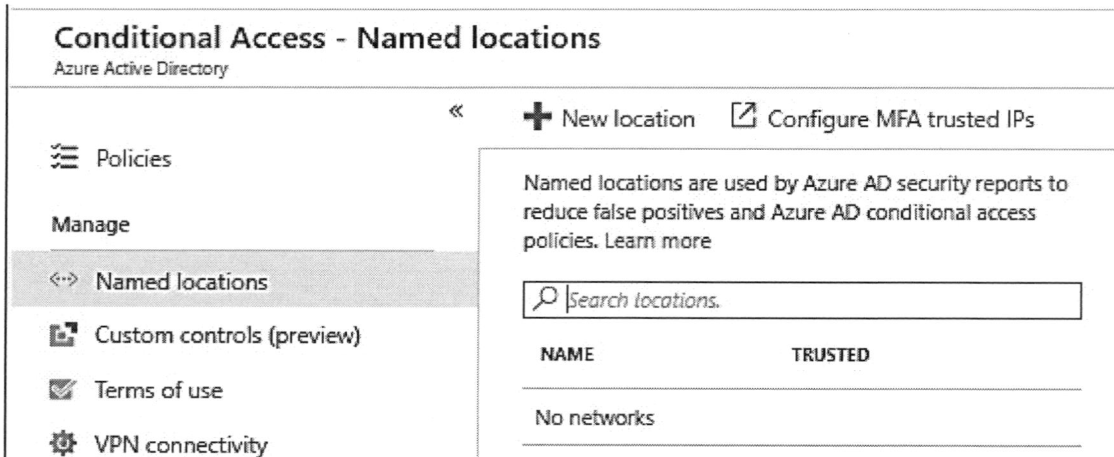

2. Click + New Location>New Location Blade opens>Enter a name, Select Countries/Region> From drop down box check select all> Deselect India> click Create (Not shown).

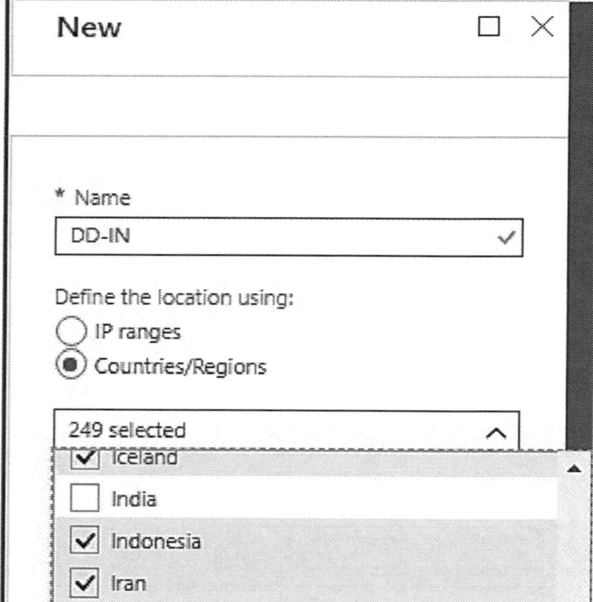

3. In Conditional Access Blade click Policies in left pane.

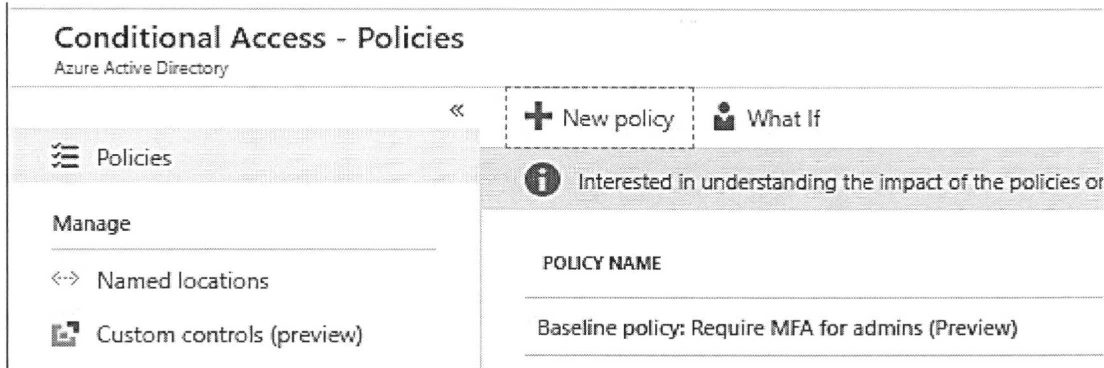

4. Click + New Policy> Create New Policy Blade opens>Enter a name>In users and groups Select **User3**>In Cloud App Select **Microsoft Azure Management**> In Conditions select Location, click Yes, Click selected Location radio Button, Click Select and then select **DD-IN** Location created in step 1& 2> Click Select>Click Done>Click Done> In Access Control select **Block** Access>Click **On** for Enable Policy> Click Create.

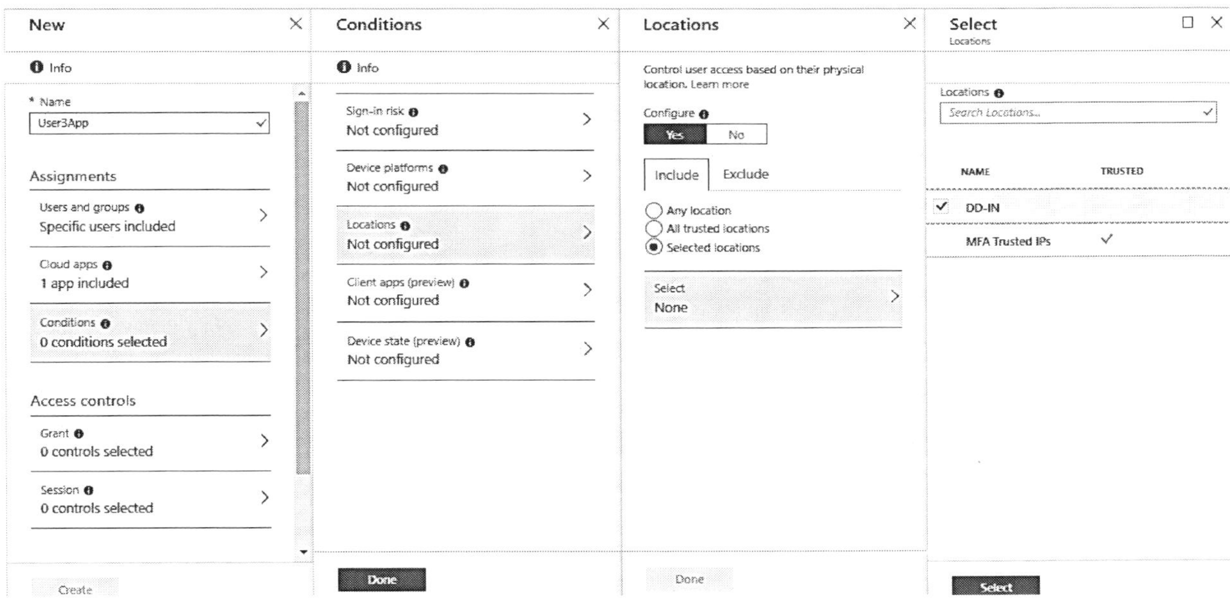

Note: Readers are advised to deselect the country from which they will be doing this Exercise.

Exercise 138:Testing CA Policy from Location outside India

For this Exercise we will use TOR Browser. You can check IP address and Location by using link https://www.iplocation.net/find-ip-address. In my case it was a European location with IP Address X.10.X.200.

1. Open Tor Browser on your laptop and go to portal.azure.com and log on with User3 Credentials> You cannot access the Azure Portal.

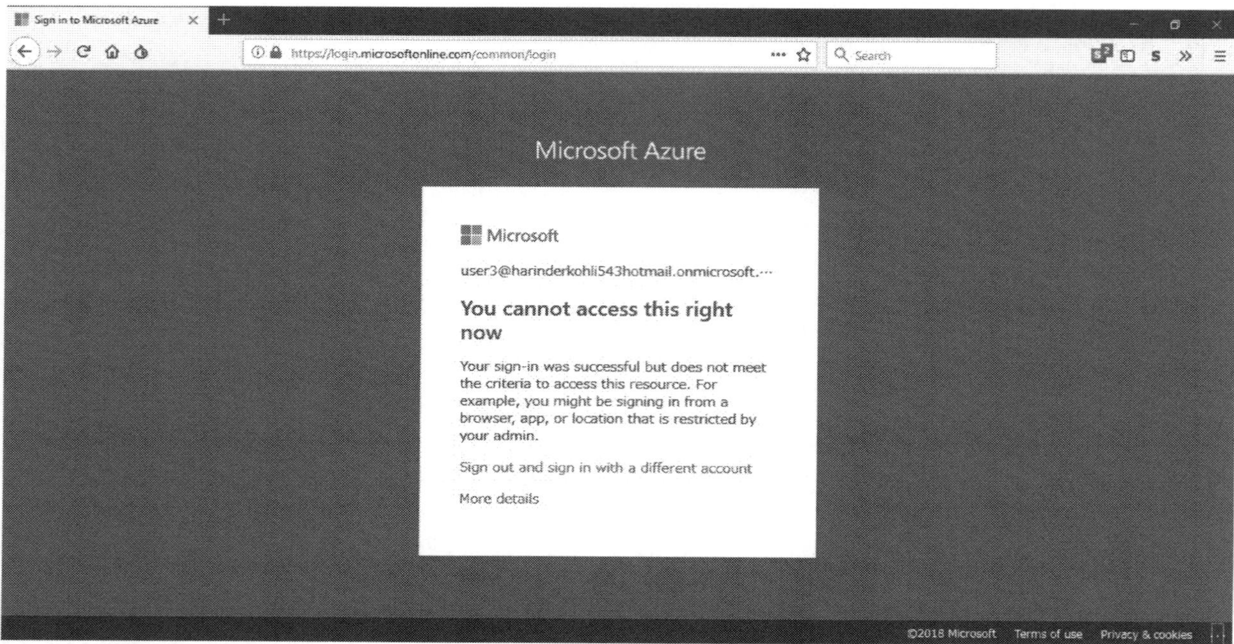

Exercise 139: Testing the CA Policy from Location in India

1. Open Firefox Browser on your laptop and go to portal.azure.com and log on with User3 Credentials> You can access the Azure Portal.

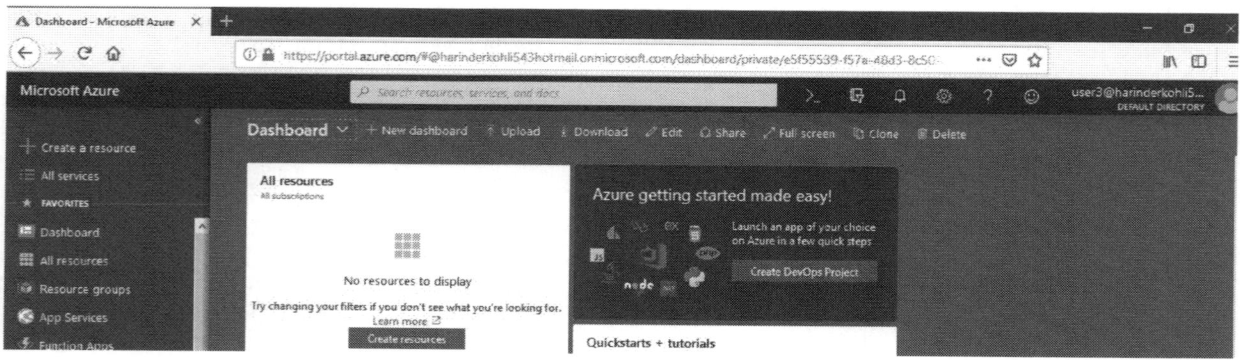

Exercise 140: Testing the Conditional Access Policy using What If option

1. In Azure AD Dashboard Click **Conditional Access** in left pane> Conditional Access Blade opens> In Conditional Access Blade click Policies in left pane>In Right pane click **What If** in Right pane>What If Pane opens>Select User3, Select Microsoft Azure Management, Select Country as Switzerland and IP Address as 176.10.99.200> click What If>Evaluation Result shows Block access.

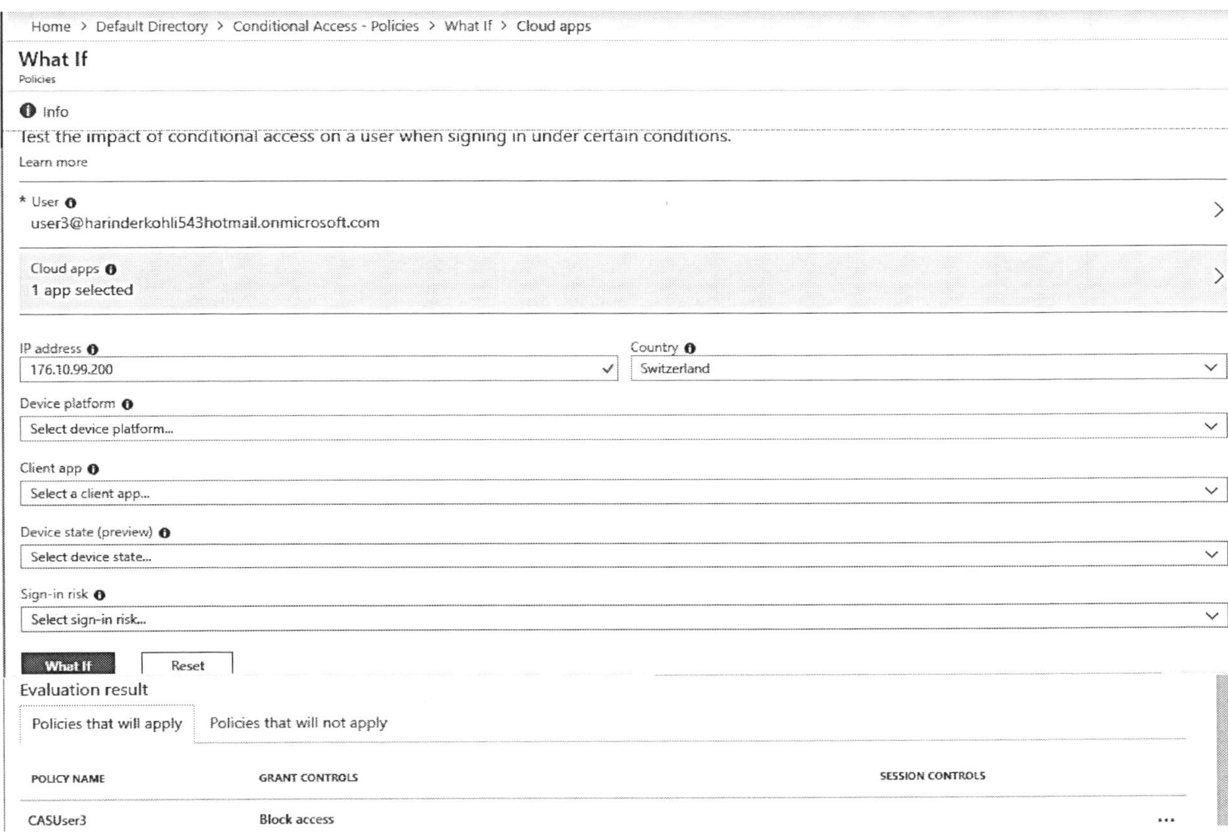

2. If I use India as Location and IP address as 139.167.240.27 then no Conditional Access Policy is applied. The reason is that in named location we did not selected India.

Evaluation result

Policies that will apply | Policies that will not apply

POLICY NAME	GRANT CONTROLS	SESSION CONTROLS
No policies		

Azure Active Directory Identity Protection

Before going into Azure AD Identity Protection let's discuss why we need it in first place. The vast majority of security breaches take place when attackers gain access to an environment by stealing a user's identity.

Azure AD Identity Protection helps in detecting and remediating compromised user identities by configuring risk-based policies that automatically respond to detected issues when a specified risk level has been reached.

Azure Active Directory Identity Protection provides risk-based conditional access to your applications and critical company data. Identity Protection uses adaptive machine learning algorithms and heuristics to detect anomalies and risk events that may indicate that an identity has been compromised. Using this data, Identity Protection generates reports and alerts that enable you to investigate these risk events and take appropriate remediation or mitigation action.

Azure Active Directory Identity Protection is a feature of the Azure AD Premium P2 edition.

Azure AD Identity Protection Functions

1. Get a consolidated view of flagged users and risk events detected using machine learning algorithms.
2. Improve security posture by acting on vulnerabilities.
3. Set risk-based Conditional Access policies to automatically protect your users from impending security breaches. Identity protection offers following 3 Risk based policies to configure.
   Azure Multi-factor Authentication registration policy.
   User risk policy.
   Sign-in risk policy.

Exercise 107: Simulate suspicious locations using TOR Browser

1. Using User2 and User3 credential log on to Azure Portal using TOR Browser. Do it couple of times using different TOR locations.

Exercise 141: Enabling Azure Active Directory Identity Protection

1. In Azure Portal Click +Create a resource> Identity>Azure AD Identity Protection> Azure AD Identity Protection Blade opens>Click Create.

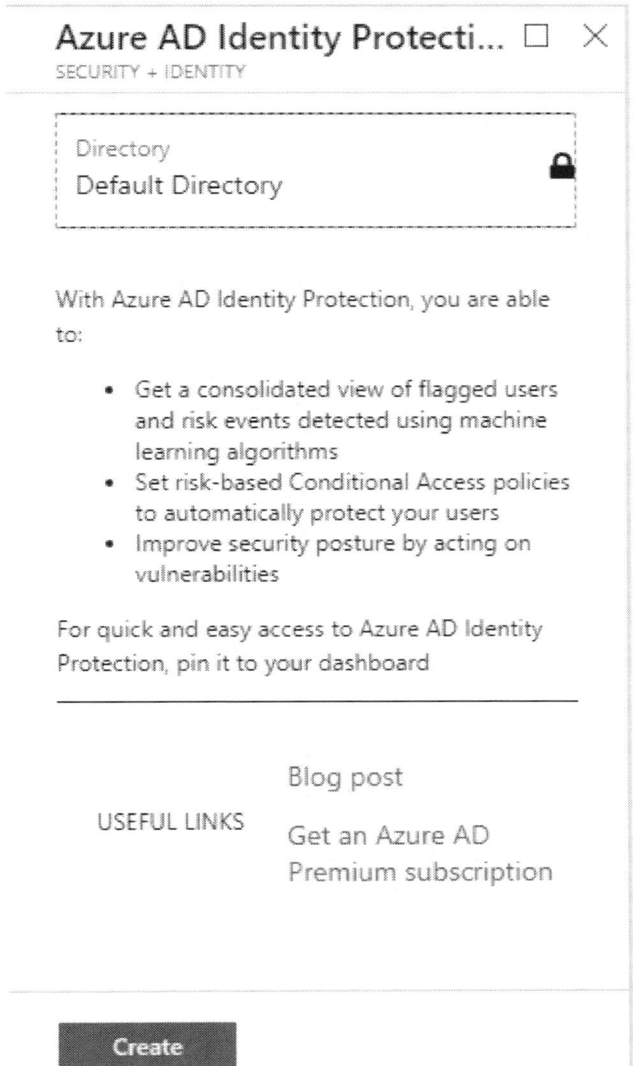

Exercise 142: Accessing Azure AD Identity Protection Dashboard

1. Open Browser and go to the AD Identity Protection Dashboard URL at https://portal.azure.com/#blade/Microsoft_AAD_ProtectionCenter/IdentitySecurityDashboardMenuBlade/Overview

2. Figure below show Identity Protection dashboard. It has 3 Mini Dashboards – **Users flagged for Risk, Risk Events and Vulnerabilities.**

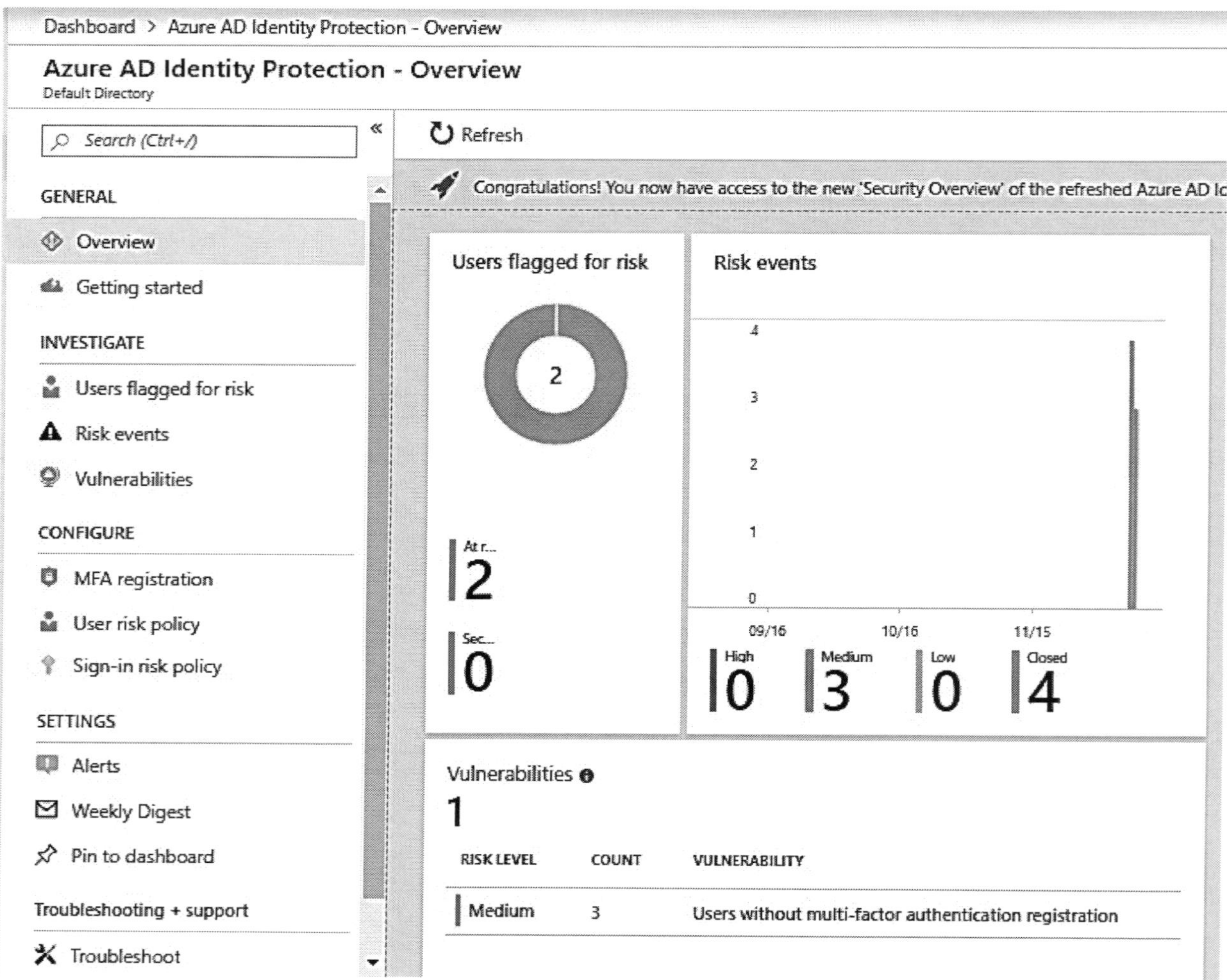

Under Configure you can see 3 risk based policies - Azure **Multi-factor Authentication registration policy, User risk policy & sign-in risk policy.**

3. Click **User flagged for Risk** in left pane>In right pane you can see security risk & status information about the user.

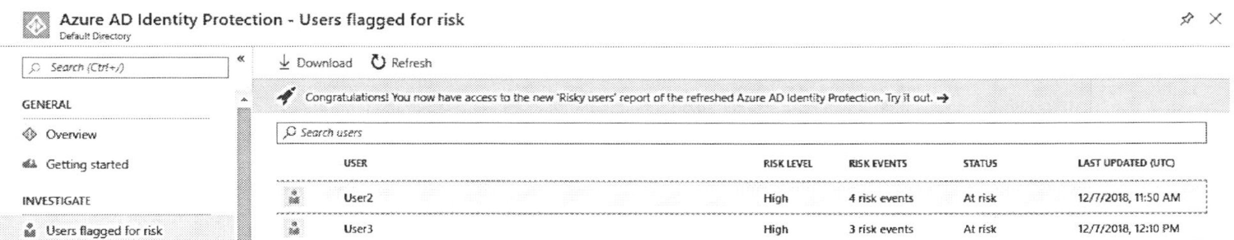

4. Click **Risk events** in left pane> You can see risk event type.

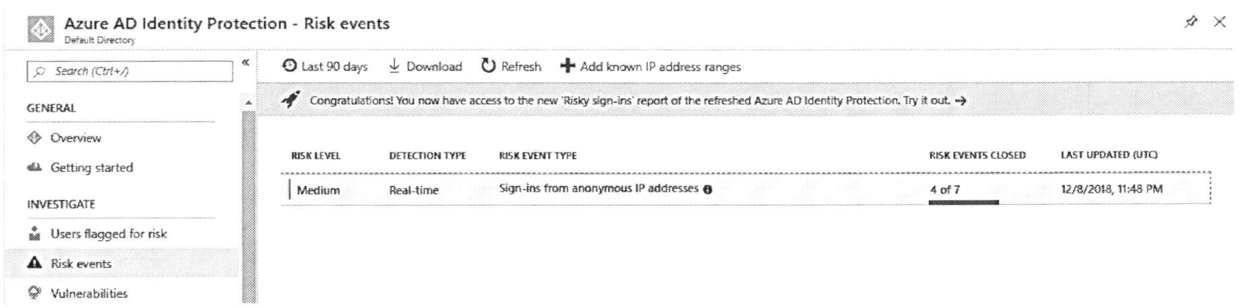

5. Click **Vulnerabilities** in left pane> You can see the risk level and type of Vulnerability which in this case is that there is no MFA for users.

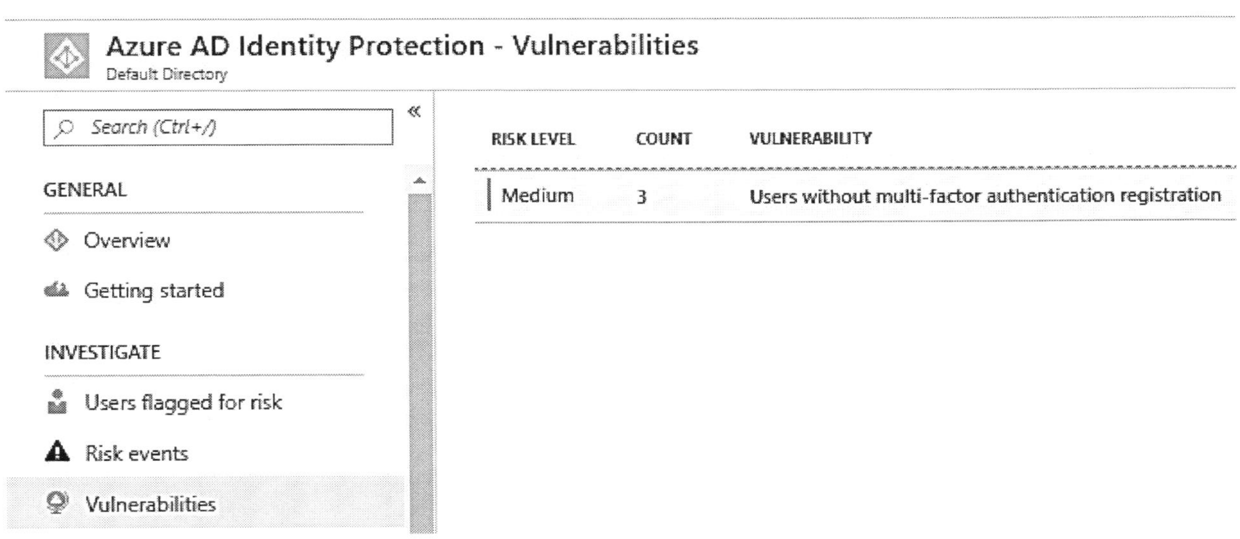

Users Flagged for Risk

These are users in your directory whose credentials might be compromised based on observed patterns of behaviour. Identity Protection Dashboard chart shows you the number of users who are currently at risk as well as users who had risk events that were already remediated.

Remediating Risk: After you have investigated, you can remediate risk events by resetting the user's password—this takes control away from any attacker who had the previous password.

Exercise 143: Demonstrating Resetting Compromised User Password

In Identity Protection Dashboard click **User flagged for Risk** in left pane.

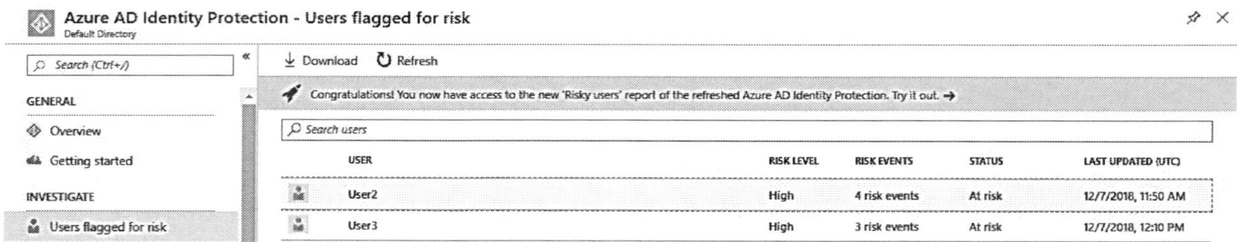

In right pane click one of the user listed. In this case I selected User3>In User3 pane click Reset password>Reset Password pane opens. From here you can reset User password.

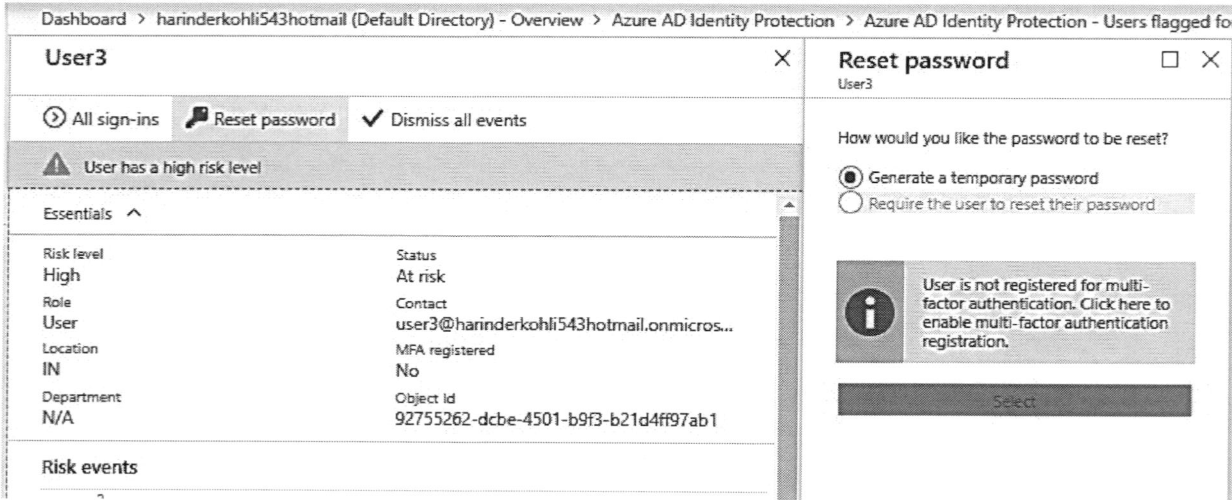

Risk events

These are events that Identity Protection has flagged as high risk and indicate that an identity may have been compromised. Some of the Risk events include:
1. Users with leaked credentials.
2. Irregular sign-in activity.
3. Sign-ins from possibly infected devices.
4. Sign-ins from unfamiliar locations.
5. Sign-ins from IP addresses with suspicious activity.
6. Sign-ins from impossible travel.

Remediating Risk Events: After you have investigated, you can remediate risk events by applying Sign-in risk policies.

Exercise 144: Investigating Risk Events

In Identity Protection Dashboard click **Risk Events** in left pane> In right pane click one of Risk Event> You can see the Risk Event- **Sign-ins from anonymous IP Addresses**. I had tried to log on with User2 & User3 using TOR Browser from one of the European locations before starting this exercise.

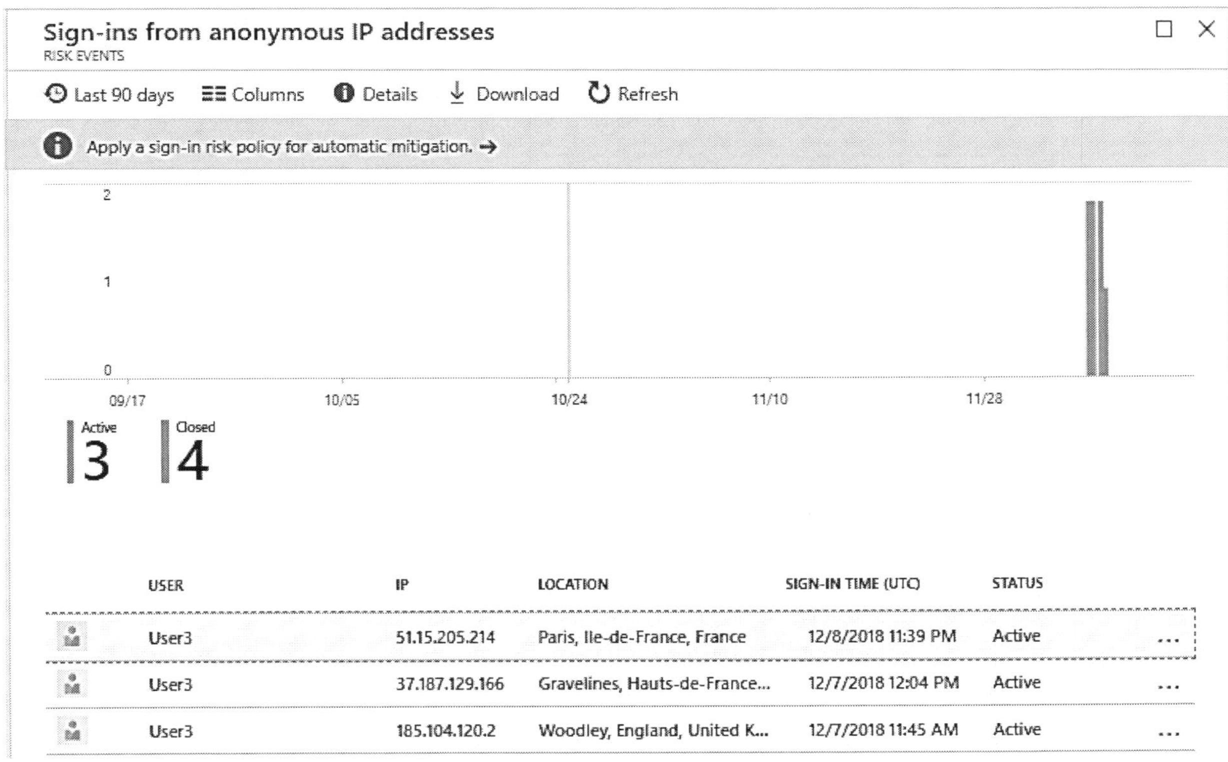

Vulnerabilities

These are weaknesses in your environment that can be exploited by an attacker. It is recommended that you address these vulnerabilities to improve the security posture of your organization and prevent attackers from exploiting these vulnerabilities. Following are some of the vulnerabilities that Identity Protection detects.

1. Users not registered for multi-factor authentication.
2. Unmanaged apps discovered in last 7 days.
3. Security Alerts from Privileged Identity Management.

Remediating Vulnerabilities: After you have investigated, you can remediate Vulnerabilities by applying MFA Registration Policy.

Exercise 145: Investigating Vulnerabilities

1. Click **Vulnerabilities** in left pane> In right pane you can see the risk level and type of Vulnerability which in this case is that there is no MFA for users.

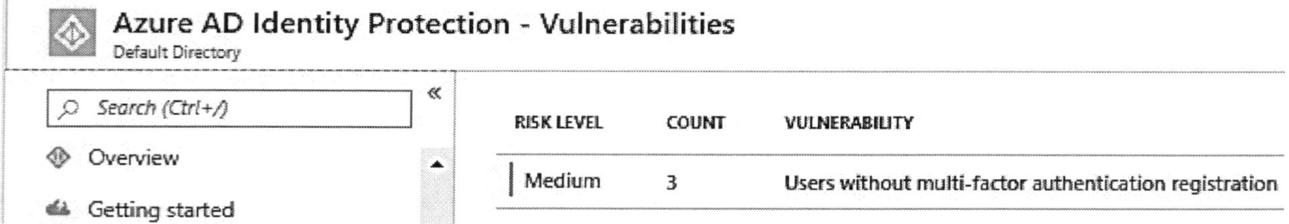

2. In right pane click on the Vulnerability discovered> MFA Policy pane opens. Here you can select MFA policy for all or selected users.

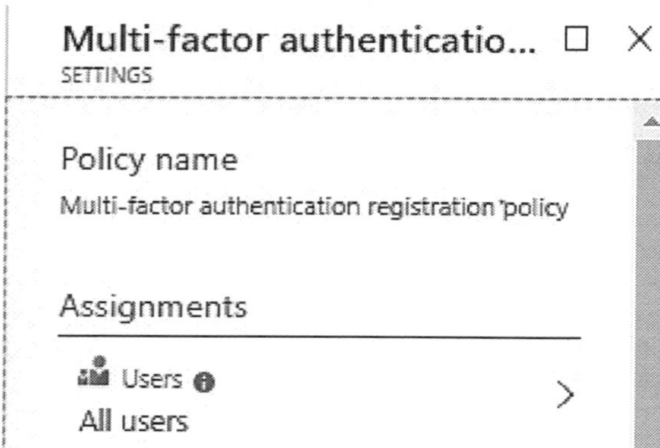

Security Policies

Identity Protection offers 3 types of security policies to help protect your organization- **Multi-factor Authentication registration policy, User risk policy & sign-in risk policy.**

Azure Multi-factor Authentication registration policy: Azure Multi-factor Authentication registration policy helps you manage and monitor the roll-out of multi-factor authentication registration by enabling you to define which employees are included in the policy and view the current registration state of impacted users.

In Identity Protection dashboard> Click MFA Registration in left pane>MFA Registration Policy opens.

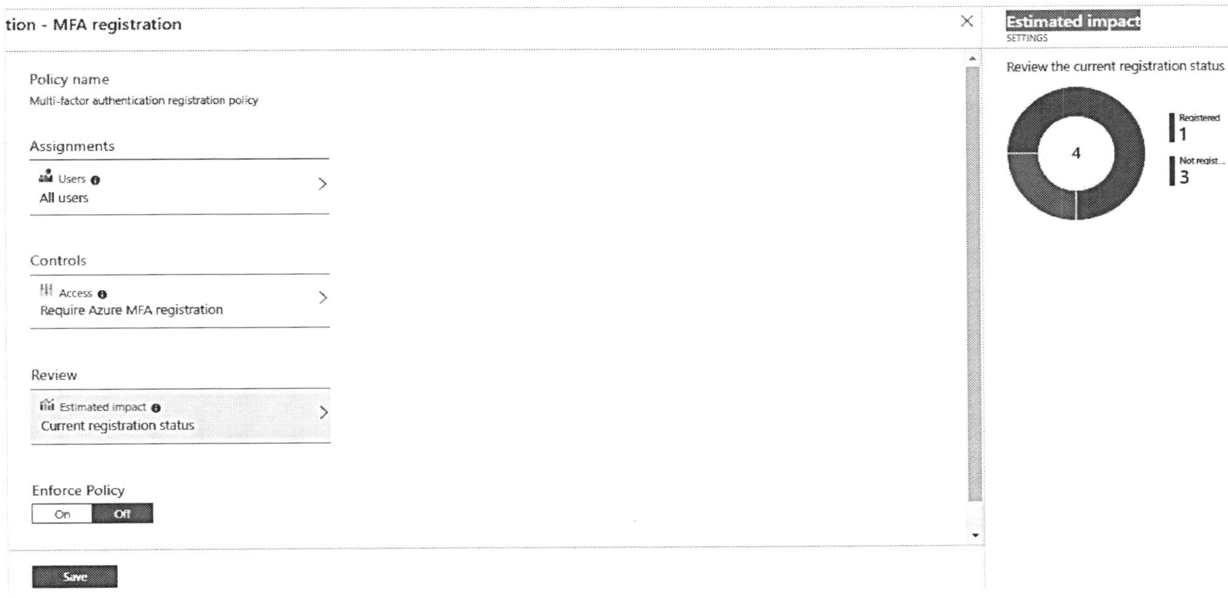

Note 1: Readers are advised to check all the options in the policy.

User risk policy: This is a Conditional Access policy which helps block risky users from signing in, or forces them to securely change their password. You can control which action (block or secure password change) is triggered at different risk levels depending your organization's risk tolerance.

In Identity Protection dashboard> Click User Risk Policy in left pane>User risk remediation Policy opens.

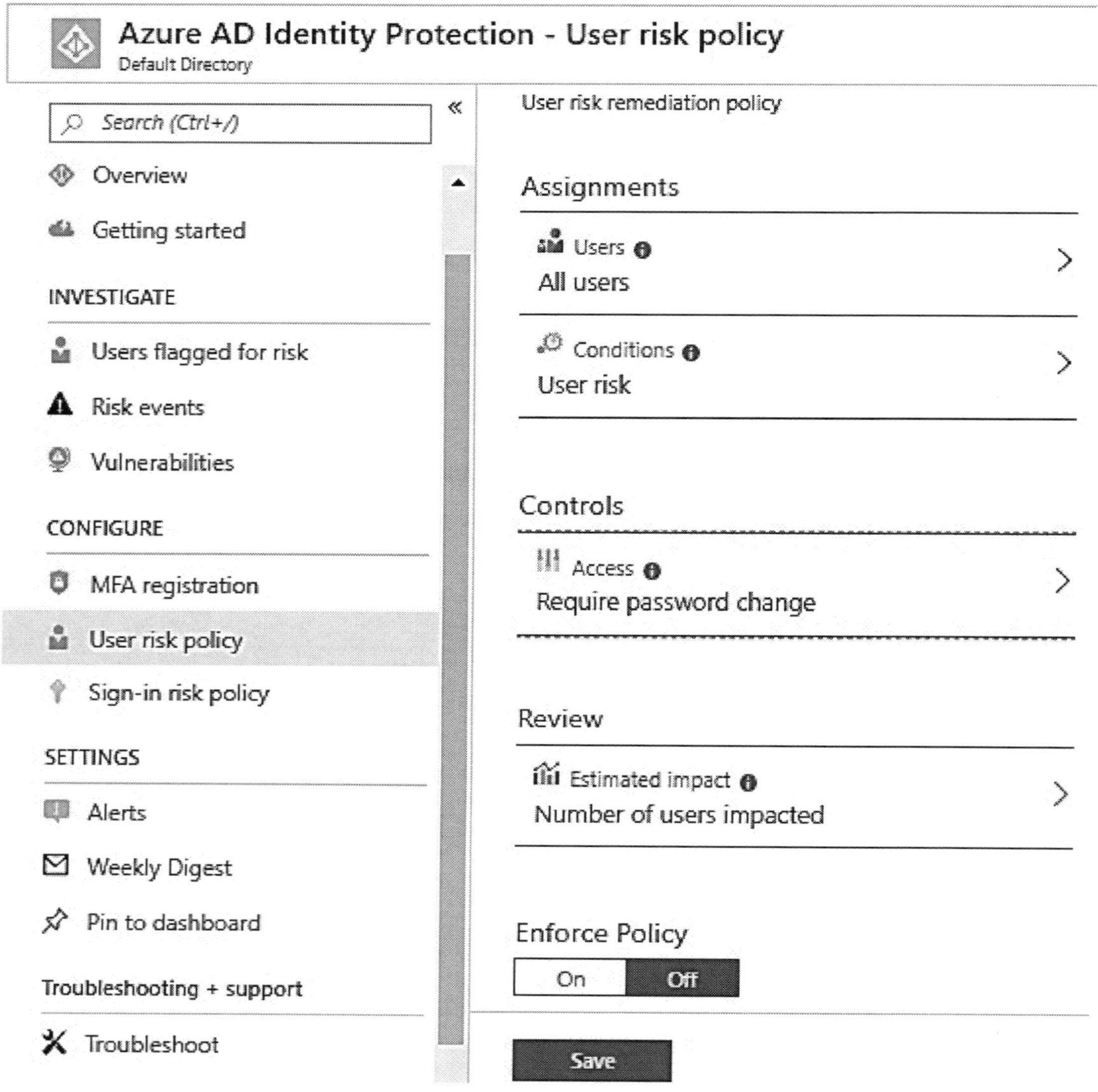

Note: Readers are advised to check all the options in the policy by clicking arrow button.

Figure below shows Condition options in User Risk Policy.

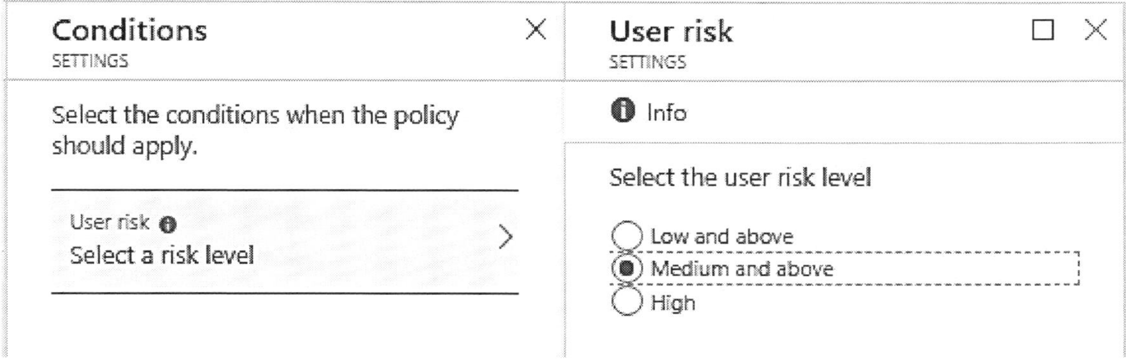

Figure below shows Control options in User Risk Policy.

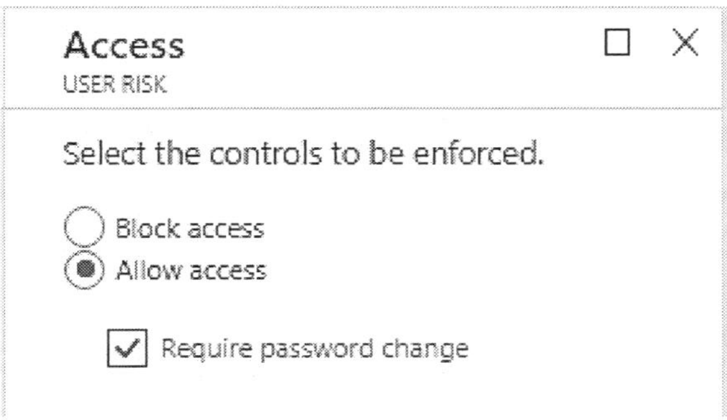

Both the above are same in User Sign-in Risk policy also.

Sign-in risk policy: You can configure a sign-in risk policy to block user sign-in or require multi-factor authentication at different risk thresholds. Click sign-in risk policy in Identity Protection dashboard to open the policy.

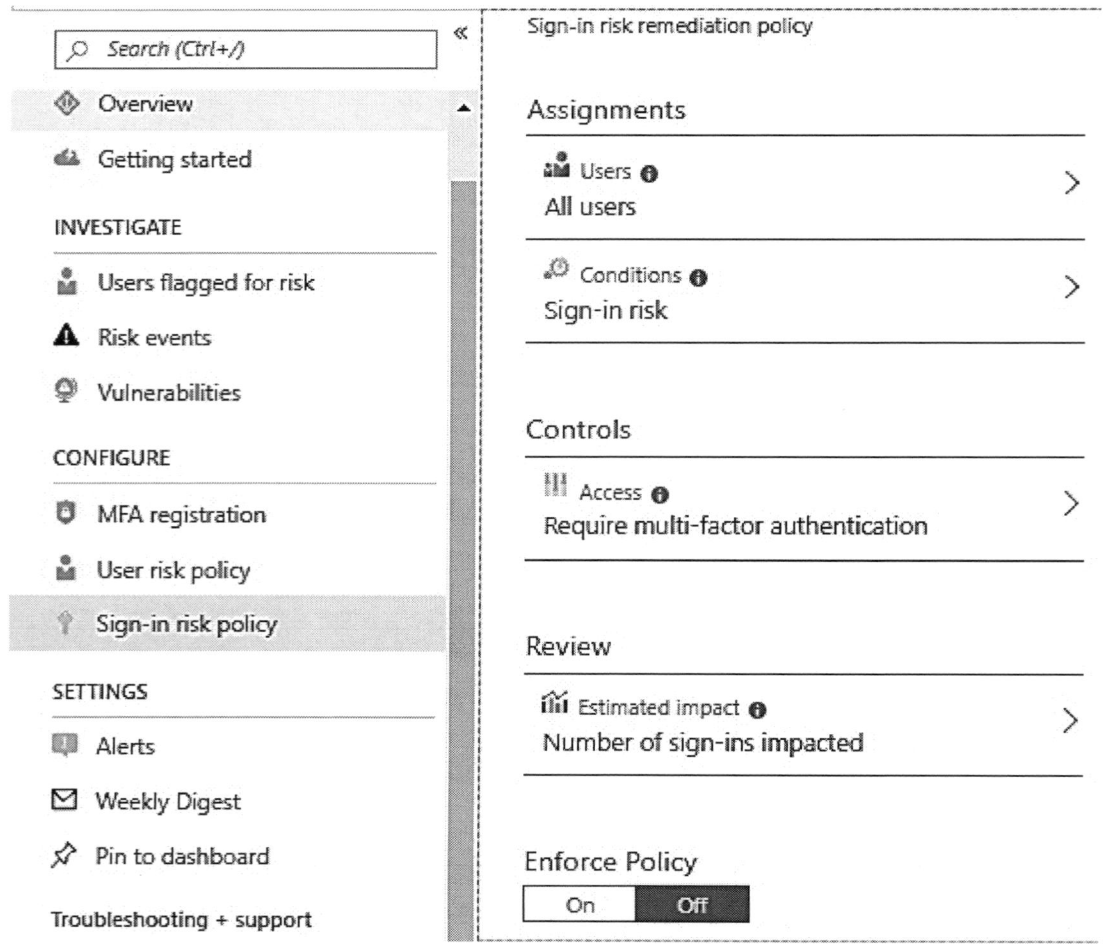

Figure below shows Condition options.

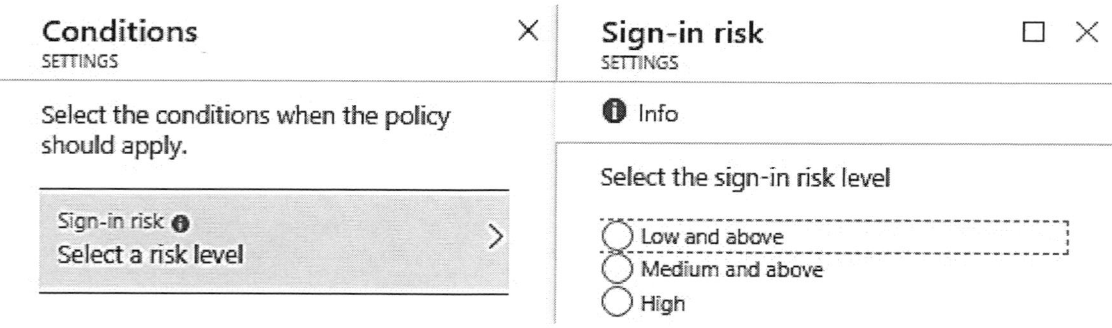

Note: Readers are advised to check Control option also.

Exercise 146: Implementing Sign-in Risk Conditional Access Policy

In this exercise we will create Sign-in Risk Conditional Access Policy which will block access if Identity Protection detects that a sign-in attempt was not performed by the legitimate owner of a user account. We will use TOR Browser for this exercise.

1. Go to Identity Protection Dashboard>Click Sign-in risk policy in left pane>Sign-in risk policy blade opens>Select **User3**>In Condition Select Medium and above> In Control Select Block Access>Click On for Enforce Policy>Click Save

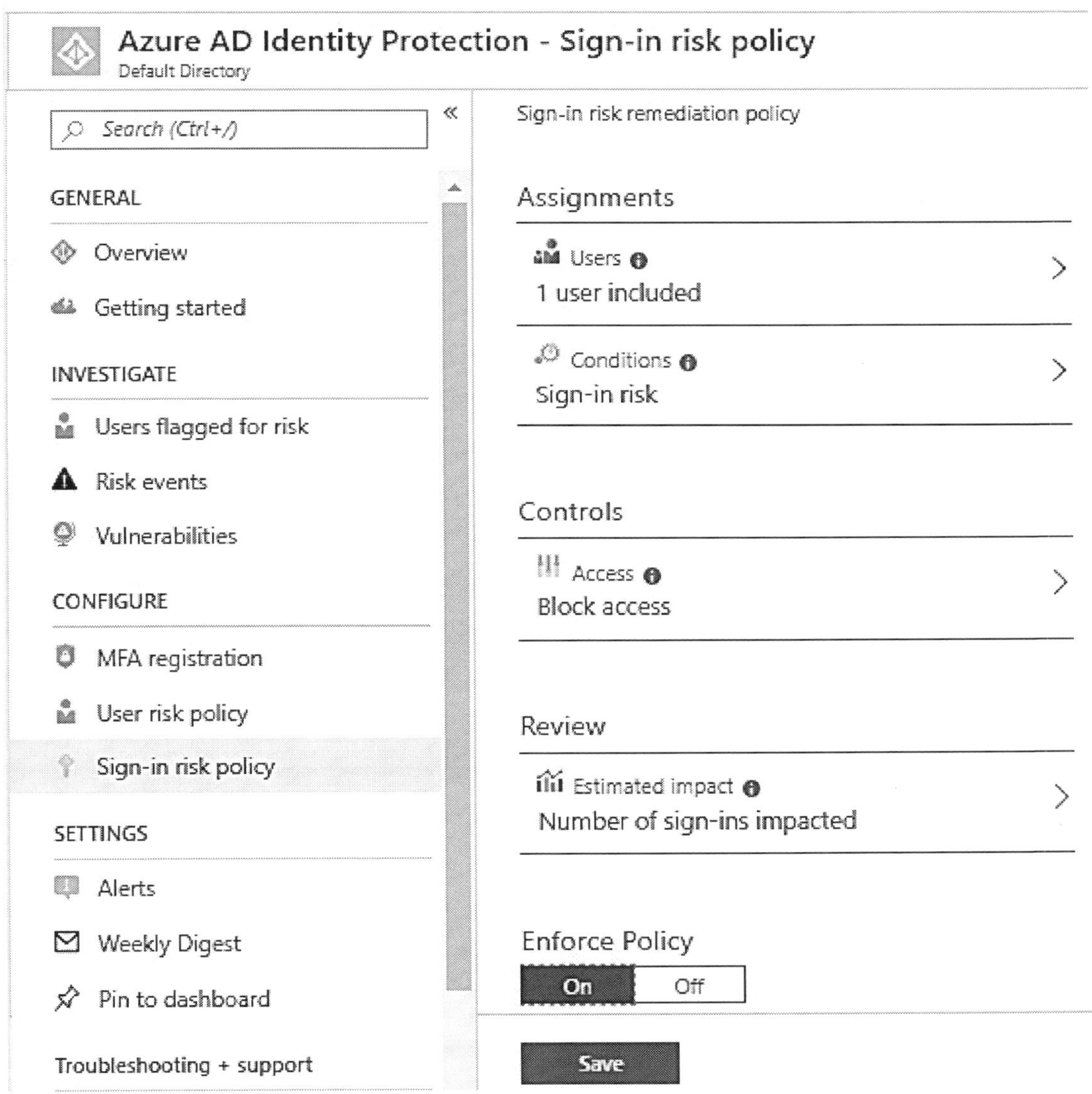

2. Open **Tor Browser** and log on to portal.azure.com with User3 credentials. Your sign-in attempt is blocked by Sign-in risk conditional access policy.

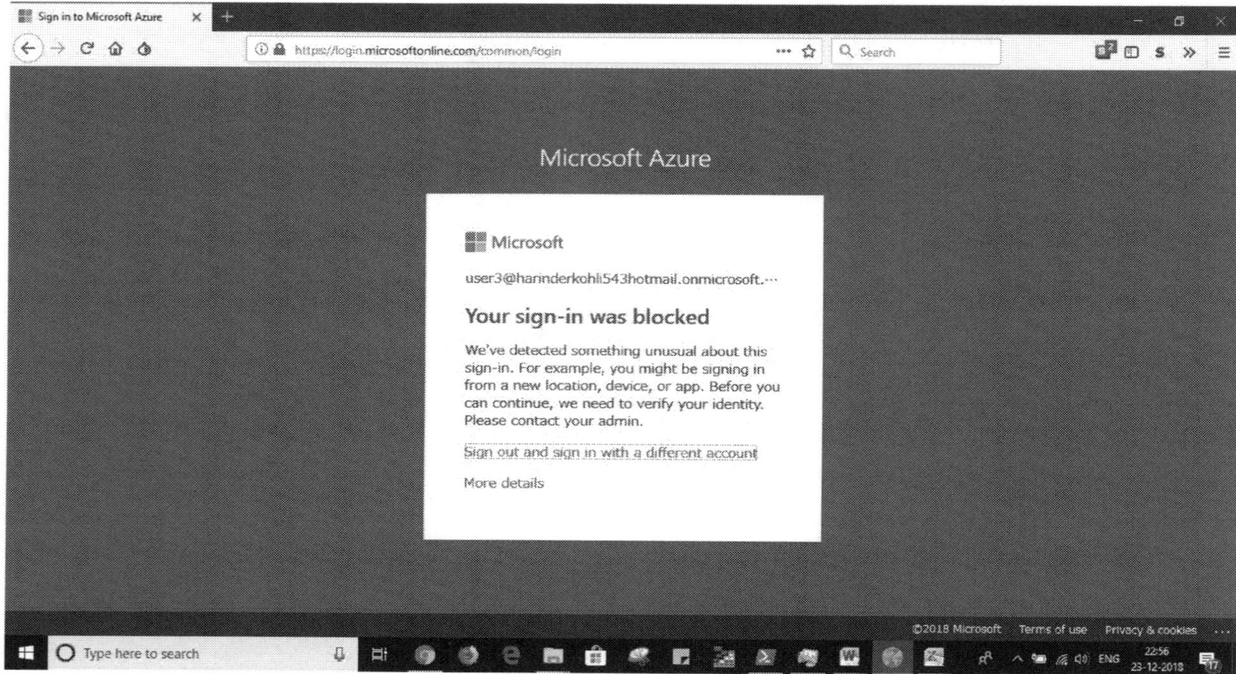

Azure AD Access Reviews

With Azure Active Directory (Azure AD) access reviews you can review user's access to enterprise applications, role assignments and group memberships on a regular basis to make sure only the right people have continued access.

Azure Active Access Reviews is a feature of the Azure AD Premium P2 edition.

Azure AD Access Reviews Use Cases

- As new employees join, how do you ensure they have the right access to be productive?
- As people move teams or leave the company, how do you ensure their old access is removed, especially when it involves guests?
- Excessive access rights can lead to audit findings and compromises as they indicate a lack of control over access.
- You have to proactively engage with resource owners to ensure they regularly review who has access to their resources.

Example of Azure AD Access Reviews

You plan to enable the application Salesforce for everyone in the Sales team group. It would be useful to ask the group owner to review the group membership prior to the group being used in a different risk content.

Where do you create Access Reviews

Access rights of users	Review created in	Reviewer experience
Security group members Office group members	Azure AD access reviews Azure AD groups	Access panel
Assigned to a connected app	Azure AD access reviews Azure AD enterprise apps (in preview)	Access panel
Azure AD role	Azure AD PIM	Azure portal
Azure resource role	Azure AD PIM	Azure portal

When to use access reviews

- **Too many users in privileged roles:** It's a good idea to check how many users have administrative access, how many of them are Global Administrators, and if there are any invited guests or partners that have not been removed after being assigned to do an administrative task. You can recertify the role assignment users in Azure AD roles such as Global Administrators, or Azure resources roles such as User Access Administrator in the Azure AD Privileged Identity Management (PIM) experience.

- **When automation is infeasible:** You can create rules for dynamic membership on security groups or Office 365 groups, but what if the HR data is not in Azure AD or if users still need access after leaving the group to train their replacement? You can then create a review on that group to ensure those who still need access should have continued access.

- **When a group is used for a new purpose:** If you have a group that is going to be synced to Azure AD, or if you plan to enable the application Salesforce for everyone in the Sales team group, it would be useful to ask the group owner to review the group membership prior to the group being used in a different risk content.

- **Business critical data access:** For certain resources, it might be required to ask people outside of IT to regularly sign out and give a justification on why they need access for auditing purposes.

- **To maintain a policy's exception list:** In an ideal world, all users would follow the access policies to secure access to your organization's resources. However, sometimes there are business cases that require you to make exceptions. As the IT admin, you can manage this task, avoid oversight of policy exceptions, and provide auditors with proof that these exceptions are reviewed regularly.

- **Ask group owners to confirm they still need guests in their groups:** Employee access might be automated with some on premises IAM, but not invited guests. If a group gives guests access to business sensitive content, then it's the group owner's responsibility to confirm the guests still have a legitimate business need for access.

- **Have reviews recur periodically:** You can set up recurring access reviews of users at set frequencies such as weekly, monthly, quarterly or annually, and the reviewers will be notified at the start of each review. Reviewers can approve or deny access with a friendly interface and with the help of smart recommendations.

Exercise 147: Create Access Review for Azure AD Group

In this exercise we will create Access Review for AZ-103 Group. AZ-103 group was created in Exercise 106, Chapter 12.

1. Go to Azure AD dashboard and click Identity Governance in left pane> Identity Governance pane opens.

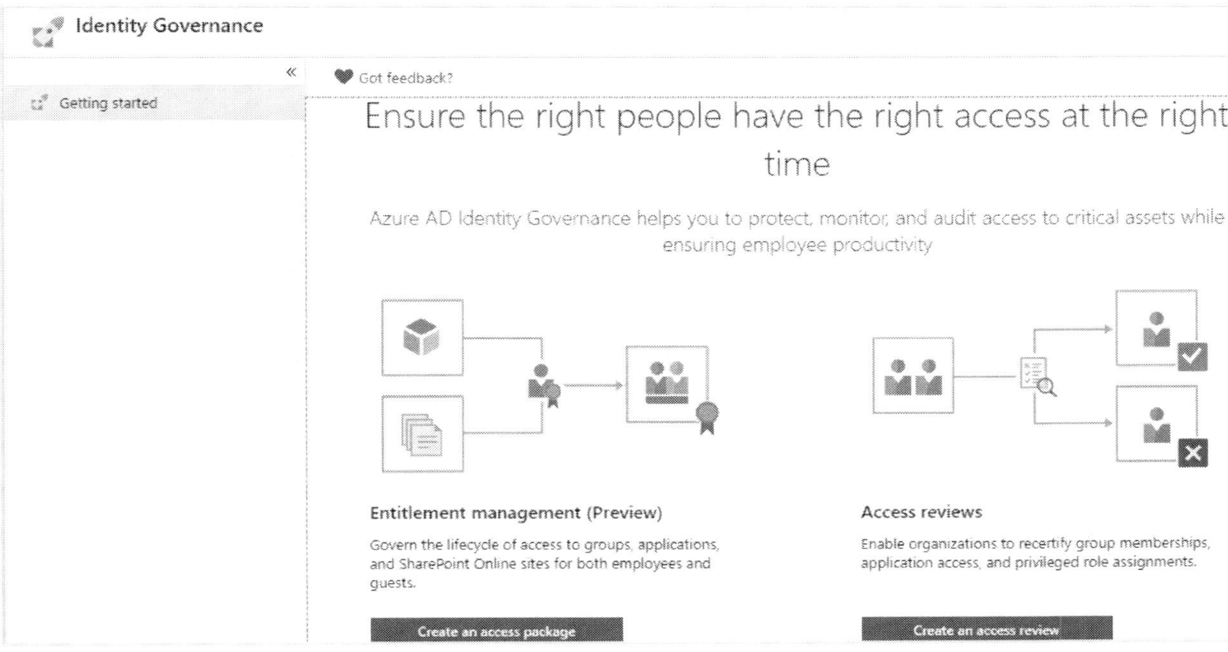

2. In Identity Governance pane Click create an access review>Create an Access review pane opens>Enter Review name, Select AZ-103 Group and select users and click start.

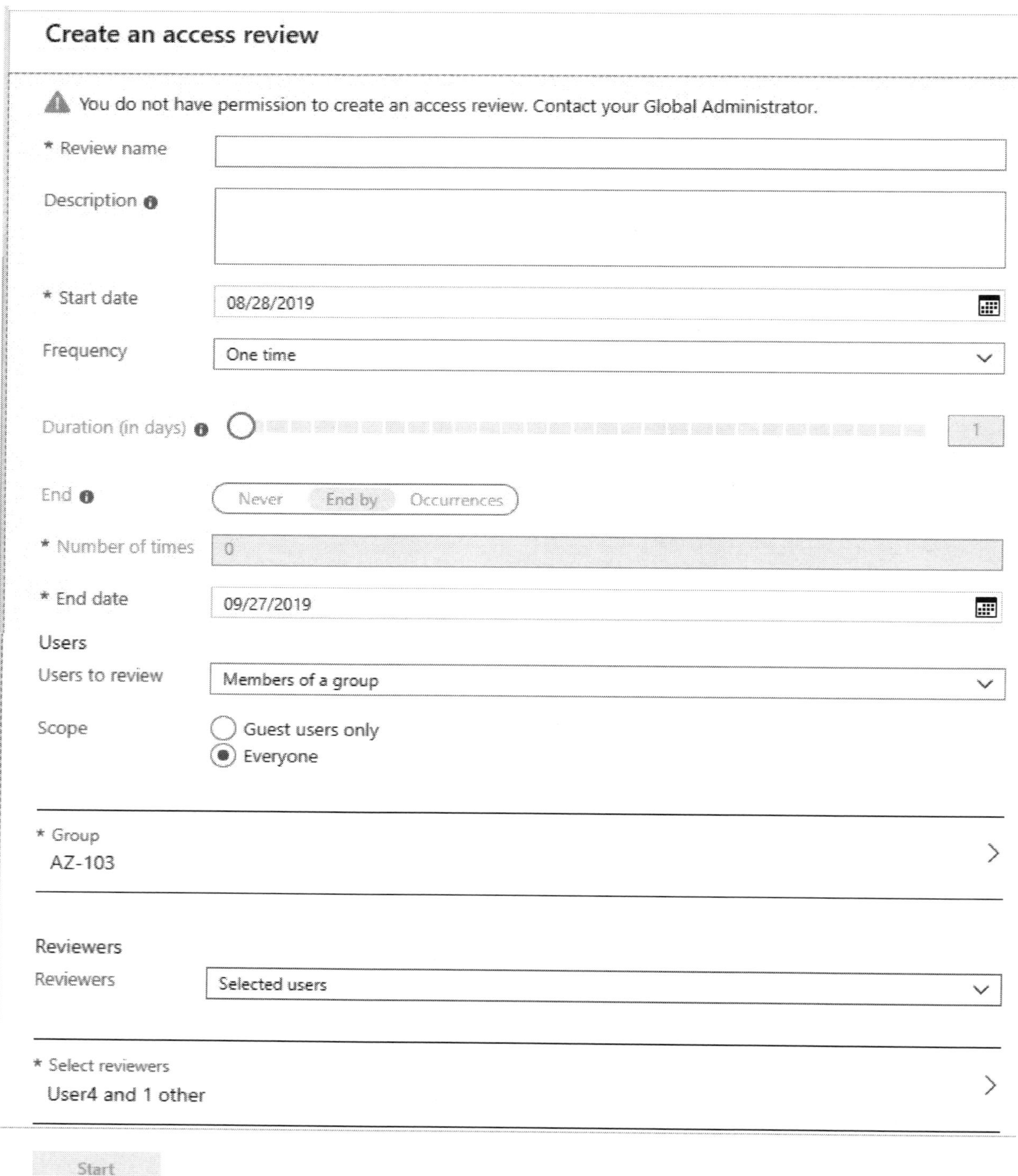

Azure AD Privileged Identity Management

Before going into Privileged Identity Management let's discuss why we need it in first place. Organizations want to minimize the number of people who have access to secure information or resources, because that reduces the chance of a malicious user getting that access, or an authorized user inadvertently impacting a sensitive resource.

Azure AD Privileged Identity Management helps you manage and protect **privileged/Administrative accounts** so that you can restrict and monitor administrators and their access to resources and provide just-in-time access when needed. Just-in-time access is only applicable for eligible admin.

Azure Active Directory Privileged Identity Management is a feature of the Azure AD Premium P2 edition. Azure AD comes in four editions – Free, Basic, Premium P1 and Premium P2.

What you can do with Privileged Identity Management

1. See which users are Azure AD administrators.
2. Enable on-demand, "**just in time**" administrative access using the concept of an **eligible admin**.
3. Get reports about administrator access history and changes in administrator assignments.
4. Get alerts about access to a privileged role.

Just in time administrator access with Eligible Admin

Azure AD Privileged Identity Management introduces the concept of an **eligible admin. Eligible admin is given just in time administrative access** for a predetermined amount of time.

Eligible admin role is inactive until the user needs access. When they need access they need to complete an activation process and become an active admin for a predetermined amount of time.

Roles managed in PIM

With Privileged Identity Management you can assign following administrator roles to users:

Global administrator has access to all administrative features. You can have more than one global admin in your organization.
Privileged role administrator manages Azure AD PIM and updates role assignments for other users.
Billing administrator makes purchases, manages subscriptions, manages support tickets, and monitors service health.
Password administrator resets passwords, manages service requests, and monitors service health. Password admins are limited to resetting passwords for users.
Service administrator manages service requests and monitors service health.
User management administrator resets passwords, monitors service health, and manages user accounts, user groups, and service requests. The user management admin can't delete a global admin, create other admin roles, or reset passwords for billing, global, and service admins.
Exchange administrator has administrative access to Exchange Online through the Exchange admin center (EAC), and can perform almost any task in Exchange Online.
SharePoint administrator has administrative access to SharePoint Online through the SharePoint Online admin center, and can perform almost any task in SharePoint Online.
Skype for Business administrator has administrative access to Skype for Business through the Skype for Business admin center, and can perform almost any task in Skype for Business Online.

Requirements to Enable Privileged Identity Management

1. To enable PIM you must be a Global Administrator with an organizational account with a verified domain name and not a Microsoft account (for example, @outlook.com), to enable PIM for a directory.

2. You must have one of the following licenses: Azure AD Premium P2 or Enterprise Mobility + Security (EMS) E5

If you're the first person to use PIM in your directory, you are automatically assigned the **Security Administrator** and **Privileged Role Administrator** roles in the directory. Only privileged role administrators can manage Azure AD directory role assignments of users. (Rewrite this)

Azure AD Application Proxy

Azure Active Directory (AD) Application Proxy publishes on-premises applications to be accessed over the internet by the remote users.

Application Proxy provides Remote Access as a Services (RASaaS).

Remote users access on-premises application through internet via Application Proxy service running in Azure cloud. Application Proxy service obviates the need to setup VPN on-premises.

Figure below shows internet users accessing on-premises application through Application Proxy service.

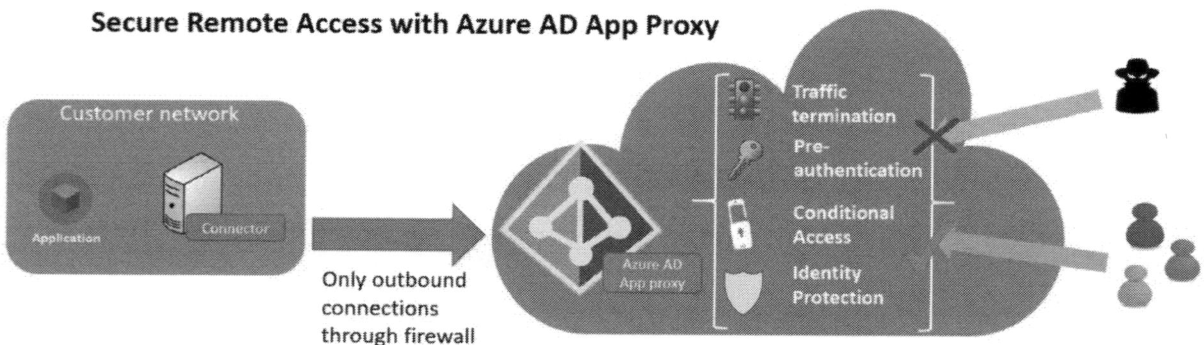

Advantages of Application Proxy

The biggest advantage of application proxy is that you don't need to configure any VPN on-premises for remote users to access the applications. Installing & Configuring VPN is a complex job and requires professional services from the system integrator.

Secondly user authentication is integrated very easily.

Thirdly application proxy solution provides enhanced security as all external user connects to on-premises application through application proxy service.

You no longer need DMZ on premises to publish your application to internet.

Azure AD Application Proxy Components

Azure AD Application Proxy consists of two components.

1. Cloud based application proxy service.
2. The Azure AD Application Proxy connector which is installed on-premises on a windows server.

Application Proxy prerequisites

1. Azure AD with Basic or Premium Subscription.
2. On-premises windows server.

Application Proxy Security Features

Authenticated access: Only authenticated connections can access the on prem network.

Conditional access: With conditional access, it is possible to further define restrictions on what traffic is allowed to access your back-end applications. You can define restrictions based on location, strength of authentication, and user risk profile.

Traffic termination: All traffic is terminated in the cloud. Back-end servers are not exposed to direct HTTP traffic.

All access is outbound: You don't need to open inbound connections to the corporate network. Azure AD connectors maintain outbound connections to the Azure AD Application Proxy service, which means that there is no need to open firewall ports for incoming connections.

Case Study 18: Secure Remote Access to on-premises Application

A regional confectionary company in USA manufactures and sells its products like cookies, cakes & chocolates to consumers in the state of California. Products are sold to consumer's indirectly through retailers.

There sales people visit the retailer for order booking every week. The stock is then delivered directly to retailers by the company. To clear the stock they also offer promotional schemes to retailers.

They have custom developed core business application which shows the stock position, retailer payment due & promotions. The application is hosted in on-premise Data Center. On-premise Data Center has one Cisco firewall.

All IT Resources are accessed from within the internal network except for core business application and Mail which accessed by sales reps and top management both on desktop & mobile (Android & Apple) from internet. To provide access to Business application from internet, SSL VPN has been setup on Cisco ASA Firewall. Total 15 users access the Business application from outside the corporate network.

Recently they had a security breach where in excel worksheet containing details of retailers and inventory was downloaded.

They don't have big IT budget. They have one system admin who manages everything. There VAR is small time IT Company which lacks skills to implement security solutions.

They recently got a quote from a big IT VAR for implementing security solutions. It consists of new firewall, IPS and identity management and cost was around 40000 USD. This was beyond their budget.

They are looking for a solution to protect their applications from security breaches. They want a simple and cost effective solution. They also don't want skilled resources and administrative overheads of managing the security solution.

Suggest a solution which satisfies above requirement with cost breakup.

Solution

We will use Azure Active Directory (AD) Application Proxy for protecting on-premises Business application.

With Azure Active Directory (AD) Application Proxy all access to Business application will happen through Application Proxy service running in Azure cloud. Application Proxy service obviates the need to setup VPN on-premises.

Figure below shows internet users accessing on-premises application through Application Proxy service.

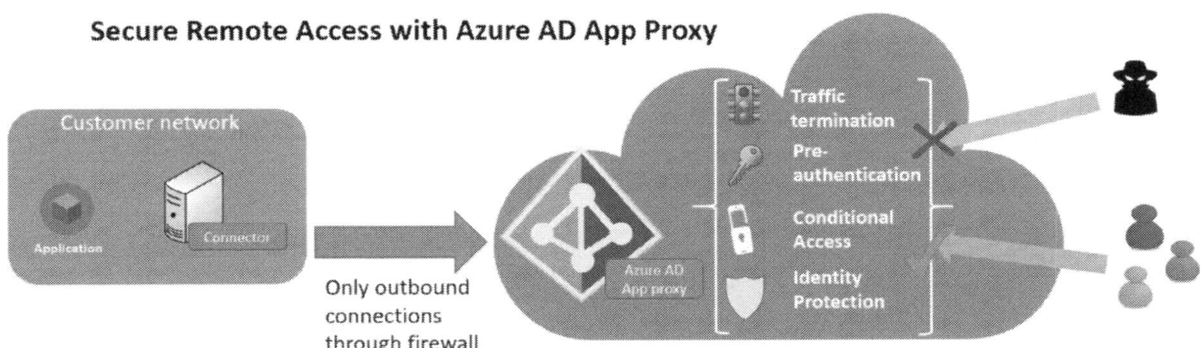

Application Proxy Security Features

Traffic termination: All traffic is terminated in the cloud. Back-end servers are not exposed to direct HTTP traffic.

All access is outbound: You don't need to open inbound connections to the corporate network. Azure AD connectors maintain outbound connections to the Azure AD Application Proxy service, which means that there is no need to open firewall ports for incoming connections.

Authenticated access: Only authenticated connections can access the on premises network. We will configure only 15 users who can access Business application from outside the corporate network.

Conditional access: With conditional access, it is possible to further define restrictions on what traffic is allowed to access your back-end applications. You can define restrictions based on location, strength of authentication, and user risk profile.

Chapter 16 Azure Active Directory B2C and B2B

Note: AZ-300 Exam syllabus does not mention's Azure AD B2C & B2B. **Use this Chapter for AZ-301 Exam Preparation only.**

This Chapter covers following Topic Lessons

- Azure Active Directory B2C
- Azure Active Directory B2C Pricing
- Azure Active Directory B2B
- Azure Active Directory B2B License Pricing
- Comparing B2C and B2B

This Chapter Covers following Lab Exercises

- Create Azure AD B2C Tenant and Link it to Azure Subscription
- Adding support for Social Account in your App (Facebook)
- Admin Adding B2B Users

This Chapter Covers following Case Studies

- Identity Management
- Licensing Case Study 1
- Licensing Case Study 2

Chapter Topology

In this Chapter we will add Azure AD B2C Tenant to the topology. We also create a Guest user in default Azure AD.

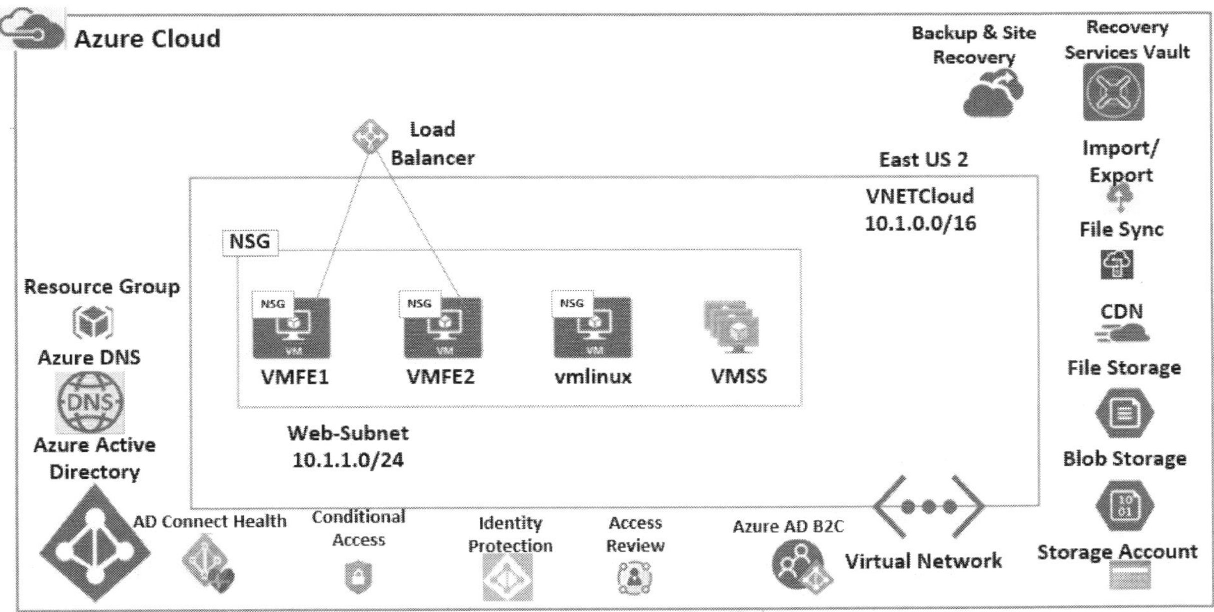

Azure Active Directory B2C

Azure Active Directory B2C is a cloud based identity and access management solution for consumer-facing web and mobile applications.

It can be easily integrated with mobile and web applications. Your customers can log on to your applications by using their existing social accounts or by creating new credentials (email & Password).

With Azure Active Directory B2C, consumers can sign up for applications by using following methods:

1. Using their Social Accounts such as Facebook, Microsoft, Google, Amazon, Linkedin etc.
2. Local Accounts by creating new credentials which can be combination of email and password or username and password.
3. Enterprise Accounts.

Working

Consumer/User authentication by application is redirected to Social accounts or Enterprise Accounts using industry standard sign-in protocols such as Oauth, WS-Federation or SAML.

Consumer facing Applications are called as Service Provider or Relying party and Social Accounts or Enterprise Accounts are called as Identity Providers.

Features and Advantages of Azure AD B2C

1. Azure Active Directory B2C is capable of supporting millions of users and billions of authentications per day.
2. Protects Consumer identities.
3. Advantage of Azure AD B2C is that it allows users to gain access to web applications and services while allowing the features of authentication and authorization to be factored out of the application code.
4. Advantage for application owner is that they don't have to create and manage infrastructure (Hardware & Software) for managing large database of B2C users.
5. Advantage for consumers is that they don't have to go through lengthy process of sign up.

Protocols and tokens

Azure AD B2C supports the OpenID Connect and OAuth 2.0 protocols for user Sign up and sign in. In the Azure AD B2C implementation of OpenID Connect, your application starts the user sign-in by issuing authentication requests to Azure AD B2C.

The result of a request to Azure AD B2C is a security token, such as an ID token or access token. This security token defines the user's identity. Tokens are received from Azure AD B2C endpoints, such as a /token or /authorize endpoint. From these tokens, you can access claims that can be used to validate an identity and allow access to secure resources.

Note: OpenID Connect and OAuth 2.0 protocols will be discussed in Part 2.

Identity Providers

An identity provider creates, maintains, and manages identity information while providing authentication services to applications also known as Service Provider.

Some of the Identity Providers supported by Azure AD B2C are as follows:

Facebook
Hotmail
Amazon
Google
Linkedin
Local Accounts

Exercise 148: Create Azure AD B2C Tenant and Link it to Azure Subscription

1. In Azure portal Click create a resource>In search box type Azure Active Directory B2C and in result select Azure Active Directory B2C and then click create> Create new B2C Tenant or Link to existing Tenant blade opens.

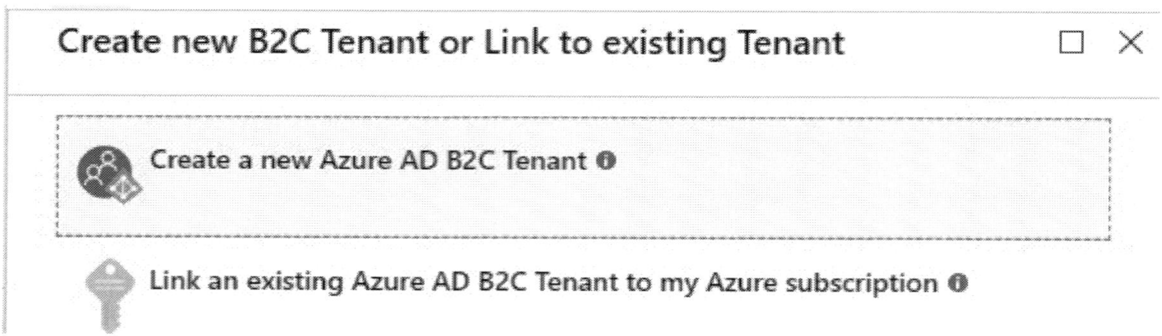

2. Select Create a new Azure AD B2C Tenant> Azure AD B2C Create Tenant blade opens> Enter organization name>Enter initial domain name>Select Country of orgin and click create (Not Shown). It will 1-2 minutes for creation.

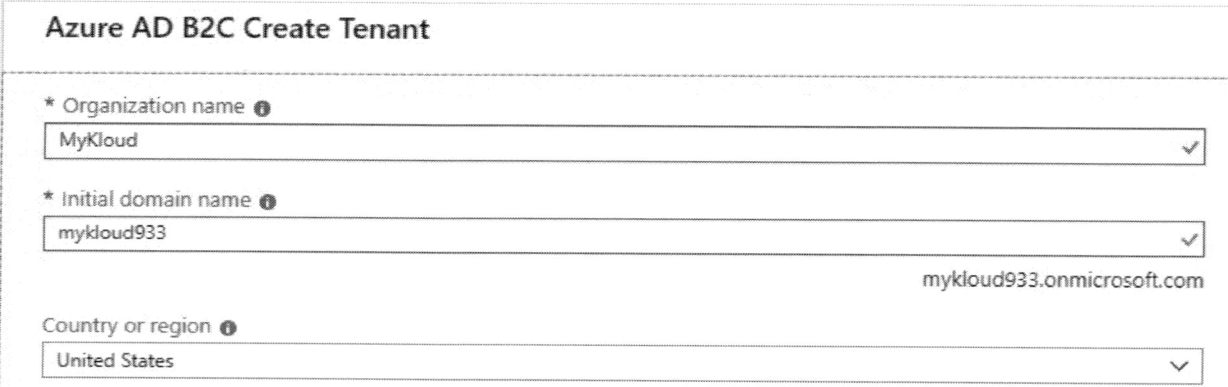

3. After you get the notification that Tenant is created, close Create Tenant Blade> In the Create new B2C Tenant or Link to existing Tenant Blade which is still open Select Link existing Azure AD B2C Tenant to Azure Subscription> Azure AD B2C Resource Blade opens>select AD B2C Tenant from Drop down box and Select Subscription> In Resource Group Select RGCloud> Click create.

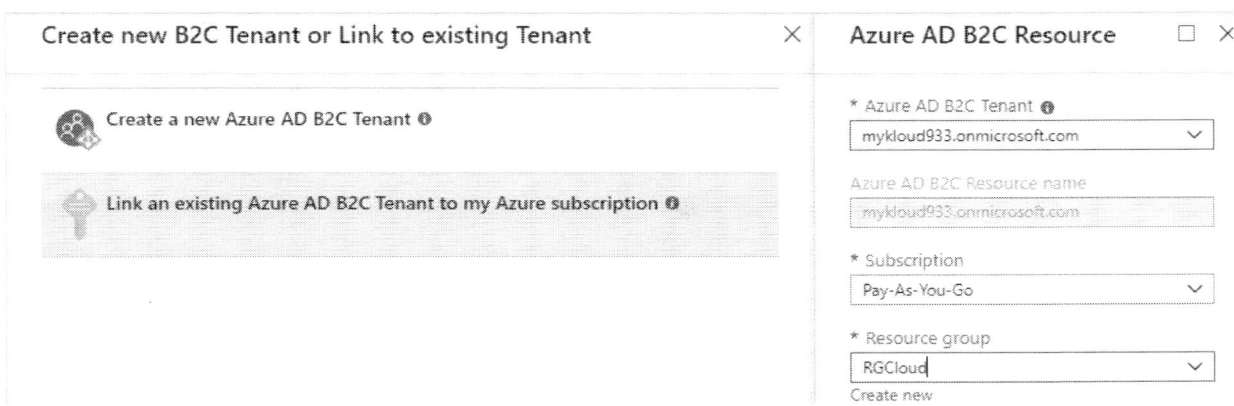

Note: mykloud933.onmicrosoft.com is B2C Tenant Domain name.

4. Figure Below shows the dashboard of Azure AD B2C Tenant.

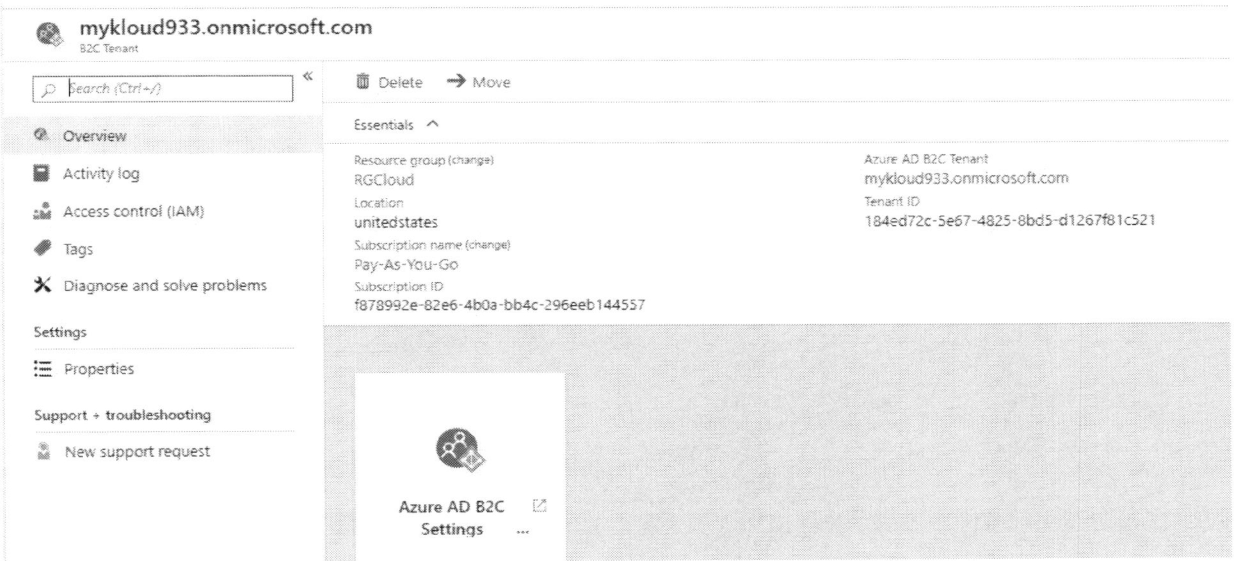

5. In Azure AD Tenant Dashboard click Azure AD B2C Settings in Right pane>A new browser window opens as shown below.

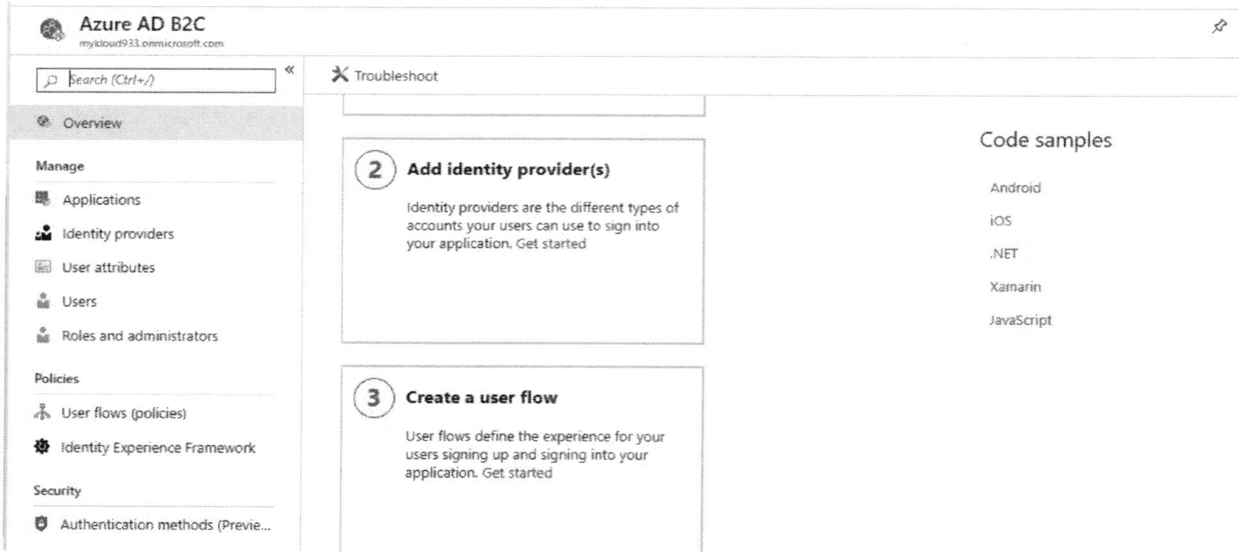

Using **Applications** option you can register your application with Azure AD B2C Tenant to provide support for Local Account. With Local Accounts Users can sign up with application using combination of email and password.

Using **Identity Providers** you can add support for Social accounts such as Facebook and Hotmail etc.

With **User Flows** You can customize consumer sign-up or sign-in when they access application.

With User Attributes you can specify **Sign-up attributes** which you want to collect from the consumer during sign-up.

Design Nugget: If you also want your application to be accessed by Azure AD users than register your application with Azure AD tenant.

Exercise 149: Adding support for Social Account (Facebook) in your App

This is a demonstration Exercise. In this Exercise we will show how to add support for Facebook in your application. For this Exercise we will use B2C tenant created in previous Exercise.

1. **Register your application with facebook** @ https://developers.facebook.com/ and generate Client id and Client Secret. Here you have to also specify the Valid OAuth redirect URIs in the form of https://login.microsoftonline.com/te/{tenant}/oauth2/authresp. Replace Tenant with B2C Tenant Domain name

2. **Configure Facebook as an identity provider.** In B2C Tenant Dashboard> Click identity providers>Identity Provider pane opens>Select Facebook. Configure social IDP pane opens> Enter a name> enter the Client ID and Client secret (of the Facebook application that you created earlier in step 1) in the Client ID and Client secret fields respectively>click save.

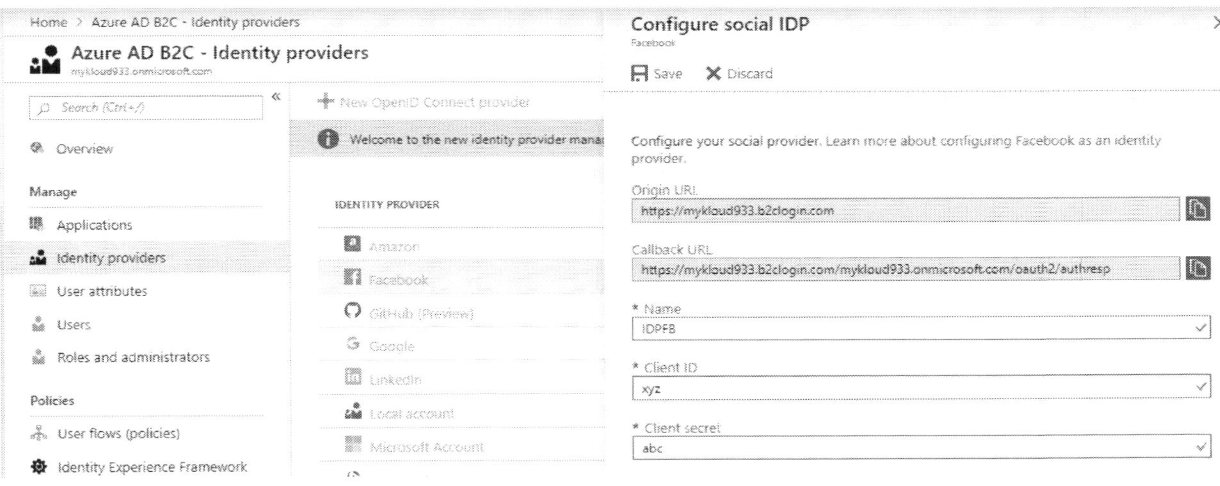

3. **Create or use existing sign-in or sign up policies.** This policy handles both consumer sign-up & sign-in with a single configuration. Here you can add depending upon your requirement single or Multiple identity Providers. In B2C Tenant Management dashboard Click User flows (policies)> Click + New user flow> Create a User flow pane opens> Click Sign up and sign in>Create Sign up and sign in opens> Enter a name>Select Facebook IDP configured in previous step>Select User Attributes and Claims as per your requirement. User attributes are values collected on sign up. Claims are values about the user returned to the application in the token>Click create.

Create
Sign up and sign in

1. Name *
The unique string used to identify this user flow in requests to Azure AD B2C. This cannot be changed after a user flow has been created.

* B2C_1_ susi

2. Identity providers *
Identity providers are the different types of accounts your users can use to log into your application. You need to select at least one for a valid user flow and you can add more in the Identity providers section for your directory. Learn more about identity providers.

Please select at least one identity provider

- [x] IDPFB
- [ ] Email signup

3. Multifactor authentication
Enabling multifactor authentication (MFA) requires your users to verify their identity with a second factor before allowing them into your application. Learn more about multifactor authentication.

Multifactor authentication Enabled Disabled

4. User attributes and claims
User attributes are values collected on sign up. Claims are values about the user returned to the application in the token. You can create custom attributes for use in your directory. Learn more about user attributes and claims.

	Collect attribute	Return claim
Given Name	☐	☐
Surname	☐	☐
City	☐	☐
Country/Region	☐	☐
Email Address	☐	☐

Show more...

Create

4. Configure your application for facebook sign-up and add information about B2C tenant name, Application id & Client secret, sign-up or sign-in policy name & Reset Password Policy name.

Azure Active Directory B2C Pricing

Azure Active Directory (Azure AD) B2C usage will be billed monthly based on the number of authentications.

Authentications: Tokens issued either in response to a sign-in request initiated by a user or initiated by an application on behalf of a user (e.g. token refresh, where the refresh interval is configurable).

AUTHENTICATIONS/MONTH	Price
First 50,000	Free
Next 9,50,000	$0.0028
Next 90,00,000	$0.0021
Next 400,00,000	$0.0014
Greater than 500,00,000	$0.0007

Case Study 19: Identity Management

A major cricket franchise of Indian Premier League (IPL) wants to engage its fans and monetize its website. The website has details of IPL matches, interview with cricket players, video highlights of the matches, Analysis by cricket experts, off field entertainment gossips, Sale of Merchandise and advertisement by their sponsors.

Fans who register with website, get access to additional contents, can post comments and are eligible for Prices.

They want fans to register with their social accounts – Facebook, Linkedin or Twitter or by registering with their email-id and password. They expect 250000 fans to register.

There requirement is that they do not want to maintain user accounts details. Another requirement is that user registration with the website should be very simple.

Suggest a solution which satisfies the above requirement.

Solution

We will use Azure Active Directory B2C for user identity Management.

With Azure Active Directory B2C, fans can sign up with website by using their existing_social accounts (Facebook, Google or Linkedin etc) or by creating new credentials (email address and password, or username and password).

One of the advantage of B2C is that you need not maintain user account and password details and associated infrastructure (Like hardware, Databases and Directory services).

Advantage for consumers is that they don't have to go through lengthy process of sign up.

Sign-in Protocol: IPL Website will redirect user authentication to Facebook, Google or Linkedin using Sign-in protocols such as oauth2 or SAML or WS-Federation.

Azure Active Directory B2B

Azure Active Directory (Azure AD) B2B collaboration enables enterprises to grant access to corporate resources and applications for partner employees by using partner-managed identities.

B2B collaboration enables partners manage their own accounts and enterprises can apply security policies to partner access.

There's no need to add external users to your directory, sync them, or manage their lifecycle; IT can invite collaborators to use any email address—Office 365, on-premises Microsoft Exchange, or even a personal address (Outlook.com, Gmail, Yahoo!, etc.)—and even set up conditional access policies, including multi-factor authentication.

Developers can use the Azure AD B2B APIs to write applications that bring together different organizations in a secure way—and deliver a seamless and intuitive end user experience.

Advantages of B2B

1. Your business partners use their own sign-in credentials, which frees you from managing an external partner directory, and from the need to remove access when users leave the partner organization.
2. You manage access to your apps independently of your business partner's account lifecycle. This means, for example, that you can revoke access without having to ask the IT department of your business partner to do anything.

Easy Azure AD B2B Setup

Easy for admin of inviting organization to send invite.
No sign-up required only sign-in for partner employee.

Secure

Azure AD security features such as MFA, conditional access, identity protection and other security feature can be extended to partner identities.

Azure AD B2B Capabilities

1. Azure AD admins can invite external users.
2. Non admins like application owner can invite external users from Access panel @ https://myapps.microsoft.com
3. Support for Security features like MFA, Conditional Access for external users.
4. External users onboarding can be customized using **B2B Invitation API.**
5. For each paid license of Azure AD (Basic or Premium) you can add 5 B2B Users.

B2B Users

An Azure Active Directory (Azure AD) business-to-business (B2B) collaboration user is a user with UserType = Guest. This guest user typically is from a partner organization and has limited privileges in the inviting directory, by default. Note: If required you can change the privileges of guest users.

In some cases UserType = members. In this case users are from Same Azure AD tenant. For example supply chain depart of a contoso company has a app which is accessed by specific workers in supply chain department and invited employees of there vendors. A contoso worker in finance department also need to access to the app. Application owner of the app can send the invite to the worker in finance department using the Azure AD B2B Invitation Manager APIs to add or invite a user from the partner organization to the host organization as a member.

B2B users sign-in options

B2B collaborators can sign in with an identity of their choice. If the user doesn't have a Microsoft account or an Azure AD account – one is created for them seamlessly at the time for offer redemption.

1. With Microsoft account like outlook/Hotmail.com
2. Gmail/yahoo mail account
3. Partner domain account (testuser@contoso.com)
4. Azure AD account (If partner has its own Azure AD tenant)

Exercise 150: Admin Adding B2B Users

1. Go to Azure AD Dashboard>Click Users> + New Guest User>Select Invite User>Enter Data as per your requirement> Enter a message>Rest select all default values>Click Invite.

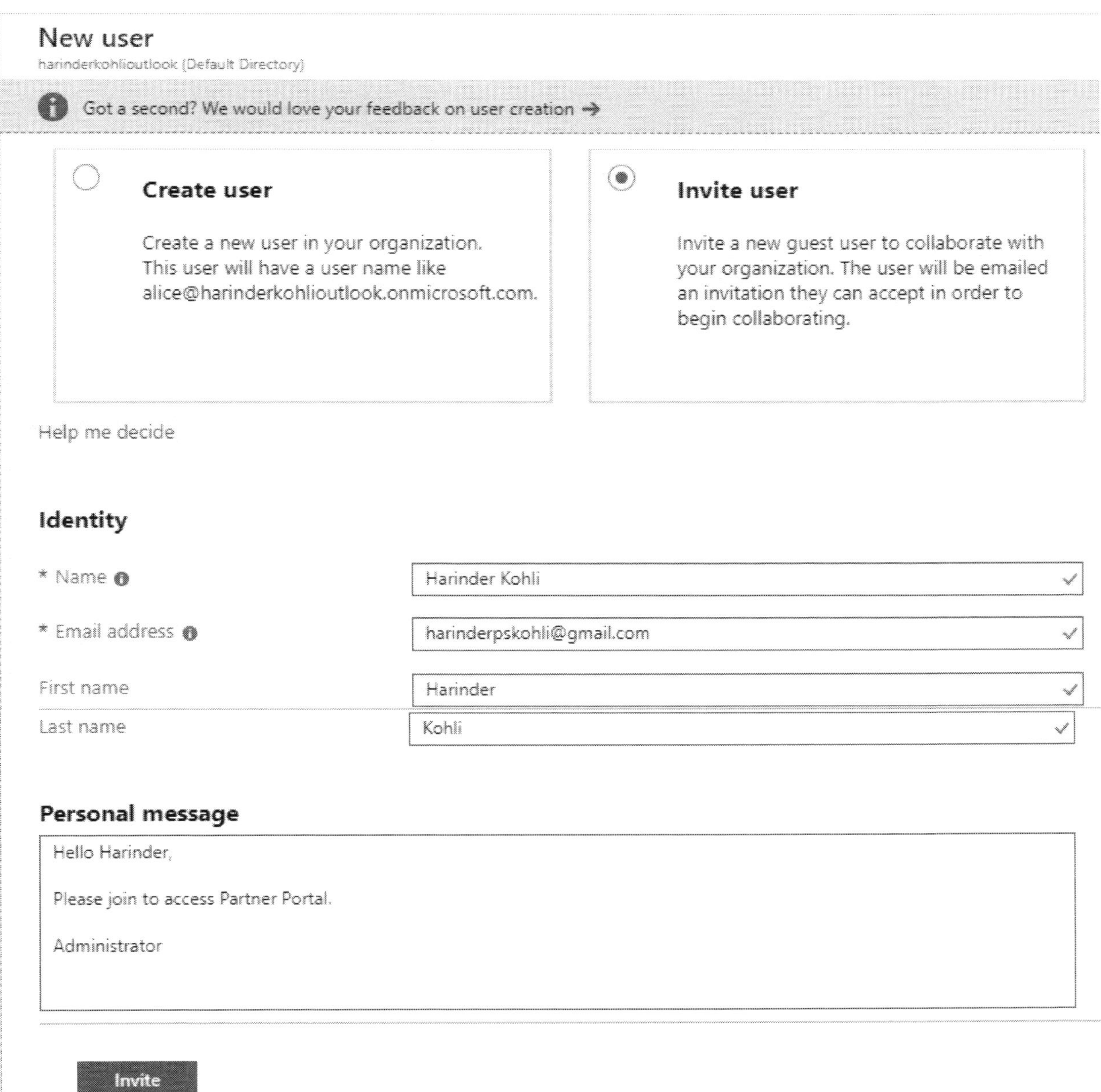

Figure below show harinderpskohli added as user type guest. Second Row from top.

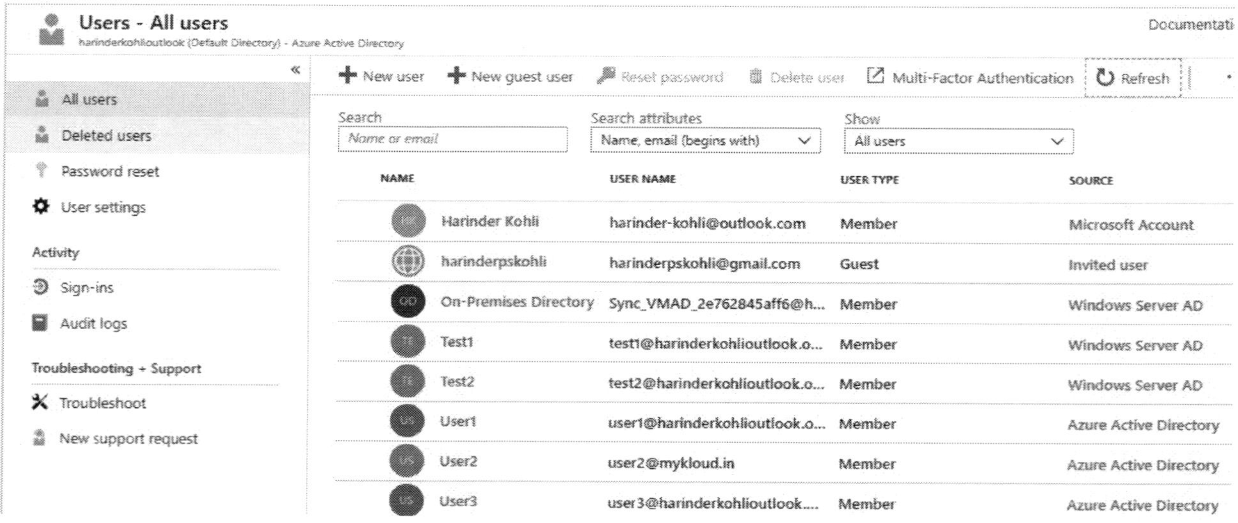

Adding B2B users directly at application level by application owner

Admins can delegate permission to add B2B users to non-admins. Non-admins can use the Azure AD Application Access Panel (https://myapps.microsoft.com) to add B2B collaboration users to applications. For this application must be enrolled for single sign-on in Azure AD Application Access Panel.

B2B License Pricing

For each paid license of Azure AD (Basic or Premium) you can add 5 B2B Users.

You can also add B2B users with Azure AD free edition without requiring any license. But in this case B2B users will be limited to features of Azure AD Free edition.

There is no need to assign licenses to B2B user accounts. Based on the 5:1 ratio, licensing is automatically calculated and reported.

If a B2B collaboration user already has a paid Azure AD license from their organization, they do not consume one of the B2B collaboration licenses of the inviting tenant.

Case Study 20: Licensing Case Study 1

A customer wants to invite 50 B2B collaboration users to its Azure AD tenant. B2B users require features of Azure AD Basic edition only. How many licenses customer should have for 50 B2B Collaboration users.

Solution: B2B licensing states that for each paid license of Azure AD (Basic or Premium) you can add 5 B2B Users.
Based on 5:1 Ratio you will require 10 licenses of Azure AD Basic Edition.

Case Study 21: Licensing Case Study 2

A customer wants to invite 100 B2B collaboration users to its Azure AD tenant. 50 of the B2B users require features of Basic edition. 30 users require MFA feature. 20 Users require both MFA & identity protection feature. How many licenses customer should have for above 100 B2B Collaboration users.

Solution: MFA feature require Azure AD Premium P1 license. Identity Protection feature requires Azure AD Premium P2 License.
Using 5:1 ratio you will require 10 licenses of Azure AD Basic, 6 licenses of Azure AD Premium P1 and 4 licenses of Azure AD Premium P2.

Comparing B2C and B2B

Both Azure Active Directory (Azure AD) B2B collaboration and Azure AD B2C allow you to work with external users in Azure AD. Table below shows difference between B2B and B2C.

Azure AD B2B collaboration	Azure AD B2C
Intended for Organizations that want to authenticate users from a partner organization, regardless of identity provider.	**Intended for** customers of your mobile and web apps, whether individuals, institutional or organizational customers into your Azure AD.
Identities supported: Employees with work or school accounts, partners with work or school accounts, or any email address.	**Identities supported:** Consumer users with local application accounts (any email address or user name) or any supported social identity with direct federation.
Directory: users from the external organization are managed in the same directory as employees, but added as guest users.	**Directory:** Managed separately from the organization's employee Directory.
Single sign-on (SSO) to all Azure AD-connected apps is supported.	**Single sign-on (SSO)** to customer owned apps within the Azure AD B2C tenants is supported.
Partner lifecycle: Managed by the host/inviting organization.	**Customer lifecycle:** Self-serve or managed by the application.
Security policy and compliance: Managed by the host/inviting organization.	**Security policy and compliance:** Managed by the application.
Branding: Host/inviting organization's brand is used.	**Branding:** Managed by application.

Chapter 17 Directory Role and RBAC

This Chapter covers following Topic Lessons

- Assign Azure AD Directory Role to Users
- Assigning Administrative Permissions using Role Based Access Control

This Chapter covers following Lab Exercises

- Assign User3 Directory role of Limited Administrator
- Check User3 Access by creating a User
- Checking User3 Access level
- Assigning User3 Role of Reader in Resource Group
- Check User3 Access level in Azure Portal
- Adding Co-Administrator to the subscription
- Check User3 Access level in Azure Portal

This Chapter Covers following Case Studies

- Design Role Based Access Control (RBAC)

Chapter Topology

In this chapter we will Assign Azure AD Directory Role to Azure AD Users. We will also assign Administrative Permissions using Role Based Access Control (RBAC) to Azure AD Users.

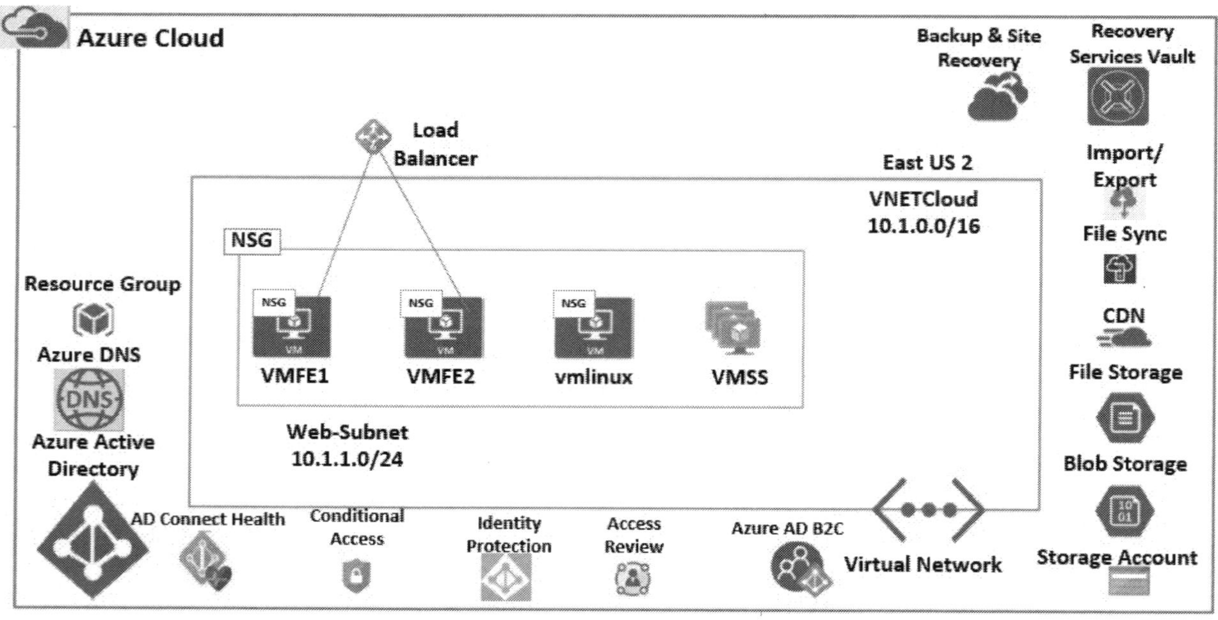

Assign Azure AD Directory Role to Users

User is assigned Directory role during user creation time. You also have the option to change user Directory role from Azure AD User Profile Dashboard.

A user can be assigned one of the following 3 directory roles:

Global Administrator: The Global administrators have full control over **all directory** resources.
Limited Administrator: Limited administrator role has full access to particular Directory feature. Following Limited Administrative roles are available in Azure.
User: User can login to Azure portal but cannot create, manage or view a resource. For a user to create, view or manage a resource in Azure Portal it needs to be assigned permissions Using Role based Access Control (RBAC).

Billing Administrator	**Exchange Service Administrator**	**Password Administrator / Helpdesk Administrator**
Compliance Administrator	**Global Administrator / Company Administrator**	**Power BI Service Administrator**
Conditional Access Administrator	**Guest Inviter**	**Privileged Role Administrator**
Dynamics 365 service administrator	**Information Protection Administrator**	**Security Administrator**
Device Administrators	**Intune Service Administrator**	**Service Support Administrator**
Directory Readers	**Mailbox Administrator**	**SharePoint Service Administrator**
Directory Synchronization Accounts	**Skype for Business / Lync Service Administrator**	
Directory Writers	**User Account Administrator**	

Exercise 151: Assign User3 Directory role of Limited Administrator

In this Exercise we will assign User3 Directory role of Limited Administrator with role of User Account Administrator. Users with this role can create and manage all aspects of users and Groups. User3 was created in Exercise 103, Chapter 12 with Directory role of User.

1. In Azure AD Dashboard>Click Users in left pane> All Users blade open>Click User3 in right pane>User3 Profile blade opens>Click Directory Role in left pane>Click +Add Assignment>Directory Roles Blade opens>Scroll down and select User administrator and click select.

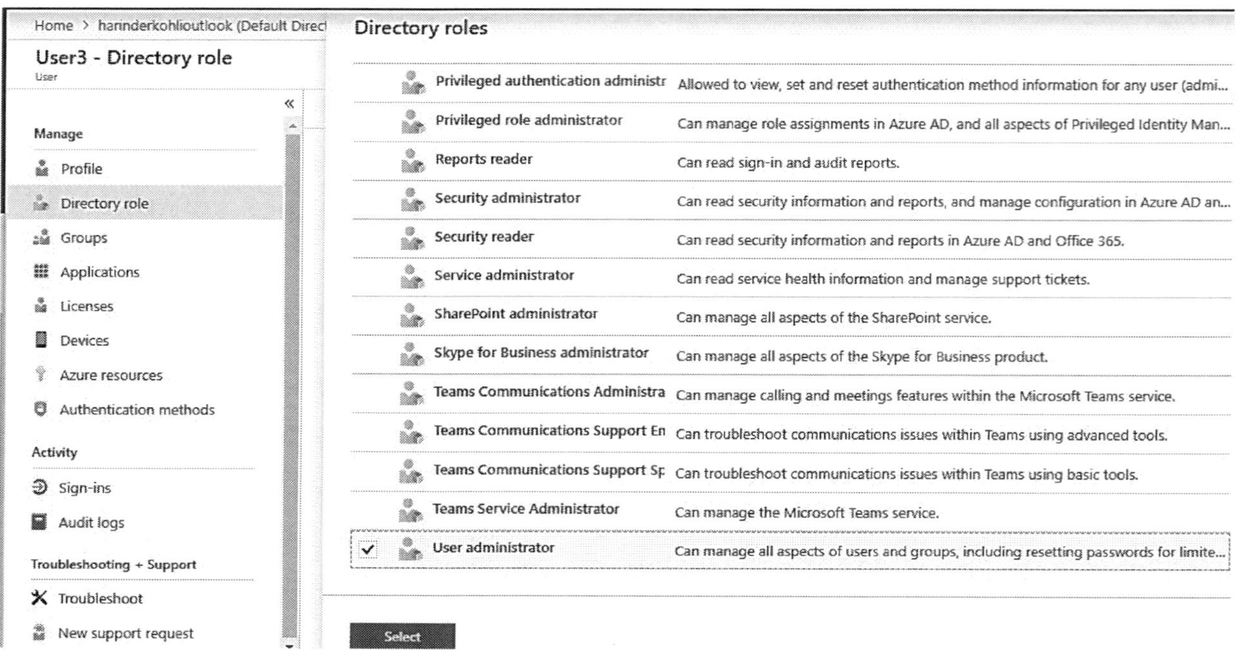

2. User3 is now assigned Directory role of User administrator.

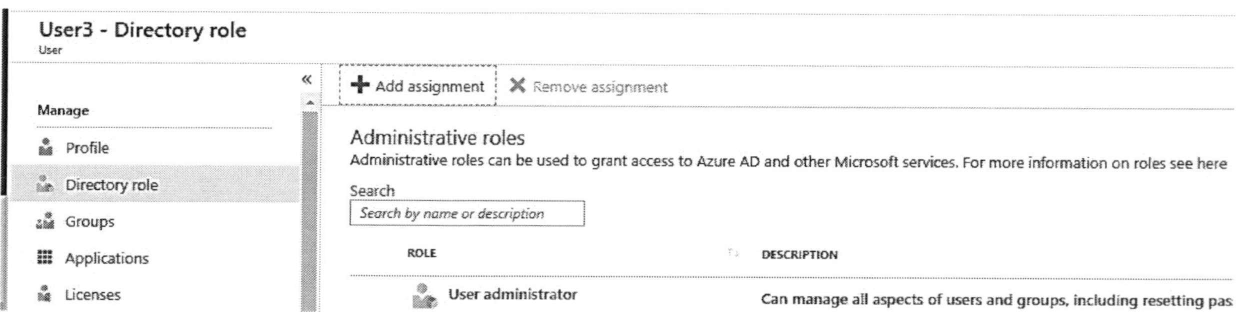

Exercise 152: Check User3 Access by creating a User

In this exercise we will log on to Azure Portal with User3 credentials and will try to create a User.

1. Open Firefox and Log on to Azure Portal @ https://portal.azure.com with User3 credentials- user3@harinderkohlioutlook.onmicrosoft.com
2. In Azure Portal click Azure Active Directory in left pane>In Azure AD Dashboard click Users in left pane>All Users blade opens>Click + New User>Create User blade opens> Enter User4 in name and user4@harinderkohlioutlook.onmicrosoft.com in user name and click create.

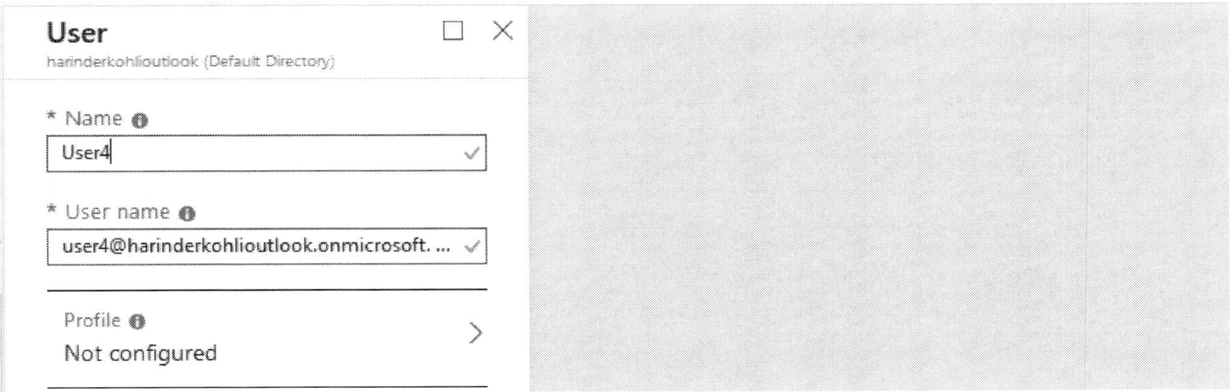

3. User4 was successfully created. Last row in below figure.

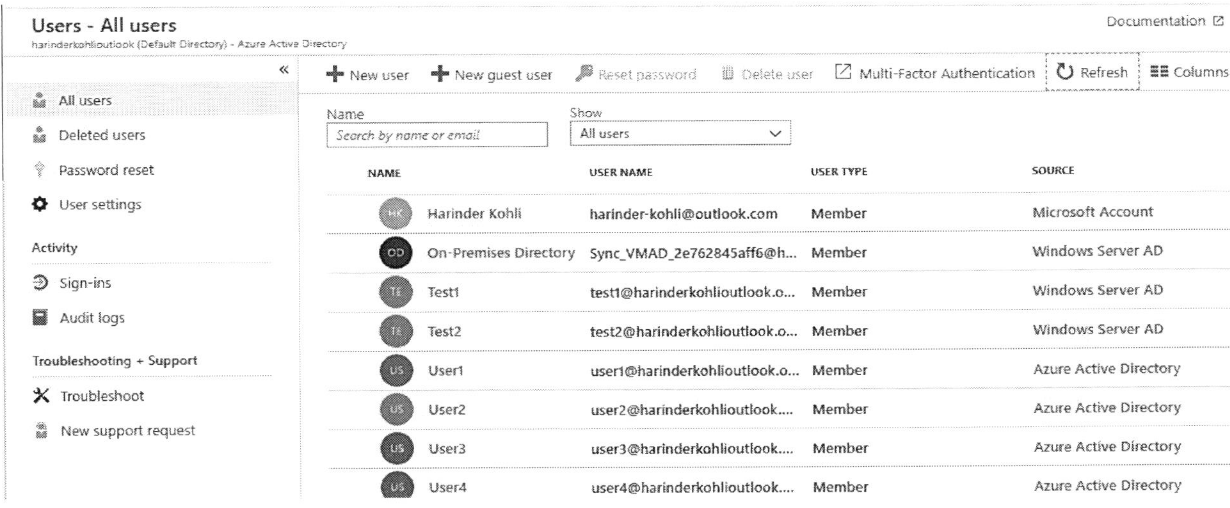

Assigning Administrative Permissions using Role Based Access Control

Before going into RBAC let's discuss why we need it in first place. Unlimited access to users in Azure can be security threat. Too few permissions means that users can't get their work done efficiently.

Azure Role-Based Access Control (RBAC) helps address above problem by offering fine-grained access management for Azure resources. With RBAC users are given amount of access based on their Job Roles. For example, use RBAC to let one employee manage virtual machines in a subscription, while another can manage SQL databases.

Role Based Access Management in Azure

You can assign roles to users, groups, and applications at a certain level. The level of a role assignment can be a subscription, a resource group, or a single resource.

Figure below shows RBAC can be assigned to User, Group & Application and can be applied at Subscription or Resource Group or single resource level.

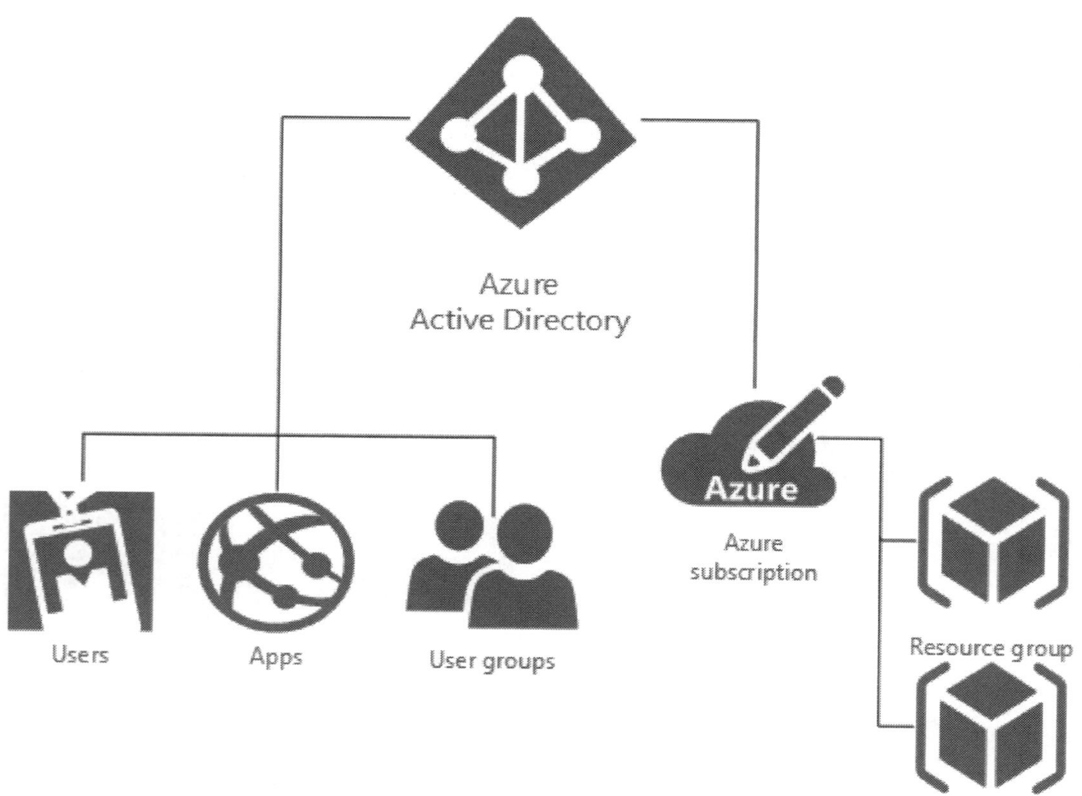

Azure RBAC Built-in roles (Important Concept)

Owner has full access to all resources including the right to delegate access to others.
Contributor can create and manage all types of Azure resources but can't grant access to others.
Reader can view existing Azure resources.

Azure RBAC Scope and Assignment

Scope: RBAC role assignments are scoped to a specific subscription, resource group, or resource.
A user given access to a single resource cannot access any other resources in the same subscription.
A role assigned at a parent scope also grants access to the children contained within it. For example, a user with access to a resource group can manage all the resources it contains, like websites, virtual machines, and Virtual Networks etc.

Role: Within the scope of the assignment, access is narrowed even further by assigning a role. Roles can be high-level, like owner, or specific, like virtual machine reader.

Following is a **partial list** of built-in roles available.

RBAC Built in Roles	Description
Backup Contributor	Can manage backup in Recovery Services vault.
Backup Operator	Can manage backup except removing backup, in Recovery Services vault.
Backup Reader	Can view all backup management services.
BizTalk Contributor	Can manage BizTalk services.
Azure Cosmos DB Account Contributor	Can manage Azure Cosmos DB accounts.
Network Contributor	Can manage all network resources.
SQL DB Contributor	Can manage SQL databases, but not their security-related policies.
User Access Administrator	Can manage user access to Azure resources.
Virtual Machine Contributor	Can create and manage virtual machines, but not the virtual network or storage.

How Administrative Permissions (RBAC) are assigned

Administrative permissions are assigned to Users using **Access Control (IAM) Tab** in Resource or Resource Group or Subscription Dashboard.

Exercise 153: Checking User3 Access level

In this exercise we will check User3 Access level in Azure Portal. User3 was created in Exercise 88, Chapter 9.

Open Firefox and Log on to Azure portal @ https://portal.azure.com with User3 Credentials (user3@harinderkohlioutlook.onmicrosoft.com) and password. You can see there are no resources to display for User3 and user has no access to resources and User cannot create any resources.

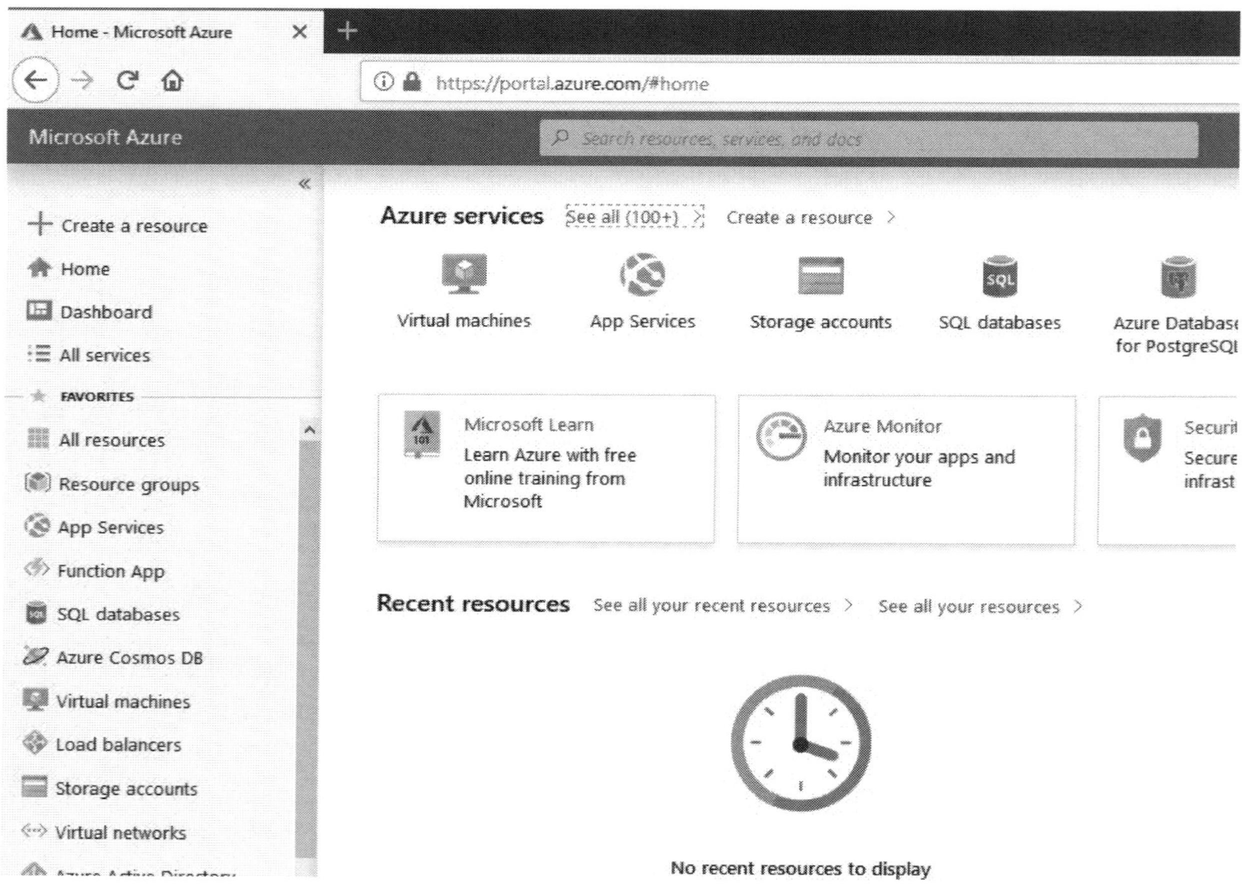

Exercise 154: Assigning User3 Role of Reader in Resource Group

In this Exercise we will assign User3, Role of Reader in Resource Group RGCloud. User3 was created in Exercise 88, Chapter 9.

1. Go to Resource Group RGCloud Dashboard>Click Access control (IAM) in left pane>In Right pane Click +Add role assignment>In Add role assignment blade select reader from down box and select User3> Click save.

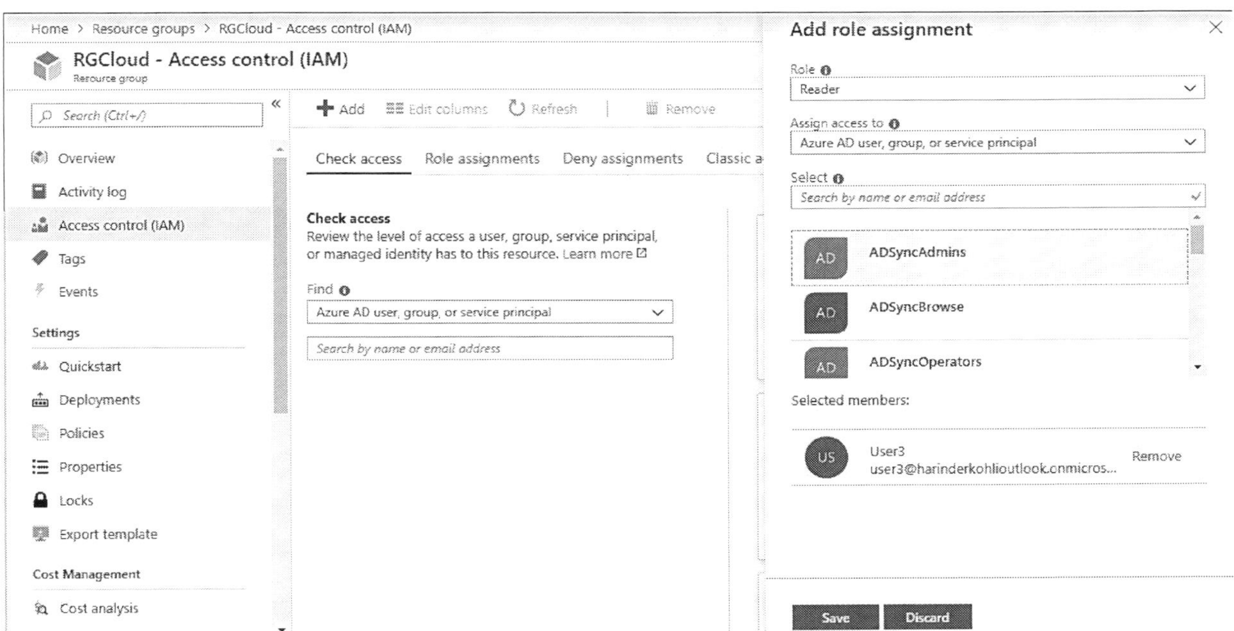

2. Click Role assignments and you can see User3 is assigned the role of Reader.

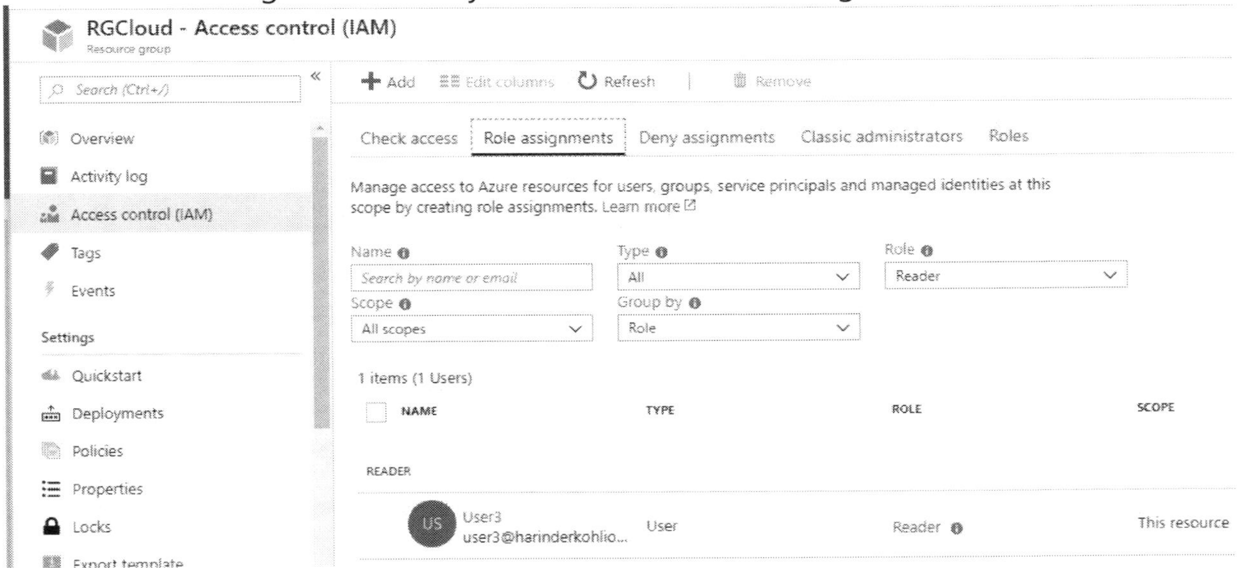

Exercise 155: Check User3 Access level in Azure Portal

1. Open Firefox and Log on to Azure Portal @ https://portal.azure.com with User3 credentials- user3@harinderkohlioutlook.onmicrosoft.com
2. Click Resource Groups in left pane> In right pane you can see User3 has access to only one Resource Group.

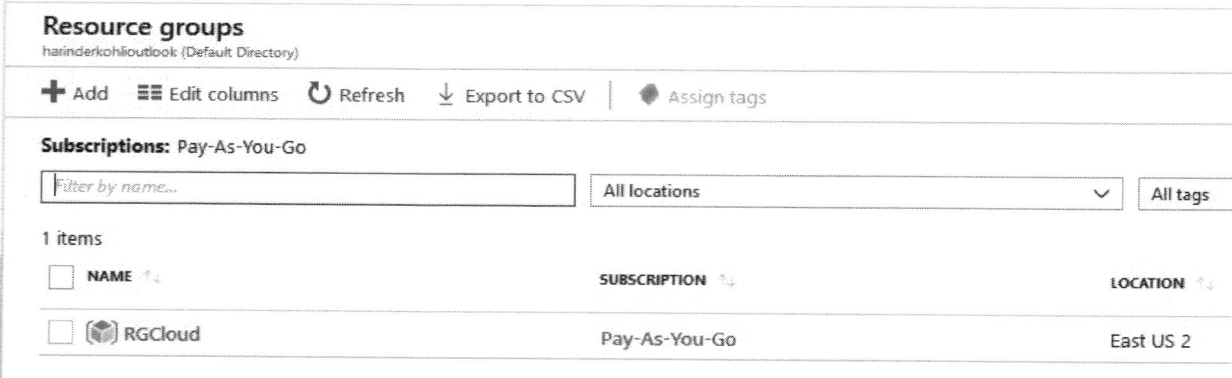

3. Click the Resource Group RGCloud. You can see all the resources created in Resource Group RGCloud.

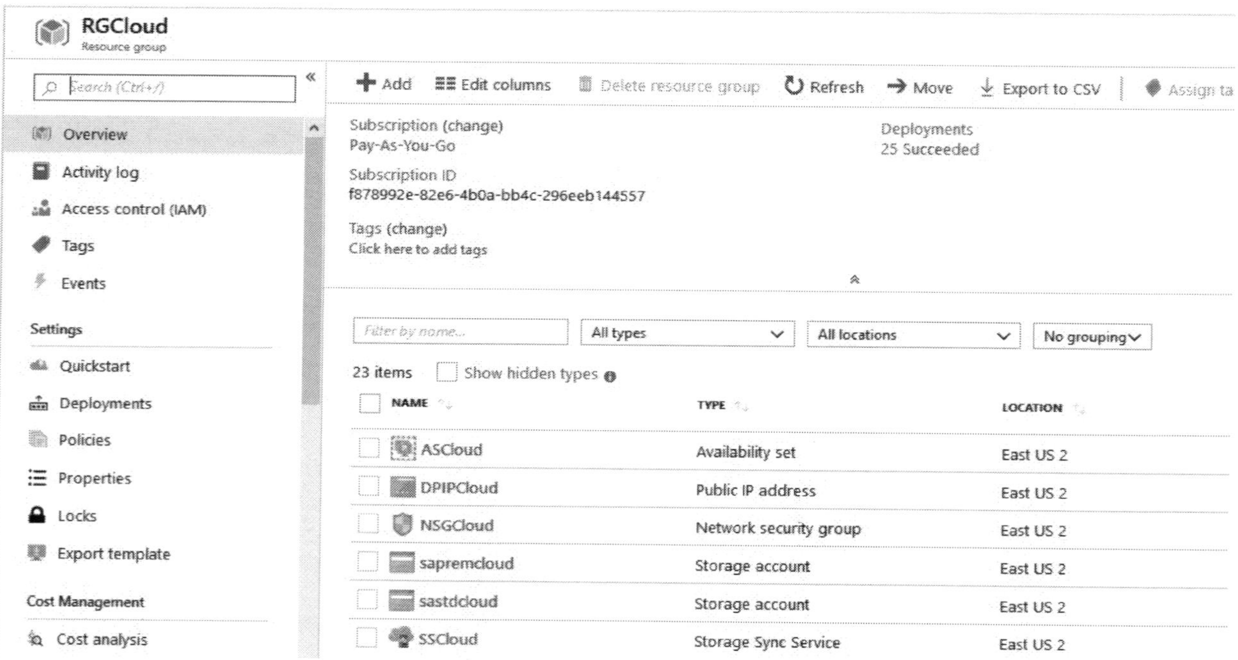

4. As an Exercise to users try to create a Resource in Resource Group RGCloud. It will fail as User3 has only Reader role assigned.

Exercise 156: Adding Co-Administrator to the subscription

In this exercise we will assign User3 role of Contributor at Subscription level. With Contributor role User3 can manage and create all resources in subscription but cannot delegate access to other users.

1. In subscription Dashboard click Access Control (IAM) in left pane> In Right pane Click +Add role assignment>In Add role assignment blade select contributor from down box and select User3> Click save.

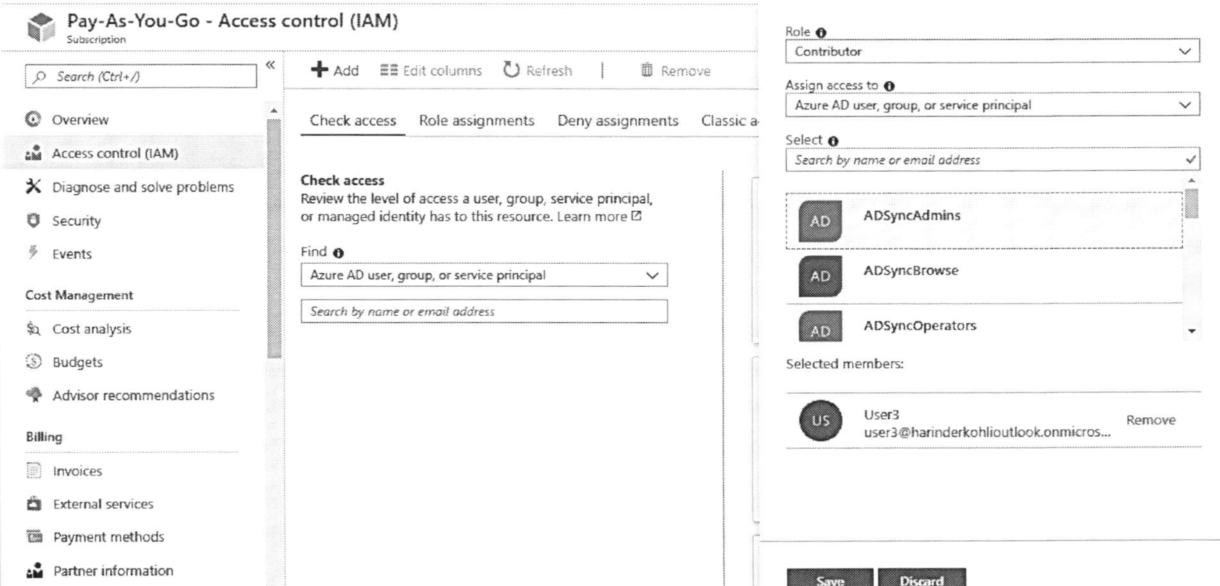

3. Click Role assignments. User3 is assigned the role of Contributor.

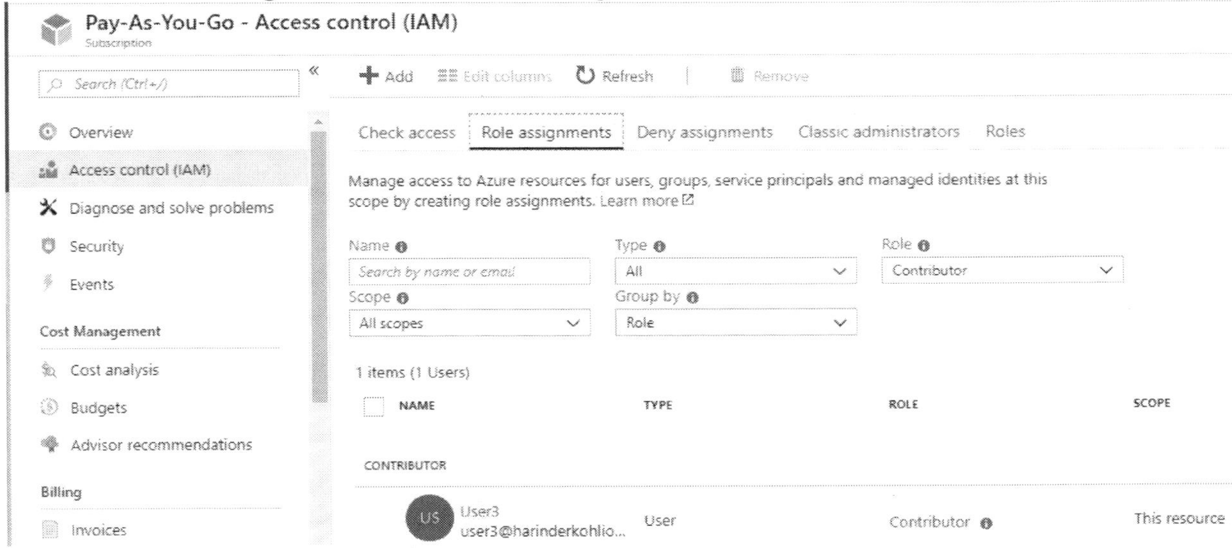

Exercise 157: Check User3 Access level in Azure Portal

1. Open Firefox and Log on to Azure Portal @ https://portal.azure.com with User3 credentials- user3@harinderkohlioutlook.onmicrosoft.com
2. Click All Resource in left pane> In right pane you can see User3 has access to All the Resources which we have created in the Subscription.

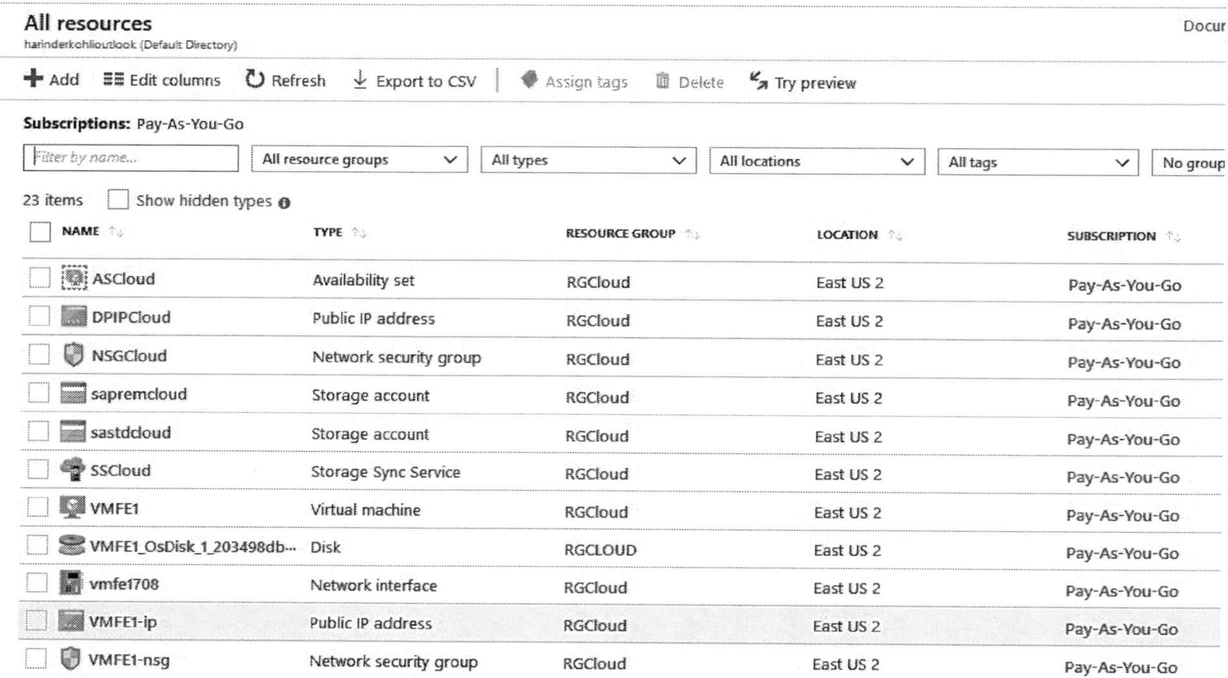

NAME	TYPE	RESOURCE GROUP	LOCATION	SUBSCRIPTION
ASCloud	Availability set	RGCloud	East US 2	Pay-As-You-Go
DPIPCloud	Public IP address	RGCloud	East US 2	Pay-As-You-Go
NSGCloud	Network security group	RGCloud	East US 2	Pay-As-You-Go
sapremcloud	Storage account	RGCloud	East US 2	Pay-As-You-Go
sastdcloud	Storage account	RGCloud	East US 2	Pay-As-You-Go
SSCloud	Storage Sync Service	RGCloud	East US 2	Pay-As-You-Go
VMFE1	Virtual machine	RGCloud	East US 2	Pay-As-You-Go
VMFE1_OsDisk_1_203498db...	Disk	RGCLOUD	East US 2	Pay-As-You-Go
vmfe1708	Network interface	RGCloud	East US 2	Pay-As-You-Go
VMFE1-ip	Public IP address	RGCloud	East US 2	Pay-As-You-Go
VMFE1-nsg	Network security group	RGCloud	East US 2	Pay-As-You-Go

As an Exercise try to create Storage Account and it will succeed.

Case Study 22: Design Role Based Access Control (RBAC)

Capstone Company is running its Applications in Azure. Azure Administrator of Capstone company assigns Azure AD User (User3) as Co-administrator with Contributor role at Subscription level. The Capstone Company has a Confidential Project running in Azure which has Applications and Resources running in Resource Group Test. Resource Group Test is being managed by a Project Manager who has been given owner role at Resource Group Test Level.

They want that User3 should have Reader level access only to Resource Group Test.

Design RBAC which satisfies above requirements.

Solution

User3 Contributor role at Subscription level will allow it to **create** and **manage** all types of Azure resources but can't grant access to others. A role assigned at a parent scope (Subscription level in this case) also grants access to the children contained within it. This means User3 will have full access to Resources in Resource Group Test.

At Resource Group Test level we will add a Role Assignment which will grant User3 the role of Reader. Though User3 has Contributor role at Subscription level but there is Explicit Permission of Reader role at child level (Resource Group Test) for User3 which will prevent User3 to Create or manage resources at Resource Group Test level. Reader role gives User3 to view resources only.

Chapter 18 Azure Subscription & Cost Management

This Chapter covers following Topic Lessons

- Azure Subscription
- Subscription Usage & Quota
- Cost Management
- Cost Analysis
- Monitor Azure Spend and Create Billing Alarms using Budgets
- Identify unused or underutilized Resources and Optimize Azure Cost
- Implementing IT Governance using Azure Policy

This Chapter covers following Lab Exercises

- Exploring Subscription Dashboard
- Checking Subscription Usage & Quota
- Accessing Cost Management Dashboard
- Cost Analysis Dashboard
- Create Budgets with Billing Notification alarms
- Advisor Recommendations
- Applying Azure Policy at Subscription Level
- Test the Allowed Virtual Machine SKU Policy

Chapter Topology

In this chapter we will explore Azure Subscription Dashboard and Cost Management + Billing Dashboard. We will monitor Azure spend through options like Cost Analysis and Budget feature. We will configure Azure policy at subscription level.

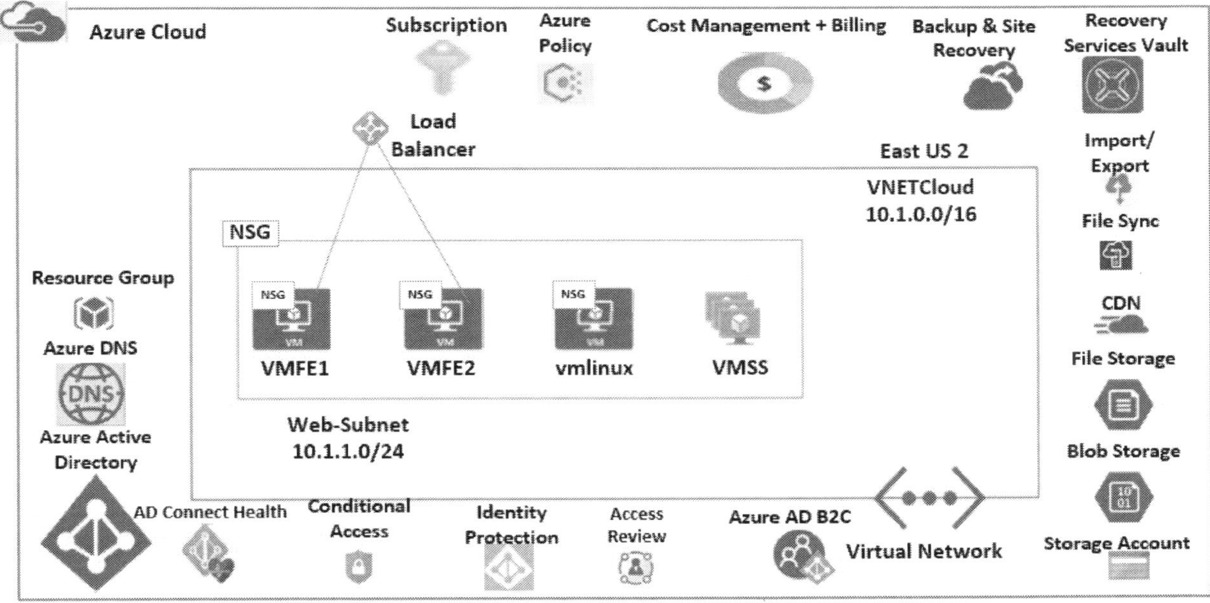

Azure Subscription

Management of Subscription happens through subscription dashboard.

Exercise158: Exploring Subscription Dashboard

1. In Azure Portal Click **Cost Management** + **Billing** in left pane> Cost Management + Billing Dashboard opens>Click Subscriptions in left pane.

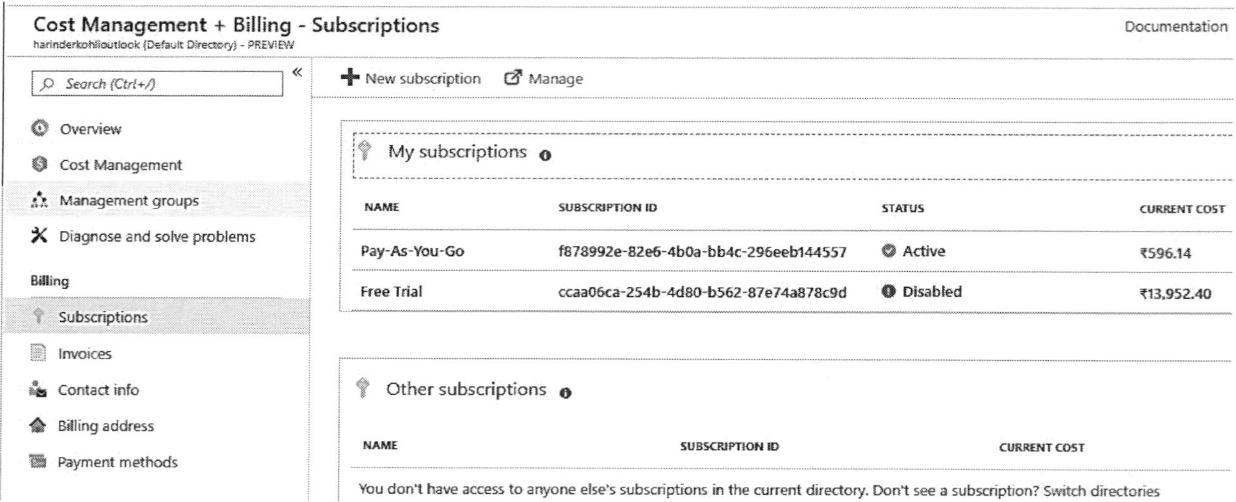

2. In right pane click your subscription>Subscription Dashboard opens.

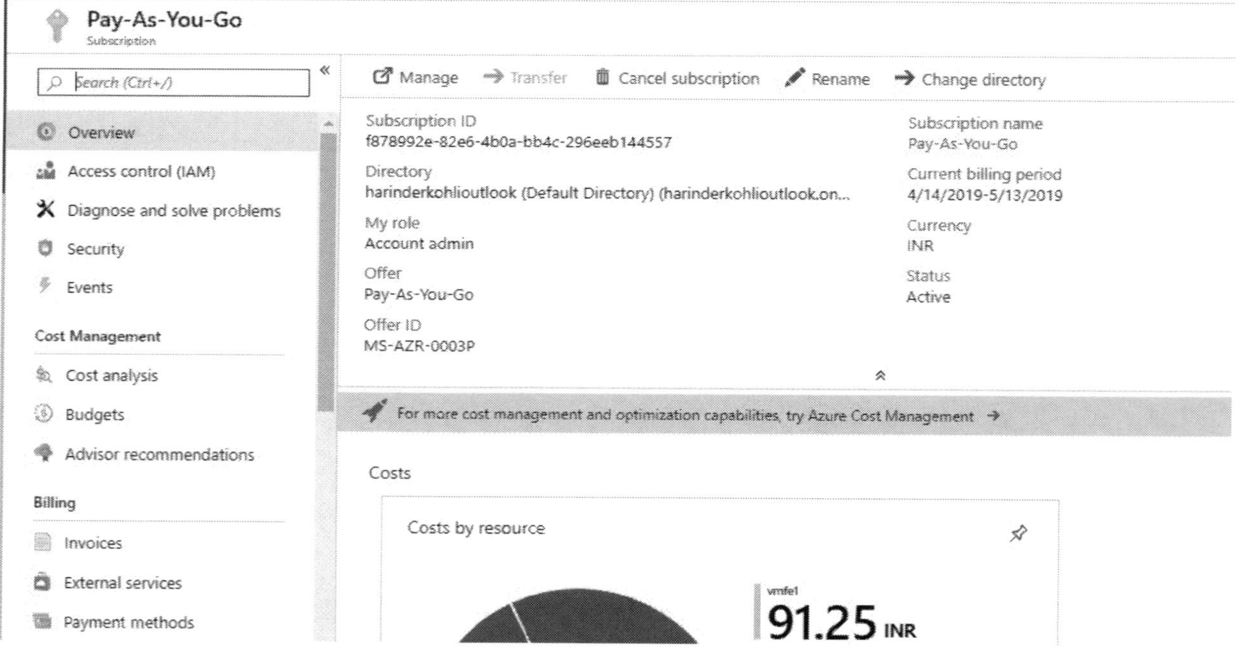

Note: Readers are advised to go through all options in Subscription dashboard and Cost Management + Billing Dashboard.

Subscription Usage & Quota

Each subscription has quota cap for resources. Resource usage is tracked per subscription. If you reach a quota cap, you can request an increase.

Usage +Quota tab in left pane will show you the usage as well as the quota associated with that resource.

Exercise 159: Checking Subscription Usage & Quota

In Subscription Dashboard Click Usage + quotas in left pane>In right pane you can see Usage + quotas for various resources> Select Microsoft.Compute from Dropdown box in Provider option.

Figure below shows usage and quota for Microsoft Compute only. You have the option to select other resources also. Readers are advised to click the drop down boxes and check other options available.

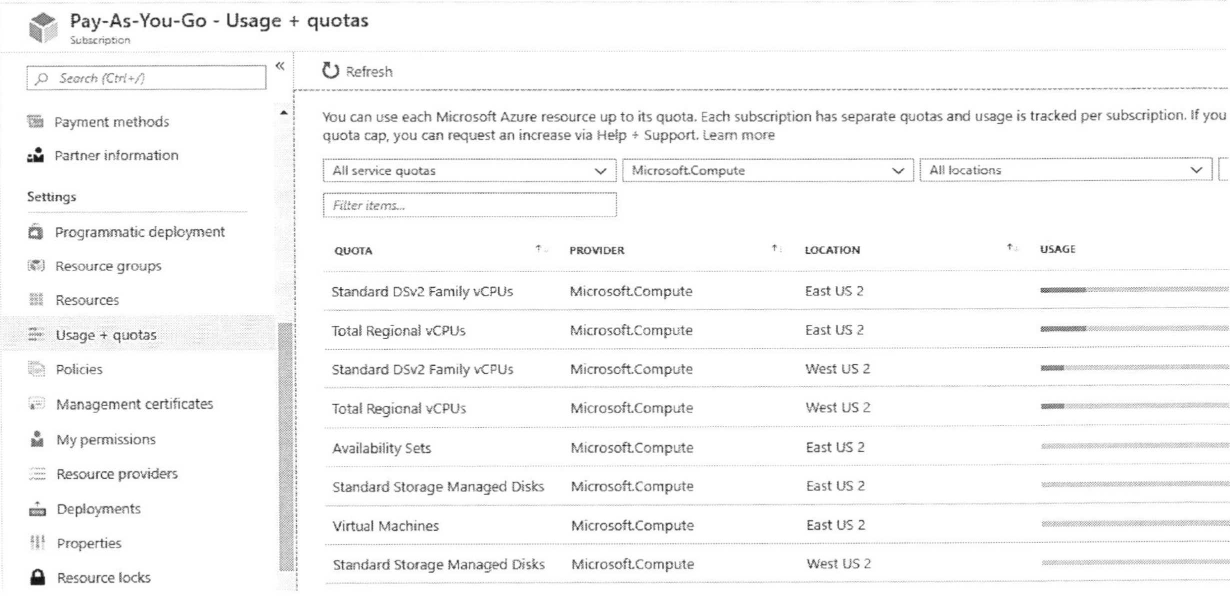

Cost Management

Using Cost Management you can visualize and monitor cloud costs and trends, improve organizational accountability and optimize cloud efficiency.

Cost Management provides following to analyze and optimize cloud costs:
Cost Analysis
Alerts
Budgets
Advisor Recommendation

Exercise 160: Accessing Cost Management Dashboard

3. In Azure Portal Click **Cost Management + Billing** in left pane> Cost Management + Billing Dashboard opens>Click Cost Management in left pane> Cost Management Dashboard opens.

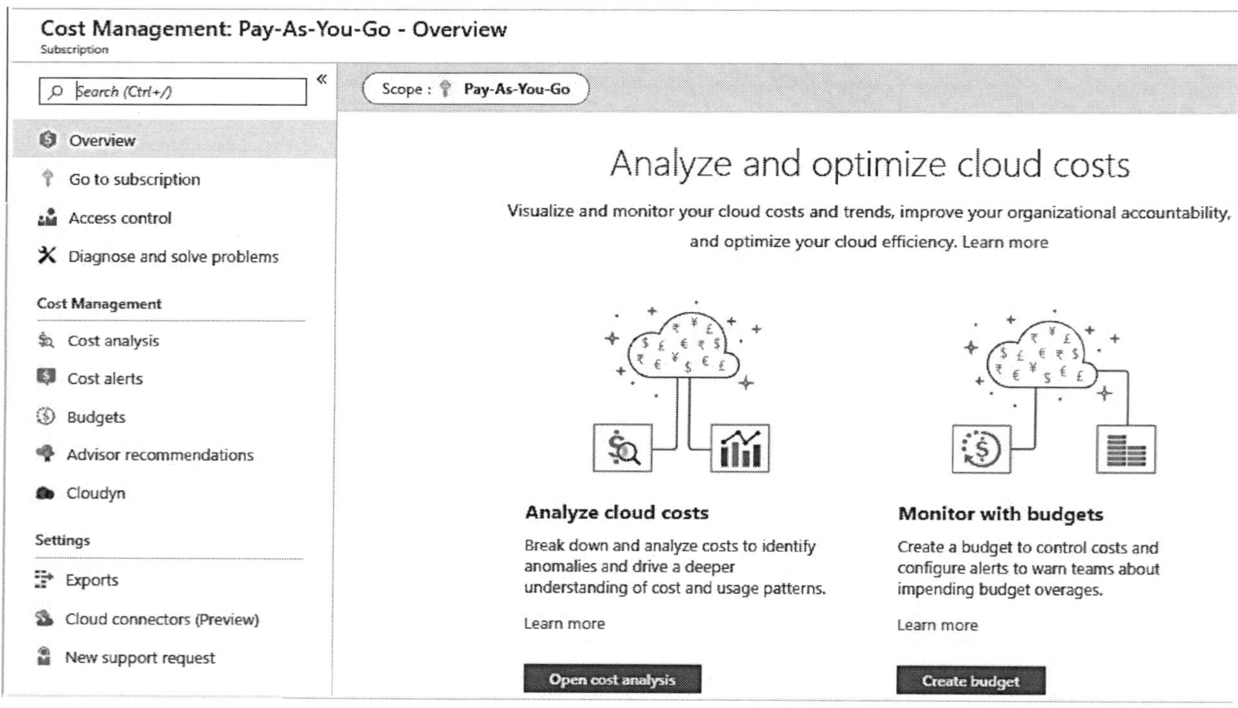

Note: Cloudyn option is being gradually replaced by Azure Cost Management. New Cloudyn registrations are limited to Microsoft CSP partner administrators

Cost Analysis

Cost Analysis helps understand where costs originated within the organization. You can view monthly, Quarterly or Custom dates cost in Cost Analysis. You can view Total cost in subscription or Cost by resource type or Resource Group or custom cost using tags.

Exercise in Resource group Chapter 15 will show how to create Cost Analysis using Tags.

Exercise 161: Cost Analysis Dashboard

1. In Azure Portal Click Cost Management + Billing in left pane> Cost Management + Billing Pane opens> Click Cost Management in left pane> Cost Management Dashboard opens>Click Cost Analysis in left pane> Cost Analysis dashboard opens. The right pane shows the total cost incurred during the billing period (April) as well as cost by resources in graphical format.

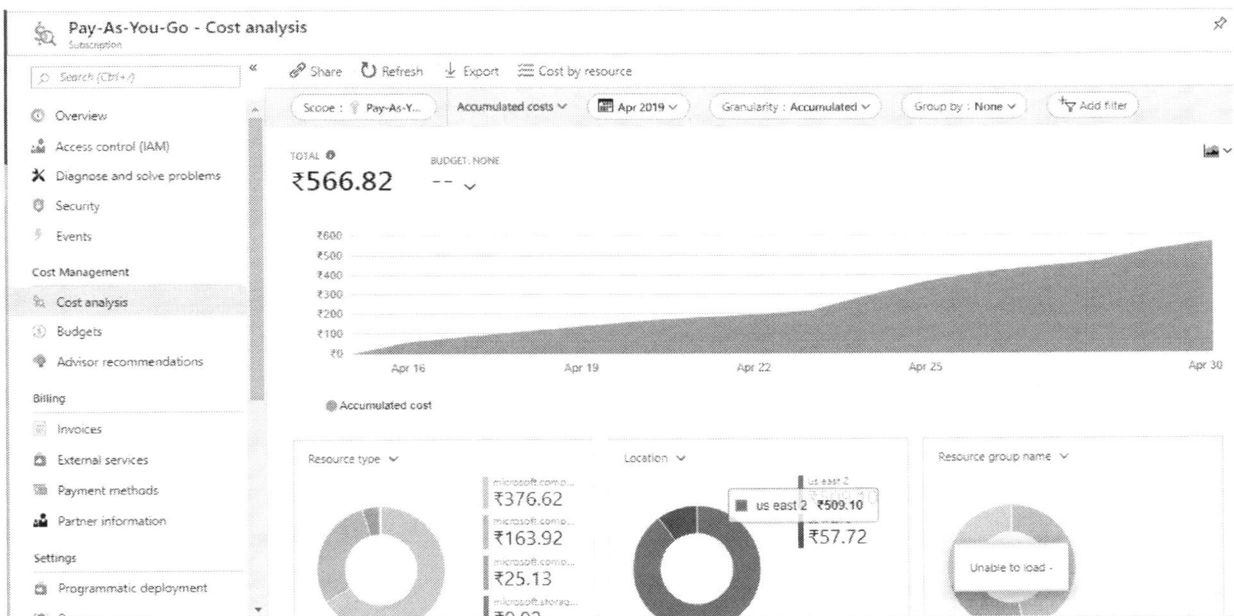

You can change dates as Last Month, this month, last Quarter, last year or custom dates from dropdown box which currently shows April 2019 in above figure.

2. **Cost Analysis by individual Resource**: You can also see individual cost of each Resource by clicking **Cost by resource** in right pane in previous figure.

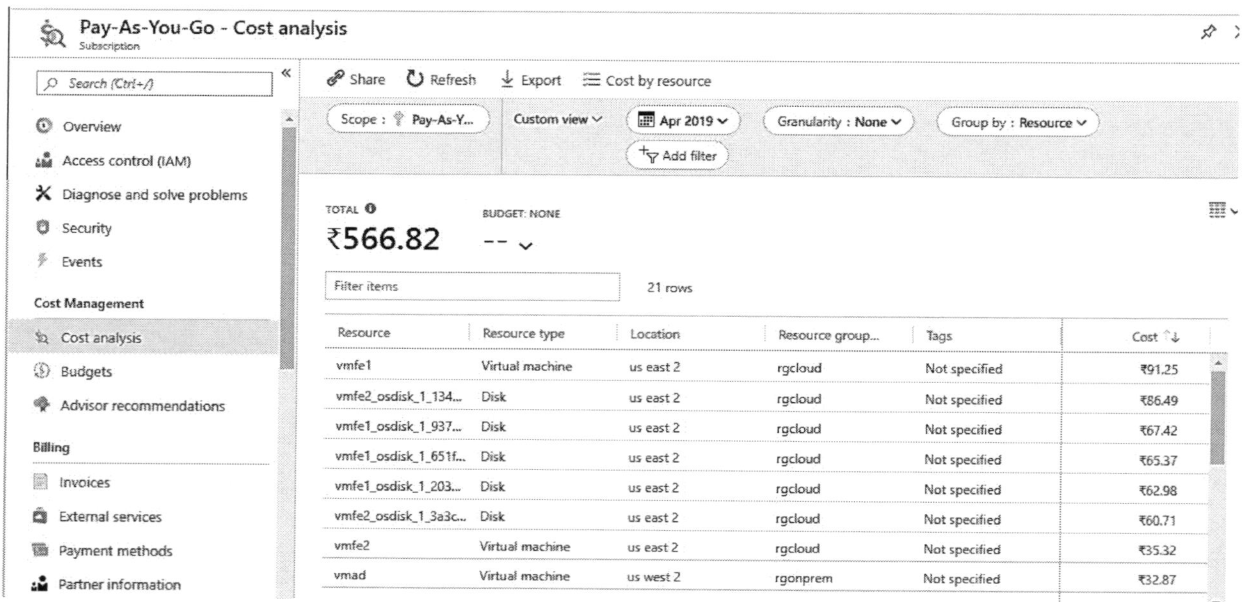

3. You can further filter to see Cost by Particular resource type, Resource Group, Location or Tags. In Filter Items Box type Virtual Machine and you can see cost of all Virtual Machines created in the subscription.

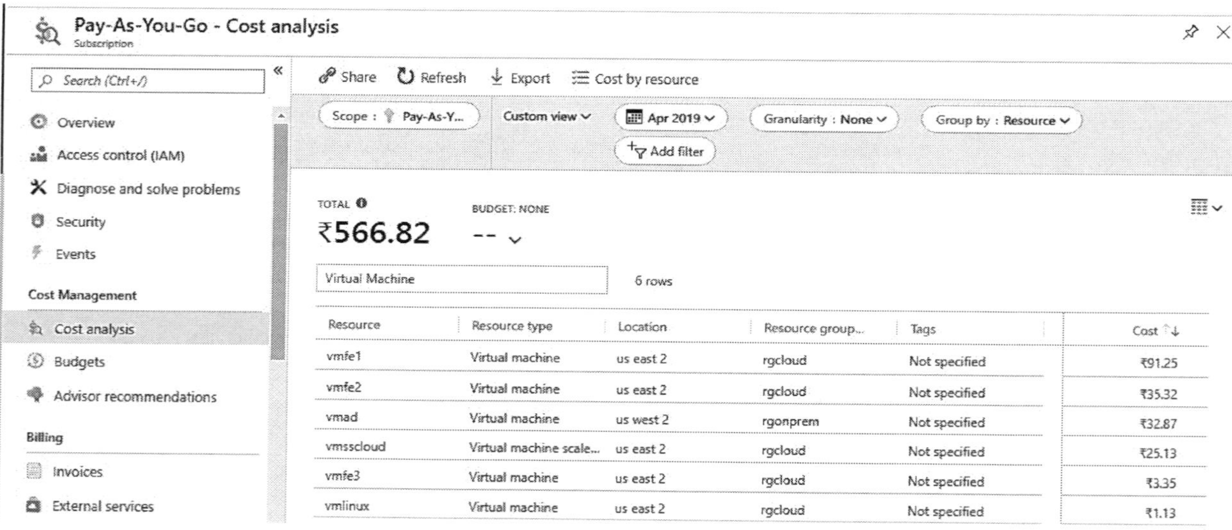

Monitor Azure Spend and Create Billing Alarms using Budgets

Budgets feature in Cost Management helps you proactively monitor Cloud cost spending over time. You can use budgets to compare and track spending as you analyze costs.

When the budget thresholds are exceeded, notifications Billing alarms are triggered. Budget feature dosen't affects consumption and none of the resources are stopped.

You can create monthly, quarterly or Yearly Budgets.

Exercise 162: Create Budgets with Billing Notification alarms

In this exercise we will create Monthly, Quarterly and Yearly Budget. If Cloud spending reaches 80% of the Budget a Billing alert email will be send.

1. **Monthly Budget:** In Cost Management Dashboard click Budgets in left pane> Click + Add in right pane> Create Budget blade opens> Enter a name> Enter Budget amount. I entered Rupees 800.> Select **Billing Month** from Resets dropdown box> Set **Billing alert condition** in terms of percentage (80%) of Budget. This will trigger an email notification alerts if the percentage threshold is reached> Add an alert email (not Shown)> click create.

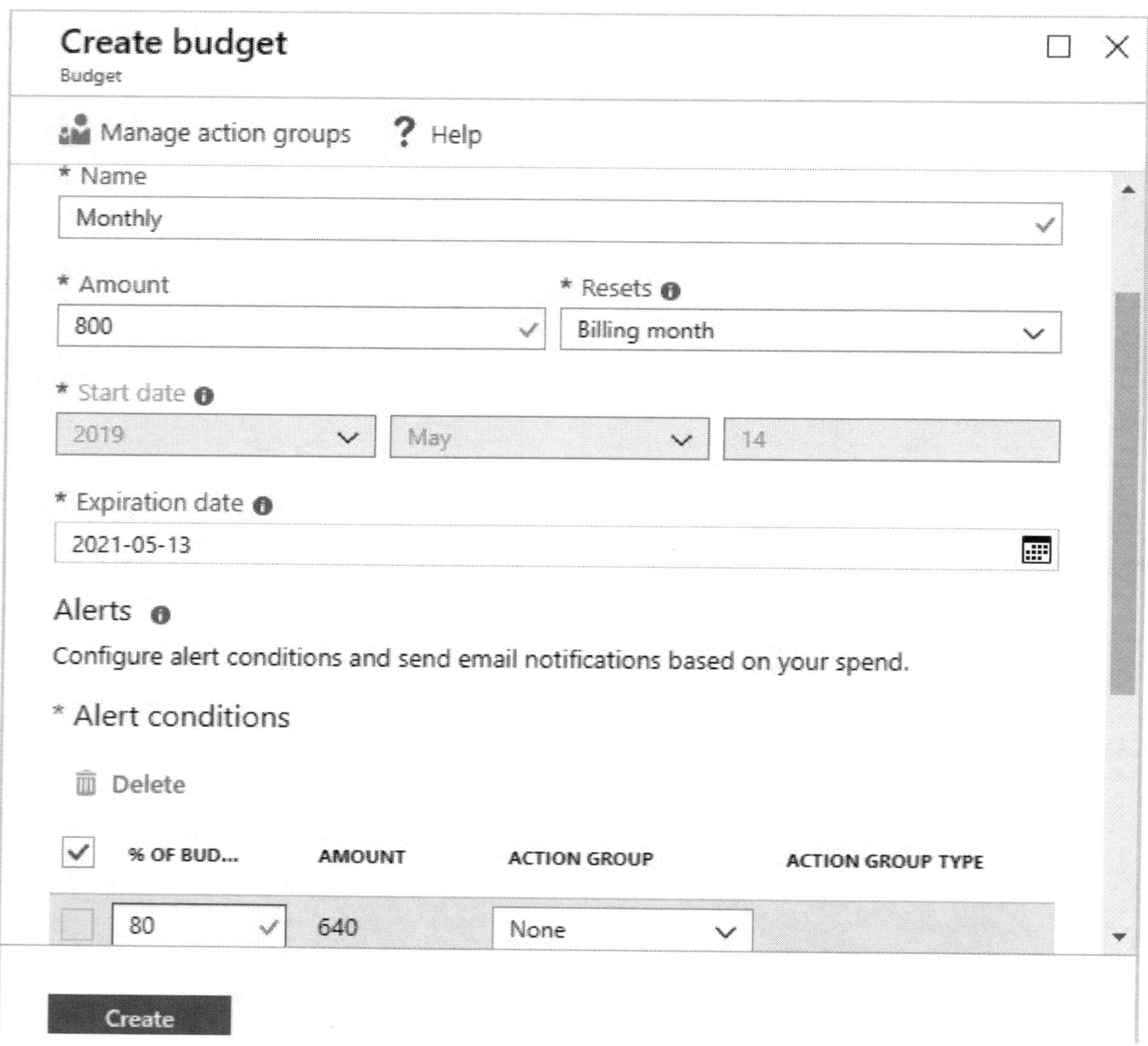

2. Figure below shows monthly budget. It shows current Monthly Cloud spend is Rupee 975.62 against a budget of Rupees 800.

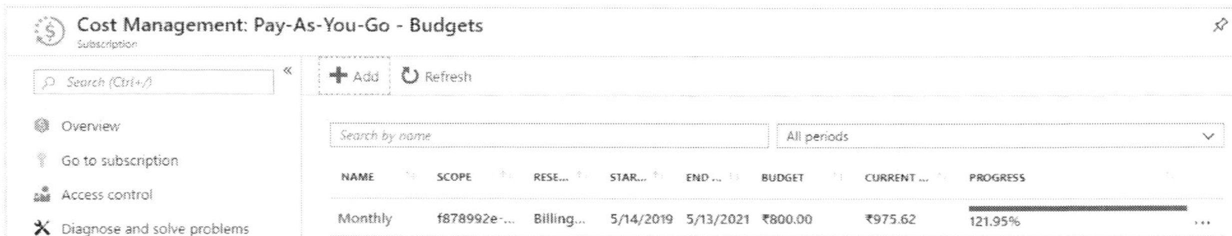

3. Similarly create Quarterly and Yearly Budget with amount 2500 and 10000 respectively. In my case currency was in Indian Rupees. Set **Billing alert condition** in terms of percentage (80%) of Budget.

4. In Budget pane you can see the current spending against the Budget. It shows current Monthly Cloud spend is Rupees 975.62 against a budget of Rupees 800. Monthly spend has exceeded the Budget. Whereas Quarterly and Yearly Budget are within budget and also have not crossed the Billing Alert threshold of 80%.

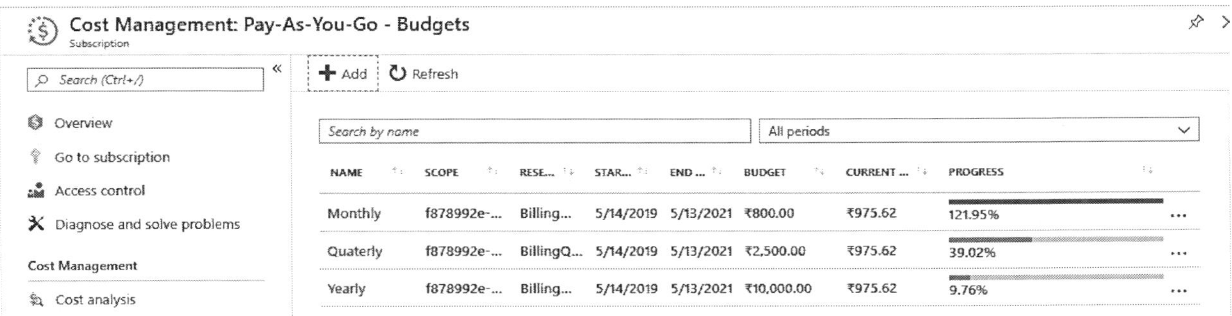

Identify unused or underutilized Resources and Optimize Azure Cost

Azure Advisor Recommendations identifies idle and underutilized resources. It then gives recommendations to optimize the Azure Cost Spend.

Example: Optimizing Azure Cost Spend on Virtual Machines

Azure Advisor monitors your virtual machine **usage for 14 days** and then identifies underutilized virtual machines. Virtual Machines whose CPU utilization is five percent or less and network usage is seven MB or less for four or more days are considered low-utilization virtual machines.
The 5% or less CPU utilization setting is the default, but you can adjust the settings.

It will then give you recommendations to change the size of the Virtual Machine to save on Potential Cost or_shutdown underutilized virtual machines to save cost.

Exercise 163: Advisor Recommendations

1. Go to Cost Management Dashboard> Click Advisor recommendations in left pane. Advisor is giving recommendation on Deleting IP Address which is not associated with any VM. This IP Address was created in Chapter 1. It is also giving Potential Yearly savings.

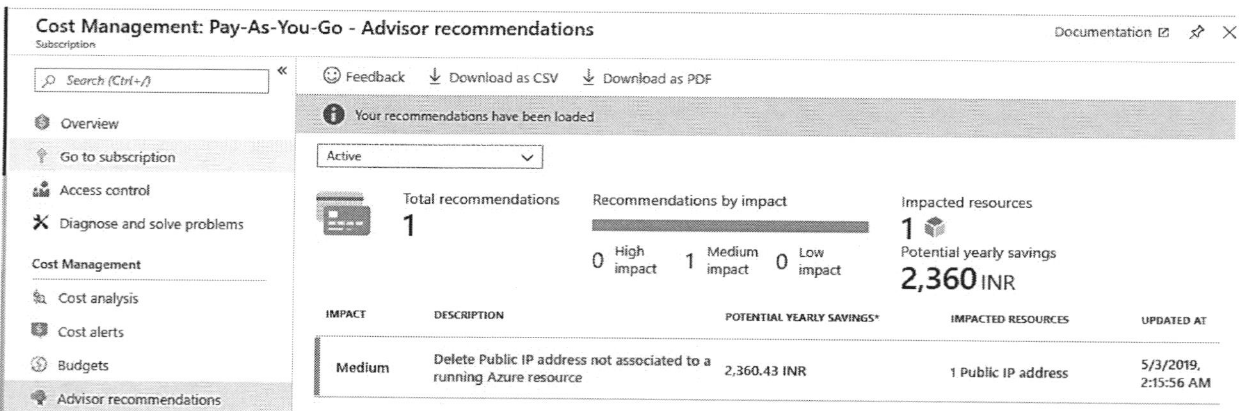

Note 1: If you access Advisor through Cost Management pane then you only get recommendation related to Cost only. Otherwise Advisor gives recommendation in 4 areas: Cost, High availability, Security and Performance.
Note 2: Advisor will be discussed in detail in Chapter 9 in Part 2 Book.
Note 3: My Subscription did not have any cost recommendation for Virtual Machines. In next step I will use screen shot from Azure Docs.

2. In the following example, the option chosen resizes current size to a **DS13_V2**. **The recommendation saves $551.30/month or $6,615.60/year.** This below screen shot is taken from Azure Docs.

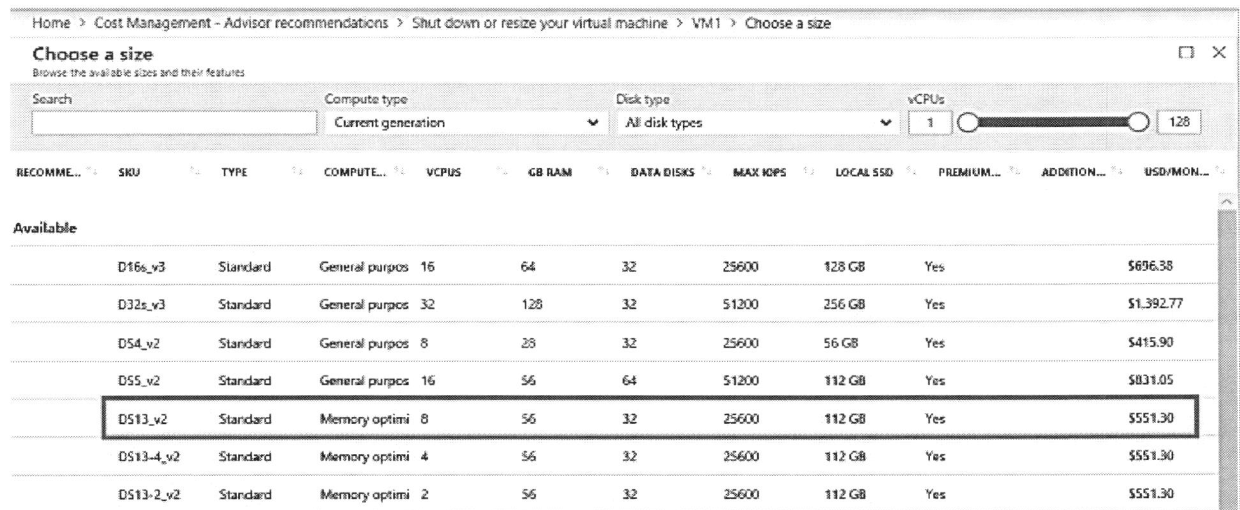

RECOMME...	SKU	TYPE	COMPUTE...	VCPUS	GB RAM	DATA DISKS	MAX IOPS	LOCAL SSD	PREMIUM...	ADDITION...	USD/MON...
	D16s_v3	Standard	General purpos	16	64	32	25600	128 GB	Yes		$696.38
	D32s_v3	Standard	General purpos	32	128	32	51200	256 GB	Yes		$1,392.77
	DS4_v2	Standard	General purpos	8	28	32	25600	56 GB	Yes		$415.90
	DS5_v2	Standard	General purpos	16	56	64	51200	112 GB	Yes		$831.05
	DS13_v2	Standard	Memory optimi	8	56	32	25600	112 GB	Yes		$551.30
	DS13-4_v2	Standard	Memory optimi	4	56	32	25600	112 GB	Yes		$551.30
	DS13-2_v2	Standard	Memory optimi	2	56	32	25600	112 GB	Yes		$551.30

Implementing IT Governance using Azure Policy

Azure Policy helps in implementing IT Governance in an organisation. IT Governance ensures that your organization is able to achieve its goals through an effective and efficient use of IT. IT Governance involves planning and initiative at strategic level to prevent IT issues from derailing IT projects.

Azure Policy is a managed service in Azure that is used to assign and manage policies. These policies enforce rules so that resources stay compliant with your corporate standards and service level agreements.

Azure Policy Example

You have assigned a policy to allow only a DSv2 SKU size of virtual machines in your environment. Once this policy has been implemented it will only allow DSv2 Size Virtual Machines to be created in your environment. Secondly any non DSv2 Virtual Machine which was their before this Policy was assigned will be marked as non-compliant. Azure Policy runs evaluations of your resources and scans for those not compliant with the policies you have created.

Policy Assignment Scope

Azure Policy can be applied at Subscription, Resource Group or at Management Group level. Policy assignments are inherited by all child resources. However, you can exclude a subscope from the policy assignment.

Built in Policies

There are Hundred built in Policies. Some of the built in policies include:

Allowed Storage Account SKUs: This policy definition has a set of conditions/rules that determine if a storage account that is being deployed is within a set of SKU sizes. Its effect is to deny all storage accounts that do not adhere to the set of defined SKU sizes.
Allowed Resource Type: This policy definition has a set of conditions/rules to specify the resource types that your organization can deploy. Its effect is to deny all resources that are not part of this defined list.
Allowed Locations: This policy enables you to restrict the locations that your organization can specify when deploying resources. Its effect is used to enforce your geo-compliance requirements.

Allowed Virtual Machine SKUs: This policy enables you to specify a set of virtual machine SKUs that your organization can deploy.
Apply tag and its default value: Applies a required tag and its default value if it's not specified by the deploy request.
Not allowed resource types: Prevents a list of resource types from being deployed.

Exercise 164: Applying Azure Policy at Subscription Level

1. Go to Subscription Dashboard>Click Policies in left pane>Policies Blade open>Click Compliance in left pane.

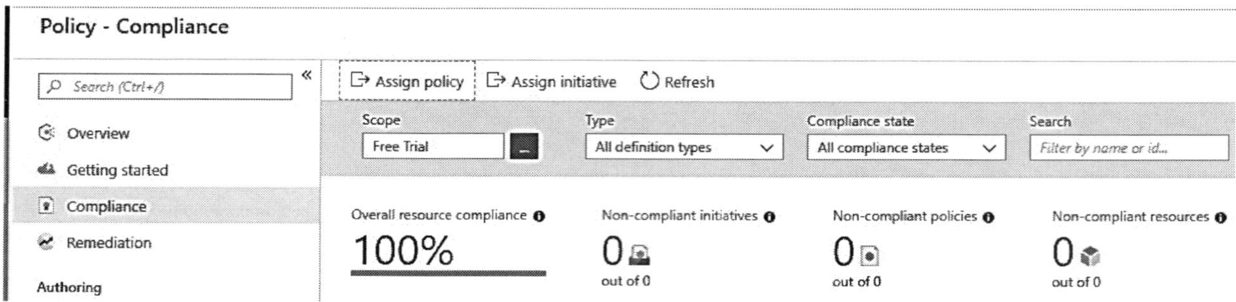

2. Click Assign Policy>Assign Policy Blade opens as shown below.

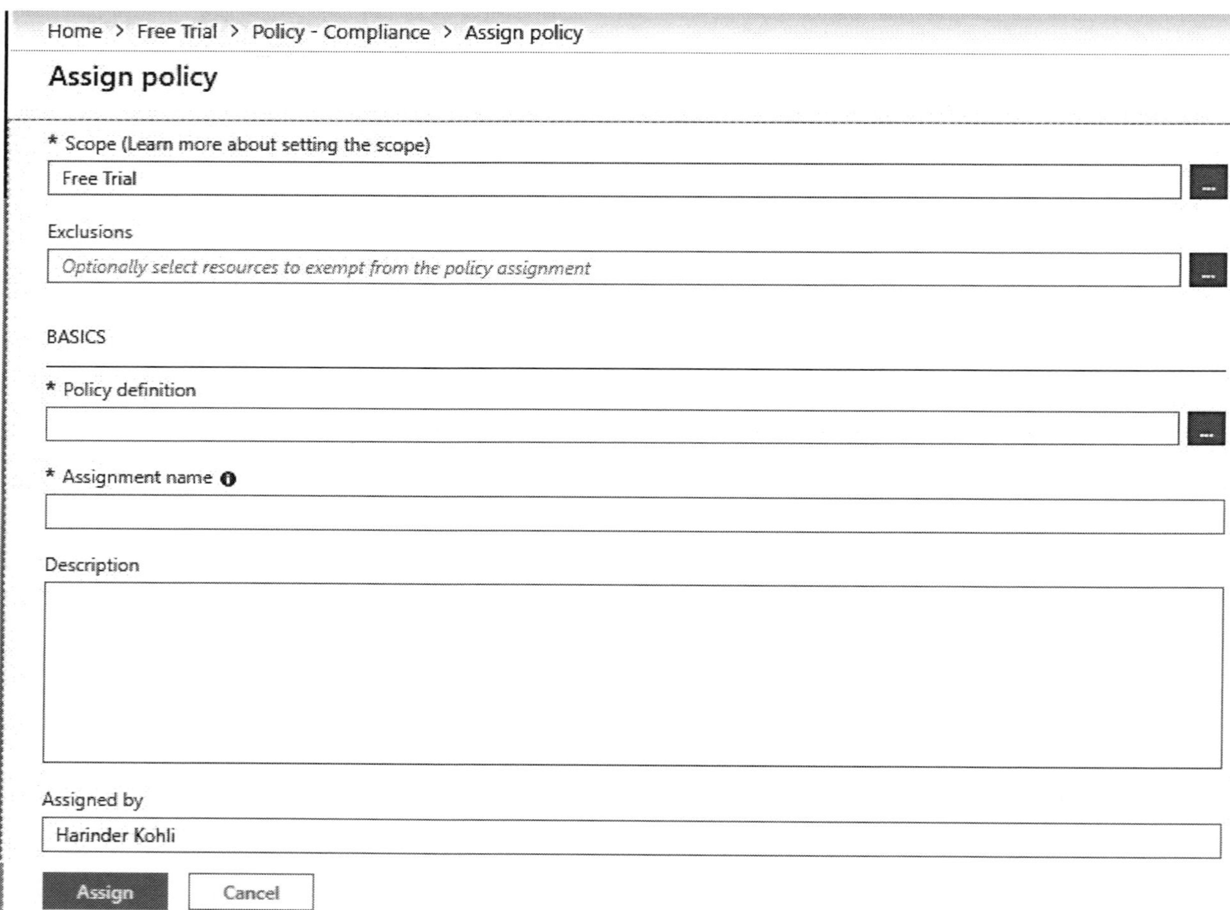

3. Under Policy Defination click ellipsis (...) Box>Available Defination Blade opens>Scroll down and select **Allowed Virtual Machine SKU**s.

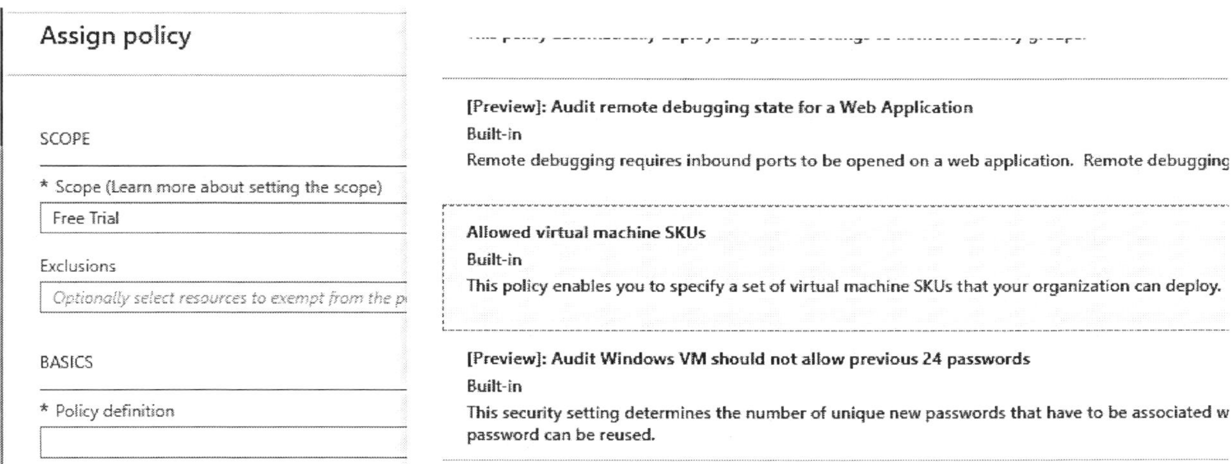

4. Select Allowed Virtual Machine SKU>Click Select> A drop down Box is created in Azure Policy Blade to select the required SKU> Here I selected Standard_D1 SKU>Click Assign in Bottom of the pane (Not shown).

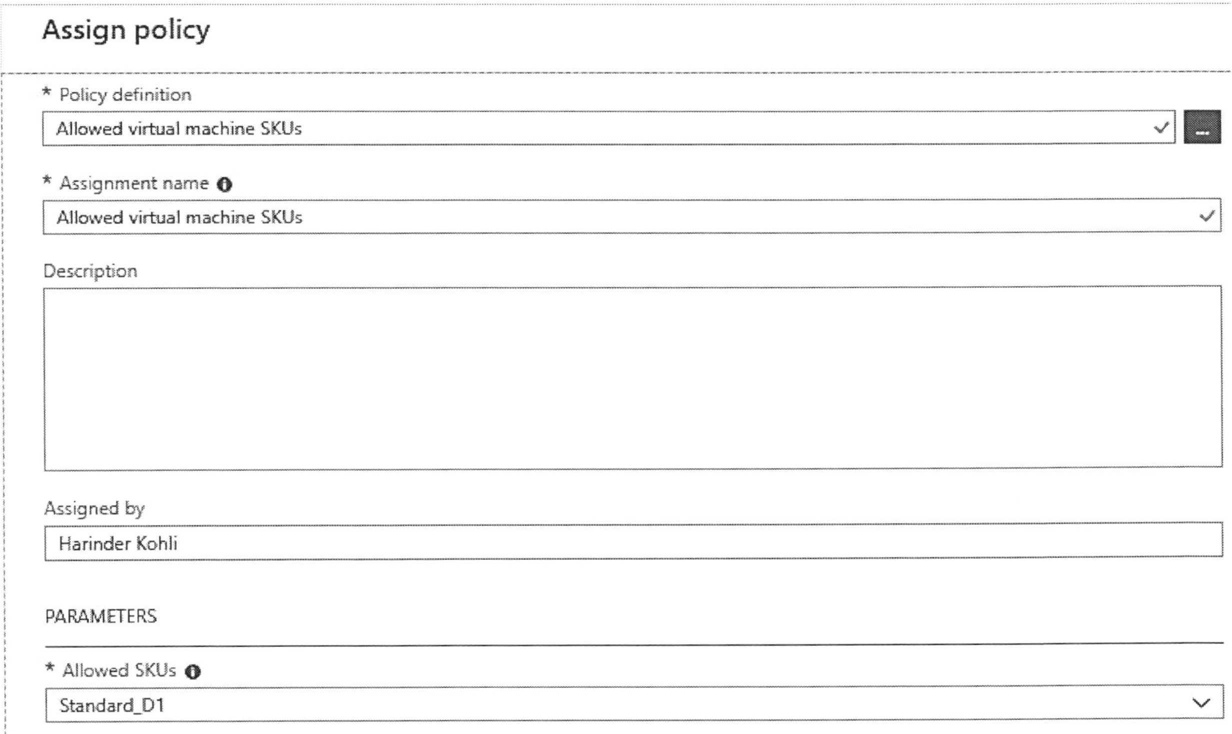

Note: An Assignment name is automatically generated. You can change it.

5. Policies dashboard shows the Policy created. It takes 15-20 minutes for Policy to take effect. You need to refresh it continuously.
   It shows 1 Resource as non-compliant.

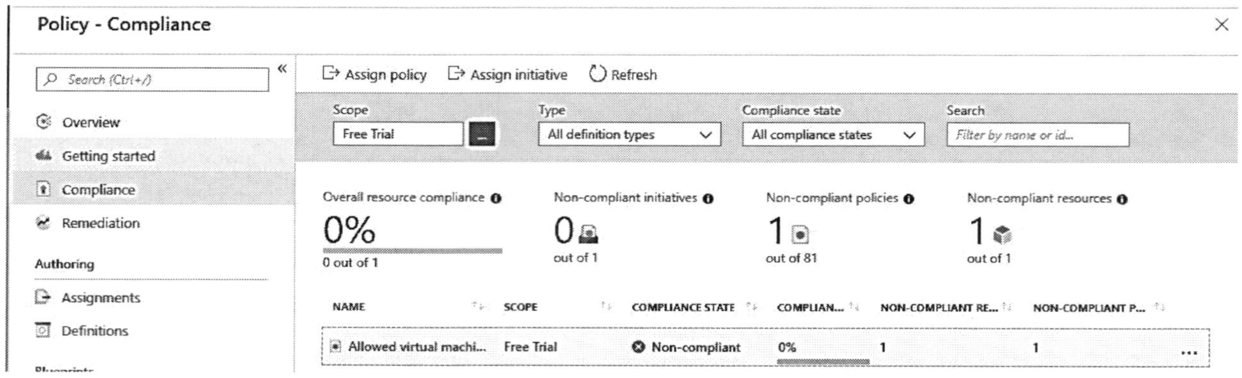

6. Click the Policy in the right pane to get the detail of Non-Compliant Resource. wvmportal VM is non-compliant. wvmportal is DS1 size SKU whereas our policy allows Standard D1 type VM.

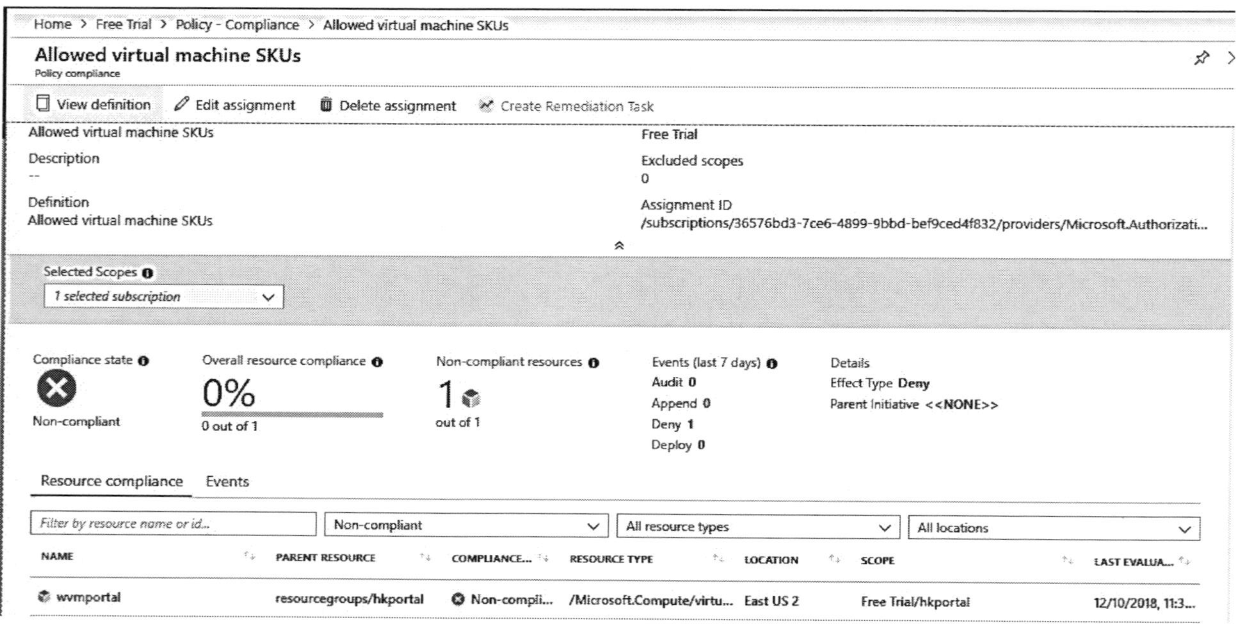

Exercise 165: Test the Allowed Virtual Machine SKU Policy

In this Exercise we will try to create A Series Virtual Machine and see whether system allows or not. Our Policy created in previous exercise at Subscription level allows Standard_D1 Machines only.

1. Click Create a Resource>Compute>Windows Server 2019 Datacenter >Create VM dashboard opens>Select Resource Group RGCloud>enter a name>In size click change size and Select VM size as A1 and enter username and password and click Review + Create> Validation fails and click on it to get the reason> Resource was disallowed by policy and Policy name was Allowed Virtual Machine SKUs. This Policy only allowed Standard_D1 Machines only.

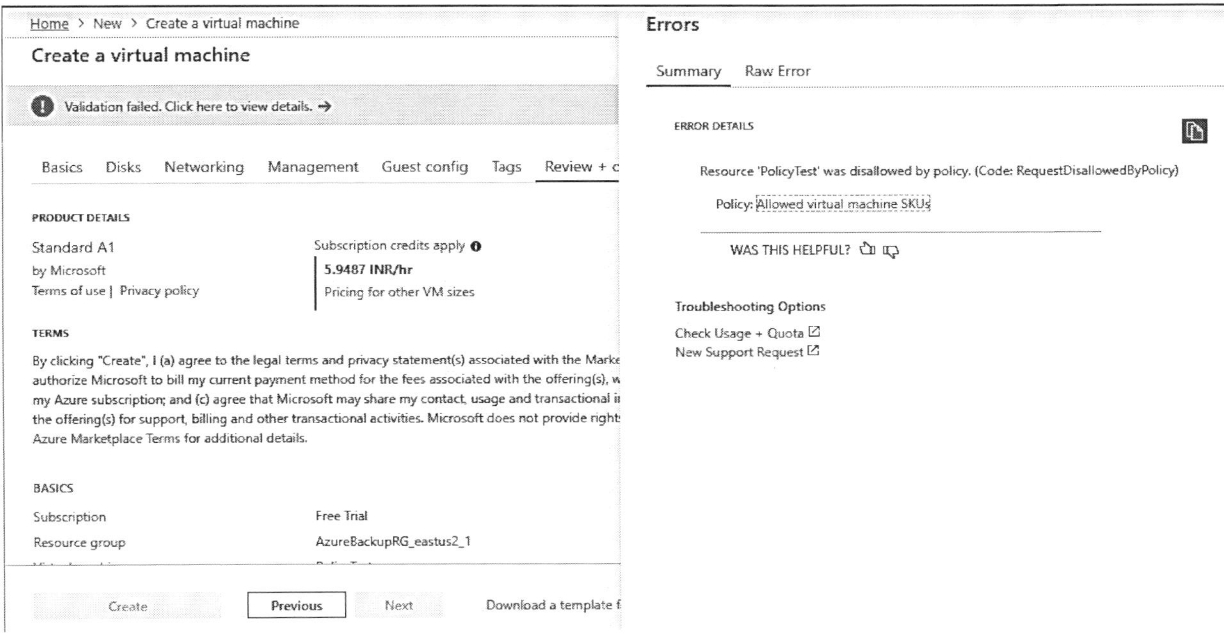

Chapter 19 Azure Resource Groups, Tags and Locks

This Chapter covers following Topic Lessons

- Resource Groups (RG)
- IT Governance at Resource Group Level using Azure Policy
- Moving Virtual Machines
- Tags
- Locks

This Chapter covers following Lab Exercises

- Create Resource Group HKTest
- Applying Azure Policy at Resource Group Level
- Test the Allowed storage accounts SKU Policy
- Move resources to new resource group
- Create Tag with name Mktg for VM wvmportal
- Create Tag with name Mktg for VM wvmportal OS Disk
- Find Cost of Resources Associated with Mktg
- Create CanNotDelete Lock on VM VMFE1
- Test the Lock

Chapter Topology

In this chapter we will add Resource Group, Tags and Locks to the Topology. We will create Azure policy at Resource Group level.

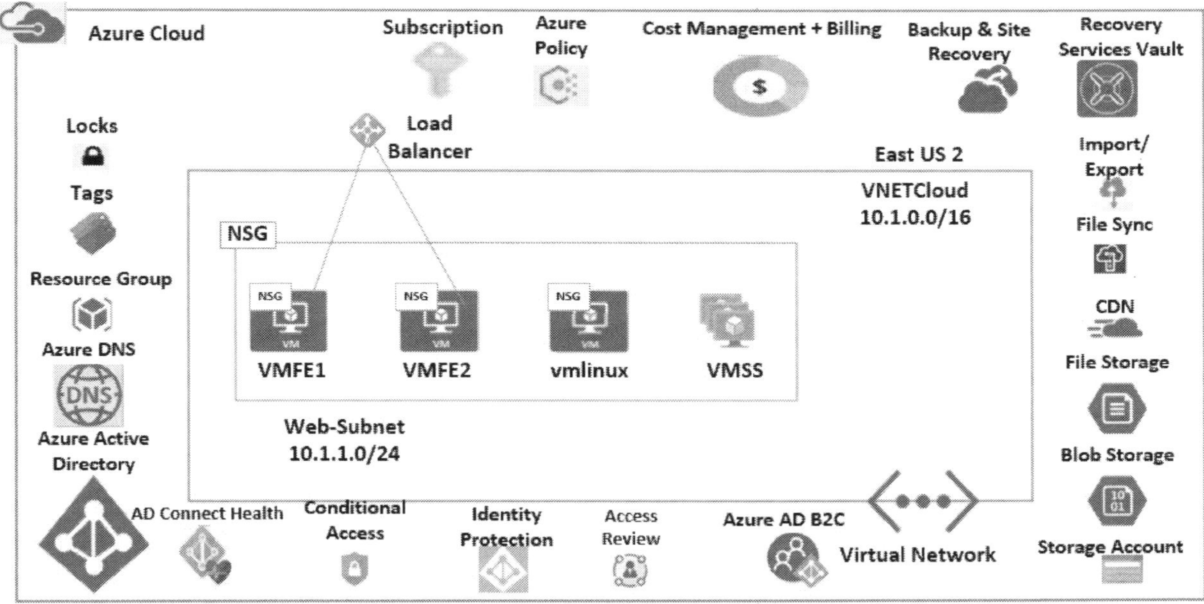

Resource Groups (RG)

Resource Groups are logical containers in which resources are grouped. All Resources in Azure are created in Resource Group. Resource Group can be created independently or can be created along with resource creation.

Resource groups allow you to manage related resources as a single unit. Using Resources Groups you can monitor, control access and manage billing for resources that are required to run an application.

Design Considerations for Resource Groups

1. A resource group can contain resources that reside in different regions.
2. All the resources in a resource group must be associated with a single subscription.
3. Each resource can only exist in one resource group.
4. You can move a resource from one resource group to another group.
5. Ideally all the resources in a resource group should share the same lifecycle. You deploy, update, and delete them together. If one resource, such as a database server, needs to exist on a different deployment cycle it should be in another resource group.
6. A RG can be used to scope access control for administrative actions.

Exercise 167: Create Resource Group HKTest

1. In Azure Portal click Resource groups in left pane>Click +Add>Add Resource Group blade opens>Enter a name and for Location select East US 2> Click Review + Create (Not Shown)> Click Create.

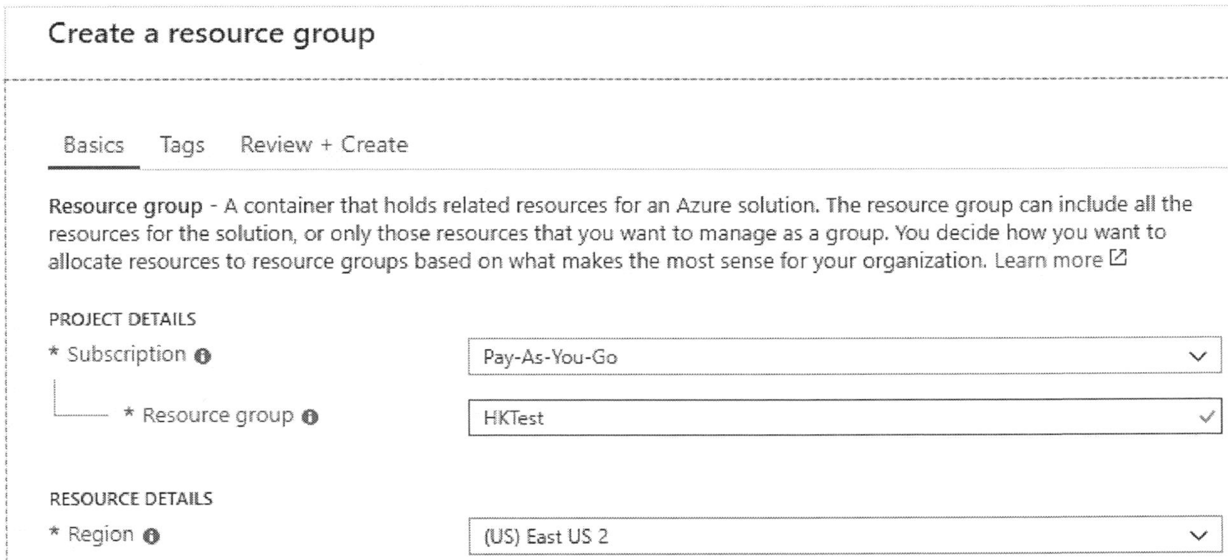

2. Figure below shows Resource Group HKTest Dashboard. Currently there are no resources to display as it is a new created group.

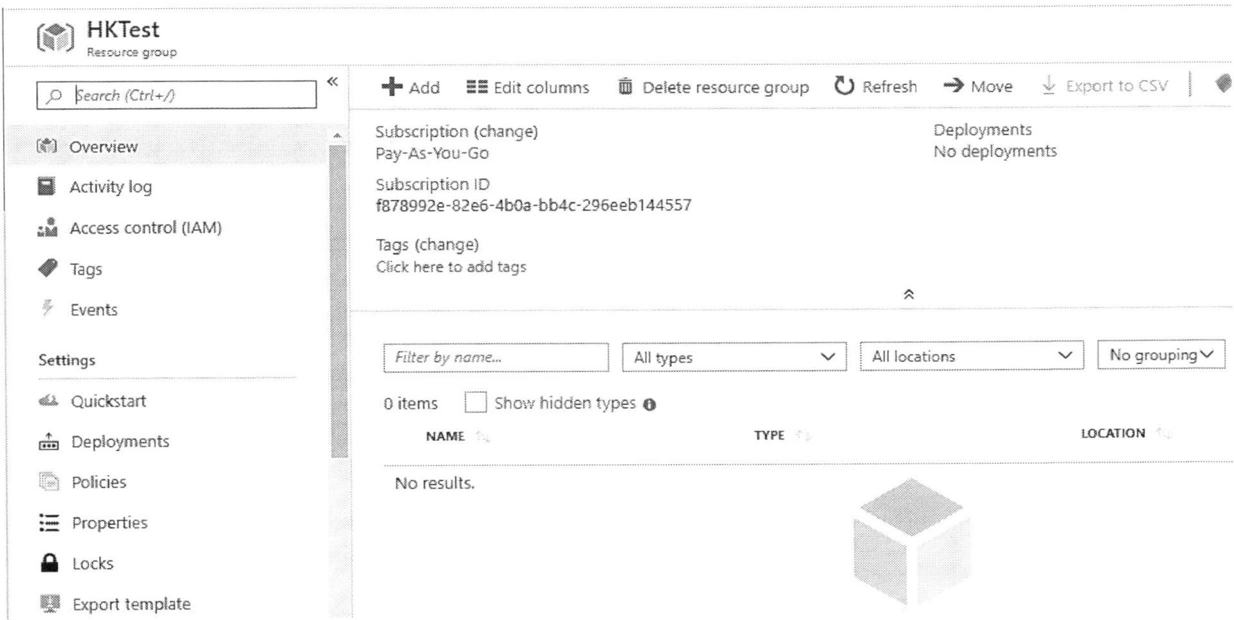

IT Governance at Resource Group level using Azure Policy

Note: Azure Policies is already discussed in Subscription Chapter. Policies can be applied at Subscription or Resource Group Level.

Azure Policy helps in implementing IT Governance in an organisation. IT Governance ensures that your organization is able to achieve its goals through an effective and efficient use of IT. IT Governance involves planning and initiative at strategic level to prevent IT issues from derailing IT projects.

Azure Policy is a managed service in Azure that is used to assign and manage policies. These policies enforce rules so that resources stay compliant with your corporate standards and service level agreements.

Policy Assignment Scope

Azure Policy can be applied at Subscription, Resource Group or at Management Group level. Policy assignments are inherited by all child resources. However, you can exclude a subscope from the policy assignment.

Built in Policies

There are Hundred built in Policies. Some of the built in policies include:

Allowed Storage Account SKUs: This policy definition has a set of conditions/rules that determine if a storage account that is being deployed is within a set of SKU sizes. Its effect is to deny all storage accounts that do not adhere to the set of defined SKU sizes.
Allowed Resource Type: This policy definition has a set of conditions/rules to specify the resource types that your organization can deploy. Its effect is to deny all resources that are not part of this defined list.
Allowed Locations: This policy enables you to restrict the locations that your organization can specify when deploying resources. Its effect is used to enforce your geo-compliance requirements.

Exercise 168: Applying Azure Policy at Resource Group Level

In this Exercise we will assign Policy to Resource Group HKTest. This Policy allows creation of Storage Account with RA GRS replication option only.

7. Go to Resource Group HKTest Dashboard>Click Policies in left pane>Policies Blade open>Click Compliance in left pane.

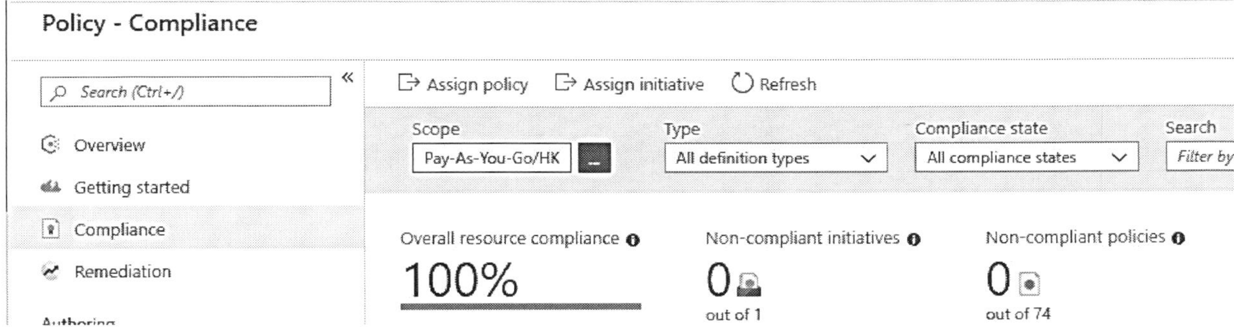

8. Click Assign Policy in right pane>Assign Policy Blade opens as shown below.

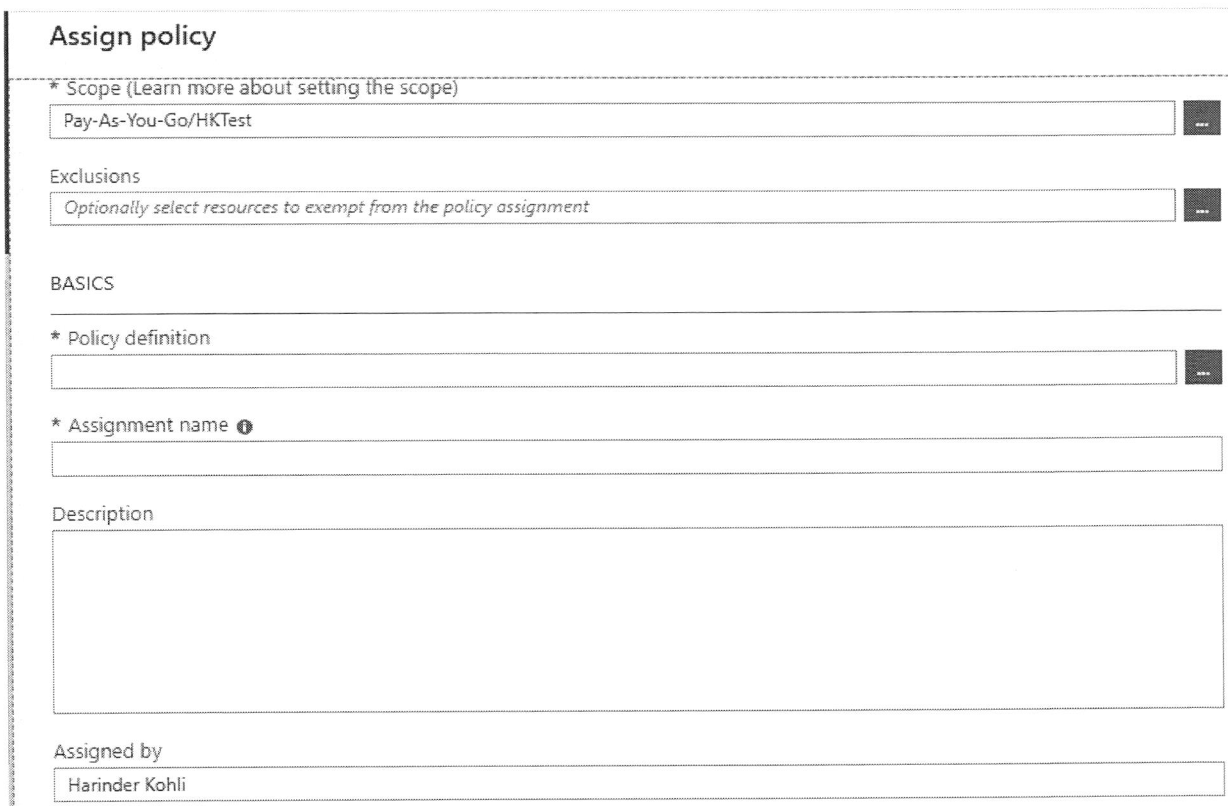

9. Under Policy Defination click ellipsis ... Box >Available Defination Blade opens>Scroll down to **Allowed storage accounts SKU**s.

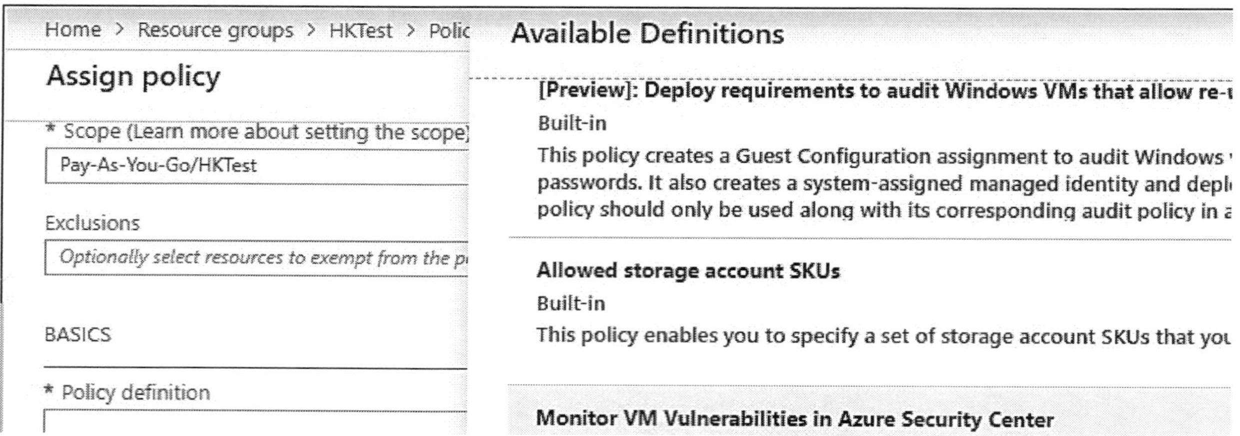

10. Select **Allowed storage accounts SKUs** >Click Select (Not shown)> A drop down Box is created in Azure Policy Blade to select the required SKU> Here I selected Standard_RAGRS>Click Assign in Bottom of the pane (Not shown).

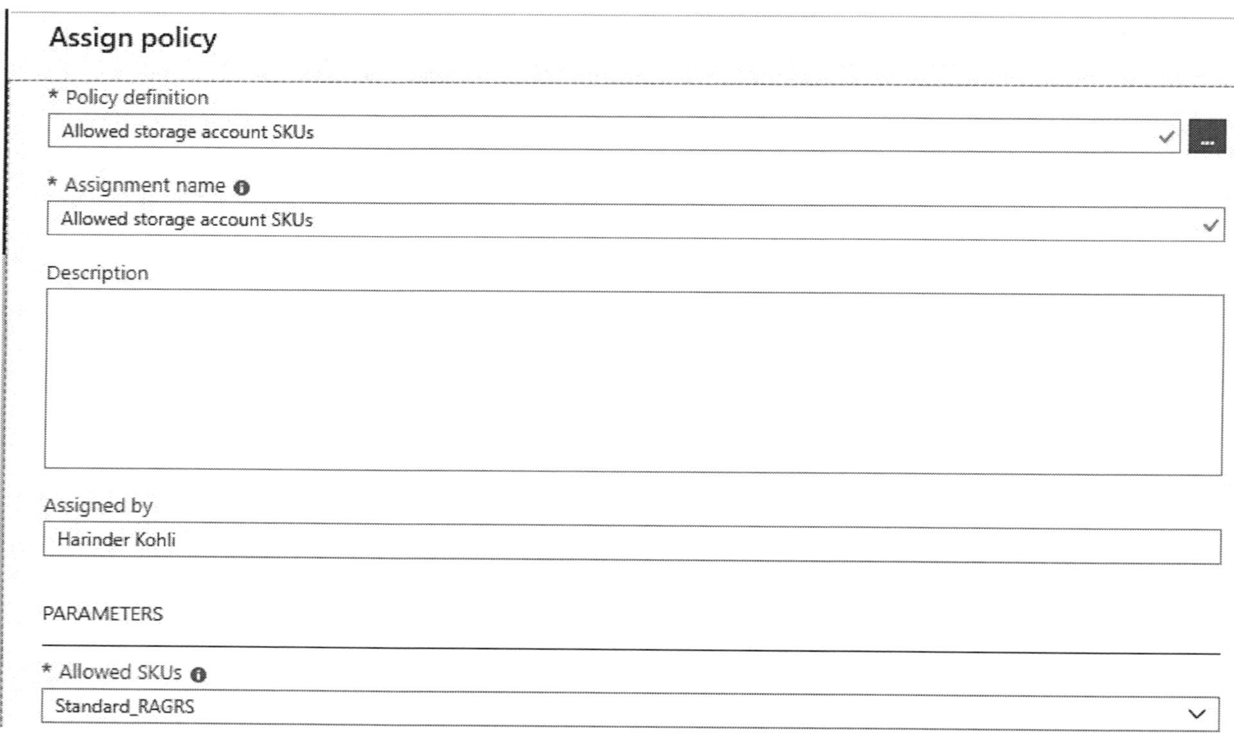

11. Policies dashboard shows the Policy created. It takes 15-20 minutes for Policy to take effect. You need to refresh it continuously.

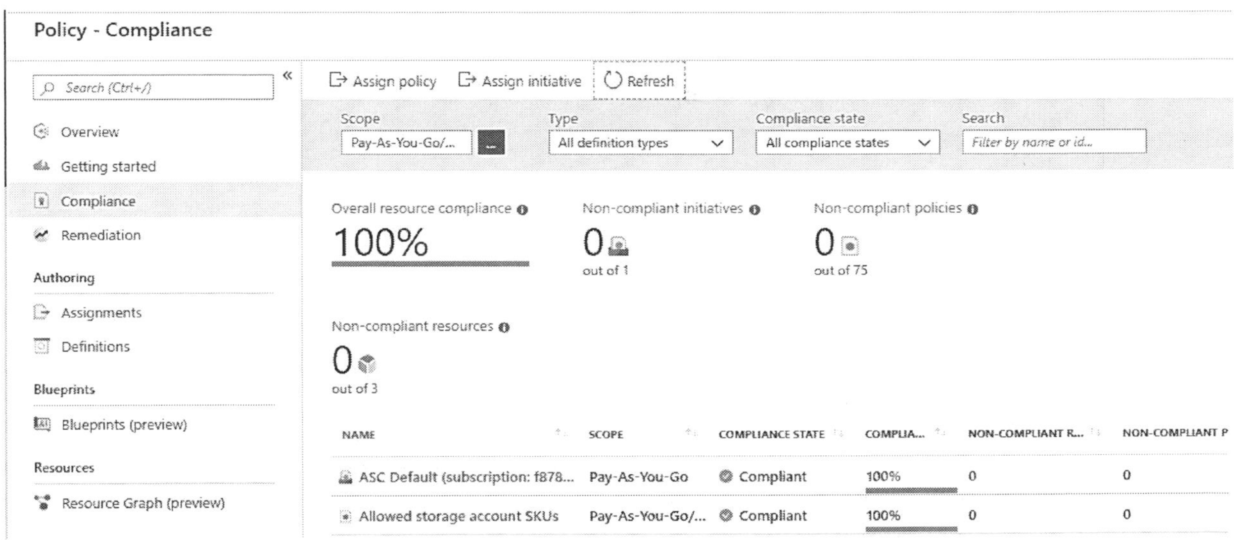

Exercise 169: Test the Allowed storage accounts SKU Policy

1. In Azure Portal click create a Resource>Storage> Storage Account>Create Storage Account Blade opens>Select Resource Group **HKTest**> Enter a name> Select Location East US 2> Make sure Replication is **LRS**.

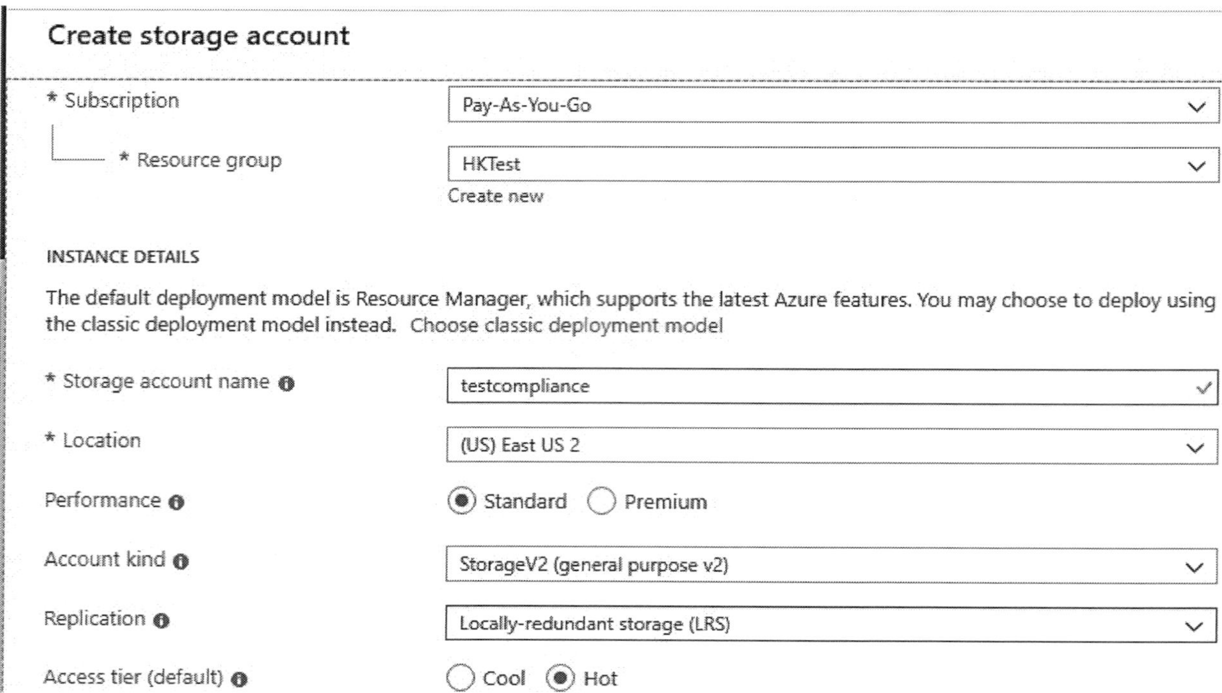

2. Click Review +Create (Not shown) in above screen>Validation fails because of Policy. Our Policy only allowed RA-GRS where as we were creating Storage Account with LRS Replication.

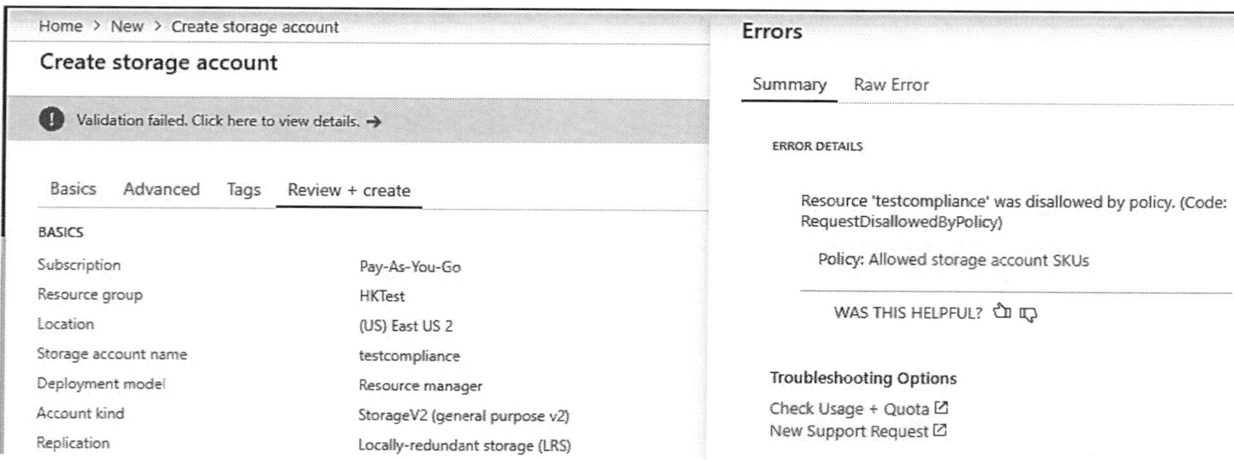

Moving Virtual Machines

You can move Azure VM to either a new subscription or a new resource group in the same subscription.

When moving resources, both the source group and the target group are locked during the operation. Write and delete operations are blocked on the resource groups until the move completes.

You can't change the location of the resource. Moving a resource only moves it to a new resource group. The new resource group may have a different location, but that doesn't change the location of the resource.

Requirement for moving resources

1. The source and destination subscriptions must exist within the same Azure Active Directory tenant.
2. The destination subscription must be registered for the resource provider of the resource being moved. If not, you receive an error stating that the **subscription is not registered for a resource type**. You might encounter this problem when moving a resource to a new subscription, but that subscription has never been used with that resource type.

Virtual Machines limitations

- You can move virtual machines with the managed disks, managed images, managed snapshots, and availability sets with virtual machines that use managed disks. Managed Disks in Availability Zones can't be moved to a different subscription.
- Virtual Machines with certificate stored in Key Vault can be moved to a new resource group in the same subscription, but not across subscriptions.
- Virtual Machine Scale Sets with Standard SKU Load Balancer or Standard SKU Public IP can't be moved.
- Virtual machines created from Marketplace resources with plans attached can't be moved across resource groups or subscriptions. Deprovision the virtual machine in the current subscription, and deploy again in the new subscription.

Exercise 170: Move resources to new resource group

In this exercise we will move Public IP DPIPCloud in Resource Group RGCloud to Resource Group HKTest. Public IP DPIPCloud was created Exercise 9, Chapter 1. **Similarly you can move VMs.**

To move resources go to the resource group with those resources, and then select the **Move** button.

1. Go to Resource Group RGCloud Dashboard>In Right pane Click Move> When You Click Move Button you get 2 options- Move to another Resource Group or Move to another Subscription.

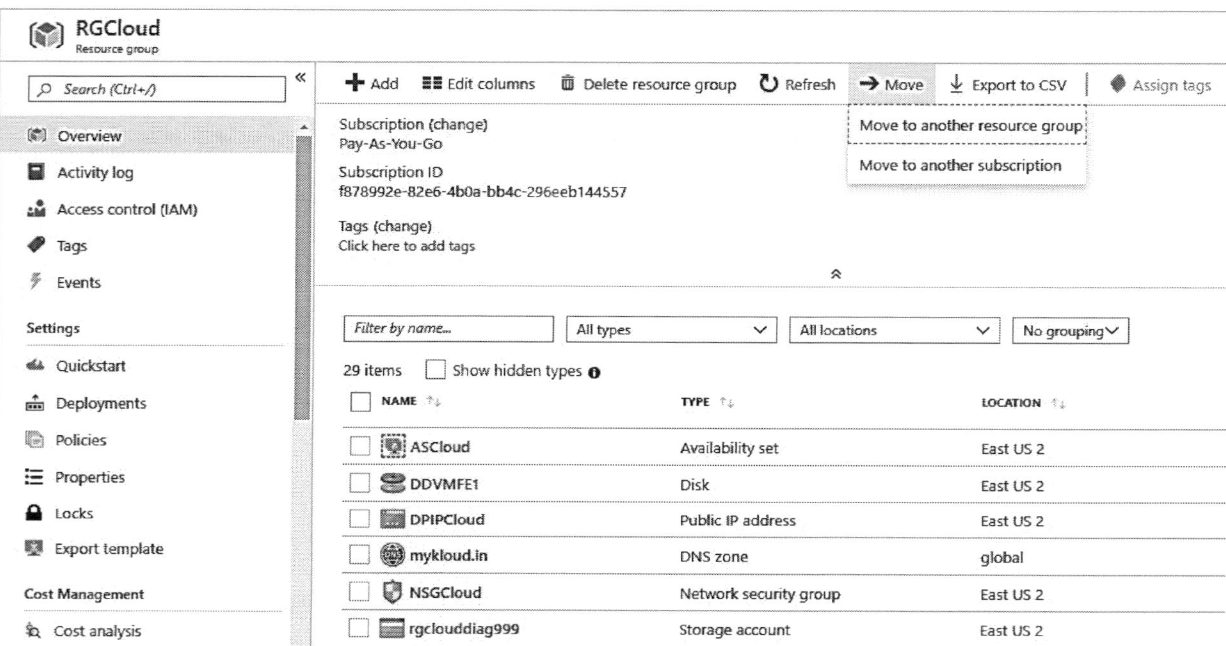

2. When You Click Move Button you get 2 options- Resource Groups or Subscription>Click Move to another Resource Group>Scroll down and Select Public IP DPIPCloud >Select Resource Group HKTest from dropdown box> Check Mark Terms & Conditions>Click OK.

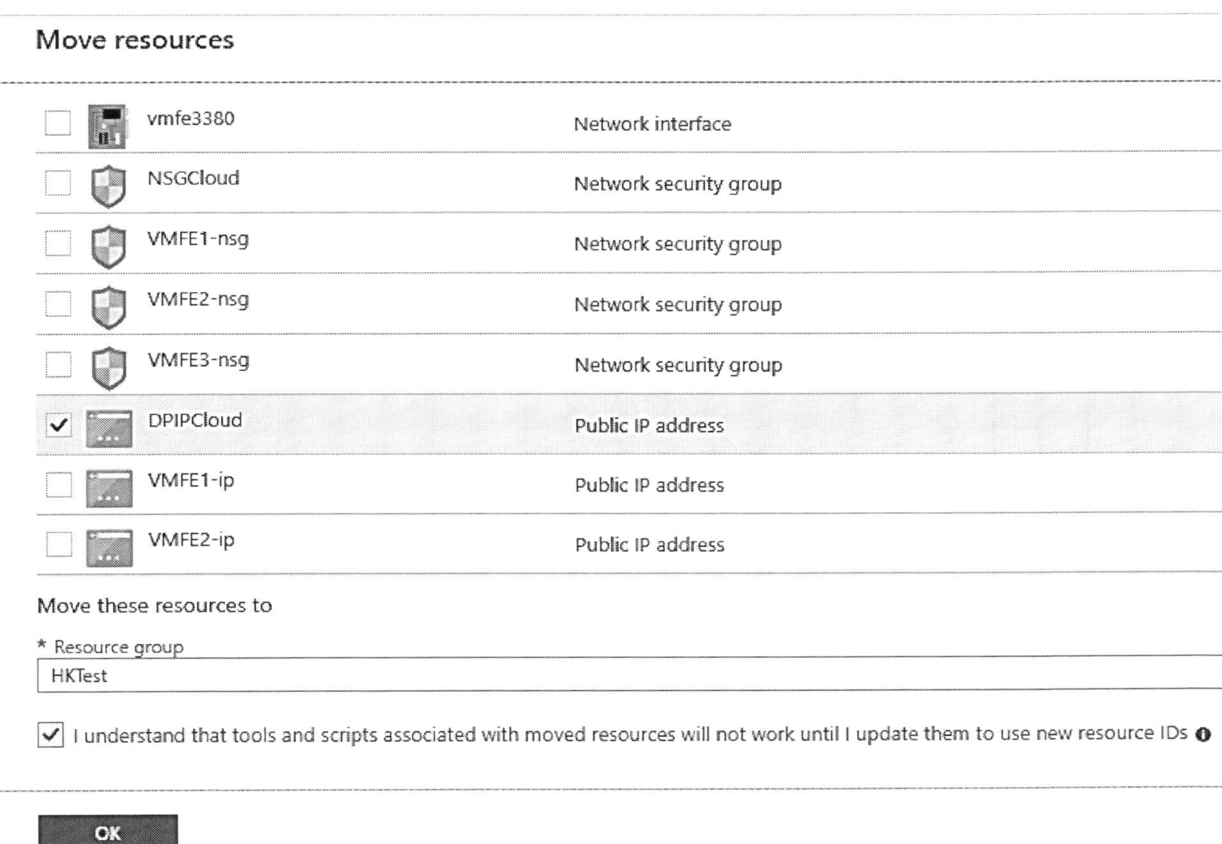

3. Go to Resource Group HKTest Dashboard>You can see Public DPIPCloud has moved from Resource Group RGCloud to Resource Group HKTest.

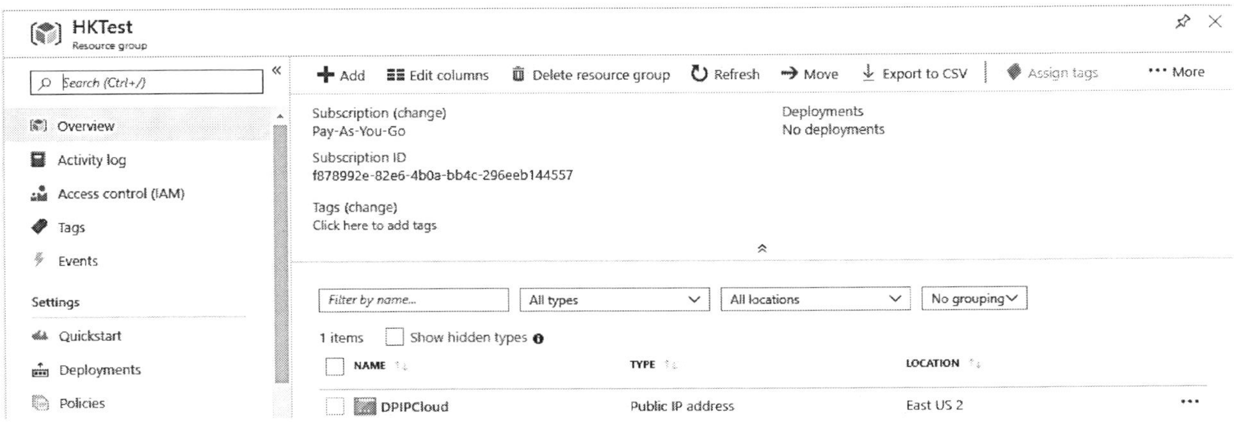

Tags

You can tag resource or resource group with name/value pairs to categorize and view resources across resource groups and across subscriptions. Using tags you can logically organize Azure resources by categories.

Each tag consists of a name and a value.

Tags enable you to retrieve related resources from different resource groups. This approach is helpful when you need to organize resources for billing or management.

Each resource or resource group can have a maximum of 15 tag name/value pairs. If you want to associate more than 15 values with a resource, use a JSON string for the tag value.

Exercise 171: Create Tag with name Mktg for VM VMFE1

Make sure that VMFE1 is running. In Azure Portal go to VM VMFE1 dashboard and click Tag in left pane>Add Tag opens in Right Pane> I entered **Mktg** in Name and **VM** in Value>Click Save.

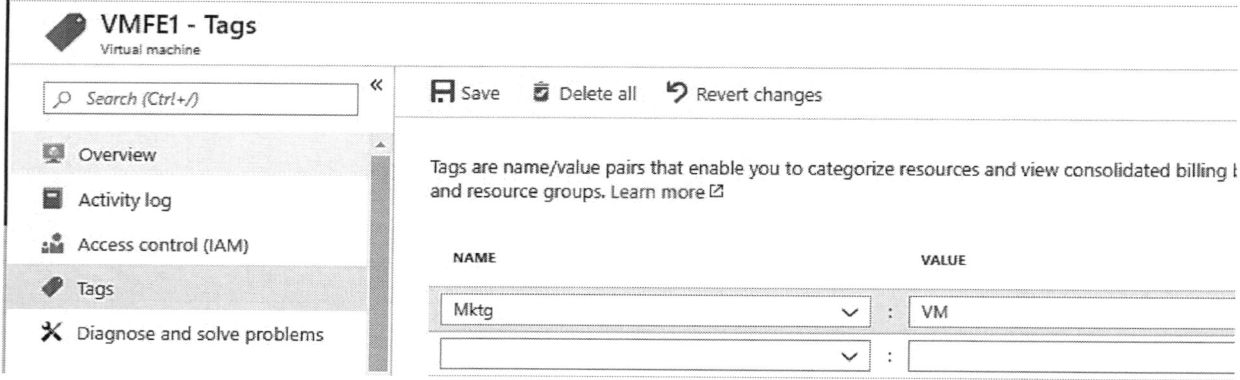

Note: VM VMFE1 was created in Exercise 25, Chapter 4.

Exercise 172: Create Tag with name Mktg for VM VMFE1 OS Disk

Go to VM VMFE1 Dashboard> In left pane Click Disks> In right pane Click VMFE1 OS Disk> OS Disk Pane opens>Click Tag in left pane>In Right pane in Name enter **Mktg** and Value Enter **OS**>Click Save.

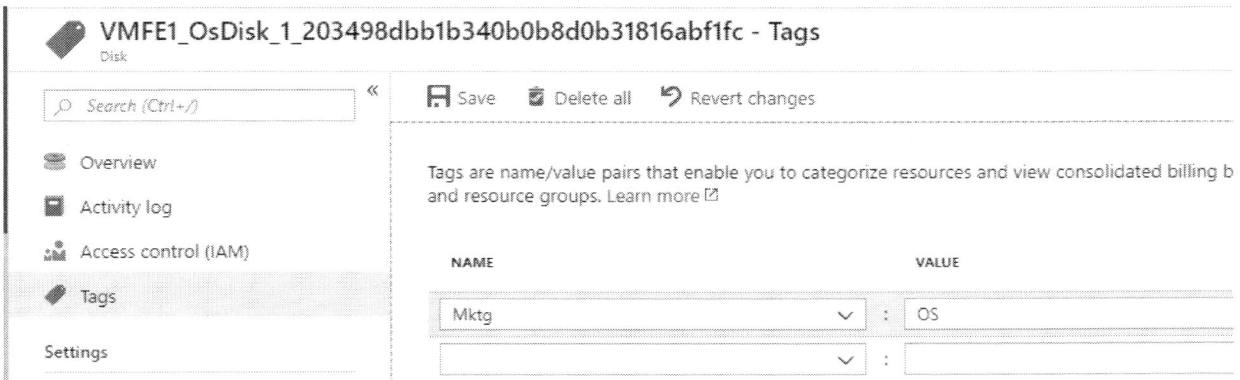

Exercise 173: Find Cost of Resources Associated with Mktg Tag

1. In Azure Portal go Cost Management dashboard>Click cost Analysis in left pane> In Right pane click **Add filter**>From Dropdown box select Tag>From Dropdown box select Mktg>From Dropdown box select os and vm> You can see total cost of VM VMFE1 and OS disk.

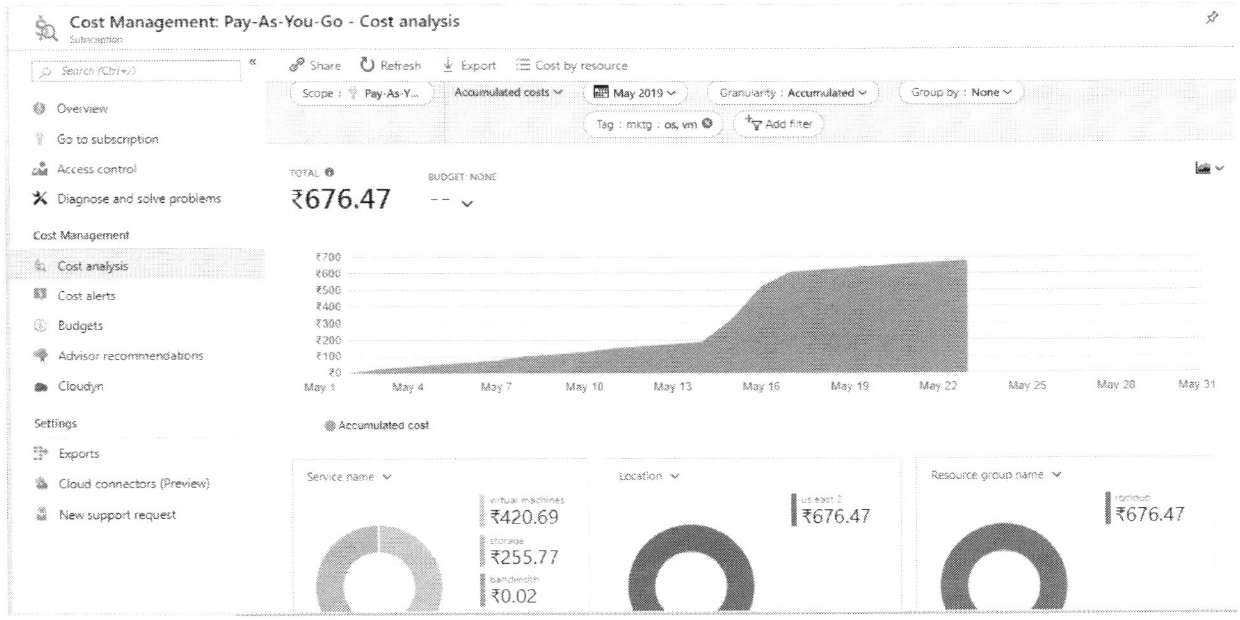

Locks

Locks are applied at subscription, resource group, or resource level to prevent users from accidentally deleting or modifying critical resources.

You can set the lock level to **CanNotDelete** or **ReadOnly**.

CanNotDelete means authorized users can still read and modify a resource, but they can't delete the resource.
ReadOnly means authorized users can read a resource, but they can't delete or update the resource.

When you apply a lock at a parent scope, all resources within that scope inherit the same lock.

Resource Manager Locks apply only to operations that happen in the management plane, which consists of operations sent to https://management.azure.com. The locks do not restrict how resources perform their own functions. Resource changes are restricted, but resource operations are not restricted.
For example a ReadOnly lock on a SQL Database prevents you from deleting or modifying the database but it does not prevent you from creating, updating or deleting data in the database. Data transactions are permitted because those operations are not sent to https://management.azure.com.

Exercise 174: Create CanNotDelete Lock on VM VMFE1

Go to VMFE1 dashboard>Click Lock in left pane>In right pane Click + Add> Add Lock blade opens>Enter a name and from dropdown box select Delete and optionally add description about lock>Click OK.

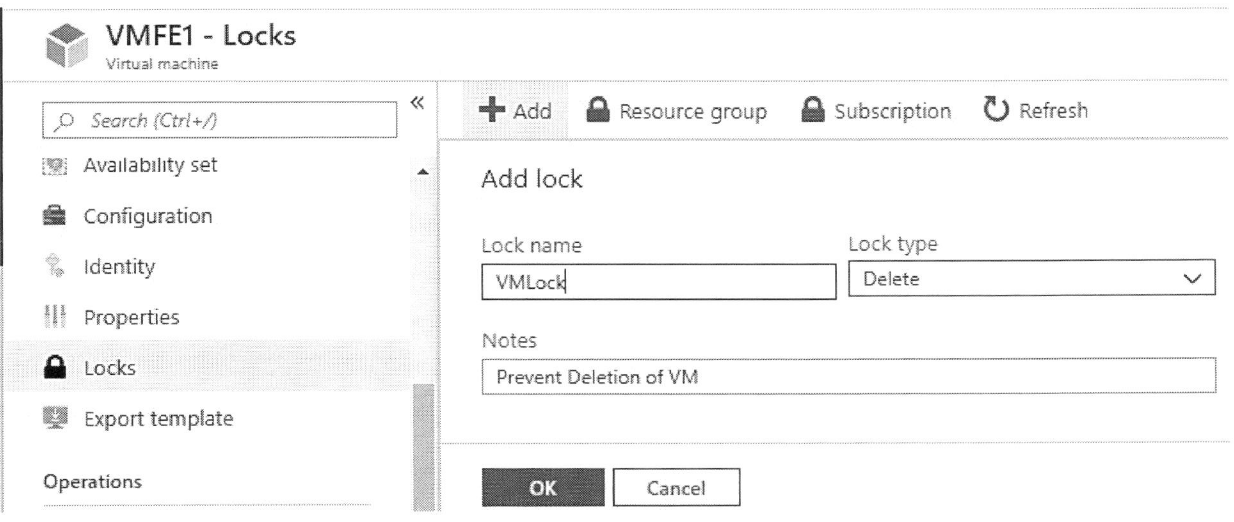

Exercise 175: Test the Lock

In VMFE1 dashboard Click overview in left pane>In Right pane Click Delete> Delete VM Box pops up>Click Yes> You get notification Failed to Delete the Virtual Machine.

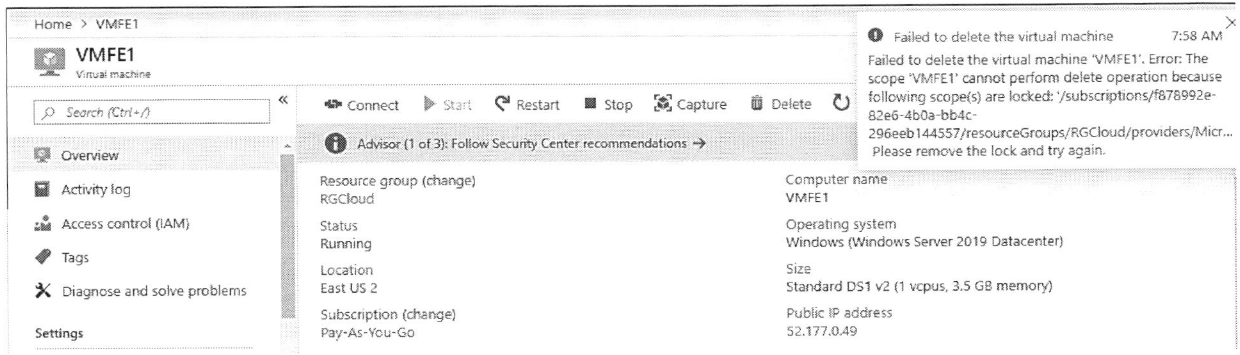

Note: VM VMFE1 was created in Exercise 25, Chapter 4.

Chapter 20 Azure Global Infrastructure

This Chapter covers following Topic Lessons

- Regions
- Geography
- Paired Regions

Azure Regions

A region is a set of datacenters (Availability Zones) deployed within a latency-defined perimeter and connected through a dedicated regional low-latency network. As of writing Microsoft has 50 Regions Worldwide.

Geography

A Geography typically contains two or more regions within the same country, that preserves data residency and compliance boundaries. There are exceptions such as some Regions with EU are considered as same geography.

Geographies allow customers with specific data-residency and compliance needs to keep their data and applications close. Geographies are fault-tolerant to withstand complete region failure through their connection to dedicated high-capacity networking infrastructure.

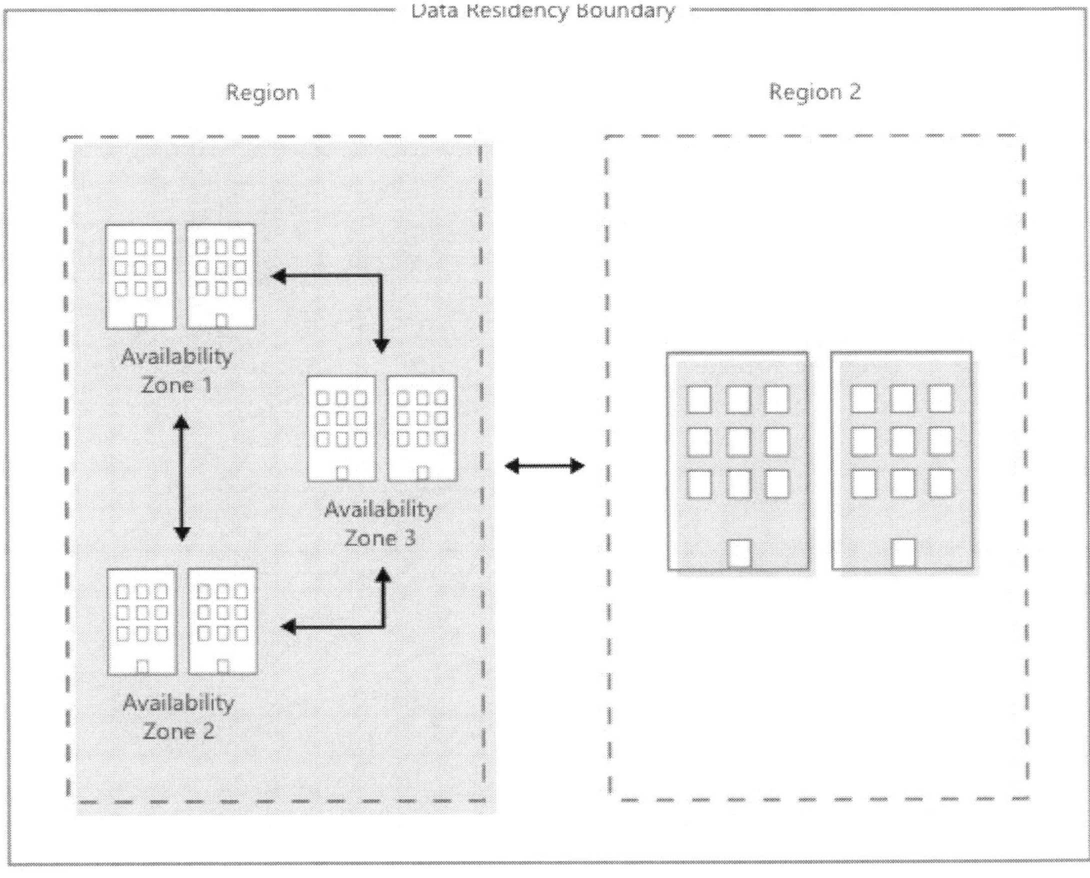

Paired Regions

Each Azure region is paired with another region within the same geography, together making a regional pair. The exception is Brazil South, which is paired with a region outside its geography.

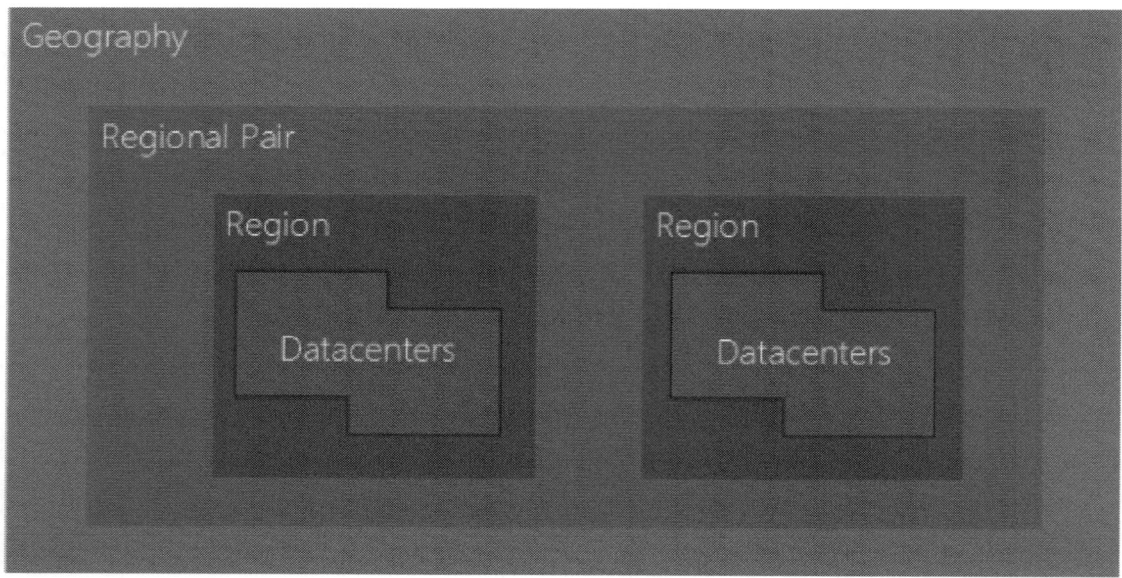

Microsoft recommends that you replicate workloads across regional pairs to benefit from Azure's isolation and availability policies. For example, planned Azure system updates are deployed sequentially (not at the same time) across paired regions. That means that even in the rare event of a faulty update, both regions will not be affected simultaneously. Furthermore, in the unlikely event of a broad outage, recovery of at least one region out of every pair is prioritized.

Table below shows some of the Azure Paired Regions.

Geography	Paired Region	Paired Region
North America	East US	West US
North America	East US 2	Central US
Canada	Canada Central	Canada East
Germany	Germany Central	Germany Northeast
India	Central India	South India
China	China North	China East
Japan	Japan East	Japan West
Korea	Korea Central	Korea South

Chapter 21 Installing Azure PowerShell Module & Azure CLI

This Chapter covers following Topic Lessons

- Azure PowerShell Module
- Azure CLI

This Chapter covers following Lab Exercises

- Install latest Version of PowerShellGet
- Install & Import Azure PowerShell Module
- Connecting to Azure using Azure PowerShell Module

Azure PowerShell

Azure PowerShell provides a set of cmdlets that use the Azure Resource Manager model for managing your Azure resources. You can use it in your browser with Azure Cloud Shell, or you can install it on your local machine and use it in any PowerShell session.

Exercise 176: Install latest Version of PowerShellGet

1. Open PowerShell in your Windows 10 Desktop and run following command.
2. Install-Module PowerShellGet -Force

```
PS C:\WINDOWS\system32> Install-Module PowerShellGet -Force

NuGet provider is required to continue
PowerShellGet requires NuGet provider version '2.8.5.201' or newer to interact with NuGet-based repositories. The NuGet
provider must be available in 'C:\Program
Files\PackageManagement\ProviderAssemblies' or 'C:\Users\Harinder Kohli\AppData\Local\PackageManagement\ProviderAssembli
es'. You can also install the NuGet provider by running
'Install-PackageProvider -Name NuGet -MinimumVersion 2.8.5.201 -Force'. Do you want PowerShellGet to install and import
the NuGet provider now?
[Y] Yes  [N] No  [S] Suspend  [?] Help (default is "Y"): y
PS C:\WINDOWS\system32>
```

3. Set the PowerShell execution policy to RemoteSigned.

```
Administrator: Windows PowerShell
Windows PowerShell
Copyright (C) Microsoft Corporation. All rights reserved.

PS C:\WINDOWS\system32> Set-ExecutionPolicy -ExecutionPolicy RemoteSigned

Execution Policy Change
The execution policy helps protect you from scripts that you do not trust. Changing the execution policy might expose
you to the security risks described in the about_Execution_Policies help topic at
https:/go.microsoft.com/fwlink/?LinkID=135170. Do you want to change the execution policy?
[Y] Yes  [A] Yes to All  [N] No  [L] No to All  [S] Suspend  [?] Help (default is "N"): y
PS C:\WINDOWS\system32>
```

Exercise 177: Install & Import Azure PowerShell Module

1. Install-Module -Name AzureRM –AllowClobber
2. Import-Module -Name AzureRM

```
PS C:\WINDOWS\system32> Install-Module -Name AzureRM -AllowClobber

Untrusted repository
You are installing the modules from an untrusted repository. If you trust this repository, cha
nge its
InstallationPolicy value by running the Set-PSRepository cmdlet. Are you sure you want to inst
all the modules from
'PSGallery'?
[Y] Yes  [A] Yes to All  [N] No  [L] No to All  [S] Suspend  [?] Help (default is "N"): y
PS C:\WINDOWS\system32> Import-Module -Name AzureRM
PS C:\WINDOWS\system32>
```

Exercise 178: Connecting to Azure using Azure PowerShell Module

1. On your desktop open Windows PowerShell App. Just type Powershell in search box and you can see Windows PowerShell App.
2. Connect-AzureRmAccount
3. This will open a browser for connecting to Azure. Enter Subscription username and password for connecting to Azure.

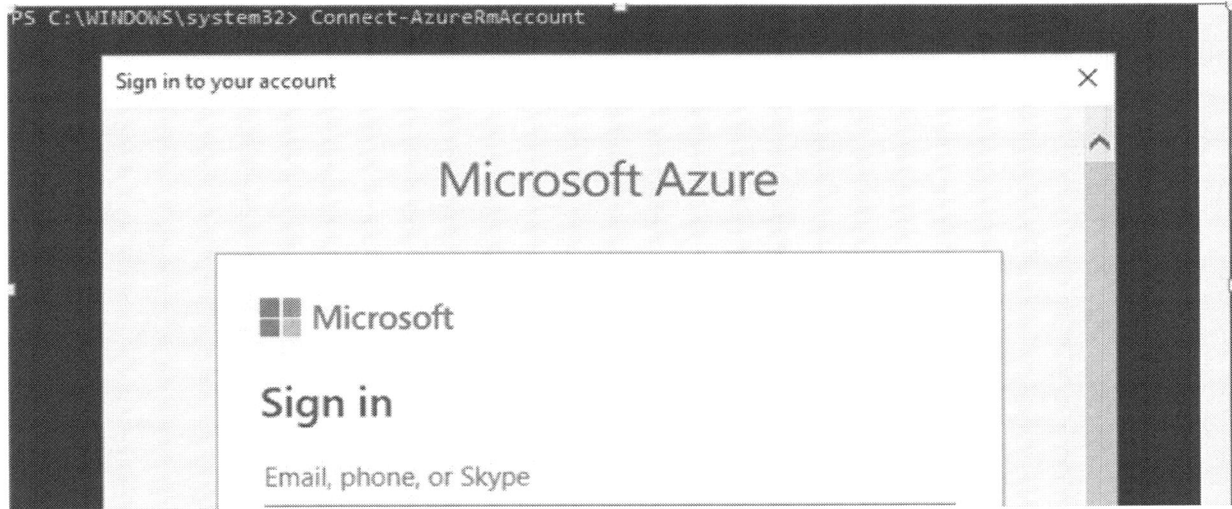

4. After you have successfully authenticated to Azure through Browser, The Powershell window will now show Azure information as shown below.

```
PS C:\WINDOWS\system32> Connect-AzureRmAccount


Account          : harinderkohli@hotmail.com
SubscriptionName : Pay-As-You-Go
SubscriptionId   : d293caf2-261c-4101-848a-c7e69524dc3a
TenantId         : 37f410dd-05ca-42c2-997a-24223270b9aa
Environment      : AzureCloud
```

5. You can also confirm above by running following command.
   Get-AzureRmSubscription

```
PS C:\WINDOWS\system32> Get-AzureRmSubscription


Name     : Pay-As-You-Go
Id       : d293caf2-261c-4101-848a-c7e69524dc3a
TenantId : 37f410dd-05ca-42c2-997a-24223270b9aa
State    : Enabled
```

Azure CLI

The Azure CLI is a command-line tool for managing Azure resources. The CLI is designed to make scripting easy, query data and support long-running operations. Azure CLI is installed via an MSI.

Note: You have the option of using Azure CLI Cloud Shell in Azure Portal instead of installing Azure CLI on Windows Machine.

Exercise 179: Install Azure CLI on Windows Machine

Download and Install Azure CLI MSI Installer
https://aka.ms/installazurecliwindows

Accessing Azure CLI
You can access Azure CLI through the Windows Command Prompt (CMD).

Exercise 180: Login to Azure with CLI

1. Open windows CMD> az login. This will open a browser. Enter your azure subscription Username and password credentials.

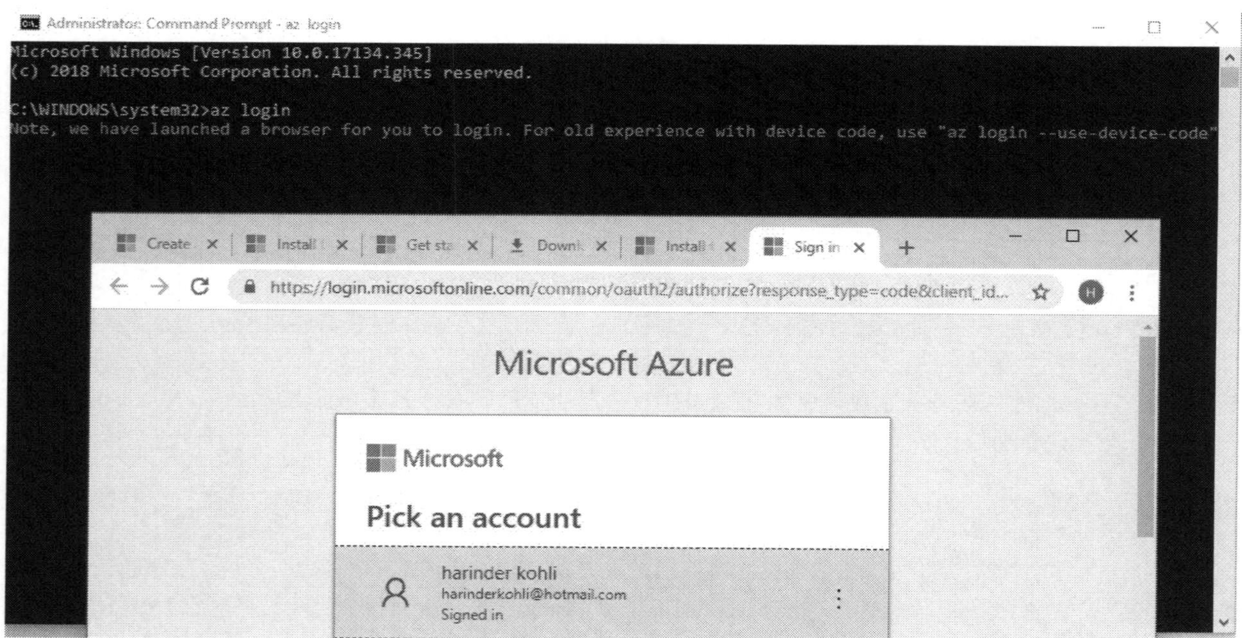

2. After you have successfully authenticated to Azure through Browser, The CMD window will now show Azure information as shown below.

```
Administrator: Command Prompt
Microsoft Windows [Version 10.0.17134.345]
(c) 2018 Microsoft Corporation. All rights reserved.

C:\WINDOWS\system32>az login
Note, we have launched a browser for you to login. For old experience with device code, use "az login --use-device-code"

You have logged in. Now let us find all the subscriptions to which you have access...
[
  {
    "cloudName": "AzureCloud",
    "id": "d293caf2-261c-4101-848a-c7e69524dc3a",
    "isDefault": true,
    "name": "Pay-As-You-Go",
    "state": "Enabled",
    "tenantId": "37f410dd-05ca-42c2-997a-24223270b9aa",
    "user": {
      "name": "harinderkohli@hotmail.com",
      "type": "user"
    }
  }
]

C:\WINDOWS\system32>
```

Chapter 22 Implementing Virtual Networks with CLI & PS

This Chapter covers following Lab Exercises

- Create Resource Group HKCLI using Azure CLI
- Create Resource Group HKPS using Azure PowerShell
- Create Virtual Network VNETCLI using Azure CLI
- Create Virtual Network VNETPS using Azure PowerShell

Exercise 181: Create Resource Group HKCLI using Azure CLI

You can either use Azure CLI on your desktop or use Cloud shell. For this lab use Azure CLI installed on our desktop. See Chapter 21 on how to use Azure CLI.

1. Open windows CMD on your desktop where Azure CLI is installed>Enter Command **az login**> This will open a browser. Select Account and Enter subscription credentials.

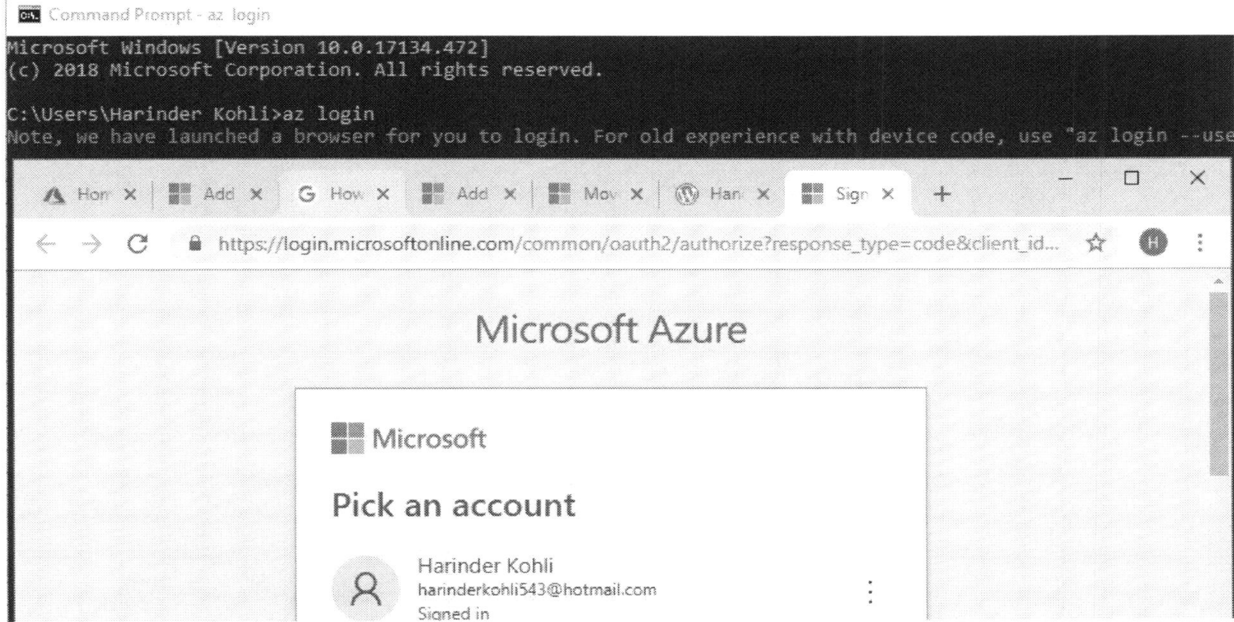

2. After you have successfully authenticated to Azure through Browser, The CMD window will now show Azure login information as shown below.

```
Command Prompt
Microsoft Windows [Version 10.0.17134.472]
(c) 2018 Microsoft Corporation. All rights reserved.

C:\Users\Harinder Kohli>az login
Note, we have launched a browser for you to login. For old experience with device co

You have logged in. Now let us find all the subscriptions to which you have access..
[
  {
    "cloudName": "AzureCloud",
    "id": "36576bd3-7ce6-4899-9bbd-bef9ced4f832",
    "isDefault": true,
    "name": "Free Trial",
```

Create Resource Group using az group command

az group create --name HKCLI –-location eastus2

```
Command Prompt

C:\Users\Harinder Kohli>az group create --name HKCLI --location eastus2
{
  "id": "/subscriptions/36576bd3-7ce6-4899-9bbd-bef9ced4f832/resourceGroups/HKCLI",
  "location": "eastus2",
  "managedBy": null,
  "name": "HKCLI",
  "properties": {
    "provisioningState": "Succeeded"
  },
  "tags": null
}

C:\Users\Harinder Kohli>
```

Check the Resource Group created

az group show –-name HKCLI or

az group show –-resource-group HKCLI

```
Command Prompt

C:\Users\Harinder Kohli>az group show --name HKCLI
{
  "id": "/subscriptions/36576bd3-7ce6-4899-9bbd-bef9ced4f832/resourceGroups/HKCLI",
  "location": "eastus2",
  "managedBy": null,
  "name": "HKCLI",
  "properties": {
    "provisioningState": "Succeeded"
  },
  "tags": null
}

C:\Users\Harinder Kohli>
```

Deleting Resource Group

az group delete –-name HKCLI –-yes

Note: Don't run above command as we need to create resources in the group.

Exercise 182: Create Resource Group HKPS using Azure PowerShell

Note: you can either install and use Azure PowerShell Module on your desktop or use Cloud shell. Refer to chapter 21 for Installing and using Azure PowerShell.

Open PowerShell on your desktop and login using Connect-AzureRmAccount.

```
PS C:\Users\Harinder Kohli> Connect-AzureRmAccount


Account          : harinderkohli543@outlook.com
SubscriptionName : Pay-As-You-Go
SubscriptionId   : 7593a7e7-0d4e-493a-922e-c433ef24df3b
TenantId         : 9dc252df-4ca2-40e7-9f9c-e2d717846ca4
Environment      : AzureCloud
```

Create Resource Group

New-AzureRmResourceGroup –Name HKPS –Location eastus2

```
PS C:\Users\Harinder Kohli> New-AzureRmResourceGroup -Name HKPS -Location eastus2

Confirm
Provided resource group already exists. Are you sure you want to update it?
[Y] Yes  [N] No  [S] Suspend  [?] Help (default is "Y"): Y


ResourceGroupName : HKPS
Location          : eastus2
ProvisioningState : Succeeded
Tags              :
ResourceId        : /subscriptions/7593a7e7-0d4e-493a-922e-c433ef24df3b/resourceGroups/HKPS
```

Check the Resource Group HKPS created

Get-AzureRMResourceGroup

Get-AzureRmResourceGroup –Name HKPS

```
PS C:\Users\Harinder Kohli> Get-AzureRmResourceGroup -Name HKPS


ResourceGroupName : HKPS
Location          : eastus2
ProvisioningState : Succeeded
Tags              :
ResourceId        : /subscriptions/7593a7e7-0d4e-493a-922e-c433ef24df3b/resourceGroups/HKPS
```

Deleting Resource Group

Remove-AzureRmResourceGroup –Name HKPS –Force

Note: Don't run above command as we need to create resources in the group.

Exercise 183: Create Virtual Network VNETCLI using Azure CLI

In this exercise we will create Virtual Network "VNETCLI" in Resource Group HKCLI using 10.2.0.0/16 address space in East US 2 Location. We will also create Subnet with name Web-Subnet with address 10.2.1.0/24.

Open cmd and enter **az login** command for Authenticating to Subscription.

Create Virtual Network using az network vnet command
az network vnet create --name VNETCLI --address-prefix 10.2.0.0/16 --resource-group HKCLI --subnet-name Web-Subnet --address-prefix 10.2.1.0/24

```
Command Prompt
C:\Users\Harinder Kohli>az network vnet create --name VNETCLI --address-prefix 10.2.0.0/16
--resource-group HKCLI --subnet-name Web-Subnet --address-prefix 10.2.1.0/24
{
  "newVNet": {
    "addressSpace": {
      "addressPrefixes": [
        "10.2.1.0/24"
      ]
    },
    "ddosProtectionPlan": null,
    "dhcpOptions": {
      "dnsServers": []
```

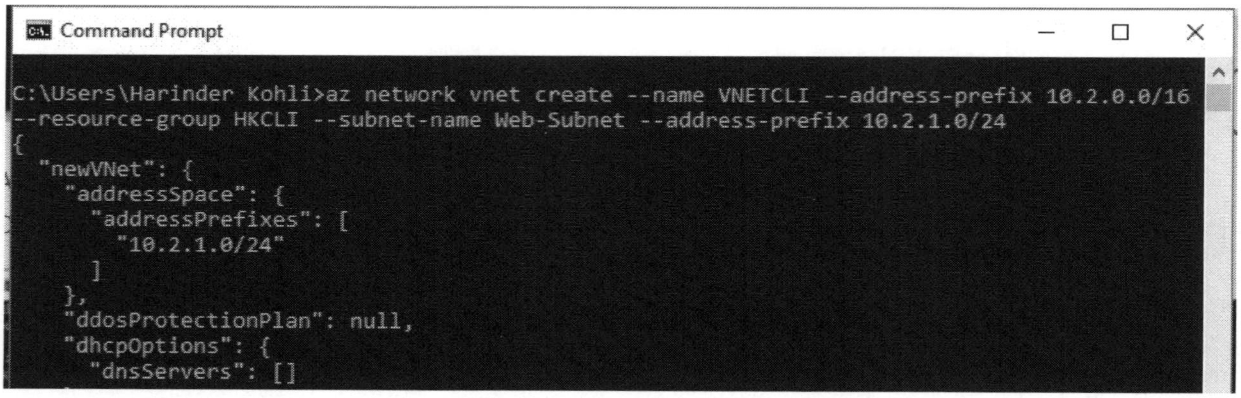

Check the Virtual Network created
az network vnet show --name VNETCLI --resource-group HKCLI

```
Command Prompt
C:\Users\Harinder Kohli>az network vnet show --name VNETCLI --resource-group HKCLI
{
  "addressSpace": {
    "addressPrefixes": [
      "10.2.1.0/24"
    ]
  },
  "ddosProtectionPlan": null,
  "dhcpOptions": {
    "dnsServers": []
```

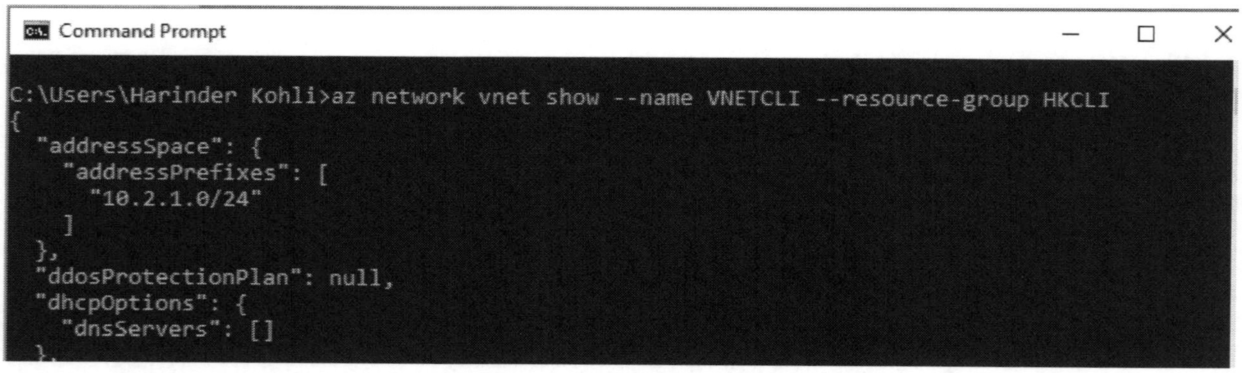

Delete Virtual Network
az network vnet delete --name VNETCLI --resource-group HKCLI
Note: Don't run above command as we need to create resources in the VNET.

Exercise 184: Create Virtual Network VNETPS using Azure PowerShell

In this exercise we will create Virtual Network "VNETPS" in Resource Group HKPS using 10.3.0.0/16 address space in East US 2 Location. We will also create Subnet with name Web-Subnet with address 10.3.1.0/24.

Open PowerShell on your desktop and login using Connect-AzureRmAccount.

Create Subnet name Web-Subnet

$subnet = New-AzureRmVirtualNetworkSubnetConfig –Name Web-Subnet -AddressPrefix 10.3.1.0/24

Create Virtual Network

New-AzureRmVirtualNetwork –Name VNETPS –ResourceGroupName HKPS –Location eastus2 –AddressPrefix 10.3.0.0/16 –Subnet $subnet

```
PS C:\Users\Harinder Kohli> New-AzureRmVirtualNetwork -Name VNETPS -ResourceGroupName HKPS -Location eastus2
-AddressPrefix 10.3.0.0/16 -Subnet $subnet
WARNING: Breaking changes in the cmdlet 'New-AzureRmVirtualNetwork' :
WARNING:  - "The output type 'Microsoft.Azure.Commands.Network.Models.PSVirtualNetwork' is changing"
 - The following properties in the output type are being deprecated :
 'EnableVmProtection'


Confirm
Are you sure you want to overwrite resource 'VNETPS'
[Y] Yes  [N] No  [S] Suspend  [?] Help (default is "Y"): Y

ResourceGroupName Name   Location ProvisioningState EnableDdosProtection EnableVmProtection
----------------- ----   -------- ----------------- -------------------- ------------------
HKPS              VNETPS eastus2  Succeeded         False                False
```

Check the Virtual Network created

Get-AzureRmVirtualNetwork –Name VNETPS –ResourceGroupName HKPS

```
PS C:\Users\Harinder Kohli> Get-AzureRmVirtualNetwork -Name VNETPS -ResourceGroupName HKPS
WARNING: Breaking changes in the cmdlet 'Get-AzureRmVirtualNetwork' :
WARNING:  - "The output type 'Microsoft.Azure.Commands.Network.Models.PSVirtualNetwork' is changing"
 - The following properties in the output type are being deprecated :
 'EnableVmProtection'


ResourceGroupName Name   Location ProvisioningState EnableDdosProtection EnableVmProtection
----------------- ----   -------- ----------------- -------------------- ------------------
HKPS              VNETPS eastus2  Succeeded         False                False
```

Delete Virtual Network

Remove-AzureRmVirtualNetwork –Name VNETPS –ResourceGroupName HKPS

Note: Don't run above command as we need to create resources in the VNET.

Chapter 23 Deploy Virtual Machines with CLI and PS

This Chapter covers following Lab Exercises

- Create Windows Server 2016 VM using Azure CLI
- Create Windows Server 2016 VM using Azure PowerShell

Exercise 185: Create Windows Server 2016 VM using Azure CLI

In this lab we will create Windows Server 2016 VM in Resource Group HKCLI and Subnet Web-Subnet in Virtual Network VNETCLI. HKCLI Resource Group was created in Exercise181 and Virtual Network VNETCLI was created in Exercise 183 in Previous Chapter.

Get the URNAlias name of the image
az vm image list

Above command is not shown in below diagram as I scrolled to locate the Windows Server 2016 image. You can see urnAlias name is **Win2016Datacenter**

Command Prompt

```
  {
    "offer": "WindowsServer",
    "publisher": "MicrosoftWindowsServer",
    "sku": "2019-Datacenter",
    "urn": "MicrosoftWindowsServer:WindowsServer:2019-Datacenter:latest",
    "urnAlias": "Win2019Datacenter",
    "version": "latest"
  },
  {
    "offer": "WindowsServer",
    "publisher": "MicrosoftWindowsServer",
    "sku": "2016-Datacenter",
    "urn": "MicrosoftWindowsServer:WindowsServer:2016-Datacenter:latest",
    "urnAlias": "Win2016Datacenter",
    "version": "latest"
  },
```

Get the name of VM Size
az vm list-sizes –location eastus2

```
C:\Users\Harinder Kohli>az vm list-sizes --location eastus2
[
  {
    "maxDataDiskCount": 1,
    "memoryInMb": 768,
    "name": "Standard_A0",
    "numberOfCores": 1,
    "osDiskSizeInMb": 1047552,
    "resourceDiskSizeInMb": 20480
```

For this lab I selected size **Standard_D2_v2** (You need to scroll down to see it).

Create Virtual Machine using az vm command

az vm create --name VMCLI --vnet-name VNETCLI --subnet Web-Subnet --resource-group HKCLI --image Win2016Datacenter --size Standard_D2_v2 --admin-username AdminAccount --admin-password Aadmin@12345

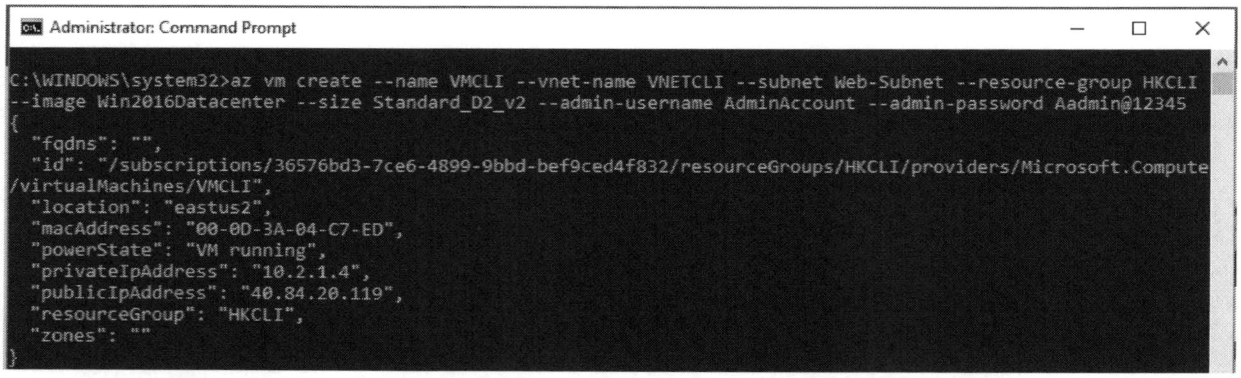

```
Administrator: Command Prompt

C:\WINDOWS\system32>az vm create --name VMCLI --vnet-name VNETCLI --subnet Web-Subnet --resource-group HKCLI
--image Win2016Datacenter --size Standard_D2_v2 --admin-username AdminAccount --admin-password Aadmin@12345
{
  "fqdns": "",
  "id": "/subscriptions/36576bd3-7ce6-4899-9bbd-bef9ced4f832/resourceGroups/HKCLI/providers/Microsoft.Compute
/virtualMachines/VMCLI",
  "location": "eastus2",
  "macAddress": "00-0D-3A-04-C7-ED",
  "powerState": "VM running",
  "privateIpAddress": "10.2.1.4",
  "publicIpAddress": "40.84.20.119",
  "resourceGroup": "HKCLI",
  "zones": ""
}
```

Check the Virtual Machine created

az vm show --name VMCLI --resource-group HKCLI

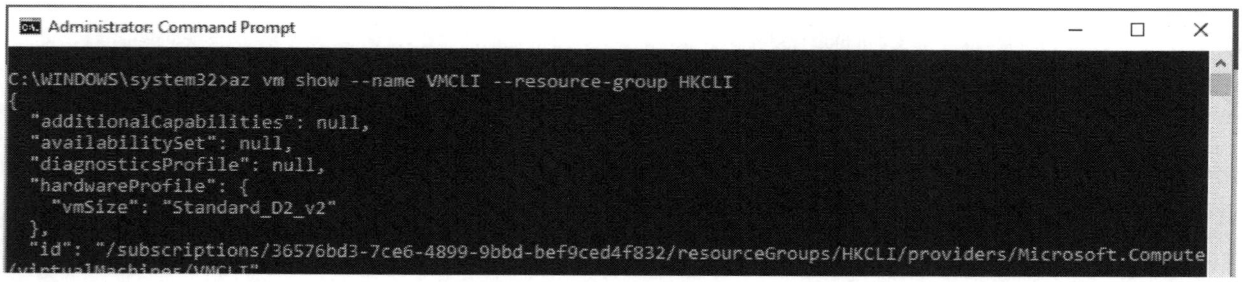

```
Administrator: Command Prompt

C:\WINDOWS\system32>az vm show --name VMCLI --resource-group HKCLI
{
  "additionalCapabilities": null,
  "availabilitySet": null,
  "diagnosticsProfile": null,
  "hardwareProfile": {
    "vmSize": "Standard_D2_v2"
  },
  "id": "/subscriptions/36576bd3-7ce6-4899-9bbd-bef9ced4f832/resourceGroups/HKCLI/providers/Microsoft.Compute
```

Delete Virtual Machine

az vm delete --name VMCLI --resource-group HKCLI

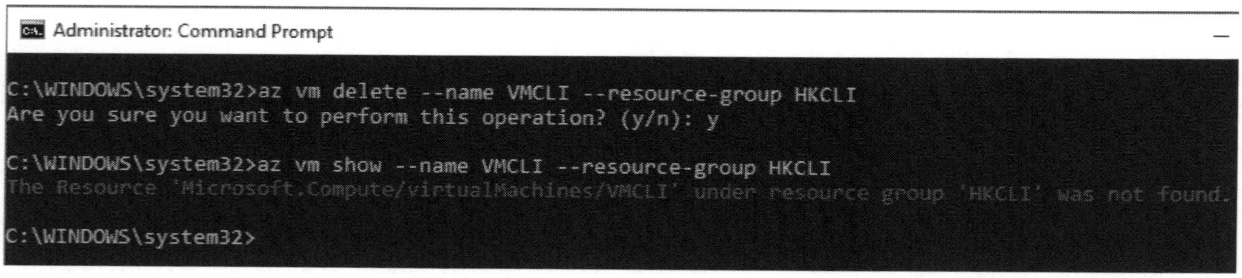

```
Administrator: Command Prompt

C:\WINDOWS\system32>az vm delete --name VMCLI --resource-group HKCLI
Are you sure you want to perform this operation? (y/n): y

C:\WINDOWS\system32>az vm show --name VMCLI --resource-group HKCLI
The Resource 'Microsoft.Compute/virtualMachines/VMCLI' under resource group 'HKCLI' was not found.

C:\WINDOWS\system32>
```

Note 1: I checked up if VM is deleted or not by using **az vm show** command.
Note 2: Make sure to delete the VM otherwise it will incur charges.

Checking VM in Portal

Go VM VMCLI Dashboard>You can see it was created in Virtual Network VNETCLI. The size is Standard D2 v2.

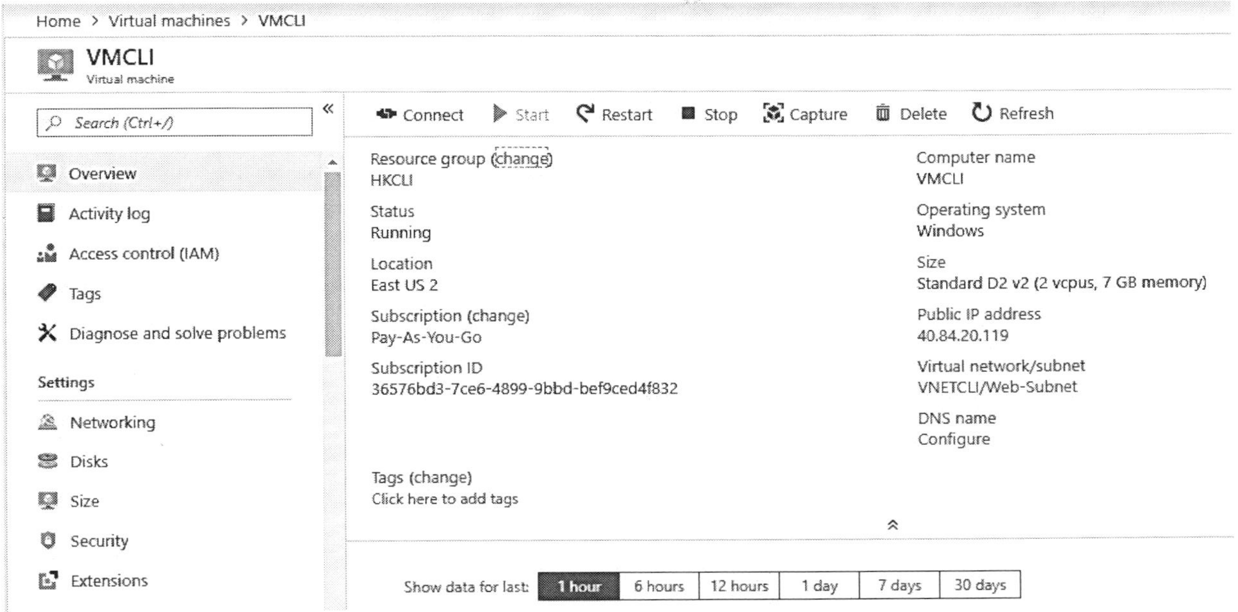

Exercise 186: Create Windows Server 2016 VM using Azure PowerShell

In this lab we will create Windows Server 2016 VM in Resource Group HKPS and Virtual Network VNETPS. HKPS Resource Group was created in Exercise 182 and Virtual Network VNETPS was created in Exercise 184 In previous Chapter.

Get the SKU, Offer & Publisher Name of the image

Get-AzureRmVMImageSku -Location EastUS2 -PublisherName MicrosoftWindowsServer -Offer WindowsServer

```
PS C:\Users\Harinder Kohli> Get-AzureRmVMImageSku -Location EastUS2 -PublisherName MicrosoftWindowsServer -Offer WindowsServer

Skus                                         Offer         PublisherName          Location Id
----                                         -----         -------------          -------- --
2008-R2-SP1                                  WindowsServer MicrosoftWindowsServer eastus2  /Subscriptio...
2008-R2-SP1-smalldisk                        WindowsServer MicrosoftWindowsServer eastus2  /Subscriptio...
2008-R2-SP1-zhcn                             WindowsServer MicrosoftWindowsServer eastus2  /Subscriptio...
2012-Datacenter                              WindowsServer MicrosoftWindowsServer eastus2  /Subscriptio...
2012-Datacenter-smalldisk                    WindowsServer MicrosoftWindowsServer eastus2  /Subscriptio...
2012-Datacenter-zhcn                         WindowsServer MicrosoftWindowsServer eastus2  /Subscriptio...
2012-R2-Datacenter                           WindowsServer MicrosoftWindowsServer eastus2  /Subscriptio...
2012-R2-Datacenter-smalldisk                 WindowsServer MicrosoftWindowsServer eastus2  /Subscriptio...
2012-R2-Datacenter-zhcn                      WindowsServer MicrosoftWindowsServer eastus2  /Subscriptio...
2016-Datacenter                              WindowsServer MicrosoftWindowsServer eastus2  /Subscriptio...
2016-Datacenter-Server-Core                  WindowsServer MicrosoftWindowsServer eastus2  /Subscriptio...
2016-Datacenter-Server-Core-smalldisk        WindowsServer MicrosoftWindowsServer eastus2  /Subscriptio...
2016-Datacenter-smalldisk                    WindowsServer MicrosoftWindowsServer eastus2  /Subscriptio...
2016-Datacenter-with-Containers              WindowsServer MicrosoftWindowsServer eastus2  /Subscriptio...
2016-Datacenter-with-RDSH                    WindowsServer MicrosoftWindowsServer eastus2  /Subscriptio...
2016-Datacenter-zhcn                         WindowsServer MicrosoftWindowsServer eastus2  /Subscriptio...
2019-Datacenter                              WindowsServer MicrosoftWindowsServer eastus2  /Subscriptio...
2019-Datacenter-Core                         WindowsServer MicrosoftWindowsServer eastus2  /Subscriptio...
2019-Datacenter-Core-smalldisk               WindowsServer MicrosoftWindowsServer eastus2  /Subscriptio...
2019-Datacenter-Core-with-Containers         WindowsServer MicrosoftWindowsServer eastus2  /Subscriptio...
2019-Datacenter-Core-with-Containers-smalldisk WindowsServer MicrosoftWindowsServer eastus2  /Subscriptio...
2019-Datacenter-smalldisk                    WindowsServer MicrosoftWindowsServer eastus2  /Subscriptio...
2019-Datacenter-with-Containers              WindowsServer MicrosoftWindowsServer eastus2  /Subscriptio...
2019-Datacenter-with-Containers-smalldisk    WindowsServer MicrosoftWindowsServer eastus2  /Subscriptio...
2019-Datacenter-zhcn                         WindowsServer MicrosoftWindowsServer eastus2  /Subscriptio...
```

Get the name of VM Size

Get-AzureRmVMSize -Location EastUS2

```
PS C:\Users\Harinder Kohli> Get-AzureRmVMSize -Location EastUS2

Name             NumberOfCores MemoryInMB MaxDataDiskCount OSDiskSizeInMB ResourceDiskSizeInMB
----             ------------- ---------- ---------------- -------------- --------------------
Standard_A0                  1        768                1        1047552                20480
Standard_A1                  1       1792                2        1047552                71680
Standard_A2                  2       3584                4        1047552               138240
Standard_A3                  4       7168                8        1047552               291840
Standard_A5                  2      14336                4        1047552               138240
Standard_A4                  8      14336               16        1047552               619520
Standard_A6                  4      28672                8        1047552               291840
Standard_A7                  8      57344               16        1047552               619520
Basic_A0                     1        768                1        1047552                20480
Basic_A1                     1       1792                2        1047552                40960
Basic_A2                     2       3584                4        1047552                61440
Basic_A3                     4       7168                8        1047552               122880
Basic_A4                     8      14336               16        1047552               245760
Standard_D1_v2               1       3584                4        1047552                51200
Standard_D2_v2               2       7168                8        1047552               102400
```

Create Virtual Machine

New-AzureRmVm -ResourceGroupName HKPS -Name VMPS -Location EastUS2 -VirtualNetworkName VNETPS -SubnetName Web-Subnet –ImageName MicrosoftWindowsServer:WindowsServer:2016-Datacenter:Latest

```
PS C:\Users\Harinder Kohli> New-AzureRmVm -ResourceGroupName HKPS -Name VMPS -Location EastUS2 -VirtualNetworkName
 VNETPS -SubnetName Web-Subnet -ImageName MicrosoftWindowsServer:WindowsServer:2016-Datacenter:Latest

cmdlet New-AzureRmVM at command pipeline position 1
Supply values for the following parameters:
Credential


ResourceGroupName        : HKPS
Id                       : /subscriptions/7593a7e7-0d4e-493a-922e-c433ef24df3b/resourceGroups/HKPS/providers/Micro
soft.Compute/virtualMachines/VMPS
VmId                     : c2fd537f-c8eb-4542-8b0c-4cd54e65749b
Name                     : VMPS
Type                     : Microsoft.Compute/virtualMachines
Location                 : eastus2
Tags                     : {}
HardwareProfile          : {VmSize}
NetworkProfile           : {NetworkInterfaces}
OSProfile                : {ComputerName, AdminUsername, WindowsConfiguration, Secrets, AllowExtensionOperations}
ProvisioningState        : Succeeded
StorageProfile           : {ImageReference, OsDisk, DataDisks}
FullyQualifiedDomainName : vmps-6bbd13.EastUS2.cloudapp.azure.com
```

Check the Virtual Machine created

Get-AzureRmVm –Name VMPS –ResourceGroupName HKPS

```
PS C:\Users\Harinder Kohli> Get-AzureRmVm -Name VMPS -ResourceGroupName HKPS
PS C:\Users\Harinder Kohli>

ResourceGroupName : HKPS
Id                : /subscriptions/7593a7e7-0d4e-493a-922e-c433ef24df3b/resourceGroups/HKPS/providers/Microsoft.C
ompute/virtualMachines/VMPS
VmId              : c2fd537f-c8eb-4542-8b0c-4cd54e65749b
Name              : VMPS
Type              : Microsoft.Compute/virtualMachines
Location          : eastus2
Tags              : {}
HardwareProfile   : {VmSize}
NetworkProfile    : {NetworkInterfaces}
OSProfile         : {ComputerName, AdminUsername, WindowsConfiguration, Secrets, AllowExtensionOperations}
ProvisioningState : Succeeded
StorageProfile    : {ImageReference, OsDisk, DataDisks}
```

Delete Virtual Machine

Remove-AzureRmVm –Name VMPS –ResourceGroupName HKPS

```
PS C:\Users\Harinder Kohli> Remove-AzureRmVm -Name VMPS -ResourceGroupName HKPS

Virtual machine removal operation
This cmdlet will remove the specified virtual machine. Do you want to continue?
[Y] Yes  [N] No  [S] Suspend  [?] Help (default is "Y"): Y


OperationId : 00a9b657-b441-49f4-9d79-0d8fca8559b2
Status      : Succeeded
StartTime   : 22-12-2018 17:07:51
EndTime     : 22-12-2018 17:08:38
```

Chapter 24 Storage Accounts with CLI and PS

This Chapter covers following Lab Exercises

- Create Storage Account Using CLI
- Create Storage Account Using PowerShell

Exercise 187: Create Storage Account Using CLI

In this exercise we will create GPv2 Storage Account "stdcli410" in Resource Group HKCLI in East US 2 Location. Resource Group HKCLI was created in Exercise 181.

Connect to Azure using Azure CLI
Open command prompt (cmd) on your desktop and enter **az login** command for connecting and authenticating to Subscription.

Create Storage Account
az storage account create --name stdcli410 --resource-group HKCLI --location eastus2 --sku Standard_LRS --kind StorageV2

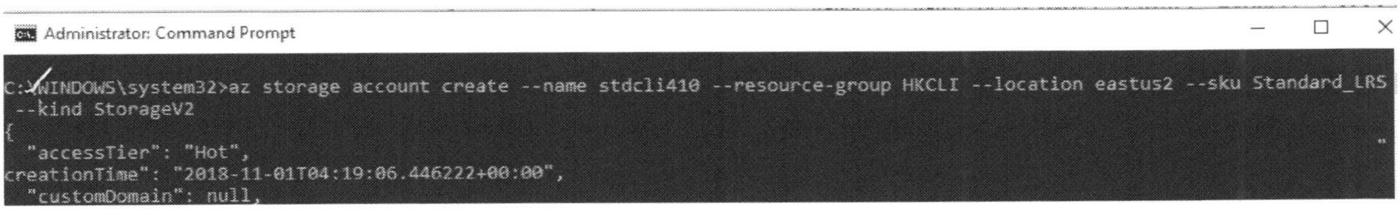

Administrator: Command Prompt

```
C:\WINDOWS\system32>az storage account create --name stdcli410 --resource-group HKCLI --location eastus2 --sku Standard_LRS
 --kind StorageV2
{
  "accessTier": "Hot",
  "creationTime": "2018-11-01T04:19:06.446222+00:00",
  "customDomain": null,
```

Check the Storage Account created
az storage account show --name stdcli410 or
az storage account show --name stdcli410 --resource-group HKCLI

```
C:\WINDOWS\system32>az storage account show --name stdcli410
{
  "accessTier": "Hot",
  "creationTime": "2018-11-01T04:19:06.446222+00:00",
  "customDomain": null,
  "enableHttpsTrafficOnly": false,
  "encryption": {
    "keySource": "Microsoft.Storage",
    "keyVaultProperties": null,
    "services": {
      "blob": {
        "enabled": true,
        "lastEnabledTime": "2018-11-01T04:19:06.539972+00:00"
```

Delete Storage Account
az storage account delete --name stdcli410
Note: Don't run above command.

Exercise 188: Create Storage Account Using PowerShell

In this exercise we will create GPv2 Storage Account "stdps410" in Resource Group HKPS in East US 2 Location. Resource Group HKPS was created in Exercise 182.

Connect to Azure using PowerShell
Open PowerShell command prompt on your desktop and login using Connect-AzureRmAccount.

Create Storage Account
New-AzureRmStorageAccount –ResourceGroupName HKPS –Name stdps410 –Location eastus2 –SkuName Standard_LRS –Kind StorageV2

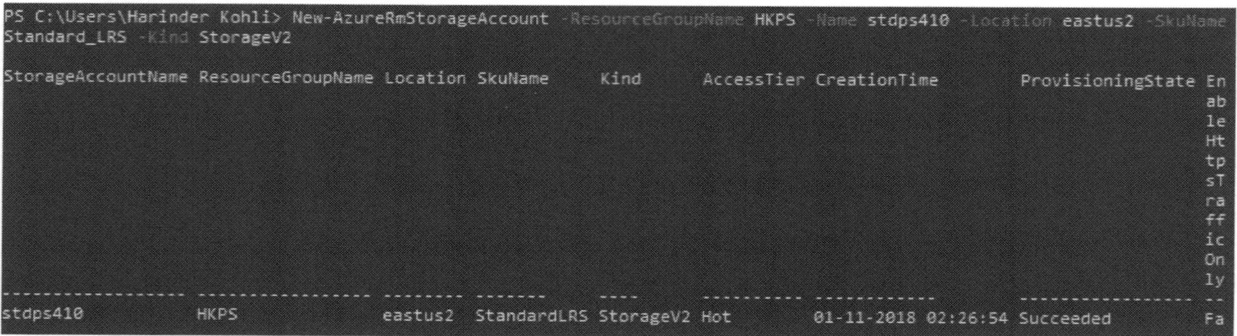

Check the Storage Account created
Get-AzureRmStorageAccount –ResourceGroupName HKPS –Name stdps410

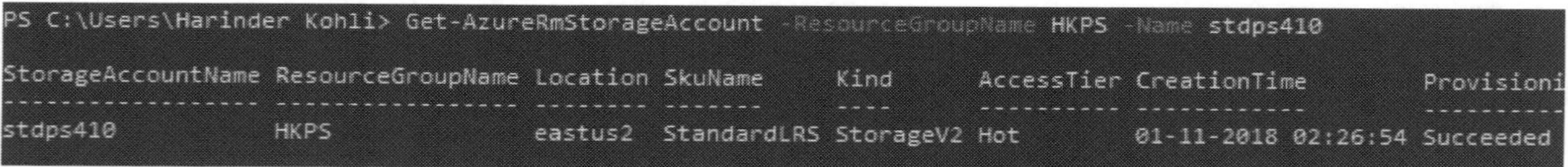

Delete Storage Account
Remove-AzureRmStorageAccount –ResourceGroupName HKPS –Name stdps410
Note: Don't run above command.

Chapter 25 Implement Storage with CLI and PowerShell

This Chapter covers following Lab Exercises

- Create Blob Storage Container using Azure CLI
- Create Blob Storage Container using PowerShell

Exercise 189: Create Blob Storage Container using Azure CLI

In this exercise we will create Blob Storage Container hk410cli in Storage Account stdcli410. Storage Account stdcli was created in Exercise 187 in previous chapter.

Connect to Azure using Azure CLI
Open command prompt (cmd) on your desktop and enter **az login** command for connecting and authenticating to Subscription.

Create Storage Container
az storage container create --name hk410cli --account-name stdcli410

Administrator: Command Prompt

```
C:\WINDOWS\system32>az storage container create --name hk410cli --account-name stdcli410
{
  "created": true
}
```

This command creates container with permission private no anonymous access.

Check the Storage Container created
az storage container list --account-name stdcli410

Administrator: Command Prompt

```
C:\WINDOWS\system32>az storage container list --account-name stdcli410
[
  {
    "metadata": null,
    "name": "hk410cli",
    "properties": {
      "etag": "\"0x8D642D93574F37D\"",
      "hasImmutabilityPolicy": "false",
      "hasLegalHold": "false",
      "lastModified": "2018-11-05T04:43:19+00:00",
      "lease": {
        "duration": null,
        "state": null,
        "status": null
```

Exercise 190: Create Blob Storage Container using PowerShell

In this exercise we will create Blob Storage Container hk410ps in Storage Account stdps410 and in Resource Group HKPS. Storage Account stdps410 was created in Exercise 188. Resource Group HKPS was created in Exercise 182.

Connect to Azure using PowerShell
Open PowerShell command prompt on your desktop and login using Connect-AzureRmAccount.

Create Storage Container
New-AzureRmStorageContainer -Name hk410ps –StorageAccountName stdps410 –ResourceGroupName HKPS

```
PS C:\Users\Harinder Kohli> New-AzureRmStorageContainer -Name hk410ps -StorageAccountName stdps410 -ResourceGroupName HKPS


ResourceGroupName     : HKPS
StorageAccountName    : stdps410
Id                    : /subscriptions/7593a7e7-0d4e-493a-922e-c433ef24df3b/resourceGroups/HKPS/providers/Microsoft.Sto
                        rage/storageAccounts/stdps410/blobServices/default/containers/hk410ps
Name                  : hk410ps
Type                  : Microsoft.Storage/storageAccounts/blobServices/containers
Etag                  :
Metadata              :
PublicAccess          :
ImmutabilityPolicy    :
LegalHold             :
LastModifiedTime      :
LeaseStatus           :
LeaseState            :
LeaseDuration         :
HasLegalHold          :
HasImmutabilityPolicy :
```

This command creates container with permission private no anonymous access.

Check the Storage Container created
Get-AzureRmStorageContainer –Name hk410ps –StorageAccountName stdps410 –ResourceGroupName HKPS or
Get-AzureRmStorageContainer –StorageAccountName stdps410 –ResourceGroupName HKPS

```
PS C:\Users\Harinder Kohli> Get-AzureRmStorageContainer -Name hk410ps -StorageAccountName stdps410 -ResourceGroupName HKPS


ResourceGroupName     : HKPS
StorageAccountName    : stdps410
Id                    : /subscriptions/7593a7e7-0d4e-493a-922e-c433ef24df3b/resourceGroups/HKPS/providers/Microsoft.Storage
                        /storageAccounts/stdps410/blobServices/default/containers/hk410ps
Name                  : hk410ps
Type                  : Microsoft.Storage/storageAccounts/blobServices/containers
Etag                  : "0x8D642FDC9386C07"
Metadata              :
PublicAccess          : None
ImmutabilityPolicy    :
LegalHold             : Microsoft.Azure.Commands.Management.Storage.Models.PSLegalHoldProperties
LastModifiedTime      : 05-11-2018 09:05:08
LeaseStatus           : Unlocked
LeaseState            : Available
```

Made in the USA
Middletown, DE
19 June 2020

10405193R00424